# Ecclesia

## A Theological Encyclopedia of the Church

Christopher O'Donnell, O.Carm.

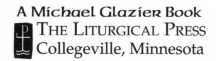

A Michael Glazier Book
THE LITURGICAL PRESS
Collegeville, Minnesota

A Michael Glazier Book published by The Liturgical Press

Cover design by Ann Blattner.

The author and publisher have made serious effort to acquire permission where necessary to reprint in this volume copyrighted material of the publishers listed below:

A. Flannery, ed., *Vatican II: The Conciliar and Postconciliar Documents.* 2 vols. (Dublin: Dominican Publications, 1973, 1982).

Canon Law Society of America, *Code of Canon Law: Latin-English Edition* (Washington, D.C., 1983).

The Lima Document, *Baptism, Eucharist and Ministry.* Faith and Order Paper No. 111 (Geneva: World Council of Churches, 1982).

N.P. Tanner, ed., *Decrees of the Ecumenical Councils.* 2 vols. (London: Sheed & Ward—Washington, D.C.: Georgetown University, 1990).

J. Neuner and J. Dupuis, ed., *The Christian Faith in the Doctrinal Documents of the Catholic Church* (London: HarperCollinsReligious, [5]1992).

M. Staniforth and A. Louth, eds. and trans., *Early Christian Writings* (Harmondsworth, England: Penguin, 1987).

G. Dix and H. Chadwick, eds., *The Treatise on the Apostolic Tradition* (Ridgefield, Conn.: Morehouse—London: Alban Press, 1992).

The Scripture quotations are from the New Revised Standard Version Bible, Catholic edition, © 1989 by the Division of Christian Education of the National Council of Churches of Christ in the USA. Used by permission. All rights reserved.

1    2    3    4    5    6    7    8

**Library of Congress Cataloging-in-Publication Data**

O'Donnell, Christopher.
    Ecclesia : a theological encyclopedia of the Church / Christopher
O'Donnell.
       p.  cm.
    "A Michael Glazier book."
    Includes bibliographical references and index.
    ISBN 0-8146-5832-6
    1. Catholic Church–Encyclopedias.   I. Title.
BX841.036  1996
262'.02'03–dc20
                                            96-12532
                                              CIP

*In Memory of John Hyde, S.J., (1909–1985)*
*and*
*With Grateful Appreciation to F.A. Sullivan, S.J.,*
*Both Teachers and Wise Guides in My Theological Quests*

# Contents

# Foreword

Studies on the Church continue to multiply. At the same time, the territory covered by ecclesiology also widens. Since Vatican II there has been a happy integration of many theological disciplines and fields which have enriched our understanding of the Church. This work seeks to make more readily available information on a wide range of topics that one may encounter when reading about the Church.

Despite its size, there have had to be limitations. It is hoped that nearly all the important subjects find some coverage in the various articles. The extensive bibliographical references seek to supplement mainly from journals the invaluable work by A. Dulles and P. Granfield, *The Church. A Bibliography* (Wilmington: Glazier, 1985). With new developments in data gathering and more sophisticated library exchanges, one's judgement of what is accessible has changed even in the past five years. As time goes on, it will be still easier for the determined researcher to track down particular works. Even within the notes there had to be some selectivity, but preference has been given to works in English and articles in other languages which have further references in English. But a decision was made at an early stage not to confine references to English. Moreover, full bibliographical information on books is normally given only for those published from 1970. A further decision was made not to include references to other dictionaries and encyclopedias, such as *Dictionnaire de théologie catholique, Lexikon für Theologie und Kirche, New Catholic Encyclopedia,* the excellent "New Dictionary" series of Glazier—The Liturgical Press, *Theologische Realenzyklopädie,* etc. The reader who has access to these works will surely use them. An exception is made for *the Dictionnaire de spiritualité,* which has much ecclesiological material where a person might not immediately think of looking.

Another limitation involves the selection of articles. While some topics suggest themselves, there could not be comprehensive treatment of ecclesiologists. The more important Church Fathers and all the general councils are briefly covered. Only a handful of contemporary writers have a short entry; my debt to them and to others will be clear from the notes and bibliography.

In a protracted work there are many people to thank. First there are libraries. I have done most work in three of them: the library at the Milltown Institute, whose librarian was D. Fleury, S.J., and is now F. O'Donoghue, S.J., assisted by Ms. Bríd O'Brien, is a model of hospitality and efficiency for any researcher or student; the library of the Gregorian University in Rome was unfailingly courteous and helpful with multiple requests for materials; the fine library at the Centro Internazionale S. Alberto in Rome was at my disposal. I was also helped greatly by the libraries at the Centro pro Unione and the Urbaniana University in Rome.

To Michael Glazier, who commissioned this work and encouraged me in its execution, my thanks are due. I express my appreciation to the staff of the Liturgical Press, especially its managing editor Mark Twomey and my copy editor, the unerring Don Molloy. Michael O'Carroll, C.SS.P., the writer of several encyclopedias, was always generously supportive of one who was trying to walk in his path, but not capable of wearing his shoes.

I owe a large debt of gratitude to several scholars. First to F.A. Sullivan, S.J., who with enormous unselfishness read almost the whole manuscript and made very many important suggestions. Colleagues at the Milltown Institute kindly read articles involving their areas of expertise: F. Clancy, S.J.; G. Corcoran, O.S.A.; J. Corkery, S.J.; W. Harrington, O.P.; J. Keating, O.Carm.; W. Kelly, S.J.; J. Macken, S.J.; R. Maloney, S.J.; P. Mullins, O.Carm.; F. O'Donoghue, S.J.; G. O'Hanlon, S.J.; the doyen of ecumenism in Ireland, M. Hurley, S.J., read several articles. I had also the help of lynx-eyed readers: my sister, Sr. Maire O'Donnell, R.S.H.M.; Sr. Áine Hayde, A.H.F.; and Pat

O'Kelly, all of whom detected errors, smoothed style, and made valuable suggestions. Successive Deans of Theology at the Milltown Institute, F. Dromey, O.M.I., and G. O'Hanlon, S.J., and its registrar, Sally Uí Chiardha, gave me very considerate timetabling to allow the work to be brought to a conclusion. Finally I wish to thank the Carmelite fraternity, Milltown Institute colleagues, and other friends for their interest, support, and prayer.

Christopher O'Donnell, O.Carm.
16 July 1995
Feast of Our Lady of Mount Carmel

# Abbreviations

| | |
|---|---|
| AA | Vatican II, *Apostolicam actuositatem* (Decree on the Apostolate of the Laity—1965). |
| AAS | *Acta Apostolicae Sedis*. Vatican. |
| AA.VV | Auctores varii (multi-authored work). |
| Abbot, Vatican II | W.M. Abbot, *The Documents of Vatican II*. London: Chapman 1967. |
| ActaRomSocIesu | *Acta romana Societatis Iesu*. Rome. |
| ActaSyn | *Acta synodalia sacrosancti Concilii Vaticani II*. 4 vols. Vatican: Polyglot Press, 1970–1978. |
| ACW | Ancient Christian Writers series. Washington, D.C.: The Catholic University of America. |
| AF | *The Apostolic Fathers*. Ed. R.M. Grant. 6 vols. (London—Camden, N.Y.—Toronto, 1964–1968). |
| AfTQ | *Africa Theological Journal*. Arusha, Tanzania. |
| AG | Vatican II, *Ad gentes* (Decree on the Missionary Activity of the Church). |
| AHC | *Annuarium historiae conciliorum*. Paderborn. |
| Alberigo, Concili | *Storia dei concili ecumenici*. Ed. G. Alberigo. Brescia: Queriniana, 1990. |
| Alberigo-Magistretti | *Consitutionis dogmaticae Lumen gentium synopsis historica*. Ed. G. Alberigo and F. Magistretti. Bologna: Istituto per le Scienze Religiose, 1975. |
| AmBenR | *American Benedictine Review*. Richardton, N.D. |
| Ambros | *Ambrosius. Strumento per il lavoro pastorale nella Chiesa di Milano*. Milan. |
| AmER | *American Ecclesiastical Review*. Washington, D.C. |
| AmplefJ | *Ampleforth Journal*. Ampleforth, England. |
| AnBoll | *Analecta bollandiana*. Brussels. |
| ANF | Ante Nicene Fathers series. Buffalo, N.Y. |
| Ang | *Angelicum*. Rome. |
| AnGreg | Analecta gregoriana series. Rome. |
| AngTR | *Anglican Theological Review*. Evanston, Ill. |
| ANL | Ante-Nicene Christian Library series. Edinburgh. |
| AnnéeCan | *L'Année canonique*. Paris. |
| AnnTheol | *Annales theologici*. Rome. |
| Antón | A. Antón, *El misterio de la Iglesia. Evolución de las ideas eclesiológicas*. BAC Maior 28, 30. 2 vols. Madrid: La Editorial Católica, 1986, 1987. |

| | |
|---|---|
| Antonian | *Antonianum.* Rome. |
| AnVal | *Anales valentinos.* Valencia. |
| Apoll | *Apollinaris.* Rome. |
| Apostolic Tradition | First number refers to B. Botte, trans. and ed., *Hippolyte de Rome. La tradition apostolique.* Sources chrétiennes 11bis. The second number is G. Dix, trans. and ed., *The Treatise on the Apostolic Tradition of St. Hippolytus of Rome.* Revised H. Chadwick. London: Alban Press— Ridgefield, Conn.: Morehouse, 1992. |
| ArcKK | *Archiv für katholisches Kirchenrecht.* Mainz. |
| ArHistDoctMA | *Archives d'histoire doctrinale et littéraire du moyen-âge.* Paris. |
| ArHPont | *Archivum historiae pontificae.* Rome. |
| ArLtgW | *Archiv für Liturgiewissenschaft.* Regensburg. |
| Asp | *Asprenas.* Naples. |
| ASS | *Acta Sanctae Sedis.* Rome 1865–1908. |
| AugL | *Augustiniana.* Leuven, Belgium. |
| AugM | *Augustinus.* Madrid. |
| AugR | *Augustinianum.* Rome. |
| AugSt | *Augustinian Studies.* Villanova, Pa. |
| AustralBR | *Australian Biblical Review.* Melbourne. |
| AustralCR | *Australian Catholic Record.* Manley, NSW. |
| Baraúna-Congar | G. Baraúna and Y. Congar, eds. *L'Église de Vatican II.* US 51 a, b, c. 3 vols. Paris: Cerf, 1966. |
| Bauer | J.B. Bauer, ed., *Encyclopedia of Biblical Theology.* 3 vols. London and Sydney: Sheed and Ward, 1970. |
| Bekenntnisschriften | H. Lietzmann, ed., *Die Bekenntnisschriften der evangelisch-lutherischen Kirche.* Göttingen: Vandenhoeck & Ruprecht, 61967. |
| Bell, Documents | G.K.A. Bell, ed., *Documents on Christian Unity. A Selection. Third Series. Fourth Series* (Oxford: UP, 1948–1958) cited not by page but by numbers which run through the three volumes. |
| Benedictina | *Benedictina.* Rome. |
| Bettenson, Documents | H. Bettenson, ed., *Documents of the Christian Church.* New York—Oxford: University Press, 21963. |
| Bib | *Biblica.* Rome. |
| BibbiaOR | *Bibbia e oriente.* Bornato in Franciacorta, Italy. |
| BibliogMiss | *Bibliografia missionaria supplemento.* Vatican Urban University. |
| BiblSac | *Bibliotheca Sacra.* Dallas, Tex. |
| BibTB | *Biblical Theology Bulletin.* New York. |
| BibTheol | *Biblical Theology.* Belfast, Northern Ireland. |
| Bijd | *Bijdragen. Filosofie en Theologie.* AA Meppel, Netherlands. |
| BJRyL | *Bulletin of the John Rylands Library.* Manchester, England. |
| BLitEc | *Bulletin de littérature ecclésiastique.* Toulouse. |
| BLtg | *Bibel und Liturgie.* Klosterneuburg, Austria. |
| Bremond | H. Bremond, *Histoire littéraire du sentiment religieux en France.* 11 vols. Paris, 1923–1933. |
| BTAfr | *Bulletin de théologie africaine—Bulletin of African Theology—Boletim de teologia africana.* Kinshasa. |

| | |
|---|---|
| BullCentUn | Centro pro Unione Rome, *Bulletin.* |
| BullPontConcDialRel | *Bulletin of Pontificum Concilium pro Dialogo inter Religiones.* Vatican. |
| Burgense | *Burgense. Collectanea scientifica.* Burgos, Spain. |
| ByzB | *Byzantion.* Wetteren, Belgium. |
| ByzSt | *Byzantine Studies.* Bakersfield, Calif.. |
| ByzZ | *Byzantinische Zeitschrift.* Munich. |
| BZ | *Biblische Zeitschrift.* Paderborn. |
| CalvinTJ | *Calvin Theological Journal.* Grand Rapids, Mich. |
| CanLawDig | *Canon Law Digest.* Milwaukee—New York, 1934–1969/Chicago, 1975– . |
| CanLawSAP | Canon Law Society of America, *Proceedings.* Washington, D.C. |
| Carlen | C. Carlen, *Papal Encyclicals 1740–1981.* 5 vols. (1740–1878, 1878–1903, 1903–1939, 1939–1958, 1958–1981) Ann Arbor, Mich.: Pierian, 1990. |
| Carmelus | *Carmelus.* Rome. |
| Carthag | *Carthaginensia. Rivista de estudios e investigación.* Murcia, Spain. |
| CathIntern | *Catholic International.* Worcester, Mass. |
| Catholica | *Catholica.* Münster. |
| Catholicisme | *Catholicisme. Hier aujourd'hui demain.* Paris, 1947– |
| CBQ | *Catholic Biblical Quarterly.* Washington, D.C. |
| CCEO | *Codex canonum ecclesiarum orientalium.* Vatican, 1990 (Canon Law of Eastern Churches). |
| CCL | Corpus christianorum series latina. Turnhout and Paris. |
| CCO | P.P. Jouannou, ed., *Les canons des conciles oecuménique.* Grottaferrata, Italy, 1962. |
| CD | Vatican II, *Christus Dominus* (Decree on the Pastoral Office of Bishops in the Church—1965) |
| ChH | *Church History.* Chicago, Ill. |
| ChicSt | *Chicago Studies.* Chicago, Ill. |
| ChQR | *Church Quarterly Review.* London. |
| CHRev | *The Catholic Historical Review.* Washington, D.C. |
| ChristJewRel | *Christian-Jewish Relations.* London. |
| CIC | *Codex Iuris Canonici.* Vatican, 1983 (The Code of Canon Law). |
| CiTom | *Ciencia tomista.* Salamanca. |
| CiuD | *Ciudad de Dios.* Madrid. |
| CivCatt | *La civiltà cattolica.* Rome. |
| CL | John Paul II, Exhortation, *Christifideles laici* (On the Vocation and the Mission of the Lay Faithful in the Church and in the World). Vatican, 1988. |
| Claret | *Claretianum.* Rome. |
| CleR | *Clergy Review.* London. |
| CollFranc | *Collectanea franciscana.* Rome. |
| ComLtg | *Communautés et liturgies.* Ottignies, Belgium. |
| Communicationes | Pontificium Consilium de legum textibus interpretandis: *Communicationes.* Vatican. |
| Communio | *Communio.* Paris. |
| ComRelM | *Commentarium pro religiosis et missionariis.* Rome. |

| | |
|---|---|
| Conc | *Concilium*. Edinburgh. |
| ConcordiaTQ | *Concordia Theological Quarterly*. Fort Wayne, Ind. |
| Congar, Augustin | Y. Congar, *L'Église. De saint Augustin à l'époque moderne*. Histoire des dogmes 111/3. Paris: Cerf, 1970. |
| Congar, L'Église une | *L'Église. Une, sainte, catholique et apostolique*. Mysterium salutus 15. Paris: Cerf, 1970. |
| Congar, Moyen-âge | Y. Congar, *L'ecclésiologie du haut moyen-âge*. Paris: Cerf, 1968. |
| Contacts | *Contacts*. Paris. |
| Coriden, CIC | J.A. Coriden, T.J. Green and D.E. Heintschel, eds., *The Code of Canon Law. A Text and Commentary*. Mahwah: Paulist—London: Chapman, 1985. |
| CredOggi | *Credere oggi*. Padua, Italy. |
| Christie-Murray, Heresy | D. Christie-Murray, *A History of Heresy*. Oxford: University Press paperback, 1989. |
| CrNSt | *Cristianesimo nella storia*. Bologna. |
| CrossC | *Cross Currents*. Dobbs Ferry, N.Y. |
| CSEL | Corpus scriptorum ecclesticorum latinorum series. Vienna. |
| CTSAP | Catholic Theological Society of America, *Proceedings*. Chicago, Ill. |
| DACL | *Dictionnaire d'archéologie chrétienne et de la liturgie*. Paris, 1907–1953. |
| Davis, Councils | L.D. Davis, *The First Seven Ecumenical Councils (325–787). Their History and Theology*. Theology and Life 21. Collegeville: Glazier—The Liturgical Press, 1983, 1990. |
| DBT | X. Léon-Dufour, ed., *Dictionary of Biblical Theology*. London: Chapman, ²1973. |
| DH | Vatican II, *Dignitatis humanae* (Declaration on religious Freedom—1965). |
| DiakMainz | *Diakonia. Internationale Zeitschrift für die Praxis der Kirche*. Mainz—Vienna. |
| Diak(USA) | *Diakonia*. Bronx, N.Y. |
| DiálEcum | *Diálogo ecuménico*. Salamanca. |
| DictDCan | *Dictionnaire de droit canonique*. Paris, 1935–1965. |
| DictEcumMov | N. Lossky et al., eds., *Dictionary of the Ecumenical Movement*. (Geneva: WCC—London: Council of Churches—Grand Rapids, Mich.: Eerdmans, 1991). |
| DirEccl | *Il diritto ecclesiastico e rassegna di diritto matrimoniale*. Milan. |
| Divinitas | *Divinitas*. Vatican. |
| DivThom | *Divus Thomas*. Piacenza, Italy. |
| DMA | *Dictionary of the Middle Ages*. New York: Scribner, 1982– |
| DocCath | *Documentation catholique*. Paris. |
| DoctCom | *Doctor communis*. Vatican. |
| DoctLife | *Doctrine and Life*. Dublin. |
| DOL | T.C. O'Brien, ed., *Documents on the Liturgy 1963–1979. Conciliar, Papal and Curial Texts* (Collegeville: The Liturgical Press, 1983). |
| Doohan, Laity | L. Doohan, *The Laity. A Bibliography*. Wilmington: Glazier, 1987. |
| DowR | *Downside Review*. Bath, England. |
| DS | H. Denzinger and A. Schönmetzer, eds., *Enchiridion symbolorum definitionum et declarationum de rebus fidei et morum*. Barcelona—Freiburg—Rome, ³⁵1973. |
| DSpir | *Dictionnaire de spiritualité ascétique et mystique*. Paris, 1937–1995. |
| DTC | *Dictionnaire de théologie catholique*. Paris, 1903–1950. |

| DublinR | *The Dublin Review.* London. |
| Dulles-Granfield | A. Dulles and P. Granfield, *The Church. A Bibliography.* Wilmington: Glazier, 1985. |
| DumbO | *Dumbarton Oakes Papers.* Cambridge, Mass. |
| DV | Vatican II, *Dei verbum* (Constitution on Divine Revelation—1965). |
| EcclXav | *Ecclesiástica xaveriana.* Bogotá, Colombia. |
| ÉchOr | *Échos d'orient.* Paris. |
| EChQ | *Eastern Churches Quarterly.* London. |
| EcOr | *Ecclesia orans.* Rome. |
| EcumBull | *Ecumenical Bulletin.* New York. |
| EcumTrends | *Ecumenical Trends.* New York. |
| EcuR | *Ecumenical Review.* Geneva. |
| EfMex | *Efemerides mexicana.* Mexico. |
| ÉglT | *Église et théologie.* Ottawa. |
| EN | Paul VI, Apost. *Exhort. Evangelii nuntiandi (Evangelization in the Modern World)*—AAS 68 (1976) 1–96. |
| Encounter | *Encounter.* Rome. |
| EncounToday | *Encounter Today.* Paris. |
| EncycEarCh | A. Di Berardino, ed., *Encyclopedia of the Early Church.* Trans. A. Walford; W.H.C. Frend, ed., 2 vols. Cambridge: Clarke, 1992. Italian *Dizionario patristico e di antichità cristiane.* |
| EncycRel | M. Eliade et al., eds., *The Encyclopedia of Religion.* 16 vols. New York: Macmillan—London: Collins, 1987. |
| EncycRelEth | J. Hastings, ed., *Encyclopedia of Religion and Ethics.* Edinburgh, 1905–1926. |
| Eno, Teaching Authority | R.B. Eno, *Teaching Authority in the Early Church.* Message of the Fathers of the Church 14. Wilmington: Glazier, 1984. |
| EphCarm | *Ephemerides carmeliticae.* Rome. |
| EphIurC | *Ephemerides iuris canonici.* Rome. |
| EphLtg | *Ephemerides liturgicae.* Rome. |
| EphMar | *Ephemerides mariologicae.* Madrid. |
| Episk | *Episkepsis.* Chambésy—Geneva, Switzerland. |
| Esprit | *Esprit.* Paris. |
| EspVie | *Esprit et vie. L'Ami du clergé.* Langres Cedex, France. |
| EstBib | *Estudios bíblicos.* Madrid. |
| EstE | *Estudios Eclesiásticos.* Madrid. |
| EstFranc | *Estudios franciscanos.* Barcelona. |
| EstTrin | *Estudios trinitarios.* Salamanca. |
| ÉtFranc | *Études franciscaines.* Blois, France. |
| ETL | *Ephemerides theologiae lovanienses.* Leuven, Belgium. |
| ETL ElenchBib | *Ephemerides theologiae lovanienses. Elenchus bibliographicus.* Leuven, Belgium. |
| ÉtMar | *Études mariales.* Paris. |
| ÉTR | *Études théologiques et religieuses.* Montpelier, France. |

| | |
|---|---|
| Études | *Études*. Paris. |
| EuntDoc | *Euntes docete*. Rome. |
| Eusebius, Hist. Eccl. | Eusebius, *The History of the Church from Christ to Constantine*. Trans. G.A. Williamson. Harmondsworth UK: Penguin, 1965. |
| ExpTim | *The Expository Times*. Edinburgh. |
| FC | Fathers of the Church series. Washington, D.C.: The Catholic University of America—Centurion Press. |
| Flannery 1, 2 | A. Flannery, ed., *Vatican II. The Conciliar and Post Conciliar Documents*. 2 vols. Dublin: Dominican Publications—New York: Costello, ²1981 and 1982. |
| Fliche-Martin | A. Fliche and V. Martin, eds., *Histoire de l'Église depuis les origines jusqu'à nos jours*. Paris, 1935–1964. |
| FoiTemps | *La foi et le temps*. Paris. |
| FoiVie | *Foi et vie*. Paris. |
| ForKTheol | *Forum katholische Theologie*. Aschaffenburg, Germany. |
| FranStAn | *Fransciscan Studies Annual*. New York. |
| FranzSt | *Franziskanische Studien*. Paderborn. |
| FreibZ | *Freiburger Zeitschrift für Philosophie und Theologie*. Freibourg, Switzerland. |
| FS | Festschrift/Festgabe/Studies in Honor of . . . |
| Fur | *The Furrow*. Maynooth, Ireland. |
| GCS | Die griechischen christlichen Schriftsteller. Leipzig. |
| GE | Vatican II, *Gravissimum educationis* (Declaration on Christian Education—1965). |
| GeistL | *Geist und Leben*. Würtzburg, Germany. |
| GI | General Instruction (Introduction to each revised liturgical book after Vatican II). |
| GlLer | *Glauben und Lernen*. Göttingen, Germany. |
| Greg | *Gregorianum*. Rome. |
| GrOrTR | *Greek Orthodox Theological Review*. Brookline, Mass. |
| GS | Vatican II, *Gaudium et spes* (Pastoral Constitution on the Church in the World of Today—1965). |
| Halton, Church | T. Halton, *The Church*. Message of the Fathers of the Church 4. Wilmington: Glazier, 1985. |
| HarvTR | *The Harvard Theological Review*. Cambridge, Mass. |
| Hefele-Leclercq | C.J. Hefele and H. Leclercq, eds., *Histoire des conciles*. Paris, 1909–1952. |
| HeilD | *Heiliger Dienst*. Salzburg, Austria. |
| HeythJ | *Heythrop Journal*. London. |
| HispSac | *Hispania sacra*. Madrid. |
| HistEcumMov | *History of the Ecumenical Movement*. Vol. 1—1517–1948, ed. R. Rouse and S.C. O' Neil. London: SPCK, ²1968. Vol. 2—1948–1968, ed. H.E. Fey. London: SPCK, 1970. |
| Horizons | *Horizons*. Villanova, Pa. |
| HoTheol | *Ho theológos*. Palermo, Italy. |
| IkiZ | *Internationale kirchliche Zeitschrift*. Bern, Switzerland. |
| IM | Vatican II, *Inter mirifica* (Decree on the Mass Media—1963). |
| IndTS | *Indian Theological Studies*. Bangalore, India. |
| InformSer | Pontifical Council for Promoting Christian Unity, *Information Service*. Vatican. |
| InterKZCommunio | *Internationale katholische Zeitschrift Communio*. Paderborn. |

| | |
|---|---|
| Interp | *Interpretation*. Richmond, Va. |
| IntRMiss | *International Review of Missions*. London. |
| IrBSt | *Irish Biblical Studies*. Belfast, Northern Ireland. |
| IrEcclRecord | *Irish Ecclesiastical Record*. Maynooth, Ireland. |
| Irén | *Irénikon*. Chevetogne, Belgium. |
| IrTQ | *Irish Theological Quarterly*. Maynooth, Ireland. |
| IslamChr | *Islamochristiana*. Roma. |
| IslamChrMusR | *Islam and Christian-Muslim Relations*. Birmingham, England. |
| Istina | *Istina*. Paris. |
| ITC | The International Theological Commission. |
| IusCan | *Ius canonicum*. Pamplona, Spain. |
| IusEccl | *Ius ecclesiae. Rivista internazionale di diritto canonico*. Milan. |
| JbAC | *Jahrbuch für Antike und Christentum*. Münster. |
| JBC | R.E. Brown, J.A. Fitzmyer and R.E. Murphy, eds., *The Jerome Biblical Commentary*. 2 vols. Englewood Cliffs: Prentice-Hall—London: Chapman,1968–1969. (See also NJBC.) |
| JBL | *Journal of Biblical Literature*. Atlanta, Ga. |
| JbLtgW | *Jahrbuch für Liturgiewissenschaft*. Münster. |
| JChuSt | *Journal of Church and State*. Waco, Tex. |
| JDhara | *Jeevadhara*. Kerala, India. |
| JDharma | *Journal of Dharma*. Bangalore, India. |
| JEcuSt | *Journal of Ecumenical Studies*. Philadelphia, Pa. |
| Jedin, Councils | H. Jedin, *Ecumenical Councils of the Catholic Church. An Historical Outline*. Freiburg—Edinburgh—London, 1960. |
| Jedin-Dolan | H. Jedin, J. Dolan and K. Kepgen, eds., *History of the Church*. 10 vols. New York: Crossroad—London: Burns & Oates, 1980–1982. |
| JEH | *Journal of Ecclesiastical History*. Cambridge, England. |
| JFemSt | *Journal of Feminist Studies in Religion*. Atlanta, Ga. |
| JRel | *Journal of Religion*. Chicago, Ill. |
| JRelSt | *Journal of Religious Studies*. Cleveland, Oh. |
| JStNT | *Journal for the Study of the New Testament*. Sheffield, England. |
| JTS | *Journal of Theological Studies*. Oxford—London. |
| Jurist | *The Jurist*. Washington, D.C. |
| Kair | *Kairos Religionswissenschaft*. Salzburg, Austria. |
| Kan | *Kanon. Jahrbuch der Gesellschaft für das Recht der Ostkirchen*. Vienna. |
| KerDo | *Kerygma und Dogma*. Göttingen, Germany. |
| KerkT | *Kerk en Theologie*. 's-Gravenhage, Netherlands. |
| Kidd | B.J. Kidd, *Documents of the Continental Reformation*. Oxford, 1911. |
| KirJb | *Kirchliches Jahrbuch für die Evangelische Kirche in Deutschland*. Gütersloh, Germany. |
| KirOst | *Kirche im Osten*. Göttingen, Germany. |
| KlassTheol | H. Fries and G. Kretschmar, eds., *Klassiker der Theologie*. 2 vols. Munich: Beck, 1981–1983. |

| | |
|---|---|
| Later | *Lateranum*. Rome. |
| Latourelle, Vatican II | R. Latourelle, ed., *Vatican II. Assessment and Perspectives Twenty-five Years After (1962–1987)*. 3 vols. New York—Mahwah: Paulist, 1988. |
| Laur | *Laurentianum*. Rome. |
| LavalTP | *Laval théologie et philosophie*. Quebec. |
| LCC | Library of Christian Classics series. London: SCM. |
| Leith, Creeds | J.H. Leith, ed., *Creeds of the Churches. A Reader in Christian Doctrine from the Bible to the Present*. Richmond: Knox Press—Oxford: Blackwell, revised ed. 1973. |
| LG | Vatican II, *Lumen gentium* (Constitution on the Church—1964). |
| LitJb | *Liturgisches Jahrbuch*. Trier, Germany. |
| LNPF | A Select Library of Nicene and Post-Nicene Fathers of the Christian Church. Buffalo—New York. |
| LouvSt | *Louvain Studies*. Leuven, Belgium. |
| LTK | *Lexikon für Theologie und Kirche*. Freiburg: Herder, 1957–1965. |
| Lumen | *Lumen. Revista de síntesis y orientación de ciencias eclesiásticas*. Vitoria, Spain. |
| LumièreV | *Lumière et vie*. Lyon, France. |
| LumVit | *Lumen vitae*. Brussels. |
| LuthJb | *Lutherjahrbuch. Organ der internationalen Lutherforschung*. Göttingen, Germany. |
| LuthQ | *Lutheran Quarterly*. Milwaukee, Wis. |
| LXX | Septuagint (Greek trans. of Old Testament) |
| MaisD | *La Maison-Dieu*. Paris. |
| Manresa | *Manresa*. Azpeitia—Guipúzcoa, Spain. |
| Mansi | J.D. Mansi, *Sacrorum conciliorum nova et amplissima collectio*. Reprint and continuation. Paris—Leipzig, 1901–1927. |
| MarSt | *Marian Studies*. Washington, D.C. |
| MedSt | *Medieval Studies*. Toronto. |
| MelitaT | *Melita theologica*. Malta. |
| MélSR | *Mélanges de science religieuse*. Lille, France. |
| MessF | Message of the Fathers of the Church series. Wilmington: Glazier. |
| MGEp | Monumenta germaniae epistolae. Hannover—Berlin. |
| MGH | Monumenta germaniae historica. Hannover—Berlin. |
| Mid-Stream | *Mid-Stream. An Ecumenical Journal*. Indianapolis, Ind. |
| MilltownSt | *Milltown Studies*. Dublin. |
| MiscCom | *Miscelánea comillas*. Madrid. |
| MiscFran | *Miscellanea francescana*. Rome. |
| ModChm | *The Modern Churchman*. Leominster, England. |
| ModT | *Modern Theology*. Oxford, England. |
| MonEccl | *Monitor ecclesiasticus*. Rome. |
| Month | *The Month*. London. |
| Mp | *Motu proprio* (of papal documents). |
| MüTZ | *Münchener theologische Zeitschrift*. Munich. |

| | |
|---|---|
| MystS | J. Feiner and M. Löhrer, eds., *Mysterium Salutis. Grundriss heilsgeschichtlicher Dogmatik.* Einsiedeln—Zürich—Cologne: Benzinger, 1965–1981. |
| NA | Vatican II, *Nostra aetate* (Declaration on the Church's Relation to Non-Christian religions—1965). |
| NBlackfr | *New Blackfriars.* London. |
| NCE | *New Catholic Encyclopedia.* New York: McGraw-Hill, 1967. Supplements, 1974– . |
| ND | J. Neuner and J. Dupuis, eds., *The Christian Faith in the Doctrinal Documents of the Catholic Church.* London—Sydney: Collins, revised ed. 1983. |
| NDictCSpir | M. Downey, ed., *The New Dictionary of Catholic Spirituality.* Collegeville: Glazier—The Liturgical Press, 1993. |
| NDictSacWorship | *The New Dictionary of Sacramental Worship.* Collegeville: Glazier—The Liturgical Press—Dublin: Gill and Macmillan, 1990. |
| NDictT | J. A. Komonchak, M. Collins and D.A. Lane, eds., *The New Dictionary of Theology.* Wilmington: Glazier—Dublin: Gill and Macmillan, 1987. |
| NDizLit | D. Sartore and A.M. Triacca, eds., *Nuovo dizionario di liturgia.* Rome: Ed. Paoline, 1984. |
| NDizMar | S. De Fiores and S. Meo, eds., *Nuovo dizionario di mariologia.* Milan: Ed. Paoline, 1985. |
| NDizSpir | S. De Fiores and T. Goffi, eds., *Nuovo dizionario di spiritualità.* Milan: Ed. Paoline, 1985. |
| NedTTs | *Nederlands theologisch Tijdschrift.* 's—Gravenhage, Netherlands. |
| Neotestamentica | *Neotestamentica. Journal of the New Testament Society of South Africa.* Pretoria, South Africa. |
| NewSchol | *The New Scholasticism.* Washington, D.C. |
| NewTR | *New Theology Review. An American Catholic Journal for Ministry.* Wilmington, Del. |
| Nicol | *Nicolas.* Bari, Italy. |
| NJB | *New Jerusalem Bible.* London: Darton, Longman & Todd—New York: Doubleday, 1985. |
| NJBC | R.E. Brown, J.A. Fitzmyer and R.E. Murphy, eds., *The New Jerome Biblical Commentary.* Englewood Cliffs: Prentice Hall—London: Chapman, 1989. (See also JBC). |
| Notitiae | *Notitiae.* Vatican. |
| NRSV | *New Revised Standard Version.* New York—Oxford: University Press, 1989. |
| NRT | *Nouvelle revue théologique.* Tournai-Namur, Belgium. |
| NT | *Novum Testamentum.* Leiden, Netherlands. |
| NTMess | New Testament Message series. Wilmington: Glazier. |
| NTS | *New Testament Studies.* London. |
| Nuntia | *Nuntia.* Vatican. |
| NVet | *Nova et vetera.* Fribourg, Switzerland. |
| O'Carroll, Theotokos | M. O'Carroll, *Theotokos. A Theological Encyclopedia of the Blessed Virgin Mary.* Wilmington: Glazier, ²1983. |
| OE | Vatican II, *Orientalium Ecclesiarum* (Decree on the Eastern Catholic Churches—1964). |
| OneChr | *One in Christ.* Turvey, England. |
| OrChr | *Oriens christianus.* Wiesbaden, Germany. |
| OrChrAn | *Orientalia christiana analecta* series. Rome. |
| OrChrPer | *Orientalia christiana periodica.* Rome. |
| Origins | *Origins.* Washington, D.C. |
| OrSyr | *L'Orient syrien.* Paris. |

| | |
|---|---|
| OrthFor | *Orthodoxes Forum. Zeitschrift des Instituts für Orthodoxe Theologie der Universität München.* St. Ottilien, Germany. |
| OssRomano | *Osservatore Romano.* Vatican. |
| OstKSt | *Ostkirchliche Studien.* Würzburg, Germany. |
| OT | Vatican II, *Optatam totius* (Decree on Priestly Formation—1965). |
| OxDCC | F.L. Cross and E.A. Livingstone, eds., *The Oxford Dictionary of the Christian Church.* Oxford: University Press, ²1983. |
| OxDPopes | J.N.D. Kelly, *The Oxford Dictionary of Popes.* New York—Oxford: University Press, 1988. |
| OxDSaints | D.H. Farmer, *The Oxford Dictionary of Saints.* New York—Oxford: University Press, ²1987. |
| Pacifica | *Pacifica. Australian Theological Studies.* Victoria, Australia. |
| Páginas | *Páginas.* Lima, Peru. |
| PatByzR | *Patristic and Byzantine Review.* Kingston, N.Y. |
| Patrology | J. Quasten, *Patrology.* 3 vols. Utrecht: Spectrum, 1950—Westminster, Md.: Christian Classics, 1986; A. de Bernardino, ed., *Patrology.* Vol. 4. Westminster, Md., 1986. |
| PC | Vatican II, *Perfectae caritatis* (Decree on the Appropriate Renewal of Religious Life—1965). |
| Periodica | *Periodica de re morali canonica liturgica.* Rome. |
| PG | Migne, *Patrologia graeca.* |
| Phase | *Phase.* Barcelona. |
| PL | Migne, *Patrologia latina.* |
| PLS | Migne, *Patrologia latina supplementum.* |
| PO | Vatican II, *Presbyterorum ordinis* (Decree on the Ministry and Life of Priests—1965). |
| PO series | Patrologia Orientalis series. Paris. |
| PraxJurRel | *Praxis juridique et religion.* Strasbourg, France. |
| PrincSemB | *Princeton Seminary Bulletin.* Princeton, N.J. |
| ProbHistChrist | *Problèmes d'histoire de cristianisme.* Brussels. |
| ProMunVit | *Pro mundi vita bulletin.* Brussels. |
| PrOrChr | *Proche-Orient Chrétien.* Jerusalem. |
| Proy | *Proyección. Teología y mondo actual.* Granada, Spain. |
| PrPeople | *Priests and People.* London. |
| QDisput | Questiones disputatae series. |
| QLtg | *Questions liturgiques—Studies in Liturgy.* Leuven, Belgium. |
| QuatreF | *Les quatre fleuves.* Paris. |
| RAC | *Reallexikon für Antike und Christentum.* Stuttgart: Hiersemann, 1950– . |
| RAfrT | *Revue africaine de théologie.* Kinshasa/Limete, Zaire. |
| Rahner, Foundations | K. Rahner, *Foundations of Christian Faith. An Introduction to the Idea of Christianity.* New York: Seabury—London: Darton, Longman & Todd, 1978. |
| Rahner, ThInvest | K. Rahner, *Theological Investigations.* 22 vols. Baltimore: Helicon—London: Darton, Longman & Todd, 1961–1991. |
| RAscétM | *Revue d'ascétique et mystique.* Paris. |
| RasT | *Rassegna di teologia.* Naples, Italy. |
| RazF | *Razón y fe.* Madrid. |

| | |
|---|---|
| RB | *Revue biblique.* Jerusalem—Paris. |
| RBén | *Revue bénédictine.* Maredsous, Belgium. |
| RClerIt | *Rivista del clero italiano.* Milan. |
| RDroitC | *Revue de droit canonique.* Strasbourg, France. |
| REB | *The Revised English Bible.* Oxford—Cambridge: University Press, 1989. |
| REBras | *Revista eclesiástica brasileira.* Petrópolis, Brazil. |
| RÉByz | *Revue des études byzantines.* Paris. |
| RechSR | *Recherches de science religieuse.* Paris. |
| RechTAncMéd | *Recherches de théologie ancienne et médiévale.* Louvain, Belgium. |
| RelLifeR | *Religious Life Review.* Dublin. |
| RelSt | *Religious Studies.* Cambridge, England. |
| RelStB | *Religious Studies Bulletin.* Sudbury, Ont., Canada |
| RelStT | *Religious Studies and Theology.* Edmonton, Canada. |
| Renovatio | *Renovatio.* Genoa, Italy. |
| REspDerCan | *Revista española de derecho canónico.* Salamanca. |
| RET | *Revista española de teologia.* Madrid. |
| RevÉtAug | *Revue des études augustiniennes.* Paris. |
| RevLitComp | *Revue de littérature comparée.* Paris. |
| RevRel | *Review for Religious.* Duluth, Minn. |
| RevSR | *Revue des sciences religieuses.* Strasbourg, France. |
| RExp | *Review and Expositor.* Louisville, Ky. |
| RHE | *Revue d'histoire ecclésiastique.* Leuven, Belgium. |
| RHPR | *Revue d'histoire et de philosophie religieuses.* Strasbourg, France. |
| RicBibRel | *Ricerche bibliche e religiose.* Milan. |
| Rites | *The Rites of the Catholic Church.* Study Edition. 2 vols. New York: Pueblo, 1980–1991. |
| RivBib | *Rivista biblica.* Bologna, Italy. |
| RivLtg | *Rivista liturgica.* Turin, Italy. |
| RivStorChItal | *Rivista di storia della chiesa in Italia.* Rome. |
| RivStorLettRel | *Rivista di storia e letteratura religiosa.* Florence, Italy. |
| RNAB | *Revised New Testament of the New American Bible.* Nashville: Catholic Bible Press/Nelson, 1987. |
| RömQ | *Römische Quartalschrift für christliche Altertumskunde und Kirchengeschichte.* Freiburg im Br., Germany. |
| Rouët de Journel | M.J. Rouët de Journel, *Enchiridion patristicum loci SS Patrum, doctorum sacriptorum ecclesiasticorum.* Barcelona—Friburg—Rome: Herder, [21]1959. |
| RRéf | *Revue réformée.* Aix-en-Provence, France. |
| RSPT | *Revue des sciences philosophiques et théologiques.* Paris. |
| RThom | *Revue thomiste.* Toulouse, France. |
| RTLim | *Rivista teológica limense.* Lima, Peru. |
| RTLv | *Revue théologique de Louvain.* Louvain, Belgium. |

| | |
|---|---|
| RTPhil | *Revue de théologie et de philosophie*. Epalinges, Switzerland. |
| RUnivOtt | *Revue de l'Université d'Ottawa*. Ottawa. |
| SacDoct | *Sacra doctrina*. Bologna, Italy. |
| Salaverri, Ecclesia | I. Salaverri, "De Ecclesia Christi" in *Sacrae theologiae summa*. 4 vols. BAC 61. Madrid: La Editorial Católica, ²1952. 1:497-953. |
| Sales | *Salesianum*. Rome. |
| Salm | *Salmanticensis*. Salamanca. |
| Sap | *Sapienza*. Naples, Italy. |
| SC | Vatican II, *Sacrosanctum concilium* (Constitution on the Sacred Liturgy—1963). |
| SC series | Sources Chrétiennes series. Paris: Cerf. |
| ScEsp | *Science et esprit*. Montreal. |
| Schaff, Creeds | P. and D.S. Schaff, eds., *The Creeds of Christendom*. 3 vols. Grand Rapids: Baker, 1990 reprint of 1931 ed. |
| Schol | *Scholastik*. Freiburg im Br., Germany. |
| ScotJT | *Scottish Journal of Theology*. Edinburgh. |
| ScR | *Sciences religieuses—Studies in religion*. Montreal, Canada. |
| ScripTPamp | *Scripta theologica*. Pamplona, Spain. |
| ScuolC | *La scuola cattolica*. Venegono Inferiore (VA) Italy. |
| SecC | *The Second Century. A Journal of Early Christian Studies*. Abilene, Tex. |
| Semeia | *Semeia. An Experimental Journal for Biblical Criticism*. Atlanta, Ga. |
| Seminarium | *Seminarium*. Rome. |
| SM | K. Rahner, C. Ernst and K. Smyth, eds*., Sacramentum Mundi. An Encyclopedia of Theology*. 6 vols. New York: Herder & Herder—London: Burns & Oates, 1968–1970. |
| Sobornost | *Sobornost*. London. |
| Speculum | *Speculum. A Journal of Medieval Studies*. Cambridge, Mass. |
| Spiritus | *Spiritus*. Paris. |
| SpToday | *Spirituality Today*. Chicago, Ill. |
| ST | St. Thomas Aquinas, *Summa theologiae*. |
| StFrances | *Studi francescani*. Florence, Italy. |
| ST series | Studi e testi series. Vatican. |
| StCan | *Studia canonica*. Ottawa. |
| StEcum | *Studi ecumenici*. Verona, Italy. |
| StimZ | *Stimmen der Zeit*. Freiburg im Br., Germany. |
| StLtg | *Studia liturgica. An International Ecumenical Quarterly for Liturgical Research and Renewal*. AB Grave, Netherlands. |
| StMiss | *Studia missionalia*. Rome. |
| StMor | *Studia Moralia*. Rome. |
| StPatav | *Studia patavina*. Padua, Italy. |
| StPatr | *Studia patristica*. Berlin. |
| StRel | *Studies in Religion—Sciences religieuses*. Waterloo, Ont., Canada. |
| StTheol | *Studia theologica. Scandanavian Journal of Theology*. Lund, Denmark. |

| | |
|---|---|
| Supp | *Le supplément*. Paris. |
| SuppDictBib | *Dictionnaire de la bible. Supplément*. Paris, 1928– . |
| SVlad | *St. Vladimir's Theological Quarterly*. Crestwood, N.Y. |
| SWJT | *South Western Journal of Theology*. Fort Worth, Tex. |
| Synaxis | *Synaxis. Annuale dell'Istituto per la documentazione e la ricerca S. Paolo*. Catania, Italy. |
| Tablet | *The Tablet*. London. |
| Tanner 1, 2. | N.P. Tanner, ed., *Decrees of the Ecumenical Councils*. 2 vols. London: Sheed & Ward—Georgetown: University Press, 1990. |
| TDig | *Theology Digest*. Duluth, Minn. |
| TDNT | G. Kittel et al., eds., *Theological Dictionary of the New Testament*. 10 vols. Grand Rapids: Eerdmans, 1964–1976. |
| Teresianum | *Teresianum*. Rome. |
| TGegw | *Theologie der Gegenwart*. Münster. |
| TGl | *Theologie und Glaube*. Paderborn. |
| Theologia | *Teologia*. Brescia—Milan. |
| Theology | *Theology*. London. |
| ThPh | *Theologie und Philosophie*. Freiburg im Br., Germany. |
| TJb | *Theologisches Jahrbuch*. Leipzig. |
| TLZ | *Theologische Literaturzeitung*. Berlin. |
| TorontoJT | *Toronto Journal of Theology*. Toronto. |
| TPQ | *Theologisch-praktische Quartalschrift*. Linz, Austria. |
| TQ | *Theologische Quartalschrift*. Tübingen, Germany. |
| Traditio | *Traditio*. New York. |
| TRE | *Theologische Realenzylopädie*. Berlin—New York, 1976– . |
| TrierTZ | *Trierer theologische Zeitschrift*. Trier, Germany. |
| TS | *Theological Studies*. Baltimore, Md. |
| TTod | *Theology Today*. Princeton, N.J. |
| TU | Texte und Untersuchungen series. Leipzig—Berlin. |
| TXav | *Theologica xaveriana*. Bogotá, Colombia. |
| TyndB | *Tyndale Bulletin*. Nottingham, England. |
| TZBas | *Theologische Zeitschrift*. Basel, Switzerland. |
| UnaSan | *Una sancta. Zeitschrift für ökumenische Begegnung*. Freising, Germany. |
| UnChrétiens | *Unité des chrétiens*. Paris. |
| UP | University Press (as publisher). |
| UR | Vatican II, *Unitatis redintegratio* (Decree on Ecumenism—1964). |
| US | Unam Sanctam series. Paris: Cerf. |
| VerkündForsch | *Verkündigung und Forschung*. Munich. |
| VerVida | *Verdad y vida*. Madrid. |
| VetChr | *Vetera christianorum*. Bari, Italy. |
| VieCons | *Vie consacrée*. Brussels. |

| | |
|---|---|
| VieSp | *La vie spirituelle*. Paris. |
| VigChr | *Vigiliae Christianae*. Leiden, Netherlands. |
| VitaCons | *Vita consecrata*. Milan. |
| VitaMonast | *Vita monastica*. Camaldoli, Italy. |
| Vorgrimler, Vatican II | H. Vorgrimler, ed., *Commentary on the Documents of Vatican II*. 5 vols. New York: Herder & Herder—London: Burns & Oates, 1967–1969. |
| VT | *Vetus testamentum*. Leiden, Netherlands. |
| VYoti | *Vidyajyoti. Journal of Theological Reflection*. Delhi, India. |
| Way | *The Way*. London. |
| WaySupp | *The Way. Supplement*. London |
| ZEvEthik | *Zeitschrift für evangelische Ethik*. Gütersloh, Germany. |
| ZKG | *Zeitschrift für Kirchengeschichte*. Stuttgart, Germany. |
| ZkT | *Zeitschrift für katholische Theologie*. Innsbruck, Austria. |
| ZMissRW | *Zeitschrift für Missionswissenschaft und Religionswissenschaft*. Münster, Germany. |
| ZNT | *Zeitschrift für Neutestamentliche Wissenschaft*. Berlin. |
| ZTK | *Zeitschrift für Theologie und Kirche*. Tübingen, Germany. |

# A

## ABEL, CHURCH FROM

Vatican II referred to the traditional theme "from the just Abel to the last of the elect" in a summary of the Father's plan (LG 2). It thus avoided a difficulty in an earlier draft that might appear to confuse the universal Church with the Catholic Church in a narrower sense.[1] The attention of the council members had earlier been drawn to the classic study by Y. Congar, *"Ecclesia ab Abel."*[2] The idea of the Church preexisting the Incarnation is present in some early Fathers,[3] especially in the context of the salvation of those who preceded Christ (v. CLEMENT, PSEUDO). Preexistence was also associated with the question first raised in the 2nd century by a pagan, Celsus, as to why the Savior came so late in history.[4] Again, the Church is seen in Hermas (q.v.) as an old woman: "Why then is she an old lady? Because, he (the angel) said, she was created the first of all things. For this reason is she old; and for her sake was the world established."[5]

It would seem to be Augustine who about 412 first used the expression "the Church from Abel" at the outset of the Pelagian controversy and when he was already thinking of his great work *City of God*.[6] He drew the conclusion that the just people in the OT were in a sense already Christians.[7] Apart from allusions to Augustine, the idea of the Church originating with Abel is not greatly in evidence in the patristic period,[8] though it was commonplace and comprehensively studied in the Middle Ages.[9] At that time, it was treated alongside theses on Christ as the sole mediator and as head of the Church and on the unicity of (partial) OT and (full) NT faith.[10] With the coming of treatises on the Church, interest shifted from a primarily spiritual view of the Church—in which the Abel theme had an important role—to a more institutional one, especially in later Counter-Reformation controversies. It was probably to counter an excessively institutional emphasis which was dominant after Pius XII's *Mystici corporis* (q.v. and v. MEMBERSHIP) that Congar revived the ancient theme of the Church from Abel.[11]

As used in Vatican II (LG 2), the theme of the Church from Abel is eschatological: it is only at the end that the Church will consist of all, and only, the just. It is the emphasis on the just, even before Christ, that led the Fathers to speak of Abel rather than Adam. The story of Abel (Gen 4:1-16, 25) also shows the ecclesiological motif of God triumphing through weakness and death.[12]

[1]ActaSyn 3/1:172—Alberigo-Magistretti 437. [2]M. Reding, H. Elfers, and F. Hofmann, eds., *Abhandlungen über Theologie und Kirche*, FS K. Adam (Dusseldorf: Patmos, 1952) 79–108 = Y. Congar, *Études d'ecclésiologie médiévale* (London: Variorum Reprints, 1983) 79–108; cf. Alberigo-Magistretti 8. [3]E.g., Nicetas of Remesiana, *De Symbolo* 10:1, in A.E. Burn, *Niceta of Remesiana. His Life and Works* (Cambridge, 1905) 48. [4]Congar (n. 2) 79–81; cf. A. Stötzel, "Warum Christus so spät erschein—die apologetische Argumentation des frühen Christums," ZKG 92 (1981) 147–160. [5]*Vis.* 2:4, 1—SC 53:96. [6]Congar (n. 2) 84–85; see *Serm.* 341:9, 10—PL 39:1449-1450; *Enar.in ps.* 90:2, 1—PL 37:1509; 142:3—PL 37:1846; *Civ.Dei.* 18:51—PL 41:614. Cf. P. Bogomeo, *L'Église de ce temps dans la prédication de saint Augustin* (Paris: Études Augustiniennes, 1972) 30–32. [7]*De bapt.* 1:15, 24—PL 43:122; see other texts in Congar (n. 2) n. 52. [8]Congar (n. 2) 87; see however Gregory the Great, *Hom. in Ev.* 1:19, 1—PL 76:1154/Halton 36; *Moralia* 3:22—PL 75:616; R. Bélenger, *"Ecclesia ab exordio mundi:* modèles et degrés d'appartenance à l'Église chez Grégoire le Grand," StRel 16 (1987) 265–273. [9] Congar, Moyen-âge, 68–69 and n. 43. [10]Congar (n. 2) 88–93. [11]Ibid., 96–99. [12]L. Vischer, "Ecclesia ab Abel," IKiZ 72 (1982) 86–91

## ACOLYTE

The second of the two restored ministries is acolyte (Greek *akolouthos*—attendant), the first being reader (q.v.). Both first appear in the Roman Church about 250 C.E. A letter from Cornelius, bishop of Rome (d. 253), indicated that there were forty-six presbyters, seven deacons, forty-two acolytes and fifty-two of other lower ministers.[1] The office of acolyte was known in North Africa in the time of Cyprian (q.v.), but not in the East. In time it became a minor order mostly associated with liturgical service. From the medieval period up to Vatican II, the tasks of acolytes were also shared by subdeacons (q.v.) and later by lay youths (altar servers). The ministry of acolyte became merely one of the steps, or minor orders, leading to priesthood.

In the post-Vatican II renewal of liturgy, Paul VI retained acolyte as a ministry in the mp. *Ministeria quaedam* (v. MINISTRY);[2] it is no longer called an "order." The functions of the acolyte are liturgical and include: aiding the deacon and being minister to the priest; serving at the altar; being extraordinary minister of the Eucharist; instructing other faithful about how to assist at liturgical functions. Paul VI insisted on cultivating a spirituality in keeping with being an acolyte. The ministry of acolyte may be conferred as a stable one on those who have no intention of progressing to sacred orders; but the *Code of Canon Law* restricts this to men (*viri laici*—CIC 230 § 1)

---

[1]Eusebius, *Hist. eccl.* 6:43.  [2]AAS 64 (1972) 529–534/Eng. trans. *The Rites of the Catholic Church,* 2 vols. (Collegeville: The Liturgical Press, study edition, 1988–1991) 2:6-11.

## ADAM, Karl (1876–1966)

The Tübingen professor K. Adam was born in Bavaria in 1876. He is one of the principal authors in the 20th-century renewal of ecclesiology.[1] His most important work on the Church was *The Spirit of Catholicism,*[2] which narrowly escaped being placed on the Index (q.v.) about 1930, due probably to his insistence on the weaknesses of the Church and on the need for renewal. He was indeed quite realistic about the mediocrity that can infect the Church's institutions and members: "As long as Catholicism lasts, it will feel the need for reform, for a more perfect assimilation of its actuality to the ideal. . . . Eminent popes, bishops of great spiritual force, theologians of genius, priests of extraordinary graces and devout layfolk: these must be, not the rule, but the exception. God raises them up only at special times, when he needs them for his Church. . . . The Church has from God the guarantee that she will not fall into error regarding faith and morals; but she has no guarantee whatever that every act and decision of ecclesiastical authority will be excellent and perfect. Mediocrity and even defects are possible."[3] The center of his ecclesiology was the Body (q.v.) of Christ: the Church is not a group of individuals but a transpersonal unity of those who belong to the true Israel, to

the sacrament of the efficacious presence of the mysteries of Christ. The Church is furthermore central to his vision of God's revelation: "The structure of Catholic faith may be summarized in a single sentence: I come to a living faith in the Triune God through Christ in the Church. I experience the action of the living God through Christ realizing Himself in His Church. So we see that the certitude of Catholic faith rests on the sacred triad: God, Christ, Church."[4] His ecumenical writing insisted that each Church take its own Confession seriously, and in the end it is only through unity with Christ that we have a foundation for unity between the Churches.[5]

---

[1]J. Laubach, "Karl Adam," in L. Reinish, ed., *Theologians of Our Time* (Notre Dame, 1964); A. Auer, "Karl Adam: 1876–1966," TQ 150 (130–143); R.A.Kreig, *Karl Adam: Catholicism in German Culture* (Notre Dame: UP, 1992); T.J. Skrabak-Edwards, *Karl Adam and the Defense of Catholicism.* Diss. (Washington, D.C.: The Catholic University of America, 1989); J. Steltzenberger, "Bibliographie Karl Adam," TQ 138 (1958) 330-347.  [2]*Das Wesen des Katholizismus* (1924), Eng. trans. (London: Sheed & Ward, 1929).  [3]Ibid. (ch. 13) 243, 249. Cf. on the self-emptying of the Church, "Le mystère de l'Incarnation du Christ et de son Corps mystique," Études 75/237 (1938) 26–48.  [4]Ibid. (n. 2, ch. 4) 51.  [5]*One and Holy* (New York, 1951) ch. 3.

## ADIAPHORA

The word *adiaphora* (Greek "indifferent things") is used mainly by Lutheran theologians from the 16th century to the present to designate laws or structures which are reversible or free, as opposed to those which are mandatory through divine law (*ius divinum*—q.v.). Apart from its historical importance, it has much relevance in clarifying issues in ecumenical dialogue.[1]

---

[1]A.C. Piepkorn, "*Ius Divinum* and *Adiaphoron* in Relation to Structural Problems in the Church: the Position of the Lutheran Symbolical Books," in P.C. Empie and T.A. Murphy, *Papal Primacy and the Universal Church.* Lutherans and Roman Catholics in Dialogue 5 (Minneapolis, Minn.: Augsburg, 1974) 119–126; H. Jedin in Jedin-Dolan 5:350-351; "Adiaphorists," OxDDC 17.

## AETERNI PATRIS

Two major Church documents carry as initial words and hence title, *Aeterni Patris.* The first was Pius IX's letter of convocation of Vatican I of June 1868.[1] It dealt with the role of the pope as protector of faith and morals and with the errors of the time.

The second was the encyclical of Leo XIII (Aug. 1879) aimed at restoring scholastic philosophy, and especially that of St. Thomas (q.v.).[2] Thomism was not dead in the late 19th century; indeed one can say that Leo was giving official approbation to an already existing movement.[3] The encyclical has four main parts: the importance of philosophy in giving the rational presuppositions for revelation and in giving theology an organic and scientific character; philosophy not opposed to divine revelation, but reason retaining its autonomy and dignity; history showing philosophy at the service of the faith; the philosophy of St. Thomas as antidote to current errors and as fostering cultural advancement. The centenary of the encyclical saw the production of numerous studies.[4]

The choice of St. Thomas as the outstanding teacher for the Church was reiterated in the 1917 *Code of Canon Law* (589 § 1). Vatican II was the first council ever to recommend globally a particular theologian: ". . . students for the priesthood should learn more deeply, with the help of speculation and with St. Thomas as teacher, all aspects of these mysteries" (OT 16). The new *Code* states that St. Thomas is especially *(praesertim)* the teacher in theological training (can. 252 § 3). These recent statements point to the fact stated by Benedict XV: ". . . the Church has made the doctrine of St. Thomas particularly its own,"[5] a sentiment reiterated by Paul VI.[6]

---

[1]*Acta Pii IX*, 4:412-423.  [2]*Acta Leonis XIII*, 1 (1878–1879) 255–285/Carlen 3:17-26, with extracts DS 3135–3140.  [3]D. Composta, "L'enciclica 'Aeterni Patris' di Leone XIII e il suo significato storico," EuntDoc 33 (1980) 299–328; B.M. Bonasea, "Pioneers of the Nineteenth Century Scholastic Revival in Italy," NewSchol 28 (1954) 1–37; O. Köhler in Jedin-Dolan 9:307-311.  [4]*Atti del VIII Congresso Tomistico Internazionale*, 3 vols. Studi tomistici 10–12 (Vatican, 1981); J. Alexander, "Aeterni Patris 1879–1979: A Bibliography of American Responses," Thom 43 (1979) 480–481; A. Bandera, "Centenario de la encíclica 'Aeterni Patris' de León XIII," CiTom 108 (1981) 575–583; G. Bortolaso, "Il significato dell'enciclica *Aeterni Patris*," DoctCom 33 (1980) 271–276; T. McGuckin, "A Century of 'Pontifical' Thomism," NewBlackfr 72 (1991) 377–384; G. Perini, "'Aeterni Patris' (1879–1979)," DivThom 82 (1979) 3–18.  [5]Encyclical *Fausto appetente die*, AAS 13 (1921) 332/Carlen 3:218.  [6]Epist. *Lumen ecclesiae* to Master General of Dominicans, AAS 66 (1974) 673–702; R. Spiazza, "La lettera del Papa Paolo VI nel settimo centenario della morte di San Tommaso d'Aquino," Divinitas 19 (1975) 5–15; idem, "La scelta di San Tommaso da parte della Chiesa," DocCom 34 (1981) 3–10; G. Perini, "'Dall' *Aeterni Patris* al Concilio Vaticano II: Le directive del Magistero sulla dottrina di San Tommaso," ScripTPamp 11 (1979) 619–658.

## AFANAS'EV, Nicolas (1893–1966)

The influence of Nicolas Afanas'ev (Afanassieff) in ecclesiology continues to grow. After studying science in Russia, he turned to theology, became a priest, and in 1930 a professor at the Orthodox Institute of St. Sergius founded by Russian émigrés in Paris in 1925.[1] Though his specializations were canon law,[2] Church history, and, above all, patristics,[3] his abiding place in the history of theology will be for his idea of "Eucharistic ecclesiology" (v. EUCHARIST). Rejecting a universalist ecclesiology which he claimed was derived from Cyrian (q.v.), he drew out the implications of NT texts on the local church (q.v.) and of the remark of Ignatius

of Antioch (q.v.): ". . . where Jesus Christ is, there is the catholic Church."[4] Thus he states: "Where there is a Eucharistic assembly, there is the Church. The Church cannot exist without Eucharistic assembly; and the Eucharistic assembly cannot but manifest the plenitude and the unity of the Church. Hence the structure and the order of the Church come from the Eucharistic assembly, which contains the whole basis of ecclesial organization."[5] The Church was instituted at the Last Supper, but actualized at Pentecost.[6] Though Afanas'ev strongly emphasized the role and ministry of the one who presides at the Eucharist,[7] he did not accept any other power or exercise of authority over the Eucharistic community. His insistence on love as the only bond between communities involves a rejection of a full notion of hierarchy,[8] a point for which he has been criticized by both Orthodox and Catholic writers.[9]

Though the Eucharistic ecclesiology of Afanas'ev is incomplete, its central intuitions, along with its profound pneumatology and insistence on charism, can hardly be ignored in any ecclesiology that would seek to be fully authentic.[10]

---

[1]A. Nichols, *Theology in the Russian Diaspora: Church, Fathers, Eucharist in Nikolai Afanas'ev (1893–1966)*—(Cambridge: UP, 1989).  [2]A. Nichols, "Nikolai Afanas'ev and the Byzantine Canonical Tradition," HeythJ 33 (1992) 415–425.  [3]A. Nichols, "The Appeal to the Fathers in the Ecclesiology of Nikolai Afanas'ev," HeythJ 33 (1992) 125–145, 247–266.  [4]*Ad Symryn.* 8:2.  [5]*L'Église du Saint-Esprit*, Cogitatio fidei 83 (Paris: Cerf, 1975) 196.  [6]Ibid., 246.  [7]"The Ministry of the Laity in the Church," EcuR 10 (1957–1958) 255–263; see N. Koulomzine, "Les rôles liturgiques dans l'assemblée de l'Église primitive selon le père Nicolas Afanassieff," in AA.VV. *L'assemblée liturgique et les différents rôles dans l'assemblée*, Conferences Saint Serge 23, Bibliotheca *Ephemerides liturgicae* 9 (Rome: Ed. Liturgiche, 1977) 209–224.  [8]"La doctrine de la primauté à la lumière de l'ecclésiologie," Istina 4 (1957) 401–420; "Le concile dans la théologie russe," Irén 35 (1962) 316–339; "Una sancta: En mémoire de Jean XXIII, le pape de l'amour," Irén 36 (1963) 436–475; "The Church that Presides in Love," in J. Meyendorff et al., eds., *The Primacy of Peter* (London: Faith Press, 1963) 57–110 = N. Afanassieff et al., *La primauté de Pierre dans l'Église orthodoxe*, Bibliothèque orthodoxe (Neuchâtel: Delachaux & Niestlé, 1960) 9–64.  [9]J.D. Zizioulas, *L'être ecclésiale*. Perspective orthodoxe 3 (Geneva: Labor et Fides, 1981) 18–21; L. Bouyer, review of L'Église (n. 5), Istina 22 (1977) 97–101; B. Mondin, *Le nuove ecclesiologie*, Teologia 29 (Rome: Ed. Paoline, 1980) 238–248.  [10]P. Plank, *Die Eucharistieversammlung als Kirche. Zur Entstehung und Entfaltung der eucharistischen Ekklesiologie Nikolaj Afanas'evs (1893–1966)*. Das östliche Christentum N.F. 31 (Würzburg: Augustinus Verlag, 1980) with review art. A. Gerhards, "Die Eucharistieversammlung als Kirche," LitJb 31 (1981) 186–192; P. McParlan, "Eucharistic Ecclesiology," OneChr 22 (1986) 314–331; idem, *The Eucharist Makes the Church: Henri de Lubac and John Zizioulas in Dialogue* (Edinburgh: Clark, 1993) 226–235.

## AGAPÊ

The Greek word *agapê* refers in the NT to the love which comes from God and which must be shared by

Christians in a brotherly and sisterly way.[1] One way of showing this love was a common meal, attested in 1 Cor 11:17-34 as preceding the Eucharist. There was also the Eucharist with a meal in the community of the *Didachê* (9–10). Ignatius of Antioch (q.v.) refers to love-feasts, but apparently in a sacramental context and requiring the presence of the bishop.[2] But here and in other early texts it is not easy to know if the reference is to the Eucharist, to a meal preceding the Eucharist, or during which the Eucharist is celebrated, or to a meal quite distinct from the Eucharist.[3]

In the *Apostolic Tradition* (q.v.), there are three meals that have *agapê* characteristics. There is a meal presided over by the bishop, who blesses bread and wine and who also instructs and answers questions. Both silence and praise are characteristics of this meal. Food is sent afterwards to the poor and the sick. This is not the Eucharist (26–29/26:1-17). There is also a solemn evening meal with the lighting of the lamp by the deacon. The bishop must be present. Psalms are recited. This meal may well combine with a Eucharist (25/26:18-32). Third, there is a meal provided for widows, at which the presence of the bishop is not envisaged (27/30).

From the time of Cyprian (q.v.), if not earlier, the Eucharist was celebrated in the morning, with a common meal sometimes taking place in the evening. From the 4th century it was gradually replaced by other forms of charity.

---

[1]E. Staffer, "Agapê," TDNT 1:21-55; C. Spicq, *Agape in the New Testament*, 2 vols. (St. Louis: Herder, 1963–1965).  [2]Ad Smyrn. 8.  [3]J.M. Hanssens, "L'agape et l'eucharistie," EphLtg 41 (1927) 525–548; 42 (1928) 545–574; 43 (1929) 177–198, 520–529; G. Dix, *The Shape of the Liturgy* (Westminster, Md., 1945) 82–102.

## ALBERIGO, Giuseppe (1926– )

Since 1967 Giuseppe Alberigo has been professor of Church history at Bologna, and, from 1962, director of the research group, Istituto per le Scienze Religiose. He has been responsible for a number of very important works on Trent (he would seem to have coined "Tridentinism"),[1] on Vatican II (q.v.),[2] on John XXIII (q.v.),[3] on reception (q.v.),[4] and on conciliar texts.[5] In the 1970s he opposed the idea of a Fundamental Law (v. LAW) for the Church.[6] In 1980 he founded the journal *Cristianesimo nella storia*. His *Synopsis historica* (with F. Magistretti), which gives in parallel columns the evolution of *Lumen gentium*[7] and related documentation, is a most valuable tool for scientific work on the Constitution, as are the linguistic indices[8] of the documents of Vatican II which he sponsored.

---

[1]"L'ecclesiologia del Concilio di Trento," RivStorChItal 18 (1964) 227–242; *La riforma protestante* (Milan:Garzanti, 1959); "Du Concile de Trente au tridentinisme," Irén 54 (1981) 192–200.  [2]*Il Vaticano II e la Chiesa*, ed., with J.P. Jossua (Brescia: Paideia,

1985).  [3]*Giovanni XXIII Profezia nella fedeltà* (Brescia: Queriniana, 1978); *Fede Tradizione Profezia: Richerche su Giovanni XXIII e sul Vaticano II* (Brescia: Paideia, 1984); ed. *Giovanni XXIII transizione del papato e della chiesa* (Rome: Borla, 1988).  [4]Ed. with J.P. Jossua and J.A. Komonchak, *The Reception of Vatican II* (Washington, D.C.: The Catholic University of America Press, 1987).  [5]*Conciliorum oecumenicorum decreta* (Bologna: Istituto per le Scienze Religiose, [3]1973) = Eng. trans. Tanner, 2 vols.  [6]E.g., "Notes sur un nouveau projet de loi fundamentale de l'Église," RSPT 62 (1978) 505–522.  [7]*Constitutionis dogmaticae Lumen Gentium synopsis historica* (Bologna: Istituto per le Scienze Religiose, 1975).  [8]*Indices verborum et locutionum decretorum Concilii Vaticani II*, 9 vols. (Florence, 1968—Bologna, 1984).

## ALBIGENSES

A closely-knit group of Cathari (q.v.) was found at Albi, from which the French Cathari were named "Albigenses."[1] In its pure form their doctrine was strongly dualistic, not unlike Manichees: from two eternal principles of good and evil, spirit and matter were respectively formed. The soul must therefore be released from its imprisonment. They rejected the Incarnation, the Church and many of its doctrines and sacramental practices.

There were two groups within the sect. The strict observers, who had received the *consolamentum* ("consolation"—a spirit baptism), were strict vegetarians, and abstained from marriage. These were called the "Perfect." The second group, called "Believers," lived a more ordinary life, some even remaining in the Catholic Church; they hoped to receive the *consolamentum* in old age or on their deathbeds. The Albigenses spread widely in France and in the North of Spain and Italy. They were much admired by the people because the austerity of their lives was in direct contrast to an often dissolute clergy.

Innocent III (q.v.) sought to convert them, but with little success. There was a crusade (q.v.) against them ca. 1208–1218. They were condemned by local councils, by Lateran III (q.v.),[2] and implicitly by Lateran IV (q.v.), which reiterated a crusade against them and other heretics, with an indulgence attached equivalent to two years service in the Holy Land.[3]

The Dominican Inquisition (q.v.) was charged in 1223 with ending the heresy, which eventually disappeared by the end of the following century. Its dualistic and rigorist characteristics reappear in various guises throughout the centuries.

---

[1]H. Wolter, in Jedin-Dolan 4:98-102, 159-166; D. Christie-Murray, *A History of Heresy* (Oxford—New York: Oxford UP, 1989) 104–108; OxDCC 31.  [2]Tanner 1:224.  [3]Tanner 1:230-231, 233-235/DS 800–802.

## ALUMBRADOS

The Alumbrados or Illuminati appeared in Spain about 1511 grouped around Isabel de la Cruz and her follower

Pedro Ruiz Alcaraz, who was to become its leader. As with much of this rather shadowy movement, it is not easy to be precise about its origins, though it is customary to point to Islamic and Jewish mysticism, the Rhineland mystics, and Erasmian ideas as its roots. A fundamental insight was that of the interior illumination of the believer by the Holy Spirit, especially in the reading of Scripture (see texts like 1 Cor 2:10-16; Matt 11:25-26) and in mental and contemplative prayer. The Alumbrados showed little interest in ascetical practices or in sacramental life apart from the Eucharist. But it is difficult to be accurate about their stand, as we have to rely excessively on hostile evidence in processes. They were quickly seen as a threat to the institutional Church and were condemned by the Inquisition (q.v.) in 1525. There is general scholarly agreement that there was false mysticism and quietism in their spirituality.[1]

Recently there have been attempts to deny any mysticism properly so-called in the early Alumbrados, and to interpret their positions in terms of the Lutheran doctrines of justification and works.[2] Their undoubted downplaying of works and of obedience to ecclesiastical authority may well be, however, a consequence of quietism rather than of positions shared with Luther. The element of quietism would certainly lead later Alumbrados to draw degenerate conclusions about moral behavior. Later in the 16th century, Alumbrados would again appear in Spain as well as in France, but by 1630 it had virtually ceased to exist as a movement. The numbers involved were never very large—only 115 were processed by the Inquisition.[3] But it would be a major threat in 16th-century Spain.[4] Accusations of Illuminism were made against all the major Spanish mystics, and it remains constantly a charge easy to make and difficult to sustain as subsequent history clearly shows. It is, too, an instance of the tension that exists between spiritual movements and the institutional Church, with the constant danger that the former may slide into unorthodox doctrines and practices.

[1]M. Bataillon, *Erasme et l'Espagne: Recherches sur l'histoire spirituelle du XVIe siècle* (Paris, 1937); Bremond 8:196-227; T.K. Connolly, "Alumbrados (Illuminati)," NCE 1:356; Eulogio de la Virgen del Carmen, "Illuminisme," DSpir 7:1382–1385; B. Llorca, "Los alumbrados españoles en los siglos XVI y XVII," RazF 34 (1934) 323–342, 467–485; A Márquez, *Los Alumbrados: orígenes y filosofía (1529–1559)* (Madrid: Taurus, 1972); P. Réginald-Omez, "Illuminés," Catholicisme 5:1221-1225. [2]Cf. J.-C. Nieto, "L'hérésie des Alumbrados," RSPR 66 (1986) 403–418; idem, "The Heretical Alumbrados dexados: Isabel de la Cruz and Pedro Ruiz de Alcarez," RevLitComp 52 (1978) 293–313; idem, *Juan de Valdés and the Origins of the Spanish and Italian Reformation* (Geneva: Droz, 1979). [3]Llorca (n. 1) 484. [4]Bremond (n. 1).

## AMBROSE, St. (ca. 339–397)

Elected bishop of Milan while still only a catechumen in 373, Ambrose pursued the study of Scripture and theology, notably the Greek Fathers, so successfully, that he became one of the four great doctors (q.v.) of the Western Church. The writings of Ambrose are generally works occasioned by events, in particular the Arian controversy and pastoral issues.[1] They are mainly sermons or derived from homilies.[2] His ecclesiology developed throughout his episcopacy.[3] Most of the major patristic themes and images of the Church continually reappear in his works: the moon, the sea, mystical vine, mystical flock, boat, people of God (q.v.), the reign of Christ, temple (q.v.), body (q.v.) and spouse (q.v.) of Christ, OT and NT women as figures of the Church, the Virgin Mary as image and model.[4] His Marian reflections largely arose out of his constant preoccupation with the Church and his consideration of virginity.[5] Of special importance is the subtle, fluid, and fluctuating notion of the heavenly Jerusalem (q.v.) already found in Origen (q.v.) and Didymus the Blind. In Ambrose it has greater breadth than in St. Augustine, who followed him.[6] In his attitude toward heretics (q.v.) and Jews (q.v.),[7] Ambrose reflects the views of his times.

Ambrose's relations with the Empire are a very significant aspect of his ecclesiology:[8] he delineated very carefully the areas of Church and Empire; he presumed that the emperor would use his power at the service of the Church when needed; the emperor was within, not above, the Church, and he could be excommunicated for wrongdoing. In this matter Ambrose is indispensable for any understanding of the later Middle Ages.

In what has been called a veritable treatise on the election of bishops, his writing to the Church of Vercelli reaffirms ascetical practices against neo-Epicurianism, recalls the Church there to discipline and virtue, and within this context speaks of the qualities needed for a bishop.[9] In this letter and frequently elsewhere, he speaks about virgins (q.v.) and widows (q.v.); here also, but more developed in his *De officiis*,[10] we find his concern for the behavior of the clergy. He was also responsible for the development of the cult of the martyrs (q.v.).[11] Ambrose has an important place in ecclesiology; in Church history he is notable for being very instrumental in the conversion of Augustine (q.v.).

[1]Life, see M.G. Mara, Patrology 4:144-180; M.R.P. McGuire, "Ambrose, St.," NCE 1:372-375; A. Paredi, *Saint Ambrose: His Life and Times* (Notre Dame: UP, 1964). Studies: see P.E. Beatrice et al., *Cento anni di bibliografia ambrosiana (1874–1974)*. Studia patristica mediolensia 11 (Milan: Vita e Pensiero, 1981); G. Piccolo, "Saggio di bibliografia ambrosiana," ScuolC 98 (1970) 187–207; G. Lazzati, ed., *Ambrosius episcopus*. Atti del congresso internazionale 1974—Studia patristica mediolanensia 6–7, 2 vols. (Milan: Vita e Pensiero, 1976). [2]PL 14–17, with many trans. and some critical texts; see Mara (n. 1). [3]G. Toscani, *Teologia della chiesa in Sant Ambrogio*. Studia patristica mediolanensia (Milan:Vita e Pensiero, 1974), with critique of E. Lamirande EglT 8 (1977) 337–368; J. Rinna, *Die Kirche als Corpus*

*Christi Mysticum beim hl. Ambrosius* (Rome, 1940); C. Morino, *Church and State in the Teaching of St. Ambrose* (Washington, D.C. 1969); J.J. Marcellic, *Ecclesia sponsa apud s. Ambrosium* (Rome, 1967). [4]Toscani (n. 3) 149–207; H. Rahner, *Symbole der Kirche. Die Ekklesiologie der Väter* (Salzburg: Mühler, 1964) Index s.v. Ambrosius. [5]See O'Carroll, Theotokos 17–22. [6]E. Lamirande, "Le thème de la Jérusalem céleste chez saint Ambroise," RevÉtAug 29 (1983) 219–232; a key text is *Expos. evang. sec. Lucam* 2:88-89—PL 15:1585-1586/SC 52:43. [7]E.g., *Epist.* 40 and 41—PL 16:1101-1121/FC 26:6-19, 385-397; G. Figueroa, *The Church and the Synagogue in Saint Ambrose:* The Catholic University of America Studies in Sacred Theology, 2nd series 25 (Washington, D.C., 1949). [8]See *Epist.* to emperors: nn. 1, 17–18, 21, 24, 40, 51, 53, 57, 61–62 and *De obitu Theodosii oratio*—PL 16:1385-1410; summary of events Mara (n. 1) 145–150; J. Gaudemet, "Droit seculier et droit de l'Église chez saint Ambroise" in *Ambrosius episcopus* (n. 1) 1:286-315; V.R. Vasey, "The Example of Naboth in St. Ambrose's Doctrine on Imperium-Sacerdotium," Jurist 44 (1984) 426–440. [9]*Epist.* 63—PL 16:1188-1220/FC 26:321-363. [10]PL 16:25-194/LNPF (2nd series) 10:1-89/M. Testard, trans. and ed., *Les devoirs,* vol. 1 (Paris: Ed. Les Belles Lettres, 1984). [11]A. Bastiaesen, "Paulin de Milan et le culte des martyrs chez saint Ambroise," in *Ambrosius episcopus* (n. 1) 2:143-150.

## AMERICANISM

See LEO XIII

## ANABAPTISTS

Anabaptists (from Greek "to baptize again") were a radical wing of the Reformation. Belonging for the most part to the lower social classes, they were far from being a homogeneous group, as they were found with differing theological positions in several countries. Common to all was a biblical literalism, originally derived from the early Zwingli (q.v.).[1] He, however, opposed their rejection of the value or validity of infant baptism, which was quickly to become their distinguishing mark. But unlike the Donatists, they did not see themselves as rebaptizing, and so they usually called themselves "Christian Brethren." They soon repudiated other doctrines which were not perceived as scriptural, especially ones concerned with Church order.[2] Christological errors were also found, for instance in the Anabaptist lay preacher Melchior Hoffman (d. ca. 1543);[3] he held some millennial views too. His influential views continued in the "Melchiorite" wing of the Anabaptists which survived him.

One of the most influential of the Anabaptists and a main leader in the Peasant War was Thomas Münzer/Müntzer (ca. 1490–1525).[4] The centenary of his birth gave rise to some significant studies.[5] Some main groups of 16th-century Anabaptists survived.[6] The Hutterites who sought refuge in Moravia under the leadership of Jacob Hutter (d. 1536) practiced common ownership, and continue still in the U.S. The Mennonites (from Menno Simons d. 1561) had their earlier origins in Holland and later, too, crossed the Atlantic.[7] The Confession of Schleitheim (1527),[8]

drawn up by the ex-Benedictine monk Michael Sattler, as well as the Mennonite Dordrecht Confession (1623) can be said to be representative of the theology of both groups:[9] an insistence on adult baptism; the "ban" or strict discipline of the community; separation from non-members; the triple refusal of oaths, of the bearing of arms, and of involvement in political life. A more radical rejection of Church organization was found in the followers of Casper Schwenckfeld (d. 1561),[10] who held a belief in an invisible church which might include all who were faithful to the "Inner Word of the Spirit," not dissimilar to the "Inner Light" earlier taught by T. Münzer. In time the Society of Friends (Quakers—q.v.) would incorporate some of the views of the Schwenckfelder Church.

At the time of the Reformation, the Anabaptists were bitterly persecuted by both Catholics and mainstream Reformers. The polemics of the time harshly judged their doctrinal positions as well as some unfortunate deviations, including polygamy, during the siege of Münster (1533–1535). It is only in the present century, particularly through their own Mennonite writers, that the depth and importance of their theology of martyrdom, patient suffering, and pacifism[11] has begun to be appreciated, as also their insistence on the community dimension of ecclesiology with an emphasis on sharing wealth.[12] Significant, too, is the search for a Christian attitude to politics in a pluralist society,[13] especially by the influential Sojourners community in Washington, D.C., and in Latin America.[14]

The Mennonites meet internationally as the Mennonite World Conference, whose 12th Assembly was in Winnipeg (1990). Formal ecumenical conversations with the World Alliance of Reformed Churches began in 1984[15] and with the Baptist World Alliance in 1989. Some of the national conferences of Mennonites are members of the WCC, and several are engaged in ecumenical discussions at local levels.

[1]J.D. Weaver, *Becoming Anabaptist: The Origin and Significance of Sixteenth Century Anabaptism* (Scottdale, Penn.: Herald Press, 1987); F. Ferrario, "L'anabattismo delle origini e il problema ermeneutico," RasT 29 (1988) 382–400; E. Iserloh in Jedin-Dolan 5:178-189. [2]G.H. Williams and A.M. Mergal, eds., *Spiritual and Anabaptist Writers,* LCC 25 (London: SCM—Philadelphia: Westminster, 1957). M. Lienhard, ed., *Les débuts et caractéristiques de l'Anabaptisme: Actes du colloque Strasbourg 1875* (The Hague: Nijhoff, 1977). [3]K. Deppermann, *Melchior Hoffman: Social Unrest and Apocalyptic Visions of the Age of Reformation* (Edinburgh: Clark, 1987). [4]*Collected Works,* P. Matheson, ed. (Edinburgh: Clark, 1988); T. Scott, "From Polemics to Sobriety: Thomas Müntzer in Recent Research," JEH 39 (1988) 557–572. [5]S. Bräuer and H. Junghams, eds., *Der Theologe Thomas Müntzer: Untersuchungen zu seiner Entwicklung und Lehre* (Göttingen: Vandenhoeck & Ruprecht, 1989); H.G. Goertz, *Thomas Müntzer. Mystiker, Apokalyptker, Revolutionär* (Munich: Beck, 1989); E.W. Gritsch, *Thomas Müntzer: A Tragedy of Errors* (Minneapolis: Fortress, 1989); B. Lohse, *Thomas Müntzer in neuer Sicht* (Göttingen: Vandenhoeck & Ruprecht, 1991); P. Matheson,

"Christianity as Insurrection," ScotJT 44 (1991) 311–324; T. Scott, *Thomas Müntzer. Theology and Revolution in the German Refor-mation* (Basingstoke UK: Macmillan, 1992); G. Vogler, *Thomas Müntzer. Schriftenreihe Geschichte* (Berlin: Dietz, 1989).  [6]G.W. Forell, "Anabaptists," NCE 1:459-460; "Anabaptists," OxDCC 47–48. [7]*The Mennonite Encyclopedia*, 4 vols. (Scottdale, Penn.: Mennonite Publ., 1955–1960); C.H. Smith—revised C. Krahn, *The Story of the Mennonites* (Newton, Kans., ⁴1957); J.C. Wenger, *The Mennonite Church in America* (Scottdale, Penn: Herald Press, 1966).  [8]Text in L. von Muralt and W. Schmidt, *Quellen für Geschichte der Täufer in der Schweiz* (Zürich, 1952) 2:26-36; Eng. trans. Leith, Creeds 282–292.  [9]A.C. Snyder, *The Life and Thought of Michael Sattler* (Scottdale, Penn.: Mennonite Publ., 1984). For Dordrecht Confession see Leith, Creeds 292–308.  [10]R. Emmet McLoughlin, *Casper Schwenckfeld: Reluctant Radical* (Yale: UP, 1986).  [11]Cf. J.A. Mihevc, *The Politicization of the Mennonite Peace Witness in the Twentieth Century.* Diss. (Toronto: St. Michael, 1988).  [12]L. Millar, "Mennonite World Conference" and "Mennonites," DictEcumMov 668–669; J. Séguy, "Un cas d'institutionalisation du croire: Les Assemblées anabaptistes-mennonites de France," ReschSR 77 (1989) 165–196.  [13]D.W. Brown, "Communal Ecclesiology: The Power of the Anabaptist Vision," TTod 36 (1979–1980) 22–29; J.R. Burkholder and C. Redekop, eds., *Kingdom, Cross and Community* (Scottdale, Penn.: Herald Press, 1976); R. Friedmann, *The Theology of Anabaptism* (Scottdale, Penn.: Herald Press, 1973); W. Klassen, *Anabaptism: Neither Catholic nor Protestant* (Waterloo, Ont.: Mellen, 1973).  [14]L.A. Rutschman, "Latin American Liberation Theology and Radical Anabaptism," JEcuSt 19 (1982) 38–56.  [15]R.T. Bender, "Baptism, Peace and the State in the Reformed and Mennonite Traditions: Phase Two," Mid-Stream 31 (1992) 41–43.

## ANGELS

Belief in angels is a feature of both OT and NT, where they are seen as having the role of praising God in heaven and of being his messengers or servants on earth.[1] They feature frequently in the teaching of Jesus (e.g., Matt 13:39, 49; 18:10 par; 24:36 par; Luke 15:10), and minister to him (e.g., Matt 4:11; Luke 22:43; cf. Matt 26:53; Rev 5:11-12; 7:11-12; 1 Tim 3:16). The names of three of them are known: Raphael ("God heals"—Tob 3:17; 12:15), Gabriel ("Hero of God"—Dan 8:16; 9:21; Luke 1:19, 26), Michael ("Who is like God"—Dan 10:13, 21; 12:1; Jude 9; Rev 12:7). Their number is vast (Heb 12:22; Rev 5:11).

Affirmations about angels were frequent, but speculation about them was sporadic in the patristic period until Dionysius the Pseudo Areopagite (q.v.), who was the first to grasp their essentially spiritual nature.[2] Various Fathers had searched the Scriptures for the different kinds of angels: Cyril of Jerusalem (d. 386),[3] John Chrysostom (d. 407),[4] Gregory of Nyssa (d. ca. 395).[5] In the OT they found seraphim and cherubim and, from the Col 1:16 and Eph 1:21, thrones, dominations, principalities, and powers, while angels and archangels were found in Jude 9 and 1 Thess 4:16. But the early Fathers ordered the ranks differently. In subsequent theology the still different order of Dionysius would dominate: in descending order were three choirs of first rank, seraphim, cherubim, thrones; of second rank dominations, powers and authorities; of third rank principalities, archangels, angels.[6] Gregory the Great retained the names but changed the Dionysian ranking,[7] leading Dante to suggest that he will be amused at his mistake after his death![8] The Dionysian order entered the schools with Peter Lombard,[9] and was adopted by St. Thomas,[10] who said that the Dionysian Order was more with respect to the spiritual perfection of angels, whereas Gregory was considering rather their ministry.[11] From St. Thomas, too, we have speculation on the nature of angels: they are not composed of matter and form; all the angels are each a species; from their immateriality follows their immortality; they can act on a place without movement by applying their power to the place where they want to be.[12] The keen interest in angels in the medieval period arose partly from their being pure spirits (and thus their existence and activity presented many metaphysical problems), partly from popular piety and partly from the notion of the Great Chain of Being in which they played out various roles between God and the cosmos, including humans.

Belief in guardian angels is based on OT experience of beneficent angels and on Matt 18:10. The rabbis held the notion of guardian angel and the idea that only the highest angels could see God face to face; Jesus states that those who have charge of the little ones see the face of the Father (Matt 18:10).[13] Many of the Fathers refer to the angels of peoples, cities, and individuals, matters taken up in the scholastic period, e.g., St. Thomas.[14]

Belief in angels has been constant in Roman Catholic and Eastern Churches, attested by iconography, hymns, prayers, and by the liturgy. In the revision of the calendar, the celebration of Sts. Michael, Gabriel, and Raphael is a feast (29 Sept.), and there is a memorial of the Guardian Angels (2 Oct.). In the liturgy of the dead, the angels are seen as companions of the departed to the throne of mercy.

The Magisterium has several times intervened to cut short aberrant ideas about angels. They are mentioned in a definition of Lateran IV (q.v.)—repeated at Vatican I—where they are said to be personal spirits which are created.[15] Though the main purport of these definitions is the fact that God is the creator of all, angels included, these texts do not allow the possibility of denial of the existence of angels.[16] Pius XII complained about the denial of the spiritual personality of angels,[17] Pope Paul VI included belief in the existence of angels in his Profession of Faith,[18] and their existence is asserted many times in the new Catechism.[19] Given the long tradition, and the continual mention of angels in the liturgy, especially in each Eucharistic preface, it is hard to see how their existence does not pertain to the faith of the Church.[20] For St. Thomas, they belong to the mystical body of the Church and have Christ as their head.[21] Provided that we keep it within a Christological perspective,[22] the angelic world broadens our vision of the Church, and draws us into a vision of divine providence, and of beauty in his creation, as yet unseen.[23]

[1]P.-M. Galopin and P. Grelot, "Angels," DBT 14–16; G. Kittel, "Angelos," TDNT 1:74-87; J. Michl, "Angel," Bauer 1:20-28. See J. Ries and H. Limet, *Anges et démons*. Actes du colloque de Liège et de Louvain-la-Neuve 25–26 novembre 1987 (Louvain-la-Neuve: Centre d'Histoire des Religions, 1989); M. García Cordero, "El ministero de los ángeles en los escritos del Nuevo Testamento," CiTom 118 (1991) 3–40. [2]OxDCC 53; J. Daniélou, *The Angels and Their Mission According to the Fathers of the Church* (Dublin: Four Courts—Westminster, Md.: Christian Classics, 1988 from 1957, Newman Press ed.); R. Roques, *L'univers dionysien. Structure hiérarchique du monde selon le Pseudo-Denys* (Paris: Cerf, 1983) 135–167; B. Studer, "Angel," EncycEarCh 1:38-40. [3]*Catechetical Letter* 23:6/*Mystagogical* 5:6—PG 33:1109-1128, perhaps by John of Jerusalem (d. 417)—Patrology 3:364-366. [4]A.M. Malingrey, in SC28bis:40-50; *Homilies on Genesis* 4:5—PG 53:44; *De incomprehensibili Dei natura* 1:6 and 2:2—PG 48:706-707, 714. [5]*Homily 15 on the Canticle of Canticles*—PG 44:1100. [6]*Celestial Hierarchy* 6:2; 7-9, in C. Luibhead and P. Rorem, trans. and eds., *Pseudo-Dionysius: The Complete Works*. Classics of Western Spirituality (London: SPCK—Mahwah: Paulist, 1987) 160–173/PG 3:200-261. [7]*XL Hom., in Ev.* 2:34, 7-14—PL 76:1249-1255; *Moralia* 32:48—PL 76:665-666; *Epist.* 5:54—PL 77:786. [8]*Paradiso* 28:130-135. [9]*Liber 2 sententiarum* d.9. [10]*In 2 Sent* d.9, q.1, a.3. [11]ST 1a, q.108, a.5. [12]ST 1a, qq.50–62; 107–108. [13]J.P. Meier, *Matthew*, NTMess 2 (Wilmington: Glazier—Dublin: Veritas, 1980) 203–204. [14]ST 1a, q.113. [15]Tanner 1:230/DS 800/ND 19 and Tanner 2:805/DS 3002/ND 412; P.M. Quay, "Angels and Demons: The Teaching of IV Lateran," TS 42 (1981) 20–45. [16]Cf. K. Rahner, "Angels," SM 1:27-35 at 32. [17]Ency. *Humani generis* AAS 42 (1950) 570. [18]AAS 60 (1968) 433. [19]Mainly 328–336, with 28 other nos. [20]AA.VV. *Angeli e demoni. Il dramma della storia tra il bene e il male*. Corso di teologia sistematica 11 (Bologna: Ed. Dehoniane, 1991); I.F. Sagüés, "De angelis" in *Sacrae theologiae summa* (Madrid: BAC, 1958) 2:560-599, 609-617. [21]ST 3a, q.8, a.4c. [22]Cf. LG 49; Rahner (n. 16) 29. [23]R. Ombres, "Sharing the Universe with Angels," NBlackfr 73 (1992) 252–256; cf. K. Rahner, "On Angels," ThInvest 19:235-274; S.R.L. Clark, "Where Have All the Angels Gone?," RelSt 28 (1992) 221–234.

## ANGLICAN COMMUNION

One of the earliest uses of the word "Anglicanism" was by J.H. Newman (q.v.) in 1838; the term "Anglican Communion" is found from 1851.[1] Some avoid the use of "Anglican Church," for what in fact exists is a communion of Churches historically derived from the Church of England. It was described by the Lambeth Conference of Bishops in 1930 as "a fellowship, within the one holy catholic and apostolic Church, of those duly constituted dioceses, provinces or regional Churches in communion with the See of Canterbury."

Historians of Anglicanism see its origins in the early and medieval Church of which it is a reformation. The separate existence of Anglicanism began in the reign of the English Henry VIII (1491-1547, king from 1509). In 1533–1534 the Convocation, i.e., clergy and bishops of the Church of England rejected the pope and recognized the king as supreme head of the Church on earth. The Church of England split from Rome during the reigns of Edward VI (d. 1553) and Elizabeth I (d. 1603) and became Protestant in doctrine and some structures,[2] retaining, however, the threefold ministry of bishop, priest, and deacon. The Protestantism of Anglicanism is rather more Calvinist than Lutheran.

Bishop Samuel Seabury of Connecticut was the first Anglican to be consecrated for work outside Great Britain and Ireland (1784). Others soon followed as the Anglican Communion became established in those areas where the British Empire flourished. There are now twenty-seven provinces in the Anglican Communion. The first Lambeth Conference of Anglican bishops took place in 1867; decennial meetings were decided in 1888.

The Anglican lawyer and author of the influential *The History of Tithes*, John Selden (1584-1654), wrote: "If you want to know how the Church of *England* serves God, go to the Common-Prayer-Book, consult not this nor that man." The prayerbook distinguished Anglican from Puritan (q.v.) and from Roman Catholic. Up to recent decades it was the principal bond of Anglicans throughout the world. The original, largely the work of Archbishop Thomas Cranmer (1489-1556), who drew on Eastern patristic sources as well as on continental Protestant ones, was published in 1549. It was revised several times until a definitive edition appeared in 1662. (Along with the Authorized Version of the Bible, the prayerbook represents one of the masterpieces of the English language.) Attempts at revision of the prayerbook were thwarted by parliament in 1927 and 1928. Guidelines for a revision were proposed by the Lambeth Conference of 1958, and led to the approval of the Alternative Service Book (1980). Other Churches within Anglicanism also have alternative service books.

In the early days of the Reformation in England, texts of Articles were published: Ten (1536), Thirteen (1538), Forty-two (1553), and, finally, Thirty-nine (1563 and 1571). These were all influenced by Continental Protestantism, especially Calvinist. The *Thirty-nine Articles*,[3] the main author/editor of which was Archbishop Parker (1504-1575), a disciple of Cranmer, show some similarities with the recently published Lutheran Confession of Würtemberg (presented to Trent in 1562).[4] The *Articles* are not a creed, nor a full exposition of doctrine: they seek to delineate the Church of England positions over and against Roman Catholic, Anabaptist, and Puritan ones. They fall into four main parts: the substance of the faith (aa. 1–5), the rule of faith (aa. 6–8), the life of faith or personal religion (aa. 9–18), and corporate religion (aa. 19–39). Article 8 states that the Nicene, Athanasian, and Apostles' Creeds "ought thoroughly be received and believed." The teaching on the Church is found in aa. 19–21: "the visible Church of Christ is a congregation of faithful men in the which the pure word of God is preached and the Sacraments be duly ministered, according to Christ's ordinance in all those things that of necessity are requisite to the same. . . . [T]he Church of Rome hath erred, not only in their living and manner of ceremonies, but also in matters of faith" (a. 19); the Church has authority, but under Scripture and never against it (a. 20); general councils may, and have, erred even in things pertaining to God (a. 21). Interpreted in their context, the Articles are not so vague or ambiguous as some have claimed; rather are they minimal and leave many secondary questions open.[5]

Early on in the English Reformation the idea of a book of homilies for an unlearned clergy was conceived. Mainly the work of Cranmer, the *Book of Twelve Homilies* appeared in 1547, to be followed by a second book, completed in 1563 and published in 1571. The majority of the latter were by Bishop John Jewel (1522–1571). Though nowadays unsuitable for preaching, the *Homilies,* along with the *Book of Common Prayer* and the *Thirty-nine Articles* became a repository of Anglican doctrine.

Anglican theology seeks to be at once Catholic and Reformed.[6] (For this and other reasons, such as the word "catholic" in the Creed, Anglicans object to being called "non-Catholic".) It is often remarked that there is no Anglican theology; there is, however, an Anglican method which applies a threefold criterion by appealing to Scripture, to tradition, and to reason.[7]

Key expressions of Anglican thought are to be found in the Anglican Divines, i.e., especially those in the 16th and 17th centuries, who have left a corpus of theological, ethical, and devotional tracts which has been received in the Anglican Communion as part of its heritage.[8] Characteristic of their teaching is the centrality of the Word of God, the *Book of Common Prayer,* a sense of tradition, and a strong emphasis on reason. They belong to a *via media,* avoiding extremes, yet at the same time showing the comprehensiveness that is such a part of the Anglican spirit. Several of these divines are regarded as saints (q.v.) by some Anglicans, e.g., Richard Hooker (d. 1600, feast 3 Nov.), Jeremy Taylor (d. 1637, feast 13 Aug.), Lancelot Andrews (d. 1626, feast 25 or 26 Sept.), William Law (d. 1761, feast 9 April).[9]

The core ecclesiology of Anglicanism may be seen as expressed in the Lambeth Quadrilateral (v. ANGLICANISM AND ECUMENISM). But more profoundly it is to be sought in the liturgy which prays God to "inspire continually the universal Church with a spirit of truth and concord" and to pray that "all they that confess thy holy name may agree in the truth of thy Word, and live in unity and godly love."[10]

The Church of England sees itself as the inheritor of a tradition going back to St. Augustine of Canterbury (d. ca. 604) and beyond. It retains a Reformed emphasis on the Word of God which itself authenticates the Creeds (*Thirty-nine Articles* 8). In liturgy and in ecclesiology there is a strong sense that some things are indifferent (Greek *adiaphora*—q.v.) and may be tolerated when not contrary to Scripture. Already in the 16th century we find Erastian ideas in circulation (from the Swiss theologian Thomas Erastus, 1524–1583), viz., some supremacy of the State over the Church in ecclesiastical matters. Such ideas became critical in the 19th century. From the 17th century in particular the importance of the episcopate in Anglicanism was much stressed.[11] There were two decisive turning points: the 17th-century rejection of the narrowness of Puritanism; the 18th-century resistance to the enthusiasm of Methodism (q.v.). Despite the variety of Church models that have been proposed, Anglicanism has not been fixated on any of them. Rather we find "comprehensiveness" as a key notion, being the willingness to hold open various interpretations of the Church.[12]

In the history of Anglicanism there are party terms which are not always clear, but have some value in identifying trends. In the 18th century there were three groups: High Church, firmly maintaining the bond between Crown and Church and believing that there should be only one Church in England; the Low Church party, liberal in politics, faithful to the Hanoverian succession, but more liberal about dissenters; the Latitudinarian group (Broad Church used as a term from 1854), weary of controversy about dogma, loyal to the National Church as an institution, but loose in dogmatic traditions and influenced by Deism. These traditions continued into the 19th century but were also used differently: Evangelicals ("Low") came into existence through 18th-century revivals and awakenings; the Tractarians ("High") rediscovered the nature of the Church of England as a spiritual society and reasserted the continuity with its pre-Reformation past, but they eschewed Roman Catholic practices, usages, devotions; Modernists ("Broad") affirmed the right and duty of the Church to restate its doctrines when necessary in the light of modern knowledge and criticism.[13]

Of these, Roman Catholics need to be sensitive to the position and restricted influence of Anglo-Catholicism; it may at times be more valued by Roman Catholics than by fellow Anglicans.[14] It is a dogmatic and sacramental position within Anglicanism which emphasizes the continuity of links with the early Church and retains elements of medieval Christianity. Rejecting the label "Protestant," it can in places be seen almost as a mirror image of Roman Catholicism, to the point of using the latter's liturgical books. Its origin is the 19th-century

Oxford Movement (q.v.), whose originator was John Keble (1772–1866). It was a reaction against Erastianism and liberalism. When J.H. Newman (q.v.) converted to Rome in 1854, the Oxford Movement lost its Oxford base and became Anglo-Catholicism.[15]

The evangelical wing of the Anglican Communion is not static. It continues to develop spiritually, to grow in influence in the Church of England, and to deepen its theology, especially on the Eucharist and on ecumenism. The Roman Catholic experience of dialogue with them has been increasingly fruitful in recent years.

Anglicanism has been to the fore in ecumenism; of some importance is the Branch Theory, along with the self-identity of being a bridge Church (v. ANGLICANISM AND ECUMENISM). In the ecumenical movement the significance of its spirituality, without which no account of Anglicanism is complete,[16] has not been sufficiently emphasized. Notable, too, is the "special position" accorded to the Anglican Communion in Vatican II because of its retention of Catholic traditions and institutions (UR 13).

Among the Catholic elements rediscovered in 19th-century Anglicanism is religious life (q.v.). Elizabeth I (queen 1558–1603) suppressed all religious orders. Some were refounded in the succeeding centuries, but none survived. In 1845 the Sisterhood of the Holy Cross was established, and the work of J.M. Neale (1818–1866) was very influential, seen in the foundation of the Sisterhood of St. Margaret (1855). By the 1960s there were over 100 female communities in the United Kingdom, but only a few male ones. Anglican religious communities of men and women are found today in many of the provinces of the Communion.

In contemporary Anglicanism there is a heightened sensitivity to the laity. They generally constitute one of the three houses of the Churches' synods, and have a role in local administration as well. But more importantly, "The Church carries out its mission through the ministry of all its members. . . . The ministers of the Church are lay persons, bishops, priests and deacons."[17]

Some position on primacy has always been found throughout Anglican history, and at the present time the primacy has great ecumenical significance.[18] A major problem facing Anglicanism, especially in ecumenical issues, arises from the independence of each province. (The ordination of women as priests and bishops in some provinces and not yet in others has for the moment increased the difficulty.) At Lambeth 1988, Archbishop Robert Runcie made a strong appeal for a move from independence to interdependence.[19]

A comprehensive picture of Anglican ecclesiology is to be sought not only in its theologians and its living tradition but also in the agreed conclusions of the many ecumenical dialogues in which the whole Anglican communion and individual provinces are engaged.

See ANGLICANISM AND ECUMENISM; ANGLICAN ORDERS

[1]J. Robert Wright, "Anglicanism, Ecclesia Anglicana and Anglican: An Essay on Terminology," in S. Sykes and J. Booty, eds., The Study of Anglicanism (London: SPCK—Philadelphia: Fortress, 1988) 424–429. [2]P. Avis, Anglicanism and the Christian Church (Edinburgh: Clark, 1989) 23–35; W.P. Haugaard, "The History of Anglicanism. From the Reformation to the Eighteenth Century," in Sykes and Booty (n. 1) 3–9. [3]Text Schaff, Creeds 3:486-516. [4]Ibid., 1:343-344, 627-629. [5]P. Tonn, "The Articles and Homilies," in Sykes and Booty (n. 1) 136; E.J. Bicknell and H.J. Carpenter, A Theological Introduction to the Thirty-Nine Articles of the Church of England (London, 1959); O. O'Donovan, On the Thirty Nine Articles: A Conversation with Tudor Christianity (Exeter: Paternoster, 1986). [6]S.C. Neil, Anglicanism (London: Penguin, 1958); Sykes and Booty (n. 1) passim. [7]H.R. McAdoo, Being an Anglican (Dublin: APCK—London: SPCK, 1977) 13. [8]J. Booty, "Standard Divines," in Sykes and Booty (n. 1) 163–174; H.R. McAdoo, The Spirit of Anglicanism (London—New York, 1965). [9]R. Symonds, Alternative Saints. The Post-Reformation British People Commemorated by the Church of England (Basingstoke—London: Macmillan, 1988). [10]P.H.E. Thomas, "Doctrine of the Church," in Sykes and Booty (n. 1) 219–231; cf. A. Hanson, Church, Sacraments and Ministry (London: Mowbray, 1975); E.G. Jay, The Church, 2 vols. (London: SPCK, 1978). [11]R.A. Norris, "Episcopacy," in Sykes and Booty (n. 1) 296–309. [12]Ibid., 230. [13]H.R.T. Brandreth, HistEcumMov 1:306; G. Carey, "Parties in the Church of England," Theology 91 (1988) 266–273. [14]W.S.F. Pickering, Anglo-Catholicism: A Study in Religious Ambiguity (London: Routledge, 1989); G. Rowell, The Vision Glorious. Themes and Personalities of the Catholic Revival in Anglicanism (Oxford—New York, UP, 1983). G.H. Tavard, The Quest for Catholicity: A Study in Anglicanism (London, 1963) 179–200; A. Wilkenson, "Requiem for Anglo Catholicism," Theology 81 (1978) 40–45. [15]L.N. Crumb, The Oxford Movement and its Leaders: A Bibliography of Secondary and Lesser Primary Sources. ATLA Bibliography 24 (London: ATLA—Scarecrow, 1988); H. Blandreth, The Ecumenical Ideals of the Oxford Movement (London, 1947). [16]A.M. Allchin, "Anglican Spirituality," in Sykes and Booty (n. 1) 313–325; L. Bouyer, A History of Christian Spirituality, Vol. 3—Orthodox Spirituality and Protestant and Anglican Spirituality (London, 1968); J.R.H. Moorman, The Anglican Spiritual Tradition (London: Darton, Longman & Todd, 1983). [17]Catechism of the American Book of Common Prayer (1979) 855. See Church of England study, All Are Called: Towards a Theology of the Laity (London: CIO Publishing, 1985); V.J. Dozier, The Authority of the Laity (Washington, D.C.: Alban Institute, 1982); F. Frost, "Les laïcs dans l'Anglicanisme," MélSR 43 (1987) 145–155. [18]G.R. Evans, "The Anglican Doctrine of Primacy," AngTR 72 (1990) 363–378. [19]"The Nature of the Unity We Seek," OneChr 24 (1988) 328–341; C.T. Greenacre, "Diversity in Unity: A Problem for Anglicans," BullCentUn 39 (1991) 4–10. Cf. G.R. Evans, "Anglican Conciliar Theory: Provincial Autonomy and the Present Crisis," OneChr 25 (1989) 34–52.

## ANGLICAN ORDERS

The condemnation of Anglican Orders as "absolutely null and utterly void" in the past and present by Pope Leo XIII (1896) had a prehistory and a subsequent history. The immediate prehistory is clearer in recent decades with the opening up of the Vatican archives on the issue;[1] the subsequent history takes in various views up to ARCIC 1 (v. ANGLICANISM AND ECUMENISM).

From the time of the Reformation it was customary to ordain "absolutely" Anglican priests who were reconciled with Rome, and who wished to enter its ministerial priesthood. By the late 19th century the invalidity of the Orders without further sacramental rite was questioned. It was asked whether Anglicans converting could at least be ordained "conditionally," there being at least a doubt that their orders were valid.

Two conflicting views were presented to Leo XIII. The Anglican Lord Halifax (1839–1934) and his French Roman Catholic friend Fr. Fernand Portal (1855–1926) saw a recognition of Anglican Orders as hastening the reconciliation between Rome and Canterbury. Cardinal Vaughan (1822–1903), whose view of unity ("unionism") was largely restricted to individual conversions, saw such recognition as removing a motive for individual conversions, which he was sure would become a flood if Anglican Orders were declared invalid.

The pope sought opinions of theologians and set up a commission to examine the matter: though some of its members accepted that the Orders were valid or at least doubtfully so, the majority would seem to have favored their nullity. The commission reached no conclusion, and its documents were placed in the hands of the papal theologian Raffaele Pierotti, who wrote a negative opinion.[2]

After a meeting of the Holy Office, 16 July 1896, which unanimously voted against validity, Pope Leo XIII issued the bull *Apostolicae curae* (13 Sept. 1896) condemning Anglican Orders.[3] The bull did not deal with the question of apostolic succession being broken in the Church of England, but took up two matters: defect of form and defect of intention. The 1552 *Ordinal* of King Edward VI was judged not to have conveyed the sacramental meaning of priesthood, as the essential words (the "form") did not express the meaning of Orders: in the case of priests, power to offer the Eucharistic sacrifice; in the case of bishops, the high priesthood, the sum total of the sacred ministry. The second defect lay in the fact that the consecrators of Matthew Parker in 1559 did not have the intention "to do what the Church does." The "innate character and spirit of the Ordinal *(nativa indoles ac spiritus)*" shows that there was no such intention, and furthermore, those using it could not have had such an intention. The bull also spoke to other issues: the decisions of the 16th-century papal legate Cardinal Pole; the custom of absolute ordination for three centuries of converts from Anglicanism; the two historical cases of a French Calvinist (1684) and of John Gordon (1704), both ordained according to the Edwardian Ritual.

The Church of England archbishops gave a reasoned reply in which they pointed to the variety of forms of ordination in the past, especially in the East;

they insisted that the intention of the Church of England in its ordinations was precisely to confer the ministry found in apostolic times; they remarked, "In overthrowing our orders, he overthrows his own, and pronounces sentence on his own Church."[4] Since 1896 there have been studies explaining or reinforcing the view of the bull,[5] and ones which are critical of its historical facts and theological limitations.[6]

The work of ARCIC (v. ANGLICANISM AND ECUMENISM) suggested that it was time to reconsider the position of Anglican Orders: the Commission "believes that [its] agreement on the essentials of eucharistic faith with regard to the sacramental presence of Christ and the sacrificial dimension of the eucharist, and on the nature and purpose of priesthood, ordination, and apostolic succession, is the new context in which the questions should now be discussed. This calls for a reappraisal of the verdict on Anglican Orders in *Apostolicae curae* (1896)."[7]

A letter of Cardinal J. Willebrands, President of the Secretariat for Promoting Christian Unity (13 July 1985), to the co-chairmen of ARCIC II gave indications that a common faith rediscovered may allow a changed view of the 1552 Ordinal, "a consideration that could lead to a new evaluation by the Catholic Church of the sufficiency of these Anglican rites as far as concerns future ordinations." He explicitly prescinded from the question of continuity by apostolic succession and mentioned the ordination of women only in passing.[8]

There have been various proposals about how Anglican Orders could be treated as the Communions of Rome and Canterbury draw closer.[9] One approach is to see apostolic succession (q.v.) as lying primarily in communities' fidelity of apostolic practice and life, rather than in a linear enumeration of their pastors.[10] Defect of intention is also reviewed, for example in the statement of O.P. Rafferty: "At the very least the Roman Catholic Church must grant that the English reformers intended to continue the ministry of priesthood that Christ had given to his Church."[11] Another possibility that is considered is the Eastern notion of economy (q.v.).[12]

Others would hold that some kind of conditional ordination is perhaps inevitable,[13] or a progressive recognition of ministries found in other unions involving Anglicans. The whole theology of validity needs careful study, one that might escape from the neoscholastic categories of the late 19th century.[14] There are also important Anglican studies which frequently treat of the matter in Anglican dialogue with non-episcopal Churches.[15]

The solution to the question of Anglican Orders will finally come about only in the context of an ever greater communion (q.v.) between Canterbury and Rome, a communion that already exists but has been given as yet too little institutional recognition. In the short-term at least, the ordination of women (v. WOMEN, ORDINATION) is a further difficulty that will not easily be surmounted.

There has not been a unified view among the Orthodox Churches: both before and after the Bucharest meeting on Anglican Orders (1935), some Churches have recognized their validity, while others have not. It is common for Orthodox Churches not to see the question in isolation but within the wider area of a common faith, or lack thereof.[16]

---

[1]G. Rambaldi, "A proposito della Bolla 'Apostolicae curae': Note di contesto e schemi preparatori," Greg 61 (1980) 677–743; idem, "La Bolla 'Apostolicae curae' sulle ordinazioni anglicane I–II," Greg 64 (1983) 631–637; 66 (1985) 53–88. [2]G. Rambaldi, "Relazione e voto del P. Raffaele Pierotti, O.P., Maestro del S. Palazzo Apostolico sulle ordinazioni anglicane," ArHPont 20 (1982) 337–388. [3]ASS 29 (1896–1897) 198–201; Acta Leonis XIII, 16:258-275. [4]"Responsio Archiepiscoporum Angliae . . ." in T.A. Lacey, *A Roman Diary and Other Documents Relating to the Papal Inquiry into English Ordinations MDCCCXCVI* (London, 1910) 354–394 at 378–379, 387. [5]E.g., E.C. Messenger, *The Reformation, the Mass and the Priesthood*, 2 vols. (London, 1936–1937); F. Clark, *Anglican Orders and Defect of Intention* (London, 1956); idem, *Eucharistic Sacrifice and the Reformation* (London, [2]1967); A.F. von Gunten, "Les ordinations anglicanes: Le problème affronté par Léon XIII," NVet 63 (1988) 1–21; 65 (1990) 46–60. [6]E.g., J.H. Evans, "The Case for Anglican Orders," Month 267/1407 (1985) 23–31; J.J. Hughes, *Absolutely Null and Utterly Void: An Account of the Papal Condemnation of Anglican Orders, 1896* (London, 1968); idem, *Stewards of the Lord: A Reappraisal of Anglican Orders* (London: Sheed and Ward, 1970); G.H. Tavard, *A Review of Anglican Orders: The Problem and the Solution* (Collegeville: The Liturgical Press, 1990). [7]"Elucidation" (1979) n. 6 in ARCIC, *The Final Report* (London: CTS-SPCK, 1982) 44–45; cf. A.F. von Gunten, "L'Église catholique pourrait-elle reconsidérer sa position sur les ordinations anglicanes?," NVet 58 (1983) 252–267. [8]OneChr 22 (1986) 199–202; reply 202–204; cf. "Anglican Orders: The Dialogue's Evolving Context," Origins 20 (1990) 136–146; DoctLife 40 (1970) 375–379. [9]J.J. Hughes, "Recent Studies of the Validity of Anglican Orders," Conc 1/4 (Jan. 1968) 68–73. [10]T. Ryan, "Reflections on 'A New Context for Discussing Anglican Orders,'" OneChr 22 (1986) 228–233; J.M.R. Tillard, "Recognition of Ministries: What is the Real Question?," OneChr 21 (1985) 31–39; M. Villain, "Can There Be Apostolic Succession Outside the Continuity of Laying on of Hands?," Conc 4/4 (April 1968) 45–53. [11]"The Case for Anglican Orders," Month 267/1409 (1985) 129–137 at 133. [12]K. McDonnell, "Ways of Validating Ministry," JEcuSt 7 (1970) 254–263 at 259; cf. E. Kilmartin, *Towards Reunion: The Orthodox and Roman Catholic Churches* (New York: Paulist, 1979) 82–88; H. Marot, "The Orthodox Churches and Anglican Orders," Conc 4/4 (April 1968) 77–81. [13]E. Yarnold, "Les ordinations anglicanes: est-il possible d'avancer?," *Unité des chrétiens* 64 (April 1984) 21. [14]H. McSorley, "Determining the 'Validity' of Orders and the Meaning of 'Validity,'" Jurist 41 (1981) 371–404. [15]H. Chadwick, "The Discussion of Anglican Orders in Modern Anglican Theology," Conc 4/4 (April 1968) 72–77. [16]H. Marot, "The Orthodox Churches and Anglican Orders," Conc 4/4 (April 1968) 77–81.

## ANGLICANISM AND ECUMENISM

Since the 19th century the Anglican Communion has been involved in what we now call ecumenism. From the beginning of the modern ecumenical movement (q.v.) the Anglican presence has been markedly strong.[1] The various initiatives are confusing unless one grasps the complexities of the Anglican Communion (q.v.) itself.

In Chicago 1886 the Protestant Episcopal Church, which was and is Anglican, adopted four statements as "inherent parts of [the] sacred deposit [of Christian faith]." Two years later at the Lambeth Conference, these were slightly altered and became known as the "Lambeth Quadrilateral." However, as the preamble shows, these were intended as a basis on which work could be undertaken towards unity: "That in the opinion of this Conference, the following articles supply a basis on which approach may be by God's blessing made towards Home Reunion: a) The Holy Scriptures of the Old and New Testaments, as 'containing all things necessary for salvation,' and as being the rule and ultimate standard of faith. b) The Apostles' Creed, as the Baptismal Symbol; and the Nicene Creed, as the sufficient statement of the Christian faith. c) The two Sacraments ordained by Christ Himself—Baptism and the Supper of the Lord—ministered with unfailing use of Christ's words of institution and of the elements ordained by Him. d) The Historic Episcopate, locally adapted in the methods of its administration to the varying needs of the nations and peoples called of God into the Unity of His Church." In time the Quadrilateral moved from being a basis on which to begin discussions to becoming more of a basis for entry into unity.[2]

The openness to ecumenical endeavor in the Anglican Communion is due in no small measure to its sense of being both Catholic and Reformed. In the past this led also to the expression of the Branch Theory, already latent in the younger J.H. Newman (q.v.): "We are the English Catholics; abroad are the Roman Catholics, some of whom are also among ourselves; elsewhere are the Greek Catholics."[3] An earlier expression was the prayer of Bishop Lancelot Andrews (d. 1626) for "the Catholic Church Eastern, Western, British." But where and when the Branch Theory was first worked out is not certain.[4] Its extreme form of stating that the Church of Christ is made up partly of Roman Catholic, Eastern Orthodox, and Anglican Churches was condemned in a letter from the Holy Office to English bishops (1864).[5]

As well as its involvement with the Life and Work movement from 1925, Faith and Order from 1927, and the World Council of Churches from 1948 (v. ECUMENICAL MOVEMENT), the Anglican Communion has been engaged in several important bilateral dialogues.

In Scandinavia dialogue with Lutherans began in 1909. Substantial agreement has been reached on most doctrinal matters, and Eucharistic hospitality is the norm (v. INTERCOMMUNION). In the l980s, discussions with some non-episcopal Lutheran Churches revolved around the notion of *episkopê*. Succession has been seen not primarily in an unbroken chain of ordinations but in the presiding ministry of a Church maintaining a continuity of apostolic faith.[6]

Originating from the Church of England, the Methodist Churches have had mixed fortunes in moves towards unity with Anglicans. In the Churches of South India (1947) and North India (1970), Methodists and Anglicans have achieved union—along with other Churches. Twice, in 1969 and 1972, the Church of England was unable to ratify a two-stage plan for Anglican-Methodist unity, a main problem in each case being the position on episcopacy of Methodists and Anglicans.[7] In 1989 there were plans to have bilateral dialogue between the Anglican Communion and the World Methodist Council, with a meeting taking place in Jerusalem (1992).

As early as 1931 there was a statement that there should be full communion between the Anglican Communion and the Old Catholics (q.v.), the "Bonn Agreement," which was finally ratified at the 1958 Lambeth Conference.[8]

Dialogue with the Oriental Orthodox Churches (non-Chalcedonian: some Armenian, Ethiopian, Syrian, and Indian) began formally in 1985 with a meeting in St. Albans, though there had been some previous contacts 1908–1920.[9] A Common Declaration on Christology was signed by the Coptic Pope Shenouda III and Archbishop Runcie of Canterbury in 1987.[10]

From the 16th to 19th centuries there were various contacts between Anglicans and the Orthodox, but mostly on individual bases. A doctrinal commission met between the two world wars, but major official dialogues began in 1973, leading to two Agreed Statements mainly covering questions of the Trinity, Church, Tradition, and spirituality.[11] The ordination of women is very much opposed by the Orthodox, and nearly led to the suspension of meaningful dialogue after 1977. At the meeting in New Valamo in Finland (1989), the name given to the dialogue was changed to International Commission for Anglican-Orthodox Dialogue.

Dialogue with the Reformed Churches (Congregationalists and Presbyterians) is of relatively recent origin. The subscription to confessional standards and episcopal ordination have been two areas of difficulty. Anglicans have joined with Reformed Churches in the Churches of South and North India (1947, 1970). There have been many examples of cooperation over the last century between Anglicans and the Reformed, with an international dialogue (1981–1984).[12]

Dialogue with the Roman Catholic Church[13] began with the Malines Conversations (q.v.). Immediately after Vatican II, Archbishop Ramsey and Pope Paul VI set up the Anglican-Roman Catholic International Commission (ARCIC) with the object to have "a serious dialogue which, founded on the gospels and on the ancient common traditions, may lead to the unity for which Christ prayed." Meeting from 1970–1981, ARCIC 1 claimed to have reached "substantial agreement" on Eucharistic doctrine, ministry, and ordination; there was a "degree of agreement" on authority and papacy.[14] The Lambeth Conference of 1988 stated that the areas of substantial agreement were sufficient "to take the next step forward"; the authority statements were seen as "a firm basis for the direction and agenda of the continuing dialogue on authority." The Congregation for the Doctrine of the Faith gave an initial response in 1982,[15] but the input of the Congregation in the official reply of the Roman Catholic Church in 1991 was in several places less than positive. Though welcoming the work of ARCIC 1, the joint response of the Congregation for the Doctrine of the Faith and the Pontifical Council for Promoting Christian Unity was cautionary and less sanguine than the Lambeth response.[16] Some disappointment was expressed at the Vatican's inability to concede the measure of agreements claimed by ARCIC; it was also suggested that the Response operated out of a different methodology than the one used by ARCIC, suggested to it by Pope Paul VI and Archbishop Ramsey.[17]

At the meeting in Canterbury between Archbishop Runcie and Pope John Paul II (1982), ARCIC 2 was set up "to examine, especially in the light of our respective judgements on *The Final Report,* the outstanding doctrinal differences which still separate us" and "to study all that hinders the mutual recognition of the ministries of our communions." Its first report was *Salvation and the Church.*[18] The response of the Congregation for the Doctrine of the Faith, though welcoming, refused to concede that there was "substantial agreement" yet on all issues.[19] The next ARCIC Report was *Church as Communion* (1991).[20]

At the meeting of Archbishop Runcie and Pope John Paul II in 1989, it was noted that the Anglican admission of women to priesthood (v. WOMEN, ORDINATION OF) "prevents reconciliation between us even where there is otherwise progress towards agreement in faith on the meaning of the Eucharist and the ordained ministry."

Apart from these various dialogues at international level, the Anglican Communion is engaged in many multilateral and national dialogues, all showing new areas of agreement. Covenanting (q.v.) with other Churches failed in the Church of England in 1982 by a few votes; it has been attempted in other provinces of the Anglican Communion, but has not had very notable results. Some of the reasons lie in Anglican problems with non-episcopal ministries, and in the Anglican preferred interest in the progress of ARCIC.[21]

In Anglicanism, as in most other communions, ecumenism at the level of the local Church is still too much neglected, and in some senses it is from this more important grass-roots dialogue and relationships that we can expect reception (q.v.) of the impressive agreements at international levels.

[1] S. Runciman et al., *Anglican Initiatives in Christian Unity* (London: SPCK, 1967); K. Sansbury, *Truth, Unity and Concord: Anglican Faith in Ecumenical Setting* (London: Mowbray, 1967); M. Tanner, "The Ecumenical Future," in S. Sykes and J. Booty, *The Study of Anglicanism* (London: SPCK—Philadelphia: Fortress, 1988) 379–393.   [2] H.R.T. Brandreth, in HistEcumMov 1:264-266, note 265 n. 2; J.R. Wright, ed., *Quadrilateral at One Hundred* (Cincinnati: Forward Movement, 1988).   [3] Sermon 29, Nov. 1829, *Parochial and Plain Sermons* (London, 1891) 3:191-192.   [4] G.V. Florovsky, in HistEcumMov 1:196, n. 3.   [5] DS 2885-2888.   [6] *Pullach Report* 1972, in H. Meyer and L. Vischer, eds., *Growth in Agreement*, Ecumenical Documents 2/Faith and Order Paper 108 (New York: Paulist—Geneva: WCC, 1984) 13–34; *Niagara Report: Consultation on Episcopé* (London: ACC—Geneva: Lutheran World Federation, 1988); G.R. Evans, *"Episcopé* and Episcopacy: The Niagara Report," OneChr 25 (1989) 281–286.   [7] J.M. Turner, *Conflict and Reconciliation: Studies in Methodism and Ecumenism in England, 1740–1982* (London: Epworth, 1985).   [8] *Growth in Agreement* (n. 6) 36–38. "Authority and Primacy in the Church (Agreed Statement of the Anglican-Old Catholic Theological Conference, Chichester 1985)," EcumBull 73 (1985) 20–23; G. Huelin, ed., *Old Catholics and Anglicans: 1931–1981* (Oxford: UP, 1984); U. von Arx, "Autorität und Primat in der Kirche, ein Nachwort zur Entstehung des Textes," IKiZ 80 (1990) 12–15.   [9] H. Hill, ed., *Light from the East: A Symposium on the Oriental Orthodox and Assyrian Churches* (Toronto: Anglican Book Centre, 1988).   [10] Irén 59 (1986) 67/OneChr 23 (1987) 341–342 ; cf. W. Taylor, "Convergence in Christology: Amba Bishoi 1990," Sobornost 12 (1990) 80–84; OneChr 26 (1990) 106–111.   [11] K. Ware and C. Davey, eds., *Anglican-Orthodox Dialogue: The Moscow Agreed Statement* (London: SPCK, 1977); *Anglican-Orthodox Dialogue: The Dublin Agreed Statement 1984* (London: SPCK, 1984); *Growth in Agreement* (n. 6) 39–59. See P.A. Baktis, "The Dublin Statement: Investigation and Analysis," OneChr 25 (1989) 169–179; C. Davey, "The Doctrine of the Church in International Bilateral Dialogues," OneChr 22 (1986) 134–145 at 141–145; V.T. Istavridis, *Orthodoxy and Anglicanism* (London: SPCK, 1966); H. Wybrew, "The Mystery of the Church in the Dublin Agreed Statement," Sobornost 7 (1985) 52–56.   [12] *God's Reign and Our Unity* (London: SPCK, 1984); see C. Davey (n. 11 OneChr) 139–141.   [13] B. and M. Pawley, *Rome and Canterbury through Four Centuries: A Study of the Relations between the Church of Rome and the Anglican Church, 1539–1981* (London: Mowbray, 1981); M.J. van Dyck, *Growing Closer Together: Rome and Canterbury* (Slough UK: St. Paul, 1992); J.W. Witmer and J.R. Wright, eds., *Called to Full Unity: Documents on Anglican-Roman Catholic Relations, 1966–1983* (Washington, D.C.: U.S. Catholic Conference, 1986).   [14] *The Final Report* (London: Catholic Truth Society—SPCK, 1982).   [15] Origins 11/47 (May 1982) 752ff; Irén 55 (1982) 3–6; cf. J. Ratzinger, *Church, Ecumenism and Politics* (New York: Crossroad—Slough UK: St. Paul, 1988) 63–98.   [16] CathInter 3/3 (1992) 125–130.   [17] F.A. Sullivan, "The Vatican Response to ARCIC I," Greg 73 (1992) 489–498 = OneChr 28 (1992) 223–231; C. Hill, "The Fundamental Question of Ecumenical Method," OneChr 28 (1992) 136–147. See D. Brown, "The Response to ARCIC—I: The Big Questions," ibid., 148–154; G.R. Evans, "Rome's Response to ARCIC and the Problem of Confessional Identity," ibid., 155–167; M. Richards, "Twenty-five Years of Anglican-Roman Catholic Dialogue—Where Do We Go from Here?," ibid., 126–135.   [18] London: Church House—Catholic Truth Society, 1987.   [19] *Observation on Salvation and the Church of ARCIC II* (London: Catholic Truth Society, 1988).   [20] CathIntern 2/7( 1–14 April 1991) 327–338, with evaluation F.A. Sullivan, 339–341; C. Hill, "'The Church as Communion': an Anglican Response," OneChr 28 (1992) 323–330.   [21] R. Greenacre, "Les dialogues bilatéraux dans lesquels la Communion anglicane est engagée," Irén 56 (1983) 34–45.

## ANOINTING OF THE SICK

Vatican II recommended that the name of the sacrament of "Extreme Unction" be changed to "Anointing of the Sick," and at the same time stated that it was not a sacrament only for those on the point of death (SC 73). The Church has always seen its scriptural basis to lie in the anointing with oil in Mark 6:13 and in the words of James 5:14-15: "Are any among you sick? They should call for the elders of the church and have them pray over them, anointing them in the name of the Lord. The prayer of faith will save the sick, and the Lord will raise them up; and anyone who has committed sins will be forgiven."[1] In the complex history of the sacrament[2] the accent was on healing until the 9th century in the West, and has largely remained so in the East;[3] the spiritual effects became very emphasized in the scholastic period, and by Trent the sacrament was seen mainly as a preparation for death.

The ecclesial dimension of the sacrament emerges from its role in the whole Church's caring for the sick,[4] and in the exercise of the common priesthood (v. PRIESTHOOD) by the sick person: "By the sacred anointing of the sick and the prayer of the priests the whole Church commends those who are ill to the suffering and glorified Lord that he may raise them up and save them. And indeed she exhorts them to contribute to the good of the people of God by freely uniting themselves to the passion and death of Christ" (LG 11; cf. GI 5). The Rite gives examples of intentions for which the sick person may offer his or her sufferings: for peace in the world; for a deepening of the life of the Spirit in the local Church; for the pope and the bishops; for people suffering in a particular disaster (GI 56). Moreover, all baptized Christians should share in the ministry to the sick, especially the family and friends of those who are ill by words of faith, by praying with them, by interceding for them, by encouraging them, and by celebrating the sacraments with them (GI 33–34). Priests minister to the sick by word and sacrament, and thus also strengthen the hope and faith of others in the Church (GI 35–37). The ecclesial and communitarian aspects are very visible in communal celebrations (GI 36) of the sacrament in a parish or at a shrine.

An important liturgical gesture in the anointing of the sick is the imposition of hands (q.v.) with prayer, which is an invocation of the power of the Holy Spirit upon the sick persons. The English language, unlike some others, allows us to distinguish between curing and healing as effects of the sacrament: a cure, or removal of the illness, sometimes does occur (GI 6); in one properly disposed there should always be healing, that is the sick, whatever their state, are brought into a fullness of life (cf. John 10:10) which will be spiritual and almost always also psychological (cf. GI 6).

The *Code of Canon Law* states that a person who is to receive the sacrament should be in danger (CIC 998 *pericolose;* 1004 § 1, in *periculo*—not "in danger of death" as a widely circulating translation states[5]). Thus the ICEL translators indicate that the sacrament "may and should be given to anyone whose health is seriously impaired (but) it may not be given indiscriminately or to any person whose health is not seriously impaired" (GI 6n).

In modern times Anglican liturgies usually provide for unction of the sick with laying on of hands. The meaning of this rite in Anglicanism, as indeed that of the practice of lay anointing in the Catholic Church up to the 9th century,[6] is in need of theological clarification. In particular the Tridentine decree, reiterated in Canon Law (CIC 1003 § 1; CCEO 739 § 1) reserving the administration to priests, is being probed in contemporary writing.[7]

[1]Cf. Trent sess. 14—Tanner 2:710, 713/DS 1695, 1716/ND 1636, 1656. [2]B. Poschmann, *Penance and the Anointing of the Sick* (New York: Herder & Herder—London: Chapman, 1964); AA.VV. *Temple of the Holy Spirit: Sickness and Death of the Christian in the Liturgy,* Twenty-first Liturgical Conference of Saint-Serge (New York: Pueblo, 1983 from French 1975); R. Béraudy, "Le sacrement des malades: Étude historique et théologique," NRT 96 (1974) 600–634; A. Cuschieri, *Anointing the Sick: A Theological and Canonical Study* (London: University Press of America, 1993); J.L. Empereur, *Prophetic Anointing: God's Call to the Sick, the Elderly and the Dying.* Message of the Sacraments 7 (Wilmington: Glazier, 1984); D. Power, "Let the Sick Man Call," HeythJ 9 (1978) 256–270; M. Ramos, "Nota para una historia litúrgica de la unción de los enfermos," Phase 161 (1987) 383–402; L.P. Rogge, *The Relationship between the Sacrament of the Anointing of the Sick and the Charism of Healing within the Catholic Charismatic Renewal.* Diss. (Ann Arbor: University Microfilms International, 1984); C. Traets, "The Sick and Suffering Person: A Liturgical/Sacramental Approach," QLtg 71 (1990) 30–49; On the Rite, see J. Stefanski, "Redaktionsarbeiten am neuen Ritus der Krankenölweihe," EphLit 103 (1989) 42–78. Conc 214 (1991/2). [3]A. Backhaus, "Heilung und Heil—die Krankenölung der orthodoxen Kirche," UnaSan 42 (1987) 201–212; T. Spácil, *Doctrina theologiae Orientis Separati de sacra infirmorum unctione,* Orientalia Christiana 74 (Rome: Oriental Institute, 1931); cf. P. Meyendorff, "The Anointing of the Sick: Some Pastoral Considerations," SVlad 35 (1991) 241–255. [4]"The Pastoral Care of the Sick"—Conc 214 (1991/2). [5]*The Code of Canon Law,* trans. Canon Law Society of Great Britain and Ireland (London: Chapman, 1983). Cf. M.J. Himes, "Getting Down to Cases," NewTR 4/1 (Feb. 1991) 64–67; C. O'Donnell, "Who Is to Be Anointed?," Fur 35 (1984) 58–60. [6]Rogge (n. 2) 187–234, who notes also 261–263 that the practice continued to be upheld in theology in the 15th century with perhaps some approval from Martin V. [7]Rogge, ibid.; J.J. Ziegler, *Let Them Anoint the Sick* (Collegeville: The Liturgical Press, 1987).

## ANONYMOUS CHRISTIANS

The radical optimism of Vatican II with regard to the salvation of non-Christians (q.v.) is one of the most significant positions of the whole council according to K. Rahner and many others.[1] We can point to several texts that cumulatively indicate not only that non-Christians may be saved (AG 3, 7; GS 22), but also suggest that the non-Christian religions may be mediations of salvation (GS 41, 92; AG 3, 9, 11, 15; LG 17; NA 2). The problem arises about how the divine plan may be understood, especially in the light of the one mediation of Christ (1 Tim 2:4) and the necessity of the Church. The council stated that such salvation is in a way "known to God" (GS 22); a full understanding of the divine plan in the matter will not open to us, but we must seek to harmonize this new development with other tenets of the faith.

The notion of "anonymous Christian" is found in K. Rahner's attempt to defend the uniqueness and necessity of Christ while admitting with Vatican II the real possibility of salvation for every person.[2] He bases his theory on his fundamental theological position about God's self-communication to men and women in their existential state. When persons on the basis of grace thus respond in freedom, this self-revelation arouses supernatural faith and love, through which they can reach salvation. Since Christ is the only mediator, this divine self-communication is Trinitarian, and therefore in reality Christian. Since the people do not recognize the character of the grace received, it can be called "anonymous." A non-Christian religion may be the means God uses to communicate with a person; there is, then, genuine mediation in such a religion, not by human efforts but through its use by the Holy Spirit.

Rahner's theory of anonymous Christian is also developed to cover the situation of those who have no real contact with religion. They can have anonymous faith arising out of love, and so come to salvation.[3]

Though most of the major Catholic theologians after Vatican II agree that non-Christians may be saved, and that their religion is used by God for salvation,[4] Rahner has been criticized for aspects of his theory.[5] Some fear that it weakens the urgency of missionary work: if people can be saved in their religion, why seek to offer them Christianity? But F.A. Sullivan has shown that the objections are not insuperable.[6]

With H. de Lubac and others, one may prefer to avoid the term "anonymous Christian," a position that Rahner himself admits.[7] The main thrust of Rahner's theory, whatever its details, seems incontestable, viz. people are saved through implicit faith based on a graced response in love to God's self-communication in the depths of their hearts, and usually mediated through religious experience. The theory probably requires a more comprehensive Trinitarian basis, and one could also argue for the term "anonymous spiritans."[8] The Holy Spirit has been operative since the beginning of creation, giving grace in virtue of the foreseen merits of Christ—the most dramatic example of which is Mary's Immaculate Conception.

---

[1]See F.A. Sullivan, "Anonymous Christians," in *Salvation Outside the Church: Tracing the History of the Catholic Response* (New York: Paulist, 1992) 162–181.    [2]"Anonymous Christians," ThInvest 6:390-398; "Observations on the Problem of Anonymous Christians," ThInvest 14:280-294; "Anonymous Christianity and the Missionary Task of the Church," ThInvest 12:161-178.    [3]"Atheism and Implicit Christianity," ThInvest 9:145-164; "Anonymous and Explicit Faith," ThInvest 16:52-59; "The Church and Atheism," ThInvest 21:137-150.    [4]Sullivan (n. 1) 181 with nn. 38–50.    [5]B. Sesboüé, "Karl Rahner et les 'Chrétiens anonymes,'" Études 361 (1984) 521–536; cf. P.J. Lynch, "Servant Ecclesiologies: A Challenge to Rahner's Understanding of Church and World," IrTQ 57 (1991) 277–298; E. Conway, *The Anonymous Christian: A Relativised Christianity? An Evaluation of Hans Urs von Balthasar's Critique of Karl Rahner's Theory of Anonymous Christian,* European University Studies (Frankfurt am M.: Lang, 1993).    [6]Op. cit. (n. 1) 173–178.    [7]H. de Lubac, *Paradoxe et mystère de l'Église* (Paris, 1967) 152–163; Rahner, ThInvest 14:281, 292.    [8]F.E. Crowe, "Son and Spirit: Tension in the Divine Missions," ScEsp 35 (1983) 153–169 at 162–163.

## ANTINOMIANISM

A term from the Greek (*anti*—against, *nomos*—law) indicating those who wished to be free of law in the name of the gospel. Appeal is made to Rom 3:8, but in a way that contradicts Gal 5:1, 13. Antinomianism appeared in the 1st and 2nd centuries and sporadically afterwards. It is often associated with Gnostic sects, and would appear to be present in New Age Neognosticism (v. MOVEMENTS, NON-CHRISTIAN).

## APOSTLES

Considering the importance of the apostles in the primitive Church (Eph 2:20), it is perhaps surprising that "there is no unified apostle-concept, so that there is a possibility of different conceptions of the apostolic ministry and of the principle of apostolicity."[1] A crucial text is the fragment of primitive kerygma in 1 Cor 15:5-7: "and that he appeared to Cephas, then to the twelve. Then he appeared to more than five hundred brothers and sisters at one time. . . . Then he appeared to James, then to all the apostles." The Twelve is clearly a group name, for only eleven were present after Judas' death. C.K. Barrett notes that "Paul is here quoting a formula that he did not himself make up, and that the notion of a group of twelve special disciples is pre-Pauline and therefore very early."[2]

Three different applications of the term "apostle" may be distinguished. First, there is a distinctive Pauline usage: Paul was at pains to defend his own apostleship in the face of some super-apostles at Corinth (2 Cor, chs. 10–12), for even though he recognized that others were apostles before him (Gal 1:17), he, too, had seen the Lord (1 Cor 9:1; 15:8) and had been given a mission to preach (Gal 1:16). Second, for Luke-Acts (with the exception of Acts 14:4, 14) only the Twelve, who were with Jesus and were witnesses of the resurrection, are called apostles (Acts 1:22-23; cf. Luke 6:13—"he called his disciples, and chose twelve of them whom he also named apostles"). For Luke "the Twelve become the bond of continuity between Jesus' kingdom preaching and the Church's preaching of God's word."[3] Compared with Mark, who uses the word "apostle" only once and this in the context of preaching (Mark 6:30 with 6:7), and Matthew, who uses *apostolos* only in naming the Twelve (Matt 10:2), Luke sees the twelve apostles as a group with a special role both in the ministry of Jesus and in the early Church. He uses the term *apostolos* 34 times (out of a total of 80 in the NT, of which 35 are Pauline). In the Gospel, Luke uses the term six times for a special group (Luke 9:1 with 9:10, 12; 11:49; 17:5; 22:14, and after the defection of Judas 24:10 with 24:9, 33). Though one can be sure that Jesus gathered a special group from amongst his disciples, the giving of the name "apostles" to them may be retrojection on the part of Luke,[4] and indeed of Matthew. In the first part of Acts the apostles are seen as resident in Jerusalem and having a decisive role in guiding the Church, both through teaching and authoritative actions.[5] But since James the brother of John, unlike Judas, is not replaced (12:1), this special role seems to have been temporary; indeed the Twelve do not appear to act collegially after the appointment of the Seven (Acts 6:1-6). Later it is James and the presbyters that we find as leaders in Jerusalem (21:18) or apostles and elders (e.g., 15:2, 4, 6, 22, 23; 16:4)—for Peter "left and went to another place" (Acts 12:17); Peter would, however, appear to have been present at the crucial meeting in Jesusalem (Acts 15:7,14). The Pauline and the Lucan notions of apostle both have the meaning of witnesses to the resurrection and of a commission from the Lord to preach. Third, there is a more general usage of the word "apostle" for others: Paul and Barnabas (Acts 14:4, 14; cf. 1 Cor 9:5-6; 2 Cor 11:13), James, brother of the Lord (Gal 1:19), probably Andronicus and Junias ("prominent among the apostles"—Rom 16:7) and possibly Apollos (1 Cor 4:6, 9), Silvanus, and Timothy (1 Thess 2:6-7 with 1:1).

Modern study on the meaning of apostleship began in 1865 with J.B. Lightfoot, who distinguished the Pauline from other usages,[6] and it has been highly controverted ever since. Secular Greek usage is of no real help for grasping the meaning of *apostolos*. A most significant contribution was by R.H. Rengstorf, who in 1933, following up a suggestion of Lightfoot, proposed the rabbinic notion of *shaliach* as a key to its understanding.[7] The *shaliach* was one sent on a commission according to the maxim: the *shaliach* is like the man himself. Since attestation of the notion of *shaliach* is later than the NT, and is also juridical in character, thus not a real correspondence, the parallel was later rejected by many scholars.[8] All of these, with the exception of W. Schmithals, whose widely rejected thesis looks to Gnostic sources, claim that the notion of apostle is of Christian origin. In recent decades the *shaliach* parallel has returned to favor; it is now seen not only in rabbinic literature, which is difficult to date, but also in OT notions of prophetic sending connected with the Hebrew root *slch* (LXX *apostellein*).[9]

In some profound way the Church is built on the apostles and prophets (Eph 2:20 with a single Greek article). We find the synoptic tradition indicating that the apostles/Twelve are given special instruction and commissions by Jesus during his ministry (Matt 10:1; 11:1) and an authoritative mission by the risen Jesus (Matt 28:18-20; Mark 16:15-16; Luke 24:45-49 with Acts 1:8; John 20:21-23; cf. Matt 16:19 with 18:18 which also may be post-resurrectional). These functions are seen to be continued in Acts and by Paul: teaching (apostles—Acts 2:14, 37, 42; 4:33; Paul—1 Cor 1:17; Gal 1:16); authoritative acts (apostles—Acts 6:2-4; 8:14; 15:2, 22 [with presbyters]; Paul—1 Cor 5:3; 2 Cor 10:1-2.8). Their significance in the Church is also eschatological, a fact attested by the synoptic tradition and the Apocalypse (Matt 19:28; Luke 22:30; Rev 21:14): since judging can mean ruling, the synoptic text could suggest that the Twelve will be rulers of the new people or that they will share in the eschatological triumph of the Lord;[10] the Twelve apostles are foundations of the Church and hence of the New Jerusalem.[11]

Crucial to the function of apostleship is the anointing with the Holy Spirit: the risen Jesus breathed his Spirit on them (John 20:22), and they were not to depart from Jerusalem until they received the Spirit (cf. Luke 24:49; Acts 1:8). Furthermore, apostleship is also first in the Pauline lists of charisms (1 Cor 12:28; Eph 4:11). Paul's own call to apostleship was charismatic (cf. Rom 1:5; Gal 1:12, 15). The charism of apostle continued after the actual time of the Twelve (v. DIDACHÊ). Other charisms are also associated with the role of apostle: signs and wonders (Acts 2:43; 4:12), the giving of the Spirit (Acts 8:14-17; 19:6), as well as persecution and tribulation (Acts 5:18, 40; cf. 8:1; 2 Cor 6:4-10; 7:4-5; 11:23-28). Except, however, for

Peter himself, and John always, however, with Peter (Acts 3:1, 4, 11; 4:1, 13, 19; 8:14), early tradition does not recall specific activities of particular members of the Twelve after the resurrection. This may account for discrepancies even in the lists of their names (Matt 9:2-4; Mark 3:18-19; Luke 9:14-16; Acts 1:13)—they were remembered as a group rather than as individuals.

In Vatican II we find extensive references to the apostles. The most important idea is that they formed a college, a notion that met with some resistance until the Biblical Commission at the request of Paul VI studied the question and agreed that the clause "in accordance with the Lord's decree *(statuente Domino),* St. Peter and the rest of the apostles constitute a unique apostolic college" (LG 22), could be proved in the Scriptures.[12] Among other assertions of the council are the following: they formed a college, or stable group, with Peter as their head (LG 19); Christ sent them forth as he himself had been sent by the Father (SC 6; LG 17, 18; AG 5; PO 2); they were given a universal mission to preach (LG 19, 32; DV 7; DH 11; AG 5); the Church was founded on them (LG 7; NA 4; AG 1, 9); they received the commission to spread the Church to all peoples and to guide it (LG 8, 20; CD 2); they received a special outpouring of the Holy Spirit (LG 19, 59; DV 20; SC 6); they were given a special legacy to transmit (UR 14; DV 19) to the end of time (LG 20); under the guidance of the Spirit they were responsible for writing down the message of salvation (DV 7, 8).

The place and function of the apostles are crucial to the understanding of apostolic succession (q.v.), the apostolicity of the Church (q.v.), and episcopal collegiality (v. BISHOP, COLLEGIALITY).

---

[1]R. Schnackenburg, "Apostolicity: The Present Position of Studies," OneChr 6 (1970) 243–273 at 251; cf. F.H. Agnew, "The Origin of the NT Apostle-concept: A Review of Research," JBL 105 (1986) 75–96; idem, "Apostle," NDictT 48–52; Congar, L'Église une . . . 182–185; J.A. Jáuregui, "Función de los 'Doce' en la Iglesia de Jerusalén: Estudio histórico-exegético sobre el estado de la discusión," EstE 63 (1988) 257–284; F.A. Sullivan, *The Church We Believe In: One, Holy, Catholic and Apostolic* (Mahwah: Paulist—Dublin: Gill & Macmillan, 1988) 152–168; H. Küng, *The Church* (London: Search, 1971) 344–354; R.E. Brown, *Priest and Bishop: Biblical Reflections* (Dublin: Chapman, 1971).   [2]*A Commentary on the First Epistle to the Corinthians* (London: Black, 1968) 341.   [3]R.J. Karris, NJBC, 694.   [4]See J. Dupont, "Le nom d'apôtres a-t-il été donné aux douze par Jésus," OrSyr 1 (1956) 267–290, 425–444 at 438–444.   [5]J. Dupont, "L'Apôtre comme intermédiare du salut dans les Actes des Apôtres," RTPhil 112 (1980) 342–358; S. Brown, "Apostleship in the New Testament as an Historical and Theological Problem," NTS 30 (1984) 474–480.   [6]*St. Paul's Epistle to the Galatians* (Grand Rapids: Zondervan, [10]1957) 92–100.   [7]TDNT 1:398-447.   [8]E.g., L. Cerfaux, "Pour l'histoire du titre apostolos dans le Nouveau Testament," RechSR 48 (1960) 76–92; B. Rigaux, "The Twelve Apostles," Conc 34 (1968) 6–7; J.A. Kirk, "Apostleship after Rengstorf: Towards a Synthesis," NTS 21 (1974–1975) 249–264 at 250–252; W. Schmithals, *The Office of Apostle in the Early Church* (Nashville: Abingdon, 1969) 98–110; fuller bibliog.

Agnew, "The Origin" (n. 1) 85 n. 44, 91 n. 76.   [9]See F.H. Agnew, NDictT 48–52 at 48–49; X. Léon-Dufour, "Apostles," DBT 24.   [10]See J.B. Meier, *Matthew.* NTMess 3 (Wilmington: Glazier— Dublin: Veritas, 1980) 223.   [11]J.-L. D'Aragon, JBC 2:492.   [12]Acta Syn 3/1: 13-14/Alberigo-Magistretti 432.

## APOSTOLATE

The word "apostle" (q.v.) lies at the root of the more recent word "apostolate," which is used about sharing in the apostolic office of the Church. The reality, if not the word, existed from the beginning: the works that we would term apostolic or being an apostolate are frequently found in the NT and in the patristic tradition.[1] In the medieval tradition the word "apostolate" tended to be used about the office of the original apostles. Some of the material nowadays pertaining to apostolate was then treated under headings like the "active life."[2]

It was not until the 19th century that the word "apostolate" was used about the laity (q.v.). In the 20th century the notion of Catholic Action became widespread.[3] The name came from an Italian group, Azione Cattolica; Pius X (q.v.) was the first pope to use it. But it was Pius XI who spoke of the value of the laity's work: ". . . when united with their pastors and bishops they participate in the works of the apostolate, both individual and social."[4] He tended to restrict Catholic Action to works or actions of the laity, which were organized, apostolic, and done under special mandate of the bishop. This strict sense of Catholic Action was mostly found in Latin Europe. By the 1950s there was a scope of meaning ranging from the strict sense above to any action of Catholic laity inspired by their faith.[5] A spirituality of lay apostolate and of Catholic Action also developed.[6]

Pius XII noted a certain confusion in language, and he sought to apply "Catholic Action" to all organized groups of the lay apostolate recognized as such.[7] The key specification of Catholic Action was its relation to the hierarchy: under its direction and sharing in its mission (Pius XI); in collaboration or cooperation (Pius XII). It took on a different profile in each country. Some countries did not have any Catholic Action in the strict sense.

Many of the interventions of the bishops in the first two sessions of Vatican II were conditioned by the notion of Catholic Action.[8] With the third session there was a change, so that we have the apostolate of the laity seen as being a commissioning from Christ through baptism and confirmation. Their apostolate has its origin in the specific gifts they have received. There can also be a call "to a more immediate collaboration in the apostolate of the hierarchy" (LG 34).

The Decree on the Apostolate of the Laity sees the apostolate of the laity as a sharing in the mission of the Church, one proper to them and indispensable (AA 1); it recalls their sharing in the priestly, prophetic, kingly office of Christ (AA 2; cf. LG 34–36); the decree notes the need for holiness in their state in life (AA 4).

Vatican II sees a wide spectrum of activity as belonging to the apostolate: "Christ's work of redemption, while it primarily concerns the salvation of human beings, also embraces the renewal of the whole temporal order. Hence the mission of the church is not only to bring the good news of Christ and his grace to men and women, but also to permeate the whole order of temporal things with the spirit of the gospel and so perfect it. Therefore laypeople, in carrying out this mission of the church, will exercise their apostolate both in the church and in the world, in the spiritual order as well as in the temporal" (AA 5). The council develops these ideas and shows how there are different fields of the apostolate in which all are to be involved according to their calling and gifts (AA 6–14); the forms of the apostolate are also multiple (AA 15–19). One form of the apostolate which retains validity in many countries is Catholic Action (AA 20). The relationship between the hierarchy and the laity involved in the apostolate is dealt with in a chapter on due order (AA 23–27). A final chapter deals with formation for the apostolate, a formation which should begin at childhood and includes not only the acquisition of attitudes and skills but also theology and spirituality (AAS 28–32). With this decree the Church finally escaped from the narrowness that is inherent in the notion of Catholic Action to a wider vision of the apostolate being the task of every lay person.

The council also called on religious to renew their apostolate (PC 8); in the post-Vatican II period many religious now prefer to use the word "mission." The *Code* speaks of religious contributing to the Church's salvific mission (CIC 574 § 2). It lays down that "the apostolate of all religious consists first in their witness of a consecrated life which they are bound to foster by prayer and penance" (CIC 637). It recognizes that "in institutes dedicated to the works of the apostolate, apostolic action pertains to their very nature"; apostolic action is to proceed from an intimate union with God and is to be exercised in the name of and by the mandate of the Church, and in communion (CIC 675; cf. 678–683). The law also acknowledges the right and duty of all the faithful to engage in the mission of the Church (CIC 216; cf. 211); the right and duty is made specific for laity (CIC 225).[9]

According to Vatican II, the apostolate is "every effort of the mystical body . . . that . . . by spreading Christ's kingdom . . . all may be brought to share in the saving work of redemption." (AA 2) In recent decades the words evangelization (q.v.) and mission (q.v.) are widely used as synonyms for apostolate.

However, one can make distinctions within the area of apostolate: strictly speaking, missionary activity consists in the effort to evangelize and plant the Church in an area in which Christ is not known; pastoral activity amongst the members of the Church seeks to deepen their faith and to expand it in the whole Christian life; ecumenical activity aims at promoting Christian unity.

The 1988 post-synodal "Vocation and Mission of the Lay Faithful in the Church and in the World" (*Christifideles laici*—CL) builds on Vatican II developments and clarifications. It asserts strongly the mission of the laity: "Lay people as well are personally called by the Lord, from whom they receive a mission on behalf of the Church and the world" (CL 2; cf. 3). It reiterates the council's emphasis on the sharing in the priestly, prophetic and kingly office of Christ, and sees this as given in baptism with a further development in confirmation (CL 14). The Exhortation stresses the secular character of the laity's involvement (CL 15; 36), though in deep communion (q.v.) with the whole Church (CL 18–19; 25; 28; 30–32). It distinguishes the ministries rooted in holy orders from those having their origin in baptism and confirmation (CL 21–23) and underscores the place of charisms (q.v.—CL 24). In line with AA it develops the variety of vocations and apostolates of laity in the Church and world (CL 45–57); it deals finally with maturation and formation (CL 57–63).

Amid all these developments there remains in some areas a place for Catholic Action in a more traditional sense.[10] The laity have a double focus in their apostolate: they share in the Church's mission within the Church; they have a special role in bringing the secular under the lordship of Jesus.[11] But one must avoid the danger of seeing the clergy as being involved with the sacred, with the laity confined to the world. The laity have a genuine apostolate in the Church. The task of pastoral theology is to recognize this apostolate and to avoid clericalizing it. The more securely it is rooted in the initiation sacraments, the less danger there will be of this aberration; clericalization emerges when we see laity doing works instead of or on behalf of the clergy, rather than in their own right as laity. Different local Churches, different cultures and times will determine the way in which bishops, priests, laity, and religious engage in the one mission of the Church through the activities of the apostolate.

[1]Y. Congar, *Lay People in the Church: A Study for a Theology of the Laity* (London, ²1965) 349–399.  [2]E.g., St. Thomas Aquinas, ST 2-2ae, qq.179–182; q.188, a.2.  [3]Congar (n. 1) 362–399.  [4]*Ubi arcano Dei*—AAS 14 (1925) 695/Carlen 3:236.  [5]J. Newman, *What is Catholic Action?* (Dublin, 1958); T.M. Hesburgh, *The Theology of Catholic Action* (Notre Dame, Ind., 1946).  [6]J.B. Chautard, *The Soul of the Apostolate* (Trappist, Ky., 1941).  [7]*Six ans se sont*—AAS 49 (1957) 929–930.  [8]I. Sanna, "Il dibattito conciliare sull'Azione Cattolica," Later 53 (1987) 398–433.  [9]E. Rinere, "Conciliar and Canonical Applications of 'Ministry' to the Laity," Jurist 47 (1987) 204–227.  [10]F. Tagliaferri, "L'azione cattolica, associazione di laici al servizio della missione della Chiesa," in AA.VV. *I laici nella Chiesa e nel mondo.* Coll. Fiamma viva 28 (Rome: Teresianum, 1987) 87–101.  [11]G. Thils, "Les fidèles laïcs: leur secularité, leur ecclésialité," NRT 109 (1987) 182–207 at 194; cf. K. Rahner, "Notes on the Lay Apostolate," ThInvest 2:319-352.

## APOSTOLIC—APOSTOLICITY

The Church is confessed in the Creed as "apostolic." The meaning of this designation is to be sought in an understanding of both apostle (q.v.) and apostolic succession (q.v.). A broad description of apostolicity is of being in harmony and in communion with the apostolic Church from the beginning. For some Churches this will involve not much more than acceptance of the Scriptures and the forms of ministry described therein, whereas for others, tradition in faith and structures, especially in ministry, is an essential characteristic involved in the notion of being apostolic. Historically, this latter view was associated with the Anglican, Old Catholic, Orthodox, other Eastern, and the Roman Catholic Churches; the former view would include all the other Churches. In recent decades ecumenical discussions have led away from a narrow view of apostolic as a "note" (q.v.) of the Church to a dynamic concept that involves growth and can likewise envisage decline. The U.S. Eastern Orthodox/ Roman Catholic Consultation states the following: "'The Church is apostolic' is not simply a statement of fact, but is an object of faith (I believe . . .). Like the Christ-event, this apostolicity is a gift of God given once for all; its content is not of our making."[1] It has a historical dimension and an eschatological one,[2] both based on the role given by Christ to the apostles. Therefore, apostolicity, as manifested in the Eucharist and in icons, belongs to the Church in its present reality.[3] The apostolic deposit is not an inert object, but a living confession by which in baptism each Christian appropriates the apostolic life and faith of the Church.[4] Furthermore, apostolic succession is to be seen within the continuity of the community as a whole in apostolic life and faith; "Apostolicity seems to consist more in fidelity to the apostles' proclamation and mission than to any form of the apostolic office."[5] Finally, the Petrine office is reflected both in the local Church (the Orthodox emphasis) and in the universal Church (the Roman Catholic emphasis), but "there is no intrinsic opposition between these two approaches."[6]

These advances in the understanding of apostolicity are to be found in other consultations between various Churches: some stress more strongly the missionary dimension of the apostolic Church which shares in the worldwide mission given by Christ to his apostles (Matt 28:18-20); others have a greater pneumatological emphasis.[7] Notable among all dialogue documents for the range of its participating authors is the Lima statement, *Baptism, Eucharist and Ministry* (1982).[8] Its fourth chapter on ministry, "Succession in the Apostolic Tradition," paragraph 34, "Apostolic Tradition in the Church," states: "Apostolic tradition in the Church means continuity in the permanent characteristics of the Church of the apostles: witness to the apostolic faith, proclamation and fresh interpretation of the Gospel, celebration of baptism and the eucharist, the transmission of ministerial responsibilities, communion in prayer, love, joy and suffering, service to the sick and the needy, unity among the local churches and sharing the gifts which the Lord has given to each." Here it would seem clear that the commission preferred to use the words "apostolic tradition" rather than "apostolicity," but the paragraph contains essential elements of the Church's apostolicity.[9]

Given the convergence of understanding of the notion of apostolicity, the more intractable difficulty remains that of apostolic succession. But the ability of both types of Churches—"Protestant" and "Catholic"—to see genuine apostolicity in each others' faith, life, and ministry is a remarkable development. The issue of apostolicity will remain a key one, for it ultimately goes back to the divine plan of redemption. The ministry and paschal mystery of Jesus are to be encountered by every age through the Pentecostal gift of the Spirit.[10] But apostolicity denotes the way in which we approach this mystery and share its fruits. It is God's plan that we encounter salvation in community (LG 9): his grace is mediated through men and women with a special activity devolving on episcopal ministers. So at its deepest level, apostolicity denotes this possibility of encountering now the Mystery through the Holy Spirit in a community which mediates the divine plan throughout history.

---

[1]H.M. Biedermann, "Apostolizität als Gottes Gabe im Leben der Kirche," OstKSt 37 (1988) 38–54—English text 38–42; T. Fitzgerald, "The Eastern Orthodox-Roman Catholic Statement on Apostolicity," GrOrTR 32 (1987) 191–199—text 194–199, n. 6. [2]J.-M. Garrigues and M.-J. Le Guillou, "Statut eschatologique et caractère ontologique de la succession apostolique," RThom 75 (1978) 395–417. [3]Text (n. 1) nn. 6–7. [4]Ibid., nn. 8–9. [5]Ibid., n. 10. [6]Ibid., n. 12. [7]Cf. F.A. Sullivan, *The Church We Believe In: One, Holy, Catholic and Apostolic* (Dublin: Gill & Macmillan—Mahwah: Paulist, 1988) 185–197; for documentation see H. Meyer and L. Vischer, eds., *Growth in Agreement:* Ecumenical Documents 2 (New York: Paulist—Geneva: World Council of Churches, 1984). [8]Faith and Order Paper 111 (Geneva: World Council of Churches, 1982). [9]Sullivan (n. 7) 197. [10]Cf. Congar, L'Église une . . . 216–222.

## APOSTOLIC COLLECTIONS OR PSEUDEPIGRAPHA

The *Didachê* (q.v.) and *The Apostolic Tradition* (q.v.) of the (Pseudo) Hippolytus are the best known canon-

ical and liturgical texts which bear the name "apostolic" or are ascribed to one of the apostles or to someone like Clement belonging to the apostolic circle. Pseudepigraphy was quite acceptable in ancient times: it was an assertion that the work claimed to be faithful to the thought or tradition of a person or school; it also facilitated distribution of a book or idea, lending to a recent work the prestige of an earlier master. The attributions to the apostles are thus without historical value but have an important meaning: the authors/compilers wish to invest their document with apostolic authority.[1] These collections are an invaluable source of information about the life of the Church in the early centuries,[2] provided that we keep in mind the warning of B. Botte: they may reflect a reforming ideal of their author/compiler that is not the actuality of the Church of their origin, and hence they must be used only with the utmost critical vigilance.[3] The literary genre of these documents varies: letters from an "apostle" or "apostles"; sermons; canons or prescriptions concerning morals, liturgy or Church institutions. Many give liturgical prayers, which were in actual use or were models for celebration.

One needs to distinguish individual texts or works and collections of texts. The most important collections are as follows:

1) *The Clementine Octateuch,*[4] a 7th-century compilation of earlier sources.[5] Its first two books contain the *Testamentum Domini,* a 4th- or 5th-century work on Church order, church building, and a complete liturgy.[6] The third book contains the *Doctrine of the XII Apostles,* an early compilation. Other books have the treatise on charisms from the *Apostolic Constitutions,* much of the material of liturgical texts of the *Apostolic Tradition,* and various canons. It is called *Octateuch* to distinguish it from the *Apostolic Constitutions,* also in eight books and likewise ascribed to Clement. Ancient translations differ quite substantially from this Syriac *Octateuch.*

2) The *Alexandrine Synodus,*[7] which includes the *Apostolic Tradition* and the *Ecclesiastical Constitution of the Apostles.*[8] This last work is also known as the *Apostolic Constitution,* and as *The Ecclesiastical Apostolic Canons,* its early title being *Ordinances of the Holy Apostles through Clement.* It is early 4th-century and presents the apostles gathered to make regulations concerning the Church: the doctrine of The Two Ways in the moral section (2–14), a disciplinary section containing norms for Church order (15–28), and a conclusion (29–30). An Arabic translation adds 56 canons, whence the title sometimes of *The 127 Canons.*[9]

3) *The Apostolic Constitutions* (q.v.)[10] is the best known of the collections. It is a late 4th-century Syro-Palestinian compilation. Books I–VI contain a text of the *Didascalia Apostolorum,* an early 3rd-century

Syrian pastoral manual dealing in a rather haphazard way with liturgical, moral, and canonical matters,[11] but notable especially for its non-rigorist position on penance (v. RECONCILIATION, SACRAMENT OF). Book VII contains the *Didachê* and various prayers. Book VIII has two chapters on charisms, *The Apostolic Tradition* and *85 Apostolic Canons*. The Trullan Synod (q.v.) condemned *The Apostolic Constitutions*, with the exception of their last part, but this action did not have any profound effect in subsequent canonical literature.

4) The Hauler Fragments from MS Verona LV (53).[12] Amid the *Sentences* of Isidore of Seville this late 4th-century text has parts of the *Didascalia Apostolorum, The Apostolic Tradition*, and the *Ecclesiastical Constitution of the Apostles*.[13]

A document which had an independent existence apart from these collections is the *Canons of Hippolytus*, comprising 38 canons and a sermon; it is a reworking of the *Apostolic Tradition*. The original Greek from the late 4th century is lost, but we have translations probably from the 6th century.[14]

The key documents contained in these collections are thus the following: the *Didachê, The Apostolic Tradition, The Didascalia Apostolorum*, and *The Ecclesiastical Constitution of the Apostles/Apostolic Canons*. Though the documents, according to their transmission—apart from the *Didachê*—show great variation since they reflect the Church in which they were transcribed, they nevertheless have major themes which can be summarized under the following headings: moral precepts, sometimes presented as The Two Ways (a theme in several early documents[15]); questions of ordination and Church institutions; issues of Christian initiation; instructions for various groups of persons in the Church; liturgical, especially Eucharistic texts. Though one cannot posit a common source for these documents, they reflect in a way not easy to determine some elements coming from the 2nd century and thus within a century of the apostles.

[1]M. Metzger, "Nouvelles perspectives pour la prétendue *Tradition apostolique*," EcOr 5 (1988) 252 citing H. Engberding, "Das angebliche Dokument roemischer Liturgie aus dem Beginn des dritten Jahrhundert," in *Miscellanea liturgica in honorem L. Cuniberti Mohlberg* (Rome, 1948) 57; W. Speyer, "Religiose Pseudepigraphie und literarische Fälschung im Altertum," JbAC 8/9 (1965–1966—Münster, 1967) 88–125; idem, *Die literarische Fälschung im heidnischen und christlichen Altertum* (Munich: Beck, 1971); A.F. Walls, "A Note on the Apostolic Claim in the Church Order Literature," *Studia Patristica*. TU 64 (Berlin, 1957) 83–92. [2]A. Faivre. "La documentation canonico-liturgique de l'Église ancienne," RevSR 54 (1980) 204–219; 273–297 at 204. [3]B. Botte, "Les plus anciennes collections canono-liturgiques," OrSyr 5 (1960) 331–350 at 346. [4]F. Nau, *La version syriaque de l'Octateuque de Clément* (Paris, 1913); J.P. Arendzen, "An Entire Syriac Text of the Apostolic Church Order," JTS 3 (1902) 59–80 (Bk. 3 only). [5]See Faivre (n. 2) 208–209. [6]Syriac edition with Latin tr. Ignatius Ephraem II Rahmani (Mainz, 1899); Eng. trans. J. Cooper and A.J.

Maclean, *The Testament of the Lord* (Edinburgh, 1902). [7]G. Horner, *The Statutes of the Apostles or Canones Ecclesiastici* (London, 1904); cf. Patrology 2:119-120. [8]Text F.X. Funk, *Didascalia et Constitutiones Apostolorum* (Paderborn, 1905) 1:564-593; Eng. trans. ANL 17:257-269. [9]Text and French trans. J. and A. Périer, *Les "127" canons des Apôtres* (Paris, 1912). [10]Text F.X. Funk, *Didascalia et Constitutiones Apostolorum*, 2 vols. (Paderborn, 1905); Metzger: SC 320, 329, 336; P. Nautin, "Apostolic Constitutions," EncycEarCh 62–63. [11]Text F.X. Funk (n. 10) 1:2-384; R.H. Connolly, *Didascalia Apostolorum* (Oxford, 1929, 1971); cf. P. Galtier,"La date de la Didascalie des Apôtres," RHE 13 (1947) 315–351; Patrology 2:147-152. [12]E. Hauler, *Didascaliae Apostolorum . . .* (Leipzig, 1900), text to be found in E. Tidner, *Didascaliae Apostolorum, Canonum ecclesiasticorum, Traditionis Apostolicae Versiones Latinae*. TU 75 (Berlin, 1963). [13]Text F.X. Funk, *Doctrina duodecim apostolorum* (Tübingen, 1987) 50–74; J.P. Arendzen, "An Entire Syriac Text of the Apostolic Church Order," JTS 3 (1902) 59–80, with Eng. trans. [14]R.-G. Coquin, *Les Canons d'Hippolyte*. PO 31, 2 (Paris: Firmin-Didot, 1966). [15]*Didachê* 4:13; *Letter of Barnabas* 18–20; Irenaeus, *Adv. haer.* 4:33, 8; 5:30, 1; Tertullian, *De praescriptione* 38, and some authors noted by Eusebius—Polycrates, *Hist. eccl.* 5:24; Denis of Corinth 4:23, 12 and an anonymous anti-Montanist 5:16.

## APOSTOLIC CONSTITUTIONS

The *Apostolic Constitutions* (AC), the apogee of the great apostolic collections (q.v.), can be dated very close to 380 C.E. and from the region of Antioch in Syria.[1] The work is written in eight books of unequal length comprising the 3rd-century *Didascalia apostolorum* (Bks. 1–6),[2] the 1st-century *Didachê* (q.v.—Bk. 7), and the early 3rd-century *Apostolic Tradition* (q.v.) of the Ps-Hippolytus, along with a version of the 4th-century *85 Apostolic/Conciliar Canons* (Bk. 8). The AC is ascribed to Clement (v. APOSTOLIC COLLECTIONS).

The AC is a compilation, and thus does not have a fully unified presentation of ideas. Moreover, its various parts are themselves largely compilations. Thus there are internal inconsistencies in the text. Moreover, scribes in later centuries attempted to harmonize its text with the orthodoxy of later councils. The charge that it is Arian has not been convincingly proved despite its condemnation by Photius in 891; "Arian," indicating the crucial Christological heresy, was a term rather loosely applied to works whose orthodoxy was in any way questioned.[3]

There are some key underlying theological ideas widely operative in the work:[4] the primacy of salvation history, for God has intervened in time; the consequence of God's intervention in salvation, which is described as knowledge, life, reconciliation; Christ, priest and mediator is the only Son of the eternal Father; the heavenly hierarchy is a model for the Church below, which supplants Israel; there are some transformed Jewish prayers, even though the work itself is strongly anti-Judaic. The pneumatology of the work is undeveloped: the Holy Spirit is not yet seen in terms of Constantinople I (380–381—q.v.); though higher than any of the angels, the Holy Spirit is not clearly asserted to be a divine person.

Ecclesiologically, the work is of great interest as indicating the reality, aspirations, or perhaps the memory of the Church in the late 4th century: since it has several ancient texts, we cannot be sure that the reality of the Church is as described in the various works that make up the AC. The fundamental images of the Church are flock and ship, in which each person has a place and role (AC 2:57, 2, 4 and 12).

Remembering the dates of the various works that make up the AC, and noting that there is some evidence of editorial or scribal retouching, we can see the main teaching on the institutions of the Church. (The matters arising in AC will be treated in the appropriate articles elsewhere.) Book 1 is largely concerned with the various moral issues mostly pertaining to the laity (q.v.). Book 2 takes up matters affecting bishops (q.v.), who are quite central in the whole AC. It also deals with priests (q.v.) and deacons (q.v.). The long 2:57 gives an ordering of the Church for liturgy: "As for you, O Bishop, be holy and irreproachable, not quarrelsome or prone to anger, not harsh, but know how to build up, convert, instruct; be amenable, kindly, patient, ready to exhort and comfort as a man of God. When you assemble the Church of God, demand like the pilot of a huge ship that everybody behave with great discipline. Tell the deacons, like sailors, to assign with great care and dignity their places to the brethren like passengers. And first, let the building be oblong facing East, with the vestries on both sides towards the East; it will then resemble a ship. In the middle will be placed the bishop's throne; on either side the priests will be seated; the deacons should be beside them, attentive and dressed in ample garments, for they correspond to the sailors and the masters of the ship. They are to see to it that the laity sit in their own area, with great discipline and composed, the women to one side keeping silence."[5] Elsewhere the treatise deals at length with bishops (q.v.), priests (q.v.), deacons (q.v.), deaconesses (q.v.), exorcists (v. EXORCISM), prophets (q.v.), charisms (q.v.), and the life state of widows (q.v.) and virgins (q.v.).

The AC gives many examples of prayers and blessings. The great blessings in Book 2:33-38 would seem to have a synagogue background but with Christian editing.[6] Central to its prayers is *anamnêsis* (recall), i.e., some invocation, no matter how short, of the divine work of creation and redemption. The request to God comes in third place after a sometimes elaborate address, and the *anamnêsis;* there are, however, blessings without supplications. The verb *eucharistein* is often used of prayers of praise and thanksgiving. Most of the prayers end with a doxology in which Christ is mediator, and some, like the conclusion of the whole work, are Trinitarian: ". . . he will give you eternal life with us through the mediation of his beloved servant Jesus Christ our God and savior, through whom be glory to him the God and Father above all, in the Holy Spirit the Paraclete, and always and for ages. Amen."[7] The imposition of hands (q.v.) is of particular importance as a liturgical gesture.

Scholars are divided about the two anaphoras of the AC: some hold them to be an original composition of the compiler,[8] others believe that they represent a stage in the evolution of the Eucharistic Prayers.[9] One anaphora is short and probably incomplete based on the *Didachê,*[10] and the other is a long, magnificent one based on the *Apostolic Tradition.*[11] This latter is sometimes called the *Clementine Anaphora.* Its parts are: opening dialogue, not very different from our modern one at the Preface; a prayer of praise; *anamnêsis* of the great works of creation; *anamnêsis* of the first covenant; the biblical trisagion—Holy, holy, holy; a Christological *anamnêsis; anamnêsis* of the Last Supper; an *anamnêsis* of the paschal mystery and prayer of offering; an *epiclêsis* over the offered elements and for the assembly; prayers of intercession for the Church, the world, for good harvest, etc. There then follow a second set of intercessions, the communion, and a long postcommunion prayer.

The compiler of the AC insists on offices to be attended by all twice daily,[12] a point made also by a contemporary, St. John Chrysostom.[13] Fasting is twice weekly, Wednesday and Friday.[14] There is a long account of the liturgical year, which amplifies material in the *Didascalia.*[15] The following feasts are celebrated: Christmas, Epiphany, Friday and Saturday of the Passion, Easter, Ascension, Pentecost, and the week after Pentecost, which is festive but includes fasting. In the area of the reconciliation of sinners (v. RECONCILIATION), the compiler is far from rigorous, and the teaching on marriage (q.v.) is very positive, even though a somewhat negative view is taken of second marriages by widows and widowers.

The *Apostolic Constitutions* remains a mine of information about the life of the early Church and provides a vivid background against which one can read patristic texts of the period.

---

[1]M. Metzger, *Les constitutions apostoliques,* SC 320, 329, 336 (Paris: Cerf, 1985–1987); other texts: PG 1:509-1156; F.X. Funk, *Didascalia et Constitutiones apostolorum,* 2 vols. (Paderborn, 1905); tr. J. Donaldson, *The Clementine Homilies, The Apostolical Constitutions.* ANL 27 (Edinburgh, 1870). [2]R.H. Connolly, *Didascalia Apostolorum, Syriac Version translated and accompanied by the Verona Fragments* (Oxford, 1929, reprint 1962); M.D. Gibson, *The Didascalia Apostolorum in English* (London—Cambridge, 1903). [3]Metzger (n. 1) 320:14-17. [4]Metzger (n. 1) 329:10-39; idem, "La théologie des Constitutions apostoliques par Clément," RevSR 53 (1983) 29–49, 112–122, 169–194, 273–294. [5]2:57, 1–4—SC 329:310-312. [6]L. Bouyer, *Eucharistie* (Paris:

Desclée, ²1968) 122–136, 245–261; cf. D.A. Fiensy, *Prayers Alleged to be Jewish: An Examination of the Constitutiones Apostolorum,* Brown Jewish Studies 65 (Chico, Calif.: Decatur-Scholars Press, 1985). ⁷8:48, 3—SC 336:310. Cf. 4:5, 4—SC 329:178. ⁸E.g., R. Cabié, "Les prières eucharistiques des 'Constitutions Apostoliques' sont-elles des témoins de la liturgie du IVe siècle?," BLitE 84 (1983) 83–99. ⁹E.g., E. Braniste, "L'assemblée liturgique dans les 'Constitutions Apostoliques' et les différentes fonctions dans son cadre," in AA.VV. *L'assemblée liturgique et les différents rôles dans l'assemblée.* Conférences Saint-Serge 23 (Rome: Ed. Liturgiche, 1977) 93–130; E. Mazza, "La 'gratiarum actio mystica' del libro VII delle 'Constituzioni apostoliche,' una tappa nella storia della anafora eucaristica," EphLtg 13 (1979) 123–187; M. Metzger, "Les deux prières eucharistiques des 'Constitutions Apostoliques,'" RevSR 45 (1971) 52–77; idem, SC 329:83-84; A. Verheul, "Les prières eucharistiques dans les 'Constitutiones apostolorum,'" QLtg 61 (1980) 129–143. ¹⁰7:25—SC 336:52-54. ¹¹8:12—SC 336:176-205. ¹²2:36, 6 and 59:1-2 and 60—SC 329:260, 324, 326-330. ¹³*Huit catéchèses baptismales* 8:18—SC 50bis:257; cf. B. Fischer, "La prière ecclésiale et familiale dans le christianisme ancien," MaisD 116 (1973) 41–58. ¹⁴5:20, 18—SC 329:284. ¹⁵5:13-20—SC 329:246-284.

## APOSTOLIC FATHERS

Since the 17th century the term "Apostolic Fathers" has been given to a number of writers belonging to the 1st and 2nd centuries.[1] They were presumed to have been in contact either with the apostles or with those who knew the apostles. Numbered among the writings of the apostolic fathers are the *Didachê* (q.v.), the Letters of Ignatius (q.v.), Barnabas (q.v.), and of Clement (q.v.) to the Corinthians and the "Second" pseudonymous Letter of Clement (v. CLEMENT, PSEUDO, SECOND LETTER), Hermas (q.v.), the Letter of Polycarp (q.v.), and the Fragments of Papias. Though it may have been written later, the Letter of Diognetus (q.v.) is sometimes included. Most of these authors are mentioned in the History of the Church by Eusebius, but their writings were in some cases lost for many centuries.

Some of these works were composed even before the last books of the NT were written. Though differing widely in form, language, and intent, there are some common themes which appear in these early writings: the two ways of light and darkness, gnosticism, Christology, and especially the refutation of docetism, relations with Judaism and with the secular world, institutions and charisms, moral norms and the Christian life, martyrdom, authority in the Church. In some cases we have already the Church order of a single bishop, presbyters, and deacons; in other cases this full development has not yet occurred. Some of them represent clear tendencies of "Early Catholicism" (q.v.). Several of these works were regarded as being scriptural (v. RECEPTION) in some Churches during the early centuries. Until the 19th century they were often disregarded for two quite different reasons: many Protestant authors were interested only in Scripture and saw these texts as a corruption of the Scripture, or

at least irrelevant; many Catholic scholars were put off by the fact that they did not show the more developed theology of the later councils. In the present day these texts are taken as they stand as important witnesses to the Church of the period from about 70 to 170 C.E.

---

[1]Texts in various patristic series—ACW, AF, ANF, ANL, LCC, SC; J.B. Lightfoot, *The Apostolic Fathers* (Grand Rapids, Baker Book House, 1974); M. Staniforth and A. Louth, *Early Christian Writings* (Harmondsworth: Penguin, ²1987). For studies, see individual writers and L.W. Barnard, *Studies in the Apostolic Fathers and Their Background* (Oxford: Blackwell, 1966); R.M. Grant, *The Apostolic Fathers,* vol. 1 (London—New York: Nelson, 1964); Patrology 1:40-105; S. Tugwell, *The Apostolic Fathers.* Outstanding Christian Thinkers (London: Chapman, 1989).

## APOSTOLIC SUCCESSION

Christians who confess the Church to be apostolic (q.v.) must have some understanding of how the Church today is in continuity with the Church of the apostles (v. APOSTLES). Crucial to this understanding will be the weight given to the developments in Church order from the close of the NT period to the middle of the 3rd century.

In the NT we find a diversity of ministries (v. MINISTRY) of the early Church. In some cases we do not know how these arose, or we are told that they are charismatic, being given by the Spirit who breathes as he wills (cf. 1 Cor 12:4-11, 28-30; Eph 4:11-12), or they are apostles (q.v.) called and sent by Christ. In other cases we see that people are appointed to ministry: the Seven who served the Hellenists (Acts 6:1-6), the *presbuteroi* (elders) appointed by Paul in each Church (Acts 14:23); the *presbuteroi* who were to have responsibility for the local Church in Ephesus, in the knowledge that they would not see Paul again (Acts 20:17-38); Timothy, on whom hands were laid by Paul (2 Tim 1:6) and by the *presbuteroi* (1 Tim 4:14); the *diakonoi* and *episkopoi* (overseers) who were selected by Timothy and Titus (1 Tim 3:1-10; Titus 1:5-9). The Pastoral Epistles portray clearly enough a transmission of duty and power to lead the Christian community even though they speak only in connection with Paul and his delegates (cf. 2 Tim 2:1-2). But if the community is to be cared for, instructed, admonished, encouraged, and presided over in such a way as to remain constant to the tradition, it would require continual and faithful leadership. The Pastoral model shows that authority has been handed on from one generation to the next.[1]

We also find a diversity of structures, though this word is somewhat anachronistic when applied to NT situations: in Jerusalem we find authority to lie with the apostles in and with the community (Acts 1–15), and later with James and the *presbuteroi* (Acts 21:18); in Philippi there were *episkopoi* and *diakonoi* (Phil

1:1); in other Churches there were one or more *presbuteroi* (Jas 5:14; 1 Pet 5:1, 5; 2 John 1; 3 John 3).

The question of succession arises when we seek to grasp the transition between the above Church order and the situation found universally at the end of the 2nd century.[2] There are two issues: the nature of the evolution and its legitimacy. In studying the evidence we need first to remember that the notion of succession was well known in both pagan and Jewish milieux, e.g., in philosophical and rabbinic schools and in politics, as well as in the OT (e.g., Moses—Num 27:18-23; Elijah—2 Kgs 2:9-15).[3] Second, we are speaking of a time when immediate eschatological expectancy had waned, but the Church was conscious of a universal mission (Matt 28:18-20; Acts 1:8).[4]

In the *Didachê* (q.v.), possibly contemporaneous with the last NT writing, *episkopoi* and *diakonoi* are to be elected apparently to supply for the absence of prophets and teachers (15:1; cf. 13:4). The author seems to feel the need to insist that these are on a par with prophets and teachers (15:2). The author knows also *apostoloi,* but these are itinerant preachers, often prophets, and not apostles in the stricter NT sense (11:3-6). Another early work, the *Epistle of Barnabas* (ca. 117–132—q.v.) has no account of ministers.[5] The *Epistle to Diognetus* (q.v.) from 150–210 C.E. does not speak of ministry either; it does, however, have a reference to "the tradition of the apostles" (11:6).

The first clear assertion of succession is in the *Epistle of Clement* (q.v.) dating from about 96 C.E.,[6] a letter of reproof from the Church of Rome to the Corinthian Church which had deposed certain *presbuteroi.* The author, named as Clement only a half century later by Dionysius of Corinth,[7] insists on the divine origin of Church office: the apostles come with a message from Christ (42:1-2); in their universal mission (42:2): "from land to land, accordingly, and from city to city they preached and from among their earliest converts appointed men whom they had tested by the Spirit to act as bishops and deacons for the future believers" (42:4); furthermore, "the apostles laid down a rule once for all to this effect: when these men die, other approved men shall succeed to their sacred ministry" (44:3).[8] These men are called indifferently *episkopoi* and *presbuteroi* (21:6; 44:5; 47:6; 54:2; 57:1). They are either appointed by the apostles or with the consent of the Church (44:3). They also offer sacrifices, clearly a liturgical function (44:4). The ministers in the Church at Corinth are still a collegial body; there is no evidence yet of a single monarchical bishop. There are two indications of the author's authority: he apologizes at the outset for not devoting his attention earlier to the Corinthian problem; God is speaking through him (59:1). But it is not clear that this latter is because of his own office or is from a prophetic impulse, though in the total context of the Epistle the former seems more probable.

The letters of Ignatius (q.v.) show a developed Church structure in the eastern Mediterranean. The seven letters written about 110 C.E.[9] show a fixed structure of one bishop *(episkopos)* and groups of both *presbuteroi* and deacons *(diakonoi):* "the bishop is to preside in the place of God, while the presbyters are to function as the council of the apostles, and the deacons, who are most dear to me, are entrusted with the ministry of Jesus Christ."[10] Everywhere he insists on respect for the bishop: he represents Christ,[11] and the presbyters the apostles;[12] there is to be unity around the bishop,[13] who celebrates the one Eucharist;[14] nothing must be done without the approval of the bishop.[15] But Ignatius does not speak of himself or of other bishops as "successors of the apostles." In Ignatius we thus find not only the fact of a monarchical episcopate but a justification for it and for the offices of priests and deacons, along with some incipient theologizing on these structures. Though commonly used, there are grounds for not employing the word "monarchical" about this period (v. BISHOPS). The hierarchy is not a mere human creation, but represents the divine volition and the positive will of Christ.

The *Letter to the Philippians* by Polycarp refers to presbyters with him (Intro.; cf. 6:1) and deacons (5:2); he does not speak of a bishop at Philippi, but of presbyters. Being in the tradition of Ignatius (13), he implies a monarchical episcopate. After him evidence not only for a monarchical episcopate but for an apostolic succession becomes ever more clear and frequent. Irenaeus (q.v.) speaks of those "who were constituted bishops by the apostles and their successors up to us,"[16] and of "a succession from the apostles."[17] He can list the bishops in various dioceses right back to the apostles.[18] Tertullian (d. ca. 225) in his pre-Montanist days argued against the heretics for a succession both in apostolic doctrine and in episcopal office.[19] Hegesippus (ca. 180), though he may not have made actual lists of bishops, was concerned to visit the apostolic Churches to ascertain their teaching.[20] He seems to link episcopacy with teaching. The argument of Irenaeus and Tertullian is threefold: the apostles committed their teaching to Churches and to those to whom they gave an office of pastoral care; the apostolic doctrine is faithfully preserved and handed down in Churches of apostolic origin through a succession of bishops; throughout the world the same doctrine, from the same apostolic source, is handed down. "In their writings the concept of apostolic succession was the regular succession of teachers of the faith one after another in the pastoral leadership of the Churches."[21]

At about the same time Ps-Hippolytus of Rome (v. APOSTOLIC TRADITION) described the rite of ordination of a bishop, which, given his conservative mind-set, probably represents the practice of the late 2nd century.[22] There are important ecclesiological, Christological, and pneumatological factors in the ordination: the bishop is chosen by the local community; he is seen to share in the mandate given by Christ to the apostles; the *epiclêsis* is a prayer for gifts of power and authority from the Spirit of leadership and high priesthood.[23]

Thus within about a century after the death of the apostles, each Church was being led by one bishop. Moreover, these bishops, in their role of pastoral leadership, were recognized as the legitimate successors of the apostles. We cannot say that this development is indicated as the sole possibility that might theoretically have arisen from the picture of the Churches in the NT. But that is not to say that this development is reversible. On the contrary, this evolution took place under the guidance of the Spirit without any apparent opposition, and with the promise of the Lord that the Church would be indefectible. The structure which emerged of monarchical bishop with priests and deacons belongs to the essential nature of the Church. This is the argument from *ius divinum* (q.v.).

Vatican II teaches that "the bishops have by divine institution *(ex divina institutione)* taken the place of the apostles as pastors of the Church" (LG 20; cf. 18; CD 2). This statement certainly implies that the episcopate is not an element of purely human and variable Church law. It also indicates some sort of apostolic succession of a sacramental and juridical nature, since the bishops have, in the traditional phrase, taken the place *(in locum successisse)* of the apostles, but it does not tell us how this succession has come about.[24] The early tradition also speaks of succession from, and in, the apostles.[25]

There is wide diversity in understanding the meaning of apostolic succession. All Churches accept that apostolicity involves a succession in the faith of the apostles and a sharing in the universal mission given to the apostles. Many Protestant Churches would in the past have been happy with the aphorism of Luther: "The true apostolic succession is the gospel. Whoever preaches the pure gospel stands in apostolic succession." The acceptability of this axiom will depend greatly on how the word "gospel" is understood and the ecclesiological presuppositions that lie behind its use. The Anglican Communion, the Orthodox, and other Eastern Churches, the Old Catholic and the Roman Catholic Churches insist also on uninterrupted succession in ministry brought about through the ordination of bishops. The classical apologetics of Catholic ecclesiology would speak of "legitimate" or "formal" succession in order to exclude Anglicans and Orthodox.[26] Orthodox views vary in the emphasis they give to apostolic faith and life, to episcopal succession

and the succession of faith communities, and to the eschatological function of the apostles. There is generally a very strong accent on the "now" of apostolicity, especially in the Eucharistic liturgy.[27]

The views of K. Barth (q.v.) are important because influential. He rejects any view of apostolicity based on historical or juridical grounds, and strongly objects to apostolic succession being based on ordination as this would be to predispose the Holy Spirit to act according to human demands, a transferring of the Holy Spirit from person to person. For him there is legitimate apostolic succession only when there is a following of the apostles in discipleship, hearing, respect and obedience, all according to Scripture.[28]

In Vatican II we find a further idea of the local Church (q.v.) also being apostolic through the power of Christ (LG 26).[29] Apostolicity is not merely chronological but also effective in each age. It is "the continuing fidelity to Christ's loving and saving work and message, to ministry and service inspired by the evangelical vision and teaching of the original apostles."[30] For a full notion of apostolic succession we have to take account of the whole Church being in actual dependence on Christ through those whom he has sent, and of the hierarchy being in a particular way successors of the apostles in a mission of sanctification, preaching, and pastoring.[31]

We should also note ecumenical convergence. In Vatican II there was some acceptance of apostolicity in the Orthodox Churches: the authentic theological traditions of the Orientals are "nourished by the living tradition of the apostles" (UR 17); they have true sacraments "through apostolic succession" (UR 15); the tradition handed down from the apostles *(tradita ab apostolis hereditas)* was differently received in the East and the West (UR 14).[32] In the various ecumenical dialogues there is also a growing convergence on the central notions about apostolicity and some willingness on the part of some Churches to recognize a genuine apostolicity in others.[33] For Churches of a more "Protestant" kind the criterion of apostolic succession had been restricted mainly to succession of apostolic doctrine. Churches of a more "Catholic" emphasis insisted too exclusively on the succession of legitimate ministers through episcopal ordination. Moreover, Roman Catholicism demanded communion with the See of Peter as essential to full apostolic succession. Recent dialogues have widened the discussion and have also shown a new readiness to agree on some essentials of the meaning of apostolic succession.[34] F.A. Sullivan sums up the situation by the 1980s, noting that "we have seen a growing recognition, on the part of Catholics, of the apostolic character of the faith, life and ministry of Protestant churches, and a growing appreciation, on the part of Protestants, of the importance of episcopal ordination as a sign of the apostolicity of ministry."[35] The Roman Catholic-Lutheran Joint Commission rightly pointed to the next crucial step, namely, the mutual recognition of ministry, and had the courage to make concrete suggestions.[36]

At the basis of apostolic succession is the question of how we today can be joined through time and space to the unique Christ event. Apostolic succession shows that the Christ event is mediated in the community of the Church through ministers who are in doctrinal and sacramental continuity with the apostles. Apostolic ministry is inseparable from apostolic doctrine, and guarantees it.[37]

[1]P. Rogers, The Few in Charge of the Many. Diss. (Rome: Gregorian University, 1977) 50–51. [2]M.M. Garijo-Guembe, "La 'sucesión apostólica' en los tres primeros siglos de la Iglesia," DiálEcum 11 (1976) 179–231; G. Mastrandrea, "Il principio di apostolicità nella chiesa romana dal I al V secolo," Nicol 6 (1978) 355–362. [3]Cf. A.M. Javierre, El tema literario de la sucesión en el Iudaismo, Helenismo y Christianismo primitivo. Bibl. theol. Salesiana 1 (Zurich: Pas, 1963); idem, "Le thème de la succession des apôtres dans la littérature chrétienne primitive," in Y. Congar and B.-D. Dupuy, eds., L'Épiscopat et l'Église universelle, US 39 (Paris, 1962) 171–221. [4]Congar, L'Église une 199–201. [5]Patrology 1:90-91; J.A. Kleist, ACW 6:31-32. [6]Patrology 1:49-50; J.A. Kleist, ACW 1:4-5. [7]Eusebius, Hist. eccl. 2:25. [8]Text in Halton 101–102; SC 167:167, 171. [9]Patrology 1:63-64; A.J. Kleist, ACW 1:53-56. [10]Magnesians 6:1; see Philadelphians Intro. [11]Ephesians 3:2; 5:3; Magnesians 2; 3:1; Trallians 2:1; 3:1; Smyrnaeans 8:2. [12]Trallians 2:2; 3:1. [13]Philadelphians Intro.; 3:2; 7:2; 8:1. [14]Philadelphians 4; Smyrnaeans 8:1-2; 9:2. [15]Smyrnaeans 9:1; Polycarp 4:1. [16]Adv. haer. 3:3, 1. [17]Ibid., 4:26, 2; cf. 3:3, 4 with B. Botte, "À propos de l'Adversus haereses III, 3, 2 de saint Irénée," Irén 30 (1957) 156–163; See E. Molland, "Irenaeus of Lugdunum and the Apostolic Succession," JEH 1 (1950) 12–28; idem, "Le développement de l'idée de succession apostolique," RHPR 35 (1954) 1–29. [18]Ibid., 3:3, 1. On lists, cf. E. Casper, Die älteste römische Bischofsliste (Berlin, 1926). [19]De praescript. haer. 20–21; 32; 36–37—Halton 100; Eno 58–59, 60–63; CCL 1:201-203, 212-213, 216-218. [20]Eusebius, Hist. eccl. 4:21-22—Eng. trans. 181; cf. Patrology 1:284-286. [21]F.A. Sullivan, The Church We Believe In: One, Holy, Catholic and Apostolic (Dublin: Gill and Macmillan—Mahweh: Paulist, 1988) 172; J.N.D. Kelly, "'Catholic and Apostolic' in the Early Church," OneChr 6 (1970) 274–287 at 283. [22]G. Dix, ed., and H. Chadwick, revised ed., The Apostolic Tradition (London: Alban Press—Ridgefield, Conn.: Morehouse, [2]1992); B. Botte, SC 11 bis. [23]Text Halton 104–105; see Sullivan (n. 21) 109. [24]See K. Rahner, in Vorgrimler 1:190-192; O. Perler, "L'évêque représentant du Christ selon les documents des premiers siècles," in Y. Congar and B.D. Duprey (n. 3) 31–66. [25]J.-M. Garrigues and M.-J. Le Guillou, "Statut eschatologique et caractère ontologique de la succession apostolique," RThom 75 (1978) 395–417 at 403–405; Javierre, op. cit. (n. 3). [26]E.g., Salaverri Ecclesia 600–601. [27]M.M. Garijo-Guembe, "Notas sobre la sucesión apostólica en la teología ortodoxa," DiálEcum 11 (1976) 131–154; J.D. Zizioulas, "La continuité avec les origines apostoliques dans la conscience théologique des Églises orthodoxes," Istina 19 (1974) 66–94. [28]Church Dogmatics 4:1 (Edinburgh: Clark, 1956) 712–725; cf. C. O'Grady, The Church in the Theology of Karl Barth (London: Chapman, 1968) 279–284; idem, The Church in Catholic Theology: Dialogue with Karl Barth (London: Chapman, 1969) 310–317. [29]E. Lanne, "The Local Church: Its Catholicity and Apostolicity," OneChr 6 (1970) 288–313.

[30]Sharing the Faith: National Catechetical Directory for Catholics of the United States (Washington, D.C.: U.S. Catholic Conference, 1979) 41; M. Vellanickal, "Apostolicity and the Individual Churches," JDhara 13 (1983) 265–278. [31]International Theological Commission, Texts and Documents (1969–1985) (San Francisco: Ignatius, 1989)—"The Apostolicity of the Church and Apostolic Succession (1973)" 93–104/DocCath 71 (1974) 613–618. [32]E. Lanne (n. 29) 302–305. [33]See Sullivan (n. 21) 186–188. [34]H. Mayer and L. Vischer, eds., Growth in Agreement. Ecumenical Documents 2 (New York: Paulist, 1984); Sullivan (n. 21) 185–209. [35]Op. cit. (n. 21) 209. [36]Text Information Service of Secretariat for Promoting Christian Unity 59 (1985) III–IV, pp. 44–72; cf. Sullivan (n. 21) 207–209. [37]Congar (n. 3) 214–215; Conc 34 (1968)4/4—"Apostolic by Succession?"; E.J. Kilmartin, "Apostolic Office: Sacrament of Christ," TS 36 (1975) 243–264.

## APOSTOLIC TRADITION

A document of the greatest importance for liturgical history and for ecclesiology, the *Apostolic Tradition,* poses enormous difficulties for historians. It was commonly attributed to Hippolytus, an author noted by Eusebius as bishop of an unknown see,[1] and known to Jerome,[2] though neither ascribe this work to him. There was also a priest Hippolytus (b. ca. 178), who opposed Pope Callistus for laxity towards penitents, and remained in schism under his two successors also. Reconciled later, he was martyred in 235 and is venerated as a saint. Some describe him as a Roman;[3] others suggest an oriental origin, e.g., Alexandria;[4] others prefer to leave aside the issue.[5] In 1551 a statue now in the Vatican Library was discovered with thirteen works inscribed on its base including the *Apostolic Tradition.* It would now seem that the statue is not in fact of Hippolytus, though the inscribed titles are from the first half of the 3rd century.[6] On the basis of the complex evidence available,[7] various scholarly positions are to be noted: with Eusebius, Jerome, and Photius, some will say that most of the works ascribed to Hippolytus in tradition, and the statue itself, are authentic;[8] two writers are involved, called Hippolytus and Jôsêpos,[9] or both called Hippolytus.[10] Authorship of the *Apostolic Tradition* is denied to Hippolytus by some,[11] but affirmed by others such as A.-G. Martimort and B. Botte, both, however, insisting on the value of the treatise irrespective of its authorship.[12]

Other works by, or ascribed to, Hippolytus have notable ecclesiology, e.g., the image of the boat in *The Antichrist,*[13] and of the key of the sealed books (Isa 29:11; Rev 3:7; ch. 5) in the commentary on Daniel.[14] These two works are also important for their explicit rejection of an imminent Parousia.[15] But the most important work, whatever about its authorship, is the *Apostolic Tradition,* which dates from the early 3rd century, even though B. Botte's reconstruction represents the text about a century later.[16] Some scholars regard it as a composite work and prefer to call it *diataxeis* (Statutes, from an 8th-century florilegium) rather than *paradosis* (Tradition).[17] A. Faivre notes that it is the most often cited ancient document in post-Vatican II theology,[18] and Martimort states that "the Church of *Lumen gentium* would recognize itself in the picture given to us in the *Apostolic Tradition*."[19] The work is one of several apostolic collections (q.v.) which establish norms for behavior, liturgy, and Church order. It is safe to hold that the text represents customs at Rome about the beginning of the 3rd century, some being unique to that city. Given the conservative character of the document, it may sometimes reflect the situation as it was several decades earlier. It must not, however, be taken as a set of norms or liturgical texts that were obligatory elsewhere, even though it was to have a profound influence in later centuries.

It opens with a reference to charisms, which may be a lost first part of the work, since the statue inscription can be read as *Apostolic Tradition on Charisms* or *On Charisms and Apostolic Tradition*. It announces that it will give the essential of the tradition *(ad verticem traditionis)* that persisted until then, and which is known by the grace of the Holy Spirit (Prologue).[20] There follow three parts: institutions in the Church (1–14), initiation (15–21/15–23), and practices of the Church (22–42/24–38). The first part (1–6) begins with the bishop (q.v.): he is chosen by the people who assemble on Sunday with the presbyterium; the bishops who gather impose hands (v. IMPOSITION OF HANDS) at the request of all (2).[21] There is silent prayer for the descent of the Spirit and then a consecratory prayer (2–3/2:4, 3; v. BISHOPS). The prayer here and elsewhere is a model: a bishop may pray spontaneously or according to a fixed form; the only condition is right doctrine *(orthodoxos—9/10:3-5)*.

There follows an anaphora, important among other reasons for being the basis of the modern Eucharistic Prayer II. Here as elsewhere it retains a primitive Christology, using *puer* (child) for Jesus. The prayer is said by the bishop but with and on behalf of the assembled people ("we"). After the narration of the Eucharistic institution, there is an *anamnêsis (memores)* and the earliest *epiclêsis* (q.v.), a prayer that the Holy Spirit come upon the offering (4/4:11-12) and fill the people, confirming their faith in truth (4/4:12). In other places, too, we find important elements of pneumatology (q.v.): in concluding doxologies the Spirit is seen as in the Church *(cum Sancto Spiritu in sancta Ecclesia—6/6:4;* cf. 7/8:5 . . .); the Spirit will give perfect grace to those who have a right faith so that they will be able to teach; the Spirit is to come also upon the priest (q.v.) and deacon (q.v.) at ordination and on the newly baptized at the post-baptismal anointing (v. INITIATION); the Spirit is present for discernment about illicit states of life for catechumens (16/16:25); the faithful are to be diligent in attending

morning instructions in the church, "where the Spirit abounds *(floret)"* (35/31:2; 41/35:3).

Two episcopal blessings follow, the Latin version of the blessing of the oil is the first appearance of the trilogy, priest-prophet-king (q.v.). There follow the rites for the ordination of presbyters and deacons (7–8/8–9; v. PRIESTS, DEACONS). Here we see clearly the unity of the presbyterium around the bishop of the local Church, a picture which complements the doctrine of Ignatius of Antioch (q.v.) a century earlier. There are several difficulties in the next section, on confessors (q.v.): some are to receive the imposition of the hand (9/10:1-2), but widows (q.v.), readers (q.v.), virgins (q.v.), subdeacons (q.v.), and healers (v. HEALING) are not to receive the imposition (10–14/11–15). These texts show a developed practice and emerging theory of the imposition of the hand (q.v.).

The second part of the *Apostolic Tradition* is concerned with initiation (q.v. and v. BAPTISM) from the first steps of the candidate to full incorporation in the Eucharist. Here, too, we have a picture of the local Church: all are involved in the presentation of the candidate, and the instruction can be given by laity.[22] This part ends with a reference to the *disciplina arcani:* matters of the faith are to be given by the bishop only to those who have communicated (21/23:14).

The third part deals with various matters of Church life, but is somewhat lacking in order and unity. The Eucharist is received on Sunday and on other days as the bishop decides (22/23:3). Norms are laid down for fasting, almsgiving, common meals, care with the Eucharistic elements, evening and other prayer times.[23] People are to attend morning instruction if there is one. It concludes with an exhortation to hold fast to this apostolic doctrine, for heresy (q.v.) has come about because of lack of teaching. If there is anything missing in this instruction, God, who directs the Church, will reveal it.

The historical importance of the *Apostolic Tradition* lies partly in its influence on other collections of norms and in its liturgical authority. But perhaps more than all else it remains a model for ecclesiology, legislation, and liturgy in being solidly founded on a Christological, soteriological, and ultimately Trinitarian basis: Church life, law, and liturgy can have no other foundation.[24]

[1]*Hist. eccl.* 6:20; 6:22; 6:45 (pp. 261–262, 286).  [2]*De viribus inlustribus* 61—LNPF 3:375.  [3]E.g., B. Botte, *La Tradition apostolique de saint Hippolyte: Essai de reconstruction,* Liturgiewissenschaftliche Quellen und Forschungen 31 (Münster: Aschendorff, 1963) xi–xvii, a view he retained SC 11bis; G. Kretschmar, "Early Christian Liturgy in the Light of Contemporary Historical Research," StLtg 16 (1986–1987) 31–53 at 32–33—cf. MaisD 149 (1982) 57–90 at 61; T.J. Harrington, "The Local Church at Rome in the Second Century: A Common Cemetery Emerges amid Developments in this 'Laboratory of Christian Policy,'" StCan 23 (1989) 167–188. For English

translation see G. Dix, ed., and H. Chadwick, revised ed., *The Apostolic Tradition* (London: Alban Press—Ridgefield, Conn.: Morehouse, ²1992). ⁴E.g., J.-M. Hanssens, *La liturgie d'Hippolyte, Ses documents—son titulaire: Ses origines et son caractère.* Orientalia christiana analecta 155 (Rome: Oriental Institute, 1959, ²1965). ⁵M. Richard, "Hippolyte de Rome (saint)," DSpir 7:531–571 at 545. ⁶See M. Guarducci, "La statua di 'Sant'Ippolito,'" in AA.VV. *Ricerche su Ippolito.* Studia ephemeridis *Augustianum* 13 (Rome: Instit. Augustianum, 1977) 17–30, who is followed by E. Prinzivelli, "Hippolytus, Statue of," EncycEarCh 1:385. ⁷See H. Leclerque, "Hippolyte (Statue et cimetière de saint)," DACL 6:2419-2483 for almost all relevant texts. ⁸E.g., Patrology 2: 163-207 (Quasten, 1950). ⁹E.g., P. Nautin, *Hippolytus et Josipe. Contribution à l'histoire de la littérature chrétienne du troisième siècle.* Études et textes pour l'histoire du dogme de la Trinité 1 (Paris: Cerf, 1947); idem, "Hippolytus," EncycEarCh 1:383-385. ¹⁰E.g., V. Loi, "L'identità letteraria di Ippolito di Roma" in *Ricerche su Ippolyto* (n. 6) 88; M. Somonetti, "Due note su Ippolito," ibid., 125, cf. 153. ¹¹E.g., J. Magne, *Tradition apostolique sur les charismes et Diataxis des saints apôtres* (Paris: n.p., 1975); idem, "En finir avec la 'Tradition' d'Hippolyte!," BLitEc 89 (1988) 5–22; M. Metzger, "Nouvelles perspectives pour la prétendue *Tradition apostolique,*" EcOr 5 (1988) 241–259. ¹²A.-G. Martimort, "La tradition apostolique d'Hippolyte," AnnéeCan 23 (1979) 159–173; idem, "Nouvel examen de la 'Tradition Apostolique' d'Hippolyte," BLitEc 88(1987) 5–25; idem, "Encore Hipployte et la 'Tradition apostolique,'" BLitEc 92 (1991) 113–137; B. Botte, *La tradition* (n. 3) xvii. ¹³N. 59—*Hippolytus* (Edinburgh, 1869) 2:35. ¹⁴*In Dan.* 19–20—*Hippolytus* (Edinburgh, 1887) 1:453-454. ¹⁵D.G. Dunbar, "The Delay of the Parousia in Hippolytus," VigChr 37 (1983) 313–327. The two works are probably authentic, but cf. Nautin, EncycEarCh 1:384. ¹⁶N. 3. ¹⁷See Magne and Metzger (both n. 11). ¹⁸"La documentation canonico-liturgique de l'Église ancienne," RevSR 54 (1980) 204–219, 273–297 at 279, n. 30. ¹⁹"Nouvel examen" (n. 12) 7. ²⁰Numbers given are Botte, SC/Dix; see *Abbreviations.* ²¹P.F. Bradshaw, "The Participation of other Bishops in the Ordination of a Bishop in the *Apostolic Tradition* of Hippolytus," StPatr 18/2 (1989) 335–338. ²²B. Botte, "Peuple chrétien et hiérarchie dans la 'Tradition apostolique' de saint Hippolyte," in AA.VV. *L'assemblée liturgique et les différents rôles dans l'assemblée.* Conférences Saint-Serge 23—Biblioteca Ephemerides liturgicae subsidia 9 (Rome: Ed. Liturgiche, 1977) 79–91, esp. 83–84. ²³L.E. Phillips, "Daily Prayer in the *Apostolic Tradition* of Hippolytus," JTS 40 (1989) 389–400. ²⁴See Martimort, "La tradition" (n. 12) 173.

## AQUINAS

See THOMAS AQUINAS, ST.

## ARMS RACE

The arms race which followed World War II was a most important challenge to Catholic moral theology, and was an instance of the positions and counter-positions that characterize the groping of the Church in its magisterium (q.v.), theologians, and believers as its teaching is stretched and develops (v. DEVELOPMENT OF DOCTRINE).[1] Vatican II laid down the principle that "peace is more than the absence of war. . . . [Peace] must be actualized by those thirsting after an ever more perfect reign of justice. . . . [P]eace is also the fruit of love, for love goes beyond what justice can ensure" (GS 78). Later, the same document condemned total warfare (GS 80) and went on to state that "the arms race is one of the greatest traps (*gravissimam plagam*) for humanity and one which injures the poor to an intolerable degree" (GS 81).

After the council, nations continued to spend a huge percentage of their gross national product (GNP) on armaments, with nations in the Third World/Socioeconomic South, spending proportionately more than the Warsaw Pact and National Atlantic Treaty Organization (NATO) blocs. Prior to 1989 these latter developed a strategy of deterrence (cf. GS 81) on which and on related matters several hierarchies offered guidance.[2] It gradually became clear that the classical "just war" morality[3] could not be neatly applied to nuclear combat.[4] Reaction to the U.S. bishops' statements was mixed, especially on the crucial issue of the qualitative difference of nuclear war and on the limits to the doctrine of deterrence.[5] Concern for these issues is an important area of ecumenical collaboration and reflection.[6] In the end one cannot escape the strong language of the Roman Synod of 1974 which, in a document presented by the Holy See to a United Nations special committee for the study of disarmament,[7] described the arms race as "insanity" and "a machine gone mad."

¹J.A. Dwyer, "Peace" in NDictT 748–753. ²M. Heirman, "Bishops' Conferences on War and Peace in 1983," CrossC 33 (1983–1984) 275–288; cf. J.R. Connolly, "The Morality of Nuclear Deterrence: Conditional or Unconditional," IrTQ 54 (1988) 1–20; O. O'Donovan, *Peace and Certainty: A Theological Essay on Deterrence* (Oxford: Clarendon, 1989). ³Going back to Augustine and forged out in Middle Ages, the just war theory is explained (with bibliog.) in U.S. Bishops' pastoral, *The Challenge of Peace: God's Promise and Our Response*—May 3, 1983 (Washington, D.C.: United States Catholic Conference, 1983) 26–34 with nn. 31–32; cf. E.A. Synan, "St. Thomas Aquinas and the Profession of Arms," MedSt 50 (1980) 404–437. ⁴D. Mieth, "On the State of Peace Discussions in the Catholic Church," Conc 195 (1988) 44–52 at 49–50. ⁵J.E. Dougherty, *The Bishops and Nuclear Weapons: The Catholic Pastoral Letter on War and Peace* (Connecticut: Archon-Shoe String, 1984); J.M. Finnis, J.M. Boyle Jr, C. Grisez, *Nuclear Deterrence: Morality and Realism* (Oxford: Clarendon, 1987); G. Weigel, *"Tranquillitas Ordinis": The Present Failure and Future Promise of American Catholic Thought on War and Peace* (Oxford—New York: Oxford UP, 1987); R.L. Barry and M.M. Murphy, "Can Deterrence be Moral?: A Review Discussion," Thom 52 (1988) 719–736; J. R. Connolly, "The Morality of Nuclear Deterrence," IrTQ 54 (1988) 1–20; cf. D. Martin and P. Mullan, eds., *Unholy Warfare: The Church and the Bomb* (Oxford: Blackwell, 1983). ⁶*Peace and Disarmament: Documents of the World Council of Churches/Roman Catholic Church* (Geneva: WCC—Vatican: Commisione Iustitia et Pax, 1982). ⁷Quoted in M.E. Jegen, "An Entirely New Attitude," Conc 165 (1983) 51–60 at n. 2.

## ASSOCIATIONS OF THE FAITHFUL

Even before the time of Constantine (d. 337—q.v.) associations or societies of various kinds were found among the faithful.[1] Guilds, societies, and lay confraternities later multiplied, necessitating legislation by

Hincmar of Rheims in 852 to curb abuses and to regulate their relationship with Church authorities. During the Middle Ages many confraternities and third orders developed, often associated with religious orders. Under Gregory XIII (1572–1585) transnational archconfraternities arose; with their Roman approval they could share their spiritual privileges with other societies. A great number of societies, many of which still exist, were founded after the Council of Trent (q.v.). The 1917 *Code of Canon Law* in an extensive treatment (CIC 684–725) distinguished associations from religious institutes and societies without vows, and noted their three main purposes: the spiritual perfection of the members, exercising works of piety or charity, and advancing public worship (CIC 685). The 1917 *Code* also laid down some conditions regulating the relationship between the Church authorities and associations,[2] but one would have to say that this section of the earlier *Code* reflected the hierarchical and institutional model of the Church then in vogue, and that the associations were seen as *lay*. Between 1917 and Vatican II, while many associations continued to be founded, two important new developments took place: Catholic Action (v. APOSTOLATE) and Secular Institutes (q.v.). A further significant factor was the special status given to one of the most successful of all lay associations, the Society of St. Vincent de Paul, which was excluded from many norms of the 1917 *Code* (CIC 686–699).[3] Vatican II warmly endorsed associations of the faithful, including some for priests and religious.[4]

The new *Code* of 1983 affirmed the establishment of associations as one of the fundamental rights of the faithful (not therefore just the laity): "The Christian faithful are free to found and to govern associations for charitable and religious purposes, or for the fostering of the Christian vocation in the world; they can come together for meetings to pursue these purposes in common" (CIC 215). This statement should also be seen in the light of the following canon, which states the right of all the faithful to share in the mission of the Church by apostolic activity (CIC 216).

A later canon explaining the right of CIC 215 is broader than the 1917 *Code:* "In the Church there are associations distinct from institutes of consecrated life and societies of apostolic life, in which the faithful, either clergy or laity, or clergy together with laity, strive to further a more perfect life by promoting public worship or Christian doctrine, or by fostering other works of the apostolate, namely attempts at evangelization, the exercise of works of charity or piety, the animation of the temporal order with a Christian spirit" (CIC 298). It might be hard to conceive of works which would not fit under one of these very open categories. But the latter may not, however, sufficiently cover associations that could lie between these lay associations and institutes of consecrated life or societies of apostolic life.[5] It has been argued that the *Code* did not take on board the variety of associations envisaged in Vatican II (AA 18–19) and that it furnished an excessively juridical framework within which associations are to be viewed.[6]

The canons governing associations (298–329)[7] have to be observed by associations which are public (CIC 301 § 3), i.e., erected by the competent authority, or are private (CIC 299), i.e., established by agreement of their members and later approved.[8] Approval will involve the acceptance of their statutes (CIC 304, 314, 333 § 2). They are subsequently subject to ecclesiastical authority in such matters as faith and morals and Church law, and are juridic persons (see CIC 114–116, and 322 in the case of private associations).[9] But though there is a preference for public (erected or subsequently adopted by authority) or private (approved) associations (CIC 298 § 2), there is no exclusion of associations which do not seek to have such status; CIC 299 § 3 refers to recognition *(agnoscitur)* of associations, not to their right to exist.[10] Those that have not sought or received approval would be bound by the obligations arising from the common good of the Church and the rights of others (CIC 223 § 1). The competent authority for approval of public associations is the Holy See for universal and international ones, the conference of bishops for national ones, and the local bishop for diocesan associations (CIC 312). Groups which share in the spirit of some religious institute are called "third orders or some other appropriate name"; these are under the higher direction of the institute (CIC 303). It should be noted that no association may call itself "Catholic" without approval from the competent authority (CIC 300), since this title is one of the marks (q.v.) of the Church (v. CATHOLIC) and thus may not be adopted by a private decision (cf. CIC 216, 803 § 3).

The further norms of the *Code* distinguish between public (312–320) and private associations (321–326). They deal with matters of organization (CIC 304–305), membership (CIC 306–308, 316), functioning (CIC 309–311, 323–325), moderators or leaders (CIC 309, 317–318, 324 § 1), chaplains and spiritual guides (CIC 317, 324, cf. 564), administration of goods (CIC 319, 325), suppression of associations (CIC 320, 326), autonomy (CIC 321), and the juridic personality of associations (CIC 322). There are also special canons about associations of clergy, i.e., with diocesan clergy as members (CIC 278 §§ 1–2), clerical associations, i.e., under the direction of clergy (CIC 302), and associations of laity (CIC 327–329). The very positive tone of these canons, as well as the flexibility allowed, would give ample room for future developments according to the charism that may be given to members of the faithful (see LG 12; PO 9; AA 3) to serve the mission of the

Church by establishing or evolving associations of the faithful. Though associations have a long history, there is need for further theological reflection on their nature[11] and for a positive attitude to future forms.

One of the most important developments in religious life in the l980s was the growth of associations connected with religious congregations. Their form and the strength of the bond with the institute varies, but there are two vital advantages: the faithful are helped to live their Christian commitment through the charism of the religious institute; the religious deepen their grasp of their own charism in the very act of sharing it.

[1]J.A. Amos, "A Legal History of Associations of the Christian Faithful," StCan 21 (1987) 271–297; S. de Angelis, *De fidelibus associationibus,* 2 vols. (Naples, 1959).  [2]Amos, 281–283.  [3]AAS 13 (1921) 135–144.  [4]AA 4, 15, 21, 22; CD 17, 29, 30; AG 15, 38, 39, 41; PC 22; GE 8; GS 90; PO 8–9.  [5]A. Jacobs, "Les associations de fidèles dans l'Église," StCan 22 (1988) 359–379 at 379.  [6]E. Corecco, "Aspects of the Reception of Vatican II in the Code of Canon Law," in G. Alberigo et al., eds., *The Reception of Vatican II* (Washington, D.C.: The Catholic University Press—Tunbridge Wells: Burns and Oates, 1987) 268–269; cf. G. Ghirlanda, "Quaestiones de christifidelium consociationibus non solutae," Periodica 80 (1991) 523–558.  [7]E. Kneal, "Associations of the Christian Faithful," in Coriden CIC 243–257; R. Pagé, "Associations of the Faithful in the Church," Jurist 47 (1987) 165–203; L. Martínez Sistach, "Asociaciones públicas y privadas de laicos," IusCan 26 (1986) 139–183; W. Schulz, "La posizione giuridica delle associazioni e la loro funzione nella Chiesa," Apoll 59 (1986) 115–130.  [8]R. Pagé, "Les associations de fidèles: reconnaissance et érection," StCan 19 (1985) 327–338; cf. J.T. Martín de Agar, "Brevi cenni sulle fondamento dei rapporti tra gerarchia e associazioni," Apoll 62 (1989) 49–58.  [9]Schulz (n. 7) 116–120.  [10]Schulz (n. 7) 122–124; Pagé (n. 8) 172–174, 199–200.  [11]L. Gerosa, "Le 'charisme originaire': Pour une justification théologique du droit des associations dans l'Église," NRT 112 (1990) 234–235.

# AUGSBURG CONFESSION

In 1530 a profession of faith[1] was presented to the Emperor Charles V at the Diet of Augsburg. Written with some help from Luther (who commented on a first draft), it was almost totally the work of Philipp Melanchthon (q.v.), and it aimed at countering the charges of John Eck (1486–1543) that Lutheranism was reviving ancient heresies. It took account of Zwingli's (q.v.) positions and opposed Anabaptist (q.v.) tenets. It is in twenty-eight articles. The first twenty-one are irenic in tone: God (1); Original Sin (2); the Son of God (3); Justification (4); Ecclesiastical Ministry (5, 14); New Obedience (6); Church (7–8); Sacraments (9–13); Ecclesiastical Rites (15); Civil Affairs (16); Eschatology (17); Free Will (18); Cause of Sin (19); Faith and Good Works (20); Veneration of the Saints (21). The second part, written first, is harsher and deals with the perceived abuses in the Church of the time: Communion under Two Kinds (22); Priestly Marriage (23); the Mass (24); Confession (25); Foods, Fast and Abstinence (26); Monastic Vows (27); Ecclesiastical Power (28). The Emperor's theologians at the Diet drew up a reply, the *Confutatio Pontificia,*[2] which approved nine articles totally, six in part or with qualifications, and rejected thirteen. Melanchthon produced a reply, *Apologie,*[3] which the Emperor refused to accept.

The *Augsburg Confession* has always been a basic document of Lutheranism.[4] Around the 1950s, in the Lutheran movement *Die Sammlung,* a more Catholic understanding of the text was proposed,[5] though without very much influence. For the 450th anniversary of the *Confession,* congresses were held and many studies appeared.[6] Catholics began to ask if their Church could not accept the document as an authentic expression of a common faith:[7] some were positive, but later drew back;[8] others were positive, but with varying nuances;[9] some were negative.[10] Other Churches, too, studied its implications.[11]

The ecclesiology[12] of the *Confession* is to be found mainly in arts. 5, 7, 8, 14 and 28, though the word *ecclesia* is found 83 times in the Latin text, with *Kirche* and derivatives 54 times. The main statement on the Church is art. 7: ". . . the one holy Church will remain forever. Now this Church is the congregation of the saints, in which the Gospel is rightly taught *(pure docetur/rein gepredigt),* and the sacraments are rightly *(recte/gereicht)* administered. And for that unity of the Church it is enough to have agreement about the doctrine of the Gospel and the administration of the sacraments. It is not necessary that the traditions of men, or rites and ceremonies instituted by men, be everywhere the same . . ." (cf. 5 on preaching). The meaning of "saints" is the NT one (e.g., Phil 1:1) and that of the Creed,[13] and it is not clear that Melanchthon is saying more than LG 15, which states that for full communion, grace and faith are necessary, when he states in art. 8, which directly envisages Donatism: ". . . the Church is properly *(proprie sit/eigentlich nicht anders ist dann)* the congregation of saints and true believers . . . in which hypocrites and sinners are mixed" *(admixti sunt/bleiben).* Moreover, the words "in which" from art. 7 imply a visible Church,[14] in which ministry is not excluded.[15] On ecclesiastical order, the *Confessio* demands that one be called in order to teach and administer the sacraments (14). At the conclusion there is a long section which is quite negative about the abuse of episcopal power, especially in secular matters (28), though Melanchthon defended a carefully delimited episcopal jurisdiction.[16]

Given the desire for unity, and the fact that the text belongs to the early days of the Reformation, it is understandable perhaps that the document is silent on matters which will later be divisive, such as the papacy, transubstantiation, purgatory, the Blessed Virgin.

But other matters that belong to a full presentation of Catholic truth are omitted, e.g., some sacraments (cf. 9–13, which deal only with baptism, the Lord's Supper, and confession). Furthermore, it must be admitted that two readings of the text are possible: a more Protestant and a more Catholic one. But unlike later Reformation documents, "it clearly accepts a Christianity in which salvation is mediated by the Church and not simply by the gospel."[17] It is also true that evangelical insights of the *Confessio,* such as the fiducial aspect of faith, tended to be neglected by polemical Catholic theology in succeeding centuries. As a Catholic presentation of evangelical Christianity, it still retains its value for ecumenical dialogue.

[1]Critical text Bekenntnisschriften 31–137, but for Latin see also H. Bornkamm, *Der authentische lateinische Text der* Confessio Augustana (1530)—(Heidelberg: UP, 1954); Eng. trans. Leith, Creeds 63–107; Schall, Creeds 3:1–73; T.G. Tappert, *The Book of Concord: The Confessions of the Evangelical Lutheran Church* (Philadelphia, 1959) 24–285; Kidd, n. 116, pp. 259–289; Bibliog. ETL ElenchBib 57 (1981) 298*–301*   [2]Text *Corpus Reformatorum* v. 27 (Halle—Berlin—Leipzig, 1859) 81–184 (Latin), 189–228 (German); M. Cassese, *Augusta 1530: Il dibattito luterano-cattolico* (Milan: Libera Facoltà Biblica Internazionale, 1981) 230–375 (Latin and Italian). See H. Immenkötter, *Die Confutatio der Confessio Augustana vom 3. August 1530.* Corpus Catholicorum 33 (Münster: Aschendorff, 1979); J. Wicks, "Abuses under Indictment at the Diet of Augsburg 1530." TS 41 (1980) 253–302 at 293–300. [3]Bekenntnisschriften (n. 1) 139–405. [4]G. Rupp, "Foundation Documents of the Faith: IV—The Augsburg Confession, 1530," ExpTim 91 (1979–1980) 99–101. [5]H. Asmussen, *Warum noch lutherische Kirche?: Ein Gespräch mit dem Ausburgerischen Bekenntnis* (Stüttgart, 1949); M. Lackmann, *The Augsburg Confession and Catholic Unity* (New York, 1963); idem, "The Call of Evangelical Christianity to Catholic Fulfillment," in H. Asmussen et al., *The Unfinished Reformation* (Notre Dame, Ind.: 1961) 70–97. [6]E.g., R. Blanc, ed., *La Confession d'Augsbourg. 450e anniversaire. Autour d'un colloque oecuménique internationale.* Le point théologique 37 (Paris: Beauchesne, 1980); Y. Congar, "Chronique oecuménique: Sur la Confession d'Augsbourg," RSPT 64 (1980) 255–264; G. Distante, "Un colloquio teologico internazionale sulla *Confessio Augustana,*" Nicol 8 (1986) 183–191; F. Heinrich and E. Ratz, eds., *Confessio Augustana: Hindernis oder Hilfe?* (Regensburg: Pustet, 1979); W.E. Langley, "The Augsburg Confession and Theological Traditions," TDig 28 (1980) 357–365; B. Lohse and O.H. Pesch, eds., *Das augsburger Bekenntnis von 1530 damals und heute* (Munich: Kaiser—Mainz: Grünewald, 1980); V. Vinay, "La confessio augustana in una visuale ecumenica," StEcum 1 (1983) 9–40. [7]"Catholic Recognition of the Augsburg Confession: A Selected Bibliography (1975–1979)," TDig 28 (1980) 120–123; R. Penaskovic, "Roman Catholic Recognition of the Augsburg Confession," TS 41 (1980) 303–321. [8]E.g., J. Ratzinger, "Prognosen für die Zukunft des Ökumenismus," *Bausteine* 17/65 (1977) 6–14, but cf. somewhat more negative "Anmerkungen zur Frage einer Anerkennung der Confessio Augustana durch die katholische Kirche," MüTZ 29 (1978) 225–237. [9]E.g., M. Cassese, "L'interpretazione cattolica della Confessiona Augustana del 1530," ScuolC 110 (1982) 272–288; A. Dulles, "The Catholicity of the Augsburg Confession," JRel 63 (1983) 337–354; W. Echermann, "Die Confessio Augustana in katholischer Sicht," TGl 68 (1978) 153–167; J.P. Kenny, "Roman Catholic Recognition of the Confession of Augsburg," IrTQ 48 (1981) 107–126; G.W. Forell and J.F.

McCue, eds., *Confessing One Faith: A Joint Commentary on the Augsburg Confession by Lutheran and Catholic Theologians* (Minneapolis: Augsburg, 1982); E. Iserloth, "450 Jahre Confessio Augustana: Eine Bilanz," Catholica 35 (1981) 1–16; P. Meinhold, ed., *Kirche und Bekenntnis: Historische und theologische Aspekte zur Frage der gegenseitigen Anerkennung der lutherischen und der katholischen Kirche auf der Grundlage der Confessio Augustana.* Institut für europäische Geschichte Mainz (Wiesbaden: Steiner, 1980); W. Kasper, "The Augsburg Confession in Roman Catholic Perspective," in H. Meyer, ed., *The Augsburg Confession in Ecumenical Perspective.* LWF Report 6/7 (Geneva: Lutheran World Federation, 1980) 163–187; H. Meyer, ed., *Lutheran/Roman Catholic Discussion on the Augsburg Confession: Documents 1977–1981.* LWF Report 10 (Geneva: Lutheran World Federation, 1982); H. Meyer, H. Schütte et al., eds., *Confessio Augustana Bekenntnis des einen Glaubens: Gemeinsame Untersuchung lutherischer und katholischer Theologen* (Paderborn: Bonifacius—Frankfurt am M.: Lembeck, 1980); R. Penaskovic, "Roman Catholic Recognition of the Augsburg Confession," TS 41 (1980) 303–321. [10]E.g., B. Gherardini, "La 'Confessio Augustana': Un Documento cattolico?," Divinitas 25 (1981) 206–218. [11]H. Meyer, ed., *The Augsburg Confession* (n. 9); V. Vajta, ed., *Confessio Augustana 1530–1980: Commemoration and Self-Examination.* LWF Report 9 (Geneva: Lutheran World Federation, 1980); W. Kahle, "Die Bedeutung der Confessio Augustana für die Kirchen im Osten," KirOst 27 (1984) 9–35; T. Nikolaou, "Zur Diskussion über die Confessio Augustana aus orthodoxer Sicht," UnaS 35 (1980) 154–160; D. Fischer, "Calvin et la Confession d'Augsbourg," RRéf 36 (1985) 72–91; G. Müller, "Die 'Confessio Augustana' im Jahre 1980," LuthJb 50 (1983) 126–149; G. Nagy (Lutheran), "Confessio Augustana: 450 anni di una confessio di fede ecumenica," Asp 27 (1980) 189–195; R.J. Neuhaus (Lutheran), "Augsburg and Catholicism: Healing the Reformation Breach," TTod 37 (1980–1981) 294–305. [12]J.S. Arrieta, "La Iglesia en la 'Confessio Augustana': su visión desde la perspectiva católica," EstE 57 (1982) 3–38; W. Beinert, "Der Kirchen und Sakraments Begriff der Confessio Augustana," TGl 69 (1979) 237–262; M. Casssese, "La concezione della Chiesa nella Confessio Augustana dal 1530," RicBibRel 14 (1980) 95–164; H. Meyer and H. Schütte, "Die Auffassung von Kirche im Augsburgischen Bekenntnis," in H. Meyer, H. Schütte et al., *Confessio Augustana* (n. 9) 168–197; R. Penaskovic, "The Ecclesiology of the Augsburg Confession," HeythJ 23 (1982) 139–152. [13]*Apologie* 7 and 8—Bekenntnisschriften (n. 1) 235. [14]Arrieta (n. 12) 13–15. [15]Ibid., 19–24, citing W. Beinert, E. Iserloh, H. Schütte, et al. [16]Ibid., 24–28; cf. J. Wicks (n. 2) 283–284. [17]A. Dulles, "The Catholicity of the Augsburg Confession," JRel 63 (1983) 337–354 at 344 and cf. Dulles (n. 9).

## AUGUSTINE OF HIPPO, St. (354–430)

Augustine, the son of a pious mother, St. Monica, was enrolled as a catechumen shortly after his birth,[1] but drifted away from the faith at Carthage where he embraced Manichaeism. He was later enthusiastic over Neo-Platonism, an influence that would be inspirational for him for the rest of his life. Ambition[2] and providential circumstances led him to Milan, where he fell under the influence of Ambrose (q.v.) and the life of the Church there.[3] On 24 April 387 he was baptized; he was ordained a priest in 391 and became bishop of Hippo in 396, where he died in 430.[4]

Augustine's complex and profound ecclesiology can be studied in many ways.[5] It had various influences:

the key events in his life;[6] his conversion journey; episcopal ministry; the main heresies he had to contend with (Manichaeism, Donatism, and Pelagianism), and the areas of theology he developed in response (Trinity, Incarnation, grace,[7] and sacraments).

He sees the Church in the widest possible context: "The right order of the confession of faith requires that the Church should be subordinated to the Trinity, just as a house is to its inhabitants, a temple to its God, and a community to its founder. The holy Church as a whole, i.e., the Church in heaven as well as on earth, is the temple of God, even the temple of the most Holy Trinity."[8] If we add the Augustinian notion of the "Church from Abel" (v. ABEL), we have here the full range of his ecclesiology, which must be kept free from reductionism if it is to be authentic. We can note with Pope John Paul II: "One may rightly say that the summit of the theological thinking of the bishop of Hippo is Christ and the Church."[9] At the heart of his ecclesiology is the notion of the whole Christ *(Christus totus),* according to which Christ is always present and active in his body, the Church; the Church and Christ form one person. "The body of this head is the Church, not only the one which is in this place, but the Church which is present in this place and spread throughout the whole earthly world; and not only those who live in this time, but all from Abel to those who will be born at the end of time and believe in Christ: hence the people of the saints who belong to the one only city, the Body of Christ, whose head is Christ."[10] The soul of the Body is the Holy Spirit: "What the soul is for the body of man, the Holy Spirit is for the Body of Christ which is the Church; the Holy Spirit operates in the whole Church what the soul works in the members of a single body."[11] "Outside this body no one is animated by the Holy Spirit."[12] Though deeply pneumatological, Augustine develops the Church and its origins in terms of the mysteries of Christ's life, e.g., Incarnation, Cross, Ascension.[13]

We have seen above the extension of the Church in time and into eternity. There is the celestial Church whose citizens are angels;[14] the Church is primarily the active gathering of the new humanity into communion with God.[15] Again, "To serve the one God is the *raison d'être* of the whole Church,"[16] of Christianity—"this is the Christian religion: to serve and worship the one God."[17] There is an eschatological tension in Augustine's ecclesiology, one that appears under a variety of images: pilgrimage-homeland, hope-reality, faith-sight, labor-praise, threshing floor-barn, Lenten penance-Easter joy, labor pains-birth, and other contrasting images.

In his early writings,[18] and on his own admission,[19] Augustine held a moderate form of millenarianism (q.v.).[20] Later he would interpret the millenarianist texts of Rev 20:4 as the time between the binding of the strong man (Mark 3:27) in Christ's redemptive work and his reigning with the just.[21]

Many ecclesiological themes come together in Augustine's great work *City of God (De civitate Dei),*[22] which was written to refute the pagans who claimed that the Church was the cause of the ruin of the Roman Empire. But as É. Lamirande remarks, "it is not easy to determine exactly the relations asserted by Augustine between the Church and the City of God. It is not a complete identity, still less a complete dissociation."[23] The two cities, heavenly and earthly, are distinguished by their loves: love of God and love by God in the former, self-love in the latter. The subjects of the earthly city are those who have an exclusive or preponderant love for earthly things, whereas the subjects of the heavenly city are all whom God has chosen: first the angels, then the just who lived from the beginning to the end of time. In the present time the two cities are indeed separable, but mainly exist in this world as intermixed *(perplexae).*[24] Paul, for example, once belonged to the earthly city before his conversion. The Church is the place where the two cities interact: "the Church is the city of God insofar as the human race is concerned."[25] There are two stages in the one Church, not two Churches.[26] But Church in the most perfect sense is the celestial Church.[27]

Such ideas are not confined to the City of God. Elsewhere Augustine contrasts Peter as representing the here and now of the Church, with John already bearing the marks of the future; these are not, however, to be separated.[28] He also uses the images of Martha and Mary in a similar way.[29]

Augustine confessed the Church to be holy: in its doctrine and sacraments, as Body of Christ, and in the works and virtues of its members. This holiness is only a preparation for one which will be more complete.[30] But the principal claim for its holiness is the Holy Spirit, the true soul of the Church, for "the love of God poured into our hearts by the Holy Spirit, makes one of many souls, and one heart of many hearts."[31] The Holy Spirit works through many of his charisms in the Church, so that "if you want to live in the Spirit, [then] preserve love, love the truth, desire unity, and in this way reach eternity."[32] Augustine speaks of an invisible Church contained in a visible one. The visible Church contains all Christians, good and bad. Augustine's neo-Platonic philosophy is kept strictly at the service of his theological thought, as in the notion of the visible and invisible Church, based on the notion of the visibility of the body and the invisibility of the soul:[33] Christians who serve the world in a life of sin are visibly members of the Church, but do not belong to the "invisible union *(compago)* of charity";[34] they enjoy the communion of saints, but only the just constitute "the congregation and society of the saints."[35] There are different levels in belonging to the House of God.[36] The Church, then, is not a pure community as the Donatists or Montanists would demand, but a mixed one *(corpus permixtum)*.[37] This idea of the "mixed Church" was, like many other important ecclesiological insights, derived from Tyconius.[38] Sinners, moreover, are many, a multitude in fact.[39] More strikingly: "The Spouse found a prostitute and made her a virgin. One must not deny that she was a prostitute, lest liberating mercy be forgotten."[40] In the Church there is both chaff and grain.[41] But one must love this Church which one realistically sees as good and bad: "we have the Holy Spirit if we love the Church."[42]

Augustine firmly maintained the other marks (q.v.) of the Church. Indeed he might be called the apostle and theologian of unity.[43] Truth and orthodoxy are found only in that Church where "there is Christian unity and the love of the Holy Spirit."[44] From Cyprian (q.v.), who greatly influenced all of his theology, especially ecclesiology, he derived the idea that the Holy Spirit is the principle of unity in the Trinity and in the Church,[45] so that the Church is a people unified by the relation of Father, Son, and Spirit. B. Mondin remarks, "According to Augustine the first principle of invisible unity is the Holy Spirit who confers on the members of the Church the grace of Christ; the first principle of visible unity is the Eucharist."[46] The unity of the Church is "a community of the faithful united among themselves through Eucharistic love" so that "since what is realized is one, preserving the one faith, loving one another . . . to be one, preserving one sole faith, one only hope, an undivided charity."[47] For Augustine catholicity meant universality, as distinct from the local Church. He owes to Optatus (fl. 370) part of his vision of catholicity and some of the arguments he used against the Donatists. His major argument against them was that they lacked catholicity: they were to be found only in Africa, whereas the true Church was everywhere.[48] Nor is catholicity a mere territorial diffusion, but it is throughout time, from Abel to the second coming of Christ.[49] It includes not only those who believe in Christ up to the present but all who will believe in the future, so that catholicity passes over time into eternity.[50] Unity and diversity are represented in the Pentecostal gift of tongues.[51] The Church is a pilgrim with continual nostalgia for its homeland,[52] a theme influenced, among other things, by Neo-Platonism.

Augustine did not emphasize apostolicity to the extent that Irenaeus (q.v.) or Tertullian (q.v.) did. But we do find some texts where apostolicity is a criterion of authenticity. He noted that in Rome there were no Donatists among them.[53] He stressed the worldwide mission of the apostles beginning from Jerusalem preaching one gospel.[54] But he believed that except among a very few tribes, there had been preaching everywhere.[55] We can understand how having this belief he could presume that those not baptized were most likely in bad faith (v. SALVATION).

Augustine's views on the institutions of the Church,[56] while scarcely innovative, retain their validity for all time: from the way he was received by Ambrose, he knew the bishop's office to be a fatherly one,[57] though on a few occasions in an anti-Donatist context, he spoke against this title.[58] For him, the bishop's ministry is essentially a ministry of communion and service;[59] the faithful are usually called Church *(ecclesia),* people *(plebs/populus),* flock *(grex).* The model for his *Rule* is the first Jerusalem community.[60]

Images for the Church abound in Augustine's writings: it was above all mother (q.v.)—J. Ratzinger is surely right in suggesting that his major development of the idea of the Church as mother (q.v.) was deeply influenced by his own mother, Monica.[61] "Whatever you are, you can rest secure, you have God as your Father and the Church as your mother," is a typical phrase,[62] echoing Cyprian.[63] Likewise, "the Church gives birth and is a virgin. And if you think about it, she gives birth to Christ, for it is his members that are baptized."[64] This fecundity of the Church is modeled on Mary's: "The Church is a virgin . . . a virgin she conceives. She imitates Mary, who gave birth to the Lord. . . . Thus the Church gives birth and is a virgin."[65] The Church is God's house.[66] It is a nest: "I as a miserable one, when I thought I could fly, I left the nest, and fell before I could fly."[67] Other images include:[68] queen (q.v.) in both his comments on Ps 44(45) and Song of Songs;[69] the moon;[70] a ship;[71] the ark of Noah,[72] love (q.v.) of the Church; new Eve and especially spouse (q.v.);[73] mother hen,[74] widow,[75] and dove, characteristic of his anti-Donatist period.[76]

St. Augustine's rich ecclesiology proved to be very influential, especially in his doctrine of the "mixed" Church of the holy and the sinful; in his teaching on the Body of Christ whose soul is the Holy Spirit; in the scope (and occasional subsequent misunderstandings) of the two cities; in his insistence, against the Donatists, of the validity of sacraments received outside the Catholic Church; in his soundings of the relation of Church and State from the Donatist controversy.[77] Moreover, his ecclesiology is in a profound sense also a spirituality.[78] There is no ecclesiology that can avoid the questions posed by Augustine, and so often given penetrating answers by him.

[1]*Confessions* (infra *Conf.* 1:11, 17).  [2]*Conf.* 5:14, 24.  [3]N. Lanzi, *La Chiesa nella conversione di S. Agostino* (Vatican, 1989) 28–31 = DoctCom 41 (1988) 257–273; 42 (1989) 42–62 at 46–47; J. O'Meara, *The Young Augustine* (London, 1954, 1980) ch. 8.  [4]P. Brown, *Augustine of Hippo* (California, 1967); G. Bonner, *St. Augustine of Hippo: Life and Controversies* (Philadelphia, 1963—

Norwich: Canterbury Press 1986); G. Lawless, *Augustine of Hippo and His Monastic Rule* (Oxford: Clarendon, 1987); A. Trapè, *St. Augustine: Man, Pastor, Mystic* (New York: Catholic Book Pub. Co., 1986); F. van der Meer, *Augustine the Bishop* (London, 1961). [5]A. Trapè in Patrology 4:445-449, with excellent bibliog.; T.J. van Bavel, "What Kind of Church Do You Want?: The Breadth of Augustine's Ecclesiology," LouvSt 7 (1979) 147–171 = TDig 26 (1978) 30–35; P. Borgomeo, *L'Église de ce temps dans la prédication de saint Augustin* (Paris: Études Augustiniennes, 1972); F.G. Clancy, *St. Augustine of Hippo on Christ, His Church and the Holy Spirit: A Study of the "De baptismo" and the "Tractatus in Ioannis evangelium."* Diss. (Oxford, 1992); Congar, Augustin 11–24; S.J. Grabowski, *The Church: An Introduction to the Theology of St. Augustine* (St. Louis—London, 1957); É. Lamirande, "Un siècle et demi d'études sur l'ecclésiologie de saint Augustin," RevÉtAug 8 (1962) 1–125; idem, "Supplément bibliographique sur l'ecclésiologie de St. Augustin," ibid., 17 (1971) 177–182; idem, *Études sur l'ecclésiologie de saint Augustin* (Ottawa, 1969); idem, "L'Église dans l'*Enchiridion* de saint Augustin," EglT 10 (1979) 195–206; B. Mondin, "Il pensiero ecclesiologico di sant'Agostino," Sap 40 (1987) 369–391; A. Schindler, "Augustins Ekklesiologie in den Spannungsfeldern seiner Zeit und heutiger Ökumene," FreiZ 34 (1987) 295–309. [6]F. Hoffmann, *Der Kirchenbegriff des hl. Augustinus in seinen Grundlagen und in seinen Entwicklung* (Munich, 1933). [7]H.U. von Balthasar, *Das Antlitz der Kirche* (Einsiedeln: Benziger, [2]1955—French: *Le visage de l'Église.* US 31. Paris: Cerf, 1958). [8]*Enchiridion* 15:56—PL 40:258-259; cf. D. Puskaric, "La Chiesa e il mistero trinitario nella predicazione di S. Agostino," AugR 19 (1979) 486–506. [9]Apost. letter, *Augustinum Hipponensem,* AAS 79 (1987) 131–170; J. Salaverri, "Presencia dinámica de Jesucristo en la Iglesia según San Agustín," MiscCom 34 (1976) 125–143. [10]*Enar.in ps.* 90:2—PL 37:1159. Cf. *Serm.* 45:6-7—PL 38:265-267; *Serm.* 341:9—PL 39:1499-1500; cf. Borgomeo (n. 5) 191–234; É. Mersch, *The Theology of the Mystical Body* (St. Louis, 1958) passim. [11]*Serm.* 267:4—PL 38:1231. [12]*Epist.* 185:11, 50—PL 33:315; *Tr. in Ioan.* 26:13—PL 35:1613. [13]W. Marrevee, "An Ecclesial Dimension of Augustine's Understanding of the Ascension of Christ," RUnivOtt 37 (1967) 322–343. [14]*Serm.* 341:9, 11—PL 39:1500. [15]*Tr. in Ioan.* 124:5—PL 35:1973-1974; *Retract.* 1:21, 1—PL 32:618. [16]*Enchir.* 15:56—PL 40:259. [17]*Tr. in Ioan.* 23:5—PL 35:1585. [18]E.g., *Serm.* 259:2—PL 38:1197. [19]"We once were of that opinion," *De civ. Dei* 20:7—CCL 48:709/PL 41:667. [20]G. Bonner, "Augustine and Millenarianism" in R. Williams, ed., *The Making of Orthodoxy.* FS H. Chadwick (Cambridge: UP, 1989) 235–254; M. Dulaey, "L'Apocalypse: Augustin et Tyconius," in A.M. la Bonnardière, ed., *Augustin et la Bible.* Bible de tous les temps 3 (Paris: Beauchesne, 1986) 369–386. [21]*De civ. Dei* 20:9—CCL 48:717/PL 41:674. [22]Bibliog. D.F. Donnelly, *Augustine's "De civitate Dei": An Annotated Bibliography of Modern Criticism 1960–1990.* Augustinian Historical Institute Service, vol. L (New York—Berne: Peter Lang, 1991); Y. Congar, *"Civitas Dei et ecclesia* chez saint Augustin: Histoire de la recherche, son état present," RevÉtAug 3 (1957) 1–14; Trapè in Patrology 4:364-368. See J.M. Langford, "El hombre y la Iglesia en la *Ciudad de Dios,"* AugM 31 (1986) 155–160; A. Lauras and H. Rondet, "Les thèmes des deux cités dans l'oeuvre de saint Augustin," in *Études Augustiniennes* (Paris, 1953) 99–160; P. Piret, "La Cité de Dieu," BLitEc 89 (1988) 116–137, 263–273; J. van Oort, *Jerusalem and Babylon: A Study of Augustine's City of God and the Sources of His Doctrine of the Two Cities* (Leiden: Brill, 1991). [23]"L'Église" (n. 5) 170, n. 75; cf. J. Dougherty, "The Sacred City and the City of God," AugSt 10 (1979) 81–90. [24]*De civ. Dei* 1:35 and 14:28—CCL 47:34; 48:451-452. [25]*De civ. Dei* 18:1; 20:9, 1—CCL 48:592, 716. [26]*Brev. coll.* 3:9, 16; 3:10, 20—PL 43:623-633, 635. [27]É. Lamirande, *L'Église céleste selon St. Augustin* (Paris, 1963); idem, "Jérusalem céleste," DSpir 8:944-958. [28]*Tr. in Ioan.* 124:5, 7—CC 35:1972-1976. [29]A.M. la

Bonnardière, "Marthe et Marie figures de l'Église d'après saint Augustin," VieSp 86 (1952) 404–427. [30]*Retract.* 2:18—CCL 57:104. [31]*Tr. in Ioan.* 39:5—PL 35:1683-1684; cf. N. Escobar, "Donatismo y santidad de la Iglesia," AugM 22 (1977) 323–330 at 326–329; idem, "Consecuencias de la santidad de la Iglesia según san Agustín," ibid., 24 (1979) 133–155; idem, "Iglesia, donatismo y santidad en la polémica agustiniana," ibid., 27 (1982) 55–77; idem, "La Iglesia y la santidad moral según san Agustín," ibid., 29 (1984) 159–172; D. Faul, "Sinners in the Holy Church: A Problem in the Ecclesiology of St. Augustine," StPatr 9 (1966) 404–415. [32]*Serm.* 267:4—PL 38:1231. [33]Mondin (n. 5) 372–373. [34]*De bapt.* 3:26—PL 43:152; cf. *Serm.* 269:2—PL 38:1235; *Tr. in Ioan.* 27:6—PL 35:1618. [35]*De civ. Dei* 10:6—CCL 47:279/PL 41:450. [36]*De bapt.* 7:51-52—CSEL 51:370-372. [37]*De doct. Christiana* 3:32, 45—PL 34:82 in context of critique of Tyconius' second exegetical rule. [38]See M. Dulaey, "Tyconius," DSpir 15:1349-1356 at 1354. [39]*Serm.* 223—PL 38:1092; Borgomeo (n. 5) 279–298. [40]*S. Guelferb* 1:8—PLS 2:541; cf. *Serm.* 10:2 CCL 41:155/PL 38:92-93; H.U. von Balthasar, "Casta meretrix," in *Explorations in Theology* (San Francisco: Ignatius, 1991) 2:193–288. [41]See *Enar.in ps.* 25:5—PL 36:190-191; *De civ. Dei* 18:49—CCL 48:647/PL 41:611. [42]*Tr. in Ioan.* 32:8—PL 35:1646; cf. *De bapt.* 3:16, 21—PL 43:148-149. [43]Trapè (n. 5) 446. [44]*Epist.* 173:6—PL 33:756; R. Eno, "Doctrinal Authority in St. Augustine," AugSt 12 (1981) 137–172. [45]See Cyprian, *De orat. Dom.* 23—CSEL 3A:284-285. [46]Art. cit. (n. 3) 377; *Serm.* 131—PL 38:730; *Serm.* 227—PL 38:1099-1100; *Serm.* 272—PL 38:1246-1248; see G. Bonner, "The Church and the Eucharist in the Theology of Saint Augustine," Sobornost 7 (1978) 448–461. O. Pasquato, "Eucaristia e Chiesa in Agostino," EphLtg 102 (1988) 46–63; C. Traets, "The Eucharist and Christian Community. Some Pauline and Augustinian Evidence," LouvSt 12 (1987) 152–171. [47]*Serm.* 229—PL 38:1103. [48]*Serm.* 46:18 and 36—PL 38:280 and 290-291. [49]*Serm.* 341:11—PL 39:1499-1500. [50]*Enar.in ps.* 90:2—PL 37:1159. [51]*Serm.* 267:3—PL 38:1230-1231; *Enar.in ps.* 147:19—PL 37:1929; 32:2, 7—PL 36:288-289; *Tr. in Ioan.* 6:3 and 32:7—PL 35:1426 and 1645. [52]*Enar.in ps.* 103:4, 4—CCL 40:1524; Borgomeo (n. 5) 146–150. [53]*Epist.* 43:7—PL 33:163. [54]*Serm.* 268:4—PL 38:1231. [55]*In epist. Ioan.* 2:2—PL 35:1990. [56]F. Genn, *Trinität und Amt nach Augustinus.* Sammlung Horizonte Neue Folge 23 (Einsiedeln: Johannes, 1986). [57]*Confess.* 5:13, 23. On bishop see *Serm.* 340—PL 38:1482-1484; *Serm. Guelf.* 32—PLS 2:637-649. G.P. Lawless, "Augustine's Burden of Ministry," Ang 61 (1984) 295–315. [58]É. Lamirande, "Cheminement de la pensée de saint Augustin sur la paternité spirituelle" (n. 5—Études) 135–148. [59]*Enar.in ps.* 72:34—PL 36:928-929; 103:3—PL 37:1364-1366. [60]*The Rule of Saint Augustine,* tr. R. Canning with intro. and commentary by T.J. van Bavel (London: Darton, Longman and Todd, 1984) 42; M.F. Berrouard, "La première communauté de Jérusalem comme image de l'unité de la Trinité. Une des exégèses d'Act 4, 32a," in C. Mayer and K.H. Chetius, eds., *Homo Spiritalis.* FS L. Verheijn (Würzburg: Augustinus Verlag, 1987). [61]*Volk und Haus Gottes in Augustins Lehre von der Kirche.* Münchener theologische Studien 11/7 (Munich, 1954). [62]*Contra litt. Petiliani* 3:9, 10—PL 43:333; *De virginitate* 5—PL 40:398-399. [63]Cf. *De unit. eccl.* 6—CSEL 3/1:214 and *Serm.* 74:7—CSEL 3:214. [64]*Serm.* 213:7—PL 38:1064; M.A. Cenzon, "Ecclesial Dimension of Baptism through the Augustinian Category 'Ecclesia Mater,'" AnnTheol 3 (1989) 315–345. [65]*Serm.* 213:7—PL 38:1064. [66]*Enar.in ps.* 131:10—PL 37:1720; see J. Gaillard, "Domus Dei," DSpir 3:1551-1567; Ratzinger (n. 61). [67]*Serm.* 51:5, 6—PL 38:537; T. Mariucci, "Il nido di Dio: Di un'immagine della Chiesa in s. Agostino," Divinitas 29 (1985) 273–280. [68]See index in H. Rahner, *Symbole der Kirche: Die Ecclesiologie der Väter* (Salzburg, 1964). [69]*Enar.in ps.* 44:24—PL 36:509; *De civ. Dei* 17: 20—PL 41:666 and 48:586; Lamirande, *Études* (n. 5) 21–31. [70]*Epist.* 55:6, 10—PL 33:209; *Enar.in ps.*10:3 and 120:12—PL 36:131-133, 1615-1616. [71]*Serm.*

83:1—PL 38:424.   [72]*De civ. Dei* 15:26—CCL 48:493-494; *De unitate Ecclesiae* 5:9—PL 43:397; *QQ in VT in Gen 7*—PL 34:229-235; *Contra Faustum* 12:20—PL 42:264-265.   [73]R. Desjardins, "Le Christ *Sponsus* et l'Église *Sponsa* chez Augustin," BLitEc 67 (1966) 241–256 and Clancy (n. 5) passim.   [74]*Enar.in ps.* 88:2, 14—PL 37:1140-1141.   [75]*Enar.in ps.* 131:23, 25—PL 37:1726–1727.   [76]*De bapt.* 6:40, 78—CSEL 51:336; 7:44, 87—CSEL 51:365; and throughout. *Tr. in Ioan.* 5–6.   [77]F. Cranz, "The Development of Augustine's Ideas on Society Before the Donatist Controversy," HarvTR 47 (1954) 255–316.   [78]V. Capánaga, "La Iglesia en la espiritualidad de s. Agustín" in AA.VV. *Mysterium ecclesiae in consciencia sanctorum* (Rome: Teresianum, 1967) 88–133 = EphCarm 17 (1966).

## AUTHORITY

Though formally distinct, authority and power may be studied together. The source of all authority is God (Dan 7:14); all power belongs to God as creator (Gen 1–2) and savior of the people. He has given a share in authority and power to humankind (Gen 1:28-30). In society authority is attributed to persons with special abilities, prestige, or an official function.[1] Authority in the Church is the right to issue commands that are to be obeyed and teaching that is to be accepted. The source of authority is Christ working through his Holy Spirit. Power is first a secular idea, arising both from a philosophy of being and from human society.[2] Power in the Church is the capacity to teach, sanctify, and govern, which is a sharing in the triple office of Christ as priest, prophet, and king (q.v.). In a wider sense, power is the achievement or control of intended effects; it also can be seen to include the ability to influence persons or groups and to control them and situations. It may also have the negative meaning of preventing or inhibiting effects or change. An important distinction can arise between the two in that the effectiveness of authority depends on subjects recognizing it and feeling obliged to respect and obey it; this might not be the case for the exercise of power.

Authority and power are two realities that are in disfavor in the Church and in our secular world. Yet they are essential to the NT.[3] Jesus taught "as one having authority" (*exousia*—Mark 1:22); he promises that the apostles will be "clothed with power from on high" (*dunamis*—Luke 24:49; cf. Acts 1:8). He taught with divine authority, superseding the law of Moses in some instances and bringing it to perfection (Matt 5:17-48). He is Lord of the Sabbath (Mark 2:28); he exercised his divine authority in forgiving sins (Matt 9:2-6), a power which he gave also to his Church (Matt 9:8; John 20:22-23). He showed that he had power over nature (Matt 8:27) and over all kinds of diseases and evil spirits. He communicated some of these powers to his followers (Matt 10:1, 8; Luke 10:1, 9, 17; Mark 16:17-18), especially to preach the kingdom (Matt 10:7; 28:18-20; Mark 16:15-16). He acknowledged human authority, but asserted its divine origin (Matt 22:21; John 19:11). His style of authority, however, was "as one who serves" (Luke 22:27; cf. Phil 2:6-8)); though Teacher and Lord, he washed his disciples' feet (John 13:13-14). He warned his disciples against acting like Gentile rulers, and commanded service and mutual slavery in imitation of himself (Matt 20:25-28). *Exousia* and *dunamis* at times seem somewhat interchangeable: Jesus called the Twelve and "gave them power and authority *(dunamin kai exousian)* over all demons and to cure diseases" (Luke 9:1); one can suggest that Jesus in his power *(dunamis)* exercises authority *(exousia):* "Endowment with the Spirit gives him *exousia,* a definite personal authority he has, in substantial terms, the *dunamis* to exercise."[4]

The early Church recognized civil and family authority (Rom 13:1-7; Eph 6:1-8; 1 Pet 2:13–3:7). It knew the power of the Spirit who gave his charisms (q.v.) and legitimized authority (Acts 1–15; 1 Cor 2:3-4; 4:19-21; 5:3). The Spirit is also active in those who perform ministry (q.v.) in the community (1 Cor 12:5-6, 28), an authority which is genuine, but must be exercised and accepted with humility (1 Pet 5:1-6). The apostles (q.v.) exercise authority as well as others (v. BISHOPS). Even in the NT the authority of the OT, as well as of apostolic writings, is acknowledged (2 Pet 1:20-21; cf. 3:15-16).[5] But above all, in its early credal formula, the Church confessed "Jesus is Lord" (1 Cor 12:3; Rom 10:9; Phil 2:11—v. CREEDS).[6]

Authority in the Church develops in tandem with the relationship of the Church to the secular world. A brief overview is not easy as the evolution is complex.[7] In the earliest post-apostolic writings we already find authority in the Church, as in Clement (q.v.), Ignatius (q.v.), and the *Didachê* (q.v.), which is both institutional and charismatic (v. CHARISM).[8] There is such an ancient emphasis on authority that some Protestants refer to the phenomenon as "Early Catholicism" (v. CATHOLICISM, EARLY). Though there is authority in teaching,[9] in liturgical celebration, and in governing, there is still in the patristic period a dominant focus on the community of believers, a feature especially evident in the ecclesiology of St. Cyprian (q.v.).

After the Edict of Constantine (q.v.) the Church was no longer persecuted, and entered into public life in the person of the bishops, who gradually over the next 700 years exercised authority also in secular affairs. But the ideal of spiritual authority and service was kept alive in such figures as Pope St. Gregory the Great (q.v.).

The decadence particularly of the 10th-century Church led to calls for reform. In the following century the conviction grew that reform would have to be "from the head" *(a capite),* i.e., from the papacy down; hence there was a concentration in theology and in law on all texts that would support the idea of a strong, centralized papacy (v. PAPACY). Various biblical texts (e.g., Jer 1:10; 1 Cor 2:15; 6:3; 1 Pet 2:9) were given a legalistic interpretation in support of a papal hegemony. Lay investiture (q.v.) and simony (q.v.), the causes of many evils in the Church, were vigorously attacked, and the Gregorian reform (v. GREGORY VII) had notable achievements. This reform was one of the major turning points in the history of the Church.[10] The notion of plenitude of power *(plenitudo potestatis)* became associated with the pope, who was seen not only as head of the Church, but of the Christian people.[11] In time bishops were seen to derive their authority from the pope; thus F. Suarez (d. 1617): "Episcopal power is nothing else but some sharing of papal power."[12] Hereinafter, the prestige and authority of the papacy would grow until Vatican I (q.v.), and only be placed in a fuller ecclesiology by Vatican II (q.v. and v. BISHOPS, COLLEGIALITY).

The radical denial of authority at the Reformation in the name of "Scripture alone" led to a reaction of a strong emphasis on authority and to what Y. Congar called a "mystique" of authority which had roots in the Middle Ages—a complete identification of the will of God with institutional authority.[13] There was increasing accent on the text "Whosoever listens to you, listens to me, and whoever rejects you, rejects me" (Luke 10:16). There was a growth in what Congar termed "hierarchology," a tendency to use the word "Church" when what was meant was its hierarchy,[14] a vision of the Church centered on its leaders instead of the Eucharist, its true heart.

From the 19th century an earlier tendency to see the magisterium (q.v.) in terms of power becomes more pronounced, culminating in the 1950 Encyclical of Pius XII, *Humani generis*.[15] The emphasis on authority was not only centralized in Rome, especially with the reform of the Curia in 1587 (v. VATICAN); at another level it affected the concept of the bishop, even the parish priest, who were seen as "governing" their flock, rather than pastoring or serving them. This arose in the Middle Ages, but was very pronounced after Trent (q.v.). Again, it was not until Vatican II that this emphasis was corrected.

The council speaks several times of secular power and public authority (GS 21, 73, 74, 87; CD 19; DH 1, 3, 11), and of international authority (GS 79, 82). It also teaches that there is sacred power in the Church (LG 18, 27, 43; OT 20): the apostles (LG 7); supreme authority in the Church (LG 27; CD 8); papal (LG 22, 45; CD 2, 3, 4, 11; AG 22, 29; OE 9), patriarchal and hierarchical (CD 11); patriarchs (OE 9, 23); in collegiality (LG 21, 22; CD 4); bishops (LG 22, 23, 27, 45; CD 4, 6, 16, 19, 20, 25, 30, 32, 34, 35; SC 26, 45, 57; AG 20, 40; PO 5, 7; OT 4; UR 8); parish priests (LG 30); priests (LG 28); laity (AA 24); finally, authority in liturgical matters (SC 22, 36, 39, 40, 53, 63, 77).

Behind all these texts are two overriding ideas: power in the Church is a sharing in the office of Christ as priest-prophet-king; authority is service, and it is to be exercised in this style.

The development of authority is also inseparable from the progress of law (q.v.). In the early Middle Ages there were collections of laws, decrees, and ordinances which culminated in Gratian (q.v.) and subsequent additions.[16] A crucial distinction between the powers of jurisdiction (q.v.) and orders *(potestas iurisdictionis/ordinis),* and the power of temporal administration began to emerge from the 12th and 13th centuries. The original word "jurisdiction" comes from classical Roman law and referred to the specific judicial authority of the praetor in trials. Gradually, jurisdiction meant the power of governing in the Church, though it also retained a judicial sense. In the 19th century the notion of teaching authority or magisterium (q.v.) was separated out from jurisdiction which was then seen more as pertaining to the area of discipline and spiritual authority. Other distinctions arose. Ordinary jurisdiction was attached to an office, and contradistinguished from delegated jurisdiction which came from a higher authority or the law. Jurisdiction could be exercised in the external forum which was public, commonly seen in juridical acts and the legal and juridical provisions for marriage. It was also found in the internal forum, the area of conscience, as in the sacrament of penance.[17] In Church law jurisdiction was required for hearing confessions. This is still the case, though the *Code* following Vatican II (except LG 25) here avoids the word jurisdiction. It speaks rather of "faculty" which is conceded by law or by a competent authority such as the local bishop (e.g., CIC 965–976).[18] Jurisdiction is normally attached to sacramental orders, though laity can in some cases cooperate in the exercise of this power. Thus canon 129 § 2 is a remarkable development in the new *Code:* "Lay members of the Christian faithful can cooperate in the exercise of power in accord with the norm of law." It is not very specific—its interpretation is much disputed—but it has significant potential for future development (v. LAITY with nn. 49–51).[19]

The supreme principle of the new *Code,* seen in the description of the Christian faithful (CIC 204), is also the triple office of priest, prophet, and king, but is only fully carried through in Book III, "The Teaching Office of the Church," and Book IV, "The Sanctifying Office in the Church." The kingly office is found throughout the *Code,* usually in such terms as the power of governing *(potestas regiminis),* and especially in Book II, "The People of God." The new *Code* uses the contemporary tripartite division of governmental authority as legislative, executive, and judicial (CIC 135 § 1).[20] Administration, which pertains to executive power, appears throughout the *Code*. The lack of clear steps to be taken when administrative procedures are questionable or unjust is a weakness of the 1983 law (salvo CIC 1732, which concerns particular acts).[21]

The vocabulary of the *Code* lacks some precision,[22] but this may provide possibility for creative interpretation, openness, juridical and theological development. With the virtual disappearance of the word "jurisdiction" (only five instances), the key words about power in the law are now: *facultas,* generally with the meaning of competence; *officium* (260 times, with 60 signifying obligation, and the majority of the rest indicating ecclesiastical office); *munus,* marking the triple office and also generally meaning "task," and sometimes interchangeable with "office" (e.g., CIC 377 § 2; 331).

There is extensive writing on authority and power in recent decades which seeks to reflect the insights of Vatican II and to root their exercise in NT categories.[23] Developments in the theology of the local Church (q.v.) should counterbalance centralizing tendencies which were largely absent in the patristic period.[24] The purpose of all authority is to serve truth and love in a catholic unity.[25] But the history of the Church, even recently, shows the use of repression, which is in tension with the liberating message of the gospel.[26] An allied problem is the possibility of dissent (q.v.) from authoritative teaching or disciplinary enactments. There is widespread rejection of the Church's authority to legislate on moral matters. Some theological studies propose radical reinterpretation not only of the exercise of authority but also of its theoretical bases. There are also accusations of authoritarianism and paternalism.[27]

Of particular importance are ecumenical studies, which share the lived experience of authority in other Churches. Authority among the Orthodox is seen in five areas: Scripture, the "sense of the faith" or general conscience of the Church, episcopate, councils, and primacy. The Fathers of the Church (q.v.) have a significant authority in both doctrinal and practical matters. Orthodox authority is far less juridical than in the Latin West.[28] Anglican theology professes to be both evangelical and catholic. It gives preeminence to the Word of God, but also stresses authority, both episcopal and synodal, with participation of the laity. Authority is also enshrined in *The Book of Common Prayer.*[29]

There is the further issue of democracy. The Church is not a democracy in the accepted meaning of the word. The magisterium has, however, frequently praised democracy as a value in secular society (cf. GS 31). Moreover, there are values in modern democracy that the Church could, and should, enshrine in its own life.[30] In 1968 Cardinal L.J. Suenens (q.v.) strongly proposed the idea of co-responsibility in the Church, which led at the time to much controversy.[31] Though he was more concerned with collegiality, the principles

can be more widely applied in the Church. The principle of Roman law, "Whatever affects everyone must be approved by everyone" *(quod omnes tangit, debet ab omnibus approbari),* cannot be universally applied to the Church. But we should make an important distinction implied by Cardinal Suenens: people can be involved in *decision-making,* even though they may be excluded from *decision-taking.*[32] E. Corecco has analyzed the consequences of applying secular categories too readily to the Church. The disquiet felt by parish councils and priests' councils ("He doesn't listen") and the parallel statement by those in authority ("It is only consultative") testify to an attempt by one group to gain power and by others to retain it. Instead of this power struggle the true theological category is communion (q.v.), which must exist between authority figures and those being pastored by them.[33]

An emphasis on communion and participation is especially important for those who feel themselves disempowered or marginalized in the Church, particularly the poor (q.v.) and women (v. FEMINISM IN THE CHURCH. The development of ministry (q.v.) and of a practical theology and pastorale of charism (q.v.) are essential if authority in the Church is not to become fossilized or self-serving. Finally, it is impossible to overemphasize the importance of the style of the exercise of authority: authority is indeed service, but this must be reflected in the way it is used at every level in the Church.

[1]W. Milinski, "Authority," SM 1:129-133.    [2]K. Hemmerle, "Power," SM 5:70-72.    [3]F.A. Amiot and P. Grelot, "Authority," DBT 36–39; J. Blank, "The Concept of 'Power' in the Church: New Testament Perspectives," Conc 197 (1988) 3–12; A. Cunningham, "Pastoral Leadership in the Early Church," ChicSt 17 (1978) 357–370; W. Foerster, *"Exestin etc.,"* TDNT 2:560-570; W. Grundmann, *"Dunamai etc.,"* TDNT 2:284-317; M.F. Lacan, "Power," DBT 438–442; J.H. Siedl, "Power," Bauer 2:673-676; J.F. O'Grady, "Power and Authority: Issues for the Contemporary Church," LouvSt 10 (1984–1985) 122–140.    [4]Grundmann (n. 3) TDNT 2:301.    [5]R. Gnuse, "Authority of the Scriptures: Quest for a Norm," BibTB 13 (1983) 59–66; D.K. McKim, ed., *The Authoritative Word: Essays on the Nature of Scripture* (Grand Rapids: Eerdmans, 1983); P. Wells, "L'autorité de la Bible: qu'est-ce que c'est?," RRéf 33 (1982) 97–107.    [6]Y. Congar, *Power and Poverty in the Church* (London, 1964) 21–39.    [7]Ibid., 40–79; R.B. Eno, "Authority and Conflict in the Early Church," EglT 7 (1976) 41–60; J.E. Lynch, "Power in the Church: An Historico-critical Survey," Conc 197 (1988) 13–22.    [8]K.B. Steinhauser, "Authority in the Primitive Church," PatrByzR 3 (1984) 89–100.    [9]R. Gryson, "The Authority of the Teacher in the Ancient and Medieval Church," JEcuSt 19 (1982) 176–187.    [10]Congar, Augustin 89–122; F. Kempf, in Jedin-Dolan 3:351-403; C. Munier, "L'autorité de l'Église dans le système des sources du droit médiévale," IusCan 16 (1976) 39–60.    [11]Ibid., 252–259, 271–281.    [12]*De legibus* 4:4, 11.    [13]Op. cit. (n. 6) 60–63, 69–71.    [14]Op. cit. (n. 6) 70; *Lay People in the Church: A Study for a Theology of Laity* (London, 1965) 48 and n.    [15]AAS 42 (1950) 561–578 with 960/Carlen, Encyclicals 4:175-184/partly DS 3875–3899. Cf. G. Alberigo, "The Authority of the Church in the Documents of Vatican I and Vatican II," JEcuSt 19 (1982) 119–145; P.F. Fransen, "Criticism of some Basic Theological Notions in Matters of Church

Authority," ibid., 48–74; idem., "The Exercise of Authority in the Church Today: Its Concrete Forms," LouvSt 9 (1982–1983) 1–25; Y. Congar, "Towards a Catholic Synthesis," Conc 148 (1981) 68–80. [16]Congar, Augustin 145–155; F. Kempf, in Jedin-Dolan 3:426-436; H. Wolter, in Jedin-Dolan 4:49-50, 93-94, 260-267.    [17]F.J. Urrutia, "Internal Forum-External Forum: The Criterion of Distinction," in Latourelle, Vatican II, 1:634-667.    [18]F.R. McManus, in Coriden, CIC 683–688.    [19]J.M. Huels, "Another Look at Lay Jurisdiction," Jurist 41 (1981) 59–80, commenting on J.J. Cuneo, "The Power of Jurisdiction: Empowerment for Church Functioning and Mission Distinct from the Power of Orders," Jurist 39 (1979) 183–219; J.H. Provost, "The Participation of the Laity in the Governance of the Church," StCan 17 (1983) 417–448.    [20]L.G. Wrenn, "The Scope of the Church's Judicial Competence," Jurist 45 (1985) 639–652; cf. P. Gaspari, "De potestate in Ecclesia," EphIurC 44 (1990) 9–32; J.K. Mallet, The Ministry of Governance (Washington, D.C.: Canon Law Society of America, 1986).    [21]M.R. Moodie, "The Administrator and the Law: Authority and Its Exercise in the Code," Jurist 46 (1986) 43–69; F.J. Urrutia, "Administrative Power in the Church According to the Code of Canon Law," StCan 20 (1986) 253–273. [22]R. Torfs, "Auctoritas-Potestas-Jurisdictio-Facultas-Officium-Munus: A Conceptual Analysis," Conc 197n (1988) 63–73; cf. B. Gangoiti, "I termini ed i concetti di 'auctoritas, potestas, iurisdictio' in diritto canonico," Apoll 51 (1978) 562–576.    [23]E. Corecco, "Aspects of the Reception of Vatican II in the Code of Canon Law," in G. Alberigo et al., eds., The Reception of Vatican II (Washington, D.C.: The Catholic University of America Press—Tunbridge Wells: Burns and Oates, 1987) 249–296; P.F. Fransen, ed., Authority in the Church. Annua nuntia lovaniensia 26 (Leuven: UP, 1983); idem, "The Exercise of Authority in the Church Today: Its Concrete Forms," LouvSt 9 (1982–1983) 3–25; E. Hill, Ministry and Authority in the Catholic Church (London: Chapman, 1988); B. van Iersel, "Who According to the New Testament Has the Say in the Church?," Conc 148 (1981) 11–17; K. Rahner, "The Theology of Power," ThInvest 4:391-409; T.P. Rausch, Authority and Leadership in the Church: Past Directions and Future Possibilities (Wilmington: Glazier, 1988); D.A. Steele, Images of Leadership and Authority in the Church: Biblical Principles and Secular Models (New York—London: University Press of America, 1986); Conc 197 (1988); Way 29 (Oct. 1989); cf. G.R. Evans, ed., Christian Authority. FS H. Chadwick (Oxford: Clarendon, 1988).    [24]Y. Congar, "Autonomie et pouvoir central dans l'Église vus par la théologie catholique," Irén 53 (291–313).    [25]J.M.R. Tillard, "Autorité et mémoire dans l'Église," Irén 61 (1988) 332–346, 481–484.    [26]F.G. Laishley, "Repression and Liberation in the Church," HeythJ 29 (1988) 157–174, 329–342, 450–460.    [27]E. Cuddy, "On Coping with Authority in the Church: A Multi-Disciplinary Perspective," CrossC 32 (1982–1983) 440–460; cf. P. Nott, "Towards a Theology of Leadership," ExpT 97 (1985–86) 138–142.    [28]B. Bobrinskoy, "How Does the Church Remain in the Truth?: An Orthodox Response," Conc 148 (1981) 18–22; C. Collins, "Authority in the Eastern Christian Churches," Diak (USA) 12 (1977) 59–70; C. Konstantinidis, "Authority in the Orthodox Church," Sobornost 3 (1981) 197–209 = ÖkRu 31(1982) 31–47; K. Ware, "L'exercice de l'autorité dans l'Église orthodoxe," Irén 54 (1981) 451–471; 55 (1982) 25–34.    [29]See passim, in ARCIC, The Final Report (London: CTS-SPCK, 1982), and in S. Sykes and J. Booty, eds., The Study of Anglicanism (London: SPCK—Philadelphia: Fortress, 1988); J. Baycroft, "An Anglican Approach to Authority," OneChr 25 (1989) 23–33; P. Sedgwick, "Recent Criticisms of the Concept of Authority in the Church of England," Theology 91 (1988) 258–266; S. Sykes, ed., Authority in the Anglican Communion. FS J. Howe (Toronto: Anglican Book Centre, 1987); idem, "Power in the Church of England," Conc 197 (1988) 123–128.    [30]P. Eyt, "Vers une Église démocratique?," NRT 91 (1969) 597–613.    [31]Co-responsibility in the Church (New York, 1968); cf. J. de Brouker, ed., The Suenens Dossier (Notre Dame, Ind.: Fides, 1970); L.J. Suenens, Memories and Hopes (Dublin: Veritas, 1992) 208–216.    [32]Cf. Memories and Hopes (n. 31) 192.    [33]"Church Parliament or Service," TDig 22 (1974) 136–142 = InterKZCommunio 1 (1972) 33–53.

## AVIGNON

Avignon, a city in the south of France, was a center for the Albigensian heresy (q.v.) in the 12th century. On the death of Benedict XI (1304), the Frenchman Bertrand de Got, archbishop of Bordeaux, was elected pope after an eleven-month conclave, and took the name Clement V (1305–1314). Although he intended to move to Rome, he settled in Avignon (1309), thus inaugurating the "Babylonian Captivity of the Papacy" (1309–1377). The popes of that period all held the title Bishop of Rome, and gave indications of going there. Only Urban V (1362–1370), however, actually did so (1367), though he returned to Avignon three years later. The definitive return to Rome was made by Gregory XI (1370–1378) early in 1377. The Avignon period[1] was marked by too great a deference to the kings of France. It also was a time when curial bureaucracy was inflated and nepotism was commonplace. The Avignon Captivity was to lead to the great schism of the West (v. SCHISM, GREAT WESTERN).

[1]OxDictPopes 212–226; K.A. Fink in Jedin-Dolan 4:291-344; N. Housley, The Avignon Papacy and the Crusades 1305–1378 (Oxford: Clarendon, 1986); W. Brandmüller, Pabst und Konzil im Grossen Schisma 1378–1431 (Paderborn—Munich—Zürich: Schöningh, 1990).

# B

## BALTHASAR, Hans Urs von (1905–1988)

Hans Urs von Balthasar was born in Lucerne, Switzerland, in 1905. He completed a doctorate on German idealism before becoming a Jesuit in 1929. He studied philosophy in Pullach, where E. Przywara taught, and theology in Lyons, where he met H. de Lubac (q.v.), from whom he derived his enduring love of the Fathers (q.v.). From 1940 to 1948 he was student chaplain at Basle, and came into contact with Adrienne von Speyr, whom he received into the Church. Together they founded a secular institute, the Community of St. John *(Johannesgemeinschaft).* His superiors saw a permanent commitment to this work as incompatible with Jesuit life, and he came to the most painful decision to leave the Society of Jesus, though he kept close spiritual bonds with it and remained thoroughly Ignatian throughout his life. A period of isolation followed; he was not called to Vatican II (q.v.) in any capacity. After the Council he gradually became accepted: he received the Paul VI prize for theology in 1984; he was a member of the International Theological Commission (from 1969); on 26 June 1988, two days before he was to have been created cardinal, he died.

K. Rahner has called his achievements "really breathtaking";[1] H. de Lubac said that he "was perhaps the most cultured person of his time."[2] His incredible productivity[3] is seen in hundreds of essays (many collected in book form); numerous patristic editions and commentaries; serious hagiographical studies; translations, especially of the Fathers and of French Catholic writers—Claudel, Péguy, Bernanos; transcriptions and editions of the voluminous mystical works of Adrienne von Speyr. Besides all this, there is the multivolumed trilogy: *The Glory of the Lord,* which investigates in seven volumes the theology of the divine beauty seen especially in the cross and resurrection; his *Theodrama* in five volumes, which deals with divine and human freedom in salvation history; the three-volume *Logic-Theology,* which treats of philosophical and divine truth revealed in Jesus Christ. A huge secondary literature is developing around his work, and many doctoral theses investigate aspects of his immense output.[4] Five retrospective essays on his own books at ten-year intervals enable us to grasp his dominant concerns.[5]

His writing on the Church is extensive[6] and impossible to summarize adequately. Significantly, he entitles an important essay, "Who is the Church?"[7] The Church must be viewed in personal terms. At the heart of his ecclesiology is love: love bestowed, love received, love returned. An early work, *Love Alone: The Way of Revelation*[8] would be more accurately, if inelegantly, entitled "Credible Is Only Love."[9]

In 1952 he wrote a bold work calling on the Church to leave the security of its bastions and face the challenges of modern society.[10] But after Vatican II he seemed to have become more conservative, being especially concerned with the contemporary rejection of the papacy, an anti-Roman sentiment that he saw sweeping the Church.[11] Some may attempt to distinguish the sweeping genius of his theological speculation from his practical judgments about the contemporary Church. But such demarcation may not be necessary. From the full perspective of divine love, which he sees revealed in the beauty of Calvary and Easter, many current ecclesiological concerns pale into quasi-insignificance. His totality of vision is such that he opposes all reductionism of the Mystery, whether in some liberation theology, or in an influential secular institute. Above all he is the determined foe of any theology or renewal which would threaten to empty the Cross of Christ of its meaning (see 1 Cor 1:17).[12]

One of Balthasar's greatest contributions to 20th-century theology—one shared with K. Rahner—was his integration of theology and spirituality.[13] More than anybody else he is responsible for the view that the writings and the lives of the saints constitute an important theological source (q.v.). It is in this way that he finds the notions of Body (q.v.), Spouse (q.v.) and Mother (q.v.) more fertile than People (q.v.) or institution (q.v.). Indeed, he subordinates the institutional dimension of the Church to its feminine Marian principle: "For the Church was already present in her before men were set in office."[14] More than that, "In Mary, in her immaculate yes to God, the Church is perfect from the outset."[15] In a more developed exposition he sees as essential four constituent traditions of the Church:[16] the horizontal Petrine witness and shepherding; the Pauline witness of revelation from above; the contemplative witness of John in the communion of the followers of Jesus, incorporating a vision that is also apocalyptic, uniting heaven and earth; the Marian witness, which grounds the other three, for the Church is to share in the experience of Mary. To the extent that the Church fails to be Marian, it fails to be the Church of Christ.

Time and again he returns to the notion of the *Catholica,* the universal truth to which the Church must bear living witness without diminution or distortion. He sees humanity as being defrauded by partial truths. It is only in the fullness of truth rooted in love that the Church can open out into the divine Mystery and thus authentically serve humankind.

[1]Quoted in M. Kehl and W. Löser, eds., *The Von Balthasar Reader* (New York: Crossroad—Edinburgh: Clark, 1982) 6–7.   [2]"Un testimonio di Cristo: Hans Urs von Balthasar," Humanitas 9 (1965) 851–869 at 853 = *Paradox et mystère de l'Église* (Paris, 1967) 180–212.   [3]Bibliog. C. Capol, ed., *Hans Urs von Balthasar: Bibliographie 1925–1990* (Einsiedeln: Johannes Verlag, 1990).   [4]Significant and helpful as introductions—T. Guarino, "Reading von Balthasar: Fundamental Themes," NTRev 4/3 (1991) 52–63; Kehl and Löser (n. 1); B. McGregor and T. Norris, eds., *The Beauty of Christ: A Introduction to the Theology of Hans Urs von Balthasar* (Edinburgh: Clark, 1994); G. Marchesi, *La cristologia di Hans Urs von Balthasar.* AnGreg 207 (Rome: Gregorian UP, 1977); J. O'Donnell, "Truth as Love: The Understanding of Truth According to Hans Urs von Balthasar," Pacifica 1 (1988) 189–211; G.F. O'Hanlon, *The Immutability of God in the Theology of Hans Urs von Balthasar* (Cambridge UK: UP, 1990); see Communio 16 (Fall 1989) 306–490 and works in n. 5.   [5]Collected in *My Work: In Retrospect* (San Francisco: Ignatius, 1993). See E. Gurriero, *Hans Urs von Balthasar* (Italian Milan: Ed. Paoline, 1991—German Einsiedeln: Johannes, 1993); J. O'Donnell, *Hans Urs von Balthasar.* Outstanding Christian Thinkers (London: Chapman, 1992); J. Riches, ed., *The Analogy of Beauty: The Theology of Hans Urs von Balthasar* (Edinburgh: Clark, 1986).   [6]Extracts in Kehl and Löser (n. 1) 205–318.   [7]*Church and World* (New York: Sheed and Ward, 1967) 112–165.   [8]London: Burns and Oates, 1968.   [9]*Glaubhaft*

*ist nur Liebe* (Einsiedeln: Johannes-Verlag, [3]1966).   [10]*Schleifung der Bastionen* (Einsiedeln: Johannes-Verlag, 1952, [5]1993—Eng. trans., *Razing the Bastions* (San Francisco: Ignatius, 1993).   [11]*Der antirömische Affekt* (Freiburg: Herder, 1974)—Eng. trans., *The Office of Peter and the Structure of the Church* (San Francisco: Ignatius, 1986).   [12]A. Peelman, "Hans Urs von Balthasar: Un diagnostic théologique de la civilisation occidentale," ÉglT 10 (1979) 257–274.   [13]"From the Theology of God to Theology in the Church," CleR 68 (1983) 79–94 = Communio (French) 6/5 (1981) 8–19. See P. Petit, *Un grand théologien spirituel: Hans Urs von Balthasar* (Montreal: Méridien, 1985).   [14]"The Marian Principle," in *Elucidations* (London: SPCK, 1975) 64–72 at 72; art. cit. (n. 12) 127–137.   [15]"From the Theology . . ." (n. 13) 86.   [16]*The Glory of the Lord: A Theological Aesthetics. Vol. 1—Seeing the Form* (Edinburgh: Clarke, 1982) 350–365, cf. 338–350.

## BAPTISM

Many accounts of baptism are to be found in recent studies;[1] there is less on the ecclesial aspects of the sacrament. The baptism instituted by Jesus was from the very beginning the rite of initiation into the community of his disciples (Acts 2:41-42; 19:1-7; Matt 28:19). Early reflection saw it as incorporation into the death and resurrection of Jesus (Rom 6:3-4), an incorporation into Christ (Gal 3:27). New Testament teaching also insisted on the necessity of baptism (Mark 16:16; John 3:5).

The catechumenate (q.v.) which took shape early in the 2nd century emphasized that those not baptized were not full members of the Church; indeed they were excluded from the sacrament-sacrifice of the Eucharist after the Liturgy of the Word.[2]

From about the 3rd century we find teaching that says martyrdom can take the place of baptism: there is reference to baptism of blood in the *Apostolic Tradition* (q.v.). If a catechumen is arrested for the Lord's name, and is killed "before his sins are remitted, he will be justified, for he has received baptism in his blood" (19). Also in the *Apostolic Tradition* there is clear reference to the baptism of infants: the parents or another member of the family speaks for them (21/21:4).

The actual ceremony of initiation as attested by the great 4th-century homilies shows a clear awareness that baptism is entry into the Church.[3] St. Augustine appealed to the liturgical practice of the Church: "Studying the scriptures and the authority of the whole Church, and the form of the sacrament itself, it is clearly seen that in infants there is a remission of sin."[4] For him, faith had an integral place within the sacrament's very structure; the Church as mother (q.v.) gives birth through baptism.[5]

The medieval synthesis[6] is well represented by St. Thomas Aquinas: baptism is the remission of sin,[7] incorporation as a member into Christ the head;[8] infants are baptized through the faith of the Church—a point also found in Augustine.[9]

The Council of Florence (q.v.), quoting a minor work of St. Thomas, taught that baptism is "the gateway to the spiritual life; by it we are made members of Christ and belong to his body, the Church." Baptism confers a character and cannot be repeated.[10] The Council of Trent (q.v.) taught the effects of baptism as really changing the person, and it defended infant baptism against some of the Reformers.[11]

Vatican II outlined the effects of baptism in the context of the priesthood of the whole Church: "Incorporated into the Church through baptism, the faithful are by the baptismal character given a place in the worship of the Christian religion; and reborn as children of God they have an obligation to profess publicly the faith they have received from God through the Church" (LG 11; cf. LG 7). It further taught the necessity of baptism (LG 14, 17) and the Church's mission to baptize (LG 17); incorporation into the paschal mystery of Christ (SC 7); the bond of unity among all Christians constituted by the sacrament (UR 3, 22, 23). Baptism alone is not sufficient for full communion in the Church (LG 15; cf. MEMBERSHIP).[12] The council called for a revision of the rites of baptism and the catechumenate (SC 64–69). In the post-Vatican II period there was a recognition of the baptism conferred in other Churches and an abandonment of the tutiorist practice of conditional baptism for those who sought reconciliation with the Catholic Church.[13]

The 1983 *Code of Canon Law* gives a succinct definition of the sacrament with its effects: "Baptism, the gate to the sacraments, necessary for salvation in fact or at least in intention, by which men and women are freed from their sins, are reborn as children of God and, configured to Christ by an indelible character, are incorporated in the Church, is validly conferred only by washing with true water together with the required form of words" (CIC 849). The subsequent canons deal with the celebration of the sacrament, its minister (ordinary: bishop, priest or deacon; extraordinary: any person), its subject, sponsors, special cases (CIC 849–871). In the case of infant baptism it is required that the parents or at least one of them give consent; there must be a founded hope that the infant will be brought up in the Catholic religion (CIC 868). The preferred time is Sunday, especially during the Easter vigil; the proper place is the parish church or other oratory (CIC 857–858).[14]

Recent ecumenical discussion of the sacrament led to the Lima. Faith and Order document, *Baptism, Eucharist and Ministry* (1982).[15] It saw baptism as a sign of the kingdom of God and of the life of the world to come (n. 7). It outlined the scriptural teaching on baptism, and notes divergences between the Churches (nn. 1–22). On the ecclesial effects of baptism it noted: "Baptism is a sign and seal of our common discipleship. Through baptism, Christians are brought into union with Christ, with each other and with the Church of every time and place. Our common baptism, which unites us to Christ in faith, is thus a basic bond of unity. . . . Our one baptism into Christ constitutes a call to the churches to overcome their divisions and visibly manifest their fellowship" (n. 6).

In Pentecostal and charismatic traditions we find a major emphasis on "Baptism in the Holy Spirit," known by a variety of terms (v. CHARISMATIC RENEWAL). It is not a second baptism but a vitalization of baptism, a conversion experience with openness to the gifts and power of the Holy Spirit. Theological explanations vary, but a centrist position would see it as an outpouring of the Holy Spirit or a mission of the Spirit.[16] There is patristic evidence to suggest that baptism in the Spirit, by whatever name, should be normative for Christian living, rather than be seen as an exceptional grace.[17] The general position of Pentecostalists is that water baptism, received after an adult experience of conversion and faith in Christ, is valid Christian baptism, but needs to be completed by the experience of baptism in the Spirit, with the gift of tongues.[18]

The sacrament of baptism is the first of the sacraments of initiation (q.v.); it looks forward to the special gifting in confirmation (q.v.) and to the fullness of incorporation into Christ and into the Church which comes through the Eucharist.[19]

[1]E.g., A. Kavanagh, *The Shape of Baptism: The Rite of Christian Initiation* (New York: Pueblo, 1978); T.A. Marsh, *Gift of Community: Baptism and Confirmation*. Message of the Sacraments 2 (Wilmington: Glazier, 1984); M. Searle, *Christening: The Making of Christians* (Collegeville: The Liturgical Press, 1980); L.G. Walsh, *The Sacraments of Initiation: Baptism, Confirmation, Eucharist* (London: Chapman, 1988); E.C. Whitaker, *Documents of the Baptismal Liturgy* (London: SPCK, [2]1970). [2]M. Dujarier, *A History of the Catechumenate: The First Six Centuries* (New York—Chicago: Sadlier, 1979). [3]E. Yarnold, *The Awe-Inspiring Rites of Initiation: Baptismal Homilies of the Fourth Century* (Slough UK: St. Paul's, 1971). [4]*De pecc. meritis* 1:34, 64—PL 44:147; *De gratia Christi* 2:16, 17—PL 44: 393. See J.-A. Vinel, "L'argument liturgique opposé par saint Augustin aux Pélagiens," QLtg 68 (1987) 209–241. [5]*De bapt.* 1:15, 23—CSEL 51:167. See M.A. Cenzon, "Ecclesial Dimension of Baptism through the Augustinian Category 'Ecclesia Mater,'" AnnTheol 3 (1989) 315–345. [6]J.D.C. Fischer, *Christian Initiation: Baptism in the Medieval West* (London, 1965). [7]ST 3a, q.69, a.2. [8]ST 3a, q.69, aa.3-6; q.68, a.1 ad3. [9]ST 3a, q.68, a.9; q.69, a.8. [10]DS 1313–1314/ND 1308, 1412. [11]DS 1614–1627/ND 1420–1433. [12]K.J. Becker, "The Teaching of Vatican II on Baptism: A Stimulus for Theology," in Latourelle, Vatican II, 2:47-99. [13]Secretariat for Promoting Christian Unity, Directory *Ad totam Ecclesiam* (14 May 1967) 9–20—Flannery 1:487-490. [14]Cf. G. Siegwalt, "Le lieu ecclésial et liturgique de l'acte du baptême," RHPR 71 (1991) 39–44. [15]Faith and Order Paper 111 (Geneva: WCC, 1982). [16]F.A. Sullivan, "Baptism in the Holy Spirit: A Catholic Interpretation of the Pentecostal Experience," Greg 55 (1974) 49–68; idem, *Charisms and the Charismatic Renewal* (Ann Arbor: Servant—Dublin: Gill and Macmillan, 1982) 59–75. [17]K. McDonnell and G.T. Montague, *Christian Initiation and Baptism in the Holy Spirit:*

*Evidence from the First Eight Centuries* (Collegeville: Glazier/The Liturgical Press, 1991); idem, eds., *Fanning the Flame: What Does Baptism in the Holy Spirit Have to Do with Christian Initiation* (Collegeville: The Liturgical Press, 1991); K. McDonnell, "Communion Ecclesiology and Baptism in the Spirit: Tertullian and the Early Church," TS 49 (1988) 471–494. [18]Cf. C.M. Robeck Jr. and J.L. Sandridge, "The Ecclesiology of Koinonia and Baptism: A Pentecostal Perspective," JEcuSt 27 (1991) 504–534. [19]St. Thomas ST 3a, q.73, a.3; A. Goosens, "Baptême et Église: Une relecture," QLtg 72 (1991) 142–158; J.M.R. Tillard, "Perspectives nouvelles sur le baptême," Irén 51 (1978) 171–185, 296.

## BAPTISTS

The Baptists form one of the largest Protestant Churches. Their origin in modern times is to be traced to John Smyth and Thomas Helwys, who proposed the separation of Church and State and rejected infant baptism. They left England to escape persecution (1607) and went to Holland, where they came under the influence of Mennonites or Anabaptists (q.v.). They soon returned to England and established the first Baptist Church in 1612. From there it spread throughout the world, and particularly to America; Roger Williams settled in Rhode Island in 1639. There have been many Baptist Churches and splinter groups in the succeeding centuries,[1] with some coming together in the Baptist World Alliance (BWA) in 1905.[2]

From the 19th century the myth grew about forebears in various marginalized groups of Baptists going back to NT times ("Landmarkism"). Knowing persecution from the beginning, they have been strong advocates of religious freedom. From early times Baptists advocated the complete separation of Church and State. The chief NT image of the Church for Baptists is probably the People of God (q.v.) lived out in the *koinônia* (v. COMMUNION) of the family of God. In the Church, worship has a basic priority, for it allows people to experience God's salvific action. Baptism is a symbolic action which is performed when the candidate has experienced saving faith. Those who have been baptized as infants in other Churches receive believer's baptism, usually by immersion, on associating themselves with a Baptist congregation. Baptists deny that this is rebaptism, as the infant baptism previously received is not seen as true baptism in the NT sense.

The authority for the administration of the Church is in the hands of the congregation, which approves the call of ministers and ordains them as either pastor or deacon in a prayer of dedication attended by ministers of nearby congregations.[3] Even though each Baptist congregation is autonomous, associations have been found as early as 1650, and have contributed to the remarkable unity of faith and confession, as well as missionary efforts.[4]

Although Baptists are happy to cooperate in works of evangelization, their congregational sense makes them uneasy when they encounter the structures of other Churches.[5] Nor are all Baptists happy with the World Council of Churches (v. ECUMENISM, WCC), which some see as too politicized, though other Baptist groups are full members. The BWA sponsors international ecumenical dialogue.

Dialogue on an international level has taken place with the Lutherans since 1986. Baptists have shown themselves concerned about condemnations of their positions in Lutheran confessions; Lutherans have been equally concerned about the non-acceptance of their baptism. Other topics dealt with are discipleship, Church and authority.[6] Similar issues had been discussed in Germany since 1979.[7]

The BWA was in dialogue with the World Alliance of Reformed Churches from 1973–1977. Both are representatives of the radical Reformation; both see themselves as renewing the local Church on a NT model; both follow a Calvinist theology; both stress lay participation and are unhappy with *episcopê*/oversight being centered in one person.[8]

Significant dialogue in the U.S. has taken place between Roman Catholics and both the American Baptist Churches (1967–1970)[9] and Southern Baptists (1982–1984,[10] 1985–1988[11]). At the international level there has been Roman Catholic and Baptist dialogue from 1984 on the theme of mission, Church, witness, and evangelism.[12] A synthesis of the conversations, *Summons to Witness to Christ in Today's World,* was published in 1988.[13]

A special contribution of Baptists to the ecumenical movement is their dedication to mission and evangelization, which, in the past, however, has not always excluded proselytism. Their courage and commitment resulted in martyrdom in the USSR prior to 1989.

[1]R.G. Torbet, *A History of the Baptists* (Philadelphia: Judson, [2]1963); W.H. Brackney, *The Baptists* (Westport, Conn.: Greenwood, 1988). [2]F.T. Lord, *Baptist World Fellowship: A Short History of the Baptist World Alliance* (London: Carey Kingsgate, 1955); E.A. Payne, *The Baptist Union: A Short History* (London: Carey Kingsgate, 1959). [3]"The Philadelphia Confession (1688)," in Schaff, Creeds 3:738–741; "New Hampshire Baptist Confession," ibid., 742–748; see C. Brownlow Hastings, *Introducing Southern Baptists: Their Faith and Their Life* (New York: Paulist, 1981); idem, "A Baptist Bibliography," GrOrTR 22 (1977) 263–265; E.F. Tupper, "A Baptist Vision of the Church," RExp 84 (1987) 617–632. [4]A.W. Graves, "The Present Role of the Baptist Association," RExp 77 (1980) 185–199; W.B. Shurden, "The Historical Background of Baptist Associations," RExp 77 (1980) 161–175. [5]W.R. Estep, *Baptists and Christian Unity* (Nashville: Broadman, 1967); J.D. Hughey, "Baptists and the Ecumenical Movement," EcuR 10 (1957–1958) 401–410. [6]*Baptists and Lutherans in Dialogue* (Geneva: BWA—LWF, 1990). [7]G. Rothermundt, "Ein Dialog beginnt: Die baptistisch-lutherischen Gespräche seit 1979," ÖkRu 36 (1987) 321–331. [8]*Baptists and Reformed in Dialogue* (Geneva: World Alliance of Reformed Churches, 1984). [9]J.A. Burgess and J. Gros, *Building Unity.* Ecumenical Documents 4 (New York: Paulist, 1989) 39–44; RExp 79 (1982/2); W.H. Porter, "Ecumenical

Concerns among American Baptists," JEcuS 17 (1980) 21–37. [10]Ibid., 45–51; SWJT 28 (1986/2); T.F. Stransky, "A Roman Catholic Perspective on Baptist Ecumenism," JEcuSt 17 (1980) 125–132. [11]AA.VV. *To Understand Each Other* (New Orleans: Baptist Seminary, 1989); "Agreed Statement," Origins 19/10 (1989) 166–168; T. Horgan, "Southern Baptist/Roman Catholic Dialogue," JEcuSt 25 (1988) 157–158. [12]InformSer 55 (1984) 2–3, 67–68; 59 (1985) 3–4, 40; 72 (1990) 5–18 = OneChr 26 (1990) 238–255; J.M. Radano, "The Catholic Church in Dialogue with Lutherans, Reformed and Baptists," OneChr 24 (1988) 71–81. [13]CathIntern 1 (1990) 237–245.

## BARMEN CONFESSION

In May 1934 representatives from Lutheran, Reformed, and United Churches met in Barmen (present-day Wuppertal) to organize Protestant resistance to National Socialism (Nazism) in Germany. Their leader was M. Niemöller, their theological mentor was K. Barth (q.v.). From the meeting came the "Confessing Church" as opposed to the "German Christians" who opted for passive resistance and those theologians—including G. Kittel—who openly supported the Nazi "moral renewal" of German society.[1] By 1937 the Confessing Church movement was largely driven underground, but its Barmen Confession[2] was a rallying standard of biblical faith in the sole Lordship of Jesus, and a condemnation of any who would subvert this Lordship. "Jesus Christ, as he is testified to us in the Scripture is the one Word we are to hear, whom we are to trust and obey in life and death" (art. 1). Though its basis is clearly Christological, the document is primarily ecclesiological in seeking to show how the Churches were to react to the Nazi ideology.[3] Thus article 3 quotes Eph 3:15-16 and continues: "The Christian Church is the community of brethren in which Jesus Christ presently works in the word and sacraments through the Holy Spirit. With her faith as well as with her ordinances, she has to witness in the midst of the world of sin as the Church of forgiven sinners that she is his alone, that she lives and wishes to live only by his counsel and comfort in expectation of his appearance." Article 6 quotes Matt 28:20 and 2 Tim 2:9 and states: "The commission of the Church, in which her freedom is founded, consists in this: in place of Christ and thus in service of his own word and work, to extend through word and sacrament the message of the free grace of God to all people." Article 5 deals with Church and State with the solemn warning: "[The Church] reminds men of God's Kingdom, God's commandment and righteousness, and thereby the responsibility of rulers and ruled."

After the war, the Barmen Confession became an official or quasi-official creed in some Churches. In the Lutheran Church in Germany it can be mentioned in Church constitutions, but not in the context of describing the Church's dependence on the 16th-century confessional statements. Rather difficult to assess is

the influence of the unity at Barmen on subsequent ecumenical endeavors.[4] Whilst the historical issues facing the Churches at Barmen were unique, the achievement of a very prompt and profound reading of the signs of the times makes Barmen a prophetic symbol for the Church at all times.[5]

[1]R.P. Ericksen, *Theologians Under Hitler* (New Haven: Yale UP, 1975, 1986). [2]Text in Leith, Creeds 518–522; F.H. Littell, *The German Phoenix* (Garden City, N.Y.: Doubleday, 1960) 184–188. E.H. Amberg, "Barmen 1934–1984: Ein Literaturbericht," TLZ 111 (1986) 161–174; C. Nicolaisen, "Barmen 1934–1984. Bibliographie der 1983–1986 erschienenen Titel," KirJb 11 (1984—ed. 1986) 3:127-146; H.V. Stephen, ed*., Das eine Wort für Alle: Barmen 1934–1984. Eine Dokumentation* (Neukirchen—Vluyn: Neukirchener Verl., 1986). [3]H. Vall, *Iglesias e idología nazi: El Sínodo de Barmen (1934)* (Salamanca: Sígueme, 1976) with rev. art. by S. Cavallotto in RasT 19 (1978) 398–405; H.G. Locke, ed., *The Barmen Confession. Papers from the Seattle Assembly.* Toronto Studies in Theology 26 (Lewiston, N.Y.—Queenston, Ont: Mellen, 1986). [4]A. Boyens, "Die theologische Erklärung von Barmen 1934 und ihr Echo in der Ökumene," ÖkRu 33 (1986) 368–378. [5]K. Blaser, "The Barmen Declaration and the Present Theological Context," EcuR 36 (1984) 299–315 = RTPhil 116 (1984) 85–103; A.C. Cochrane, "Barmen: the Church Between Temptation and Grace," PrincSemB 6 (1985) 68–77; D.J. Hall, "Barmen: Lesson in Theology," TorontoJT 1 (1985) 180–199; H.G. Locke, ed., *The Church Confronts the Nazis: Barmen Then and Now* (New York—Toronto: Edwin Mellen, 1984); A.J. Reimer, "The Theology of Barmen: Its Partisan-political Dimension," TorontoJT 1 (1985) 155–174.

## BARNABAS, LETTER OF

The *Letter of Barnabas*[1] was ascribed to Barnabas by Cyril of Alexandria. The fact that it was attested in the city of Alexandria alone in the 3rd and 4th centuries may indicate its origin as from there. We know nothing about its author except that the letter itself seems to indicate that he was a convert from Judaism. It can be argued that he wrote in the first half of the 2nd century, though some scholars put it as early as 70 C.E.[2]

The letter, or rather treatise, for it is not in epistolary form, has two parts (some would say three[3]). There is a doctrinal first part and a practical second part. The doctrinal first part seeks to prove that the Jews completely misunderstood the teaching of the OT by interpreting it literally. This consists of an allegorical account of the OT: the various elements of Hebrew religion are either rejected or given a fuller meaning in the light of Christ; its sacrifices described as human offerings (2:6; cf. 7-8); its fasting, which should have been deeds of righteousness (3:2-5); its covenant, which belongs rather to Christians (4:7; 14:1-9); likewise its temple, "for the dwelling of our hearts is a temple sacred to the Lord (6:15; cf. 16:1-10); its circumcision, for "he circumcised our ears that we might hear the word and believe. But the circumcision in which they (the Jews) trust has been abolished" (9:3-4);

its clean and unclean animals, for "Moses received three decrees concerning food, and spoke of them in a spiritual sense, but the Jews received them as referring to food in the carnal desires" (10:9); even the law (15:2-4). It is Christ who is the fulfillment of the whole OT (5:1-14; 7:1-11).

Its teaching on baptism in this first part is significant: "Blessed are those who put their hope in the cross and descended into the water . . . we come up bearing fruit in our hearts, fear and hope in Jesus in the Spirit" (11:8, 11); thus we are temples of God, "when we received forgiveness of sins and put our hope in the Name, we were renewed, totally recreated, and so God truly dwells in us as in his habitation" (16:8). Important, too, is the teaching about Sunday: "Therefore we also celebrate with joy the eighth day on which Jesus also rose from the dead, was made manifest, and ascended into heaven" (15:8-9). This is the earliest text explaining why Christians observe Sunday rather than Saturday as a holy day.

The practical second part is a traditional exposition of the Two Ways, quite similar to the *Didachê,* both perhaps coming from a common source. There are notable features here: the prohibition of abortion (19:5); the eschatological view of the kingdom of God (21:1), and a certain imminent sense of its coming (21:3).[4]

The *Letter of Barnabas* deals with the perennial question of the relationship between the two testaments by spiritualizing and allegorizing the OT. Others, like the heretic Marcion (d. ca. 160), will go further and deny totally the validity of the OT.

---

[1]Texts: PG 2:727-782; F.X. Glimm, FC 1:185-222; R.A. Kraft, AF 3:80-162; J.B. Lightfoot, *The Apostolic Fathers* (Grand Rapids: Baker, 1974) 137–156; J.A. Robinson (R.H. Connolly, ed.), "The Epistle of Barnabas and the Didache," JTS 35 (1934) 113–146. [2]S. Tugwell, *The Apostolic Fathers.* Outstanding Christian Thinkers (London: Chapman, 1989) 21–46; Kraft (n. 1) 17–56.   [3]B. Robillard, "L'Epître de Barnabé: trois époques, trois théologies, trois rédacteurs," RB 78 (1971) 184–209.   [4]A. Hermans, "Le Pseudo-Barnabé est-il millénariste?," ETL 35 (1959) 849–876.

## BARTH, Karl (1886–1968)

One of the leading theologians of the 20th century, the Swiss Calvinist Karl Barth[1] was born in Basle in 1886. After theological studies in various universities, he was a pastor for an extended period (1909–1921). He became professor at Göttingen in 1921 and later taught at Münster and Bonn. With the advent of Nazism, he became a leader of the Confessing Church and a principal author of its great Barmen Declaration (1934—q.v.). He was forced to leave Germany, and taught at Basle until retirement in 1962.

Though Barth had studied under Adolf von Harnack, as a pastor he began to react against Protestant liberalism. He returned to a theology of the Word of God with

a new discovery of the Bible. A fruit of his early intuitions was his commentary on Romans (1919; revised 1922). The bibliography of his works, and of studies about him, is vast.[2]

He was involved in the Church in many ways: as believer, as pastor, as a defender of purity of divine revelation especially against Nazism, as theologian, as ecumenist with a major input into the First General Assembly of the World Council of Churches (v. ECUMENISM, WCC) at Amsterdam (1948), as friendly but firm critic of Vatican II.[3] His ecclesiological thought is written not in an organic or complete form,[4] but is found throughout his vast works, especially in his monumental *Church Dogmatics,*[5] and in essays from 1932 to 1957.[6] It rests on his fundamental positions about the transcendence of God, the nature of revelation, creation, reconciliation, and atonement, and about autonomy being only under the Word of God, who is an acting subject rather than an object for theology.[7] From his positions on these central issues he concludes to the impossibility of natural theology, to the ultimate irrelevance of merely human achievements, to total dependence on grace, and to the radical incapacity of humanity or the Church to cooperate in any way with the divine action without grace. God's sole revelation is in Jesus Christ, and the Word of God is his one and only means of communication with men and women. Barth therefore rejects any mediation of the Church, except insofar as it echoes God's Word. The Church community is gathered by the Word of God and built up by the Holy Spirit: "A congregation is the coming together of those who belong to Jesus Christ through the Holy Spirit."[8]

The ecclesiology of Barth at times coheres well with Vatican II developments; at other times it is in sharp contrast with Catholic positions. It can never be ignored. His exposition of the four marks (q.v.) of the Church, significantly to be found during his treatment of reconciliation, can show us some important points of divergence, as well as key Barthian themes.[9] The immediate context[10] is the Church seen as an event, gathered by the Holy Spirit into community, so that the Church is more accurately said to take place rather than to exist. It is a visible community involved in worship, teaching, preaching, instruction, theology, and confession. This community is the Body of Christ through the Spirit.

The Church is one:[11] the visible and invisible Church are one; the Church on earth *(ecclesia militans)* and the Church in heaven *(ecclesia triumphans)* are one; the people of Israel before and after Christ are one inseparable community; the various Churches that exist in different places are one. Any other plurality, such as Christians not recognizing other Churches, is a scandal and in contradiction with Ephesians, chapter 4.

Instead, confessing "one Church" means placing Jesus Christ at the center and allowing him to question our divisions.

The Church is holy[12] because God sets it apart. Its holiness is a reflection of its Head, a free gift. Though the Church is always in need of reform *(semper reformanda),* it can never be other than holy too, the bride of Christ; it is therefore always a responsible and dangerous matter to criticize the Church, though it may at times be necessary to do so. The true holy members of the Church are known to the Lord alone; obedience is a necessary consequence and expression of the Church being holy.

The Church is catholic:[13] this means that the Church has a character by virtue of which it is always and everywhere the same; catholicity is implicitly the contrast between the true Church and a false one that is heretical, schismatic, or apostate. The word "catholic" must not be ceded to the Roman Church, for either a Church is catholic or it is not the Church. The catholicity or variety of the Church is geographical, in different societies, in diverse times, comprehending individual members who must not set themselves apart from the community. It cannot be presumed that either a majority or a minority in the Church will necessarily reflect the *catholica.* Like the other marks of the Church, catholicity as a spiritual and qualitative predicate can only be believed.

The Church is apostolic:[14] the word "apostolic" does not add to the above three predicates, but gives a spiritual criterion—to be used in faith—identifying the one, holy, catholic Church. Apostolic means discipleship in the school of, and under the normative authority, instruction, and direction of the apostles, listening to them and accepting their message. Apostolic does not mean a visible succession of ministers, which would be a juridical rather than spiritual norm; apostolic authority cannot be passed on, for one cannot control the Spirit or force the Spirit to anoint a particular person. The authority of apostolicity is that of service; the forms of Church structure are altogether secondary, but they must be loose so as not to encroach on the lordship of Jesus. Apostolicity is found when the Church takes the direction of Scripture in its preaching and theology, making them Christocentric, and when the Church is faithful to its commission to be a herald in prayer, sacraments, inner fellowship, and theology.

The Church is not an end in itself but exists for the world, in which it is to be herald as an ambassador in the service of proclamation and *kerygma.*[15] The goal of the Church is the kingdom: "If we really hope for the kingdom of God, then we can also endure the Church in its pettiness."[16]

In general, Barth faults the Catholic Church for what he sees as its going beyond faith alone and hav-ing too high a regard for what is juridical and merely human. Nonetheless, some of his most insightful and sympathetic critics have been Catholics.[17]

Since the 1920s Barth has been described as "neo-orthodox." In the English-speaking world this term has been sometimes understood as meaning "traditional." In fact, it also means that Barth was profoundly modern.

[1]E. Busch, *Karl Barth: His Life from Letters and Autobiographical Texts* (Philadelphia: Fortress, 1976); E. Jüngel, *Karl Barth: A Theological Legacy* (Philadelphia: Westminster, 1986). [2]See C. von Kirchbaum, in *Antwort.* FS zum 70. Geburtstag (Zurich, 1965) 945–960; E. Busch, in *Parrhesia.* FS zum 80. Geburtstag (Zurich, 1966) 709–723; see also M. Kwiran, *Index to Literature on Barth, Bonhoeffer and Bultmann.* Theologische Zeitschrift. Sonderband VII (Basel: Reinhardt, 1977); A. Moda, "Karl Barth (1886–1968): Una selezione bibliografica," ScoulC 104 (1976) 370–405; G. Hunsinger, *How to Read Karl Barth: The Shape of His Theology* (New York: Oxford UP, 1991). [3]*Ad limina apostolorum: An Appraisal of Vatican II* (Richmond, Va.: John Knox Press, 1968—German 1967); *How I Changed My Mind* (Edinburgh: St. Andrew's Press. 1969). [4]J.A. Estrada, "El elemento carismático de la Iglesia en la eclesiología de Karl Barth," EstE 59 (1984) 53–83; W. Greive, *Die Kirche als Ort der Wahrheit: Das Verständnis der Kirche in der Theologie Karl Barths.* Forschungen zur systematischen und ökumenischen Theologie 61 (Göttingen: Vandenhoech and Ruprecht, 1991); C. Journet, "L'ecclésiologie de Karl Barth," in *L'Église du Verbe Incarné* (Bruges, 1961) 2:1129-1171; B. Mondin, *Le nuove ecclesiologie.* Teologia 29 (Rome: Paoline, 1980) 56–63; C. O'Grady, *The Church in the Theology of Karl Barth* (London: Chapman, 1968); idem, *The Church in Catholic Theology: Dialogue with Karl Barth* (London: Chapman, 1969); M.B. Schepers, "The Work of the Spirit: Karl Barth on the Nature of the Church," TS 23 (1962) 625–642. [5]Eng. trans. 13 vols (New York—Edinburgh: Clark, 1936–1969) of *Die kirchliche Dogmatik* (Zurich, 1932–1967). See K. Barth, *How I Changed My Mind* (Edinburgh: St. Andrew Press, 1969). [6]*L'Église* (Geneva, 1964). [7]J. Macken, *The Autonomy Theme in the "Church Dogmatics": Karl Barth and his Critics* (Cambridge: UP, 1990). [8]*Dogmatics in Outline* (London: SCM, 1966, from 1949) ch. 22, p. 141. [9]*Church Dogmatics* 4/1: 668-725 (*Die kirchliche Dogmatik* 4/1:746-809). Cf. "The Notion of the Church," in *Catholiques et Protestants* (Paris, 1963); "The Living Congregation of the Living Lord Jesus Christ," in *The Universal Church in God's Design.* The Amsterdam Assembly Series (London, 1948) 1:67-76. [10]*Dogmatics* 4/1:643-668—*Dogmatik* 4/1:718-746. [11]*Dogmatics* 4/1:669-685—*Dogmatik* 4/1:746-765. [12]*Dogmatics* 4/1:685-701—*Dogmatik* 4/1:765-783. [13]*Dogmatics* 4/1:701-712—*Dogmatik* 4/1:783-795. [14]*Dogmatics* 4/1:712-725—*Dogmatik* 4/1:795-809. [15]*Dogmatics in Outline* (n. 7) ch. 22, pp. 146–147. [16]Ibid., 148. [17]E.g., H. Urs von Balthasar, *The Theology of Karl Barth* (New York: Holt, Reinhart and Winston, 1971 from German 1951/1976); H. Bouillard, *Karl Barth.* 2 vols. (Paris: Aubier, 1957); G. Foley, "The Catholic Critics of Karl Barth in Outline and Analysis," ScotJT 14 (1961) 136–155; idem, "Das Verhaltnis Karl Barths zur römischen Katholizmus," in G. Busch et al., eds., *Parrhesia.* FS K. Barth (Zurich: EVZ, 1966) 598–616; H. Fries, "Kirche als Ereignis: Zu Karl Barths Lehre von der Kirche," Catholica 11 (1957) 81–108; J. Hamer, *Karl Barth* (London: Collins—New York: Alba, 1962); J. Macken, "The Catholic Reception of Karl Barth's Theology," MilltownSt 25 (1990) 95–113; P.J. Rosato, *The Spirit as Lord: The Pneumatology of Karl Barth* (Edinburgh: Clark, 1981). See above O'Grady (n. 4), Macken (n. 7) and B. Reymond, *Théologien où*

*prophète: Les Francophones et Karl Barth avant 1945* (Lausanne: L'Age d'Homme, 1985).

## BASIC CHRISTIAN COMMUNITIES

In a broad sense, A.F. McGovern notes, "the basic ecclesial communities can be considered as a general expression of liberation theology in practice." Both are born from the same impetus of concern for the poor: the basic Christian communities (BCC) embody the spirit of liberation theology, and they in turn provide theologians with a major source for theological reflection.[1]

The term "Basic Christian Community" (*Comunidades Eclesiales de Base*—CEB) is not univocal. The word "basic" tends to refer to those who are at the bottom of the socio-economic heap, and who are at the base of a pyramidically conceived Church. It would often be well translated as "grass-roots." Though the term is applied to very many kinds of Christian-based groups among the poor, for this article the term is largely restricted to small, Scripture-centered reflection and action groups among the poor in Latin America. In Peru the term is Committed Christian Communities (*Comunidades Cristianas Comprometidas*).

The BCCs began to appear in Brazil about 1963. Their inspiration arose partly from work in the field of education, particularly that of P. Freire,[2] as well as from groups concerned with the Church's social teaching. The shortage of priests for regular liturgical celebrations also contributed to their development.

A common form of BCC is a group of between ten and thirty people in a rural area or a slum shantytown coming together regularly to reflect on their situation in the light of Scripture, to sing and to pray together, and to propose action for the life problems of its members. Each word in "basic Christian community/basic ecclesial community" is significant: it is a community, not a discussion group, but one in which members care for, and share with, one another; it is Christian/ecclesial and so related to the Church; it is of the base, that is comprising the marginalized in society.[3]

Following G. Cook we can see four fundamental orientations in BCCs.[4] They have a new way of seeing reality, i.e., from the perspective of the poor. At the same time their main paradigm for the Church is that of the People of God, and there is some greater emphasis on moral values than on religious practice. Second, there is a new way of being Church. Though the institutions are generally given their proper role, there is a stress on the radical equality of all believers, on participation by all, in their different ways, in the teaching and sanctifying role of the Church as well as in decision-making.[5] Third, there is a new way of approaching Scripture.[6] The key methodology is that of a community reading the Scripture in the light of its own situations and life experience. Scripture is no longer a book, the only key-holder of which is the priest or the educated person. The Bible belongs to all the people of God, and all have a Spirit-given ability to come to know themselves, their circumstances, and God's plan from its teaching. Fourth, the BCCs show a new way of understanding mission. They are a concrete realization of the Puebla statement, "preferential option for the poor" (v. POOR).[7] The poor are to be evangelized, but perhaps more significantly, they in turn are also evangelizers in the Church and the world.

The relation of BCCs to the parish structure is complex and diverse. Where the parish is weak, the BCC is obviously very important for the religious and social welfare of the people. There need not be any conflict in theory or practice between parish and BCC, though a healthy tension can exist: the parish is an administrative center largely concerned with sacramental ministry; the BCC is the place where there is a primary experience of community.

Official Church teaching shows an ever greater openness to BCCs. The Second Conference of Latin American Bishops (CELAM) at Medellín (1968) spoke positively of BCCs as "the first and fundamental ecclesiastical nucleus."[8] In the interim before the Third Conference of CELAM at Puebla (1979) there were National Conferences of the BCCs beginning with Vitória in 1975, at which there was a significant number of bishops present. In that year Paul VI issued his great exhortation on evangelization in which he warned against communities that were anti-hierarchical, but welcomed those which were truly ecclesial, stating the conditions under which they could truly be a "hope for the Church."[9] Puebla welcomed the growth in BCCs since Medellín and spoke extensively and warmly of their value and possibilities, while at the same time being aware of deviations.[10] The extraordinary Synod of 1985 spoke very positively of BCCs in its final report: "Since the Church is communion, the new 'basic Christian communities,' if they truly live in communion with the Church, are an authentic expression of communion and a way of building a more profound communion. They are then a reason for great hope for the life of the Church."[11] In his post-synodal exhortation, *The Vocation and Mission of the Lay Faithful* (1988), Pope John Paul II gave criteria for discerning lay groups and for recognizing a true ecclesiality in them. Though of wider application within the Church, these "Criteria of Ecclesiality" apply also to BCCs. Such are: the primacy of the call of every Christian to holiness; the responsibility of professing the Catholic faith; the witness of authentic communion with the Church's pastors; conformity to, and participation in, the Church's apostolic goals; a commitment to a presence in human society at the service of the total dignity of the person.[12] These criteria reflect a different ecclesiology and starting point than those of the majority of BCCs. Still they suggest some indispensable conditions for the BCCs to remain within the catholic unity of the Church. There is a danger that the groups could be manipulated to radical activism, and be so concerned with social change that they might lose sight of the spiritual aspect of that integral liberation which is at the heart of Christ's message. But there is another threat to the effectiveness of BCCs. They could be so protective of their autonomy that they would not be sufficiently aware that profound social change will not come about solely through individual conversion of heart. They need a corporate commitment to renewal of, even change in, political and Church institutions.[13]

Originally a phenomenon in Latin America, where they are numbered in hundreds of thousands, BCCs have spread to other countries where the basic insight is adapted for differing cultures and situations.[14]

BCCs remain one of the richest concrete expressions of post-Vatican ecclesiology, and they have important lessons for the Church in every place. They have also an important contribution to make in the area of spirituality (v. LIBERATION THEOLOGIES), through their vision of holiness seen from the perspective of the poor.[15] They hold out possibilities for the renewal of parish (q.v.) life throughout the world.

[1]A.F. McGovern, *Liberation Theology and Its Critics: Toward an Assessment* (Maryknoll: Orbis, 1989) 199; REBras 46/183 (1986) 481–669.  [2]P. Freire, *Pedagogy of the Oppressed* (Harmondsworth: Penguin, 1972); D. Collins, *Paulo Freire: His Life, Works and Thoughts* (New York: Paulist, 1977); S. Mainwaring, *The Catholic Church and Politics in Brazil 1916–1985* (Stanford: UP, 1986) 66–70.  [3]M. de C. Azevedo, *Basic Christian Communities in Brazil* (Washington, D.C.: Georgetown UP, 1987); R. van der Ploeg, "As CEBs na fase da adolescncia," REBras 51 (1991) 29–64.  [4]G. Cook, *The Expectation of the Poor: Latin American Basic Ecclesial Communities in Protestant Perspective* (Maryknoll: Orbis, 1985); cf. G. Deelen, "The Church on Its Way to the People: Basic Christian Communities in Brazil," CrossC 30 (1980–1981) 385–408 = Pro Mundi Vita Bulletin (April 1980).  [5]L. Boff, *Ecclesiogenesis: The Base Communities Reinvent the Church* (Maryknoll: Orbis—London: Collins, 1986—Portuguese 1977); idem, *Church: Charism and Power—Liberation and the Institutional Church* (New York: Crossroad, 1986—Portuguese 1981).  [6]C. Mesters, "The Use of the Bible in Christian Communities of the Common People," in S. Torres and J. Eagleson, eds., *The Challenge of Basic Christian Communities* (Maryknoll: Orbis, 1981) 197–210 = A.T. Hennelly, ed., *Liberation Theology: A Documentary History* (Maryknoll: Orbis, 1990) 14–28. Cf. also Mester's many books, especially *Defenseless Flower: A New Reading of the Bible* (Maryknoll: Orbis, 1989).  [7]*Puebla: Official English Edition* (Washington, D.C.: National Conference of Catholic Bishops—Slough UK: St Paul, 1980) nn. 382, 733, 769, 1134, 1165, 1217. See CELAM, Santa Domingo (1992) arts. 54–64, 259.  [8]L.M. Colonese, ed., *The Church in the Present-day Transformation of Latin America in the Light of the Council* (Washington, D.C.: U.S. Catholic Conference, 1968–1969) "Joint Pastoral Planning, Medellín," in Vol. 2, 15:10-11.  [9]*Evangelii nuntiandi*, n. 58—Flannery 2:738-740.  [10]Puebla (n. 7) nn. 96–98, 617–657.  [11]*The Final Report 6—Synode extraordinaire* (Paris: Cerf, 1986) 562.  [12]*Christi-fideles laici*, n. 30.  [13]McGovern (n. 1) 212; Azevedo (n. 3) 82–88, 139–142.  [14]E.g., M. de C. Azevedo, "Basic Ecclesial Communities: A Meeting Point of Ecclesiologies," TS 46 (1985) 601–620; T.A. Kleissler, M.A. LeBert and M.C. McGinnes, *Resources for Small Christian Communities* (New York—Mahwah: Paulist, 1991); idem, *Small Christian Communities* (ibid., 1991); P. Lefebvre, "Les communautés ecclésiales de base à Kinshasa: Éléments d'analyse critique," BTAfr 6 (1984) 5–16; M.S. Martin, "New Christian Communities and the Post Vatican Theology of the Laity," IndTS 19 (1982) 210–225; D. Martinez, "Basic Christian Communities: A New Model of Church within the U.S. Hispanic Community," NewTR 3/4 (Nov. 1990) 35–42; L. Mascarenhas, "Basic Christian Communities in an Islamic Setting," VYoti 44 (1980) 216–226; K. Rahner, "Basic Communities," ThInvest 19:159-165.  [15]M. O'Neill, *God Hears the Cry of the Poor: The Emerging Spirituality in the Christian Communities in Peru (1965–1986).* Diss. (Rome: Gregorian, 1990).

## BASIL THE GREAT, St. (ca. 330–379)

Basil was a member of an extraordinary family. Six of his relatives are venerated as saints, the best known being his brother Gregory of Nyssa (q.v.), who with Basil's very close friend, Gregory of Nazianzus, formed the trio of the Cappadocian Fathers. He was born in Caesarea in Cappadocia about 330.[1] After a good education in secular studies, especially rhetoric, he experienced a conversion and became a monk and a hermit. About six years later (364) he was called by his bishop to come to defend the Church against the Arian emperor Valens. He became bishop of Caesarea in 370 and devoted himself to service of the poor, the defense of the Church against heresy, and the care of his diocese. He died in 379 just before the Council of Constantinople I (q.v.), which vindicated his theological positions.

Basil was one of the greatest Fathers of the Church, leaving an indelible mark on the East, as well as being highly influential in the West. He was the principal monastic legislator, and his longer and shorter rules, *Regulae fusius tratatae* and *Regulae brevius tratatae* were authoritative in the East, and in the West through St. Benedict.[2]

Basil's major dogmatic treatises are a work against Eunomius (only the first three books are considered authentic),[3] and his book *On the Holy Spirit,* from about 375.[4] *The Liturgy of St. Basil*[5] used on the greater feasts in the East goes back to him: he did not so much create it as revise it; changes were subsequently made to it in the Church. In addition he has left a very large number of sermons and letters on theological and spiritual topics.

In ecclesiology the canons of Basil are important. They are letters written about Church order, and they passed into the Eastern corpus of law.[6] The Arian controversy involved also important issues of Church and Empire.[7] Basil asserted the Church's independence in the face of the emperor Valens' persecution of

Catholics; Basil stood firm.[8] The meeting of the emperor's prefect gives a classical vignette recorded by Gregory Nazianzus. When Modestus angrily stated that nobody had ever dared speak to him the way Basil had done, the latter replied, "Perhaps you have never yet had to deal with a bishop."[9] His misunderstandings with Pope Damasus on the succession of Antioch and his approach to Rome were based on two different views: the Roman primacy was quite evolved in the West; Basil was not aware of this.

His ecclesiology stresses the unity of the Church, which is a work of the Spirit; thus to be separated from unity is to be detached from the Spirit.[10] Ecclesiology for him is inextricably linked with pneumatology.

[1]M.M. Fox, *Life and Times of St. Basil* (Washington, D.C., 1939); G.L. Prestige, *St. Basil the Great and Apollinaris of Laodicea* (London, 1956); Patrology 3:204-236. [2]Longer PG 31:889-1052; Shorter 1079–1306/FC 9. [3]PG 29:497-669/SC 299 and 305. [4]PG 32:67-217/LNPF ser. 2, 8:2-50/SC 17bis. [5]PG 31:1629-1656/J.N.W.B. Robertson, *The Divine Liturgies of Chrysostom and Basil* (London, 1894); G. Ferrari, "La dimensione teologica nella liturgia di S. Basilio," Nicol 8 (1980) 138–144; E. Lanne, "Les anaphores eucharistiques de saint Basile et la communauté ecclésiale," Irén 55 (1982) 307–331. [6]*Epp.* 188, 199, 217; see D. Salachas, "Le lettere canoniche di san Basilio," Nicol 8 (1980) 73–84. [7]G.F. Reilly, *Imperium and Sacerdotium According to St. Basil the Great* (Washington, D.C., 1945). [8]K. Baus, in Jedin-Dolan, 64–68, 85–86. [9]Gregory Nazianzus, *Oratio 43*—trans. J.H. Newman, *The Church of the Fathers* (London: [4]1968) 14–17. [10]*De Spiritu Sancto* 26—PG 32:181; *Reg. fus.* 7:2—PG 31:929. See S. Manna, "L'ecclesiologia di S. Basilio," Nicol 10 (1982) 47–74; P.J. Fedwick, *The Church and the Charisma of Leadership in Basil of Caesarea* (Toronto: Pontifical Institute of Medieval Studies, 1979); A. Rauch and P. Imhof, eds., *Basilius: Heiliger der einen Kirche.* Koinonia. Schriftenreihe des ostkirchlichen Instituts Regensburg 1 (Munich: Kaffke, 1981); T. Špidlík, "'Sentirsi chiesa' nella catechesi di Basilio Magno," in S. Felici, ed., *Ecclesiologia e catechesi patristica.* Biblioteca di scienze religiose 46 (Rome: LAS, 1982) 113–122.

## BASLE, Council of (1431–1449)

The Council of Basle (Basel)[1] was convoked by Martin V (1417–1431), who died before it opened on 23 July 1431. Earlier, in obedience to the decree *Frequens* of the Council of Constance (q.v.), he had summoned a poorly attended council at Pavia, later transferred to Siena (1423–1424). Eugenius IV (1431–1447)[2] appointed Julian Caesarini as legate and president of the council, but actively tried to oppose it and attempted in November 1431 to transfer it to Bologna. The 1st session of the council (14 Dec. 1431) recalled Constance, and set out three aims: the extirpation of all heresy, peace in the Christian people, and reform.[3]

In its 2nd and 3rd sessions (February and April 1432) the council refused the dissolution demanded by Eugenius IV, who eventually had to accede to some of its wishes (*Dudum sacram,* 10 Aug. 1433). He had the support of only six out of twenty-one cardinals, and many of the secular powers also opposed him. Though some reforms were decreed, viz. election of bishops,[4] and provincial and synodal councils,[5] most of the time up to the 17th session (26 April 1434) was taken up with polemics between the pope and the council. A worthwhile period of conciliar discussions, however, was the dialogue with the Bohemians (January–April 1433).[6] It was a rare example in the second millennium of those thought of as heretics being given the right to appear and speak at a council. After further discussions at Prague, the *Compactata* were drawn up, and these answered the main Hussite gravamina. Though approved by Basle in 1437, they were not ratified by the curia, and were annulled in 1462.

The second and most fruitful phase of the council was its 19th to 25th sessions (7 Sept. 1434–7 May 1437). In the 19th session (7 Sept. 1434) legates from the Greek emperor and patriarch were received and plans were made for conciliar meetings. It also issued a decree on Jews (q.v.) and infidels (Muslims?), which was a quite restrictive form of apartheid.[7] However, those converting to the faith received the protection of law concerning their property.[8] Other sessions were devoted to reforms: concubinage was condemned and ecclesiastical penalties regulated (20th);[9] annates, or the first year's revenue of a benefice payable to the Roman curia, were suppressed; decrees for right order in worship were laid down (21st);[10] legislation was enacted about papal elections, the duties of the pope, and about cardinals (23rd).[11]

After dealing with arrangements for the meeting with the Greeks in the 24th session (14 April 1436), the council did nothing for a year. Meanwhile Eugenius IV found his position somewhat strengthened and he moved against the council again. At the 25th session (7 May 1437) a majority favored Basle, Avignon, or Savoy for the forthcoming ecumenical council with the Greeks, but a minority siding with Eugenius IV chose Florence or Udine.[12] This session was to be the last that would be received (v. RECEPTION) by the Catholic Church as authentic. Pope Eugenius dissolved Basle on 18 September 1437. A minority of bishops transferred to the Council of Florence (q.v.), while the majority continued to meet at Basle until 1448, when they transferred to Lausanne, eventually closing the council on 25 April 1449.

There was some notable activity while the council was thus in schism. It met again with the Bohemians, conceding their demands about communion with the chalice (30th session). It laid down the "three truths" on 16 May 1439 (33rd session): "It is a truth of the catholic faith that the holy general council holds power over the pope and anyone else. The Roman pontiff of his own authority cannot dissolve, transfer or prorogue the general council when lawfully assembled without its own consent, and that is part of the same truth. Whoever obstinately opposes these truths must be deemed a heretic."[13] This statement was designed to justify the intended deposition of Eugenius IV; it was an assertion that the decree *Haec sancta* of Constance (q.v.) was a matter of faith.[14] The council moved against Eugenius at its next session on 25 June 1439, deposing him and electing the Duke Amadeus of Savoy in his place, the antipope Felix V (1439–1449). Meanwhile one of several condemnations of Basle, the decree *Moyses,* emanated from the papal council of Florence.[15]

In the midst of all this political maneuvering, the schismatic council found time to define the Immaculate Conception of Mary (36th session—17 Sept. 1439), and to introduce the feast of the Visitation of Mary (1 July 1441).

The council transferred to Lausanne in 1448 and dissolved itself at the 5th session there on 25 April 1449. Felix had been looking for a way out of his situation from 1445. He found accommodation with the new pope Nicholas V (1447–1455): he solemnly abdicated on 7 April 1449 and was created cardinal bishop of Santa Sabina and papal vicar and legate in Savoy. He died two years later.

The lasting significance of Basel is tied up with that of Constance. Together they represented the high point of conciliarism (q.v.). Both, moreover, were reform councils, and the failure of their reforms would in time open the way to the more radical reform propounded by the 16th century Protestants.

---

[1]J. Gill, *Constance et Bâle-Florence.* Histoire des conciles 9 (Paris: Ed. Orante, 1965); K.A. Fink, in Jedin-Dolan 4:473–479; D.J. Geanakoplos, "An Orthodox View of the Councils of Basel (1431–1449) and Florence (1438–1439) as Paradigm for the Study of Modern Ecumenical Councils," GrOrTR 30 (1985) 311–334 = TZBas 38 (1982) 330–359; J. Helmrath, *Das Basler Konzil 1431–1439. Forschungsstand und Probleme* (Cologne—Vienna: Böhlau, 1987); E. Meuthen, "Das Basler Konzil in römisch-katholischer Sicht," TZBas 38 (1982) 274–308; J. Wohlmuth in Alberigo, Concili 240–259, with bibliog. 277–281; idem, *Verständigung in der Kirche: Untersucht an der Sprache des Konzils von Basel* (Mainz: Matthias Grünewald, 1983); cf. A. Black, *Council and Commune: The Conciliar Movement and the Fifteenth-century Heritage* (London: Burns and Oates—Shepherdstown: Patmos, 1979). [2]L. Bilderback, "Eugene IV and the First Dissolution of the Council of Basel," ChH 36 (1967) 243–253; J.W. Steiber, *Pope Eugenius IV, the Council of Basel, and the Secular and Ecclesiastical Authorities in the Empire: The Conflict Over Supreme Authority and Power in the Church* (Leiden: Brill, 1978). [3]Tanner 1:455-456. [4]Sess. 12—Tanner 1:469-472. [5]Sess. 15—Tanner 1:473-476. [6]Sess 4 safe-conduct—Tanner 1:460-462; G. Christianson, "Wyclif's Ghost: The Politics of Reunion at the Council of Basel," AHC 17 (1985) 193–208. [7]Tanner 1:483-484. [8]Tanner 1:484-485. [9]Tanner 1:485-488. [10]Tanner 1:488-492. [11]Tanner 1:494-504. [12]Tanner 1:510-513. [13]Mansi 39:178-180. [14]Tanner 1:408-409. [15]Sess. 7—Tanner 1:529-534.

## BEA, Cardinal Augustine (1881–1968)

One of the most important figures at Vatican II, Augustine Bea tends to be remembered most for the last eight years of his life, after he was created Cardinal at the age of seventy-nine. Yet his earlier life was a preparation for his quite extraordinary service of the Church in his final years.[1]

He was born in South Baden (Germany) in 1881 of a very poor family. He was never to enjoy good health, beginning with childhood tuberculosis. He entered the Society of Jesus in 1902 and was ordained priest in 1912. A very wide range of studies and assignments followed until his appointment as provincial superior of the newly founded Jesuit province of Upper Germany (1921). Assigned to Rome in 1924, he lectured on Scripture at the Gregorian University and the Biblicum, becoming rector of the latter for nineteen years (1930–1949). He was editor for twenty years of its prestigious journal, *Biblica,* and wrote over 260 articles and eight books.[2] He was a key author of the encyclical on biblical studies, *Divino afflante Spiritu* (1943),[3] and for thirteen years personal confessor to Pius XII until the pope's death in 1958.

During the 1940s and 1950s Bea was a consulter of several Vatican congregations, and he became more and more involved in ecumenical matters. It was for some a surprise when in 1960, at the age of seventy-nine, he was appointed President of the Secretariat for Promoting Christian Unity,[4] even though he had indeed been well prepared for it. Almost immediately he began to emphasize the baptism common to all Christians, an insight later given prominence at the council.[5]

During Vatican II he played a vital role, the significance of which could hardly be exaggerated. He addressed the council nineteen times in his own right as a member, and presented four texts on behalf of the Secretariat for Promoting Christian Unity. Throughout the council he held a watching brief for ecumenism and was responsible for many insertions into, and amendments of, texts. This applied particularly to the documents on the Church, Revelation, Ecumenism, Religious Freedom and Non-Christian Religions (LG, DV, UR, NA, DH). After the council he worked tirelessly for ecumenism until his death in 1968.

His concerns reached beyond Christian ecumenism to relations with Jews, and indeed to wider issues affecting the whole of humanity. His passion for integrity led him to remark at the outset of the council when the Biblicum was being fiercely attacked by people on the right: "There are some who do not remember that the truth, the gospels and Christ cannot be defended by means condemned by the truth, the gospels and Christ."[6] He was to know plenty of opposition, but he was supported by a deep spirituality, which we can glimpse in his retreat notes.[7]

[1]S. Schmidt, *Agostino Bea, il cardinale dell'unità* (Rome: Città Nuova, 1987), on which see A. Rolla and G.M. Pizzuti, Asp 36 (1989) 80–87, and H. Fries, StimZ 208 (1990) 569–572; B. Leeming, *Augustine Cardinal Bea* (Notre Dame, 1964); AA.VV. *Augustin Kardinal Bea: Wegbereiter der Einheit* (Augsburg: Winfried-Werk, 1971); M. Gilbert, "Le cardinal Augustin Bea 1881–1968," NRT 105 (1983) 369–383; J. Grootaers, *I protagonisti del Vaticano II* (Milan: San Paolo, 1994) 67–81; R.A.F. MacKenzie, "Augustin Bea 1881–1968," Bib 49 (1968) 453–456; S.Schmidt, "Il cardinale Bea: sua preparazione alla missione ecumenica," ArHPont 16 (1978) 313–336. [2]Bibliography Bib 43 (1962) 265–276. [3]AAS 35 (1943) 297–326/Carlen 4:65-78. [4]AAS 52 (1960) 495. [5]E. Lanne, "La contribution du cardinal Bea à la question du baptême et l'Unité des chrétiens," Irén 55 (1982) 471–499. [6]In mimeographed text in various languages circulated to council members, 1962, *The Historicity of the Gospels.* [7]S. Schmidt, ed., *Augustin Cardinal Bea: Spiritual Profile. Notes from the Cardinal's Diary* (London—Dublin, Chapman, 1971).

## BEDE, St. (673–735)

Born near Sunderland in the North of England in 673, Bede led a singularly uneventful life, perhaps never traveling outside Northumbria where he was a monk. He was ordained priest about 703 and devoted his life to monastic observance. He died in 735. He was declared Doctor of the Church in 1899. The centenary of his birth gave rise to renewed interest in his life and works.[1]

An early medieval polymath, his works[2] range widely over the area of exegesis, science, education, chronology. His achievement in the field of history was especially significant with the *Ecclesiastical History of the People of England,* belonging to a new kind of religious history: it had a deep interest in miracles, which bridges the natural and supernatural, and points to divine providence at work in the world.[3]

His ecclesiology is marked by typology, foreshadowed in many OT realities and illustrated and made concrete in NT ones.[4] The view of the Church is one of universality, with the heavenly Church comprising all the elect, even before Christ: "a catholic multitude of all the elect through all places and all the times of this world."[5] In the patristic tradition he sees the Church as the New Eve born from the side of the Crucified, and thus his spouse;[6] But as Y. Congar notes, following the Augustinian line, he passes from spouse to body with the theme of one flesh *(una caro),* and from spouse to mother:[7] "the Church is spouse and wife which, remaining immaculate, continually gives birth to spiritual children for God."[8] A distinction which he popularized between the key of knowledge and the key of power *(clavis scientiae . . . potestatis),* would be taken up in early scholasticism.[9] He did not show much interest in questions of the papacy, though he had great respect for the see of Peter.[10] The works of Bede can still be read for a rich ecclesiology within the patristic tradition which draws its theology primarily from Scripture.

[1]G. Bonner, "Bede Studies in 1973," CleR 58 (1973) 689–696; cf. W.F. Bolton, "A Bede Bibliography 1935–1960," Trad 10 (1962) 436–445; T. Eckenrode, "The Venerable Bede: A Bibliographical Essay 1970–1981," AmBenR 36 (1985) 172–194; P.H. Blair, *The World of Bede* (London: Secker and Warburg, 1970) 310–317; B. Ward, *The Venerable Bede.* Outstanding Christian Thinkers (London: Chapman, 1990). [2]Texts: PL 90–95; CCL 118A, 135B, 175; English 12 vols. J.A. Giles, ed. (London, 1843–1844). [3]B. Colgrave and R.A.B. Mynors, *Bede's Ecclesiastical History of the English People.* Oxford Medieval Texts (Oxford: Clarendon, 1992); J.M. Wallace-Hadrill, *Bede's Ecclesiastical History of the English People: A Historical Commentary.* Oxford Medieval Texts (Oxford: Clarendon, 1988); L.W. Bernard, "Bede and Eusebius as Church Historians," in idem, ed., *Studies in Church History and Patristics* (Thessloniki: Patriarhikon Idruma Paterikon Meleton, 1978) 354–372. [4]Congar, Augustin 44–48; idem, *L'ecclésiologie du haut moyen-âge* (Paris: Cerf, 1968) 61–166 passim; J. Beumer, "Das Kirchenbild in den Schriftkommentaren Bedas des Ehrwürdigen," Schol 28 (1953) 40–56; E.P. Echlin, "Bede and the Church," IrTQ 40 (1973) 351–363. [5]*In Cant.* 5:6—PL 91:1182. [6]*Hexameron* 1—PL 91:52. [7]Ibid., Congar, Augustin 46. [8]*Expos. Apoc.* 3:21—PL 93:195. [9]Congar, Augustin 47 citing *In Matt. hom.* 16—PL 94:222. [10]Congar, Augustin 47–48; idem, Moyen-âge (n. 4) 152.

## BELLARMINE, St. Robert (1542–1621)

Robert Bellarmine was born in Tuscany in 1542.[1] He became a Jesuit in 1560 and was ordained a priest ten years later. For a time he taught at Louvain, lecturing on St. Thomas' *Summa theologiae,* and refuting the theories on grace of Baius. In 1576 he was appointed "Professor of Controversial Theology" at the Jesuit Roman College, where his lectures became the basis of his *Disputations on the Controversies of the Christian Faith* (3 vols. 1586–1593). His wide range of scholarship and busy life included work on the Vulgate, Hebrew grammar, a catechism that went into an astonishing 400 printings (v. CATECHETICS), preaching and pastoral care, especially of the poor. He became cardinal in 1598, archbishop of Capua in 1602, resigning in 1605 on his appointment as Prefect of the Vatican Library and member of various Roman congregations. He was not unsympathetic to Galileo (q.v.), though advising caution.[2] He died in 1621 after a very pious and austere life, producing fine devotional writings in his last years.[3] He was canonized in 1930, and declared a Doctor of the Church (q.v.) in 1931.[4]

The approach of his greatest work, *The Controversies,* stands out from that of many of his contemporaries: though it is polemical, it avoided abuse, seeking to convince by its arguments. Its three books consider: the sources of revelation and Scripture, the Church (I); the sacraments (II); grace and justification (III). In treating the Church he treats Christ as its head, the supreme pontiff, head of the Church militant; the Church united in councils and dispersed throughout the world; members of the Church militant—clergy, monks and laity.[5]

For him the burning question was where the true Church was to be found—an issue which arose in controversies with Wycliffe (q.v.), Hus (q.v.), and the Reformers. His narrow apologetic definition of the Church was to become classical: "the assembly of people *(coetus hominum)* bound by the same faith and communion of the same sacraments under the government of legitimate pastors and especially the Roman Pontiff."[6] Against views of the Reformers, especially Calvin, he stressed the visibility of the Church in another equally famous assertion: "The Church is as visible and palpable as the assembly of the Roman people, or the kingdom of France, or the republic of Venice."[7] But his view of the Church was more universal than these quotations suggest. At the beginning of *The Controversies* he outlines his plan: "I will discuss the universal Church, which is on earth, in purgatory, and in heaven; I will begin with Christ the supreme head and principle of the Church." On the papacy he held that the pope had only indirect power in temporal matters,[8] a view that probably delayed his canonization.

Bellarmine's ecclesiology is much richer than selective quotations often suggest.[9] He developed the theology of the Body of Christ (q.v.), and of the papacy. He was sensitive to several pneumatological aspects of the Church. He further popularized the list of ecumenical councils (q.v.) which has become accepted in the Catholic Church, without however any formal statement of the magisterium on the matter.[10]

[1]OxDSaints 38; J. Broderick, *Robert Bellarmine: Saint and Scholar* (London, 1961); G. Galeota, ed., *Roberto Bellarmino arcivescovo di Capua, teologo e pastore della riforma cattolica.* 2 vols. (Capua: Istit. Superiore di Scienze Religiose, 1990); P. Giustiniani, "Roberto Bellarmino teologo e pastore della riforma cattolica," Asp 36 (1989) 88–92. [2]Cf. R.J. Blackwell, *Galileo, Bellarmine and the Bible* (Notre Dame—London: Notre Dame UP, 1991). [3]*St. Robert Bellarmine: Spiritual Writings.* Ed. and trans. J.P. Donnelly. Classics of Western Spirituality (New York—Mahwah: Paulist, 1989). [4]Works: *Opera omnia* 7 vols. (Naples, 1851–1861), 12 vols. (Paris: Vivès, 1870–1874); *Opera oratoria posthuma.* 11 vols. (Rome: 1942–1950). [5]Antón 1:879-893; J. Beumer, "Die kirchliche Gliedschaftin der Lehre des hl. Robert Bellarmine," TGl 38 (1948) 243–257; J.M. Boves, "Las notas de la Iglesia según el B. Belarmino," EstE 2 (1923) 225–235; Congar, Augustin 371–375; J. Corboy, *The Doctrine of the Infallibility of the Pope in Bellarmine and His Influence on the Definition of the Vatican.* Diss. (Rome: Gregorian, 1961); G.A. Harden, "Robert Bellarmine's Concept of the Church," in J.E. Sommerfeldt, ed., *Studies in Medieval Culture.* 2 vols. (Michigan: West Michigan UP, 1966) 2:120-127; H. Jedin, in Jedin-Dolan 5:540-541, 724; M. Navascués, "La eclesiología de S. Roberto Belarmino," EcclJav 8–9 (1958–1959) 1–85. [6]*De controversiis. De conciliis et ecclesia* 3:2. [7]Ibid. See Congar, Augustin 372–373. [8]*De romano pontifice* Bk. 5; J. Courtney Murray, "St. Robert Bellarmine on the Indirect Power," TS 9 (1948) 491–535. [9]Antón (n. 5); S. Tromp, "De biformi conceptu cum 'Christi mystici' tum 'Corporis Christi mystici,' in Controversiis S.R. Bellarmini," Greg 23 (1942) 279–290. [10]*De conciliis et ecclesia militante* (1586).

## BERNARD, St. (ca. 1090–1153)

St. Bernard was born near Dijon about 1090. At the age of twenty-two he went with 31 companions to the languishing reformed monastery of Cîteaux. After a few years he was made abbot of a new foundation, Clairvaux. From it before his death Bernard had made 66 more foundations throughout Europe, while there were 700 monks in the motherhouse alone. Although his was a monastic soul, he became deeply involved in all the Church affairs of the day, being especially concerned with Church reform. He was a close confidant of popes, especially one of his pupils and former Cistercian, Eugenius III (1145–1153), to whom he sent a book of good advice, *On Consideration.* He was an eloquent preacher of the disastrous 2nd Crusade (q.v.). His influence on monasticism was profound and lasting, especially his encouragement of mysticism, which would have its seedbed in the ordinary framework of monastic observance. He was canonized in 1174 and proclaimed a Doctor of the Church (q.v.) in 1830.[1]

The bibliography on his life and works is enormous,[2] and includes some important studies of his ecclesiology.[3] His main contribution to ecclesiology can be summarized under three headings. First, he takes up the idea of spouse (q.v.) in his sermons on the Song of Songs. Following in the patristic tradition that goes back to Origen (q.v.), the spouse is sometimes the human soul, sometimes the Church.[4] The center of his ecclesiology is "The Church or the soul loving God" *(Ecclesia seu anima diligens Deum).*[5] There is, however, only one spouse who is the Church; others share in the blessings of being spouse through association with the Church—indeed every member of the Church shares in the blessings to some degree.[6] One may note in passing that Bernard, the "Marian Doctor" par excellence never uses bridal images about Mary, whom in some sense he places above the Church.[7] Coming from a monastic culture in which each one is vowed in the service of God and should be reaching towards holiness of life, Bernard's primary idea of the Church is that of holy people in spiritual combat. The heart of the Church is charity. But sinners belong to the Church.[8]

Second, Bernard is a keen reformer of the Church, with particular attention to the abuses arising from exemption (q.v.) and with special regard for the papacy. He writes to Eugenius III: "In this finery you are the successor not of Peter but of Constantine. I suggest that these things must be allowed for the time being, but are not to be assumed as a right."[9] He sees the Roman Church transformed into a Curia (v. VATICAN): "Every day laws resound the palace, but these are the laws of Justinian, not of the Lord."[10] But if he recognizes that these externals are unavoidable, he wishes Pope Eugenius to keep his high spiritual ideals in the midst of corrupting forces: "Before all else you should consider that the Holy Roman Church, over which God has established you as head, is the mother of Churches, not the mistress; furthermore you are not lord of bishops but one of them."[11] He takes up the notion of fullness of power *(plenitudo potestatis)* already found in Leo the Great (q.v.). But in decrying the abuse of excessive exemptions he comments: "In doing this you demonstrate that you have the fullness of power, but perhaps not of justice. You do this because you have the power; but the question is whether you ought to do it."[12] He recognizes the fullness of power, but he does not consider the theoretical applications of the notion.

Third, Bernard held a theory of the two swords, but, as a reading of his texts shows, it is not in the hierocratic manner frequently attributed to him. Thus: "Both swords, that is, the spiritual and the material belong to the Church; however, the latter is to be drawn for the Church, the former by the Church. The spiritual sword should be drawn by the hand of the priest; the material sword by the hand of the knight, but at the bidding of the priest *(ad nutum sacerdotis)* and at the command of the emperor."[13] Other references to the two swords are also passing ones, but they do acknowledge that a sword may be used for the defense of the religion.[14] It is clear that Bernard is not evolving a socio-political theory, but stating in practice that the Church has the power to excommunicate (spiritual sword) and the right to indicate to the emperor that coercion is needed in a particular case for the defense of the Church.[15]

Sometimes called "the Last of the Fathers (q.v.)," St. Bernard stands at the dawn of the scholastic period, but the sapiential character of his theological reflection shows him to lie in the great patristic tradition rooted in the monasteries rather than in the newer style of theologizing that would soon emerge in the universities.

[1]OxDSaints 44–45; H. Daniel-Rops, *Bernard of Clairvaux* (New York, 1964); G.L.C. Frank, "St. Bernard of Clairvaux and the Eastern Tradition," SVlad 36 (1992) 315–318; B.S. James, *St. Bernard of Clairvaux: An Essay in Biography* (London, 1957); D. Knowles, "Saint Bernard of Clairvaux, 1090–1153," DublinR 227 (1953) 104–121; J. Leclercq, *Recueil d'études sur saint Bernard.* 3 vols. (Rome: Ed. Storia e letteratura, 1962–1969); J. Regnard, "La voie théologale de saint Bernard," VieSp 145 (1991) 43–57. [2]Works: PL 182–183; J. Leclercq et al., *Sancti Bernardini Opera* (Rome: Ed. Cistercienses, 1957–); Eng. trans. Cistercian Fathers Series (CF); cf. L. Janauschek, *Bibliographia Bernardina* (Vienna, 1891, rpt. Hildesheim: Olms, n.d.); J. Bouton, *Bibliographie Bernardine 1891–1957* (Paris: Lethielleux, 1958); E. Manning, "Bibliographie Bernardine (1957–1970)," *Documentation Cistercienne* 6 (1972); H. Wolter in Jedin-Dolan 18–22 with bibliog. 639–641. [3]Y. Congar, "L'ecclésiologie de S. Bernard," Anal. sac. ord., Cisterciensis 9 (1953) 136–190; Congar, Augustin 125–129; M. Casey, "Bernard of Clairvaux: The Man Behind the Mask," Pacifica 3 (1990) 269–287; E. Kennan, "The *De consideratione* of St. Bernard of Clairvaux and the Papacy in the Mid-Twelfth Century: A Review of Scholarship," Trad 23 (1967) 73–115; K. Kilga, "Der Kirchenbegriff des hl. Bernard von Clairvaux," Cistercienser-Chronik 54 (1947) 46–64, 149–179, 253–271; 55 (1948) 39–55, 88–114; 156–187. [4]Congar, "L'ecclésiologie . . ." (n. 3) 138; C. Dumont, "La spiritualité de saint Bernard," NRT 112 (1990) 502–515. [5]*Cant* 29:7—PL 183:932/CF 7:108. [6]*Cant* 68:4—PL 183:1110/CF 40:20. [7]Congar, "L'ecclésiologie . . ." (n. 3) 138–139, 152–154. [8]*Cant* 25:2—PL 183:899/CF 7:51. [9]*Consideration* 4:3, 6—PL 182:776/CF 13:117. [10]Ibid., 1:4, 5—PL 182:732/CF 13:32. [11]Ibid., 4:7, 23—PL 182:788/CF 13:137. [12]Ibid., 3:4, 14—PL 182:766-767/CF 13:97-98. [13]Ibid., 4:3, 7—PL 182:7764/CF 37:118; cf. *Epist.* 256:1—PL 182:463-464. [14]*Ad milites Templi* 3:5—PL 182:924-925/CF 19:135. [15]Congar, Augustin 142–145; B. Jacqueline, "Le pouvoir pontifical selon saint Bernard: L'argument des deux glaives," AnnéeCan 2 (1953) 197–201.

## BISHOPS

There are three Greek words in the NT that lie behind the evolution of the notion of bishop: *episkopein*—to supervise, oversee, care for (1 Pet 5:2); *episkopê*—position or function of supervision (Acts 1:20; 1 Tim 3:1); *episkopos*—supervisor, overseer, "bishop" (Acts 20:28; Phil 1:1; 1 Tim 3:2; Titus 1:7; 1 Pet 2:25). This last was in NT times interchangeable with *presbuteros* (elder—Titus 1:5-7; 1 Tim 3:1; 5:17; Acts 20:17, 28), whence we eventually get presbyter/priest (q.v.).[1] Though many authors hold that *presbuteros* came from the Jewish tradition, while *episkopos* came from a gentile environment, it is arguable that both are from Jewish sources.[2]

In the NT we find the plural *episkopoi* along with *diakonoi* (Phil 1:1). The picture given in the Pastoral Epistles is of Timothy and Titus setting up authority structures to deal with the vacuum left by the death of the apostles. This would suggest that Luke in Acts 14:23 is anachronistic.[3] Neither *episkopos* nor *presbuteros* appear in any of the lists of charisms (q.v.) in the NT; administrators (*kubernêseis*—1 Cor 12:28) come late in the list of charisms/officials. The qualifications for an *episkopos* are listed in Titus 1:7-11; 1 Tim 3:1-7. We are not clear about the exact functions of the presbyter-bishops: they teach (1 Tim 5:17); they are to refute false doctrine (Titus 1:9); the qualification of managing their own homes well can suggest that they are administrators of the community's goods (1 Tim 3:3-5; cf. 1 Pet 5:2). Elsewhere we have the image of shepherd (Acts 20:28; 1 Pet 5:2). We find accord between the Pauline view of the presbyter-bishop and the Petrine one in 1 Peter. No cultic role, no function with regard to the Eucharist, is ascribed to them. The nearest we can find is Jas 5:14-15, where the presbyters are to be called to pray and anoint the sick.

In the letters of Ignatius (q.v.) the bishop has unique authority with regard to both baptism and the Eucharist. In the NT, apart from the dominical command to the

Eleven (Matt 28:19; cf. Mark 16:16), we have baptizing ascribed to various people (Acts 2:41; 8:38; 9:18; 10:48; 1 Cor 1:14-17). In Acts 13:2 we find the prophets and teachers apparently worshiping *(leitourgountôn),* which may be the same as the action of the prophets in the *Didachê* (q.v.): "Let the prophets give thanks *(eucharistein)* as they will." But this community is also to appoint *episkopoi* and *diakonoi*.[4]

The structure of the Churches in the letters of Ignatius is that of one bishop, several presbyters *(presbuteroi),* and several deacons *(diakonoi).* It has been customary to refer to its head as a "monarchical bishop," but the term is not quite accurate as the bishop does not act alone, but always with his presbyters and deacons. Furthermore, we have evidence in Ignatius of a function of the bishop as being the center of unity, a unity which is primarily found and fostered through the Eucharist.[5]

The *Apostolic Tradition* (q.v.) is a most important witness of early 3rd century practice and theology. There are interpretations which are in more Catholic[6] or more Protestant[7] vein. But the text must be said to be in harmony with the other early evidence about the development of the episcopate. Bishops are to be chosen by the people and there is some unspecified ratification (2/2:2).[8] The people request bishops to lay hands on the one chosen, while all the rest pray silently that the Spirit come upon him (2/2:4). The prayer of consecration is addressed to the Father, who does not leave the sanctuary without ministers and "who knows hearts" and who has chosen his servant for the episcopacy, that he might pour out the power that is from him, the princely Spirit *(dunamin tou hêgemonikou pneumatos*—Spirit of leadership,[9] 3/3:4). The prayer asks that the candidate feed the holy flock, serve as high priest, minister blamelessly day and night, propitiate God's countenance, and offer the gifts of the holy Church.[10] By the high priestly Spirit *(tô pneumati tô archieratikô)* he is to have the power to forgive sins, to administer *(didonai klêrous),* to loose every bond by the power given to the apostles, to offer a pleasing perfume (3/3:5). In the ordination of priests (q.v.) the bishop prays for the "Spirit of grace and counsel" and for deacons (q.v.) the "Spirit of grace and diligence" (7/8:2 and 8/9:11). It is clear then that the episcopal ministry has its origin in God who chooses and empowers, and its power, one different from that of priests and deacons, is from the Holy Spirit. The two titles given to the bishops are "high priest" *(archiereus)* and "leader" *(proistamenos),* and the verb "feed/tend" *(poimainein)* is used as a general description of his ministry (3/3:4). The dignity of the episcopate is implied in the kiss of peace he receives, "for he has been made worthy of this" (4/4:1). Again, in the *Apostolic Tradition* (q.v.

for texts) all other ministers and offices are constituted by the bishop; the priest is his fellow-councillor (8/9:2), but the deacon and subdeacon are appointed for his service (8/9:2,4; 34/30). Apart from the offices or ministries in the prayer of consecration, there are several others: the bishop seems to be the normal celebrant of the Eucharist (4,21, 22/4, 23,2 4); he presides and teaches at the Agapê (q.v.), and at baptism (21/21–23); he is the chief exorcist (v. EXORCISM) at baptism (20/20:3), and the phrase above "to loose every bond," apparently citing Matt 18:18, may also refer to exorcism (3/3:5); as head he is to maintain pure doctrine (1/1:5; 43/38:3), and he gives explanations at baptism (21/23:4, 14); he receives and blesses the offerings of the people (5–6/5–6; 31–32/38:1-6). Although the bishop is said to receive the same Spirit as the apostles, and although episcopal ordination by other bishops is clearly through the divine will to act in the authority given to the apostles (3/3), there is no emphasis on an unbroken chain of valid episcopal ordinations.[11] It is clearly right to see with F.A. Sullivan ecclesiological, Christological, and pneumatological factors in the apostolicity of faith and ministry found in the *Apostolic Tradition.*[12]

By the time of Cyprian (d. 258—q.v.) a decisive change occurred in the role of the bishop, one which was beginning to emerge in the *Apostolic Constitutions* (q.v.). Whereas in Ignatius the sole minister of the Eucharist was the bishop, now with quasi-parishes being established in rural areas, priests become ministers of the Eucharist and the bishop becomes more and more an administrator, but with special concern for doctrine.[13] In some places, however, the care, and above all the Eucharistic celebrations, of the new administrative units still remained with a bishop called *chôrepiskopos* (rural bishop in dependence on the bishop of the diocese), a practice which still obtains in the Orthodox Church. From the beginning the bishop attended councils representing the faith of his Church and linking in to the catholicity of the whole Church.

The late 4th century *Apostolic Constitutions* retain much of the norms of earlier legal texts, but it is more specific in some matters: apparently following the norm of Nicaea (q.v.),[14] all or at least three bishops ordain, and the metropolitan must give his consent.[15] Three cases are "invalid," though we must beware of using technical language of a more developed theology:[16] ordinations conferred by heretics, the orders of those who pass into heresy or schism, or an ordination arranged by nepotism.[17] In the *Didascalia apostolorum* found in the *Apostolic Constitutions* bishops hold a central place, the whole of book two being devoted mainly to them. There is a variety of titles given: father, lords, masters, teachers, presidents, prophets, doctors, etc.[18] Following the *Didascalia,* itself depending on the Pastoral Epistles, the *Constitutions* lay down carefully the qualities required in a bishop and in his behavior.[19] Great emphasis is placed on study of the Scriptures, compassion for the poor,[20] and for repentant sinners.[21] He is to be impartial, neither unduly flattering the rich nor despising or oppressing the poor:[22] "He is to be prudent, humble, knowing how to admonish with the Lord's teaching, mature in elevated concerns, one who has renounced the base things of this world and all pagan desires. He is to be capable in ruling, sharp in recognizing the wicked and being on his guard with them, but yet a friend to all, just and discerning; whatever are fine human qualities, the bishop should have them."[23] Since the Church is menaced by heresies, the bishop's teaching role is stressed: "He is to be indulgent, patient in his admonitions, well capable of instruction, diligent in meditating the Lord's books, reading frequently the better to interpret the scriptures, expounding the prophets in accordance with the gospel."[24] His care extends to all, especially the widows (q.v.); he is to be diligent in the liturgy.[25] Such is his authority that the clerics and laity owe him respect.[26]

The views of Jerome (q.v.) are important because often misunderstood. Jerome was objecting to the pretensions of some deacons who placed themselves above priests. Jerome asserts that they cannot consecrate the Eucharist, unlike bishops and priests, both of whom are equal *in this respect*.[27]

From the 4th century we find an increasing number of bishops chosen from among the ranks of monks. But in the late patristic period and early Middle Ages we find an assimilation between the life and function of the nobility and that of the bishop,[28] a development which in time would lead to the investiture controversy (q.v.).

In the scholastic period major authors both asserted and denied the sacramentality of the episcopate.[29] Trent distinguished three hierarchical orders, stated the superiority of the episcopate,[30] and initiated reforms especially on preaching and on the residence of bishops.[31] The reforms were rather fragmentary and did not emanate from a completely unified vision of the episcopate, but rather from a conviction that non-residence and over-commitment to secular affairs by bishops was utterly detrimental to the Church and therefore needed to be at the center of a reform program.[32] The Tridentine renewal of the episcopate finds an outstanding model in St. Charles Borromeo of Milan (1538–1584).[33] After Trent the sacramentality of episcopal orders was generally accepted, except for some Thomists who held the views of the early St. Thomas, who had not, however, treated the episcopate in his unfinished *Summa theologiae*.[34]

Vatican I had time only to make definitions about the papacy (q.v.). Bismarck later tried to cause dissension by asserting that the bishops had been radically demeaned by the teaching of this council on the primacy of the pope. The German bishops denied this claim and stated that episcopal power remained intact after Vatican I. Their position won the wholehearted praise of Pius IX.[35]

Vatican II devoted most of the third chapter of the Constitution on the Church to the episcopate: the bishops are successors of the apostles (LG 18, 20), of the college of the apostles (LG 22); bishops receive the fullness of the sacrament of orders and taking on the functions of Christ, the teacher, shepherd and pontiff, they act in his person (LG 21); along with the pope, and never apart from him, the bishops constitute a college (LG 22; v. BISHOPS, COLLEGIALITY); each bishop has the task of pastoral government of his own diocese, but as a member of the college he also has care for the universal Church (LG 23; CD 6); each bishop has a teaching mission (LG 25), a sanctifying mission (LG 26), and authority to govern in the name of Christ (LG 27); a principal manifestation of the Church is the liturgy presided over by the bishop surrounded by his presbyterate and ministers (SC 41). The Decree on the Pastoral Office of Bishops in the Church developed the pastoral and practical implications of the *Lumen gentium* text: teaching office (CD 12–14); sanctifying office (CD 15), pastoral office (CD 16–21; diocesan boundaries (CD 22–24); coadjutor and auxiliary bishops (CD 25–26); intra-diocesan matters (CD 27–32) and religious (CD 33); inter-diocesan matters and notably Bishops' Conferences (q.v.—36–43). Vatican II called for a Synod of Bishops (q.v.—CD 5). An important role of the bishop is teaching, which is authoritative in his own diocese (v. MAGISTERIUM).[36] Such teaching is not infallible. The bishops are, however, infallible as a college in the cases specified in LG 25 (v. INFALLIBILITY).

The task of the bishop is primarily to ensure the unity, holiness, and witness of the local Church both within and towards the world (see LG 26).[37] But the fullness of the priesthood enjoyed by the bishop does not demand that we see all ministry and gifts as deriving from him; rather he is their center of unity and inspiration.[38]

Vatican II took further steps in the prickly question of the appointment of bishops. In the early Middle Ages bishops were often appointed by secular princes. In 1215 the 4th Lateran Council (q.v.) formally prohibited the participation of secular authorities in episcopal elections.[39] Up to the 13th century bishops were elected, usually by the cathedral chapter. From then on we find Rome strengthening its position: from confirming elections, it began to nominate or appoint bishops in various places in the Latin Rite. When agreements or concordats were being signed between the Church and secular authorities, it was quite common from the 15th to late 19th centuries to give the secular power the rite to nominate or appoint bishops: in canonical language the head of state conferred the *ius ad rem,* while the pope gave the *ius in re.*[40] With one exception, the last such concession was to Monaco in 1887. The 1917 *Code* affirmed the principle that appointment of bishops belonged to the pope (can. 329). After that time, even where there was the approved custom of election, it was usual for the canons to be allowed to elect the bishop from a list of three candidates supplied by Rome. In the interim before Vatican II the Holy See obtained some voluntary renunciation of the right of appointment—mostly in Latin America. In the name of religious liberty (v. FREEDOM, RELIGIOUS), the council wanted the pope to have the right and liberty of appointment, and expressed the wish that states would voluntarily give up their rights after negotiation (CD 20). This right of the Church was reaffirmed by the 1983 *Code* (c. 377).[41] The various heads of state have all renounced their rights, except for the case of two dioceses in France, Strasbourg and Metz. In current Church law it is the apostolic legate who sends a list of three names to the Holy See with his own recommendation (CIC 364 § 4) after widespread consultation among the hierarchy, the cathedral chapter in the diocese in which there is a vacancy, and possibly also other clergy and laity (CIC 377). The pope then makes an appointment, on hearing the advice of the Congregation for Bishops (v. VATICAN).[42] In the Catholic Churches of the East it is the patriarchs and their synods that appoint bishops, subject to the right of Rome to intervene in a particular case (OE 9).[43] It could be argued that the appointment of bishops in the Western Church/Latin Rite is an activity of the bishop of Rome as patriarch (q.v.) rather than as pope or supreme pontiff.

The new *Code* of canon law deals with the bishop in an extended series of canons which are found in the section of the book on the People of God dealing with The Local Church (can. 368–502). The *Code* takes up matters from the 1973 Directory on the Pastoral Office of Bishop.[44] Though many themes and principles from Vatican II are very marked,[45] it would have to be said that a tension observable between two ecclesiologies in the Council, viz. juridical and communion, are carried over into the *Code.*[46]

There are possibilities both in Vatican II and in the *Code* for synodal functioning in the local Church (q.v.) which have not yet found widespread or effective expression, viz. diocesan synod, pastoral council, presbyteral/priests' council, college of consulters, chapter of canons (v. SYNODS AND COUNCILS, LOCAL). It would seem clear that there is obvious and widespread reluctance on the part of bishops of the Latin Rite to take up with any enthusiasm all the possibilities of synodal government open to them by Vatican II and current law. There has plainly been a lack of reception (q.v.). A further major synodal body is the bishops' conference (q.v.), which may be based on national boundaries or be transnational; this one has been generally more effective.

The meaning of the episcopate[47] can be deduced from the Rite of Ordination, especially the prayer of consecration or *epiclêsis* (q.v.). The consecrating prelate recalls the OT priesthood, and the three bishops pray: "So now pour out upon this chosen one the power that is from you, the governing Spirit whom you gave to your beloved Son, Jesus Christ, the Spirit given by him to the holy apostles who founded the Church in every place to be your temple for the unceasing glory and praise of your name." This sentence is the heart of the ordination. The main celebrant goes on to ask for the gifts that the newly consecrated bishop will need and to recall the service he is to give in the Church: a shepherd, a high priest and blameless, one with the power to loose sins and other bonds, and one who is to be pleasing to God "by his gentleness and purity of heart," thus "presenting a fragrant offering."

The significance of the visit *ad limina apostolorum*[48] is seen from its complex history. Historically it refers to pilgrimages, from the time of the Middle Ages "to the threshold of the apostles," viz. to the tombs of Peter and Paul. The canonical meaning originated in the 8th century, when all bishops consecrated at Rome had to visit its bishop. Later Gregory VII (q.v.) extended it to all metropolitans, and Sixtus V required it from all bishops in 1584; it was to be every three to ten years. In the current *Code* it is enjoined on all bishops every five years (CIC 400).[49] It is an exercise in communion (q.v.),[50] a bond of union between the bishop of Rome and all the bishops. It allows the bishop to report on his diocese; it promotes good relations with the Vatican offices, and alerts the pope to the situation of the Church worldwide.

The main symbols of the episcopal office in the West are the crosier and miter. The former, a crook-shaped staff, used by bishops (also by many abbots and abbesses), may have its origins as a walking-stick. It became a liturgical symbol from the 7th century on, and later obtained the symbolism of a shepherd's staff as a sign of the pastoral office. The miter (Greek *mitra,* turban), worn on the head, is crown-shaped in the East, but shield-shaped in the West. It became part of the papal insignia by the 11th century, and quickly spread to bishops (and abbots). It is a symbol of honor, a visual enrichment in liturgical celebrations. Bishops can use the miter and crosier in their own diocese, but not in another diocese without at least the presumed consent of the local bishops (CIC 390). A series of decrees in the 1960s simplified pontifical vestments and insignia.[51]

The conferral of the pallium is another symbol pertaining to episcopacy, in this case the metropolitan or bishop of the chief diocese in an area.[52] It is a liturgical garment, not unlike a stole, worn by metropolitans at liturgical functions within their area. It originated in the East where bishops still wear it *(omophorion)*. In the West it was a papal vestment, of uncertain origin, but before the 9th century. By then it had become mandatory for metropolitans to seek it from the pope. In the Middle Ages it was considered a sign that the metropolitan power was from the pope; nowadays it signifies that the metropolitan exercises his power in communion with the pope.[53] In this sense it can be seen as a symbol of collegiality (v. BISHOPS, COLLEGIALITY).

The theology of the episcopate in the Orthodox Churches relies heavily on the ancient tradition found in Ignatius of Antioch and in the *Apostolic Tradition* of Ps-Hippolytus.[54] The bishop is another Christ *(alter Christus)*, thus ensuring the unity of the Church in the Eucharist. He is also another apostle *(alter apostolus)*, thus ensuring the continuity of the Church in history. Even when the priest celebrates the Eucharist, he must do so on the Antimension, a cloth containing relics and having representations of Christ but carrying the bishop's signature. This is parallel to the Western custom from the 5th to the 8th centuries of the Fermentum, viz., particles of the consecrated bread from the papal Mass were sent to neighboring parishes. Both emphasize the unity of the Eucharist and consequently of the Church.

In the ecumenical movement there is some special difficulty in relating churches which have bishops with those who have none. But even non-episcopal Churches have a sense of *episkopê* and on this basis dialogue continues.[55]

---

[1]R.E. Brown, *"Episkopê* and *Episkopos* in the New Testament,"* TS 41 (1980) 322–338 at 333–334; B. Cooke, *Ministry to Word and Sacrament* (Philadelphia: Fortress, 1976); J. Delorme, ed., *Le ministère et les ministères selon le Nouveau Testament* (Paris: Seuil, 1974); J.H. Elliott, "Ministry and Church Order in the New Testament: A Traditio-historical Analysis (1 Pet 5:1-5 and parallels)," CBQ 32 (1970) 367–391; A. Fernández, "Obispos y presbíteros: Historia y doctrina acera de la diferenciación del ministerio eclesiástico," Burgense 18 (1977) 357–418; A. Lemaire, *Les ministères aux origines de l'Église.* Lectio divina 68 (Paris: Cerf, 1971). [2]Brown, op. cit. (n. 1) 333–334. [3]Ibid., 331. [4]*Didachê* 10:7 and 15:1-2; cf. Brown 336. [5]J. Zizioulas, "Épiskopè et Épiskopos dans l'Église primitive: Bref inventaire de la documentation," Irén 56 (1983) 484–502, found also in *Episkopé and Episcopate in Ecumenical Perspective.* Faith and Order Paper 102 (Geneva: WCC, 1980); A. Brent, "History and Eschatological Mysticism in Ignatius of Antioch," ETL 65 (1989) 309–329; A. Cunningham, *The Bishop in the Church: Patristic Texts on the Role of the Episkopos.* Theology and Life 13 (Delaware: Glazier, 1985). [6]E.g., J. Lécuyer, "Épiscopat et presbytérat dans les écrits d'Hippolyte de Rome," RechSR

41 (1953) 30–50. [7]E.g., J.E. Stam, *Episcopacy in the Apostolic Tradition of Hippolytus.* Bd 111 der theologischen Dissertationen (Basel, 1969). [8]Cf. R. Gryson, "Les élections épiscopales en Occident au IVe siècle," RHE 75 (1980) 257–283; P. Stockmeier, "The Election of Bishops by Clergy and People in the Early Church," Conc 123 (1980) 3–9. [9]F.A. Sullivan, *The Church We Believe In: One, Holy, Catholic and Apostolic* (Dublin: Gill & Macmillan—Mahwah: Paulist, 1988) 177. [10]Stam (n. 7) 30–39. [11]Ibid., 101–104. [12]Sullivan (n. 9) 177–180. [13]Zizioulas (n. 5) 495–499; J.E. Lynch, "The Changing Role of the Bishop: An Historical Survey," Jurist 39 (1979) 289–312 at 292–294. [14]Nicaea (325) canon 4—Tanner 7. [15]8:27; 8:4, 6; 8:47, 34—SC 336: 228; 142; 284; cf. R. Gryson, "Les élections épiscopales en Orient au IVe siècle," RHE 74 (1978) 301–345. [16]C. Vogel, "Chirotonie et chirothésie," Irén 45 (1972) 207f. [17]VI:15, 3—SC 329:342; VIII, 47, 68—SC 336:300; VIII:2, 4 and 6—SC 336:136; VIII: 47, 76—SC 336:302-304. [18]M. Metzger, SC 329:45; cf. 2:20, 1-2—SC 320:196-198; 2:25, 7—SC 320:230-232; 2:26:3-4—SC 320:236-238, etc. [19]2:2—SC 320:146-148. [20]2:4, 2—SC 320:150. [21]2:15, 3-4; 2:18; 2:20, 6; 2:24; 2:41, 5—SC 320:182-184; 190-196; 200; 222-226; 272-274. [22]2:5, 1—SC 320:150. [23]2:5, 3—SC 320:154. Cf. 2:21, 1; 2:24, 7—SC 320: 204; 320:226. [24]2:54—SC 320:152; cf. 2:44, 1-2—SC 320:282. [25]2:57, 2—SC 320:310-312. [26]2:28, 9—SC 320:248. [27]*Epist. ad Evangelum* 146—PL 22:1193-1194; cf. O. Rousseau, "La doctrine du ministère épiscopal de ses vicissitudes dans l'Église d'Occident," in Y. Congar and B.-D. Dupuy, *L'Épiscopat et l'Église universelle.* US 39 (Paris, 1962) 279–308 at 280–282; Y. Bodin, *Saint Jérôme et l'Église.* Théologie historique 6 (Paris, 1966) 174–204; L. Lécuyer, "Aux origines de la théologie de l'épiscopat," Greg 35 (1955) 56–89 at 57–58. [28]J.A. Estrada, "El episcopado en el alto medievo (siglos VI–X), Anotaciones históricas," EstE 62 (1987) 27–47. [29]Rousseau (n. 27) 282–283. [30]DS 1776–1777/ND 1719–1720/Tanner 2:744; G. Alberigo, "Le potestà episcopali nei dibattiti tridentini," in AA.VV. *Il Concilio di Trento e la riforma tridentina.* Atti del convegno storico internazionale, Trento 2–6 sett. 1963 (Rome—Freiburg: Herder, 1965) 2:471-523; G. Fahrnberger, "Episkopat und Presbyterat in den Discussionen des Konzils von Trent," Catholica 30 (1976) 119–152. [31]Sess. 5 on Reform n. 9—Tanner 2:669; Sess VI on Reform 1—Tanner 2:681-682; Sess. 23 on Reform—Tanner 2:744-753; Sess. 25 on General Reform—Tanner 784-796. [32]32. G. Alberigo, "L'episcopato nel cattolicesimo post-tridentino," CrNSt 6 (1985) 71–91 at 76–77. [33]Ibid., 82–87. [34]Lécuyer, art. cit. (n. 27); idem, "Les étapes de l'enseignement thomiste sur l'épiscopat," RThom 57 (1957) 29–52; S. Wood, "The Sacramentality of Episcopal Consecration," TS 51 (1990) 479–496. [35]DS 3112–3117/ND 841; O. Rousseau, "La vraie valeur de l'épiscopat dans l'Église d'après d'importants documents de 1875" in Congar-Dupuy (n. 27) 709–736. [36]R.J. Barrett, "The Bishop as Ordinary Teacher of the Faith," MonEccl 117 (1992) 231–281; F.G. Thomas, "The Bishop in his Teaching Office and Those who Assist Him," StCan 21 (1987) 229–238. [37]J.M.R. Tillard, "L'évêque, le diocèse et l'unité de l'Église," Kan 7 (1985) 242–254; A. Jones, "New Vision for the Episcopate?," Theology 81 (1978) 281–287. [38]J.M.R. Tillard, "The Bishop and Other Ministers," OneChr 14 (1978) 50–54; cf. B. Cooke, "'Fullness of Orders': Theological Reflections," Jurist 41 (1981) 405–421. [39]Can. 25—Tanner 1:247. [40]R. Metz, "L'indépendance de l'Église dans la choix des évêques à Vatican II et dans le Code de 1983, aboutissement d'un demi siècle d'effort diplomatique," RDroitC 37 (1987) 143–170 at 145; idem, "Innovation et anachronismes au sujet de la nomination des évêques dans de récentes conventions passées entre le Saint-Siège et divers États (1973–1984)," StCan 20 (1986) 197–219. [41]Metz, "L'indépendance" (n. 40) 162–166 for interpretation, and T.J. Green in Coriden CIC 320–323. [42]J.T. Ellis, "The Selection of Bishops," AmBenR 35 (1984) 111–127; F. Sarrazin, "La nomination des évêques dans l'Église latine," StCan 21 (1987)

367–407; Conc 137 (1980).   ⁴³CCEO 180–189; cf. J. Khoury, "The Election of Bishops in the Eastern Churches," Conc 147 (1981) 20–27; "La scelta dei vescovi nel Codice dei Canoni delle Chiese Orientali," Apoll 65 (1992) 77–91.   ⁴⁴Sacra Congregatio de Episcopis, *Directorium de pastorali ministerio episcoporum* (Vatican, 1973).   ⁴⁵T.J. Green, "The Diocesan Bishop in the Revised Code: Some Introductory Reflections," Jurist 42 (1982) 320–347; J. Herranz Casado, "The Personal Power of Governance of the Diocesan Bishop," Communicationes 20 (1988) 288–310.   ⁴⁶J.M.R. Tillard, art. cit. (n. 38) 243, n. 3; cf. A. Acerbi, *Due ecclesiologie: ecclesiologia juridica ed ecclesiologia di comunione nella Lumen gentium* (Bologna: Ed. Dehoniane, 1975); cf. T.J. Green, "The Church's Sanctifying Mission: Some Aspects of the Normative Role of the Diocesan Bishop," StCan 25 (1991) 245–276.   ⁴⁷See K. Rahner, "The Episcopal Office," ThInvest 6:313-360; idem, "Pastoral-Theological Observations on Episcopacy in the Teaching of Vatican II," ThInvest 6:361-368; idem, "Aspects of the Episcopal Office," ThInvest 14:185-201.   ⁴⁸G. Ghirlanda, "La visita 'ad limina apostolorum,'" CivCatt 140 (1989) 3:359-372.   ⁴⁹Congregation for Bishops, "Direttorio per la visita 'ad limina,'" Apoll 61 (1988) 556–566 with observations 566–590.   ⁵⁰W. Bertrams, "De origine et significatione notionis 'hierarchica communio,'" Periodica 69 (1980) 23–30.   ⁵¹AAS 50(1968) 374–377, 406–412; 51(1969) 334–340.   ⁵²H. Orioli, "La collazione del pallio," Nuntia 4 (1976) 88–96.   ⁵³J.H. Provost, in Coriden, CIC 355.   ⁵⁴J. Zizioulas, "The Bishop in the Theological Doctrine of the Orthodox Church," Kan 7 (1985) 23–35; J. Meyendorff, *Catholicity and the Church* (Crestwood, N.Y.: St. Vladimir's Seminary Press, 1983) 49–64; Emilianos Timiadis, "Meaning of the Ministry-Episcopacy," PatByzR 1 (1982) 81–99; P. Menevissoglou, "La signification canonique et ecclésiologique des titres épiscopaux dans l'Église orthodoxe," Kan 7 (1985) 74–90; G. Wagner, "The Bishop in Eastern Orthodox Theology," Conc 1/8 (Jan. 1972).   ⁵⁵See Lima Document, *Baptism, Eucharist and Ministry.* Faith and Order Paper 111 (Geneva: WCC, 1982) 21–30.

## BISHOPS, COLLEGIALITY

Of all the matters treated at Vatican II, one of the most controversial was the collegiality of bishops. Though there was not yet full maturity on all aspects of collegiality at the time, on the level at which the council taught the doctrine there had been ample investigation; reflection on the topic continues to be ongoing.¹ Collegiality first appeared in the Vatican II schema, *Concilium duce Spiritu,* in November 1962, and later in drafts of the Constitution on the Church (LG).

Fears were expressed by many council members that the primacy of the pope defined at Vatican I might be impugned. The council members were reminded of the ancient terminology in the April–July 1963 draft of LG: *ordo* in Tertullian (q.v.),² body and college *(corpus . . . collegium)* in Cyprian (q.v.),³ and the technical use of *collegium* in Optatus of Milevis (fl. 370).⁴

There were other historical precedents that raised apprehensions: there was a Protestant collegial theory in the 17th and 18th centuries; collegial theories were found in canon lawyers infected with Josephinism (q.v.) and Febronianism (q.v.), though these had been eliminated in the 19th century by the triumph of the idea of the Church as "perfect society" (q.v.).

In the second session there was a test vote on 29 October 1963 on whether the episcopal body or college *(corpus seu collegium)* was the successor of the college of apostles in the evangelical task of sanctifying and pastoring; 1808 positive, 336 negative votes resulted.⁵ In May 1964 Paul V1 consulted the members of the Biblical Commission on whether it could be proved from Scripture that it was the Lord's disposition *(statuente Domino)* that Peter and the other apostles constituted one apostolic college, and whether the Roman Pontiff, successor of Peter, and the bishops, successors of the apostles, were united in the same way *(inter se coniunguntur).* The replies were positive, and were distributed in the council in September 1964.⁶

The theological commission went to great pains to reassure the council members that the primacy of the pope was safeguarded. A rearguard action was fought by the minority of the council against both the sacramentality of the episcopate and above all collegiality.⁷ The commission also reiterated that the word *"collegium"* is not to be taken in a secular sense of a body of equals. Furthermore, it occasionally used the idea of body *(corpus)* and order *(ordo)* so that "college" would not be the only expression employed. Eventually Msgr. G. Philips, the main author of LG, produced a Preliminary Explanatory Note *(Nota explicativa praevia),* which was published along with the Constitution as an appendix. Some points are of importance with regard to this note: it is in no small part drawn from the reservations expressed by the minority, often to exact wording; it was never voted upon by the council; the Note should be interpreted by *Lumen gentium,* and not the other way round; the publication of the Note ensured the near unanimity of the passage of chapter 3 of LG.⁸

The main lines of the Council's teaching on collegiality are to be found in LG 19 and 22: Christ formed the apostles as a college or permanent group *(ad modum collegii seu coetus stabilis—*LG 19); Peter was placed at the head of the college (LG 19); the office of apostles was made permanent in the order of bishops (LG 20); the college of bishops succeeds the college of apostles (LG 22); the collegial character and nature of the episcopal order is evidenced in various practices of the early Church (LG 22); "a person is constituted a member of the episcopal body by virtue of sacramental consecration and by hierarchical communion with the head and members of the college" (LG 22); the college has authority only when in union with the Roman Pontiff, its head (LG 22); the multiplicity of the membership of the college expresses the universality and unity of the flock of Christ (LG 22); the college's supreme power in the Church is solemnly expressed in an ecumenical council, but collegial acts are also possible on the part of bishops dispersed throughout the world (LG 22).

The text of chapter 3 of the Constitution contains frequent nervous reminders that the college of bishops cannot act except in communion with the head, the pope. The pope has supreme and universal power in the Church (Vatican I and LG 22) and so, too, does the college of bishops united with him. The theological question arises whether there are one or two sources of supreme power in the Church. Solutions are variously proposed. The view of the minority at the council would in effect deny power to the college of bishops in any real sense: there is but one power, the pope's; for solemnity, he may join with the bishops in some act.[9] It seems best to assert that there is only one source of supreme and universal power in the Church, which is the college of bishops united with the pope. The pope has supreme and universal power, which he can always exercise alone, but he does so, not as an individual, but as head of the college of bishops. This view stresses one and undivided power in the one ministry given by the Lord. It echoes tradition, especially Cyprian, who strongly held that episcopal power was one and undivided.[10] Others would see two sources of supreme power inadequately distinct: the pope as vicar of Christ for the universal Church and the college, which must include the pope as bishop of Rome. This is the view, it is claimed, that harmonizes best with the council,[11] and possibly with *The Final Report* of the 1985 Extraordinary Synod.[12]

Placing together LG 22 and 23, a theological understanding of collegiality and papacy emerges: the principle of unity is the universal primacy of Jesus Christ exercised through the Spirit in both the college with its head and in the head of the college alone.[13]

It has become customary to speak of both effective and affective collegiality: the former is determined by theological statements and juridical norms about collegiality by the council and later by the *Code of Canon Law;* the latter cannot be juridically determined, for it lies in a sense of collegiality manifested in the collegial acts that bishops choose to perform for the benefit of the whole Church, or for example, needy dioceses (cf. LG 21, 23).[14]

In 1969 an extraordinary synod (q.v.) took place to explore the relations between the episcopacy and the primacy. It issued no document, but made recommendations about communications between the Holy See and bishops.[15]

Bishops' conferences (q.v.) and post-Vatican II general synods (q.v.)[16] are limited expressions of collegiality. In the post-conciliar years the notion of collegiality has been extended to other situations in which there is authority and coresponsibility, or the possibility of a more synodal style of government, e.g., diocese, parish (q.v.), religious congregations. But like episcopal collegiality itself, this interesting development or extension of the council's thought tends to be a matter of language, rather than to have found concrete expression through communion (q.v.) in government at various levels.[17] In the diocese, structures exist, if seldom put to full use, whereby the spirit of collegiality can be made both affective and effective (v. SYNODS AND COUNCILS).

In the new *Code* it would seem that there is a strong, if not undue, influence of the "Preliminary Explanatory Note."[18] Along with LG 20, 22, and CD 4, it underlies the description of the college: "The college of bishops, whose head is the Supreme Pontiff and whose members are the bishops by virtue of sacramental consecration and hierarchical communion with the head and members of the college, and in which the apostolic body endures, together with its head, and never without its head, is also the subject of supreme and full power over the universal Church" (CIC 336.) The *Code* goes on to deal with the exercise of power by the college: ecumenical councils (v. COUNCILS) cc. 337–341; synod of bishops (q.v.) cc. 342–348.

Since Vatican II it appears that there has been a limited reception (q.v.) of the notion of collegiality. Emphasis has been more on the primacy, and this is how Protestant ecumenists would also judge the matter.[19] A deepened development in the theology and in the living out of communion would seem necessary before there can be a full reception of all that is taught and implied in the conciliar teaching on collegiality.

[1]A. Montana, "Comunione, collegialità, primato . . . conferenze episcopali. Rassegna bibliografica," Later 54 (1988) 467–482; Baraúna—Congar, six arts (J. Ratzinger, U. Betti, J.C. Groot, S. Lyonnet, J. Hajjar, G. Dejaifve) 3:736-890; Y. Congar, "Introduction" to Y. Congar, ed., *La collégialité épiscopale: Histoire et théologie.* US 52 (Paris 1965) 7–8; A. Calvo Espiga, "El ejercicio de la colegialidad en el gobierno de la Iglesia universal," Lumen 32 (1983) 300–320; H. Coathalem, "Un horizon de Vatican II: L'autorité suprême du pontife romain et celle de l'évêque," NRT 92 (1970) 1009–1023; C. Colombo, "Il significato de la collegialità episcopale nella Chiesa secondo la 'Lumen gentium,'" RasT 21 (1980) 177–188; P. Granfield, "The Uncertain Future of Collegiality," Proceedings CTSA 40 (1985) 95–106; R.P. McBrien, "Collegiality: State of the Question," in J.A. Coriden, ed., *The Once and Future Church* (New York: Alba, 1971) 1–24; G. Mazzoni, *La collegialità episcopale. Tra teologia e diritto canonico.* Ricerche sul diritto ecclesiale 1 (Bologna: Ed. Dehoniane, 1986); C.M. Murphy, "Collegiality: An Essay Toward Better Understanding," TS 46 (1985) 38–49; L.J. O'Connell, "Collegiality: Theology and Practice for the 80s," TDig 29 (1981) 319–328; K. Rahner, "On the Relationship between the Pope and the College of Bishops," ThInvest 10:50-70; J. Ratzinger, "The Pastoral Implications of Episcopal Collegiality," Conc 1/1 (1965) 20–34; D.M. Stanley, "The New Testament Basis for Collegiality," TS 25 (1964) 197–216 = TDig 13 (1965) 222–227; L. Vischer, "After the Debate on Collegiality," EcuR 37 (1985) 306–317; K. Walf, "Collegiality of Bishops without Roman Centrism?," TDig 34 (1987) 145–148 = Diakonia (Germany) 17 (1986) 167–173; Conc 210 (1990/4).   [2]*Adv. Marcion* 4:5—CSEL 47:490; *Praescr. haer.* 32—PL 2:44.   [3]*Epist* 68:3-4—CSEL 3/2:746-747/Halton 107 (part).   [4]*Contra Parmen. Donat.* 1:4; 3:12; 7:6—

CSEL 26:5, 99-100, 179-180. Cf. Alberigo-Magistretti 108.
[5]ActaSyn 2/3:574-575, 670—Alberigo-Magistretti 429–430.
[6]ActaSyn 3/1: 13-14—Alberigo-Magistretti 432–433. [7]ActaSyn 3/1:234-241; 3/8:57-81—Alberigo-Magistretti 450–453, 519–529.
[8]J. Grootaers, *Primauté et collégialité: Le dossier de Gérard Philips sur la Nota explicativa praevia (Lumen Gentium III)*. Bibliotheca ETL (Louvain, 1986); cf. G. Alberigo, "L'episcopato al Vaticano II: A proposito della Nota explicativa praevia e di mgr. Philips," CrNSt 8/1 (1987) 147–163; U. Betti, *La dottrina dell'episcopato nel Vaticano II: Il cap. III della costituzione dommatica Lumen gentium* (Rome: Città Nuova, [1]1968, [2]1984) 441–539. See also G. Dejaifve, *Un tournant décisif de l'ecclésiologie à Vatican II*. Le point théologique 31 (Paris: Beauchesne, 1978) 25–42. [9]See A. Acerbi, *Due ecclesiologie: Ecclesiologia giuridica ed ecclesiologia di comunione nella "Lumen gentium"* (Bologna: Dehoniane, 1975) 243–245, 444–457. [10]*De eccl. cath. unitate* 5 with M. Bévenot, "In solidum and St. Cyprian" JTS 6 (1955) 244–248; Y. Congar in V. Faglio and G. Concetti, eds., *La collegialità episcopale per il futuro della Chiesa* (Florence, 1969) 43–61; G. Dejaifve, "Peut-on concilier le collège épiscopale et la primauté?" in Congar, ed. (n. 1) 289–303; K. Rahner in Vorgrimler, Vatican II, 1:201-204; idem, "On the Relationship Between the Pope and the College of Bishops," ThInvest 10:50-70; idem, in K. Rahner and J. Ratzinger, *The Episcopate and the Primacy*. Q. Disput. 4 (Freiburg—London, 1966—German 1962) 75–108. [11]See arts by G.[W.] Bertrams in CivCatt 113 (1962) 2:213-222; 115 (1964) 1:436-455; 116 (1965) 2:568-572; idem, *The Papacy, the Episcopacy, and Collegiality* (Westminster, Md., 1964); idem, *Questiones fundamentales iuris canonici* (Rome: Gregorian UP, 1969); idem (W. Bertrams), "De subjecto supremae potestatis Ecclesiae," Per 54 (1965) 173–232, 490–499; K. Mörsdorf, "Bishop. 4.—Canon Law," SM 1:231-232. [12]*Extraordinary Synod of Bishops* (Washington, D.C.: NCCB, 1986) 19; *Synod extraordinaire: Célébration de Vatican II* (Paris: Cerf, 1986) 560–561—cf. ibid., 27–28 (J.A. Komonchak). [13]C. Colombo, "Il significato della collegialità episcopale nella Chiesa," IusCan 19 (1979) 13–28 at 24; cf. idem, art. cit. (n. 1) 186. [14]Colombo (n. 1) 181–184. [15]A. Antón, *Primado y colegialidad: Su relaciones a la luz del primer Sínodo extraordinario* (Madrid: BAC, [2]1970). [16]Cf. A. Antón, "Sinodo e collegialità extraconciliare dei vescovi," in Faglio and Concetti (n. 10) 62–78. [17]See A. Antón, "Postconciliar Ecclesiology: Expectations, Results, and Prospects for the Future," in Latourelle, Vatican II, 1:407-438. [18]E. Corecco, "Aspects of the Reception of Vatican II in the Code of Canon Law," in G. Alberigo et al., eds., *The Reception of Vatican II* (Washington, D.C.: The Catholic University Press—Tunbridge Wells: Burns and Oates, 1987) 277–278, 284–286. [19]L. Vischer, "The Reception of the Debate on Collegiality," in G. Alberigo et al. (n. 18) 233–248.

## BISHOPS' CONFERENCES

Meetings or conferences of bishops in France and elsewhere appeared from the middle of the 16th century, probably to avoid the restrictions that surrounded the holding of councils (q.v.). The number of conferences increased in the 19th and 20th centuries. The 1917 *Code* gave some little role to meetings (*conventus*) of bishops (cc. 292, 1507, 1909). Though mainly confined to national boundaries, conferences now also take in wider areas, most notably CELAM (1955), the Latin American Conference.[1]

In view of the positive history of their conferences,[2] the bishops at Vatican II saw the need for territorial bodies (SC 22; UR 8) and decreed the establishment of conferences (CD 37–38). During the conciliar discussion two issues predominated: the theological basis for the conferences and their capacity to enact obligatory decisions.[3] The council adopted a positive, if guarded position (CD 38.4). Initial legislation for conferences appeared in 1966,[4] and the *Code of Canon Law* dealt with them in cc. 447–459 stating, "The conference of bishops, a permanent institution, is a grouping of bishops of a given nation or territory whereby, according to the norms of law, they jointly exercise certain pastoral functions on behalf of the Christian faithful of their territory in view of promoting that greater good which the Church offers humankind, especially through forms and programs of the apostolate which are fittingly adapted to the circumstances of the time and place" (CIC 447). This text adds the limiting word "certain" to the Vatican II text, "exercise their pastoral functions" (CD 38), and the norm that the conference is a permanent institution, a juridic person. Whereas Vatican II sees conferences as having also a missionary outreach to the world (see CD 36), the *Code* sees them mainly as interecclesial.[5]

It belongs to the Holy See to erect or suppress conferences (cc. 448–449). Membership is determined by two main criteria: membership of the college of bishops (or of the equivalent in law) and pastoral responsibility (CIC 450).[6] Conferences are to have statutes, regular meetings (CIC 451–454), and appropriate permanent structures (CIC 457–458). Mutual relations between conferences are encouraged (CIC 459).[7]

The most contentious area concerns the decrees of conferences, and their binding force. First, there are at least 82 matters which by law are committed to action by episcopal conferences.[8]

Second, there are cases which the Holy See may commit to the conference, or for which the conference may request a mandate. In these two cases there must be a two-thirds majority of the members of the conferences whether they are present or not. In other decrees each bishop must give his consent before it is a binding act of the conference (CIC 455). The decrees and the acts of the conference are to be sent to the Apostolic See for its attention and possible revision (*recognosci possint*—CIC 456). History shows that in the case of provincial councils and synods (CIC 446), the revision by the Holy See has been both substantive and often additional to what was decreed at local level.[9]

There are two distinct attitudes to episcopal conferences in the Church today: one, represented among others by the later writings of Cardinal J. Ratzinger,[10] by Cardinal H. de Lubac,[11] and the Vatican 1988 draft document on Bishops' Conferences.[12] These would insist on the essentially pragmatic nature of episcopal conferences: they are not by divine authority (*ius divinum*—q.v.); they are at best only analogously an exercise of collegiality; they risk downgrading the individual bishop's duty to teach in his diocese, or letting bishops hide behind the bureaucratic institution of the conference and evading this duty; furthermore, they can give rise to the hazard of excessive nationalism, thus attacking the basis of that communion (q.v.) which is the Church; there is no theologically justified intermediate body between the local bishop and the Petrine See; the very large number of episcopal conferences can lead to a contradictory or fragmentary witness in the world. In particular this viewpoint insists strongly that the role of the conference is not a teaching or magisterial one, but only pastoral.

But there is, however, another position forcefully represented at the 1988 Salamanca Colloquium:[13] episcopal conferences are in continuity with provincial and regional councils in the history of the Church;[14] the categories of *ius divinum* and merely ecclesiastical law are not entirely suitable for the theological underpinning (or rejection) of bishops' conferences, for otherwise we risk impugning important past councils of the Church;[15] bishops' conferences are a true, if partial, expression of collegiality;[16] their theological basis is to be sought in the episcopate being a sacred order and hence facing towards God and outward towards the Church and the world; they are an organic body which is marked by solidarity between its members in their sacred functions; they are a manifestation of the solicitude towards all the Churches, which is an essential mark of the episcopal college.[17]

The question of the magisterial power of bishops' conferences became a live issue only in the mid-1980s. The negative arguments[18] of the writers cited above do not seem apodictic, and there is a body of opinion among respected ecclesiologists and canonists that would ascribe at least a limited magisterial function to bishops' conferences.[19] In their arguments they do not proceed directly by way of collegiality (v. BISHOPS, COLLEGIALITY), which requires that bishops teach in conjunction with the head of the episcopal college, the pope. It is legitimate, however, to speak of partial collegiality (cf. "collegial spirit"—*collegialis affectus*—LG 23). Instead, they argue from the Vatican II debates and the ensuing text (CD 38 interpreted by CD 11), from the 1969 Synod of Bishops, from CIC 447, 753 and 838 § 3 of the 1983 *Code*. The theological basis is based more on insights into the implication of the Church being a communion (q.v.), and of having the obligation of adaptation to various places in ways that at times are beyond the capacity of local bishops alone, adaptations which may not be suitable matters for a general edict coming from Rome. Many point to the basic equivalence in fact between modern episcopal conferences and particular or provincial councils and synods from earliest times up to the reformation.[20]

If there is magisterial teaching by episcopal conferences, the question of assent naturally arises. Further necessary questions would look at the nature of the teaching: Is it merely repeating what has already been taught by the universal or papal magisterium? Is it giving guidance in some new and difficult area, and if so, is this guidance provisional or definitive? Is it alerting Catholics to social issues on which there may be a diversity of practical opinions? The nature of the document will determine the obligation, if any, to assent.[21]

During the council and immediately afterwards the new status of bishops' councils was welcomed by bishops and theologians,[22] as well as by the 1969 and 1985 Synods of Bishops (q.v.). There has been a development with a healthy tension between the conference and the local bishops, between the conferences and the Holy See. If these elements are kept in tension, then the new phenomenon, with its ancient conciliar and synodal roots, will be a valuable experience for the Church, one open to forms and developments that perhaps we cannot as yet see. The collegial spirit finds concrete application in episcopal conferences (cf. LG 23). No one can doubt their pastoral utility and still less their necessity in the current situation.[23] The whole Church would be the poorer without the Latin American Bishops' Conference's statements at Medellín (1968), Puebla (1979), Santo Domingo (1992), and other documents emanating from various hierarchies, notably of the U.S., Germany, and France.

[1]J. Soria-Vasco, "Le C.E.L.A.M. ou Conseil Episcopal Latino-Americain," AnnéeCan 18 (1974) 179–220. [2]Y. Congar, "The Apostolic College, Primacy and Episcopal Conferences," TDig 34 (1987) 211–215 = EspVie 96/27 (1986) 385–390; P. Eyt, "Autour des conférences épiscopales," NRT 111 (1989) 343–359; B. Franck, "La conférence épiscopale et les autres institutions de collégialité intermédiaires," AnnéeCan 27 (1983) 67–120; A. García y García, "Las conferencias episcopales a la luz de la historia," Salm 13 (1976) 555–570; J.A. Komonchak, "Episcopal Conferences," ChicSt 27 (1988) 311–328; H. Legrand et al., eds., *The Nature and Future of Episcopal Conferences* (Washington, D.C.: The Catholic University of America Press, 1988) = Jurist 48 (1988); L. Mistò, "Le conferenze episcopali dalle origini al nuovo Codice di diritto canonico," ScuolC 117 (1989) 415–451; H. Müller and H.J. Pottmeyer, eds., *Die Bishofskonferenz: Theologischer und juridischer Status* (Düsseldorf: Patmos, 1989); H. Pottmeyer, "Was ist eine Bischofskonferenz?: Zur Diskussion um den theologischen Status der Bischofskonferenzen," StiZt 206 (1988) 435–446; J.H. Provost in Coriden CIC 363–364; K. Rahner, "On Bishops' Conferences," ThInvest 6:369-389. [3]ActaSyn 2/4:364-925; 2/5:9-176, 193-401. [4]*Motu proprio* of Paul VI, *Ecclesiae sanctae* 1:41—Flannery 1:609-610; Cong. for Bishops Directory, *Ecclesiae imago*, "On the Pastoral Ministry of Bishops" (Feb. 1973). [5]Provost (n. 2) 365. [6]Ibid., 366. [7]R. Lettmann, "Episcopal Conferences in the New Canon Law," StCan 14 (1980) 347–367; J. Sánchez y Sánchez, "Episcopal Conferences and the Roman Curia," Conc 127 (1979) 104–114. [8]List in Provost (n. 2)

370–372; F.G. Morrissey, "Decisions of Episcopal Conferences in Implementing the New Law," StCan 20 (1986) 105–121.  [9]Provost, ibid., 362, 372.  [10]*The Ratzinger Report* (San Francisco: Ignatius, 1985) 58–63.  [11]*The Motherhood of the Church Followed by Particular Churches in the Universal Church* (San Francisco: Ignatius, 1982) 257–273; cf. S. Wood, "The Theological Foundations of Episcopal Conferences and Collegiality," StCan 22 (1988) 327–338.  [12]Origins 17 (7 April 1988) 731–737.  [13]H. Legrand et al. (n. 2).  [14]H.J. Sieben, "Episcopal Conferences in the Light of Particular Councils During the First Millennium," Jurist 48 (1988) and H. Legrand (n. 2) 30–56; cf. A. García y García, "Episcopal Conferences in Light of Particular Councils During the Second Millennium," Jurist 48 (1988) = Legrand (n. 2) 57–67.  [15]A. Antón, "The Theological 'Status' of Episcopal Conferences," Jurist 48 (1988) = Legrand (n. 2) 185–219; idem, *Conferencias episcopales ¿instancias intermedias? El estado teológico de la cuestión*. Verdad e imagen 111 (Salamanca: Sígueme, 1989); idem, three arts. Greg 70 (1989) 205–232, 439–494, 741–778.  [16]W. Kasper, "Der theologische Status der Bischofskonferenzen," TQ 167 (1987) 1–6; cf. T. Eselman, "The Study of Episcopal Confer-ences: An Application of the Principle of Functionality," Jurist 51 (1991) 311–325; G. Famerée, "Au fondement des conférences épiscopales: la 'communio ecclesiarum,'" RTLv 23 (1992) 343–354; F. Guillemette, "Les conférences épiscopales sont-elles une institution de la collégialité épiscopale?," StCan 25 (1991) 39–76.  [17]Legrand (n. 2); D.B. Murray, "The Legislative Authority of the Episcopal Conference," StCan 20 (1986) 33–47; J. Salaverri, "Teología de la conferencia episcopal," EstE 50 (1975) 255–268.  [18]See also G. Ghirlanda, "De episcoporum conferentia deque exercitio potestatis magisterii," Periodica 87 (1987) 573–604; J.P. Green, *Conferences of Bishops and the Exercise of the "munus docendi" of the Church*. Diss. (Rome: Gregorian University, 1987); G. Mucci, "Le conferenze episcopali e l'autorità di magistero," CivCatt 138 (1987) 1:327–328; A. Naud, "Le magistère contesté des conférences épiscopales," ScEsp 41 (1989) 93–114.  [19]Antón, op. cit. (n. 15); A. Dulles, *The Reshaping of Catholicism: Current Challenges in the Theology of the Church* (San Francisco: Harper and Row, 1988) 207–226 = Origins 14 (1985) 528–534; idem, "What is the Role of a Bishops Conference?," Origins 17 (1988) 789–796; J. Manzanares, "The Doctrinal Authority of Bishops' Conferences," Legrand (n. 2) = Jurist 48 (1988) 234–263; P.J. Urrutria, "De exercitio muneris docendi a conferentiis episcoporum," Periodica 76 (1987) 605–636.  [20]E.g., Y. Congar—B. Lauret, *Fifty Years of Catholic Theology* (London: SCM, 1988) 11–13; idem, "Collège, primauté . . . conférences épiscopales: Quelques notes," EspVie 96/27 (1986) 385–390 = TDig 34 (1987) 211–215; see n. 14 above.  [21]Dulles (n. 19) 219–220; Komonchak (n. 2) 315.  [22]E.g., J. Hamer, "Les conférences épiscopales, exercice de la collégialité," NRT 85 (1963) 966–969; J. Ratzinger, "The Pastoral Implications of Episcopal Collegiality," Conc 1/1 (1964) 39–67.  [23]1985 Synod of Bishops, *The Final Report* 5.

# BLACK THEOLOGY

Black theology has three related sources: the Civil Rights movement of the 1950s in the U.S., a key figure being Martin Luther King, Jr.; the Black Power movement of the 1960s, which began within Civil Rights but changed course; the publication of a book by Joseph R. Washington in 1964.[1] The author's intent was to criticize the white Churches for not integrating black religious societies into the mainstream of American Protestantism. He proceeded by way of questioning the existence of a genuine black theology, calling it rather an instrument of social progress. Various reac-

tions followed, but it was to be James H. Cone, an American Methodist Episcopalian, who would write the first major book on black theology[2] and be one of the movement's most articulate spokespersons.[3]

Black theology quickly evolved,[4] and it soon adopted some of the key insights of liberation theologies (q.v.). It sought first to explain to blacks what it means to be black and Christian, and only later to address the wider Christian world. Black theology saw from an early stage that not only individual white Christians but the white Churches played a part in oppressive structures. In the formative experience of slavery, blacks found the white Churches to be the institutions of the slavemasters, whereas their God was found in story, song, and prayer.

Black theology soon took root in Africa, a first book being banned in South Africa.[5] Like some liberation theologies, black theology seeks to transform the Church by demanding that it show in fruits of justice its transcendent origins in Jesus Christ.[6] It must be the agent for the liberation which is its message. In Christology there is an emphasis on Jesus being black, not in his skin pigmentation but in bearing the burdens of the black peoples all the way to the Cross and transforming them in his resurrection. Black theology is also taken up in the special perspective of feminist theology (q.v.).[7]

Black theology is only slowly being accepted within Catholicism, though Paul VI said, prophetically, in 1969, "You must now give your gifts of Blackness to the whole Church."[8]

There is some danger of a sect mentality if black theology becomes too exclusively the domain of special groups, like those of Negro ethnicity, or if its center does not embrace the core values of Christianity, as some Protestant commentators have noted.[9]

[1]*Black Religion: The Negro and Christianity in the United States* (Boston: Beacon, 1964).  [2]*Black Theology and Black Power* (New York: Seabury, 1969).  [3]*A Black Theology of Liberation* (Philadelphia: Lippincott, 1970); *God of the Oppressed* (New York: Seabury, 1975); "Black Religion in American Religion," TTod 43 (1986–1987) 6–21; cf. D.L. Hayes, "James H. Cone, Black Historical Experience and the Origins of Black Theology," LouvSt 12 (1987) 245–260; S. Molla, "James H. Cone, théologien noir américain," RTPhil 116 (1984) 217–239 with bibliog.  [4]G.S. Wilmore and J.H. Cone, eds., *Black Theology: A Documentary History 1966–1979* (Maryknoll: Orbis, 1979) with bibliog. 609–623 (J.H. Cone), 624–637 (V.T. Eason); J.H. Evans and G.E. Gorman, *Black Theology: A Critical Assessment and Annotated Bibliography*. Bibliographies and Indexes in Religious Studies 10 (Westport, Conn.: Greenwood Press, 1987).  [5]Mokgethi Motlhabi, ed., *Essays in Black Theology* (Johannesburg: UGM, 1972) republ. ed. B.S. Moore, *The Challenge of Black Theology in South Africa* (Atlanta: Knox Press, 1974); M. Motlhabi, "The Historic Origins of Black Theology," BTAfr 6 (1984) 211–226; I. Hexham, "A Short History of Black Theology in South Africa," RAfrT 6 (1982), # 12, 189–203.  [6]J.H. Cone, "What Is the Church?: A Black Perspective," BTAfr 5 (1983) 21–33.  [7]P. Murray, "Black Theology and

Feminist Theology: A Comparative Vision," AngTR 60 (1978) 3–24; *Black Theology: A Documentary History* (n. 4) 363–442. [8]"To the Heart of Africa," The Pope Speaks 14 (1969) 219; cf. Black Bishops of U.S. pastoral, "What We Have Seen and Heard," Origins (18 Oct. 1984); J. Bosch, "Apuntes para una aproximación a la 'Teología Negra,'" CiTom 114 (1987) 623–652; C. Davis, "Black Spirituality: A Roman Catholic Perspective," RExp 80 (1983) 97–108. [9]E.g., H. Wayne House, "An Investigation of Black Liberation Theology," BiblSac 139 (1982) 159–176; cf. E.K. Braxton, "Toward a Black Catholic Theology," in *Black Theology: A Documentary History* (n. 4) 325–328.

## BODY OF CHRIST

The Pauline theme of Body of Christ is central to ecclesiology, and still retains its importance after Vatican II, though superseded in many people's minds by the concept of the Church as the People of God (q.v.). The publication in 1943 of the encyclical *Mystici Corporis* (q.v.) was a major event in the history of ecclesiology, marking a stage in a development which lasted over a century. The rediscovery of the theme of the Body of Christ dates from Möhler (q.v.) and later the Roman School (q.v.) and Scheeben (q.v.).[1] Möhler went back to the Fathers, especially the Greek ones, to find the grounds for a view of the Church as the continuing incarnation: "The Church is the Body of the Lord: it is in its universality, his visible form—his permanent everrenovated, humanity—his eternal revelation."[2] From the Roman School, specifically C. Schrader, we have the draft of a document on the Church prepared for Vatican I, but never discussed, in which the doctrine of the Body of Christ was prominent.[3] Towards the end of the century Leo XIII spoke of the Mystical Body in the encyclicals *Satis cognitum* (1896) and *Divinum illud* (1897).[4] After the First World War there was increased theological interest in the notion of the Body of Christ.[5] Some of the more influential writers should be noted. The first important work of E. Mersch (1890–1940), *Le corps mystique du Christ* (1933),[6] was a historical study, in the Scriptures and in the Fathers, of the Mystical Body, from which he concluded: "The very nature of the doctrine makes it both the center of resistance against error and the heart of the Church's positive teaching," and "since it is inseparable from the dogma of Christology, the doctrine of the Mystical Body is one with the central truth of Christianity."[7] He then published in 1934 an article that would be quite influential: he put forward the idea that the Mystical Body was the center of all theology.[8] His synthetic study of the doctrine of the Body of Christ was published posthumously.[9] Whereas Mersch's vision is aptly summarized in the Augustinian phrase "the whole Christ," which stresses above all the interiority of the gifts given in the Body,[10] others like R. Guardini (q.v.) and K. Adam (q.v.) accented also the personalist and communitarian dimensions of the doctrine: the

Church is an organic community, for "the 'many,' the sum total of all who are redeemed in Christ, are in their inner relationship to one another, in their interrelation and correlation, in their organic communion, objectively and finally the Body of Christ."[11] E. Przywara sought to find a mean between two faulty developments: on the one hand an excessive emphasis on the notion of "mystical," which would either confuse the divine and the human, or lead to a quietism; on the other hand the tendency exemplified by M.D. Koster (v. PEOPLE OF GOD) to reject the concept of the Body of Christ.[12]

The most significant writer of the period 1930–1950 was to be S. Tromp (q.v.),[13] as he had a key responsibility for the contents of the 1943 encyclical *Mystici Corporis*. The encyclical is, unfairly indeed, mainly remembered today for its positions that were not followed by Vatican II. The Pope identified the Mystical Body with the Roman Catholic Church: "To describe the true Church of Christ—which is the Holy, Catholic, Apostolic, Roman Church—there is no name more noble, none more excellent, none more divine, than 'the mystical Body of Jesus Christ.'"[14] Hence, on the question of membership (q.v.) of the Church: visible unity was a prerequisite, with others ordered to the Church only by some unconscious yearning and desire *(quodam desiderio ac voto)*.[15] The pope repeated the idea in *Humani generis* a few years later: "That the Mystical Body of Christ and the Catholic Church in communion with Rome are one and the same thing is a doctrine based on revealed truth."[16] Further, the encyclical, as did Tromp, sought to integrate the ecclesiology of the perfect society (q.v.) with the biblical and patristic traditions. These questions were all hotly debated in the following decades, along with the meaning of the word "mystical" as applied to the Church. The term was not used by Paul. Indeed, until the Middle Ages the "mystical Body of Christ" was the Eucharist, while the Church was the Body, or the real Body,[17] the change in terminology being brought about by the controversy with Berengar of Tours (d. 1088) on Eucharistic presence. St. Thomas spoke of Christ and the Church forming one mystical person.[18] From the 19th century "mystical" was used with a variety of meanings, some, between the two world wars, quite exaggerated. Pius XII explained the word as distinguishing the physical body of the glorified Christ from the Church, as indicating that the Church is not a mere moral or purely juridical union.[19] But after 1943 theologians would ask if Mystical Body of Christ was a true definition of the Church,[20] and they often understood "mystical" as also having a sacramental meaning.[21]

The first schema prepared for Vatican II, *Aeternus Unigeniti Pater*[22] was very much in the line of the 1943 encyclical. But the final text (LG 7) is much richer, one, moreover, which follows the evolution of NT theology on the Body.[23] Vatican II does not follow Augustine and some modern exegetes in seeing the origin of the notion of the Body of Christ in Paul's conversion experience on the road to Damascus (Acts 9:5).[24] It begins rather with texts from Gal 6:15 and 2 Cor 5:17 on the new creation through the death of Christ and his communication to us of his Spirit. The next two paragraphs treat of the doctrine as found in 1 Cor and Rom. There have been many suggestions about the origin of the concept of the Body of Christ. In 1 Cor 12:14-26 Paul does not seem to go beyond the allegory of the human body to describe the social order found, for example, in Menenius Agrippa. But vv. 12 and 27 show that Paul has already pondered deeply the relationship of the Corinthian community with Christ. Earlier in the letter he argues to the unlawfulness of prostitution from their being members of Christ in the Spirit (cf. 1 Cor 6:15-17, and esp. v. 17 where the parallelism with v. 16 might lead us to expect "one body," but states instead "one spirit"). In 1 Cor 10:16-17 Paul is concerned to keep Christians away from meals associated with pagan rites. He states that the common sharing in the one Eucharistic bread, and so in the Body of Christ, brings about a unity in the one Body of Christ. Gnostic texts are of uncertain date, and it is not possible to establish a direct influence of them on Paul. We are then left with four main suggestions as to the origin of Paul's concept of Body of Christ: first, the Greek social metaphor, which he has already transcended in 1 Cor; second, his reflection on the Eucharist;[25] third, Jewish reflections on Adam, including the whole human race,[26] a point which, however, is difficult to establish; fourth, and more probably, his doctrine of the Christian being "in Christ" *(en Christô).*[27] In these texts, and in Rom 12:5, also cited in LG 7, the vision of Paul does not seem to go beyond that of the local community.

With the captivity epistles, Col and Eph quotations from which follow in LG 7, the vision broadens in three ways. Now the Church is not the local community but the whole Church. Second, Christ is the head of the Church: "He is the head of the Body, the Church" (Col 1:18; cf. Eph 1:22). Head has two meanings: it signifies authority (Eph 5:23-24; Col 2:10); in Greek medicine the head was seen as the source of vital influence (Col 2:19; Eph 4:15-16). The third development is the assertion of total fullness *(plêrôma)* dwelling in Christ (e.g., Col 2:9; Eph 1:22-23; 3:19; 4:12-13).[28] P. Benoit argues that in Col the author was concerned to show that Christ was supreme over all beings. Since spiritual beings were also involved, the notion of Head of the Body would not have been appropriate. In Eph the notion becomes more fully cosmic.[29] The origin of the concept is more surely to be found in OT wisdom than in Gnostic sources. [30] Finally, there are texts in LG 6 which can be said to approximate to the Body of Christ in LG 7: the vine (John 15:1-5), the household of God (Eph 2:19, 22), the living stones (1 Pet 2:5)—to which might be added the texts where Christ assimilates his followers to himself (cf. Matt 10:40; 25:40).

A most difficult question remains, one on which authors differ enormously: What is the meaning of Body of Christ used in the Scriptures, in tradition, and in the magisterium? Scholars speak of allegory, metaphor, symbol, moral union, realism, etc. One must always observe a distinction between the physical risen body of Christ and his body which is the Church. By including at least twenty ecclesiological themes in a broad framework, LG 7 may be said to indicate an approach. The Body of Christ points to a reality which can only be a set of relationships which are brought about by the Christ's redemption and by his sending of the Spirit. These relationships are expressed in the sacramental life and in the other activities of the Church. The Church is bonded into Christ and lives in him through the Spirit, and it must grow into its head by submission in a spousal relationship. Through Christ all the members of the Church are bonded to one another. The Holy Spirit is said to vivify the Body in a way comparable to the soul in the human body. There was some opposition in the council to the idea that the Spirit is the "soul" of the mystical Body: it is not scriptural; it could lead to ecclesiastical monophysitism by suggesting a substantial union between the Spirit and the Church; one could fear an ecclesiastical Apollinarianism, so that if the Spirit were the soul of the Church, sin and failure predicated of the Church would also be attributed to the Holy Spirit. An earlier tradition was more positive towards the analogy: Augustine wrote, "What our spirit, that is our soul, is to our members, the Holy Spirit is to the members of Christ, the Body of Christ which is the Church";[31] St. Thomas sees the analogy in terms of the unity of the Church: "Just as it is to the unity of the soul that the unity of the Body is attributed, so too it is the unity of the Holy Spirit which constitutes the unity of the Church."[32] The thought of Augustine was taken up by Leo XIII in *Divinum illud,*[33] and Pius XII spoke of the Spirit being the soul of the Body as the "divine principle of life and power."[34]

The Body of Christ is not a static notion, for the Body itself is continually in growth until it reaches the fullness of God. The concept of Body does not say everything about the Church; it needs other ideas,[35] People of God (q.v.), and Temple (q.v.) to bring out more fully the Trinitarian dimensions of the Church (LG 17). But Body more fully illustrates some aspects of the mystery of the Church than these last two can do alone.

[1]A. Kerkvoorde, "La théologie du 'Corps Mystique' au dix-neuvième siècle," NRT 67 (1945) 417–430; Antón 2:612-615. Bibliog. on Body of Christ in Dulles-Granfield 67–68.    [2]Symbolik ed. 5, sect. 38, cf. 37, trans. Symbolism (London, 1906) 278.    [3]Kerkvoorde (n. 1) 425. [4]ASS 28 (1895–1896) 709–739 and ASS 29(1896–1897) 644–658/ Carlen, 2:387-408 and 2:409-417; see Antón 2:480-490, 612-613. [5]J.J. Bluett, "The Mystical Body of Christ: 1890–1940," TS 3 (1942) 261–289—an extensive bibliog. but confined to English and French titles; J.E. Scully, "The Theology of the Mystical Body of Christ in French Language Theology 1930–1950: A Review and Assessment," IrTQ 58 (1992) 58–74.    [6]2nd ed. (1936) trans. The Whole Christ (Milwaukee—London, 1938); Antón 2:620-621.    [7]The Whole Christ (n. 6) 577 and 579–580.    [8]"Le Christ mystique centre de la théologie comme science," NRT 5 (1934) 449–475.    [9]The Theology of the Mystical Body (St. Louis—London, 1951). See G. Dejaifve, "La théologie du Corps Mystique du P. Em. Mersch," NRT 67 (1940–1945) 408–416 [1016–1024]; G.E. Malanowski, "Émile Mersch, S.J. (1890–1940). Un christocentrisme unifié," NRT 112 (1960) 44–66. [10]E.g., In Ps. 90, Serm 2—PL 37:1159.    [11]K. Adam, The Spirit of Catholicism (London, 1934) ch. 3, p. 39.    [12]E.g., "Theologie der Kirche," Schol 16 (1941) 321–334.    [13]Corpus Christi quod est Ecclesia, 4 vols. (Rome, 1937–1962).    [14]Par 13—AAS 35(1943) 199/Carlen 4:39-40.    [15]Pars 21–22, 102—Ibid., AAS 199 and 242/ Carlen 41, 58.    [16]Par 27—AAS 42(1950) 571/Carlen 4:179.    [17]H. de Lubac, Corpus Mysticum (Paris, ²1948) 23–46.    [18]ST 3a, q.19, a.4.    [19]Pars 58–66—AAS 35(1943) 221–225/Carlen 4:48-51.    [20]See Antón 2:642-643.    [21]Thus J. Ratzinger, "Leib Christi," LTK 6:911-912.    [22]ActSyn 1/4:12-91.    [23]On NT see B.M. Ahern, "The Christian's Union with the Body of Christ in Cor, Gal, and Rom," CBQ 23 (1961) 199–209; F. Amiot, "Body," DBT 53–56; P. Benoit, "L'Église Corps du Christ," in Exégèse et théologie. 4 vols. (Paris: Cerf, 1961–1982) 4:205-262; L. Cerfaux, The Church in the Theology of St. Paul (New York—London, 1959) 262–286; J.A. Fitzmyer, "Pauline Theology," JBC 2:823-824; idem, "Pauline Theology," NJBC 1409–1410; P.S. Minear, Images of the Church in the New Testament (Philadelphia: Westminster, 1960) 173–220; W. Pesch, "Body," in Bauer 1:81-84; J.A.T. Robinson, The Body: A Study in Pauline Theology (London, 1952)—but cf. Benoit's reservations RB 64 (1957) 581–583; H. Schlier, "Leib Christi," LTK 6:907-910; R. Schnackenburg, The Church in the New Testament (London: Burns and Oates, 1974) 165–176; E. Schweitzer, "Soma," TDNT 7:1067-1094, but with reservations—cf. Benoit (n. 23) 4:219.    [24]See authors in Cerfaux (n. 23) 262, n. 1.    [25]E.g., Cerfaux (n. 23) 263–265.    [26]See Schlier (n. 23) 908–909.    [27]Benoit (n. 23) 220–227.    [28]Cf. Benoit (n. 23) 230–237; I. de la Potterie, "Le Christ, Plérôme de l'Église (Eph 1:22-23)," Bib 58 (1977) 500–524; A. Feuillet, "L'Église plérôme du Christ d'après Ephés., 1, 23," NRT 78 (1956) 449–472, 593–610; K. Usami, Somatic Comprehension of Unity: The Church in Ephesus. Analecta biblica 101 (Rome: Biblical Institute, 1983).    [29]Art. cit (n. 23) 233–237.    [30]Feuillet, art. cit. (n. 28).    [31]Serm. 268:2—PL 38:1232.    [32]In Col. 1, lect. 5 (46).    [33]Divinum illud—ASS 29 (1896–1897) 650/Carlen 2:412.    [34]Encyl. Mystici corporis—AAS 35 (1943) 218–220/Carlen 4:48.    [35]Cf. A. Dulles, Models of the Church (Dublin: Gill and Macmillan, ²1988) 50–57.

## BOFF, Leonardo (1938– )

Leonardo Boff entered the Order of St. Francis in Brazil, where he was born in 1938. He studied under K. Rahner (q.v.) in Germany and became professor of theology at Petropolis. His book, *Church: Charism and Power:*

*Liberation Theology and the Institutional Church*[1] was negatively viewed by the Congregation for the Doctrine of the Faith in 1985. Boff was commanded to refrain from lecturing or writing for a year (April 1985–March 1986), which he accepted at the time, saying "I prefer to walk with the Church rather than walk alone with my theology," and noting that his work was not deemed heretical, but classed as "dangerous."[2] After his period of silence he began to write further, but eventually he felt compelled to leave his Franciscan Order in 1992.

All of Boff's theology shows him to be extremely well-read in European and Latin American writers. His ecclesiology is deeply influenced by the concerns of liberation theologies (q.v.). He sees the Church as especially the Church of the poor: walking with the poor and learning from them.[3] His earlier writings tended to favor charismatic elements of the Church over institutional ones.[4]

His remarkable volume concerned mainly with the Virgin Mary,[5] which pursues profound insights of feminism, has received a mainly hostile reception from established Mariologists; he would seem not to have preserved the necessary distance between the Holy Spirit and the creature, and to have used language like Hypostatic Union rather too loosely. The recent introduction to liberation theology, which he wrote with his brother, Clodovis, is a valuable pointer to current positions.[6] Intuitive rather than closely argued, the theology of L. Boff, like that of so many liberation theologians, deeply challenges the whole Church.

[1]New York: Crossroad, 1986—Portuguese 1981.    [2]Tablet, 30 March 1985. See Sacred Congregation for the Doctrine of the Faith, "Statement of Notification on Church: Charism and Power, by Leonardo Boff," Origins 14 (1985) 684–687; D. Flanagan, "Two Visions of Church: The Boff-Ratzinger Encounter," DoctLife 40 (1990) 517–520; H. Cox, The Silencing of Leonardo Boff: The Vatican and the Future of World Christianity (Oak Park, Ill.: Meyer-Stone Books, 1988); M. Kehl, "Kirche: 'Charisma und Macht,' Zum Streit um Leonardo Boff," GeistL 58 (1985) 337–350    [3]L. Boff, New Evangelization: Good News to the Poor (Maryknoll: Orbis, 1991 from Portuguese 1990).    [4]Ecclesiogenesis: The Base Communities Reinvent the Church (Maryknoll: Orbis—London: Collins, 1986 from Portuguese 1977); C. Ménard, "L'ecclésiologie des théologiens de la libération: Contexte général et analyse de quelques questions ecclésiologiques discutées par Leonardo Boff," EglT 19 (1988) 349–372; G. Mucci, "Il ministero ordinato nell'Ecclesiogenesi di L. Boff," CivCatt 137 (1986) 3:119-129; T. Rodríguez, G.I., "Una eclesiología de comunión y participación de los pobres: Estudio de la relación CEBs-jerarquía de Leonardo Boff," TXav 38 (1988) 369–388.    [5]The Maternal Face of God: The Feminine and Its Religious Expressions (San Francisco, etc.: Harper and Row, 1987 from Portuguese 1979). [6]L. Boff and C. Boff, Introducing Liberation Theology (Maryknoll: Orbis, 1987 from Portuguese 1986).

## BOLDNESS

The word "boldness" *(parrêsia)* has a rich range of meaning in the NT.[1] In classical Greek it meant the freedom of speech enjoyed by the citizen of the city state. Later it would mean the openness which friends enjoy in speaking to one another: between them bold speech will not cause offense.

In the NT there are some neutral occurrences of the word, where it just means "openly" (e.g., John 7:4, 13; Col 2:15). But there are several significant usages. Boldness characterizes the preaching of Jesus (Matt 8:32; John 11:14; 16:25, 29; 18:20). The apostolic preaching, too, is noted for its boldness (Acts 2:29; 4:13; 4:29, 31). Boldness is a mark of intimacy and love (2 Cor 7:4; Phlm 8). Faith and hope are characterized by their boldness (1 Tim 3:13; Heb 3:6). Boldness is a gift for which one must pray (Eph 6:19); indeed prayer itself is marked by boldness (1 John 3:25; 5:14). The Christian has boldness in approaching God through Christ (Eph 3:12). A remarkable notion is that the Christian can even face the parousia with boldness (1 John 2:28; 4:17). The cognate verb "to speak boldly" (parrêsiazomai) is a mark of the apostolic preaching (Acts 9:27-28; 13:46; 18:26; 19:8; Eph 6:20; 1 Thess 2:2).

In the patristic tradition boldness is often associated with various virtues, e.g., prayer, wisdom, truth.[2] Boldness belongs to the gift of fortitude received in confirmation (q.v.), and is a gift of the Spirit.[3] St Thomas speaks of a moderating boldness which is neither presumption nor pusillanimity.[4]

The Church always requires boldness; it is the gift that is found in its martyrs (q.v.).[5] It is also needed in times of change and turmoil. The Church is to look to the Spirit rather than withdraw in fear behind institutional bulwarks or its own human powers. Some manifestations of excessive conservatism, integralism (q.v.), and fundamentalism (q.v.) are in the last analysis a failure of biblical parrêsia, that boldness which is a gift continually to be sought (Eph 6:19).

[1]H. Schlier, "Parrêsia, parrêsiazomai," TDNT 5:871-886; M. Boutier, "Sur la parrhesia dans le Nouveau Testament," in C.C. Marcheselli, ed., Parola e spirito. FS S. Cipriani. 2 vols. (Brescia: Paideia, 1987) 1:611-621; H. Jaeger, "Parrêsia et fiducia. Étude spirituelle des mots," StPatr 1/1 (1957) 221–239; K. Rahner, "Parresia (Boldness)," ThInvest 7:260-267; cf. idem, "Courage for an Ecumenical Community," ThInvest 20:3-12; E. Vallauri, "La preghiera per la parresia (Atti 4, 24-31)," Laur 27 (1986) 185–216. [2]H. Jaeger, "Parrêsia et fiducia," StPatr 1 (1957) 221–239. [3]St. Thomas, ST 2–2ae, q.139, a.1c. [4]ST 2–2ae, q.130, a.1c and q.133, a.2c.; In Eph. prol. [5]C. Noce, "La parrhesia terrestre del martire," EuntDoc 39 (1986) 321–340.

# BONAVENTURE, St. (ca. 1217–1274)

Bonaventure was born about 1217 (perhaps 1221) near Orvieto (Italy). Probably in 1243 he entered the Franciscans and studied theology in Paris under Alexander of Hales, becoming Master of Theology there. Almost certainly in 1257, he was elected Master General of the Franciscan Order, of which he is sometimes called "the second founder." St. Francis of Assisi (d. 1226) was not an organizer, and after his death his order was rent in factions, each group claiming to be his authentic followers. Bonaventure adopted a moderate position in the various disputes about poverty, rejecting the extremes of the "Spiritual Franciscans."[1] Against the position of Francis, Bonaventure insisted on the need of studies for the sake of the Church, which involved possessing books, houses, attending universities, and holding teaching posts. He was forced by Gregory X to accept the cardinalate in 1273. He played a prominent role at the Council of Lyons II (1274—q.v.) and died the same year. Canonized in 1482, he was declared Doctor of the Church in 1588. In the medieval schools he was called the "Seraphic Doctor."

Bonaventure's extensive works[2] cover most areas of theology and spirituality. In contrast with the more Aristotelian Thomas Aquinas (q.v.), Bonaventure remained deeply Augustinian. His ecclesiology[3] is profoundly Christological: Christ the Incarnate Word draws people into the plenitude of grace. But we contemplate truth through wisdom received from the Spirit who continually binds the Church in faith and love to its head. The mission of the Spirit is threefold: to sanctify the Church, to give it the grace of Christ, to teach it divine truth.[4] The Church continues the salvific work of Christ through the sacraments; it is the visible presence of Christ's mediatory role; the Church is formed by the sacraments.[5]

Y. Congar asserts that Bonaventure was the principal theoretician of the papal monarchy in the 13th century.[6] Though he did not use the expression, Bonaventure held a doctrine largely equivalent to papal infallibility.[7] He also held not only a primacy of the Roman Church but also of the pope: "He is one, first and supreme spiritual father of all spiritual fathers, indeed of all the faithful. He is the supreme hierarch, the one spouse, undivided head, supreme pontiff, vicar of Christ, fount, source and rule of all ecclesiastical headships (principatuum), which as from the head is each ordered power down to the lowest member of the Church derived."[8] Bonaventure is, however, rather reserved about drawing political implications from the papal monarchy or from his views of The Two Swords, which he seems to have derived from Bernard (q.v.).[9]

In common with the great scholastics, Bonaventure did not write an ex professo ecclesiology. His views of the Church have a richness coming from his integration of the Church into the unified vision of his theology, a theology which is also so often a spirituality.

[1]H. Wolter in Jedin-Dolan 4:241-246; E. Iserloh, ibid., 369–375; cf. DS 908. [2]Critical ed., 10 vols. (Quaracchi, 1882– ); Eng. trans. J. de Vinck, 5 vols. (Paterson, 1960–1970). [3]Congar, Augustin 221–224; H. Berresheim, *Christus als Haupt der Kirche nach dem hl. Bonaventure: Ein Beitrag zur Theologie der Kirche* (Bonn, 1939). [4]J.F. Quinn, "The Role of the Holy Spirit in St. Bonaventure's Theology," FranSt 33 (1973) 273–284. [5]A. Pompei, "Ecclesia et sacramenta: Ecclesia peregrinans, fundamentum sacramentorum, formatur sacramentis," in A. Pompei, ed., *San Bonaventura maestro di vita francescana e di sapienza cristiana.* Atti congresso internazionale per il VII centenario di san Bonaventura da Bagnoreggio. 3 vols. (Rome: Pont. Fac. S. Bonaventura, 1976) 2:363-379; D. Culhane, *De corpore mystico doctrina Seraphici* (Mundelein, 1934); S. Simonis, "De causalitate Eucharistiae in Corpus mysticum doctrina S. Bonaventurae," Antonian 8 (1933) 143–228. [6]Op. cit. (n. 3) 222. [7]J.F. Quinn, "St. Bonaventure and the Magisterium of the Church," MiscFran 75 (1975) 597–610. [8]*Breviloquium* 6, 12— *Opera omnia* 5:150. [9]Congar, op. cit. (n. 3) 222.

## BONHOEFFER, Dietrich (1906–1945)

Born in 1906, Dietrich Bonhoeffer was the son of a professor of psychiatry at Berlin. He studied there as well as in Tübingen, Barcelona, and Union Theological New York (1928–1929).[1] Deeply influenced by K. Barth (q.v.), he began teaching and pastoral work in Berlin in 1931. Opposed to Nazism from the beginning, he joined the Confessing Church and in 1934 signed the Barmen Declaration (q.v.). He felt it his duty to return to Germany at the outbreak of the Second World War. After trying to mediate between England and German opponents of Hitler, he was arrested in 1943, and eventually hanged in the concentration camp at Flossenbürg in 1945.

His first thesis, *Sanctorum Communio,*[2] was praised by K. Barth (q.v.), who was struck by the originality of its author. His other substantial works include *The Cost of Discipleship*[3] and *Ethics.*[4] However, his best-known and most influential work was the posthumous *Letters and Papers from Prison,*[5] occasional pieces smuggled out of prison.

Though his published corpus is not large, Bonhoeffer is notable among 20th-century theologians.[6] His early work shows his ecclesiology to be radically Christological: the Church is where Christ through the Holy Spirit takes form among humans; it is Christ existing in community—an imperfect community indeed. In his later work Bonhoeffer inveighed against "cheap grace" which would be our achievement, as opposed to the "costly grace" through which God draws us in discipleship. His posthumous prison papers showed new developments as he pondered the meaning of religion itself ("religionless Christianity"), the Incarnation (Jesus "the man for others"), the Trinity (God "suffering" in humanity). Some of his theological ideas—not always in context—were much in vogue in the 1960s and 1970s in various "Death of God" and secularization theologies among some mainline Lutheran theologians, and having an influence at least indirectly on some important liberation theologians. The significance of Bonhoeffer lies not only in the questions he raised but in his being an enduring symbol of theology personalized in an authentic life leading to martyrdom.

[1]E. Bethge, *Dietrich Bonhoeffer: Theologian—Christian—Contemporary* (London: Collins Fount pb—New York: Harper and Row, 1977). [2]*The Communion of Saints: A Dogmatic Inquiry into the Sociology of the Church* (New York, 1963). [3]New York, 1963—London, 1964. [4]Rearranged ed. London, 1964—New York, 1965. [5]Enlarged edition by E. Bethge (London, 1971—New York, 1972). [6]J.J. Alemany, "Actualidad de Dietrich Bonhoeffer. Boletín," MiscCom 45 (1987) 197–238; C. Green and W. Floyd, eds., *Bonhoeffer Bibliography: Primary and Secondary Sources in English* (Hartford: Hartford Seminary, 1986); E. Bethge, "Religionless Christianity—A Mistake?" StRel 12 (1983) 19–26; J. De Gouchy, *Dietrich Bonhoeffer: Witness to Jesus Christ.* The Making of Modern Theology 4 (London: Collins, 1988); J.D. Godsey, "Dietrich Bonhoeffer," in D.F. Ford, ed., *The Modern Theologians.* 2 vols. (Oxford—New York: Blackwell, 1989) 1:50-70; G. Kretschmar, "Dietrich Bonhoeffer (1906–1945)," in KlassTheol 2:376-403; M.E. Marty, *The Place of Bonhoeffer: Problems and Possibilities in His Thought* (London: SCM, 1963).

## BONIFACE VIII, Pope (1294–1303)

On the abdication of Pope St. Celestine V (1294), the able canonist Benedetto Caetani was elected, taking the title of Boniface VIII.[1] He began to tidy up the administration of his saintly, but somewhat incompetent predecessor. He supported the mendicant orders, though he would later reduce their sphere of influence with his decree *Super cathedram* (1301). He constantly intervened in international affairs, but his politics were not often successful, since he was impulsive and held a concept of the pope as universal arbitrator which was no longer acceptable in the early 14th century. A long quarrel with Philip IV of France (1285–1314) dominated most of his pontificate. He was the first pope to proclaim a Jubilee Year (1300) with indulgences for visiting the tombs of the apostles. He made a lasting contribution to canon law, publishing in 1298 the *Liber sextus,* which formed a third part of the canonical *Corpus.* He was a patron of learning and of the arts, but his pontificate was marred by family acquisitiveness and his character defects which made him singularly unlikeable.

He is remembered most for the bull *Unam sanctam* (1302).[2] It is an extreme but, for the time, not a novel exposition of the temporal power of the pope. It affirms the total freedom of the Church from interference on the part of temporal powers, by asserting the subservience of the temporal to the spiritual power, which is identified with that of the pope; the pope has plentitude of power.[3] Boniface stresses strongly the unity of the Church: it has only one head. The bull then takes up the theme of The Two Swords found in

St. Bernard (q.v.): the material sword is used *for* the Church, the spiritual one *by* the Church; the material sword is in the hands of kings and soldiers but at the discretion of the *sacerdos*. The spiritual power can institute (*instituere,* which can be "institute" or "instruct") the secular and judge it, if it transgresses. If the earthly power is deviant, it is judged by the spiritual; the spiritual power is judged only by God.[4]

The bull concludes with the words: "Furthermore we declare, state and define that it is absolutely necessary for the salvation of all men that they submit to the Roman Pontiff."[5] The meaning of this conclusion is not agreed among scholars. G. Tavard holds that it teaches papal supremacy over temporal rulers, but not infallibly.[6] There are several reasons for denying that this statement, despite its apparent solemnity, is in fact an infallible one. First, it has not been universally received as such, either at the time of its launching or later. Second, it lacks the technical word *"pronuntiamus"* (we proclaim); the formula used, *"declaramus, dicimus, diffinimus,"* is the one used by consistorial decisions at the time.[7] Third, the text is taken from St. Thomas Aquinas, and can be seen to state no more than does the beginning of the bull, viz., the necessity of the Church for salvation.[8] F.A. Sullivan concludes: "It is safe to say that if his bull defined anything, it was simply the traditional doctrine that there is no salvation outside the Catholic Church."[9] It is therefore to be interpreted in accordance with the theology of "outside the Church" (q.v.). The text was recalled at the 5th Lateran Council (q.v.).[10] *Unam sanctam* may be said to represent an apogee of papal absolutism.

[1]OxDPopes 208–210; H. Wolter, in Jedin-Dolan 4:269-281.    [2]DS 870–875/ND 804.    [3]G.H. Tavard, "The Bull *Unam sanctam* of Boniface VIII," in P.C. Empie and T.A. Murphy, eds., *Papal Primacy and the Universal Church.* Lutherans and Catholics in Dialogue 5 (Minneapolis: Augsburg, 1974) 105–119.    [4]DS 873.    [5]DS 875/ND 804.    [6]Art. cit. (n. 3).    [7]J. Willebrands, "Roman Catholic/Lutheran Dialogue in the U.S.A. Papal Primacy: An Appraisal," OneChr 13 (1977) 207–219 at 211–212, following K.A. Fink, TQ 146 (1966) 500.    [8]*Contra error. Graec.* 2:32; but cf. E. Gallina, "De potestate ecclesiae in temporalibus iuxta doctrinam Bonifacii VIII," EphIurC 45 (1989) 9–37 with bibliog.    [9]*Salvation Outside the Church? Tracing the History of the Catholic Response* (New York—Mahwah: Paulist, 1992) 63–66 at 66.    [10]Sess. 11 (1516)—Tanner 1:643-644.

## BRANCH THEORY

See ANGLICANISM AND ECUMENISM

## BROTHERS AND SISTERS

The "fraternity" *(adelphotês)* is a NT name for the Church (1 Pet 2:17; 5:9). Despite the desirability of using inclusive language, the notion underlying fraternity must be retained in any theoretical or lived ex-

pression of Church. Since sorority is still a neologism, some will prefer to speak of "sisters and brothers" as a translation for "fraternity." Even the sectarian or ideological abuse of "fraternity" should not prevent us from experiencing its richness in a Christian context.[1]

The Greek word *adelphoi* (brothers/brethren) can include sisters, even though there is a word *adelphê* meaning sister. In the NT the common word for the community is "brethren" or "brothers and sisters" (as in the NRSV trans.).[2] It is based on baptism, which makes us adopted children of the Father and gives us Jesus as our brother, the "firstborn among many brothers ["within a large family"—NRSV] (Rom 8:29; Heb 2:2:11-17). This relationship to Jesus is further specified as those who do the will of the Father (Mark 3:35). Various consequences are drawn from this relationship of brother and sister: love of enemies who are children with us of a common Father (Matt 5:44-45); without distinction of dignity all are to accept one teacher, the Christ (Matt 23:8); there is to be no distinction based on riches or poverty (1 Cor 11:20-22, 33), or based on race, social status, or sex (Gal 3:28; Col 3:11); the Easter Jesus restored the dignity of those who had abandoned him when he called them "brethren" (Matt 28:10; John 20:17; cf. Heb 2:11); Ananias recognizes a brother in the persecutor Saul (Acts 9:17; 22:13). Since Paul acknowledges that the Jews who have not accepted Jesus are still "brothers" ["kindred"—NRSV] (Rom 9:3), the Church has to be careful not to place limits on sisterhood and brotherhood. Apart from the common bond of humanity, recognized by ancient Stoic philosophers, by the Enlightenment and French Revolution, the Christian vision accepts that all humans are children of the one Father. This can be seen to lie behind the teaching of Vatican II about the relationship of the People of God with the whole of humanity (LG 14–16).

Augustine (q.v.) has a developed theology of fraternity and sorority: "Our first parents were Adam and Eve: the former father, the latter mother; hence we are brothers and sisters *(fratres).* Let us lay aside our first origin: God is our Father, the Church is our mother; hence we are brothers and sisters *(fratres).*"[3] Elsewhere he states that we are to acknowledge the baptism of those in heresy or schism: as we do not rebaptize them we are to accept them as our brothers, show them great love, and pray for unity with them.[4]

The medieval mendicant movement was a response to the signs of the times. Society was becoming more urbanized and stratified. The friars (from *frater,* a brother) evangelized both in the towns and villages, while other religious were perceived as more remote in their monasteries. Their fraternity was seen as twofold: within the convent and with the people they served. Theirs was a "mixed life" of prayer and apostolate, while the monasteries were mainly contemplative.[5] Religious life (q.v.) has as one of its functions the proclamation of lived fraternity and sorority as a sign of the deepest values of the Church (PC 15; LG 44).

Dating as it does from the early 1960s, one cannot expect Vatican II to have used inclusive language. The word "fraternity" occurs 26 times in Vatican II: GS (12 times), LG (4), PO (2), AA (2), and once each in AG, OE, PC, and UR. It has a range of meanings: the Church gathered around the Eucharist (LG 26) or the Christian community (LG 28; PO 6); the bond uniting Christians with each other (PO 9; AA 23); the love of brothers and sisters (caritate fraternitatis) is to exist between Christians of the East and West (OE 30); Trinitarian union will give an increase of mutual love of brothers and sisters (mutuam fraternitatem—UR 7); the bonds between those already in a particular body are described as fraternal—priests (LG 28; PO 28), the same religious congregation (PC 15), the family builds up the brotherhood/sisterhood of love (LG 41); apart from any ecclesial reference, it is also used to indicate the ideal of living together in the human family (all 12 references in GS; AA 14; AG 8). The word brother/sister (frater) is found 105 times and always with a Christological basis, explicit or implied (26 in UR; 20 in LG; 17 in GS; 14 in PO, 11 in AA, 6 in AG, 5 in PC, once each in DV, SC, CD, OT, NA, GE). Of particular importance are the designation of other Christians as fratres separati in ecumenical texts, the meaning of universal brotherhood in GS, and the brotherhood that should exist between priests. By such usages of fraternitas/fratres, Vatican II stresses the fundamental equality of all in the Church (even in PO 9 which speaks of priests as brothers among brothers and sisters (fratres inter fratres).

In an early preconciliar book, J. Ratzinger developed the note of a theology of brotherhood which is still valid: fraternity and sorority have faith as their only foundation; they must seek to remove barriers; they are built on the Eucharist and will always be frail in implementing in community what is received in sacrament; finally, they are at the service of the world through mission, love, and redemptive suffering.[6]

Christian fraternity and sorority are not merely given, but they are tasks that the disciples of Jesus must undertake: they have to be continually built up and are under constant threat from sin, division, and the temptation to dominate others (cf. Matt 20:25-28; 1 Pet 1:22; 3:8).

---

[1]M. Dujarier, L'Église-fraternité: Les origines de l'expression "adelphotes-fraternitas" aux trois premiers siècles du christianisme. Théologies (Paris: Cerf, 1991); R. Hoet, "Omnes autem fratres estis": Étude du concept ecclésiologique des "frères" selon Mt 23:8-12. Analecta Gregoriana 232 (Rome Gregorian UP, 1982); J. Ratzinger, "Fraternité," DSpir 5:1141-1167; idem, The Open

Circle: The Meaning of Christian Brotherhood (New York, 1966) = Christian Brotherhood (London, 1966); G. Ruggieri, "The Rediscovery of the Church as an Evangelical Brotherhood," Conc 146 (1981) 22–29.  [2]H. von Soden, "Adelphos," TDNT 1:144-146. [3]Serm. 56:10, 14—PL 38:384.  [4]In Ps. 32:29—PL 36:299-300. [5]O. Steggink, "Fraternità apostolica: Storia e rinnovamento," in B. Secondin, ed., Profeti di fraternità: Per una visione rinnovata della spiritualità carmelitana (Bologna: Ed. Dehoniane, 1985) 41–65. [6]Op. cit. (n. 1).

# BUDDHISM

Buddhism[1] is of Indian origin beginning with Siddharta Gautama (ca. 563–480 B.C.E.), the first Buddha ("the enlightened one"). After enforced luxury at his father's house, he escaped to become a wandering hermit, and finally found the Middle Way between his early hedonism and the violent asceticism he practiced for a while. One day under a fig tree he received enlightenment (bodhi), which he later taught the many disciples who surrounded him (dharma). Central to Buddhism are the Four Holy Truths (v. HOLY):[2] everything is suffering (dukkha, which also includes imperfection and impermanence); the source of this suffering is desire (for sensual pleasure, for an afterlife, even for annihilation, for thought); there is an escape from this suffering through the cessation of desire in the final state of bliss and perfection (nirvana); the escape consists of the Noble Eightfold Path: Right Understanding, Right Thought (these are Wisdom), Right Speech, Right Action, Right Livelihood, Right Effort (these are Morality), and finally Right Mindfulness, Right Concentration (Meditation). Another essential doctrine in Buddhism is karma, literally "action." It refers to the consequences of our good and evil actions found in our lives, and which can also resurface in later rebirths. There are Ten Perfections which are to be cultivated by anyone seeking enlightenment: generosity, morality, renunciation, wisdom, energy, patience, truthfulness, determination, loving kindness, equanimity. The Four Sublime States are kindness, compassion, sympathetic joy, and equanimity.

There are several traditions of Buddhism, the best-known to the West being Ch'an in China, called Zen in Japan. This represents a practical, more down-to-earth tradition, which has great emphasis on the essentials, especially on sitting in meditation to cultivate stillness and to devote all one's energies to achieving enlightenment.[3]

Vatican II spoke positively about religions such as Buddhism in the Constitution on the Church: "There are others who search for the unknown God in shadows and images; God is not far from people of this kind since he gives to all life and breath and everything (see Acts 17:24-28), and the Savior wishes all to be saved (see 1 Tim 2:4—LG 16)." More explicit is the Declaration on Non-Christian Religions: "In Buddhism, according to its various forms, the radical inadequacy of this changeable world is acknowledged, and a way is taught whereby those with a devout and trustful spirit may be able to reach either a state of perfect freedom or, relying on their own efforts or on help from a higher source, the highest illumination" (NA 2).

It will be seen that Buddhism is a difficult calling, with features that belong more to monastic rather than ordinary life. Dialogue (q.v.) with Buddhism has grown in recent decades, especially between monks of East and West. There are specific difficulties with Buddhist dialogue. It does not easily take the form of both parties wishing to learn from one another; Buddhists tend to see themselves as the possessors of wisdom which they will share with, without learning from, Christians. Some Christians will accept Buddhism as only a philosophical system, rather than as a religion; they mistake the Buddha's silence about religion and the gods for atheism. Most seriously, no common religious language is shared by East and West, so that misunderstandings are very common. At a superficial level Buddhism can seem to Western eyes very Pelagian: the main emphasis seems to be on human effort without much attention paid to divine help.[4]

Since Vatican II there have been many dialogues at various levels in most of the countries in which Buddhism is strong.[5] Dialogue between Christian and Buddhist leaders can be quite esoteric in language and thought; at the level of ordinary Christians and Buddhists there can be substantial agreement about what constitutes the good life well lived. A key area for dialogue is holiness.[6] Another area in which a common vision between Buddhists and Christians is possible is ecology:[7] Buddhist compassion and Christian love reach also to our world and environment.

The Church has much to gain from dialogue with Buddhists.[8] Christians need to learn a language and concepts with which to dialogue with the East. Both Buddhists and Christians have to realize that all talk about the Godhead is either by analogy or by negation; the Christian Church indeed knows the apophatic way of speaking about God, while Buddhists extend the use of negation to many areas of the spiritual life. It is in the areas of soteriology, theodicy, and sacramentology that the greatest difficulties of mutual comprehension arise. To some extent the new language will have to reflect religious experience, for it is here that Buddhists and Christians meet at the deepest level. Some of the most fruitful dialogue has taken place between monks of the Christian West and Buddhist monks.[9] Dialogue with Buddhists can help the Church to appreciate more deeply the Mystery which is revealed in Christ Jesus, and to hold together in a healthy tension both immanence and transcendence. Such dialogue is unlikely to bring about many conversions from Buddhism to Christianity. Its aim rather will be to make each dialogue partner appreciate the other more fully, and indeed to help both partners to deepen their grasp of the riches of their own tradition.

[1]D. Gira, *Comprendre le Bouddhisme* (Paris: Centurion, 1989); P. Harvey, *An Introduction to Buddhism* (Cambridge: UP, 1990); J. Masson, *Le Bouddhisme: Chemin de libération. Approches et recherches.* Museum Lessianum. Sect. Miss. 59 (Paris: Desclée de Brouwer, 1975); J. Snelling, *The Buddhist Handbook* (London: Century Hutchinson, 1987); Y. Yoo, *Books on Buddhism: An Annotated Subject Guide* (Metuchen, N.J.: Scarecrow, 1976); Communio (Paris) 13/4 (1988); Concilium 116 (1978); LumièreV 38/193 (1989) 1–123.   [2]J. Spae, "Sanctity in Buddhism," JDharma 8 (1983) 182–191; idem, "Buddhist Models of Holiness," Conc 129 (1979) 79–87.   [3]*Zen Buddhism in North America: A History and Directory* (Toronto: Zen Lotus Society, 1986).   [4]F. Chenderlin, "A Christian View of Buddhist Thought and Practice," DivThom 80 (1977) 24–92; R. Costet, "Dialogue entre chrétiens et bouddhistes en Thaïlande," Spiritus 33/126 (1992) 84–91; D. Gira, "Regard chrétien sur le bouddhisme: Réflexions sur le dialogue interreligieux et la mission," Spiritus 32/122 (1992) 26–38; A. Pieris, *Love Meets Wisdom: A Christian Experience of Buddhism* (Maryknoll: Orbis, 1988).   [5]E.J. Harris, "Buddhist-Christian Dialogue," DictEcumMov 112–113; P.O. Ingram and F.J. Streng, *Buddhist-Christian Dialogue: Mutual Renewal and Transformation* (Honolulu: Hawaii UP, 1986); P. Massein, "Les chrétiens face au bouddhisme," ETR 66 (1991) 87–98; M. Zago, "Dialogue with Buddhists in Asia," in W. Jenkinson and H. O'Sullivan, *Trends in Mission: Towards the Third Millennium* (Maryknoll: Orbis, 1991) 280–287. See journals: *Buddhist-Christian Studies* (University of Hawaii), Society for Buddhist-Christian Studies, *Newsletter* (Berkeley, Calif.: Graduate Theological Union).   [6]J. Spae, "Buddhist Models of Holiness," Conc 129 (1979) 79–87 = "Sanctity in Buddhism," JDharma 8 (1983) 182–191.   [7]R. Atkins, "Buddhism and Ecology," Bulletin 27 (1992) 58–65; A. Hunt Badiner, ed., *Dharma Gaya: A Harvest of Essays in Buddhism and Ecology* (Berkeley: Parallax Press, 1990).   [8]P.F. Knitter, "Horizons on Christianity's New Dialogue with Buddhism," Horizons 8 (1981) 40–61.   [9]Bulletin 28 (1988) 1–67; T. Merton, *The Asian Journal of Thomas Merton* (New York: New Directions, 1975); C. MacCormick, "The Zen Catholicism of Thomas Merton," JEcuS 9 (1972) 812–817; M. Wijayaratna, *Buddhist Monastic Life According to the Texts of the Theravâda Tradition* (Cambridge: UP, 1990).

## BUGNINI, Annibale (1912–1982)

More than anybody else, Annibale Bugnini[1] was responsible for the liturgical reforms of Vatican II. Born in Umbria in 1912, he was ordained in 1936 as a Vincentian priest. From 1948 to 1960 he was secretary of the Commission for General Liturgical restoration. In the wake of Pius XII's encyclical on the liturgy, *Mediator Dei* (1947), this period saw important changes, especially the reform of the Holy Week liturgy. During this work Bugnini learned the value of multidisciplinary study of liturgy by liturgical historians, theologians, exegetes, canonists, rubricists, artists, musicians, pastoral clergy, and monks; later in the post-Vatican II period he would draw on such diverse skills.[2] In the years 1960–1964 he was involved in Vatican II. In 1964–1969 he was secretary of Consilium

(Council for the Implementation of the Constitution on the Sacred Liturgy). Suffering much opposition and misunderstanding, he skillfully secured the revision of the liturgical books. He became secretary of the Congregation for Divine Worship (1969–1975). In circumstances the exact details of which are not widely known, he seems to have lost the support of Paul VI, and was transferred from Rome to be Pro-Nuncio Apostolic in Iran (1976), a position he held at his death in Rome (1982). He himself considered two epitaphs for his tomb, *Liturgiae cultor et amator* (Worker for, and lover of, the Liturgy) and "He served the Church." Indeed he remarked in 1979, "I have served the Church, I have loved the Church, I have suffered for the Church."

---

[1]P. Jounel, "Monseigneur Bugnini," MaisD 152 (1982) 187–192; B. Fischer et al., "In memoriam," EphLtg 97 (1983) 3–75; F.R. McManus, "Bugnini, Annibale," NCE 18:46-48. [2]A. Bugnini, *The Reform of the Liturgy 1948–1975* (Collegeville: The Liturgical Press, 1990) 944–952.

## BULGAKOV, Sergii (1871–1944)

After an early commitment to Marxism, Bulgakov was converted to Orthodoxy on the eve of the Russian Revolution. Exiled in 1922, he went to Paris where he became Dean of the new Russian Orthodox Seminary of St. Sergius. There he developed the teaching of Solov'ev on sophiology (q.v.) and returned to the important theme of *sobornost'* (q.v.). He associated Sophia with the substance of God, and he sought to avoid any residue of pantheism by using (and perhaps coining) the word "panentheism," which expresses the ideality of the world in God while avoiding any further identification of God and the world. "Sophia in Bulgakov's system appears both as an intermediate between God and creatures and as identical with God and creatures. It possesses a 'double face,' one turned towards God as the image of God and the other turned towards the world and hence the eternal foundation of the world."[1] On what were largely personal grounds, Bulgakov was denounced as a heretic by Orthodox hierarchs in the 1920s and 1930s, but he always professed his Orthodox faith. The obscurity of his writing led to several misinterpretations of his thought.

Though he stresses the incarnational foundation of ecclesiology,[2] Bulgakov here, as in all of his theology, is wary of a Christocentricism[3] that would neglect the Holy Spirit: "The Church, in her quality of Body of Christ, which lives with the life of Christ, is by that fact the domain where the Holy Spirit lives and works. More than this, the Church is life by the Holy Spirit be-cause it is the Body of Christ. This is why the Church may be considered as a blessed life in the Holy Spirit, or as life of the Holy Spirit in humanity."[4] Again: "We may say that in the present age the Church is the body of Christ precisely as being the eucharistic body on which are bestowed the eucharistic gifts of the Holy Ghost, the giver of life in Christ."[5] Tradition (q.v.) also depends on the Holy Spirit: "From an exterior point of view tradition expresses itself by all that is impregnated with the Spirit of the Church, and in this sense is inexhaustible. . . . In the interior life of the Church its tradition assumes many forms, literature, liturgy, canonical documents, memorials. . . . Tradition is not a book which records a certain moment in the development of the Church and then stops, but a book always being written by the Church's life."[6] Though he accepts hierarchical ministry, he is rather unwilling to see it as above the people.[7] Following Khomiakov (q.v.) he stresses *sobornost'*, which "is opposed both to authoritarianism and to individualism; it is a unanimity, a harmonious sharing of authority. It is the liberty of love which unites believers."[8] His vision widens out into the all-encompassing range of *Sophia* or Wisdom, disclosed in the Incarnation and in the power of Pentecost. Indeed, contemplating institutional Catholicism, modern Protestantism, the social gospel, and secularization, Bulgakov states: "The future of living Christianity rests with the sophianic interpretations of the world and of its destiny. All the dogmatic and practical problems of modern Christian theology seem to form a knot, the unraveling of which inevitably leads to sophiology."[9] The work of Bulgakov provides a rich vein which ecclesiology cannot afford to neglect.

---

[1]G.A. Maloney, *A History of Orthodox Theology Since 1453* (Belmont, Mass.: Nordland, 1976) 64–65. See R. Williams, "Eastern Orthodox Theology," in D.F. Ford, ed., *The Modern Theologians.* 2 vols. (Oxford—New York: Blackwell, 1989) 2:156-159; H.-J. Ruppert, "Sergej N. Bulgakov" in KlassTheol 2:262-276; N. Zernov, *Three Russian Prophets: Khomiakov, Dostoevsky, Soloviev* (London, 1944). [2]"Die Lehre von der Kirche in orthodoxer Sicht," IKiZ 47 (1957) 168–200 at 176–179, 184. [3]S. Swierkosz, *L'Église visible selon Sergej Bulgakov: Structure hiérarchique et sacramentelle,* OrChrAn 211 (Rome: Oriental Institute, 1980). [4]*The Orthodox Church* (London, 1935—Crestwood, N.Y.: St. Vladimir's Seminary, [2]1988) 2. [5]*The Wisdom of God: A Brief Summary of Sophiology* (New York—London, 1937) 206. [6]Op. cit. (n. 4) 26–27. [7]Ibid., 60; M. Semeraro, "Sacerdozio di Cristo e sacerdozio dei fedeli nel pensiero di Sergej Bulgakov," Later 47 (1981) 212–221. [8]J. Pain and N. Zernov, eds., *A Bulgakov Anthology* (London: SPCK, 1976) 127. [9]Ibid., 145–156 at 153, a text taken from *The Wisdom of God* (London, 1937); cf. W.F. Crumm, *The Doctrine of Sophia According to Sergius N. Bulgakov* (Cambridge, Mass., 1965); A. Walker, "Sophiology," Diak (USA) 16 (1981) 40–54; L. Zander, "Die Weisheit Gottes im russischen Glauben und Denken," KerDo 2 (1956) 29–53.

# C

## CALVIN, John (1509–1564)

John Calvin was born at Noyon in Picardy in 1509.[1] From an early age he intended to pursue a Church career, but a religious experience in 1533 convinced him that he had a mission to restore the Church to its original purity. His first visit to Geneva 1536–1538 revealed him to be a rigorist religious reformer, but opposition to his disciplinary norms, and his conflict with Church authority in Berne, led to his leaving Geneva. He returned in 1541, set up a somewhat theocratic state on OT lines, with a very strict morality, and he became the sole arbitrator of what is genuine Christianity.

Calvin's output was huge.[2] He was extremely learned; there were several important influences on his thought: Occamism, medieval mystical movements, Christian humanism, and of course Augustine; he was also a careful exegete.

His doctrine on the Church is found throughout his works,[3] especially in his scriptural commentaries;[4] there is a more systematic treatment in his often revised *Institutes of the Christian Religion*.[5] His doctrine of the divine transcendence powerfully influenced his scriptural aptitude. He strongly affirmed the role of the laity (q.v.). His identification of the Church is typically Reformation: "Wherever we see the Word of God purely preached and heard, and the sacraments administered according to Christ's institution, there, it is not to be doubted, a church of Christ exists . . . for it is certain that such things are not without fruit."[6]

The Church, which he calls Mother (q.v.),[7] "stands by God's election and cannot waver or fall any more than his eternal providence can."[8] Though he is conscious of flaws and failings in the Church, he nevertheless states: "In the Church alone is kept safe and uncorrupted the doctrine in which piety stands sound and the use of the sacraments ordained by the Lord is guarded."[9] Within the visible Church there are those who are Christian only in name. The Church of the elect is invisible to us, is seen with the eyes of God alone; we have in the meantime to keep communion with the visible Church.[10]

He takes over much NT symbolism, especially the favored image of the Body of Christ. He derives a ministerial structure from the NT and notes: "So also today it is (God's) will to teach us through human means." He sets great store by the ministry of word and sacrament, clearly indicating some kind of mediation through them.[11] "We see how God, who could in a moment perfect his own, nevertheless desires them to grow up into manhood solely under the education of the Church."[12]

He had a strong sense of the need of Church discipline, not so much to combat heresy, which is self-evident, but for moral lapses.[13] He refutes at length in the *Institutes* the errors he perceived in the Roman Church,[14] a long section which can still challenge this Church to incarnate gospel values in every aspect of its life. Apart from his ecclesiology, perhaps the lesson that Calvin has above all to teach our age is his sense of the transcendence of God. An age that does not appreciate talk of sin, needs today perhaps to hear more about the holiness of God and his incomparable majesty.

[1]W.J. Bouwsma, *John Calvin: A Sixteenth-Century Portrait* (New York—Oxford: Oxford UP, 1988); A.E. McGrath, *A Life of John Calvin: A Study in the Shaping of Western Culture* (Oxford: Blackwell, 1990); T.H.L. Parker, *John Calvin* (Batavia, Ill.: Lion, 1988—London: Dent, 1975); G.R. Potter and M. Greengrass, *John Calvin. Documents of Modern History* (London: Arnold-Hodder & Stoughton, 1983); E. Iserloh, in Jedin-Dolan 5:361-390. [2]*Corpus Reformatorum,* vols. 29–77; English LCC 20–23. See annual bibliog. CalvinTJ. [3]Anton 2:648-708; A. Ganoczy, "L'Église, communauté ou institution": L'héritage ecclésiologique de Calvin,"

RTPhil 22 (1977) 222–234; T. George, ed., *John Calvin and the Church: A Prism of Reform* (Louisville, Ky.: Westminster-Knox, 1990); B.C. Milner, Jr., *Calvin's Doctrine of the Church.* Studies in the History of Christian Thought 5 (Leiden: Brill, 1970); K. McDonnell, *John Calvin, the Church and the Eucharist* (Princeton, 1967); L. Schummer, "Pour redécouvrir l'Église selon Jean Calvin," RRéf 42/4 (1991) 23–28; R.S. Wallace, *Calvin, Geneva, and the Reformation* (Grand Rapids, Mich.: Baker, 1991).   [4]Anthology LCC 23:361-406   [5]1538 ed. (London: Collins 1988); 1559 ed. LCC 20–21.   [6]*Institutes* (1559) 4:1, 9—LCC 21:1023-1024.   [7]Ibid., 4:1, 1; 1, 4—1011–1012, 1016.   [8]Ibid., 4:1, 3—1015.   [9]Ibid., 4:1, 12—1026.   [10]Ibid., 4:1, 7—1021–1022; cf. 4:1, 2—1013.   [11]Ibid., 4:1, 2—1013; 4:3, 1-14—1053–1064.   [12]Ibid., 4:1, 5—1017; cf. 4:1, 5-6—1016–1021.   [13]R. White, "Oil and Vinegar: Calvin on Church Discipline," ScottJT 38 (1985) 25–40.   [14]*Institutes* 4:2-20—1041–1521.

## CANON OF SCRIPTURE

See RECEPTION

## CARDINALS

The origins of the cardinalate are obscure. Two etymologies have been proposed: *incardinare,* from Gregory I (q.v.), who transferred into vacant dioceses bishops whose own dioceses had been overrun by invasions; *cardo* (hinge), implying one on whom the administration turns. In earlier times "cardinal" could be applied to priests permanently attached to a church. Later cardinal-priests were the priests assigned to various Roman churches, 25 from the 6th century, but later raised to 28. Cardinal-deacons looked after the poor in the seven districts of Rome. About the 8th century cardinal-bishops were appointed as the pope's representatives. The cardinals were a loosely knit body until the time of Leo IX (1049–1054). In time they would rank as Roman princes, taking precedence immediately after the pope. United as a college (consistory), they were the pope's immediate advisors.[1] Canon 1 of the Synod of Rome (1059) under Nicolas II laid down that cardinals elect the pope,[2] a decree implicitly endorsed at Lateran III (1179—q.v.), whose first canon referred to earlier decrees on the subject.[5]

After the schism, when thirteen cardinals created the antipope Clement II in 1084, reflection on the role of cardinals gradually grew into an ideology. It was one which would last until the victory of the papacy at the councils of Florence (q.v.) and Trent (q.v.). St. Peter Damian (q.v.) had seen cardinals as a senate like that which in ancient Rome shared sovereignty with the emperor.[4] Others during the Middle Ages saw the cardinals as constituting the "Roman Church" along with the pope, and he could not act independently of them.[5] By the time of the Council of Florence, the notion of cardinal was quite inflated; it was thought that the cardinalate was of divine origin, and cardinals ranked in precedence above patriarchs.[6]

Cardinals are appointed by the pope. Their number was fixed at 70 by Sixtus V in 1586. John XXIII derogated from this rule in 1958, so that there is now no upper limit. The latter also decided in 1962 that all cardinals should be consecrated bishops, a move which reflected the doctrine of the collegiality of bishops in the government of the Church. Pope Paul VI twice reorganized the College of Cardinals, most notably restricting the right to enter the conclave for the election of a new pope to those under eighty years old.[7]

The *Code of Canon Law* deals with cardinals mainly in cc. 349–359. It envisages primarily two kinds of cardinal: those who exercise office in the Curia (v. VATICAN), who must reside in Rome and, moreover, relinquish their office at the age of 75 (CIC 354); those who are diocesan bishops and come to Rome when summoned by the pope (CIC 356). They have three major functions: election of a new pope; collegially assisting the pope when called together about some grave matter; serving the pope through various offices (CIC 349). On the death of a pope, the College of Cardinals takes over the government of the Church during the interregnum *(sede vacante),* according to norms set down in the apostolic constitution, *Romano Pontifici eligendo* (1975), of Paul VI.[8]

[1]G. Alberigo, *Cardinalato e collegialità: Studi sull'ecclesiologia tra l'XI et il XIV secolo* (Florence, 1969); M. Andrieu, "L'origine du titre de Cardinal dans l'Église romaine," *Miscellanea Giovanni Mercati.* ST 125 (Vatican, 1946) 5:113-144; T. Bertone, "Il servizio del cardinalato al ministero del successore di Pietro," Sales 48 (1986) 109–121; S. Kuttner, "Cardinals. A History of a Canonical Concept," Trad 3 (1945) 129–214; C. Lefebvre, "Le cardinalat et la communio," in I. d'Ercole and A.M. Stickler, eds., *Comunione interecclesiale—collegialità—primato—ecumenismo. Communio 12.* 2 vols. (Rome: LAS, 1972) 983-1001; P.A.B. Llewellyn, "Le premier développment du collège des cardinaux," ReschSR 67 (1979) 31–44; J.H. Provost in Coriden, CIC 286–287.   [2]Mansi 19:879, 907.   [3]Tanner 1:211.   [4]*Opusc.* 31:7—PL 145:540.   [5]Congar, Augustin 115–116.   [6]Alberigo (n. 1) 79 and n. 45.   [7]*Sacro cardinalis consilio* (26 Feb. 1965) and *Ingravescentem aetatem* (21 Nov. 1970)—AAS 57 (1965) 296–297; 62 (1970) 143–145/CanLawDig 6:312-313; 7:143-145.   [9]AAS 67 (1975) 609–645 at 611–613.

## CASEL, Odo (1886–1948)

Born in 1886 at Koblenz-Lützel, during his university days at Bonn he met Dom Herwegen, future abbot of Maria-Laach, an acquaintanceship which would determine his monastic entry there in 1913. In a letter of uncertain date he noted that he had his first intuition of the doctrine of the mysteries *(Mysterienlehre)* at a High Mass, an intuition that would deepen during thesis work on the Eucharistic doctrine of St. Justin (q.v.).[1] Sent subsequently to Bonn for philological studies, he was in an atmosphere in which the study of religions, especially Greco-Roman, influenced him deeply and led to a doctoral thesis on "The Mystical Silence of the Greek Philosophers" (1918).

His output was substantial: over 100 articles, several books, and over 20,000 letters—all of which are needed to grasp his thought, which he never presented in a systematic way. Studies constantly appear.[2] His central insight about the Mystery would not be exceptional in the post-Vatican II period, but was highly significant when first penned. First, the Mystery is the Godhead itself, infinite, inaccessible, threefold, holy. God is revealed to his creatures in a veiled way, and they have an obscure sense of his presence. Second, the Mystery is revealed in the Incarnation; Christ is the Mystery in person, manifested in human flesh. The apostles preach this Mystery, so that by faith and the mysteries, Christ ever lives in the Church. The first two, then, are bound up in a third sense of mystery: the person of the Savior, his redemptive work and the work of grace are ours through the mystery of worship. There is for the believer a real sharing in the actual saving acts that constitute the mystery of Christ. He lays great stress on Rom 6:1-11, in which he sees the death of Jesus present in the baptismal action[3][6]

Casel continued his interest in mystery religions right up to his death, seeing parallels or analogies, though not dependence, between them and Christianity; rather they were both expressions of the same human spirit which reaches within and without to express the divine mystery which is apprehended by the religious person. In the mystery religions he saw a conviction that their god reaches down to human misery and by his presence transforms it.

Though scholars have since found faults in his interpretations of all his key sources[4]—mystery religions, Scripture, and the Fathers—his basic intuitions have not been reversed.[5] His insights have indeed been honed, modified, corrected. Part of the difficulty is that he eschewed the current scholastic language and method and was misinterpreted by those of this tradition. There is continuing difficulty in understanding how Christ is present in his mysteries as celebrated in the liturgy, but the fact is now part of our present liturgical heritage (cf. SC 2, 5, 7, 10–13, 41).[6]

A deepened theology of *anamnêsis* (remembrance) is necessary to render Casel's thought more systematic and to deal with the *how* question, addressed somewhat differently, for example, by St. Thomas.[7] The contribution of Casel to liturgy is immense; his value for ecclesiology is also significant. Ecclesiology can never again be separated from liturgy, its highest expression (SC 10); in some sense the Eucharist (q.v.) is at the very heart of the Church (LG 11); contemplation and liturgy belong together in the Christian life; mysticism belongs to the life of the Church in such a way that it is seriously impoverished when the mystical is ignored or downplayed. Finally, his work is not without ecumenical significance: for the Protestant tradition, his emphasis on one offering of Christ is important; for the East, his centrality of the Eucharist and his sense of liturgical epiphany could strike deep chords.[8]

[1]*Lettre d'automne 1948, in Le Mystère de l'Église* (Paris: Mame, 1965) 9, 41, cited I.-H. Dalmais, "La liturgie célébration du mystère: Dom Odo Casel (1886–1948)," QuatreF 21–22 (1985) 65–78, n. 1. [2]O.D. Santagada, "Dom Odo Casel: Contributo monografico per una bibliografia generale delle sue opere, degli studi sulla sua dottrina e della sua influenza nella teologia contemporanea," ArLtgW 10 (1967) 7–77; A. Haüssling, "Bibliographie Odo Casel 1967–1985," ArLtgW 28 (1986) 26–42; idem, "Bibliographie Odo Casel" (1986), ArLtgW 29 (1987) 189–198; cf. 105–106; A. Gozier, "L'Influence de Dom Odo Casel en France," ArLtgW 28 (1986) 22–25; see M.J. Krahe, *Der Herr is der Geist: Studien zur Theologie Odo Casels.* Pietas liturgica 2–3, 2 vols. (St. Ottilien: EOS, 1986) [A. Schilson, ArLtgW 29 (1987) 375–384; B. Neunheuser, MüTZ 38 (1987) 275–288]; A. Schilson, *Theologie als Sakramententheologie: Die Mysterientheologie Odo Casel.* Tübingen theologische Studien 18 (Mainz: Matthias-Grünewald, 1982); A. Triacca, "Dom Burhard Neunheuser, intreprete di Dom Odo Casel: Rassegna bibliografica," Sales 40 (1978) 625–632. [3]*The Mystery of Christian Worship* (Westminster, Md., 1962—German 1932); "Mysteriengegenwart" JbLtgW 8 (1929) 145–224. [4]Surveys T. Filthaut, *Die Kontroverse über die Mysterienlehre* (Warendorf, 1947 = French *La théologie des mystères. Exposé de la controverse,* Paris 1954); H.B. Meyer, "Odo Casels Idee der Mysteriengegenwart in Neuer Sicht," ALtgW 28 (1986) 388–395; B. Neunheuser, ArLtgW 3 (1953) 104–122; 4 (1956) 316–324; 5 (1958) 333–353. [5]A. Gozier, *La porte du ciel: Réactualiser le mystère avec Odo Casel* (Paris: SOS, 1987); B. Neunheuser, "Odo Casel in Retrospect and Prospect," Worship 50 (1976) 489–503; T.F. Koernke, "Mystery Theology," NewDict-SacWorship 883–891; MaisD 14 (1948) 1–106; M. McMahon, "Towards a Theology of the Liturgy: Dom Odo Casel and the *Mysterientheorie,*" StLtg 3 (1964) 129–154; A.M. Triacca, "Odo Casel e il movimento liturgico," EphLtg 101 (1988) 153–181; E. von Severus, "Der Werdegang und die Grundgedanken O. Casels," EcOr 5 (1988) 165–175. [6]A.A. Häussling, "Odo Casel—Noch von Aktualität?," ArLtgW 28 (1986) 357–387; "La théologie des mystères de Dom Casel dans la tradition catholique," in A. Pistoia and A.M. Triacca, *L'économie du salut dans la liturgie.* Bibliotheca Ephemerides liturgicae subsidia 25 (Rome: CLV-Ed. Liturgiche, 1982) 143–156; G. Lafont, "Permanence et transformation des intuitions de Dom Casel," EcOr 4 (1987) 261–284. [7]M. Matthijs, "'Mysteriengegenwart' secundum S. Thomas," Ang 34 (1957) 393–399. [8]H.-J. Schulz, "Odo Casel," UnaSan 39 (1984) 52–55.

## CATECHISMS

The word "catechism" comes from Greek, meaning "to speak so as to be heard," hence "to instruct." For many people it suggests a method of learning through question and answer, and there have indeed been many such catechisms. In the OT there are short summary texts of Israelite faith that are often called catechetical (e.g., Deut 6:1-15; 7:7-11; 30:15-17); likewise in the NT, e.g., the Eucharist (1 Cor 11:23-26; the resurrection (1 Cor 15:3-7), the mystery of Christ (1 Tim 3:16). Other books are often seen as catechetical instructions (Jas, 1 Pet).

Even before the close of the NT period there were handbooks of moral and liturgical instruction, such as the *Didachê.* As the catechumenate (q.v.) developed, so too did formal teaching, especially in the times immediately preceding and following the actual initiation ceremonies.[1]

Soon comprehensive treatments of the faith appeared, e.g., Augustine's *Enchiridion* on faith (Creed), hope (Lord's Prayer) and love (moral precepts),[2] and his *De catechizandis rudibus,* a work of catechetical instruction for simple people.[3] In the Middle Ages such works multiplied; some were in question-and-answer format. St. Thomas taught that catechesis *(catechismus)* should precede baptism;[4] and he gave a series of sermons on the Creed as well as writing a work on the articles of faith (Apostles' Creed) and the sacraments.[5]

At the time of the Reformation there were several very significant catechisms: Luther's *Small Catechism* in questions and answers, which was meant for parish priests and preachers, and his *Larger Catechism,* which was a theological treatise on all aspects of the faith.[6] Sts. Peter Canisius and Robert Bellarmine (q.v.) both wrote catechisms which went into over a hundred editions in succeeding centuries. Very influential, too, was the Catechism which emerged after Trent, often called the "Roman Catechism," but the full title of which is self-explanatory: *Catechism Ordered by the Decree of the Council of Trent for Parish Priests and Published by Command of the Supreme Pontiff Pius V* (1566).[7] It had the structure which by then was common: Creed, sacraments, commandments, prayer.

At Vatican I it was proposed to have a universal catechism to replace the myriad diocesan ones. It was to be a small catechism, not displacing, however, the Roman one. But even then the debate showed that some bishops feared a Romanizing tendency which would not respect cultural diversity, evident, for instance, in the contrast between Latin views and Germanic and Anglo-Saxon ones.[8] There were various suggestions made after this council up to Vatican II.[9] In particular, Pius X produced a catechism for the Roman province, *Catechism of Christian Doctrine,*[10] modeled on one by an Italian bishop, M. Casati (1782).

The catechisms until the 1930s were of the doctrinal kind.[11] From then, in Germany, under the influence of people like the liturgist J.A. Jungmann, it was proposed that catechesis should be kerygmatic, following the approach of salvation history. At the Bangkok Study Week on Mission Catechetics (1962), it was further realized that before evangelization (q.v.) there is often a need for pre-evangelization, which is characterized by listening to where people really are before evangelization proper can begin.[12] By the 1970s the thrust of catechetics had become anthropological,

following the theological approach that is characteristic of K. Rahner (q.v.) and many others.[13]

New catechisms for adults appeared, notably the controversial "Dutch Catechism" (1967), which in subsequent editions had to carry a supplement with revisions approved by a commission of cardinals.[14] A more successful venture was the "German Catechism," largely drafted by W. Kasper.[15] It lacks any extensive treatment of sin or commandments.

At Vatican II there were calls not for a new catechism but for a catechetical directory (CD 44), which was eventually published in 1971 by the Congregation of the Clergy.[16] Paul VI made important statements on catechetics to the First International Catechetics Congress[17] and in the post-synodal exhortation on evangelization.[18] He determined that the Fourth Synod of Bishops (1977) would be devoted to catechesis.[19] At this synod there was a request by many of the bishops for a new universal catechism. John Paul II issued a post-synodal exhortation *Catechesi tradendae* in 1979[20] which was a rich exploration of all aspects of catechesis.

Meanwhile some in the Church awaited with apprehension[21] the appearance of the new *Catechism of the Catholic Church,* which appeared in French in 1992. Responsibility for the catechism rested with a commission of cardinals, but a main drafter was Bishop C. Schönborn.

This new *Catechism* is meant primarily for bishops, for those writing catechisms, and others in the Church. It is not meant to displace more popular catechisms but to be their theological basis. It is a long work, 676 pages in the French text which, as the original one, will retain importance even after the Latin text appears.

It follows the Tridentine model in its four parts: I. "The Profession of Faith" (faith, revelation, the Apostles Creed); II. "The Celebration of the Christian Mystery" (sacramental economy, the seven sacraments, sacramentals, funerals); III. "Life in Christ" (the human vocation, moral principles, the human community, law and grace, the decalogue); IV. "Christian Prayer" (teaching on prayer, commentary on the Our Father.) The work is admirably cross-referenced, and must be taken as four interlinking parts. A strong feature is its constant scriptural basis (over 3000 references) and the fact that it draws heavily on the liturgies of both East and West (over 100 references). There are quotations from over 50 Eastern and Western authors, the most frequent being Augustine (88 times), St. Thomas (65 times) and St. Irenaeus (32 times). But lesser authors are also featured, e.g., St. Thérèse of Lisieux, Bl. Elizabeth of the Trinity, and two writers who have not been beatified (Julian of Norwich and Cardinal Newman).

The *Catechism* generally avoids taking up theological positions. It is an exposition of the teaching of the

Church, which remains largely at the level of verbal explanation. A serious difficulty arises from the sheer comprehensiveness of the book. It contains Church teaching of very different levels, often without an indication of the status of the teaching: revealed faith, matters connected with revelation, binding teaching of the universal magisterium, common Church teaching, positions fairly unanimously adopted by theologians. No hierarchy of truths (q.v.) is easily detectable. A hermeneutic of the *Catechism* will be a task for the years ahead.

Teaching on ecclesiology appears passim in the *Catechism;* the main treatment is in the context of the 8th and 9th articles of the Creed, "I believe in the Holy Spirit, the Holy Catholic Church" (nn. 683–975).

The new *Catechism* will be a most important document if it is not misused: it must not stifle but rather encourage theology; its purpose is more to present the truth than to condemn errors; it is a resource book for preachers and bishops, rather than a text to be quoted in undigested form; it is to be inculturated in different places, rather than be imposed everywhere as a uniform and static text. The Church will have to await the reception (q.v.) of the *Catechism* in the years ahead. Commentaries and subsidiary studies are already pouring out in various languages.[22]

There has been much controversy about the English translation. A competent translation into idiomatic English with awareness of the need for inclusive language was made by an American priest, reportedly Douglas Clark. After representations to Rome, another translation was commissioned, and made apparently by the Australian bishop Eric Darcy. It is more literal, with a harsh insensitivity to inclusive language. For example, "man," etc., is found when it could easily have been avoided, sometimes added even when not in the original French. Many would regard this translation as a serious pastoral mistake which ultimately can be laid only at the door of the highly placed Church officials; it provoked much anger and negativity toward the *Catechism* at the time of its publication, and not only among those of strongly feminist views.

Very interesting will be the attitude of the Churches of the East, and the Anglican and Protestant Churches of the West. Some initial reactions have been positive.

[1]E.g., E. Yarnold, ed., *The Awe-Inspiring Rites of Initiation: Baptismal Homilies of the Fourth Century* (Slough UK: St. Paul's, 1971). [2]PL 40:231-290/ACW 3/LNPF 3, Ser. 1: 237-276. [3]PL 40:309-348/ACW 3/LNPF 3, Ser. 1:282-314. [4]ST 3a, q.71, a.1. [5]*Collationes super Credo in Deum,* trans. *The Three Greatest Prayers* (London, 1937); *De articulis fidei et Ecclesiae sacramentis*—trans. in part, *Catechetical Instructions of St. Thomas* (New York, 1939, 1953). [6]Bekenntnisschriften 499–527 and 543–733. [7]Latin text ed., P. Rodríguez (Vatican—Barañain—Pamplona: Navarra UP, 1989). [8]Mansi 50:699-702. [9]M.T. Donnellan, *Rationale for a Universal Catechism* (Washington, D.C.: The Catholic University of America, 1972); cf. E. Kevane, "Vatican I, St. Pius X and the Universal Catechism," Divinitas 31 (1987) 291–330. [10]Trans. E. Kevane (Arlington, Va.: Center for Family Catechetics, 1986). [11]M. Warren, ed., *Sourcebook for Modern Catechetics* (Winona, Minn.: St. Mary's Press, 1983). [12]A. Nebreda, "East Asian Study Week on Mission Catechetics," LumVit 17 (1962) 717–730. [13]A. Exeler, "Catechesis as the Proclamation of a Message and the Interpretation of Experiences," LumVit 25 (1970) 561–573. [14]*A New Catechism: Catholic Faith for Adults* (New York: Herder & Herder—London: Burns & Oates, 1967). Edition with Supplement (London: Search Press, 1970). [15]*The Church's Confession of Faith: A Catholic Catechism for Adults* (San Francisco: Ignatius, 1987 from German 1985). [16]Flannery 2:529-605. [17]AAS 63 (1971) 758-764. [18]*Evangelii nuntiandi* (1975) n. 44 with 45-48, 54—AAS 68 (1976) 34-35, 35-38, 43/Flannery 2:729-730, 730-732, 735. [19]C. Dooley, "Catechesis in Our Time," LvSt 7 (1978–1979) 194–204. [20]AAS 71 (1979) 1277–1340/Flannery 2:762-814; J. Laforest, "Une étape importante dans l'histoire de la catéchèse," LavalTP 38 (1982) 9–18. [21]Cf. Conc 204 (1989). [22]E.g., in English: B. Hill and W. Madges, *The Catechism: Highlights and Commentary* (Mystic, Conn.: Twenty-third Publications, 1994); B.L. Marthaler, ed., *Introducing the Catechism of the Catholic Church: Traditional Themes and Contemporary Issues* (London: SPCK—Mahwah: Paulist, 1994); J.E. Regan et al., *Exploring the Catechism* (Collegeville: The Liturgical Press, 1994); M.J. Walsh, ed., *Commentary on the Catechism of the Catholic Church* (London: Chapman, 1994).

## CATECHISTS

The word "catechists" does not appear in the NT, but their functions were probably undertaken by those called "teachers" (q.v.). Catechetical schools *(didaskaleion)* existed from the 2nd century, famous being those of Justin at Rome (before 165) and of Clement of Alexandria (from 189 though the school was earlier) and of Origen who took over the Alexandrian school about 204 C.E. These seemed also to present secular subjects, especially dialogue with Greek philosophy. They were nearer to being a high school or even theological faculty than a place for elementary instruction.

Among the most ancient texts relative to the function of the catechist are to be found in the *Pseudo-Clementine Writings.* Under this designation are grouped together several apocryphal texts comprising *The Letter of Peter to James, The Letter of Clement to James, The Homilies, The Recognitions.*[1] The dating of these texts is a delicate matter: they are formed of various strata and rereadings. In their final form, one can place them in the 4th century, but their core was probably from the time of Origen in the first half of the 3rd century, and using still earlier material. The passages about the catechists seem to belong to earlier strata.[2] The catechist was independent of what we would later call the clergy. In the *Letter of Clement to James* (14) he was called a recruiting officer. By the time of the Pseudo-Clementine homilies it was a presbyter-catechist; in the *Recognitions,* the catechist has disappeared. In the *Apostolic Tradition* (q.v.) the catechist could be lay or ecclesiastic. Shortly afterwards catechesis became a priestly, above all an episcopal task, and so remained for many centuries.[3] Many of the Fathers produced catechetical works (v. CATECHISMS).[4] There was always an insistence on the duty of parents in passing on the faith to their children. From the Middle Ages, manuals to help pastors and parents in the catechetical task emerged (v. CATECHISMS).

In modern times there were several developments. From the 19th century the educational system as we know it evolved. In Catholic schools religious instruction was given. But in state schools in many countries this was not possible, and the Church sought various ways of teaching young people the faith and of preparing them for the sacraments. A prime example of this kind of instruction, the Confraternity of Christian Doctrine (CCD), which had roots in the 16th century, received its *magna charta* from Pius X in 1905,[5] and became mandatory in the 1917 canon law (CIC 711 § 2). From the 1930s there was an awareness of the need of special training for catechists, and centers became established from then on. The American CCD set up its own formation courses for laity.[6]

A parallel development was the rise of the catechist in missionary territories. Since, of necessity, missionary priests traveled continually to many Mass stations, the key figures in villages were the catechists; Vatican II acknowledged their importance (AG 17; cf. 15). It implied a spiritual leadership of the catechists in the local community, in which they teach doctrine and preside over prayers in their community. The council also spoke of a possible canonical mission being bestowed on them in a liturgical function (AG 17). Later Pope Paul VI, in his apostolic letter on renewing the ministries of reader (q.v.) and acolyte (q.v.), explicitly suggested that a conference of bishops might seek to have catechist as a ministry liturgically established in an area.[7] Soon afterwards he praised the work of catechists in his apostolic exhortation on evangelization.[8]

The 1983 *Code of Canon Law* devotes several canons to catechesis and the role various people assume in it (CIC 773–780).[9] The concern for catechetics "pertains to all members of the Church in proportion to each one's role" (CIC 774 § 1), with parents having a special responsibility (§ 2). The obligation of providing for proper catechesis falls primarily on the bishop, and second on the local pastor; catechists have a special role, and must receive adequate training (CIC 776, 780).

The new *Catechism* notes that times of renewal in the Church were times of strong catechesis (n. 4); the challenge to catechists may never have been greater than at this present time.

[1]PG 1:1157-1474; 2:19-646/ANF 8:73-212, 223-246; Patrology 1:59-63; R. Trevijano in EncycEarCh 1:179.   [2]A. Faivre, "Les fonctions ecclésiales dans les Écrits Pseudo-clémentines," RevSR 50 (1976) 97–111.   [3]M. Sauvage, *Catéchèse et laïcat: Participation des laïcs au ministère de la Parole* (Paris, 1962).   [4]F. Cocchini, "Catechesis," EncycEarCh 1:150-151.   [5]Encyc. *Acerbo nimis* ASS 37 (1905) 613–625/Carlen Encyclicals 3:29-35.   [6]J.E. Kraus, NCE 4:155-156; B.L. Marthaler, "The Rise and Decline of the CCD," ChicSt 29 (1990) 3–15.   [7]*Ministeria quaedam* (1972). [8]*Evangelii nuntiandi* (1975) nn. 44, 72—Flannery 2:729-730, 747-749.   [9]J.A. Fuentes, "The Active Participants in Catechesis and Their Dependence on the Magisterium (Canons 773–780)," StCan 23 (1989) 373–386.

## CATECHUMENATE

In the post-Vatican II revision of liturgy, the *Rite of Christian Initiation of Adults* (RCIA) uses the term "catechumenate" only for the period from inscription to the Lent preceding baptism, when the term "elect" replaces "catechumens" for those undergoing the scrutinies and other final rites. But it is common to refer to the whole process of initiation (q.v.) up to baptism as the catechumenate.

In the NT we do not have indications about preparations demanded before baptism; on the contrary, it would seem that faith, that is, a confession of the lordship of Jesus (e.g., Acts 2:36-41) and his resurrection, was the basic requirement, and that after baptism there would be teaching (q.v.). In the 2nd century there were indications of some preparation of candidates, but it was only with the *Apostolic Tradition* (q.v.) in Rome that there was a process of initiation of considerable complexity.[1] It began with an examination of the candidates by the teachers (*doctores*—q.v.) concerning their motivation. Their manner of living had also to be attested: certain trades and professions had to be abandoned before admission to the catechumenate (15–16/16). The catechumenate lasted three years, but behavior was a more important criterion than the time requirement (17/17:1-2). Always after instruction there was prayer for the catechumens (18/18:1). Catechumens had to stay apart: during prayers (18/18:1-2); they could not give the kiss of peace (*pacem*), for their kiss (*osculum*) was not yet holy (18/18:3); they were dismissed after the prayer (*precem*—prayer of the faithful?) after hand imposition (q.v.) by the teacher (19/19:1); they were not to sit at table at the Lord's Supper (*cenadeipon*) with the faithful (27/26:5). In the Holy Week preceding baptism the chosen were again examined, and there were special prayers and exorcism (q.v.) by the bishop (20/20:1-9).

From the beginning of the 3rd century there was a catechumenal structure also in Egypt and North Africa, and there is evidence of similar structure soon afterwards in Palestine, Syria, and Spain. The careful account of the final states of instruction of the candidates in the journal of Egeria (ca. 381–384—q.v.)[2] may indicate that this had already fallen into disuse in her native Galicia (NW Spain or Gaul). During Lent there was daily instruction about the whole of Scripture for those who were to be baptized; other catechumens who were still in an initial stage were excluded. This teaching, she said, was called "catechetics" (*cathecisis*)—an indication perhaps that the word was novel to her. The Creed was also given and explained by the bishop; in Holy Week it had to be recited, "given back," to the bishop. Egeria did not seem to know about a similar handing over of the Our Father. She mentioned that the most sacred mysteries were explained only during Easter Week.[3]

During this 4th century there is evidence that people became catechumens for secondary motives, e.g., to marry a Christian, to enter public office in the empire. They endlessly postponed baptism, and at Epiphany time each year bishops sought to awaken the slumbering catechumens.[4] Later, by the 5th century, the only period of preparation was the season of Lent itself, and by the next century the classical catechumenate was no more.[5]

Traces of the catechumenate remained in medieval theological writing and in some liturgies. In the sixteenth and following centuries there were often mass baptisms of converts in mission territories, but there was also a movement, which steadily gathered momentum, requiring serious preparation and instruction before baptism. But unlike the ancient catechumenate, these latter were not in a liturgical setting.

In the 20th century, there was growing emphasis on baptismal preparation. The Sacred Congregation of Rites, without waiting for Vatican II, restored the conferring of baptism by stages; it divided up the existing rite of baptism into seven parts.[6] The council called for the reestablishment of the catechumenate (SC 64–66; CD 14).

The *Rite of Christian Initiation of Adults* (RCIA) which appeared in 1972 is one of the most mature documents of the whole liturgical reform.[7] It is explicitly very adaptable to different situations. It consists of three main stages. First, the catechumenate proper, which is in several steps: rites of acceptance into catechumenate (41–74); rites of the catechumenate, mostly celebrations of the Word, exorcisms and blessings (75–117). Second, the catechumenate is followed by the election or enrollment of names at the beginning of the Lent preceding actual baptism (nn. 118–137). Henceforth the candidates are called "the elect," and the stage is called "The Period of Purifi-cation and Enlightenment." It consists of scrutinies, which are liturgies around the great Gospel readings from John, chapters 4, 9, and 11, celebrated on the 3rd–5th Sundays of Lent. The scrutinies are readings, homily, intercessions, and exorcisms (nn. 150–156, 164–177). During this final period there is the Presentation of the Creed (nn. 157–163), and of the Our Father (nn. 178–184). Other preparatory rites are celebrated on Holy Saturday (nn. 185–205). Third, the whole process of initiation concludes during the Easter Vigil with the celebration of baptism, confirmation (by the priest presiding at the Vigil if no bishop is present), and the reception of the Eucharist. The RCIA envisages a further "Period of Postbaptismal Catechesis or Mystagogy" (nn. 244–251; cf. AG 15; CIC 789).[8]

The RCIA seeks conversion at three levels: cognitive development as the faith is unfolded; affective growth in attitudes and spirituality; behavioral change in turning from sin, in the acquisition of virtue, and in acts of love.[9] The Copernican revolution of the RCIA places baptism not at the beginning of conversion but as the outcome of a conversion process which is begun well before the sacrament and will continue after it.

The rite is marked by a significant role of the Holy Spirit or pneumatology (q.v.).[10] The notable ecclesiological aspect of the RCIA is its insistence on initiation being carried out in the community, with various contributions from catechists, deacons, priests, and laity, all under the pastoral care of the local bishop.[11] It is a rite of the whole believing community, which is active through ministries, prayer, and example in the upbuilding of the catechumens. Various hierarchies have laid down norms for the catechumenate in their area, taking advantage of the flexibility envisaged by the rite.[12]

The catechumen, even though not fully initiated, is said to "belong to the Church" and to be "part of Christ's household" from the first acceptance into the order of catechumens (RCIA 47), a position that reflects Vatican II (LG 14; AG 10) and the *Code* (CIC 206; cf. 788; 851).[13] This sense of belonging to the Church is particularly important for those who, for example because of marital situations, cannot be admitted to baptism.[14]

The RCIA will probably take decades to become completely inserted into the life of the Church and to influence profoundly the way we think about conversion and grace. In the meantime partial evaluations have been found generally favorable.[15] Since its publication in 1972 the RCIA has also been the basis or model for various programs of Church and particularly parish renewal. This reflects the versatility of the rite and its power, as well as stressing the fact that initiation is lifelong until at death the Eucharist becomes Viaticum.

[1]M. Dujarier, *A History of the Catechumenate: The First Six Centuries* (New York: Sadlier, 1979). [2]*Itinerarium/Peregrinatio/Pilgrimage*, ch. 46. [3]Cf. E. Yarnold, *The Awe-Inspiring Rites of Initiation. Baptismal Homilies of the Fourth Century* (Slough UK: St. Paul, 1971). [4]Dujarier (n. 1) 78–84. [5]Ibid., 96–111 [6]AAS 54 (1962) 310–338. [7]See *The Rites of the Catholic Church*. Vol. 1A. Initiation (New York: Pueblo, 1988) nn. 36–251; M. Dujarier,

*The Rites of Christian Initiation: Historical and Pastoral Reflections* (New York &c.: Sadlier, 1979); J.B. Dunning, *New Wine: New Wineskins, Exploring the RCIA* (New York &c.: Sadlier, 1981); A. Kavanagh, "The Norm of Baptism: The New Rite of Christian Initiation of Adults," Worship 48 (1974) 143–152; idem, "Christian Initiation of Adults: The Rites," ibid., 318–335; W.J. Reedy, ed., *Becoming a Catholic Christian* (New York: Sadlier, 1979); Conc 122 (1979).    [8]See E. Mazza, *Mystagogy: A Theology of Liturgy in the Patristic Age* (New York: Pueblo, 1989).    [9]R.D. Duggan, "Conversion in the 'Ordo initiationis christianorum adultorum,'" EphLtg 96 (1982) 57–83, 209–252; 97 (1983) 141–223; R. Duggan, ed., *Conversion and the Catechumenate* (New York—Ramsey, 1984).    [10]G. Celada, "Prescencia del Espíritu Santo el la celebración de la iniciación cristiana," Nicol 16 (1989) 53–86. [11]G.S. Worgul, "The Ecclesiology of 'The Rite of Christian Initiation of Adults,'" LouvSt 6 (1976–1977) 159–169.    [12]B. Fischer, "The National Statutes for the Catechumenate Approved by the Conference of Bishops of the USA on November 11, 1986," StLtg 19 (1989) 125–132.    [13]J.H. Provost, in Coriden, CIC 129–130.    [14]M. Dujarier, "Sur le statut du catéchumème dans l'Église," MaisD 152 (1982) 143–173; cf. M. Legrain, "Les ambiguïtés actuelles du statut catéchuménal," NRT 94 (1972) 1053–1064; 95 (1973) 43–59.    [15]R.B. Kemp et al., "The Rite of Christian Initiation of Adults at Ten Years," Worship 56 (1982) 309–335; B. McEvoy, "The Rite of Christian Initiation of Adults: A Progress Report," CleR 69 (1984) 22–26.

## CATHARI

Cathari (Greek *katharos*—pure) is the name applied to several sects beginning with the Novatians (q.v.) at the Council of Nicaea.[1] They had in common a separatist impulse, generally with a rejection of sinners from their communities. The name is mostly associated with a sect in Germany in the second half of the 12th century, who were known in France as the Albigensians (q.v.).[2]

[1]Canon 8—Tanner 1:9-10.    [2]L. Duvernoy, *Le catharisme: La religion des Cathares* (Paris: Privat, 1976); G. Gonnet, "Cathars and Waldenses within the Church in the Middle Ages," Conc 200 (1988) 89–93; M. Lambert, *Medieval Heresy: Popular Movements from the Gregorian Reform to the Reformation* (Oxford: Blackwell, [2]1992) 105–146; S. Runciman, *The Medieval Manichee* (Cambridge, 1947) 116–170; J. Russell, "Interpretations of the Origin of Medieval Heresy," MedSt 25 (1963) 26–53; J. Ventadour, *Les mystéres de la tradition cathare: Le fantastique enseignement des albigeois* (Paris: Ed. Vecchi, 1988).

## CATHERINE OF SIENA, St. (1347–1380)

Caterina Benincasa[1] was born in Siena probably about 1347. At the age of six she had the first of her significant visions as she walked in Siena: a vision of Christ in pontifical attire, accompanied by Peter, Paul, and John the Evangelist; Christ gazed at her, smiled, and blessed her. This vision contains elements that would be foundational in her life. Christ appears not as in Bethlehem, or as the Crucified, but as pontiff.[2] Her first biographer, Raymond of Capua, notes that from that time she was given to asceticism, making a vow of virginity a year later.[3]

At about the age of eighteen she became a Dominican tertiary, a member of the *mantellate* who wore the Dominican habit but lived at home, coming together for various prayers. Though the tertiaries engaged in works of charity, Catherine herself remained at home in solitude for three years, at the end of which she received the grace of mystical marriage. After this she moved out and became more and more active in service of others. Later she became involved in public affairs, seeking to bring peace to Florence, and advising popes. She traveled to Avignon and later to Rome, where she died in 1380. She was canonized in 1461.

Her writings comprise 382 letters, 26 prayers, and the book of *The Dialogue*.[4] There is a huge bibliography on her works.[5] This centers on her mystical experience and her ecclesiology, which is our interest here.[6] Though her education was at best spasmodic, she is regarded by H.U. von Balthasar (q.v.) as the most metaphysical of the mystics,[7] and she was declared a Doctor (q.v.) of the Church in 1970.[8]

She was intensely concerned with renewal and reform of the Church.[9] She did not hesitate to rebuke popes and ecclesiastics in her letters; her prayers show her appreciation both of the beauty and the frailty of holders of ecclesial office. She was passionately solicitous for the unity of the Church. Through Christological and Trinitarian mysticism she penetrated deeply into the mission of the Church, which is to make effective the blood of Christ in humanity. She commits all to the three Persons to whom she attributes Power, Wisdom, and Clemency, respectively.[12]

At the beginning of the more political and ecclesiastical part of her career, she shows four deep commitments: salvation of others, fidelity to the papacy, adherence to Christ crucified, and work for the unity of the Church. The great ecumenical vision of 1 April 1376 may seem to contrast with current ecclesiology. She writes: "I saw the people, Christians and unbelievers, entering the side of Christ crucified."[11] Six decades later the Council of Florence would still presume the culpability and non-salvation of those outside the Church (v. OUTSIDE THE CHURCH). However, it is probable that Catherine envisaged the conversion of non-Christians before their salvation.

The rich ecclesiology, both explicit and implicit, in her works stresses above all the theme of love: love received by the Church; love returned by the Church; love for the Church. Her teaching and life give deep insights into the role of intercession for the Church and the world.[12]

[1]M.A. Fatula, *Catherine of Siena's Way* (Delaware: Glazier—London: Darton, Longman & Todd, 1987); J.M. Perrin, *Catherine of Siena* (Westminster, Md., 1965).    [2]L. Tincani, *Santa Caterina da Siena per la Chiesa e per il Papa* (Rome: Ed. Cateriniane, 1977) 23.    [3]*Legenda maior* 1:3—Eng. trans. G. Lamb, *The Life of St.*

*Catherine of Siena* (London: Harvill, 1960)—C. Kearns (Delaware: Glazier, 1980).    [4]*Il Dialogo della divina providenza ovvero Libro della divina dottrina*, G. Cavallini, ed. (Rome: Ed. Catheriniane, [2]1980)—Eng. trans. S. Noffke, *Catherine of Siena: The Dialogue* (New York: Paulist, 1980); *Le lettere di S. Caterina da Siena*, P. Misciatelli, ed. 6 vols. (Florence, 1940)—Trans. S. Noffke (Binghamton, N.Y.: Medieval and Renaissance Studies, 1988); K. Foster and M.J. Ronayne, *I Catherine: Selected Writings of Catherine of Siena* (London: Collins, 1980); *Le orazioni*. G. Cavallini, ed. (Rome: Ed. Cateriniane, 1978)—trans. S. Noffke, *The Prayers of Catherine of Siena* (New York: Paulist, 1983).    [5]L. Zanini, *Bibliografia analitica di S. Caterina da Siena, 1901–1950* (Rome: Centro Naz. di Studi Cateriniani, 1971) supplemented 1951–1975 by L. Zanini and C. Paterna (1985) and 1975–1985 by C. Paterna (1989).    [6]M.V. Bernadot, "Au service de l'Église," VieSp 18 (1928) 129–160; R. Moretti, "Il dramma della chiesa in Caterina da Siena," in *Mysterium ecclesiae in conscientia sanctorum*. Bibliotheca carmelitica 2:6 (Rome: Ed. Teresianum, 1967) 231–283 = EphCarm 17 (1966) 231–283; S. Noffke, "Catherine of Siena: Mission and Ministry in the Church," RevRel 39 (1980) 183–195; D. Orsuto, *St. Catherine of Siena: Trinitarian Experience and Mission in the Church*. Diss. exc. (Rome: Gregorian, 1990); L. Tincani, *Caterina da Siena per la Chiesa e per il papa* (Rome: Ed. Cateriniane, 1977).    [7]"Lineamenti della dottrina di S. Caterina da Siena," Quaderni cateriniani 24 (Siena: Cantagalli, 1980) 1–15.    [8]AAS 62 (1970) 673–678.    [9]*Dialogue* 1 and passim, there and in Letters.    [10]Passim, e.g., *Prayers* 5—Eng. trans. (n. 4) 45–50.    [11]*Letter* 219—Noffke (n. 4); *Letter* 65, p. 207.    [12]M. O'Driscoll, "Mercy for the World: St. Catherine's View of Intercessory Prayer," SpToday 32 (1980) 46–56.

## CATHOLIC

The word "catholic" (Greek *kath'holon*—according to the whole) makes its first appearance in Christian literature in Ignatius of Antioch (q.v.) about 110 C.E.: "Where Jesus Christ is present, there we have the catholic Church."[1] Scholars dispute whether the meaning here is "universal" or "true/authentic," with the majority favoring the former,[2] just as the bishop presides in the local Church, Jesus Christ presides in the universal Church. The *Martyrdom of Polycarp* (v. POLYCARP), written about 50 years later, uses the word in both senses: three times meaning the universal Church[3] and once in the sense of authentic or fullness of the Church, when it describes Polycarp as "bishop of the catholic Church at Smyrna."[4] The idea is more developed by Cyril of Jerusalem (d. 386): the Church is catholic because it is spread throughout the world; it teaches in fullness all the doctrines people should know; it brings all people into religious obedience; it is a universal cure for sin; it possesses all virtues.[5] The two meanings that persist most in the patristic period are those of universality and orthodoxy. Indeed, one of St. Augustine's major arguments against the Donatists (q.v.) was that they were, far from being universal, confined to North Africa; the Eunomians on the other hand were found only in the East.[6] The division of Christ's clothes on Calvary symbolized the spread of the Church to the four corners of the earth.[7] In his writings Augustine uses the noun *"catholica"* 240 times between 388 and 420 C.E.[8] The Donatists' reply was naturally to appeal to the other meaning of "catholic," viz., purity of doctrine. The two meanings coexisted for a thousand years,[9] but with the split from the East, the Latin Church adopted the name "Catholic," while the East called themselves "Orthodox."

In the medieval period we find the basis for a deeper theology of catholicity emerging, helped by the dominant expression of the Church as a gathering of the faithful *(congregatio fidelium),* which is readily open to universal notions. Thus in St. Thomas Aquinas we have the various elements for a theology of catholicity: the thesis of the grace of Christ as head of the Church—all are one in him and under him at least potentially.[10] Furthermore, the Church is universal in three senses: unlike the Donatists, it is found in every place (cf. Rom 1:8), having three parts—on earth, in heaven, and in purgatory; it includes persons of all states (cf. Gal 3:28); it is boundless in time from Abel (q.v.) to the consummation of the ages.[11] Again, because, apart from heretics, the one faith believed by all the Church is catholic, shown in universal precepts and worship throughout the world.[12]

The two basic meanings of "catholic" in tradition have their foundation in Scripture. The disciples of Jesus knew that they were in receipt of a universal mission (Matt 28:19; Mark 16:15; Acts 1:8), even though Jesus' own mission was largely confined to the Jews of his time (see Matt 15:24; 10:6);[13] they sedulously preserved the tradition handed on (see 1 Cor 15:3; Gal 1:6-8; 1 Tim 3:15; Jude 3); they knew Christ as the *plêrôma* (see Eph 1:23; 3:19; 4:13; Col 1:19; 2:9; John 1:16; v. BODY), or fullness of divine gifts, and the center of the universe.[14] Since we are dealing with catholicity in the Church when we consider diversity in unity, we can thus see as an expression of catholicity the varying ecclesiologies within the unity of the NT itself (v. NT ECCLESIOLOGIES).

After the geographic expansions of the 15th century, another aspect of catholicity arose, one that would be worked out only in the 20th century, viz., a qualitative catholicity, or the ability of the Church to belong truly to each culture and period of history.[15] After the Reformation, "catholic" became one of the four notes (q.v.) of the Church.[16]

The three aspects of catholicity currently recognized are taken up by Vatican II, but within a theology of communion (q.v.). In LG 13 we find an overall view of catholicity: the notion, dear to orthodox theologians among others, of the source of catholicity being the Trinity;[17] the universality of races, nations, and cultures; unity in diversity of members of the Church and of local churches vis-à-vis the whole Church; catholicity as reaching out to all of humanity.

This concluding reference to all people everywhere leads into a treatment of various categories of persons precisely as related to the Church: the catholic faithful (LG 14); other Christians (LG 15); those who are not Christian (LG 16). The final article of the chapter considers the role of evangelization "so that the fullness of the whole world may move into the people of God, the body of the Lord and the temple of the Holy Spirit" (LG 17).

Since Vatican II there has been notable interest in inculturation (q.v.). We can summarize the contribution of Vatican II through a quotation from B. Kloppenburg, who uses the council's own words: "The Church does not destroy or reject, but considers attentively and respectfully, examines in a benevolent spirit, acknowledges, preserves intact, fosters, cultivates, develops, purifies, heals, strengthens, elevates, takes into Christian life, and even at times into the liturgy, and brings to perfection in Christ—all that is not indissolubly bound up with superstition and error, all that is good, just, holy, lovable and beautiful, whether in the minds and hearts of persons and in their spiritual endowment, or in the abilities, resources, temporal and spiritual goods, socio-cultural values, customs, cultures, rates, ascetical and contemplative traditions, arts, teachings, and ways of acting of peoples, nations, and religions. Note well, even religions! for all this ('precious elements of religion and humanity' GS 92) is a preparation for the gospel, a guidance towards the true God, a secret presence of God, a hidden seed of the word, rays of truth which enlightens every man."[18]

A full grasp of the *Catholica* demands a true universalist spirit open to all that is good, excluding no one and no good value. Just as languages led to confusion among peoples (see Gen 11:1-9), so at Pentecost, the Holy Spirit brings people of different languages and cultures into a new unity (see Acts 2:1-11). The many voices today must be subsumed into a unity; freedom must not, however, prove detrimental to truth.[19] But each new set of questions posed to the Church is an invitation to a deeper catholicity; moreover, those who answer the critical questions of our time will tend more and more to be laity and the dispossessed, in addition to professional theologians and Church pastors.[20]

A developed catholicity will be modeled on Trinitarian love, which embraces all in the cross and resurrection of Christ.[21] If the Mystery is being lived out, then there is no room for a deadening uniformity: rather there must be a catholic life, namely of unity in diversity. First, there is a universality based on peoples: the Church was born in diversity (Acts 2:5-11), but became one in mind and heart (Acts 4:32). Second, there is unity of patrimony: the Church must not just make the nations hers, but the nations must make the Church

theirs. Two striking quotations by Y. Congar make the point: "One writer on missiology has said that the definitive commentary on the gospels cannot be written until China, Japan and India have become Christian." He then quotes C. Journet: "The expansion of the Church reveals her to herself."[22] A similar notion is found in B. Kloppenburg: "To the extent that the Church does not in fact become Brazilian, the Brazilian will not be of the Church."[23] Third, there is unity in the diversity of Church life and government: different states, different ministries, offices, and charisms show forth the Church's diversity, which should be in healthy tension with the call to unity.

We have been using the word "catholicity," which at base is rather abstract, even though it refers to very concrete situations and aspects of the life of the Church. "Catholicism" is more concrete, yet in our time quite ambiguous. We can speak of catholicism even where the norms of adherence to the Church are extremely tentative, or where, as in situations of liberation and grass-roots ecclesial communities, there is a strong adherence to values and to people's needs, if not always to an institution. We can speak of "popular catholicism" if we retain the root meaning of the adjective, viz., of the people.[24] The whole area of popular religiosity (q.v.) can be destructive of a full unity in faith and sacraments, or it can be evidence of the tradition of a people living intensely high moments of religious commitment. The particular, or what belongs only to one people or area, can be divisive, if it is not open to wider values and the whole of the *Catholica*.

In the ecumenical movement one finds descriptions of Churches as being of the "Catholic" or "Protestant" type, a distinction that has roots in the 18th century, surfacing again at the opening meeting of the WCC (Amsterdam 1948), and that has had P. Tillich as popular exponent. While the adjective "catholic" may be predicated of all Christian Churches which profess Christ and confess the Creed, there are nonetheless certain facets of Catholicism which are less at home in various Protestant Churches. ". . . the term catholic (usually with a capital C) is predicated of those Churches which are conspicuous for their sacramental, liturgical, hierarchical, and dogmatic features, and those which stress continuity with the institutional and doctrinal developments of the patristic and medieval periods."[25] Quite central to the catholic view is historical mediation of God's grace and message through sacraments and institutions. Roman Catholicism (q.v.)[26] adds communion with the supreme pontiff as an essential feature of the Church (LG 14). The "protestant" type of Christianity places greater emphasis on the initiative of the Word of God and the response of faith, focused on the doctrine of "faith alone," and the freedom of the believer to follow the inspiration of the Holy Spirit even at the price of conflict with ecclesiastical authority.[27] It tends, moreover, to reject absolute claims for any relative or finite reality; structures are seen as impediments or as unnecessary for Christian life, which is characterized by the immediacy of God's Word and the response of faith.[28]

Furthermore, in the ecumenical movement, the notion of "Unity in Diversity" is widely accepted—indeed, uniformity was rejected at the first World Conference of Faith and Order (Lausanne, 1927). But some would see a crisis over the concept of unity in diversity: some stress a unity which approaches uniformity; others emphasize diversity so intensely that unity in the sense of fully committed communion inevitably disappears.[29] Even the Lutheran World Federation's "Unity in Reconciled Diversity" (1977) presents difficulties: the Churches are not at one with regard to authority; the nature of the consensus of faith needed in a genuine communion is not clear; the relation between Church structure and credal consensus is too often left vague.[30]

Catholicity poses several challenges: the ordained and the non-ordained ministries must work in unity; charism (q.v.) must be fostered; the local (q.v.) Church must be developed without a particularism that would impinge on unity; the central authority of the Church must respect the legitimate demands and aspirations of local Churches. It is clear that while catholicity is a gift of the Spirit deep within the Church, it remains also a task (see UR 4). In the end, catholicity will be protected only in an ecclesiology of communion which is rooted in the Eucharist and in the lives of each people. Orthodox ecclesiology is very concerned to stress the Eucharistic center of catholicity, but with due attention to the hierarchical structure of the local Church. Furthermore, we should see the emergence of local and general councils as being concerned with the issue of the local and the universal Church.[31] A full treatment of the Orthodox theology on catholicity also involves a consideration of *sobornost'* (q.v.).

Theological pluralism (q.v.) is an especially difficult area for the emergence of a truly catholic expression or understanding fitted to the needs and visions of particular peoples. Again, catholicity will be an essential element in the correct transmission of authentic tradition;[32] or in the celebrated tessera of Vincent of Lérin (d. ca. 450), we are to hold what is believed everywhere, always, and by everyone *(quod semper, quod ubique, quod ab omnibus).*[33] In theology, as in other matters, the institutional structures can try to impose unity (and also unfortunately uniformity); but catholicity remains always an activity of the Spirit working through the concrete situation of each local Church. Catholicity embraces the *whole* Church *(ec-*

*clesia universa)* and the Church everywhere *(ecclesia universalis).*[34]

The Church always learns from the past. Its history has shown that "Catholicism is characterized by a radical openness to all truth and every value. It is comprehensive and all embracing towards the totality of Christian experience and tradition, in all the theological, doctrinal, spiritual, liturgical, canonical, institutional, and social awareness and diversity of that experience and tradition."[35] The full notion of catholicity is found only alongside the other gifts and tasks of unity, holiness and apostolicity within an eschatological perspective.[36] The new *Catechism* (nn. 830–843) shows much of the richness of the notion.

[1]*Ad Smyr.* 8:2.  [2]Views in A. de Halleux, "'L'Église catholique' dans la lettre ignacienne aux Smyrniotes," ETL 58 (1982) 5–24; J.N.D. Kelly, "'Catholic' and 'Apostolic' in the Early Centuries," OneChr 6 (1970) 274–287. [3]Salutation, 8:1; 19:2. [4]16:2. [5]*Catechesis* 18:23—PG 33:1044/Halton 84–85. [6]*Serm.* 46:8, 18—PL 38:280-281; *Tr. in Ioan.* 13:3—CCL 33:131. [7]*Tr. in Ioan.* 118:4—CCL 36:656. [8]Congar, L'Église une 153, n. 14. [9]Ibid., 152–158. [10]*4 Sent.* q.13, q.2, sol. 1; ST 3a, q.8, a.3. [11]*In Symbol. apostolorum* 9; cf. C. Lepelley, "Le catholicisme dans le temps," QuatreF 25–26 (1988) 142–153. [12]*In Eph.* 4, lect. 2 (199); *Super 1 decret.* 1; *In Boeth. de Trinitate* 2, q.3, a.3. [13]F.A. Sullivan, *The Church We Believe In. One, Holy, Catholic and Apostolic* (Dublin: Gill and Macmillan—Mahweh: Paulist, 1988) 88–91. [14]S.S. Verhovskoy, "Catholicity and the Structures of the Church," SVlad 17 (1973) 19–40 at 24–28; J. Witte, "Die Katholizität der Kirche: Eine neue Interpretation nach alter Tradition," Greg 42 (1961) 193–241 at 201–222 (cf. comment Congar, L'Église une 163, n. 46). [15]Congar, L'Église une 159–160; F.A. Bednarski, "Il problema della specificità della cultura cattolica alla luce della dottrina del Concilio Vaticano II," Ang 57 (1980) 10–31; J. Bosc, "The Catholicity of the Church," OneChr 6 (1970) 338–347. [16]H. Moureau, DTC 2:1999-2012; see J.W. O'Malley, ed., *Catholicism in Early Modern History: A Guide to Research* (St. Louis: Center for Reformation Research, 1988). [17]Cf. Y. Congar, L'Église une 161–165; J. Meyendorff, *Catholicity and the Church* (Crestwood, N.Y., St. Vladimir's Seminary Press, 1983); Verhovskoy (n. 14) 21; T. Ware, *The Orthodox Church* (Harmondsworth: Pelican, [6]1983) 244–249; Sullivan (n. 13) 88–93. [18]*The Ecclesiology of Vatican II* (Chicago: Franciscan Herald, 1974) 150. The Council texts are LG 13, 16, 17, 23; GS 42, 92; SC 37; AG 3, 9, 11, 18, 22; NA 2; UR 4. [19]W. Beinert, "Die Katholizität der Kirche," in W. Baier et al., eds., *Weisheit Gottes—Weisheit der Welt.* FS J. Ratzinger. 2 vols. (St. Ottilien: EOS, 1987) 2:1021-1037. [20]F. Bussini, "Changes in Theology and the New Contours of the Church's Catholicity," Conc 115 (1978) 33–45; A.T. Sanon, "Où est l'Église universelle? Promesses anciennes et attentes nouvelles," LumièreV 137 (1978) 63–79. [21]H.U. von Balthasar, *Catholique* (Paris: Fayard, 1976) 17–35. [22]Cited in *The Mystery of the Church* (London, 1960) 146, n. 2. [23]Op. cit. (n. 18) 153. [24]C. Jungo, "Du catholicisme à la communauté catholique: La recherche d'une identité," FreibZ 30 (1983) 425–445. [25]A. Dulles, *The Catholicity of the Church* (Oxford: Clarendon, 1985) 169. [26]Y. Congar, "Romanité et catholicité: Histoire de la conjonction changeante des deux dimensions de l'Église," RSPT 71 (1987) 161–190. [27]A. Dulles, "Catholicity and Catholicism," TDig 34 (1987) 203–207 at 204 = ConcordiaTQ 50 (1986) 81–93. [28]Dulles (n. 25) 166 and 5–8. [29]H. Meyer, "'Unity in Diversity,' a Concept in Crisis: Lutheran Reflections,"

OneChr 24 (1988) 128–141.    [30]Ibid., 135–139; cf. "Catholicité et apostolicité: Documents d'études préparés par la Commission 'Catholicité et Apostolicité,'" Irén 43 (1970) 163–200 at 168–171. [31]J. Meyendorff, "The Catholicity of the Church: An Introduction," SVlad 17 (1973) 5–18; J.D. Zizioulas, "The Eucharistic Community and the Catholicity of the Church," OneChr 6 (1970) 314–337; cf. replies to Verhovskoy (n. 14) by Archbishop Basil of Brussels 41–52 and Metropolitan John of Helsinki 53–59.    [32]N. Denyer, "Catholic and Apostolic," ScotJT 38 (1985) 515–528; J.A. Möhler, Symbolism (London, 1906) sections 37–39.    [33]PL 50:639; see J. Mados, El concepto de la tradición en S. Vicente de Lerins. Analecta Gregoriana 5 (Rome, 1933).    [34]G.P. Montini, "Ecclesia universalis an ecclesia universa?," Periodica 74 (1985) 43–62. [35]R. P. McBrien, Catholicism (London: Chapman, Study Edition, 1984) 1173; cf. A. Dulles, op. cit. (n. 25).    [36]H. Wagner, "Aspekte der Katholizität," Catholica 30 (1976) 55–68; cf. W. Beinert, Um das dritte Kirchenattribut. 2 vols. (Essen, 1964).

## CATHOLIC ACTION

See APOSTOLATE

## CATHOLICISM, EARLY

Early Catholicism (Frühkatholizismus/Protocatholicisme/Précatholicisme) formerly was a pejorative term found in some 19th- and 20th-century Protestant writers[1] to describe the developments in the subapostolic age (c. 95–150 C.E.) which are seen as retrograde steps compared with the pristine evangelical character of the original message.[2] Such are: concern for tradition and apostolic literature; emerging distinction between laity and clergy; hierarchical rather than charismatic organization; development of a monarchical episcopate; emerging principle of transmitted authority or apostolic succession; a conception of faith in objective rather than subjective categories; an emphasis on sound doctrine; a moralization of faith which tends towards legalism; concern for ecclesiastical consolidation and unity; a growing emphasis on sacraments which mediate salvation; waning of apocalyptic eschatology.[3] Some authors such as E. Käsemann[4] trace "early catholicism" to the later writings of the NT, such as the Pastoral Epistles, 2 Pet, and Luke, which they compare unfavorably with the more charismatic situation of the Church found in the undoubtedly genuine letters of Paul. Such a position easily, if not inevitably, leads to an assertion of a "canon within the canon," that is, a list of books of the NT which are more reliable witnesses and of greater value to the historian and theologian than others in the acknowledged canon. In the face of this view, the Catholic Church would insist on the inspired nature of all the NT books, even if they portray a diversity in theology.[5]

[1]K.H. Neufeld, " 'Frühkatholizismus'—Idee und Begriff," ZkT 94 (1972) 1–28; idem, "Cattolicesimo nascente: Proposta di un termine," RivBib 36 (1988) 255–258.    [2]J.C. Turro and R.E. Brown, JBC 2:533; R.E. Brown and R.F. Collins, NJBC 1053.    [3]C.C. Black II, "The Johannine Epistles and the Question of Early

Catholicism," NT 28 (1986) 131–158 at 132; J.D.G. Dunn, Unity and Diversity in the New Testament: An Enquiry into the Character of Earliest Christianity (Philadelphia: Westminster, 1977) 341–366; J. H. Elliott, "A Catholic Gospel: Reflections on 'Early Catholicism' in the New Testament," CBQ 31 (1969) 213–223 at 214; V. Fusco, "Sul concetto di protocattolicesimo," RivBib 30 (1982) 401–434; D. Harrington, "The 'Early Catholic' Writings of the New Testament: The Church Adjusting to World History," in Light of All Nations. Good News Studies 3 (Wilmington: Glazier—Dublin: Veritas, 1982) 61–78 = The Word in the World. FS F.L. Moriarty (Cambridge, Mass.: Weston College Press) 97–113. L. Sabourin, "Traits 'protocatholiques' dans le Nouveau Testament," ScEsp 38 (1986) 301–315 = TDig 35 (1988) 237–243.    [4]Essays on New Testament Themes. Studies in Biblical Theology 41 (London: SCM, 1964) 169–195.    [5]P. Grech, "Unità e diversità nel Nuovo Testamento," RivBib 30 (1982) 289–445.

## CELESTINE V, Pope St. (1294)

After the death of Nicholas IV (1288–1292), a conclave lasting over twenty-seven months eventually elected a hermit, Pietro del Morrone. He was hailed in the circles of the Spirituals as the "Angel Pope" expected by the Joachimite movement. Some saw his election as the beginning of a new era for the Church. He proved to be a disappointment, turning out to be easily manipulated by Charles II the Lame, king of Naples. After six months he abdicated, in December 1294, and for fear of a schismatic movement of Spirituals gathering around him, he was not allowed to return to his beloved solitude but was kept in quite honorable confinement until his death two years later. Apart from setting a precedent in abdicating, Celestine showed that personal holiness does not guarantee an impressive papacy. His ineffectual pontificate laid the way open for the energetic Boniface VIII (q.v.). Dante had a low opinion of Celestine, probably referring to him as "the coward who made the great refusal."[1] Later history has been kinder, and there is some revisionist writing.[2] He was canonized in 1313.

[1]"Che fece per viltà il gran rifiuto"—Inferno 3:59-60.    [2]P. Herde, Cölestin V. 1294. Päpste und Papsttum Bd 16 (Stuttgart: Hiersemann, 1981) [S.M. Pagano, Benedictina 29 (1982) 257–260; W. Imkamp, RömQ 78 (1983) 127–133]; H. Wolter, in Jedin-Dolan 4:267-269; OxDPopes 206–208. See O. Gurgo, Celestino V (Novara: Istit. Geografica de Agostini, [2]1988).

## CELIBACY OF CLERGY

Clerical celibacy is a complex issue with a history which is not yet fully agreed upon among scholars. The modern problematic gives an urgency to historical, theological, psychological, and sociological studies. The celibacy of the Catholic clergy can be paralleled in other religions, in which continence, if not perpetual celibacy, is demanded of priests and religious dedicants.[1]

The OT, as well as other religions, sets a high store on the virginity of brides (Deut 22:14-29—v. VIR-

GINS). Though the OT has a most positive view of sexuality and marriage, yet there are laws of ritual purity for priests and for those entering the sanctuary (Lev 15:1-18, 31; 22:4-9; 1 Sam 21:4-5).

The elaborate laws of OT purity were annulled by the NT. Since the ministers of the NT were not called priests, nor was there hieratic language used about them (V. PRIESTS, MINISTERIAL), conditions for those having a specialized function at worship were not detailed in the NT. Teaching about celibacy is found in various places. In Matt 19:12 there is the statement by Jesus about eunuchs for the kingdom. Though some exegetes have recently sought to interpret this logion in its immediate context of marriage and *porneia*,[2] the majority still hold that here there is an invitation to celibacy extended to those to whom God grants the ability.[3]

Paul in 1 Cor 7:25-40 is concerned with issues of celibacy and marriage. He envisions those not married, widowed, those who for faith motives have left their spouse, and those abstaining within marriage. There is a preference for celibacy (vv. 7-8, 40).[4] The majority of exegetes would still hold that some of the apostles lived married lives (1 Cor 9:5), but a few would argue that the Greek "sister [as] wife" indicates celibacy or continence. Another NT text perhaps indicative of celibacy is the addition found only in Luke of "wife" in the list of abnegations for the sake of the kingdom (18:29).[5]

In the Pastoral Epistles there is an insistence on an *episkopos* or *diakonos,* being "the husband of one wife" (1 Tim 3:2, 12; Titus 1:6). This has been traditionally interpreted as being negative towards second marriages, but it may only mean fidelity to one's actual wife, and not be a prohibition of a widow/widower remarrying.[6]

The issue of celibacy in the pre-Nicene period is highly controverted, largely because of paucity of evidence. Some assert that there was a tradition about clerical celibacy back to apostolic times, or at least that there was a demand for continence in the context of liturgical celebration.[7] The more common view is that in this period there were indeed some celibates, such as Origen, Tertullian; other bishops and priests were married, and it is not possible to assert a norm of continence in their case.[8] But all of the early texts are difficult to interpret.[9]

The earliest legislation on celibacy was given by the Spanish Council of Elvira (ca. 306). The eighty-one canons, perhaps only one-quarter of which may be genuine, with the remainder being late 4th century, are generally rigorist, and seek in particular to direct the behavior of the clergy. The famous 33rd canon reads: "It is decreed that bishops, presbyters, and deacons, or *(vel)* all clergy placed in the ministry, are to abstain completely *(in totum)* from their wives, and not beget sons. Whoever does so, let him forfeit his rank among the clergy."[10] The translation of the canon is controverted:[11] Does the *vel* explain who those in the ministry are (bishops, etc.) or does it refer to others as well? Does *in totum* refer to the council, to partial, or to total abstinence? A further problem dividing scholars is whether this prohibition was novel at the time. Legislation tends to be conservative, and there is then a prima facie case for suggestions that this canon reflects an earlier tradition of law or practice. But the lack of evidence leaves the question open.

Current scholarship tends to dismiss the account of the Church historian Socrates (Scholasticus), who stated that a celibate bishop, Paphnutius, appealed at Nicaea (q.v.) that celibacy should not be imposed on the clergy.[12] The supposed incident had scarcely any influence in the patristic period, though it would be used by Gratian.[13] The Council of Nicaea (325—q.v.) in canon 3 forbade the clergy to have women living with them who are not above suspicion (v. VIRGINS).[14]

In the late 4th-century *Apostolic Constitutions* (q.v.) we see that though a person once married could be ordained bishop, priest, or deacon, no marriage was allowed after ordination.[15] It further laid down: "A bishop, a priest or a deacon shall not repudiate his wife on the pretext of piety; if he does so he is to be excluded *(aphorizesthô),* if he persists he is to be deposed."[16] Leo the Great (440–461—q.v.) reiterated this latter prescription but bade them live as brother and sister. But from about the time of Popes Damasus I (366–384) or Siricius (384–399), clerical continence was being insisted upon in the West. The reasons given were ascetical and also included cultic purity for sacred ministers, paralleled in OT and in paganism.[17] From the 5th century celibacy or at least continence would seem also to be urged on subdeacons because of their sacred liturgical ministry.[18] And henceforth many regional councils reiterated legislation on celibacy. Such repetition leads one to suspect that the ideal or norms of clerical celibacy were meeting practical resistance.

From about the Gregorian reform (v. GREGORY VII) there was frequent legislation against concubinage, continuing into the medieval councils.[19] Lateran II (q.v.) declared orders to be an impediment to matrimony.[20] In the period of High Scholasticism, canonists and theologians disputed whether this was of divine or ecclesiastical law; St. Thomas Aquinas held the latter.[21]

At the eve of the Reformation, clerical marriage and concubinage were common. The Reformers condemned clerical celibacy in theory and practice, and this led to enforcement decrees at Trent (q.v.).[22] The picture in the West from Trent to Vatican II was of general insistence on clerical celibacy, with all attempts to change the law being rebuffed.[23]

The history of the East follows a different tradition. Though revisionist historians like R. Cholij[24] seek to

establish that celibacy actually belongs to the more authentic tradition in the East also, the practice has been
fairly constant since the Council of Trullo (q.v.), also
called Quinisext (692). The custom in many places for
some centuries before Trullo was a demand for absolute continence in the case of bishops.[25] If a bishop-
elect was married, his wife was to live at his expense
at a remote monastery, or become a deaconess. This
was reenacted also in Trullo.[26] The 13th canon of this
council covered several issues.[27] Clerics were permitted to marry only before orders. The legislation showed
some anti-Latin feelings. It criticized those who would
forbid a married priest, deacon, or subdeacon the use
of marriage. But sexual relations were forbidden before the celebration of liturgy, viz., Saturdays. The council appealed to apostolic tradition, which by that time
would scarcely be apodictic; it utilizes the 3rd canon of
the Council of Carthage (390 C.E.), which hardly more
convincingly had also appealed to apostolic tradition.
But there is a difference: the Council of Carthage was
insisting on perpetual celibacy or continence; Trullo
was insisting only on periodic continence.[28]

Strangely, the Council of Trullo gave rise to an insistence on marriage for the lower clergy, so that if a
priest's wife died, he had to cease from ministry. In
time greater frequency of Eucharistic celebration led
to a demand for monk-priests who would be able to
celebrate daily. The Uniate Churches (q.v.) generally
retained the Eastern tradition and allowed married
clergy; such provision still prevails in the new *Code*
for the Eastern Churches.[29]

At Vatican II there was some discussion about
celibacy. It was recognized as a gift to the Church (LG
45; AA 4), and the celibacy of religious was praised
(PC 12). The issuing of statements on clerical celibacy
was complicated by the danger that the Eastern practice could be denigrated, even as the Western or Latin
dispensation is being advocated (LG 29; OT 10). The
council allowed the ordination of married men to the
diaconate (LG 29—v. DEACONS).

Paul VI reserved to himself an extended statement
on clerical celibacy, which appeared as the encyclical
*Sacerdotalis caelibatus* (1967).[30] It places celibacy
within a Christological, ecclesiological, anthropological, and eschatological framework. The objections to
clerical celibacy are outlined and given a preliminary
answer based on tradition and the experience of the
Church (nn. 7–11). The law of celibacy is confirmed
(nn. 14–16) and the reasons for it are presented (nn.
17–34). The discipline of the Western Church is described (nn. 36–37). The differing practice of the
Eastern Churches is noted with some significant observations: the Holy Spirit has providentially and super-
naturally influenced that part of the Church; there is an
appropriateness between celibate priesthood and min-

isterial priesthood; "these venerable Churches also
possess to a certain extent the principle of a celibate
priesthood" (nn. 39–40). This last assertion is based on
the law that only celibate priests are ordained bishops,
and marriage is forbidden to those already in orders.
The encyclical gives substantial treatment to human
values (nn. 50–59) and to formation in celibacy (nn.
60–72). The role of celibacy in priestly life, the question of defections, and the roles of the bishop and of
the faithful in supporting celibate priests are dealt with
extensively (nn. 73–97). It is noteworthy that though
the pope notes the traditional arguments about cultic
purity (n. 6), he does not adopt them. Furthermore, he
is careful to present celibacy as a special vocation
which in no way denigrates marriage (n. 20).

The encyclical did not put an end to discussion, and
the topic of celibacy was taken up again at the 1971
Synod of Bishops. Its document on priestly ministry
avoids any suggestion that celibacy involves a negative
view of sex or is based on the notion of ritual purity. By
a huge margin (168 to 3), the synod voted that the law
of celibacy be retained in the Latin Church; the vote
recommending that the pope should not make exceptions in particular cases was also decisive (107 to 87).[31]

The current *Code of Canon Law* lays down norms
for celibacy in line with Vatican II and the encyclical
of Paul VI.[32] Since 1972 there has had to be a public
profession of celibacy by unmarried candidates for
permanent diaconate and priesthood unless they are
religious in perpetual vows.[33] Rare in the past, dispensation from celibacy with laicization[34] became common after Vatican II; with the pontificate of Pope John
Paul II (1978– ), such dispensations were less frequent
at the beginning of his pontificate, not to say quite difficult to obtain;[35] since the early 1990s they have been
given a little more freely. The Vatican Congregation
for Christian Education gave important guidelines
(1974) on formation for priestly celibacy.[36]

Despite the Latin law of priestly celibacy, from the
time of Pius XII (1950) there have been some ordinations of non-Catholic pastors who have been married
and have come into full communion with the Catholic
Church.[37] This is now somewhat more frequent as
more Anglican priests, unhappy with the ordination of
women and other matters, have come to Rome.

Since the 1960s the arguments for and against compulsory clerical celibacy have been repetitively debated.[38] Clerical celibacy is called into question for
various reasons: it is not intrinsic to priesthood; it is
not essentially more perfect than married love; its historical origins are suspect, coming from a neo-Platonic
view of sexuality and OT ideas of ritual purity; there is
evidence that its observance has always been problematic, at least for a significant minority, leading to the
adage, *si non caste, tamen caute* ("if unchaste, be dis-

creet"); celibacy, being a charism, cannot be imposed; it can, and again for a significant number does, lead to a stunted affective life, and immaturity in relationships. The most significant argument against a law of celibacy, however, is the assertion that because of it the Christian people are in places being seriously deprived of the Eucharist. Hence there are appeals for a married clergy at least in some parts of the world.[39]

No one argument in favor of clerical celibacy is itself fully compelling, though the cumulative force of the various reasons is impressive: it answers a call to loving intimacy with God in a way sanctioned by a long tradition of East and West; it is a counter-cultural sign and a striking challenge in modern society, which needs the witness that celibacy offers; it seeks to allow apostolic availability for the needs of the Church and the world; it aims at, and frees the heart for, non-selfish love of all to whom the celibate ministers; it is a way of loving; it is a mature choice of a high ideal. It is, however, of the utmost importance that there be no downgrading of marriage when advocating celibacy; indeed, it has been argued that if marriage were to be taken really seriously, it would be hard to combine its demands with a wholehearted dedication to priesthood.[40]

The debate continues, and it will only be through the "sense of the faith" (q.v.) that the current practices in the East and West will either continue or be changed. A judgment, or discernment, by the Church at large that there is indeed an inner logic binding priesthood and celibacy will lead to the continuance of the law. Conversely, a judgment that the Spirit had ceased to bestow the gift of celibacy widely in the Church would in time inevitably have to result in a change of legislation.

[1]D. Gold, "Celibacy," EncycRel 3:144-148. [2]J. Dupont, *Mariage et divorce dans l'Évangile. Mt 19,3-12* (St.-André-les-Bruges, 1959); Q. Quesnell, "'Made Themselves Eunuchs for the Kingdom of Heaven' (Mt 19,12)," CBQ 30 (1968) 335–358 = TDig 17 (1969) 222–226; cf. P.-R. Côte, "Les eunuques pour le Royaume (Mt 19,12)," EglT 17 (1986) 321–334. [3]T. Matura, "Le célibat dans le Nouveau Testament," NRT 97 (1975) 481–500, 595–604 at 487–496; F.J. Moloney, "Matthew 19, 3-12 on Celibacy," JStNT 2 (1979) 42–60. [4]Matura (n. 3) 595–598. [5]Ibid., 496–498. [6]R.A. Wild, in NJBC 894, 897. [7]R. Cholij, "Celibacy: A Tradition of the Eastern Church," PrPeople 2 (1988) 208–221; C. Cochini, *Apostolic Origins of Priestly Celibacy* (San Francisco: Ignatius, 1992—French 1981); for reservations, see R. Balducelli, TS 43 (1982) 693–705. [8]P. Delhaye, "Celibacy, History of," NCE 3:369-374; J.E. Lynch, "Marriage and Celibacy of the Clergy: The Discipline of the Western Church: An Historical-Canonical Synopsis," Jurist 32 (1972) 14–38, 189–212 at 15–23. [9]E.g., M.D. Hart, "Gregory of Nyssa's Ironic Praise of the Celibate Life," HeythJ 32 (1992) 1–19. [10]Mansi 2:11; Hefele-Leclercq 1:239. [11]R. Gryson, "Dix ans de recherches sur les origines du célibat ecclésiastique," RTLv 11 (1980) 157–185 at 161–164. [12]Socrates, Historia ecclesiastica 1:11—PG 67:101-104/Nicene and Post-Nicene Fathers 2:18. See R. Cholij, *Clerical Celibacy in East and West* (Leominster UK: Fowler Wright, 1988) 85–92; Gryson (n. 11) 164–165, reversing opinion in his *Les origines du célibat ecclésiastique du premier au septième siècle* (Louvain: Gembloux, 1970)

87–93, on which see H. Crouzel, NRT 92 (1990) 649–653. [13]Pars 1, d.31, c.12. [14]Tanner 1:7. [15]6:17, 1 —SC 329:346. [16]8:47, 5—SC 336:276. [17]Lynch (n. 8) 25–29; D. Callam, "Clerical Continence in the Fourth Century: Three Papal Decretals," TS 41 (1980) 3–50. See Innocent I, *Epist.* 2:9-10—PL 20:475-477. [18]Leo I, *Epist.* 14:4—PL 54:672. [19]E.g., Lateran I (1123), can. 7—Tanner 1:191; Lateran III (1179), can. 11—Tanner 1:217. See Delhaye (n. 8) 372–373; A.M. Stickler, "The Evolution of the Discipline of Celibacy in the Western Church from the End of the Patristic Era to the Council of Trent," in AA.VV. *Priesthood and Celibacy* (Rome—Milan: Ancora, 1972) 503–597. [20]Canon 7—Tanner 1:198. [21]ST 2–2ae, q.88, a.11c. [22]Sess. 24, can. 9 on marriage, Tanner 2:755/DS 1809/ND 1816; sess. 25 on general reform, ch. 14—Tanner 2:792-793. [23]*Priesthood and Celibacy* (n. 19) 729–743; Lynch (n. 8) 210–212. [24]Op. cit. (nn. 7 and 12). [25]P. l'Huillier, "Episcopal Celibacy in the Orthodox Tradition," SVlad 35 (1991) 271–300. [26]Can. 48—P.P. Joannou, *Discipline générale antique,* 2 vols. (Grottaferrata, 1962) 1:186; Hefele-Leclercq 3:560-581 at 569; Cholij (n. 12) 106–107. [27]Joannou, ibid., 140–143; Hefele-Leclercq 3:565; Cholij, ibid., 115–116. [28]Cholij, ibid., 117–124. [29]CCEO 758 § 3, 804. Cf. R.D. Lee, "An Eastern Christian Overview on Sexuality, Remarriage and Divorce, Celibacy," Diakonia USA 15 (1980) 263–270. [30]Letter, 10 Oct. 1965—ActSyn 4/1:40; Encyc. AAS 49 (1967) 657–697/Carlen, Encyclicals 5:203-221. See D. Marzotto, "Sulla natura del celibato sacerdotale. Analisi degli ultimi documenti del magistero (1964–1974)," ScuolC 107 (1979) 591–628. [31]C. Caprile, *Il sinodo dei vescovi II. Assemblea generale 1971.* 2 vols. (Rome: Civiltà cattolica, 1972). [32]Can. 277, 1394–1395; cf. R. Cholij, "Observaciones críticas acera de los cánones que tratan sobre el celibato en el Código de Derecho Canónico de 1983," IusCan 31 (1991) 291–305. [33]Can. 1037. [34]Can. 290/3; 291–292. [35]E. Colagiovanni, "De dispensatione a caelibatu sacerdotali juxta novas normas," MonEccl 106 (1981) 209–238; E. Kneal, "Laicization: CLSA Survey, 1982," CanLawSAP 47 (1982) 247–250; J.L. Lynch in Coriden CIC 232–237; M. O'Reilly, "Canonical Procedures for the Laicization of Priests," CanLawSAP 44 (1982) 233–246; M. Zalba, "De sacerdotalis caelibatus dispensatione normae hodiernae," Periodica 70 (1981) 237–256. [36]*A Guide to Formation in Priestly Celibacy* (11 April 1974). [37]P.L. Golden, in Coriden, CIC 209–210 with n. 97. [38]Summary in D.J. Goergen, "Celibacy," NDictT 174–176. See N. Echivard, "Le sens du célibat consacré dans l'Église," VieCons 59 (1987) 7–20; C.A. Gallagher and T.L. Vandenberg, *The Celibacy Myth: Loving for Life* (New York: Crossroad, 1987); J.S. Kachuba, "Imposed Celibacy: Is It Ethical?," Diak USA 12 (1977) 145–156; S.R. Kenzig, "Can Priestly Celibacy Have Symbolic Value for Christian People?," LouvSt 6 (1976–1977) 273–287; J.A. Komonchak, "Celibacy and Tradition," ChicSt 20 (1981) 5–17; P. O'Leary, "Is Celibacy Essential to Priesthood?," DoctLife 40 (1990) 467–472; M.W. Pable, "Priesthood and Celibacy," ChicSt 20 (1981) 59–77; E. Schillebeeckx, *Celibacy under Fire* (London, 1968). L.W. Weber, "Celibacy," SM 1:275-280; AA.VV. *Priesthood and Celibacy* (n. 19) 623–973; Concilium 78[8/8] (1972); Supp 166 (1988). [39]R. Hickey, *A Case for an Auxiliary Priesthood* (Maryknoll: Orbis, 1982); cf. E. Schillebeeckx, *The Church with a Human Face: A New and Expanded Theology of Ministry* (London: SCM, 1985) 240–251. [40]M.J. Nicolas, *La grâce d'être prêtre* (Paris: Desclée, 1986) 183–186.

## CENSORSHIP OF BOOKS

Censorship of written material is found in many cultures and in many ages. In Christian history there have been examples of books being prohibited or destroyed: there was book-burning at Ephesus (Acts 19:19-20); the works of Arius were destroyed at Nicaea, and those of Manichaeus by Leo the Great, etc. The review of books before publication, which is pre-censorship, or more commonly called *imprimatur* (Latin: "let it be printed"), has roots in the Middle Ages, in which various religious orders and universities required that books be vetted before being divulgated.[1]

With the invention of printing, the Church attempted to have all books submitted for pre-censorship;[2] later the demand for *licentia,* or permission, was restricted to books involving religion.[3] In the 16th century the *Index* (q.v.) was established; it contained regulations about pre-censorship. In his edition of the *Index* in 1664, Alexander VII was the first to use the word *censores* for those who examined books. Benedict XIV laid down that censorship was not to be used to settle or suppress legitimate theological differences.[4] A simplification of the law by Leo XIII in 1897 was mostly carried over into the 1917 *Code of Canon Law* (CIC 1384–1394). Though what was required was variously called "permission/approval/authorization," which are positive expressions, the action of the censoring authority was essentially negative: it merely provided an assurance that the book was judged not to be harmful to faith or morals.

In 1975 the Congregation for the Doctrine of the Faith issued a new decree which contained a radically new approach to censorship.[5] Its norms have been largely incorporated into the new *Code* (CIC 822–832). The kinds of publication requiring pre-censorship are now restricted: books of the Sacred Scriptures in original or translation; liturgical books and books of private prayers; catechisms and catechetical writing; textbooks on Scripture, theology, canon law, Church history and religious or moral disciplines which are used as a basis of instruction in elementary, 2nd or 3rd level schools, and colleges; books treating of religion or morals which are displayed, sold, or distributed in churches or chapels (CIC 825–827). These are "printed books which, for diverse reasons, require a maximum of accuracy and reliability: basic, officially sanctioned Church books."[6] It follows that the censor "in carrying out this office . . . is to consider only the teaching of the Church about faith and morals as it is proposed by the ecclesiastical magisterium" (CIC 831 § 2). A norm for censorship is not therefore the consensus of theologians or even good theology. On the other hand the term ecclesiastical magisterium (q.v.) is a wide term encompassing a large number of various kinds of documents of varying binding power. All the norms about pre-censorship restrict rights and therefore must be interpreted strictly, viz., minimally (CIC 18). Thus textbooks *(textus, quibus institutio nititur)* should be narrowly understood as books which courses follow and are built upon them in a systematic way; it does not mean supplementary or required reading.[7]

Approbation can be sought for works already published, and the recent practice of the Congregation for the Doctrine of the Faith shows that approbation may be later withdrawn after it has already been given.[8]

The new element in the *Code* would not seem to involve an approbation much stronger than the "nothing harmful" of the 1917 *Code* and previous legislation. There are two standards of approval: the Scriptures and liturgical publications must show textual accuracy and conformity with approved editions or translations; catechisms, textbooks, pamphlet rack material, and books sold in churches, must represent the teaching of the Church as set forth by the magisterium.

Finally, the *Code* gives a rather wide authority to bishops to have other kinds of works submitted for their judgment (CIC 823 § 1), and it is recommended that books not falling within the list of obligatory pre-censorship should be submitted to the local ordinary (CIC 827 § 3). In 1992 the Congregation for the Doctrine of the Faith issued an instruction, *Supervising the Written Media,* which summarized the law and gave norms for its implementation.[9]

---

[1]J.A. Coriden, "The End of the Imprimatur," Jurist 44 (1984) 339–356; J.C. Calhoun, "Censorship of Books (Canon Law)," NCE 3:392-394; E. Jombert, "Censure des livres," DictDCan 3:157-169. [2]Lateran V—Tanner 1:632-633 [3]Trent, sess. 4—Tanner 2:664-665. [4]Coriden (n. 1) 346. [5]Decree *Ecclesiae pastorum*—AAS 67 (1975) 281–284; E. Baragli, "Una costante preoccupazione della Chiesa," CivCatt 126 (1975) 2:436-449. [6]Coriden (n. 1) 351. [7]Ibid., 353. [8]Ibid., 354–355. [9]30 March 1992—CathIntern 3 (1992) 756–770.

## CHALCEDON, Council of (451)

The Council of Chalcedon had a complicated prehistory. After the Council of Ephesus (431—q.v.), the monk Eutyches developed a Monophysite doctrine, according to which before the union of the Incarnation there were two natures, divine and human, but only one afterwards. Eutyches was condemned by a synod of Constantinople (444), and he appealed to various other synods, including Rome. Pope Leo the Great (q.v.) replied with the *Tome* written to Flavian, Patriarch of Constantinople; it was a Western Christology, broadly in line with Antioch. A council met at Ephesus in 449, called the "Robber Council" (*latrocinio*) by Leo; 150 bishops met and rehabilitated Eutyches.[1]

Leo at first was not enthusiastic about the idea of a new council; he wanted the *Tome* accepted and signed by the bishops. The emperor Marcion nevertheless convoked a council at Nicaea, later changed to Chalcedon (451).[2] The difference in view between the pope who wanted a council in the West, and the emperor who summoned one in the East is evidence of the correlative dialectic between papacy and empire;

there is no indication that Leo did not recognize the emperor's right to summon a council.

The council was traditionally said to comprise 600 members. Today the figure is calculated at about 350, with two African bishops being the only Western representatives apart from the papal delegation of two bishops, one priest, and the pope's representative at Constantinople. In its early sessions it received the creed of Constantinople (v. CONSTANTINOPLE I). The reading of Leo's *Tome* was received enthusiastically by the majority with cries of "Peter has spoken through Leo."

The definition drawn up at Chalcedon was not a full profession of faith, but was concerned with disputed issues of the time. It had various antecedents: the formula of union of 433; the second letter of Cyril to Nestorius; the *Tome* of Leo; the profession of faith of Flavian at the local council of Constantinople (448). It shows a dialectic of unity in the divine and human: "The one and the same Lord Jesus Christ" is "perfect in divinity and perfect in humanity," "true God and true Man," "consubstantial with God according to divinity and consubstantial with us according to humanity." Jesus Christ is "to be acknowledged in two natures" *(en duo phusesin* not *ek duo phuseôn),* "without confusion, without change, without division, without separation" *(asugchutôs, atreptôs, adiairetôs, achôristôs)*—the first two excluding Monophysitism, the second two excluding Nestorianism; the diverse natures *(phuseôn)* with their respective properties are not less after union, but come together to form only one person *(eis hen prosôpon)* and only one subsistent being *(mian hupostasin).*[3] Far from being a hellenization of dogma or an ontological determination, the definition is very open to further elaboration.[4] However, as it did not define the terms it used, it was liable subsequently to varying interpretations.

The council also passed 28 canons—the Greeks have taken a 29th canon from the minutes of the 19th session, and a 30th from the minutes from the 4th session.[5] The best known is the 28th canon, which accords Constantinople, the "second Rome," a primacy of honor equal to Rome because of its status as imperial capital.[6] The papal legates rejected this, and it led to Leo's late approval of the council (only in 453 and without this canon). Of the other 27 disciplinary canons, many were directed at the ordering of the lives of monks, especially their appropriate submission to the bishop (cc. 4, 8; cf. cc. 3, 16, 18, 23, 24).[7] Other canons took up various issues: the validity of the canons of previous councils (c. 1); condemnation of simony (c. 2); extension of earlier conciliar decrees on clergy, and prohibition of their engagement in temporal affairs (c. 3), in military service (c. 7); prohibition of the transfer of clergy from diocese to diocese (cc. 5, 20); permanence in one's province (c. 19); the

responsibilities of bishops (cc. 6, 12, 21, 25, 26); rural parishes (q.v.) subject to bishop (c. 17).

Chalcedon is important for its influence on Eastern canon law. It represents a high point of Christology "from above," but one which still cannot be ignored in any future statements about the Incarnation, even those which by preference begin "from below."[8] Nevertheless, the council left various problems unresolved: issues of Christology, of ecclesiology, and of Church-State would cause difficulties in succeeding centuries.[9]

---

[1]W. de Vries, "Das Konzil von Ephesus 449, eine 'Räubersynode'?," OrChrPer 41 (1975) 357–398. [2]K. Baus, in Jedin-Dolan 2:114-121; P.-T. Camelot, *Éphèse et Chalcédoine.* Histoire des conciles 2 (Paris: Ed. de L'Orante, 1961); L.D. Davis, *The First Seven Ecumenical Councils (325–787): Their History and Theology.* Theology and Life 21 (Wilmington: Glazier, 1983) 170–206; W. de Vries, *Orient et occident: Les structures ecclésiales vues dans l'histoire des sept premiers conciles oecuménique* (Paris: Cerf, 1974) 101–160; A. Grillmeier and H. Bacht, eds., *Das Konzil von Chalkedon.* 3 vols. (Würzburg, 1951–1954); A. Grillmeier, *Christ in Christian Tradition* (London: Mowbray, ²1975); L. Perrone, in Alberigo, Concili 85–107; P. Stockmeier, "Das Konzil von Chalkedon: Probleme der Forschung," FreibZ 29 (1982) 140–156. [3]Tanner 1:83-86/DS 300–302/ND 613–615; A.J. Festugière, *Actes du concile de chalcédoine. Sess. III–IV. La définition de la foi* (Geneva: Cramer, 1983); see A. de Halleux, "La définition christologique à Chalcédoine," RTLv 7 (1976) 3–23, 155–170; M. Slusser, "The Issues in the Definition of the Council of Chalcedon," TorontoJT 6 (1990) 63–69. [4]B.J.F. Lonergan, "The Hellenization of Dogma," in W.F.J. Ryan and B.J. Tyrrell, eds., *A Second Collection* (London: Darton, Longman & Todd, 1974) 11–32—TS 28 (1967) 336–351. [5]Tanner 1:87-102. [6]A. de Halleux, "Le vingt-huitième canon de Chalcédoine," StPatr 19 (1989) 28–36; idem, "Les deux Romes dans la définition de Chalcédoine sur les prérogatives du siège de Constantinople," in *Patrologie et oecuménisme: Receuil d'études* (Leuven: UP, 1990) 504–519; T.O. Martin, "The Twenty-eighth Canon of Chalcedon: A Background Note," in Grillmeier—Bacht (n. 2) 2:459-450; A. Wuyts, "Le 28e canon de Chalcédoine et le fondement du primat romain," OrChrPer 17 (1951) 265–282. [7]L. Ueding, "Die Kanones von Chalkedon in ihrer Bedeutung für Mönchtum und Klerus," in Grillmeier and Bacht (n. 2) 2:569-676. [8]R. Butterworth, "Coping with a Council: Christology after Chalcedon," Month 258 (1987) 455–460; G. Havrilak, "Chalcedon and Orthodox Christology Today," SVlad 33 (1989) 127–145. [9]E. Ludwig, "Chalcedon and its Aftermath: Three Unresolved Crises," Laur 27 (1986) 98–120.

## CHARISM

Charism, word and role, was the subject of a clash of viewpoints in the second session of Vatican II. Cardinal E. Ruffini objected to the emphasis being given to charism in the Constitution on the Church. He held a view, termed "dispensationalist," according to which charism, though widespread in the early Church, ceased after the first few centuries to be given apart from exceptional cases and persons. The opposing view was expressed by Cardinal L.J. Suenens in a noteworthy speech (22 Oct. 1963).[1] His view that charism belonged to the nature of the Church reflected important writing in the 1950s; it eventually prevailed in the council. The council teaching demands careful rereading of the NT evidence.

The word "charism" (Greek *charisma,* plur. *charismata*) is derived from the Greek word *charis,* meaning grace. Its precise denotation must in each case be sought from its context.[2] In Paul it can mean the fundamental gift of redemption and eternal life (e.g., Rom 5:15-16) or particular gifts such as those given to the Israelite people (Rom 11:29). The special Pauline usage is plural and is used mainly about gifts given in the Body or community.[3] In 1 Pet 4:10-11 the various gifts are divided in two: speaking gifts and serving gifts. Both must be used for the benefit of others and for the glory of God. It is also implied that each person has received a gift, which is Paul's presumption too (cf. 1 Cor 7:7; 12:7, 11). Paul is extremely positive about the gifts, despite the confusion and disorder they occasioned at Corinth (1 Cor 12–14): "strive for the spiritual gifts" (*pneumatika*—1 Cor 14:1).

There are four lists of charisms in the NT. The Church in Corinth was particularly favored (1 Cor 1:4-7; cf. 1 Cor 12:4-11; 1 Cor 12:27-30). Before he visited Rome (Rom 1:10-13; 15:24, 32), Paul had heard of, or expected to find, charismatic gifts in their Church (Rom 12:4-8). Finally, there is a further list in Eph 4:11-13. The context of these charisms is the Body, which is enriched by their diversity. Their purpose is "for profit" (*pros to sumpheron*—1 Cor 12:7; cf. 14:12), that is, the upbuilding of the community. There is no reason to think that the NT anywhere gives an exhaustive list of charisms;[4] Paul deals with actual charisms at Corinth, and with ones he expects to be found in Rome. Neither do we get an evaluative order of the charisms, but there are some indications of their relative importance: apostle and prophet are listed first; prophecy is higher than tongues, which comes last (cf. 1 Cor 12:10, 28 with 14:1-5). It is not always clear in the NT lists where the author is speaking of an office in the Church with its gift, and where there is merely reference to a gift. Love is not enumerated among the gifts; it is "a more excellent way" within which the charisms have their true scope (1 Cor 12:31–13:10). From the evidence of the Church at Corinth, it is clear that the possession of charism is no guarantee of personal holiness. The charism-bearers (*pneumatikoi*—1 Cor 3:1-3; 14:37) and the whole charismatic community there give ample evidence of sin and frailty. Again in Matthew's time (ca. 85) some bearers of powerful charisms are warned that by their personal behavior they may be found outside the eschatological kingdom (Matt 7:21-23).[5] In Mark the presence of charism is associated with faith (*pisteusasin*—16:17). The gift is given to those who believe and is to be used in faith; genuine gifts may be exercised by those who are morally unworthy. Though St. Paul knew a charism of discernment (1 Cor 12:10—*diakriseis pneumatôn*), we soon find, as in the *Didachê* (q.v.), a discernment of gifts, especially prophecy (q.v.), based very much on the behavior of their bearers.

The charisms are in evidence in the post-NT period.[6] *The Didachê* gives norms for apostles and prophets. The only charism mentioned by Ignatius of Antioch (q.v.) is of a prophetic utterance by himself.[7] The Smyrnaens remember Polycarp as an apostolic and prophetic teacher.[8] Several early writers refer to the "prophetic Spirit," meaning the Holy Spirit who inspired either the OT prophets or NT ones.[9] The lost first part of the 3rd century *Apostolic Tradition* (q.v.) was a treatise on charisms. The idea of a charism of office (*Amtscharisma*) is incipient in this work, but developed in Cyprian, Firmilian, and others.[10] Irenaeus knew charisms such as are found in the NT, especially prophecy and healings.[11] He uses the words *charisma, charis,* and *dôrea* for any gift of divine grace, including the Holy Spirit itself. He emphasized the vital bond between the Holy Spirit and the Church. The *charismata* of the Spirit are placed in the Church and are found only within her bosom.[12] Origen knew only traces *(ichnê)* of the NT charisms.[13]

But gradually the charisms declined: Montanism made the Church wary of extraordinary phenomena; the episcopacy became stronger and drew into itself most of the initiatives of the Church's life.[14] By the time of Augustine, charisms were little in evidence. In an early work he observed that the Holy Spirit no longer came visibly at the imposition of his hands;[15] he also interpreted the gift of tongues as the large number of actual languages spoken by the Church throughout the world.[16] But in his later work he said that he had heard of numerous healings in his area.[17]

In the Middle Ages we can take St. Thomas Aquinas as a representative figure. After *De veritate* q.27 (1258–1259) he distinguishes *gratia gratum faciens* (grace making holy or sanctifying grace) from *gratia gratis datum* (grace freely given, viz., for others). To the latter he assigns charisms.[18] He treats them in different works,[19] seeking to relate the scriptural teaching to the primitive Church and to the Church which he knew; inevitably in this latter case, his experience and hence his understanding is restricted, though it is not without deep insights and perceptive observations.[20]

The institutional ecclesiology of the Reformation and post-Reformation period had little time for reflection on charism; the main stress was on authority and the visibility of the Church. Charism belonged to hagiography rather than to ecclesiology. In the 20th century R. Sohm (1841–1917) viewed the Church as a purely spiritual and charismatic body, and rejected canon law as an abandonment of the primitive ideal of

Christianity. M. Weber (1864–1920) studied charism primarily from a sociological stance, but applied his findings also to religion. Authority is of three kinds: traditional, based on the past; rational, on the need for administration; charismatic, founded on the inspiration of a leader.[21] As the century progressed, charism and institution were increasingly seen as in opposition. There are two important references to charism in the teaching of Pius XII: in the encyclical *Mystici corporis* (1943) and on the occasion of the canonization of Pius X. He noted the temptation to see in the Church two orders of activity, the hierarchic and the charismatic (often called prophetic); both are foreseen and ordered by Christ and both are equally informed by the Holy Spirit.[22]

Vatican II has some general references to charism: the Holy Spirit instructs and directs the Church through a diversity of gifts both hierarchical and charismatic (LG 4; cf. LG 7). The main treatment is in LG 12: there is the Spirit's activity in sanctifying the Church apart from sacraments, ministries, and virtues for "he also apportions his gifts 'to each individually as he wills' (1 Cor 12:11), and among the faithful of every rank he distributes special graces by which he renders them fit and ready to undertake the various tasks and offices which help the renewal and building up of the Church, according to that word: 'to each is given the manifestation of the Spirit for the common good' (*ad utilitatem*—1 Cor 12:7)." The text goes on to speak of the gifts which are outstanding or simpler and more widely diffused, and adds: "The judgment about their (charisms') genuineness and ordered use belongs to those who preside over the Church, to whom it belongs especially not to extinguish the Spirit but to test everything and hold fast to what is good (cf. 1 Thess 5:12, 19-21)." These graces are called "special" because of the *way* in which they are given—directly by the Spirit, and because of their *purpose* which is service of the Church and the world.[23] While charism in the NT can be described as "free gifts of the Spirit intended for the building up of the Church, the Body of Christ,"[24] more broadly in the council documents a charism can be described as "a grace-given capacity and willingness for some kind of service that contributes to the renewal and upbuilding of the Church."[29]

There are two other texts on charism that particularly concern the laity: "(priests) must discern with a sense of faith the manifold gifts, both exalted and ordinary, that the laity have, acknowledge them gladly and foster them with care" (PO 9); "Through receiving these gifts of grace, however unspectacular, every one of the faithful has the right and duty to exercise them in the Church and in the world for the good of humanity and the building up of the Church" (AA 3; cf. AG 28). The charisms of the laity are not to be seen as a threat by the clergy, but as a gift to the Church, which they must foster and steward.

In the revision of the *Code of Canon Law* these texts are surprisingly absent from the list of rights and duties of the faithful and laity (cc. 208–231), especially in the light of Pope John Paul II's document, *Sacrae disciplinae leges,* which, in introducing the *Code,* speaks of it as providing an order for the fruitful exercise of love, grace, and charisms. Charism did feature in the drafts of the law until 1982, when it was suppressed; AA 3 was judged good but not juridical, so treatment of charism was left to the Introduction of the *Code.*[26]

Since Vatican II there has been an extensive literature on charism. Part of this stemmed from the Charismatic Renewal (q.v.), and reflects the rediscovery in the life of the Church of the charisms listed in the NT. The Pentecostal Churches (q.v.) have wide experience of charisms and have much reflection on their wise and unwise use. But the main discussion has centered around the tension between charism and institution or office. Such tension is already found in the NT.[27] In the earliest NT book (ca. 50) Paul warns the Thessalonians to be discerning about gifts, but on the other hand they must not stifle the Spirit or reject prophecy (1 Thess 5:19-21). Moreover, as one with authority in Corinth, he makes provision for the discernment, and ordered use of the charisms in the Church there (1 Cor 14).

Around the turn of the century, R. Sohm saw the Church primarily as charismatic. He saw institutional elements, and especially law, as secular and unevangelical, indeed as evidence of corrupting catholicism (V. CATHOLICISM, EARLY).[28] Though Sohm's precise positions are rarely found nowadays, the problem he articulated lies behind ecclesiologies which express a clear preference for the Corinthian model of Church over others, notably that of the Pastoral Epistles.

Some authors, in protecting and promoting the role of charism, seem ultimately to say less than is necessary about the role of institution.[29] But the contrary fault is much more common in practice: charism is not allowed its full and proper role in the Church, especially at the local level. There is an awareness of this problem in various liberation theologies (q.v.)[30] and generally in the Churches, both Protestant and Catholic.[31] There are problems both practical and theological. In practice there is a widespread need for conversion on the part of pastors so that they welcome and foster the charismatic gifts of the laity (PO 9; AA 3),[32] and acknowledge their ministry (q.v.) in the Church.[33] Even if there is an enlightened approach on the part of pastors, there is the danger of clericalization in their attitude. The laity are not free from a clericalized mentality when they look to pastors to initiate, to guide, or to approve their work in areas in which they already have a calling, a competence, and appropriate charisms. Probably most of those who are not concerned with avoiding clericalization are themselves infected with it.

The theoretical question regards the relation of charism and institution. The solution lies in strongly affirming that both institution and charism come from the same Holy Spirit. Indeed, if there is no tension between charism and institution, then probably either charism is being suppressed or the institutions of the Church are not being given the opportunity of playing their Spirit-given role. The Church as institution must naturally be conservative; it needs charism and the activity of the Holy Spirit to vivify it (AG 4). Charisms need to be discerned by pastors (LG 12; PO 9; AA 3). But pastors need charism to fulfill their own function. Formerly called "the grace of office," charism is the only ultimate guarantee that authority and institution will operate healthily in the Church. Authority, for example, is truly given in the Church, but only charism will ensure that it is wisely exercised in love. Finally, it needs to be stressed that initial opposition of Church authority to apparent charism is no guarantee that genuine charism is not present or that the Holy Spirit is not at work. History has many lessons to teach in this matter: the ecumenical movement was ignored for decades by the Catholic Church; many saints and heroic figures in the past spent time under a cloud, or were actively persecuted, e.g., St. John of the Cross, St. Joan of Arc, Newman, and some outstanding theologians in the 1950s. Discernment is itself a charism, but may be misused. The only ultimate criterion is the one given by the Lord: "You will know them by their fruits" (Matt 7:20). For an interim period the bearer of charism may be misunderstood and have to suffer patiently. The tension between charism and institution should never be resolved, but rather lived creatively under the Spirit who gives both of these gifts to the Church.

[1]"The Charismatic Dimension of the Church," in Y. Congar et al., eds., *Council Speeches at Vatican II* (London—New York, 1964) 18–21 = L.J. Suenens, *Coresponsibility in the Church* (New York, 1968) 214–218. [2]H. Conzelmann, "Charisma," TDNT 9:402-406; A. George and P. Grelot, "Charisms," DBT 68–71; K.S. Hemphill, *Spiritual Gifts: Empowering the New Testament Church* (Nashville, Tenn.: Broadman, 1988); R. Koch, "Charisma," Bauer 1:96-101; R. Laurentin, "Charisms: Terminological Precision," Conc 109 (1978) 3–12; H.E. Lona, "Carisma e institución: Reflexiones sobre la eclesiología y los ministros en san Pablo y en la tradición paulinas," Proy 2 (1990) 135–163; V. Scippa, "I carismi per la vitalità della Chiesa: Studio esegetico su 1 Cor 12–14; Rm 12,6-8; Ef 4,11-13; I Pet 4,10-11," Asp 38 (1991) 5–25; F.A. Sullivan, *Charisms and the Charismatic Renewal: A Biblical and Theological Study* (Ann Arbor: Servant—Dublin: Gill and Macmillan, 1982) 17–46; B.M. Wambacq, "Le mot charisme," NRT 97 (1975) 345–355; idem, "Il termine 'carisma'," VitaCons 13 (1977) 615–624. [3]E.E. Ellis, "Spiritual Gifts in the Pauline Community," NTS 20 (1974) 128–144; J.J. Kilgallen, "Reflections on Charisma(ta) in the New Testament," StMiss 41 (1992) 289–325. [4]Sullivan (n. 2) 27–29. [5]D. Hill, "False Prophets and Charismatics: Structure and Interpretation in Mt 7:15-23," Bib 57 (1976) 327–348; M. Krämer, "Hütet euch vor den falschen Propheten," Bib 57 (1976) 35–377. [6]D. Grasso, "I carismi nella Chiesa antica," AugR 20 (1980) 671–686; N. Baumert, "Zur Semantik von *charisma* bei den frühen Vätern," TPhil 63 (1988) 60–78. [7]*Philadelph.* 7:1-2. [8]*Martyrdom of Polycarp* 16:2—LCC 1:155. [9]E.g., Athenagoras, Plea 7 and 18—LCC 306–307, 316; Justin, *1 Apol.* 6—LCC 1:245; Irenaeus, *Adv. haer.* 3:6, 1-3; 4:26, 2, 5. [10]J.E. Stam, *Episcopacy in the Apostolic Tradition of Hippolytus.* Bd. 111 der theologischen Dissertationen (Basel, 1969) 62 and n. 134. [11]*Adv. haer.* 2:32, 4—PG 7:828-829/ANL 5:245-246; 3:11, 9—PG 7:828-829/ANL 5:295-296. [12]*Adv. haer.* 4:26, 5; cf. 2:32, 4; 3:24, 1; 4:26, 2; 5:6, 1 —PG 7:1055-1056, 830, 966, 1053-1054, 1137-1138. [13]*Contra Celsum* 1:2; 1:46; 2:8; 7:8; R. Kydd, "Origen and the Gifts of the Spirit," EglT 13 (1982) 111–116. [14]J.L. Ash, "The Decline of Ecstatic Prophecy in the Early Church," TS 37 (1976) 227–252. [15]*De bapt.* 3:16, 21—PL 43:149. [16]*Serm.* 268:2—PL 38:1232; *Serm.* 87:7 (9)—PL 38:535. [17]*Retract.* 12:7; 13:5—FC 60: 55, 61–62; J. Bentivegna, "The Witness of St. Augustine on the Action of the Holy Spirit in the Church and the Practice of Charismata in his Times," StPatr 22 (1989) 188–201; idem, "La praxis de los carismas de la iglesia di san Agustín," AugM 36 (1991) 15–37. [18]ST 1–2ae, q.111, a.4. [19]ST 1–2ae, q.111; 2–2ae, qq.171–174, 176–178; *Summa c. gentiles* 3:154; *In Rom* 12, lect. 2 (976–982); *In 1 Cor* 12 and 14; *In Eph* 4, lect. 4 (210–212); *In Heb 2*, lect. 1 (99). [20]P. Fernandez, "Los carismas en Santo Tomás de Aquino," in *Credo in Spiritum Sanctum.* Atti del Congresso Teologico Internazionale di Pneumatologia. 2 vols. (Vatican, 1983) 1:473-488, expanded as "La gracia carismática en Santo Tomás de Aquino," Ang 60 (1983) 3–39; id. "Teología de los carismas en la 'Summa Theologiae' de Santo Tomás," CiTom 105 (1978) 177–223; E. Stiegman, "Charism and Institution in Aquinas," Thom 38 (1974) 723–733; see I. Biffi, "La teologia medievale dei 'carismi,'" Teologia 15 (1990) 198–225. [21]M. Weber, *On Charisma and Institution-Building,* S. Eisenstadt, ed. (Chicago, 1968). [22]AAS 46 (1954) 313–317; cf. *Mystici corporis* AAS 35 (1943) 200, 224/Carlen, 4:16, 50. [23]Sullivan (n. 2) 11–14; J.M. Rovira Belloso, "Los carismas según el Concilio Vaticano II," EstTrin 10 (1976) 77–94; P. Mullins, "The Theology of Charisms: Vatican II and the New Catechism," MilltownSt 33 (1994) 123–164. [24]Laurentin (n. 2) 8. [25]Sullivan (n. 2) 13. [26]E. Corecco, "Aspects of the Reception of Vatican II in the Code of Canon Law," in G. Alberigo et al., eds, *The Reception of Vatican II* (Tunbridge Wells UK: Burns & Oates—Washington, D.C.: The Catholic University of America, 1987) 249–296 at 266–268; Communicationes 12 (1980) 43–44; L. Vela, "Dialecta eclesial: carismas y derecho," EstE 65 (1990) 19–57. [27]A. Brent, "Pseudonymity and Charisma in the Ministry of the Early Church," AugR 27 (1987) 347–376; F. Hahn, "Charisma und Amt: Die Diskussion über das kirchliche Amt im Lichte der neutestamentlichen Charismenlehre," ZTK 76 (1979) 419–449; S. Muñoz Iglesias, "Carismas y comunidad en el Nuevo Testamento," CiTom 106 (1979) 623–654; E.D. O'Connor, "Charisme et institution," NRT 96 (1974) 3–19; C. Osiek, "Relation of Charism to Rights and Duties in the New Testament Church," Jurist 41 (1981)295–313; R. Schnackenburg, "Charisma und Amt in der Urkirche und heute," MüTZ 37 (1986) 233–248; idem, "Charisma und Amt in der gegenwärtigen neutestamentlichen Forschung—Aspekte, Tendenzen und Fragestellungen aus römisch-katholischer Sicht," in T. Rendtorff, ed., *Charisma und Institution* (Gütersloh: Mohn, 1985) 350–367; E. Schweizer, "Konzeptionen von Charisma und Amt im Neuen Testament," ibid., 316–334. [28]See Y. Congar, "Rudolf Sohm nous interroge encore," RSPT 57 (1973) 263–294; E. Nardoni, "Charism in the Early Church since Rudolph Sohm: an Ecumenical Challenge," TS 53 (1992) 646–662. [29]E.g., G. Hasenhüttl, *Charisma: Ordnungsprinzip der Kirche* (Freiburg, 1969). [30]L. Boff, *Ecclesiogenesis: The Base Communities Reinvent the Church* (London: Collins—Maryknoll:

Orbis, 1986 = Petrópolis, Brazil, 1977); E. Dussel, "The Differentiation of Charisms," Conc 109 (1978) 36–55; R. Vidales, "Charisms and Political Action," ibid., 67–77. [31]B. Cooke, *Ministry to Word and Sacrament: History and Theology* (Philadelphia: Fortress, 1976); B. de Margerie, "Los carismas otorgados a la Iglesia por el Espíritu Santo, don de Dios," EstTrin 9 (1975) 401–424 = Divinitas 21 (1977) 357–382; J.A. Estrada, La Iglesia: *¿Institución o carisma? Verdad e imagen* 88 (Salamanca: Sígueme, 1984); B. Gherardini, "Istituzione e carismi," Divinitas 25 (1981) 247–258; J.-L. Leuba, "Carisma e institución," EstTrin 10 (1976) 187–202; K. Rahner, *The Dynamic Element in the Church.* QDisput 12 (Freiburg—London, 1964) 42–83; idem, "Observations on the Factor of the Charismatic in the Church," ThInvest 12:81-97; L. Sartori, "The Structure of Juridical and Charismatic Power in the Christian Community," Conc 109 (1978) 56–66. Cf. also n. 27 above. [32]See John Paul II, Apost. Exhort. *Christifideles laici* ("The Vocation and Mission of the Laity" 1988) 24—AAS 81 (1989) 433–435. [33]Ibid., 23—AAS 429–433.

## CHARISMATIC RENEWAL

Charismatic Renewal is a movement for the revitalization of the Church. It is known by different names: (Neo)Pentecostalism, Renewal, Spiritual Renewal, Renewal in the Spirit. None of these is fully satisfactory, as they may seem to preempt renewal or movements of the Spirit in favor of one group. Nomenclature apart, the movement has an identity in the mainline Churches. This article focuses on the movement in the Catholic Church.

Its roots lie in Classical Pentecostalism, which arose in the USA at the turn of the century. It was on 1 January 1901 that Agnes Ozman had hands laid on her at the Bible School of Charles F. Parnham in Topeka, Kansas; she began to "speak in tongues" and experienced what would soon be called "Baptism in the Spirit." Those who were open to charismatic gifts of the Spirit, and received them, were not accepted in their Protestant Churches, and gradually Pentecostal Churches came into being.

In the 1960s the mainline Protestant Churches began to have members with Pentecostal-style gifts; this time they were able to remain in their Churches. The beginnings of such gifting in the Catholic Church happened in 1967, when two Catholic laymen at Duquesne University attended a Neo-Pentecostal prayer meeting and had hands laid upon them, after which they had Pentecostal kinds of experience. Soon there were similar occurrences at Notre Dame, Indiana. Within a few years the movement was worldwide within the Catholic Church. While many episcopal conferences warned of the dangers of the movement, their overall evaluation was positive—a discernment that the Holy Spirit was truly at work in the movement.[1] In a memorable address in 1975, Pope Paul VI described the movement as "a chance for the Church and the world," a phrase reechoed by John Paul II in 1981.[2] Pope Paul commended the movement to the care of Cardinal L.J. Suenens, who for more than a decade was one of its most prominent spokespersons and guides, especially through widespread travel and a series of books called the *Malines Documents*,[3] which he authored or sponsored on various aspects of the movement.

There is an extensive literature on all aspects of the movement;[4] a further major research resource is the thousands of cassette tapes of conferences and lectures by leaders and prominent speakers. There is at every stage a problem of both theology and of language. Since the charismatic phenomenon was new to the Catholic Church, the only language available was Protestant and Pentecostal; with the use of their language there was sometimes also a transfer of their theology.

At the heart of Charismatic Renewal is the phenomenon of a special conversion and gifting known by different names, the most common being "Baptism in the Holy Spirit," and in Italy and France "Outpouring of the Spirit"; in Protestant Churches "born again Christian" often corresponds to the same reality. F.A. Sullivan (q.v.) describes it as "a religious experience which initiates a decisively new sense of the presence and working of God in one's life, which working usually involves one or more charismatic gifts."[5] There are two main ways of understanding this experience. One is that of Sullivan: basing himself on St. Thomas,[6] he sees it as a special grace, a new imparting of the Spirit not necessarily related to any immediate sacramental context.[7] The other main view is to relate the experience to sacramental baptism in one of several ways: a release of the power of the Spirit already given in baptism; a conscious experience of what was received sacramentally. Recently it has been argued by Catholics that "Baptism in the Spirit" was normative in the reception of sacramental baptism in NT and patristic times.[8]

However it is explained, people in Charismatic Renewal usually receive "Baptism in the Holy Spirit" on the occasion of laying-on of hands and prayer; there is commonly a period of preparation of some eight weeks called the "Seminar."

The gifts or charisms (q.v.) received correspond closely to the NT ones described by Paul, but are not limited to these. Perhaps the most common gift is a new love of, and ability to read, the Scriptures, along with a deepened or renewed prayer life. For Catholics there is also a new appreciation of sacraments and liturgy. But it is the Lordship of Jesus, not the gifts, that is central in Charismatic Renewal.

The place where Charismatic Renewal is encountered is usually the prayer meeting, a loosely structured time of praise, singing, Scripture reading, testimony, silence, often with a quasi-formal input ("a teaching") being given by a designated speaker. Leadership of the prayer group is mainly lay, and is exercised by a small number of persons variously called "a core group" or "pastoral team" or some such name.

In places there has been a move towards community formation by those involved in the movement. Communities can be very close-knit or more informal. In both cases there is an attempt at some mutual support and at giving guidance in Christian living.

Charismatic Renewal has spread widely throughout the world, and it takes on different qualities in the local Churches. The charge is made, especially by those more drawn to liberation theology (q.v.), that the movement is too inward-looking and vertical, with insufficient horizontal commitment to issues of justice and peace. Leaders and theologians of the movement would reply that the special role of Charismatic Renewal is to evangelize: to exist so that people may come into the experience of the "Baptism in the Holy Spirit," to an acceptance of the Lordship of Jesus, to an awareness of the power of the Holy Spirit. The movement as such is not drawn to specific horizontal endeavors, though if those involved in it are authentic, they will surely care for their suffering brothers and sisters. In short, Charismatic Renewal has a precise function in the Church and need not answer every need, however urgent. The experience of local Churches is that many people find a new commitment in Charismatic Renewal, and even though they may cease to be deeply involved in the movement, they then move to other ways of service of the Church and world. Charismatic Renewal has as its aim to move, in the expression of John Paul II, "to the heart of the Church," and ultimately to sink into a renewed Church. The deepest concerns of Charismatic Renewal are not an optional extra, but part of what it means to be authentic and fully alive as a Christian.

Charismatic Renewal has important ecumenical dimensions.[9] Many prayer groups are composed of members of different Churches, so that there is prayer together and a common sharing of Scripture (UR 8, 21). But there is another bond that is not always found in ecumenical contacts. Since the presence of the power and gifts of the Spirit, and the proclamation of the Lordship of Jesus are found wherever members meet, there is a deeply felt unity of shared religious experience which transcends differences. At the same time, false irenicism (UR 11) is not commonly a problem. Just as there are those in the Catholic Church who are either hostile to, unaffected by, or deeply committed to Charismatic Renewal, the same range of attitudes, from enthusiasm to antagonism, is found also in the other Christian Churches.

[1]K. McDonnell, ed., *Presence, Power, Praise: Documents on the Charismatic Renewal*. 3 vols. (Collegeville: The Liturgical Press, 1980). [2]19 May 1975 and 7 May 1981. Nineteen papal texts in K. McDonnell, ed., *Open the Windows: The Popes and Charismatic Renewal* (South Bend, Ind.: Greenlawn, 1989). [3]L.J. Suenens, *Memories and Hopes* (Dublin: Veritas, 1992) 266–320, 371–377. [4]K. McDonnell, ed., *The Holy Spirit and Power* (New York:

Doubleday, 1975); R. Laurentin, *Catholic Pentecostalism* (London: Darton, Longman & Todd, 1977); C. O'Donnell, "Neo-Pentecostalism in North America and Europe," Conc 161 (1983) 35–41; F.A. Sullivan, "Pentcôtisme," DSpir 12:1035-1052—Eng. trans. without notes, *Pentecostalism and the Charismatic Renewal* (Dublin: Veritas, 1986); L.J. Suenens, *A New Pentecost* (New York: Seabury, 1975); V. Synan, *In the Latter Days: The Outpouring of the Holy Spirit in the Twentieth Century* (Ann Arbor: Servant, 1984). [5]*Pentecostalism* (n. 4) 12. [6]ST 1a, q.43, a.6c and ad 2. [7]*Charisms and the Charismatic Renewal: A Biblical and Theological Study* (Ann Arbor: Servant, 1982) 59–75; idem, "'Baptism in the Holy Spirit': A Catholic Interpretation of the Pentecostal Experience," Greg 55 (1974) 49–68. [8]K. McDonnell and G.T. Montague, *Christian Initiation and Baptism in the Holy Spirit: Evidence from the First Eight Centuries* (Collegeville: Glazier—The Liturgical Press, 1991). [9]A. Bittlinger, ed., *The Church is Charismatic* (Geneva: WCC, 1981); P. Hocken, "Charismatic Renewal, the Churches and Unity," OneChr 15 (1979) 310–321; idem, "Charismatic Movement," DictEcumMov 145–149; K. McDonnell, *Charismatic Renewal and the Churches* (New York: Seabury, 1976); idem, "Charismatic Renewal and Ecumenism," OneChr 14 (1978) 247–258; P.F. O'Mara, "Ecumenism in the Catholic Charismatic Renewal Movement," JEcuSt 17 (1980) 647–657.

## CHURCH, The Term EKKLÊSIA

In some Western languages the word "church" comes either from a Germanic root *kirika,* itself derived from Greek, with the idea of "house of God," hence English *church,* German *Kirche,* Dutch *kerk,* etc., or in other languages it comes from the Greek *ekklêsia,* often via the Latin *ecclesia,* thus, French *église,* Italian *chiesa,* Spanish *iglesia,* Irish *eaglais,* etc. The more difficult question is how the NT communities chose *ekklêsia.*[1] Some scholars suggest that *ekklêsia* was chosen deliberately in opposition to the Jewish *sunagôgê* (used of the Christian community only in Jas 2:2); evidence is somewhat lacking for a firm conclusion. We also find in the LXX *ekklêsia tou theou* (of God) to refer to the assembly of the people at Sinai and other religious occasions. It seems likely that such use of the phrase influenced use of it by the early Christians. Whatever the Semitic background of the word *ekklêsia* (*qehalâ, kenishtha,* or *'edâ),* the NT idea is originally that of an eschatological people gathered together by Jesus.[2] Furthermore, *ekklêsia* first referred to the local community, and only in the later Deutero-Pauline Colossians and Ephesians was used of the universal Church. Thus R. Bultmann saw an evolution in several stages: Christians began as a sect within Judaism; even the admission of pagans did not fundamentally alter the continuity with the OT people; the theology of the Body of Christ (q.v.) in time led to a sense of being distinct; finally, the delay in the parousia ushered in structures, and the Church became an institution of salvation. The evidence, however, would force a more nuanced treatment of the issue.[3]

The vast majority of references in Paul to the *ekklêsia* are in the context of a particular assembly in a house (e.g., Aquila and Prisca—1 Cor 16:19), city (e.g., Thessalonica—1 Thess 1:1), or area (e.g., Gal 1:2, 22). The OT *qahal*—the liturgical assembly of Israel (LXX *ekklêsia*)—and the Greek social, political, and familial assemblies both probably lie behind the choice of the word by the Christian communities. But 1 Cor 1:2—the phrase "those in every place"—would urge caution about any suggestion that in early writings *ekklêsia* had a purely restricted usage. Moreover, it would seem that the term "Church of God" (1 Cor 15:9; Gal 1:13; Phil 3:6), while primarily referring to the Church at Jerusalem, had already some universalist overtones.[4] Indeed, a careful study of these texts along with others in 1 Cor (1:1; 12:28; 14:34-35; 16:1, 19) makes it unlikely that a wider use of the work *ekklêsia* is to be sought only in the deutero-Pauline Colossians and Ephesians. Again the quasi-name, "called saints," (Rom 1:6; 1 Cor 1:2), and the qualifying *"tou Theou"* (Church of God) transcend local designation. Further, both individuals (2 Cor 5:17) and Churches (Churches of Judea—Gal 1:22; 1 Thess 2:14) are said to be "in Christ." The formula *en Christô* "expresses the newness of the Christian reality established by Christ's action that has taken place in the past and is now taking place in the Spirit. God's action has taken place in Christ; the Christian community now lives in Christ in the power of that saving action and in the likeness of Christ."[5] Finally, the early designation of the followers of Christ as "the way" (Acts 9:2; 19:2, 23; 22:4; 24:14, 22) would seem to imply a consciousness of being a community which is fulfilling the divine plan, and hence not to be restricted to one place.[6] Another word *koinônia* (v. COMMUNION) seems in the light of Qumran to have a similar more universalist meaning.[7] When we come to Ephesians and Colossians it is clear that there is a vision of the Church that is universal (e.g., Col 1:18-24; 2:19; Eph 1:23; 5:22-27). The conclusion of R.E. Brown is judicious: "In tracing how Christians understood themselves as church, one could argue for a logical progression from original unity to regional or ideological diversity and finally to universality."[8] The whole question must be seen in the light of NT ecclesiologies (q.v.), which show the particular concerns and limits of each author.

[1]F. Schüssler Fiorenza, *Foundational Theology: Jesus and the Church* (New York: Crossroad, 1985) 122–132; J.Y. Campbell, "The Origin and Meaning of the Word *Ekklesia*," JTS 49 (1948) 130–142.  [2]J.P. Meier, *Matthew*. NTMess 3 (Wilmington: Glazier—Dublin: Veritas, 1980) 182; K.L. Schmidt, "Ekklêsia," TDNT 3:502-539.  [3]Ibid., and W.A. Meeks, *The First Urban Christians* (New Haven—London: Yale UP, 1983) 74–110.  [4]F. Schüssler Fiorenza (n. 1) 127–128 with nn.; R.E. Brown, *Biblical Exegesis and Church Doctrine* (New Jersey: Paulist—London: Chapman, 1985) 114–134.  [5]F. Schüssler Fiorenza (n. 1) 131.  [6]Brown (n. 4) 117–118.  [7]Ibid., 118–119.  [8]Ibid., 119.

## CLEMENT OF ROME, Pope St. (fl. ca. 96)

Though various traditions describe him as the second or third successor of Peter, Clement may have been only one of several *episkopoi* in Rome ca. 91—ca. 101 C.E. These traditions, attested by such as Tertullian and Irenaeus, witness also to his importance and influence; his *Letter to the Corinthians*[1] was for over a century read in Church and regarded in some places as scriptural. The *Letter* was an occasional piece reacting to the expulsion of presbyters at Corinth, but it allows us to glimpse at some important ecclesiological issues at the end of the 1st century.

The *Letter* opens with an apology for the delay in addressing the dispute. Whether the intervention of the Roman Church was solicited or not, there is no doubt that it felt it had some authority to intervene in the matter. It would be anachronistic to see in this text a full-blown notion of papal primacy, but as S. Tugwell notes, "It does look as if the Roman Church was already conscious of having, and was accepted as having, some sort of responsibility for the well-being of churches other than its own local congregation."[2] It is not clear what the causes of the schism were, but Clement clearly regards the ousting of the elder leaders as unjustified, and he calls on the Church to reestablish Church order (19–20; 46:9; 56–57). He appeals to the order found in the OT (40:1–41:1), before describing the order laid down by the apostles in two key passages that would later be cited by Vatican II (LG 20): "Now, the Gospel was given to the Apostles for us by the Lord Jesus Christ; and Jesus the Christ was sent from God. That is to say that Christ received his commission from God, and the apostles theirs from Christ. . . . And as they went through the territories and townships preaching, they appointed their first converts—after testing them by the Spirit—to be bishops and deacons for the believers of the future" (42:1 and 4). Again, ". . . our apostles knew, through our Lord Jesus Christ, that there would be dissensions over the title of bishop. In their full foreknowledge of this, therefore, they proceeded to appoint the ministers I spoke of, and they went on to add an instruction that if these should fall asleep, other accredited persons should succeed them in their office" (44:1-2).[3] Clement also cites the Pauline analogy of the body (37:4–38:1; cf. 1 Cor 12:14-26). If the suggestion is right that what was at issue in Corinth was the principle of meritocracy, we find a continuing relevance in Clement's insistence on respect for the authority which we find in the Church. His praise of harmony in the Church (19:1–20:12) represents another value, but one in which discernment is necessary; we must not seek peace at any cost; peace must be creative and not a dead absence of conflicting viewpoints.

The prestige of Clement in the early Church is attested by the very many pseudonymous works ascribed to him (v. CLEMENT, PSEUDO), especially the "Second Letter," the Clementine homilies, and the *Apostolic Constitutions* (q.v.).

[1]Texts and commentaries: F.X. Glimm, FC 1:3-58; C.C. Richardson, LCC 1:33-73; R.M. Grant and H.H. Graham, *The Apostolic Fathers*. Vol. 2 (London: Nelson, 1965); J.B. Lightfoot, ed., J.R. Harmer, *The Apostolic Fathers* (Grand Rapids: Baker, 1956 from tr. 1891); M. Staniforth and A. Louth, *Early Christian Writings* (Harmondsworth: Penguin, ²1987) 17–51. See B.E. Bowe, *A Church in Crisis: Ecclesiology and Paraenesis in Clement of Rome*. Harvard Dissertations in Religion 23 (Minneapolis: Fortress, 1988); R.E. Brown and J.P. Meier, *Rome and Antioch: New Testament Cradles of Catholic Christianity* (Mahwah: Paulist—London: Chapman, 1983) 159–183; S. Tugwell, *The Apostolic Fathers*. Outstanding Christian Thinkers (London: Chapman, 1989) 89–103. [2]Op. cit., 90. See Bowe (n. 1); A. Faivre, "Le système normatif dans la lettre de Clement de Rome aux Corinthiens," RevSR 54 (1980) 129–152. [3]Trans. Staniforth—Louth (n. 1) 40–41.

## CLEMENT, PSEUDO- , SECOND LETTER

Several important early documents are ascribed to Clement (q.v.) of Rome, attesting his importance and to the prestige of the Roman Church in the early Church. One of these, the oldest example of Christian preaching is the 2nd *Letter*.[1] It is still used in the liturgy for Office of Readings (Week 32), which rightly describes it as a homily of a 2nd century author. Since it cites the NT as Scripture, and, despite its emphasis on false doctrine, does not refer clearly to Gnosticism, it is likely to date early in the 2nd century.[2] The liturgical context of the homily is clear, but it is not certain whether the author is a presbyter.[3] The homily is an exhortation to moral purity, to steadfastness in persecution, and to repentance. It inveighs against a disjunction between liturgy and life: "And let us not merely seem to pay attention and to believe now, while being admonished by the presbyters, but also when we have gone home, let us remember the commandments of the Lord and let us not be carried away by worldly lusts."[4] A somewhat obscure passage in chapter 14 clearly alludes to "the first Church, the spiritual one, established before the sun and moon" (v. ABEL, CHURCH FROM) and develops the bridal idea found in Eph 5:23-32: "For the scripture says: God made man male and female; the male is Christ and the female is the Church. The sacred books, moreover, and the apostles say that the Church is not of the present time, but existed from the beginning. For she was spiritual, as also our Jesus. . . . And the Church, being spiritual, was revealed in the flesh of Christ showing us that if any of us guard her in the flesh and do not corrupt her, he will receive her again in the Holy Spirit."[5] The author seems to be saying that the Church is incarnate in Christ; hence we must have respect for the flesh of the Church, its exterior, bodily existence, in ourselves and others, if we are to belong to the spiritual Church created before the sun and moon. Such a doctrine of the Church, at once both practical and mystical, is a strong antidote to the paganism which surrounded the author and his audience.

Also ascribed to Clement are two letters to virgins (v. VIRGINS), but which, however, date from about the end of the 3rd or beginning of the 4th century.[6]

[1]Texts and commentaries: F.X. Glimm, FC 1:61-79; R.M. Grant and H.H. Graham, *The Apostolic Fathers*. Vol. 2 (London: Nelson, 1965) 109–135; J.B. Lightfoot, ed., J.R. Harmer, *The Apostolic Fathers* (Grand Rapids: Baker, 1956, tr. of 1891) 43–52; C.C. Richardson, LCC 1:183-189. [2]S. Tugwell, *The Apostolic Fathers*. Outstanding Christian Thinkers (London: Chapman, 1989) 147, n. 3. [3]Cf. Letter 15:1 with 17:3; 19:1. [4]17:3—trans. FC 76. [5]14:2-3—trans. 74. [6]E.S. Cirici, "Las 'Cartas a las virgenes' atribuidas a Clemente romano," EfMex 8/22 (1990) 71–91.

## COMMUNICATIO IN SACRIS (SHARING IN SACRED THINGS)

See INTERCOMMUNION and UNIATE CHURCHES

## COMMUNION—KOINÔNIA

Communion translates the Greek word *koinônia*, which cannot be rendered exactly in English. The root *koin-* suggests what is common, hence words such as "fellowship," "participation," "communion," and "solidarity," always with a personal element, contribute to the sense of *koinônia*. There is no consensus about the origin of the word: OT parallels and Hellenistic ones are both suggested.[1]

In the NT there are several strands of thought.[2] The concept of *koinônia* may of course be present, even when the word is not used. In the texts where it occurs, though there is some overlapping, one can distinguish those which are broadly Christological and pneumatological from those which are also ecclesiological.

We are called into fellowship of the Son (1 Cor 1:9), into communion in the body and blood of Christ (1 Cor 10:16); we have fellowship in the sufferings of Christ (Phil 3:10; 1 Pet 4:13). We are being drawn into fellowship in Christ and with the Father (1 John 1:3, 6). We already have some share in the glory that is to be revealed (1 Pet 5:1), in the divine nature (2 Pet 1:4). There is participation in the gospel, which is either through faith, or through collaboration in or for evangelization (Phil 1:5; cf. 1 Cor 9:23). A most important idea is *koinônia* of the Spirit (2 Cor 13:13; Phil 2:1).[3]

Other texts have a more ecclesiological tone.[4] Paul's collection for the poor in Jerusalem is an act of fellowship (2 Cor 8:4; 9:13; cf. Rom 15:26.) Ministry has overtones of fellowship (2 Cor 8:23.) There is fellowship in faith (Phlm 6; cf. v. 17; 1 John 1:7; Heb 10:33), from which comes sharing (Heb 13:16). Though the more obvious meaning of the fellowship in Acts 2:42

is a sharing of material goods (v. 45; 4:32-37),[5] its placement between teaching and Eucharist would seem to indicate sharing in other ways too, so that a mark of the early Church was that of brothers and sisters who shared with one another and in divine gifts.

*Koinônia* and cognate words in the NT have rich Trinitarian and ecclesiological meaning. Along with such reflections there was a practical building up of communities throughout the Mediterranean basin from NT times.[6] Confession of faith is also a realization of *koinônia*.[7]

Though the word is not always found, the nature of the Church in the early centuries can be summarized by *communio/koinônia*. We frequently find the reality when people speak of the Church as one (q.v.) and catholic (q.v.). The Church is a Church of Churches, a communion of communions; local Churches throughout the world in communion with each other, and each one being a communion of the baptized brought together as a community through the Eucharist. But the communion is not merely horizontal; its baptismal and Eucharistic basis means that it is rooted in the Trinity, in the mystery of God.[8]

In the course of history the scriptural meaning has been largely retained, but in the West especially there was a tendency towards a rather restricted notion of communion more in terms of juridical bonds between bishops and the faithful, bishops among one another, and the faithful among themselves.[9] The reality of communion was an important element in patristic reflection, mostly in the context of Church and of the Eucharist.[10] It was fostered in the ways that Vatican II suggested were expressions of collegiality: councils and the cultivation of bonds of communion (LG 22; v. BISHOPS, COLLEGIALITY). The liturgies of East and West all reflect the double focus of communion: horizontal between the members of the Church; vertical through the Spirit in Christ to the Father.[11] Excommunication (q.v.) was exclusion from communion, especially from the Eucharist.

In the Middle Ages there were developments in law (q.v.) and reforms (v. GREGORY VII and PAPACY) which led to more juridical categories being applied to the Church. But the notion of, though not always the word, communion remained. Thus St. Thomas, for instance, could see the Church not so much as an institution but as constituted by faith and the sacraments of faith.[12] The notion, again not always the word, also survived in the Church's constant teaching and experience of evangelical love, of spirituality, and principally of liturgy. All these emphasized horizontal and vertical communion even when institutional ideas predominated from the later Middle Ages, in Counter-Reformation writings and subsequently in the manuals.

Around the time of Vatican II there was a growing interest in the idea of communion.[13] The council spoke about it in a large number of important texts. In 1975 A. Acerbi published a study which has been fairly well received by theologians.[14] Its thesis is that there are two ecclesiologies in the Constitution on the Church, a juridical ecclesiology and one of communion; the book, however, may oversimplify the reality. Communion, at any rate, is clearly one key to the understanding of the council's ecclesiology. The internal bond between the faithful is described as communion (LG 13; DV 10; UR 2.) It is brought about by the Holy Spirit (LG 4; UR 2; GS 32). Though there is diversity, there are bonds of intimate communion with regard to spiritual riches, apostolic workers and temporal assistance (LG 13).

One essential element of full incorporation into the Church is the bond of ecclesiastical government and communion (LG 13). The visible principle of the unity of faith and communion is Peter and his successors (LG 8, 18; OE 24); bishops are to be in communion with him to assume office (LG 24) and to teach (LG 25). Particular Churches exist in communion with each other (LG 13). Episcopal collegiality (v. BISHOPS, COLLEGIALITY) is an instance of communion. The offices of bishop (LG 22) and priests (PO 7) are to be exercised in "hierarchical communion."[15] This neologism was introduced at a late stage in the elaboration of LG to counteract certain ways of speaking by council members which would have communion as something nonobligatory, and divorced from juridical bonds. Founded on the sacrament of orders, in its fullest reality it is a work of the Spirit, being both spiritual and juridical. The *Nota praevia* (n. 2) of LG distinguishes functions *(munera)* and powers *(potestates):* the former are given in ordination, the latter by juridical commission (cf. LG 21.) The same Note emphasizes that hierarchical communion is not a vague disposition *(quodam affectu),* but requires a juridical form and animation by charity.

Communion is the main operating notion in the decree on ecumenism. The situation of estranged Churches is seen as a separation from full communion (UR 3), which previously existed (UR 14, 19). Though differences are an obstacle to full ecclesiastical communion (UR 3, 4), for those who believe in Christ and are baptized, there is some real though imperfect communion with the Catholic Church (*in quadem cum ecclesia catholica communione, etsi non perfecta, constituuntur*—UR 3; LG 15); there is a communion in prayers and other spiritual benefits (LG 15). The aim of ecumenism is full communion (UR 14, 18, 22; cf. OE 4) in the Eucharist (UR 4). The Churches of the East know that through liturgy and the outpouring of the Spirit they enter into communion with the Trinity (UR 15). The Churches of the East seek to preserve family ties of common faith and charity (*fraternas illas in fidei caritatis que communione necessitudines*—UR 14). Some in the East are already living in full communion with their brothers and sisters who follow the traditions of the West (UR 17). The decree distinguishes two works of the Spirit: ecumenism and the situation of individuals wishing full catholic communion (UR 4). The word "communion" is also used instead of "Churches and ecclesial communities" in relation to religious bodies in dialogue (UR 4). All celebrations of the Lord's Supper, even if imperfect through lack of orders, signify life in communion with Christ (UR 22). Whereas there is communion with other Christians, the council only says that "those who have not yet received the gospel" are related to the people of God in various ways (*diversis rationibus ordinantur*—LG 16).

For Vatican II, then, communion is an internal spiritual reality with visible expression. To speak about this external aspect would not necessarily mean an imposition of juridicism on the spiritual constituent of the Church; the Church is both "a visible assembly and a spiritual community" (LG 8). The gift of catholicity is seen in that "the whole and individual parts grow greater through the mutual communication of all *(ex omnibus invicem communicantibus)*" towards fullness in unity (LG 13); the unity of the Church is a unity of communion, a unity in communion. The Church has essentially two poles; this elliptical structure of episcopal and papal poles is of divine institution.[16]

Communion is so much at the heart of the Church that it signifies the desired aim of ecumenism. It is a dynamic unifying principle of the Church. It is possible to find in Vatican II the basis for a Eucharistic ecclesiology (v. EUCHARIST). The normal expression for sharing in the gift of the Eucharist is communion, a usage retained in Vatican II (SC 55). In the breaking of bread we enter into communion with the Lord and with one another (cf. LG 3; UR 2; AA 8; PO 6).

After the council the notion of communion was studied briefly at the 1969 Synod of Bishops (q.v.) in the context of collegiality. There was more extensive exploration at the 1985 synod celebrating the 20th anniversary of Vatican II. It was seen as a determinant notion of the ecclesiology of the council.[17] In view of some misuse of the notion of People of God, the synod tended to play up the notion of communion in its Final Report.[18] Under the rubric "The Church as Communion," it dealt with the meaning of communion, unity and pluriformity of the Church, Eastern Churches, collegiality, bishops' conferences, participation and co-responsibility in the Church, and ecumenical communion.

The International Theological Commission (q.v.) in 1984 dealt briefly with communion in its document "Select Themes of Ecclesiology." It was at pains to stress that People of God and communion did not impugn the external structures of the Church: "The communion that gives definition to the new people of God is therefore a social communion of a hierarchically ordered sort."[19]

The *Code* of canon law does employ the notion of communion, but it is a somewhat reduced usage. At one time it was proposed that communion be used for the restructuring of the entire *Code*. Mainly for practical reasons this was not followed: it would lose all reference to the 1917 law, which would be against the guidelines given by Paul VI; it would be a radical innovation detached from the historical evolution of Church law and the rich legislative-canonical tradition of the Church.[20] It can be argued that the theological notion of communion and the socio-philosophical notion of society do not really harmonize fully.[21] As a book of law, it had to use juridical categories and language, but its exposition of ecclesial communion (CIC 209) ignored the richness of LG 14 and has no pneumatological reference. It gave the basis of communion in can. 204, dealing with the notion of the Christian faithful, and then proceeded: "Those baptized are fully in communion with the Catholic Church on this earth who are joined with Christ in its visible structure by the bonds of profession of faith, of the sacraments, and of ecclesiastical governance" (CIC 205).[22] This canon is not intended as a full definition of communion; it lacks the crucial demand of LG 14 that one be in grace *("Spiritum Christi habentes")* for full communion.[23] It lays down only what is necessary from a juridical point of view: "on this earth" and "visible structure."

The *Code* uses the term "communion" about 34 times: except for a few instances, it is employed in a univocal sense.[24] It is used generically usually in relation to the Catholic Church (14 times). The term "hierarchical communion" is found twice (CIC 336; 375 § 2), and its equivalent eight times. In the strict sense it is the organic and structural knot which binds together the members of the hierarchy in the episcopal college with one another and with the pope (CIC 336); it can also be seen to determine the relationships of priests (CIC 245 § 2; 275 § 1) and deacons (CIC 757). The parish priest is to work hard "so that the faithful be concerned for parochial communion and that they realize that they are members both of the diocese and of the universal Church and participate in and support such communion" (CIC 529 § 2). This is a specification of a cardinal duty of each member of the Church: "always to maintain communion with the Church" (CIC 209 § 1).

In 1992 the Congregation for the Doctrine of the Faith sent to all bishops a letter entitled "Some Aspects of the Church as Communion."[25] It states that the concept of communion "can certainly be a key for the renewal of the Church" (n. 1). It seems that the reason for the document is that "some approaches to ecclesiology suffer from a clearly inadequate awareness of the

Church as a mystery of communion" (n. 1). It largely follows Vatican II in its five-part exposition: The Church, a Mystery of Communion; Universal Church and Particular Churches; Communion of the Churches, Eucharist and Episcopate; Unity and Diversity in Ecclesial Communion; Ecclesial Communion and Ecumenism. But there are extensions, based on recent papal addresses: the concept of communion "lies at the heart of the Church's self-understanding" (n. 3); "The primacy of the Bishop of Rome and the episcopal college are proper elements of the universal Church that are 'not derived from the particularity of the Churches' [John Paul II] but are nevertheless interior to each particular Church" (n. 13); "Every valid celebration of the Eucharist expresses this communion with Peter and the whole Church, or objectively calls for it, as in the case of Christian Churches separated from Rome" (n. 14); "the formula of the Second Vatican Council: The Church is formed in and out of the Churches (Ecclesia in et ex Ecclesiis), is inseparable from this other formula: The Churches in and formed out of the Church (Ecclesiae in et ex Ecclesia—n. 9)." The letter warns against exaggerations in the way of conceiving the particular Church (n. 9), and of some Eucharistic ecclesiologies (n. 11—v. EUCHARIST). This letter raises a difficult problem of hermeneutics. It seeks "to recall briefly and clearly some of the fundamental elements that are to be considered already settled also by those who undertake the hoped-for theological investigation" (n. 2). It is difficult to see that everything in the letter should be considered as "already settled"; there is some theologizing that at this stage would seem tentative or need further elaboration or even refining.

It is impossible to understate the ecumenical importance of the notion of communion.[26] The World Council of Churches is an example of Churches being in some communion; it also embraces the idea of conciliarity.[27] Communion is central to Orthodox ecclesiology,[28] to its abiding in truth.[29] Communion also features prominently in the various dialogues (q.v.) taking place between the Churches,.[30] and particularly between the Catholic Church and the Anglican Communion (q.v.).[31] The fifth World Conference on Faith and Order (Santiago de Compostela, Spain 1993) was devoted to the topic of communion.

Communion is the way of grounding ecclesiology firmly into the saving Incarnation and the mystery of the Trinity: the Church in its relation to Christ and the Spirit, in its internal unity between local and universal reality, can be seen as a reflection of the Trinitarian perichôrêsis, or mutuality in reciprocal presence.[32] The theology of communion underlies the attempts to build up community within the Church (v. BASIC CHRISTIAN COMMUNITIES and COUNCILS). Communion points to the Eucharistic center of the Church; it is its life principle.[33] The Church through communion is a community of worship, mission, and service.

[1]P.C. Bori, Koinonia: L'idea della comunione nell'ecclesiologia recente e nel Nuovo Testamento (Brescia: Paideia Ed., 1972) 107–113. See J.D.M. Derrett, "Koinos, koinoô," Filología neotestamentaria 5 (1992) 69–78.    [2]Bori (n. 5); F. Hauck, "Koinos etc." TDNT 3:789-809; M. McDermott, "The Biblical Doctrine of Koinônia," BZ 19 (1975) 64–77, 219–233; G. Panikulam, Koinônia in the New Testament. Analecta biblica 85 (Rome: Gregorian UP, 1979); L. Sabourin, "Koinonia in the New Testament," RelStB 1 (1981) 109–115; H.J. Sieben et al., "Koinonia," DSpir 8:1743-1769; L.S. Thornton, The Common Life in the Body of Christ (London, [3]1950).    [3]A. di Marco, "Koinonia-Communio: Flp 2,1," Laur 21 (1980) 376–403.    [4]J.M.R. Tillard, "What Is the Church of God?," OneChr 20 (1984) 226–242. See, with caution, S. Brown, "Koinonia as the Basis of New Testament Ecclesiology?," OneChr 12 (1976) 157–167.    [5]M. Manzanera, "Koinonia en Hch 2, 42. Notas sobre su interpretación y origen histórico-doctrinal," EstE 52 (1977) 307–329.    [6]J. Dunn, "'Instruments of Koinonia' in the Early Church," OneChr 25 (1989) 204–216; J. Eckert, "The Realization of Fellowship in the Earliest Christian Communities," Conc 130 (1979) 21–28; L. Hertling, Communio: Church and Primacy in Early Christianity (Chicago: Loyola UP, 1972).    [7]J.M.R. Tillard, "Koinonia—Sacrament," OneChr 22 (1986) 104–114; idem, "Communion and Salvation," ibid., 28 (1992) 1–12.    [8]J.M.R. Tillard, Église d'églises: L'ecclésiologie de communion (Paris: Cerf, 1987) 47–48.    [9]Cf. M.A. Fahey, "Ecclesiastical 'Economy' and Mutual Recognition of Faith: A Roman Catholic Perspective," Diakonia (USA) 11 (1976) 204–223 at 209.    [10]H.-M. Legrand, "Communion ecclésiale et Eucharistie aux premiers siècles," AnnéeCan 25 (1981) 125–148; H.J. Sieben, "Communion: Chez les pères," DSpir 8:1750-1754; J.M.R. Tillard, "Koinonia," DictEcuMov 572–573.    [11]R.C.D. Jasper and G.J. Cuming, eds., Prayers of the Eucharist: Early and Reformed (New York: Pueblo, 1975).    [12]ST 3a, q.64, a.2; see M. Useros Carretero, "Statuta ecclesiae" y "Sacramenta ecclesiae" en la eclesiología de St. Tomás. Analecta Gregoriana 119 (Rome: Gregorian UP, 1962).    [13]E.g., J. Hamer, The Church Is a Communion (New York, 1964).    [14]Due ecclesiologie: Ecclesiologia giuridica ed ecclesiologia di comunione nella "Lumen gentium." Nuovi saggi teologici 4 (Bologna: Ed. Dehoniane, 1975).    [15]G. Ghirlanda, "Hierarchica communio": Significatio della formula nella Lumen gentium. Analecta gregoriana 216 (Rome: Gregorian UP, 1980); idem, "La notion de communion hiérarchique dans le concile Vatican II," AnnéeCan 25 (1981) 231–254; J. Beyer, "'Hierarchica communio': Una chiave dell'ecclesiologia della 'Lumen gentium,'" CivCatt 132 (1981) 2:464-473.    [16]W. Kasper, "L'Église comme communion: Un fil conducteur dans l'ecclésiologie de Vatican II," Communio 12/1 (1987) 15–31 at 26; cf. Conc 127 (1979); Jurist 36 (1976); I. d'Ercole and A.M. Stickler, eds., Comunione interecclesiale: Collegialità-primato-ecumenismo. Communio 12–13 (Rome: LAS, 1972).    [17]Conc 188 (1986); G. Danneels, "Le synode extraordinaire de 1985," NRT 108 (1986) 161–173; K. McDonnell, "Vatican II (1962–1964), Puebla (1979), Synod (1985). Koinonia/Communio as an Integral Ecclesiology," JEcuSt 25 (1988) 399–427; J.M.R. Tillard, "The Church of God Is a Communion: The Ecclesiological Perspective of Vatican II," OneChr 17 (1981) 117–131 = Irén 53 (1980) 451–468; idem, "Corps du Christ et Esprit Saint: Les exigences de la communion," Irén 63 (1990) 163–185; J. Willebrands, "Vatican II's Ecclesiology of Communion," OneChr 23 (1987) 179–181.    [18]Synode extraordinaire. Célébration de Vatican II (Paris: Cerf, 1986) Rapport finale II, C: 549–567 at 559–563; A. Danaux, "L'Église comme communion. Réflections à propos du rapport final du synode extraordinaire de 1985," NRT 110 (1988) 16–37, 161–180; J.A. Komonchak, "The Synod of 1985 and the Notion of the Church," ChicSt 26 (1987) 330–345.

[19]International Theological Commission, *Texts and Documents 1969–1985* (San Francisco: Ignatius, 1989) 287.   [20]R. Castillo Lara, "La communion ecclésiale dans le nouveau Code de droit canonique," StCan 17 (1983) 331–355 at 332–333.   [21]H. Müller, "Utrum 'communio' sit principium formale-canonicum novae codificationis iuris canonici ecclesiae latinae," Periodica 74 (1985) 85–108.   [22]V. de Paolis, "Communio in novo codice iuris canonici," Periodica 77 (1988) 521–552.   [23]Acta Syn 3/1:203—Alberigo-Magistretti 446.   [24]Castillo Lara (n. 20) 340–341.   [25]CathIntern 3 (1992) 761–767, with ecumenical reactions 767–776; C. Hill, " 'The Church as Communion': An Anglican Response," OneChr 28 (1992) 323–330.   [26]J.M.R. Tillard, "Ecclésiologie de communion et exigence oecuménique," Irén 59 (1986) 201–230.   [27]*Councils and the Ecumenical Movement.* WCC Studies 5 (Geneva, 1968).   [28]O. Clément, "Orthodox Ecclesiology as an Ecclesiology of Communion," OneChr 6 (1970) 101–122; J.D. Zizioulas, "Verité et communion dans la perspective de la pensée patristique grecque," Irén 50 (1977) 451–510; idem, *Being as Communion: Studies in Personhood and the Church* (London: Darton, Lonman & Todd, 1985).   [29]J.D. Zizioulas, "Verité et communion dans la perspective de la pensée patristique grecque," Irén 50 (1977) 451–510.   [30]See H. Meyer and L. Vischer, eds., *Growth in Agreement: Reports and Agreed Statements of Ecumenical Conversations on a World Level.* Ecumenical Documents 2—Faith and Order Paper 108 (New York: Paulist—Geneva: WCC, 1984) passim; J.A. Burgess and J. Gros, *Building Unity: Ecumenical Dialogues with Roman Catholic Participation in the United States.* Ecumenical Documents 4 (New York: Paulist, 1989) passim.   [31]ARCIC II Report, "Church as Communion" (1991), CathIntern 2 (1991) 327–338 with evaluation by F.A. Sullivan, 339–341.   [32]R. Kress, "The Church as Communio: Trinity and Incarnation as the Foundation of Ecclesiology," Jurist 36 (1976) 127–158; idem, *The Church: Communion, Sacrament, Communication* (New York—Mahwah: Paulist, 1985) 30–107.   [33]P. Franzen, "La comunione ecclesiale principio di vita," CrNSt 2 (1981) 165–185; H. Rikhof, *The Concept of the Church* (London: Sheed & Ward, 1980) 232, 234.

## COMMUNION OF SAINTS

The words "Communion of Saints" *(communio sanctorum/koinônia tôn hagiôn)* are first attested in the late 4th century.[1] The underlying reality is older. In the NT itself, the members of the Church are called the "saints" (v. HOLY) and the notion of communion (q.v.) is well developed. Both of these ideas are found in the pre-Nicene Fathers.[2]

There is an ambiguity in the genitive plural which, being masculine or neuter in Greek or Latin, can mean "of holy persons/things." The earliest Greek usages seem to refer to sharing in the Eucharist, a meaning also found in the West. However, the West more frequently refers to holy persons, often with the denotation of those in glory, those on earth, and later occasionally also those in purgatory (q.v.). J.N.D. Kelly suggests that from the 5th to 8th centuries the primary meaning is "fellowship with holy persons," with sacramental meanings being secondary, perhaps arising from the apparent silence about sacraments, especially the Eucharist, in the creeds. For Augustine, the key to the communion of saints is his idea of the whole Christ *(totus Christus).*[3]

To be an operative word for modern theology and especially ecumenical dialogue, the notion of communion of saints needs some explanation. It touches on several ecclesiological themes: the Church as the sacrament of salvation (q.v.); Trinitarian life shared by its members; its communitarian dimension;[4] the three states of the Church—heaven, earth, purgatory (LG 49);[5] the role of Mary (q.v.)—Mother, model, and intercessor.[6]

At the Reformation the term "Communion of Saints" was retained in some form. The reference to the Communion of Saints in the Apostles' Creed is retained in Luther's *Shorter Catechism*[7] and is developed in the *Larger Catechism,* where it is interpreted as a holy communion *(ein heilige Gemein)* meaning the holy ones who make up the Church who are endowed with spiritual gifts used in love and concord.[8] Calvin (q.v.) holds a similar doctrine, explicitly disavowing the intercession of the saints.[9] The *Augsburg Confession* (q.v.) spoke of the Church as "the congregation of saints and true believers" (a. 8), but rejected the cult of the saints (a. 21).[10] The *Heidelberg Catechism* answers question 55, What dost thou understand by the communion of saints?: "First, that believers, all and every one, as members of Christ, have part in him and in all his treasures and gifts. Second, that each must feel himself bound to use his gifts, readily and cheerfully, for the advantage and welfare of other members."[11] The Communion of Saints also features in the *Anglican Catechism* of 1549 and 1662,[12] the *Westminster Confession of Faith* (1647),[13] and the *Articles of Faith* of the Presbyterian Church of England (1890).[14] A measure of agreement was reached between Anglicans and the Orthodox on the Communion of Saints in the 1980 Llandaff Statement.[15] The difficulties of the Catholic position as perceived by Lutherans are found in the U.S. Dialogue 1983–1990; they are still substantive[16]

The sense of the Communion of Saints is very strong in Orthodoxy, even though the expression seems originally Western.[17] It is seen in solidarity between the members of the Church, mutual sharing in faith, sacraments, love, prayer; those in heaven share with those on earth. Whereas in the West we are warned that religious images should not distract from liturgical celebration,[18] in the East the centrality in the liturgical area of the iconostasis is a potent reminder that the saints, far from being a distraction, are profoundly involved in the liturgical celebration.[19] It is especially the *anaphora* (Eucharistic Prayer) in the East and in the Catholic West that gives a primary experience of the Communion of Saints: the Eucharist is celebrated with the explicit memory of Mary and the saints, with commemoration of the dead (v. PURGATORY), as well as for the living.

One of the significant deductions from the doctrine of the Communion of Saints is a rich theology of intercession and exchange of merits. It also opposes any tendency to see salvation purely in personal terms.[20] The doctrine of the Communion of Saints gives rise to the idea of the treasury of the Church (q.v.), itself the basis of indulgences (q.v.).[21] A developed understanding of the Communion of Saints will help to integrate the vertical and horizontal dimensions of the Church; it also has the possibility of opening up new perspectives for ecumenical discussion on the person and role of the Virgin Mary.

[1]J.N.D. Kelly, *Early Christian Creeds* (London: Longman, [3]1972) 388–397. Bibliog. Y. Congar, *I Believe in the Holy Spirit,* 3 vols. (New York: Seabury—London: Chapman, 1983) 3:63, n. 24; see many aspects in QuatreF 25–26 (1988) 3–131.   [2]B. Testa, "La comunione dei santi: Riflessioni teologiche," Communio 97 (Jan.–Feb. 1988) 10–30; F. Bolgiani, "Sanctorum communio: Le nouveau testament et les premiers siècles de la théologie patristique," QuatreF 25–26 (1988) 17–48.   [3]R. Brunet, "Charité et communion des saints chez saint Augustin," RAscétM 31 (1955) 386–398.   [4]Testa (n. 2) 17–25.   [5]C. Schönborn, "La 'communio sanctorum' e i tre 'stati di vita' della Chiesa," Communio 97 (Jan.–Feb. 1988) 31–45.   [6]N. Bux, "La presenza di Maria nella 'communio sanctorum' della Chiesa," Ibid., 67–73; A.M. Triacca and A. Pistoia, *La Mère du Jésus-Christ et la communion des saints dans la liturgie.* Biblioteca Ephemerides Liturgicae subsidia 37 (Rome: CLV—Ediz. Liturgiche, 1986).   [7]Bekenntnisschriften 511.   [8]2:3—Ibid., 657–658.   [9]*Institutes of Christian Religion* 4:1, 3—LCC 21:1014-1016; 3:20, 24—LCC 21:882-883.   [10]Schaff, Creeds 3:12, 26; G. Kretschmer—R. Laurentin, "Der Artikel vom Dienst der Heiligen in der Confession Augustana," in H. Meyer and H. Schütte, eds., *Confession Augustana Bekenntnis des einen Glaubens* (Paderborn: Bonifacius—Frankfurt a. M.: Lembeck, 1980) 256–280.   [11]Ibid., 3:325.   [12]Ibid., 3:518.   [13]Ch. 26—Ibid., 3:659-660.   [14]Art. 17—Ibid., 3:918.   [15]H. Meyer and L. Vischer, *Growth in Agreement.* Ecumenical Documents 2—Faith and Order Paper 108 (New York: Paulist—Geneva: WCC, 1984) 57–59.   [16]H.G. Anderson et al., eds., *The One Mediator, the Saints and Mary.* Lutherans and Catholics in Dialogue VIII (Minneapolis: Augsburg, 1992).   [17]P.N. Trembelas, *Dogmatique de l'Église orthodoxe catholique,* 3 vols. (Chevetogne: Desclée de Brouwer, 1967) 2:439-453; M. Basarb, "Communio sanctorum nach orthodoxem Verständnis," UnaSan 43 (1988) 284–288, 308.   [18]*Roman Missal* GI 278.   [19]A. Vicini, "L'iconostasi come 'communio sanctorum,'" Communio 97 (Jan.–Feb. 1988) 74–85.   [20]H. de Lubac, "Credo sanctorum communionem," Communio (Milan) 1 (1972) 22–31; P. Emmanuel, "Je crois à la communion des saints aujourd'hui," VieSp 134 (1980) 228–249; cf. S. Benko, *The Meaning of Sanctorum Communio.* Studies in Historical Theology 3 (London, 1964).   [21]Paul VI, *Indulgentiarum doctrina* (1967)—AAS 59 (1967) 5–14/Flannery 1:62-79, ch. 2, nn. 4–5.

## CONCILIARISM

Conciliarism arose as a theory during the Great Schism (1378–1417), when the Latin Church was divided in allegiance between two and, for a time, three popes. It held the proposition that the supreme authority was vested in an ecumenical council independently of the pope, and that the council was superior to him. The high points of conciliarism were the councils of Constance (q.v.) and Basle (q.v.). The great achievement of Constance was the reestablishment of unity. The fact that neither Constance nor Basle wished to abolish the papacy shows that they were rooted in Catholic constitutional principles.

A judgment on medieval conciliarism depends largely on how one interprets the decree, *Haec sancta,* of the 5th session of the Council of Constance (6 April 1415), and its reception by the Council of Basle.[1] First of all, we have to agree that it was *Haec sancta* that led to the end of the schism. Interpretations of its significance vary.[2] B. Tierney sees the decree as giving a foundation to a moderate constitutionalism in the Church.[3] G. Alberigo stresses: the self-understanding of the council as being legitimately united in the Holy Spirit; the immediate presence to the council of Christ; the duty of obedience of all the faithful, including the pope, in matters of reform, especially the ending of schism. In particular, Constance sees its power as immediately from God, and not one mediated by the pope.[4]

Basle, in turn, allows for a papal convocation of a council; but once it is assembled, its power comes from Christ, so that the pope cannot dismiss it in the way he convoked it. The council now represents the universal Church. The "three truths" (v. BASLE) are an assertion that the Church is the pillar and ground of truth, and one who does not conform to it is heretical.

A later development, again showing independence from the papacy, was Gallicanism (q.v.). The orthodox response became clarified over the centuries. Key points in this development were Vatican I (q.v.), with its doctrine of papal primacy, and the Vatican II (q.v.) teaching on collegiality of bishops (q.v.) with and under the pope. The permanent issue raised by conciliarism is the tension which exists in the Church between its papal, monarchical principle, and its corporate principle of dialogue and shared responsibility. The solution lies in a deepened theology of communion (q.v.).

[1]Tanner 1:409-410; J. Beck, *Le Concile de Basle (1434): Les origines du theatre reformiste et partisan en France.* The History of Christian Thought 18 (Leiden: Brill, 1979) 47–62; A. Black, *Council and Commune: The Conciliar Movement and the Fifteenth-century Heritage* (London: Burns & Oates—Shepherdstown: Patmos, 1979); M. Fois, "Il concilio di Costanza nella storiografia recente," CivCatt 126 (1975) 2:11-27; idem, "Il valore ecclesiologico del decreto 'Haec sancta' del Concilio di Costanza," ibid., 3:138-152; T.E. Morrissey, "After Six Humdred Years: The Great Western Schism, Conciliarism and Constance," TS 40 (1979) 495–509; Bibl. J. Wohlmuth in Alberigo, Concili 177–281.   [2]J. Wohlmuth (n. 1) 268–276.   [3]"Hermeneutics and History: The Problem of Haec sancta," in T. Sandquist and T. Powicke, eds., *Essays in Honour of Bertie Wilkinson* (Toronto, 1969) 354–370; cf. idem, *Foundations of the Conciliar Theory: The Contributions of the Medieval Canonists from Gratian to the Schism* (Cambridge, 1955).   [4]*Chiesa conciliare: Identità e significato del conciliarismo* (Brescia: Paideia, 1981) 165–205.

## CONCORDATS

The current Catholic usage of "concordat" is that of an agreement between the Holy See and a sovereign state.[1] The first concordat was that of Worms (1122), which ended the investiture (q.v.) controversy. But it is largely a 19th- and 20th-century phenomenon, beginning with the concordat of 1801 between Pius VII and Napoleon Bonaparte which restored the Catholic Church in France. In the following years the publication by the emperor of the Organic Articles sought to regulate further the relation of State and Church to the disadvantage of the latter. These were not repealed until the formal separation of Church and State in France (1905).[2]

In the redrawn map of Europe after the 1914–1918 World War, the Church entered into a variety of agreements with countries of various political structures.[3] In general the Holy See sought, but did not always obtain in practice, the free nomination of bishops, of teachers, and seminary staff; freedom for clergy in their ministry; the legal rights and liberties of religious institutions; recognition of Church marriages; the right to have Catholic schools; the right of ecclesiastical legal persons to acquire, possess, and administer property.

A most difficult concordat to achieve was the one with the fascist Italian state under B. Mussolini which, with the Lateran Treaty (1929), finally ended the decades-long hostility of the Church to a united Italy. The Italian concordat became in some ways a model for subsequent concordats,[4] several of which were later signed with Latin-American states. The concordat signed with Hitler in 1933 would be controversial. It did have the effect in the beginning of mitigating Nazi oppression of the Church, but as time went on it gradually became less effective.

In the period after World War II, several concordats were signed, notably with Spain (1953). However, where a full concordat proved impossible, the Holy See tried to get in place some other legal document, such as the protocols with states in Eastern Europe, and the "Modus vivendi" treaty with Tunisia in 1964.

It would seem likely that such treaties will be the way ahead in Church-state relations, when these require legal instruments.[5] However, as late as 1977 there was a revision of the concordat with Italy.[6]

The appropriate body of the Holy See in dealing with these matters is the Secretariat of State. Church law leaves concordats untouched (CIC 3); such matters of Church-state are handled by papal legates, not by local bishops, whose advice is, however, to be sought (CIC 365).

[1]J. Julg, L'Église et les états: Histoire des concordats (Paris: Nouvelle Cité, 1990).   [2]R. Aubert, in Jedin-Dolan 7:50-82.   [3]G. May, in Jedin-Dolan 10:177-228.   [4]R. Coppola, "Le concordat italien comme modèle des concordats modernes," Kanon 10 (1991) 89–104.   [5]C. Corral, "The Concordat and Other Conventions Between the Roman Catholic Church and Various States 'in vigore' at the Present," Kanon 10 (1991) 77–88.   [6]L. Guerzon, "La revisione del Concordato: Un occasione per un profondo ripensamento della problematica relativa ai rapporti tra stato e chiesa," DirEccl 88 (1977) 263–281.

## CONFESSORS

The NT stresses the need of confessing the faith (1 John 2:23; 1 Tim 6:16). Denial of the faith risks denial by Christ himself before the Father (Matt 10:32). In the early centuries confession and martyrdom went together, and there is some evidence of martyrs being called "confessors."[1] From the 3rd century until the "Edict" of Constantine (q.v.), the terminology becomes clearer: martyrs died for the faith; confessors were those who suffered for it but were not put to death, a distinction recorded by Eusebius.[2] When peace came to the Church, confessors were those who were distinguished by virtue and asceticism.

In the *Apostolic Tradition* (9/10:1-2—q.v.) we read of two kinds of confessors: those who had suffered seriously for the faith; those whose punishment had been slight or private. The bishop's hand is not to be laid on the first "for deaconate or priesthood" (*non imponetur manus super eum ad diaconatum vel presbyteratum*— v. IMPOSITION OF THE HANDS). Many Catholic,[3] but fewer Protestant,[4] scholars are embarrassed by this text. The solution of B. Botte commends itself: it seems impossible that the author of the text would envisage the sending of the Spirit for ministry to occur at public profession of faith. It would be more likely that confessors that have publicly professed have the *dignity* of priesthood or deaconate, and hence do not need imposition of the hand. But lesser confessors need the imposition of hand for the dignity of each order. The problem is control or ordering of the confessors who, if numerous, could cause confusion, not only by their issuing of a *libellus* (petition) but in obtaining personal places of honor.[5]

The custom of confessors giving this *libellus* led to abuses. It was originally a document from a martyr or confessor which was given in favor of one who had apostasized and might be doing public penance. It seems to have caused particular difficulties at Carthage, and Cyprian (q.v.) complained about the laxity which arose from overfree bestowal of the *libellus pacis*. There may also have been a problem arising from the confessors being peremptory in their request that a lapsed person be reconciled (v. RECONCILIATION).[6] As the confessors thought that their own sufferings were of avail also to the lapsed before God, the *libellus* can be seen as an early form of indulgence (q.v.).

After the age of the martyrs the Fathers did not hesitate to see the ascetical life in terms of martyrdom, for example, Athanasius speaking about Anthony did so.[7] Just as the martyrs rejected the world through death, the confessors, especially through asceticism, were also considered dead to the world. In the West the first confessors to be venerated were bishops: Sylvester at Rome (d. 335), Martin in Gaul (d. 397),

Severus at Naples (d. ca. 409), Augustine (d. 430—q.v.). In the East the early confessors were: Anthony (d. 373), Hilarion (d. 371), Athanasius (d. 373). Later the term was used generally about holy persons; King Edward of England (1003–1066), for example, was declared a confessor by Alexander III in 1161.

In the post-Vatican II revision of the liturgy the category of confessor is no longer used in the common of saints; it is replaced by commons of pastors, and of holy men and women.

---

[1]E. Day, "Confessor," NCE 4:141-142; B. Köttling, "Die Stellung des Konfessors in der alten Kirche," JbAC 19 (1976) 7–23.    [2]*Hist. eccl.* 5:2, 2-3, p. 204.    [3]E.g., J. Coppens, *L'imposition des mains et les rites connexes* (Paris, 1925) 152.    [4]E.g., J.E. Stam, *Episcopacy in the Apostolic Tradition of Hippolytus.* Bd. 111 der theologischen Dissertationen (Basel, 1969) 50–58.    [5]SC 11bis:27-28; cf. E.R. Hardy, "The Decline and Fall of the Confessor-Presbyter," StPatr 15/1 (1984) 221–226.    [6]*Epist.* 33—PL 4:226/Library of Fathers 17 (Oxford, 1884) 75–77; cf. *De lapsis* CSEL 3/1:235-265.    [7]*Vita Antonii* 46–47—PG 26:911/Athanasius, *The Life of Anthony.* Classics of Western Spirituality (New York: Paulist, 1980) 65–66; cf. Sulpicius Severus about St. Martin of Tours, *Epist.* 2—CSEL 1:143-144; John Chrysostom, *Hom. in epist. ad Heb.* 11:3—PG 63:93; Augustine, *Serm.* 286—PL 38:1300; *Serm.* 118—PL 38:1439-1440.

## CONFIRMATION

There is an enormous amount of writing on almost every aspect of confirmation:[1] its origins;[2] its rite;[3] the recipient, especially the age at which it is to be received;[4] the effects of the sacrament, particularly the giving of the Holy Spirit[5] and its ecclesial dimension;[6] the practice of other Churches.[7] This article concentrates on the ecclesial dimension of the sacrament and takes as its main sources Vatican II, the Apostolic Constitution which introduced the revised rite, and the liturgical text.

Vatican II called for a renewal of the sacrament of confirmation, to show its place in the total rite of initiation (SC 71). In LG 11 there are three comparatives (given here with italics) which show the key issue of confirmation, viz., its relation to baptism: "With the sacrament of confirmation they are bound *more perfectly* to the Church; they are enriched by a *special strength* of the Holy Spirit, and in this way they are under *more pressing* obligation *(arctius obligantur)* to spread the faith by word and deed." Here there would seem to be one primarily individual effect (strengthening) and two ecclesial effects (binding to Church and obligation of witness). Almost all works on confirmation point to the (Pseudo) Faustus of Riez (5th c.) as the originator of the notion of strength *(ad robur)*.

In the 1971 apostolic constitution *Divinae consortium naturae* (DCN), with which he introduced the revised rite,[8] Pope Paul VI retained this basic theology of Vatican II, as did the General Instruction (GI) and the rite (R) themselves.[9] The revised rite was almost totally the work of B. Botte with some contribution from B. Kleinheyer, hence the importance of their studies.[10] The traditional scriptural basis for confirmation (Acts 8:15-17) is strengthened in DCN by an account of the Spirit in the life of Jesus and at Pentecost. After a historical study of the rite, Paul VI adopted a modified Byzantine formula: *accipe signaculum Doni Spiritus Sancti* (ICEL "Be sealed with the Gift of the Holy Spirit"). To the dismay of some liturgists the pope further declared that the traditional imposition of the hand was contained in the anointing with the bishop's thumb. They were even more upset by the fact that the imposition of hands over all those to be confirmed with the ancient prayer "All powerful God" is not part of the essence of the sacrament.[11] In the revised rite great care is taken to link confirmation with baptism: there are many references in DCN and GI as well as in the rite. There are also clearly seen individual effects such as grace and strengthening of the recipient, as well as an ecclesial role of spreading the Christian message (GI 9).

The theological problems arise when we begin to ask how precisely confirmation is related to baptism, especially as LG 11 seems to give a similar task of witnessing to both sacraments. There are also major theological questions about the relation of the sacrament to the Eucharist, particularly as in many countries children receive the Eucharist before the second sacrament of initiation. One way forward is to focus on the traditional doctrine of sacramental character. The three sacramental characters give a state in the Church: member, official witness, ordained minister. It is the character that determines the kind of grace received; the reception of the character of confirmation gives an expanded capacity to receive grace, grace which in this case is for a public mission in the Church. It is the same character that allows the Eucharist to have more profound effects in one confirmed than in one merely baptized. It can be argued that this view has solid grounds in the teaching of St. Thomas.[12]

One could go further and state that confirmation will have a different effect (within the category of public witness) depending on the state of life of the individual who has received it: single, married, widowed, religious, deacon, priest, or bishop. In each state there are new possibilities for the sacrament to be effective.

The main theological problems affecting confirmation arise from poor pneumatology and the neglect of the sacramental character. The main pastoral problems come from the fact that expediency, rather than theology, often governs questions of reception, age, suitable preparation, and catechesis.[13]

Practical issues about the minister are covered in the GI and by law (CIC 879–896): the *Code* refused the Vatican II teaching that bishops are the originating minister *(ministri originarii—LG 26)*, preferring the formula of Trent, ordinary minister (*ordinarium ministrum*—CIC 882).[14] A priest may, however, assist the bishop, administering the sacrament if there is too great a number of candidates (GI 8; R 28; CIC 814). A priest who baptizes one who is no longer an infant, or receives an already baptized person into full communion with the Church, also confirms at the same time (CIC 883). Priests may also confirm in danger of death and in some other situations (CIC 883 § 3; 884). The Latin Church therefore sets great store by the episcopal minister who admits the candidate into fuller life in the Church, and who in his person represents the apostolic link with Pentecost (GI 7). In the Churches of the East there was more concern with the integrity of the three sacraments of initiation, even though the link with the bishop is preserved through the necessity of having the myron (chrism) confected by him (CCEO 693). In the East "Chrismation with Holy Myron," as it is called, can be validly conferred by all priests (CCEO 696 § 1). Most Churches of the East celebrate together the three sacraments of initiation. It follows that an extensive theology of Chrismation is not found in the East; with some exceptions those in the East look to the whole sacramental initiation. Indeed so diverse are the liturgies both ancient and modern, Eastern and Western, that about all that can be affirmed with certainty concerning every text is that there is always some gifting by the Holy Spirit, and some connection with a bishop.

The Church is still in the process of coming to an understanding of this second, and secondary, sacrament of initiation, in which the varying agendas of theologians, liturgists, and pastoral agents all are important contributions.

---

[1]Bibliog., A. Caprioli, "Saggio bibliografico sulla confermazione nelle ricerche storico-teologiche dal 1946 al 1973," ScuolC 103 (1975) 645–659; L. Leijssen, "Confirmation: Status Quaestionis with an Overview of the Literature," QLtg 70 (1989) 1–28; A.M. Triacca, "Per una trattazione organica sulla 'confermazione': verso una teologia liturgica (Rassegna e ragguaglio)," EphLtg 86 (1972) 128–179. Studies: G. Austin, *Anointing with the Spirit. The Rite of Confirmation: The Use of Oil and Chrism.* Studies in the Reformed Rites of the Catholic Church 3 (New York: Pueblo, 1985); T. Marsh, *Gift of Community: Baptism and Confirmation.* Message of the Sacraments 2 (Wilmington: Glazier, 1984); L. Walsh, *The Sacraments of Initiation: Baptism, Confirmation, Eucharist* (London: Chapman, 1988) 111–164; Conc 122 (1979). [2]C. Munier, "Initiation Chrétienne et rites d'onction (IIe–IIIe siècles)," RevSR 64 (1990) 115–125. See controverted A. Kavanagh, *Confirmation: Origins and Reform* (New York: Pueblo, 1988) with P. Turner, "The Origins of Confirmation: An Analysis of Aidan Kavanagh's Hypothesis," Worship 65 (1991) 320–336 with reply 337–338; A. Kavanagh, "The Origins and Reform of Confirmation," QLtg 70 (1989) 69–80 = SVlad 70 (1989) 69–80. [3]G.-H. Baudry, "La réforme de la confirmation de Vatican II à Paul VI," MélSR 45 (1988) 83–101; L. Ligier, *La confirmation: Sens et conjoncture oecuménique hier et aujourd'hui.* Théologie historique 23 (Paris: Beauchesne, 1973). [4]M. Balhoff, "Age for Confirmation: Canonical Evidence," Jurist 45 (1985) 549–587; M. Gwinnell, "Confirmation: Sacrament of Initiation," CleR 69 (1984) 126–135; J. Nuttal, "Confirmation: At What Age?," CleR 57 (1982) 278–281. [5]K.J. Becker, "Le don de la confirmation," MaisD 168 (1986) 15–32; A. Elberti, "Accipe signiculaum doni Spiritus Sancti. La confermazione: fonte del sacerdozio regale dei fedeli?," Greg 72 (1991) 491–513; A. Nocent, "La confirmation: Questions posées aux théologiens et aux pasteurs," Greg 72 (1991) 689–704. [6]P. van den Berghe, "La confirmation dans la vie ecclésiale d'aujourd'hui," Qltg 70 (1989) 117–126; E. Doyle, "Confirmation for Commitment to Mission," CleR 57 (1982) 161–165; C. O'Donnell, *The Ecclesial Effect of Confirmation: A Study in Saint Thomas and in the Revised Rite.* Diss. exc. (Rome: Gregorian UP, 1987)—full text 2 vols. (Ann Arbor: UMI, 1988). [7]R. Bornet, "La confirmation dans le protestantisme et dans l'anglicanisme," MaisD 168 (1986) 77–105; idem, "La confirmation dans les Églises de la Réforme: Tradition luthérienne, calvinienne et anglicane," Qltg 70 (1989) 51–68; J.D.C. Fischer, *Confirmation: Then and Now.* Alcuin Club (London: SPCK, 1978; M. Hackett, "The Rite of 'Confirmation' in the Book of Common Prayer and in Authorized Services 1973," AngTR 56 (1974) 292–310. [8]Text: *The Rites of the Catholic Church. Vol. 1A—Initiation* (New York: Pueblo, 2,1988) 472–478. [9]Ibid., GI 479–486; R 487–494. [10]B. Botte, "Problèmes de la confirmation," Qltg 53 (1972) 3–10; B. Kleinheyer, "Le nouveau rituel de la confirmation," MaisD 110 (1972) 51–71. [11]*Rites* (n. 8) DCN 477; GI 9—482. [12]C. O'Donnell, "Confirmation: Light from St. Thomas," MilltownSt 25 (1990) 76–94; 27 (1991) 62–81. [13]See bibliog. (n. 1) and P. De Clerck, "La confirmation, moyen de catéchèse?," QLtg 70 (1989) 89–100. [14]DS 1630/ND 1436.

## CONGAR, Cardinal Yves M.J. (1904–1995)

Born in the French Ardennes in 1904, Yves Congar studied under J. Maritain at the Institut Catholique in Paris, before entering the Dominican Order; after his profession in 1925 he studied at Le Saulchoir (then in Belgium). There he found a new approach to St. Thomas, one which relied more on the actual text of the author than on the use of his text for apologetic purposes and for support of narrow positions of the magisterium. Its method was described by M.D. Chenu in a book subsequently placed on the Index in 1942.[1] Congar was introduced to the writings of J.A. Möhler (q.v.) by Chenu. He was to have a lasting influence on Congar for several reasons: his pioneering work in ecumenism; his erudition in patristics; his advocacy of *ressourcement;* his concern to balance both Christological and pneumatological dimensions of the Church.

At the time of his ordination in 1930 Congar was convinced of a calling to work for Christian unity;[2] he was confirmed in his ecumenical vocation by a meeting in 1932 with Abbé P. Couturier (v. ECUMENISM, SPIRITUALITY); he had lasting associations with the ecumenical monastery of Chevetogne. He undertook study of Reformation and of Orthodox authors. He became concerned with problems of presenting the faith as a contemporary message, and founded and edited the series *Unam Sanctam.* Its first volume was his classic work on ecumenism, *Chrétiens-désunis,* translations of which were afterwards forbidden by the Vatican.[3]

After wartime incarceration he returned to teaching in Le Saulchoir. By then storm clouds were gathering for the bitter campaign about the so-called "New Theology." In 1950 he published another classic, this one on true and false reform in the Church.[4] In the same year Pius XII moved against the "New Theology" in his encyclical *Humani generis.*[5] The pope warned against a dangerous historicism and false irenicism, but without naming any author. The finger was pointed at Congar among others, and he suffered irksome restrictions before being relieved of teaching in 1954. He recalls the period in an important introduction to his collected essays, *Dialogue Between Christians.*[6]

After the war he developed an interest in the laity, which produced the path-finding *Lay People in the Church.*[7] In it he used as a major unifying notion the trilogy Priest-Prophet-King (q.v.), which would afterwards be significant at Vatican II.

From 1954 to 1960 he was more or less in exile: Jerusalem, Cambridge, Strasbourg. He found favor with John XXIII and was a consultant in the preparatory work for Vatican II, becoming a peritus in 1962. During the council he contributed to at least eight documents (LG, UR, NA, DV, DH, AG, PO, and GS).[8] After the council he wrote extensively on its texts and teaching, as well as producing notable historical studies in ecclesiology.[9] His interest in the thought of the East eventfully bore fruit in substantial volumes on pneumatology.[10]

It is very difficult to classify the enormous output of Congar, more than 30 books and 1200 articles, not including reviews.[11] In an important study W. Henn suggests three categories under which his works can be classified: ecumenism, questions of fundamental theology, ecclesiology.[12] Nor is it easy to name the main influences of his thought apart from his beloved St. Thomas, though some can be suggested. From 1932 he kept in contact with current writing on ecclesiology through regular bulletins and reviews, particularly in *La vie intellectuelle, Bulletin Thomiste, Revue des sciences philosophiques et théologiques,* adding pneumatology in later years. His researches in the history of ecclesiology brought him deeply into the Fathers, the medieval theologians, and medieval councils. He was especially drawn to Luther (q.v.), J.A. Möhler (q.v.), M. Blondel, K. Barth (q.v.), all of whom he interpreted with critical sympathy. He had a remarkable grasp of Anglican, Protestant, and Orthodox thought. The liturgy of East and West was also an important influence.

Congar's work would seem to keep in tension two poles: tradition and the actual situation of the Church. He sought to serve the Church and its faith by a contemporary exposition rooted in the riches of the past. Now that studies begin to appear,[13] and more than a dozen doctoral theses, an evaluation of his place in 20th-century ecclesiology is emerging;[14] it is certainly a very significant one. Few questions about the Church have not been treated by him, always with critical judgment and enormous erudition. As a theologian he may be best described as historian and renewer. Reflecting on his work he stated simply, "I am no philosopher," and asserted that K. Rahner's program of rethinking the Church's message for today's pagan world was not his particular gift. However, as he thought of his cultivation of the *Unam sanctam* series and of his own writings, he added, "But I was not to know—Another knew it on my behalf!—that this would pave the way for Vatican II. I was filled to overflowing. All the things to which I gave quite special attention issued in the Council: ecclesiology, ecumenism, reform of the Church, the lay state, mission, ministries, collegiality, return to the sources and Tradition."[15] It could be a worthy epitaph, though he might prefer the title of the book he wrote in 1969, *This Church Which I Love.*[16] In an interview about 1985 he stated: "The study of theology, in which I have been engaged all my life . . . has always been inseparably linked for me with the celebration of the liturgy. I find it essential to 'celebrate' the Mysteries that I am studying. The two are for me one single thing."[17] Of his replete work one can say that anything he wrote is worth reading and still relevant, either in itself or for an understanding of Vatican II and of the contemporary Church.

[1]*Un école de théologie: Le Saulchoir* (Kain: Le Saulchoir, 1937); cf. G. Alberigo et al., *Une école de théologie: Le Saulchoir* (Paris: Cerf, 1985). [2]J.P. Jossua, "L'oeuvre oecuménique du Père Congar," *Études* 357 (1982/2) 543–555. [3]*Chrétiens-désunis: Principes d'un "oecuménisme" catholique* (Paris, 1937)—Eng. trans. *Divided Christendom: A Catholic Study of the Problem of Reunion* (London, 1937—Ann Arbor: University Microfilms, 1967). See J. Famerée, "*Chrétiens désunis* de P. Congar: 50 ans après," NRT 110 (1988) 666–686. [4]*Vrai et fausse réforme dans l'Église.* US 20 (Paris, 1950). [5]AAS 42 (1950) 561–578/Carlen, Encyclicals 4:175-183. [6]Autobiographical information, in *Dialogue Between Christians: Catholic Contributions to Ecumenism* (London: Chapman, 1964) 1–51; "Letter from Father Yves Congar O.P.," TDig 30 (1985) 213–216; *Fifty Years of Catholic Theology: Conversations with Yves Congar, Edited and Introduced by B. Lauret* (London: SCM, 1988). See A. Stacpoole, "Early Ecumenism, Early Congar," Month 259 (1988) 502–510, 623–631; E. Fouilloux, "Recherche théologique et magistère romain en 1952: Une 'affaire' parmi d'autres," ReschSR 71 (1983) 269–286; G. Weigel, "The Historical Background of the Encyclical Humani Generis," TS 12 (1951) 208–230. [7]London: Chapman, ²1965—First French ed. 1953. [8]J. Puyo, *Yves Congar: Une vie pour la verité* (Paris: Centurion, 1975) 149. [9]Congar, Augustin; Congar, Moyen-âge. [10]*I Believe in the Holy Spirit.* 3 vols. (London: Chapman—New York: Seabury, 1983—French 1979–1980). [11]Bibliog. P. Quattrocchi, in J.P. Jossua, *Yves Congar: Theology in the Service of God's People* (Chicago, 1968) 185–241, supplemented by A. Nichols, "An Yves Congar Bibliography 1967–1987," Ang 66 (1989) 422–466. [12]*The Hierarchy of Truths According to Yves Congar, O.P.* AnGreg 246 (Rome: Gregorian UP, 1987) 22–24. [13]R. McBrien, "Church and Ministry: the Achievement of Yves Congar," TDig 32 (1985) 203–211; B. Mondin, "La ecclesiologia di Yves Congar," EunDoc 32 (1979) 409–432; A. Nicols,

*Yves Congar.* Outstanding Christian Thinkers (London: Chapman, 1989). [14]J. Famerée, "L'ecclésiologie du Père Yves Congar," RSPT 76 (1992) 377–419; idem, *L'ecclésiologie d'Yves Congar avant Vatican II. Histoire et église: Analyse et Reprise Critique.* Bibliotheca Ephemeridum Theologicarum Lovaniensium 107 (Leuven: UP—Peeters, 1992); T.I. MacDonald, *The Ecclesiology of Yves Congar: Foundational Themes* (New York—London: Lanham—University Press of America, 1984); J.M. Connolly, *The Voices of France: A Survey of Contemporary Theology in France* (New York, 1961). [15]"Reflections on Being a Theologian," NewBlackfr 62 (1981) 405–409 at 405. [16]Denville, N.J.: Dimension, 1969. [17]*Called to Life* (Slough UK: St. Paul's, 1987) 3.

# CONGREGATIONAL CHURCHES

Congregationalism is a form of Church institution which is characterized by the independence and autonomy of each local Church. It is strongly democratic in government, reflecting thus the truth that Christ alone is head of the Church. This polity (q.v.) is shared by, among others, Baptists and some Pentecostalists.

But there are also Congregational Churches whose roots are found in the Reformation emphasis on the priesthood of all believers, and in England among those Puritans who despaired of Church reformation under either episcopal or presbyterian establishment. Two booklets of R. Brown in 1582 laid the foundation for Congregationalism (hence earlier "Brownists"). Congregationalism spread throughout England in the 17th century, where it was persecuted. A number of their members fled to the New World, where they played a major part in shaping its religion and politics. Congregational Churches came together in England in 1832 in the Congregational Union of England and Wales, an advisory body without legislative power, which became in 1966 the Congregational Church in England and Wales. Union with the Presbyterian Church of England led to the United Reformed Church (1972). The International Congregational Council first met in London in 1891, and united with the World Presbyterian Alliance in 1970 to form The World Alliance of Reformed Churches.[1]

The ecclesiology of Congregationalists tends to be both biblical and Calvinist. Those who are holy, showing themselves in practical sainthood, belong to Christ. The Church is the covenanted people of God, which one normally enters through baptism. It is a worshiping community whose prayers are inseparable from its prophetic and diaconal service; it is a sign of God's love for all his creation and of his liberating purpose for all.[2]

Ecumenical dialogue is taking place at international levels with several Churches: Anglicans (q.v.) from 1981; Baptists (q.v.) from 1974; Disciples of Christ (q.v.) from 1987; Lutherans (q.v.) from 1985; Methodists (q.v.) from 1985; Orthodox (q.v.) from 1988.

The first series of conversations with the Roman Catholic Church began with a study of "The Presence of Christ in Church and World" (1977).[3] A second phase worked on the topic "Towards a Common Understanding of the Church."[4]

Congregationalism brings several gifts to ecumenism: it insists that the lordship of Jesus is superior to any Church order; membership of the Church is lived at the local level and one cannot be an authentic Christian without belonging to a Church; since all Christians are members of the Church catholic, all sectarianism is to be avoided.

[1]G.G. Atkins and F.L. Fagley, *History of American Congregationalism* (Boston, 1942); P.T. Forsyth, *Congregationalism and Reunion* (London: Independent, 1952); idem, *Faith, Freedom and the Future* (London: Independent, 1955); R.T. Jones, *Congregationalism in England 1662–1962* (Hull: Independent, 1962); E. Routley, *The Story of Congregationalism* (London: Independent, 1961); J.W.T. Youngs, *The Congregationalists* (London: Greenwood, 1991). [2]A.P.F. Sell, *Saints: Visible, Orderly and Catholic: The Congregational Idea of the Church* (Princeton: UP, 1986). [3]H. Meyer and L. Vischer, eds., *Growth in Agreement.* Faith and Order Paper 108 (New York: Paulist—Geneva: WCC, 1984) 434–463. [4]L. Vischer and A. Karrer, eds., *Reformed and Roman Catholic in Dialogue* (Geneva: World Alliance of Reformed Churches, 1988).

# CONSECRATED LIFE

The term "consecrated life" is often used generically to cover special vocations in the Church, through which people seek the perfection of charity. In Church law consecrated life includes only religious institutes (q.v.), hermits (q.v.), consecrated virgins (v. VIRGINS), and secular institutes (q.v.).[1] Associated in the popular mind with these, but not in law called consecrated life, are societies of apostolic life (q.v.).

The new law for all of these has been careful to allow room for the charism of each, avoiding the strait-jacketing that was a tendency of the 1917 law. The *Code* gives norms for all institutes of consecrated life (CIC 573–606). These are marked by the profession of the evangelical counsels and a stable lifestyle in an institute canonically erected by competent Church authority (CIC 573). The competent authority may be the local bishop (CIC 579, 595) or the Holy See (CIC 589). Consecrated life is by its very nature neither clerical nor lay: some institutes are recognized by the Church as clerical (even though they may also have lay members); others are recognized as lay (CIC 588). Exemption (q.v.) from some aspects of the governance of the local bishop in favor of the Holy See or other ecclesiastical authority is retained (CIC 591). Each institute must itself spell out its understanding of the evangelical counsels (CIC 598–601). Two canons are added on hermits and consecrated virgins.

All forms of consecrated life in the wide sense have sought renewal after Vatican II. In general they have some problem with identity in view of the council's insistence on the universal call to holiness (LG ch. 5).

Some have sought to downplay their distinction from the Christian faithful in general, thereby at times increasing the crisis of identity. Others continue to search for expression of the way in which their life is distinct from that of the rest of the Christian faithful. The council was anxious to affirm the validity of religious life (LG ch. 6; PC) and other forms of radical commitment. A feature of the post-Vatican II Church is the emergence of other forms of committed Christian life (v. ASSOCIATIONS OF THE FAITHFUL; MOVEMENTS), and even of consecrated life in the strict sense, for which last the law has made provision (CIC 605).

The key theological point to be made about consecrated life is that it is a way of living more radically the foundational consecration, which is through baptism. Strictly speaking it should be said that it is God who consecrates: it is God who gives the initial vocation to baptism and all subsequent callings. The response by vows in consecrated life has throughout history taken many forms, all of which are an enrichment of the Church, as each emphasizes in its own way some aspect of the mystery of Christ and of the one holiness which has a myriad of forms (LG 41).

[1]M.A. Trapet, "Les dangers d'une réduction de la vie consacrée à la vie religieuse," AnnéeCan 30 (1987) 83–89.

## CONSTANCE, Council of (1414–1417)

The Council of Constance[1] was summoned by the antipope John XXIII (1410–1415) and the emperor Sigismund. Its aims were to settle the Great Western Schism (v. SCHISM, GREAT WESTERN), to reform the Church, and to combat heresy. It faced the fact of three popes: Gregory XII in the (authentic) Roman line from Urban VI; Benedict XIII in the Avignon line going back to Clement VI; John XXIII in the line which began with the Council of Pisa. When he saw that things were moving against him, John XXIII fled, hoping thereby to wreck the council, but Sigismund held it together. In its fifth session the council then enacted the decree *Haec sancta* (one of several in the council bearing that incipit): "legitimately assembled in the Holy Spirit, constituting a general council and representing the catholic church militant, it (the council) has power immediately from Christ; and that everyone of whatever state or dignity, even papal, is bound to obey it in those matters which pertain to the faith, the eradication of the said heresy and the general reform of the said church of God in head and members."[2] John XXIII was returned to the council and deposed.[3]

Gregory XII insisted on convoking the council himself in July 1415 before resigning. The Avignon pope Benedict was intractable and was deposed in July 1417.[4] Martin V was elected on the 11th and crowned on the 26th November, thus putting an end to the schism.

In the interval, the council dealt with several issues. It forbade the administration of the Eucharist to the faithful under the species of wine; it appealed to the real and full presence of Christ under the appearance of bread.[5] It also condemned over 200 propositions of Wycliffe (q.v.).[6] The council then treated the case of John Hus (q.v.). Proving to be obstinate, he was condemned as a heretic. He was handed over to the secular power and burned at the stake.[7] His friend and disciple Jerome of Prague suffered the same fate a year later.[8] The council also condemned the opinion of John Petit who had justified tyrannicide.[9]

At its 39th session it made a statement on general councils and the avoidance of future schisms; it laid down a profession of faith to be made by the pope.[10] It listed 18 needed reforms at its 40th session, 30 October 1417.[11] After the election of Martin V the council issued some reform decrees.[12] It ordained that there should be a council after five, then seven, then every ten years. The next council was settled for Pavia.[13]

There is a lack of scholarly agreement on the ecumenicity of this council.[14] Some will hold that the council became ecumenical either with the second convocation by Gregory or the election of Martin, thus avoiding having the apparently conciliarist *Haec sancta a*s part of an ecumenical council (v. CONCILIARISM). A form of approval for what the council enacted *conciliariter* by Martin V is not fully clear:[15] it certainly covers the final decrees in the pope's name, viz., session 43. Others will hold that the Council of Constance was ecumenical in its entirety.[16]

[1]K.A. Fink, in Jedin-Dolan 4:448-468; J. Gill, *Constance et Bâle-Florence*. Histoire des conciles 9 (Paris: Ed. de l'Orante, 1965); A. Franzen and W. Müller, *Das Konzil von Konstanz: Beitrage zu seiner Geschichte und Theologie*. FS H. Schäfele (Freiburg—Basel—Vienna, 1964); J. Wohlmuth in Alberigo, Concili 222–239. [2]Tanner 1:409. [3]Sess. 12—Tanner 1:417-418. [4]Tanner 1:437-438. [5]Ibid., 1:418-419/DS 1198–1200. [6]Ibid., 1:421-426/DS 1151–1195. [7]Ibid., 1:426-431/DS 1201–1230; M. Spinka, *John Hus and the Council of Constance* (New York, 1965). [8]Tanner 1:433-434. [9]Ibid., 1:432/DS 1235. [10]Ibid., 1:438-442. [11]Ibid., 1:444. [12]Ibid., 1:447-450. [13]Ibid., 1:438-439, 450. [14]A. Franzen, "The Council of Constance: Present State of the Problem," Conc 7 (1965) 29–68; J. Gill, "Il decreto Haec Sancta Synodus del Concilio di Costanza," RivStorChItal 21 (1967) 123–130; J.H. Mundy and K.M. Woody, eds., *The Council of Constance: The Unification of the Church* (New York—London: Columbia UP, 1961); B. Tierney, "Constance, Council of," NCE 4:219-223. [15]Tanner 1:450, n. 4; DS p.315 after DS 1146. [16]Fink (n. 1) 468.

## CONSTANTINE, Emperor (ca. 274/288–337)

Son of the emperor Constantius Chlorus and St. Helena, the date of Constantine's birth is uncertain.[1] He became emperor in 306 and senior ruler in the empire after the defeat of his rival Maxentius (312). In that battle he is reported to have adopted the *labarum,* a military standard composed of a monogram of Christ.

His very gradual conversion to Christianity seems to have begun then (312–313).[2] But like many people of his time Constantine was baptized only on his deathbed. Shortly afterwards toleration and imperial favor were given to the Christian religion. Some toleration had been given to the Christians by Galerius in 311, though it was followed by renewed persecution in some places under Maximinius. It is disputed if there was ever a formal declaration such as the so-called "Edict of Milan" (313), which, if genuine, did not establish the Christian religion but tolerated all religions equally.[3]

Constantine seems at an early stage to have become determined to unite the Church and state by close bonds. In 313 the Donatists appealed to him; he referred the matter to Church synods (including Arles in 314), and heard the matter himself in 316. He found against the Donatists, and when they rebelled, he repressed them sternly.

Various imperial norms continued to favor the Christians; notable was his decree forbidding work on Sunday (321). Parallel with these moves were various restrictions on pagan worship, beginning with decrees against augury (319 and 320). After the defeat of the Eastern Augustus Licinius (324), he more and more saw himself as defender of Christianity.

Another Church conflict was referred to him, a major one on the Person of the Son. He summoned the Council of Nicaea (q.v.) and presided over it himself. Though sincerely wanting to foster the Church, his choice of advisors was not always happy.

He transferred the imperial capital to Constantinople about 330. The prominence of the Eastern Church around the new capital paradoxically led to advancement of the bishop of Rome as the most significant figure in the West, the only one to stand comparison with Eastern bishops.

An equitable judgment on the long-term effects of the Constantinian epoch is difficult.[4] A popular anti-Catholic view represented by the English historian E. Gibbon (1737–1794) saw the triumph of Christianity arising mainly from the decadence of the Empire.[5] Not more convincing is the Marxist view that saw the triumph as one of the proletariat; from the beginning, Christianity had been preached to, and accepted by, all social classes. The support of Constantine was crucial, but the moral and ethical values espoused by the Church, seen even in the courage of its martyrs, was even more significant. The incarnational faith of Christians, their genuine mutual love and forgiveness, and the more complete salvation offered by their faith is probably the most decisive reason for the triumph of the faith.

Constantine's actions and attitudes certainly led to enormous growth and the possibility of religious development at every level: liturgy, preaching, teaching, missionary work, etc. But there is some limited element of truth with those who use "Constantinian" as a pejorative catch-cry: the danger was of making the Church subservient to the needs of the state, not always avoided. The Christianizing of secular culture and public life was inevitably uneven. Caesaropapism became a troublesome manifestation, especially in the East; there even to this day, the relation of Church and state is often ambiguous. Constantine was certainly a key figure in one of the great turning-points of Church history. Before him the world outside the Church was basically hostile; after him it became friendly, at times too friendly.

His reign included negative as well as many positive features. He was on the whole a humane emperor. He is venerated as a saint in the Eastern Church, with a feast shared with his mother (21 May).

[1]K. Baus, in Jedin-Dolan 1:405-432; R. MacMullan, *Constantine* (New York, 1969—London, 1970).   [2]Baus (n. 1) 410–416; cf. P. Keresztes, "The Phenomenon of Constantine the Great's Conversion," AugR 27 (1987) 85–100.   [3]Baus (n. 1) 416–418; cf. J.-R. Palanque, "A propos du prétendu édit de Milan," ByzB 10 (1935) 607–616.   [4]S.L. Greenslade, *Church and State from Constantine to Theodosius* (London, 1954); J. Pelikan, *The Excellent Empire: The Fall of Rome and the Triumph of the Church* (San Francisco: Harper & Row, 1987); cf. L.W. Bernard, "Church-State Relations AD 313–337," JChurSt 24 (1982) 337–355; R. MacMullan, *Christianizing the Roman Empire AD 100–400* (New Haven—London: Yale UP, ca. 1984).   [5]*History of the Decline and Fall of the Roman Empire* (many eds.).

## CONSTANTINOPLE I, Council of (381)

In the decades following Nicaea (325—q.v.) the Arians and Semi-Arians gradually consolidated their position, e.g., by exiling Athanasius from the See of Alexandria. After the death of Constantine (361), Constantius II favored the Semi-Arians in the East, while the West unified under Constance remained faithful to Nicaea. A long series of local councils in the East were aimed at undermining the First Council. In this period two new issues arose: the divinity of the Holy Spirit and the full humanity of the Word, compromised by the Apollinarians who denied him a human soul.

Summoned by Theodosius, Constantinople I, "the council of the 150 fathers," comprised only bishops of the East.[1] It regularized the position of the bishop of Constantinople itself. Gregory Nazianzus was ratified as bishop, only to be forced to resign later in the council. The council passed four canons.[2] The first was a comprehensive condemnation of the Arian heresy and its sects.[3] The second limited the power of bishops within fixed areas. The third, which reflects an anti-Roman and anti-Alexandrian feeling, gave a primacy of honor to Constantinople in the East as the new Rome. Maximus the Cynic and his followers were condemned in the fourth canon. Canons five and six were from a synod of Constantinople held a year later, and the seventh canon comes from a letter of the Church of Constantinople to the bishop Martyrius of Antioch.

The most important creed in Christendom is clearly the Nicene-Constantinopolitan.[4] The present text made its appearance at Chalcedon, where it was recognized as an authentic expression of the faith. It is not the Nicene Creed with a few additions, but probably was based on a Jerusalem or Antioch creed which expressed the faith of Nicaea. Though scholarly opinion varies,[5] there are strong grounds for suggesting that the creed was produced by Constantinople I. There are important additions to existing creeds: the addition of the words "of his kingdom there will be no end" and the indirect affirmation of the divinity of the Holy Spirit—he is "Lord" and "giver of life," he "proceeds from the Father" and along with the Father and the Son he is to be "adored and glorified".[6]

The consequence of the council was the definitive reception (q.v.) of Nicaea in both the East and the West. Though it was in fact only a local council, its ecumenical status was recognized in its later reception by the whole Church.[7] Pope Gregory I wrote: "I confess, accept and venerate the four councils (Nicaea, Constantinople, Ephesus, and Chalcedon) in the same way as I do the four books of the holy gospel."[8] The canons, however, were not formally accepted in the West for 900 years. On the occasion of the centenary of the council, John Paul II issued a letter *A concilio Constantinipolitano I*[9] devoted largely to pneumatology (q.v.).

---

[1]L.D. Davis, Councils 81–133; W. de Wries, *Orient et occident: Les structures ecclésiales vues dans l'histoire des sept premiers conciles oecuméniques* (Paris: Cerf, 1974) 43–60; J. Ortiz de Urbina, *Nicée et Constantinople.* Histoire des conciles 1 (Paris: Ed. de l'Orante, 1963); L. Perrone in Alberigo, Concili 57–70. IrTQ 48/3-4 (1981) commemorative issue.    [2]Tanner 1:31-32.    [3]Tanner 1:31/DS 151/ND 13.    [4]Davis (n. 1) 121–126; J.N.D. Kelly, *Early Christian Creeds* (London: Longman, [3]1972) 296–367; J. Lebon, "Les anciens symboles dans la définition de Chalcédoine," RHE 32 (1936) 809–876; J. Ortiz de Urbina, "La struttura del symbolo Constantinopolatano," OrChrPer 12 (1946) 275–285.    [5]For creed originating at council, see Kelly, Davis, Lebon (n. 4); for negative view, see D.L. Holland, "The Creeds of Nicaea and Constantinople Reexamined," ChH 38 (1969) 1–14.    [6]A. de Halleux, "La profession de l'Esprit-Saint dans le symbole de Constantinople," RTLv 10 (1979) 5–39.    [7]AA.VV., *La signification et l'actualité du IIe concile oecuménique pour le monde chrétien d'aujourd'hui* (Chambésy—Geneva, 1982); H. Chadwick, "The Origin of the Term 'Oecumenical Council,'" JTS 23 (1972) 132–135; A. de Halleux, "Le IIe concile oecuménique: Une évolution dogmatique et ecclésiologique," CrNSt 3 (1982) 297–327; A.M. Ritter, *Das Konzil von Konstantinopel und sein Symbol.* Studien zur Geschichte des II. Ökumenischen Konzils (Göttingen, 1965).    [8]*Reg. epist.* 1—MGH Epist 1:36.    [9]AAS 73 (1981) 513–527/DocCath 78 (1981) 367–371.

## CONSTANTINOPLE II, Council of (553)

In the aftermath of Chalcedon (451, q.v.) there were charges and countercharges: the West stressed two actions in Christ—divine and human—and was thus accused of Nestorianism; the East emphasized the unity of Christ and was seen in the West as Monophysite. The Monophysites attempted to weaken or reject Chalcedon, and so were rejecting the conciliar institution of the Church; they were also resisting the emperor. In the same period tenets of Origenism were circulating, such as the *apokastasis* of the world and reincarnation. Political rivalry paralleled the theological differences between Rome and Constantinople. The emperor Zeno (474–476) attempted reconciliation, and the patriarch Acacio, along with the emperor, sought unity with a document called the *Henotikon* (482) which, however, made important concessions to Monophysitism and led to the Acacian schism (484–519).[1]

The main issue became the status of the *Three Chapters,* an edict of Justinian (543–544 C.E.) condemning three dead theologians as Nestorian: Theodore of Mopsuestia, Theodoret of Cyprus, and Ibas of Edessa. The emperor, seeking to reconcile the Monophysites, was making a veiled attack on Antiochene theology and on Chalcedon. Pope Vigilius (537–555) at first refused to concur, but after a time of house arrest in Constantinople and intimidation, his resistance crumbled and he issued his *Judicatum* or "Judgment" condemning the *Three Chapters* (548), though without prejudice to Chalcedon. This papal action was bitterly opposed in the West, especially in Africa, so that the pope withdrew it. He agreed with the emperor to call a council, but the emperor insisted that it be in Constantinople and not as the pope wished in Italy, which would have ensured a greater Western participation. Thus the fifth ecumenical council, Constantinople II, opened on 5 May 553.[2] It numbered 160 bishops, eight of whom were African.

Alleging the inadequacy of Western representation, the pope refused to attend. In a letter of 14 May 553, the *First Constitution,* the pope, supported by 16 bishops mostly from the West, condemned 60 propositions of Theodore, but did not condemn him personally, nor did he condemn Theodoret or Ibas; he wished to avoid any appearance of rejecting Chalcedon. The council nonetheless condemned the *Three Chapters* at its 8th session (2 June 553) in a lengthy judgment followed by 14 anathemas.[3]

The emperor then sought to intimidate the pope, and within six months had broken his spirit. In December, Vigilius wrote to Euthycius, the new patriarch of Constantinople, and recalling Augustine's *Retractations,* revoked his earlier defense of the *Three Chapters,* stating that they should be condemned. But that did not satisfy the emperor, who demanded and obtained the pope's approval of the council with the *Second Constitution* of February 554. A schism followed in the West. Reception (q.v.) of this council was thus to be slow there.[4]

The council did not have any discussion of Church discipline, nor did it issue any canons. It is not clear what Origenist positions, if any, were condemned by the actual council.[5]

---

[1]W.H.C. Frend, *The Rise of the Monophysite Movement: Chapters in the History of the Church in the Fifth and Sixth Centuries* (Cambridge: UP, 1972); P.T.R. Gray, *The Defense of Chalcedon in the East, 451–553* (Leiden: Brill, 1979). [2]H.G. Beck, in Jedin-Dolan 2:450–457; L.D. Davis, *Councils* 207–257; W. de Vries, *Orient et occident: Les structures ecclésiales vues dans l'histoire des sept premiers conciles oecuméniques* (Paris: Cerf, 1974) 161–194; G.L.C. Frank, "The Council of Constantinople II as a Model Reconciliation Council," TS 52 (1991) 636–650; C. Moeller, "Le Ve concile oecuménique et le magistère ordinaire au Ve siècle," RSPT 34 (1951) 413–423. F.X. Murphy and P. Sherwood, *Constantinople II et Constantinople III,* Histoire des conciles 3 (Paris: Ed. L'Orante, 1974); P.A. Yannopoulos, in Alberigo, Concili 121–133. [3]Tanner 1:107–122; anathemas only DS 421–438/ND 620:1–14. [4]R.B. Eno, "Papal Damage Control in the Aftermath of the Three Chapters Controversy," StPatr 19 (1989) 52–56. [5]Cf. Davis (n. 2) 245–247.

## CONSTANTINOPLE III, Council of (680–681)

After the Second Council of Constantinople (Constantinople II—q.v.) the Monophysites parted from the unity of the Church and from the domain of the empire. After 628 the Emperor Heraclius (610–641) sought from Sergius, patriarch of Constantinople, a formula that would unite all in the Greco-Roman world. He proposed the idea, with which Pope Honorius (625–638—q.v.) agreed, that in Christ there was one operation (*energeia*—Monoenergism); going further, the pope spoke of one will *(thelêsis)* in Christ (Monothelitism).[1] Heraclius imposed this last view on the empire by the edict *Ecthesis* (Exposition) in 636. Maximus the Confessor (ca. 580–662—q.v.) was the major theologian attacking the innovation. Various synods in the 7th century condemned Monothelitism, including the local Lateran synod in Rome (649),[2] and a Roman synod under Pope Agatho (678–681) in 680.

The emperor Constantine IV (668–685) convoked what was to be the sixth ecumenical council, Constantinople III (680–681).[3] At its 8th session it accepted the teaching of Pope Agatho, and at its 17th session condemned Monothelitism in a decree signed by 174 council fathers. Honorius was censured by name.[4]

The council did not promulgate any disciplinary decrees; this was to be done at the Council of Trullo (q.v.). Pope Leo II, successor to Agatho, approved the council proceedings in 682.

---

[1]P. Galtier, "La première lettre du pape Honorius," Greg 29 (1948) 42–61; V. Grumel, "Recherches sur l'histoire du monothélisme,"

ÉchOr 27 (1928) 6–16, 257–277; 28 (1929) 19–34, 158–166, 272–282; 29 (1930) 16–28; P. Vergesse, "The Monothelite Controversy—A Historical Survey," GrOrTR 13 (1968) 196–211. [2]DS 500–522/ND 627:1-16. [3]R. Riedinger, ed., *Concilium universale constantinopolitanum tertium: Concilii actiones I–IX.* Acta conciliorum oecumenicorum. Series 2. Vol. 2. Pars 1a. (Berlin—New York: De Gruyter, 1990); H.G. Beck, in Jedin-Dolan 2:462-463; Davis, Councils 258–289; W. de Vries, *Orient et occident: Les structures ecclésiales dans l'histoire des sept premiers conciles oecuméniques* (Paris: Cerf, 1974) 195–220; F.X. Murphy and P. Sherwood, *Constantinople II et Constantinople III,* Histoire des conciles 3 (Paris: Ed. l'Orante, 1974); P.A. Yannopoulos in Alberigo, Concili 134–140. [4]Tanner 1:125-130/DS 550–559/ND 635–637.

## CONSTANTINOPLE IV, Council of (869–870)

The Fourth Council of Constantinople was accepted as the eighth ecumenical council in the West only from about the 11th century, but it was never so received in the East. It comes at a phase of extreme complexity in the Eastern Empire, the details of which are not fully clear to scholars even today.[1]

The immediate context can be taken as the accession of the quarrelsome Ignatius to the patriarchate of Constantinople in 847. He was forced to abdicate in 858 and he accepted, under some fairly reasonable conditions, that he be succeeded by Photius. Trouble soon arose. Photius repudiated this accommodation with his predecessor, and the legitimacy of his own appointment was contested. A political issue was also involved: both Rome and Constantinople claimed jurisdiction over Bulgaria. In 863 a Lateran synod in Rome deposed Photius. The pope, Nicholas II (858–867), showed himself to be very ignorant of, and unsympathetic to, the Byzantine Church, especially its rite.[2]

Photius responded by two significant moves: he complained about the addition to the Creed of the words "and the Son" (v. FILIOQUE); he held a synod in 867 which claimed to depose the pope.[3] Photius was overthrown by the emperor Basil in 867 and Ignatius was reinstated. Hadrian II (867–872), when appraised of Photius' condemnation of his predecessor, held a synod at Rome in 867 which anathematized Photius and his associates. The pope was soon in correspondence with the emperor, who wanted a general council to determine the situation of those ordained by Photius.

The council met from November 869 to February 870.[4] It made a profession of faith and upheld the Roman condemnation of Photius.[5] Twenty-seven canons are associated with the council:[6] it again approved icons (c. 3);[7] the acts of Photius were invalidated (cc. 4, 6, 9, 25); it sanctioned the Eastern order of patriarchs, viz., giving precedence to Constantinople before Alexandria (c. 21); it asserted a primacy of the Roman See in a text that would be used later by Vatican I (c. 21).[8]

Within days of the conclusion of the council, the delegates of the patriarchs, despite the protestations of the papal envoys, ruled that Bulgaria should fall under the jurisdiction of Constantinople, and not of Rome as Nicholas I had claimed.

In the East this council was seen as a humiliation of the Byzantine Church and a betrayal of its autonomy to Rome. So when Ignatius died in 877, Photius could once again become patriarch (878–886). A synod held at Constantinople in 879–880[9] under the presidency of Photius, attended by almost 400 bishops, showed Photius' rehabilitation; the papal envoys insisted that this was by an act of John VIII (872–882). This pope clearly wanted peace and unity with the East, and was prepared to make compromises for their attainment.

The lasting significance of the Photian saga was the precedent it set for explicit anti-Romanism and ultimately schism. Though his direct influence on the 1054 schism was slight, the activities and works of Photius provided an arsenal that would be drawn upon by Eastern protagonists in the years ahead.

[1]H.G. Beck, in Jedin-Dolan 3:174-193.   [2]G.T. Dennis, "The 'Anti-Greek' Character of the Responsa ad Bulgaros of Nicholas I," OrChrPer 24 (1958) 165–174, but cf. Beck (n. 1) 179 n. 20.   [3]F. Dvornik, "The Patriarch Photius and the Roman Primacy," ChicSt 2 (1963) 94–107.   [4]W. de Vries, *Orient et occident: Les structures ecclésiales vues dans l'histoire des sept premiers conciles oecuménique* (Paris: Cerf, 1974) 245–282; F. Dvornik, *The Photian Schism: History and Legend* (Cambridge, 1948); L. Perrone in Alberigo, Concili 157–181; D. Stiernon, *Constantinople IV,* Histoire des conciles 5 (Paris: Ed. l'Orante, 1967); See V. Peri, "C'è un concilio oecumenico ottavo?," AHC 8 (1976) 53–79, with response C. Leonardi, "Das achte ökumenische Konzil," AHC 10 (1978) 53–60 [= Renovatio 12 (1977) 493–498] and Peri reply 61–66.   [5]Tanner 1:160-168   [6]Tanner 1:166-187.   [7]DS 653–656/ND 1253.   [8]DS 661–664; Vat. I—DS 3066/ND 832.   [9]J.L. Boojamra, "The Photian Synod of 879–80 and the Papal Commonitorium," ByzSt 9 (1982) 1–23; A. van Bunnen, "Le concile de Constantinople de 879–880," Contacts 33 (1981) 6–40, 211–234; 34 (1982) 47–61; P. Stephanou, "Deux conciles, deux ecclésiologies? Les conciles de Constantinople en 869 et en 879," OrChrPer 39 (1973) 363–407.

## COPTIC CHRISTIANITY

The word "Coptic" comes from an Arabic pronunciation *(qubti)* of the Greek for Egyptian *(aiguitoi)*. When the Arabs came to Egypt (639–641) they assumed that this was the local usage. Today there are other Christian communities in Egypt, but the most significant are the Copts, who form perhaps 9 percent of the population.

The heritage of the Church of Egypt associates its origin with St. Mark, martyred in Alexandria about 63 C.E. Alexandria became an important Christian and theological center. It was, moreover, enriched by the proximity to the Desert Fathers (v. HERMITS), and developed a strong monastic tradition.

The Christological teaching of Chalcedon (451—q.v.) was not accepted by the Egyptian bishops and laity, who became at least verbally Monophysite. They were persecuted in order to force their acceptance of the council. From the 5th to the 9th centuries Greek patriarchs lived in Alexandria, with their Coptic counterparts being found in the desert monastery of St. Macarius. With the Muslim invasions, Arabic replaced Coptic, which, however, remained the liturgical language. Coptic liturgy is a modification of the Greek Alexandrian rite, with some monastic traits.

The spirituality of the Coptic Church[1] is most marked by its monastic inheritance of the 4th and following centuries, with some characteristic features: work and prayer, a radical choice of God, an avoidance of excesses, the importance of the spiritual father, and a primacy of love. Modern Coptic spirituality stresses Scripture read in church and in the home, and memorized; there is a central emphasis on the liturgy; important, too, are fasting and popular feasts; monasticism is being revitalized.

Modern ecumenical contacts (V. ECUMENISM, ORTHODOX) have shown that the monophysitism of the Copts is rather nominal and need not be a barrier to unity, at least with the Orthodox, if not also with Anglicans.[2] In 1974 a joint commission of the Catholic Church and the non-Chalcedonian Coptic Orthodox Church began to meet, and produced a declaration on Christology in 1976, further refined in 1988.[3] Following meetings between Pope John Paul II and the Coptic Pope Shenouda in 1988, it would seem that Chalcedon need not be a barrier to unity[4]

A union with the Coptic Orthodox Churches was signed at the Council of Florence (1442),[5] but it did not last. Franciscan and Jesuit missionaries went to Egypt in the 17th century. The conversion of a Coptic bishop, Amba Athanasius, in 1741, gave rise to a small community of Uniates (q.v.), but a patriarchate was not established until 1895.[6] These Catholics do not have the strong monastic tradition of the Orthodox Copts, but have several religious institutes on Latin models.

[1]K. Samir, "La spiritualità copta ieri e oggi," in AA.VV. *La spiritualità delle Chiese Cristiane orientali.* Corso breve di ecumenismo 7 (Rome: Centro pro Unione, 1986) 65–76.   [2]P. Gregorios et al., eds., *Does Chalcedon Divide or Unite? Towards Convergence in Orthodox Christology* (Geneva: WCC, 1981); H. Hill, ed., *Light from the East: A Symposium on the Oriental Orthodox and Assyrian Churches* (Toronto: Anglican Book Centre, 1988); M.P. Martin et al., "Les nouveaux courants dans la communauté copte orthodoxe," PrOrChr 40 (1990) 245–259.   [3]*Four Vienna Consultations* (Vienna: Pro Oriente, 1988).   [4] See SPCU *Information Service* 76 (1991/1) 13, and F.A. Sullivan, "Lessons We Have Learned from the Participation of Rome in Ecumenism," MilltownSt 34 (1994) 13–30.   [5]Tanner 1:567-583/DS 1330–1353.   [6]C. Suetens, "Origine et développment de l'Église copte catholique," Irén 65 (1992) 42–62.

# COUNCILS

A council is a formal meeting of bishops, often with representatives from other Churches, for the purpose of regulating discipline or doctrine. This description is sufficiently wide to cover all of the meetings which in the past have been called councils or sometimes synods (q.v.).[1] The *Code of Canon Law* deals with diocesan councils (v. SYNODS AND COUNCILS).

Apart from the ecumenical councils, which began with Nicaea (q.v.) in 325, there were many gatherings of bishops and representatives; the meeting of the Church of Jerusalem, which dealt with the problem of Judaic practices and the role of the Law, has often been called the "Council of Apostles" (Acts 15:1-30). From the end of the 2nd century, councils are to be found throughout the Church, first those dealing with the date of Easter (ca. 196) and with Montanism. From the 3rd century they are found in Asia Minor, Rome, North Africa, and in Spain from the 4th century. Many of these were purely local; some, like the councils against Pelagianism, Carthage XV or XVI (418) and at Orange II (529), assumed special importance from their apparent approval of their decisions by the bishop of Rome and their wide acceptance in the West.[2]

During the early centuries the regional councils in the West regularly sent copies of their decrees to Rome, where they were explicitly or tacitly accepted. An exception was the Council of Carthage (252), which deliberately repudiated the Roman doctrine on the question of the (re)baptism of heretics. A further stage in the development of the relationship between pope and councils was the action of Julius I at the Roman synod (341) which rehabilitated Athanasius of Alexandria, who had been condemned by the Synod of Tyre. At the Synod of Rome (382) in the time of Damasus (366–384), the text of Matt 16:18 was used to assert papal power, in a demand that the approval of the Roman bishop was necessary for the validity of an Imperial Synod. In fact synods or councils lacking that approval would never be influential in the future.[3]

Of crucial importance for the history of the Church and of dogma were the seven great councils of the first millennium.[4] These were summoned by the imperial power; they were called in a time of perceived crisis; they were preponderantly Eastern. Most of them were attended by papal representatives, and almost all of their decrees were approved by a pope subsequent to the council; they certainly do not, however, fulfill the conditions for an ecumenical council in current Church law. They saw themselves as examining Scripture and presenting the living traditions of their Churches. In general there was a difference in attitudes between the Roman delegates and the Eastern bishops: the former saw themselves as presenting the position that should be adopted; the latter considered themselves judges of the tradition, and ended up by agreeing with the Roman position not because it was Roman, but because they perceived it to be the tradition, and true, after their examination of the evidence. It would be the 9th century before infallibility was ascribed to the decisions of the major councils. The seven great councils, now called ecumenical, achieved a consensus with the past (Scripture and Tradition), and in communion with the rest of the Church, especially manifested in papal approval of its decrees. In a word these councils were received (v. RECEPTION) as divinely guided and as enshrining true teaching, which we would today, following Vatican I and II, call "irreversible." The seven are each given an entry in this volume (q.v.): Nicaea I (325), Constantinople I (381), Ephesus (431), Chalcedon (451), Constantinople II (553), Constantinople III (680–681), Nicaea II (787).

The common Orthodox view is that a council is ecumenical only if received by the five patriarchs (q.v.); hence no council since Nicaea II (787—q.v.) has been, or could be, ecumenical in the full sense.[5] The Orthodox generally call other assemblies "local" *(topikai);* the decrees of some of them feature in their canonical collections, though there is evidence that some synods have been given the epithet "ecumenical."[6] Only the first three councils have in the past been recognized by the Oriental Orthodox Churches (v. EASTERN CHURCHES).[7] Synods are, however, an important feature of the Eastern Churches (q.v.).[8]

Councils did not act by majority rule. The first seven ecumenical councils were not representative by modern standards. It was rather their unanimous reception by the leaders of the apostolic sees, as explicated later in a theory of Pentarchy (i.e., the notion that the Church of the first centuries was guided through the five ancient sees of Rome, Constantinople, Alexandria, Antioch, and Jerusalem).[9]

The Catholic Church has never definitively taught the number of ecumenical or general councils. Nor at the beginning was there a self-reflection by the councils themselves about their ecumenicity. Only at Nicaea II was there discussion about what constituted the ecumenicity of previous councils. These included: 1) concordance and homogeneity with previous councils acknowledged as ecumenical; 2) the concourse of competent authorities, with special emphasis on the Roman Church. Later at Lyons I (q.v.) we get a description of the participants of medieval councils: "kings, prelates and princes both ecclesiastical and lay, whether by themselves or by official representatives."[10]

The seven papal councils of the Middle Ages are clearly different from the first seven great councils. Nowadays they are often called by historians "general" councils, but many theologians continue to call them "ecumenical," with all that this last implies with regard to the infallibility of their teaching. These are: Lateran I–IV, Lyons I–II, Vienne. (Articles on each appear in this volume.) Their status was very much questioned in the 16th century. Indeed, Y. Congar is on record as stating that "the purely Latin Councils are not ecumenical councils but councils of the patriarchy of the West."[11] And in 1974 Paul V1, commenting on the 700th anniversary of Lyons II, called it, "the sixth among the general synods held in the West."[12] The profession of faith for popes proposed by the Council of Basle (q.v.) distinguished between the "eight holy universal councils" (Nicaea I to Constantinople IV) and the "general councils" of the Middle Ages.[13] The Council of Constance (1415—q.v.), which ended the Western Schism, claimed to represent the universal Church. The Council of Florence (q.v.), due to its greater representation of the East, was in the late medieval period called the 8th council (9th for those who counted Constantinople IV). It was called the eighth council by a Roman edition of its acts published in 1526. But this was not to be for long, nor to obtain in the East.

Nearly a century later Robert Bellarmine (1542–1621—q.v.) was concerned to give the strongest possible background to Trent. During his theological career he produced several lists, not all of them published. Eventually he gave a full, but by no means original, list of the councils, drawing on various earlier writers, particularly A. de Pontac writing in 1566–1567. Bellarmine published his inventory in the controversial tract *De conciliis et ecclesia militante* (1586). He regarded Constance and Basle as one, and included seven medieval councils (four Lateran, two of Lyon, and that of Vienne). Not only were they acknowledged for their influence in the Western Church, as their decrees had been taken into canon law, but they were given the status of ecumenical. Bellarmine denied that the presence of the Eastern patriarchs was necessary for a council to be ecumenical, judging rather on their papal inspiration and approbation. After some hesitation, and attempts at correction of Bellarmine's list, it is now common to speak of twenty-one general councils from Nicaea I to Vatican II.[14]

The present law of the Church is found in the *Code* (cc. 338–341). The principal points are: the pope alone can convoke, preside over (personally or through others), transfer, suspend, or dissolve a general council; he prepares and approves the agenda; only bishops have the right and duty to take part, though others may be called by the "supreme authority of the Church" (pope, or pope and council); the decrees of the council require approval by the pope and council members, confirmation by the pope, and promulgation at his order.

A difficult area, one in which Catholic scholars are frequently careless, is the hermeneutics of conciliar statements: the tools of exegesis so well developed in scriptural studies can be absent in dealing with councils, so that one encounters rather fundamentalist readings.[15]

But important as ecumenical and general councils undoubtedly are, there is another sense of conciliarity,[16] which is a characteristic of Church government. Its supreme authority lies with the College of Bishops (q.v.) united with the pope; conciliar or synodal structures are provided in law, ranging from councils of bishops to parish councils. A failure of the post-Vatican II Church has been the inability to translate a theology of conciliarity into practice. Instead, what is proposed by those not in authority is often a democratic mode, and by those with authority a process of consultation that does not often give a sense of participation. Though conciliarism (q.v.) must be rejected in its absolute form, it did seek to enshrine genuine values for a Church whose main attribute must always be communion (q.v.).[17]

The Reformers did not ascribe any infallibility to the councils. Where these were accepted, it was because their doctrine was judged consonant with Scripture. But basically they were human events, and liable to error.[18]

In recent ecumenical dialogue there are several developments. A first is to look again at the ancient councils, especially the first four, as normative for belief: in condemning error and in proposing truth in accord with Scripture.[19] A second is to look to what might constitute a council in the future.[20] The role of the papacy in some future council is obviously a neuralgic point.[21] The recent legislation in the revised *Code* would not seem to provide a helpful model. A third is to see ways in which conciliarity is in fact exercised in the various Churches, especially within the WCC (q.v.). The New Delhi General Assembly expresses the idea that "It (the WCC) is the Churches in continuing council."[22] After the WCC General Assembly at Uppsala (1968) there was a fresh study, with the idea of the World Council as "a transitional opportunity for eventually actualizing a truly universal, ecumenical, conciliar form of life."[23] Another expression of conciliarity has been the formation of local, national, and regional councils of Churches.[24] When we speak of "councils of Churches" in English, there is ambiguity. The WCC and regional councils are of another nature than the ancient ecumenical councils or the councils of the Roman Catholic Church, or the governing body of any other Church. (The German *Rat* and French *conseil* both differ from *Konzil/concile*.)[25]

It is clear that the World Council of Churches and other similar regional and local councils are not in this full sense councils of the Church. They are meeting places for Churches which are not yet in full communion and do not accept a common authority. They do, nevertheless, provide a framework within which true conciliarity and communion can develop.[26]

Of particular importance is the theology and experience of conciliarity in the Churches of the Christian East with the ongoing debates on the notion of *sobornost'* (q.v.).[27] Significant, too, if extremely diverse, are the evaluations of Vatican II by Orthodox theologians; some will see this council as paving the way for a truly ecumenical council.[28] It is unlikely that there could be such a council without the Churches already being in a state of Eucharistic sharing, though some Protestant writers would wish to see Eucharistic sharing as a step on the road to full conciliarity.[29]

For Catholics, Orthodox, and Protestants alike, it is important to realize the partial nature and limited aims of the councils of the past. With the exception of Vatican II, they were all called to deal with some crisis or difficulty in the Church. Their teaching is limited, conditioned by their history. They do not so much close questions as represent a particular stage, and they are open to further development.[30] Even granted the real achievements of councils, the faith of the Church is incomparably richer than what has been taught in them (v. SOURCES OF THEOLOGY). Nonetheless, for the present, the development of conciliarity[31] within the Churches and between them is a key task, one that will build up unity even if a fully ecumenical council of all the Churches seems to belong to a very distant future.

[1]J.D. Mansi, *Sacrorum conciliorum nova et amplissima collectio* (Florence, 1759–1798. Reprint and continuation, Paris and Leipzig, 1901–1927); Ecumenical Councils, Tanner vols. 1–2. Survey: J. van Laarhoven, "The Ecumenical Councils in the Balance: A Quantitative Review," Conc 167 (1983) 50–60. History: G. Alberigo, *Storia dei concili ecumenici* (Brescia: Queriniana, 1990); H. Jedin, *Ecumenical Councils of the Catholic Church: An Historical Outline* (Freiburg: Herder—Edinburgh: Nelson, 1959). [2]DS 222–230; 370–398. [3]H.-J. Sieben, "On the Relation Between Council and Pope Up to the Middle of the Fifth Century," Conc 167 (1983) 19–24; V. Peri, "Le synergie entre le pape et le concile oecuménique: Note d'histoire sur l'ecclésiologie traditionnelle de l'Église indivise," Irén 56 (1983) 163–193. [4]H.J. Sieben, *Die Konzilsidee der alten Kirche* (Paderborn: Schöningh, 1979); W. de Vries, *Orient et Occident: Les structures ecclésiales vues dans l'histoire des sept premiers conciles oecuménique* (Paris: Cerf, 1974); P. Duprey, "Conciliarité et primautés," PrOrChr 39 (1989) 225–236; J. Roche, "Conciles, Empereurs et Papes," PrOrChr 28 (1978) 85–104. [5]F.A. Sullivan, *Magisterium. Teaching Authority in the Catholic Church* (Dublin: Gill and Macmillan, 1983) 84–88; L.D. Davis, *The First Seven Ecumenical Councils (325–787): Their History and Theology* (Collegeville: Glazier—The Liturgical Press, 1983, 1990); cf. J. Boojamra, "The Byzantine Notion of the 'Ecumenical Council' in the Fourteenth Century," ByzZ 80 (1987) 59–76. [6]M. Jugie, "Le nombre des conciles oecuméniques reconnus par l'Église gréco-russe," EchOr 18 (1919) 305–320; Peter L'Huillier, *The Church of the Ancient Councils* (New York: St. Vladimir's Seminary Press, 1989). [7]Mar Severius Zakka Iwas, "Wann ist ein Konzil ökumenisch?" in AA.VV., *Okumene, Konzil, Unfehlbarkeit* (Innsbruck—Vienna—Munich: Tyrolia, 1979) 48–56.

[8]J. Hajjar, "The Synod in the Eastern Church," Conc 8/1 (Oct. 1965) 30–34. [9]See H. Marot, "Note sur la pentarchie," Irén 32 (1959) 436–442; P. L'Huillier, "The Development of the Concept of an Ecumenical Council (4th–8th Centuries)" GkOrTR 36 (1991) 243–262. [10]Tanner 1:278. [11]Y. Congar—B. Lauret, *Fifty Years of Catholic Theology: Conversations with Yves Congar* (London: SCM, 1988) 56. [12]Letter to his legate, Card. Willebrands AAS 66 (1974) 620; see "Septième Centenaire du Concile de Lyon," PrOrChr 25 (1975) 51–62 at 55. [13]Tanner 1:496. [14]H.J. Sieben, "Robert Bellarmin und die Zahl der Ökumenischen Konzilien," ThPh 61 (1986) 24–59; J.G. Gaztambide, "El número de los concilios ecuménicos," in *Ecclesia Militans: Studien zur Konzilien-und Reformationsgeschichte*. FS R. Bäumer, 2 vols. (Paderborn: Schöningh, 1988) 1:1-21; V. Peri, *I concili e le chiese: Ricerca storica sulla tradizione d'universalità dei sinodi ecumenici* (Rome, 1965); H.J. Sieben, *Die Konzilsidee des lateinischen Mittelalters (847–1378)* (Paderborn: Schöningh, 1984). [15]H.E. Mertens and F. de Graeve, eds., *Piet F. Fransen, Hermeneutics of the Councils and Other Studies*. Bibliotheca Epemeridum theologicarum lovaniensium 69 (Leuven: UP—Peeters, 1985); P. Fransen, "On the Need for the Study of the Historical Sense of Conciliar Texts," in J. Todd, ed., *Problems of Authority* (London, 1962); G. Bof, "L'ermeneutica delle definizione conciliari," Asp 29 (1982) 109–140, 223–255. See F.A. Sullivan, *Creative Fidelity* (New York: Paulist, 1996). [16]Y. Congar, "The Conciliar Structure or Regime of the Church," Conc 167 (1983) 3–9. [17]J. Wohlmuth, "Conciliarism and the Constitution of the Church," Conc 167 (1983) 31–36. [18]E.g., *Thirty-nine Articles,* art. 21 in Leith, Creeds 273–274; *Westminster Confession* 1:10, ibid., 196. See P. Ricca, "Le conciliarità e la concezione dell'autorità nelle prospettive della Riforma," Nicol 15 (1991) 175–182. [19]ARCIC, *The Final Report* (London: SPCK—CTS, 1982) 62–64 (Venice V:19-23) 97–98 (Windsor Statement 33); G. Tavard, "What Elements Determine the Ecumenicity of a Council?," Conc 167 (1983) 45–49. [20]"Councils, Conciliarity and a Genuinely Universal Council," *Study Encounter* 10:2 (Geneva: WCC, 1974); P. Ricca "Should the Ecumenical Council be an Expression of the Collegiality of Bishops, of the *Communio Ecclesiarum* or even a Representation of the Whole Community of the Faithful?," Conc 167 (1983) 85–91. [21]G. Alberigo, "The Papacy in the Ecumenical Council," Conc 167 (1983) 69–75. [22]*The New Delhi Report*. Sect. 11, n. 49 (New York: Association Press, 1961) 132. Cf. *Councils and the Ecumenical Movement*. WCC Studies 5 (Geneva, 1968, completed before the RCC became a full member of Faith and Order). [23]*Faith and Order: Louvain 1971*. Faith and Order Paper 59 (Geneva, 1971) 225; cf. B. Forte, "Consiliarità: quale future? La Consultazione teologica delle Chiese Europee a Sofia (3–8 ottobre 1977)," RasT 18 (1977) 615–621. [24]T.F. Best, "Councils of Churches," DictEcumMov 231–238; R. Rouse in HistEcumMov 1:620-630; T. Short in HistEcumMov 2:93-113. [25]P.C. Rodger and L. Vischer, eds., *The Fourth World Conference on Faith and Order*. Faith and Order Paper 42 (London, 1964) 48–49; A. Keshishiak, *Conciliar Fellowship a Common Goal* (Geneva: WCC, 1992). [26]Faith and Order: Louvain (n. 23) 227–228; J.M.R. Tillard, "Une ecclésiologie des 'Conseils d'Églises'," PrOrChr 32 (1982) 3–13. [27]M. Aghiorgoussis, "Theological and Historical Aspects of Conciliarity: Some Propositions for Discussion," GkOrTR 24 (1979) 5–19; Y. Congar, "Church Structures and Councils in the Relations Between East and West," OneChr 11 (1975) 224–265; J. Madey, "Ecumenical Council and Pan-Orthodox Synod: A Comparison," Conc 167 (1983) 61–68; J. Meyendorff, "Was ist ein ökumensiches Konzil?" in *Okumene, Konzil, Unfehlbarkeit* (Innsbruck: Tyrolia, 1979) 36–47. [28]N. Nissiotis, "Towards a New Ecumenical Age," EcumR 37 (1985) 326–335 at 335. [29]G. Wainwright, "Conciliarity and Eucharist," OneChr 14 (1979) 30–49. [30]G. Dejaifve, "Pour un bon usage des

conciles," NRT 101 (1979) 801–814.  [31] D. Radu, "Autorité et conciliarité dans la pratique actuelle de l'Église: convergence et tensions," Nicol 18 (1991) 277–304.

## COVENANTING

"Covenanting" is a term in ecumenism, meaning a state of less than full organic union between two or more Churches.[1] Each Church maintains for some time its own structures, worship, and ministry, but shares in "sacred things" *(communicatio in sacris):* faith, baptism, Eucharist, ministry, and mission. After the Faith and Order meeting in Nottingham, England (1964), Welsh Churches moved to form a covenant which was brought about in 1975, based on a sevenfold "recognition": same faith, same calling from God, acknowledgement of being one Church of Jesus Christ, common baptism and membership, ordained ministries, patterns of worship and sacramental life that are gifts of Christ, same concern for Church government. Members of this covenant in Wales are the Anglican, Presbyterian, Methodist, and United Reformed Churches.

A similar move in England failed when the Church of England synod narrowly missed the requisite two-thirds majority in the House of Clergy. The problem was partly with non-episcopal ministries, and partly a fear of thwarting the ARCIC dialogue which at the time seemed very promising (v. ANGLICANISM AND ECUMENISM).

Covenanting has been attempted in other countries, most notably in the USA. Though non-theological factors may militate against covenanting, there is need for substantial agreement in matters of faith and ministry before a covenant can hope to succeed.

Interchurch marriages (v. MARRIAGE, INTERCHURCH) are a living laboratory in which models of covenanting can be truly tested in the pain of disunity and the joy of some achieved unity.

[1]P.A. Crowe, "Covenanting," DictEcumMov 244–245; P. Hocken, "Covenants for Unity," OneChr 25 (1989) 3–13, 155–162, 273–280.

## CREEDS AND PROFESSIONS OF FAITH

The Greek word *sumbalon* meant a token, like half a coin, which was put together as a sign of recognition. In Christian terms it became a sign of recognition or communion between believers, and then a summary of principal truths of the faith. Occasionally one encounters the word "symbol" for a profession of faith.[1]

The English word "creed" ultimately derives from the Latin *credo* (I believe). Creeds are brief formulae giving the essential elements of the faith. They are to be found in the OT (e.g., Deut 6:4-7, 21-23; 7:7-11), and in the NT as something handed on (1 Cor 11:23-26; 15:3-7; 1 Tim 3:16). The earliest creeds of the Church were a confession that Jesus was Messiah (Mark 8:29; Acts 9:22;

John 20:31) in Judaeo-Christian circles, or in Hellenistic ones, that "Jesus is Lord" (1 Cor 12:3; Rom 10:9).

Soon creeds arose in the context of baptism. These local creeds were brief, doxological statements, at first in interrogative form ("Do you believe . . . ? I do/I believe") and Trinitarian in structure, as in the *Apostolic Tradition* (21/21:12-18), which represents a form earlier than those of the 4th century.[2]

From the early 3rd century the custom of *traditio/redditio* of the baptismal creed arose at the end of the catechumenate (q.v.): the candidates were "given" the creed, which they later "gave back" by publicly reciting it before the bishop, and later professing its truth ("I do/I believe") during the actual baptism itself.

Creeds in time became declarative ("I believe . . ."). The so-called Apostles' Creed usually labeled T *(textus receptus)* is a development of the ancient Roman creed called R. It probably arose in SW France in the late 6th or early 7th century. It would gradually become definitive in the Western Church from about the 9th century, was regarded as authoritative by the 12th, and has been unchanged since the 16th century.[3]

In the early Church another kind of doctrinal formula arose, usually called the *Rule of Faith (regula fidei)* but having other names as well. The terminology appears first in Irenaeus (q.v.); we then find it in several 3rd- and 4th-century authors. It was not a baptismal creed, but a summary of the Christian faith taught in a local Church. Early writers see the rules of faith as embodying the teaching of Scripture, and use them as a test of orthodoxy.

With the Christological and Trinitarian controversies, new universal creeds arose which were a test of orthodoxy. These were in technical language and to an extent limited by and to the issue disputed. They were "bishops' creeds," and did not supplant the more primitive baptismal creeds in local use.[4]

The "Nicene Creed," originally an anti-Arian profession promulgated in a modified form at Constantinople I (q.v.) and adopted at Chalcedon (q.v.), eventually entered the liturgy of the Eucharist. In various places, occasionally with slight variants, it was also used from an early time in the East as a baptismal creed.[5] The so-called Athanasian Creed *(Quicumque)* was aimed at the heresies of Arius, Nestorius, and Apollinaris. Its author was not Athanasius, but it probably originated at Lérins sometime between ca. 440 and ca. 520.[6]

It is important to note that creeds do not express fully the faith of the Church, but only those main truths that are appropriate for baptism or for counteracting some heterodox positions. Thus the crucially important truth of God's unconditional love for all his human creatures is found in no creed until the recent one of Paul VI.[7]

At the time of the Reformation and afterwards many Churches adopted creeds or professions of faith, which did not however displace the ancient creeds, for example: the Tridentine Profession of Faith;[8] the Lutheran Augsburg Confession (q.v.);[9] the Anglican *Thirty-nine Articles of Religion;*[10] the Puritan, later Presbyterian, *Westminster Confession* (1647).[11] These Reformation era credal statements all emphasize the issues controverted, and represent the particular Church's position in response.

After Vatican II Paul VI issued a creed to close the Year of Faith commemorating the 19th centenary of the death of the apostles Peter and Paul. The pope did not intend a dogmatic definition, but asserted that the creed "repeats in substance the Creed of Nicaea with some developments called for by the spiritual condition of the times."[12] The emphasis on divine love in this profession is notable; the ecclesiological and Eucharistic statements reflect issues then current. There has been some Orthodox criticism of a pope devising a credal profession alone.

Up to 1967 those undertaking various offices in the Church were bound to make a profession of faith and take an anti-Modernist oath.[13] The current *Code* states specifically those bound to make a profession of faith, normally on entry into an office: members of councils and synods; those promoted to be cardinals or bishops; diocesan officials of various specified kinds (e.g., vicars general, vicars judicial, pastors); rectors of seminaries; professors of theology and philosophy; those entering the diaconate; superiors in clerical religious institutes according to the constitutions of the institute (CIC 833). The law also specifies carefully the person before whom the Profession of Faith is to be made.[14]

A new formula for the Profession of Faith was promulgated by the Congregation for the Doctrine of the Faith and published as a new Profession of Faith in 1989.[15] Its first part consists of the Nicene-Constantinopolitan Creed as used in Western liturgy. The second part is in three paragraphs "in order better to distinguish the type of truth and the appropriate assent required" *(il tipo di verità e il relativo assenso richiesto).*[16]

Thus there are three questions to be asked about each paragraph, viz., the kind of doctrine involved, the way in which it is taught, the kind of assent required.[17]

The first paragraph covers the "deposit of faith," taught solemnly by pope or council, or by the ordinary and universal magisterium. The assent is an act of divine faith. The second paragraph covers the secondary object of the Church's teaching authority, viz., doctrines concerning faith or morals which are not themselves revealed but are required for the safeguarding or exposition of what is contained in the deposit of faith. It is not clear that secondary determinations of the natural law are necessarily included here.[18] The assent is contained in the words "I firmly accept and hold" *(Firmiter . . . amplector ac retineo).* Neither

the word "faith" or "believe" is used. It is a firm interior assent to the proposition as true.

The third paragraph covers authoritative teaching of the pope or college of bishops, which is not intended to be definitive. The response is "I adhere with religious submission of will and intellect" *(religioso voluntatis et intellectus obsequio adhaereo).* This involves a docility to assent to teaching or a sustained attempt to reject any tendency to obstinacy in an opposed view.[19] This paragraph should be interpreted according to the position of LG 25 and the clarification made at the council by the Doctrinal Commission.[20]

At the same time, in 1989, the Congregation for the Doctrine of the Faith also published the oath to be taken on the assumption of office.[21] The oath pertains to the responsibilities of the office being taken up, preserving the deposit of faith in its entirety, following and fostering the discipline of the Church, preserving communion with the Church's pastors, and helping the rulers *(rectores)* and bishops of the Church. The oath is a new obligation not found in the 1983 *Code of Canon Law.* It could be suggested that the oath is sufficiently vague and general both to allow people to take it without undue anxiety and paradoxically to leave the way open to subsequent scrupulosity. It can be argued that it does not impose any obligation not already in Church law and other magisterial enactments. It has had a mixed reception.[22]

Mainly in an ecumenical context, but also for pastoral reasons, there have been attempts recently to produce new formulas of faith.[23] Given the pluralism (q.v.) of theology in the Church,[24] it is not envisaged that new credal formulas would necessarily be universal. It would have to be a collaborative venture involving the magisterium, theologians, and those pastoring and being pastored in the Church, for it can only be an articulation of the sense of the faith (q.v.).[25] Indeed, we do not know the author of any of the great creeds that have nourished the Church.

There has been a recent ecumenical commentary on the Nicene-Constantinopolitan Creed,[26] as well as much discussion about the possibility of creating new confessions of faith.[27] But here, too, we should probably rather expect that a creed would well up from Christians rather than be the creation of any group, even if they be ecumenical theologians. An ecumenical creed must avoid the danger of minimalism (taking away all differences and being left with a meager remnant) as well as be alert to the possibility of weakening catholicity. It must also respect the hierarchy of truths (q.v.), and avoid undue highlighting of secondary or sectarian issues.

The purpose of creeds is the self-expression of the community, doxology, instruction in the faith, witness, identity of the community, and a test of orthodoxy.[28] At different times one or the other of these may be more to the fore. The value and indeed the authenticity of any creed will eventually be evidenced by its reception (q.v.) in the Churches.

---

[1]J.N.D. Kelly, *Early Christian Creeds* (London: Longman, [3]1972) 52–61.   [2]DS 1–64.   [3]Kelly (n. 1) 368–434; E. Lanne, "Le Symbole des Apôtres, expression de la foi apostolique et le Symbole de Nicée," Irén 56 (1988) 467–483; P. Smulders, "Some Riddles in the Apostles' Creed I–III," Bijd 31 (1970) 234–261; 32 (1971) 350–366; 41 (1980) 3–14.   [4]DS 71–76; 125; 139; 150; 357–359; 441–443; 490–493; 525–541; 546–548 . . . ND 12–17. D. Papandreou, "Le confessioni della Chiesa primitiva: origine, funzione, recezione," StEcum 4 (1986) 131–148; F.M. Young, *The Making of the Creeds* (London: SCM—Philadelphia: Trinity, 1991).   [5]Kelly (n. 1) 296–331.   [6]J.N.D. Kelly, *The Athanasian Creed* (London, 1964).   [7]P. Chirico, "The Relation of Values to Ecclesiology," ChicSt 19 (1980) 291–304 at 299.   [8]Schaff, Creeds 2:207-210/DS 1862–1870/ND 30–38; G. Alberigo, "Profession de foi et doxologie dans le catholicisme des XVe et XVIe siècles," Irén 47 (1974) 5–26.   [9]Schaff, Creeds 3:7-73.   [10]Ibid., 3:486-516; G. Rowell, "Le confessioni di fede della Chiesa primitiva nella tradizione classica anglicana," StEcum 4 (1986) 149–180.   [11]Schaff, Creeds 3:600-673.   [12]AAS 60 (1968) 433–435—Profession of Faith 436–445/ND 39:1-23.   [13]DS 3537–3550; cf. AAS 59 (1967) 1058.   [14]J.A. Coriden in Coriden CIC 585–586; L. DeFleurquin, "The Profession of Faith and the Oath of Fidelity: A Manifestation of Seriousness and Loyalty in the Life of the Church," StCan 23 (1989) 485–499.   [15]AAS 81 (1989) 105/Origins 16 (1989) 663.   [16]AAS ibid., 104.   [17]F.A. Sullivan, "Some Observations on the New Formula for the Profession of Faith," Greg 70 (1989) 549–558.   [18]Sullivan (n. 17) 553–554, uneasy with U. Betti Osservatore Romano (25.2.1989).   [19]Sullivan (n. 17) 557.   [20]G. Thils, "La nouvelle 'Profession de foi' et *Lumen gentium,* 25," RTLv 20 (1989) 336–343; cf. more negative U. Betti, "L'ossequio al Magistero Pontificio 'non ex cathedra' nel n. 25 della 'Lumen gentium,'" Anton 62 (1987) 423–461.   [21]AAS 81 (1989) 106/Origins 16 (1989) 663.   [22]F.J. Urrutia, "Iusiurandum fidelitatis," Periodica 80 (1991) 529–578; J. Galot, "La profession de foi et le serment de fidelité," EspVie 99 (1989) 694–698; J.F. Keenan, "Compelling Assent: Magisterium, Conscience and Oaths," IrTQ 57 (1991) 209–227; L. Örsy, *The Profession of Faith and the Oath of Fidelity: A Theological and Canonical Analysis* (Wilmington: Glazier—Dublin: Dominican Publications, 1990).   [23]Bibliog., "The Creed in the Melting Pot," Conc 6/1 (1970) 131–153; K. Rahner, "The Need for a 'Short Formula' of Christian Faith," ThInvest 9:117-126 (= 1965); idem, "Reflections on the Problems Involved in Devising a Short Formula of the Faith," ThInvest 11:230-244.   [24]K. Rahner, "Pluralism in Theology and the Unity of the Creed in the Church," ThInvest 11:3-23.   [25]P. Fransen, "Unity and Confessional Statements: Historical and Theological Inquiry into Traditional R.C. Conceptions," Bijd 33 (1972) 2–38.   [26]*Confessing the One Faith: An Ecumenical Explication of the Apostolic Faith as It Is Confessed in the Nicene-Constantinipolitan Creed (381).* Faith and Order Paper 153 (Geneva: WCC, 1991); S.M. Heim, *Faith to Creed: Ecumenical Perspectives to Creed Consultation.* Commission on Faith and Order NCCCUSA 1989 (Grand Rapids, Mich.: Eerdmans, 1991). Cf. H. Schlink, ed., *Confessing Our Faith Around the World.* 5 vols. (Geneva: WCC, 1983–1986).   [27]G.J. Békés and H. Meyer, eds., *Confessio fidei.* International Ecumenical Colloquium, Rome 3–8 Nov. 1980. Studia anselmiana—Sacramentum 7 (Rome: Ateneo Anselmo, 1982); J. Guhrt, "Professione di fede e confessioni di fede oggi," StEcum 4 (1986) 203–224; L. Sartori, "Verso una professione comune di fede tra le confessioni cristiane?," StPatav 29 (1981) 257–269; Conc 118 (1978).   [28]A. Dulles, "Modern Credal Affirmations," ExpTim 91 (1980) 291–296.

## CRUSADES

The crusades were military expeditions from Western Europe to the Eastern Mediterranean, aimed at recovering the Holy Land from Islamic domination and returning it to Christian hands.[1] There were five major crusades. The threat of Islam was felt in Spain especially in the 11th century and gave rise to wars of liberation. Gregory VII (q.v.) embraced the idea of holy wars also for the purposes of reform. A military ideology in Christian terms gradually developed and was responsive to the calling of the first crusade by Urban II (1088–1099) at the Council of Clermont in 1095.[2]

By 1099 Jerusalem was captured, and for the next twenty years, the Christians sought to consolidate their victory by establishing a series of Latin states. When Edessa fell in 1144 a second crusade was called, preached notably by St. Bernard (q.v.).[3] It set out in 1147 and failed to ease the situation for the Franks in the East. When in 1187 Saladin captured Jerusalem and overran much of the Latin territory, a third crusade (1189–1192) was called, in which the emperor Barbarossa, Richard I of England, and Philip II of France all took part.[4] Much Latin territory was recovered, but they failed to recapture Jerusalem.

The fourth crusade set off in 1202.[5] Its original destination was Egypt, but it was deflected to Constantinople, which it sacked in April 1204, leaving an indelible memory in the East and animosity towards the Latin West which was to remain for centuries. The interest of the West would henceforth be divided between the new Latin Empire, Romania, and the needs of the Franks under increasing pressure from the Muslims.

At the opening of Lateran IV (1215—q.v.), Innocent III (1198–1216) stressed reform of the Church and the crusade as the chief topics of the council. The final constitution deals in great detail with the crusade proposed for 1 June 1217.[6] But before it could take place, Innocent III had died, and the crusade was to be ineffectual.

There were several other crusades. Many groups, partly military, partly pilgrim, went in support of the Latin states. Jerusalem was in Christian hands from 1229–1244. Slowly the Latin states succumbed to Muslim power and in 1291 the last Latin state fell. For the next 150 years there would be many expeditions against the Turks and much talk of crusades. The Greeks came to the Council of Florence (q.v.) at least as intent on securing help against the Turks as on seeking unity in faith with the West. But with the West not providing practical help, Constantinople fell to the Turks in 1453. Pius II (1458–1464) was very keen to organize a crusade, but failed to get support.[7] With him, if not indeed earlier with the Turkish victory at Nicopolis in 1396, the classical crusading ideal finally died.

The effect of crusades on the Church needs nuanced evaluation. Their early popularity among popes, bishops, clergy, and laity betokened a spirituality of heroism and sacrifice and a love of the Holy Places. The associated penance and prayer, the granting of indulgences to those who took up the crusader cross, all point to spiritual values.[8] Crusading was seen as a valid expression of the Christian vocation. The secular knights and the various orders of knights were to be found united in values shared in Christendom; the orders of hospitaler knights also cared for pilgrims and those who became sick in the Holy Land. Even the crusade taxes were usually willingly paid, at least in the beginning. But the brutality of the crusades, the venality of some of those taking part, the political ambitions and the quest for wealth in the East are negative features. Worse still was the massacre of Jews (q.v.) carried out by crusaders on their way through Europe. Long before they had ended, the abuses had led to a disillusionment with the notion of crusades. A further reason was the sense of disappointment: Why were those fighting for God's cause so unsuccessful?

More ambiguous was the extension of the notion of crusade to offensives against heretics and infidels. Thus there was evangelization by the sword in Central Germany and the Baltic area. The crusades against the Albigensians (q.v.) were theoretically justified as struggles for the faith. In 1208 Innocent III proclaimed a crusade against them, one which would be marked by great cruelty. Lateran IV (q.v.) and later popes extended the same spiritual privileges to those undertaking these crusades as those enjoyed through expeditions to the Holy Land.[9] But this extension of the notion of crusade became too easily confused with local political aims and factions: a secular war became a religious one, and the papacy sometimes used the notion of crusade for political ends.

The term "crusade" has been used in the 19th and 20th centuries about various religious movements of special fervor, often where there is a focus on evangelization.

[1]H.E. Mayer, *The Crusades* (Oxford: Clarendon, ²1988); cf. S. Impellizzeri, "Aux racines de l'idée de croisade et sa survive dans les idéologies politiques," Nicol 12 (1985) 339–348; S. Runciman, *The Crusades.* 3 vols. (Harmondsworth UK: Penguin, 1965); Bibliog. Jedin-Dolan 3:545-546.    [2]F. Kempf, in Jedin-Dolan 3:445-452; P.J. Cole, *The Preaching of the Crusades to the Holy Land 1095–1270* (Cambridge, Mass.: Medieval Academy of America, 1991); J. Riley-Smith, *The First Crusade and the Idea of Crusading* (Philadelphia: Pennsylvania UP, 1986); idem, *The Crusades: A Short History* (London: Athlone Press, 1987).    [3]H. Wolter, in Jedin-Dolan 4:35-39.    [4]Ibid., 82-85.    [5]Ibid., 154-158.    [6]Tanner 1:267-271; T.C. Van Cleve, "The Fifth Crusade," in K.M. Setton, ed., *A History of the Crusades.* Vol. 2 (Philadelphia, 1962) 377–428; cf. Lyons I—Tanner 1:297-301.    [7]G. Raynaud, "Observations sur l'idée de croisade au XVe siècle: De la chute de Byzance (29 mai 1453) à la mort de Pie II (14 août 1464)," BLitEc 89 (1988) 274–290.    [8]H. Wolter, in Jedin-Dolan 4:86-88.    [9]E.g., Lateran IV, Constit. 3—Tanner 1:234.

## CYPRIAN, St. (ca. 200–258)

Born about 200 C.E. at Carthage, Thascius Caecilianus Cyprianus[1] was an orator and legal advocate before becoming a Christian ca. 245. By 248 he had been chosen by the people as their bishop, with the consent of neighboring bishops. The Decian persecution broke out almost immediately and he went into exile. During the persecution a number apostatized, the *lapsi.* Cyprian took a moderate view: they could be reconciled after a period of penance. But he opposed the over-lax view which allowed confessors (q.v.) to grant a *libellus* too readily (v. RECONCILIATION).[2] His position was upheld by the local council of Carthage in 251.

He was not, however, so orthodox on the question of the Novatians (q.v.) and baptism. At the time, and afterwards, many refused to accept heretical baptism if the heresy denied the Trinity. Cyprian's position was to refuse to accept the validity of any baptism performed outside the *Catholica,* whether heretical or schismatic. He was thus in serious conflict with Pope Stephen I (254–257). The pope saw Cyprian's position as novel, and replied with the magisterial *Nihil innovetur nisi quod traditum est* (No innovations, tradition alone).[3] Cyprian's response was "custom without truth is the antiquity of error."[4] Only the death of Stephen and the martyrdom of Cyprian a year later (258 C.E.) avoided a serious breach of communion. The *passio,* or account of his martyrdom, is one of the classics of the genre (v. MARTYRS).[5]

The writings of Cyprian are pastoral,[6] in answer to the questions that arose in his diocese and in North Africa in his time. He is in many places influenced by Tertullian (q.v.) whom he acknowledges as his master. In addition to his work on the lapsed, two groups of his writings are significant from the point of view of ecclesiology.[7] His greatest contribution is *The Unity of the Catholic Church.*[8] He stresses the need for preserving the unity of the Church against heresies: "He who does not keep to the true way of salvation will inevitably falter and stray."[9] The Church is necessary for salvation: "You cannot have God for your Father if you do not have the Church for your mother"; just as there was no escape outside the ark of Noah, likewise now with the Church.[10] More bluntly, "There is no salvation out of the Church" *(salus extra ecclesiam non est).*[11]

There has been much controversy about chapter 4 relating to the Church being founded on Peter: there are two versions of the text, the second, the shorter one, is now widely accepted as being a revision by Cyprian himself, since in the controversy with Pope Stephen he would have been embarrassed by his earlier emphasis on the Church being built on, and giving

Peter a primacy.[12] The existence of two editions, even if not by Cyprian, shows that in the 3rd century the doctrine of Petrine and papal primacy was still in process of development.[13] Another important feature of this work is the emphasis on the unifying role of the bishop. "The authority of the bishops forms a unity, of which each holds his part in its totality."[14]

The other important contribution of Cyprian to ecclesiology is the letters: 65 by him, and 16 addressed to him.[15] They give a vivid picture of the North African Church in the 3rd century. He deals with the lapsed in several letters.[16] The primacy of Rome is indicated in various places: "The Church founded by Christ the Lord on Peter."[17] He does not seem to accept what later would be seen as a primacy of Rome, even though he recognizes a unifying role for its bishop.[18]

His views of the episcopate are quite developed: "The authority of the bishops forms a unity, of which each holds his part in its totality."[19] Again, "The Church is established upon the bishops and every action of the Church is governed through these same prelates."[20] Unity with the bishop is essential: "The bishop is in the Church and the Church is in the bishop, and if there is anyone who is not with the bishop, he is not in the Church."[21]

Cyprian as bishop is given the title *papa* in letters to him from the Church of Rome.[22] This title was given to bishops in many places in the West; it gradually became restricted, and from 1073 was reserved for the bishop of Rome; in the East it seems confined to the bishop of Alexandria in the patristic period.

Very significant is Cyprian's emphasis on consultation and dialogue. Writing to his priests and deacons he states: "From the beginning of my episcopate, I decided to do nothing of my own opinion privately without your advice and the consent of the people."[23] This is the classical form of Church "democracy," which is dialogical in communion, flowing from the structure and ordinance of the Church itself.[24]

An important epithet for the Church in Cyprian is "catholic" (q.v.),[25] and the reality of "catholic" is frequently present even if the word is not used.[26] He also speaks of the Church as mother (q.v.)[27] and queen (q.v.).[28] His views are important for an understanding of early councils as representing "a double consensus, one horizontal and the other vertical, which in the end is God's work."[29]

The writings of Cyprian have been an important source for Church law. His commentary on the Our Father remains a significant spiritual document, quoted seven times in the new Catechism and reproduced almost in its entirety in the *Liturgy of the Hours*.[30]

[1]K. Baus, in Jedin-Dolan 1:252-254; Patrology 2:340-383; A.A. Ehrhardt, "Cyprian, Father of Western Christianity," ChQR 133
(1941) 178–196; P. Hinchcliff, *Cyprian of Carthage and the Unity of the Catholic Church* (London: Chapman, 1974); J.C. Plumpe, *Mater ecclesia* (Washington, D.C., 1943) 81–108. [2]*De lapsis*—CSEL 1:235-264/ACW 25:13-42. [3]DS 110/ND 1401. [4]*Epist.* 74:9—FC 51:292; M. Bévenot, "Cyprian's Platform in the Rebaptism Controversy," HeythJ 12 (1978) 123–142; F. Cardman, "Cyprian and Rome," Conc 158 (1982) 33–39. [5]ANF 5:267-274. [6]S. Cavallotto, "Il magistero episcopale di Cipriano di Cartagine: Aspetti metodologici," DivThom 91 (1988) 375–407; 92 (1989) 33–73; B.C. Butler, "St. Cyprian and the Church," DowR 71 (1952–1953) 1–13, 119–134, 258–272. [7]L. Dattrino, "L'ecclesiologia di san Cipriano nel contesto della chiesa del III secolo," Later 50 (1984) 127–150; A. Davids, "One or None: Cyprian on the Church and Tradition," Conc 1/8 (Jan 1972) 46–52; S. Folgado Flórez, "Estructura sacramental de la Iglesia según san Cipriano," CiuD 195 (1982) 189–222. [8]*De ecclesiae unitate*—CSEL 3/1:207-233/ANF 5:421-429/ACW 25:43-68/LCC 5:124-142. C.A. Bobertz "The Historical Context of Cyprian's *De unitate*," JTS 41 (1990) 107–111; Hinchliff (n. 1). [9]Ibid., 2—ACW 25:44. [10]Ibid., 6—ACW 25:48-49. [11]*Epist.* 73:21—FC 51:282. [12]Patrology 2:352-353; M. Bévenot ACW 25:7-8, 46-47, 102-107. [13]M. Bévenot, "A Primacy Is Given to Peter: *primatus Petro datur*," JTS 5 (1954) 19–35; idem, "Épiscopat et primauté chez St. Cyprian," ETL 42 (1966) 176–195; P. Camelot, "Saint Cyprian et la primauté," Istina 4 (1957) 421–434; R. Minnerath, "La position de l'Église de Rome aux trois premiers siècles," in *Il primato del vescovo di Roma nel primo millennio: Ricerche e testimonianze*. Atti e documenti 4 (Vatican, 1991) 139–171 at 162–168. [14]*De ecclesiae unitate* 4—ACW 25:47. [15]CSEL 3/2; FC 51/ACW 43–44. [16]*Epist.* 15–17, 33—FC 43–51, 85–87. [17]*Epist.* 70:3—FC 51:261. [18]*Epist.* 68—FC 239–243. [19]*De ecclesiae unitate* 4—ACW 25:47. See M. Bévenot, "*In solidum* and St. Cyprian," JTS 6 (1955) ) 244–248; M. Guerra Gómez, " 'In solidum' o 'colegialmente'(De unit. eccl. 4). La colegialidad episcopal y el Primado romano según S. Cipriano obispo de Cartago (aa. 248–258), y los papas de su tiempo," AnnTheol 3 (1989) 219–285. [20]*Epist.* 33:1—FC 86. [21]*Epist.* 66:8—FC 229; see 71:3—FC 51:264. [22]*Epist.* 8 and 30 addresses and 30:8—FC 51: 20, 72, 78. [23]*Epist.* 14—FC 51:43; cf. 38:1—FC 51:97. See P. Granfield, "Episcopal Elections in Cyprian: Clerical and Lay Participation," TS 37 (1976) 41–69. [24]J. Ratzinger, *Democratisation dans l'Église?* (Paris: Apostolat des Éditions, 1972) 51–52. [25]*Epist.* 54:4—FC 51:133. [26]*De ecclesiae unitate* 8—ACW 25:50-51. See S. Folgado Flóres, "La catolicidad, fórmula de identifición de la Iglesia en San Cipriano," CiuD 202 (1989) 593–611. [27]E.g., *Epist.* 46—51:118. [28]*De ecclesiae unitate* 14—ACW 25:56. [29]H.J. Sieben, "Episcopal Conferences in the Light of Particular Councils During the First Millennium," in H. Lagrand et al., *The Nature and Future of Episcopal Conferences* (Washington, D.C.: The Catholic University of America Press, 1988) = Jurist 48 (1988) both 30–56 at 33. [30]CSEL 3/1:265-294/ANF 5:447-457/Office of Readings, week eleven.

## CYRIL OF ALEXANDRIA, St. (d. 444)

The first certain date of St. Cyril's life is that of his succession to his uncle in the patriarchal See of Alexandria in 412.[1] His life and writings can be divided in two. Up to 428 he was mostly concerned with the Novatians (q.v.) and with extirpating the last remnants of paganism. After that date he was the champion of orthodoxy against Nestorius, bishop of Constantinople. A synod of Rome (430) arising from an appeal of both protagonists led to the condemnation of Nestorius and the approval of Cyril's theology.

Cyril then drew up twelve anathemas which he sent to Nestorius with a covering letter. To try to avoid a split in Eastern Christendom the emperor summoned a council at Ephesus in 431. Before the arrival of the Antiochene supporters of Nestorius, Cyril had the orthodox doctrine approved. The 2nd letter of Cyril to Nestorius was approved as orthodox, and his 3rd letter with twelve anathemas of the latter were included in its proceedings.[2] A rival council, set up by late arriving John of Antioch, which excommunicated Cyril, led to the emperor deposing both Cyril and Nestorius. Cyril was soon reinstated. His remaining years were taken up with restoring peace between his Church and Antioch and with Christological questions.

In his extensive works,[3] he is the first to develop as a theological source the witness of the preceding Fathers of the Church;[4] he also often used arguments from reason. Apart from his Christological concerns, which includes his championing of the term *Theotokos* (God-bearer) for the Virgin Mary, he is an important witness to contemporary attitudes to the Roman Church. He certainly regarded it as an authoritative See, and was both anxious that his position be accepted in Rome, and was deferential to the bishops of that Church.[5] His concern for the unity of the Church was marked in his later years by an insistence on charity for the separated and erring:[6] he claimed that he was second to none in his love for Nestorius himself.[7] He saw the Holy Spirit as active in every area of the Church's existence, and notably contributed to a theology of communion (q.v.).[8] He was proclaimed Doctor of the Church (q.v.) in 1882.[9]

[1]Quasten, Patrology 3:116-142; W.J. Burghardt, "Cyril of Alexandria," NCE 4:571-576; J. Mahé, "Cyrille d'Alexandrie, saint," DTC 3:2476-2527; M. Simonetti, "Cyril of Alexandria," EncycEarCh 1:214-215.    [2]Tanner 1:40-61/DS 250-263/ND 604-606.    [3]PG 68-77.    [4]*In Ioan* 10—PG 74:419; *Epist.* 55—PG 77:202-203; cf. Quasten 3:135-136.    [5]See Pius XII, Encyc. *Orientalis Ecclesiae decus* on St. Cyril in Celebration of 15th centenary of his Death. AAS 36 (1944) 129-144/Carlen 4:81-88.    [6]J. Capmany, "La comunicatión del Espíritu Santo en la Iglesia-Cuerpo Místico como principio de su unidad según san Cirilo de Alejandría," RES 17 (1957) 173-204; H. du Manoir, "L'Église, Corps du Christ chez saint Cyrille d'Alexandrie," Greg 20 (1939) 83-100, 161-188, 481-506; L. Malavez, "L'Église dans le Christ: Étude de théologie historique et théorique," RechSR 25 (1935) 257-291; 418-440.    [7]*Epist.* 9—PG 77:62.    [8]C. Scanzillo, "Lo Spirito Santo e la comunione ecclesiale in Cirillo di Alessandria," Asp 30 (1983) 47-61.    [9]B. de Margerie, "Centenaire du doctorat ecclésiale de S. Cyrille d'Alexandrie (1882-1982)," EspVie 92 (1982) 377-379.

# D

## DEACONESS—WOMEN DEACONS

It is clear from the NT that women (q.v.) served Jesus (Mark 1:31; Luke 8:2-3; cf. chs. 22:55–24:12), a fact that would have caused no little surprise at the time. They are also found with particular roles in the early Church, but apart from possibly two texts, we do not get evidence of this role being that of deacon. However, in Rom 16:1 Phoebe is called *diakonos.* (The word did not have a feminine form until much later when *diakonissa,* a neologism, was created; before that a feminine article prefaced the noun *diakonos.*) We cannot know what might have been the assistance *(pro-statis)* she rendered Paul and others. There is no way of being sure that the word *diakonos* is being used in a generic sense as in 1 Thess 2:2; 2 Cor 3:6; 11:23 or as indicating a specific group or function, as in Phil 1:1; 1 Tim 3:8, 12.[1] The other text is 1 Tim 3:11 in the middle of a passage devoted to deacons where the author speaks of women: exegetes from antiquity to the present have found the text difficult; it cannot be excluded that it refers to women deacons even though no precise role is assigned to them in this passage. The text in the same letter dealing with widows (1 Tim 5:9-10) in the early centuries influenced the lifestyle and tasks proposed for deaconesses.

When we look to the history of deaconesses in the Church, the picture is very complex.[2] The famous letter of Pliny to Trajan (111–113) speaks of slaves *(an-cillae)* who were servants *(ministrae),* but there is no indication of the nature of their service. Ignatius (q.v.), at about the same time, has a curious phrase, "The virgins called widows,"[3] but there is no reason to suppose that they were deaconesses. There is no evidence of deaconesses in the *Didachê,* in Ignatius, in Tertullian, or in the *Apostolic Tradition.* In the *Didascalia apostolorum,* probably from the early 4th century[4] and con-tained in the late 4th century *Apostolic Constitutions* (q.v.), we have a developed typology and the functions of the deaconess: the bishop takes the place of God, the deacons are the type of Christ, the deaconesses are the type of the Spirit, priests are to be honored as the apostles.[5] This kind of typology is already found in Ignatius;[6] it is understandable, since the Spirit is femi-nine in Syriac. Except for this passage, the *Apostolic Constitutions* place deaconesses last in lists of clergy,[7] but they precede the widows who owe submission to the deaconesses.[8] Later in the work we find an account of the function of the deaconesses: they are to minister materially and possibly spiritually to women, mainly the sick, in their homes; they are to anoint the bodies of women at baptism (but not baptize them—this is the role of the bishop); they are to instruct and educate the women after baptism.[9] They also have some function as intermediaries between women and the male clergy.[10] In the institution of deaconesses, by the impo-sition of hands by the bishop, the only task mentioned in the consecratory prayer is custody of the church doors.[11] As scriptural evidence, the text does not cite Rom 16:1 or 1 Tim 3, but the women who were "dea-cons of Jesus" and stood beneath the cross (Matt 27:55).[12] The Council of Nicaea, in a much disputed and variously interpreted canon, seems to indicate that deaconesses do not receive hand imposition, and that they are moreover to be counted among the laity.[13]

In Syria, where the *Didascalia apostolorum* was in circulation, the impulse for the creation of dea-conesses was social pressure: men could not visit the homes of women to minister to them; modesty was to be fostered at the baptism of immersion in which the recipients were nude.

In the *Testamentum Domini* (v. APOSTOLIC COLLEC-TIONS) it is widows who are assigned these tasks

119

mentioned above, and other ministries.[14] Deaconesses are also mentioned: they are listed in the laity after the men; they are to bring Paschal Communion to pregnant women; they are to stand guard at the door of the church; they are to be supervised by the widows.[15] These norms of the *Didascalia* and of the *Testamentum Domini* are taken up by other Churches, sometimes with local modifications. In the section on widows we find in the *Didascalia* and in *the Apostolic Constitutions* a prohibition against women preaching, though deaconesses are not explicitly mentioned.[16]

When the various liturgies are examined, one constant difficulty emerges. Liturgical mss. are notably conservative: copyists will retain what was no longer the actual practice of a particular Church. This factor also makes the dating of a particular ceremonial or prayer very difficult. The Byzantine and Chaldean rites have deaconesses: their function was mainly for baptism of women, and to install superiors of women's monasteries. Whether or not there were deaconesses in Egypt is disputed.[17] In the Syrian Church we find an added ministry of anointing sick women.[18] A.-G. Martimort concludes that by the 11th century deaconesses had all but disappeared in the Eastern Church.[19]

In the Latin Churches deaconesses do not appear at all in the early centuries. In the late 5th-century *Statuta Ecclesiae antiquae* widows or female monks were to be instructed in order to prepare women for baptism, but there were strong prohibitions against women preaching or baptizing.[20] Though not mentioned in the Carolingian reformed liturgies, deaconesses made an appearance in Italy in the 7th to 9th centuries,[21] but their role seems mostly to have been to care for monastic women. Later there would be a confusion between deaconesses and abbesses;[22] furthermore, the term *"diaconissa"* could mean a deacon's wife. In the later Middle Ages there was an institution of deaconesses in order to have somebody in women's monasteries able to read the Gospel and the homily at the night offices.

Though one can draw various conclusions from some rite in a particular Church at a particular time,[23] the overall conclusion of Martimort, after quite an exhaustive survey of the patristic and liturgical literature, seems valid: he notes that there was not a parity in the functions of the deaconess and of the deacon. In other words he argues that there were not simply male and female deacons; rather male deacons functioned in the Church's ministry in one way, while female deaconesses functioned in another. Only very occasionally do we find deaconesses associated with the clergy: their more usual place was with the women, and rarely in the ranks of the widows (q.v.) and virgins (q.v.).

The current position in some Churches of the Anglican Communion would reflect the historical conclusions of Martimort. From 1861 there have been deaconesses in the Church of England, but it is stated that they do not constitute one of the Holy Orders of the Church of England. Where the ordination of women is accepted, a deaconess would have to be ordained deacon to progress to priesthood. The position is not, however, fully clear, as deaconesses can, in case of need, fulfill many of the roles, including liturgical ones, of the ordained deacon.

A restoration of the office of deaconess is always a possibility for the Catholic Church. The German hierarchy spoke about it in 1976, and in 1981 requested the Holy See to investigate the possibility of the restoration of the order.[24] A common argument against such a move is that it would take away from the idea that all women should be involved in the life of the Church and bear witness in the world as believers. But much the same argument can be adduced against the permanent diaconate. Deaconesses died out in the Church when their major though rather restricted ministry at adult baptism came to an end; they will only come back if there is reflection and agreement on the need for a special ministry in the Church today. There could be a possibility of such a restoration if the notion of *diakonia* or service were more fully developed. Then the Church might see the need for a strong symbol and focus for the distinctively feminine contribution to the following of Jesus the Servant.

[1]J.A. Fitzmyer, NJBC in loc.; K. Romaniuk, "Was Phoebe in Rom 16, 1 a Deaconess?," ZNW 81 (1990) 132–134.   [2]A.-G. Martimort, *Deaconesses: A Historical Study* (San Francisco: Ignatius, 1986 = French orig. 1982); J.D. Davies, "Deacons, Deaconesses and Minor Orders in the Patristic Period," JEH 14 (1963) 1–15; H. Frohnhofen, "Women Deacons in the Early Church," TDig 34 (1987) 149–153 = StimZ 111 (1986) 269–278; R. Gryson, Le ministère des femmes dans l'Église ancienne. Recherches et synthèses 4 (Gembloux: Duculot, 1972); B. Kleinheyer, "Zur Geschichte der Diakonissen: Ein bibliographischer Hinweis," LitJb 34 (1984) 58–64; C. Vagaggini, "L'ordinazione delle diaconesse nella tradizione greca e bizantina," OrChrPer 40 (1974) 146–189.   [3]Ad Smyr. 13:1.   [4]Patrology 2:147-152.   [5]Apostolic Constitutions 2:26, 6—SC 320:238—R.H. Connolly, Didascalia Apostolorum: The Syriac Text Translated (Oxford, 1929) 88.   [6]Ad Magnes. 6—SC 10A:98-99.   [7]2:26, 3; 8:28:7; 31:2—SC 320:236; 336:230, 234.   [8]8:13, 14; 3:8, 1—SC 336:210; 329:140.   [9]Didascal. 16—Connolly trans. (n. 5) 146–147; Apostolic Constitutions 3:16, 1–2—SC 329:154–156.   [10]Apostolic Constitutions 2:26, 6—SC 320:238-240.   [11]Apostolic Constitutions 8:20, 1-2—SC 336: 220–222.   [12]Didascalia apostolorum 16—Connolly (n. 5) 147–149.   [13]Canon 19—Tanner 1:15.   [14]Testamentum Domini 2:8, 12—J. Cooper and A.J. Maclean, The Testament of Our Lord (Edinburgh, 1902) 127.   [15]Ibid., 1:19, 7; 1:23, 1; 1:35, 1; 1:36, 4; 1:40-43—Cooper and Maclean 64, 70, 101, 103, 105–111.   [16]Constit. apost. 3:6, 1-2—SC 329:132; Didascalia 15—F.X. Funk, Didascalia et Constitutiones apostolorum. 2 vols. (Paderborn, 1905) 1:191—Connolly (n. 5) 133.   [17]Martimort (n. 2, ch. 3; K. Zanetti, "Y en a-t-il des diaconesses en Égypt?," VetChr 27 (1990) 369–373.   [18]G. Orioli, "Il testo dell'ordinazione delle diaconesse nella chiesa di Antiochia dei Siri," Apoll 62 (1989) 633–640.   [19]Op. cit. (n. 2) ch. 8.   [20]C.

Munier, ed., *Les Statuta Ecclesiae antiqua*. Bibliothèque de l'Institut de droit canonique de l'Université de Strasbourg 5 (Paris, 1960) nn. 10, 37, and 41, pp. 86, 100, 136–138. [21]J. Ysebert, "The Deaconesses in the Western Church of Late Antiquity and Their Origins," in G.J.M. Bartelink et al., eds., *Eulogia*. FS A.A.R. Bastiaensen. Instrumenta Patristica 24 (Steenbrugge: Abbatia S. Petri, 1991) 421–436. [22]Sr. Teresa [J. White], "The Development and Eclipse of the Deacon Abbess," StPatr 19 (1989) 111–116. [23]See A. Cunningham, "Deaconess," NDictT 270–271. [24]DocCath 78 (1981) 1079. Cf. E. Theodorou, "L'Institution des diaconesses dans l'Église orthodoxe et la possibilité de sa rénovation," Contacts 41 (1989) 124–144.

## DEACONS

In the NT[1] we find *diakonoi* along with *episkopoi* about 55 C.E. at Philippi (Phil 1:1), and instructions about their recruitment and behavior in the later pastoral letter, 1 Tim 3:8-12.[2] These texts point to a specific group in the early Church. In addition, there is a generic use of the term in which it may not mean much more than minister, e.g., 1 Thess 3:2; 2 Cor 3:6; 11:23. A particular difficulty arises about Phoebe (Rom 16:1): is the term *diakonos* applied to her in virtue of a special function, or only generically? (v. DEACONESS). Acts 6:1-6 has long been favored in liturgical usage as the origin of the diaconate; modern exegesis, however, does not concur. In this text there is probably the appointment of the Seven as leaders and ministers for the Greek-speaking Christians in the early Church, more or less parallel with the structure of the Twelve for the Hebrew converts (v. PRIMITIVE CHURCH).[3] We do not get a clear picture of the role and function of the deacon from the NT, except that the word "deacon" *(diakonos)* connotes service. The other early texts do not add to clarity, apart from reinforcing the NT idea that some form of leadership/service as well as liturgical functions is implied.[4] By the end of the 1st century we find deacons in the Churches visited by Ignatius (q.v.),[5] in the *Didachê* (q.v.) and in the *Letter of Clement* (q.v.).[6] The Letters of Ignatius seem to suggest some preaching of the word.[7]

Towards the beginning of the 3rd century the figure of the deacon begins to emerge more clearly. In the *Apostolic Tradition* (q.v.) only the bishop (and not the priests) lays hands on the candidate, who is said not to receive the Spirit common to the presbyters, for he is ordained not into the priesthood, but into the service of the bishop *(in ministerio episcopi)*. (One could note that Ignatius was accompanied by a deacon, Burrus, who was either his amanuensis or messenger.[8]) Behind this mainly liturgical norm in the *Apostolic Tradition* may lie an attempt by some deacons to achieve greater dignity and authority.[9] The *epiclêsis* (q.v.) of the ordination rite prays for the Spirit of grace and zeal. The Verona Sacramentary for ordination of a deacon includes a prayer that he will receive the grace to minister at the altar and to be an example to the people.[10] The typology of the rite is that of Jesus the servant.[11]

The *Apostolic Tradition* showed the deacon as clearly distinct from the presbyters. About the same time the deacon was described as specially related to the bishop: "Let the bishop and deacon, then, be of one mind. . . . Let the deacon be the hearing of the bishop, and his mouth and his heart and his soul."[12] In time one deacon, the archdeacon, would be especially associated with the bishop and had extensive powers up to the 13th century; it is now an honorific title. Meanwhile there was a long series of canonical texts which clearly demanded a subordination of deacons to presbyters.[13] Their role incorporated both liturgy and service, especially social work and ministry to the poor.

In the late 4th century the *Apostolic Constitutions* (q.v.) give an important place to the deacon,[14] third in rank after, and subject to, the priests: he does not exercise the priesthood *(hierôsunê)* reserved to bishops and priests, but he is at their service;[15] he is described as the bishop's prophet and messenger *(angelos)*;[16] the language about his relationship to the bishop in the *Apostolic Tradition* is repeated;[17] an important function is to lead the people in prayer.[18] In Ps-Dionysius (q.v.) the task of the deacon is to purify especially those approaching the initiation sacraments.[19]

The later history of the diaconate shows a decline after the 4th century.[20] Before that time a bishop might be chosen from among the deacons, and in Rome a priest might not always be ordained a deacon first. Gradually the diaconate became merely a step on the path to priestly ordination, and by the 9th century the deacon's functions were almost entirely liturgical.[21] However, St. Thomas Aquinas in one place refers to the proclamation of the Gospel as the highest task of the deacon,[22] but notes other tasks as well: he disposes the people for the sacraments by holy admonitions;[23] he dispenses the chalice as one who is between the priest and the people.[24] By the time of Trent future priests spent only a very short time as deacons. The council wanted to reestablish the traditional offices, including that of deacon,[25] but its decree remained a dead letter.

There was a movement in Germany in the 1950s to confer the diaconate on deeply committed Church workers, and it was largely through the German bishops that the call for a restoration of the permanent diaconate was first made at Vatican II.[26] One can detect a double motivation for this restoration: the shortage of priests; a desire to complete the hierarchical structure by regaining a valued ministry.[27] But the restoration was not approved merely for the pragmatic reason of shortage of priestly vocations. Vatican II in chapter 3 of LG dealing with the hierarchy stated that the functions of deacons are "extremely necessary for the life of the Church"; it was left to local hierarchies to determine the possibility in their area of a permanent diaconate (LG 29; OE 17). The acts of the council show that there was much discussion about this restoration and about the issue of married deacons.²⁸ But the clearest assertion comes in AG 16: "It would help those men who carry out the ministry of a deacon—preaching the word of God as catechists, governing scattered communities in the name of the bishop or pastor, or exercising charity in the performance of social or charitable works—if they were strengthened by the imposition of hands which has come down from the apostles. They would be more closely bound to the altar, and their ministry would be made more fruitful through the sacramental grace of the diaconate."

The theology of the diaconate is not yet very fully developed. One difficulty stems from the fact that lay persons can perform, at least exceptionally, most of the duties listed for the deacon given in LG 29 (baptism, distribution of Holy Communion, marriage, Viaticum, reading Scripture, sacramentals, funeral services, presiding at worship and prayers, works of charity and functions of administration) and given in the *Code of Canon Law* (preaching, baptizing, distributing Holy Communion—CIC 764, 861, 910), to which can be added one given by Paul VI: "to foster and aid the lay apostolate."²⁹ The key to understanding the diaconate should be sought not in what the deacon does, but what he is: the sacramental representative of Christ the Servant such that he "cooperates" with the pastors, whereas the laity are said "to assist" (CIC 519). Deacons "serve the people of God in union with the bishop and his clergy" (CD 15; cf. LG 20, 41). Rather than stressing his traditional place lower than priests, we need to understand his role both in relation to the bishop and priests as collaborator, and to the faithful as servant in an ecclesiology of communion (q.v.). It is in this context that we can understand the triple service of the deacon (LG 29 reflecting the functions of Priest, Prophet, and King (q.v.): service of the liturgy in everything that does not pertain to the ministerial priest alone; thus the deacon can give benediction (CIC 943); service of the word (reading the Scripture, instruction and exhortation), service of charity (which includes the whole range of caring activity of the Church). It should be noted that since Vatican II the deacon is an ordinary minister of baptism and of Holy Communion: this is a doctrinal and canonical development. One may also see in the distinction between deacons who cooperate with, and the laity who assist, the pastor a new development in understanding the ministry of deacons; their activity is a function of the sacrament of orders.³⁰

The canon law affecting the permanent diaconate entails the following: unmarried candidates are bound to celibacy (CIC 1037); a married man must be at least 35 years of age and have the consent of his wife (CIC 1031 § 2)—should his wife die he cannot remarry (CIC 1087); he should receive adequate formation (CIC 1027–1028; 1032. A candidate for diaconate must be accepted by a bishop for his diocese or be a member of a religious institute (CIC 1015–1016; 1018–1019; 1025 § 3). A person becomes a cleric through reception of the diaconate (CIC 266 § 1).

The spirituality of the diaconate can be seen especially in the post-Vatican II decrees of Pope Paul VI³¹ and in the Rite of Ordination: deacons are ordained for the service of the altar; they receive the sevenfold gift of the Spirit to fulfill their ministry; the consecratory prayer asks, "May they excel in every virtue: in love that is sincere, in concern for the sick and the poor, in unassuming authority, in self-discipline and in holiness of life. . . . May they in this life imitate your Son who came, not to be served but to serve." In giving them the Book of the Gospels the bishop says, "receive the Gospel of Christ whose herald you now are. Believe what you read, teach what you believe, and practice what you teach" (cf. DV 25).

There has been much interest for the permanent diaconate in the United States and in some European countries. Only time will show the value to the Church of the restoration of this order and will lead the whole Church to understand its meaning and function more completely;³² time is also needed to determine the manner of formation for permanent deacons in each country;³³ time, too, will show if marriage contributes to an enriched ministry in the Church.

Finally, one should note the Lima statement (q.v.), which invites Churches that do not have the diaconate to reflect on it, and at the same time seeks to give some common understanding of the order for those Churches which possess it: "Deacons represent to the Church its calling as servant in the world. By struggling in Christ's name with the myriad needs of societies and persons, deacons exemplify the interdependence of worship and service in the Church's life. They exercise responsibility in the worship of the congregation: for example, by reading the Scriptures, preaching and leading the people in prayer. They help in the teaching of the congregation. They exercise a ministry of love within the community. They fulfill certain administrative tasks and may be elected to responsibilities for governance." If there were clarification on this last matter of governance, the Lima text would seem acceptable in a Catholic theology of the diaconate.³⁴

¹D.E. Hiebert, "Behind the Word 'Deacon': A New Testament Study," BiblSac 140 (1983) 151–162; L.R. Hennessey, "*Diakonia and Diakonoi:* Early Christian Perspectives on Service and the Servants," NewTR 4/4 (Nov. 1991) 5–23. ²G. Deiana, "Il diacono in 1 Tim 3:8-13" in AA.VV. Il *diaconato permanente.* Teologia e confronto 2 (Naples: Dehoniane, 1983) 219–226; H.W. Beyer,

"Diakoneô," TDNT 2:81-93.   [3]S. Cipriani, "Sono davvero 'diaconi' i 'Sette' di Atti 6, 3-6?'in *Il diaconato permanente* (n. 3) 227–236. R.J. Dillon in NJBC in loc., n. 43; B. Domagalski, "Waren die 'Sieben' Diakone?," BZ 26 (1982) 21–33; J.T. Lienhard, "Acts 6:1-6: A Redactional View," CBQ 37 (1975) 228–236.   [4]*I Clement* 40:5, 42; G. Bentivegna, "Il 'terzo sacerdozio': rilieve sul diaconato nella storia della Chiesa," RasT 20 (1979) 144–154.   [5]E.g., *Philadelphians,* Pref.; 4; 7:2; 10:2. . . .   [6]44:4-5.   [7]*Philadelph.* 11:1; cf. 10:1. [8]*Eph.* 2:1 with *Philadelph.* 11:2   [9]See J.E. Stam, *Episcopacy in the Apostolic Tradition of Hippolytus.* Bd 111 der theologischen Dissertationen (Basel, 1969) 46–48.   [10]M.S. Gros, "Les plus anciennes formules romaines de bénédiction des diacres," EcOr 5 (1988) 45–52.   [11]*Apostolic Tradition* 8/9:4-12.   [12]*Didascalia* 2:44, 2 and 4—R.H. Connolly, tr. and ed., *Didascalia apostolorum: The Syriac Version Translated and Accompanied by the Verona Latin Fragments* (Oxford, 1929) 109 = *Apostolic Constitutions* 2:44, 4—SC 320:284. [13]J.W. Pokusa, "The Diaconate: A History of Law Following Practice," Jurist 45 (1985) 95–135 at 99–115. B. Domagalski, "Römische Diakone im 4. Jahrhundert: Zum Verhaltnis von Bischof, Diakon und Presbyter," in J.G. Plöger and H.J. Weber, *Der Diakon: Wiederentdeckung und Erneuerung seines Dienstes.* FS A. Frotz (Freiburg—Basel—Vienna: Herder, 21981) 44–56; J.G. Davis, "Deacons, Deaconess and Minor Orders in the Patristic Period," JEH 14 (1963) 1–15; L.R. Hennessy, "*Diakonia* and *Diakonoi* in the Pre-Nicene Church," in T. Halton and J.P. Williamson, eds., *Diakonia.* FS R.T. Meyer (Washington, D.C.: The Catholic University of America Press, 1986) 160–186.   [14]Cf. M. Metzger, SC 329:50-53.   [15]8:28, 4; 46:10-11—SC 336:230, 268-270.   [16]2:30, 2—SC 329:248-250. [17]2:44, 4—SC 320:284.   [18]8:10; 8:13, 3-9—SC 336:166-172, 204-206.   [19]*Ecclesiastical Hierarchy* 5:6 and 8—PG 3:508, 516 [20]J.M. Barnett, *The Diaconate: A Full and Equal Order* (New York: Seabury, 1981); W. Croce, "Aus der Geschichte des Diakonates," in K. Rahner and H. Vorgrimler, eds., *Diaconia in Christo: Über die Erneuerung des Diakonates.* Q. Disputatae 15–16 (Frieburg Br.: 1962) 92–128; J.G. Davies, "Deacons, Deaconesses and Minor Orders in the Patristic Period," JEH 14 (1963) 1–15.   [21]R.E. Reynolds, "An Early Medieval Tract on the Diaconate," HarvTR 72 (1979) 97–100.   [22]*Summma c. gent.* 4:75.   [23]ST 3a, q.64, a.1 ad 1. [24]Ibid., q.82, a.3 ad 1.   [25]Sess. 23, Decree on Reform canon 17— Tanner 2:750.   [26]P. Beltrando, *Diaconi per la Chiesa: Itinerario ecclesiologico del ripristino del ministerio diaconale.* Fede e cultura (Milan: Istit. Propagando Libreria, 1977); E.J. Fiedler, "The Permanent Diaconate," TTod 36 (1979–1980) 401–411 at 403–404; J. Hornef and P. Winninger, "Chronique de la restauration du diaconat (1945–1965)," in *Le diacre dans l'Église et le monde d'aujourd'hui* (Paris, 1966) 205–222; H. Krimm, ed., *Das diakonische Amt der Kirche* (Stuttgart, 21965); idem, ed., *Quellen zur Geschichte der Diakonie* (Stuttgart, 1960–1964); J. Ludwig, "Theologische Überlungen zur Weiterwicklung des Diakonats," MüTZ 40 (1989) 129–143; Rahner-Vorgrimler, *Diakonia in Christo* (n. 20).   [27]J. Galot, "Le diaconat permanent—sa valeur," EsprVie 94 (1984) 433–440; K. Rahner, "The Theology of the Restoration of the Diaconate," ThInvest 5:268-314; idem, "On the Diaconate," ThInvest 12:61-80; E. Royón Lara, "El ministerio del diácono en una Iglesia ministerial," EstE 62 (1987) 3–25; A. Weiss, "Diaconat, un nouveau clergé," PraxJurRel 7 (1990) 31–43.   [28]ActsSyn 3/1:259-269/ Alberigo-Magistretti 462–466. See K. Rahner, "The Teaching of the Second Vatican Council on the Diakonate," ThInvest 10:222-232. [29]*Sacrum diaconatus ordinem* (18 June 1967) AAS 59 (1967) 697–704—DOL 2533-2546 (excerpt).   [30]CIC 519 with 1008 and see LG 20. See Pokusa (n. 13) 116–119.   [31]Motu proprio General Norms for Restoring the Permanent Diaconate (18 June 1967) *Sacrorum diaconatus ordinem* in AAS 49(1967) 697–704—Flannery 1:433-440; Norms for the Order of Diaconate (15 Aug. 1972) *Ad pascendum* in AAS 64 (1972) 534–540.   [32]J. Alves, "The Ministry of Deacons," ChicSt 16 (1977) 203–208. Bishops Committee on the Permanent Diaconate, *Permanent Deacons in the United States* (Washington, D.C.: USCC, 1971); idem, *A National Study of the Permanent Diaconate in the United States* (Washington, D.C.: USCC, 1981); M. Cancouët, "Les diacres" Communio 13/2 (1988) 94–105; K. Rahner (n. 27).   [33]E.g., V. Oteiza, *Diáconos para una Iglesia en renovación: Manual de formación ascético-teólogico de los candidatos al diaconado.* 2 vols. (Bilbao: Ed. Mensajero, 1982). [34]Cf. H.-M. Legrand, "Bulletin d'ecclésiologie: Le diaconat: renouveau et théologie," RSPT 69 (1985) 101–124 at 124.

## De LUBAC, Cardinal Henri (1896–1991)

Henri de Lubac was born at Cambrai (France) on 20 February 1896. He entered the Society of Jesus and became professor of theology at Lyon-Fourvière in 1929. Enormously prolific, with over forty books and innumerable articles, his first major work was *Catholicisme: Les aspects sociaux du dogme (1938)*.[1] With J. Daniélou in 1942 he founded the important series of patristic texts, *Sources Chrétiennes,* now nearly 400 volumes.

On the publication of *Surnaturel: Études historiques,*[2] he came under a cloud. He was widely seen as being one of the people censured by Pius XII's critique of the "New Theology" in 1950. Prohibited from teaching, he devoted himself to writing. He was vindicated in 1960 when John XXIII appointed him a *peritus,* or expert, for Vatican II;[3] still greater satisfaction was seen to be done when in 1983 he was appointed a cardinal by John Paul II. He died in 1991.

His enormous work output[4] ranges over patristics, the medieval and modern period, and many authors past and present for whom he has been a positive revisionist.[5] His rich and complex ecclesiology must be sought throughout his extensive corpus.[6] It is deeply rooted in tradition, with a profound sense of the historicity of the Church; it is profoundly both Christological and Trinitarian. A basis for a Eucharistic ecclesiology (q.v.) may be found in his work.[7] Refined by suffering and harassment, his ecclesiology breathes a serene love (q.v.) for the Church, about which he once remarked: "It is not enough to suffer for the Church, unless one has learned to suffer from the Church."

[1]Paris, 1938,   [4]1947; Eng. trans. *Catholicism: A Study of Dogma in Relation to the Corporate Destiny of Mankind* (New York, 1950). [2]Paris, 1948.   [3]K.H. Neufeld, "Henri de Lubac als Konzilstheologe," TPQ 134 (1986) 149–159.   [4]Bibliog., K.H. Neufeld and M. Sales, *Bibliographie Henri de Lubac 1925–1974 (*Einsiedeln: Johannes Verlag, 1974); updated idem, in appendix to H. de Lubac. *Théologie dans l'histoire.* 2 vols. (Paris: Desclée de Brouwer, 1990) 2:408-416; also H. de Lubac *Théologies d'occasion* (Paris: Desclée de Brouwer, 1984) 473–475. See A. Santos Hernánez, "Cardenal Henri de Lubac (1896–1991). Nota bio-bibliográfica," EstE 66 (1991) 327–335.   [5]H.U. von Balthasar, "L'Henri de Lubac. L'oeuvre organique d'une vie," NRT 97 (1975) 879–913; 98 (1976) 33–59. AA.VV. "Henri de Lubac," RechSR 80 (1992) 321–408; A. Dulles, "Henri de Lubac: In Appreciation," *America* 165 (1991) 180–182.   [6]*The Splendor of the Church* (New York, 1956 —San Francisco: Ignatius, 1986); *Corpus Mysticum: L'Eucharistie*

*et l'Église au moyen-âge* (Paris, 1944); *Paradoxe et mystère de l'Église* (Paris, 1967); *The Motherhood of the Church Followed by Particular Churches in the Universal Church* (San Francisco: Ignatius, 1982). See B. Mondin, *Le nuove ecclesiologie: Un'immagine attuale della Chiesa* (Rome: Paoline, 1980) 250–261; M. Pelchat, *L'ecclésiologie dans l'oeuvre de Henri de Lubac.* Diss. Abs. (Rome: Gregorian, 1986); G. Trapani, "Aspetti ecclesiologici dal pensiero di Henri de Lubac," HoTheol 7 (1989) 223–274.   [7]P. McParlan, *The Eucharist Makes the Church: Henri de Lubac and John Zizioulas in Dialogue* (Edinburgh: Clark, 1993).

## DENZINGER, Heinrich Joseph (1819–1893)

Heinrich Joseph Denzinger was born in Liège (Belgium) in 1819. After ordination in 1844 he taught theology at Würzburg. He wrote many works on historical theology, especially on Eastern rites. He is best remembered for his *Enchiridion* ("Handbook of Creeds, Definitions and Declarations about Faith and Morals"), which first appeared in 1854. It has gone through at least 35 editions with several editors, including C. Bannwart (hence abbrev. DB in older writings) and K. Rahner.

In 1963 A. Schönmetzer published a profound revision of the work for its 32rd edition (generally abbreviated DS).[1] The first 76 numbers of the work are devoted to creeds, and from n. 100 magisterial documents are presented in chronological order. Texts are given in the original Latin, with Greek ones having a Latin translation. The later editions continue the tradition of superb indices. The popular English translation by J. Neuner and J. Dupuis (ND)[2] is incomplete, and since it deals with the material by subject rather than chronologically, comparison between DS and ND is sometimes difficult.

For nearly a century and a half the Church has been indebted to what is called simply "Denzinger," a modestly priced, reliable, and quite comprehensive collection of papal and conciliar statements. What is sometimes called "Denzinger theology" is an inadequate theological method rather than a problem with Denzinger.[3] Manual theology before Vatican II saw itself primarily as giving the grounds for, and explaining, the teaching of the Church found in Denzinger. This position is found in Pius XII's *Humani generis,* where he echoes Pius IX: "It is for the theologian to show how and where the teaching given by the living magisterium of the Church is contained in Scripture and in our sacred tradition," and later he refers to his predecessor's statement that tracing the Church's defined doctrines to their source was the highest office of theology.[4] Properly used as one of several theological sources (q.v.), Denzinger (at least in translation) will always be an essential companion for every theologian and all serious students of theology.

---

[1]*Enchiridion symbolorum definitionum et declarationum de rebus fidei et morum* (Barcelona &c.: Herder, [35]1973).   [2]*The Christian*

*Faith: Doctrinal Documents of the Catholic Church* (London: HarperCollins Religious, [5]1992).   [3]Y. Congar, "Du bon usage de Denzinger," in *Situations et tâches présentes de la théologie* (Paris, 1967) 111–113; B.J.F. Lonergan, *Method in Theology* (London: Darton, Longman & Todd, 1971) 330–333.   [4]AAS 42 (1950) 568/DS 3886/Carlen 4:178-179.

## DEVELOPMENT

The notion of development became prominent in the 1960s, seen for instance in the setting up in 1964 of the United Nations Conference on Trade and Development (UNCTAD). In the face of the poverty of the "Third World"—the phrase dates from this time—sociologists, economists, and also theologians[1] saw a solution in development. Something of the optimism of development is to be found at Vatican II in the Constitution on the Church in the Modern World (GS 63–66, 69, 85).

Pope Paul VI in his major encyclical *Populorum progressio* (1967)[2] is critical of a "trickle down" theory of development which is a surrender to market forces with a hope that the poor will ultimately benefit; in economics, a rising tide does not necessarily lift all boats.[3] But he also coined a lapidary phrase, "development[:] the new name for peace."[4] Within a few years *of Populorum progressio* Paul VI wrote what amounted to an encyclical, but in the form of an open letter to Cardinal M. Roy, a commemoration of Leo XIII's *Rerum novarum,* called *Octogesima adveniens.*[5] In this letter he has already moved away from any latent utopianism of the earlier document, showing much more awareness of the complexity of political, social, and economic issues.

Even though liberation theology (q.v.) was soon to take the stage in Latin America, later extending to Asia and Africa, the positive insights of the development phase of Catholic social teaching retain validity, and are still being studied especially in Europe and Third World countries.[6]

---

[1]G. Baver, *Towards a Theology of Development: An Annotated Bibliography* (Cartigny Switzerland: Sodepax, 1970); AA.VV. *In Search of a Theory of Development* (Cartigny: Sodepax, 1969); P. Land, ed., *Theology Meets Progress* (Rome: Gregorian UP, 1971); P. Land, "What Is Development? Questions Raised for Theological Reflection," Greg 50 (1969) 33–62.   [2]AAS 59 (1967) 257–299/ Carlen 3:183-201.   [3]See ibid., 58.   [4]Ibid., n. 76; see R. Coste, "L'encylique *Populorum progressio* vingt ans après," NRT 109 (1987) 161–181.   [5]AAS 67 (1971) 401–441.   [6]E. Boné, "Pour une théologie du développment," RAfrT 11 (1987) 179–201; H. Carrier, "Chiesa, cultura e sviluppo," Greg 62 (1981) 661–679; V. Cosmao, "Problématique du développment; défi à l'Église,"LavalTP 44 (1988) 3–18; R. Dickinson, *Poor Yet Making Many Rich* (Geneva: WCC, 1983); idem, "Development," DictEcumMov 268–274; W. Fernandes, "Christians and Development in India Today,"VYoti 44 (1980) 64–75, 98–107; P. Laurent, "Le développment des peuples," Études 368/4 (1988) 459–462; R. Laurentin, *Liberation, Development and Salvation* (New York: Orbis, 1969); S.A. Martinez, "Development, People's Participation and Theology,"

EcuR 30 (1978) 266–275; W.S. Mooneyham, "The Church and Development: Caring Can't Wait," IntRMiss 59 (198–1981) 56–70; Conc 117 (1978), 140 (1980).

## DEVELOPMENT OF DOCTRINE

The development of doctrine is clearly a fact: there has been growth in the Church's teaching since NT times. Development is clearly instanced in the area of Christology by the move from the NT texts to Nicaea (q.v.) to Constantinople III (q.v.). Further examples are numerous, as in the whole area of sacramental theology, the papacy (q.v.), the Marian dogmas. There is always a progression in the understanding of the faith: the Spirit constantly teaches the Church (John 14:25; 16:13); Vatican I asserts that reason can obtain a limited but most fruitful understanding of the sacred mysteries.[1] We speak of a development of dogma when such a theological understanding becomes normative and irreversible through a solemn intervention of the magisterium (q.v.) or the sense of the faith (LG 12—q.v.) of the whole Church guided by the ordinary universal magisterium.[2]

The issue of development was little raised in patristic times. There were rather static affirmations of a constant identity: Pope St. Stephen against Cyprian (q.v.), "Let no innovation be made except what has been handed down";[3] Vincent of Lérins maintained that what was to be held was "what was believed everywhere, always, and by all."[4] A common patristic image was that of the identity despite change found in a child who becomes an adult. In that time the factors most responsible for development were the need to clarify the truth in combating error, and the liturgy. The councils and creeds went beyond the exact expression of Scripture; likewise did worship. Leo I (q.v.) considered Chalcedon not a new faith, but a clarification of what was already believed.[5]

The patristic and later scholastic sense of tradition allowed a development to take place without much reflection on the process.[6] Trent affirmed that truth and rules of right conduct "are contained in written books and unwritten traditions which were received by the apostles from the mouth of Christ himself or else have come down to us, handed on as it were from the apostles themselves at the inspiration of the Holy Spirit."[7] But given the wide range of Catholic opinion represented at the council, it would be unwise to give a restrictive interpretation of this text.

We have to wait for the 18th and 19th centuries for illumination on the meaning of development and its processes. The Catholic Tübingen school developed what was germinal in late medieval times: the notion of living tradition. Crucial, too, at the time was the beginning of a historicist approach. It was now possible to deal with the issue of development. The first was

J.S. Drey (1777–1853), who studied particularly the development which occurred in the conflict between orthodoxy and heterodoxy.[8] J.A. Möhler (q.v.) saw tradition as vital and growing in both his pneumatological and more internal *Die Einheit der Kirche* (1825) and his Christological and more institutional *Symbolik* (1832, definitive 5th ed., 1838).

The main theoretician of development in the 19th century was J.H. Newman (q.v.), especially in his *Essay on the Development of Doctrine* (1845), which was not, however, his first joust with the topic.[9] Before his conversion to Roman Catholicism (1845), Newman was concerned with a double problem: Catholic "additions" after NT times; Anglican inconsistency in following the principle of "Scripture alone." The main thrust of his master work was to explain that the Catholic "additions" were not accretions, but legitimate development. He begins with the notion of a living idea: unlike mathematical ideas, it grows, changes, becomes more accurate when encountering other ideas in different places and times. His task is to find grounds for discernment of legitimate growth from accretions. He enumerates seven "notes" or tests:[10] unity of type, which remains despite change; continuity of principles in various stages; a unitive power of assimilation of other ideas; logical sequence, not that development is a logical deduction, but it must not contradict logic; previous anticipations or intimations; conservation of past positions, illustrating and corroborating them; chronic vigor or duration, an energy over a long period in countering error and evolving into formal statements. Newman's masterly exposition remains on the phenomenological level; a systematic understanding of development must still be sought.

Vatican I took up the question of development, but in a limited context: it eliminated the idea that past dogmas can have in a later time a completely different meaning, and cites Vincent of Lérins to the effect that despite growth and progress in understanding, it be "only in its own proper kind, that is to say, in the same dogma, the same sense, and the same understanding."[11]

With the help of intervening studies by Y. Congar and others, Vatican II was able to advance the position of the previous two councils. There is now clear acceptance of a living and growing tradition: "There is growth in understanding of what has been handed down, both the words and the realities they signify. This comes about through contemplation and study by believers, who 'ponder these things in their hearts' (see Luke 1:19 and 51); through the intimate understanding of the spiritual things they experience; and through the preaching of those who, on succeeding to the office of bishop, receive the sure charism of truth" (DV 8; cf. GS 44).

With the council, then, we are committed to seeing at least one modus of development as a growth in

---

understanding. The explanation of development will depend on one's position on the nature of theology, theological method, and hermeneutics.[12]

We can eliminate quickly two views: an anachronist one would see as earlier implicit what was later defined as dogma;[13] an archaic position would deny the legitimacy of any statement not clearly in the NT. The latter is the classical Protestant position, as seen verbally in the *Thirty-nine Articles* of the Anglican tradition (art. 6); in practice the exposition of faith was not thus confined (arts. 8, 25).[14] More nuanced Protestant positions point to development taking place at a primal stage; some would dub primitive developments as Early Catholicism (q.v.) and see them as a deviation, with roots even in the NT itself. Both of these views are contradicted either by the way in which dogmas developed, or by the fact of development itself. The Marian dogmas are touchstones for any theory of development: their history is well researched; they represent an ecumenical problem which Catholics will have to help Protestants solve, but within a wider context of the meaning of revelation and tradition.[15]

Whereas few Catholics would be happy with a theory of ongoing revelation in the sense that new truths are continually being revealed to the Church through the Spirit, there is a sense in which the same Spirit is unfolding to the Church new depths of the mystery revealed in Christ Jesus. The deepest problem here is the older view of revelation as propositions, rather than the unfolding of the Mystery which is ultimately the Trinity and the saving plan manifested in Christ Jesus and in the sending of the Spirit. Perhaps the best expression of development for the late 20th century is one of Spirit-guided dialogue between the Mystery and the whole Church from which may emerge issues in time-conditioned dogmatic statements which can, however, be normative in the sense that what they assert cannot later be denied.[16]

Development cannot be conceived apart from contemplation of the Word, the understanding that arises from spiritual experience rooted in historical situations, and the proclamation of the magisterium.[17] A theology cut off from spirituality, from liturgy, from the struggles of people, can neither give rise to development nor hope to explain it.

[1]Tanner 1:808/DS 3016/ND 132. [2]Z. Alszeghy, "The *Sensus Fidei* and the Development of Dogma" in Latourelle, Vatican II, 1:138-156. [3]DS 110/ND 1401. [4]*Commonitorium* 2—PL 50:639. [5]*Epist.* 104:1—PL 54:991-993. [6]Y. Congar, *Tradition and Traditions: An Historical Essay and a Theological Essay* (New York, 1966). [7]Sess. 4—Tanner 2:663/DS 1501/ND 210. [8]J.E. Thiel, "J.S. Drey on Doctrinal Development: The Context of the Theological Encyclopedia," HeythJ 27 (1986) 290–305. [9]I. Ker, *John Henry Newman: A Biography* (Oxford: UP, 1988) 257–315; see O. Chadwick, *From Bossuet to Newman: The Idea of Doctrinal Development* (Cambridge: UP, 1957) with response I.T. Ker,

"Newman's Theory—Development or Continuing Revelation," in J.D. Bastable, ed., *Newman and Gladstone Centennial Essays* (Dublin: Veritas, 1978) 145–149; N. Lash, *Newman on Development: The Search for an Explanation in History* (London: Sheed & Ward—Shepherdstown, W.Va: Patmos, 1975); A. Nichols, *From Newman to Congar: The Idea of Doctrinal Development from the Victorians to the Second Vatican Council* (Edinburgh: Clark, 1990); T. O'Loughlin, "Newman, Vincent of Lerins and Development," IrTQ 57 (1991) 147–166. [10]*An Essay on the Development of Christian Doctrine* (London, Longmans, 1878) 169–205. [11]Tanner 2:809/DS 3021/ND 136. [12]F.S. Schüssler Fiorenza, "Systematic Theology: Task and Methods," in F.S. Schüssler Fiorenza and J.P. Galvin, eds., *Systematic Theology: Roman Catholic Perspectives.* 2 vols. (Minneapolis: Fortress, 1991) 1:1-87; see H. Hammans, "Recent Catholic Views on the Development of Dogma," Conc 1/3 (Jan. 1967) 53–63; N. Lash, *Change in Focus: A Study of Doctrinal Change and Continuity* (London: Sheed & Ward, 1973); B.J.F. Lonergan, *Method in Theology* (London: Darton, Longman & Todd, 1972) 295–333; K. Rahner, "The Development of Dogma," ThInvest 1:39-77; idem, "Considerations on the Development of Dogma," ThInvest 4:3-35; idem, "Yesterday's History of Dogma and Theology for Tomorrow," ThInvest 18:3-34; J. Walgrave, *Unfolding Revelation* (Philadelphia: Westminster, 1972). [13]See E. Dhanis, "Révélation explicite et implicite," Greg 34 (1953) 187–237. [14]Schaff, Creeds 3: 487-516. [15]See W.H. Marschner, "Criteria for Doctrinal Development in Marian Dogmas," MarSt 28 (1977) 47–100. [16]Cf. A. Dulles, "Doctrinal Renewal: A Situationist View," in *The Resilient Church: The Necessity and Limits of Adaptation* (Dublin: Gill and Macmillan, 1978) 45–62. [17]J. Ratzinger, Interview on Luther and the Unity of the Churches, DocCath 81 (1984) 126.

## DIALOGUE

Dialogue is very much a 20th-century word, even though the reality has been known to all ages and peoples. Dialogue derives central insights from personalist philosophies, and especially that of M. Buber (1878–1965). It has also become in this century a key word in the ecumenical movement (q.v.). It entered the magisterium with Vatican II (q.v.). At the beginning of its 2nd session, Paul VI (q.v.) gave the council as two of its four aims the promotion of Christian unity and dialogue with the contemporary world.[1] A year later, in his first encyclical,[2] he spoke at length about dialogue as the mental attitude which the Catholic Church must adopt regarding the contemporary world (n. 58). With theological depth he showed that dialogue must be patterned on the divine dialogue of salvation (nn. 70–77). He repeatedly gave as the reason for dialogue the message that the Church has for the world (nn. 65, 69, 78, 80 . . .). He outlined as in concentric circles those who are to be addressed in dialogue: separated Christians, Jews and Moslems, all humanity, including atheists. Though he did mention that dialogue "will result in the discovery of elements of truth in the opinions of others and make us want to express our teaching with great fairness" (n. 83), the idea of the Church learning from dialogue does not really surface in the encyclical.

Vatican II so developed the notion of dialogue, in various ways, that it became one of the significant words associated with the council. Dialogue is a means whereby people attain truth (DH 3); it has to be learned and so emphasis is to be placed on developing in seminarians gifts that favor dialogue with people (OT 19) and with non-Christians (AG 16); the Catholic school has a role in fostering dialogue with the human community (GE 8); seats of ecclesiastical higher studies have as their function that "dialogue with our separated fellow Christians and with non-Christians may be promoted" (GE 11); there is a special importance of dialogue in the context of missionary activity (AG 11, 20, 34, 41);[3] the Church seeks dialogue with cultures, and with all of humanity, to build in true peace (GS 28, 56, 92); the approach of dialogue is courtesy, love of truth, and charity (GS 28).

Only at the very end of the council do we find the clearest indication of the significance of dialogue within the Church and of the characteristics of the Church's approach. It is the norm given before the council by John XXIII, "there should be unity in essentials, freedom in doubtful matters and charity in everything" (GS 92).[4]

Some key characteristics of ecumenical dialogue and its field are found in the Decree on Ecumenism: there is dialogue between experts (UR 4); it takes place in a religious spirit (UR 4); its result is that "everyone gains a truer knowledge and more just appreciation of the teaching and life of each communion" (UR 4); dialogue is needed "to acquire a more adequate understanding of the respective doctrines of other Christians, their history, their spiritual and liturgical life, their religious psychology and culture" (UR 9). Dialogue involves both sides being on an equal footing (*unusquisque par cum pari agat*—UR 9); in ecumenical dialogue there is to be love of the truth, charity, and humility. . . . "The way will be opened to incite all . . . to a clearer manifestation of the unfathomable riches of Christ" (UR 11).

Understanding of the origin of the Eastern Churches and of the relations of East and West in the first millennium "will greatly contribute to the dialogue in view" (UR 14); there is urgent need for "fraternal dialogue with the east" (UR 18). Because of special difficulties, bases of dialogue with other Christians are set down (UR 19): Sacred Scripture, which is treasured by Protestants, is "an outstanding instrument in the hand of God" for the work of dialogue (UR 21); dialogue "should include among its subjects the Lord's Supper and other sacraments, worship and the church's ministry" (UR 22); "ecumenical dialogue might start with discussion of the application of the gospel to moral questions" (UR 23).

More specific guidance about dialogue is given in post-conciliar documents. It has been a time of grow-

ing ecumenical dialogue between all the Churches, including the Catholic Church (v. ECUMENISM AND THE ROMAN CATHOLIC CHURCH and other arts. on ECUMENISM). It has been pointed out that there are two fundamentally different, though not exclusive, understandings of dialogue in the council's documents. The first, "explicative," has the aim of mutual understanding between Christians. The other, "investigative," is a reflection together, a listening together, to the message of Christ in order to express it more profoundly (see UR 4, 9, 11).[5] One of the tasks of the newly erected Council of the Laity (1967) was to promote dialogue within the Church between hierarchy and laity, and between the various forms of lay activity.[6]

The first part of the 1967 Ecumenical Directory of the Secretariat for Christian Unity[7] commits to diocesan and territorial ecumenical commissions the task of fostering dialogue.[8] The whole theology and practice of baptism is to be examined in dialogue between the Churches, as is the matter of sharing in spiritual things *(communicatio in spiritualibus)*.[9]

The second part from 1970[10] dealing with ecumenism and higher education has some important statements: people are to be educated in their Catholic faith the better to take part in ecumenical dialogue;[11] examination of "the spiritual treasury and wealth of doctrine which each Christian community has for its own . . . can lead all Christians to a deeper understanding of the nature of the Church";[12] institutes of higher education have an important role in dialogue, for though false irenicism is to be avoided, there is an aim "to have a mind open and ready to base life more deeply on one's own faith because of the fuller knowledge derived from dialogue with others."[13] Here we see clearly expressed what up to then had been tentative, viz., that Catholics can deepen their own faith through what they learn in dialogue. In a text of the Secretariat for Christian Unity *Reflections and Suggestions Concerning Ecumenical Dialogue* issued in 1970,[14] the idea of learning from others is again stressed.[15] This wide-ranging document also insists that dialogue must be learned,[16] that it takes place in many different ways and circumstances,[17] and that "it will be conducted between the participants as between equals."[18] Notable is the recognition that genuine and valuable ecumenical dialogue can take place spontaneously when Christians meet, and in an unstructured way at various centers of study.[19]

In the post-conciliar documentation the main stress was on loving, respectful relationships in which both sides of dialogue can learn more about the positions of others. In his letter to Patriarch Athenagoras of Constantinople, Pope Paul VI drew attention to the need to have "a sincere dialogue made possible by the reestablishment of fraternal charity in order to know one another and to respect the diverse liturgical, spiritual, disciplinary and theological traditions."[20] There is also fruit for the Catholic participants in learning more about their own faith. The Catholic Church is currently engaged in international dialogue with eleven Christian world confessional bodies.

But dialogue is not restricted to Christian communities. Texts above show that Vatican II advocated dialogue with non-Christians. Twenty-five years after the council's Declaration on Non-Christian Religions (NA), the Pontifical Council for Interreligious Dialogue issued, in collaboration with the Congregation for the Evangelization of Peoples, a major document, *Dialogue and Proclamation: Reflections and Orientations on Interreligious Dialogue and the Proclamation of the Gospel of Jesus Christ.*[21] It noted at the outset that the interreligious dialogue envisaged by Vatican II "is only gradually coming to be understood. Its practice remains hesitant in some places."[22] Dialogue and proclamation are not mutually exclusive: both belong to the Church's mission.[23] Dialogue can be understood in various ways: on a human level, reciprocal communication ; an attitude of respect and friendship in the evangelizing mission of the Church; in the context of religious plurality, "all positive and constructive interreligious relations with individuals and communities of other faiths which are directed at mutual understanding and enrichment in obedience to truth and respect for freedom."[24] It is asserted very clearly that the Church can learn from dialogue: "While keeping their identity intact, Christians must be prepared to learn and to receive from and through others the positive values of their traditions. Through dialogue they may be moved to give up ingrained prejudices, to revise preconceived ideas, and even sometimes to allow the understanding of their faith to be purified."[25] The document outlines four forms of dialogue: the dialogue of life, in which people share their joys and sorrows in a neighborly spirit; the dialogue of action, in which people collaborate in the integral liberation of people; the dialogue of theological exchange, "where specialists seek to deepen their understanding of their respective religious heritages, and appreciate each other's spiritual values;" the dialogue of religious experience, "where persons . . . share their spiritual riches, for instance with regard to prayer and contemplation, faith and ways of searching for God or the Absolute."[26] There is, furthermore, dialogue at the level of culture.[27] The disposition required for dialogue is to be "neither ingenuous nor overly critical, but open and receptive," holding on to one's own religious conviction with openness to truth.[28] There are obstacles to interreligious dialogue: unlike inter-Church dialogues in which the participants are appointed by, or somehow represent, their Churches, dialogue with other faiths cannot easily find representative or authoritative figures; difficulties, too, stem "from a lack of understanding of the true nature and goal of interreligious dialogue."[29]

The post-conciliar years have seen an increase in dialogue with non-Christian religions (v. NON-CHRISTIANS) at all levels. Dialogue remains the continuing agenda for the Churches, with an aim toward mutual understanding and the promotion of Christian unity. It remains a task of the missionary Church as it approaches the great religions of Asia and Africa and seeks to discover the preparation of the gospel already implanted in them (cf. LG 16).[30] But it is a dialogue in which the Church must be self-critical and respectfully critical of others in a common search for truth. A new need in what is often called a "post-Christian age" is dialogue within the culture of pluralistic societies.[31]

Considering the interest in dialogue at all levels of Church life since the council,[32] one can be surprised at the dearth of texts about dialogue, except for religious dialogue with other Christians and people of other faiths. But the essentials are stated: there is to be dialogue with people of good will concerning matters of the common good of society (AA 14, 29; GE 1; GS 23, 25, 43, 56, 92); bishops are to have regular dialogue with their priests (CD 28); bishops are to choose priests who have special ability to help with the lay apostolate and to dialogue with the laity (AA 25); in seminarians, aptitudes conducive to dialogue with people are to be cultivated (OT 19). In dealing with religious obedience there is probably an oblique reference to dialogue, "superiors must listen to their subjects" (PC 14); dialogue is explicit in the post-conciliar apostolic exhortation on the renewal of religious life.[33] Though not very frequently expressly mentioned, dialogue is at the heart of the important 1978 document on the relations between bishops and religious, *Mutuae relationes* (nn. 38, 40, 49, conclusion).[34]

Canon Law does not mention dialogue very often except for dialogue with non-Christians (CIC 787). It is, however, implicit in the very many statements on consultation in both pastoral and contentious issues. Indeed, one could say that without a spirit of dialogue, the whole book of laws, instead of fostering Christian freedom under the law of Christ in his Church, could be quite oppressive.

Finally, it is in trusting dialogue in communion (q.v.) that authority (q.v.) in the Church is best exercised at every level; such dialogue protects authority from being a power-struggle, domination, manipulation, and from rejection by those whom authority is seeking to serve. Dialogue must be patterned on the eternal divine dialogue, on the model of the discourse of the Incarnate Word with humanity, and on the tentative steps people take in a dialogical search for intimacy with God.[35]

[1]29 Sept. 1963—ActaSyn 2/1:193-199.  [2]*Ecclesiam suam*—AAS 56 (1964) 609–659/Carlen 5:135-160; Cf. AA.VV. *"Ecclesiam suam": Première lettre encyclique de Paul VI.* Colloque international Rome 24–26 octobre 1980 (Brescia: Istituto Paolo VI—Rome: Ed. Studium Vita Nova, 1982)—summary A. Amato, Sales 43 (1981) 149–159; K. Gawron, *Dialogue as a Pastoral Method in the Teaching of Pope Paul VI.* Diss. exc. (Rome: Gregorian University, 1982).  [3]M. Dhavamony, "Evangelization and Dialogue in Vatican II and in the 1974 Synod," in Latourelle, Vatican II 3:264-281.  [4]Encyc. *Ad Petri cathedram* (29 June 1959)—AAS 51 (1959) 513/Carlen 5:12.  [5]H. Witte, cited by W. Henn, "The Hierarchy of Truths," ETLv 66 (1990) 111–142 at 115–116; cf. A. Birmelé, "Les dialogues entre Églises chrétiennes: Bilan et perspectives," Études 373 (1990) 679–690; K. Rahner, "On the Theology of the Ecumenical Discussion," ThInvest 11:24-67.  [6]Mp. *Catholicam Christi ecclesiam* (6 Jan. 1967)—AAS 59 (1967) 25–28.  [7]AAS 59 (1967) 574–592/Flannery 1:483-501.  [8]Ibid., nn. 6, 8/Flannery 1:485, 486.  [9]Ibid., n. 16, 25–27/Flannery 1:489, 492–493.  [10]16 March 1970—Flannery 1:515-532.  [11]Ibid., 68/1:517.  [12]Ibid., 72/1:520.  [13]Ibid., 76/1:524.  [14]15 Aug. 1970—Flannery 1:535-553.  [15]Ibid., V, 1 and V, 3/Flannery 1:547, 549.  [16]Ibid., IV, 3/Flannery 1:543-544.  [17]Ibid., VII, 1–10/Flannery 1:550-553.  [18]Ibid., IV, 2/Flannery 1:542.  [19]Ibid., VII, 1–2/Flannery 1:550.  [20]25 July 1967—AAS 59 (1967) 852–854/E.J. Stormon, ed., *Towards the Healing of Schism.* Ecumenical Documents III (New York-Mahwah: Paulist, 1987) 157–161.  [21]Pontifical Council for Interreligious Dialogue *Bulletin* 26 (1991) 210–250 text of 19 June 1991/OssRomano (English) 1 July 1991/DocCath 88 (1991) 874–890; cf. Secretariat for Unbelievers, *Humanae personae dignitatem.* "Dialogue with Unbelievers" (28.8.1968)—DocCath 45 (1968) 1665–1676/Flannery 1:1002-1014; Secretariat for Non-Christians, *The Attitude of the Church Towards the Followers of Other Religions. Reflections and Orientations on Dialogue and Mission* (Vatican: Pentecost, 1984)/DocCath 81 (1984) 844–849.  [22]Pontifical Council for Interreligious Dialogue (n. 21) 4b, pp. 211–212.  [23]Ibid., 4c, p. 212; 77–80, pp. 245–246; cf. Encyc. *Redemptoris missio.* "The Permanent Validity of the Church's Missionary Mandate" (7 Dec. 1990), nn. 55–57—AAS 83 (1991) 302–305/CathInter 2 (1991) 277–278.  [24]Pontifical Council (n. 21) 9, p. 214.  [25]Ibid., 49, p. 230; cf. 34, p. 224; 40, p. 227.  [26]Ibid., 42, p. 228  [27]Ibid., 45–56, p. 229.  [28]Ibid., 47–49, p. 230.  [29]Ibid., 53, cf. 52, 54, pp. 231–232; cf. B. Groth, "From Monologue to Dialogue in Conversations with Nonbelievers, or the Difficult Search for Partners in Dialogue," in Latourelle, Vatican II, 3:184-198.  [30]J. Dupuis, "Interreligious Dialogue in the Church's Evangelizing Mission: Twenty Years of Evolution of a Theological Concept," in Latourelle Vatican II, 3:237-263; L. Swidler, "Interreligious Dialogue: A Christian Necessity," CrossC 35 (1985–1986) 129–147; W. Teasdale, "Dialogue as a Spiritual Resource," JDhara 13 (1983) 343–353.  [31]K. Rahner, "Reflections on Dialogue Within a Pluralistic Society," ThInvest 6:31-42.  [32]K. Rahner, "Dialogue in the Church," ThInvest 10:103-121.  [33]*Evangelica testificatio* (29 June 1979) n. 25—Flannery 1:692.  [34]*Mutuae relationes*—AAS 70 (1978) 473–506/Flannery 2:209-243.  [35]K. Rahner, "Dialogue with God?," ThInvest 18:122-131.

## DICTATUS PAPAE

In 1075 Pope Gregory VII (1073–1085) dictated a list of 27 propositions which claimed near absolute power for the pope, e.g., "That the Roman Pontiff alone is rightly called universal"(2); "That he may depose emperors" (12); "That he may transfer bishops, if neces-

sary from one see to another" (13); "That no synod may be called general without his order" (16); "That no chapter or book may be regarded as canonical without his authority" (17); "That no sentence of his may be retracted by anyone; and that he, alone of all, can retract it" (18); "That he himself may be judged by no one" (19); "That to this See the more important cases of every Church should be submitted" (21); "That the Roman Church has never erred, nor ever, by witness of Scripture, shall err to all eternity" (22); "That he should not be considered a catholic who is not in conformity with the Roman Church" (26); "That the Pope may absolve subjects of unjust men from their fealty" (27).[1]

Scholars are not unanimous about the precise function the statements were to serve. They have been variously seen as: a list of conditions for the reestablishment of communion with the East; an outline for a Lenten synod in Rome (1075); chapter headings for a collection of texts; an outline of headings under which canonists were to seek authoritative texts.[2] Even when they are not cited, the ideas of the *Dictatus papae* were to recur continually up to the Reformation and beyond.

[1]Latin text E. Casper, ed., *Das Register Gregors VII,* in MGEpist. sel. 2:55a, 201–208. Eng. trans. S.Z. Ehler and J.B. Morrall, eds., *Church and State Through the Centuries* (Westminster, Md., 1954) 43–44; also P. Granfield, *The Limits of the Papacy: Authority and Autonomy in the Church* (London: Darton, Longman & Todd—New York: Crossroad, 1987) 34–35.  [2]Congar, Augustin 104, n. 7; F. Kempf, in Jedin-Dolan 3:369.

## DIDACHÊ

Though it was known to the Fathers, usually under the title "The Instruction of the Twelve Apostles," the text of the *Didachê* was discovered only in 1873, and then with the additional title of *The Lord's Instruction to the Gentiles Through the Twelve Apostles.* It is probably a composite work dating almost certainly from the lst century; it cannot be dated after 150 C.E. In some Churches it was regarded for a time as belonging to the scriptural canon. It comes most probably from Syria,[1] though Egypt has also been suggested.[2] The *Didachê* is extremely important for a study of the sub-apostolic Church, as the vast amount of scholarly writing testifies.[3]

The text, which contains sixteen short chapters, begins with a pre-baptismal catechesis, the way of life and the way of death (1–6), a theme common in Judaeo-Christian writing. Its presence also in the *Letter of Barnabas* (q.v.) and in the very early *The Doctrine of the Apostles*[4] would seem to indicate independent witnesses to a complex teaching of Jewish origin on "The Two Ways" (cf. Deut 30:15-20).[5] Chapters 7–10 deal with liturgical norms commencing with baptism (7), its sacramental form recalling Matt 28:19. Fasting is specified for Wednesday and Friday, apparently against Judaizing Christians (v. PRIMITIVE CHURCH), who would seem to have fasted like pious Jews on Mondays and Thursdays.[6] The Our Father (with a doxology, "for thine is the power and the glory") is enjoined thrice daily (8). Reconciliation (q.v.) is regarded as very important: it is both vertical, through communitarian confession of sin to God, and horizontal, in relation to the offended person. In the work we have the beginning of an evolution of a penitential discipline (4:6; 8:2-3; 14; 15).[7]

The ninth chapter raises many interpretative difficulties: it begins "Now about the eucharist," but scholarly opinion is divided as to whether it is a Eucharist, an agape meal, or a combination of both.[8] Acceptance of a Eucharistic interpretation is more common, especially among Catholic authors, though not all will see a sacrificial dimension as clear.[9] The "Vine of David" may refer to the Church, whose unity is symbolized by the broken bread: "As this broken bread, once dispersed over the hills, was brought together and became one loaf, so may thy Church be brought together from the end of the earth into thy kingdom" (9:4). A prayer after that asks: "Be mindful of thy Church, O Lord; deliver it from all evil, perfect it in thy love, sanctify it, and gather it from the four winds into the kingdom which thou hast prepared for it" (10:5). Thus we have both an awareness of the Church being gifted, and awaiting eschatological perfection.

Later chapters contain some disciplinary norms, which raise further ecclesiological issues. Apostles are mentioned, not the twelve, rather itinerant preachers who go around spreading the Christian message; since the Didachê audience is an established community, there is no reason why they should stay more than one day (11:5). The role of the prophets (q.v.) is more complex: the apostles may be also prophets (11:3);[10] there are stable prophets who give thanks at the Eucharist (10:7), and as high priests are supported by the community; there are wandering prophets; the community might not in fact, however, have a prophet (13).

The fact that prophets preside at the Eucharist, without any reference to ordination, may make for difficulties. We have, it would seem, to seek behind ordination to find what is at its core: a divine choice of a person designated by the Spirit-guided institutional Church. In an earlier period the Spirit chose leaders charismatically, and thus prophets were at that time the appropriate ministers of the Eucharist. If no prophets were raised up, officials were to be provided (see below). That does not mean that the transitional dispensation of the sub-apostolic age could again today be reinstated by human choice.

Prophets are to be tested by their way of life more than by their teaching (11). Further, there are teachers (didaskaloi, v. TEACHERS) mentioned alongside the prophets (13:2; 15:1-2), so all instruction would not seem to be given by these latter.

Chapters 14–15 are seen by many as a separate body of text. The gathering on the Lord's Day for the breaking of bread, almost certainly the Eucharist, is accompanied by an admission of sin and reconciliation of differences in the assembly (14). Chapter 15 deals with the provision of ministers: the community must then (oun) elect bishops and deacons (episkopoi kai diakonoi; cf. Ph 1:1) since there is a question of worship (leitourgia). The text does not mention presbyters (presbuteroi), who belong more usually to Churches established in Jewish milieux, whereas episkopos was a Greek civil office assumed into Christian language;[11] the Qumrân literature, however, is a warning against making this distinction absolute (v. BISHOPS). The bishops and deacons are on a par with the apostles and teachers (15:2). It is not clear, however, that the former two are elected only in the absence of apostles and teachers.[12] Fraternal correction is enjoined and exclusion from the community for some unnamed offenses (15). The final chapter (16) is a warning to stand firm in faith and to be on guard against the Deceiver at the end-time, and finally it looks forward to the parousia, the glorious coming of the Lord.

The Didachê is then a precious witness to Church life before the established institutions found in Ignatius of Antioch (q.v.). Its situation in some ways resembles the Church in Corinth when it was addressed by Clement (q.v.). The Didachê has, moreover, affinities with Matthew's Gospel, both in content and style, possibly also in milieu.[13]

[1]Thus J. Quasten, Patrology 1:29-39 at 37; W. Rordorf and A. Tuilier, SC 248:97; J.A. Kleist ACW 6:4-6; S. Tugwell, The Apostolic Fathers. Outstanding Christian Thinkers (London: Chapman, 1989) 1-21. Trans. used here M. Staniforth and A. Louth, Early Christian Writings: The Apostolic Fathers (Harmondsworth UK: Penguin, ²1987). [2]Thus C.C. Richardson, Early Christian Fathers. LCC 1 (London: SCM, 1953) 161-166; cf. SC 248:97 for adherents of this view. [3]See bibliog. in nn. 1, 2; K. Baus, in Jedin-Dolan 1:139, 472; OxDCC 401; K. Niederwimmer, Die Didache. Kommentar zu den Apostolischen Vätern 1 (Göttingen: Vandenhoeck & Ruprecht, 1989). [4]Text most probably of the 1st century is extant only in Latin trans. SC 248:207-210. [5]J.P. Audet, La Didachè: Instructions des apôtres (Paris, 1958) 158. [6]Cf. Rordorf—Tuilier (n. 1) 36-37. [7]W. Rordorf, "La rémission des péchés selon la Didachè," Irén 46 (1973) 283-297. [8] SC 248:37-48; K. Gamber, "Die Eucharistia der Didache," EphLg 101 (1987) 3-23; B. Grimonprez-Damm, "Le 'sacrifice' eucharistique dans la Didachè," RevSR 64 (1990) 9-25. [9]Grimonprez-Damm (n. 8). [10]A. de Halleux, "Les ministères dans la Didachè," Irén 53 (1980) 5-29 at 13. [11]Rordorf-Tuilier (n. 1) 73-78; cf. C.N. Jefford, "Presbyters in the Community of the Didache," StPatr 21 (1989) 122-128. [12]A. de Halleux (n. 10) 21-24; cf., however, Rordorf-Tuilier (n. 1) 72, 75. [13]J.M. Court, "The Didachê and St. Matthew's Gospel," ScotJT 34 (1981) 109-120.

## DIDASCALIA APOSTOLORUM

See APOSTOLIC CONSTITUTIONS

## DIOCESE

The word "diocese" has both a secular and an ecclesiastical history. In the Roman Empire it was a large unit of administration comprising a number of provinces. The Church, which began in towns, gradually extended into the surrounding rural areas. In the NT the local Christian community, e.g., in Corinth, was called the *ekklêsia* that is in Corinth (see 1 Cor 1:2). But *ekklêsia* was also used of the whole Christian Church, as in Ephesians and Colossians. Later the name "parish" was used for the local Church (still retained in the East today). Beginning in Africa in the 4th century, "diocese" became the name for the local Church under its bishop, though "parish" would also be found in the West until the 9th century.[1]

In the current *Code of Canon Law* dioceses are the first instance of particular Churches (CIC 368; see LG 23; v. PARTICULAR CHURCH). The word in the Eastern Churches is "eparchy." The law describes the diocese thus: "A diocese is a portion of the people of God which is entrusted for pastoral care to a bishop with the cooperation of the presbyterate so that, adhering to its pastor and guided by him in the Holy Spirit through the gospel and the Eucharist, it constitutes a particular Church in which the one, holy, catholic and apostolic Church is truly present and operative" (CIC 369; see CD 11). The *Code* deals at length with the structure of the diocese and of comparable entities in the Church in a way that recognizes the complexity of many present-day urban dioceses (460–514) and the role of the bishops in being their pastors (CIC 375–402). The bishop in charge of a diocese is called a "local ordinary"; a provincial superior or general of a clerical congregation is also an ordinary, but with jurisdiction over only his own members.

A diocese is not merely an administrative subdivision of a wider unit which would be the universal Church. It is fully the Catholic Church as it is present in this place if it is in communion with all other dioceses and with the Church of Rome and with its bishop, the pope. The bishop is head of the diocese in his own right, and not by delegation of the pope or as his representative (LG 27). The local ordinary as member of the College of Bishops (q.v.) is, moreover, to have a concern for all the Church.

Just as the bishop is not isolated from the rest of the Church, but in communion with it, so too he is to be in communion with, and foster communion with his clergy and all the people of the diocese. Some structures are provided by law for promoting such communion (v. SYNODS AND COUNCILS AND DIALOGUE).

Most modern dioceses consist of a number of parishes (q.v.), the place where the mass of people actually encounter the Church. A number of dioceses constitute a province in which there is a metropolitan, usually an archbishop pastoring his own archdiocese (CIC 435). Not all archbishops are metropolitans, since the title archbishop can be a personal one given by the Holy See. The metropolitan has very little authority in the suffragan sees, i.e., the dioceses that make up the province. His is generally an office of vigilance, and he may act only in cases specified by law (CIC 436). In some countries the most ancient metropolitan see has the title "primatial"; its archbishop is usually a cardinal. The primatial see is sometimes not the present political capital, and may not be the most significant city in the country; thus in France Lyons, in Germany Munich, in Ireland Armagh.

---

[1]OxDCC 404; T.J. Green, J.H. Provost and J.A. Alesandro in Coriden, CIC 311–413.

## DIOGNETUS, EPISTLE TO

We cannot determine either the intended recipient of this apology for the Christian faith or its author,[1] though there is some probability that it may have originated in Asia Minor. The weight of scholarly opinion would suggest a date between 150–210 C.E. It existed in only one ms, containing treatises by Justin (q.v.), destroyed during the shelling of Strasbourg in 1870; various copies had fortunately been made after its discovery in the 16th century. The letter sets out to answer three questions: what kind of cult is Christianity, which differs from paganism (2) and Judaism? (3–4); what is the secret of their mutual love? (6–8); why did the new religion come so late in human history? (9). Chapter 10 is a call to conversion and to imitation of God. Some suggest that the final two chapters are by another hand; recently the unity of the text has been defended with serious arguments:[2] pages may have been lost before them in the original ms, so that what seems to be a homily on the mystery of faith could be a conclusion of the original work. Their author describes himself as having been a disciple (*mathêtês*) of the apostles and becoming a teacher (*didaskalos*) of the Gentiles (11:1).

Interest today in the text does not lie in the rather crude refutation of paganism, in the anti-Jewish polemic,[3] or in its relationship to current Greek philosophy,[4] but rather in its Christology, which is primitive in 8:9—beloved Son (*agapêtou paidos*, cf. 9:1) and more developed in terms of the *Logos* in n. 11, in its ecclesiology and its theology of participated divine life (10:5-7). The text is remarkable for its eloquent description of the Church in the world: "Christians are not distinguished from the rest of humanity by either country, speech or customs. They do not live in cities of their own; they use no peculiar language, they do not follow an eccentric manner of life. . . . They reside in their own countries, but only as aliens; they take part in everything as citizens, and endure everything as foreigners. Every foreign land is their home, and every home a foreign land. They marry like everyone else; they beget children; but they do not expose their offspring. They share their table with one another, but not their marriage bed. . . . They obey the established laws, but in their own lives they go beyond the law. . . . In a word: what the soul is in the body, that Christians are in the world. The soul is spread through all the members of the body, and Christians are scattered through all the cities of the world. The soul dwells in the body, but does not belong to the body, just so Christians live in the world, but are not of the world."[5] A somewhat obscure passage in concluding chapters is evidence of a Christological vision of the Church: "He (the Logos) is the Eternal One who today is accounted a Son, by whom the Church is enriched, grace unfolds in the saints and multiplies in them—the grace that gives understanding, reveals mysteries, announces seasons, rejoices in believers, gives freely to seekers, such as do not break the pledges of their faith, nor transgress the bounds fixed by the fathers. Then the reverence taught by the law is hymned, and the grace given to the prophets is recognized, the faith in the gospels is strengthened, the tradition of the apostles is preserved, and the grace of the Church is exultant" (11:5-6).

Neither part of the work gives any indication of institutions in the Church, except for the reference to the tradition (paradosis) of the apostles above.

---

[1]H.I. Marrou, A Diognète, SC 33:241-268; J.A. Kleist, ACW 6:127-134; C.C. Richardson, ed., LCC 1:205-212; Patrology 1:248-253; T. Baumeister, "Zur Datierung der Schrift an Diognet," VigChr 42 (1988) 105–111; D. Grasso, "Un saggio di evangelizzazione nel secondo secolo: La Lettera a Diogneto," in C.C. Marcheselli, ed., Parola e Spirito. FS S. Cipriani. 2 vols. (Brescia: Paideia, 1982) 1:777-788.  [2]M. Rizzi, La questione dell'unità dell'Ad Diognetum. Studia Patristica Mediolanensia 16 (Milan: Vita e Pensiero, 1989); cf. E. Cattaneo, "L'enigma dell'Ad Diognetum," RasT 32 (1991) 327–332.  [3]P.H. Poirier, "Elements de polémique anti-juive dans l'Ad Diognetum," VigChr 40 (1986) 218–225.  [4]R.G. Tanner, "The Epistle to Diognetus and Contemporary Greek Thought," StPatr 15/1 (1984) 495–508.  [5]Nn. 5–6; fuller text Halton 148–149.

## DIONYSIUS/DENIS THE AREOPAGITE, PSEUDO-

An unknown Syrian monk at the turn of the 5th and 6th centuries[1] was destined to have quite exceptional influence in theology,[2] but especially in liturgy and spirituality[3] as well as ecclesiology.[4] Purporting to be Dionysius, the convert of Paul (see Acts 17:34), the pseudonymous author of the Corpus Dionysianum/ Corpus Areopagiticum wrote four short treatises, The Celestial Hierarchy (CH), The Divine Names (DN), The Ecclesiastical Hierarchy (EH), and Mystical Theology (MT), ten letters, and perhaps seven other lost works to which he himself refers.[5]

At first his Christology was suspect, until a magisterial gloss by Maximus the Confessor (q.v.) showed him in orthodox light. His language and forms of thought are markedly Neo-Platonic. This is seen especially in his continual use of the categories of procession and return (proodos/epistrophê), as well as his penchant for triads and enneads ('nines') and his use of theourgia for a divine act. But he is most definitely a Christian writer. His influence was enormous in the Middle Ages (he is quoted 1600 times by St. Thomas Aquinas, q.v.), and in the mystical writing of the 14th to 17th centuries.[6] The attitude of the Reformers towards him vacillated.[7]

In spirituality he gave a Christian understanding to the three ways—purgative, illuminative, and unitive or perfective—already encountered in Neo-Platonism.[8] Though the words had already been used by the Neo-Platonists in a religious sense, his was the first Christian use of apophatic (knowing God in the mysticism of dark loving, "in the dazzling darkness of hidden silence.")[9] and cataphatic (knowing by affirmation):[10] "God is therefore known in all things and as distinct from all things. He is known through knowledge and through unknowing . . . the most divine knowledge of God, that which comes through unknowing is achieved in a union far beyond mind. . . ."[11]

For ecclesiology his teaching on the hierarchies is central; he may well have been the one to coin the word hierarchia.[12] He writes: "In my opinion a hierarchy is a sacred order, a state of understanding and an activity approximating as closely as possible to the divine. And it is uplifted to the imitation of God in proportion to the enlightenment divinely given to it."[13] Hierarchy is more than a rank: it includes the activity necessary to come into divine likeness or deification within the rank or order. Creatures normally remain within their rank and are perfected within it by purification, illumination, and union: "Hierarchy is the outreach of God's love, it is not a ladder we struggle up by our own efforts."[14] The first hierarchy is that of angels (q.v.). Their nine choirs are a paradigm for the earthly hierarchy, which Dionysius calls "our hierarchy": "This arrangement is copied by our own hierarchy, which tries to imitate angelic beauty as far as possible, to be shaped by it, as in images, and to be uplifted to the transcendent source of all order and all hierarchy."[15] In The Ecclesiastical Hierarchy he deals first with sacraments (cc. 2–4): illumination or baptism, synaxis or Eucharist, and the sacrament of oil. In each case he gives a triad: an introductory chapter; a description of the mystery or rite; the contemplation or understanding of the mystery, which he regards as the most important of the expositions.

The next part is a triad of clerical orders: the hierarch or bishop, priest, and deacon (c. 5). "The holy sacraments bring about purification, illumination and perfection. The deacons form the order which purifies. The priests constitute the order which gives illumination. And the hierarchs (bishops), living in conformity with God, make up the order which perfects."[16] In the lowest triad (c. 6) we find those preparing for initiation (catechumens) who are being instructed by the deacons, then sinners who are still being drawn along the road to holiness and the possessed.[17] Higher we find those who have been well purified; these, the laity, are being illumined by the priests. The highest rank, which "possesses full power and complete holiness in its activities" is that of monks.[18] This order is entrusted to the perfecting power of the bishops.

The hierarchical notion, most clearly seen in his exposition on angels (CH), contains the cardinal principle of the interaction of the rank above on the one below, in continuous mediation of illumination. This was seized by the medievals to support their views of the great chain of being and of universal order. The abiding importance of Dionysius is surely his strong liturgical sense, which sees the Church at its highest in worship, and his union of profound mysticism, along with the practicalities of Church life: those who would instruct should themselves be holy.[19] To view Dionysius' theology as excessively individualistic would seem to neglect its essential liturgical coloring, the sense of sharing and interaction between all the hierarchies, as each brings others along with it in a never-ending communion of divine life received and shared.[20]

[1]S. Lilla, "Dionysius the Areopagite, Pseudo," EncycEarCh 1:238-240; A. Louth, *Denis the Areopagite.* Outstanding Christian Thinkers (Wilton CT: Morehouse-Barlow—London: Chapman, 1990). [2]H. Urs von Balthasar, *The Glory of the Lord.* 7 vols. (San Francisco: Ignatius—New York: Crossroad, 1982–1992) 2:144-210; C.A. Bernard, "Les formes de la théologie chez Denys l'Aréopagite," Greg 59 (1978) 41–69; S. Lilla, "Introduzione allo studio dello Ps. Dionigi l'Areopagita," Augustianum 22 (1982) 533–577 with bibliog.; R. Roques, *L'univers dionysien: Structure et monde selon le Pseudo-Denys* (Paris: Cerf 1983). [3]C.A. Bernard, "La doctrine mystique de Denys l'Aréopagite," Greg 68 (1987) 523–566; A. Louth, "Denys the Areopagite," in C. Jones et al., eds., *The Study of Spirituality* (London: SPCK, 184–189; R. Roques et al., "Denys Aréopagite (Le Pseudo-)," DSpir 3:244-429; cf. J. Auxentios-Thornton, "Three Byzantine Commentaries on the Divine Liturgy: A Comparative Treatment (Dionysius, Maximus, Germanos)," GkOrTR 32 (1987) 285–308. [4]Y. Congar, Augustin 224–230; B. Mondin, "I modelli ecclesiologici di Agostino, Pseudo-Dionigi, Bernardo e Tommaso," in *Cinquant'anni di magistero teologico.* FS A. Piolanti—Studi tomistici 26 (Vatican, 1985) 75–98 at 82–86; C. Pera, "Il mistero della chiesa nello Pseudo-Dionigi," in AA.VV. *Mysterium Ecclesiae in conscientia sanctorum* (Rome: Ed. del Teresianum, 1967) 134–157. [5]C. Luibheid and P. Rorem, tr. and eds., *Pseudo-Dionysius: The Complete Works.*

The Classics of Western Spirituality (Mahwah: Paulist—London: SPCK, 1987); PG 3:119-1122—critical edition forthcoming from Göttingen. [6]J. Leclercq, "Influence and Noninfluence of Dionysius in the Western Middle Ages," in Luibheid and Rorem (n. 5) 25–32. [7]K. Froehlich, ibid., 33–46. [8]T. Špidlík, *The Spirituality of the Christian East* (Kalamazoo: Cistercian Publications, 1986) 70. [9]MT 1:1—Luibheid-Rorem 135/PG 3:997; cf. Von Balthasar (n. 2) 204–207. [10]Louth (n. 1) 87. [11]DN 7:3—Luibheid-Rorem 108–109/PG 3:872; cf. MT 1–5 and CH 2—Luibheid-Rorem 49–54, 147–152/PG 3:585–593, 136–145. [12]Louth (n. 1) 38. [13]CH 3:1—Luibheid–Rorem (n. 5) 153/PG 3:164; cf. 3:2 154/PG 3:165; EH 1:3 197/PG 3:373; EH 5:2/234-236/PG 3:500-504. [14]Louth (n. 1) 41. [15]CH 8:2—Luibheid-Rorem 169/PG 3:241; cf. 9:2—170/PG 3:260; 10:1—173/PG 3:272; I.P. Sheldon-Williams, "The Ecclesiastical Hierarchy of Pseudo-Dionysius," DowR 82 (1964) 293–302. [16]Luibheid-Rorem (n. 5) 248/PG 3:536. [17]Cf. for lowest EH 3:6-7—Luibheid-Rorem 214–217/PG 3:432-436. [18]EH 6:3—Luibheid-Rorem (n. 5) 244/PG 3:532. [19]Cf. EH 3:3, 14—Luibheid-Rorem (n. 5) 223/PG 445. [20]Cf. EH 1:2—Luibheid-Rorem (n. 5) 196/PG 3:373.

## DISCIPLES OF CHRIST

The establishment of the Disciples of Christ, formerly the Christian Church, can be attributed to the presbyterian preacher M.W. Stone about 1801, and later to a father and son, Thomas and Alexander Campbell. Followers of both Stone and Campbell came together in 1832. An early conviction of theirs was the need for Christian unity as the foundation of mission, evangelism, and renewal. They held a narrow New Testament ecclesiology. Today still, all creeds are rejected. The weekly celebration of the Lord's Supper is the central act of worship. They practice believer's baptism and are congregationally organized.[1]

The Disciples of Christ have two international bodies. The World Convention of Churches of Christ is an inspirational global fellowship of members meeting every four years. The Disciples Ecumenical Consultative Council deals with official Church-to-Church relations: it appoints representatives for ecumenical meetings, and is a clearing house for information about worldwide ecumenical relations. At present it is engaged in three international dialogues.

There have been meetings with the Roman Catholic Church since 1977, mostly dealing with the search for unity and in particular with spiritual ecumenism (v. ECUMENISM, SPIRITUAL). The first series of discussions centered on "Apostolicity and Catholicity" (1977–1982), a second from 1983 on "The Church as Koinonia in Christ."[2] The methodology used in these talks has attracted some interest on the part of other Churches: it does not seek agreed statements, but rather lines of convergence.

There were warm relations with the Russian Orthodox Church even during the cold-war period, and formal dialogue began in 1987. Themes have included: "Baptism, Eucharist and Ministry," "Peace-making,"

"The Renewal of Parish Life," and "The Church's Diaconal Ministry in Society."[3]

Official dialogue with the World Alliance of Reformed Churches began in 1987 with the discussion of common roots, baptism and communion, ministry, and models of unity.[4]

The Disciples of Christ have a strong sacramental sense to contribute to ecumenical dialogue. The Church is both the local congregation of believers and it is universal in comprising all Christians bound together in community *(koinônia)*.

---

[1]W.E. Garrison, *Christian Unity and Disciples of Christ* (St. Louis: Bethany, 1955); A.T. de Groot, *The Disciples of Christ: A History* (St. Louis, [2]1958); K. Lawrence, ed., *Classic Themes of Disciples Theology* (Fort Worth: Christian UP, 1986); K.L. Teegarden, *We Call Ourselves Disciples* (St. Louis: Bethany, 1979).   [2]H. Meyer and L. Vischer, eds., *Growth in Agreement.* Faith and Order Paper 108 (New York: Paulist—Geneva: WCC, 1984) 154–166. Subsequent meetings Mid-Stream 25 (1986) 339–425; 26 (1987) 582–585; 27 (1988) 337–427; 29 (1990) 199–303; N.M. Lahutsky, " 'All Roads Lead to Rome': the 1991 Meeting of the Disciples of Christ/Roman Catholic Commission for Dialogue," Mid-Stream 31 (1992) 139–145; See J.M.R. Tillard, "The Contribution of the Disciples of Christ/Roman Catholic Dialogue for the Ecclesiology of the Ecumenical Movement," Mid-Stream 31 (1992) 14–25; "The Church as Communion in Christ: Report of the Disciples of Christ/Roman Catholic International Committee for Dialogue," Mid-Stream 33 (1994) 219–239; W. Henn, "An Evaluation of 'The Church as Communion,'" ibid., 159–172.   [3]*The Russian Orthodox Church and the Disciples of Christ in Dialogue* (Indianapolis: Council on Christian Unity, 1981); "Disciples and Russian Orthodox in Dialogue," Mid-Stream 27 (1988) 295–298.   [4]Mid-Stream 27 (1988) 89–182; A.P.F. Sell, ed., *Reformed and Disciples of Christ in Dialogue* (Geneva: World Alliance of Reformed Churches, 1985).

## DISCIPLINA ARCANI

In the early Church there was a custom of keeping from catechumens and pagans the innermost mysteries of the faith, especially initiation, Eucharist, the Lord's Prayer, and the Creed. Since the 17th century this custom has been known as the *disciplina arcani* ("discipline of the secret").[1] Its practice arose only gradually: Justin (q.v.) did not observe it; Irenaeus indeed charged the Gnostics (q.v.) of secrecy about their doctrines.[2]

The *disciplina arcani* developed with the catechumenate (q.v.), in which there was a dynamic of gradual unfolding of the mysteries of the faith. The *disciplina arcani,* which was strong in the 3rd and 4th centuries, disappeared as the Church spread throughout Europe, and the catechumenate itself began to collapse.

---

[1]P. Batiffol, "L'arcane," in *Etudes d'histoire et de théologie positive.* Vol. 1, Ie ser. (Paris, [8]1926) 1–41.   [2]*Adv. haer.* 3:3, 1; 15, 1.

## DISSENT

The possibility of dissent arises because most Church teaching does not fall into the narrow category of in-

fallible, irreformable doctrine (v. INFALLIBILITY). Only what is revealed, or taught as infallible, can claim unconditional assent. All other teaching could be faulty, although it would be quite wrong either to hold that most teaching is flawed, or to approach magisterial teaching suspiciously, presuming it to be in error. A Catholic will rather assume that Church teaching is correct and to be accepted. But ecclesiology must face the possibility of dissent, given the undoubted fact that there has in the past been erroneous teaching by the magisterium (q.v.). The question must be answered according to theological and ecclesiological principles, even though the issue is a most practical one, given the instances in the 1970s and 1980s involving conflict between individual theologians and the Holy See.[1]

The question of dissent came up during Vatican II: four bishops cited the possibility of a learned person who could not internally assent to non-infallible teaching. The Doctrinal Commission refused to deal with this in LG 25 but said: "About this matter approved theological treatments are to be consulted *(probatae expositiones theologicae)*."[2] At that time what was almost certainly meant were the manuals of theology being used in the theological schools. Some of these granted that internal assent can in exceptional circumstances be withheld, but they did not allow public dissociation from authoritative teaching of the Holy See.[3]

After Vatican II, in the wake of the encyclical on the regulation of births *Humanae vitae* (1968), a new phenomenon was found of a substantial number of theologians, and an even greater number of laity, publicly rejecting the papal teaching. Though some of the dissent may have rested on non-theological grounds, such as the difficulty or impossibility of observing the norms proposed by the pope, there was a body of opinion that rejected the teaching as erroneous or non-apodictic.[4] The dissent on the issue of birth regulation concerned moral matters. There was also dissent on doctrinal matters by Archbishop Lefebvre (q.v.), which ended in schism (q.v.). Some quite widespread dissent has also greeted the declaration "On the Admission of Women to the Priesthood."[5] In addition, some theologians were censured or called to order by the Holy See, notably H. Küng (q.v.), L. Boff (q.v.), and E. Schillebeeckx (q.v.).

We can in practice distinguish dissent in a moral matter from dissent in teaching. In moral matters people are bound to follow their conscience, which is a practical judgment about the rightness or wrongness of following a particular course of action. According to Vatican II, "In forming their consciences, the Christian faithful should give careful attention *(diligenter attendere)* to the sacred and certain teaching of the Church" (DH 14). The new *Catechism* states that in the formation of conscience we are "guided by" the authoritative teaching of the Church (n. 1785). The council did not approve a more restrictive wording, viz., they should form their conscience "according to" the teaching of the Church.[6] In this delicate matter of the formation of conscience, there are many possibilities for unauthentic behavior: people may not consider sufficiently the teaching of the Church; they may not approach such teaching with a desire to give a sincere assent; they may not be in possession of sufficient reasons or knowledge to warrant dissent; they may be imprudent or arrogant, etc. Thus while it is possible that a person may have to dissent from moral teaching of the magisterium in order to follow the dictates of conscience, it is easy to envisage instances of dissent which would proceed from an erroneous conscience, even one culpably erroneous. With regard to dissent on doctrinal matters, it would probably be extremely rare that a person would be in possession of such knowledge as would make dissent obligatory. More common would be the case in which the question not of obligation but of the right to dissent could arise. It must be kept in mind that the pursuit of truth is a process, that at a particular stage a definitive answer may not yet be available. The magisterium may give guidance that it thinks appropriate, even thinking that it is closing discussion on a matter. But there may be other issues, facts, arguments, circumstances that are not taken into consideration by the theologians employed by the magisterium, so that a directive seems flawed, if not erroneous.

A general observation is that Church authorities have been more successful in telling theologians what they are not to do than in developing a genuine process for dialogue on issues on which dissent occurs. The Instruction of the Congregation for the Doctrine of the Faith "On the Ecclesial Vocation of the Theologian" (1990) is an important reflection on the role of theologians (q.v.).[7]

A serious problem with the document is the lack of clarity and even careless writing (n. 15) in the issue of infallible and non-infallible teaching. To be a Catholic in good standing, one must of course accept infallible pronouncements. An important observation is made in n. 17: "One must therefore take into account the proper character of every exercise of the Magisterium, considering the extent to which its authority is engaged." This is a need long recognized in theology, but the document goes on immediately to blur distinctions: "It is also to be borne in mind that all acts of the Magisterium derive from the same source, that is, Christ who desires that His People walk in the entire truth. For this reason, magisterial decisions in matters of discipline, even if they are not guaranteed by the charism of infallibility, are not without divine assistance and call for the adherence of the faithful." The problem here is the appeal to Christ. His help is presumed present, but there is another source for acts of the Magisterium, namely frail

human cooperation, which in disciplinary acts is not protected by charism of infallibility; the Instruction could be seen to imply that there is little difference in the adherence demanded, whether the Magisterium is acting infallibly or not.

Though the Instruction claims to be guidance on the ecclesial role of theologians, some have suspected that had the issue of dissent not arisen so sharply in the 1980s, the Church would not have received such an Instruction. Over a quarter of the document is devoted to dissent (nn. 32–41), which it seems to want to eliminate. Some of the points it makes are surely beyond cavil. It deals with dissent which arises from "the ideology of philosophical liberalism" (n. 32), from "a model of protest which takes its inspiration from political society" (33), from a hermeneutic that would not recognize the special position of magisterial teachings (n. 34), from a sociological understanding of the sense of the faithful (n. 35; v. SENSE OF THE FAITH), from an appeal to human rights (n. 36). *As presented by the Instruction,* none of these is an adequate basis for public dissent.

Arising as it does in the context of problems of the preceding decade, the Instruction is thus at great pains to eliminate many grounds that are alleged for dissent. It strongly opposes attempts to manipulate public opinion in the Church against positions of the magisterium (n. 39).[8] Indeed it seems to envisage dissent mainly in terms of public disclaimers in the media. But would it be "exerting the pressure of public opinion" to publish dissenting views in scientific reviews? One of the important ways in which theological positions are evaluated is by the judgment of other theologians, and this presumes that opinions are circulated or published. However, many scholarly journals are routinely surveyed by theologically literate religious affairs journalists of the media. Some conclude that dissent can never have even the limited publicity of theological journals. The Instruction does not really deal with the practical issue at this level, nor its theoretical basis.

For the theologian who has difficulty in assenting to teaching of the magisterium, there are two proposals. "Faced with a proposition to which he feels he cannot give his intellectual assent, the theologian nevertheless has the duty to remain open to a deeper examination of the question. For a loyal spirit, animated by love for the Church, such a situation can certainly prove a difficult trial. It can be a call to suffer for the truth, in silence and prayer, but with a certainty, that if the truth is really at stake, it will ultimately prevail" (n. 31).

The second solution proposed might, like the first, give the impression that, if there are problems, it is most probably the theologian who will be at fault: "If it happens that they [theologians] encounter difficulties due to the character of their research, they should seek their solution in trustful dialogue with the Pastors in the spirit of truth and charity which is that of communion of the Church" (n. 40).

It would be fair to say that the Church has not yet found a way of dealing constructively with dissent. There is the problem of a certain "double-think." Whereas people will readily accept that teaching of the magisterium was flawed, even erroneous, in the past, there is a tendency to speak and to act as if this could not happen in the present or in the future. The Instruction, however, seems also to imply that previous defective teaching was providentially effective in the life of the Church (n. 24).

Some practical points might be made. Theologians may need to learn appropriate styles of dissent, ones which do not seem to impugn the authoritative teaching office of the Church itself. One thinks of Y. Congar's sidestepping the ultimately unfruitful teaching of Pius XII on membership of the Church; he indirectly critiqued the papal position when he studied the theme of the Church from Abel (q.v.).

A distinction must be made between the research of theologians and what is appropriate to teach in theological faculties, particularly at the undergraduate level.[9] Church authorities have the right to ensure the transmission of official Church teaching, which they do by having a profession of faith (v. CREEDS), censorship of books (q.v.), and the licensing of members of ecclesiastical faculties by a canonical mission (CIC 229, 812, 818)[10] or its equivalent. This right of Church authorities cannot be dismissed by appeals to academic freedom, a rather recent notion that even in secular disciplines is not absolute.

Those charged with authoritative teaching in the Church must not only consult experts (which they undoubtedly do), but they could profitably be seen to do so. The system of "green papers" in some parliamentary democracies is not without interest: proposals for government action are published and opened to discussion and comment. (The later "white paper" contains the actually proposed legislation after the process of consultation.) The outline or *lineamenta* for the synods of bishops is not unlike a "green paper." The rather obsessive secrecy surrounding much Church consultation is not helpful. The worst possible scenario for the Church would be to have a magisterium that is fearful, defensive, or repressive, and theologians who are marginalized and thus either passive or overly contentious. The stage of the Instruction is an important one; much study still needs to be done by both the magisterium and by theologians. Happily this is ongoing.[11] The virtual silencing of theologians in the 1950s should hopefully not arise again.

[1]C.E. Curran and R.A. McCormick, *The Magisterium and Morality.* Readings in Moral Theology 3 (New York—Ramsey, 1982); idem, *Dissent in the Church.* Readings in Moral Theology 6 (New York—Mahwah: Paulist, 1988); R.A. McCormick, "Notes on Moral Theology," TS 42 (1981) 74–121; "The Right to Dissent," Conc 158 (1982); L. Orsy, "Magisterium: Assent and Dissent," TS 48 (1987) 473–598. [2]ActaSyn 3/8:88—Alberigo-Magistretti 532. [3]E.g., authors in I. Salaverri, Ecclesia 719–720. [4]See J.A. Komanchak, "Humanae vitae and Its Reception: Ecclesiological Reflections," TS 39 (1980) 221–257. Cf. D.M. Cowdin, "Religious Liberty, Religious Dissent and the Catholic Tradition," HeythJ 32 (1991) 26–61; J.F. Kippley, Continued Dissent: Is It Responsible Loyalty?," TS 32 (1971) 48–65. [5]Cong. Doctrine of the Faith, *Inter insigniores* (1976)—AAS 69 (1977) 98–116/Flannery 2:331-345. [6]F.A. Sullivan, *Magisterium: Teaching Authority in the Church* (Dublin: Gill and Macmillan, 1983) 169–170. [7]Vatican City, 1990. See J.A. Komonchak, "The Magisterium and Theologians," ChicSt 29 (1990) 307–329; M. Lefebvre, "Quelle est la mission du théologien?," EglT 22 (1991) 177–190; cf. n. 4; A. Dulles, L. Örsy and C. Duquoc, "Place of Theologians," *Tablet* 18 Aug., 25 Aug., and 1 Sept. 1991, pp. 1033–1034, 1066–1069, 1097–1098; F.A. Sullivan, "The Theologian's Ecclesial Vocation and the 1990 CDF Instruction," TS 52 (1991) 51–68. [8]Cf. K. Rahner, "Opposition in the Church," ThInvest 17:127-138. [9]A. Dulles, *The Craft of Theology: From Symbol to System* (Dublin: Gill and Macmillan, 1982) 105–118, 165–178. [10]J.A. Coriden, in Coriden, CIC 575–576. [11]U.S. Bishops, "Doctrinal Responsibilities: Approaches to Promoting Cooperation and Resolving Misunderstandings Between Bishops and Theologians," Origins 19 (1989) 97–110.

## DIVINE RIGHT

In medieval social theory the words "Divine Right" indicated a doctrine that a monarch in a hereditary succession had a divine and non-voidable right to the royal throne. Allied to this was the idea that rebellion against the monarch was the worst of all political crimes. The subject was supposed to suffer passively the punishments meted out for disobedience to immoral commands of an evil ruler. The theory developed during the contest between the medieval papacy and the emperor.[1]

In modern theology divine right mainly concerns the legitimacy of developments, especially in Church order, e.g., pope, bishops, and priests. In this context the Latin *ius divinum* (q.v.) is more commonly used.

[1]D. Wolf, "Divine Right of Kings," NCE 922–923; OxDCC 412.

## DOCTORS OF THE CHURCH

Apart from modern academic degrees, there are two senses in which the term "doctor" is used in the Church. In the medieval schools various theologians were called "doctor" with a sobriquet, e.g., *Doctor angelicus/communis* (Thomas Aquinas), *Doctor mellifluus* (Bernard of Clairvaux), *Doctor seraphicus* (Bonaventure), *Doctor subtilis* (Duns Scotus), *Doctor universalis* (Albert the Great).[1]

More important is the title "Doctor of the Church" given to the outstanding theologians of the past. In modern times the conditions were laid down by Benedict XIV before becoming pope: they must be canonized, renowned for learning, and proclaimed "doctor" by an ecumenical council or the pope.[2] Some outstanding and influential theologians like Origen (d. 254) are not doctors of the Church because they are not known as saints.

From the 8th century, four doctors of the West were acknowledged: Ambrose (d. 397), Augustine (d. 430), Jerome (d. 420) and Gregory the Great (d. 604). In time four great Eastern doctors were recognized: John Chrysostom (d. 407), Basil the Great (d. 379), Gregory of Nazianzus (d. 389), Athanasius (d. 373). There was no addition to this list of eight until the time of Pius V (1566–1572).

Afterwards 24 more have been added: in 1556, Thomas Aquinas (d. 1274); in 1588, Bonaventure (d. 1274); in 1720, Anselm (d. 1109); in 1722, Isidore of Seville (d. 636); in 1729, Peter Chrysologus (d. ca. 450); in 1754, Leo the Great (d. 461); in 1828, Peter Damian (d. 1072); in 1830, Bernard of Clairvaux (d. 1153); in 1851, Hilary of Poitiers (d. ca. 368); in 1871, Alphonsus Liguori (d. 1787); in 1877, Francis de Sales (d. 1622); in 1882, Cyril of Alexandria (d. 444) and Cyril of Jerusalem (d. 386); in 1890, John Damascene (d. ca. 749); in 1899, Bede the Venerable (d. 735); in 1920, Ephrem (d. 373); in 1925, Peter Canisius (d. 1597); in 1926, John of the Cross (d. 1591); in 1931, Robert Bellarmine (d. 1621); in 1932, Albert the Great (d. 1280); in 1946, Anthony of Padua (d. 1231); in 1959, Laurence of Brindisi (d. 1619); in 1970, Teresa of Avila (d. 1582); and Catherine of Siena (d. 1380).

There are, then, twenty-four from the West, and eight from the East: two popes, eighteen bishops, nine priests, one deacon, and two women. As evidence of the breakdown between spirituality and dogmatic theology, one can notice that apart from controversialists, the last dogmatic theologian to have been declared a Doctor of the Church was Albert the Great, who died in 1280. Of those who died after him, one would note the four doctors in the area of spirituality (Francis de Sales, John of the Cross, Teresa of Avila, and Catherine of Siena), one moralist (Alphonsus Liguori), but no major exegete. Two of the more recent nominations (Anthony of Padua and Lawrence of Brindisi) would not seem to have had a major influence in the history of theology.

---

[1]List in NCE 4:935-938.    [2]*De servorum Dei beatificatione et beatorum canonizatione* 2:11, 8—2:12, 9 (Bonn, 1738); U. Betti, "A proposito del conferimento del titolo di dottore della Chiesa," Antonian 63 (1988) 278–291.

## DÖLLINGER, Johann Joseph Ignaz von (1799–1890)

Born in Bavaria 1799, J.J. Ignaz von Döllinger, became professor of church history at Aschaffenburg in 1823, and from 1826 to 1873 at Munich. His earlier leanings were conservative, even Ultramontane, but gradually he espoused German nationalism in his views on the Church; he became critical of the papacy, first of its temporal power, then of the infallibility decree at Vatican I (q.v.). Refusing to accept the council, he was excommunicated in 1871. He worked closely with the Old Catholic Churches, though he never joined them.[1]

Earlier an implacable foe of Protestantism, in his later years he became interested in, and worked for, Christian unity. Though some would challenge his originality, his vast erudition is beyond question. His contribution to Church history is that he insisted on high standards of scholarship and showed Catholic historians that, while being loyal to their faith, they must write history scientifically unencumbered by any prejudice that might arise from a narrow theological vision. At the same time, his was one of the voices that called on theologians to a sense of history in their discipline. Not without some revisionism, his life and works are presently (1996) enjoying renewed interest in Germany.[2]

---

[1]V. Conzemius, "Aspects ecclésiologiques de l'évolution de Döllinger et du Vieux Catholicisme," RevSR 34 (1960) 247–279; G. Schwaiger, "Ignaz von Döllinger (1799–1890)," KlassTheol 2:127-150; S.J. Tonsor, Döllinger, Johann Joseph Ignaz von," NCE 4:959-960; Jedin-Dolan, vol. 8 passim.    [2]P. Neuner, "Ignaz von Döllinger als Theologe der Ökumene," MüTZ 41 (1991) 245–260; G. Schwaiger, "Ignaz von Döllinger: Der Apologet—Jahre der Wandlung," MüTZ 41 (1990) 197–214; M. Weitlauff, "Ignaz von Döllinger—Im Schatten des Ersten Vatikanums," MüTZ 41 (1990) 215–243.

## DONATION OF CONSTANTINE

Since the work of Lorenzo Valla (ca. 1406–1457), the *Donation of Constantine* has generally been acknowledged as spurious.[1]

Suspicions about its genuineness had previously been voiced by Nicholas of Cusa (d. 1464). In many mss the document claimed to be a decree of the emperor Constantine (d. 337) conferring on Sylvester I (314–335) primacy over Antioch, Constantinople, Alexandria, and Jerusalem, as well as dominion over all Italy; the pope was also given supreme power over the clergy. The *Donation* was incorporated into the *False Decretals* (q.v.) and was used by popes from St. Leo IX (1049–1054). The *Donation* is part of a larger work, *Constitutio Constantini*, also called *Vita Sylvestri*.

In recent years it has become clear that Valla's refutation, based on a very corrupt text of the *Donation*, was itself not devoid of errors.[2] Moreover, critical texts show that early versions of the *Donation* did not give supreme secular authority to the popes, and did little more than grant to the Church independence and special protection in a time when the empire was still pagan.[3] It gave some territory to the Roman Church

138    DONATISM

and acknowledged and extended the rights already acknowledged by the Council of Nicaea in 325 (q.v.). Spurious or not, the *Donation* was more a reflection of the existing situation of the medieval Church than a direct cause or basis for new papal aggrandizement.

[1]W. Setz, *Lorenzo Valla Schrift gegen Konstantinische Schenkung* (Tübingen: Niemeyer, 1975).  [2]Text *Fontes iuris germanici antiqui* 10 (1968); H. Fuhrmann, "Die kanonistische Überlieferung des Constitutum bis zum Dekret Gratians," *Deutsches Archiv* 30 (1974) 356–449; S.Z. Ehler and J.B. Morall, eds., *Church and State Through the Centuries* (Westminster, Md., 1954) 16–22; cf. I. Boba, "La 'Donatio Constantini' e l'Oratio' del Valla a confronto," Ang 67 (1990) 215–239.  [3]F. Masai, "La politique des Isauriens et la naissance de l'Europe," Byzantion 33 (1963) 191–221 at 210–219.

## DONATISM

Donatism,[1] a schismatic movement in North Africa, now dated from 308–310/311, had its remote origin in the edict of Diocletian that the Scriptures were to be handed up. Those who did so were called *traditores* (from *tradere*—to give up). A group of Catholics refused to accept Bishop Caecilian as bishop of Carthage on the grounds that he had been consecrated by a *traditor,* Felix of Aptunga. The Numidian bishops supported the objectors and consecrated a rival who was soon succeeded by Donatus, from whom the schism took its name. The followers were attacked both by the State and by theologians, notably Optatus, and St. Augustine (q.v.).[2] The movement remained in North Africa until it petered out when the Church there was destroyed by the Arabs in the 7th and 8th centuries.

At the center of Donatism were conflicting personalities, people eager to escape suspicion of having themselves been *traditores,* and all of them unwilling to dialogue. Theologically, Donatism showed the tendency to restrict membership of the Church only to those who are holy (v. HOLY), and hence to discount the value of the sacraments administered by those perceived as sinners. St. Augustine pointed to the validity of such sacraments and attacked the practice of (re)baptism by the Donatists of those who came to their side. The issues involved in this schism reoccur whenever a rigorist attitude is adopted to membership (q.v.) of the Church.

W.F. Frend, *The Donatist Church: A Movement of Protest in Roman North Africa* (Oxford, 1952); N. Escobar, "Donatismo y santidad de la Iglesia," AugM 22 (1977) 323–330; B. Kriegbaum, *Kirche der Traditorem oder Kirche der Märtyrer? Die Vorgeschichte des Donatismus.* Innsbrucker theologische Studien 16 (Innsbruck—Vienna: Tyrolia, 1986); J.L. Maier, *Le dossier du Donatisme.* 2 vols. Texte und Untersuchungen zur Geschichte der altchristlichen Literatur 134–135 (Berlin: Akademie Verlag, 1987, 1989); A. Schindler, *L'histoire du donatisme du point de vue de sa propre théologie.* Bibliothèque de la Revue d'histoire ecclésiastique 67 (Louvain-la-Neuve, 1983).  [2]É. Lamirande, *La situation ecclésiastique des Donatistes d'après saint Augustin: Contribution à l'histoire doctrinale de l'oecuménisme* (Ottawa: UP, 1972).

## DULLES, Avery (1918– )

Born in 1918 of Presbyterian background, Avery Dulles became a Catholic while a student at Harvard, and a Jesuit in 1946. He completed a doctorate at the Gregorian University, Rome, on the prophetic dimension in Anglican theology. He has written over fifteen books, mostly on the area of revelation and ecclesiology. His work, *Models of the Church,*[1] has been highly influential, and its approach has been applied by others in different areas of theology (v. MODELS).[2] It remains largely on a phenomenological level, which is a step towards a systematic understanding of the Church. The second edition of the book shows Dulles moving from a preference for a sacramental model to that of a community of disciples.

His collections of essays on various aspects of ecclesiology all show some common traits: rigorous analysis, balanced positions, exact scholarship.[3] All can be read with profit by those concerned with ecclesiological questions. He has made an important contribution to ecumenism not only in his general ecclesiology but in official dialogues including the Lutheran-Roman Catholic ones. Doctoral theses are now appearing on his work.[4] For many years teaching at The Catholic University of America in Washington, he afterwards became professor of religion and society at Fordham University.

[1]*Models of the Church: A Critical Assessment of the Church in All Its Aspects* (Dublin: Gill and Macmillan, ²1988).  [2]E.g., J.F. O'Grady, *Models of Jesus* (New York: Doubleday, 1981).  [3]E.g., *The Resilient Church: The Necessity and Limits of Adaptation* (Dublin: Gill and Macmillan, 1978); *A Church to Believe In: Discipleship and the Dynamics of Freedom* (New York: Crossroad, 1983); *The Catholicity of the Church* (Oxford: Clarendon, 1985); *The Reshaping of Catholicism: Current Challenges in the Theology of the Church* (San Francisco, 1988); *The Craft of Theology: From Symbol to System* (Dublin: Gill and Macmillan—New York: Crossroad, 1992).  [4]E.g., A.-M.R. Kirmse *The Church and the Churches: A Study of Ecclesiological and Ecumenical Developments in the Writings of Avery Dulles, S.J.* Diss. (Fordham University, 1989).

# E

## EASTERN CHURCHES

The Eastern Christian Churches are a very complex reality for which there is no fully satisfactory classification:[1] historical descriptions of the Churches is one approach;[2] a categorization on the basis of communion is also possible.[3] Any cataloguing will inevitably have overlapping; accuracy is hard to achieve, as dates and facts can be variously interpreted. One method, which shows clearly the complexity and the overlaps, is to divide them by using four questions based on rite, doctrine, ethnic group, and communion.

What is their *rite* (q.v.)? A rite is not merely a liturgical distinction, but it involves also a system of jurisprudence, institutions, and spirituality (OE 3; UR 14). Each Church will belong to one of five Eastern rites: Alexandrian, Antiochene, Armenian, Chaldean, Byzantine.

What is their *doctrine?* At the Council of Ephesus (431—q.v.) Nestorius was condemned. Some groups formed the Nestorian Churches and are Chaldean Rite. These are mainly found in Iraq, Iran, Syria, and South India, but it would not be right to ascribe Nestorian positions to all of them today. At the Council of Chalcedon (451—q.v.) Monophysitism was condemned and gave rise to the Monophysite Churches, though again it may not represent their current beliefs. They belong to the Alexandrian, Antiochene, and Armenian rites. The Churches which accepted the first seven councils are called Orthodox Churches. From the Middle Ages, some Christians from all five rites became reconciled with Rome and are called the Uniat(e) Churches (q.v.).

What is their *country of origin or ethnic group?* In the Alexandrian Rite we have Uniate and Monophysite Churches which are Coptic and Ethiopian. In the Antiochene Rite there are Uniate and Monophysite Churches that are Malankar (Syrian and Indian), and Uniate Maronites[4] (Lebanon). In the Armenian Rite there are Catholic and Monophysite Armenians in the former USSR, and in Iran, Iraq, Egypt. In the Chaldean Rite there are Nestorian Churches comprising Assyrian (in Iraq) and Indian Melusian groups, and Uniate Churches in Iraq, as well as Malabar groups in India. Except for a small number of Churches which are hard to classify, all the rest belong to the Byzantine Rite, which comprises both Catholic and Orthodox Churches in Eastern Europe, and Orthodox Churches of Chinese, Finnish, Japanese, and Ugandan peoples. Most of the Eastern Churches have members, and usually a bishop, in the USA.

The above three questions are enough to place any of the major Eastern Churches; a fourth question reviews them all again and adds further clarifications. With whom are they in *communion?* This question indicates the relationship of the Church with other Churches of the East. An illustration of communion (q.v.), which is always reciprocal, is that the Church of Rome is not in communion with Protestant Churches or with the Orthodox, but is in communion with the Uniates who accept Catholic doctrines and the primacy of the pope, even though they retain their own rites and are largely confined to certain ethnic groups.

The Assyrian Church is in communion with no other Church.[5] It is Nestorian in origin, and is to be found in Iran and the USA. Some 15,000 Thomas Christians (q.v.) belong to the Assyrian Church of the East.

There are five ancient Christian Churches in communion with one another, but otherwise separate in rite and jurisdiction. They are variously called The Oriental Orthodox Churches, The Lesser Eastern Churches, The Ancient Oriental Churches, the Non-Chalcedonian or Pre-Chalcedonian Churches. Their origin was a refusal to accept Chalcedon, for which reason they are also called Monophysite, even though their Christological positions are not now heretical, but differ verbally from Orthodox confessions of the unity of Christ in two natures. They comprise the following: the Armenian Orthodox Church (former USSR), whose liturgy is a synthesis of Byzantine and Syrian traditions; the Coptic Orthodox Church (Egypt, Middle East), with a liturgy developed from Alexandria, and with monastic influences; the Ethiopian Orthodox Church, which retains some Jewish practices (circumcision, dietary laws, and Saturday as well as Sunday sabbath) and has a strong monastic tradition; the Syrian Orthodox Church (Syria, Lebanon, Turkey, Israel), which has a rich theological and spiritual tradition, is also known as the Jacobite Church, though this epithet should be avoided;[6] the Malankar Orthodox Syrian Church (India), a group of Thomas Christians (q.v.) who broke away from a Portuguese Latinization campaign in 1665.

These five Churches also have the following Uniate counterparts, with the date of their hierarchy being recognized by Rome (the dates given for their union will vary in authors depending on the criteria employed to determine it): Armenian Catholic Church (abortive reunion in 1439 at the Council of Florence [q.v.], some reunited, 1742); Coptic Catholic Church (1824, 1895); Ethiopian Catholic Church (1626, but collapsed due to Latinization—metropolitan see, 1961); the Syrian Catholic Church (1662, 1782); Syro-Malankara Catholic Church (1930).

There are two Uniate Churches deriving from the Assyrian Church: the Chaldean Catholic Church (1553); the Syro-Malabar Catholic Church (1662, 1886). There is also a group of Uniate Christian Churches which originally were part of the Orthodox Church. These are sometimes called "Byzantine Catholic" or "Greek Catholic." With their dates of union, or of the establishment of their hierarchy in communion with Rome, they are: Melkite Catholic Church (1744); Ukrainian Catholic Church (16th to 18th c.); Ruthenian Catholic Church (1646, 1664, 1713); Romanian Catholic Church (1698–1700); Greek Catholic Church (1878ff); Byzantine Catholics in former Yugoslavia (1611, 1777); Bulgarian Catholic Church (1861); Slovak Catholic Church (1646, 1968); Hungarian Catholic Church (from Middle Ages, 18th c., and 1912). Other Byzantine Catholic Communities are: Russians (19th c.); Byelorussians (1595–1596); Albanian (1628); Georgian (1329). These last four were suppressed by secular authorities or incorporated into Orthodox Church, but may reemerge in the changed political situations of the late 20th century.

Though the Maronite Catholic Church and the Italo-Albanian Catholic Church never lost commu-

nion with Rome, in many ways they can be considered along with the Uniate Churches.

The presence of the Uniate Churches is very much resented by the Orthodox, especially when a bishop or patriarch is appointed for the same area as an Orthodox one.[7]

The Orthodox Churches (q.v.) are by far the most numerous of the Eastern Churches and are in dialogue (v. ECUMENISM) with several Churches of the West. The Orthodox Churches follow the Byzantine rite, and have Uniate counterparts in most Eastern European countries, but not where the Orthodox have expanded to China, Estonia, Finland, Japan, Latvia, and Uganda.

For various reasons the Churches of the Christian East tended to be isolated until the 19th and 20th centuries. We are now becoming aware through scholarly and popular publications, through translations and the publication of their classical works, congresses, and ecumenical contacts, of the rich theology and spirituality that have been protected from Latinization or destruction by the very fact of schism and seclusion for many centuries (v. ORTHODOX CHURCH).[8]

John Paul II celebrated the centenary of the apostolic letter of Leo XIII, *Orientalium dignitatus* (1895), by issuing an apostolic letter which spoke warmly of the theological and spiritual heritage of the Eastern Churches, and encouraged ecumenical activity.[9]

[1]H.-M. Legrand, "Introduction aux églises d'orient: Bulletin," RSPT 56 (1972) 661–713. [2]D. Attwater, *The Christian Churches of the East.* 2 vols. (London, [2]1961); G.A. Maloney, "Eastern Churches," NCE 5:13-21. [3]R.G. Roberson, *The Eastern Christian Churches: A Brief Survey* (Rome: Oriental Institute [3]1986). [4]L. Wehbé, "L'Église maronite," EspVie 96 (1986) 17–23, 41–46. [5]B. Dupuy, "Essai d'histoire de l'Église 'assyrienne,'" Istina 34 (1990) 159–170. [6]B. Dupuy, "L'Église syrienne d'Antioche des origines à aujourd'hui," Istina 34 (1990) 171–188, n. 1. [7]Ignace Hazim, "Une vision antiochienne de l'unité de l'Église," PrOrChr 29 (1979) 202–208. [8]M.M. Garijo-Guemble, "Boletín de teología oriental," DiálEcum 12 (1977) 433–446; P.D. Peterson and R.F. Frazer, eds., *Eastern Christianity: A Bibliography Selected from the ATLA Database* (Chicago: ATLA, rev. 1986). [9]*Orientale lumen* (2 May 1995)— DocCath 92/2117 (1995) 517–531; AAS 87 (1995) 745–774.

# ECCLESIOLOGY

The Church existed before there was an ecclesiology. If we take this last to mean doctrine or theology about the Church, then already in the NT there is ecclesiology (v. NEW TESTAMENT ECCLESIOLOGIES). Likewise there is much ecclesiology from the time of the *Didachê* (q.v.) or the letters of Ignatius (q.v.). There is a fertile patristic ecclesiology, which is not yet fully exploited by scholars; indications appear in various articles of this volume.[1]

The medievals had a rich ecclesiology (v. THOMAS AQUINAS). But the first tractate specifically on the Church was probably *De regimine christiano* by James of Viterbo (ca. 1301), with the first really complete one being that of John of Torquemada (d. 1468), *Summa de ecclesia*, which was papalist against a conciliarist ecclesiology. The Avignon schism (q.v.) occasioned many writings on the Church.[2] In the centuries after Trent the main interest in ecclesiology was apologetic (v. NOTES). But systematic works were nevertheless written by major theologians like J.A. Möhler (q.v.) and M. Scheeben (q.v.); others like J.H. Newman (q.v.) have a profound ecclesiology in various places in their works.

The placing of the tract on the Church already gives an indication of the ecclesiology of the author. Thus, M. Scheeben treats the Eucharist, then Church, then other sacraments; M. Schmaus deals with redemption, then Church, then grace; Y. Congar at one stage leaned towards dealing with Christology and then having a tract on Christian anthropology, within which Church ecumenism and Mary would also be treated; some Orthodox writers place the Church after sacraments and before eschatology; perhaps the majority of Roman Catholics place the Church after redemption and before sacraments.[3]

A simple question, but not admitting an easy answer, is why the Church? The answer includes its being a sacrament (q.v.) of salvation, and being the place of a Trinitarian economy. At the experiential level of religious experience it focuses on Jesus, its Lord, being power and wisdom.[4]

At some stage, then, one must also ask what is the Church? There are many possible answers,[5] and many have been given throughout history. The various answers operate at different levels. We can *describe* the Church as "local Churches throughout the world united with each other and with the successor of Peter in a common life of apostolic faith supported by apostolic ministry." Such an answer does not bring us into an understanding of the Church. An advance is the phenomenological approach of A. Dulles (q.v.).[6] He takes five paradigms, central insights about the Church, and shows that other ideas can cluster around them. But in the end, the method of models (q.v.) fails to give a comprehensive grasp of the Church, since each model needs to be complemented by the others; Dulles himself states that the five "are in fact permanent characteristics of the Church";[7] "There is no super-model that does full justice to all the characteristics of the Church."[8] Dulles would later propose yet another model, viz., the Church as Community of Disciples, though he eventually admits that this model, too, needs to be complemented by the others.[9] The servant model has, moreover, been recently developed beyond the stage noted by Dulles.[10] It would seem that philosophical models[11] are no more successful in presenting a unified understanding: each makes a contribution only.

In the past there have been many attempts at unifying the truths about the Church.[12] The dominant pre-Vatican II one was *societas perfecta:* the Church, like the state, is a perfect society (q.v.) in that it contains within itself all that is necessary to achieve its finality. In *Mystici corporis* (1943), Pius XII (q.v.) attempted to integrate this vision of the Church with the Pauline doctrine of the Body of Christ (q.v.). Other integrations were sought, e.g., by C. Journet (q.v.), in terms of the Church being one, holy, catholic, and apostolic.[13] It is commonly thought that People of God (q.v.) is a unifying understanding, but it needs to be complemented by other insights.

Modern ecumenism affords insights about the Church[14] both from the Protestant West[15] and above all from the Orthodox East.[16] Also germane is the question of whether the Church is a subject or a person.[17] The tendency to hypostasize the Church is very often implicit in theology.

Many ecclesiologists warn against the danger of paralleling Christological heresies in ecclesiology. An ecclesiological Monophysitism can so stress the divine in the Church that it destroys the economy and overlooks what is human. The temptation of Nestorianism emphasizes the economy in the world, but it sees the Church as celestial and terrestrial, with only an abstract unity. Against these deviations we have to hold a Chalcedon-based view of ecclesiology: inseparable union of the divine and the human without division or confusion (see LG 8).[18] Christology gives another set of insights: just as it can begin "from below," from humanity to Jesus, who is ultimately the Incarnate Word, or "from above," as initiating from the descent of the Word into humanity, so too, ecclesiology may begin "from below" in the historical community, or "from above" as beginning in the divine economy and in Trinitarian relations.[19]

We attempt a unified understanding, one which must take account of ecclesiology and the situation of the Church in the late 20th century. We begin with a list of some criteria that should be used to judge an understanding of the Church. First, there are general criteria which would apply to any time in the Church's history. These can be used to judge any ecclesiology, from any period, and they can point to deficiencies in former attempts to speak in a comprehensive way about the Church. Some such criteria are: the centrality of Jesus Christ and his mission; a Trinitarian perspective of the Church's existence; sin and frailty; the essential characteristics of unity, holiness, catholicity, and apostolicity; a gathering of people; the role of law and authority; the Church in the world.

Second, there are criteria that stem from our late 20th century perspective. Among them are: the identity of the Church in Vatican II—People of God (LG 13; NA 4), Body of Christ (LG 7, 14, 48 . . . AA 2; AG 6), temple of the Holy Spirit (PO 1; LG 17; AG 7); the insights of liberation theologies; the role of the laity; charism; spirituality; ecology. In recent decades there is a new emphasis on the law of the Cross; G. O'Collins writes: "A genuine theology of the cross would call into question much of the talk about a 'successful' Church, a 'well-run' diocese, a 'flourishing' congregation, a parish 'in good shape.' The Christian community in its various groupings should be reminded of the principle, 'power made perfect in weakness.' Moltmann's *Church in the Power of the Spirit* rightly speaks of 'the community of the cross (Kreuzgemeinde).' For the most part, however, ecclesiologies—or at least Roman Catholic ones—do not take up this theme."[20]

The search for a unified understanding can be assisted by recent Eucharistic ecclesiologies (q.v.) whose modern prime originator was Afanas'ev (q.v.), and whose influence continues to grow.[21] We can be alerted to the significance of a Eucharistic ecclesiology by the statements of Vatican II that the Eucharist is the source and summit *(fons et culmen)* of the whole Christian life (LG 11) and a principal manifestation of the Church (SC 41). A Eucharistic ecclesiology may well be the most satisfying available. But it involves a deep appreciation of the meaning of the Eucharist, one that many people in the West may not yet have achieved. A view of the Eucharist as a purely cultic act, divorced from actual Christian living, would not sufficiently underpin an ecclesiology. As a pastoral strategy, it might be better to present what is involved in a Eucharistic ecclesiology but in different terms, ones which might lead people to develop their understanding of the Eucharist and hence of the Church. At Vatican II the words "to the praise of the creator and redeemer" (LG 31) were added at the request of several council members to make clearer the cultic aspect of the whole Church, and to focus attention on creation and redemption.[22]

The most apposite approach would seem to be through *koinônia* or communion (q.v.), which is central to Vatican II ecclesiology.[23] The term itself is not readily translatable: J.M.R. Tillard suggests "partnership," "shared life," or "joint partaking" for the *koinônia* of the early Church in Acts 2:42-47.[24] The notion of *koinônia* includes a vertical dimension of divine life and gifts received by the Church, and a horizontal dimension in sharing this life and gifts with others. Moreover, the Church exists to internalize this *koinônia*, and so to share it that others in turn may internalize it too.[25]

The following is offered as a unified understanding: The Church on earth is a community of the disciples of Christ on pilgrimage to the eschatological kingdom, patterned on the person and mission of Mary and knowing its Lord as incarnate power and wisdom. In a secular world it is the sacrament of universal salvation, called upon to unfold and actualize the values of the

kingdom and to work for the unity of all the followers of Christ. It is filled with the Holy Spirit, who dwells in it as in a temple, makes its members the Body of Christ and the People of God, the adopted children of the Father. The Spirit provides the one, holy, catholic, and apostolic Church with its institutional and charismatic gifts, and calls it into ever deeper conversion. The Church, through the communion of all its members with their differing ministries (Petrine, hierarchical, and lay), is to respond to the gifts it has received by a worship which brings all humanity and the whole of creation before the Father in praise and intercession, and which opens the Church to receive still greater gifts through sacramental life, prayer, and the self-offering of its members under the sign of the Cross. Continually strengthened by this worship, the Church stands in faith under the Word of God and perseveres in its authentic Tradition, so that despite sin and weakness, it lives in hope and continues the mission of Christ as priest, prophet, and king, in spreading the liberating good news of the kingdom, and thus in love serves the world and all creation at the level of their deepest needs. The Church is marked by love among its members; it cares for its members being purified after death in purgatory, and rejoices in communion with them, with its members on earth, and with those already in glory.

[1]See H. Rahner, *Symbole der Kirche: Die Ekklesiologie der Väter* (Salzburg, 1964). Cf. W. Knoch, *Die Früscholastik und ihre Ekklesiologie: Eine Einführung* (Paderborn: Bonifatius, 1992). [2]Congar, Augustin 269–275; 340–344. [3]Y. Congar, "Traditio thomistica in materia ecclesiologica," Ang 43 (1966) 405–428 at 427–428; A. Antón, "El tratado 'de ecclesia' en la enseñanza de la teología, " Greg 50 (1969) 651–688. [4]F. Schüssler Fiorenza, "The Church's Religious Identity and Its Social and Political Mission," TS 43 (1982) 197–225; M.C. Cherian, "Jesus Christ our Wisdom," VYoti 41 (1973) 430–444; cf. P.D. Hanson, "The Identity and Purpose of the Church," TToday 42 (1985–86) 342–352. [5]W. Breuning, "Wie 'definiert' sich Kirche heute?" in J. Schreiner, ed., *Unterwegs zur Kirche.* QDisput 110 (Freiburg—Basel—Vienna: Herder, 1987) 11–32; S. Dianich, *Ecclesiologia: Questioni di metodo e una proposta* (Milan: Ed. Paoline, 1993); A.T. and R.P.C. Hanson, *The Identity of the Church: A Guide to Recognizing the Contemporary Church* (London: SCM, 1987); E. Jay, *The Church: Its Changing Image Through Twenty Centuries* (Atlanta: John Knox, 1980); M. Kehl, *Die Kirche: Eine katholische Ekklesiologie* (Würzburg: Echter, 1992); R. Michiels, "The Self-Understanding of the Church After Vatican II," LouvSt 14 (1989) 83–107; T.H. Sanks, *Salt, Leaven and Light: The Community Called Church* (New York: Crossroad, 1992); G. Tavard, *The Church, Community of Salvation: An Ecumenical Ecclesiology.* New Theology Studies 1 (Collegeville: The Liturgical Press, 1992); J.M.R. Tillard, "Qu'est-ce que l'Église de Dieu?," PrOrChr 34 (1984) 3–20; D. Valentini, "Autocomprehensione di Chiesa, impegno di evangelizzazione e profezia," Sales 49 (1987) 3–63. [6]*Models of the Church* (Dublin: Gill and Macmillan, [2]1988). [7]Ibid., 204. [8]Ibid., 206. [9]Ibid., 226. [10]J.Y. Calvez, "La funzione diaconale della Chiesa," RasT 29 (1988) 217–234; S. Sabugal, "La iglesia: Sierva de Dios, al servicio de los hombres," RET 46 (1986) 127–179; [11]T.F. O'Meara, "Philosophical Models in Ecclesiology," TS 39 (1978) 2–21. [12]P. Chirico, "Dynamics of Change in the Church's Self-Understanding," TS 39

(1978) 55–75; B. Cooke, "The Church: Catholic and Ecumenical," Today 36 (1979–1980) 353–367; A. Dulles, "A Half Century of Ecclesiology," TS 50 (1989) 419–422; A. Grounelle, "Définitions de l'Église," ETR 63 (1988) 67–73; R. Haight, "On Systematic Ecclesiology," TorontoST 8 (1992) 220–238; J.A. Komonchak, "Lonergan and the Tasks of Ecclesiology," in M.L. Lamb, ed., *Creativity and Method.* FS B. Lonergan (Milwaukee: Marquette UP, 1981) 265–273; B. Mondin, *Le nuove ecclesiologie: Un'immagine attuale della chiesa.* Teologia 29 (Rome: Ed. Paoline, 1980); S. Pie I Ninot, "Eclesiología fundamental: 'Status quaestionis,'" RET 49 (1989) 361–403.    [13]C. Journet, *L'Église du Verbe Incarné.* 3 vols. (Paris 1951–1969).    [14]C. Cereti, "Contributo dei dialoghi fra le chiese per un trattato di ecclesiologia, "StEcum 6 (1988) 167–181; B. Forte, "Il trattato di ecclesiologia: una impostazione ecumenica," StEcum 6 (1988) 153–165; L. Sartori, "L'ecclesiologia cattolica dal Vaticano II ad oggi e l'ecumenismo," Asp 31 (1984) 227–250.    [15]E. Jüngel, "Thèses dogmatiques sur l'ecclésiologie," FoiVie 38/2 (1989) 5–11.    [16]H. Biedermann, "Gotteslehre und Kirchenver-ständnis: Zugang der orthodoxen und der katholischen Theologie," TPQ 129 (1981) 131–142; P. Ferlay, "Trinité, Église, monde: Tâches actuelles en ecclésologie," NRT 102 (1982) 227–234; G. Limouris, "The Understanding of the Church Emerging in the Bilateral Dialogues—Coherence or Divergence," GrOrTR 36 (1991) 1–10; N.A. Nissiotis, "The Theology of the Church and Its Accomplish-ment," EcumR 29 (1987) 62–76.    [17]S. Wiedenhofer, "Die Kirche als 'Subjekt' oder 'Person,'" in W. Baier et al., eds., *Weisheit Gottes—Weisheit der Welt.* FS J. Ratzinger. 2 vols. (St. Ottilien: EOS, 1987) 2:999–1020.    [18]V. Lossky, "The Temptations of Ecclesial Consciousness," SVlad 32 (1988) 245–254.    [19]Cf. R. Haight, "Historical Ecclesiology: An Essay on Method in the Study of the Church," ScEsp 39 (1987) 27–46, 345–374.    [20]In G. O'Collins, R. Faricy and M. Flick, *The Cross Today* (Rome-Sydney: Dwyer, 1977) 46–47.    [21]P. McPartlan, "Eucharistic Ecclesiology," OneChr 22 (1986) 314–331; idem, *The Eucharist Makes the Church: Henri de Lubac and John Zizioulas in Dialogue* (Edinburgh: Clark, 1993).    [22]ActaSyn 3/1:283—Alberigo-Magistretti 468.    [23]Cf. Apost. Exhort., *Christifideles laici* ("The Vocation and the Mission of the Lay Faithful in the World"—1988) 19–20.    [24]"Koinonia—Sacrament," OneChr 22(1986) 104–114 at 109.    [25]Cf. P. Chirico, "The Relationship of Values to Ecclesiology," ChicSt 19 (1980) 291–304.

## ECONOMY (OIKONOMIA)

The word "economy" has several meanings in theology. From the Greek *oikonomia* it has a basic sense of house management (*oikos/nomos*—house/law). It refers to God's saving plan revealed above all in the redemptive work of Jesus Christ. Theology contrasts the immanent Trinity—the absolute mystery of the eternal life of the Godhead, and the economic Trinity—seen in the missions of Son and Spirit (Gal 4:4-6) and thus fulfilling the divine plan (Eph 1:10; 3:9) in salvation history.

There is another use of the term "economy" which has ecclesiological and ecumenical significance. The concept and use of *oikonomia* is very important for the Orthodox Church. But its meaning has never been officially defined.[1] Rather than the management suggested by the Greek root, the Church use of the word implies more condescension and mercy, and it is opposed to *akribeia*, which is the strict application of

canons and laws in a situation. Both, however, are needed in the life of the Church. The need for *oikonomia* arises when there is an apparent conflict between the claim of the law and the call of the Christian spirit.[2] Orthodox theologians point to the canons of the early councils, and especially to two canonical letters of St. Basil (nn. 188 and 199), for examples of, and a basis for, the exercise of economy. In the past two centuries, economy has become important, especially in relation to Orthodox-Anglican relations.[3] In general, one can say that in dogmatic matters the Orthodox Churches lean towards *akribeia,* whereas in moral and sacramental matters they are more open to economy, with the Greek Orthodox being perhaps less open.

Economy is closely linked with Orthodox ecclesiology; this Church's consciousness of being the one, true Church has meant that in practice economy is exercised only when there is a question of a person or a group of persons embracing Orthodoxy. The Orthodox Churches have not considered very much the ecclesial situation of the non-Orthodox Churches and individuals. There are theologians and Churches who favor Cyprian over Augustine in the matter of (re)baptism of converts to Orthodoxy. In the past two centuries the possible application of economy in sacramental matters is seen in four very different positions adopted: economy can make what is invalid to be valid and what is valid to be invalid; economy can make what is valid to be invalid, but not what is invalid to be valid; economy cannot make what is valid to be invalid, but can make what is invalid to be valid; economy can neither make what is valid to be invalid, nor what is invalid to be valid.[4] There is generally a refusal to apply economy to inter-communion with other Churches. Different Churches, even the same Church at different times, take up quite contrary positions about the application of economy, e.g., recognizing or not the validity of the baptism or ordination of persons coming to Orthodoxy.

While there is no unanimous or agreed position on economy,[5] an attempt to discuss it at a Pan-Orthodox Synod in the 1970s failed when the preparatory document[6] gave rise to much criticism and divergent views. The American Eastern Orthodox-Roman Catholic Bilateral Consultation produced a Joint Statement in 1976 which noted the variety of opinions on economy and stated that its proper understanding involves the exercise of spiritual discernment, and not a mere legalistic procedure. It looked forward to the day when there would be mutual recognition of sacraments and full communion.[7]

The theology of economy invites the Catholic Church to examine what may be the possibilities in its own tradition:[8] dispensation; *epikeia* (a prudential judgment about the non-applicability of the law in a particular case); the concept of *Ecclesia supplet* (the

Church supplying what is missing in some sacramental disciplines); *sanatio in radice* (CIC 1161–1165 with 1107).[9] But in the West these are juridical and definable procedures, whereas *oikonomia,* a work of the Spirit guiding the *oikonomos* or bishop, remains less definable and more theological.[10]

---

[1]M. Azkoul, "Oikonomia and the Orthodox Church," PatByzR 6 (1987) 65–79; Bartholomeos Archondonis, "The Problem of Oikonomia Today," Kan 6 (983) 39–50; at 39–40; Chrysostomos of Oreoi, "Some Theological Reflections on Economy and Non-Orthodox Baptisms," PatByzR 6 (1987) 130–135; J.H. Erickson, "Oikonomia in Byzantine Canon Law," in *Law, Church and Society.* FS S. Kuttner (Pennsylvania: UP, 1977) 227–236; M.A. Fahey, "Ecclesiastical 'Economy' and Mutual Recognition of Faith: A Roman Catholic Perspective," Diak (USA) 11 (1976) 204–223; J. Kotsonis, *Problèmes de l'économie ecclésiastique* (Gembloux: Duculot, 1971); P. L'Huillier, "L'économie dans la tradition orthodoxe," Kan 6 (1983) 19–38; D. Salachas, "'Oikonomia' et 'akribeia' nella ortodossia greca odierna," Nicol 4 (1976) 301–340; C.N. Tsirpanlis, "Doctrinal 'Oikonomia' and Sacramental Koinonia in Greek Patristic Theology and Contemporary Orthodox Ecumenism," PatByzR 6 (1987) 30–43. [2]L. Örsy, "In Search of the Meaning of *Oikonomia:* Report on a Convention," TS 43 (1982) 312–319 at 313. [3]F.J. Thomson, "Economy: An Examination of the Various Theories of Economy Held in the Orthodox Church, with Special Reference to the Economical Recognition of Non-Orthodox Sacraments," JTS 16 (1965) 368–420; J.N. Bailev, "Validity and Authenticity: The Difference between Western and Orthodox Views on Orders," SVlad 8 (1964) 86–92; J. Kotsonis, "The Validity of Anglican Orders According to the Canon Law of the Orthodox Church," GrOrTR 3 (1957) 182–196; 4 (1958) 44–65. [4]Thomson (n. 3) 384. [5]Ibid., 394; see G. Florovsky, "The Orthodox Churches and the Ecumenical Movement Prior to 1910," HistEcumMov 1:171–215; P. Rai, "L'écomomie chez les Orthodoxes depuis 1755," Istina 3 (1973) 359–368. [6]*Towards the Great Council* (London: SPCK, 1973). [7]Text in J.A. Burgess and J. Gros, eds., *Building Unity: Ecumenical Dialogues with Roman Catholic Participation in the United States.* Ecumenical Documents 4 (New York—Mahwah, Paulist, 1989) 332–334. [8]Y. Congar, "Propos en vue d'une théologie de l'Économie dans la tradition latine," Irén 46 (1972) 155–206, 312; A. Nihal, "Sacraments—An Insight from the Orthodox Church," ChicSt 14 (1975) 252–259; K. Duchatelez, "La notion d'économie et ses richesses théologiques," NRT 92 (1970) 267–292. [9]See T.P. Doyle, in Coriden CIC 826–829 with 792 (bibliog. 833). [10]Örsy (n. 2) 316–319; idem, in Coriden CIC 43–44; J.H. Erickson, "Sacramental 'Economy' in Recent Roman Catholic Thought," Jurist 48 (1988) 653–667.

## ECUMENICAL MOVEMENT

The word "ecumenism" is from the Greek *oikoumenê* meaning the inhabited world.[1] In this and the following articles it will be used about qualities, attitudes, actions which express the consciousness of, and desire for, Christian unity. Departures from that meaning will be noted. There have been ecumenical activities immediately after each rupture in ecclesiastical communion (q.v.), from the time, therefore, of the early councils (q.v.). There have been notable efforts dating from the 16th century.[2] But it is customary to date the birth of the modern ecumenical movement from the meeting of the World Missionary Conference (of mission-sending societies) at Edinburgh in 1910.[3]

The scandal of disunity was being acutely felt in mission territories, in the divided witness of Christian Churches. The impetus of Edinburgh led to the establishment of the Life and Work movement which met for the first time in Stockholm 1925.[4] Its aim was to study the application of Christian principles to international relations and to economic, social, and industrial life; it coined the phrase "service unites but doctrine divides." At the same time the Faith and Order movement came into being, meeting at Lausanne in 1927.[5] It concentrated on questions of doctrine and ministry. These two movements are both necessary, as Churches are divided by both theological and non-theological factors,[6] the latter in some cases are more intractable.

At the Life and Work meeting at Oxford (1937) and the Faith and Order one at Edinburgh the same year, it was agreed that the two movements should merge about 1942 to form the World Council of Churches (WCC—v. ECUMENISM, WORLD COUNCIL OF CHURCHES). As the war intervened, the union did not take place until 1948, in Amsterdam.[7]

The Roman Catholic Church refused invitations to all of these meetings. The inspiration of Edinburgh 1910 led also to the establishment of the International Missionary Council (Jerusalem 1928),[8] which became part of the WCC in 1961 as its Department of Mission and Evangelism.

In this first period of ecumenism (1910–1948) there were several unions on the national or international level of Churches of the same background or denomination; some of these date back to the previous century: there are now world associations of Anglicans (q.v.), Baptists (q.v.), Congregationalists (q.v.), Disciples of Christ (q.v.), Lutherans (q.v.), Methodists (q.v.), Pentecostalists (q.v.), and Presbyterians (q.v.).

There was also a development of the Christian Unity Week of Prayer, which originated as a week at Pentecost and later was fixed as 18–25 January (v. ECUMENISM, SPIRITUALITY).

Significant, too, were conversations and dialogue (v. ECUMENISM, DIALOGUE) between Churches of different kinds, but unions were few except, for example, the Church of South India (Anglicans, Congregationalists, Methodists, and Presbyterians) in 1947,[9] and the United Church of Canada. Elsewhere episcopacy, non-theological factors, and doctrinal differences have blocked unions. From the 1960s, negotiations with a view to Church unions at national and international levels, both confessional and intraconfesssional, increased enormously. The key inspiration in these years of Faith and Order was the goal articulated by its secretary, O. Tomkins: "One Church Renewed for Mission." But by the 1970s interest in schemes of unity tapered off; there was more interest in process than in plans.

In the period up to 1949, with the exception of the Malines Conversations (q.v.), there was no formal involvement of the Roman Catholic Church in the ecumenical movement (v. ECUMENISM, ROMAN CATHOLIC CHURCH). The Holy Office Instruction of 1949 gave some formal recognition to the ecumenical movement in terms which were somewhat guarded, if not grudging. In 1960 the establishment of Secretariat for the Promotion of the Unity of Christians prepared the way for the Vatican II Decree on Ecumenism *(Unitatis redintegratio)* in 1964. The Roman Catholic Church became a full member of Faith and Order in 1968.

After the establishment of the WCC, relations between the Churches steadily improved. Since the New Delhi general assembly (1961), Catholics have attended as observers. The number of ecumenical dialogues (q.v.) increased in a dramatic manner. Also, the number of unions between Churches multiplied (v. ECUMENISM, UNIONS).[10]

In the ecumenical movement after 1948 some issues were clarified, and the nature of the obstacles to unity became more obvious. It became apparent to all that the unity we seek must be a visible unity, that it must seek to include all Churches, that it is not to be uniformity with rigid structures. At the same time difficulties have become evident: friendliness and good relations cannot be allowed to cloak or minimize the real differences that exist; the Eucharist is central to Christian unity, and thus involves the issue of ministry; purely classicist or fundamentalist interpretations of doctrines soon lead to a blind alley; at the Faith and Order meeting at Lund (1952), it was realized that "comparative ecclesiology"—comparing and contrasting different convictions—had reached its useful limit and offered no prospect of advancement.[11] Instead, it proposed to study together the relationship between God and the Church, with the Montreal meeting (1963) stressing the Trinitarian dimension of the Church.[12] The fifth world conference of Faith and Order, Santiago, Spain (1993), took up the theme "Towards *Koinonia* in Faith, Life and Witness" at a time when the ecumenical movement was showing some loss of self-confidence and direction, and seeing yet more clearly the serious difficulties ahead. Nonetheless, the placing of *koinônia* at the heart of the ecumenical quest was itself a major advance.

Many important studies were to follow the Lund and Montreal meetings of Faith and Order, the most significant being probably *Baptism, Eucharist and Ministry* (BEM) at the Conference in Lima (1982).[13]

In the meetings of the WCC and of Faith and Order, and other ecumenical statements and documents, we find the important concept of reception (q.v.). Unless and until statements and studies are received by the Churches at institutional or central level, as well as by the Churches' grass-roots, such statements do not produce their intended fruits.

The ecumenical movement continues in a multifaceted way, but it continually questions its direction and health. After the initial enthusiasm of Edinburgh (1910), of Amsterdam (1948), and of Vatican II in the Roman Catholic Church (1962–1965), the movement has had to return to its slow progress and limited achievements in ongoing work for unity. Its direction and aims approaching the close of the 20th century should be noted. There are three fields for ecumenical activity by the Church of Rome: with the so-called Monophysite churches (v. EASTERN CHURCHES), where there is almost full accord; the schism with the East, about which official dialogue began in 1980; the Churches of the Reform and later, with which there are eight current dialogues.

The ecumenical movement can be said not to have one center, but like an ellipse to have two foci, Geneva (WCC) and Rome.[14] The former prefers multilateral dialogue, the latter bilateral. Moreover, there are, broadly speaking, two ecclesiologies. Protestantism conceives the Church as arising from the free association of the faithful, brought together by the Word. Catholicism and the Eastern Churches see the Church as constructed from above with the structures left by Christ or taught to the primitive Church by the Spirit. Because of the importance of reception, ecumenism at the grass-roots level needs more development: the agreed statements between the various Churches have not yet been sufficiently reflected in their ongoing life. But it is only when we recall the situation in the first half of this century that we see just how much progress has been made on many fronts (v. other ECUMENISM arts.).[15]

At the beginning of the ecumenical movement in each Church, there was an early advance as the problems at the affective, psychological level decreased, and trust grew between the Churches. After this initial stage, the hard theological issues have to be tackled in patient dialogue. The issue of method will always be crucial.[16] But the discovery of existing unity in theology, in vision, in common religious experience of the lordship of Christ and of the power of the Holy Spirit is a solid foundation for further progress.

It is common to use the term "wider ecumenism" for dialogue and relations with Judaism (v. JEWS), Islam (q.v.), Buddhism (q.v.), Hinduism (q.v.), and generally the non-Christian (q.v.) religions. This term is furthermore loosely applied to various forms of dialogue with the world and culture, with society and groups especially disadvantaged. Finally, the word "ecumenics" is growing in currency, as in the "Irish School of

Ecumenics" (Dublin) founded in 1970 by M. Hurley: it refers to the scientific and practical study of all issues associated with a divided Christendom, and particularly with reflection on ecumenism itself.[17]

[1]E. Fahey, *Ecumenism: A Bibliographical Overview* (London: Greenwood Press, 1993); see BullCentUn for bibliog. on books and dialogues. [2]HistEcumMov 1:1-349. [3]K.S. Latourette, ibid., 1:355-363; P.A. Crowe, *The Ecumenical Movement in Bibliographical Outline* (New York: National Council of the Churches of Christ, 1965). [4]N. Karlström, HistEcumMov 1:509-542. [5]T. Tallow, ibid., 1:405-441; L. Vischer, ed., *A Documentary History of Faith and Order 1927-1963* (St. Louis: Bethany, 1963); G. Gassmann, *Documentary History of Faith and Order 1963-1993*. Faith and Order Paper 159 (Geneva: WCC, 1993). [6]M. Hurley, *Theology of Ecumenism*. Theology Today 9 (Cork, Ireland: Mercier, 1969). [7]W.A. Visser 't Hooft, HistEcumMov 1:697-731. [8]K.S. Latourette, ibid., 1:366-373. [9]S.C. Neill, ibid., 1:473-476; K.C. Abraham, "CSI Ecclesiology: Some Issues and Challenges," JDhara 19 (1989) 249-266. [10]M. Cressey, "Notable Unions— Additional Gifts: United Churches and the WCC," EcuR 40 (1988) 446-457. [11]M.B. Handspicker, HistEcumMov 2:151; cf. Y. Tesfai, "The Church in Focus: Ecclesiology in Contemporary Ecumenical Discussion," OneChr 27 (1991) 134-143. [12]Ibid., 2:147-162. [13]Faith and Order Paper 111 (Geneva: WCC, 1982). See M. Thurian, *Churches Respond to BEM*, 6 vols. (Geneva: WCC, 1986-1989); cf. F. Glendon-Hill, "The Call to Unity: On Growing Together Through Worship," OneChr 27 (1991) 49-56. [14]C.J. Dumont, "Analyse critique rétrospective et prospective de l'oecuménisme post-conciliaire," EspVie 93 (1983) 225-231. [15]E.I. Cassidy, "The Catholic Church and Ecumenism as We Approach the Third Millennium," BullCentUn 39 (1991) 11-20. [16] C. Hill, "The Fundamental Question of Ecumenical Method," OneChr 28 (1992) 136-147; M.T. Thangaraj, "Is Full Church Unity Possible or Desirable?," EcuR 44 (1992) 91-99. [17]M. Hurley, "Ecumenism, Ecumenical Theology and Ecumenics," IrTQ 45 (1978) 132-137.

## ECUMENISM, ORTHODOX AND OTHER EASTERN CHURCHES

From the late Middle Ages there was a geographical, cultural, theological, and psychological separation between East and West (v. ORTHODOX). There was especially a gulf between old patristics and the new scholasticism. Ecumenism scarcely existed, as F. Florovsky neatly summarizes: "To the Easterner, union presented itself as the imposition of Byzantinism on the West; to the Westerner, as the Latinization of the East. Each world chose to go its own way; the Western neglecting the Greek patristic tradition . . . the Greeks taking no account of anything that happened in the West since the separation."[1]

The Council of Florence (q.v.) showed that union with Church leaders would not be effective unless the whole Church received (v. RECEPTION) the negotiations. But from that time there were individuals both from the West and the East who looked to a truly ecumenical council to bring about union. Moreover, there were many local and individual efforts at dialogue and rapprochement, some involving Roman Catholics, but the majority were Protestants or Orthodox who had studied in western Europe.[2]

From the 17th century, some Anglicans with their interest in the ancient tradition were noteworthy for their curiosity about, and open approach to, the East. When more official discussions took place in the 19th century, Orthodox opinion was divided: some felt that the Anglican Communion was in schism and could only "return" to the true Church by fully accepting its doctrines. On the question of the validity of Anglican Orders (q.v.), some theologians and bishops held that economy (q.v.) could be applied; others insisted on re-ordination.[3]

Discussions with the Old Catholics (q.v.) began soon after 1871, but did not come to any conclusion.[4] The key issue in contacts with Old Catholics and Anglicans was the distinction between faith and worship. Gradually the Orthodox came to the conclusion that there was not sufficient unity in faith to justify union with these Churches.

In 1920 a Letter was sent from the locum tenens of Constantinople and eleven Metropolitans "unto all the Churches of Christ wheresoever they be," inviting them to renounce proselytism and form a league of Churches for mutual assistance. This Letter represents a formal entry of the Orthodox into the ecumenical movement.[5]

Orthodox representatives were to be found in the formation of Faith and Order (1927) and Life and Work (1925—v. ECUMENICAL MOVEMENT). The major contribution of the Orthodox was surely to remind ecumenists of the need for unity in faith as a condition for reunion.[6] Ecumenical developments were much helped by the establishment of the Russian Institute of Orthodox Theology founded in Paris in 1925, with help from western Churches, mainly Anglican.[7] The Moscow Consultation of representatives of autocephalous churches in 1948 discouraged further participation in the ecumenical movement by the Orthodox. The reasons would seem to be partly political—representing the then USSR view of initiatives in the West. They were also partly theological; the proposed World Council of Churches (WCC) appeared to have a definite Protestant ethos, and partly an ecclesiological misunderstanding of what the WCC sought to be. This meant that at the inauguration of the WCC in Amsterdam the same year, only a few Eastern Churches were present (Greek-speaking Churches, the USA Orthodox, Russian Exarchate in Western Europe—20 delegates). By the late 1960s all the Orthodox Churches except for the Albanian had become members of the WCC.

Notable in the ecumenical involvement of the Eastern Churches have been the Ecumenical Institute at Bossey (1946), the Fellowship of St. Alban and St. Sergius in England (1928), as well as various movements involving youth from East and West.[8]

The small group of Oriental Orthodox Churches (v. EASTERN CHURCHES) began to meet at first informally from 1948, leading to a World Conference of Oriental Orthodox Churches at Addis Ababa (1965). From the First Pan Orthodox Conference (Rhodes 1961), relations between the Oriental Orthodox Churches and the Orthodox Churches have been discussed. Starting with unofficial conversations, 1964–1971, it soon became evident that doctrinal differences lay more in terminology than in substance. Official dialogue began at Addis Ababa (1971) and continued.[9] By the late 1980s little seemed to prevent a union.[10] By 1990 these Oriental Orthodox Churches were also involved in international dialogue with Anglicans and the Roman Catholic Church.[11]

Relations between the main Orthodox Churches and Rome began to improve in the reigns of John XXIII (1958–1963) and Patriarch Athenagoras (1948–1972). The exchanges of messages between Constantinople and Rome were published in 1971 under the traditional Greek title *Tomos Agapis* (Volume of Charity).[12] The Churches of Russia and Georgia were the only ones to send observers to the first two sessions of Vatican II (1962, 1963), but by the end, Constantinople, Alexandria, Serbia, and Bulgaria were represented. Paul VI and Patriarch Athenagoras lifted the mutual 11th-century anathemas in 1965. Formal dialogue between Rome and Constantinople began with the setting up of the Joint Catholic-Orthodox Commission, in 1979, which envisages "an advance towards the reestablishment of full communion between the Catholic and the Orthodox sister Churches."[13] By common agreement it was decided not to begin with the most difficult issues; the opening topic was "The Mystery of the Church and the Eucharist in the Light of the Mystery of the Holy Trinity." Discussion continues both at international and more local levels and reveals both possible agreements and tensions that have deep roots in history.[14]

By 1990 there were many examples of local or national dialogue between Orthodox Churches and other denominations, with the following being international: Anglican (q.v.), Disciples of Christ (q.v.), Lutheran (q.v.), Methodist (q.v.), Old Catholic (q.v.).[15]

There have been a series of contacts with Protestants from the time of the Reformation, and several local dialogues with the Reformed (q.v.) in the 20th century. From 1988 there has been an international dialogue with the World Alliance of Reformed Churches, discussing the doctrine of the Trinity as based on the Nicene Creed.[16]

In the 20th century the involvement of the Orthodox Churches in the WCC has proved to be most significant both for them and for the world body (v. ECUMENISM, WCC): it has helped Orthodoxy out of isolation; it has

given to the Churches of the West the witness of a tradition going back to the primitive Church, one that has been characterized by spirituality as much as by doctrine. At the same time, the doctrinal differences between Constantinople and Rome are not huge, but non-doctrinal factors may be intractable for some time. With the new freedom of religion in Eastern Europe after 1989, the appointment of Latin Rite bishops in the East has been particularly resented, and it has led to some cooling in ecumenical relations.[17] The issue of the papacy, too, remains without any resolution in sight; the recent encyclical on ecumenism shows some openness to a new vision of the Petrine ministry.[18]

---

[1]G. Florovsky, "The Orthodox Churches and the Ecumenical Movement Prior to 1910," HistEcumMov 1:171-172. [2]Ibid., 172–196. [3]Ibid., 177, 196–202, 209–213. [4]Ibid., 205–209. [5]Bell, Documents n. 13; T. Fitzgerald, "The Patriarchal Encyclicals on Christian Unity 1902–1973," GkOrTR 22 (1977) 299–318. [6]N. Zernov, "The Eastern Churches and the Ecumenical Movement in the Twentieth Century," HistEcumMov 1: 654-656. [7]Ibid., 661–662. [8]Ibid., 649–668. [9]Istina 31 (1986) 396–412; P. Gregorios et al., eds., *Does Chalcedon Divide or Unite?: Towards Convergence in Orthodox Christology* (Geneva: WCC, 1981). [10]"Anba Bishoy Statement," Istina 34 (1990) 225–230; GrOrTR 34 (1989) 393–397; J. Meyendorff, "Chalcedonians and Non-Chalcedonians: Last Steps to Unity," SVlad 33 (1989) 319–329; T. Fitzgerald, "Towards Reestablishment of Full Communion: The Orthodox-Oriental Orthodox Dialogue," GrOrTR 36 (1991) 169–182—Agreed Statement 183–188. [11]"Communiqué," StVladTQ 34 (1990) 78–83/Sobornost 12 (1990) 78–90/GkOrTR 34(1989) 393–397; cf. A. de Halleux, "Orthodoxes orientaux en dialogue," Irén 64 (1991) 332–358; M. an Parys, "Les Églises orientales orthodoxes et l'oecuménisme," Irén 64 (1991) 323–331. [12]E.J. Stormon, ed., *Towards the Healing of Schism: The Sees of Rome and Constantinople 1958–1984* (New York: Paulist, 1987); J. Meyendorff and E. Lanne, two arts.: "Églises-soeurs: Implications ecclésiologiques du Tomos Agapis," Istina 20 (1975) 35–46, 46–74. [13]30.11.1979—Stormon (n. 12) 367. Texts OneChr 19 (1981) 188–197; 23 (1987) 330–340; 24 (1988) 367–377. [14]Orthodox-Roman Catholic Consultation 1989, "Primacy and Conciliarity," Origins 19 (1989) 469–472; "Le document d'Ariccia," Irén 65 (1992) 491–498; cf. J. Borelli, "A Critical Moment in Orthodox and Catholic Relations," Ecumenism 27 (1992) 25–27; E. Clapsis, "The Roman Catholic Church and Orthodoxy: Twenty-Five Years after Vatican II," GkOrTR 35 (1990) 221–236; C. Davey, "Clearing a Path Through a Minefield: Orthodox-Roman Catholic Dialogue," OneChr 27 (1991) 8–23; C. Moeller, "A New Ecumenical Movement?," Diak(USA) 18 (1983) 54–67; M. Daniel de Moldavie, "Le dialogue orthodoxe-catholique entre l'échec et l'espoir," Episk 22 (1991) 12–14; P. McPartlan, ed., *One in 2000: Towards Catholic-Orthodox Unity, Agreed Statements and Parish Papers* (Slough UK: St. Pauls, 1993); idem, "Towards Catholic-Orthodox Unity," Communio 19/2 (1993) 305–320. [15]Bibliog. See Bull CentUn yearly updates; OneChr; Irén; Istina. [16]"Relations entre les Communions," Irén 59 (1986) 231–233; T.F. Torrance, ed., *Theological Dialogue between Orthodox and Reformed Churches* (Edinburgh: Scottish Academic Press, 1985); L. Vischer, "The Legacy of Kyrill Loukaris: A Contribution to the Orthodox-Reformed Dialogue," Mid-Stream 25 (1986) 165–183. [17]H. Legrand, "Le dialogue catholique-orthodoxe: Quelques enjeux ecclésiologiques de la crise actuelle autour des Églises unies," BullCentUn 43 (1993) 3–16; cf. V. Poggi, ed., *"Le travail futur*

d'après le Père Philippe de Régis (1897–1955)," OrChrPer 58 (1992) 5–21.    [18]*Ut unum sint* (25 May 1995)—DocCath 92/2118 (1995) 567–597 at nn. 88–96 with 50–63; AAS 67 (1995) 921–982 at 973–980.

## ECUMENISM AND THE ROMAN CATHOLIC CHURCH

The Roman Catholic Church (RCC) was not involved in what may be called the founding meeting of the ecumenical movement, the World Conference on Mission in Edinburgh 1910. Indeed the RCC refused all invitations to attend organizations stemming from Edinburgh until 1961 (v. ECUMENICAL MOVEMENT and ECUMENISM, WORLD COUNCIL OF CHURCHES). An exception to RCC non-involvement in ecumenism was the Malines Conversations (1921–1925—q.v.).

Pius XI's encyclical *Mortalium animos,* "Fostering True Religious Union,"[1] provided a brake on any incipient ecumenical activities. Among its concerns: that there was a danger of indifferentism, of giving the impression that one Church was as good as another; that the Catholic Church might be seen to be tacitly accepting some of the Protestant ecclesiologies of the day; that supporting or encouraging ecumenical meetings would be "to countenance a false Christian religion quite alien to the one true Church of Christ." Hence the pope concluded: "There is only one way in which the unity of all Christians may be fostered, and that is by promoting the return to the one true Church of Christ of those who are separated from it; for from that one true Church they have in the past unhappily fallen away." For Rome at the time "reunion" meant "return." Such sentiments were often found in subsequent popes up to and including John XXIII.[2]

Though it did not allow Catholics to attend the first meeting of the World Council of Churches at Amsterdam (1948), the Holy Office in the following year gave permission under careful restrictions for Catholics to be involved in ecumenism.[3]

An event of major importance was the establishment of the Secretariat for the Promotion of Christian Unity 1960.[4] Originally set up in order to prepare for Vatican II, it afterwards became a permanent organ.[5] In the 1988 reform of the Curia (v. VATICAN) it received a new title, Pontifical Council for the Promotion of Christian Unity.

A highlight of Vatican II was the presence of observers from other Christian bodies, some officially sent by their Churches, others invited by the Secretariat for Unity. These observers included some members of Orthodox Churches, various Protestant groups, the Anglican Communion, and the World Council of Churches. They had access to all council documentation and had a place of honor at conciliar sessions. Though they did not have the right to address the

council, they communicated their views to the Secretariat for Unity, which frequently passed them on to the relevant conciliar commissions. The importance of these observers cannot easily be exaggerated. as by their presence they were a daily reminder to the council fathers of the ecumenical aim of the council.

In the first session of Vatican II, a schema on the unity of the Church was discussed briefly; it dealt also with Eastern Churches. In opening the second session, Pope Paul VI gave as one of the four aims of the council the restoration of unity among all Christians.[6]

In the second session, the first three chapters of the schema on ecumenism were discussed (18.11—2.12.1963) and were approved, subject to revision. The other two chapters, later to be the Declarations on Non-Christian Religions and on Religious Liberty, were postponed. In the third session, the decree on ecumenism to become *Unitatis redintegratio* (UR) was further discussed, and just before its final approval, 19 modifications were made at the request of the pope.[7] The final vote in favor of the decree was quasi-unanimous (2137 to 11).

The Decree on Ecumenism presumes the Constitution on the Church (UR 1), and Paul VI stated in approving both that the Decree complements the Constitution.[8] Both documents are then interdependent. The Constitution on the Church makes some important contributions to an ecumenical theology: the use of the word "subsists" (LG 8; cf. UR 4—v. SUBSISTS); the assertion that "many elements of sanctification and of truth" are to be found outside the structure of the RCC (LG 8; cf. UR 3); the notion of full and imperfect communion (LG 14; cf. UR 3, 14, 22) in place of the language of being really members *(reapse)* of Pius XII's *Mystici Corporis;* the application of the words "churches" and "ecclesial communities" for bodies not in full communion with the RCC (LG 15; cf. UR 19).[9]

The introduction to the Decree notes the scandal of disunity, and states that the ecumenical movement is a grace of the Holy Spirit (UR 1). Since there is only one ecumenism in which various Christians are differently engaged according to their convictions, especially ecclesiological, the title of the first chapter was changed from "Principles of Catholic Ecumenism" to "Catholic Principles of Ecumenism." This chapter gives the self-identity of the RCC (UR 2–3); the words "we believe" in it are to be taken in a strong sense meaning the faith of the Church. It is admitted that in history there have been faults on both sides which have fostered disunity (UR 3). There are gifts and graces outside the visible boundaries of the Catholic Church "which properly belong to the one Church of Christ" (UR 3). The ecumenical movement is briefly described with a stress on charity and truth (UR 4), and developed in the second chapter, "The Practice of Ecumenism": "the restoration of unity is the concern of the whole Church, faithful and clergy alike" (UR 5); "renewal is of notable ecumenical importance" (UR 6); "there can be no ecumenism worthy of the name without a change of heart," and living holier lives is a furthering of Christian unity (UR 7); "spiritual ecumenism," or prayer, especially with other Christians, is highly praised (UR 8); mutual understanding is very important, and dialogue "where each side can treat the other on equal footing" (*par cum pari agat)* is strongly recommended (UR 9); in dialogue it must be remembered that there is a "hierarchy of truths" (UR 11—v. HIERARCHY OF TRUTHS); cooperation is particularly lauded (UR 12).

The third chapter, "Churches and Ecclesial Communities Separated from the Roman Apostolic See," deals first with the Churches of the East. It begins with a historical observation of great importance: "For many centuries the churches of the east and the west followed their separate ways though linked in a union of faith and sacramental life; the Roman See by common consent acted as guide when disagreements arose between them over matters of faith and discipline" (UR 14). The full implications of this text have not yet been fully grasped, especially if taken in conjunction with the citation of Acts in art. 18: "this holy synod solemnly repeats the declaration of previous councils and Roman pontiffs, that for the restoration or the maintenance of unity and communion it is necessary 'to impose no burden beyond what is essential'" (Acts 15:28). This chapter lists important features of the life of the Churches of the East: basic dogmas of faith; liturgy; Marian devotion; true sacraments; monasticism; the discipline of various rites; a pluralism of theological expression. The council declares "that all this heritage of spirituality and liturgy, of discipline and theology, in its various traditions, belongs to the full catholic and apostolic character of the church" (*ad plenam catholicitatem et apostolicitatem . . . pertinere*—UR 17). This recognition of two of the marks (q.v.) of the Church in the life of the Eastern Churches is clearly significant.

The second part of this chapter deals with "Separated Churches and Ecclesial Communities in the West." The use of "Churches and ecclesial communities" leaves room for theological interpretation. The *relatio* of the Decree on Ecumenism, however, indicates that validity of orders and a valid Eucharist are key factors in ascribing the term "Church".[10] Thus, at least for the Council, the Orthodox and Oriental Churches and the Old Catholics are certainly deserving of the name "Church". The Decree lists important gifts of the Western Churches and ecclesial communities: echoing the Basis of the World Council of Churches, "open confession of Jesus Christ as God and Lord . . . to the glory of the one God, Father, Son and Holy Spirit," it

notes, however, that there are divergences in the doctrines of the Incarnation and Redemption (UR 20); it praises the love and reverence of these bodies for the Scriptures (UR 21); baptism is already a bond of union (UR 22); worship, prayer, and moral rectitude are also recognized (UR 23). In conclusion the Decree warns against unhealthy ecumenical activities; it urges that measures taken by Catholics may "place no obstacle to the ways of divine providence and . . . avoid prejudging the future inspirations of the holy Spirit," and since Christian unity is beyond human powers, it "grounds its hope deeply on Christ's prayer for the Church, on the Father's love for us, and on the power of the Holy Spirit" (UR 24).

Thus the decree stresses love, upholds legitimate diversity, and emphasizes the spiritual dimension of ecumenism. In the period after Vatican II there were many reforms which should themselves be contributions to unity. Moreover, dialogue, which is mentioned by the decree ten times, but mainly with the aim of greater reciprocal knowledge, takes on a new meaning as a quest for unity through the study of contentious issues. But the decree proposes no model for unity, though it implies unity in essentials (UR 4, 16, 18).[11]

In the period immediately after the council, relations with the World Council of Churches grew closer, but have stopped short of membership (v. ECUMENISM, WCC). The Catholic Church became a full member of Faith and Order in 1968. The Secretariat for Unity produced a Directory on ecumenism in two parts (1967, 1970).[12]

In addition, the Secretariat brought out a Declaration on Eucharistic intercommunion (1972), which had to be followed by another (1973) due to the former being interpreted too widely.[13] It produced a document on the many forms of dialogue (q.v.) in 1970.[14] The Pontifical Council for Promoting Christian Unity issued, in 1993, *The Directory for the Application of Principles and Norms on Ecumenism*.[15] This wide-ranging document is in five chapters: I. "The Search for Christian Unity" (nn. 9–36)—the Church's commitment to ecumenism, especially at Vatican II; II. "Organization in the Catholic Church at the Service of Christian Unity" (nn. 37–53)—structures and activities at all levels; III. "Ecumenical Formation in the Catholic Church" (nn. 55–91)—means of formation, and the formation of all the faithful, with particular emphasis on future ministers; IV. "Communion in Life and Spiritual Activity Among the Baptized" (nn. 92–160)—the communion which exists and how it is to be fostered; V. "Ecumenical Cooperation, Dialogue and Common Witness" (nn. 161–218)—norms for cooperation with a view to dialogue and witness. In general, this new directory brings together existing norms and legislation, rather than breaking much significant new ground.

Ecumenical dialogue has taken place at every level in the years after Vatican II. Of particular importance is the dialogue which springs up spontaneously when Christians meet one another,[16] and dialogues at national and regional level. But it is perhaps the international dialogues that have most caught the imagination of the Churches. Since Vatican II there has been international bilateral theological dialogue with eleven world confessional bodies including the following: the Orthodox Churches, the Anglican Communion, the Lutheran World Federation, the World Methodist Council, some Evangelicals, the Baptist World Alliance, the World Alliance of Reformed Churches, Disciples of Christ, the Pentecostals (v. RELEVANT ARTICLES).[17]

The 1991 Vatican response to the Anglican-RCC dialogue (ARCIC) showed how difficult, and how slow, is the road to doctrinal agreement; even within the Vatican it would appear that different stances are adopted by the Secretariat for Unity and by the Congregation for the Doctrine of the Faith.[18] But there are also other avenues opening up for ecumenical advances. We see the RCC at the national level joining local Councils of Churches as full members, rather than with the former observer status. Apart from the obvious problems inherent in ecumenical activity, the 1990s showed several other difficulties: frustration with the slowness of progress—documents pile up, the right things are continually being said, but to some it appears that nothing worthwhile has been achieved; failure to understand the ecumenical method in ongoing dialogues, and thus some are tempted to look for a quick affective communion; problems with sects in places lead pastors to be wary of any interchurch contacts; abuses in ecumenical work has led people to a disenchantment with ecumenism, which is then rejected outright by those of the extreme right, or quietly ignored as people get on with other ecclesial tasks and ministries.[19] A further problem is the slowness in giving concrete expression to the unity that is perceived already to exist between the Catholic Church and other Churches or ecclesial bodies. Some Catholic theologians suggest that more progress could be made (v. ECUMENISM, UNION), and that some of the hesitations on the part of the Churches, including the Catholic Church should be overcome.[20]

Change of heart, openness to new perspectives, and a willingness to be surprised by the Spirit will remain crucial ecumenical virtues. Spiritual ecumenism (q.v.) is vital since the obstacles to unity can be surmounted only by the power of the Holy Spirit.

The encyclical of Pope John Paul II on ecumenism has been initially welcomed for its tone and open spirit.[21]

---

[1]*Mortalium animos* AAS 20 (1928) 5–16/Carlen 3:313-319. [2]Encyc. *Ad Petri cathredram* (19 June 1959)—AAS 51 (1959) 498–531/Carlen 5:5-20. [3]Instr. Holy Office *Ecclesia Catholica* (20 Dec. 1949)—AAS 42 (1950) 142–147. [4]AAS 52 (1960) 433; Motu proprio *Superno Dei nutu,* ibid., 436; cf. 495. [5]Paul VI, Mp, *Finis concilio*—AAS 58 (1966) 37–40; J. Willebrands, "Réflexions sur les vingt années de travail du Secrétariat pour l'Unité des Chrétiens," Irén 54 (1981) 5–24. [6]Alloc. 29 Sept. 1963—ActSyn 2/1:189–199. [7]L. Jaeger, *A Stand on Ecumenism: The Council's Decree* (London, 1965) 51–55. [8]Discourse (21 Nov. 1964)—ActSyn 3/8:914. [9]F.A. Sullivan, "The Decree on Ecumenism: Presuppositions and Consequences," OneChr 26 (1990) 7–19 = RasT 31 (1990) 231–246. [10]ActaSyn 3/2: 335. See UR 22c, which uses only "ecclesial communities." [11]E. Lanne, "Le décret sur l'Oecuménisme vingt ans après," Irén 57 (1984) 451–468. [12]*Ad totam Ecclesiam*—AAS 59 (1967) 574–592/Flannery 1:483-501; *Spiritus Domini*—AAS 62 (1970) 257–263/Flannery 1:515-532. [13]AAS 64 (1972) 518–525/Flannery 1:554-559; AAS 65 (1973) 616–619/Flannery 1:560-563. [14]DocCath 67 (1990) 876–882/Flannery 1:535-553. [15]25 Mar. 1993—AAS 85 (1993) 1039–1119/CathIntern 4 (1993) 351–399. [16]Document (n. 14) VII/I—DocCath 881/Flannery 550. [17]See OneChr and Irén for regular reports, BullCentUn for bibliog; "The Catholic Church in Dialogue Today," OneChr 18 (1982) 192–247; J.M.R. Tillard, "Église catholique et dialogues bilatéraux," Irén 56 (1988) 5–19. [18]See F.A. Sullivan, "The Vatican Response to ARCIC 1," Greg 73 (1992) 489–498. [19]E.I. Cassidy, "The Catholic Church and Ecumenism as We Approach the Third Christian Millennium," BullCentUn 39 (1991) 11–20; A. Dulles, "The Decree on Ecumenism: Twenty-five Years After," in T.D. Horgan, ed., *Walking Together: Roman Catholics and Ecumenism Twenty-five Years After Vatican II* (Grand Rapids: Eerdmans, 1990) 17–25; J.-M. R. Tillard, "Regard sur l'oecuménisme: où en sommes-nous?," FreibZPT 29 (1982) 252–263. [20]E.g., K. Rahner, "Pseudo-Problems in Ecumenical Discussion," ThInvest 18:35-53; idem, "Some Problems in Contemporary Ecumenism," ThInvest 14:245-253; idem, "Ecumenical Theology in the Future," ThInvest 14:254-269; T. Ryan, "Ecumenism: Dead or Alive? An Unofficial Investigation," OneChr 27 (1991) 121–133; cf. G.H. Tavard, "Lessons of Ecumenism for Catholic Theology," OneChr 27 (1991) 346–351, and G. Lindbeck, "Two Kinds of Ecumenism: Unitive and Interdenominational," Greg 70 (1989) 647–660. [21]*Ut unum sint* (25 May 1995)—DocCath 92/2118 (1995) 567–597; AAS 67 (1995) 921–982.

## ECUMENISM, SPIRITUALITY

Abbé Paul Couturier (1881–1953)[1] initiated in Lyons the celebration of an octave of prayer for Christian unity in 1934 from 18 January (Feast of the Chair of Peter) to 25 January (Feast of the Conversion of St. Paul). This was a development of the Church Unity Octave founded in 1908 by two Anglicans, Rev. Spencer Jones and Rev. Paul J.F. Wattson; the latter soon afterwards became Roman Catholic. From 1939 the Week was observed as the "Week of Universal Prayer" for the unity of all baptized Christians "as and how Christ wills." The inspiration of Couturier is seen in the fact that the week is not just a week of intercession, but has incorporated in it elements of repentance, conversion, and the recognition of fault in disunity. Since 1968 the Week has been prepared by both the Church of Rome and the World Council of Churches (WCC—q.v.).

Vatican II made a notable observation in the context of approving prayer for unity: "This change of heart and holiness of life, along with public and private prayer for the unity of Christians, should be regarded as the soul of the whole ecumenical movement, and merits the name 'spiritual ecumenism'" (UR 8). But the council warns that intercommunion (q.v.) or common worship *(communicatio in sacris)* is a means for the restoration of Christian unity, but not one to be used indiscriminately (v. EUCHARISTIC SHARING).

From the birth of the modern ecumenical movement (q.v.) in Edinburgh (1910), common prayer and worship have been a feature of all major meetings. Of great importance has been the spiritual experience of different forms of worship,[2] not least the tradition of the Eastern Churches. The Vancouver General Assembly of the WCC (1983) gave worship a more central role, and the WCC later took up the issue of spirituality in various initiatives, including a new compilation of prayers which have a strong element of ecumenical intercession.[3]

The establishment of the ecumenical community at Taizé by Roger Schutz and Max Thurian in 1940,[4] and various interdenominational Bible and prayer groups all highlight the importance of spirituality in the ecumenical movement. Such gatherings come to be aware of a unity in the Spirit which crosses denominational boundaries. Important, too, are common translations of the Bible, not only for what they produce but also for the cooperation involved, which itself forges bonds of trust and communion or fellowship. Hymnody is another area in which there have been notable advances, with many traditional settings as well as new compositions—such as Taizé chants—now shared among Christians.[5]

In recent years there has been a growing realization of the need for both an ecumenical spirituality and for spirituality in ecumenism.[6] Ecumenism that is merely at the level of discussion or common activity fails on several counts: it does not incorporate sufficiently the reality of unity being beyond human power; it does not enrich the participants with gifts to be shared mutually; it does not allow for both the expression and experience of already existing, if partial, unity in the Spirit. Spirituality appears as soon as people ask what before God are the consequences for them of ecumenical activity or new insights. The recognition of the lives of holy persons and saints (q.v.) in different Churches is a neglected, but major, source of edification and ecumenical insights.[7] A sincere commitment to the holy work of ecumenism cannot take place without spirituality. An ecumenical spirituality will in turn help participants to also grow in the Spirit within their own religious affiliation.

[1]G. Curtis, *Paul Couturier and Unity in Christ* (London: SCM, 1964); M. Villain, *The Life and Work of Abbé Paul Couturier* (Haywards Heath UK, 1959). [2]F. Glendon-Hill, "The Call to Unity: On Growing together Through Worship," OneChr 27 (1991) 45–56. [3]J.B. Carden, comp., *With All God's People: The New Ecumenical Prayer Cycle.* 2 vols (Geneva: WCC, 1989). [4]J.L. Balado, *The Story of Taizé* (London: Mowbray, [3]1988); R. Brico, *Taizé. Brother Roger and His Community* (London: Collins, 1978). [5]*Cantate Domino: An Ecumenical Hymn Book* (Oxford: UP, 1980). [6]A.J. van der Bent, "The Concern for Spirituality: An Analytical and Bibliographical Survey of the Discussion Within the WCC Constituency," EcuR 38 (1986) 101–114; J. Hüttenbügel, "Über ökumenische Spiritualität," Catholica 35 (1981) 211–222; P. Lengsfeld, "Ökumenische Spiritualität als Voraussetzung von Rezeption," in P. Lengsfeld and H.G. Stobbe eds., *Theologischer Konsens und Kirchenspaltung* (Stuttgart: Kohlhammer, 1981) 126–134. [7]Cf. D.H. Farmer, *The Oxford Dictionary of Saints* (Oxford: UP, [2]1987) and R. Symonds, *Alternative Saints: The Post-Reformation British People Commemorated as Saints by the Church of England* (Basingstoke-London: Macmillan, 1988).

## ECUMENISM, UNION

The expression "ecumenism and union" covers several matters: the union of Churches that have a common faith and tradition; united Churches from several traditions;[1] requirements for unity.

Since the 19th century there have been a growing number of unions between Churches on the basis of common confessions, *formulae concordiae,* communion of word and sacrament, and recognition of ministries worldwide.[2] Such bodies with their dates for early international meetings of their confession (sometimes under slightly different names) are: the Anglican Communion (Lambeth 1867), the International Old Catholic Bishops Conference (1889), the World Alliance of Reformed Churches (1877), the Lutheran World Federation (1923), the Friends World Committee for Consultation (1920), the Disciples Ecumenical Consultative Council (1930), the World Methodist Council (1881), the Baptist World Alliance (1905), and the World Pentecostal Conference (1947). Some of these have their central offices at or close to the World Council of Churches (q.v.) in Geneva. Since 1957 fourteen world families have generally met annually under the auspices of the WCC in Geneva. From 1979 their self-designation has been changed from "World Confessional Families" to "Christian World Communions."

Also since the 19th century there have been unions, traditionally called "organic unity," across denominational lines, made up of four distinguishable groups: 1) Churches in Germany and in what was the Austro-Hungarian Empire, e.g., Evangelische Kirche der Pfalz (1818), die Union (1817), Evangelische Kirche von Kurhessen-Waldeck (1820); 2) Churches of European settlement in the British Commonwealth and USA, mostly of Methodist and Reformed traditions, e.g., United Church of Canada (1925), United Church of Christ (USA 1957); 3) Churches of similar origins which have roots in African and Asian cultures, e.g., Church of Christ in Zaire (1970), United Church of Zambia (1965); 4) the South Asian group, e.g., Church of South India[3] (1947), Churches of North India and of Pakistan (both 1970). To these should be added the United Church of Japan (1941). A majority of these unions have been made up of two traditions, Reformed and Methodist, sometimes also Baptist. Outside South Asia no scheme involving Anglicans has been brought to fruition, and Lutheran participation has been minimal. The Roman Catholic Church and the Orthodox Churches have been generous in praising such unions but have held themselves apart; they prefer to wait for unions to take place so that more united partners in dialogue might be found. The Lutherans[4] and others have feared the loss of the Reformation emphases on grace and faith, and have been more interested in a reconciled diversity of tradition rather than structural unions which call for the death of the older identities.[5] But even in Lutheran circles there is an admission that reconciled diversity may not be the end of the ecumenical road.

In the U.S., the Consultation on Church Union (from 1962) explored the issues that needed clarification: 1) the historical basis for the Christian ministry that is found in the Scriptures and the early Church; 2) the origins, use, and understanding of creeds and confessional statements; 3) a restatement of the theology of liturgy; 4) the relation of word and sacrament.[6] In its development the Consultation discovered both the difficulty of, and plans for, the reconciliation of ministries, but also encountered the problem of Churches being less ecumenical than their ecumenists.[7] The Consultation of United and Uniting Churches has met regularly since 1967 (Bossey; cf. Limuru 1970, Toronto 1975, Colombo 1981, Potsdam 1987), and shows a growing number of Churches achieving or approaching union with one another. There is an emphasis on organic union, but in some cases the united Church has become a new denomination. The role of the WCC in all recent unions has been quite significant, at least in providing encouragement, expertise, and experience.[8]

Since the late 1960s we find a new unity across denominational boundaries in the experience of the power of the Holy Spirit in charismatic and pentecostal encounters. Similarly, we find new accords between evangelicals of various churches. Human distortions of this new gift of God to the Churches are possible: individualism, when the religious experience can lead to a downplaying of the importance of structures; some indeed claim that the Churches are an obstacle to union with God.[9]

It is clearly affirmed by those engaged in ecumenism that for Church union a measure of doctrinal accord is a prerequisite. There is also a second principle, which states that complete agreement on all matters of doctrine is unattainable and ought not be regarded as necessary, or may not be even desirable. Since Vatican II in Catholic life, both worship and theology, there is an added sensitivity to the fact that unity does not require uniformity. Similarly in ecumenism the ideal is perhaps best expressed as unity in diversity. In his encyclical *Ad Petri cathedram* (1959), John XXIII quoted the maxim, "In necessary things unity, in doubtful things liberty, in all things charity."[10]

Furthermore, Vatican II taught that there is a hierarchy of truths (UR 11—q.v.), but theologians are not agreed about its concrete role in ecumenical dialogue.[11] The question then arises about how much unity is needed in order to allow Churches, especially the Roman Catholic and Orthodox, to unite. At the level of ministry there is agreement between the RCC, the Orthodox, as well as Old Catholics and Anglicans, that there must be episcopacy. At the level of faith it is easy to agree that there must be unity in essentials, but there is no agreement on their specification. A specific problem for Catholics, and hence for others, is the development of doctrine (q.v.). Thus the description of the unity of East and West in the first millennium with a limited role for the successor of Peter, found in Vatican II (UR 14), seems to contrast strongly with the developed doctrine of papal primacy (q.v.) and infallibility (q.v.) of Vatican I (q.v.).

With some notable exceptions, there are too few theologians in the Catholic Church reflecting on the form that unity might take.[12] Such guidance, or reactions, as have emerged from the Vatican, do not offer very much hope for unity with a major denomination in any foreseeable future, except perhaps with the Oriental Eastern Churches.[13] At the close of the century the main energy of the ecumenical movement is not devoted to making plans for union but is focused rather on the coming together of Churches at various levels of their life and doctrine.

---

[1]M. Kinnamon, "United and Uniting Churches," DictEcumMov 1032–1036. [2]Cf. V.A. McClelland, "Corporate Reunion: A Nineteenth Century Dilemma," TS 43 (1982) 3–29. [3]K.C. Abraham, "CSI Ecclesiology: Some Issues and Challenges," JDhara 19 (1989) 249–266. [4]G. Gassmann, "Non sans difficultés: L'attitude des Luthériens à l'égard des Églises unies et des négociations d'union," Irén 55 (1982) 363–366. [5]M. Cressey, "Notable Unions— Additional Gifts: United Church and the WCC," EcuR 40 (1988) 446–457; *Survey of Church Union Negotiations* (Geneva: WCC from 1955– ). [6]*Consultation on Church Union—The Reports of the Four Meetings* (Cincinnati, 1966) 18. [7]J.T. Ford, "A Plan and a Process: The Pilgrimage of the Consultation on Church Union," Jurist 44 (1984) 247–275. [8]M. Kinnamon and T.F. Best, eds., *Called to Be One in Christ: United Churches and the Ecumenical Movement.* Faith and Order Paper 127 (Geneva: WCC, 1985). [9]See J.-M.R. Tillard, "Regard sur l'oecuménisme: où en sommes-nous?," FreibZPT 29 (1982) 252–263; J. Zizioulas, "Implications ecclésiologiques de deux types de pneumatologie," in *Communio Sanctorum.* FS J.J. von Allmen (Geneva: WCC, 1982) 141–154; R. Cantalamessa, "That They May All be One so That the World May

Believe," OneChr 27 (1991) 201–208. [10]J. Lecler, "À propos d'une maxime citée par Jean XXIII: *In necessariis unitas, in dubiis libertas, in omnibus caritas,*" RechSR 49 (1961) 549–560; 52 (1964) 432–438. [11]H. Chadwick, "'Substantial Agreement': A Problem in Ecumenism," LouvSt 16 (1991) 207–219. [12]E.g., A. Dulles, "Paths to Doctrinal Agreement: Ten Theses," TS 47 (1986) 32–47; Y. Congar, *Diversity in Communion* (Mystic, Conn.: Twenty-third, 1985); H. Fries and K. Rahner, *Unity of the Churches: An Actual Possibility* (New York: Paulist, 1985); A. Houtepen, "Towards an Ecumenical Vision of the Church," OneChr 25 (1989) 217–237; K. Rahner, "Third Church?," ThInvest 17:215-227; idem, "Is Church Union Dogmatically Possible?," ThInvest 17:197-214; Y. Tesfai, "The Church in Focus: Ecclesiology in Contemporary Ecumenical Discussion," OneChr 27 (1991) 134–143; G. Wainwright, "La confession et les confessions: vers l'unité confessionelle et confessante des chrétiens," Irén 57 (1984) 5–26. [13]See F.A. Sullivan, "Lessons We Have Learned from the Participation of Rome in Ecumenism," MilltownSt 34 (1994) 13–30.

## ECUMENISM AND THE WORLD COUNCIL OF CHURCHES

The World Council of Churches (WCC) came about in 1948 through a union of the Life and Work and the Faith and Order movements (v. ECUMENICAL MOVEMENT).[1] Its first general assembly, in which 147 Churches participated, took place in Amsterdam. The number arises from giving equal emphasis to confessional and regional principles; thus, e.g., the Church of England and the Church of Ireland (both Anglican) could be members. Only a few churches of the Christian East were represented (v. ECUMENISM, ORTHODOX). There were no Roman Catholics present, since the permission to attend as observers was not forthcoming from Rome. Nonetheless, there were Catholics associated with its participants, and praying for, its success.[2]

The "Basis" of the WCC at Amsterdam was that "The World Council of Churches is a fellowship of Churches which accept our Lord Jesus Christ as God and Savior."[3] The Amsterdam assembly passed four statements and commended them to the Churches for their serious consideration and appropriate action, a procedure which reflects the nature of the WCC. It is not a body having power or jurisdiction over any member Church. One of the more significant features of this assembly was that it faced what it called "our deepest difference," namely, the nature of the Church, and detected a division between a "Protestant" emphasis on the initiative of the Word of God and the response of faith, and a "Catholic" emphasis on the visible continuity of the Church. This distinction still has some value, though it oversimplifies a complex situation.

The second general assembly was held at Evanston, Illinois (1954), and subsequent ones were at New Delhi (1961)—the first at which there were Roman Catholic observers and the occasion when the majority of Orthodox Churches joined, Uppsala (1968), Nairobi (1978), Vancouver (1983), and Canberra (1991).

Between the general assemblies, which are attended by delegates of all the member Churches, there are meetings of the Central Committee, comprising some 100 delegates. The WCC has, besides Faith and Order, a large number of departments and sections which produce statements and documents which are published regularly. They get additional status if "adopted" or "received" by the Central Committee or the General Assembly. Some of the most important documents have appeared as "Faith and Order Papers."

From its early days there was discussion of the nature of the WCC itself, that was largely resolved at the Central Committee meeting in Toronto (1950) which produced "The Church, the Churches and the World Council of Churches." It stated: "The WCC is not and must never become a Super-Church"; its purpose is "to bring the Churches into living contact with each other"; the WCC has no ecclesiology of its own, therefore no Church is obliged to change its ecclesiology, nor "to accept a specific doctrine concerning the nature of the Church"; Churches belonging to the WCC recognize "that the membership of the Church of Christ is more inclusive than membership of their own Church body"; but this does not mean "that each Church must regard the other member Churches as Churches in the true and full sense of the word" but that they (member Churches of the WCC) recognize one another as serving the one Lord."[4] The general assembly in New Delhi confirmed this Toronto report, adding the idea that the WCC "is the Churches in continuing council." Over the years the WCC would develop several studies on conciliarity. A further clarification arose at the Faith and Order meeting at Montreal (1963): "The Council is not the Church; it is not seeking to be a Church or *the* Church," but it "offers itself as a servant of the Churches and of the Church."[5]

From 1950 there were requests, especially from the Orthodox Churches, to modify the Amsterdam "Basis" to make it Trinitarian. It was generally agreed that the Basis was not a full statement of Christian faith but said merely what held the Churches together in the WCC, providing the starting point of conversation and the foundation of collaboration. At New Delhi (1961) the Basis was emended to: "The World Council of Churches is a fellowship of Churches which confess the Lord Jesus Christ as God and Savior according to the Scriptures and therefore seek to fulfill together their common calling to the glory of the one God, Father, Son, and Spirit."[6]

As a fellowship of Churches, the WCC has no authority over any Church. Its many statements are commended to its members for their consideration. The only authority of these statements is, then, their intrinsic wisdom as perceived by, and received in, the Churches. The meetings of the Central Committee over the years have shown strong leadership to the Churches, especially in the area of racism and social issues.[7] Its support for movements of liberation in the 1970s has been controversial, leading some Churches to leave the WCC or openly criticize it to the point of publicly dissociating themselves from some programs.

Matters concerning mission are dealt with by the Department of Mission and Evangelism, which was created when the International Missionary Council (itself a child of Edinburgh 1910) joined the WCC at the New Delhi Assembly (1961).

The relationship of Geneva (WCC) and the Church of Rome (RCC) has substantially grown. The RCC did not have any part in the movements that led up to Amsterdam, Faith and Order, and Life and Work. Invitation to attend at the first two assemblies with observer status were not accepted by the RCC. The establishment of the Secretariat for Promoting Christian Unity in 1960, as well as the formal commitment of the RCC to the ecumenical movement with the Vatican II decree on Ecumenism, both led to a change in attitudes, so that since New Delhi there have been official observers at all general assemblies. Moreover, the RCC has been a full member of Faith and Order since 1968.

In the period immediately after Vatican II, there were important developments as Rome and Geneva drew closer. Collaboration in the Unity Week of Prayer began in 1966 (v. ECUMENISM, SPIRITUALITY).[8] In 1965 a Joint Working Group (JWG) was set up between the RCC and the WCC. This produced a number of significant reports,[9] in particular a common rejection of proselytism (q.v.).[10] But a three-year study by the JWG led to the conclusion that the RCC would not apply for membership of the WCC in the near future.[11] Moreover, three areas of collaboration between the RCC and the WCC ceased after some initial promise: Christian Medical Commission, Women's Ecumenical Liaison Group, and the Joint Committee on Society, Development, and Peace (SODEPAX). In 1971–1972 the JWG made an important survey of the Week of Prayer for Christian Unity.[12] After 1975 the JWG turned its attention more to local ecumenism, mission, and social issues, though theological study has been ongoing.[13]

The initial reaction of Eastern Christianity to the WCC was caution; it appeared too Western and Protestant. But the Toronto Statement removed obstacles and paved the way for full participation. Since 1961 the contribution of the Orthodox members to the WCC has been very significant: they shared their doctrines, especially Trinitarian ones, with Faith and Order; they gave their particular input into the Life and Work activities of the WCC; they highlighted the role and meaning of worship, especially of the Eucharist; they expressed mystical and ascetic concepts from the living tradition of the faithful; they contributed to the ongoing debate on the unity of the Church as it is understood theologically and historically (v. ECUMENISM, ORTHODOX).[14]

The WCC continues to evolve both in its self-understanding and in its activities.[15] Canberra (1991) saw the assembly of representatives of 318 Churches. It may well be the last of the series of General Assemblies in that format. The WCC will have to seek new ways; it may have confused tolerance and the much richer notion of communion (q.v.).[16]

Geneva remains with Rome one of the two foci of an ecumenical movement perhaps best seen not as a circle but an ellipse. The WCC remains committed to a view of ecumenism that is not restricted to doctrinal issues; it maintains its heritage from both Life and Work and Faith and Order.[17] It needs perhaps to focus more sharply on the theological and practical issues concerning Church unity (v. ECUMENISM, UNION).

[1]W.A. Visser 't Hooft, "The Genesis of the World Council of Churches" in HistEcumMov 1:697–724; idem, The Genesis and Formation of the World Council of Churches (Geneva: WCC, 1982). [2]Y. Congar, Dialogue Between Christians (London: Chapman, 1966) 36–38; "Some Roman Catholic Voices about the First Assembly," EcuR 1 (1948) 202–212. [3]Visser 't Hooft, art. cit. (n. 1) 705. [4]EcuR 3 (1950–1951) 47–53; V. Borovoy, "The Ecclesiastical Significance of the WCC: The Legacy and Promise of Toronto," EcuR 40 (1988) 504–518; T.F. Stransky, "A Basis Beyond the Basis: Roman Catholic/World Council of Churches Collaboration," EcuR 37 (1985) 213–222; W.A. Visser 't Hooft, "The Super-Church and the Ecumenical Movement," EcuR 10 (1957–1958) 365–385. [5]H. Krüger, HistEcumMov 2:29-30. [6]Ibid., 33–36; K. Raiser, "Confessing the Lord Jesus Christ as God and Savior," EcuR 37 (1985) 182–188; W. Theurer, Die trinitarische Basis des Ökumenischen Rates der Kirchen (Bergen-Enkheim bei Frankfurt/Main: Kaffke, 1967); W.A. Visser 't Hooft, "The Basis: its History and Significance," EcuR 37 (1985) 170–174; L. Newbigen, "A Fellowship of Churches," EcuR 37 (1985) 175–181. [7]J. Ellul, "Some Reflections on the Ecumenical Movement," EcuR 40 (1988) 382–390. [8]L. Vischer, HistEcumMov 2:311–352; see A. Houtepen, "Towards Conciliar Collaboration: The WCC and the Roman Catholic Communion of Churches," EcuR 40 (1988) 473–487; W.A. Visser 't Hooft, "WCC-Roman Catholic Relations: Some Personal Reflections," EcuR 37 (1985) 336–344. [9]1) EcuR 18 (1966) 243–252; 2) EcuR 19 (1967) 461–469; 3) EcuR 23 (1971) 44–69; 4) Breaking Barriers: Nairobi 1975 (London: SPCK—Grand Rapids: Eerdmans, 1976) 271–282; 5) EcuR 35 (1983) 198–218; 6) OneChr 27 (1991) 246–293. See W. Bildstein, "Protestant-Catholic Engagement: The Case of the Joint Working Group," EcuR 42 (1990) 24–34; K. Raiser, "Beyond Collaboration: Perspectives on the Work of the Joint Working Group Between the Roman Catholic Church and the World Council of Churches 1972–1982," EcuR 35 (1983) 179–194; T. Sabev, "The Joint Working Group: Twenty-five years in Service of Unity," EcuR 42 (1990) 17–23; L. Vischer, "The Activities of the Joint Working Group between the Roman Catholic Church and the World Council of Churches 1965–1969," EcuR 22 (1970) 36–69. [10]EcuR 23 (1971) 9–20. [11]Breaking Barriers (n. 9) 275; see Study Document EcuR 24 (1982) 247–288; G. Bavaud, "L'Église catholique pourait-elle entrer au Conseil oecuménique?," NVet 15 (1990) 99–111 = TDig 38 (1991) 9–14; N. Nissiotis, "Towards a New Ecumenical Era," EcuR 37 (1985) 326–335; Visser 't Hooft (n. 8). [12]OneChr 9

(1973) 84–102.  [13]Raiser (n. 9) 184–187.  [14]"Declaration of the Ecumenical Patriarch on the Occasion of the Twenty-fifth Anniversary of the World Council of Churches," EcuR 25 (1973) 475–481; G. Tsetsis, "The Meaning of the Orthodox Presence," EcuR 40 (1988) 440–445; Archb. Iakovos, "The Contribution of Eastern Orthodoxy to the Ecumenical Movement," EcuR 21 (1959) 394–404; I. Sviridov, "25 Years of the Russian Orthodox Church in WCC Membership," EcuR 39 (1987) 347–351.  [15]A. Keshishian, "Towards a Self-understanding of the WCC," EcuR 43 (1991) 11–21; L.S. Mudge, "The World Council at the Crossroads," EcuR 43 (1991) 79–85.  [16]J.-M.R. Tillard, "L'Esprit Saint était-il à Canberra?," Irén 64 (1991) 163–204. On Canberra see also M. Kinnamon, ed., *Signs of the Spirit: Official Report, Seventh Assembly, Canberra, Australia 7–20 February 1991* (Geneva: WCC—Grand Rapids: Eerdmans, 1991); EcuR 43 (1991) 161–261; Istina 36 (1991) 363–378; ÖkRu 40 (1991) 245–400; TS 52 (1991) 607–635.  [17]J.S. Conway, "Images of the WCC," EcuR 36 (1984) 391–403; J. Deschner, "Amsterdam's Vision of Church Unity Today," EcuR 40 (1988) 349–358; C. Scouteris, "The Ecclesiastical Significance of the WCC: The Fusion of Doctrine and Life," EcuR 40 (1988) 519–527.

## EDUCATION

From the beginning the Church has been concerned with education. There are other articles on education and theology (v. MAGISTERIUM, THEOLOGIANS); other aspects are covered here. In the early centuries Christians used the secular schools for basic education: *ludus litterarius* to learn to read, write, and count; *grammmaticus,* which studied the ancient classics; rhetoric was studied from about the age of eighteen.

Schools of catechesis soon arose, with such illustrious teachers as Justin (q.v.), Origen (q.v.), Ephrem (q.v.). These schools often taught scientific subjects and also philosophy.[1] From the 4th century education was provided for some children at the monasteries, but it is hard to know how organized or extensive such schooling was before the 6th century. From the Middle Ages schools were found associated with cathedrals. From that time, too, religious began to be involved in education in some places. After the Reformation we have the establishment of religious institutes whose primary apostolate was teaching, a trend very marked in the 19th century.

From this century. too, we have the growth of secular schools, in which there may not have been place for religious education. The Church was always eager to ensure the Christian education of children, and tried for example through concordats (q.v.) to ensure freedom of, or provision for, Catholic education.

Vatican II produced a Declaration on Christian Education, *Gravissimum educationis* (GE). Declarations of this council were addressed not only to the Church but to the world, seeking to explain the Church's position. It is not the finest of the council's documents. The third session (1964), when it was debated, was dominated by other concerns—religious freedom (q.v.), collegiality (q.v.), ecumenism (q.v.). It

labors under another disadvantage, as do all subsequent Vatican documents on education: the difference of culture, of socio-economic conditions, of traditions, all lead to great diversity in education, so that the council and other documents have to remain at the level of principles and cannot descend to practical particularities. For the same reason bibliographies on education must be formulated according to country or region, and have a unity arising from dealing with one level or aspect of education.

Matters concerning education appear in several documents of the council: the right to education; the duty incumbent on various people to ensure proper education; forms of Christian education; the nature of social and political education (GS 48–52, 69, 87, 89; AG 12; CD 15, 35; AA 30; DH 3, 8; PC 10; OT 11). The declaration alone does not give, therefore, a full picture of the council's teaching on education.[2]

The preface to GE places education within the mandate to announce the mystery of salvation to all, and to renew all things in Christ. It then asserts education as a universal right (GE 1), before going on to give a definition of Christian education: "This indeed aims not only at the maturity of the human person . . . but has this objective principally in view: that, while the baptized are being introduced gradually to the knowledge of the mystery of salvation, they may daily become conscious of the gift of faith . . . that they may learn to adore God the Father in spirit and truth (see John 4:23) . . . and may be formed to lead their own lives according to the new person in true righteousness and holiness (Eph 4:22-24); that thus they may attain to mature adulthood, according to the measure of the stature of the fullness of Christ (see Eph 4:13), and that they exert themselves for the increase of the mystical body" (GE 2).

The declaration throughout focuses on persons and on the Christian vision of their goal in the Church, in the world, and for eternity. There is constant reference to the right and duty of education. The center of the document is not the school as such but, more widely, education. It gives a key position to the family (GE 4), and it is only in arts. 5–7 that the school is treated, and the Catholic school in arts. 8–12. The school's aim is specified: "While it improves the intellectual faculties with assiduous care, it develops the capacity for judging correctly, introduces pupils to the cultural heritage acquired by previous generations, promotes a sense of values, and prepares for professional life" (GE 5). The role for education in the area of faith is greater in the Catholic school (GE 8–12). The declaration deals with higher education and universities, particularly Catholic ones (GE 10–11), before concluding with the topic of cooperation between educational establishments (GE 12).

In the years after the council education suffered severely through the economic recessions which began in the 1970s. The situation varied from country to country. In the U.S. the support of the Catholic parochial schools became ever more burdensome, and their identity has been explored. In some countries basic literacy is still a major problem. The growth in population causes serious difficulties elsewhere. In Latin America at Puebla[3] education was studied within the context of the needs of the poor, the necessity of developing vibrant Christians who will be committed to the betterment of society as well as to the needs of the Church.

The post-Vatican II period saw three significant documents from the Holy See. In 1977, the Sacred Congregation for Christian Education gave norms about Catholic schools.[4] Five years later it addressed the question of lay Catholics in schools. By then Catholic schools were being staffed by an ever-diminishing number of priests, religious brothers, and sisters; many lay Catholics taught in secular schools. The document seeks the positive opportunities that this new challenge affords and sets out guidelines.[5] As situations continued to change, the Congregation published in 1988 another document on the Catholic school, this time with a focus on its religious dimension.[6] In 1990 John Paul II issued an apostolic constitution on Catholic Universities.[7] The document covers institutions which vary widely from country to country, and it is of interest also to Catholics involved in college ("third level") education, even when their institute does not fall under the category of "Catholic university/faculty."

The *Code of Canon Law* (CIC 793–821) deals with Catholic education by symbolically beginning its first canon, as J.A. Coriden notes, with the word "parents," and then proceeding to indicate their rights and duties.[8] The tone throughout reflects Vatican II and post-conciliar documents on the wholeness of the person being educated: spiritual, intellectual, social, moral, and physical. There follow specific norms about the role of the bishop. The section ends with some canons on Catholic universities and other institutes of higher learning (CIC 807–814)[9] and with a chapter on ecclesiastical universities and faculties (CIC 815–821).[10] The new law for the Eastern Churches has its own discipline on education (CSEO 627–650) which may be found under the title Ecclesiastical Magisterium.

One must consider the question of catechetics (q.v.) for a fuller understanding of the Church's concern for education. Its position on education is always changing with constant adherence, however, to basic principles.

[1]S. Pricoco, "School," EncycEarCh 2:759-762.  [2]M. Léna, "L'éducation à la lumière du Concile Vatican II," NRT 109 (1997) 564–586; F. Guerella, "A vent'anni dalla dichiarazione conciliare *Gravissimum educationis*," RasT 27 (1986) 338–351.  [3]*Puebla: Evangelization at Present and in the Future of Latin America—Conclusions* (Washington, D.C.: National Conference of Catholic Bishops—Slough: St. Paul, 1980) nn. 1012–1050.  [4]*Malgré les déclarations* (24 June 1977)—DocCath 74 (1977) 705–716/Flannery 2:606-629.  [5]*Les laïcs catholiques* (15 Oct. 1982)—DocCath 79 (1982) 979–991/ Flannery 2:630-661; J. Marmion, "Catholic Traditions in Education," CleR 71 (1986) 260–264, 294–299, 329–333.  [6]*The Religious Dimension of Education in a Catholic School* (Dublin: Veritas— Vatican, 1988); J. Malone, "The Religious Dimension of Catholic Education," ChicSt 28 (1989) 264–276; Seminarium 28 (1988/2). [7]*Ex corde Ecclesiae*—AAS 82 (1990) 1475–1509/CathIntern 1 (1990) 202–217.  [8]J.A. Coriden in Coriden, CIC 564–578; F.G. Morrissey, "The Rights of Parents in the Education of their Children (Canons 796–806)," StCan 23 (1989) 429–444.  [9]P. Valdrini, "Les universités catholiques: exercise d'un droit et contrôle de son exercise (canons 807–814)," StCan 23 (1989) 445–458.  [10]F.J. Urrutia, "Ecclesiastical Universities and Faculties," StCan 23 (1989) 459–469.

# EGERIA

The discovery in 1884 of the *Itinerarium/Peregrinatio ad loca sancta,* the travelogue of Egeria (earlier called Aetheria or Sylvia) has raised questions still unresolved.[1] There is now some general agreement on the name of the author and on the date of her pilgrimage from Galicia (NW Spain—though Gaul was previously suggested) to Egypt, Sinai, Palestine, and Constantinople (381–384). She was apparently some kind of religious, and her work is in the form of letters to her "sisters." Her *latina vulgaris* with its mixture of classicisms and Grecisms fascinates philologists.

The holy places of the OT and NT were clearly known in her time, and they were the sites of churches and liturgical ceremonies. Her testimony about the liturgy she observed at Jerusalem (ch. 24 to incomplete end at ch. 49) is of exceptional interest.[2] The Church there had monks and virgins (q.v.) who had some specific liturgical roles; she also distinguishes those liturgical offices attended by a great crowd of laity from those in which only a few lay people were present. The offices consist of psalms and prayers, as well as readings. Catechumens (q.v.) attended some of them. There were ceremonies for catechumens that are similar to ones found elsewhere (ch. 46).

She found monks in each place, usually as hermits, and often with a priest who celebrated the liturgy. She saw women in monastic cells (chs. 23, 28). The many bishops she met in her travels were frequently former monks. Egeria was continually impressed with the holiness of monks and bishops; the Churches she described give no evidence of the laxity which followed the age of persecutions. The Church with a committed laity revolved around the liturgy, and radically drew life from the Scriptures.

[1]*Egeria: Diary of a Pilgrimage.* FC 38 (New York—Ramsey: 1970)/SC 21; 296/CCL 175; bibliog. Patrology 4:561-562; C. Baraut, HispSac 7 (1954) 203–215; M. Starowieyski, AugR 19 (1979) 297–318. See P. Devos, "Egeriana III," AnBoll 109 (1991) 363–381; A. Linage Conde, "El monacato femenino entre la

clausura y peregrinación en torno a Egeria," *Studia monastica* 34 (1992) 29–40.  [2]M. Augé, "La asamblea litúrgica en la 'Itinerarium Egeriae'," EcOr 7 (1990) 43–60.

## EPHESUS, Council of (431)

After the councils of Nicaea (q.v.) and Constantinople I (q.v.) the Christological issue was mainly how to express the integrity of the divine and the human in the Incarnate Son. The Johannine Christology of Alexandria saw the mystery in terms of the Word *(logos)* and the flesh *(sarx)*. The Antiochean school looked to the model of Word and man *(logos anthropos)*. The first ran the danger of fusing the two elements; the second was open to an equivalent assertion of two Christs. Nestorius (381–ca. 451), bishop of Constantinople from 428, saw the Incarnation in terms of redemption. He sought a median position in statements about Mary made for a Christological purpose: he proposed *Christotokos* (Christ-bearer) instead of either *Theotokos* (God-bearer) or *anthrôpotokos* (man-bearer). He was thus led in the direction of seeing Christ as two persons. Cyril, bishop of Alexandria from 412, wrote a circular letter against Nestorius and then a second letter to him in 430. The same year, Nestorius was condemned by a Roman synod, and at Alexandria.

The Emperor Theodosius II called a council to meet at Ephesus on Pentecost.[1] Cyril began the council a fortnight later without waiting either for the Roman delegates or for the Nestorian party. This Cyrillian council, which was later accepted as an ecumenical one, acted as follows:[2] it decided that Cyril's second letter to Nestorius and not the latter's reply was in conformity with Nicaea; it heard Cyril's third letter to Nestorius containing twelve anathemas, but it is doubtful whether the council formally approved them in the sense that the contradictory propositions would be dogmas of faith;[3] it confirmed the Nicene creed and forbade the production of new creeds (v. FILIOQUE); it formulated a definition against the Messalians; it produced a circular letter, informing clergy and laity about the condemnation of John of Antioch; it decreed the autonomy of the Church of Cyprus; it produced six canons against those associated with Nestorius and some other heretics.

The late arriving John of Antioch and the Eastern bishops set up an alternative council and attempted to excommunicate Cyril. The Roman legates joined the Cyrillian council, whose acts were approved by Sixtus III in 432. It would be 433 before Cyril and John of Antioch were reconciled; the latter made a profession of faith accepted by the former. About 436 Nestorius was sent into exile. The Christological work of Ephesus had to be complemented by Chalcedon (q.v.) in 451.

[1]K. Baus, in Jedin-Dolan 2:103-107; P.-T. Camelot, *Éphèse et Chalcédoine.* Histoire des conciles 2 (Paris: Ed. l'Orante, 1962); L.D.
Davis, Councils, 134–169; R. Deuresse, "Les actes du concile d'Éphèse," RSPT 18 (1929) 233–242, 408–431; W. de Vries, *Orient et occident: Les structures ecclésiales vues dans l'histoire des sept premiers conciles oecuméniques* (Paris: Cerf, 1974) 61–100; A.J. Festugière, ed., *Éphèse et Chalcédoine, Actes des conciles* (Paris: Beauchesne, 1982); I. Ortiz de Urbina, "Il dogma di Efeso," RÉByz 11 (1953) 233–240; L. Perrone in Alberigo, Concili 71–85; T. Sagi-Bunic, "Documentatio doctrinalis Ephesino-Chalcedonensis," Laur 3 (1963) 499–514.  [2]Tanner 1:40-74; DS 250–266/ND 604–606.  [3]See J. Lebon, "Autour de la définition de foi au Concile d'Éphèse," ETL 8 (1931) 393–412 at 402; A. de Halleux, "Les douze chapitres cyrilliens au concile d'Éphèse (430–433)," RTLv 23 (1992) 425–458.

## EPHREM OF SYRIA, St. (ca 306–373)

Born at Nisibis, Mesopotamia, about 306 C.E., Ephrem was baptized about 324 and became a deacon.[1] He was later head of a cathedral catechetical school. After Nisibis was captured by the Persians (361) he retired to become something of a monk or hermit near Edessa, though he continued teaching and charitable work. He wrote extensive commentaries on the Scriptures, earlier in the style of Jewish midrash, and later in the Antioch fashion. His hymns have an enormous influence on Eastern liturgy. He was proclaimed Doctor of the Church (q.v.) in 1920.

Ephrem did not write a specific treatise on the Church, but he often alludes to it under an enormous variety of symbols drawn from Scripture, language, nature, and the sacraments. The Church is the bride and mother, the ark, the Body, Eucharist, vineyard, temple, rock; it is filled with the warming presence of the Spirit. The Church is on pilgrimage, which he called way or voyage, to the eternal kingdom.[2] The Church is in a sense the sacramental restoration of paradise. Virginity transforms the Church into a new paradise.[3] A strong sense of eschatology allows him to see the Church both as a re-creation of paradise and already partly in triumph.[4] His kind of patristic ecclesiology, mostly in verse, shows great richness and warmth.

His poetic style can be appreciated in a volume of the "Classics of Western Spirituality" series, which does not, however, contain very much on ecclesiology.[5] From his other works we know that his Church was episcopal, with strong apostolic roots; it had a vibrant sacramental life; martyrs were venerated and commemorated. Ephrem's writings show him writing against three foes of the Church: Jewish proselytism, Gnostic sects, and Arians.

[1]F. Rilliet, "Ephrem the Syrian," EncycEarCh 1:276-277.  [2]R. Murray, *Symbols of Church and Kingdom: A Study in the Syriac Tradition* (Cambridge: UP, 1975); idem, "St. Ephrem the Syrian on Church Unity," EChQ 15 (1963) 164–176.  [3]A. de Halleux, "Saint Éphrem le Syrien," RTLv 14 (1983) 328–355 at 353–354.  [4]*Hymns on Paradise* 2:13; 6:7, 9, 10; 11:2—Trans. S. Brock (Crestwood, N.Y.: St. Vladimir's Seminary Press, 1990) 89, 111–112, 154.  [5]K.E. McVey, trans., *Ephrem the Syrian: Hymns* (New York—Mahwah: Paulist, 1989).

# EPICLÊSIS

The Greek word *epiklêsis* originally meant invocation, and in time came to mean prayer in general. In recent decades there is a tendency to restrict its use to an invocation to the Father to send the Holy Spirit or—rarely—as a prayer directly to the Holy Spirit. Its most frequent use concerns the Eucharist, in which it is a prayer for the Holy Spirit to change the bread and wine into the Body and Blood of Christ, or a prayer that those assembled be drawn into communion, unity, and love.[1] Though Eucharistic Prayer I has no *epiclêsis* (except perhaps for the prayer *Quam oblationem,* "Look with favor . . ."), the new Eucharistic Prayers after Vatican II all have such an invocation. There are also prayers of *epiclêsis* in the various sacraments: in the blessing of the water at baptism and during the rites of confirmation and ordination. Many revised service books of Anglican or Protestant Churches also have prayers of *epiclêsis.*[2] A remarkable insight about both *epiclêsis* and ecclesiology is to be found in Y. Congar, who stated: "Everywhere that there should be an intervention of the Holy Spirit, his coming must be implored. . . . Under one form or another an *epiclêsis* is necessary for the Spirit's concelebration with the Church, giving her operations a divine approbation."[3]

[1]J. Lamberts, "Eucharistie et Esprit Saint," QLtg 326 (1986) 33-52 = TDig 34 (1987) 51-55.    [2]OxDCC 463.    [3]*Le concile et les conciles* (Paris, 1960) 313-314; cf. P.P. O'Leary, *The Triune Church: A Study in the Ecclesiology of A.S. Xomjakov* (Dublin: Dominican—Freiburg Switz.: UP, 1982) 133-139 with 164-182.

# ESCHATOLOGY

Eschatology (Greek *eschatos* = last, and *logos* = discourse) pertains to the last things. Traditionally these were four: death, judgment, hell, heaven. Purgatory (q.v.) is also considered in this context. There has been from the mid-20th century some developments in the understanding and presentation of these truths. The theology of death has been influenced by personalist and other philosophies.[1] The relationship between judgment after death and the parousia (Greek = presence/arrival) has been explored.[2] Though the existence of hell is retained as an integral part of the Christian message, some theologians are now taking a much more optimistic position about many people actually ending up there.[3] There has been a renewed interest in Christian hope, especially since J. Moltmann developed its implications for the Church and society.[4]

But these issues mainly concern the last things for the individual. They pertain to issues that at present can be freely discussed by theologians, provided that revealed matters are not impugned. They are, moreover, complicated issues, as the scriptural texts are in very symbolic language and require careful hermeneu-tics to discern.[5] Any detailed account of individual eschatology is outside the scope of this work, which focuses on ecclesiology.

The eschatological dimension of the Church has been present from the beginning (v. JERUSALEM). The promise that the gates of Hades will not prevail against the Church (Matt 16:18) already looks to the Church as having an indefinite future. The intermingling of the Church with the symbol of the kingdom (q.v.) also points to a future identity after the final decisive triumph of Christ (1 Cor 14:24-28). The doctrine of the communion of saints (q.v.) is an affirmation, too, of an other-worldly existence of the Church, one not yet consummated. The threefold division of the Church as militant, suffering, and triumphant is a similar indication.

But classical works on ecclesiology did not tend to include eschatology, which was a separate tract in theology, *De novissimis,* the Last Things. In the 20th century questions of eschatology came into ecclesiology through the controversy about the position of Jesus vis-à-vis the kingdom which he preached: Did he expect its imminent realization? At the same time theologians returned to questions about the parousia and the meaning for the believer of the eventual triumph of Christ.

At Vatican II the idea of a chapter on eschatology in the Constitution on the Church—absent in the first draft—seems to have come from John XXIII, who was concerned about the place of the saints. The titles of the various drafts show a rapid development in the thinking of the Doctrinal Commission: "The Relation of the Pilgrim Church with the Church in Triumph" (Feb. 1964); "The Consummation of Holiness in the Glory of the Saints" (March 1964); the final title, "The Eschatological Character of the Pilgrim Church and Its Union with the Heavenly Church" (July 1964). In the discussion of the council (15–16 Sept. 1964) three points were emphasized: a clearer statement on the role of the Spirit; the place of the Eucharist in eschatology; the collective, historical, and cosmic aspects of the Christian vocation.[6] At a late stage a reference to our having only one, single terrestrial life (*unico . . . cursu*—Heb 9:27) was added (LG 48) to exclude reincarnation theories.[7]

In its four articles, LG chapter 7[8] deals with issues of individual eschatology, but it is more concerned with the ecclesial aspect, with the Church on pilgrimage to its eternal home. It stresses that the final age has dawned and that the Church already celebrates in liturgy the glory that lies ahead (LG 48, 50). It develops, especially by means of the parables of Jesus, the attitudes of watching, hope, and love that ought to characterize the pilgrim Church (LG 48). It exposes the doctrine of the three stages of the one Church: triumphant, being purified, still struggling on earth (LG 49). Two articles deal with the saints (q.v.): the tradition of venerating them is vindicated (LG 50); the marks of true devotion are avoidance of abuses and an emphasis on the imitation of the saints. Throughout the chapter there is constant reference to the reality of the communion of saints. In the Constitution eschatology is at once realized, for the future age is already breaking out through the Spirit, and still to be achieved.[9]

In the post-conciliar period the renewed liturgy is notable for the eschatological note which is sounded in all the revised rites.[10] The International Theological Commission gave some attention to the eschatological character of the Church in 1984.[11] It noted that it had not aroused much interest in commentators on the council, but observed that it was integral to an understanding of chapter 2 on the People of God (LG 9; cf. 48 and GS 40). The Commission stressed the eschatological finality of the Church which, however, "does not lead to any downplaying of temporal responsibility."

The eschatological dimension needs stressing for those whose focus is strongly horizontal, as in liberation theology (q.v.); but it cannot be so exclusively accented that earthly commitment (GS 43) or working in and for the renewal of the Church is weakened (LG 8). At the same time, the realization that the eschaton, or kingdom, is already present and at work in the Church (LG 3) is a corrective for undue pessimism about the Church.

---

[1]L. Boras, *The Theology of Death* (New York, 1965); K. Rahner, *On the Theology of Death.* QDisput 2 (Herder: Freiburg—London: Burns & Oates, 1961). [2]S. Cong. Doctrine of the Faith, *Recentiores episcoporum synodi,* "Life after Death"—AAS 71 (1979) 939–943/Flannery 2:500-504; cf. K. Rahner, "The Intermediate State," ThInvest 17 (1981) 114–124; idem, "The Life of the Dead," ThInvest 4:347-354. [3]H.U. von Balthasar, *Dare We Hope "That All Men Be Saved"?* (San Francisco: Ignatius, 1988); J.R. Sachs, "Current Eschatology: Universal Salvation and the Problem of Hell," TS 52 (1991) 227–254. [4]*The Theology of Hope* (New York, 1967); see M. Hellwig, *What Are They Saying about Death and Hope?* (New York: Paulist, 1978); G.W. McRae, "Eschatology," ChicSt 17 (1978) 59–74. [5]K. Rahner, "The Hermeneutics of Eschatological Assertions," ThInvest 4:327-346; cf. Z. Hayes, "Visions of a Future: Symbols of Heaven and Hell," ChicSt 24 (1985) 145–165; Conc 41 (1969/1:5). [6]ActaSyn 3/5:59, 63. [7]ActsSyn3/8:150. [8]P. Molinari, "Caractère eschatologique de l'Église pérégrinante et ses rapports avec l'Église céleste," in Baraúna-Congar, L'Église 2:1193-1216. [9]G. Kretscham, "The Eschatological Tension in the Life of the Church Today," Conc 146 (1981) 36–41; H.-E. Mertens, "An Ecclesiology in Eschatological Perspective," LouvSt 7 (1978–1979) 55–60; K. Rahner, "Immanent and Transcendent Consummation of the World," ThInvest 10:273-289; A.C. Thiselton, "Realized Eschatology at Corinth," NTS 24 (1978) 510–526. [10]W. Rordorf, "Liturgie et eschatologie," AugR 18 (1978) 153–162. [11]"Select Themes of Eschatology" (1984) X:1, ITC 300–301; see Catechism 988–1060 on all aspects of eschatology.

## EUCHARIST AND THE CHURCH

The years since World War II have seen a vast amount of theological reflection on the Eucharist.[1] Through the liturgical movement (v. LITURGY) in the various Churches ancient texts have been studied and new ones composed.[2] Important theological studies continue to appear.[3] The Eucharist is the focus of many ecumenical dialogues and conversations.[4] The 1982 Faith and Order "Lima" document, though deficient in ways from a Catholic viewpoint, has, nonetheless, a remarkable statement about the total understanding of the Eucharist: thanksgiving to the Father; memorial *(anamnêsis)* of Christ, invocation of the Spirit; communion of the faithful; meal of the kingdom.[5]

There are innumerable liturgical and pastoral studies, both books and articles, dealing with the Eucharist and its celebration. In the Catholic Church there have been many decrees and instructions about the Eucharist since Vatican II.[6] The fourteen articles in *The New Dictionary of Sacramental Worship*[7] and in other recent reference works[8] provide a summary of current developments. The matter treated here is confined to the relation of Eucharist and Church, a patristic and medieval theme which is arousing much attention in contemporary ecclesiology.

In the NT Eucharist and Church are already closely linked. The Last Supper is clearly foundational for the Church, which immediately after Pentecost had as one of its key distinguishing marks the breaking of bread (Acts 2:42). The tradition about the Lord's Supper is one of the main catechetical formulae given to Paul at his conversion (1 Cor 11:23-25). Paul then reflects on the implications of the Eucharist for the Corinthian community (1 Cor 10:16-21; 11:17-34).[9]

In the Early Church it would seem that the one who presided over the Church in a place also presided over the Eucharist (v. PRIESTHOOD).[10] In the *Didachê* (q.v.), the letters of Ignatius of Antioch (q.v.), St. Justin (q.v.), the *Apostolic Tradition* (q.v.), and in the *Apostolic Constitutions* (q.v.) the Eucharist has a central position in the life of the Churches.[11] Membership of the Church could be said to comprise communion and access to the Eucharist.[12]

In the patristic period there is a tendency in liturgies for the West to be more Christological, stressing the meeting with the Lord, and for the East to follow more a salvation history direction; these can be illustrated respectively in the first and fourth Eucharistic Prayers of the current Roman liturgy. But the ecclesial aspect is found in both West and East. In particular there is intercession for the universal Church—clearer, however, in the East (Liturgy of St. Basil) than in the West.[13]

St. Augustine in his celebrated *Sermon* 272 said, "It is your mystery that is placed on the altar. It is your mystery that you receive. To that which you are, you reply Amen."[14] The often quoted statement by Augustine, "Nor do you change me into you, as food of your flesh, but you are changed into me," does not occur originally in a Eucharistic context, but is about the Word of God.[15] In the East, St. Maximus the Confessor (q.v.) has a profound sense of both liturgy and Church. J. Zizioulas (q.v.) summarizes his teaching "in the same Spirit the very structure of the Church becomes the existential structure of each person."[16] The commentary on the liturgy, *The Church's Mystagogy*,[17] of Maximus sees the Church's Eucharistic liturgy as both reflecting heavenly realities and anticipating their final accomplishment; the Church in the Eucharistic mysteries is joined to, and similar to, the angels in their heavenly liturgy.

The medieval synthesis of St. Thomas Aquinas (q.v.) is both in harmony with, and a development of, patristic intuitions.[18] In a dense article he states that the sacraments are a triple sign: commemorative of what has taken place, namely, the passion of Christ; demonstrative of what is effected in us by the passion of Christ, namely, grace; prognostic, that is, the announcing of future glory.[19] His treatment of the structure of the Mass shows that it commemorates the passion, touches those present and involves those already in glory.[20] In an earlier article he uses the triple structure of the sacrament: the sacrament alone *(sacramentum tantum)* is the bread and wine; the intermediate reality *(res et sacramentum)* is the body and blood of Christ; the ultimate reality *(res tantum)* is the unity of the mystical body;[21] indeed this final effect of the sacrament makes it necessary for salvation, at least *in voto,* viz., a person to be saved must in some way have the intention of receiving the sacrament and be thus incorporated into the unity of the Church.[22] All of the sacraments have their finality in the Eucharist,[23] which contains the entire mystery of our salvation.[24] Though Aquinas accepts that an effect of the sacrament is individual strengthening through spiritual food,[25] the more profound significance of communion is the unity of the Church,[26] which in the Eucharist is by charity.[27] The Eucharist as offered, and as representing the passion of Christ, is a sacrifice;[28] it is preeminently a sacrifice,[29] offered to God,[30] a sacrifice that is of benefit to the Church,[31] and is joined to the heavenly Church.[32]

After St. Thomas the vision of the Eucharist significantly narrowed to a predominantly individual one. At the Council of Florence the decree *Pro Armenis* is largely based on St. Thomas' little work *On the Articles of Faith and the Sacraments*. It is still stated that the effect of the sacrament is "the union of the Christian people to Christ,"[33] reflecting St. Thomas' statement there that the ultimate reality *(res)* of the sacrament is "the unity of the mystical Body."[34]

At Trent only disputed matters were normally treated and the council was anxious to allow the pluralism of the theological schools to persist. Hence the ecclesial effect of the Eucharist was not much to the fore. The 13th session refers to the Eucharist "which our Savior has left his Church precisely as a symbol of the unity and charity with which he desired all Christians to be joined together and united."[35] In the 22nd session, on the sacrifice of the Mass, it taught that the Lord left "his beloved Spouse the Church a visible sacrifice," which was himself, "to be offered by the Church through her priests."[36] It reinforces the decree of Florence that water is to be added to the wine, which signifies "the union of Christ with his faithful people."[37]

But from St. Thomas until the 19th century, though it was clear that the Eucharist as sacrament and sacrifice was indeed a high point of the Church's life, there was little attempt to see it as encompassing the whole mystery of salvation, and hence of the Church. This rediscovery is largely the work of N. Afanas'ev (q.v.); we have from him a rich seam of "Eucharistic ecclesiology," a term which he seems to have coined.[38] His key insight is that "where there is a Eucharistic assembly, there Christ abides, and there is the Church of God in Christ."[39] The intuition of pioneers need not be fully worked out; Afanas'ev has been criticized for such an emphasis on the local community that other ecclesial factors such as communion with other Churches, hierarchy, and the position of the universal Church are not adequately secured.

J. Zizioulas (q.v.)[40] develops the insight of Afanas'ev, which he commends as an authentically Orthodox principle. He brings to Eucharistic ecclesiology the notion of the corporate Christ, Christ never separated from the Church. Rather than a commemoration of the passion, the Eucharist is most fully understood in its eschatological future in which is the whole Christ. The Church is fully realized as the Body of Christ each time it celebrates the Eucharist; it ceases to have this fullness until it celebrates again; in the eschaton it will be abidingly the Body. In short "the Church constitutes the Eucharist while being constituted by it."[41]

Meanwhile in the Catholic Church Eucharistic ecclesiology was also coming to the fore. Already in 1953, in a chapter significantly entitled "The Heart of the Church," H. de Lubac had seized the insight that the Church and Eucharist stand "as cause to each other" so that "the Church makes *(fait)* the Eucharist, but the Eucharist also makes the Church."[42] Later he boldly concluded the chapter: "Christ in his Eucharist is truly the heart of the Church."[43] Since De Lubac did not hold the eschatological and corporate positions of Zizioulas, he was much better able to integrate other ecclesial themes such as Spouse (q.v.), hierarchy (q.v.), and the notes (q.v.) of the Church. But on the other hand he did not seem able to develop fully the sense of the Eucharist as bringing all of creation to God, a point characteristic of Eastern theology, or to integrate his Eucharistic ecclesiology as fully as Zizioulas.[44]

The Eucharistic theology of Vatican II is difficult to present in a synthetic way. It undoubtedly continues the tradition which emerged in the post-medieval period, of the Eucharist being a sacrament for the individual. But it also has a certain number of key statements which are susceptible of ecclesiological development.[45] A key choice was made by the council to use the category of memorial; here it follows O. Casel (q.v.) and many others (see SC 47, 102, 106 . . . ). The unique sacrifice of the Lord is enacted until he comes again (see LG 28); Word and sacrament are inextricably linked (SC 7). The Holy Spirit gathers the people around the Eucharist (CD 11), making alive and life-giving the flesh of the Lord (PO 5); the pneumatology of SC is, however, weak (three references only in SC 5–6). The council develops a strong sense of the local (q.v.) or particular (q.v.) Church around the Eucharist (LG 26; CD 11); the liturgy is not the action of the priest alone but of the whole assembly (SC 26). The Eucharist celebrated by the bishop is a principal manifestation of the Church (SC 41); "the Eucharistic sacrifice is the source and culmination of the whole Christian life" (LG 11; cf. PO 2); "the most holy Eucharist holds within itself the whole spiritual treasure of the Church" (PO 5); yet the liturgy which announces the transfiguration of all things (GS 38) does not exhaust the entire activity of the Church (SC 9).

Since the council there has been extensive writing on the relationship of Church and Eucharist.[46] A full Eucharistic ecclesiology will have to include the idea of the Eucharist as sacrifice[47] and sacrament, a sacred meal.[48] The relation of the invisible/visible, divine/human, charismatic/institutional (cf. LG 8) will have to be integrated into a Trinitarian and pneumatological vision of the Church.[49] There will have to be an emphasis on the community actually celebrating, one, however, open to the wider *catholica*.[50] The idea of communion (q.v.) will have to be quite central;[51] likewise conciliarity.[52] Such an ecclesiology will have to include the cosmic dimension of the Eucharist found in the East and in Teilhard de Chardin.[53] It needs also to see the Eucharist in terms of confession of faith and service,[54] viz., in the liturgy of life after the liturgy in Church.[55] It will necessarily have to be done in dialogue with Eastern theology.[56]

It remains to be seen if a Eucharistic ecclesiology can be made comprehensive enough to give a unified understanding of the Church. H. de Lubac has expressed the opinion that in itself it is too narrow in not explaining structures, and that there is the need of the Church to spread throughout the world.[57] However, if the teaching of Vatican II on the common and ministerial priesthood (q.v.), along with the trilogy of priest-prophet-king were to be integrated into a Eucharistic ecclesiology, then it might prove a very rich and comprehensive one. The whole issue needs much more study and research than it has yet received.

[1]*Eucharist. International Bibliography 1975–1984* (Strasbourg: Cerdic, 1985); R. Cabié (A.G. Martimort, ed.), *The Church at Prayer: The Eucharist.* Vol. II (Collegeville: The Liturgical Press, 1986). [2]J.M. Barkley, *The Worship of the Reformed Church:* Ecumenical Studies in Worship 15 (London: Lutterworth, 1966); R.C.D. Jasper and G.J. Cuming, eds., *Prayers of the Eucharist: Early and Reformed* (New York: Pueblo, ³1987); F.C. Senn, *New Eucharistic Prayers: An Ecumenical Study of Their Development and Structure* (New York—Mahwah: Paulist, 1987). [3]E.g., C. Giraudo, *Eucaristia per la Chiesa: Prospettive teologiche sull'Eucaristia a partire dalla "lex orandi."* Aloisiana 22 (Brescia: Morcelliana—Rome: Gregorian UP, 1989)—see A. Pelti, Asp 37 (1990) 484–492; D.N. Power, *The Eucharistic Mystery: Revitalizing the Tradition* (Dublin: Gill and Macmillan—New York: Crossroad, 1992). [4]J. Reumann, *The Supper of the Lord: The New Testament, Ecumenical Dialogues, and Faith and Order on Eucharist* (Philadelphia: Fortress, 1985). [5]E.g., *Baptism, Eucharist, Ministry.* Faith and Order Paper 111 (Geneva: WCC, 1982) 10–15. [6]See DOL and the official journal *Notitiae.* [7]P.E. Fink, ed. (Collegeville: The Liturgical Press—Dublin: Gill and Macmillan, 1990) 391–462. [8]E.g., R. Moloney, "Eucharist," NDictT 342–355; idem, *The Eucharist.* Problems in Theology (London: Chapman, 1995). [9]M. Gourgues, "Eucharistie et communauté chez saint Paul et les synoptiques," EglT 13 (1982) 57–78. [10]H.-M. Legrand, "La présidence de l'Eucharistie selon la tradition ancienne," Spiritus 18 (1977) 409–431. [11]C.N. Tsirpanlis, "The Structure of the Church in the Liturgical Traditions of the First Three Centuries," PatByzR 1 (1982) 44–62. [12]H.-M. Legrand, "Communion ecclésiale et Eucharistie aux premiers siècles," AnnéeCan 25 (1981) 125–148. [13]E. Lanne, "Les anaphores eucharistiques de saint Basile et la communauté ecclésiale," Irén 55 (1982) 307–331; idem, "L'Église une dans la prière eucharistique," Irén 50 (1977) 326–344, 511–519, 555. [14]PL 38:1247-1248; O. Pasquato, "Eucaristia e Chiesa in Agostino," EphLtg 102 (1988) 46–63; C. Traets, "The Eucharist and Christian Community: Some Pauline and Augustinian Evidence," LouvSt 12 (1987) 152–171. [15]*Confessions* 7:17, 23; 7:10, 16—PL 32:744-745, 742. [16]"The Pneumatological Structure of the Church," Communio 1 (1974) 142–158 at 152. [17]*Maximus the Confessor: Selected Writings.* Classics of Western Spirituality (New York—Mahwah: Paulist, 1985) 183–225. [18]Power (n. 3) 208–240. [19]ST 3a, q.60, a.3. [20]ST 3a, q.83, a.5; cf. q.73, a.4c. [21]ST 3a, q.73, a.3; q.80, q.4; q.82, a.2 ad 3; *In 1 Cor* 11, lect. 4 (654). [22]ST 3a, q. 73, a.3; q.80, a.11; J.-M.R. Tillard, "Le *votum Eucharistiae*: L'Eucharistie dans la rencontre des chrétiens," in *Miscelanea liturgica in onore di Sua Eminenza Giacomo Lercaro* (Rome, 1967) 2:143-194. [23]ST 3a, q.65, a.3; q.73, a.3c; see F.A. Loughery, *The Eucharist: The End of all Sacraments According to St. Thomas and His Contemporaries* (Fribourg: UP, 1972). [24]ST 3a, q.83, a.4c. [25]ST 3a, q.79, a.1; q.73, a.1. [26]ST 3a, q.73, a.4; a.79, a.5c.; q.80, a.4c. [27]*In 1 Cor* 11, lect. 7 (697). [28]ST 3a, q.79, a.5c; a.7c. [29]ST 3a, q.79, a.7 ad 1; q.83, a.1. [30]ST 3a, q.82, a.10. [31]See ST 3a, q.79, a.7c; a.83, a.4 ad 3, 5–6, 9; *In 1 Cor* 11, lect. 6 (682). [32]See ST 3a, q.83, a.4 ad 9. [33]Tanner 1:546/DS 1320/ND 1509. [34]*De art. fid. et sacr.* 2. [35]Tanner 2:693/DS 1635/ND 1512. [36]Tanner 2:733/DS 1740–1741/ND 1546. [37]Tanner 2:735/DS 1748. [38]"Réflexions d'un orthodoxe sur la collégialité des évêques," Le messager orthodoxe 29–30/1–2 (1965) 5–15. [39]"Una sancta," Irén 36 (1963) 436–475. [40]"La vision eucharistique du monde et de l'homme contemporain," Contacts 19 (1967) 83–92; idem, *Being as Communion* (London: Darton, Longman & Todd, 1985); see P. McPartlan, *The Eucharist Makes the Church: Henri de Lubac and John Zizioulas in Dialogue* (Edinburgh: Clark, 1993) with Zizioulas bibliog., 316–321. [41]J.D.Zizioulas, "The Ecclesiological Presuppositions of the Holy Eucharist," Nicol 10 (1982) 333–349 at 341; see idem, "The Eucharistic Community and the Catholicity of the Church," OneChr 6 (1970) 314–337 = Istina 14 (1969) 67–88. [42]*Méditation sur l'Église*

= *The Splendor of the Church,* ch. 4 (San Francisco: Ignatius, 1986) 134 [1956 trans. New York: Sheed & Ward—p. 92]. See E. Koma, *Le mystère de l'Eucharistie et ses dimensions ecclésiales dans l'oeuvre de Lubac.* Diss. excerpt (Rome: Gregorian, 1990); B. Medina Carpentero, "Eucharistiá y comunión en la eclesiología de Henri de Lubac," Comunio (Spain) 25 (1992) 167–212. [43]Ibid., 1986:161/1956:113. [44]McPartlan (n. 40) passim, esp. 239–305. [45]A. Caprioli, "L'eucaristia al centro della comunità. Rilettura della 'Sacrosanctum concilium,'" Ambros 67 (1991) 574–584; B. Forte, *La Chiesa nell'Eucaristia: Per un'ecclesiologia eucaristica alla luce del Vaticano II* (Naples: D'Auria, 1975); J. Ratzinger, "La collégialité épiscopale: Développement théologique," in Baraúna-Congar 3:763–790; idem, "The Ecclesiology of the Second Vatican Council," in Church, *Ecumenism and Politics: New Essays in Ecclesiology* (New York: Crossroad—Slough UK: St. Paul, 1988) 3–20; *Principles of Christian Theology* (San Francisco: Ignatius, 1987) 285–298; A. Tourneux, "L'affirmation progressive du lien entre l'Église et l'Eucharistie à Vatican II," QLtg 69 (1988) 1–25; idem, "Église et Eucharistie à Vatican II," NRT 112 (1990) 338–355; idem, "Vatican II et l'Eucharistie," QLtg 71 (1990) 81–98. [46]Bibliog. D. Valentini in L. Sartori, ed., *Eucaristia e comunità locale* (Rome: EDB, 1978) 201–214; see I. Biffi, "Eucaristia e Chiesa: Espressioni sintomatiche e punti di riferimento," ScuolC 110 (1982) 517–539; Italian Bishops' *Eucaristia, comunione e comunità* (1983); W.J. Jeanrond, "The Church: Eucharistic Community," DoctLife 38 (1988) 330–337; P. McPartlan, "Eucharistic Ecclesiology," OneChr 22 (1986) 314–331; L. Martínez Sistach, "La eucaristía manifestación principal de la Iglesia," Phase 170 (1989) 105–121; P. Martuccelli, "L'eucaristia e la chiesa: Unità e santità della chiesa in prospettiva eucaristica," RasT 29 (1988) 20–36; MaisD 137 (1979); B. Sesboüé, "Y a-t-il une différence séparatrice entre les ecclésiologies catholiques et protestantes?," NRT 109 (1987) 3–30 at 9–10; J. Theisen, "Images of the Church and the Eucharist," Worship 58 (1984) 118–129; J.M.R. Tillard, "Qu'est-ce que l'Église de Dieu," PrOrChr 34 (1984) 3–20 at n. 23. [47]A. Sicari, "Eucaristia. Sacrificio di Cristo, della Chiesa, dell'umanità," Communio 14/3 (1985) 26–36. [48]T. Guzie, "The Church as a Eucharistic Community," ChicSt 22 (1983) 283–296 (weak on sacrificial aspect). [49]J. Lamberts, "Eucharistie et Esprit Saint," QLtg 67 (1986) 33–52; J.M.R. Tillard, "L'Eucharistie et le Saint-Esprit," NRT 90 (1968) 363–387; A. Ahlers, "Eucharistie und Kirche: Kirchenrechtliche Implikationen einer eucharistischen Ecclesiologie," TPQ 14 (1992) 35–40. [50]L. Leijssen, "La communauté eucharistique: communauté de personnes en action," QLtg 64 (1983) 123–144. [51]O. Treanor, *The Relationship Between Ecclesial Communion and Eucharistic Communion since Vatican II.* Diss. (Rome: Gregorian UP, 1985); M. Gesteira Garza, *La eucaristía misterio de comunión.* Verdad e Imagen 123 (Salamanca: Sígueme, [2]1991). [52]B. Forte, "Eucharist and Conciliar Fellowship," OneChr 15 (1979) 231–237; G. Wainwright, "Conciliarity and Eucharist," OneChr 14 (1978) 30–49. [53]J. Fitzer, "Teilhard's Eucharist: A Reflection," TS 34 (1973) 251–264; M. Hottenbroth, "The Eucharist as Matrix in the System of Thought of Teilhard de Chardin," AmBenR 31 (1970) 98–121; G. Martelet, "Les grandes intuitions chrétiennes de Teilhard," RTLv 13 (1982) 186–204 at 197–200; C. Scordato, "La dimensione cosmica dell'Eucaristia nella riflessione di Teilhard de Chardin," Asp 33 (1986) 123–148. See further, G. Mantzarides, "The Divine Liturgy and the World," GkOrTR 36 (1981) 62–70. [54]J.M.R. Tillard, "Il n'est d'Église qu'Eucharistique," Nicol 10 (1982) 233–262; I. Barruffo, "L'Eucaristia è missione," RasT 25 (1984) 314–327. [55]I. Bria, "The Liturgy after the Liturgy," in AA.VV. *Martyria, Mission: The Witness of the Orthodox Churches Today* (Geneva: WCC, 1980) 66–74. [56]See International Orthodox-Roman Catholic Dialogue, "Le mystère de l'Église et de l'Eucharistie à la lumière du mystère de la Sainte Trinité," Irén 55 (1982) 350–362; I. Dura, "L'Eucharistie dans l'Église orthodoxe," FoiTemps 17 (1987) 195–214; N. Lossky, "The Eucharistic Life: The Church as a Eucharistic Community at the Local Level," EcuR 31 (1979) 69–71; T. Stylianopoulos, "Christ, Church and Eucharist," Diak (USA) 18 (1983) 100–127; E. Timiadis, "The Eucharist: The Basis of all Sacraments and of Union with God," PatByzR 3 (1984) 177–207; 4 (1985) 20–32. [57]In conversation with McParlan (n. 40) 98 with n. 3.

## EUCHARISTIC HOSPITALITY/SHARING

See INTERCOMMUNION

## EVANGELICALS

The word "evangelical" (Greek *evangelikos* = concerning good news) has been used in a wide variety of contexts. Originally it was used as a term of reproach to Luther for the narrowness of his views. He in turn used it of all Christians who accepted the doctrine of *sola gratia* (grace alone). In continental Europe *evangelisch/évangélique* may simply mean Lutheran or Protestant, often in opposition to Calvinist/Reformed. In the English-speaking world it usually indicates a special position, trend, or party within one of the mainline non-Roman Churches. Some Roman Catholics call themselves "evangelical," but they are not as yet numerous.

Evangelicalism[1] is very much associated with 18th- and 19th-century revivals, which in both England and the U.S. were marked by conversion, deep moral convictions and piety, and social commitment. But by the 20th century the emphasis was more on personal illumination, the evangelical experience of personal salvation through faith. Always easily confused with fundamentalists, evangelicals in the mid-20th century set themselves apart from fundamentalism (q.v.) and espoused what they called "new evangelicalism." This was marked by confession of the infallibility of the Bible, the Trinity, vicarious atonement, the personality and work of the Holy Spirit, and the personal return of Christ. In this century, too, evangelicals are, as in the past, deeply involved in mission or, to use their favored term, "evangelism."[2]

A key distinction between evangelicals and fundamentalists is that the former are part of mainline Churches, whereas fundamentalists usually group themselves under a charismatic leader, forming or supporting their own Christian community. Again, evangelicals are more, even if not always fully, open to scientific study of the Scriptures.

Evangelicals meet across denominational lines in the World Evangelical Fellowship (dating from 1951). This would tend to be critical of the Catholic Church, seeing it still as too little reformed in the areas of Bible and charism, even after Vatican II. The strong evangelical position on the uniqueness of Jesus Christ and the necessity of faith makes evangelicals uneasy at interfaith dialogue. The Fellowship is also an opponent of what it sees as liberalism.

Anglican evangelicals associate with evangelicals from other Churches. Moreover, their major stress is on Scripture and preaching. In the Anglican Communion (q.v.) they are in some places called "Low Church" in contrast to the "High Church," which has a greater emphasis on liturgy and tradition.

The wide spectrum of evangelical views gives different perspectives on the Catholic Church: some reject it outright and regard Catholics as unbelievers; at the other end of the spectrum there is very full cooperation with Catholics, especially in mission.

The ecumenical dialogue has indicated some points of agreement, and quite a number of disagreements.[3] Indeed the fact of dialogue at all with the Catholic Church has not been welcomed everywhere. A main contribution of the evangelicals to the ecumenical movement, including the WCC (v. ECUMENISM, WCC) is their stress on evangelism.[4]

[1]P.M. Bassett, "Evangelicals," DictEcumMov 393–395; D.W. Dayton, *Discovering an Evangelical Heritage* (New York: Harper & Row, 1976). [2]D.A. Carson, ed., *The Church in the Bible and the World*. World Evangelical Fellowship (Exeter: Paternoster—Grand Rapids: Baker, 1987). [3]M. Meeking and J. Stott, eds., *The Evangelical-Roman Catholic Dialogue on Mission 1977–1984: A Report* (Exeter: Paternoster, 1986). [4]Cf. H.T. Hoekstra, *Evangelism in Eclipse: World Mission and the World Council of Churches* (Exeter: Paternoster, 1979).

## EVANGELIST

Traditionally "evangelist" (from *euaggelion*[1] = "good news") has been the term applied to the four Gospel writers: Matthew, Mark, Luke, and John. Towards the end of the 2nd century the evangelists were associated with the four cherubim in Ezek 1:4-14 and the four living creatures of Rev 4:6-8. In iconography the tetramorph is found from the 5th century: lion, ox, eagle, and man for Mark, Luke, John, and Matthew, respectively.

The term *euaggelistês* is found three times in the NT to refer to an office and charism bearer: Philip (Acts 21:8—one of the "Seven" 6:5?); Timothy (2 Tim 4:5); one probably engaged in preaching the gospel to those not yet Christian (Eph 4:11).

[1]G. Friedrich, "Evaggelion," TDNT 2:721–737; D. Mollat, "Gospel," DBT 215–217.

## EVANGELIZATION

The word *euaggelion* meaning "gospel" or "good news," occurs 72 times in the NT, 54 of which are in the Pauline corpus.[1] It has a wide range of meaning: the whole Christian message (Mark 1:1); the good news of Jesus (2 Cor 4:4) or of Paul (2 Cor 4:3); it is for all (Mark 13:10; 16:15); it is a revelation of God (Gal 1:11-12) which is to be believed (Mark 1:15) and

proclaimed (1 Cor 9:14, 16, 18). One must risk all for the gospel (Mark 8:35; Rom 1:16), serve it (Rom 1:1; 15:16), defend it (Phil 1:7, 16); one can hinder (1 Cor 9:12) or refuse (Rom 10:16), or distort it (Gal 1:6-7). *Euaggelion* is the good news of truth (Gal 2:5, 14), of hope (Col 1:23), of peace (Eph 6:15), of God's promise (Eph 3:6), of immortality (2 Tim 1:10), of the risen Christ (1 Cor 15:1ff; 2 Tim 2:8) and of salvation (Eph 1:13). The mature thought of St. Thomas Aquinas sums up the gospel as containing only what pertains to the grace of the Holy Spirit.[2]

The word "evangelization," which does not occur in the NT, came into frequent use with Vatican II. It is especially the work of bishops to promote evangelization by the faithful (CD 6); it is associated with sanctification in the mission that belongs to the laity (AA 2, 6, 20, 26; LG 35); priests are to learn methods of evangelization (PO 19), and to realize that the Eucharist is the source and summit of all evangelization (PO 5). But it is particularly in the decree on the missions that the main contours of evangelization emerge: "the special end of missionary work is evangelization and implanting of the Church (AG 6); "the Church has the obligation and the sacred right to evangelize" (AG 7); catechumens are to engage in the Church's work of evangelization (AG 14); catechists have an important task to evangelize (AG 17), as do the laity (AG 21); evangelization by individuals and institutes arises from a charism of the Spirit (AG 23); missionary institutes are lauded for their evangelization (AG 27) and the role of the then Congregation of Propaganda Fidei is outlined (AG 29); "evangelization is a fundamental office of the people of God" (AG 35, 36); bishops are to send priests for missionary evangelization (AG 38), priests are to stimulate evangelization amongst the faithful (LG 39); contemplative and active religious institutes, as well as secular institutes, have a major role to play in the evangelization of the world (AG 40). Finally, the missionary task is described as building up young Churches so that they in turn can continue the work of evangelization (LG 17).

The 3rd ordinary Synod of Bishops (1974) took up the topic of evangelization; it was followed by the great apostolic exhortation of Paul VI, *Evangelii nuntiandi* (1975—abbrev. EN).[3] One of the finest papal documents of the century, EN recapitulates the teaching of Vatican II but sharpens its focus: the first evangelizer is Christ (EN 6-13, 15); "Evangelization is the special grace and vocation of the Church. It is her essential function. The Church exists to preach the gospel" (EN 14). Again, "evangelization is inherent in the very nature of the Church" (EN 15). Evangelization is a complex process involving a renewal of human nature, witness, public proclamation, wholehearted acceptance of, and entrance into, the community of the

Church, the adoption of the outward sign, and of apostolic works (EN 24). The exhortation lays great emphasis on witness (EN 21, 41, 66, 69, 76 . . .), but stresses that "There is no true evangelization if the name, the teaching, the life, the promises, the kingdom, and the mystery of Jesus of Nazareth, the Son of God, are not proclaimed." (EN 22) The pope also relates evangelization to important issues which have emerged in the post-Vatican II Church: culture (EN 18–20), liberation—q.v. (EN 29–39), popular religiosity or piety—q.v. (EN 48), basic communities—q.v. (EN 58), inculturation—q.v. (EN 63–64), pluralism—q.v. (EN 65–66). A long, beautiful passage deals with the work of the Holy Spirit in evangelization (EN 74–75).[4]

In 1979 the Third General Conference of Latin American Bishops (CELAM) met at Puebla to discuss evangelization.[5] There were notable advances on EN, which had already embodied a key insight about the poor (EN 76). Starting with the current reality of oppression and dependence, it espoused liberation and liberative evangelization as a critical response (nn. 470–506). In important passages, basic communities (nn. 96–97, 619–643) and popular religiosity (nn. 444–469) are positively evaluated. The conference stated a preferential but not exclusive option for the poor (nn. 1134–1165) and for youth (nn. 1166–1205). The poor are both objects of evangelization and its agents (nn. 707, 1130, 1141–1147). The potential of the poor to enrich the Church will be developed in the years following Puebla. The theme of evangelization was taken up further by the CELAM Conference at Santo Domingo (1992),[6] itself reflecting some of the self-searching occasioned by the 500th anniversary of the discovery/oppression/exploitation/evangelization of Latin America.[7]

Pope John Paul II called for a decade of evangelization preceding the year 2000.[8] One result was the Roman Evangelization 2000 office, which encourages the establishment of schools of evangelization in various parts of the world. Another is Lumen 2000 which makes use of electronic media. Both have been criticized for some neglect of the social dimension of an integral evangelization.

The pope seems to have used the term "New Evangelization" for the first time in 1979.[9] In 1983 he characterized it as new in its vigor, methods, and expression.[10] He further developed this idea a few years later:[11] it is to be new in its ardor coming from a greater unity with Christ and confidence in his power; new in methods as it involves all in the Church; new in its expression, as people learn from a heightened sense of their Christian identity to speak a relevant message which also includes a commitment to justice. The postsynodal exhortation on the vocation and mission of the laity, *Christifideles laici,* 1988, abbrev. CL) speaks of re-evangelization (CL 34, 64). The language of evangelization finds a new clarity in the encyclical on the Missions (*Redemptoris missio,* abbrev. RM).[12] Three situations are envisaged in the Church's one mission (q.v.). There are peoples, groups, and socio-cultural contexts in which Christ and his gospel are not known; this is the mission *ad gentes* in the proper sense of the term. Second, there are Christian communities with adequate and solid ecclesial structures; in these the Church carries out pastoral care. Third, "there is an intermediate situation, particularly in countries with ancient Christian roots, and occasionally in the younger Churches as well, where entire groups of the baptized have lost a living sense of the faith, or no longer consider themselves members of the Church, and live a life far removed from Christ and his gospel. In this case what is needed is a 'new evangelization' or a 're-evangelization'"(RM 33). Though there is a new clarity in the encyclical, the ideas are already to be found seminally in Vatican II (AG 6).

However, this terminology of "new/re-evangelization" is not in universal use. Many speak of "new evangelization" in the context of liberative evangelization in the Latin American situation.[13] Indeed, the call to evangelization takes different forms in various places. Without being exclusive one could sketch various key issues in diverse places: in the First World there is an emphasis on science, technology, and capitalism, and so evangelization needs to stress evangelical and transcendental values;[14] in the former socialist countries of Eastern Europe there is rapid social change in cultures that had been officially atheistic, and so evangelization must emphasize the transforming dynamism of the faith; in Latin America there is the oppression of the poor, and therefore evangelization must be seen as transformative and liberating; in Asia the great religions (v. NON-CHRISTIAN) need to be evangelized through dialogue and the witness of Christian spirituality, as well as through increasing consciousness about injustice; in Africa, former colonial countries are asserting their proud African identity, and so evangelization must be through deep inculturation (q.v.) of the gospel.

Again, without being exclusive, one can distinguish several models of evangelization. Evangelization is an ecclesial act.[15] Traditionally evangelization was by the missionaries led by priests who brought a gospel that was very European in character. The points of insertion were frequently education and health care, and there was an emphasis on conversions and later on indigenous priests. In recent decades there has been an accent on dialogue with the culture of the peoples and an attempt to build up community. In this model of evangelization those who came to a people were more aware of the "seeds of the Word" already prepared by the Holy Spirit. The encyclical of John Paul II on the missions stresses the value of dialogue but insists that it cannot displace evangelization (RM 55–57 with 33). The most recent model is the liberative one in which the gospel message is seen as good news for the whole of life. Here the poor are in a special position: they are the privileged recipients of the good news (see Luke 4:17; 7:22) and they also evangelize the evangelizers.

In the history of catechetics (q.v.) a distinction has been made since the East Asia Study Week (Bangkok 1962) between three stages: pre-evangelization, a listening phase which arouses interest and prepares the ground; evangelization proper, which leads to conversion; catechesis, which forms the Christian.[16]

From the 1960s and 70s there has been much interest on the part of Protestants in evangelization, their preferred term, however, being "evangelism." It has been much discussed in various meetings of, or under the auspices of, the World Council of Churches.[17] It is an area where there is much room for collaboration and ongoing dialogue.

[1]G. Friedrich, "Evaggelion," TDNT 2:721-737; D. Mollat, "Gospel," DBT 215-217.    [2]ST 1-2ae, q.106, a.1 ad 1.    [3]AAS 68 (1976) 1-96—Flannery 2:711-761. See A. Furioli, "A 10 anni dalle *Evangelii nuntiandi:* Nota ascetico-pastorale," EuntDoc 38 (1985) 99-114.    [4]J. Saraiva Martins, "Dimensione pneumatologica dell'evangelizzazione," EuntDoc 32 (1979) 3-32.    [5]*Puebla: Evangelization at Present and in the Future of Latin America—Conclusions* (Slough: St Paul, 1980).    [6]*Santo Domingo Conclusions* (London: CIIR, 1993); see G. Gutiérrez et al., *Santo Domingo and After: The Challenge for the Latin American Church* (London: CIIR, 1993) Conclusions 2:1, nn. 23-156.    [7]J.O. Boezzo, "Evangelização e V Centenário," REBras 50 (1990) 556-617; M. Herrera and J. Vidal, "Evangelization: Then and Now," NewTR 3/4 (Nov. 1990) 6-21.    [8]R. Guelluy, "A propos de la 'nouvelle évangélization' de l'Europe," RTLv 21 (1990) 343-347; P. Lynch. *Awakening the Giant: Evangelism and the Catholic Church* (London: Darton, Longman & Todd, 1990); P. Vanzen, "Quali linee e soggetti per una nuova evangelizzazione del mondo post moderno?," CivCatt 139 (1988) 2:245-258.    [9]Cracow, Poland (8 June 1979)—DocCath 76/13 (1979) 639 cf. 636. See A. Dulles, "John Paul II and the New Evangelization," America 166 (1992) 52-59, 69-72.    [10]Port-au-Prince, Haiti (9 March 1983)—AAS 75 (1983) 778/DocCath 80/8 (1983) 437-438.    [11]Salto, Uruguay (9 May 1988)—DocCath 85/11 (1988) 546-549.    [12]7 Dec. 1990 - AAS 83 (1991) 249-340/CathIntern 2/6 (1991) 252-292.    [13]L. Boff, *New Evangelization: Good News to the Poor* (Maryknoll: Orbis, 1991); A. Escallada Tijero, "Algunos rasgos, en clave eclesiológica de la nueva evangelización (Al hilo del Documento 'Corbán 88' sobre Pastoral Indígena)," CiTom 117 (1990) 611-627; R.M. Grácio das Nieves, "Aportes al debate sobre la nueva evangelización desde una pastoral indígena liberadora," CiTom 117 (1990) 516-533; REBras 47 (1987) 5-181.    [14]A. Krass, *Evangelizing Neo-Pagan North America* (Scottdale, Penn.: Herald Press, 1982); B.J. Leonard, "Evangelism and Contemporary American Life," RExp 77 (1980) 493-506.    [15]R. Rossignol, "Evangelization is an Ecclesial Act," IndTS 27 (1990) 321-332.    [16]A. Nebreda, "East Asian Study Week on Mission Catechetics," LumVit 17 (1962) 717-730; idem, *Kerygma in Crisis?* (Chicago, 1965).    [17]E. Castro, "Evangelism" in DictEcumMov 396-400; R.E. Coleman, "The Theology of Evangelism," RExp 77 (1980) 473-481; G.-P. Widmer, "Quelques repères d'une théologie de l'évangélization," RTPhil 114 (1982) 383-394.

## EVDOKIMOV, Paul (1901–1970)

Born at St. Petersburg in 1901, Paul Evdokimov emigrated to Paris in 1923. His first academic work was on Dostoevsky; later he came under the influence of the theologians of Saint-Serge, especially S. Bulgakov (q.v.) and N. Berdyaev. A layman, he published extensive works on Orthodox and ecumenical themes.[1] His major works on Orthodoxy[2] and on the Holy Spirit[3] show him to be profoundly Trinitarian in his approach. Remarkable works on woman in salvation history and on marriage[4] show the broad range of his thought at once patristic and scholarly, intuitive and poetical. In spirituality he advocated for all, laity and clergy, the interiorization of the monastic ideal.[5] His bold Trinitarian theology sought to accept the *Filioque* (q.v.) along with a *Spirituque:* the Spirit is a condition for the generation of the Logos.

His doctrine on the Church is strongly Trinitarian and pneumatological: it is through the Holy Spirit that the Church, especially in its local, Eucharistic manifestation, is one, holy, catholic, and apostolic.[6] In ecumenism he moved from a rather rigid Orthodox stance to more open positions, especially after being an official observer at the fourth session of Vatican II (1965). He often repeated that we know where the Church is, but it is not given to us to know where the Church is not. He would seem to have coined the expression "ecumenical epiclesis" to stress that unity is a work of the Spirit and must be sought in humble prayer, and to emphasize that it is only when the Spirit is given its rightful place in the Church that we can gain a proper understanding of Tradition, a crucial problem for ecumenism.[7] For true ecumenical dialogue one must be utterly faithful to one's own Church. Though Evdokimov rejected any Branch Theory (v. ANGLICANISM AND ECUMENISM), he emphasized the elements that characterize the main Christian bodies: the Johannine—Orthodox; Petrine—Catholicism; Pauline—Protestantism. Hence there is a reduced value in any ecumenical dialogues which do not include all three legacies. Though the Church suffers divisions there is a basic unity that still exists, which ultimately is eschatological.[8] It is arguable that this sense of the end, of all in unity, led him deeply into a theology of beauty,[9] which is essential to an integral ecclesiology.

[1]Cho D. Phan, "Paul Evdokimov-A Bibliography," Sales 44 (1982) 751–766; P.G. Gianazza, *Paul Evdokimov cantore dello Spirito Santo.* Biblioteca di scienze religiose 52 (Rome: LAS, 1983) bibliog. 169–179. See O.Clément, "La vie et l'oeuvre de Paul Evdokimov: Quelques approches," Contacts 23 (1971) 11–106; idem, "L'Eucharistie dans la pensée de Paul Evdokimov," *Pain et parole* 8 (1971) 133–147.    [2]*L'Orthodoxie* (Neuchâtel-Paris: Delachaux et Niestlé, 1959—Paris: Desclée de Brouwer, 1979).    [3]*L'Esprit saint dans la tradition orthodoxe.* Bib. Oecumén. théologie sans frontières (Paris: Cerf, 1969); *Présence de l'Esprit saint dans*

*la tradition orthodoxe* (Paris: Cerf, 1977).    [4]*La femme et le salut du monde: Étude d'anthropologie chrétienne sur les charismes des femmes* (Paris: Casterman, 1958—Desclée de Brouwer, 1979) and *Le sacrement de l'amour: Le mystère conjugal à la lumière de la tradition orthodoxe* (Paris: Epi, 1962).    [5]*Les âges de la vie spirituelle: Des pères du désert à nos jours* (Paris: Desclée de Brouwer, [2]1980).    [6]Gianazza (n. 1) 76–83; J.S. Gajek, *Il ministero della Chiesa nel pensiero di Pavel N. Evdokimov* (Rome: Pont. Instit. Orientale, 1983).    [7]Cho D. Phan, "The Eschatological Dimensions of Unity: Paul Evdokimov's Contribution to Ecumenism," Sales 42 (1980) 475–499 at 478.    [8]Ibid.    [9]*L'art de l'icône: Théologie de la beauté* (Paris: Desclée de Brouwer, 1970).

# EXCOMMUNICATION

Excommunication has a long and complex history.[1] Matthew 18:17 gives some power to shut a person out from the Christian community. In Corinth we find Paul excluding a sinner from the community for an incestuous sin (1 Cor 5:1-13). He did so in order to guard the holiness of the community and to avoid giving offense to the Holy Spirit who dwelt in the community as in a temple (q.v.). It was also meant to facilitate the sinner's conversion and return to the community.[2]

In the early patristic period virtual excommunication or exclusion from activities, and especially from the liturgical life of the community, followed on public grave sin. The term "excommunication" itself appears first in the 4th century. Even before that we see popes and other bishops refusing communion to those whose faith or practice was regarded as deviant. Thus Pope Stephen I (254–257) refused communion to the African delegates who came wishing him to approve the rebaptism of heretics, and he extended this refusal to anybody else who shared their views.[3]

In the early councils the declaration of anathema (v. HERESY) was in many ways an excommunication. But the term "excommunication" was widely used to include various forms of ecclesiastical penalty. Excommunication was not only an act against a person. Churches excommunicated one another, sometimes in the person of their bishop. Councils anathematized heretics. The most serious excommunications in the Middle Ages were surely the anathemas hurled at one another by the Eastern and Western Churches in the 11th century. The exact circumstances and meaning of these were clarified only during Vatican II.[4] They were lifted by Paul VI and Patriarch Athenagoras on 7 December 1965.[5]

The early history of excommunication is also closely tied to the history of the sacrament of reconciliation (q.v.), and it is not always easily distinguishable from it. Persons who committed grave sin were subject to a liturgical excommunication which consigned them to the ranks of the penitents. They were barred from taking part in the Eucharist until they were reconciled. As the earlier penitential discipline relaxed by the 7th century, we see emerging a discipline of excommunication for serious offenses, but this was applied not to repentant but to impenitent sinners or to those who were obdurate.

In the Middle Ages a detailed theory and practice surrounded excommunication.[6] The canonist, Pope Innocent III, gave some precision when he distinguished between excommunication, interdict, and suspension.[7] At the Council of Lyons (1245—q.v.) Innocent IV described the nature of excommunication as medicinal,[8] an idea, repeated by Trent, which demanded restitution and absolution before the lifting of an anathema.[9] The law at the time distinguished between a major excommunication which separated one from the Church and a minor one which only excluded from the sacraments.[10] There was also an insistence that no bishop could receive a person excommunicated by another.[11] In the Middle Ages excommunications, even by lower prelates, were frequent, and became an abuse. Lateran III and IV laid down some procedures and balance in the matter of penalties.[12] Trent sought more discretion relating to them, a recommendation taken over into the 1917 *Code of Canon Law.*[13]

From the Middle Ages people were forbidden to have any religious or even profane intercourse with an excommunicated person, under the pain of incurring the same excommunication themselves. In time this matter was clarified so that only certain classes of excommunicated persons were to be avoided *(vitandi).* This is the origin of the distinction between *vitandi* and *tolerati,* that was modified, but retained by the 1917 *Code,* which specified, however, that a *vitandus* had to be thus named by the Holy See (CIC 2258 § 2).

From the Middle Ages until the *Code* of 1917 there was otherwise little change in the theory or practice of excommunication. In this *Code* there was an elaborate series of excommunications of varying severity indicated by the kind of reservation, that is, the person/body who could lift the excommunication: those most specially, specially, or simply reserved to the Holy See; those reserved to bishops; those without reservation (CIC 2314–2392). The 1917 *Code* also distinguished between automatic excommunications *(latae sententiae)* which were incurred by the perpetration of the crime and excommunications by sentence *(ferendae sententiae),* which were operative only on being pronounced by the competent authority. The 1983 *Code* did not define penalties, but only gave their application and effects. The general effects of excommunication are thus outlined: "An excommunicated person is forbidden: 1) to have any ministerial participation in celebrating the Eucharistic sacrifice or in any other ceremonies whatsoever of public worship; 2) to celebrate the sacraments and sacramentals and to receive the sacraments; 3) to discharge any ecclesiastical offices, ministries, or functions whatsoever, or to place acts of governance." (CIC 1331).[14] The revised law abandoned the imposition of an excommunication *vitandus*. The bishops at the 1967 Synod (q.v.) sought a reduction of the cases of automatic excommunication *(latae sententiae)*. In the 1983 *Code* these are reduced to seven.[15] Five are reserved to the Holy See: violation of the Eucharistic species (CIC 1367); physical attack on the pope (CIC 1370 § 1); absolution by a priest of his accomplice in a sexual sin (CIC 1378 § 1); unauthorized episcopal consecration (CIC 1382); direct violation of the seal (secrecy) of confession by a priest (CIC 1388 § 1). Non-reserved are apostasy, heresy, or schism (c. 1364 §1) and procuration of abortion (CIC 1398). There are other crimes which may result in excommunication after a sentence has been pronounced *(ferendae sententiae)*. The reduction of excommunications reflects a drastic overhaul of the penal norms of the Church. The 1983 *Code* reduces the 220 canons on penalties of the 1917 law to 89; the number of penalties themselves is reduced from 101 (CIC 2314–2414) to 35 (CIC 1364–1398).

The imposition of ecclesiastical penalties always has a salvific purpose in mind: the good of the community and the conversion of the offender. The imposition of penalties is to be seen as a last resort.[16] It has been suggested that excommunication is not to be viewed in penal terms, but only as a salvific action for the sake of the individual and the Church community.[17] But this matter is controverted.[18] Moreover, excommunication is treated in that part of the *Code* which deals with penalties (Bk VI).

The 1983 *Code* does not give a definition of excommunication. But one can be deduced from a careful examination of the law; thus A. Borras writes: "Excommunication is a penal sanction of positive ecclesial law, with a specifically medicinal finality; it is established to oppose very serious delicts; its indivisible effects consist in a prohibition of exercising rights and duties according to the dispositions of the *Code* (cc. 1331, 171 § 1, n. 3, 316, 915, 996 § 1 and 1109) to such an extent that it constitutes an (almost) total exclusion from the spiritual goods of the Church."[19] An excommunication does not, therefore, exclude one from belonging to the Church, for the external bonds which give communion can remain intact (CIC 205). Since it involves serious sin (CIC 1321), the communion with the Church is not full (v. MEMBERSHIP) because grace, the internal condition necessary for full communion (LG 14), would be lacking.[20]

Excommunication is concerned with external crimes; it is an external juridical act of the Church. It does not necessarily mean that the offender is deprived of God's grace. In theory, at least, an excommunicated person can be in good faith, even while being legally excluded from aspects of the life of the Church.

Excommunications are lifted by the appropriate authority, usually the Holy See or the local bishop, depending on the reservation. Offenders normally begin to seek the remission of this censure in the sacrament of reconciliation, though recourse has usually to be made later to the relevant authority (CIC 1354–1358).

[1]F.E. Hyland, *Excommunication: Its Nature, Historical Development and Effects* (Washington, D.C., 1928); É. Jombart, "Excommunication," DictDCan 5:615-628; J.E. Lynch, "The Limits of *Communio* in the Pre-Constantinian Church," Jurist 36 (1976) 159–190.  [2]A.Y. Collins, "The Function of 'Excommunication' in Paul," HarvTR 73 (1980) 251–261; J. Murphy O'Connor, 1 *Corinthians*. NTMess 10 (Delaware: Glazier, 1979) 40–45; idem, NJBC in loc. See J. Jeremias, "Kleis," TDNT 3:744-753 at 752–753.  [3]OxDPopes 20–21.  [4]Text in E.J. Stormon, ed., *Towards the Healing of Schism: The Sees of Rome and Constantinople*. Ecumenical Documents 3 (New York—Mahwah: Paulist, 1987) 123–125.  [5]Ibid., 126–129.  [6]E.g., St. Thomas, *In 4 Sent.* d.18; *Supp.* qq. 21–24.  [7]*Decr.* 10: 5, t.40, c.20.  [8]*Decret.* 6:5, t. 11, c.1 in 6; cf. 6:2, t.12, c.1. St. Thomas, ST 2-2ae, q.31, a.2 ad 3.  [9]Sess. 22, can. reform. 11—Tanner 2:741.  [10]St. Thomas, *In 4 Sent.* d.18, q.2, a.1, qla 1.  [11]Lateran I, can. 2—Tanner 1:190; Lateran II, can. 3, 12—Tanner 1:197, 199.  [12]Lateran III can. 6 and Lateran IV Constit. 47—Tanner 1:214, 255–256.  [13]Sess. 25, Decree on General Reform, 3—Tanner 2:748; cf. CIC (1917) c. 2241 § 2.  [14]A. Borras, *L'excommunication dans le nouveau Code de droit canonique: Essai de définition* (Paris: Desclée, 1987).  [15]A. Borras, "De excommunicatione in vigenti Codice," Periodica 79 (1990) 713–732.  [16]T.J. Green, in Coriden, CIC 896.  [17]L. Gerosa, *La scominica è una pena? Saggio per una fondazione teologica del diritto penale canonico*. Studia Friburgensia (Freibourg: UP, 1984) summarized "Ist die Exkommunikation eine Strafe?," ArcKK 154 (1985) 83–120; cf. T. Green, "The Future of Penal Law in the Church," Jurist 35 (1975) 212–275.  [18]P. Le Gall, "L'excommunication est-elle une peine?," RDroitC 37 (1987) 106–117; cf. A. Borras, "Appartenance à l'Église, communion ecclésiale et excommunication," NRT 110 (1988) 801–824 at 815–821; J. Sanchis, "Sulla natura e gli effetti della scomunica," IusEccl 2 (1989) 633–661.  [19]Borras (n. 18) 821.  [20]Ibid., 821.

## EXEMPTION

Exemption is a privilege in law which removes from a superior some subject(s) who would otherwise be under his jurisdiction. Individuals, such as cardinals enjoy in law exemption from the local ordinary. But it is the exemption of religious that has been the most common, and occasionally fractious. It concerns the relationship of religious with the local bishop (v. RELIGIOUS). Originally religious were subject to the bishop. But beginning with the monastery of Bobbio in 628, exemption was granted by the pope to various monasteries and religious orders. In time abuses would arise: the authority of the local bishop was seriously diminished; confusion arose about rights and duties. The Fifth Lateran Council (q.v.) attempted to restore order,[1] but its decree was ineffectual. Trent further attempted to reduce the incidence of exemption and its abuse.[2]

The Canon Law of 1917 distinguished between exempt and non-exempt religious (CIC 488, cf. 615–616). At Vatican II the rationale for exemption was given: "To meet the needs of the Lord's flock more effectively, any institute of perfection and its individual members can, for the general good of the Church, be exempted by the supreme pontiff from the jurisdiction of local ordinaries and subjected to him alone; this is possible by reason of his primacy over the universal Church" (LG 45; cf. CD 35.3). The new *Code* took up this statement and added that an additional reason can be the good of the institute itself (CIC 591).[3] But it added important matters concerning rights and role of the local Ordinary (CIC 611, 678–679, 681, cf. 394).

Vatican II called on religious to show "reverence and obedience, towards the bishops in accordance with canon law" (LG 45). The *Code* specifies in particular that bishops coordinate the apostolic works in their diocese (CIC 394) and, in particular: "religious are subject to the authority of bishops, whom they are obliged to follow with devoted humility and respect, in those matters which involve the care of souls, the public exercise of divine worship and other works of the apostolate" (CIC 678). This canon takes up matters already found in the statement *Mutuae relationes* of 1978 on relations between bishops and religious. This document attempted to redress the balance somewhat in favor of the bishops but stressed the needs for dialogue in communion.[4] A healthy tension is to be expected between the institution of the hierarchy and the more charismatic institution of religious life. But both in harmony ought to further the good of the whole Church and of each religious institute.

---

[1]Tanner 1:645-649.  [2]Session 24, c. 11—Tanner 2:765.  [3]D. Kay, "The Historical Origins of Canon 591 of the Code of Canon Law," StCan 25 (1991) 451–464; G. Ghirlanda, "Iusta autonomia et exemptio institutorum religiosorum: Fundamenta et extensio," Periodica 78 (1989) 113–142.  [4]S. Cong. Religious and Secular Institutes, "Directives for Mutual Relations Between Bishops and Religious in the Church—*Mutuae relationes*" (1978) passim and nn. 22, 67—AAS 70 (1978) 473–506/Flannery 2:209-243.

## EXORCISM

It is common today to deny or to play down excessively the existence of hostile spiritual powers. There is clearly a reaction to mythical, exaggerated, and morbid interest in Satan and exorcism. But the existence of evil spirits is part of Catholic tradition,[1] reiterated in a study commissioned by the Congregation for Divine Worship and published in 1975.[2]

The overcoming of evil spirits, or exorcism (*ex* = out, *horkos* = oath), had a major place in the ministry of Jesus, though we would not today consider as exorcism each of the actions thus described in the Gospels.[3] Nonetheless, the ministry and teaching of Jesus point

to a struggle that is not merely against flesh and blood (see Eph 6:10-16) but against unseen and hostile spiritual powers. His exorcisms are a proclamation of the victory of the kingdom over all malevolent powers (cf. John 12:31). Exorcism was practiced by Jews at the time of Jesus (cf. Luke 11:19; Acts 19:13-14) and by his apostles (cf. Matt 10:1; Luke 10:17-20). Jesus left to his Church the power of overcoming evil spirits in his name (cf. Mark 16:17; cf. Acts 16:18), and this power was used. But, like any charism (q.v.), it did not guarantee the holiness of the recipient (cf. Matt 7:22).

The *Apostolic Tradition* (q.v.) has an elaborate series of exorcisms for catechumens. Even for a prospective catechumen it is laid down: "But if there is some one who has a devil (*daemonium habet),* let him not hear the word from the teacher until he be cleansed" (15/16:8). From the time they have been chosen (*separati sunt)* they are to be exorcised (*exorkizein)* daily; as the time for baptism draws near they are to be exorcised by the bishop "to make sure that each one is pure" (20/20:3). The reason given for the non-admittance of a person to baptism is significant: "But if there is someone who is not good or pure, then he is to be sent away, for he did not hear the word with faith, for it is impossible that the Strange One (*ho antikeimenos)* be always concealed" (20/20:4). On the Friday or Saturday before baptism there is a further exorcism by the bishop: "A hand shall be laid on them, and the bishop will adjure every alien spirit to leave them and never return. When he has finished exorcising, he breathes in their face and after having signed their forehead, ears and nose, he raises them up" (20/20:7-8). At the actual baptism there is exorcism of a second oil (*exorkismos)* in addition to the Oil of Thanksgiving (*eucharistia* 21/21:6-7). After the renunciation of Satan, the priest anoints him with the Oil of Exorcism, saying "Let every spirit depart far from thee" (*omnis spiritus abscedat a te*—sic, the adjective "evil" is not appended in Latin 21/21:9-10).

The catechumens are not to give the kiss of peace, for their kiss is not yet pure (18/18:3. At the agape (q.v.) the catechumen is to be given exorcised bread (*panis exorcismi/exorkismos*—26/26:4). For the faithful the sign of the cross is a defense: "If you are tempted sign (*consignare/sphragizein)* your forehead reverently; for it is the sign of the Passion known and proven against the devil, provided that you do it with faith. . . . For the Adversary when he sees the heart . . . is put to flight by the Spirit which is in you" (42/37:1-2).

In the *Apostolic Constitutions* (q.v.) there is some attempt to limit the importance of exorcists: it is made clear that theirs is a charismatic function and not an ordained ministry.[4] By the Middle Ages[5] and in Trent,[6] the office of exorcist was merely a step on the road to priesthood. As such, it was abolished by Pope Paul VI in 1972.[7]

Exorcism takes two forms: imprecation and deprecation. In the first, the powers of evil are addressed and commanded to leave the possessed person. Such a form of exorcism is comparatively rare, and the fact of possession must be carefully established before an exorcism is performed by a priest who has authority from the local bishop so to proceed on a case.[8] Places that have been associated with very evil practices may need treatment: usually having Mass in the house or place will banish evil influences. In other specific situations, such as involvement in voodooism, witchcraft, or other behavior that may leave people particularly open to the incursion of evil, the episcopal conference may decide on a solemn adjuration of evil during the rites of the catechumenate. Otherwise the exorcisms in the Rite of Christian Initiation of Adults (RCIA) are deprecatory in the form of prayers to the Father or to Jesus to set the catechumens or the elect free from evil of every kind. The main author of the RCIA, B. Fischer, writes that "we no longer speak to the devil (considered as being present); we speak with God about the Devil (still considered as personal)".[9] During the rites of the catechumenate, exorcisms of the deprecatory form are continual; the minister may be a catechist up to the time of the scrutinies. During the scrutinies sin is considered as closely clinging to the human heart (1st scrutiny), as being social (2nd scrutiny), as being death (3rd scrutiny). There are exorcisms in each of the scrutinies corresponding to these facets of sin and reflecting the great Gospel texts of John, chapters 4, 9, and 11, respectively.

In the classical Pentecostal Churches there is at times an excessive interest in and concern about evil spirits leading to a too frequent use of the ministry of exorcism. Ordinary sickness and misfortune tend to be ascribed to Satan. The Catholic Charismatic Renewal learned a lot from Pentecostal Churches but sought to integrate it into Catholic tradition. Thus, in an early book, F. MacNutt[10] spoke of "obsession" rather than of "possession," and rightly pointed out that "obsession" or some disturbance less than possession can be treated by anyone who believes in the power of the name of Jesus. Such ministry he termed "deliverance." But the style of prayer used was scarcely distinct from the formal exorcism of the Roman Ritual. More discreet

books followed,[11] notably, a perhaps overcautious one by Cardinal Suenens.[12] The Congregation for the Doctrine of the Faith issued instructions to bishops about exorcism in a document of 29 September 1985: it reiterated the canon law (CIC 1172); it forbade the use of an exorcism prayer dating from the time of Leo XIII; it limited certain forms of imprecation; it recalled the traditional means in the Church against evil—sacraments, the Our Father (Matt 6:13) and prayer to the Virgin Mary, the angels and saints for protection.

The importance of the exorcisms in the RCIA is that they alert the catechumens and the Christian community about the nature of the spiritual struggle in the Christian life: while we must not shirk responsibility for sin by blaming all on Satan, we still need to know that we have powerful enemies that can only be subdued in the power of the risen Lord.[13] The embolism, or prayer "Deliver us Lord . . ." inserted after the Our Father at Mass, is a deprecatory prayer which daily protects the Christian worshipers from the powers of evil.

[1]W. Kasper and K. Lehmann, eds., *Teufel—Dämonen—Besessenheit: Zur Wirklichkeit des Bösen* (Mainz: Matthias-Grünewald, [2]1978—Italian trans. *Diavolo—demoni—possessione: Sulla realtà del male* [Brescia: Queriniana, [2]1985]); B. Marconcini et al., *Angeli e demoni: Il dramma della storia tra il bene e il male.* Corso di teologia sistematica 11 (Bologna: E. Dehoniane, 1991). [2]*Les formes multiples de la superstition* ("Christian Faith and Demonology")—Flannery 2:456-485/Italian text OssRomano, 25 June, 1975. Cf. W. Beinert, "Müssen Christen an den Teufel glauben?," StimZ195 (1977) 541-554; J. Galot, "Satan," EspVie 99 (1989) 209-216; F. Reckinger, "'In meinem Namen werden sie Dämonen austreiben': Zur Reform des Exorzismus," ForKTheol 5 (1989) 137-145. [3]E. Best, "Exorcism in the New Testament and Today," BibTheol 27 (1977) 1-9. [4]8:1, 3-4; 8:23—SC 336:126-128; 224-226. [5]E.g., St. Thomas, *Summa* c. *gentiles*, 4:75. [6]Sess. 23—Tanner 2:742-743/DS 1765, 1772/ND 1708, 1715. [7]Mp. *Ministeria quaedam*—AAS 64 (1972) 529-534/DOL 340/Flannery 1:427-432. [8]CIC 1172. [9]B. Fischer, "Baptismal Exorcism in the Catholic Baptismal Rites After Vatican II," StLtg 10 (1974) 48-55 at 55. [10]*Healing* (Notre Dame: Ave Maria, 1974) ch. 15. [11]E.g., M. and D. Linn, eds., *Deliverance Prayer: Experiential, Psychological and Theological Approaches* (New York: Paulist, 1981); J. McManus, *The Ministry of Deliverance in the Catholic Tradition* (London: National Service Committee for Charismatic Renewal, 1980). [12]*Renewal and the Powers of Darkness* (London: Darton, Longman & Todd, 1983). [13]A.M. Triacca, "Esorcismo: Un sacramentale discusso. Alcune piste di riflessione in vista di ulteriori richerche—Sette gruppi di interrogativi," EcOr 4 (2987) 285-300. See MaisD 183-184 (1990) 5-261.

# F

## FAITH AND MORALS

The traditional phrase "faith and morals" is of importance particularly in the context of infallibility (q.v.); the pope's infallibility is identical to that of the Church's, and extends to "doctrine about faith and morals *(doctrinam de fide vel moribus)* to be held by the whole Church."[1] Moreover, his primacy is not confined only to those things that concern faith and morals, but it also includes what pertains to the discipline and government *(ad disciplinam et regimen)* of the Church dispersed throughout the world.[2] At the council, the relator, Bishop V. Gasser, told the fathers that *"fides et mores"* were perfectly well known *(vox notissima).*[3]

The meaning of the phrase is not quite self-evident in Christian literature. We can begin with Augustine who, in two letters, distinguished faith *(fides)* from good usages *(mores).*[4] The former is the body of doctrines universally accepted by the Church, the living concrete life of faith of Christian communities under their bishops. The latter has nothing to do with morals in the modern sense or with ethical principles. It refers to the manifold forms of Christian life, especially liturgical and sacramental, which express the living tradition of the Church.[5]

In the Middle Ages we rarely find the expression "faith and morals," though it was used by Gratian (d. 1159), the first compiler of Church law (q.v.), and some canonists after him. The reason is clear. Faith, the *fides quae,* or object of belief, was not the same as we now interpret it, viz., a series of truths revealed by God and presented as such by the teaching magisterium.[6] At the time, faith was generally taken to mean "articles of faith and sacraments": the articles of faith were the summaries in the three great creeds—Apostles', Nicene-Constantinopolitan, and Athanasian; the sacraments impinged on the whole area of Christian life. These two comprised the core of belief necessary for saving faith, and came under the rubric of *fides,* whereas *et mores* covered other aspects of the life of the faithful.[7]

When we come to Trent, we find that the Church receives the Scriptures, as well as traditions concerning faith and morals, as coming from Christ or the Holy Spirit.[8] The phrase "faith and morals" at Trent refers to the Apostolic Tradition in its different but not separate aspects, viz., the doctrine and forms of Christian life. Trent did not understand by *mores* merely "moral principles," though these latter are certainly included. In addition to Scripture, the tradition from Christ and the apostles concerns saving truth and the ordering of morals—*"disciplina morum."* The council understood by *mores* many things that are covered by the phrase "unwritten traditions," but the council also speaks of unwritten traditions that pertain to faith; however, most of the examples that the Tridentine theologians give of "unwritten traditions" pertain to practice rather than dogma. At the same time it must be noted that one can be guilty of heresy (q.v.) not only in rejecting apostolic doctrine, but also in obdurately refusing anything that belongs to Catholic life in general.[9]

After Trent another meaning of *mores* began to appear, so that by the time of Vatican I, the modern meaning is found: *mores* are a part of faith, as an extension of it in matters of moral responsibility.[10] This meaning of Vatican I is retained in Vatican II (LG 12, 25). At the same time the meaning of Trent would seem to be operative in the statement that the gospel is "the source of all saving truth and ordering of behavior" *(salutaris veritatis et morum disciplinae*—DV 7).[11] The context of the whole article makes the equation *morum = of morals* too restrictive: what is being treated is truth and the whole richness of the Christian life.

This history of the terms "faith and morals" is evidence once again of the need to be careful in reading early texts through the perspective of language meanings current in the time of the contemporary reader.

---

[1]Vatican I—Tanner 2:816/DS 3074/ND 839.  [2]Tanner 2:814/DS 3064/ND 830.  [3]Mansi 52:1224.  [4]*Ad inquisit. Ianuarii, Epist.* 54 and 55—PL 199–223.  [5]P. Fransen, "A Short History of the Meaning of the Formula *Fides et Mores,*" LouvSt 7 (1978–1979) 270–301 at 276–277.  [6]Ibid., 279.  [7]Ibid., 281–286.  [8]Tanner 2:663/DS 1501/ND 210; see also Tanner 2:664/DS 1507/ND 217. Cf. Fransen (n. 5) 289–291; Y. Congar, *Tradition and Traditions: An Historical and Theological Essay* (London: Burns & Oates, 1966, from French 1960–1963) 158, n. 3 with 50–64.  [9]M. Bévenot, "'Faith and Morals' in the Councils of Trent and Vatican 1," HeythJ 3 (1962) 15–30 at 21; P. Fransen, "Réflexions sur l'anathème au Concile de Trente," ETL 29 (1953) 657–672.  [10]Fransen (n. 5) 295.  [11]Fransen (n. 5) 299–300.

## FALSE DECRETALS

The False Decretals[1] are a collection of documents compiled about 850 in France. They were ascribed to St. Isidore of Seville (d. 636). They contain three kinds of documents: letters of pre-Nicene popes, all spurious; a collection of canons of various councils, mostly genuine; a large number of letters of popes, ranging from Sylvester I (314–335) to Gregory II (715–731), of which thirty-five or so are spurious.

The False Decretals were accepted in the Middle Ages and their conciliar canons especially became incorporated into law (q.v.). Their authenticity was first seriously disputed in 1558 by Lutheran historians, the Centuriators of Magdeburg. Subsequently they were seen to have much bogus material mingled with genuine documents.

The skillful compilation of the False Decretals was made to serve a number of purposes. At the time of composition they were used as a defense of bishops against archbishops, and as an assertion of Church rights against lay interference. At the time of their reception in Rome (864) they were little used, but from the 11th century they were much utilized in supporting papal government and reforms. The earlier inauthentic papal documents gave the prestige of the Church of the martyrs to the strengthening of papal authority throughout the Middle Ages, beginning with Gregory VII (1073–1085—q.v.).

---

[1]Congar, Augustin 62–63; E. Ewig, in Jedin-Dolan 3:145-147, 167–169; B. Leeming, "The False Decretals, Faustus of Riez and the Pseudo-Eusebius," StPatr 2 (1957) 122–140; S. Williams, "The Pseudo-Isidorian Problem Today," Speculum 29 (1954) 702–707.

## FATHERS OF THE CHURCH

The term "Fathers" was first used about bishops because of the paternal aspect of their pastoral ministry.

It was then used of bishops assembled in councils, since they determined the rule of faith and made provision for the life of the Church. Later it came to have its present-day significance: writers of antiquity, who were of undisputed orthodoxy, holiness, and communion with the Church. Those who do not fulfill the last three conditions have since Jerome (q.v.) been called "ecclesiastical writers," e.g., Tertullian, Origen.

There is a certain fluidity about the identification of the Fathers. Unlike "Doctor of the Church" (q.v.), it is a popular title, not one that is formally conferred by Church authority.[1] In a stricter sense the Fathers are usually considered to end with Gregory the Great (d. 604—q.v.) or Isidore (d. 636) in the West, and with John Damascene (d. ca. 749) in the East. Sometimes Bede (d. 735—q.v.) or even Bernard (d. 1153—q.v.) are called Fathers.

The great collections of J.-P. Migne extend still further: the 221 volumes of the *Patrologia latina* (usually abbreviated as PL or ML) reach to the time of Innocent III (d. 1216); the 162 volumes of the Greek *Patrologia graeca* (usually abbreviated PG or MG) go as far as the Council of Florence (1439—q.v.). The extraordinary industry of the Abbé Migne has left all theologians in his debt;[2] though many of his texts now have more critical editions,[3] the comprehensive range of PL and PG remains unsurpassed. With PL now appearing on database, its value is further enhanced.[4] Other collections of note are those of the Fathers writing in Syriac, Armenian, and other languages.[5]

The study of the Fathers has seen several high points. In the scholastic period the Fathers were seen as "authorities," who could be introduced significantly into theological debate. At that time, too, the Greek Fathers were being translated into Latin. There were many *Florilegia patrum,* or collections of texts of the Fathers, in the Middle Ages. From the time of the Renaissance, textual study arose, and more critical texts began to appear. The 19th century saw a new awakening in patristics, led by such theologians as J.A. Möhler (q.v.), M. Scheeben (q.v.) and J.H. Newman (q.v.). As texts became more readily available, theology continued to benefit. Around the 1950s there was some unease in magisterial circles about patristics: it was becoming clearer that the Fathers could not always be relied upon to support manual theology or even some statements of the magisterium (q.v.). By the time of Vatican II there was a well-developed theology of the Fathers, and adequate knowledge of sources, to be used at the service of the council.[6]

The important 1989 *Instruction on the Fathers* from the Congregation for Christian Education[7] reiterates the distinction between patrology (the historical and literary study of the Fathers), a term coined by the Lutheran J. Gerhard in 1653, and patristics (the study of their theological thought). It stresses the abiding role of the Fathers in theology and theological education, a point made several times by Vatican II (DV 23; OT 16) and subsequent documents.[8]

The Fathers of the Church are a *locus theologicus* (v. THEOLOGICAL SOURCES). Their unanimous consent in matters of doctrine or exegesis is considered by theologians to give certainty; in practice such unanimity would be hard to establish on a particular point. At various times it was held that in some general or wide sense the Fathers were inspired.[9]

The English-speaking world is quite well served by collections of translations of the Fathers made in the 19th[10] and 20th centuries.[11] Collected patristic texts on specific topics are found in many languages.[12] Study aids for patristics and patrology continually appear in all of the major languages. Of particular importance are those by J. Quasten[13] and the recent Italian patristic dictionary now in English.[14] In addition, all theological dictionaries and encyclopedias have relevant entries.

The present work has articles dealing mainly with the ecclesiology of some of the more important Fathers and ecclesiastical writers: Ambrose, Augustine, Basil, Bede, Bernard, Clement of Rome, Ps-Clement, Cyprian, *Didachê*, Ps-Dionysius, Gregory the Great, Gregory Nazianzus, Ps-Hippolytus (v. APOSTOLIC TRADITION), Hilary, Hermas, Ignatius of Antioch, Irenaeus, Leo the Great, Maximus, Origen, Polycarp, Tertullian.

---

[1]Patrology 1:1.  [2]A.-G. Hamman, *Jacques-Paul Migne: Le retour aux pères de l'Église.* Le point théologique 16 (Paris: Beauchesne, 1975); L.C. Sheppard, "The Abbé Jacques-Paul Migne," AmBenR 7 (1956) 112–128.  [3]*Corpus christianorum*—series latina CCL and series graeca CCG (Paris, 1953–); *Corpus scriptorum ecclesiasticorum latinorum* (Vienna, 1866–)—CSEL; *Die griechischen christlichen Schriftsteller* (Leipzig, 1897–)—GCS; *Sources chrétiennes* (Paris, 1941–)—SC. Innumerable other individual texts have critical editions.  [4]From 1993 by Chadwyck-Healey Ltd—Cambridge UK 4—Alexandria, Va.—Paris—Madrid.  [5]*Corpus scriptorum christianorum orientalium,* over 350 volumes (Paris, 1903–); *Patrologia orientalis,* over 30 volumes (Paris, 1907–).  [6]A.M. Triacca, "L'uso dei 'loci' patristici nei documenti del concilio Vaticano II: Un caso emblematico e problematico," Sales 53 (1991) 219–253.  [7]30 Nov. 1989; see M. Angel Flores R., "Los padres de la iglesia en el estudio de la teología," EfMex 8/24 (1990) 341–358; Sales 52 (1991) 3–148.  [8]E.g., Congregation for Christian Education, *The Theological Formation of Future Priests* (1976) nn. 30–33, 74, 85–88, 92. See Istituto Patristico Augustinianum, *Lo studio dei Padri della Chiesa oggi* (Rome: Lateran UP, 1977) = Seminarium 17 (1977); AA.VV. *Conferenze patristiche in occasione dell'inaugurazione dell'Istituto Patristico Augustianum Roma, 4–7 maggio 1970* (Rome: Augustianum, 1970); C. Kannengiesser, "The Future of Patristics," TS 52 (1991) 128–139; M. Pelligrino, "I padri della Chiesa hanno qualcosa da dire all'uomo d'oggi," AugR 17 (1977) 453–460.  [9]G. Bardy, "L'inspiration des Pères de l'Église," RechSR 40 (1952) 7–26.  [10]Ante-Nicene Library (Edinburgh, 1886–1892) and Ante-Nicene Fathers (Buffalo and New York, 1884–1886); Library of the Fathers (Oxford, 1838–1888); Nicene and Post-Nicene Fathers (Buffalo and New York, 1886–1890).  [11]*Ancient Christian Writers* (Westminster, Md.: 1946– ); *The*

*Fathers of the Church* (New York, 1947– ); Loeb Classical Library (London and Cambridge, Mass., 1912– ).  [12]E.g., T. Halton, general ed., Message of the Fathers of the Church. 22 vols. (Wilmington: Glazier, from 1984).  [13]*Patrology.* 3 vols. (Utrecht: Spectrum, 1950—Westminster, Md.: Christian Classics, 1986) with vol. 4, A. de Bernardino, ed. (Westminster, Md.: Christian Classics, 1986).  [14]A. de Bernardino, ed., *Dizionario patristico e di anticichità cristiane.* 3 vols. (Rome: Institutum Patristicum Augustinaum—Marietti, 1983–1988). Eng. trans. A. Walford, with additions by W.H.C. Frend, *Encyclopedia of the Early Church.* 2 vols. (Cambridge UK: Clarke, 1992).

## FEBRONIANISM

Febronianism in some ways can be seen as a German version of Gallicanism (q.v.). It represents anti-papal views and includes a theory of Church-State relations. In 1742, at the request of the three archbishop-electors, the bishop of Trier, J.N. von Hontheim (1701–1790), studied their grievances against Rome, and in 1763 wrote *The State of the Church and the Legitimate Power of the Roman Pontiff.*[1] The book was written with ecumenical intent also. It appeared under the penname of "Justinus Febronius." The book acknowledges the pope as head of the Church, but the power of the keys is given to the whole Church. The pope is to seek the unity of the Church but is not infallible, and is inferior to a general council. All bishops are equal, and infallibility resides in the whole Church. The author attacks the medieval accretions to the papacy, especially those which came through the *False Decretals* (q.v.). His views would have led to the creation of a German Church, largely independent of Rome, and subject to the prince, almost as a part of his government. The book, however, was placed on the *Index* (q.v.) in 1764. Von Hontheim may have recanted by 1778. His ideas, as disseminated by V. Eybel in a book *What Is the Pope* (1782), were condemned by Clement XIV in 1786.[2] With the French Revolution and the lack of support among the German bishops, Febronianism collapsed at the end of the 18th century.

---

[1]Antón 2:34-36, 84–87, 105–108; Congar, Augustin 407–408; M. O'Callaghan NCE 5:868-869; OxDCC 506.  [2]DS 2592–2597; cf. ND 812.

## FEENEY, Leonard (1903–1978)

The Jesuit Leonard Feeney taught at the St. Benedict Center at Cambridge, Mass. In the 1940s he proposed a rigorist interpretation of the doctrine "Outside the Church There is No Salvation" (q.v.).[1] He held that anyone who was not a Roman Catholic—except catechumens with the intention of entering the Church—could not be saved. A group of his followers were called the Slaves of the Immaculate Heart of Mary. He saw the archbishop of Boston as being in heresy in allowing that non-Roman Catholics could be saved. Eventually he was expelled from the Jesuits and excommunicated, but was reconciled before he died on 30 January 1978.

The controversy had the beneficial effect of a clarification in the Church teaching by the then Holy Office in an open letter to Archbishop Cushing, *Suprema haec sacra* (1949).[2]

---

[1]F.A. Sullivan, *Salvation Outside the Church? Tracing the History of the Catholic Response* (New York—Mahwah.: Paulist—London: Chapman, 1992) 3–4, 115–116, 134–136.  [2]AmER 127 (1952) 308–315/DS 3866–3872/ND 854–857.

## FEMINISM AND THE CHURCH

Feminism is a huge and developing area, not only of theology but also of history, sociology, psychology, philosophy, economics, and other disciplines. Here we seek to contextualize it briefly, showing some of the implications for theology, particularly ecclesiology; left to a special article, to be read along with the present one, is the question of women's ordination (q.v.).

The vast literature on feminism[1] is mostly in English and German; so far there is not so much in the Latin languages.[2] As a rapidly developing area of research, reflection, and praxis in many cultures and countries, feminism does not yet have a universally accepted vocabulary or set of symbols. As it is not thus far a fully coherent movement, but one witnessing to a variety of positions, any broad survey will be liable to criticism from any number of different perspectives. For the purpose of this article the categories of S. Schneiders will be used.[3]

There is a general term, "women's movements," which can apply to many efforts by women throughout history to better their situation or to set right the wrongs they perceive themselves to suffer precisely because they are women. These include individual women[4] as well as groups. A second term is "women's emancipation," which in a narrow sense refers to the movement from the 19th century to allow women a vote in democratic societies; it finally succeeded in the 20th century: e.g., United Kingdom (1918), USA (1920). The agenda of this movement was often more extensive than mere universal suffrage, and included other elements concerned with women's rights. Feminism in a stricter sense comes in the 1960s with such books as B. Friedan's *The Feminine Mystique* (1963) and later G. Greer's *The Female Eunuch* (1970). Christian feminism can be dated from the publication of Mary Daly's *The Church and the Second Sex*.[5]

There are a number of factors which are usually found in feminist thinkers: women's experience of patriarchy; lack of equality; discrimination. There is a division about the tactics to be employed for securing the aims of feminism. Should it pursue human rights by insisting on the same humanity that women and men

share together, or should it emphasize the difference arising from gender and thus focus on women's rights?

The final goal is clear, expressed thus by S. Schneiders: ". . . a human social order in which women are fully self-determining, fully participating members."[6] She describes the phenomenon of feminism as "a comprehensive ideology which is rooted in women's experience of sexual oppression, [which] engages in a critique of patriarchy as an essentially dysfunctional system, embraces an alternative vision for humanity and the earth, and actively seeks to bring this vision to realization."[7] She notes four forms of feminism, each having a different stance towards patriarchy and evaluation of perceived discrimination: liberal feminism, which seeks a social order in which women will have political and legal rights equal to those of men; cultural feminism, which looks for a world enriched by the mutual and equal contributions of men and women; social feminism, in which all discrimination would cease; radical feminism, in which a basic egalitarianism is sought, one much more comprehensive than equal individual rights. This last, more clearly than the others, is sensitive to oppression in all its forms, and is committed to a fundamental change in society.[8]

The oppression of women is seen by feminists as crossing all social and religious divides, even though it may be expressed with extra pain in feminist writings by or about black women;[9] the pain of color discrimination can be mingled with, and confused with, the pain of sexual discrimination.[10]

Throughout specialist journals[11] and the extensive literature from a vast array of perspectives,[12] it is obvious that feminist theology shares much with liberation theologies (q.v.).[13] Quite crucial in both is a new hermeneutic which examines classical texts like the Bible and Tradition from the perspective of women's experience and their analysis of patriarchy.[14] A narrow view of hermeneutics will almost inevitably lead to the biblical text seeming too negative, even oppressive, concerning women.[15] But the hermeneutic of suspicion is not without problems for a Catholic theology: to see the Scriptures solely as a text written by the victors of a class struggle can run the risk of denying the incarnational way in which God's revelation is mediated to us.[16]

Early works of R.R. Ruether examine the whole range of Catholic theology from a feminist stance.[17] Very significant feminist readings of the Scripture exist, written by both women and men, as well as scriptural studies by men sensitive to feminist issues.[18] The OT tradition about women, and passages indicating the maternal aspect of God, like Hosea chapter 11, have been well researched.[19] It is, however, quite astounding that the new *Catechism* can instance the OT prayers of Abraham, Moses, Elijah, David, and Solomon[20] without any allusion to the great prayers of women in the OT, e.g., Hannah (1 Sam 2:1-10), Esther (Esth 14:3-19); Judith (Jdt 9:1-14).

The origins of the Church and the expressions of its life in NT times are clearly crucial.[21] Here feminist scholars and others can clearly see the socio-cultural conditioning of Church structures in the NT patriarchal society.[22] They reasonably argue that texts like 1 Cor 11:2-16 or 1 Tim 2:12 are not normative for succeeding ages. They take full account of the portrait of Jesus and women in John[23] and especially Luke.[24] They emphasize the role of women as resurrection witnesses. They are more alert to possible implications of various texts: the persecution of women as well as men by Saul (Acts 9:2 with 5); the role played by Priscilla (Acts 18:2, 18, 26; Rom 16:3); the prophesying of the daughters of Philip (Acts 21:9); the position of Lydia (Acts 16:14-15); the consequences of Phoebe being called a deacon (Greek *diakonos* is masculine—Rom 16:1); the implications of the ministries of women in Rom 16.[25] They can sense with some probability that the companion of Cleopas on the road to Emmaus was his wife (Luke 24:13-18). They see clearly that some ministry belonged to women in the NT (v. WOMEN'S ORDINATION). The abolition of differences, including gender, for all who are one in Christ (Gal 3:28) is seen as particularly important.

But though the deeper significance of these and other texts has been overlooked in the past, and still needs further reflection, there remain three profound problems for feminist Christians. The first is the patriarchal language and symbolism about the Trinitarian Godhead itself. Many feminists do not reject the naming of God as Father: it can serve for an indication of divine creativity, protection, delight, and care, rather than patriarchy.[26] But they will often insist that the notion of Father needs to be complemented by other symbols, e.g., Mother, even while acknowledging its limitations too.[27] But it can be argued that much of this debate involves a distortion in both linguistics and theology: linguistic gender cannot be equated with sex; analogies about the Godhead theologically deny what many people see affirmed in them—rather than God is like a male human father, the point is that I am truly a child in relation to God.[28] There remains also the problem of speaking to or about God in liturgy, a matter which is being carefully studied by the International Commission on English in the Liturgy (ICEL).[29] The identification of God with Sophia-Wisdom (v. SOPHIOLOGY)[30] is important in giving other insights into the mystery of the Godhead and into the Church.

The second problem centers around the maleness of Christ. Given the fact that an incarnation of the Divine Word involved the choice of one sex, the choice of the male sex need not cause insuperable difficulties, provided the image of Christ is not manipulated in favor

of patriarchy; the precise problem lies in the fact that men are insufficiently like Christ in that they support patriarchy.[31]

The third problem is the development and persistence of patriarchal structures of Church ministry, apparently having in some sense their origins in the ministry of Jesus himself, who chose only male apostles (q.v.) for his closest associates, even though he had women as disciples who ministered to him (Luke 8:2-3—v. WOMEN'S ORDINATION).

The Tradition is hard to analyze critically and objectively. Undoubtedly outrageous things are said about women by Greek philosophers and by some Fathers and Doctors of the Church. One would also have to point to some less than forthright selectivity of quotations by feminist writers, often without any advertence to context; the much abused Augustine, while no feminist, was not a narrow misogynist either.[32] Though one would not wish to defend the many negative statements by distinguished witnesses to Christian tradition, it is important to understand some of the reasons. Society in Europe was undoubtedly patriarchal: philosophy and theology reflected society; the patriarchy in the early centuries had roots also in Greek philosophy and Roman law.[33] The socio-economic climate explains why women were seldom called "laity" (q.v.). But there was also profound misunderstanding about women: the processes of conception, and critically the existence of the ovum, were understood only in the 19th century (generally credited to E.V. Baer, in 1827); gynecological matters were treated by midwives rather than by the ancient or medieval doctors; men, even doctors, were left in ignorance about many matters. The more pessimistic writers focused on the earlier "Yahwist" Genesis chapters 2–3 rather than on the later "Priestly" account of Gen 1:27-28, which teaches the radical equality of men and women as in the image and likeness of God. Even granted all the ambivalence of the Fathers towards women, there are many passages of great depth and value about women in the patristic tradition.[34] There is evidence of women theologians such as the patrician women on the Aventine who assisted Jerome in his work, especially by criticism, and the women who asked Augustine quite sophisticated questions.[35] But the negative picture of women has still been operative in theology and teaching even after Vatican II.

The medieval tradition carried on from the patristic era: one encounters the same kinds of affirmation, both positive and negative. Even into modern times the German three Ks (*Kinder-Kirche-Küche* = children, Church, kitchen) fairly accurately summed up the place of women in society and the Church.

The magisterium since the 1960s is becoming aware of feminism and the situation of women. An early witness was John XXIII who, in his encyclical

*Pacem in terris,*[36] noted the emergence of women into public life as an important sign of the times.

Since Vatican II largely preceded the modern feminist movement,[37] its teaching on women is still rather tentative. The first substantial intervention on the role of women in the Church and society at the council was by Msgr. Coderre (28 Oct. 1964); on Schema 13, which would become GS, there were fifteen interventions on women in the third session and ten in the fourth. There are some important statements by the council on women: GS 60 condemns discrimination of all kinds, including discrimination on the grounds of sex (cf. GS 9); AA 9 observes, "Since women are increasingly taking an active part in the whole life of society, it is important that their participation in the various fields of the Church's apostolate should also increase (cf. GS 55, 60)"; AA 32 wishes that both men and women should have available study centers, not only in theology but also in anthropology, psychology, sociology, and methodology "to help develop aptitudes . . . for every field of the apostolate"; GS 52 shows awareness of "legitimate advancement of women in society." Often ignored is the closing message of the council, in which there is a long section addressed to women, characterized by openness to women's special contribution to the world.[38]

The developing magisterium on women is instanced further by the address of Paul VI in 1975, the International Year of Women. Along with many encouraging statements, there is, however, a tendency still evident to see women too much in terms of states in life specified by their sexuality: girls, mothers, wives, widows, and virgins.[39] The Pastoral Commission of the Congregation for the Evangelization of Peoples issued a significant document in 1976, "The Role of Women in Evangelization."[40] It is an attempt to identify women's specific gifts and contribution to the work of evangelization.

The new *Code of Canon Law* notably carries forward the conciliar teaching. In its important titles on the rights and duties of all the Christian faithful (CIC 208–223) and of the lay Christian faithful (CIC 224–231), women and men are equal, except for the exclusion of the former from the permanent ministries of acolytes and readers (CIC 230 § 1—*viri laici*). Compared with previous Church practice, there are a number of welcome innovations: discrimination in the matter of domicile (CIC 104) and transfer of rite (CIC 112); regulations concerning the confessional (CIC 964), the place of marriage (CIC 1115) or burial (CIC 1177); the possibility of women acting as judges in tribunals (CIC 1421 § 2); and preaching in Church (but not a homily—CIC 766–767).[41]

Pope John Paul II addressed questions about women in his apostolic letter "On the Dignity and Vocation of Women on the Occasion of the Marian Year" (MD).[42] Since many feminists have problems with the Church's presentation of Mary (v. MARY AND THE CHURCH), the Marian context and opening chapters on her may not make for an immediately receptive readership. The Pope decided "to give this text the style and character of a meditation" (MD 2).[43] He reinterprets texts traditionally used to suggest a secondary role for women to bring out the radical equality of men and women: Gen 2–3 (MD 6–7); Eph 5:25-32 (MD 23–26, 29). The anthropomorphic notion of fatherhood in God must include also what is maternal; indeed even "fatherhood" in God is completely divine and free of the "masculine" bodily characteristics proper to human fatherhood" (MD 8). Male domination was brought about by human sin and must be overcome by conversion and grace (MD 10). The Eve-Mary analogy is given a very positive interpretation (MD 9–11). The Gospel picture of women has extended treatment (MD 12–16). There is a warning that women should not abandon their own "feminine originality" in seeking to assume masculine characteristics (MD 10).[44] The document has disappointed some by its ruling out of women's ordination (q.v.). A weakness would seem to lie in its tendency to see women primarily in terms of marriage relationship or virginity, rather than in all that is constitutive of being a woman; the treatment of the feminine values shared by men is hesitant; a fuller treatment of women's proper sharing in masculinity could be desired.[45] It would, however, be unjust to regard the document as regressive. It is in many respects a significant development in Church teaching about women. Though it is not perfect, and its treatment of the issues may not always be fully satisfactory, it is a valuable contribution to a dialogue that must be ongoing within the Church. The document is not perhaps sufficiently forthright about other values found in feminist writing: concern for ecology, for deep human values, for a holistic spirituality.

A still more open document of the present pope is his 1995 letter to "Women Throughout the World." Significant points are: the wider scope and more positive tone than MD; the pope's formal apology for the Church's failures in its relation to women; its deeper sensitivity to the cultural factors that work against the full dignity of women; the strong assertion of the equality of men and women and their essential complementarity.[46]

The serious problem of the place of women in the Church is only a more acute aspect of the practical failure of the post-Vatican II Church to take the laity (q.v.) really seriously. If we leave aside married deacons (q.v.), who, though significant, are not yet a major feature of the Church's life, only a tiny percentage of men belong to what is perceived as the patriarchal hierarchy; the rest of men in the Church are quite as disenfranchised as women.

Feminism will always be a deep challenge to faith for those who see its vision. It can scarcely be denied that the Church in actual practice does manifest patriarchal features in its life, and especially in the way in which the clerical hierarchy functions. These belong to the unrenewed, sinful dimension of the Church called upon to be holy (q.v.). This sinfulness is such that a growing number of women in the Church find themselves psychologically and spiritually outside it. Not only the Church, but Christianity itself is not an option for a growing number of women.

There is further the problem that authority (q.v.) in the Church is at times exercised more like secular power than gospel service (Matt 20:25-28). The laity, both men and women, see themselves excluded from power. The consequence is that both then seek a share in power. Rather they should be led to true participation in communion (q.v.) in the Church at all levels and to the experience of authority which succeeds in empowering others for the service of the kingdom. To the extent that the clergy not only are, but are seen to be, real servants of the whole people, some diminution of patriarchal attitudes will evolve.

The most serious problem of the patriarchal features of the Church is that women especially can feel alienated from the very heart of the Church—the Eucharist (q.v.). Instead of being the source of the Church's life, indeed its ultimate meaning, the Eucharist can be perceived as a negative symbol of patriarchy. An important, but rather recent, development is the creation of women's liturgies, new types of symbol and ritual which allow women (and men) to express creatively fuller dimensions of humanity in communion with others.[47] But while welcoming such initiatives, one would wish to make two serious observations. First, such liturgies should allow openness to the Eucharist celebrated by an ordained priest, which alone fully expresses the *Catholica,* or universal Church of men and women of all times and places, with members struggling on earth and some already in glory. Second, there are liturgies which use symbols and language which belong more to New Age (v. MOVEMENTS, NON-CHRISTIAN) than to Christian values; such are those involving Mother Earth/Gaia, Wicca or witchcraft, which would have no place in an authentic Catholic worship. But the Church must heed valid insights about the meaning for the Church of redemption arising from feminist writers, even if these are still exploratory and debatable in some respects.[48]

Questions of feminism are now arising also in the Orthodox Church, in which there has been as little participation by women as in the Catholic Church.[49] Some evangelical Christians are producing significant studies,[50] though other evangelicals in the name of biblical literalism show themselves hostile to feminist

thought. But the greater participation of women from all states in the life, ministry, and especially decision-making of Protestant Churches has perhaps left the feminist agenda less acute in them than in the Catholic and Orthodox Churches. There is also a growing literature on feminism in other religions.[51]

In an imperfect world in which no utopia is in sight, feminists who strive for the true place of men and women will inevitably experience the Cross, which is the inescapable consequence of Christian discipleship (see Mark 8:34-38). At the heart of the Church lies the proclamation of Jesus as power and wisdom for every human situation.[52] For feminists experiencing the pain of a Church as yet unrenewed, there is an absolute necessity for spiritualities that express this central truth about Jesus for them,[53] and that express more fully the genuine human values that are to be found in the Church's tradition, especially its mystical inheritance. New Age or secular spiritualities will not suffice.[54]

There is a problem arising from the almost universal acceptance of human experience as a starting point for feminist theology; the danger is that theology starting from experience can tend to remain there. Theology "from below," ascending from the human to the divine, has distinguished protagonists—K. Rahner springs to mind—and is the dominant approach today. But there are also profound values in a theology "from above" which descends from the Trinitarian God to humanity. Some of the apparently intractable problems encountered in feminism related to the Church may have more profound solutions if we begin with the eternal Mystery instead of with human experience. There is need for a deeper exploration of Trinitarian life reflected in women and men being in the image of God;[55] the divine image in humanity can serve to interpret experience.

Feminism is a graced challenge for the Church today. It cannot be ignored by ecclesiology or any other branch of theology, including morality.[56] It is perhaps the most radical of the justice issues that must be faced by the Church.[57]

---

[1]Most books in following notes have bibliog. See also early works: A.E. Patrick, "Women and Religion: A Survey of Significant Literature 1965–1974," TS 36 (1975) 737–765; M.A. Warren, *The Nature of Woman: An Encyclopedia and Guide to the Literature* (Inverness, Calif.: Edgepress, 1980); *The Woman in the Church. La femme dans l'Église. Bibliographie internationale 1975–1982. International Bibliography.* RIC Supplément 70–71 (Strasbourg: Cerdic, 1982). [2]See CredOggi 68 (1992/2) for Italian and French titles. [3]*Beyond Patching* (New York—Mahwah, 1991) 5–36. [4]E.g., D. Spender, *Feminist Theorists: Three Centuries of Women Thinkers* (New York: Pantheon, 1983); M. Schneir, *Feminism: The Essential Historical Writings* (New York: Random, 1972). [5]San Francisco: Harper & Row, 1968. [6]N. 3, p. 15. [7]Ibid., 15; see Conc 182 (1985) and 1991/6; H. Mayer-Wilmes, "Women's Nature and Feminine Identity. Theological Legitimations and Feminist Questions," Conc 194 (1987) 93–101. [8]N. 3, pp. 25–30. [9]E.g., B. Hooks, *Ain't I a Woman: Black Women and Feminism* (Boston:

South End, 1981); P. Giddings, *When and Where I Enter: The Influence of Black Women on Race and Sex in America* (Toronto—New York: Bantam, 1985); R. Ruether, "Crisis in Sex and Race: Black Theology vs. Feminist Theology," in G.H. Anderson and T.F. Stransky, eds., *Liberation Theologies*. Mission Trends 4 (New York—Ramsey: Paulist—Grand Rapids, Mich.: Eerdmans, 1979) 175–188. [10]S. Thistlethwaite, *Sex, Race and God: Christian Feminism in Black and White* (New York: Crossroad, 1989). [11]E.g., *Feminist Studies* (Sheffield); *Feminist Theology* (Sheffield UK); *Femmes et hommes dans l'Église* (Paris); *Journal of Feminist Studies in Religion* (Atlanta, Ga.), *WomanSpirit* (Dublin). [12]B. Booten and N. Greinacher, eds., *Frauen in der Männerkirche* (Munich: Kaiser—Mainz: Grünewald, 1982); L. Bouyer, *Women in the Church* (San Francisco: Ignatius, 1979); W. Burghardt, ed., *Women: New Dimensions* (New York: Paulist, 1977); A.E. Carr, *Transforming Grace: Christian Tradition and Women's Experience* (San Francisco: Harper & Row, 1990); R. Coll, *Women and Religion: A Reader for Clergy* (New York—Ramsey: Paulist, 1982); R.A. Coll, *Christianity and Feminism in Conversation* (Mystic, Conn.: Twenty-Third Publications, 1994); G. Dautzenberg et al., eds., *Die Frau im Urchristentum*. QDisput 95 (Freiburg—Basel—Vienna: Herder, 1983); J. Galot, "La femme dans l'Église," Greg 68 (1987); M. Grey, "Has Feminist Theology a Vision for the Christian Church?," LouvSt 16 (1991) 27–40; M. Humm, ed., *Feminisms: A Reader* (New York—London: Harvester-Wheatsheaf, 1992); A. Loades, *Feminist Theology: A Reader* (London: SPCK, 1990); J.L. Wiedman, *Christian Feminism: Visions of a New Humanity* (San Francisco: Harper & Row, 1984); Conc 1991/6; TS 36 (1975) 557–724. [13]W. Beinert, ed., *Frauenbefreiung und Kirche: Darstellung—Analyse—Dokumentation* (Regensburg: Pustet, 1987); M.I. Buckley, "Feminist Perspectives on a Faith that Liberates," ChicSt 19 (1980) 129–143; E. Schüssler-Fiorenza, "Feminist Theology as a Critical Theology of Liberation," TS 36 (1975) 605–626 = eadem, *Discipleship of Equals: A Critical* Ekklesia-*logy of Liberation* (London: SCM, 1993) 53–80; M.J. Ress, "Feminist Theologians Challenge Church (May 31, 1984)," in A.T. Hennelly, ed., *Liberation Theology: A Documentary History* (Maryknoll: Orbis, 1990) 385–389. [14]A.Y. Collins, ed., *Feminist Perspectives in Biblical Scholarship* (Chico, Calif.: Scholars Press, 1985). [15]S.M. Schneiders, "Feminist Ideology Criticism and Biblical Hermeneutics," BibTB 19 (1989) 3–10; E.J. Johnson, "Feminist Hermeneutics," ChicSt 27 (1988) 123–135; E. Wainwright, "In Search of the Lost Coin: Towards a Feminist Biblical Hermeneutic," Pacifica 2 (1989) 135–150; J. Zumstein, "Liminaire: (Pourquoi s'intéresser à l'exégèse féministe?)," FoiVie 88/5 (1989) 1–11. [16]J.A. Little, "Sexual Equality in the Church: A Theological Resolution to the Anthropological Dilemma," HeythJ 28 (1987) 165–178. [17]*Sexism and God-Talk: Towards a Feminist Theology* (London: SCM, 1983, [2]1992) with companion volume *Womanguides: Readings Toward a Feminist Theology* (Boston: Beacon, 1985). [18]See J.S. Kselman NJBC 1129; S.M. Schneiders, ibid., 1162; L. Russell, ed., *Feminist Interpretation of the Bible* (Philadelphia: Westminster, 1985); E. Schüssler Fiorenza, "'You Are Not to Be Called Father': Early Christian History in a Feminist Perspective," CrossC 29 (1979–1980) 301–323. [19]M.-T. Wacker, "God as Mother? On the Meaning of a Biblical God-Symbol for Feminist Theology," Conc 206 (1989) 103–111; P. Trible, *God and the Rhetoric of Sexuality* (Philadelphia: Fortress, 1978); eadem, *Texts of Terror* (Philadelphia: Fortress, 1984). [20]Nn. 2568–2584. [21]*Women in the New Testament: A Select Bibliography*. Bibliography Series 1 (Oslo: Oslo UP, 1990); E. Schüssler Fiorenza, *In Memory of Her: A Feminist Theological Reconstruction of Christian Origins* (New York: Crossroad—London: SCM, 1983); B. Witherington III, *Women in the Earliest Churches*. Society for NT Studies 59 (Cambridge UK: UP, 1989); idem, *Women and the Genesis of Christianity* (Cambridge UK: UP, 1990). [22]P. Perkins, *Ministering in the Pauline Churches* (New York—Ramsey: Paulist, 1982). Cf. A.M. Dubarle, "Paul et l'antiféminisme," RSPT 60 (1976) 261–280. [23]R.E. Brown, "Roles of Women in the Fourth Gospel," TS 36 (1975) 688–699; J. Rena, Women in the Gospel of John," EglT 17 (1986) 131–147 = TDig 34 (1987) 241–245; S.M. Schneiders, "Women in the Fourth Gospel and the Role of Women in Contemporary Society," BibTB 12 (1982) 35–45. [24]D.C. Sim, "The Women Followers of Jesus: The Implications of Lk 8:1-3," HeythJ 30 (1989) 51–62. [25]P. Richardson, "From Apostles to Virgins: Romans 16 and the Roles of Women in the Early Church," TorontoJT 2 (1986) 232–261. [26]E.A. Johnson, *She Who Is: The Mystery of God in Feminist Theological Discourse* (New York: Crossroad, 1993) 282 n. 57; cf. Conc 143 (1981)—critical. [27]S. McFague, *Models of God: Theology for an Ecological, Nuclear Age* (Philadelphia: Fortress—London: SCM, 1987) 91–123, abbreviated Conc 206 (1989) 138–143; U. King, "The Divine as Mother," Conc 206 (1989) 128–137. [28]G.H. Tavard, "Sexist Language in Theology?," TS 36 (1975) 700–724; cf. S. Thistlethwaite, "Inclusive Language and Linguistic Blindness," TTod 43 (1986–1987) 533–539. [29]M. Collins, Naming God in Public Prayer," Worship 59 (1985) 291–304; L. Roy, "Inclusive Language Regarding God," Worship 65 (1991) 207–215; cf. B. Wren, *What Language Shall I Borrow? God-Talk at Worship: A Male Response to Feminist Theology* (New York: Crossroad, 1989); R.M. Frye, "On Praying 'Our Father:' The Challenge of Radical Feminist Language for God," AngTR 73 (1991) 388–402. [30]Johnson (n. 26) 124–187. [31]M.L. Cook, "The Image of Jesus as Liberating for Women," ChicSt 27 (1988) 136–150; E.A. Johnson, "Jesus, the Wisdom of God: A Biblical Basis for a Non-Androcentric Christology," ETL 50 (1985) 261–294; eadem, "The Maleness of Christ," Conc 1991/6: 108-116; R.R. Ruether, "The Liberation of Christology from Patriarchy," NBlackfr 66 (1985) 324–335. [32]N. Blásquez, "Feminismo agustiniano," AugM 27 (1982) 3–53; T.J. van Bavel, "Augustine's View on Women," AugL 39 (1989) 5–53. See K.E. Børresen, "In Defense of Augustine: How *femina* Is *homo?*," AugL 40 (1990) 411–428, correcting her *Subordinance et équivalence: Nature et rôle de la femme d'après Augustin et Thomas d'Aquin* (Paris-Oslo, 1968) revised ed., *Subordination and Equivalence: The Nature and Role of Woman in Augustine and Thomas Aquinas* (Washington, D.C., University Press of America, 1981). [33]M. Collins, "The Refusal of Women in Clerical Circles," in M. Kolbenschlag, ed., *Women in the Church* (Washington, D.C.: Pastoral Press, 1987) 1:51-63. [34]E.A. Clark, *Women in the Early Church*. Message of the Fathers of the Church 13 (Collegeville: Glazier-Liturgical Press, 1983). [35]A. Faivre, "Théologiens 'laïcs' et laïcs théologiens: Position des problèmes à l'époque paléochrétienne," Irén 60 (1987) 193–217; 350–377 at 354–360. [36]AAS 55 (1963) 267–268/Carlen 5:111 at n. 41. [37]R. Goldie, "La participation des laïcs aux travaux du Concile Vatican II," RevSR 62 (1988) 54–73. [38]Abbott, Vatican II 732–734. [39]AAS 67 (1975) 264–267. [40]*Dans le cadre*—DocCath 73 (1976) 612–618/Flannery 2:318-330. [41]See J.H. Provost, in Coriden, CIC 140–141; J.I. Bañares "La consideración de la mujer en el ordenamiento canónico," IusCan 26 (1986) 242–265; E. de Montebello, "La femme et la religieuse: Situation dans le Code de 1983," VieCons 53 (1953) 173–185; P. Martinez Sastre, "La mujer en el Nuevo Código de Derecho Canónico," Carthag 1 (1985) 69–78; M.E. Olmos Ortega, "La participación de los laicos en los órganos de gobierno de la Iglesia (con especial referencia a la mujer)," REspDerCan 46 (1989) 89–114. [42]*Mulieris dignitatem*—AAS 80 (1988) 1653–1729. [43]G. Baum, "Bulletin: The Apostolic Letter *Mulieris dignitatem*," Conc 206 (1989) 144–149; E. García Alvarez, "Ser mujer ahora: Glosa crítica a 'Mulieris dignitatem,' de Juan Pablo II," CiTom 116 (1989) 535–552; D. Lucarella, "Mulieris dignitatem," RasT 29 (1988) 513–526; M. Toso, ed., *Essere donna: Studi sulla lettera apostolica "Mulieris dignitatem" di Giovanni Paolo II* (Turin: Elle Di Ci—Leumann, 1989). [44]See A.-M Pelletier, "Le signe de la femme,"

NRT 113 (1991) 665–689.   [45]See F. Giardini, "The 'Femininity' of Christian Holiness According to 'Mulieris dignitatem' of John Paul II," Ang 67 (1990) 539–554.   [46] OssRomano (English) 17 July 1995.   [47]See T. Berger, "Women and Worship: A Bibliography," StLtg 19 (1989) 96–110; E. Gately, *Psalms of a Laywoman* (Trabuco Canyon: Source Books—Wheathampstead: Clarke, 1992; M. Procter-Smith, *In Her Own Rite: Constructing Feminist Liturgical Tradition* (Nashville: Abingdon, 1990); S. Roll, "Traditional Elements in New Women's Liturgies," QLtg 72 (1991) 43–59. See the various books by M.T. Winter, *Woman Prayer Woman Song: Resources for Ritual/WomanWord/WomanWisdom/WomanWitness* —all New York: Crossroad, 1990–1992.   [48]M. Gray, *Redeeming the Dream: Feminism, Redemption and Christian Tradition* (London: SPCK, 1989).   [49]*Men and Women in the Church* (Syosset, N.Y: Dept. of Religious Education Orthodox Church in America, 1980); E. Behr-Sigel, *Le ministère de la femme dans l'Église* (Paris: Cerf, 1987); eadem, "Les Églises orthodoxes s'interrogent sur la place de la femme dans l'Église," Irén 61 (1988) 523–529; eadem, "La place de la femme dans l'Église," Irén 56 (1983) 46–53, 194–214; E. Timiadis, "The Concern for Women in the Orthodox Tradition," Diak (USA) 12 (1977) 8–23.   [50]S.T. Foh, *Women and the Word of God: A Response to Biblical Feminism* (Grand Rapids, Mich.: Baker, 1979); K. Keay, ed., *Men, Women and God* (London: Marshall Pickering, 1987).   [51]D.L. Carmody, "Feminism and World Religions," Horizons 9 (1982) 313–322; S. Heschel, ed., *On Being a Jewish Feminist* (New York: Schocken Books, 1983).   [52]F. Schüssler Fiorenza, "The Church's Religious Identity and Its Social and Political Mission," TS 43 (1982) 197–225.   [53]L. Byrne, *Women Before God* (London: SPCK, 1988); S. Cady, M. Ronan and H. Taussig, *Sophia: The Future of Feminist Spirituality* (San Francisco: Harper & Row, 1986); R. Chinnici, *Can Women Re-Image the Church?* (New York—Mahwah: Paulist, 1992); J. Chittister, *WomanStrength: Modern Church, Modern Women* (Kansas, Mo.: Sheed & Ward, 1990); J.W. Conn, ed., *Women's Spirituality: Resources for Christian Development* (New York—Mahwah: Paulist, 1986); K. Fischer, *Women at the Well: Feminist Perspectives on Spiritual Direction* (New York—Mahwah: Paulist, 1988); M. Furlong, *A Dangerous Delight: Women and Power in the Church* (London: SPCK, 1991); U. King, *Women and Spirituality: Voices of Protest and Promise.* Women in Society (Basingtoke UK: Macmillan ²1993); J. Leonard, "Teaching Introductory Feminist Spirituality: Tracing the Trajectory Through Women Writers," JFemSt 6 (1990/2) 121–135; C. Osiek, *Beyond Anger: On Being a Feminist in the Church Today* (New York—Mahwah: Paulist—Dublin: Gill and Macmillan, 1986); Schneiders (n. 3) 72–112; eadem, "Feminist Spirituality," NDictCSpir 394–406; Schüssler Fiorenza (n. 13) Discipleship 91–103.   [54]E.g., C. Spretnak, *The Politics of Women's Spirituality: Essays on the Rise of Spiritual Power Within the Feminist Movement* (Garden City, N.Y.: Doubleday-Anchor, 1982).   [55]J.J. O'Donnell, "Man and Woman as *Imago Dei* in the Theology of Hans Urs von Balthasar," CleR 68 (1983) 117–128; M.C. Horowitz, "The Image of God in Man—Is Woman Included?," HarvTR 72 (1979) 175–206.   [56]L.S. Cahill, "Notes on Moral Theology 1989: Feminist Ethics," TS 51 (1990) 49–64; M.A. Farley, "New Patterns of Relationships: Beginnings of a Moral Revolution," TS 36 (1975) 627–646.   [57]J. Chittister, *Women, Ministry and the Church* (New York: Paulist, 1983) 6–8.

## FILIOQUE

First appearing in the 5th and 6th centuries, the addition to the Creed of the words "and from the Son" (*Filioque*) became common in the Frankish Empire from the early 9th century.[1] The formula "from the Father through the Son" (*a Patre per Filium*) surfaced at Nicaea II (787—q.v.). When introduced into their liturgy by Frankish monks at Jerusalem, the words were opposed by some Eastern monks. Charlemagne in 810 appealed to Pope Leo III (795–816), who approved the doctrine but disapproved of additions to the Creed. Photius, Patriarch of Constantinople, condemned both the content and the fact of an addition to the Creed in 860. He saw it as a destruction of the Father's role as sole principle in the Trinity. But this was an attack on the Latin missionaries in Bulgaria rather than against Rome, which had not yet admitted the addition into its liturgical use. At the Photian Synod in 879–880 (v. CONSTANTINOPLE IV), a group anathematized any addition of "false words" to the Creed, but without mentioning the *Filioque*.[2] In the mid-880s Photius again attacked the addition in a letter to the archbishop of Aquileia.[3] In 1014 Benedict VIII officially inserted the *Filioque* into the Creed, which was normally recited during Mass. The *Filioque* issue played a significant role in the mutual excommunications of 1054.

The problem at this early stage of the controversy was a difference in Trinitarian language between the theology of the East and a Western theology which was still somewhat flexible in terminology. The West, following Augustine, tended to begin with the unity of God; the East began with the Trinity manifested in salvation history, and then struggled to affirm the unity of the triune Godhead.[4] As positions hardened, the *Filioque* became the chief gravamen of the Eastern Church against the West. It became not just an issue in Trinitarian theology, but a quarrel about the role of the papacy. In the Latin Church the addition was defended. Anselm[5] appreciated but rejected the Greek formula "From the Father through the Son" and accepted the *Filioque*, but other theologians such as St. Thomas Aquinas pointed out the essential equivalence of different formulae used in the East and the West.[6]

After an abortive attempt at resolving the controversy at Lyons II (q.v.) in 1274, it was agreed at the Council of Florence (q.v.) that the Latin and Eastern formulae were both sound; the Greeks allowed that the Latins were not in heresy, but the *Filioque* was not imposed on the East.[7] Following the rejection of Florence by the Greeks, the *Filioque* has remained a most contentious issue between East and West. While the West called on the East to accept the *Filioque*, it never repudiated the legitimacy of the Eastern expression "through the Son."

Eastern positions are generally extremely negative towards the *Filioque*, though there is renewed interest in the view of the Orthodox theologian B. Bolotov (1854–1900), which regarded the *Filioque* as a legitimate Western theologoumenon, by which he meant a legitimate speculative position rather than a necessary dogmatic truth.[8] Bolotov's position was accepted by S. Bulgakov (q.v.) and P. Evdokimov (q.v.), but is rejected by V. Lossky (1903–1958), N. Nissiotis, and J.D. Zizioulas (q.v.).

At present the magisterium of the West uses the *Filioque* but distinguishes between usage and the common faith of East and West. In the ecumenical dialogue there have been various advances:[9] the Lutheran and Anglican Churches are prepared to drop the *Filioque* in liturgical celebration in some circumstances. The Catholic Church allows it to be omitted in ecumenical services with the Orthodox.[10] There is some evidence of softening on the part of the Moscow Patriarchate, which would not see the *Filioque* as absolutely impeding union.[11] Further study is needed to grasp both the values that the West wanted to protect by the insertion and retention of the *Filioque*, and also the truths which the East wishes to guard by its rejection of the formula.

[1]B. Bobrinskoy, "Le 'Filioque' hier et aujourd'hui," Contacts 34 (1982) 7–27; Hegumen Boniface, "The Filioque Question," Diak (USA) 15 (1980) 74–81; M. O'Carroll, *Veni Creator Spiritus: A Theological Encyclopedia of the Holy Spirit* (Collegeville: Glazier-Liturgical Press, 1990) 81–84; D. Ritschel, "The History of the Filioque Controversy," Conc 128 (1979) 3–14. [2]V. Grumel, "Le Filioque au concile photien de 879–80 et le témoignage de Michel d'Anchialos," ÉchOr 29 (1930) 257–263; idem, "Le décret du synode photien de 879 à 880 sur le symbole de la foi," ÉchOr 37 (1938) 357–372. [3]PG 102:793-821. [4]E. Clapsis, "The Filioque Question," PatByzR 1 (1982) 127–136. [5]*De processione S. Spiritus*—PL 158:309-310. [6]ST 1a, q.36, aa. 2–4. [7]Tanner 1:525-527/DS 1300–1302/ND 322–324. [8]*Anglican-Orthodox Dialogue: The Dublin Agreed Statement 1984* (Crestwood, N.Y.: St. Vladimir's Seminary Press, 1985) 26–28. See S. Virgulin, "Il Filioque nel pensiero del teologo russo V.B. Bolotov," in *Credo in Spiritum Sanctum*. Atti del Congresso teologico internazionale di pneumatologia (1982). 2 vols. (Vatican, 1983) 1:355-363. [9]J.C. Bauerschmidt, "'Filioque' and the Episcopal Church," AngTR 73 (1991) 7–25; M.E. Chapmen, "A Lutheran Proposal for the Neuralgic Question of the *Filioque:* The LWF at Curitiba, Brazil, 1990," JEcuSt 28 (1991) 239–259; L.J. James, "Theological Indifferentism and the Filioque Heresy," PatByzR 19 (1991) 183–192; T. Stylianopoulos, "An Ecumenical Solution to the Filioque Question?," JEcuSt 28 (1991) 260–280. [10]Origins 17 (1988) 749. A. de Halleux, "Pour un accord oecuménique sur la procession de l'Esprit Saint et l'addition du 'Filioque' au symbole," Irén 51 (1978) 451–469, 535; L. Vischer, ed., *Spirit of God, Spirit of Christ: Ecumenical Reflections on the Filioque Controversy*. Faith and Order Paper 103 (Geneva: WCC, 1981); cf. *Confessing One Faith: An Ecumenical Explication of the Apostolic Faith as It Is Confessed in the Nicene-Constantinopolitan Creed* (381). Faith and Order Paper 153 (Geneva: WCC, 1991). [11]"The Filioque in the Ecumenical Perspective," *The Journal of the Moscow Patriarchate* 3 (1982) 66–68.

## FLORENCE, Council of (1438–ca. 1445)

The Council of Florence is unique in setting out to be a council of reunion.[1] Opening in Ferrara on 8 January 1438, it was transferred to Florence in 1439 and to Rome about 1444. Like Lyons II (q.v.), which was also concerned with reunion, the official acts of Florence are lost, and we have to rely on texts of speeches, bulls, unofficial acts, and indirect evidence.[2] Also, as at Lyons II, a principal motive for Eastern participation was the need for military assistance; on doctrinal matters the Greeks intended to prove the Latins to be in error. Eugenius IV (1431–1447), who summoned the council, saw in union a support in the struggle with the conciliarist Council of Basle (q.v.); at various stages of the council there are condemnations of the contemporaneous Council of Basle.[3]

The opening session (9 April 1438) led to a discussion about purgatory (q.v.). Though agreement on this was not reached in Ferrara, it was already clear that two theologies and methods were clashing: the logical scholastic one of the Latins and the patristic argumentation of the Greeks. In October 1438 the key issue of the whole council was touched on, viz., the addition of the words "and the Son" (*Filioque*—q.v.) to the "Nicene" Creed (q.v.). For nearly three months there was an impasse. The Greeks sustained the canon of Ephesus (q.v.), which forbade additions to the Creed.[4] The Latins claimed that it was legitimate to clarify the faith. With the transfer to Florence, discussion was renewed in March 1439, mainly between the two official orators, the intransigent anti-unionist Mark Eugenicus and the scholastic theologian John of Montenero, O.P. By May the latter had adopted a more patristic argumentation, and the Greeks saw that the Greek and Latin Fathers supported both Trinitarian formulae. All at Florence held the axiom "between the Western and Eastern Fathers there can be no contradiction, since they are all illuminated by the Holy Spirit." Though this principle is insufficiently nuanced, it proved to be vital for the solution of difficulties. Thus the Greeks had to admit that while the addition to the Creed might be irregular, since it was added without consultation, it was not a dogmatic error.

In June the council considered the question of the papal primacy. While the Latins insisted on a series of papal titles and prerogatives, the Greeks emphasized the fact that the pope was *in* the Church and one of a group of patriarchs (q.v.).

The decree of union, *Laetentur coeli,*[5] is composed of an introductory part which gives the underlying ecclesiology, one of love and of divine gift and mercy, for the second, more dogmatic part.[6] This latter outlines the Trinitarian dogma of East and West with an explanation of the *Filioque*.[7] A brief section follows about the bread, leavened or unleavened, in the Eucharist: the Churches are to follow their own traditions. The section on purgatory (q.v.) defines its existence and the value of the prayers of the living for those being purified there.[8] The beatific vision is also treated—a vision of God, one and three, but unequally contemplated according to the merits of the beholder. The formula on the primacy notes the role of the pope in the Church—head, father, and teacher *(caput, patrem, doctorem)* of all Christians, but evokes the context of the ecumenical councils and sacred canons. This section was to be the basis for the teaching of Vatican I (q.v.).[9] A section on the patriarchs (q.v.) is added, repeating the ancient privileges.

After the Greeks departed, delegations from other Eastern Churches arrived. At Florence and later at Rome they concluded acts of union. With the Armenians there was *Exultate Deo* mostly on Christological matters repeating earlier councils, and on the sacraments (22 Nov. 1439).[10] The treatment of the sacraments for the most part follows a minor work of St. Thomas, *The Articles of Faith and the Sacraments of the Church,* dating from after 1261.

The bull *Cantate Domino* (4 Feb. 1442) marked union with Copts who were of Monophysite tendency; it is quite a full exposition of the faith.[11] Union with the Syrians was effected with the bull *Multa et admirabilia* (30 Nov. 1444), when the council had transferred to Rome.[12] Finally, *Benedictus sit Deus* (7 Aug. 1445) marked union with the Chaldeans and Maronites of Cyprus.[13] We do not know when exactly the council ended in Rome, but 1445 is a probable date.[14]

After the death of Eugenius IV, we enter the Renaissance with Nicholas V (1447–1455) and Pius II (1458–1464). When Constantinople fell to the Turks in 1453, the ecclesial scene was totally changed. Any evaluation of the council must be nuanced.[15] There were three significant periods after it. From 1439 to 1444 there was indecision on the part of the Greek leaders: opposition was growing with Mark Eugenicus, and soon would be greater with the future patriarch Gennadius II (George Scolarius), but support for the union was also strong. From 1444 to 1453 there was a failure of military and political support and growing hostility to the union. After 1453 the union continued only in a few areas under Venetian influence. The causes for the failure were complex: the Greeks saw military help as part of the union agreement, but in this were disappointed; ethnic and polemic matters were also significant factors. Most significantly, the union was the result of an intellectual and spiritual process for those who attended the council; others who lacked this experience rejected its conclusions. But the union was not, as some would assert, either bought by money and honors or imposed by force or threats.

The council's success therefore was limited. In the East its name even today provokes negative reactions. But it did lead to renewed interest in the Fathers on the part of the West. Its decrees on the papacy put a brake on conciliarism. Its aim of unity without insisting on uniformity remains valid today.[16] Unlike Lyons II it was a real meeting of minds and not a passive accept-

ance of a papal document previously compiled. Its ultimate failure lay in the fact that two ecclesial models, scholastic and patristic, were accepted but never acknowledged by each side as complementary and thus not integrated into a higher vision.

---

[1]J. Gill, *The Council of Florence* (Cambridge, 1959); idem, *Constance et Bâle-Florence.* Histoire des conciles 9 (Paris: Ed. l'Orante, 1965); idem, "Greeks and Latins in a Common Council: The Council of Florence 1438–1439," OrChrPer 25 (1959) 265–287; G. Alberigo, ed., *Christian Unity: The Council of Ferrara-Florence 1438/39–1989.* Bibliotheca Ephemeridum theologicarum lovanensium 97 (Leuven: UP—Peeters, 1991; E. Iserloh, in Jedin-Dolan 4:473–487; H. Jedin, Councils 132–136; U. Proch, in Alberigo, Concili 300–319. [2]*Concilium Florentinum documenta et scriptores* (Rome: Pont. Instit. Orientale, 1940–1977). [3]Tanner 1:514–520, 529–534, 559–567. [4]Tanner 1:65. [5]Tanner 1:524–528. [6]DS 1300–1308/ND 322–324, 1508, 2308–2309, 809. [7]J. Gill, *Personalities of the Council of Florence* (Oxford, 1964) 254–263; M.A. Fatula, "The Council of Florence and Pluralism in Dogma," OneChr 19 (1983) 14–27. [8]A. d'Ales, "La question du purgatoire au concile de Florence en 1438," Greg 3 (1922) 9–50; E. Boulardand, "Processus discussionis de novissimis in Concilio Florentino," OrChrPer 19 (1953) 303–349; J. Jorgenson, "The Debate Over the Patristic Texts on Purgatory at the Council of Ferrara-Florence 1438," SVlad 30 (1986) 309–334. [9]J. Gill, "The Definition of the Primacy of the Pope in the Council of Florence," HeythJ 2 (1961) 14–19. [10]Tanner 1:534–559; in part DS 1310–1328/ND 1412–1418, 1509–1511, 1612–1613, 1705, 1803. [11]Tanner 1:567–582 in part DS 1330–1353/ND 208, 325–326, 408–409, 810, 1003–1005, 1419. [12]Tanner 1:586–589. [13]Tanner 1:589–591. [14]G. Hofmann, "Das Konzil von Florenz in Rom," OrChrPer 15 (1949) 83–84. [15]H.-G. Beck, in Jedin-Dolan 4:479–498; G. Cereti, "Il concilio di Ferrara-Fierenze e la Riconciliazione fra Oriente e Occidente," ScoulC 120 (1992) 377–401; A.de Halleux, "Le Concile de Florence: union ou uniatisme?," PrOrChr 1 (1991) 209–219. [16]H. Mühlen, "Das Konzil von Florenz als vorläufiges Modell eines kommenden Unionskonzil," TGl 63 (1973) 184–197.

## FRANCIS OF ASSISI, St. (1181–1226)

The son of a wealthy cloth merchant of Assisi was christened John but later called Francesco because he was born in 1181 while his father was in France.[1] He had a rather profligate youth, but after being injured in a local war, he experienced a religious conversion. He heard a voice from a crucifix in a semi-derelict church saying "Francis, go and repair my house, which you see is totally destroyed." He renounced his inheritance and proceeded to repair this and other churches. He lived a wandering mendicant existence for a few years; then he was joined by seven companions. They used to go preaching the gospel. What distinguished the preaching of Francis and his companions from that of other itinerant preachers was his doctrinal orthodoxy and respect for Church authority. The lay character of the initial impulse was in time changed: many of his followers became clerics; Francis himself was ordained a deacon. His *Regula prima,* the primitive first rule, obtained a degree of papal approval in 1210. When Francis was on pilgrimage in the Holy Land, his order grew and needed organization, which Francis himself could not provide. He renounced his role of leadership but did oversee the drawing up of a formal rule, *the Regula bullata*, which was approved by Honorius III in 1223. He continued preaching but with no official position in his order. He became seriously ill and died at the age of forty-five in 1226. He was canonized in 1228 by Gregory IX.

The charismatic movement, which drew inspiration from Francis, was a powerful force for renewal in the Church. His dedication to "Lady Poverty" was a countercultural stance in the heyday of the Middle Ages. In time Franciscan tradition saw ever more clearly that it was not only churches which were in need of repair but the Church itself.[2] In this matter, as in others, the historical figure of Francis and the legends that grew around him became fused, and subsequently confused.

These legends need to be corrected by an appreciation of Francis' deeply Christological piety, and by his implicit ecclesiology, which was one of service of the Church in poverty, in preaching, and in devotion to the sacraments. When he refers to the Church in his writings,[3] it is with love; his images are Trinitarian, Christological, and Marian.[4] There is also his devotion to the Scriptures,[5] though it is not clear how much he and the earliest friars had direct access to the actual book of the Bible.[6]

His order, which at his death was still perhaps more of a movement than an institution, was, through Francis' foresight, closely integrated with the Curia and the Pope. In time the Franciscan Order would suffer tensions between those who clung to a simpler ascetical ideal of absolute poverty and the more moderate group exemplified by its later general, St. Bonaventure (q.v.), who saw that if the order was to serve the Church, it would need not only the freedom of movement that was characteristic of the friars but also a devotion to theological study as a support for its missionary and evangelistic preaching. Like the Dominicans, the Franciscans were a strong support to the popes in combatting heresy by preaching, and in being emissaries of peace between feuding cities and states. The hugely diverse Franciscan family of friars, religious congregations, and laity retains for the Church the profound intuitions of Franciscan spirituality.[7]

[1]M. Habig, ed., *St. Francis of Assisi: Writing and Early Biographies: English Omnibus of the Sources for the Life of St. Francis* (Chicago: Franciscan Herald Press, 1973); see R.B. Brooke "Recent Work on St. Francis of Assisi," AnBoll 100 (1982) 654–676; E. Doyle, "Select Bibliography on the Life and Message of St. Francis," Conc 149 (1981) 73–77; R. Manselli, *St. Francis of Assisi* (Chicago: Franciscan Herald, 1988); H. Wolter, in Jedin-Dolan 4:177-181; Conc 149 (1981). [2]E. Peters, "Restoring the Church and Restoring Churches: Event and Image in Franciscan Biography," FranzSt 68 (1986) 213–236; G. Cañellas, "San Francisco y la reforma de la Iglesia," VerVida 40 (1972) 55–70. C.

del Zotto, "S. Francesco d'Assisi, riformatore nella Chiesa cattolica," StMiss34 (1985) 257–319.   [3]T. Matura, "L'Église dans les écrits de François d'Assise," Anton 57 (1982) 94–112.   [4]H. Pyfferoen, "Ave Dei Genetrix Maria, quae es Virgo, Ecclesia facta," Laur 12 (1971) 412–434.   [5]I. Schlauri, "Saint François et la Bible: Essai bibliographique de sa spiritualité évangélique," CollFranc 40 (1970) 365–437.   [6]T. Desbonnets, "The Franciscan Reading of the Scriptures," Conc 149 (1981) 37–45.   [7]F. Vandenbroucke, "The Franciscan Spring," in L. Bouyer, ed., *A History of Christian Spirituality*. 3 vols. (Tunbridge Wells UK: Burns & Oates, 1968, repr. 1982) 2:283-314; see arts. in DSpir 5:1210-1422.

## FRATERNITY

See BROTHERS AND SISTERS

## FRATICELLI

The word "Fraticelli" (diminutive of Italian *frate* = friar) was originally applied to members of mendicant orders, but became restricted to an extreme Franciscan faction condemned by John XXII in 1317 and 1318.[1] These last seem to have advocated two Churches: one carnal and possessing riches; the other embracing absolute poverty. Their works also gave rise to Donatist (q.v.) and Waldensian (q.v.) positions on the invalidity of sacraments administered by sinners.

[1]DS 910-916; cf. D.L. Douie, *The Nature and Effects of the Heresy of the Fraticelli* (Manchester, 1932); M.D. Lambert, *Franciscan Poverty: The Doctrine of the Absolute Poverty of Christ and of the Apostles in the Franciscan Order 1210–1323* (London: Church History Society, 1961); G. Lett, *Heresy in the Later Middle Ages: The Relation of Heterodoxy to Dissent c. 1250–c. 1450*. 2 vols. (Manchester: UP—New York: Barnes and Noble, 1967) 1:230-238.

## FREE CHURCHES

The Free Churches are also called Non-Conformist, a term which originally meant, and still today signifies, a refusal to conform to the doctrines, disciplines, or polity (q.v.) of any Established Church. In the 17th century Non-Conformist meant Churches which, accepting the doctrines of the Church of England, declined in the main part its ceremony. "Dissenters" was another term used at this time, which included Presbyterians (in England), Baptists, Congregationalists (q.v.), Methodists (q.v.), and Quakers (q.v.).[1]

[1]H. Davier, *The English Free Churches* (London: Oxford UP, [2]1963). E. Routley, *The Story of Congregationalism* (London: Independent Press, 1961).

## FREEDOM, RELIGIOUS

The Vatican II declaration on religious freedom, *Dignitatis humanae* (DH), had a tortured history: it was worked over for two years; it was the subject of three debates in the aula; there were five versions of the text, with over 2000 amendments proposed by the council members. That is not surprising considering the strongly opposing views which were held, at times passionately, by council members.

The conservative view, though it had many nuances and variants, can be summarized in four propositions: as there is only one true Church, it alone has the right to religious freedom; all other religious bodies are in error and do not have rights; if Catholics are in a majority, they should oppose public and external freedom for those in error; if the Church is in a minority, it should seek religious freedom.

Though St. Thomas did not say that an unbeliever had a right to religious practice, he did condemn the use of force in the case of those who had never been Christian, and he allowed that religious toleration could be lawful.[1] At the time of the Reformation there was little tolerance in the principle *"cuius regio eius religio"*—only one religion was recognized, that of the ruler, to the exclusion of all others. In the New World there was some practical tolerance for Catholics and Protestants—in Maryland, founded by Lord Baltimore in 1632, and in Rhode Island, founded by Roger Williams (d. 1684). In 17th-century England there were demands for tolerance for Baptists and Quakers but not for Catholics. The Act of Toleration (1689) excluded only Catholics and Unitarians. The prevalent religious indifferentism of the Enlightenment led to calls for equal liberty for all religions. The Bill of Rights (1776) made religious liberty general in America. Thomas Jefferson (1743–1826) was a major champion of religious freedom. The 19th-century Catholic Church was too conscious of being the one true Church to be able to see wider principles.

Because of the Church-State relations in the U.S., debate on the issues of religious liberty began to take place there from the 1940s, especially through the writings of J.C. Murray (q.v.). Before the matter was debated at Vatican II, John XXIII had asserted the right to religious freedom based on the dignity of the human person: "Every human being has the right to honor God according to the dictates of an upright conscience, and therefore the right to profess his religion in private and in public."[2]

At the council the argument of the minority against the proposed document can be broadly summarized: the draft favored religious and doctrinal indifferentism; it was opposed to Catholic doctrine, in particular 19th-century papal teaching;[3] it ignored the "principle" that error has no rights; it moved from the subjective area of conscience to the objective area of right.

When finally promulgated, the document "Declaration on Religious Freedom" (DH) carried the significant subtitle "On the dignity of persons and communities to social and civil liberty in religious matters." It reflects above all the thought of J.C. Murray (q.v.), one of its main authors.

The declaration lays down the principle of freedom as a basic human right: "The human person has a right to religious freedom. Such freedom consists in this, that all should have such immunity from coercion by individuals, or by groups, or by any human power, that no one should be forced to act against his conscience in religious matters, nor prevented from acting according to his conscience, whether in private or in public, whether alone or in association with others, within due limits." (DH 2).[4]

The rest of the declaration spells out the consequences and grounds for these rights: people have an obligation to seek truth (DH 2), to follow their conscience (DH 3); "wrong is done to the human person and to the order established for people by God, if they are denied the free and corporate practice of their religion within the limits set by due public order" (DH 3), because religious acts transcend the earthly order; this right belongs to communities as well (DH 4), and also to the family which, moreover, has the right to choose in the area of religious education for children (DH 5). The consequences for civil law are spelled out: "It is an integral part of the duty of every civil authority to safeguard and promote inviolable human rights" (DH 6); the rights are to be seen within the wider context of the rights of others and the common good, for which the state should provide the relevant safeguards (DH 7–8).

The second part of the declaration looks to the basis in revelation and the magisterium of the council's teaching about the human right it has explained: it is based on the freedom of the act of faith itself (DH 10); God is to be served in human freedom, not by coercion (DH 11); even though there have been aberrations in the past, "nevertheless the church's teaching that no one's faith should be coerced has held firm" (DH 12). The Church claims freedom for itself as a spiritual authority established by Christ the Lord, which has the duty by divine command of preaching to the whole of creation (DH 13). The Church claims the right to propagate the teaching it has received from Christ, but "always without recourse to means that go against the spirit of the gospel" (DH 14), so that "account must be taken of one's obligations to the proclamation of Christ, the life giving Word, of the rights of the human person, and of the measure of the grace of Christ given to each by God to summon him to the free acceptance and profession of the faith" (DH 14). Finally the council welcomes the religious freedom in legal systems and acknowledged in international documents; it notes the absence of religious freedom under some regimes; it calls for adequate legal protection of religious freedom everywhere (DH 15).

The years after Vatican II saw extensive study of freedom and associated issues:[5] expositions of the conciliar doctrine on religious freedom;[6] accounts of problems especially under Marxist regimes;[7] broader questions of human rights,[8] including the 1981 United Nations "Declaration on the Elimination of all Forms of Intolerance and of Discrimination Based on Religion or Belief"[9] and its "Universal Declaration on Human Rights" (1948).[10] Furthermore, there was exploration of other more internal concerns: the relation of the conciliar teaching to an earlier tradition;[11] the rights of the Church;[12] religious liberty and politics;[13] freedom in the Church;[14] most recently the rights of women (v. FEMINISM); the possible relevance of the council's teaching in the issue of dissent (q.v.) within the Church.[15]

The basic rights of religious and human liberty are reiterated in both the *Code of Canon Law* (CIC 215; 218–219; 226 § 2; 227; 748) and the new *Catechism* (nn. 450; 1907; 2211; 2245). The Church's teaching on religious freedom is one of the clearer instances of a true doctrinal development, if not a Copernican revolution.[16] Religious liberty is a notable theme in ecumenical dialogue.[17]

---

[1]ST 2–2ae, qq. 10–12. [2]*Pacem in terris*—AAS 55 (1963) 260/ Carlen 5:108. [3]Gregory XVI, *Mirari vos*—DS 2730/ND 1007; Pius IX, *Syllabus*—DS 2915/ND 1013/15. [4]G. Thils, "Le fondement naturel et universel de la 'liberté religieuse,'" RTLv 20 (1989) 59–66. See J. Hamer and Y. Congar, eds., *La Liberté Religieuse: Déclaration "Dignitatis humanae personal."* US 60 (Paris: Cerf, 1967); É Poulat, "Le grand absent de 'Dignitatis humanae': L'État," Supp 175 (1990) 5–27. [5]A. Gianni, *Religious Liberty: International Bibliography 1918–1978* (Strasbourg: CERDIC, 1978); Le supplément 175 (1990) 3–149; K. Rahner, "Theology of Freedom," ThInvest 6:178-196. [6]E. Binet and R. Chenu, eds., *La liberté religieuse dans le Judaisme, le Christianisme et l'Islam.* Cogitatio fidei 110 (Paris: Cerf, 1981); M. Carter, "Dignitatis humanae: Declaration on Religious Freedom," Jurist 36 (1976) 338–352; J.C. Murray, "The Declaration on Religious Freedom," Conc 5 (May 1966) 3–10; idem, "The Declaration on Religious Freedom," in J.H. Miller, ed., *Vatican II: An Interfaith Appraisal* (Notre Dame, 1966) 565–585. [7]Conc 154 (1982); P. Mojzes, *Church and State in Postwar Eastern Europe: A Bibliographical Survey* (London: Greenwood, 1987); F. House, "The Witness of the Russian Church," OneChr 19 (1983) 219–226; V. Kouriedov, "La législation soviétique sur la religion et la liberté de conscience," Istina 32 (1978) 20–31; F. Rouleau, "Religious Persecution in the USSR and Its Special Dialectic," Communio 12/2 (1987) 51–61; K. Rousselet, "Les chrétiens évangéliques baptistes en Union Soviétique," Études 368 (1988) 257–268. [8]Conc 124 (1979); D. Hollenbach, *Claims in Conflict: Retrieving and Renewing the Catholic Human Rights Tradition* (New York: Paulist, 1979); Card. Koenig, "Droits de l'homme et liberté religieuse," Istina 26 (1981) 228–232; cf. A. Falconer, ed., *Understanding Human Rights: An Interdisciplinary and Interfaith Study* (Dublin: Irish School of Ecumenics, 1980); K. Rahner, "The Dignity and Freedom of Man," ThInvest 2:235-263 (1963). [9]Text—T.C. van Boven, "Religious Liberty in the Context of Human Rights," EcuR 37 (1985) 345–355. [10]R. Coste, "La foi chrétienne et la 'Déclaration Universelle des Droits de l'Homme'," NRT 111 (1989) 710–727. [11]B. de Margerie, *Liberté religieuse et règne du Christ* (Paris: Cerf, 1988); J. Hendriks,

"De libertate religiosa in Concilio Vaticano II disceptata: Num mutata est doctrina," Periodica 76 (1987) 83–98; F. Ocáriz, "Sulla libertà religiosa: Continuità del Vaticano II con il magistero precedente," AnnalT 3 (1989) 71–97. [12]R. Minnerath, *Le droit de l'Église à la liberté.* Le point théologique 39 (Paris: Beauchesne, 1982); L. Mistò, "'Libertas religiosa' et 'libertas ecclesiae': De quaestionis solutione lineamenta," Periodica 71 (1982) 637–661. [13]H. Madelin, "La liberté religieuse et la sphère du politique," NRT 97 (1975) 110–126, 914–939; J. Medina Orozco, "La libertad religiosa y la autoridad civil: Una perspectiva," EfMex 8 (1990) 5–15. [14]J. Coriden, ed., *The Case for Freedom: Human Rights in the Church* (Washington, D.C., 1969); A. Dulles, *A Church to Believe In: Discipleship and the Dynamics of Freedom* (New York: Crossroad, 1983) 66–79; J. Neumann, *Menschenrechte auch in der Kirche?* (Zurich: Benziger, 1976); K. Rahner, "The Church's Responsibility for the Freedom of the Individual," ThInvest 20:51-64; cf. "Freedom in the Church," ThInvest 2:89-107 (1963); J. Ratzinger, *Church, Ecumenism and Politics: New Essays in Ecclesiology* (Slough UK—New York: Crossroad, 1988) 182–203; J.-F. Six, *Church and Human Rights* (Slough UK: St. Paul, 1992). [15]D.M. Cowdin, "Religious Liberty, Religious Dissent and the Catholic Tradition," HeythJ 32 (1991) 26–61. [16]P. Colella, "La 'Dignitatis humanae' a vent'anni dal Concilio," RasT 25 (1984) 413–421; R. Coste, "Vers une élucidation du développment de la doctrine de l'Église catholique concernant la liberté religieuse," EspVie 98 (1988) 465–477; J.C. Murray, "Vers une intelligence du développment de la doctrine de l'Église sur la liberté religieuse," Hamer and Congar (n. 4) 111–147. [17]JEcuS 14 (1977) 588–729; *Religious Freedom: Main Statements by the WCC, 1948–1975* (Geneva: WCC, 1976); J.A. Hebly, "Religionsfreiheit und der Ökumenische Rat der Kirchen," ÖkRu 32 (1983) 41–56; N. Koshy, "Religious Liberty," DictEcumMov 859–863; F.H. Littell, ed., *Religious Liberty in the Crossfire of Creeds* (Philadelphia: Ecumenical Press, 1978); P. Potter, "Religious Liberty in Ecumenical Perspective," EcuR 30 (1978) 42–49.

## FUNDAMENTALISM

Towards the end of the 19th century, certain American Protestants attempted to state the essentials of strict conservative belief in opposition to liberalism and modernism. They agreed on the following five truths: the inerrancy of the Bible, the deity of Jesus Christ, the Virgin Birth, Christ's substitutionary atonement, his physical resurrection and his future bodily return. These were aggressively defended in a series of twelve booklets entitled *The Fundamentals: A Testimony to the Truth* (1910–1915), written by two wealthy brothers, Lyman and Milton Stewart, and distributed free; the series might be called the Magna Carta of fundamentalism. Christians espousing these fundamentals came to be called fundamentalists, from 1920.

Within the category "fundamentalist," there is a wide variety of differences, and some varying 19th-century roots.[1] In the complex physiognomy of fundamentalism there are many generally common features:[2] as a reaction to unwelcome modern trends, fundamentalists are permanently in opposition; they also reject modern hermeneutics, since the classical text, Bible, or Qur'an, has one meaning and is accessible to people of good will; they insist on what they call the "literal meaning" of the text, viz., it says what it seems clearly to say, and modern exegetical methods are both unnecessary and to be rejected; they lack a true sense of history, seen in their belief that ancient texts need no transposition for other ages; they tend to reject pluralism, which they equate with relativism or liberalism; they often have a strong conversion experience. Among Protestant fundamentalists evolution is rejected in favor of "creationism" based on the apparently clear meaning of Gen 1–3.

Catholic fundamentalists have not shown the same interest in this last issue. They tend to stress what they see as the literal and unchanging teaching of Trent and the anti-Modernist *Syllabus of Errors*;[3] or, like Archbishop Lefebvre (q.v.), they reject Vatican II texts and its renewal, especially liturgical.[4] There are also movements within the Catholic Church that outsiders might to a greater or lesser degree consider as fundamentalist, even if the groups in question would not welcome such a designation. Integralism (q.v.) can be seen as a form of fundamentalism.

Fundamentalism can be confused with evangelism (v. EVANGELICALS), a charge sometimes made against J. Barr's important study.[5] There are many studies of the psychology of fundamentalism:[6] Common features that emerge include: the need to be anchored; the craving in the face of complex issues to have simple answers, above all certain ones; anxiety about the political and/or Church situation; a quest for perfectionism.

T.F. O'Meara describes Christian fundamentalism as "an interpretation of Christianity in which a charismatic leader locates with easy certitude in chosen words, doctrines and practices the miraculous actions of a strict God saving an elite from an evil world."[7] Fundamentalism is found in all of the Christian Churches but with different orientations and nuances: Protestant,[8] Orthodox,[9] and Catholic.[10]

Dialogue with fundamentalists is extremely difficult because of their perception of retaining truth neglected or denied by the mainline Church.[11] Dialogue is also problematic because most fundamentalist groups are anti-Catholic, and there is a significant exodus from the Catholic Church—indeed, from all of the mainline Churches—to fundamentalists who are hostile to the Church's positions on human nature, sacraments, tradition, and Church authority.[12] But the Churches cannot afford to ignore the significant values that the fundamentalist positions seek to enshrine: a commitment to truth, a trenchant criticism of modern liberalism and secular humanism, a sincerity about religious dedication. But though in some form these are values needed for our age, the whole package of fundamentalism seriously narrows the Mystery at the heart of Christianity; rejecting pluralism, it leads very easily to a constricted and intolerant Christianity and unhealthy polarization. The Churches may perhaps need to take up more convincing positions between humanism and its opponent, fundamentalism. The very popularity of fundamentalist groups is a question and a challenge to all the Churches.

But fundamentalism is not confined to the Churches. In the late 20th century there are many indications of fundamentalism in the world of Islam (q.v.), in Japanese New Religions, and elsewhere in the Orient, as well as in many places among Christians. It has political as well as religious manifestations.[13] Fundamentalists see themselves as fighting back against the forces of secularism or modernism. In political fundamentalism violence is not uncommon, and religious symbols are often exploited for political purposes.

[1]B.J. Leonard, "The Origin and Character of Fundamentalism," RExp 79 (9182) 5–17. [2]M.E. Marty, "What is Fundamentalism? Theological Perspectives," Conc 221 (June 1992/3) 3–13. [3]DS 2901–2980. [4]D. Menozzi, "Opposition to the Council (1966–1984)," in G. Alberigo et al., eds., *The Reception of Vatican II* (Washington, D.C.: The Catholic University of America Press, 1987) 325–348. [5]*Fundamentalism* (London: SCM, [2]1981-Philadelphia: Westminster, 1978); cf. G. Marsden, *Fundamentalism and American Culture: The Shaping of Twentieth-Century Evangelicalism, 1870–1925* (New York: Oxford UP, 1980). [6]G. Hole, "Fundamentalism, Dogmatism, Fanaticism: Psychiatric Perspectives," Conc 221 (June 1992/3) 22–35; G. Müller-Fahrenholz, "What is Fundamentalism Today? Perspectives from Social Psychology," ibid., 14–21. [7]T.F. O'Meara, *Fundamentalism: A Roman Catholic Perspective* (New York: Paulist, 1990) 18. [8]S. Bruce, *The Rise and Fall of the Christian New Right: Conservative Protestant Politics in America, 1978–1988* (Oxford: Clarendon, 1990); A.D. Falconer, "Protestant Fundamentalism," DoctLife 33 (1983) 4–13; J. A. Sanders, "Fundamentalism and the Church: Theological Crisis for Mainline Protestants," BibTB 18 (1988) 43–49; M. Volf, "The Challenge of Protestant Fundamentalism," Conc 221 (June, 1992/3) 97–106. [9]V.N. Makrides, "Aspects of Greek Orthodox Fundamentalism," OrthFor 5 (1991) 49–72; C. Yannaras, "The Challenge of Orthodox Traditionalism," Conc 221 (June, 1992/3) 81–87. [10]A. Blanch, "La tentación fundamentalista," RazF 224 (1991) 387–392; R. Franco, ¿Fundamentalismo católico?," Proy 37 (1990) 251–270; L.J. White, "Fundamentalism and 'Fullness of Christianity': Catholicism's Double Challenge," BibTB 18 (1988) 50–59. Cf. U.S. Catholic Bishops, Pastoral Statement for Catholics on Biblical Fundamentalism," Origins 17 (1987) 376–377. [11]E.G. Hinson, "The Influence of Fundamentalism on Ecumenical Dialogue," JES 26 (1989) 468–482. [12]O'Meara (n. 7) 7–8 ; cf. K. Keating, *Catholicism and Fundamentalism: The Attack on "Romanism" by "Bible Christians"* (San Francisco: Ignatius, 1988). [13]M. Marty, ed., with Chicago UP for American Academy of Arts and Sciences: *Fundamentalisms Observed* (1991), *Fundamentalisms and Society* (1993), *Fundamentalisms and the State* (1993); L. Caplan, ed., *Studies in Religious Fundamentalism* (London: Macmillan, 1987); N.J. Cohen, *The Fundamentalist Phenomenon: A View from Within; A Response from Without.* Starkoff Institute Studies (Grand Rapids: Eerdmans, 1990); B.N. Lawrence, *Defenders of God: The Fundamentalist Revolt Against the Modern Age* (London: Tauris—New York: Harper & Row, 1990); LumièreV 186/37 (March 1988).

# G

## GALILEO (1564–1642)

Galileo Galilei was born at Pisa in 1564. By the age of twenty-five he held the chair of mathematics at its university; after three years he moved to the University of Padua. All his life he remained a Catholic, but with anti-clerical leanings not unusual for his time. He had a gift for making friends and especially enemies. This was probably as significant in his downfall as were his intellectual positions.[1] His treatment by Rome, however, led to the Church being pilloried for centuries.

When Galileo turned the newly invented telescope on Venus and discovered that this planet has phases like those of the moon, he realized that this fact provided a strong argument for the theory of Copernicus, who proposed that the sun was the center around which the earth and other planets revolved. He published his findings in a pamphlet, *Sidereus nuntius* ("The Starry Messenger"). When challenged that his view contradicted Scripture, he wrote to prove that it was compatible with Scripture, insisting that it was not the intention of Scripture to give answers to scientific questions. He was correct on this point, but no doubt he would have had fewer problems if he had left it to theologians to discuss. The matter came to the attention of the Roman Congregation of the Index, which decreed in 1616 that the Copernican theory was indeed contrary to Scripture. No writings of Galileo were put on the Index (q.v.), but he was informed of the decision by Cardinal Bellarmine (q.v.), and warned not to teach or defend this theory in the future. It was subsequently alleged that on this occasion an official of the Inquisition (q.v.) had put him under a formal injunction which would involve severe penalties if he were ever again to teach or defend that theory. For some years Galileo kept his peace about the Copernican theory, but after the election of his friend Cardinal Maffeo Barberini as Pope Urban VIII in 1623, Galileo felt free enough to begin writing his *Dialogue on the Two Chief World Systems,* which was a thinly disguised defense of the Copernican theory. When this work was published in 1632, it was denounced to the Inquisition. The charge then brought against Galileo was that he violated a formal injunction of the Inquisition. A document was presented in evidence against him, which lacks the official signatures that would have been required, and is most likely a forgery. As Bellarmine had since died, he could not corroborate Galileo's claim that he had not been put under such an injunction. Galileo was condemned for having violated the injunction, and sentenced to house arrest at his estate near Florence. There he wrote his greatest work on mechanics, which is the foundation of modern physics. His *Dialogue,* which had led to his condemnation, was placed on the *Index of Forbidden Books,* where it remained until the 19th century. He died in Florence in 1642. After 360 years the 1633 condemnation was quashed by the Holy See. The Church avoided any similar mistake when evolutionary theories began circulating in the 19th century. The Galileo case remains a warning to the Church for all questions relating to science and faith.

[1] N. Porter, "Galileo & the Inquisition," DoctLife 43 (1993) 349–357; cf. R.J. Blackwell, *Galileo, Bellarmine and the Bible* (Notre Dame—London: Notre Dame UP, 1991); J. Broderick, *Galileo: The Man, His Works, His Misfortunes* (London, 1964); H. Jedin, in Jedin-Dolan 5:642-643 with bibliog. 738–739; A. Finocchiaro, *The Galileo Affair: A Documentary History* (Berkeley: Calif. UP, 1989); W.R. Shea, "Galileo and the Church," in D.C. Lindberg and R.L. Numbers, eds., *God and Nature: Historical Essays on the Encounter between Christianity and Science* (Berkeley—Los Angeles—London: California UP, 1986) 114–135.

## GALLICANISM

Gallicanism was a French theological movement with roots going back to the Middle Ages.[1] Essentially, it was an attempt to limit the power of the papacy in France through the "liberties of the French Church" (*de l'Église gallicane*—hence Gallicanism). In 1516 the Pragmatic Sanction (q.v.) was superseded by a concordat, which allowed the French king the right to nominate bishops. There were two forms of Gallicanism: "royal Gallicanism" limiting the power of the papacy over national Churches; "episcopal Gallicanism" limiting the power of the papacy over individual bishops. Fear of Gallicanism was one of the reasons that Trent (q.v.) did not bring out a document on the Church.

France refused reception (q.v.) to some of the reform decrees of Trent (q.v.).[2] In 1663 the Sorbonne in Paris, which had Gallican tendencies almost from its foundation (1257), published a declaration which in substance was taken up by an assembly of the French clergy in 1682 in a formula known as the Four Gallican Articles, drawn up by the great orator and bishop, J.B. Bossuet (1627–1704).[3] They were condemned by Pope Alexander VIII in 1680,[4] and by King Louis XIV in 1693.

The first article denied any temporal power to the pope and rejected his authority over temporal or civil matters. The second upheld the decrees of the Council of Constance (q.v.), which assert the supremacy of a council over the pope. The third insisted on the inviolability of the ancient liberties of the Gallican Church. The fourth asserted that the decrees of the pope were not irreformable without the consent of the Church.

Gallicanism would remain a tendency for more than a century, appearing as independence from Rome even in more minor matters, such as the issuing of liturgical books.[5] Though it was no longer a real problem after 1830, when Ultramontanism (q.v.) was in the ascendant,[6] the *Syllabus* of Pius IX (1864—q.v.) and Vatican I (q.v.) crushed totally any remnant of Gallicanism. For an interpretation of Vatican I, it is important to remember that the council had Gallicanism in mind when formulating its definitions on the papacy.

At the beginning of the 20th century in SW France there arose a small dissident Gallican Church with its own schismatic bishops; it still exists, but shows signs of internal division.[7]

Something of the mentality of Gallicanism appeared in Germanic countries as Febronianism (q.v.) and Josephinism (q.v.); the Enlightenment was a more dominant inspiration of the latter.

[1]L. Cognet, in Jedin-Dolan 6:57-70; Congar, Augustin 394–402; V. Martin, *Les origines du gallicanisme.* 2 vols. (Paris, 1939); J.-C. Meyer, "La tradition gallicaine dans l'Église réfractaire," BLitEc 90 (1989) 163–184. [2]V. Martin, *Le gallicanisme et la réforme catholique: Essai historique sur l'introduction en France des décrets du Concile de Trente* (Paris, 1919). [3]A.G. Martimort, *Le gallicanisme de Bossuet.* US 24 (Paris, 1953). [4]DS 2281-2285. [5]W. Müller, in Jedin-Dolan 6:547-548. [6]A. Gough, *Paris and*

*Rome: The Gallican Church and the Ultramontane Campaign (1848–1853)* (Oxford: Clarendon, 1986). [7]O. Laroza, "L'Église gallicane," AnnéeC 25 (1981) 399–430.

# GNOSTICISM

Gnosticism (Greek *gnôsis* = knowledge) is a philosophical and religious system in which the communication of secret knowledge is salvific. It arose as a religious movement in the 1st century C.E. While it has been known throughout Christian history, from surviving Gnostic documents, often partly Christian,[1] and from its opponents like Irenaeus (q.v.), the discovery in Egypt in 1945 of the Nag Hammadi Gnostic library has added immensely to modern understanding of Gnosticism.[2]

The origin of Gnosticism is still a disputed matter among scholars:[3] at one time it was thought to have come from Iranian dualism; later the view grew that it developed from dissident Jewish sources; at present many scholars see it as a deformation of Christianity. In its myriad forms Gnosticism was markedly syncretistic: it borrowed from Greek philosophy, Judaism, Christianity, various pagan sources, and by the 4th century it had acquired elements of Eastern religion and magic. At its core, perhaps more central than knowledge, is a rejection of the material world. Its views are generally dualist: there are two eternal principles, one good, and the other the evil Demiurge who created the world; humans are composed of spirit and the matter which imprisons it; there is light and darkness, sometimes with a third principle, spirit, interposed. Salvation is through knowledge, which is the secret of true life and light passed on amongst Gnostic initiatees; in some texts this knowledge is a preparation for the final separation of the spiritual principle from the body.

Though it was a problem particularly of the early centuries of Christianity, the concerns of Gnosticism reappear under various guises in the course of history.[4] Some modern cults, as well as several New Age manifestations, could with some justice be termed Neo-Gnostic (v. MOVEMENTS, NON-CHRISTIAN).

[1]Patrology 1:254-277. [2]G. Filoramo, EncycEarCh 2:579 with bibliog. D.M. Scholer, *Nag Hammadi Bibliography 1948–1969* (Leiden: Brill, 1971) with annual supplements NT 13 (1971) following; R. van den Broek, "The Present State of Gnostic Studies," VigChr 37 (1981) 41–71; M. Scopello, "Bulletin sur la gnose," RechSR 77 (1989) 281–304. [3]M.J. Edwards, "New Discoveries and Gnosticism: Some Precautions," OrPerChr 55 (1989) 251–272; G. Filoramo, *A History of Gnosticism* (Oxford: Blackwell, 1990); M. Krause, *Gnosis and Gnosticism.* Papers read at Eighth International Conference on Patristic Studies Oxford 1979. Nag Hammadi Studies 17 (Leiden: Brill, 1981); P. Perkins, *The Gnostic Dialogue: The Early Church and the Crisis of Gnosticism. Theological Enquiries.* Studies in Contemporary Biblical and Theological Problems (New York—Ramsey—Toronto: Paulist, 1980); J. Ries and J.M. Sevrin, eds., *Gnosticisme et monde hellénistique.* Colloque de Louvain-la-Neuve, 11–14 mars 1980. Publications de l'Institut

Orientaliste 27 (Louvain-la-Neuve: Institut Orientaliste, 1982); K.W. Tröger, "Christianity and Gnosticism," TDig 34 (1987) 219–225.   [4]G. Hanratty, "Gnosticism and Modern Thought I–III," IrTQ 47 (1980) 3–23, 119–132; 48 (1981) 80–92.

## GRATIAN

Practically nothing is known about the life of Gratian: he was a Camaldolese monk, and he must have died before 1159. Though he is regarded as the "Father of Canon Law,"[1] his achievement must be seen in the light of compilations of law already begun in previous centuries,[2] especially the 9th-century Carolingian forgeries, including those ascribed to Isidore (d. 636).[3]

His great work, *Concordia discordantium canonum* (Concordance of Discordant Canons), was subsequently known as the *Decreta* or *Decretum gratiani.*[4] As it cites Lateran II (1139—q.v.), it cannot be dated before 1140.[5] It included nearly 4,000 conciliar decrees, patristic texts, and papal statements covering the whole area of Church discipline. His achievement in the birth of the science of law was to attempt to resolve into harmony the contradictions and inconsistencies of these sources, bringing legal principles to the task. The *Decretum* was not a simple compilation of texts, but it employed a dialectic in which, not unlike the Scholastic disputations, he proposed a problem, drew up authorities, and advanced a solution.

Not all of his sources were authentic, but though never officially approved, his text became the handbook of the papal curia and of the universities before the end of the century (v. LAW). Commentators, the decretists, soon began to work on the *Decretum;*[6] many of them became bishops and three became popes: Alexander III (1159–1181), Gregory VIII (1187), and Innocent III (1198–1216). Others became cardinals. The largely unknown monk was to exert enormous influence on the Church, not least in the centralizing use made of his work by the new canonists who directed the life of the Church. It is an exaggeration to say that the sacramental dimension of the Church was surrendered to the juridical, but the presence of law would henceforth be significant for ecclesiology.

[1]S. Kuttner, "The Father of the Science of Canon Law," Jurist 1 (1948) 2–19.   [2]F. Kempf, in Jedin-Dolan 3:426-436.   [3]E. Ewig, in Jedin-Dolan 3:167-170.   [4]A.E. Friedberg, ed., *Corpus iuris canonici.* Vol.I (Leipzig, 1879, reprint Graz 1959); H. Wolter, in Jedin-Dolan 4:93-94.   [5]G. Fransen, "La date du décret de Gratien," RHE 51 (1956) 521–531.   [6]P. Erdö, *Introductio in historiam scientiae canonicae: Praenotanda ad Codicem* (Rome: Gregorian UP, 1990) 43–74.

## GREGORY I—Pope St. GREGORY THE GREAT (590–604)

Born about 540 C.E., Gregory[1] was the son of a Roman senator and in the service of the State until 573, when he entered one of several monasteries established by himself. A nostalgia for monastic life would remain with him throughout his busy life. He was appointed a Roman deacon in 578, and apocrisiarius, or ambassador, to Byzantium a year later. He returned to Rome 585/586 and re-entered a monastery, but was elected pope in 590. A reluctant pope, he became one of the outstanding ones, earning the sobriquet "the Great" in later history. He adopted the title "servant of the servants of God" *(servus servorum Dei),* one still in use by popes.

His papacy was marked by his service to the poor, and tireless work for peace in Italy; he is remembered for his commitment to the evangelization of England, sending St. Augustine (d. ca. 604) with 40 monks in 596 and reinforcements five years later. His name is associated with liturgical reform *(Gregorian Sacramentary)*[2] and Church music (Gregorian chant), but his exact input in these areas is hard to establish.

One of the four great Western Doctors of the Church (q.v.), his works[3] comprise some 850 letters,[4] scriptural commentaries,[5] a work on bishops, *Pastoral Care,*[6] and a spiritual and allegorical commentary on Job, the *Moralia;*[7] these last two would be highly influential throughout the Middle Ages. A recent attempt by F.C. Clark to impugn the authenticity of the *Dialogues,*[8] a book on the miracles of Benedict and other Italian saints, has not been well received.[9]

His place in the history of spirituality[10] and of the papacy[11] is assured; not less significant was his influence on the medieval papacy[12] and on ecclesiology, this last being found throughout his works.[13] A dominant idea of his ecclesiology is that of the universal Church, not merely originating from Abel (q.v.) but from Adam to the last of the elect,[14] including apparently angels (q.v.) as members of Christ.[15] As a spiritual master he stresses sanctity, the "holy Church of the elect," who should by their works of love and humility ascend towards heaven.[16] But sinners remain within the Church; God discerns the good and the evil.[17] The Church as Bride includes not only those in glory but holy people on earth: "The bride in fact is the Church herself in her perfection. . . . One who already loves God with perfection represents the bride," but others who struggle for spiritual growth are those who accompany Christ the Spouse.[18] His view of the kingdom of God (q.v.) is a spiritual and moral one, yet as Y. Congar points out, his missionary zeal sought the spread of the actual Church.[19]

His attitude to temporal rulers is at times unclear: he seems somewhat obsequious in requesting temporal rulers to call local councils;[20] yet he sees the role of monarchs as essentially subservient to religious ends, and in quite a peremptory way demands justice.[21] His influence in succeeding centuries was felt in the view that temporal rulers are in the end subservient to a higher call proclaimed by the Church. But perhaps his main contribution to ecclesiology lies in the effect his spiritual works have had on bishops and monks throughout the Middle Ages, preventing institutional views from excessively prevailing in the theory and practice of Church life. A measure of his contemporary standing might be the small number of citations—only six—in the new Catechism, despite much scholarly industry about all aspects of his life and works.

[1]P. Battifol, *St Gregory the Great* (London, 1929); P.T. Camelot, "Un pape du VIe siècle: Saint Gregoire le grand," VieSp 141 (1987) 395–409; C. Dagens, *Gregoire le grand: Culture et expérience chrétiennes* (Paris: Ed. Augustiennes, 1977); F.H. Dudden, *Gregory the Great: His Place in History and Thought.* 2 vols. (London, 1905); V. Paronetto, *Gregorio Magno: Un maestro alle origini cristiane d'Europa* (Rome: Ed. Studium, 1985); J. Richards, *Consul of God: The Life and Times of Gregory the Great* (London:Routledge & Kegan Paul, 1980). See B. Colgrave, ed. and trans., *The Earliest Life of Gregory the Great* (Cambridge: UP, 1988).   [2]H. Ashworth, "Did Gregory Compose a Sacramentary?," StPatr 2 (1957) 3–16.   [3]PL 75–79; AA.VV. *Gregorio Magno e il suo tempore.* Studi ephemeridis augustinianum 34 (Rome: Augustinianum, 1991); G.R. Evans, *The Thought of Gregory the Great.* Cambridge Studies in Medieval Life and Thought 2 (Cambridge: UP, 1986); R. Godding, *Bibliografia di Gregorio Magno 1890–1989* (Rome: Città Nuova, 1990). H.J. Vogt, in Jedin-Dolan 2:744-750.   [4]MGEp 1–2/CCL 140–141.   [5]CCL 142, 144/SC 314, 327.   [6]PL 77:9-126/SC 381–382.   [7]CCL 143/SC 32bis, 212, 221.   [8]SC 251, 260, 265.   [9]F.C. Clark, *The Pseudo-Gregorian Dialogues.* Studies in the History of Christian Thought 37–38. 2 vols. (Leiden: Brill, 1987). Critiques: A. de Vogüé, RHE 83 (1988) 281–348; R. Godding, AnBoll 106 (1988) 201–229; P. Mayvaert, JEH 39 (1988) 335–381; P. Verbraken, RBén 98 (1988) 272–277. Response F.C. Clark, HeythJ 30 (1989) 257–272; JEH 40 (1089) 323–346.   [10]R. Gillet, "Gregoire le Grand," DSpir 6:872-910; idem, SC 32bis, 7–113; C. Straw, *Gregory the Great: Perfection in Imperfection* (Berkeley: Calif. UP, 1988).   [11]OxD Popes 65–68; K. Baus, in Jedin-Dolan 2:629-633.   [12]N. Sharkey, *St. Gregory the Great's Concept of Papal Power* (Washington, D.C., 1956).   [13]Congar, Augustin 33–36; C. Bonomo, *Chiesa: Corpo di Cristo secondo S. Gregorio Magno* (Rome, 1961); C. Dagens, "L'Église universelle et le monde oriental chez saint Grégoire le Grand," Istina 20 (1975) 457–475.   [14]*Moralia* Praef. 8:17-18; 3:17, 32; 5: 5, 7—PL 75: 526–527, 616, 805. See R. Bélanger, *"Ecclesia ab exordio mundi:* Modèles et degrés d'appartenance à l'Église chez Grégoire le Grand," StRel 16 (1987) 265–273.   [15]*In Ezech.* 1, hom. 8:28—PL 76:867; *In ev.* 34:11—PL 76:1252.   [16]*In Ezech hom.* 2:3:1 & 2:5, 21—PL 76: 959, 997; *Moralia* 2:56, 91; 25:8, 20–21; 34:23, 56—PL 75:598-599; 76:332-334, 750; V. Recchia, "Gregorio Magno: Lo Spirito Sancto nella vita della chiesa e delle singole anime (dalla *Hom XXX in Ev.* e dai *Dialogi*)," in S. Felici, ed., *Spirito Sancto e catechesi patristica.* Biblioteca si scienze religiose 54 (Rome: LAS, 1983) 154–194.   [17]*Moralia* 29:2, 2–4; 31:15, 28—PL 76:478-479, 589.   [18]*In Cant.* 10—CCL 144:13-14.   [19]Op. cit. (n. 13); 35–36; see *In ev.* 38:2 with 32:6—PL 76:1282, 1236.   [20]Ep 9:213, 218—MGEp 2: 199, 10; 209, 30.   [21]Congar (n. 13) 36.

## GREGORY VII, Pope St. (1073–1085)

Hildebrand was born in Tuscany about 1020. From his early 20s he was, except for a short period, in papal service until he, himself, became pope in 1073, taking the name Gregory VII. He made reform of the Church his highest goal;[1] in this he built on the work of his predecessors.[2] He had a mystical vision of the presence of St. Peter to the Church, especially to the pope. He was responsible for the famous *Dictatus papae* (q.v.) in 1075, and made use of them as appropriate. His life was well summarized in his citing, shortly before his death in exile from Rome, "I have loved justice and hated iniquity" (cf. Ps 45:7). As a reformer he attacked clerical concubinage (v. CELIBACY), simony (q.v.), and lay investiture (q.v.). His reforms met with much opposition but were significant in England, France, Spain, and Germany.[3] He obtained a confession of faith from Berengarius (ca. 1010–1088), who had held heterodox views on the Eucharist.[4]

For ecclesiology[5] his significance lay in his development of papal power in line with his predecessors, though he respected the rightful role of bishops in their own diocese.[6] He was convinced that reform must come from the top. In his time the meaning of Matt 16:19 was extended: the pope could bind and loose all; Gregory, unlike his predecessors, drew consequences from this text for papal supremacy over temporal rulers. In his conflict with Henry IV, he not only excommunicated the king but claimed the right to depose him and free his subjects from allegiance.

As pope and reformer, he saw a profound struggle between God's kingdom and that of Satan. All were called upon to be involved in this battle. The kingdom of God was the universal Church, which had the double authority of secular and priestly power *(Regnum et Sacerdotium).* Of the two, the latter had higher rank as both had the same end; as the need arose the pope could command or abrogate the secular princes. But he did not go so far as to substitute papal for secular power: the temporal retained its own finality, though ultimately it was subject to the spiritual.

One cannot remain indifferent to Gregory. Some have seen his pontificate as tyrannical and theocratic; modern historians tend to see that his motivation was a high one and that the reforms he carried through were not only institutional but deeply spiritual as well.[7]

[1]H.X. Arquillière, "La signification théologique du pontificat de Grégoire VII," RUnivOtt 20 (1950) 140–161; F. Kempf, in Jedin-Dolan 3:367-373; M.J. MacDonald, *Hildebrand: Life of Gregory VII* (London, 1932); I.S. Robinson, "Bibliographical Surveys II, Pope Gregory VII (1073–1085)," JEH 36 (1985) 439–483; W. Ullmann, *The Growth of Papal Power in the Middle Ages* (London, [2]1962) 262–309.   [2]F. Kempf, in Jedin-Dolan 3:351-366; B.V. Hergemöller, "Die Namen der Reformpäpste (1046–1145)," ArHPont 24 (1986) 7–47.   [3]F. Kempf, in Jedin-Dolan 374–385; G.B. Borino, ed., *Studi gregoriani per la storia di Gregorio VII e della riforma gregoriana.* 3 vols. (Rome: Abbey of St. Paul, 1948).   [4]DS 700/ND 1501.   [5]See works, mostly letters: PL 148:283-645/MGEp sel 2, ed. E. Casper. 2 vols. (1920–1923/1955); for local councils Mansi 20:55-630; Congar, Augustin 102–107; A. Murray,

"Pope Gregory VII and His Letters," Traditio 22 (1966) 149–201. [6]L. Meulenberg, "Gregory VII and the Bishops: Centralization of Power," Conc 1/8 (Jan. 1972) 65–78.   [7]G. Fornasari, "Coscienza ecclesiale e storia della spiritualità: Per una ridefinizione della riforma di Gregorio VII," Benedictina 33 (1986) 25–50; J. Leclercq, "Gregorio VII nel nostro secolo," ibid., 117–123; G. Ruggieri, "Santità ed ecclesiologia al sorgere della cristianità gregoriana," CrNSt 6(1985) 245–261.

## GUARDINI, Romano (1885–1968)

Born in Verona, Italy, in 1885, Romano Guardini spent most of his life in Germany.[1] After university studies in chemistry and economics, he changed to theology and was ordained a priest in 1910. A professorship of "Religion and Catholic Worldview," was created for him at Berlin (1923–1939). After the war comparable chairs were established for him at Tübingen and later at Munich. He died in 1968.

Between the two wars Guardini was very influential in the renewal of Catholic theology. His main writings[2] were on liturgy,[3] homiletics, and the relation of the Church to the world. His most famous book was a life of Christ, *The Lord,*[4] written to integrate theological questions and more modern exegesis.

In ecclesiology he emphasizes the need for "awakening the Church in souls,"[5] for overcoming individualism so that the person is committed to the community of the Church, which is more than the sum total of its individuals. He stresses a thinking or experiencing with the Church *(sentire cum Ecclesia)*. In the Church is the perfect equilibrium between the personal and the communitarian, between liberty and authority.[6] "In spite of the human, one may say too human character of the Church, we may say that it is the divine life which is acting in the life of the Church, in its manifestations of itself, and in its history."[7] And again: "The individual bears the Church in his faith, both its dynamic power and its weight; the Church is present to him as it is. It bears him and weighs him down. Its life nourishes him. Its immensity humbles him. Its breadth enlarges his horizon; its wisdom gives him a rule of life; its power enlarges his field of activity. Its formalism blocks him, its coldness hardens him; and whatever is violent, selfish, hard, or vulgar about the Church has an influence on the faith of the individual, so that the latter sometimes feels obliged to sustain the cause of God not only in the darkness of the world, but also in that of the Church."[8]

In an age of ecclesiological triumphalism, Guardini speaks always for truth, with candid realism if need be, but with love for the Church he so often calls "mother."[9]

[1]H.-B. Gerl, *Romano Guardini 1885–1968: Leben und Werk* (Mainz: Matthias Grünewald, 1985); W. Dettloff, in KlassTheol 2:318-330.   [2]*Bibliographie Romano Guardini. Guardinis Werke. Veröffentlichungen über Guardini. Rezensionen.* Harausgegeben von der Katholischen Akademie in Bayern (Paderborn: Schöningh, 1978).   [3]B. Neunhauser, "La liturgie dans la vision de Romano Guardini," in A. Pistoia and A.M. Triacca, eds., *La liturgie, son sens, son esprit, sa méthode: Liturgie et théologie.* Conférences Saint-Serge 28—Bibliotheca Ephemerides liturgicae Subsidia 27 (Rome: CLV—Ed. Liturgiche, 1982) 179–189; S. Maggiani, "Rileggere Romano Guardini: L'importanza del pensiero liturgico guardiniano per un rilancio del 'Movimento liturgico,'" RivLtg 74 (1987) 375–386.   [4]Chicago, [5]1954.   [5]*Vom Sinn der Kirche* (Mainz, 1923) 1.   [6]Antón 2:618; W. Schmidt, "Kirche in den Seelen: Zur Beziehung von Kirche und Mensch bei R. Guardini," in W. Baier et al., eds., *Weisheit Gottes—Weisheit der Welt.* FS J. Ratzinger. 2 vols. (St. Ottilien: EOS, 1987) 2:953-969.   [7]*The Life of Faith,* ch. 9 (Glen Rock, N.J.: Paulist, 1960) 118.   [8]Ibid., 119.   [9]M. Lutz-Bachmann, "'Kirche in der Seele der Gläubigen'— Romano Guardinis Kirchenverständnis und der Begriff der Kirche in der zeitgenössischen Theologie," ThPh 62 (1987) 22–42; A. Schilson, "Mahnung und Wegweisung: Zur überraschenden Aktualität Romano Guardinis," GeistL 61 (1988) 324–336.

## GUTIÉRREZ, Gustavo (1928– )

Gustavo Gutiérrez was born in Lima, Peru, in 1928. In his youth he experienced discrimination because of his mestizo (part-Native American) stock. He was drawn to medicine and psychiatry before turning to theology. His quite varied studies in Lima, Santiago (Chile), Louvain, Lyons, and the Gregorian University in Rome, ensured a wide philosophical and theological culture. His lecture at Chimbote, Peru, in 1968, when he used the term "liberation theology," is often seen as the birth of liberation theology (q.v.). (He himself would give the credit to the 16th-century liberator-priest Bartolomé de Las Casas.) That same year the Bishops' Conference at Medellín incorporated in the document on peace some of his key intuitions.

Gutiérrez has always been a pastoral priest, although he has lectured widely throughout the world. His *Theology of Liberation,* published in Lima in 1971, has become a classic.[1] Though he has used Marx to analyze the social situation in Latin America, he is unequivocally not a Marxist. He is concerned with a Christian response to the oppression of the poor, and he proposes conversion and the struggle for human dignity rather than revolution. He has always insisted on spirituality as an integral part of liberation theology.[2] He often uses the expression "liberating praxis," by which he means concrete actions done in solidarity with the poor and oppressed which are to lead to a transformed world. Along with other liberation theologians like C. Mesters, he insists that the Bible yields new insights when read from the perspective of the poor.[3]

His output is mainly in the form of articles, together with some books and collections.[4] Doctoral theses and other secondary literature on his thought are increasing;[5] particularly noteworthy is the volume arising from a Maryknoll seminar on his work and its implications.[6]

[1]Revised ed. Maryknoll: Orbis, 1988.   [2]*We Drink from Our Own Wells* (Maryknoll: Orbis, 1984).   [3]*On Job: God-Talk and the Suffering of the Innocent* (Maryknoll: Orbis, 1987).   [4]*Liberation*

*and Change* (Atlanta: Knox, 1977); *The Power of the Poor in History* (Maryknoll: Orbis 1983); *The Truth Shall Make You Free: Confrontations* (Maryknoll: Orbis, 1990); *En busca de los pobres de Jesucristo* (Salamanca: Sígueme, 1993). [5]C. Cadorette, *From the Heart of the People: The Theology of Gustavo Gutiérrez* (South Humphrey: Meyer Stone, 1988); R. Chopp, *The Praxis of Suffering* (Maryknoll: Orbis, 1986); F. Guibal, "La force subversive de l'Évangile: Sur la pensée théologique de Gustavo Gutiérrez," RechSR 77 (1989) 483–508; R. McAfee Brown, *Gustavo Gutiérrez: An Introduction to Liberation Theology* (Maryknoll: Orbis, 1990). [6]M. Ellis and O. Maduro, eds., *The Future of Liberation Theology.* FS G. Gutiérrez (Maryknoll: Orbis, 1989).

# H

## HERESY

Heresy has various meanings and different manifestations throughout history.[1] In the *Code of Canon Law* heresy is described as "the obstinate post-baptismal denial of some truth which must be believed with divine and catholic faith, or it is likewise an obstinate doubt concerning the same" (c. 751). But this modern canonical definition cannot be applied to the complex realities covered in Christian history by the word "heresy" (Greek *hairesis* = choice/thing chosen). Originally applied to members of a particular philosophical school,[2] it had the notion of "group" or "party" in Acts (e.g., 5:17); the Christian community is perceived by the Jews as a special group or sect (Acts 24:5.14). It also had a negative sense of "factions" in Gal 5:20 and in the crux of 1 Cor 11:18-19— "I hear that there are divisions *[schismata]* among you . . . there have *[dei]* to be factions *[haireseis]* among you, for only so will it become clear who among you is genuine." The meaning is somewhat obscure, but it certainly implies a negative judgment on those party to the faction.[3]

From the time of Ignatius (q.v.) the word "heresy" became applied to doctrinal error,[4] a reality already found in the NT Church, which commended orthodoxy in belief and practice and shunned deviation in doctrine and ethics (Rev 2–3; 1 John 2:22, 27).[5] In an early letter Paul would be so insistent on the orthodoxy of his gospel that even an angel teaching otherwise was to be accursed (Gal 1:8—*anathema estô*). This curse formula is found elsewhere in the NT, and it implies that the person is to be given up to the judicial wrath of God because of sin.[6] It would appear regularly in conciliar condemnation, but with varied significance.

From the beginning of the 2nd century we find tracts against, and lists of, heretics and heresies, the most fa-

mous being by Tertullian (q.v.),[7] Irenaeus (q.v.),[8] Epiphanius of Constantia,[9] and Augustine (q.v.).[10]

The early writers are mostly concerned with docetic heresies that would deny a genuine Incarnation, with Judaizing tendencies, with Marcion, who rejected in the name of a God only of love most of the Scriptures except St. Paul and some parts of Luke, and with Gnostic heresies (v. GNOSTICISM). Their response is to cling to the teaching of the apostolic Churches.[11] In the *Apostolic Tradition* (q.v.) many heresies are said to have come about because Church leaders have not taught the intention (*sententiam* from *proaipesis*) of the apostles; no heretic can induce into error the one who follows the apostolic tradition. Error indeed comes from ignorance and the ignorant.[12] Heresy in the early Church is seen as having intellectual causes, and to have its roots in pride and other vices; it is presumed that every heretic is in bad faith.[13]

Heresy and schism (q.v.) are not always clearly distinguishable in the writings of the Fathers. Basil the Great (q.v.) gives a clear difference between them: heretics are outside the deposit of faith; schismatics are groups who are dissident for ecclesiastical reasons. The baptisms of the former are invalid, but not those of the latter. He adds a third grouping, the *parasynagoga,* liturgical celebrations of rebellious bishops or priests or of those improperly instructed.[14] But this third, which seems to have originated with him, did not have much influence and was generally subsumed into schism.[15]

The process of reconciling heretics was not uniform.[16] In 253–257 C.E. there was a controversy between Pope Stephen and the African Church led by Cyprian (q.v.). The latter wanted approval for their practice of rebaptizing heretics who sought reconciliation. Stephen rejected this innovation and insisted that they receive only a hand imposition (v. IMPOSITION) in penance. The Council of Nicaea (q.v.) did not lay down any general norm, but dealt individually with each heresy. Those heretics which had an orthodox faith also had true baptism; they received an imposition of the hand. Those whose Trinitarian or Christological faith was unsound were to be rebaptized.[17] There are some doubts about the authenticity of canon 7 of Constantinople I (q.v.), which prescribed an anointing with chrism to receive the Holy Spirit for some heretics, while others of deviant Trinitarian and Christological faith were to be rebaptized.[18] The *Apostolic Canons* (v. APOSTOLIC COLLECTIONS) did not recognize the baptism of heretics in its 46th and 47th canons. Of the two modes of procedure *akribeia* (strictness) and *oikonomia* or *sygkatabasis* (condescension/mercy, v. ECONOMY), the *Canons* preferred the latter, while the two councils above took the former attitude. The Synod of Laodicea (2nd half of 4th century) took the approach of Nicaea and Constantinople. Basil (q.v.) generally did not recognize the validity of heretical baptism on account of the prevalent unorthodox Trinitarian faith (especially about the Holy Spirit) at the time.

In the patristic times, it is not always easy to know the precise opinions of heretics or the reasons why they adopted their positions. Our knowledge of their writings is often from the works of their opponents, and heretical works would scarcely be laboriously copied in the monastic scriptoria.

After the Arian and Pelagian heresies and their aftermath, there is little heresy in the West until about the 11th–12th century. The word heresy was quite equivocal at the time: it was applied to doctrinal deviations like that of Berengarius on the Eucharist or any recrudescence of Manichaeanism; sometimes it indicated disciplinary aberrations, such as simony or Nicolaïsm, the latter usually meaning clerical marriage or concubinage; it also covered unlawful preaching, especially by laity. Much of the heresy of the Middle Ages was a reaction against clerical laxity, or against the institutional Church by "spiritual" movements, or by those which stressed evangelical poverty. Important in the Middle Ages were the Cathari (q.v.) and Waldensians (q.v.).[19]

St. Thomas represents the views of his day: he distinguishes infidelity and heresy: the former was a rejection of Christ, the latter of his teaching;[20] heresy is properly about faith or those things which pertain to faith;[21] heretics are not to be tolerated, for if they do not recant, they are to be given over to the civil authority to impose the death penalty.[22] We will find this last even more intolerable unless we recall that in Christendom heretics were seen not just as enemies in the Church but a civil menace as well, and a threat to peace and order in society. It is in this context that we must understand the Inquisition (q.v.), the most brutal suppression of heretics (and of many innocents) ever devised.

In the Middle Ages heresies were more often movements rather than merely wayward beliefs of individuals, that is, until the time of John Wycliffe (q.v.). He set out from disenchantment with corruption in the Church to clear heresy. His views spread to Bohemia (Czechoslovakia), where they were taken up by John Huss (q.v.), who was condemned by the Council of Constance and burned 1415.[23]

The Reformation, as its name suggests, was an attempt by Luther (q.v.) and others to reform the Church, now in a state of some corruption. The reform within the Catholic Church was the Council of Trent (q.v.), which condemned the perceived (not always the exact) errors of the reformers. In its condemnations it used the traditional formula *anathema sit* ("let him/her be accursed") for heresy. The greatest care was taken to avoid condemning matters freely disputed among theologians. If an error were not perceived to be held by a Protestant, the council avoided *anathema sit,* and dealt with the issue in the reform decrees which were being prepared pari passu with the canons. But heresy included more than statements against divine faith: it was to cover obdurate refusal to accept the positions of the Church also in matters of discipline. The formula *anathema sit* was applied to expressions of such refusal.[24] After Trent the use of the word heresy tended to be narrower, and refer to what is contrary to divine truth; at the same time *anathema sit* was restricted to expression of heresy (v. THEOLOGICAL NOTES).

Traditional catholic theology has distinguished between material and formal heresy. The former was the adoption of a heretical position in good faith. The latter has the element of pertinacity, as in the definition of heresy in CIC 751 above: one willfully refuses to believe what is revealed by God and proposed as such by the Church. Though such pertinacity can be established about external actions, it is psychologically improbable that one would accept God's revelation in many areas, and deliberately reject his authority in some specific instance(s). Formal heresy can thus be seen as being somewhat unrealistic.[25] Implicit or hidden heresy can be seen to be continually present even within the Church, not least today.[26] Heretics see themselves as the real upholders of truth, even to the point of dying for their beliefs. Apostasy is extreme heresy, a complete abandonment of faith.

The *Code of Canon Law* has a number of provisions regarding heretics: heresy incurs an automatic excommunication (c. 1364 § 1—q.v.); notorious heretics are denied ecclesiastical funeral rites (c. 1184 § 1); past heresy is an impediment to orders (c. 1041 § 2) and to their exercise (c. 1044 § 2), with dispensation reserved to the Holy See (c. 1047); a cleric in heresy is liable to loss of clerical state (c. 290 § 2) and a religious to dismissal (c. 694).

W. Bauer has claimed that orthodoxy was only one of the currents of early Christianity: because it survived, other forms became deemed as heretical. Though useful as a corrective to simplistic examination of early sources, his famous thesis has not won wide acceptance.[27] There is also a sense that the history of orthodoxy and heresy is told as the story of winners and losers, and the positive contribution of heresy to dogmatic development and Church renewal is often not acknowledged.[28] We can see that heresy has had an important role in the development of dogma. The classical case of heresy fostering dogmatic development was Arianism: it was only when Arius asked the right question ("Is the Son a creature?"), but answered it wrongly, that the development of Nicaea could take place.[29]

Heresy always contains a truth, usually underemphasized or forgotten. The heretic pursues this facet of truth, often in an exaggerated and exclusive way. When orthodoxy eventually wins out, the vital insight of the heretic is often forgotten at the expense of the fullness of Catholic truth.

[1]Congar, L'Église une 85–121.  [2]H. Schlier, "Hiereomai," TDNT 1:180–185.  [3]I. Perez Fernandez, "Oportet haereses esse," CiTom 92 (1965) 291–311; J. Moingt, "Oportet et Haereses esse," Conc 192 (1987) 64–72; J. Murphy-O'Connor, NJBC in loc.  [4]*Trallians* 6:1; *Ephesians* 6:2; cf. P. Prigent, "L'hérésie asiate et l'Église confessante de l'Apocalypse à Ignace," VigChr 31 (1977) 1–22.  [5]G. Ghiberti, "Ortodossa e eterodossa nelle Lettere giovannee," RivBib 30 (1982) 381–400.  [6]J. Behm, "Anathema," TDNT 1:354-357.  [7]*De praescriptione haereticorum*—SC 46; cf. C. Munier, "Les conceptions hérésiologiques de Tertullien," AugR 20 (1980) 257–266; idem, "Analyse du traité de Tertullien *De praescriptione haereticorum*," RevSR 59 (1985) 12–33.  [8]*Adversus haereses*—SC 100, 152–153, 210–211, 263–264, 293–294.  [9]*Panarion*—PG 41:172-42:831/GCS 25; 31; 37.  [10]*De haeresibus*—PL 42:21-50/G. Müller, trans. The *"De haeresibus" of St. Augustine*. Patristic Studies 90 (Washington, D.C., 1956).  [11]Irenaeus, *Adv. haer.* 3:3, 1; Tertullian, *De praescr. haer.* 20:6-7; cf. Hegesippus, in Eusebius *Hist. eccl.* 4:22, 4–5; H. Chadwick, *Heresy and Orthodoxy in the Early Church*. Collected Studies 342 (Hampshire UK: Variorum, 1991); R. Lyman, "Heresy and Orthodoxy: Ancient and Modern," AngTR 74 (1992) 125–132; L. Peters, ed., *Heresy and Authority in Medieval Europe: Documents in Translation* (Philadelphia: UP, 1980); R. Williams, ed., *The Making of Orthodoxy: Essays in Honour of Henry Chadwick* (Cambridge: UP, 1989).  [12]41/38 and prologue.  [13]E.g., Tertullian, *De praescr. haer.* 8–12; Irenaeus *Adv. haer.* 4:26, 2; cf. 2 Pet 2:1-3.  [14]*Epist.* 188, canon 1—PG 32:665/S. *Basile: Lettres.* 3 vols., Y. Courtonne, ed. (Paris: Collection des Universités de France, 1957–1966) 2:121.  [15]M. Girardi, "Nozione di eresia, scisma e parasinagoga in Basilio di Cesarea," VetChr 17 (1990) 49–77.  [16]D. Salachas, "La legislazione della chiesa antica a proposito delle diverse categorie di eretici," Nicolaus 9 (1981) 315–347.  [17]Nicaea, cc. 8, 19—Tanner 1:9-10, 15;  [18]Constantinople I, c. 7—Tanner 1:35.  [19]F. Blanchetière, "Contestation des structures ecclésiales et hérésie au XIIe siècle," RHPR 67 (1987) 241–249.  [20]ST 2-2ae, q.11, a.1.  [21]Ibid., a.2.  [22]Ibid., a.3.  [23]Tanner 1:426-431/DS 1201–1230; cf. G. Leff, *Heresy in the Later Middle Ages: The Relation of Heterodoxy to Dissent c. 1250-1450.* 2 vols. (Manchester: UP—New York: Barnes & Noble, 1967) 2:606-708; M. Lambert, *Medieval Heresy: Popular Movements from the Gregorian Reform to the Reformation* (Oxford: Blackwell, ²1992).  [24]M. Bévenot, "'Faith and Morals' in the Councils of Trent and Vatican I," HeythJ 3 (1962) 15–30; cf. P. Fransen, "A Short History of the Meaning of the Formula *Fides et mores*," LouvSt 7 (1978–79) 270–301; H. Lennerz, "Notulae tridentinae: 1. Primum anathema in Concilio Tridentino," Greg 27 (1946) 136–142; S. Privitera, "Sull'eresia: Chiarificazioni etico-concettuali da analisi terminologiche," HoTheol 7 (1989) 119–170.  [25]G.A. Buckley, "Heresy, Sin of," NCE 6:1069–1070.  [26]K. Rahner, *On Heresy.* QDisput 14 (Freiburg: Herder—London: Burns & Oates, 1964) = ThInvest 5:468-512; idem, "Heresies in the Church Today?," ThInvest 12:116-141; Conc 192 (1987).  [27]J. McCue, "Bauer's *Rechtgläubigkeit und Ketzerei*," Conc 192 (1987) 28–35; cf. W. Bauer, *Orthodoxy and Heresy in Earliest Christianity* (Philadelphia: Fortress, 1971 = German ²1964).  [28]D. Christie-Murray, *A History of Heresy* (New York—Oxford, UP, 1976); W.H.C. Frend, *Saints and Sinners in the Early Church: Differing and Conflicting Traditions in the First Six Centuries* (Delaware: Glazier—London: Darton, Longman & Todd, 1985); P. Parvis, "On the Function of Heresy," NBlackfr 70 (1989) 96–104; N. Ring, "Heresy," NDictT 459–462.  [29]B.J.F. Lonergan, *The Road to Nicaea: The Dialectical Development of Trinitarian Theology* (London: Darton, Longman & Todd, 1976); Q. Quesnell, "The Foundations of Heresy," in F. Lawrence, ed., *Lonergan Workshop.* Vol. 2 (Chico CA: Scholars Press, 1981) 55–79. See passim F.A. Sullivan, *Creative Fidelity: Weighing and Interpreting Documents of the Magisterium* (New York: Paulist, 1996).

## HERMAS, The Shepherd

Hermas portrays himself as an ex-slave who was a member of the Church of Rome. The book ascribed to him, the *Shepherd,* records visions and revelations he received, mostly about the problem of sin in the Church and the issue of repentance and reconciliation. But his works also allow us to have some precious insights into his Church at a time of very scarce documentation.[1] His work is divided into five Visions, twelve *Mandates (entolê),* and ten parables *or Similitudes (parabolê).* It is variously dated with most scholars assigning it to about 140 C.E., often on the basis of a comment in the *Muratorian Fragment* (q.v.) which, while denying it to be scriptural, speaks of the *Shepherd* as having been written by Hermas, the brother of Pius, bishop of Rome.[2] The lack of clear evidence on there being one bishop in Rome at the time Hermas was writing has inclined some scholars to suggest an even earlier date in the 1st century.[3] An early date would harmonize with the statement of Origen that Hermas is the person in Rom 16:14, as well as the commission to communicate a booklet to Clement (at Rome ca. 91–ca.101?).[4] Such an early date would also account for the fact that the work was regarded as Scripture by Irenaeus, the pre-Montanist Tertullian, and Origen.

Some scholars see it as a 2nd-century composite work from two 1st-century documents: the first being by Hermas, viz., *Visions* 1-4; the second being anonymous, viz., *Vision* 5 with *Precepts* and *Parables*.[5]

Apart from being an important document in the evolution of the sacrament of reconciliation (q.v.),[6] the *Shepherd* gives some significant teaching about the Church.[7] The Church appears as an elderly lady, old because "she was created before all and it is for her that all was created" (v. ABEL, CHURCH FROM).[8] But later visions show her growing young and beautiful as her children are converted.[9]

The Church is also a spouse,[10] the house of God,[11] his vine,[12] his people,[13] and eschatological kingdom of God.[14] But the most prominent figure, one which appears twice, is of the Church as a tower.[15] The tower is being built for the Lord. Some stones are quite suitable, others have to be purified, while others are rejected. The Church here is eschatological, with a certain sense of imminence or presence. The rock on which it is built is the Son of God;[16] the stones come out from water,[17] namely baptism.

There is no detailed account of Church order, though we have mention of apostles, bishops, presbyters, teachers *(didaskoloi),* and deacons.[18] Bishops and presbyters are not spoken of together, which may suggest that they are synonymous. For a text of Roman origin, it is difficult to account for the absence of any reference to a single bishop, especially if a mid-2nd century date is accepted. There is a long section on the discernment between false and true prophets (q.v.).[19] As in the *Didachê* (q.v.), prophets are tested by their behavior.

The work of Hermas has deep roots in Judaeo-Christianity,[20] and its central concern is that of repentance and conversion. There is an urgency about conversion: there is a set time for Christians to repent, though pagans can repent any time before the end.[21] The author is very concerned with the danger of riches: the ideal situation is that the rich support the poor with material things, and the poor support the rich by their prayer.[22]

By the 4th century the authority of this ancient text had waned. This could be due to its visionary-apocalyptic approach and to the undeveloped character of its Christology and pneumatology.[23]

[1]Texts R. Joly, SC 53; J.M.-F. Marique, FC 1:235-352; G.F. Snyder AF 6. [2]Joly (n. 1) 14–15; Snyder (n. 1) 22–24; Marique (n. 1) 227–228. [3]S. Tugwell, *The Apostolic Fathers.* Outstanding Christian Thinkers (London: Chapman, 1989) 63, n. 1. [4]Vis. 2:4, 3 (8). [5]P. Nautin, "Hermas, Shepherd of," EncycEarCh 1:377. Cf. P. Henne, *L'unité du "Pastor" d'Hermas: Tradition et Rédaction.* Cahiers de la Revue biblique 31 (Paris: Gebalda, 1992) and "Un seul 'Pastor' un seul Hermas," RTLv 23 (1992) 482–488. [6]K. Rahner, "The Penitential Teaching of the Shepherd of Hermas," ThInvest 15:57-113. [7]S. Folgado Flórez, *Teoría eclesial en el Pastor de Hermas* (El Escorial: Bib. "La Ciudad de Dios," 1979) 41–70 = "Teoría teórico-descriptiva sobre la Iglesia en el 'Pastor' de Hermas," CiuD 191 (1978) 217–246; L. Pernveden, *The Concept of the Church in the Shepherd of Hermas.* St. Theol. Lundensia 27 (Lund: Gleerup, 1966). [8]Vis. 2:4, 1 (8). Folgado Flórez (n. 5) 73–99 = "La Iglesia, anterior a los siglos en el "Pastor"

de Hermas," CiuD 191 (1978) 365–391. [9]Vis. 3:11-13 (19–21). [10]Vis. 4:2, 1–2 (23). [11]Simil. 9:13, 9 (90). [12]Simil. 5:2-3 (55–56); 5:6, 2–3 (59). [13]Simil. 5:6, 2–3 (59) [14]Simil. 9:15, 2 (92); 16, 2 (93), 20, 2–3 (97); 29, 2 (106). [15]Vis. 3:1-10 (9–18); Simil. 9:2-9, 12–16 (79–86, 89–93). [16]Simil. 9:12, 1–3 (89) [17]Simil. 9:16, 1–6 (93); cf. Vis. 3:3, 5 (11). [18]Vis. 2:4, 3 (8); Simil. 9:25, 2 (102); 9:26, 2 (103); 9:27, 10, 2 (104). [19]Man. 11:1-21 (43). [20]J. Daniélou, *The Theology of Jewish Christianity* (Chicago, 1964) 10, 117–376. [21]Vis. 2:2, 5 (6). [22]Simil. 2:1-9 (51); cf. Mand. 10, 5 (40); Simil. 9:20, 1–4 (97). C. Osiek, *Rich and Poor in the Shepherd of Hermas.* CBQ Monograph 15 (Washington, D.C.: Catholic Biblical Association of America, 1983). [23]Joly SC 53:31-33.

# HERMITS

Hermits (Greek *erêmos* = solitary), also called anchorites (Greek *anachôrêtês* = withdrawn apart), began to appear in Egypt and elsewhere around the Mediterranean from the 3rd century. Egeria (q.v.) in her travels found many of them, men and women, from Sinai up through modern Palestine. An archetypical hermit was St. Anthony (251–356), who was also in a sense a monastic founder.[1] Particularly important were the Desert Fathers, many of whom were hermits.[2] They left a rich heritage of spiritual wisdom called the *Apophthegms* or Sayings of the Fathers, consisting of pithy stories and instruction.[3]

The hermits left the world in order both to seek God and to serve the world at the level of its deepest need. Though monasticism would develop from the eremitical life,[4] hermits were never entirely absent from the history of the Church, with special flowerings of the vocation in the 10th and 11th centuries in Europe, and hermitages for both men and women, e.g., Richard Rolle, Julian of Norwich, arising especially in 14th-century England. After World War II there was a renewal of interest in the solitary life.[5]

Hermits were mentioned during Vatican II[6] in a text referring to eremitical life implicitly: life in solitude (LG 43; PC 1).

The *Code* places its one canon on hermits within those on consecrated life (q.v.). It is not referring to those who, while remaining religious and under the authority of their superiors, live an eremitical life apart from community—a practice recognized from the time of St. Benedict.[7] It first describes the eremitical life, before laying down norms: "The Church recognizes the eremitic or anchorite life by which the Christian faithful devote their life to the praise of God and salvation of the world through a stricter separation from the world, the silence of solitude and assiduous prayer and penance. A hermit is recognized in the law as one dedicated to God in the consecrated life if he or she publicly professes the three evangelical counsels, confirmed by a vow or other sacred bond, in the hands of the diocesan bishop and observes his or her own plan of life under his direction" (CIC 603). The language used in the *Code* echoes the paragraph on contemplatives in PC 7. The Eastern Church has its own legislation for hermits (CCEO 481–485).

In the Latin Church canonical provision for the eremitical life is thus recent. The main responsibility in law rests with the diocesan bishop. There are many important issues that will vary from country to country and culture to culture:[8] physical and psychological maturity and health, formation, medical insurance, financial support, discernment, spiritual direction, physical safety, and the provision of the necessary structures to support this unique call.

The place for the modern hermit may be in a place apart or may be in the solitude of a modern city. The Church has still much to learn about this vocation which the Spirit has revived in its midst.

---

[1]Athanasius, *The Life of Anthony.* Classics of Western Spirituality (New York: Paulist, 1980)/ACW 10.  [2]H. Wadell, *The Desert Fathers* (London, 1936).  [3]PG 65:71-400—B. Ward, ed. and trans., *The Sayings of the Desert Fathers: The Alphabetical Collection* (London: Mowbray—Kalamazoo: Cistercian Publications, 1975); systematic collections PL 73:855-1022 and 73:1025-1066.  [4]L. Bouyer, *History of Christian Spirituality.* 3 vols. (London, 1968) 1:305-330.  [5]S. Bonnet and G. Gouley, *Les ermites* (Paris: Fayard, 1980); E. Wagner, "Eremitism in the Church," RevRel 46 (1987) 582–589.  [6]E.g., Bishop Remi de Roo, ActaSyn 3/7:609.  [7]*Rule,* c. 1.  [8]J. Beyer, "La vita eremitica o anacoretica," VitaCons 23 (1987) 565–574; H.L. MacDonald, "Hermits: The Juridical Implications of Canon 603," StCan 26 (1992) 163–189 from Diss., Ottawa 1990; E. Sastre Santos, "La vida eremítica diocesana forma de vida consagrada: Variaciones sobre el can 603," ComRelM 68 (1987) 99–124, 245–267, 331–358; 69 (1988) 145–170, 307–312.

## HIERARCHY OF TRUTHS

The phrase "hierarchy of truths" at Vatican II (UR 11) has given rise to substantial literature about its meaning and significance, especially in the area of ecumenism.[1] The idea was proposed by Archbishop Pangrazio, who asked that in the context of ecumenism attention be paid to the "hierarchical order of revealed truths."[2] Eventually a formula furnished by Cardinal Koenig was approved.[3] "When comparing doctrines with one another *(in comparandis doctrinis),* they [Catholic theologians] should remember that there exists an order or 'hierarchy' of truths *(ordinem seu 'hierarchiam' veritatum),* since they vary in their connection with the foundation of the Christian faith" (UR 11). Some textual matters call for comment. The immediate context is ecumenical dialogue. The word "hierarchy" has inverted commas in the Latin text, and this highlights the fact that it is not being precisely used in its normal sense; indeed it is there to explain or expand on the word "order." The reason given for the order or hierarchy is "their connection with the foundation of the Christian faith."

In the extensive commentaries that have followed, some points are usually made. First, though the expression is entirely new,[4] the reality is not. All catechesis (v. CATECHISMS) or synopses of the faith emphasized some truths more than others, which are not even mentioned. Creeds (q.v.) are surely an example of truths that are closely connected "with the foundation of the Christian faith"; and they are selective in what they propose. Second, the tradition as represented for example by St. Thomas Aquinas distinguished truths that are directly or *per se* objects of faith from those which are indirectly or *in ordine ad alia.*[5] Third, there can be two kinds of truths: those which concern the end, or finality, such as Trinity, or eternal life; those which concern the means, such as sacraments and Church structures. This point made by Archbishop Pangrazio was not taken up by the council; it is not without problems. Fourth, Catholic commentators noted the teaching of Pius XI: "It is nowise licit to use that distinction which some have seen fit to introduce between those articles of faith which are *fundamental* and those which are not fundamental, as they say, as if the former are to be accepted by all, while the latter may be left to the free assent of the faithful: for the supernatural virtue of faith has a formal cause, namely the authority of God revealing, and this is patient of no such distinction." Hence he concludes that we believe with the same faith the Immaculate Conception, the Trinity, the Incarnation, and papal infallibility as defined at Vatican I.[6] This distinction between fundamental (obligatory) articles and non-fundamental (free) articles had been made since the Reformation.

With these points, unanimity among commentators seems to end, and authors take different paths. Y. Congar points to a distinction in the medievals between the *quod*—the truth involved—and *quo*—the subjective act of faith. Whereas there will not be a differentiation in the latter, since faith is based on God's authority and one must believe all that God has revealed, the former will admit a difference, since the importance of the objective truths revealed obviously varies. Typically, Congar is concerned to emphasize, where possible, legitimate diversity in communion.[7] Thus it would seem that for him the Trinity is incomparably more weighty than papal infallibility, and a rejection of the former would be a greater breach of communion than refusal of the latter. There are other interpretations. H. Mühlen takes the person of Jesus as the center with regard to which truths are ranked; following Rahner he posits three basic mysteries—Trinity, Incarnation, grace; he draws out ecumenical implications of the council teaching.[8] The most extensive overview of the issue is by the Lutheran U. Valeske, which seems, however, to underestimate the possibilities open to Catholics consequent on holding a hierarchy of truths. For him the central truths are soteriological.[9] G. Tavard[10] gives a survey of the issues involved in the question, noting the significance of two subsequent documents of the Secretariat for Christian Unity (1970): "Although they [truths] all demand a due assent of faith, [they] do not all occupy the same principal or central place in the mystery revealed in Jesus Christ, since they vary in their relationship to the foundation of the Christian faith";[11] and "neither in the life nor in the teaching of the whole Church is everything presented on the same level."[12] P. O'Connell[13] suggests that the hierarchy of truths should be evidenced in the Church's life, and seen in a reduction of emphasis on ecclesiological truths about the papacy compared with the fundamental Christological and Trinitarian truths. Somewhat similar is K. Rahner's insistence on the distinction between an objective and an existential hierarchy of truths.[14] D. Carroll notes the importance of the hierarchy of truths for the composition of necessary short formulae of faith; those truths not mentioned are not denied and will be clarified in turn by the formulation of the foundational truths.[15] F. Jelly sees the Trinitarian and Christological truths as central, and the Marian dogmas as dependent on and illustrative of them.[16] Helpful in this context is W. Kasper's description of three types of dogmatic statement: those relating to God's salvific purpose (e.g., Trinity, Incarnation, salvation is only in Christ); those relating to the means of salvation (e.g., sacraments); those which proclaim paradigmatic truths expressing other truths (e.g., the Marian dogmas exemplify Christological, soteriological, and ecclesiological pronouncements).[17] There have only been a few Catholics who explicitly suggest that the hierarchy of truths could lead to a cutting back on some doctrines.[18] G. Thils, who in an early article referred to the useful psychological shock of the notion of a hierarchy of truths,[19] took the opportunity of commenting again in order to explore the mediations of truth, especially the sense of faith (q.v.) in the believing of the people;[20] most other commentators speak in the context of the magisterium (q.v.).

Much still needs to be done on the whole issue. For a Catholic, the notion of the "hierarchy of truths" cannot be an excuse for dropping truths of the faith. But it would seem that commentators have dwelt perhaps excessively on the word "hierarchy," which is not being used in an exact sense by the council, rather than on the word "order," which it somehow qualifies. The Vatican I teaching about the way in which we achieve a limited understanding of the mysteries through their interconnection is perhaps a way forward in grasping the order of the mysteries which are in some kind of hierarchy.[21] The existential order in which the graced believer attains to the Mystery will involve an ever-changing subjective hierarchy of propositional truths.[22]

Cardinal J. Ratzinger, writing in defense of the new Catechism (q.v.) against the objection that it paid too little attention to the hierarchy of truths, stated: "What the term hierarchy of truths seeks to express is that the faith of the Church is not a continually increasing sum of propositions, some of which could be put in brackets because otherwise the whole package could become too heavy. Rather faith is an organic whole in which every individual element obtains its meaning from being seen from within its proper place within the whole. The principle of the hierarchy of truths runs counter to the tendency to isolate things and break them up; instead it relates individual elements to the whole, from which they take their meaning."[23]

In ecumenical dialogue (q.v.)[24] it is necessary, as some, like Jelly, have demanded that Catholics show how they relate the more peripheral truths to the core foundation of the faith. But more could perhaps be said. If each Church were to attempt to show how it orders doctrines to one other, we might find that some underlying difficulties between the Churches are operative and that dialogue on specific issues has so far been unable to unearth or face. Again the order between the mysteries is not only a matter of rigorous intellectual truth but rather a reflection of the living experience of praise, worship, and spirituality of the Churches; ecumenical dialogue has been slow to enter these last areas.

[1]Survey: W. Henn, "The Hierarchy of Truths Twenty Years Later," TS 48 (1987) 439–471; idem, *The Hierarchy of Truths According to Yves Congar.* AnGreg 246 (Rome: Gregorian UP, 1987) 213–239. See A. Kremer, "'Hierarchia veritatum': Deutungs Möglichkeiten und ökumenische Relevanz," Catholica 46 (1992) 1–30. [2]ActaSyn 2/6: 32–35; English, in H. Küng et al., eds., *Council Speeches at Vatican II* (New York, 1964) 188–192. [3]G. Tavard, *"Hierarchia veritatum:* A Preliminary Investigation," TS 32 (1971) 278–289 at 279. [4]H. Mühlen, "Die Lehre des Vaticanum II über die 'hierarchia veritatum' und ihre Bedeutung für den ökumenischen Dialog," TGl 57 (1966) 303–335 at 316. [5]ST 2–2ae, q.1, a.6 ad 1. [6]Encyc. *Mortalium animos*—AAS 20(1928) 5–16 at 13/Carlen 3:313–319 at 317. [7]"On the 'Hierarchia veritatum,'" in D. Neiman and M. Schatkin, eds., *The Heritage of the Early Church.* FS G.V. Florovsky. OrChrAn 195 (Rome: Pont. Orientale, 1973) 409–420; idem, *Diversity and Communion* (London: SCM, 1983) See W. Henn, Congar (n 1.) 197–212, 241–252. [8]Art. cit. (n. 4). [9]*Hierarchia veritatum: Theologiegeschichtliche Hintergründe und mögliche Konsequenzen eines Hinweises im Oekumenismusdekret des II. Vatikanischen Konzils zum zwischenkirchlichen Gespräch* (Munich, 1968). [10]Art. cit. (n. 3). [11]*Directory,* Part II, 2:74—Flannery 1:522. [12]*Reflections and Suggestions Concerning Ecumenical Dialogue* IV:4b—Flannery 1:545. [13]"Hierarchy of Truths," in P.S. de Achutegui, ed., *Cardinal Bea Studies 2: The Dublin Papers* (Manila: Ateneo UP, 1972) 83–117. [14]"A Hierarchy of Truths: Central Truths and Remote Truths," ThInvest 21:162-167; cf. Rahner, Foundations 382–384. [15]"Hierarchia veritatum: A Theological and Pastoral Insight of the Second Vatican Council," IrTQ 44 (1977) 125–133. [16]"Marian Dogmas Within Vatican II's Hierarchy of Truths," MarSt 27 (1976) 17–40. [17]*An Introduction to Christian Faith* (London: Burns & Oates, 1980) 92–114. [18]W. Hryniewicz,

"La hiérarchie des verités: Implications oecuméniques d'une idée chrétienne," Irén 51 (1978) 470–491, 577; cf. A. Houtepan, *"Hierarchia Veritatum* and Orthodoxy," Conc 192 (1097) 39–52. [19]"'Hierarchia veritatum' (Décret sur l'oecuménisme, n° 11)," RTLv 10 (1979) 209–215. [20]"Hiérarchie des vérités de la foi et dialogue oecuménique," RTLv 15 (1984) 147–159. [21]Tanner 2:808/DS 3016/ND 132. [22]Cf. K. Rahner, Foundations 382–384; idem, "A Hierarchy of Truths: Central Truths and Remote Truths," ThInvest 21:162-167; idem, "Paying Due Heed to the Hierarchy of Truths," ibid., 14:37-40; A. Bodem, "Hierarchie der Wahrheiten," Sales 52 (1990) 857–869. [23]Tablet (18.8.1990) 1055, from *Herder-Korrespondenz* July, 1990. [24]W. Henn, "The Hierarchy of Truths and Christian Unity," ETLv 66 (1990) 111–142.

## HILARY OF POITIERS, St. (ca. 315–ca. 368)

Born of pagan parents in Poitiers at an uncertain date, Hilary became an orator, and married. Later, after much study, he had a conversion to Christianity. He was chosen bishop ca. 353. For the rest of his life he was an outstanding champion of orthodoxy against Arianism. He was exiled for his defense of the faith, and died about 368.

His main works are a volume against the Arians on the Trinity, *De Trinitate,*[1] and an address to the bishops of Gaul, which, however, was meant especially for the Easterners and sought to show that East and West were in unison against Arianism and must not be divided by misunderstanding over words.[2] He also wrote commentaries on the psalms[3] and on Matthew's Gospel,[4] as well as some short works, including one on the mysteries, notably of salvation history.[5]

He wrote especially on Trinitarian issues, and he did not deal professedly with the Church; nonetheless, a rich ecclesiology may be gleaned from his works.[6] He developed OT typology: Christ and the Church are prefigured in Adam and Eve; Cain symbolizes the passion of Christ; Abel represents the Church; the patriarchs up to Joshua symbolize Christ or the Church; the harlot Rahab points to the Church.[7]

Several of the common patristic images of the Church are found in Hilary:[8] God's tent;[9] the ark with Noah representing Christ and the dove the Spirit;[10] a ship,[11] the calm after Jesus enters the boat being a symbol for eschatological peace;[12] a secondary or derived light from Christ the true light,[13] mother (q.v.),[14] so that the commandment to love father and mother is interpreted as loving the Heavenly Father and Mother Church;[15] heavenly and earthly aspects;[16] Jerusalem,[17] and God's house.[18] Living stones are placed on the twelve precious stones prepared for building by Moses, the prophets, the Lord, the apostles in martyrdom, and by the Spirit through his wonderful actions.[19] Hilary's view of the Church is profoundly Trinitarian: "So this is proper to God's people, to be brothers under one Father, to be one under one Spirit, to advance harmoniously in one family, to be members of the one body under the head."[20]

The ecclesiology of Hilary is also found in his actions. He sought to unify East and West;[21] he rejected the appeasement synod of bishops at Rimini; he sought the unity of the Church in faith, "faith" being a word that is found over 1300 times in his works.[22] Unity is based ultimately on the union between Father and Son.[23]

Because of his Trinitarian theology, he has been described as "The Athanasius of the West." He was declared Doctor of the Church (q.v.) by Pius IX in 1851.

[1]*De Trinitate*—PL 10:9-472/FC 25. [2]*De synodis*—PL 10:471-546/LNPF, 2nd series 9. See P. Galtier, "Saint Hilaire: trait d'union entre l'Occident et l'Orient," Greg 40 (1959) 609–623. [3]*Comm. in ps.*—PL 9:221-908 and PLS 1:241-246/CSEL 22. [4]*In Matt.*—PL 9:917-1076/SC 254, 258. [5]*De mysteriis*—PLS 1:246-270/SC 19bis. [6]M. Figura, *Das Kirchenverständnis des Hilarius von Poitiers.* Freiburger theologische Studien (Freiburg—Basle—Vienna: Herder, 1984).; R.L. Foley, *The Ecclesiology of Hilary of Poitiers.* Diss. (Cambridge, Mass.: Harvard, 1968). [7]*De mysteriis* 2:5—SC 196bis 148; see Figura (n. 6) 114–140. [8]See H. Rahner, *Symbole der Kirche: Die Ekklesiologie der Väter* (Salzburg, 1964). [9]*In ps.* 51:16—PL 9:317-318. [10]*De myst.* 1:14—PLS 1:254-255. [11]*In Matt.* 13:1—PL 9:995. [12]Ibid., 14:18—PL 9:1003. [13]*In Matt.* 4:13; 27:4—PL 9:953, 1059-1060. [14]*De Trin.* 7:4—PL 10:202. [15]*In Matt.* 19:5—PL 9:1025. [16]*In ps.* 124:4—PL 9:681-682. [17]Ibid., *In ps.* 2:26—PL 9:276. [18]*In ps.* 14:17—PL 9:308. [19]*In ps.* 121:3—PL 9:662. [20]*In ps.* 122:15—PL 9:667. [21]G. Morrel, "Hilary of Poitiers: A Theological Bridge Between the Christian East and the Christian West," AngTR 44 (1962) 312–316; D.H. Williams, "A Reassessment of the Early Career and Exile of Hilary of Poitiers," EH 42 (1991) 202–217. [22]Figura (n. 6) 312. [23]Ibid., 327–344.

## HINDUISM

One of the ancient religions of India, Hinduism[1] has sacred books dating from about 900 B.C.E. These are, notably: the *Vedas,* containing hymns and ritual formulae; the *Brâhmanas,* dealing with cult; the *Aranyakas,* being religious reflections of forest-dwelling ascetics; the *Upanishads,* which are mystical and philosophical treatises on the Brahman, the supreme power in the universe known by meditation and asceticism. Salvation from the world is possible through mystical absorption of the one true reality, the Absolute or Brahman, later, as Brahmâ, to be identified as creator. Other figures in time became joined to Brahma, viz., Vishnu the preserver and Shiva the destroyer. Krishna is a form in which Vishnu appears in the *Bhagavad Gita,* which arrives at the idea of a personal god to be worshiped not by sacrifice but by love and devotion *(bhakti).* The law books or *Dharmashastras* laid down the four classes into which society was divided: the priests *(brahmins),* warriors and merchants, all of whom were "twice-born"—these alone could be initiated into the wisdom of the Vedas—and, fourth, the workers who had no right to learning. These classes would eventually evolve into the caste system.

Key ideas in Hinduism are *karma,* the condition of soul as a result of actions in a past life, and liberation *(moksa)*, which is freedom from the endless cycle of rebirths. Yoga is a system of practical philosophy, of physical and spiritual discipline aimed at liberation. The core of Hindu religion and philosophy is found in the *Vedânta*, which is variously commented upon in different schools. Modern Hinduism continues to reflect profoundly on the human condition and on relations with the transcendent.[2] Its influence on the West is significant, e.g., in the Hare Krishna movement and New Age spiritualities (v. MOVEMENTS, NON-CHRISTIAN).

Hinduism is a profound search for holiness (v. HOLY). Seven stages of wisdom are seven steps to holiness: the desire for the good, derived from detachment, study, the company of good people; inquiry with the practice of detachment; thinness of mind due to a wearing away of attachment to sense objects; the attainment of purity/light, in which the mind has rest; loss of contact with objective sphere as a result of the preceding stages; an absence of concepts by virtue of fusion of the objective and subjective world; the stage of pure transcendence.[3]

B. Griffiths noted: "To a Christian, Hinduism presents on the whole the most profound *preparatio evangelica* that the world has seen."[4] Vatican II speaks positively about Hinduism: "Thus in Hinduism the divine mystery is explored and propounded with an inexhaustible wealth of myths and philosophical investigations, and liberation is sought from the distresses of our state either through various forms of ascetical life or deep meditation or taking refuge in God with loving confidence" (NA 2).

The earliest dialogue with Hinduism could be said to be that of the Jesuit Robert De Nobili (1577–1656). Noting that conversion to Christianity was extremely difficult for Hindus, as converts were immediately regarded as of the lowest caste, he lived like a brahmin, in a penitential mode. He himself largely avoided public contact with other castes, believing that each caste should have its own missionaries. As a result of his efforts, the prejudices against Christianity among the higher castes were lessened. In addition, he advocated strongly what we would now call inculturation (q.v.).[5] Others, like Brahmabandhav Upadhyaya (1861–1907), sought to present Christianity as the flowering of the wisdom, heritage, and truths of Hinduism; the Hindu *Vedas* were the Old Testament of India. He held that theology was to be presented in Indian categories.[6]

There has been dialogue with Hinduism, especially at the level of spirituality. The ashram movement[7] incorporated such a dialogue. Some of its leaders, e.g., B. Griffiths (1906–1993),[8] and Henri Le Saux (Swami Abishiktananda),[9] were Western monks who, in the habit of the Hindu *sannyasi*—one who renounces the world in order to seek God—sought to integrate their Christian vision with Hinduism.

From the 1960s there has also been dialogue initiated by the WCC.[10] Dialogue (q.v.) with Hinduism[11] needs to proceed at four levels: daily life, social concern, theology, and religious experience, the last being perhaps the most fruitful.[12] As in the case of Islam (q.v.) and Buddhism (q.v.), there are few converts to Christianity. The task of mission (q.v.), therefore, will be undertaken largely through dialogue. This will help to remove misunderstandings and lead to a deepened vision of the truths in both faiths.

[1]A. Hiltebeitel, "Hinduism," EncycRel 6:336-360; B. Griffiths, "Hinduism," NCE 6:1123-1136; R. Boyd, *Indian Christian Theology* (Madras: CLS, 1976); M. and J. Stutley, *A Dictionary of Hinduism: Its Mythology, Folklore and Development 1500 B.C.- A.D. 1500* (London: Routledge & Kegan Paul, 1977). [2]G. Richards, ed., *A Sourcebook of Modern Hinduism* (London: Curzon, 1985). [3]Ibid., 213–214. [4]NCE 6:1136. [5]S. Rajamanickam, "Robert de Nobili: Christianity in the Indian Version," JDhara 17 (1987) 304–321. [6]J. Vetticatil, "Brahmabandav Upadhyaya," JDhara 17 (1987) 322–343. [7]Sr Vandana, "The Ashram Movement and the Development of the Contemplative Life," VYoti 47 (1983) 179–192; idem, *Social Justice and Ashrams* (Bangalore: Asian Trading Co., 1982). [8]*Christian Ashram: Essays Towards a Hindu and Christian Dialogue* (London: Darton, Longman & Todd, 1966); *The Marriage of East and West* (London: Collins, 1982). See Th. Matus, "Bede Griffiths, Monk (1906–1993): The Universal in the Specific," *Bulletin of the Pontificium Consilium pro Dialogo Inter Religiones* (Vatican) 23 (1993) 285–292. [9]*La rencontre de l'hindouisme et du christianisme* (Paris: Seuil, 1965); *La montée au fond du coeur: Le Journal intime dumoine chrétien-sannyasi hindou 1948–1973.* Les Deux Rives (Paris: O.E.I.L., 1986); *Intériorité et révélation: Essais théologiques* (Paris: Ed. Présence, 1982); cf. M.M. Davy, *Henri Le Saux: Le passeur entre deux rives* (Paris: Cerf, 1986); A. Gozier, *Le père Henri Le Saux à la rencontre de l'hindouisme: Une introduction à l'oeuvre d'Henri Le Saux, Swami Abhishiktananda* (Paris: Centurion, 1989). [10]K.K. Klostermaier, "Hindu-Christian Dialogue," Dict EcumMov 459–461. [11]A.M. Cocognac, *Ces pierres qui attendent: Pour un dialogue entre l'hindouisme et le christianisme* (Paris: Desclée, 1979); J. Dupuis, "Le dialogue avec l'Hindouisme dans la mission de l'Église en Inde," Bulletin 24 (1989) 257–269 = CivCatt 139 (1988) 4:336-347; P. Devanandan, *Preparation for Dialogue* (Bangalore: CISRS, 1964); A.M. Mundadan, "Hindu-Christian Dialogue: Past Twenty Years," JDhara 11 (1981) 375–394; J.D. Redington, "The Hindu-Christian Dialogue and the Interior Dialogue," TS 44 (1983) 587–603. [12]S.W. Ariarajah, "Hindu Spirituality: An Invitation to Dialogue," EcuR 38 (1986) 75–81.

## HIPPOLYTUS, St.

See APOSTOLIC TRADITION

## HOLY

"Holy" is the most ancient and the most universally attested epithet for the Church to be found in the earliest creeds. But there is some variation of expressions not easily captured in English. These affect the relation of the believer to the Church and do not condition its characteristic of holiness: I believe in the existence of a holy Church *(credo in sancta Ecclesia);* I give intellectual assent and commitment to the holy Church *(credo in sanctam Ecclesiam);* I believe the holy Church *(credo sanctam ecclesiam).*[1] In many of the creeds there is an association with the Holy Spirit, who immediately precedes the article on the holy Church so that one can say with St. Thomas Aquinas, "I believe in the Holy Spirit sanctifying the Church."[2]

The adjective "holy" is not applied to the Church in the NT, but there is abundant evidence that the creeds are soundly based on the Scripture.[3] In the OT the holy was what was separated and consecrated by God: the temple and its furnishings, sacrifices and prayers were therefore holy. God is the Holy One: this is not only an assertion of transcendence but a statement that all power, goodness, and beauty belong to God. Because God is in the midst of the people as the holy One (Hos 11:9), the people are consequently holy. They must be purified and lead lives of ethical goodness. For the NT Jesus is the Holy One of God (Mark 1:24; cf. Luke 1:35), the well-beloved Son anointed with the Holy Spirit (Luke 3:22; Acts 10:38). He, the transcendent one (Rev 3:7; 6:10), sanctified himself in sacrifice that his followers might be sanctified too (John 17:19-24). After Pentecost his followers, first in Jerusalem (Acts 9:13; 1 Cor 16:1), then elsewhere, are called (to be) "saints" (Rom 1:7; 16:15; 1 Cor 1:1-2; 7:14; Eph 2:19).[4] They are moreover "chosen and precious in God's sight . . . a royal priesthood, a holy nation, God's own people" (1 Pet 2:4, 9). The Church is the Body (q.v.) of Christ and the temple (q.v.) of the Holy Spirit. The members of the Church are consecrated to the Trinity *(eis to onoma*—Matt 28:19) in baptism, sealed with the Holy Spirit (Eph 1:13-14), and share the one Eucharistic bread (1 Cor 10:16-17).[5] From their consecration and sharing in the divine nature (2 Pet 1:4), ethical holiness should follow (Rom 6:12-14). Indeed the Pauline letters end with a chapter or more of moral exhortation; the lives of Christians are to be a spiritual sacrifice (Rom 12:1-2).

But sin is not absent from the NT Church: the primitive community saw the sin of Ananias and Sapphira (Acts 5:1-11) and bickering (6:1); Paul and other apostolic writers constantly warn against sin, even of the grossest kind (1 Cor 5:10-11; Gal 5:19-21; Col 3:5-8; 1 Pet 4:3-4; James passim); the parables of the wheat and the tares, of the good and bad fish, point to sin being present (Matt 13:24-30, 36–43, 47–49); the constant call of Jesus to mutual forgiveness is a reminder that sin and offense persist among his followers (Matt 5:23-24; 6:12, 14; 18:21-35) (v. RECONCILIATION).

Since the credal expression of the holiness of the Church is universal, patristic affirmations are commonplace. More difficult is the issue, present from the beginning, of sin and sinners.[6] Throughout history there have been attempts to restrict membership of the Church to such as are holy, predestined, or even occa-sionally to the unmarried.[7] The response of the Church has always been to defend the reality of what Augustine (q.v.) called the "mixed Church" *(Ecclesia permixta)* comprising good and evil.[8] Thus we have a rejection of the views of the Novatians (q.v.),[9] the Pelagians (qv),[10] the Donatists (q.v.),[11] the Luciferians (q.v.),[12] the Albigensians (q.v.),[13] the Fraticelli (q.v.),[14] Huss (q.v.),[15] Paschasius Quesnel (q.v.),[16] the Synod of Pistoia (q.v.).[17] Indeed for Augustine an authentic sign of the true Church is that it comprised both sinners and the holy.[18]

In Vatican II the Constitution on the Church spoke of a universal call to holiness addressed to all members of the Church (ch. 5), and referred to it as being indefectibly holy (LG 39), endowed with a true but imperfect holiness (LG 48).[19] Many of the council members wanted a statement of the notion and the nature of holiness itself. But the Doctrinal Commission refused to give a scholastic-type description or definition: rather, it gave various elements, especially from Scripture, which illustrated the ontological and dynamic nature of holiness.[20]

Some distinctions are in order as we ask how the Church is holy, remembering always that holiness is a sharing in the divine, and is a gift to the Church.[21] First, the Church is holy in what can be called its formal elements: St. Thomas Aquinas states that the Church is constituted by faith and sacraments;[22] the Church is holy through the word of God which is the basis of its faith; the Church is holy through the institutional and charismatic gifts given to its members (LG 12); above all, it is holy through being the Body of Christ (q.v.) and his Bride, and the temple (q.v.) of the Holy Spirit. Furthermore, many of the Church's members are already in glory. This objective holiness is indefectible and is not subject to sin. Second, the Church is holy through consecration (LG 9) and by being God's priestly people (LG 10). This holiness, too, is indefectible. Third, the Church is holy through the grace, virtues, and actions of its members, that is the personal holiness of individuals (LG 40). All are called to holiness, which is expressed in the double love of God and neighbor. We can speak of this as ethical holiness, and it should flow from encounter with God through the first, formal elements, and from baptismal consecration and the helps provided by Christ through his Spirit.

Though there is but one holiness (LG 41), there are many forms of life in which the call to holiness and the imitation of Christ (LG 40) must be lived out. This has given rise to schools of spirituality and to varying ideals in the course of history.[23] In the early Church the highest model of holiness was the martyr (q.v.): one who freely chose to die for Christ and his gospel. After the persecutions the monastic ideal came to the fore, and remained until recently the prime model of a consecrated and holy life: indeed, Vatican II gave special treatment to the form of Christian living marked by the adoption of vows (LG 42 and ch. 6; PC passim).[24] In recent years there has been a growing awareness that in some places, at least, holiness must be seen as having a social or political dimension.[25]

After Vatican II there was renewed interest in the theme of holiness, with many attempts to foster renewed, non-monastic forms of holiness, especially for diocesan priests[26] and laity.[27] Many new and vigorous movements (q.v.) arose which gave evidence of profound renewal.[28] Furthermore, prophetic figures of holiness, and causes being introduced for beatification, show evidence of a rich diversity in the forms of holiness today.[29] In addition, we have a new vision in the revised *Code of Canon Law* (v. LAW): instead of a book on "Things in the Church" *(De rebus),* we now have the same material under the rubric "Book IV. The Church's Office of Sanctifying" *(De Ecclesiae munere sanctificandi).*[30] With the important Marian documents of Popes Paul VI and John Paul II (v. MARY) we have a reinforcement of the notion of Mary as model of holiness set out in Vatican II (LG 67–69; cf. SC 103).

In the Churches of the Christian East[31] we do not find schools of spirituality as we know them in the West. Sanctity is seen as appropriation of the divine life celebrated in the liturgical mysteries; it is very explicitly Trinitarian and "in Christ." The attitude of the Christian is one of humble response in the face of the divine folly of love.

In the history of the Church a problem arises, one indeed to be seen in the NT itself. Although the Church is indefectibly holy, it still is a Church of sinners. Can we then assert that the Church is sinful?[32] H. Küng rightly points out that we cannot assume that everything in the Church which is imperfect, erroneous, or misguided is sinful, for there are many things that can be seen to have developed in a seemingly inevitable way, without individuals being able to do very much about them.[33] Most theologians shy away from a bald assertion that the Church is sinful; so, too, does Vatican II. The most usual solution is to say somehow that the Church is holy, but its members are sinful. Thus Vatican II: "While Christ 'holy, blameless, unstained' (Heb 7:26) knew no sin (see 2 Cor 5:21), and came only to expiate the sins of the people (see Heb 2:17), the Church, containing sinners in its own bosom, is at one and the same time holy and always in need of purification, and it pursues unceasingly penance and renewal" (LG 8). Some solutions are unsatisfactory as they do not take sufficient account of all of the evidence or of the full reality of the Church both in holiness and sin: sinners are *in* the Church, though not of the Church, largely only a verbal solution that leaves the problem intact;[34] again, the eschatological Church is

the true one, the present earthly Church laden with sin—there is, however, only one Church; one should distinguish the holy Church of the Body of Christ and a Church burdened with sin, but St. Augustine asserts that the real Church is lame, with one strong leg and one powerless one.[35] Moreover, the Decree on Ecumenism admits guilt in the Church by asking pardon for sins against unity (UR 7). Many proposed solutions are vitiated by their notion of sin[36] implicit in the posing of the problem. Sin is a culpable privation, *non-ens,* not ultimately intelligible.[37] Therefore, to speak about sin and holiness in the Church is not to speak about two simultaneously present, contradictory realities, but of sanctity and its privation. The word "is" about sin is grammatically and logically, but not ontologically, identical with the verb "is" about grace. Only if we are clear about the privative character of sin can we speak truthfully about the Church being sinful, for we are asserting only that despite its indefectible holiness, there is an element of holiness sometimes missing in the functioning of its holy institutions, in the lives of its members. Finally, it is best to speak about the Church being partly sinful, yet indefectibly holy. If a good analogy for sin is a puncture—the damaging absence of rubber in one spot of a tire, then the image for the Church would be a tire with a slow leak, constantly being refilled with air, and hence quite roadworthy through the grace continually being bestowed on it. Here we would seem merely to be restating the patristic teaching summarized in the phrase "the chaste prostitute" *(casta meretrix),*[38] or the patristic image of the Church as the moon, unstable yet always receiving light from the sun.[39]

Holiness is a mark or note (q.v.) of the Church. Vatican I stated: "The Church herself by reason of her astonishing propagation, her outstanding holiness and her inexhaustible fertility in every kind of goodness, by her catholic unity and unconquerable stability, is a kind of great and perpetual motive of credibility and an uncontrovertible evidence of her own divine mission."[40] But with Vatican II we assert that the sinner is not fully in communion with the Church. "Having the Holy Spirit," which we know from the *Acta* of the Council refers to being in the state of grace, is a necessary element for full communion in the Church (LG 14).[41]

Vatican II accepted that there are important elements of holiness not only in other Christian Churches (LG 15; UR 3, 14–23) and Judaism (LG 16; NA 4) but in the great religions of the East (NA 2). Holiness is of the essence of Buddhism (q.v.). Vatican II comments: "In Buddhism according to its various forms, the radical inadequacy of this changeable world is acknowledged and a way is taught whereby those with a devout and trustful spirit may be able to reach either a state of perfect freedom, or relying on their own efforts or on help from a higher source, the highest illumination" (NA 2). Of Hinduism (q.v.) we can say: "The condition of holiness is the perfect transparency of the Supreme in a human being. The saint is one who is completely integrated in the Absolute and is aware of his oneness with God and creation; his behavior will be, necessarily, the consequence of his realization."[42] Vatican II states: "in Hinduism the divine mystery is explored and propounded with an inexhaustible wealth of myths and penetrating philosophical investigations, and liberation is sought from the distress of our state either through various forms of ascetical life or taking refuge in God with loving confidence" (NA 2). The five pillars of Islam (q.v.) are paths to holiness. Vatican II declares: "The Church looks on Muslims with respect. They worship the one God living and subsistent, merciful and almighty, creator of heaven and earth, who has spoken to humanity and to whose decrees, even the hidden ones, they seek to submit themselves wholeheartedly . . . they have regard for the moral life and worship God especially in prayer, almsgiving and fasting" (NA 2; cf. LG 16).

When we assert that the Roman Catholic Church is the one, true Church (v. ONE), we are asserting institutional fullness. The means available in the Church can bring men and women to the height of holiness. As we marvel at the work of the Holy Spirit outside the confines of the Catholic Church, we are being challenged to use the great means of sanctity provided by Christ for his Church, and to give thanks for the examples of sanctity we receive from other Christians and from other faiths.

---

[1]DS 1–63.150/ND 1–12; P. O'Callaghan, "The Holiness of the Church in Early Christian Creeds," IrTQ 54 (1988) 59–65.   [2]ST 2–2ae, q.1, a.9 ad 5.   [3]G. Delling, "Merkmale der Kirche nach dem Neuen Testament," NTS 13 (1966/67) 297–316 at 303–306; J. de Vaulx, "Holy," DBT 236–239; A. Diez Macho, "Iglesia santa en la sagrada escritura," ScriptTPamp 14 (1982/3) 733–756; M. du Buit, "La sainteté du peuple dans l'Ancien Testament," VieSp 143 (1989) 25–37; L. Scheffczyk, "La santidad de Dios, fin y forma de la vida cristiana," ScripTPamp 11 (1979) 1021–1035.   [4]P. Jovino, "L'Église communauté des saints dans les 'Actes des Apôtres' et dans les 'Épîtres aux Thessaloniciens,'" RivBib 16 (1968) 495–526.   [5]P. Martucelli, "L'eucaristia e la chiesa: Unità e santità della chiesa in prospettiva eucaristica," RasT 29 (1988) 20–36.   [6]J.J. Machielsen, "Le problème du mal selon les pères apostoliques," EglT 12 (1981) 195–222; cf. J. Doignon, "Peccatrix ecclesia: Une formule d'inspiration origénienne chez Hilaire de Poitiers," RSPT 74 (1990) 255–258.   [7]R.B. Eno, "Holiness and Separation in the Early Centuries," ScotJT 30 (1977) 523–542.   [8]P. Borgomeo, L'Église de ce temps dans la prédication de saint Augustin (Paris: Études Augustiniennes, 1972) 277–298; D. Faul, "Sinners in the Holy Church: A Problem in the Ecclesiology of St. Augustine," StPatr 9 (1966) 404–415; F. Refoulé, "Situation des pécheurs dans l'Église d'après saint Augustin," StTheol 8 (1954) 86–102; cf. J. Doignon, "Peccatrix ecclesia: Une formule d'inspiration origénienne chez Hilaire de Poitiers," RSPT 74 (1990) 255–258.   [9]Nicaea canon 8—Tanner 1:8-9.   [10]Council of Carthage (418)—DS 228–230/ND 1904–1906; works of St. Augustine in Patrology 4:386-392.   [11]St. Augustine, Contra epistolam Parmeniani libri III—PL 43:33-108 and other works, Patrology 4:383-386.   [12]See M. Simonetti, Patrology 4:64-69.   [13]Tanner 1:230-231/DS 802/ND 21.   [14]DS 911.   [15]Tanner 1:429/DS 1201-1206.   [16]DS 2474–2478.   [17]DS 2615.   [18]Borgomeo (n. 7).   [19]C. Boureux, "Du particulier à l'universel: La sainteté à Vatican II," VieSp 143 (1989) 533–543; A. Guerra, "Llamada universal a la santidad en el Vaticano II," Manresa 60 (1988) 63–82; P. O'Callaghan, "The Holiness of the Church in Lumen gentium," Thom 52 (1988) 673–701; M. Labourdette, "La sainteté, vocation de tous les membres de l'Église," Bauaúna-Congar 3:1105-1117; L. Ravetti, La santità nella "Lumen gentium." Corona lateranensis 29 (Rome: Lateran UP, 1980); idem, "La santità nella Lumen gentium," DivThom 57 (1980) 344–355.   [20]ActSyn 3/1:326—Alberigo-Magistretti 477.   [21]F.A. Sullivan, The Church We Believe In: One, Holy, Catholic and Apostolic (Dublin: Gill and Macmillan—Mahwah: Paulist, 1988) 69–78; B. Gherardini, "Sulla teologia della santità," Divinitas 32 (1988) 601–605; I. Iparraguirre, "Nature de la sainteté et moyens pour l'obtenir," Baraúna-Congar 3:1119-1135; K.V. Truhler, "Holiness," SM 3:47–50; J. Splett and K. Hemmerle, "Holy," ibid., 50–53.   [22]ST 3a, q.64, a.2 ad 3.   [23]C. Duquoc, "Models of Holiness," Conc 129 (1979) vii–xiv; G. Holotik, "Les sources de la spiritualité catholique selon Vatican II," NRT 109 (1987) 66–77. See C. Cary-Elwes, Experiences with God: A Dictionary of Spirituality (London: Sheed & Ward, 1986); C. Jones, G. Wainwright and E. Yarnold, eds., The Study of Spirituality (London: SPCK, 1986); S. De Fiores and T. Goffi, eds., Nuovo dizionario di spiritualità (Milan: Ed. Paoline, 1985) and histories of spirituality.   [24]A. Bandera, "Santità della Chiesa e vita religiosa," VitaCons 23 (1987) 280–294, 378–391; P. Molinari and P. Gumpel, Chapter VI of the Dogmatic Constitution "Lumen gentium" on Religious Life (Rome: Gregorian UP, 1987).   [25]L. Boff, "The Need for Political Saints: From a Spirituality of Liberation to the Practice of Liberation," CrossC 30 (1980–81) 369–375, 384; D. Dorr, Spirituality and Justice (Maryknoll: Orbis—Dublin: Gill and Macmillan, 1984); idem, Integral Spirituality (Dublin: Gill and Macmillan, 1990); A. Giordano, "Politica," Nuovo Diz. Spiritualità (n. 23) 1225–1241; G. Gutiérrez, We Drink from Our Own Wells (Maryknoll: Orbis—London: SCM, 1984); M. Gutiérrez, "¿Un nuevo modelo de santidad para los laicos en América Latina?," TXav 38 (1987) 165–178; E. Hoonaert, "Models of Holiness Among the People," Conc 129 (1979) 36–45; C. Leonardi, "From 'Monastic' Holiness to 'Political' Holiness," Conc 129 (1979) 48–55; M. O'Neill, The Cry of the Poor: The Emerging Spirituality in the Christian Communities in Peru (1965–1986). Diss. (Rome: Gregorian University, 1989); P. Sheldrake, Images of Holiness: Explorations in Contemporary Spirituality (London: Darton, Longman & Todd, 1987) 91–104.   [26]F. Urbina, "Models of Priestly Holiness: A Bibliographical Review," Conc 129 (1979) 88–98.   [27]L. Doohan, The Laity: A Bibliography (Delaware: Glazier, 1987) 115–122.   [28]R.K. Seasoltz, "Contemporary American Lay Movements in Spirituality," Communio 6 (1979) 339–364; B. Secondin, Segni di profezia nella Chiesa: Comunità gruppi movimenti (Milan: Ed. O.R., 1987); A. Favale, ed., Movimenti ecclesiali contemporanei: Dimensioni storiche, teologico-spirituali ed apostoliche (Rome: Salesianum, [4]1980).   [29]B. Peyrous, "La sainteté dans l'Église depuis Vatican II," NRT 107 (1985) 641–657; B. Gherardini, "La santità della Chiesa nella catechesi di Paolo VI," DoctCom 40 (1987) 29–42.   [30]T.J. Green, "The Church's Sanctifying Office: Reflections on Selected Canons in the Revised Code," Jurist 44 (1984) 357–411; L. Misto, "Il libro IV: La funzione di santificare della Chiesa," ScuolC 112 (1984) 279–307.   [31]O. Clément, "La santità nella Chiesa ortodossa," Communio (Milan) 5 (1973 [299–308]) 3–12; P. Evdokimov, "La santità nella tradizione della Chiesa ortodossa," VitaCons 14 (1978) 234–260, 302–322 = Contacts 73–74 (1971) 119–190; T. Špidlik, The Spirituality of the Christian East: A Systematic Handbook. Cistercian Studies 79

(Kalamazoo, Mich.: Cistercian Publications, 1986) = vol 1 of *La spiritualité de l'Orient chrétien*. 2 vols. OrChrAn 206, 230 (Rome: Pont. Instit. Orientale, 1978, 1988). [32]A. Baxter, "Holiness and Sin," NBlackfr 70 (1989) 506–517; A. Birmelé, "La peccabilité de l'Église comme enjeu oecuménique," RHPR 67 (1987) 399–419; Y. Congar, L'Église une, 136–144; E. Cothenet, "Sainteté de l'Église et péché des chrétiens," NRT 96 (1974) 449–470; G. Cottier, "Église sainte: l'Église sans péché; non sans pécheurs," NVet 66/4 (1991) 9–27; G. Ligas, "Peccato 'ferita della Chiesa': la dimensione antiecclesiale del peccato secondo la *Lumen gentium*," Later 57 (1991) 71–107; P. McGoldrick, "Sin and Holy Church?," IrTQ 32 (1965) 3–27; J. Murphy-O'Connor, "Péché et communauté dans le Nouveau Testament," RB 74 (1967) 161–193 = TDig 16 (1968) 120–125; P. Neuner, "Die Kirche als Gemeinschaft der heiligen Sünder oder der sündigen Heiligen?," UnaSan 40 (1985) 93–103; K. Rahner, "Le péché dans l'Église," Baraúna-Congar 2:373-391; idem, "The Church of Sinners," ThInvest 6:253-269; idem, "The Sinful Church in the Decrees of Vatican II," ThInvest 6:270-294; Sullivan (n. 21) 79–83; B. Secondin, "Santità ecclesiale e peccato collettivo," in AA.VV. *Peccato e santità* (Rome: Teresianum, 1979) 225–251. [33]*The Church* (London: Search Press, 1971) 320. [34]C. Journet, *L'Église du Verbe Incarné*. 3 vols (Paris, 1941, 1951, 1959) 2:1117-1120; id. "Note sur l'Église sans tache ni ride," RThom 49 (1949) 208–211. [35]*Serm*. 5:8—CCL 41:59. [36]R. Bracchi, "Il concetto di 'peccato' nei nomi che lo definiscono," EphLtg 103 (1989) 221–268, 368–405; T.E. O'Connell, "A Theology of Sin," ChicSt 21 (1982) 277–292. [37]B.J.F. Lonergan, *Insight: A Study in Human Understanding* (London, 1957) 666–669. [38]H. Urs von Balthasar, *Explorations in Theology: II. Spouse of the Word* (San Francisco: Ignatius, 1991) 193–288. [39]H. Rahner, *Symbole der Kirche: Die Ekklesiologie der Väter* (Salzburg, 1964) 91–173. [40]Tanner 2:807-808/DS 3013/ND 123. [41]ActSyn 3/1:202—Alberigo-Magistretti 446. [42]C. Conio, "Jivanmukti as Holiness in Hinduism," JDharma 8(1983) 205–216 at 205.

## HONORIUS I, Pope (625–638)

Little is known about the early career of Honorius, except that he came from a wealthy aristocratic family. He became pope after a vacancy of only two days. He modeled himself on Gregory I (q.v.) and, like him, turned the papal mansion into a monastery. A pope of many achievements in the area of missions, politics, reform, and generally good administration in Rome, Honorius is, however, best remembered as the pope who was later condemned by an ecumenical council.[1] His case is the clearest blot on the Roman record for constancy in apostolic doctrine, and it is usually cited in arguments against papal infallibility.

About 634, the patriarch of Constantinople, Sergius, sent a letter to Honorius asking him about the position of stating that there is in Christ "one energy" *(mia energeia)*, viz., that while confessing two natures in Christ (Chalcedon—q.v.), there was only one single mode of activity, that of the divine Word in Christ. Sergius had found this formula useful in reconciling the Monophysites, who held that there was only one nature in Christ. Honorius sent a favorable reply, in which he used the ill-fated expression "one will." He died in the year in which the emperor Heraclius issued the *Ecthesis* (Greek "statement of faith") which be-

came the charter of Monothelitism, the doctrine that in Christ there is only a single will. Honorius' authority was used by the Monothelites in the controversy which ensued. His successors repeatedly condemned this heresy and the Council of Constantinople III (680–681—q.v.) formally censured Honorius. This condemnation was ratified by Leo II, when he approved the acts of the council in 682.

Honorius was wrong in his doctrine, at least when seen through Eastern eyes, though within the Western tradition he may well have been orthodox for his time;[2] he was certainly imprudent and ignorant of the subtleties of Christology in the Eastern Church. But because the question of the two wills in Christ was just emerging at that time, it was only after the council that, strictly speaking, one could be accused of heresy. Honorius had then been dead 43 years. The teaching he put forward had no lasting influence in the Church; it lacked reception (q.v.) in both East and West.

[1]OxDPopes 70–71; É. Amann, "Honorius," DTC 7:93-131; A Di Bernardino, "Honorius, Pope," EncycEraCh 1:396-397; P. Galtier, "La première lettre du Pape Honorius," Greg 29 (1948) 42–61. [2]E. Zocca, "Onorio I e la tradizione occidentale," AugR 27 (1987) 571–615. Cf. G. Kreuzer, *Die Honoriusfrage in Mittelalter und in die Neuzeit*. Päpste und Papsttum 8 (Stuttgart: Hiersemann 1975)—see RivStorChItal35 (1981) 152–158.

## HUMAN RIGHTS

The "Universal Declaration of Human Rights" of the United Nations on 10 December 1948 is surely a turning point of 20th-century history. It had initial precedents both in the U.S. *Declaration of Independence* (1776) and in the French Revolution *Declaration of the Rights of Man and of the Citizen* (1789).[1] In the Church, too, there had been important pronouncements before and after 1948.

Confining ourselves only to the last hundred years, we might, following F. Biffi,[2] note the highlights of the impressive body of papal teaching with a phrase indicative of the contribution and personality of each pope. Leo XIII was a prophet. With his lapidary statement "No one is allowed to violate with impunity the dignity of man, whom God himself treats with such respect," he set up, in *Rerum novarum* (1891), a program in favor not of abstract humanity, but of concrete persons threatened by both capitalism and collectivism in the following century. Pius XI (1922–1939) was a defender of personal rights menaced by totalitarianism: in his first encyclical *Ubi arcano* (1922) he had already been convinced that the neglect of the human person is the root of evil in society; in *Quadragesimo anno* he developed still further the teaching of Leo XIII; in the three encyclicals against totalitarianism—*Non abbiamo bisogno* (1931, against Fascism), *Mit brennender Sorge*

(1937, against Nazism) and *Divini Redemptoris* (1937, against atheistic communism)—he asserted religious and other freedoms and the possibility of living with personal dignity, free from dehumanizing coercions. Pius XII (1939–1958) was a builder of democracy. In a long pontificate, the pope explored questions of democracy, peace, and human rights. His Christmas radio message of 1942 was the most comprehensive papal statement yet on human rights. In it he spoke of five stars that must guide the world into peace the work of justice *(opus justitiae pax):* the person, the family, work worthy of the person, civil rights and duties, service in a Christian spirit. John XXIII (1958–1963) was an evangelist of human rights. The dignity, rights, and duties of men and women are a key to his important magisterium: the "signs of the times" (q.v.), both positive and negative, are to be read. In *Pacem in terris* (1963) he asserted that human rights are the foundation of peace, and he stressed active solidarity. In *Mater et magistra* (1961) his thought revolved around two poles: a personalist view of society, and the desire for equilibrium between the human family and personal rights and duties. Vatican II and the service of humanity: this theme is seen principally in *Gaudium et spes* (GS) and *Dignitatus humanae* (DH). Paul VI (1963–1978) was a champion of peace and a herald of human rights. The pope inherited from his predecessor and the council a double passion for peace and the human person: he established the World Day of Peace; he set up the Pontifical Commission for Justice and Peace; he chose "Justice in the World" as a theme for the 1971 Synod and commemorated Leo XIII's encyclical by the apostolic letter *Octogesima adveniens* (1971); he established the Pontifical Council "Cor Unum" (1971) for the promotion of the Third World; he addressed the issue of full and true development and social justice in *Populorum progressio* (1967). In addition he began a series of papal visits during which he constantly emphasized human rights. John Paul II (1978– ), as a pilgrim, loses no opportunity of speaking about human rights in each of the more than sixty pastoral visits he has made around the world. His major post-synodal letters rarely fail to show that peace and justice must begin with a proper appreciation of the human person, e.g., in *Sollicitudo rei socialis* (1987). He continues to insist on the practice and real implementation of human rights in all countries, even when he pays pastoral visits to countries ruled by totalitarian and oppressive regimes. In the encyclical *Centesimus annus,* to commemorate the centenary of Leo XIII's *Rerum novarum,* Pope John Paul II notes that in this century the imbalances between the nations has shifted the center of the social question from the national to international level.[3] Individual nations are no longer of themselves able to guarantee even the most basic human rights to their citizens. Hence the

popes' strong support for the United Nations in their pronouncements. A thread running through all the papal teaching on human rights is a demand for the basic human right of religious freedom (v. FREEDOM, RELIGIOUS).

Along with this rich corpus of papal teaching there is an evolving theology.[4] Though the expression "human rights" is a modern one, arising in the 17th century, the patristic and medieval traditions speak a lot about what we now understand by this term. In 1983 the International Theological Commission (ITC—q.v.) along with the Pontifical Commission Justitia et Pax studied "Proposition on the Dignity and the Rights of the Human Person,"[5] and published its working papers.[6] The ITC pointed out a hierarchy of rights: first, the right to life, the dignity which inheres in the human person, fundamental equality, liberty of thought or conscience and of religion; second, at a lower level, are civil, political, economic, social, and cultural rights of individual persons; third, rights which aim at an ideal of human situations. In speaking of human rights we have to avoid any absolute autonomy which would deny a relationship with God; the reality is more complex, for a relative autonomy, one respectful of God, can be maintained (GS 12, 14–16, 36). The perspectives of salvation history give other insights (GS 22, 32, 38, 45).

The ITC exposition of human rights[7] begins with the Scriptures: God expects that we practice mercy and fidelity to others; injustice must be foresworn; the kingdom preaching of Jesus demands a conversion of heart; as children of the one heavenly Father, we are all brothers and sisters; Jesus lived out his life and died for others; the Spirit descended on his disciples to make them a new creation; hence there are sins to be avoided and fruits that must be found in our lives (Gal 5:19-23). The ITC has a Christological vision of human rights: "It is in the light of the Word assuming the human condition and the demands of his paschal sacrifice that the foundation and extent of human rights are shown." Further clarification is found in salvation history: the human composite (1 Thess 5:23) is in the image and likeness of God (Gen 1:27), not as isolated beings, but as social and sexual beings (Gen 1:27; 2:24; GS 25) with duties and dominion over the earth (Gen 1:26; GS 34); sin must be recognized so that men and women may come into freedom from it and recover human dignity; it is in their relation to Christ and his paschal mystery that the true dignity of men and women is based and to be sought. Finally the ITC document addresses the special problems of the 1st, 2nd, and 3rd worlds, and proposes a personalist philosophy as a basis for human rights. Within such a philosophy, and founded on Christian principles, we can seek the triad of liberty, equality, and participation, which includes other rights and excludes various unilateral views of human rights.

The Church, which has preached so many fine sentiments about human rights, is itself challenged to uphold these within its own internal sphere of action; it does not consistently do so at every level from local parishes to its central administration. The listing of rights and duties in the new *Code of Canon Law* (CIC 208–231) is an important juridical innovation.[8]

Finally, one should note the ecumenical dimension of human rights. This is an area in which all Christians can cooperate and dialogue, not only among themselves but with other religions and also with non-believers.[9]

[1]R. Coste, "La foi chrétienne e la 'Déclaration Universelle des droits de l'Homme,'" NRT 111 (1989) 710–727; T.P. Fenton and M.J. Heffron, *Human Rights: A Directory of Resources* (Maryknoll: Orbis, 1989); G. Filibeck, "Quelques réflexions autour du 40e anniversaire de la Déclaration universelle des droits d'homme," Apoll 62 (1989) 699–720; E.H. Lawson, *The Sourcebook of Human Rights* (New York: Taylor and Francis, 1988); J.M. Laboa, "Iglesia y Declaración de los derechos del hombre," MiscCom 47 (1989) 473–493; M. Torelli and R. Baudoin, *Les droits de l'homme et les libertés publiques par les textes* (Montreal: Quebec UP, 1972); L.S. Wiseberg and H.M. Scoble, eds., *Human Rights Directory: Latin America, Africa, Asia Human Rights Internet* (Washington, D.C.: Human Rights Internet, 1981). [2]F. Biffi, "Il magisterio dei papi," Seminarium 34 (1983) 346–369; idem, "I diritti umani da Leone XIII a Giovanni Paolo II," in G. Concetti, ed., *I diritti umani: Dottrina e prassi* (Rome: A.V.E., 1982) 199–243; D. Hollenbach, *Claims in Conflict: Retrieving and Renewing the Catholic Human Rights Tradition* (New York: Paulist, 1979); J.-F. Six, *Church and Human Rights* (Slough UK: St. Paul, 1992). [3]*Centesimus annus* (1 May 1991) n. 21, citing Paul VI, *Populorum progessio* nn. 61–65—AAS 59 (1967) 287–289. [4]*Droits de l'homme, bibliographie internationale 1975–1981, RIC Supplément* (Strasburg: Cerdic, 1982); G.-H. Baudry, "Note sur les fondements théologiques des droits de l'hommme," MélSR 44 (1987) 15–28; R. Coste, "L'Église et les droits de l'homme," EspVie 93 (1983) 625–631; P. Daubercies, "Théologie et droits de l'homme," EspVie 99 (1989) 305–313; idem, "Égalité et droits de l'homme," RTLv 12 (1981) 187–211; É. Hamel, "The Foundations of Human Rights in Biblical Theology in Developments following on the Constitution *Gaudium et spes,*" in Latourelle, Vatican II, 2:460-478; W. Kasper, "The Theological Foundations of Human Rights," Jurist 50 (1990) 148–166; D. Murray, "The Theological Basis for Human Rights," IrTQ 55 (1990) 81–101; R. Pizzorni, "Fondazione religiosa dei diritti umani," EuntDoc 40 (1987) 567–580; G. Thils, *Droits de l'homme et perspectives chrétiennes.* Cahiers de la Revue théologique de Louvain 2 (Leuven: Peeters, 1981); Conc 124 (1979). [5]International Theological Commission, *Texts and Documents 1969–1985* (San Francisco: Ignatius, 1989) 251–266; DocCath 82 (1985) 383–391. [6]Greg 65 (1984) 231–481. [7]Op. cit. (n. 5). [8]Can. 208–231; G.V. Lobo, "Human Rights in the New Code," VYoti 48 (1984) 486–499; cf. P. Toulat, "Expérience de la pratique des Droits de l'Homme et la question des Droits dans l'Église," AnnéeCan 25 (1981) 313–320; P. Delhaye, "Diritti dell'uomo e libertà nella Chiesa," VitaCons 23 (1987) 575–592; P. Hebblethwaite, "Human Rights in the Church," JES 19 (1981) 190–201. [9]A. Falconer, "The Churches and Human Rights," OneChr 13 (1977) 321–350; idem, ed., *Understanding Human Rights* (Dublin: Irish School of Ecumenics, 1980); I. Brownlie, ed., *Basic Documents on Human Rights* (Oxford: Clarendon, [2]1981); A. Kniazeff, "Les droits de l'homme dans la perspective chrétienne," OrthFor 4 (1990) 229–233; W. Laquer and B. Rubin, eds., *The Human Rights Reader* (New York: Meridian, 1979); E. Lorenz, ed., *How Christian Are Human Rights?* (Geneva: Lutheran World Federation, 1981). A. Yannoulatos, "Eastern Orthodoxy and Human Rights," IntRMiss 73 (1984) 454–466; Conc 1990/2.

## HUSS, John (ca. 1372–1415)

John Huss (Hus) was born at Husinec (hence Huss/ Hus) in Bohemia, ca. 1372.[1] Ordained a priest in 1400, he was dean of the philosophy faculty in the university of Prague in 1401. About this time the writings of Wycliffe (q.v.) were becoming known there. Huss, who was concerned with both reform and nationalism, eagerly took up the English reformer's thought, but was also innovative in his own right. He condemned the vices of the clergy with asperity in vernacular sermons. By 1409 he was rector of the university, then a center of Wycliffite thought. He was excommunicated in 1411 and had to leave Prague. Befriended by the nobility, he began his chief work, a book on the Church *(De ecclesia),*[2] the first ten chapters of which are Wycliffite: the Church is the community of the predestined; the hierarchical structure of the Church is brought into question.

In a tense situation the emperor Sigismund suggested that Huss attend the Council of Constance (q.v.), promising him some kind of safe passage, notwithstanding which he was imprisoned at Constance. He seems to have failed to appreciate his position: he was not a free member of the council but excommunicated, suspected of heresy and called upon to answer for himself. The German king demanded that he be given a public hearing, in the course of which, in June 1415, he complained that many of the views ascribed to him were not his.

Friends tried to have him make a moderate abjuration, but he refused and was handed over to the secular arm and burned at the stake on 6 July 1415.

John Huss has been variously understood: nationalist, heretic, martyr for freedom of conscience. It seems clear that he did not hold all the views imputed to him at Constance.[3] His position on the Church was spiritual and Augustinian in flavor, but he denied important institutional features, and his views on the papacy are not tenable. His disciple, Jerome of Prague, was burned a year later at the same council.

[1]K.A. Fink, in Jedin-Dolan 447–448, 456–459; F. Leoncini, "Jan Hus e la rivoluzione hussita," RivSLetR 21 (1985) 282–298; M. Spinka. *John Hus: A Biography* (Princeton, 1968); P. De Vooght, *L'hérésie de Jean Hus.* 2 vols. (Louvain: Bibliothèque de l'Université, 1975); idem, *Hussiana* (Louvain, 1960). [2]S. Harrison, ed., *Magistri Ioannis Hus Tractatus De ecclesia* (Cambridge, Mass.: 1956); M. Spinka, *John Hus' Concept of the Church* (Princeton, 1966). [3]Tanner 1:429-431/DS 1151–1195.

# I

## ICONS

See NICAEA II, COUNCIL OF

## IGNATIUS OF ANTIOCH (d. ca. 107)

The *Letters* of Ignatius are a most important witness to the development of institutions and to the life of the immediate post-apostolic age of the Church.[1] They are also spiritual documents of rare quality. But they are not without controversy and problems. They are found in three recensions: a longer one comprising thirteen letters and many interpolations; a medium text of the seven letters known to Eusebius;[2] a shorter text. Ignatian research is a vast field with many divergent viewpoints.[3] Two recent studies have sought to prove that the letters are a forged work of the mid to late 2nd century,[4] or that the genuine Ignatian corpus comprises only four letters.[5] But the majority of scholars still hold with the genuinity of the middle recension established by J.B. Lightfoot in the last century,[6] and regard the longer text as a 4th-century work, and the shorter Syrian text as an abridgement of the middle text made about 500 C.E.,[7] though there have been attempts to show that the longer recension is the more authentic.[8]

Ignatius is often said to have been the third bishop of Antioch after Peter and Evodius. In his letter to Polycarp (q.v.) he states that peace has come to Antioch, a statement that is difficult to understand with the available evidence: perhaps it was a Church with divisions now healed;[9] perhaps persecution has now ceased there. He is being sent to Rome to be martyred. On the way he visits several Christian communities in Asia Minor, and he writes before or after his meeting with their community or leaders; he also writes to the Roman Church. Six such letters are generally consid-

ered genuine as well as one to Polycarp (q.v.), bishop of Symrna. He was martyred in Rome in the reign of Trajan (98–117), perhaps about 107 C.E.

Ignatius is very much concerned with two main errors:[10] Judaizing, which features especially in the letters to the Magnesians and Philadelphians, and Docetism, which figures largely in the letters to the Trallians and Smyrnaeans. He is opposed to Jewish practices and doctrines: "To profess Jesus Christ while continuing to follow Jewish customs is an absurdity."[11] Docetists (Greek *dokein* = to appear) denied that the Son had really become man; they held that he only appeared to have a human body. Against them Ignatius insists on the full reality of the Incarnation: "Christ was of David's line. He was the son of Mary; He was verily and indeed born, and verily and indeed persecuted in the days of Pontius Pilate, was truly crucified and gave up the ghost. . . . He was also verily raised from the dead."[12]

In the area of ecclesiology three Ignatian themes are paramount: unity, the Eucharist, and the bishop with his presbyters and deacons. Unity is explicitly mentioned sixteen times in the letters. He does not, however, exhort the Roman Church to unity, which at the very least indicates some deference to its apostolic origins. His readers in the other Churches are "to cherish unity and shun division,"[13] "abjure all factions,"[14] "hold aloof from all disunion and misguided teaching,"[15] "have no truck with the alien herbs of heresy."[16] Unity is especially important in worship: "Have a single service of prayer which everybody attends; one united supplication, one mind, one hope, in love and innocent joyfulness, which is Jesus Christ, than whom nothing is better. All of you together, as though you were approaching the only existing temple of God and the only altar, speed to the one and only Jesus Christ."[17]

The second theme is the Eucharist, which is central in Ignatius' ecclesiology; it is, moreover, intimately connected with his concern for unity and his theory of Church organization around the bishop. Thus: "Make certain therefore that you observe one common Eucharist, for there is but one Body of our Lord Jesus Christ and one cup of union with his blood, and one single altar of sacrifice—even as also there is but one bishop, with his clergy and my own fellow-servitors the deacons."[18] Again, "The sole Eucharist you should consider valid is one that is celebrated by the bishop himself, or by some person authorized by him."[19] There are five markedly Catholic ideas in Ignatius' Eucharistic theology: he uses sacrificial terms; "Eucharist" is applied to the elements; the power of the Eucharist is stressed; only the Eucharist of the bishop or his authorized delegate is valid; the celebration is of a corporate nature, a liturgical celebration.[20]

The third major ecclesiological theme is that of a single bishop, with presbyters and deacons.[21] Though it is common to refer to the "monarchical episcopate" in Ignatius, the epithet is too ambiguous: there certainly is only one bishop in the Churches to which he writes about the bishop; the bishop does not rule absolutely like a monarch, but in communion with his presbyters.[22] The bishop has primary liturgical functions: the Eucharist as above; the *agapê* (q.v.), and baptism require his presence;[23] the solemnization of marriage should have his consent.[24] The bishop presides[25] but Jesus Christ is "our sole teacher."[26] Since God's power is conferred on him, "we must regard the bishop as the Lord himself."[27] The bishop reflects the mind of Jesus Christ;[28] he is to be loved,[29] respected, and obeyed.[30]

There is a strange reference about the silence of bishops: "The more reserved a bishop is seen to be, the more he ought to be respected,"[31] a statement for which there may be several explanations. Some can be suggested. One simple reason might be support for a quiet bishop, or one who is not eloquent in dealing with heresy;[32] he is not to be thought less of because of his disposition. But there may be a deeper idea. Ignatius refers several times to the divine silence: "(God's) Word from silence proceeding";[33] Christ's silence.[34] The bishop may be seen as reflecting with power the divine silence.[35]

The presbyters surround the bishop and are like a council. "Let the bishop preside in God's place, and the presbyters take the place of the apostolic council, and let the deacons (my special favorites) be entrusted with the ministry of Jesus Christ."[36] He has a special place in his heart for deacons, and speaks of them with warmth.[37] He asserts that the bishop, presbyters, and deacons "whose appointment . . . is approved by Jesus Christ,"[38] but unlike Clement (q.v.), he gives no indication anywhere about succession (v. APOSTOLIC SUCCESSION).

There is a profound theology of martyrdom (v. MARTYR) in Ignatius, one which has been misunderstood by some who see his desire to die as morbid. But these have missed the theme of love, of union with, and imitation of Christ, which permeates the letters.[39] By martyrdom Ignatius hopes to be "a real disciple":[40] "My spirit is now all humble devotion to the Cross."[41] The whole purport of the letter to the Roman Church is that he wishes it to abstain from doing anything that would deprive him of martyrdom: "Suffer me to be a libation poured out to God."[42] We find an ecstatic longing: there is in him "only a murmur of living water that whispers within me, 'Come to the Father'";[43] "for much as I yearn for martyrdom, I am not at all sure of being found worthy of it";[44] "it is only in the name of Jesus Christ, and for the sake of sharing his sufferings that I could face all this."[45]

Much of the scholarly interest in Ignatius centers around his view of the Church at Rome. The letter to that Church is quite different in character from the others: the address to the Church which "presides in the district of the Romans" *(prokathêtai en topô chôriou Rômaiôn)* is more lavish—it is also said to "rank first in love" or to "preside in love" *(prokathêmenê tês agapês),* and to have filtered out what is alien; he does not presume to give practical advice to this Church. While there is clearly some precedence here of this Church, it is not clear where it may lie: quite probably it is seen in its Petrine and Pauline head. At most, we have here a piece of indirect evidence of the emergence of a Roman primacy (q.v.) which will take several more centuries to evolve.

In the letters of Ignatius we have great insights into the Church at the beginning of the 2nd century, but we also have questions which cannot be answered by the text of these same letters.

[1]M.T. Morse, "The Mystery of the Church in the Letters of St. Ignatius of Antioch," RevRel 39 (1980) 929–934.  [2]*Hist. eccl.* 3:36.  [3]G. Trentin, "Rassegna di studi su Ignazio," StPatav 19 (1972) 75–87.  [4]R. Joly, *Le dossier d'Ignace d'Antioch* (Brussels: UP, 1979); cf. G. Pelland in ScEsp 32 (1980) 261–297; R. Gryson in RTLv 10 (1969) 446–453.  [5]J. Ruis-Camps, *The Four Authentic Letters of Ignatius, the Martyr: A Critical Study Based on the Anomalies Contained in the Textus Receptus* (Rome: Pont. Instit. Orientale, 1979).  [6]J.B. Lightfoot, *The Apostolic Fathers.* 3 vols (London, 1885) 2/1:70–414. Other texts and translations: P.-T. Camelot, SC 10A; R.G. Grant, *The Apostolic Fathers.* Vol. 4 (London: Nelson, 1966); C. Kannengiesser, "Bulletin de théologie patristique. Ignace d'Antioche et Irénée de Lyon," RechSR 67 (1979) 559–623; J.B. Lightfoot—J.R. Harmer, *The Apostolic Fathers* (Grand Rapids: Baker, 1974); C.C. Richardson, LCC 1:74–120; W.R. Schoedel, *A Commentary on the Letters of Ignatius of Antioch* (Philadelphia: Fortress, 1985); G.G. Walsh, FC 1; M. Staniforth—A. Louth, *Early Christian Writings: The Apostolic Fathers* (London: Penguin, [2]1987)—this last is used here for trans-

lations. [7]P.-T. Camelot, "Ignace d'Antioche," DSpir 7:1250-1266; P. Meinhold, *Studien zu Ignatius von Antiochien* (Wiesbaden: Steiner, 1979); S. Tugwell, *The Apostolic Fathers*. Outstanding Christian Thinkers (London: Chapman, 1989). [8]See R. Weijenborg, *Les lettres d'Ignace d'Antioch: Étude de critique littéraire et de théologie* (Leiden: Brill, 1969) 15–21. [9]*Ad Polycarp.* 7:1. See Tugwell (n. 7) 108, 123; F.W. Schlatter, "The Restoration of Peace in Ignatius' Antioch," JTS 35 (1984) 465–469. [10]C. Trevett, "The Much-maligned Ignatius," ExpTim 93 (1981–1982) 299–302. [11]*Ad Magnes.* 10:3; cf. 8:1; *Ad Philadel.* 6:1; cf. P.J. Donahue, "Jewish Christianity in the Letters of St. Ignatius of Antioch," VigChr 32 (1978) 81–93. [12]*Ad Trall.* 9:1-2; cf. *Ad Smyrn.* 1:1-4:1; *Ad Magnes.* 1:2; 11:1. [13]*Ad Philadel.* 7:2. [14]*Ad Smyrn.* 8:1. [15]*Ad Philadel.* 2:1. [16]*Ad Trall.* 6:1. [17]*Ad Magnes.* 7:1-2. [18]*Ad Philadel.* 4:1. [19]*Ad Smyrn.* 8:1; cf. *Ad Philadel.* 4:1 [20]S.M. Gibbard, "The Eucharist in the Ignatian Epistles," StPatr 8/2 (1963) 214–218. [21]A. Brent, "History and Eschatological Mysticism in Ignatius of Antioch," ETL 65 (1989) 309–329; B. Dupuy, "Aux origines de l'episcopat: Le corpus des Lettres d'Ignace d'Antioche et le ministère d'unité," Istina 27 (1982) 269–277; A. McArthur, "The Office of a Bishop in the Ignatian Epistles and in the Didascalia Apostolorum Compared," StPatr 4 (1961) 298–304; A. Marranzini, "Lineamenti della figura del vescovo secondo S.Ignazio di Antiochia," Asp 23 (1976) 303–318; R. Padberg, "Das Amtsverständnis in der Ignatiusbriefe," TGl 62 (1972) 47–54; H.J. Vogt, "Ignatius von Antiochien über den Bischof und seine Gemeinde," TQ 158 (1978) 15–27. [22]*Ad Trall.* 12:2. [23]*Ad Smyrn.* 8:2. [24]*Ad Polycarp.* 5:2. [25]*Ad Magnes.* 6:1. [26]*Ad Magnes.* 9:1. [27]*Ad Eph.* 6:1; *Ad Trall.* 2:1. [28]*Ad Eph.* 3:2. [29]*Ad Eph.* 1:3 [30]*Ad Eph.* 2:2; *Ad Magnes.* 3:1; *Ad Philadel.* 7:1-2; *Ad Smyrn.* 9:1. [31]*Ad Eph.* 6:1. [32]*Ad Philadel.* 1:1; Schoedel (n. 6) 56–57, 77, 91, 120–122, 196. [33]*Ad Magnes.* 8:2; cf. *Ad Eph.* 19:1. [34]*Ad Eph.* 15:1. [35]H. Chadwick, "The Silence of Bishops," HarvTR 43 (1950) 169–172; cf. Schoedel (n. 6) 56–57; Tugwell (n. 7) 118–120. [36]*Ad Magnes.* 6:1; cf. *Ad Trall.* 2:1-3:1; *Ad Smyrn.* 8:1; cf. M. Mees, "Ignatius von Antiochien über das Priesterum," Later 47 (1981) 53–69. [37]*Ad Mag.* 6:1; *Ad Trall.* 2:2; *Ad Philadel.* 11:1. [38]*Ad Philadel.* prol.; cf. 1:1. [39]Cf. Meinhold (n. 7) 10–18. [40]*Ad Eph.* 1:3. [41]*Ad Eph.* 18:1. [42]*Ad Rom.* 2:2. [43]Ibid., 7:2. [44]*Ad Trall.* 4:2. [45]*Ad Smyrn.* 4:2.

## IGNATIUS OF LOYOLA, St. (1491–1556)

Born in 1491 of Basque nobility, Iñigo López de Loyola was first a courtier, then a soldier.[1] Wounded at the siege of Pamplona (1521), he received a first conversion during a long convalescence at Loyola, and later a deep mystical transformation in Manresa (1522–1523). He studied at Barcelona, Alcalá, Salamanca, and Paris. In Paris he gathered a few companions who were afterwards ordained priests. Though the idea of a pilgrimage to Jerusalem suggested itself, they eventually went to Rome to place themselves at the service of the pope. The Society of Jesus was approved in 1540. In addition to the customary vows, it had a fourth: to obey without hesitation every mission given by the pope "for the sake of matters pertaining to the worship of God and the welfare of the Christian religion."[2] What is particularly significant about this vow, apart from its novelty, is the fact that from the time of Ignatius' conversion to the year before his death, the occupants of the See of Peter were hardly very in-

spiring, and were indeed distinctly worldly (Clement VII, Paul III, Julius III); the final pope of his lifetime, Paul IV, was hostile to Ignatius.

It would be almost impossible to exaggerate the importance of Ignatius and his order in the Counter-Reformation, in the spread of mission, in education at all levels, and in the history of spirituality. The contribution of Ignatius to ecclesiology lies primarily in the order he founded, in its commitment to ecclesiastical learning, in the spirituality he espoused and taught his followers. This last was one of service to Christ in the Church militant. The apostolic aim of the Society was given to it by Julius III in wide terms: "To strive especially for the defense and propagation of the faith and for the progress of souls in Christian life and doctrine, by means of public preaching, lectures and any other ministration whatever of the word of God, and further by means of the *Spiritual Exercises,* the education of children and unlettered persons in Christianity, and the spiritual consolation of Christ's faithful through hearing confessions and the administration of other sacraments . . . [and] in performing any other works of charity."[3]

Ignatius seems to have coined the expression "our holy mother the hierarchical Church."[4] Despite the degenerate state of the Church, Ignatius has a strong ecclesial focus in his *Spiritual Exercises*[5] on it. Decision-making should be "of positive advantage to our Holy Mother the Hierarchical Church, or at least not contrary to her interests" (n. 170). In his "Rules for Thinking with the Church" (nn. 352–370), he seeks obedience, love, approval, and submission with regard to the Church. It is disputed whether these rules are anti-Reformation or anti-Erasmus. He does not seem to have studied Luther in any detail, and he was certainly disturbed by Erasmus' criticism of the Church and of its piety.[6] In Ignatius' mind there seems to be a dynamic movement from God to Church, to obedience, to mission.[7] At the time of the Ignatian centenary, John Paul II emphasized especially the contribution which Ignatius' *Spiritual Exercises* had made to the Church.[8]

[1]Bibliog. *Archivum historicum Societatis Jesu* from 1932. See J. Broderick, *St. Ignatius Loyola: The Pilgrim Years* (New York, 1956); C. Dalmases, *Ignatius of Loyola: Founder of the Jesuits* (St. Louis, Mo.: Institute of Jesuit Sources, 1985); H. Jedin, in Jedin-Dolan 5:446-455; H. Rahner, *Ignatius the Theologian* (London—New York, 1968); K. Rahner and P. Imhof, *Ignatius of Loyola* (London—Cleveland: Collins, 1979). [2]*Constitutions* [7]—*The Constitutions of the Society of Jesus.* Trans. and ed., G.E. Ganss (St. Louis, Mo.: Institute of Jesuit Sources, 1970) 80. [3]*Constitutions* [3]—Ganss (n. 2) 66–67; cf. [642, 645, 650] 282–284. [4]Congar, Augustin 369–370 with nn. [5]L.J. Puhl, ed., *The Spiritual Exercises of St. Ignatius* (Chicago: Loyola UP, 1950); most recent G.E. Ganss, *The Spiritual Exercises of Saint Ignatius: Translation and Commentary* (Chicago: Loyola UP, 1992); F. Evain, "Dynamique des Exercises de saint Ignace et sens de l'Église," NRT 112 (1992) 696–707; R. Maloney, "Ignatius the Theologian and His Legacy to Theology," MilltownSt 29 (1992) 34–50; J.C. Scannone: "Los Ejercicios Espirituales: Lugar

teológico," *Stromata* 47 (1991) 231–247. See J. Corella, "Bibliografía sobre las Reglas para el sentido de Iglesisa," MiscCom 49 (1991) 521–53.  [6]P.H. Kolvenbach, "'Pietas' et 'eruditio' nella ricerca teologica," CivCatt 140 (1989) 3:252-264.  [7]Ibid., 370; K. Rahner, "The Ignatian Mysticism of Joy in the World," ThInvest 3:277-293.  [8]Apost. Letter to Superior General, P.H. Kolvenbach, 31 July 1990—CathIntern 1 (1990) 152–154.

## IMAGES OF THE CHURCH

In the NT there is a profusion of images of the Church. P.S. Minear points to 95,[1] though one may question whether some are genuine figures of the Church. Vatican II notes that images are taken mainly "from the life of the shepherd or from cultivation of the land, from the art of building or from family life," and gives special prominence to some of these biblical figures: sheepfold, gateway, flock, cultivated field, vineyard, vine, building, house and household of God, temple, bride, Jerusalem from above, pilgrim, and exile (LG 6). More particular attention is paid to Kingdom (q.v.), People (q.v.), Body (q.v.) and Temple (q.v.—LG 5, 7, 9, 17).

An image is an analogy in which there is a similarity between it and the reality to which it refers. An image becomes a symbol if it moves from being a mere logical comparison to touching the area of feeling or affectivity.[2] Kingdom, People, Body, and Temple—and several others, are clearly symbols. A symbol may also function as a model (q.v.), especially if it helps to explain or explore data. In the biblical symbols of the Church we are not only told a truth about the Church, but we are drawn towards a commitment to the truth contained in the symbol. Of their nature symbols cannot be exhausted in a logical deduction, but are open-ended and heuristic as well as having a range of meanings. Each symbol of the Church will focus on some particular aspect, or aspects, of the mystery.

Patristic ecclesiology often proceeded by way of symbols. The following are particularly important: the Church as moon—waxing and waning and drawing its light from the sun; the water flowing from the side of Christ (John 7:37-38 with 19:34); the Christian on a sea journey to the heavenly homeland; the Church as ship, with the cross as its mast; the Church as the boat of Peter; the ark of Noah.[3]

Though the biblical and patristic images and symbols retain their validity, they may have little impact on modern urban dwellers, or in Asian or African cultures. Symbols can become mere images if they have to be interpreted in detail. Artists, poets, preachers, and theologians of every era and culture are challenged to present images of the Church suited for each time and place. A further, no less vital task is the appropriation of liturgical symbols along with the creation of new ones to draw people into the meaning of liturgical celebrations.

[1]*Images of the Church in the New Testament* (Philadelphia: Westminster, 1960); cf. H. Rikhof, *The Concept of Church: A Methodological Inquiry into the Use of Metaphors in Ecclesiology* (London: Sheed & Ward—Shepherdstown, W.Va.: Patmos, 1981).  [2]B.J.F. Lonergan, *Method in Theology* (London: Darton, Longman & Todd, 1972) 64–69; K. Rahner, "The Theology of Symbol," ThInvest 4:221-252.  [3]H. Rahner, *Symbole der Kirche: Die Ekklesiologie der Väter* (Salzburg, 1964).

## IMPOSITION OF THE HAND(S)

In various religions we find the most impressive symbolic action of laying a hand/hands on a person. It is often found in healing rituals, usually indicating that the healer is a person of power (cf. Mark 5:27-30—reverse, the healer is touched).[1] It is found in the OT as a sign of blessing (Gen 48:13-16), as a sign of consecration, setting apart, or gifting (Num 8:10; 27:15-23; Deut 34:9), as a sign of identification in the case of sacrificial offerings (Lev 1:4; 3:2) and of the scapegoat (Lev 16:21-22).[2]

In the NT[3] we find Jesus laying his hands on children as a sign of blessing (Mark 10:16; Matt 19:13). He frequently lays his hands on the sick for healing (e.g., Mark 1:41; 8:23-26; Luke 4:40; 13:13), but sometimes he exorcises or heals with a word alone (e.g., Mark 2:9-11; 5:8-13; 9:25). The Church was given a ministry of healing, which was often exercised by the laying on of hands (Mark 16:18; Acts 9:12,17; 28:8), but not exclusively so (cf. Jas 5:14; Acts 5:15).

The apostolic laying on of hands gave the gift of the Holy Spirit (Acts 8:17-19; 19:6). We also find hand-imposition in setting people apart for an office or task (Acts 6:6; 13:3; 2 Tim 1:6-7). The occasion or meaning of some particular impositions (1 Tim 4:14; 5:22; Heb 6:2) is not always clear. In NT texts the apostolic imposition of hands can be seen to have a double meaning: it is an *epiclêsis* (q.v.) or prayer for the Spirit or divine gifts; it implies communion between the one touching and the one touched.

In the *Apostolic Tradition* (q.v.) there is quite a developed practice of, and an emerging theory about, the imposition of the hand. The bishop lays his hand on the candidates for episcopacy, priesthood, and diaconate, as well as on some confessors (q.v.). It is stated explicitly that there is no hand-imposition for subdeacons (q.v.), widows (q.v.), virgins (q.v.), readers (q.v.), healers (v. HEALING). Only the bishop lays hands on the candidate for diaconate. The reason for this last is that "the deacon is not ordained to the priesthood" (8/9:2) and "he does not receive the spirit common to the presbyterium, in which the priests share" (8/9:4). On the other hand, the members of the presbyterium sign the candidate *(sphragizein)* by laying their hand on him, while the bishop ordains *(cheirotonein)*. This is because of the common spirit they have; the priest has the power to receive but not to give the Spirit (8/9:5-8). The imposition of the hand is an important feature of the catechumenate: the teacher (q.v.) lays his hand on the candidates after prayers (19/19:1); hands are laid on them for exorcism daily in the period immediately preceding baptism (20/20:3); the bishop performs a final exorcism with the laying on of his hand (20/20:3, 8). The one who baptizes lays a hand on the candidates confessing their faith in the actual moment of baptism (21/21:14).

In the late 4th-century *Apostolic Constitutions* (q.v.), there is a careful distinction between two forms of hand-laying: *cheirotonia* is for the ordination of bishops, priests, deacons, and sub-deacons;[4] *cheirothesia* indicates other impositions of hand(s) for baptismal ritual,[5] for the reconciliation of penitents,[6] or in blessings.[7] The difference between the two is explicit and conscious: the baptized are not ordained, and only the bishop uses *cheirotonia*, whereas priests can use *cheirothesia*.[8] The meaning for Augustine of hand-laying at baptism was that of prayer: "What else is it other than prayer upon a person?"[9]

In the mid-20th century a major reorientation of sacramental understanding occurred: sacraments were seen as saving actions of Christ;[10] there was a pneumatological dimension so that the Spirit is said to be operative, or else given, in each sacrament. These two insights find apt expression in the renewed emphasis on the imposition of hands.[11]

Imposition of hands is central in the post-Vatican II liturgy: there is a silent imposition of hands in the ordination of a deacon, priest, or bishop, and in the anointing of the sick (q.v.); there is a solemn imposition of hands over the confirmed (v. CONFIRMATION) preparatory to the anointing, which is itself seen as a hand-imposition; the sacrament of reconciliation (q.v.) has a hand-imposition in the act of absolution; at Mass the first *epiclêsis* over the bread and wine is said with an imposition of hands, and concelebrants extend their hands over the host and chalice at the consecration; the final solemn blessing at Mass is also with an imposition of hands over the assembly; a blessing with the sign of the cross may also be seen as an imposition of the hand.

The symbol of imposition of hands is always to be interpreted by the prayer that accompanies it.[12] It may be a sacramental form or it may be a prayer for blessing or healing. There is no reason to suggest that imposition of hands is to be restricted to clergy. It is used, and legitimately so, in prayer for healing, by lay persons, especially in charismatic groups.

The theological question must be asked about how imposition of hands is to be understood. Is the one laying hands seen to be a source of power, or is it a gesture of prayer, an *epiclêsis?* Though scholars hold

various viewpoints,[13] it is perhaps preferable to see hand-imposition as a symbol of *epiclêsis*. In the case of the sacraments we have a guarantee that the prayer will be answered if the recipient is properly disposed (an *ex opere operato* effect); in the case of healing prayer and non-sacramental uses of imposition, there is no such guarantee (it is *ex opere operantis*).[14]

Those in healing ministry in the Churches often speak of sensing healing power passing from them to a person. Others with equally remarkable gifts do not seem to have such sensations, or to have had them only at the outset of their ministry. Such perceptions still await appropriate investigation. It may still be asserted that the primary symbolism of hand-imposition is that of invocation or *epiclêsis,* even though God may use the healer as a physical instrument, or some psychic powers may be involved in a particular case.

Important as the theological questions are, we need also to see as highly significant the human warmth of the symbol of hand-imposition both in sacramental and non-sacramental contexts.

---

[1]F.W. Denny, "Hands," EncycRel 6:188-191; G. Defretin, "Main," Catholicisme 8:184-187; J.C. Didier, "Imposition des mains," ibid., 5:1356-1361; J.A. McCulloch, "Hand," EncycRelEth 6:492-497. [2]J.-B. Brunnon, DBT 254–255; M.C. Sansom, "Laying on of Hands in the Old Testament," ExpT 94 (1982–1983) 323–326; R. Peter, "L'imposition des mains dans l'ancien testament," VT 27 (1977) 48–55. [3]J. Coppens, *L'imposition des mains et les rites connexes dans le nouveau testament et dans l'Église primitive* (Paris, 1925); idem, "Imposition of Hands," NCE 7:401-403; E. Lohse, "Cheir etc.," TDNT 9:424-432; C. Maurer, "Epitithêmi," TDNT 9:159-161. [4]8:4-5 and 16–17 and 21 and 23–28—SC 336: 140–150, 216–220, 222, 224–232. [5]2:32, 3—SC 320:252; 3:16, 3—SC 329:1567:43, 3—SC 336:104. [6]2:18, 7 and 41, 2—SC 320:192, 272. [7]E.g., 8:37, 4—SC 336: 248. [8]3:16, 3—SC 329:156; 8:28, 2–3—SC 336:228-230. Cf. C. Vogel, "'Chirotonie et chirothésie': Importance et relativité du geste de l'imposition des mains dans la collation des ordres," Irén 45 (1972) 7–21, 207–238. [9]*De bapt.* 3:16, 21—CSEL 51:213. See G. Bavaud edition, *De baptismo libri VIII.* Bibliothèque augustinienne 29—Traités Anti-Donatistes, Vol. 2 (Paris, 1964)—"Note complémentaire 15: Le don de l'Esprit par l'imposition des mains," 2:600-605. [10]E.g., E. Schillebeeckx, *Christ the Sacrament of Encounter with God* (London, 1963). [11]G. Diekmann, "The Laying On of Hands: The Basic Sacramental Rite," CTSAP 29 (1979) 339–351 with responses by J.M. Powers 353–356 and E.J. Kilmartin 357–366. [12]P. Galtier, "Imposition des mains," DTC 7:1302–1432 at 1338–1339. [13]J.K. Coyle, "The Laying on of Hands as Conferral of the Spirit: Some Problems and a Possible Solution," StPatr 18/2 (1989) 339–353; J.-T. Maertens, "Un rite de pouvoir: L'imposition des mains," ScR 6 (1976–77) 637–649; 7 (1978) 25–39; C. Vogel, "La chirotonie presbytérale du liturgie comme condition de la célébration eucharistique," in AA.VV. *L'assemblée liturgique et les différents rôles dans l'assemblée.* Conferences Saint-Serge 23. Bibliotheca *Ephemerides liturgiae* 9 (Rome: Ed. Liturgiche, 1977) 307–319; V.E. Fiala, "L'imposition des mains comme signe de la communication de l'Esprit-Saint dans les rites latins," ibid., 87–103. [14]F.A. Sullivan, "The Laying on of Hands in Christian Tradition," in M.W Wilson, ed., *Spirit and Renewal.* FS J. Rodman Williams (Sheffield: Academic Press, 1994) 42–54.

## IMPRIMATUR

See CENSORSHIP OF BOOKS

## INCULTURATION

The neologism "inculturation" came into Catholic theology in the mid-1970s, especially in the writings of the Jesuit General, P. Arrupe.[1] It appears in a Roman document for the first time in the message of the fifth Synod of Bishops (1977). But from two years earlier we have what has been called the "Charter of Inculturation," viz., the exhortation on evangelization, *Evangelii nuntiandi* (1976)[2] of Pope Paul VI (see nn. 20, 63). The term "inculturation" has been frequently used by Pope John Paul II.

As a neologism its meaning and employment have not yet been standardized by repeated usage,[3] and other terms have been suggested, e.g., "inter-culturality" by Cardinal J. Ratzinger in an important address, "Christ, Faith, and the Challenge of Cultures." It is to be distinguished from the sociological term "enculturation," apparently coined by M.J. Herkovits,[4] which means the same as "socialization," namely, the process by which an individual becomes part of a culture; in this case it is a learning process for the person. It is further to be distinguished from "adaptation," which refers either to the missionary seeking to conform personally to the culture on the model of Paul, who became all things to all (cf. 1 Cor 9:21-22), or to the attempt to make the universal, immutable message intelligible to people of another culture. Adaptation is largely exterior, whereas inculturation is mainly interior.

The International Theological Commission (ITC) noted in 1984 that inculturation reflects incarnation: "Just as God the Word assumed a concrete humanity in his own Person and lived out all the particularities of the human condition in a given place and time, and in the midst of a single people, so the Church, following Christ's example and through the gift of his Spirit, has to become incarnate in every place, every time, and every people (cf. Acts 2:5-11)."[5] Inculturation is a new expression of revelation, of the mystery of Christ, arising from its assimilation by the local Church.

In the discussion of inculturation in the late 1970s and 1980s, one can detect two interpretations of Vatican II on Mission (*Ad gentes* 22—hereafter AG): these are a more minimalist one—frequent in the magisterium—and a maximalist one, with a wide spectrum between them.[6] The minimalist tends to interpret this text of AG in terms of the evangelization of culture. Other interpretations speak more about the inculturation of the gospel. Again the ITC is insightful: "In the evangelization of cultures and the inculturation of the Gospel a wondrous exchange is brought about: on one hand the Gospel reveals to each culture and sets free within it the final truth of the values that the culture carries. On the other hand each and every culture expresses the Gospel in an original fashion and manifests new aspects of it. This inculturation is an aspect of the recapitulation of all things in Christ (Eph 1:10), and of the catholicity of the Church (Vatican II, *Lumen gentium,* LG 16, 17)."[7]

In practice, the issue of inculturation arises in three key areas. First, in theology, in which the one faith seeks new expressions.[8] Second, in catechetics (q.v.), which seeks to present the faith in a specific culture and to reflect that culture in the mystery of Christ.[9] Third, in liturgy which gives expression to Christian worship in the concrete worship of a particular people.[10]

The International Theological Commission returned to the topic of inculturation in 1987–1988, giving it a deeper basis: the magisterium; nature, culture and grace; inculturation in the history of salvation; current problems of inculturation—popular piety, non-Christian religions, young Churches, modernity.[11]

Inculturation faces the problem of changing cultures and the potential intrusion of alien cultures in local Churches. Not only in countries like the USA, England, and Australia do we find multicultural phenomena, but cultural diversity and challenges to inculturation are widely experienced in the countries of Africa,[12] Latin America,[13] and Asia.[14] The Cameroon theologian J.-M. Ela sees inculturation as liberation: missionaries cannot carry out inculturation; they can only start the process. But Africans cannot carry out inculturation as long as they are in cultural and socio-economic bondage to non-Africans. There is a danger that Africa will opt for a second-rate inculturation or indigenism, a preoccupation with the unimportant, the superficial, and the non-controversial.[15] The other danger is that the Church will be rejected as alien by the younger countries as they seek to protect and foster their cultural identity.[16]

The urgency and the perennial nature of a commitment to inculturation may be intuited through three quotations from works written long before the word inculturation was created. Y. Congar cites two, one unnamed: "One writer on missiology has said that the definitive commentary on the Gospels cannot be written until China, Japan and India have become Christian. Cf. Journet: 'The expansion of the Church reveals her to herself.'"[17] A third is from B. Kloppenburg: "To the extent that the Church does not in fact become Brazilian, the Brazilian will not be of the Church."[18] What is involved in inculturation is the very catholicity (v. CATHOLIC) of the Church. With so much at stake, the Church dare not err on the side of caution.

[1]"Lettre et document de travail sur l'inculturation," ActaRomSocIesu 17 (1978) 282–309. See AA.VV. *Inculturation: Its Meaning and*

*Urgency* (Nairobi: St. Paul, 1986); A. Amato, "Inculturazione—contestualizzazione—teologia in contesto: Elementi di bibliografia scelta," Sales 43 (1983) 79–111; G. Arbuckle, *Earthing the Gospel: An Inculturation Handbook for Pastoral Workers* (Maryknoll: Orbis—London: Chapman, 1990); A.A. Roest Crollius, "What Is So New About Inculturation? A Concept and its Implications," Greg 59 (1978) 721–738; A. Pieris, *An Asian Theology of Liberation* (Maryknoll: Orbis, 1988); A. Shorter, *Toward a Theology of Inculturation* (London: Chapman, 1988); N. Standaert, "L'histoire d'un néologisme: Le terme 'inculturation' dans les documents romains," NRT 110 (1988) 555–570; *Inculturation. Working Papers on Living Faith and Cultures* 1 (Rome: Gregorian UP, 1982–); Seminarium 32 (1992) 3–193. [2]AAS 68 (1976) 1–96/Flannery 2:711-761. [3]A.A. Roest Crollius (n. 1) 721. For Ratzinger, see OssRomano (English) 26 April 1995. [4]*Man and His Works* (New York, 1952) 39. [5]"Select Themes in Ecclesiology," 4.2 in International Theological Commission, *Texts and Documents 1969–1985* (San Francisco: Ignatius, 1989) 280. [6]Standaert (n. 1) 564–567; see. P.M. Guglielminetti, "Dall'inculturazione alla transculturazione: Rapporti tra evangelizzazione e cultura alla luce del Decreto conciliare 'Ad gentes.'" RasT 25 (1984) 211–226. [7]ITC (n.5) 280. [8]P. Drego, "The Mission of the Local Church and the Inculturation of the Gospel," VYoti 45 (1981) 258–265, 423–435; J.-N. Revet and D. Mitrani, "Théologies nouvelles dans trois continents," ETR 58 (1983) 27–52; J. Saldanha, "Theological Inculturation as a Missiological Problem," IndTS 14 (1977) 333–348. [9]Pope John Paul II, *Catechesi tradendae*—AAS 71 (1979) 1277–1340/Flannery 2:762-814; see n. 53 at 794–795. [10]G. Arbuckle, "Inculturation not Adaptation: Time to Change Terminology," Worship 60 (1986) 511–520; H. Bernh, "Zur Frage der Inkulturation der Liturgie," ZkT 105 (1983) 1–31; A.J. Chupungco, "Inculturation and the Organic Progression of Liturgy," EcOr 7 (1990) 7–21; idem," A Definition of Liturgical Inculturation," EcOr 5 (1988) 11–23; G. Gispert-Sauch, "Liturgical Inculturation Questioned," VYoti 46 (1982) 546–552. [11]"Fides et inculturatio," Greg 70 (1989) 625–646. [12]Shorter (n. 1) 251–260; see T. Okure et al., *32 Articles Evaluating Inculturation of Christianity in Africa* (Eldoret, Kenya: Ameca Gaba, 1990); J. Parrot, ed., *A Reader in African Christian Theology* (London: SPCK, 1987). [13]W. Weber, "Christum auf Lateinamerikanischentwicklungen, Chancen, Gefahren," ZMissRW 62 (1978) 241–251. [14]AA.VV., "Indian Ecclesiology: A Rereading of the Pioneers," JDhara 17 (1987) 261–343; A. Pieris, *An Asian Theology of Liberation* (Maryknoll: Orbis, 1988); A. Pushparajan, "Sociological Aspects of Inculturation," IndTS 18 (1981) 271–288; G. van Leeuwen, ed., *Searching for an Indian Ecclesiology* (Bangalore: Asian Trading Co., 1984). [15]*Ma foi d'africain* (Paris, 1985) quoted Shorter (n.1) 247–248. [16]B. Bujo, "Au nom de l'Evangile refus d'un christianisme neo-coloniste," BTAfr 6 (1984) 117–127. [17]*The Mystery of the Church* (London, 1960—French 1956) 146, n. 2 with C. Journet cited as *The Church of the Word Incarnate*, Vol. 2. [18]*The Ecclesiology of Vatican II* (Chicago: Franciscan Herald, 1974) 153.

## INDEX OF PROHIBITED BOOKS

The *Index librorum prohibitorum* first appeared in 1559 under Paul IV. Pius V created the Congregation of the Index in 1571. Benedict XIV reorganized the discipline of the *Index* to make it less harsh. Norms given by Leo XIII were incorporated into the 1917 *Code of Canon Law*.[1] The *Index* proscribed whole categories of books: unauthorized versions of the Scriptures; books promoting heresies or attacking good morals or catholic dogmas; those teaching superstitions or magic; those condoning duelling, suicide, divorce; those which were lascivious or obscene, etc. It also contained a long list of individual books and authors whose complete output was banned.

The *Index* was abolished in 1966.[2] Censorship (q.v.) of certain kinds of books is still in force, and the Holy See occasionally gives a warning *(monitum)* about particular works.

[1]G. Alberigo, "Institutional Defence of Orthodoxy," Conc 192 (1987) 84–93; D. Dario Composta, "L'Indice dei libri proibiti." EuntDoc 45 (1992) 375–407. J.A. Coriden, "The End of the *Imprimatur*," Jurist 44 (1984) 339–356. [2]Notification of S. Cong. Doctrine of the Faith, *Post apostolicas litteras,* AAS 58 (1966) 1186; R. Bortolotti, "Librorum prohibitio iuxta notificationem S.C. Pro D.F., die 14 iunii 1966," Periodica 56 (1967) 116–138.

## INDULGENCES

An indulgence is the remission of the temporal punishment due to sin in virtue of the infinite merits of Christ, together with the merits of the saints, which are available to the Church through the Communion of Saints (q.v.). Its basis is then the notion of the Church's treasury (q.v.) of goods and merits.

The origin of indulgences is to be sought in the practice of a confessor (q.v.) or martyr (q.v.) giving a *libellus*—a letter asking for clemency—to one who had to undergo canonical penance as a result of inconstancy of faith in the face of persecution (v. RECONCILIATION). Another stage was the growth of intercession for the dead. A third stage was a developing understanding of the remission of sin. These dogmatic truths gradually became clear. With baptism, all sin is remitted. For sins after baptism there was the sacrament of reconciliation/penance. With this second sacrament there was associated the idea of personal penance as well as conversion. Penitential practices were in time seen to cover any remaining punishment or penalty due to sin, any residue of disordered affections or desires. The power of the keys was seen to extend also over this remnant, and the Church called upon the merits of Christ and of the saints, especially Mary, to assist the sinner in coming into full spiritual integrity.

By the Middle Ages indulgences were attached to various practices such as going on a crusade (q.v.). For such an act there was a plenary indulgence, viz., one taking away all expiation due to remnants of sin. These were seen as transferable to the departed, but only by way of intercession: as an offering to God, they did not guarantee that a particular person would be released from purgatory as a result.

The scholastics developed the theory of indulgences, St. Thomas, for example, wrote on it at considerable length in his early work,[1] and he had to deal with it in disputed questions during his teaching career.[2]

An important stage in the development of indulgences was the jubilee bull of Clement VI. The jubilee, with a plenary indulgence attached to a pilgrimage to Rome, had been decreed by Boniface VIII to take place every hundred years, beginning with 1300. Clement decided that it should be every fifty years, beginning with 1350. In his bull he set out the scholastic theology of indulgences: Christ's merits are superabundant; to his merits, those of the saints are added; this treasury is entrusted to the Church.[3] The growth of interest in indulgences in the later Middle Ages led to many abuses, including what appeared to be the selling of indulgences: they were dispensed by a professional "pardoner" in return for an alms. As is well known, such a practice was the occasion which sparked the Reformation. There were attempts at reform beginning with Trent, which outlined Catholic teaching[4] and demanded that any association of money with indulgences cease.[5]

Indulgences were discussed at Vatican II, but the reform was to await the apostolic constitution of Paul VI in 1967.[6] The pope sets out in some detail the above theology of indulgences before stating: "In granting an indulgence the Church uses its power as minister of Christ's redemption. It not only prays. It intervenes with its authority to dispense to the faithful, provided they have the right dispositions, the treasury of satisfaction which Christ and the saints won for the remission of temporal punishment" (n. 8). Indulgences, far from being a claim based on our merits, are a gift we receive from the merits of Christ on the performance of specified conditions. Indulgences deepen our bond with the whole Church (nn. 9–10).

The papal document also reduced drastically the number of plenary indulgences: a plenary indulgence can be gained only once a day, and it always requires sacramental confession, Holy Communion, and prayer for the pope's intentions (the Our Father and the Hail Mary once). Though one confession may suffice for several plenary indulgences, Communion must be received for each. Furthermore, "it is necessary to be free from all attachment to any sin at all, even venial sin" (nn. 6–9). This last condition makes it extremely difficult to gain a plenary indulgence, and heightens its significance. A most valuable plenary indulgence is the one which can be gained at the moment of death, even in the absence of a priest to give the Apostolic Pardon, provided the person was in the habit of saying some prayers during his or her life (norms 18). An important dimension of indulgences is that of purgatory (q.v.). Those who are being purified or healed in that state can have their purgation mitigated by the prayer of the Church, and by indulgences gained for the deceased by the living who offer them to God "by way of suffrage" (n. 10 and norms 3). Partial indulgences

are no longer indicated in "days" or "years" (norms 4); it is the love of the person who performs the act and the value of the act itself that determines a partial indulgence (n. 12). The Church's manual of indulgences is to be updated.[7] The teaching of Paul VI is carried over into the new *Catechism* (para. 1471–1479) and made specific in law (CIC 992–997).

Since indulgences were such an issue at the Reformation, and still are with the Churches of the Reform, it is important that a careful theology of indulgences be presented, one which does not seem to bear a semi-commercial emphasis on works rather than being a gift of grace mediated by the Church and received through faith. In the matter of indulgences we need to stress the dispositions of contrition, love, and faith to avoid any impression of an "automatic favor" being dispensed by Church authorities.[8]

---

[1]*In 4 Sent.* d. 20, a.3 = Supp. qq. 25–27; q.71, a.10.  [2]E.g., *Quodlibet* 2, q.8, a.2 (38).  [3]DS 1025–1027/ND 1681–1683.  [4]Sess. 25—DS 1835/ND 1686/Tanner 2:796-797.  [5]Sess. 21—Tanner 2:731-732.  [6]*Indulgentiarum doctrina*—AAS 59 (1967) 5–24/Flannery 1:62-79/part in ND 1687–1690.  [7]*Enchiridion indulgentiarum. Normae et concessiones* (Vatican, 1968).  [8]P.T. Beer, "What Price Indulgences? Trent and Now," TS 39 (1978) 526–535; K. Rahner, "Remarks on the Theology of Indulgences," ThInvest 2:175-201; idem, "A Brief Theological Study on Indulgences," ibid., 10:150-165; idem, "On the Official Teaching of the Church Today on the Subject of Indulgences," ibid., 166–198.

## INFALLIBILITY

Infallibility is a major issue in ecumenical discussion[1] and within the Catholic Church, where we find denials or such profound reinterpretation that it is in practice rejected.[2] It involves us in questions of history, of dogma, and of hermeneutics. The word "infallible" means immunity from error. It is a negative term but refers to something positive: the Church (and various persons and organs of the Church) is said to be infallible insofar as it is assured of abiding in the truth of the gospel.[3]

We begin with Christ: he is infallible. As he faces towards God as man and on behalf of humanity, and as he faces humanity as God and on behalf of God, he shows indefectible faith and infallible testimony. The Church which is constituted by the gift of his Spirit and guaranteed his abiding presence (Matt 28:20) is likewise indefectible in faith and is infallible (1 Tim 3:15).[4] The Church shares in the infallibility of Christ, who in turn reflects the divine attribute of infallibility. The Church which is infallible, because indefectible in faith, is not an abstraction but the concrete People of God (q.v.). Infallibility has to be seen in the context of the biblical notion of truth: it is not an abstraction but is within the mission given by Christ to his Church.[5]

The Church is infallible in believing and in teaching. First, faith, as St. Thomas Aquinas pointed out, cannot be deceived.[6] The faith of the Church is sustained by the Spirit in giving the supernatural appreciation of the faith (*sensus fidei*—v. SENSE OF THE FAITH) to the whole people of God (LG 12). Second, it is the conviction of the Church from NT times that it teaches the truth without error, to the extent that those who reject its normative teaching are to be excluded (v. HERESY and EXCOMMUNICATION). It is argued that if God did not endow the Church with unfailing faith, the stringent demands made on the believer would be insupportable (cf. Gal 1:6; Mark 16:16; Luke 10:16). While the whole community of the Church is thus infallible in its belief, i.e., in the acceptance and profession of its normative faith, each individual is not, however, infallible.[7]

It is the conviction of the Catholic Church that God will preserve the whole community in truth as it faces towards him in worshiping faith and in facing towards the world with his message and on his behalf. God will also share his infallible truth with its official teachers in the fulfillment of their office. People can err in matters of faith, both as individuals and as teachers in the Church.

From the time of Irenaeus (q.v.) there was a conviction that what was taught in all the Churches could not be false.[8] Vincent of Lérins (d. before 450) summed up the conviction of the Church in the lapidary statement that universality, antiquity, and unanimous consent are the guarantors of truth (*quod ubique, quod semper, quod ab omnibus*).[9] Soon certain councils (q.v.) were regarded as normative for belief. Some of these were later called ecumenical councils, but there were other local councils, e.g., the second Council of Orange (529), that also became touchstones for orthodoxy. In the first millennium, universality of teaching and certain gatherings of bishops, along with subsequent papal approval, were received (v. RECEPTION) by the Church as being both binding and free from error. The conviction arose that radical revision of this universal or gathered teaching was impossible.[10]

In 19th-century terminology these would be called, respectively, an exercise of the ordinary and extraordinary magisterium (q.v.). These two modes of teaching, viz., the bishops throughout the world or gathered in council, have been held to be infallible to the present day, a conviction reiterated in Vatican II. But in the case of the ordinary magisterium, it is not enough for a truth to be universally taught; it must be taught so as to be definitively held (*tanquam definitive tenendam*—LG 25).[11]

In an early ecumenical council there was usually a papal legate(s) present and, in time, a pope subsequently approved its teaching. The question arose in the Middle Ages about the guarantee of truth given to the pope when teaching alone. St. Thomas Aquinas asserted papal infallibility in some sense when he taught that the pope could issue a creed to be held by the whole Church.[12] But the roots for such teaching stretch further back. In the first millennium there was a near universal conviction that the Roman Church had never erred. From the time of Pope Gelasius I (d. 496) we find approximations to the assertion that the Roman Church cannot err.[13] Earlier than that, with Popes Damasus I (d. 384) and Siricius (d. 399), we find the idea of an almost mystical presence of Peter in the papacy. This idea was strongly felt in Leo I, but though it faded, it never quite died out, emerging at times very strongly, as in the case of Gregory VII (q.v.); on solemn occasions the popes still see themselves as united with, and successor of, Peter, fulfilling his role in the Church.[14]

Along with these reflections there is an insistence on the fact that there can be no reconsideration of Roman decisions (from Zosimus, d. 418, and Boniface I, d. 422), and that at Rome there was unbroken and faithful preaching of apostolic doctrine.[15] The views of Leo I (q.v.) are well known: he did not see a council as necessary, in view of the fact that he had spoken with clarity in his *Tome*; he saw Chalcedon (q.v.) merely as accepting his views.[16] The statement that the first see is judged by no one (*prima sedes a nemine judicatur*) began to appear in the 6th century; it was indeed of suspect origins—a nonexistent council (Sinuessa); however it became a commonplace in canonical legislation, and later in conciliar theory.[17]

The behavior of three popes, Liberius (q.v.), Vigilius (q.v.), and Honorius I (q.v.) was not up to the high standards expected of the bishop of Rome. But the complex issues of their reigns were quickly forgotten and left no lasting impression in the Western Church, which increasingly accepted the Roman norms as a reliable rule of faith. The Petrine See retained in the eyes of the Church a doctrinal purity in its faith. Thus it is clear that the convictions of St. Thomas mentioned above were in line with an ancient tradition which increasingly held a special position for teaching of the popes, and a sense of their security in the orthodox faith. The roots of papal infallibility are thus much earlier than a cursory reading of the well-known study of B. Tierney might suggest.[18]

This scholar is right in seeing a new emphasis on papal inerrancy in the late 13th and early 14th centuries with Peter Olivi (d. 1298) and Guido Terreni (d. 1342). The former, for partisan reasons, wanted to limit popes to follow the teaching of their predecessors: he did not want a future pope to change the approval Nicholas III gave in 1279 to views on extreme poverty held by Spiritual Franciscans. He used the term "faith and morals" (q.v.) and taught that the pope was an unerring teacher when he spoke "magisterially."[19] Guido, a staunch papalist, taught that the pope could not err in "determining" (*determinando*) in faith; this technical word means that a controversy or an issue is being settled beyond doubt on the authority of the master, here the pope.[20] But his view would seem to allow too much papal teaching to come under the rubric of inerrancy.

In the Middle Ages, contemporaneously with the growing assertion of the purity of the faith of the Roman See, and also of the pope, theologians and canonists were very clear that a pope could fall into heresy as an individual; in this case he would automatically cease to be pope.[21]

Later in the 14th century and right through to the Reformation there were many factors that ensured that the doctrine of infallibility did not develop smoothly: the Avignon (q.v.) captivity, the Western Schism (q.v.), conciliarism (q.v.), the need for reform at every level, the Protestant revolt. In the period of the Counter-Reformation, papal infallibility was defended by many theologians, though the rise of Gallicanism (q.v.) ensured that it did not make a very steady progress in the centuries after Trent.[22]

With the 19th century it was felt that a declaration of papal infallibility was necessary for the promotion of the spiritual authority of the papacy. Though Vatican I (q.v.) made various pronouncements, it was dominated by the issue of infallibility. There was an "infallibilist" group whose leaders were Manning (England), Descamps (Belgium), Senestrey (Germany), and Pie (France). These were the Ultramontane (q.v.) party.[23] Aided and supported by Pius IX, this group used its numerical strength ruthlessly to crush the minority whom in practice it regarded as heretical. The minority was headed by Rauscher (Austria), Simor (Hungary), Dupanloup (France), and the conciliar historian Hefle (Germany).[24] The German theologian J.J.I. von Döllinger (d. 1890—q.v.), who opposed papal infallibility even to the point of incurring a postconciliar excommunication, supplied them with ammunition for their cause. Though the infallibilist majority won out against the minority view that either infallibility could not be defined or was inopportune, the infallibilist extremists failed in their further aim to have a definition that the pope was infallible in administrative acts. In the debates the council members were aware of historical difficulties posed against the definition; they were also conscious of the exercise of papal power in defining the Immaculate Conception sixteen years earlier (1854).

Infallibility is treated in the fourth chapter of the Constitution *Pastor aeternus* (v. VATICAN I). The text requires careful hermeneutics involving a knowledge of the precise object of the definition. Above all it is necessary to remember that it is Gallican positions that the council wants to exclude, and this central fact gives the key to the interpretation of the definition. In the chapter introducing the definition[25] it is made clear that infallibility is an aspect of the papal primacy (q.v.) already defined. It appeals to Matt 16:18 and Luke 22:32 and to earlier councils, Constantinople IV (q.v.), Lyons II (q.v.) and Florence (q.v.). The council goes on to state that it judges it absolutely necessary to make the definition. The vital expressions of the definition are: it is "a divinely revealed doctrine"—hence not a novelty; "the Roman Pontiff"—each single pope, thus avoiding the Gallican idea that only the line of popes generally taught truthfully; "when he speaks *ex cathedra,*" immediately explained in the following clause, "when, in the exercise of his office as shepherd and teacher of all Christians, in virtue of his supreme apostolic authority, he defines . . .'"—hence it is only in very specific situations that the pope is infallible; "he defines" governs the object: "a doctrine concerning faith or morals (q.v.) to be held by the whole Church"—hence infallibility does not operate in the area of politics, matters of administration, or of temporal power; the infallibility enjoyed by the pope is the same infallibility which "the divine Redeemer willed his Church to enjoy"—the meaning here is not developed, but it is not a new thing, though the ecclesial gift can even reside in an individual, viz., the pope; "by the divine assistance"—the source of infallibility is God, it does not ultimately depend on human endeavors, consultation, or theological investigations. In the debates there was much discussion whether infallibility is personal or belonging only to the statements made. The council spoke carefully of the infallible magisterium of the Roman Pontiff.[26] It is clear that when teaching *ex cathedra* the pope enjoys a charism of the Holy Spirit; infallibility is not merely God's prevention of error, but a gracing in truth.[27]

It was the final clause of the declaration, the one which caused most difficulty at the council and most misunderstanding since: the definitions are "irreformable of themselves (*ex sese . . . irreformabiles)* and not by the consent of the Church." The reason for this addition was to avert every vestige of Gallicanism (q.v.) and especially its 4th article in 1682, whose language is echoed while its assertion is contradicted.[28] Vatican I is asserting that infallible statements are "irreversible," not that they could not be better formulated. The council also denies that the source of infallibility lies in the consent of the Church. In interpreting the document it is important to note that the doctrine is presented largely in juridical categories characteristic of the majority of bishops at the council; the minority tended to speak more in terms of tradition, of the witness of the faith.

Vatican II receives this teaching and presents it in LG 25. Its context is, however, significant: the article deals respectively with the infallibility of bishops, of the Church,[29] of the pope, and once again of bishops. Though it retains much of the language of the earlier council, there are some changes which represent both clarifications and some development in understanding: the Roman Pontiff is called "head of the college of bishops"—this reduces the danger that one might see the pope as somehow "above" the Church in definitions rather than "within" the Church and the college as he teaches infallibly;[30] the object of infallibility "extends just as far as the deposit of divine revelation that is to be guarded as sacred and faithfully expounded"—there is a clear limit to infallibility, it cannot propose new doctrines that do not pertain to the deposit of revelation;[31] the exercise of infallibility is seen more clearly in the light of Luke 22:32 as confirming in faith; the "divine assistance" of Vatican I becomes "the assistance of the Holy Spirit promised to him in blessed Peter"—there is here perhaps a light echo of the Petrine presence to the pope found in an earlier tradition; the notion of reception is specified in a negative and positive sense—definitions "have no need of approval from others nor do they admit any appeal to any other judgment," but "the assent of the Church, however, can never fail to be given to these definitions on account of the activity of the same Holy Spirit"; "the Church's own charism of infallibility individually exists" in the pope—another indication of the ecclesial nature of infallible definitions. Vatican II further adds: "When the Roman Pontiff or the body of bishops together with him define a decision, they do so in accordance with revelation itself, by which all are obliged to abide and to which all must conform"—infallible decisions cannot therefore be something alien in the Church, but are rather the expression of its authentic faith. It is worth noting that the new *Code of Canon Law* did not reproduce some added nuances of LG 25 in CIC 749–750; neither did it integrate its own canon 212 § 1 into the question of infallibility.[32]

The re-presentation of the doctrine of Vatican I by the later council contains several points made in the official *relatio,* or explanation of the text, by Bishop V. Gasser just before voting on the definition.[33] It also shows itself to be sensitive to points that were made in important studies of infallibility in the early 60s,[34] studies which would continue after the council.[35]

In the period after Vatican II there were several developments. An important document of the then-called Sacred Congregation for the Doctrine of the Faith drew attention to the need for hermeneutics of the texts of Church teaching,[36] and specified somewhat the object of infallibility: "According to Catholic doctrine, the infallibility of the magisterium extends not only to the deposit of faith, but also to those things, without which this deposit of faith cannot be properly safeguarded and explained."[37] F.A. Sullivan

comments that the Congregation does not use the vague "connected with revelation," but more restrictive "things without which the deposit cannot be properly safeguarded and explained."[38] Here we are faced with what is called the secondary objects of infallibility, viz., truths which are not revealed, but are necessary to protect revelation. To find out what the secondary objects would be, we have to consult a theological consensus. Some of what were thus regarded before Vatican II would no longer command serious support (e.g., canonization of saints and approbation of religious orders).[39] Many centrist theologians would probably agree on the following: 1) the condemnation of propositions contrary to revealed truth—such power could be necessary to preserve revealed truth; 2) propositions that necessarily follow from revealed truth (a proposition itself not revealed, but follows as a strict conclusion, and thus sometimes called "virtually revealed")—not being revealed, they do not belong to the deposit of faith, but it is conceivable that an infallible statement might be required to elucidate a revealed truth; 3) "dogmatic facts," which are of two kinds: a) historical facts connected with revelation, e.g., the ecumenicity of a council; b) the compatibility or incompatibility of published opinions with revealed truth—an author might try to escape condemnation by saying that he meant something else, in which case the magisterium might have to say, even infallibly, "the objective meaning of this statement is heretical." To reject secondary objects of infallibility would be to go against Catholic teaching, but would not fall under the anathema of Vatican I.[40]

There is a dispute about whether or not particular norms of the natural law can be the object of infallible teaching. Sullivan[41] represents the opinion of a wide consensus: while holding that basic principles of the natural law can be infallibly taught, he disagrees with those who in practice seem to defend the definability of particular norms.[42] The urgency of the question is that it concerns the encyclical of Paul VI, *Humanae vitae,* on the regulation of births.[43] Some theologians affirm that the sinfulness of contraception has been so taught by the popes and by the ordinary magisterium of bishops throughout the world that it is infallible teaching.[44] Though constantly reaffirmed by Pope John Paul II, both in Rome and in his pastoral journeys, it would seem that the reception (q.v.) that one must expect to be given to an infallible teaching is not as yet forthcoming.

One must not merge what is true with what is infallible: there is much true teaching in the Church which does not fulfill the conditions for infallibility. One would have a very impoverished faith if one confined oneself only to what has been infallibly taught: the liturgy constantly proclaims truths not infallibly taught; significant papal teaching in encyclicals and exhortations does not fall under infallibility.

There is, however, a real danger of what has been called "creeping infallibility." Though everyone admits that the conditions for papal infallibility are extremely exacting and narrow, there can be an approach to the ordinary magisterium which would demand the type of assent which properly belongs only to infallible teaching (v. MAGISTERIUM, DISSENT).

In his controversial book *Infallible? An Enquiry*, H. Küng stated that the conditions for the infallibility of the ordinary magisterium were fulfilled in the case of contraception, but as he presumed it and the teaching of Paul VI to have been misguided, he proceeded to strike at the heart of the whole doctrine of infallibility.[45] Though he had both defenders—albeit some with reservations[46]—and opponents,[47] the real service he contributed to the understanding of infallibility has been highlighted only by a few, most notably P. Chirico's dispassionate *sic* and *non* dialogue with him.[48] In particular, Küng has made it very difficult to retain a simplistic textbook a priori approach to infallibility, which merely looks to the verification of four conditions: pastor and teacher of all the faithful; use of supreme authority; definition of a doctrine of faith and morals; binding teaching. If the pope then intends to settle a matter definitively and seems to fulfill these conditions, he would be regarded as teaching infallibly. But there is plenty of evidence of the fact that there have been occasions when all these conditions would seem to have been fulfilled, but the Church does not bow to these decisions as exercises of infallibility.

This has moved theologians to look once again at the Orthodox insistence on reception (q.v.). To make reception the cause or source of infallibility would be Gallican, and directly against Vatican I. It is quite another thing to say that reception may be the only conclusive evidence that infallible teaching has actually been propounded.[49]

There has never been an official list of infallible papal teaching. The instances culled from theologians by F. Dublanchy in 1927, writing therefore before the Assumption in 1950, probably represent the upper limit at thirteen, many of which would not be considered infallible by mainstream theologians today.[50] At the lower limit it is asserted that no papal statement exactly fulfills the situations given by the official relator, V. Gasser, at Vatican I: he argued that papal infallibility is necessary when there are divisions and scandals and dangers to the unity of the Church, conditions which were not fulfilled in the case of the Marian dogmas.[51] Nonetheless, most theologians would accept the definition of the Immaculate Conception (1854) and of the Assumption (1950) as exercises of infallible teaching authority,[52] perhaps with some other statements

from the past, such as the *Tome* of Leo (q.v.). The number of papal infallible statements is at any rate extremely small. To some it may appear as a trifle ironic that the magisterium has up to now relied on theologians to establish what doctrines have in fact been infallibly taught. An important forthcoming book by F.A. Sullivan surveys all Church teaching that may be infallible, both papal and conciliar.[53]

[1]P.C. Empie et al., eds., *Teaching Authority and Infallibility in the Church*. Lutherans and Catholics in Dialogue VI (Minneapolis: Augsburg, 1978); ARCIC, *Authority in the Church II*. Windsor Report 1981, nn. 23–33. [2]E.g., L.M. Bermejo, "The Alleged Infallibility of Councils," Bijd 38 (1977) 128–162; H. Küng, *Infallible? An Enquiry* (London: Collins Fontana, 1972). [3]A. Dulles, "Infallibility: the Terminology," in Empie (n. 1) 69–80 at 71. [4]R. Murray, "Who or What is Infallible?" in AA.VV. *Infallibility in the Church: An Anglican-Catholic Dialogue* (London, 1968) 26–30; F.A. Sullivan, *Magisterium: Teaching Authority in the Catholic Church* (Dublin: Gill and Macmillan—New York: Paulist, 1983) 4–9. [5]C.J. Dumont, "Sur la pleine acceptation biblique du mot 'verité' et ses implications en matière d'infallibilité," RSPT 67 (1983) 87–96. [6]ST 2–2ae, q.1, a.3; cf. G. Bavaud, "Les deux manières de justifier l'infallibilité de l'Église," NVet 58 (1983) 161–167. [7]Sullivan (n. 4) 9–17. [8]*Adv. haer.* 1:10, 1–2; cf. Eno, Teaching Authority 42–50. [9]*Commonitorium* 2—PL 50:639; cf. Eno, Teaching Authority 142–152; idem, "Ecclesia Docens: Structures of Doctrinal Authority in Tertullian and Vincent," Thom 40 (1976) 96–115. [10]R.B. Eno, "Some Elements in the Pre-History of Papal Infallibility" in Empie (n. 1) 238–258 at 247. [11]Sullivan (n. 4) 125–127; K. Rahner, "Magisterium," SM 3:356. [12]ST 2–2ae, q.1, a.10; cf. Y. Congar, "St. Thomas and the Infallibility of the Papal Magisterium (Summa Theol. 11–11, q.1, a.10)," Thom 38 (1974) 81–105; U. Horst, "Kirche und Papst nach Thomas von Aquin," Catholica 31 (1977) 151–167. [13]Eno (n.10) 243–244; cf. Eno, Teaching Authority 163–167. [14]Eno (n. 10) 252. [15]Ibid., 242–243, 245–247, 252. [16]*Epist.* 36–37—PL 54: 809–812; 44:1—PL 54: 829; 103—PL 54: 992. [17]Eno (n. 10) 246. [18]B. Tierney, *Origins of Papal Infallibility 1150–1350: A Study on the Concepts of Infallibility, Sovereignty and Tradition in the Middle Ages* (Leiden: Brill, 1972). [19]Ibid., 96, 119–120. [20]Ibid., 249–250, 268–269. [21]Congar, Augustin 245–246; R. Manselli, "Le cas du pape hérétique vu à travers les courants spirituels au XIVe siècle," in E. Castelli, ed., *L'infallibilité: Son aspect philosophique et théologique* (Paris: Aubier, 1970) 113–130; Tierney (n. 18) 49–54. [22]Sullivan (n. 4) 93–94. [23]H.J. Pottmeyer, *Unfehlbarkeit und Souveränität: Die päpstliche Unfehlbarkeit im System der ultramontanen Ekklesiologie des 19. Jahrhunderts* (Mainz: Grünewald, 1975). [24]M. O'Gara, *Triumph in Defeat: Infallibility, Vatican I and the French Minority Bishops* (Washington, D.C.: The Catholic University of America Press, 1988) with review G. Thils, ETL 65 (1989) 412–419. [25]Tanner 2:815–816/DS 3065–3072/ND 831–838; cf. U. Betti, "Dottrina della costituzione 'Pastor aeternus,'" in *La costituzione dommatica "Pastor aeternus" del Concilio Vaticano I* (Rome, 1961) 627–647 = AA.VV., *De doctrina Concilii Vaticani primi. Studia selecta annis 1948–1964 scripta* (Vatican, 1969) 343–360; A. Chevasse, "La véritable conception de l'infallibilité papale d'après le Concile du Vatican," in *Église et unité* (Lille, 1948) 57–91 = ibid., 559–575. [26]J.P. Torrell, "L'infallibilité pontificale est-elle un privilège 'personnel'? Une controverse au premier Concile du Vatican," RSPT 45 (1961) 229–245 = De doctrina (n. 25) 559–575. [27]K. McDonnell, "Infallibility as Charism at Vatican I," in Empie (n. 1) 270–286. [28]DS 2284; cf. G. Dejaifve, "Ex sese, non autem ex consensu

Ecclesiae," Sales 24 (1962) 283–295 (in French) = De doctrina (n. 25) 506–520. [29]W. Dantine and J. Hamer, arts on "Die Unfehlbarkeit der Kirche," in AA.VV. Ökumene, Konzil, Unfehlbarkeit (Innsbruck: Tyrolia, 1979) 27–35, 13–26. [30]P. Duprey, "Some Reflections on Infallibility," OneChr 24 (1988) 196–201. [31]K. Rahner, "On the Concept of Infallibility in Catholic Theology," ThInvest 14:66-84. [32]K. Walf, "L'infallibilité, comme la voit le 'Code de droit canonique' (canons 749–750),'" StCan 23 (1989) 257–266. [33]V. Gasser, ed. J.T. O'Connor, The Gift of Infallibility (Boston: St. Paul, 1986) = Mansi 52:1204-1230. [34]AA.VV. L'infallibilité de l'Église (Chevetogne, 1961); De doctrina (n. 25); R. Aubert, Vatican I. Histoire des conciles oecuméniques 12 (Paris, 1963); G. Thils, L'infallibilité du peuple chrétien "in credendo." Notes de théologie posttridentine (Paris-Louvain, 1963). [35]E. Castelli, ed. (n. 21); G.H. Tavard, "Infallibility: A Survey and a Proposal," OneChr 22 (1986) 24–43; G. Thils, L'infallibilité pontificale (Gembloux: Duculot, 1968); idem, Primauté et infallibilité du Pontife Romain à Vatican I et autres études d'ecclésiologie (Leuven: Peeters, 1989). Cf. J.T. Ford, "Infallibility: A Review of Recent Studies," TS 40 (1979) 273–305. [36]Declaration Mysterium Ecclesiae (24 June 1973)—Flannery 2:433-435. [37]Ibid., 432. [38]Op. cit. (n. 4) 134. [39]Sullivan (n. 4) 136; cf. E. Pacentini, "L'infallibilità papale nella canonizzazione dei santi," MiscFran 91 (1991) 187–225 and manuals, e.g., Salaverri, Ecclesia 741–744. [40]Ibid., 135–136; cf. A. Dulles, "Moderate Infallibilism: An Ecumenical Approach," in A Church to Believe In (New York: Crossroad, 1983) 133–148 [= Empie (n. 1) 81–100] 138. [41]Op. cit. (n. 4) 148–152. [42]E.g., J.C. Ford and G. Grisez, "Contraception and the Infallibility of the Ordinary Magisterium," TS 39 (1978) 258–312. But cf. F.A. Sullivan, "The 'Secondary Object' of Infallibility," TS 54 (1993) 536–550. [43]AAS 60 (1968) 481–503—Flannery 2:397-416/Carlen 5:223-233. [44]Ford and Grisez (n. 42); cf. E. Lio, Humanae vitae e infallibilità: Il concilio, Paolo VI e Giovanni Paolo II (Vatican, 1986); M.L. Ciappi, "'Humanae vitae' e infallibilità," Divinitas 32 (1988) 595–600. [45]Op. cit. (n. 2). [46]J.J. Kirvan, ed., The Infallibility Debate (New York: Paulist, 1971); H. Küng, ed., Fehlbar? Eine Bilanz (Einsiedeln: Benziger, 1971). [47]K. Rahner, ed., Zum Problem Unfehlbarkeit: Antworten auf die Anfrage von Hans Küng. QDisput 54 (Freiburg: Herder, 1971); cf. TDig 19 (1971) 107–123; cf. C.J. Peter, "A Rahner-Küng Debate and Ecumenical Possibilities," in Empie (n. 1) 159–168. [48]"Infallibility: Rapprochement Between Küng and the Official Church?," TS 42 (1981) 529–560; G. Dejaifve, "Où en est le problème de l'infallibilité," NRT 100 (1978) 373–388 = TDig 27 (1979) 107–110; cf. J.J. Hughes, "Hans Küng and the Magisterium," TS 41 (1980) 376–392.2234. [49]P. Chirico, Infallibility: The Crossroads of Doctrine (Delaware: Glazier, 1983) 239–242 with "Infallibility: A Reply," Thom 44 (1980) 128–135; idem, "Infallibility—Another Approach," HeythJ 21 (1980) 376–392 at 389; Dulles (n. 29) 139; Sullivan (n. 4) 106–109. [50]"Infallibilité du pape," DTC 7:1638-1717 at 1703; K. Schatz, "Welche bisherigen päpstlichen Lehrentscheidungen sind 'ex cathedra'?" in W. Löser et al., eds., Dogmengeschichte und katholische Theologie (Würzburg: Echter, 1985) 403–422. [51]Mansi 52:1213, 1217; cf. Vatican I, Tanner 2:816/DS 3071/ND 837; F. Kerr, "Vatican I and the Papacy 5," NBlackfr 60 (1979) 357–366; Dulles (n. 29) 147–148 (nuanced). [52]E.R. Carroll, "Papal Infallibility and the Marian Definitions: Some Considerations," Carmelus 26 (1979) 213–250; J.L. Heft, "Papal Infallibility and the Marian Dogmas: An Introduction," OneChr 18 (1982) 309–340. [53]Creative Fidelity: Weighing and Interpreting Documents of the Magisterium (New York: Paulist, 1996).

# INITIATION

In the post-Vatican II renewal of the liturgy, the Rite of Christian Initiation of Adults (RCIA—1972) notes that the rite of adult initiation includes not only the celebration of the sacraments of baptism (q.v.), confirmation (q.v.), and Eucharist (q.v.) but all of the rites belonging to the catechumenate (q.v.).[1] Initiation is "a gradual process that takes place in the community of the faithful . . . suited to a spiritual journey of adults which varies according to the many forms of God's grace."[2] The whole initiation may stretch over years, culminating in the reception together of the three sacraments of baptism, confirmation, and Eucharist—all administered by a priest if no bishop is present. All three are required for full initiation (CIC 842 § 2). Initiation may be seen as having several dimensions: it is initiation into Christ, into the life of the Spirit, into the Church.[3]

The initiation of infants varies between the East and the Latin West. In the East the three sacraments are administered together in infancy. In the Latin West baptism is administered in infancy (CIC 867), with confirmation and the reception of the Eucharist being postponed until the child reaches the use of reason, or later. Though for pastoral reasons the conference of bishops may allow confirmation to be administered after First Communion, for example at the age of 12 or later, there is a clear preference in the liturgical books[4] and in law (CIC 891) for the traditional order of baptism, confirmation, and Eucharist.

A difficult theological question arises about the relationship of initiation to the Church. In itself initiation is into the Catholic Church. In the case of an adult who is baptized into a Church or ecclesiastical communion which lacks fullness of faith, initiation does not confer full incorporation into the Catholic Church. An infant will later come into full, or defective, profession of faith at a more mature age. This profession of faith will determine the degree of incorporation into the Church: full, if there is complete Catholic communion in faith, sacraments and Church discipline; partial, if one of these elements is missing.[5]

There is a sense in which we can say that initiation is ongoing throughout life, as there can be an indefinite growth in the appropriation of, and life through, the sacraments of initiation. In the Apostolic Tradition (q.v.) we read that after receiving the Eucharist the newly initiated "are to apply themselves to good works, to pleasing God, to good conduct, to being zealous for the Church (vacans ecclesiae), doing what they have learned, and advancing in piety (in pietate—21/23:12)." Clearly, initiation is the beginning of a lifelong journey. The Eucharist is both a sacrament of initiation, and, as Viaticum, the final preparation for death.

[1]General Instruction n. 2.   [2]Ibid., 4–5.   [3]Cf. H. Bourgeois, "L'Église est-elle initiatrice?," MaidD 132 (1977) 103–135.   [4]GI for Rite of Confirmation n. 11.   [5]See K.J. Becker, "The Teaching of Vatican II on Baptism: A Stimulus for Theology," in Latourelle, Vatican II 2:47-99.

## INNOCENT III, Pope (1198–1216)

Lotario de' Conti di Segni was born of a patrician family at Anagni in 1160/61.[1] He studied theology at Paris and law at Bologna. As a young man he composed learned, if unoriginal, treatises on contempt of the world and on the Mass. Aged only thirty-eight, he was unanimously elected pope on the second ballot at the conclave of 1198.

Innocent had an exalted idea of the papacy; he began to make customary the title "Vicar of Christ" (v. PAPAL TITLES).[2] He recovered control over some of the papal states. He was actively involved in European politics wherever the interests of the Church were at stake. Though he did not confuse Church and State, he held that the pope was not only head of the Church but head also of the Christian people, and in a real sense the pope was, therefore, the possessor of the fullness of power *(plenitudo potestatis)*.[3] He saw the exercise of this power appropriate whenever there was a state of emergency, problems arising from the sin of Christian rulers, or disputes between them which required arbitration or a judgment in favor of one of the clashing monarchs.

His pontificate was dominated, however, not so much by politics as by a concern for the fourth crusade (q.v.), reform, and the combatting of heresy. To these ends he convoked the Fourth Lateran Council (q.v.). He also contributed to Roman centralization by enormous legislative activity (more than 6,000 letters, many of them decretals), and by his insistence that bishops should visit Rome every four years.

In Innocent, papal power probably reached its apogee. The centuries which immediately followed would continually face the problem of harmonizing in practice the theoretical distinction between the power of the Church and of the State, admirably formulated under him by Lateran IV.[4]

[1]OxDPopes 186–188; Congar, Augustin 192–197; H. Wolter, in Jedin-Dolan 4:136-172. J. Clayton, *Pope Innocent III and His Times* (Milwaukee, 1941); J.M. Powell, ed., *Innocent III: Vicar of Christ the Lord of the World* (Washington, D.C.: The Catholic University of America Press, [2]1994); J. Sayers, *Innocent III* (London—New York, Longman, 1994); Works: PL 214–217.   [2]S. Kuttner, "Universal; Pope or Servant of God's Servants: The Canonists, Papal Titles and Innocent III," RDroitC 31 (1981) 109–149.   [3]B. Tierney, "The Continuity of Papal Political Theory in the Thirteenth Century: Some Methodological Considerations," MedSt 27 (1965) 227–245; J.A. Watt, *The Theory of Papal Monarchy in the Thirteenth Century* (London, 1965).   [4]Constit. 42—Tanner 1:253.

## INQUISITION

The Inquisition was a juridical persecution of heresy by special Church courts.[1] Constituting some of the more shameful pages of Church history, it began only gradually.[2] In the 12th century there were many heresies, notably the Cathari (q.v.), and their offshoot the Albigenses (q.v.). It was no longer a matter of a few individuals but of extensive movements. The initial reaction of the Church was to preach against them, even to hold discussions. With the local Council of Tours (1163) a policy of moving directly against heretics began, seeking them out instead of waiting for them to be denounced. Heresy was seen not only as a threat to the Church's doctrine and the unity of its organization but also a civil threat to the well-being of the state. Under Innocent III (1198–1216) heresy became described as an act of treason.[3] By the early 13th century inquisitors were appointed, mostly from the Dominican and Franciscan Orders, though seculars were also to be found. They were de facto subject only to the pope. Manuals to guide inquisitors were found chiefly in the following century. At Lateran IV (1215—q.v.) it was decreed that heresy was to be sought out, and reluctant bishops and secular lords were subject to canonical penalties, but by the Council of Vienne (q.v.) some controls were established.[4]

By the beginning of the 13th century, the practice was established of turning over to the secular arm for punishment—often the pyre—those found guilty of heresy by the bishop's or inquisitor's court. These measures were accepted by Gregory IX in 1231. In succeeding years other deplorable elements were gradually added: torture, and the punishments of infamy, banishment, loss of civil and political rights as well as death. A particularly onerous feature was the demand that the accused prove their innocence against accusations often made secretly and without the possibility of effective legal representation or reply. Though the scandal of the medieval inquisition cannot be justified, it can perhaps be understood in its context, in which Christendom was a unity of faith and social order: an attack on the former was a threat to the latter.

The inquisition continued in existence in many places throughout Europe during the later Middle Ages. There were several reforms, notably under Clement V (1305–1314). It was much less active by the mid-15th century. But Paul III (1534–1549) established the Congregation of the Inquisition in 1542 as the final court of appeal in trials for heresy; it was also named the Holy Office. Though set up to ensure doctrinal purity, it soon became a tribunal for moral offenses, and the frequency with which it led to the death penalty was significant.[5] It was most active in the second half of the 16th century. The case of Galileo (q.v.)

was not typical of the Inquisition. He was tried and condemned for disobeying a purported injunction of the Holy Office. Had he been tried and found guilty of heresy, he would not have been given the mild punishment of being consigned to house arrest at his villa near Florence. The Inquisition was even extended to India, and it was active in Goa from 1560–1812: as in the Americas, it was frequently used for protecting patronage rights, and possibly active more often in cases such as alleged sorcery than of heresy.

The Spanish Inquisition was of a different kind, in that its sponsor was the state, in the persons of Ferdinand V and Isabella, and it was set up with papal approval in 1479.[6] It was originally directed against *marranos,* Jews who had been baptized but were thought to have returned to former practices. It was also used against *moriscos,* Moors who had been forcibly baptized. Later it sought out Protestants and Alumbrados (q.v.). This last category led to people of deep spirituality, like the Spanish mystics, being under threat. Ignatius of Loyola (q.v.) was imprisoned for forty-two days, suspected of being an Alumbrado.

The Spanish Inquisition was most active under Philip II (king 1556–1598). He saw Protestants as a threat to the state, and feared that the Moors would obtain a European bridgehead through Granada. Even after the Inquisition had passed its height, there were still 782 *autos-da-fé* under Philip V (1683–1746); the last was in Seville (1781). Abolished in 1808, the Spanish Inquisition was briefly reintroduced 1814–1834.

The process leading to the death penalty was known by its Portuguese title *auto-da-fé* (act of faith): a procession, Mass, sermon, reading of sentence, and handing over of the accused to the secular power. The Church authority "exhorted mercy" from the secular power, even though the Bull of Innocent IV *Ad extirpanda* (1252) laid heavy canonical penalties on those secular authorities which did not proceed with the death sentence within five days; many would see this apparently cynical appeal for mercy as symptomatic of deeply problematic features of the whole system of inquisition. Even when all allowances are made for the political, cultural, and religious influences which led to the establishment and evolution of the Inquisition, it has ultimately to be deplored for the way in which it operated; it is one of the darker features of Church history.

[1]E. van der Vekené, *Bibliographie der Inquisition* (Hildersheim, 1963); idem, *Bibliotheca bibliographica historiae sanctae Inquisitionis.* Bibliographisches Verzeichnis der gedruckten Schriftums und Literatur der Inquisition. 2 vols. (Vaduz: Topos Verlag, 1983). [2]H. Wolter, in Jedin-Dolan 4:98-104, 159–166, 208–216; Y. Dossat, NCE 7:535-541; B. Hamilton, *The Medieval Inquisition.* Foundations of Medieval History (London: Arnold-Hodder and Stoughton, 1981); H. Maisonneuve, *Études sur les origines de l'Inquisition* (Paris, [2]1960); E. Peter, *Inquisition* (New York: Free Press—London: Collier Macmillan, 1988). Cf. B. van Hove, "Oltre il mito dell' Inquisizione," CivCatt 143 (1992) 4:458-467, 578–588. [3]Decretal, *Vergentis in senium* (1199). [4]Lateran IV—Tanner 1:233-235; Vienne—1:380-383. [5]H. Jedin, in Jedin-Dolan 5:487; M. Kroch and A. Skybová, *Die Inquisition im Zeitalter der Gegenreformation* (Stuttgart-Berlin: Kohlhammer, 1985). [6]B. Bennassar et al., *L'Inquisition espagnole XVe-XIXe siècle* (Paris: Hachette, 1979); H. Kamen, *The Spanish Inquisition: The Iron Century.* History of Civilization (London: Weidenfeld & Nicolson, 1965); idem, *Inquisition and Society in Spain in the Sixteenth and Seventeenth Centuries* (London: Weidenfeld and Nicolson, 1985).

# INSTITUTION

Sometimes used in a pejorative sense, institution referring to the Church has a wide range of meanings. In general it means the Church seen in its doctrinal, sacramental, and governmental structures.[1] "Institutional" can therefore include credal statements, the magisterium (q.v.), councils (q.v.), sacraments and law (q.v.), Church membership (q.v.), structures such as hierarchy, and religious life. One could also state that, in a sense, Scripture belongs to the institutional area of the Church.

An obverse of institution is charism (q.v.). Seen in a more profound light, institution refers to everything in the Church that involves human mediation; charism depends rather on the direct intervention of the Spirit. For instance, a bishop decides who should be ordained in his diocese, but not who should receive charismatic gifts. He can, however, regulate their use.[2] Charism requires institution for order; institution requires charism and the working of the Spirit for dynamism and life.

Grace is normally mediated by institutional means, that is, through word and sacrament. But the Spirit frequently works independently of institutions. The medieval adage "God is not bound by the sacraments" grasps this intuition.

Institutionalism is a deviation in ecclesiology whereby what is institutional is seen as primary,[3] especially office holders and their activities. The pyramid image of the Church, with the pope and bishops at the top and a passive, merely receptive laity at the bottom, is an institutionalist perception. The view of the Church as a perfect society (q.v.) is an institutional one. Vatican II broke away from an overly institutionalist view of the Church, though traces of institutionalism can be found in its documents. If we are careful to avoid institutionalism, we can then treasure the essential and valuable elements of institution in the Church. If one holds that the heart of the Church is the Eucharist (q.v.), then one is at once both accepting an institution and relying on the Spirit to vivify the Church through this institution which reveals the Church's deepest reality.

[1]A. Dulles, *Models of the Church* (Dublin: Gill and Macmillan, [2]1988) 39. [2]K. Rahner, "The Charismatic Element in the Church" in *The Dynamic Element in the Church.* QDisput. 12 (Freiburg—

London, 1964) 42–83; "Institution and Freedom," ThInvest 13:105-121; idem, "On the Structures of the People of God Today," ThInvest 12:218-228. See G. Angelini, "Forme storiche della Chiesa," Ambros 68 (1992) 78–94.   [3]See Dulles (n. 1) 34–46.

## INTEGRALISM

The term integralist was a term applied to those who considered themselves "integral Catholics," opposing liberal Catholics and modernists. Integralism/integrism, strictly speaking, is a movement which arose in response to Pius X's encyclical *Pascendi* against Modernism (q.v.) in 1907. The pope urged bishops to be wary about doctrinal errors taught by priests and in seminaries, and exhorted them to set up vigilance committees in their dioceses.[1]

Integralism,[2] which had been a tendency in the closing years of the 19th century, became organized in the time of Pius X. An Italian priest, Umberto Benigni, later attached to the Secretariat of State, founded the *Sodalitium Pianum* (in France, *La Sapinière*), which was very small but highly influential. It conducted bitter attacks, not always with intellectual honesty, against those whom it decided were Modernists. Some of the ablest scholars in France and Italy, several cardinals, and many bishops were the objects of their denunciations. The organization disbanded for a while after the death of Pius X (1914); it reappeared again and was suppressed by the Holy Office in 1921.

The Integralists had few outstanding theologians, apart from E. Barbier, who campaigned against Leo XIII and published extensively.[3] They collaborated with the royalist right-wing French political movement *Action française,* led by an agnostic, Charles Maurras, who supported Pius X's anti-modernist attitudes.[4]

Though belonging to the Modernist period, strictly speaking, integralism as a tendency can lie beneath the statements and actions of some of those who would seek to protect the Church.[5]

It manifests itself in a view of Tradition that is frozen in the past, that sees modern thought and research as always a potential threat from which Catholics must be protected by Church authority or alert guardians of orthodoxy. Integralist aspirations were not absent around the time of the encyclical *Humani generis* (1950) and of the post-Vatican II reforms, especially liturgical.[6] Integralist attitudes were also found among some of those who openly or covertly supported the ideas of Archbishop M. Lefebvre (q.v.).

[1]ASS 40 (1907) 593–650/Carlen 3:71-97.   [2]R. Aubert, in Jedin-Dolan 9:467-480, 619–620; idem, "Mgr Benigni, un intégriste aux antécédents progressistes: une interprétation nouvelle du 'catholicisme intégral,'" RTLv 8 (1977) 461–468; Y. Congar, *Vrai et fausse réforme dans l'Église* (Paris, [1]1950) 604–622 omitted by author in 1969 edition; C. Ledré, "Intégrisme," Catholicisme 5:1822-1834; G.J. O'Brien, "Integralism," NCE 7:552-553; É. Poulat, *Intégrisme*

*et catholicisme intégral* (Tournai-Paris, Desclée, 1969); R. Rémond, "L'intégrisme catholique: Portrait intellectuel," Études 370 (1989) 95–105.   [3]Notably, *Histoire du catholicisme libéral et du catholicisme social en France: Du Concile du Vatican à l'avènement de SS Benoît XV (1870–1914).* 5 vols. (Bordeaux, 1923). G.J. O'Brien, *Integralism: An Historico-Critical Study of this Phenomenon in France as Seen in the Writings of Emmanuel Barbier.* Diss. exc. (Woodstock, 1963).   [4]Cf. E. Weber, *The Action Française* (Stanford, 1962); M. Garrigou-Lagrange, "Integrisme et national-catholicisme," Esprit 27 (1959) 515–543.   [5]Cf. H. Urs von Balthasar, "Integralismus heute," Diak (Mainz) 18 (1988) 221–229.   [6]M. Olivi, "L'Integralismo francese e la riforma liturgica del Concilio Vaticano II," EphLtg 106 (1992) 38–67, 117–152.

## INTERCOMMUNION

The term "intercommunion" is commonly used for the sharing of the Eucharist among Christians whose Churches are not in full communion with one another. However, given the variety of situations that can be present, one can profitably attend to the distinctions which were introduced by the Faith and Order meeting at Lund in 1952:[1] *Full Communion* between Churches of the same confessional family; *Intercommunion with Intercelebration* "where two Churches not of the same confessional family by agreement allow communicant members freely to communicate at the altars of each, and where there is freedom of ministers to officiate sacramentally in either Church, e.g., Lutheran and Reformed Churches in France";[2] *Intercommunion* in which the freedom of ministers to celebrate is absent, e.g., Old Catholics and Anglicans; *Open Communion* where one Church invites members of other Churches to receive communion; *Mutual Open Communion* where two or more Churches on principle invite each other's members to receive communion; *Limited Open Communion* where there is admission in cases of emergency or other special circumstances; *Closed Communion,* where a Church limits participation in the Lord's Supper to its own members.[3]

The practice of Churches varies enormously in this matter: there are not only positions held worldwide by Churches, but there are also individual agreements between Churches at universal or more local levels.[4] At the heart of each position adopted is usually one of two theological positions about the Eucharist; some see the Eucharist as such a sign of unity that intercommunion would be a lie; others stress that the Eucharist is a means to unity, and so practice some form of "Eucharistic hospitality." This last term can at times be more accurate than "intercommunion," since some Churches will invite other Christians to share in the Eucharist, while not being themselves prepared to receive at the latter's worship. Another reason here can be doubt about the validity of orders: Roman Catholics, Orthodox, and some Anglicans will not consider as definitely valid the orders of non-episcopal Churches.

What follows is mainly concerned with the practice and theology of the Roman Catholic Church. Vatican II approved of prayer together with other Christians (UR 9), but it immediately added: "Worship in common *(communicatio in sacris)* is not to be considered as a means to be used indiscriminately *(indiscretim)* for the restoration of Christian unity. There are two main principles governing the practice of this common worship: first, the bearing witness to the unity of the church, and second, the sharing in the means of grace. Witness to the unity of the Church generally forbids common worship *(communicatio),* but the grace to be had from it *(gratia procuranda)* sometimes commends this practice. The course to be adopted, with due regard to all circumstances of time, place and persons, is to be decided by local episcopal authority, unless it is otherwise determined by the bishops' conference according to its own statutes, or by the holy see" (UR 8).

In its decree on the Catholic Eastern Churches, Vatican II spelled out how these principles should be applied in the case of Eucharistic and other sharing between Catholics and members of separated Eastern Churches. It declared: "The sacraments of penance, holy eucharist and anointing of the sick may be conferred on eastern Christians who in good faith are separated from the catholic church, if they make the request of their own accord and are properly disposed. Indeed, it is also permitted for Catholics to ask for the same sacraments from those non-catholic ministers in whose church there are valid sacraments, whenever necessity or real spiritual advantage suggest it and access to a catholic priest becomes physically or morally impossible" (OE 27). The 1993 *Directory for Ecumenism*[5] adds a word of caution about exercising this freedom: "Eastern churches, on the basis of their own ecclesiological understanding, may have more restrictive disciplines in this matter, which others should respect. . . . A Catholic who legitimately wishes to communicate with Eastern Christians must respect the Eastern discipline as much as possible, and refrain from communicating if that Church restricts sacramental communion to its own members to the exclusion of others" (nn. 122, 124).

While Vatican II itself spelled out the application of its principles to the sacramental sharing between Catholics and Eastern Christians, it was left to the Secretariat for Christian Unity to apply these principles to the case of such sharing between Catholics and separated Christians of the West. In its 1967 *Directory for Ecumenism* and in further clarifications issued in 1970, 1972, and 1973,[6] the Secretariat laid down conditions under which a Catholic priest could lawfully administer the Eucharist to members of the Anglican and Protestant Churches. Finally, the 1983 *Code of Canon Law* adopted the guidelines laid down by the Secretariat and made them the law of the Church. Canon 844 §§ 2, 3 confirms what was said by Vatican II in OE 27 about sacramental sharing between Catholics and members of Eastern Churches (see CCEO 671). Canon 844 § 4 lays down the following conditions under which a Catholic priest may administer the sacraments of penance, Eucharist, and anointing of the sick to Anglicans and Protestants: "If the danger of death is present or other grave necessity *(alia urgeat gravis necessitas)* in the judgment of the diocesan bishop or the conference of bishops, Catholic ministers may licitly administer these sacraments . . . (to those) who cannot approach a minister of their own community and on their own initiative ask for it, provided they manifest Catholic faith in these sacraments and are properly disposed."

The *Code* leaves it up to local bishops or episcopal conferences to spell out the kind of "grave necessity" that is required. It would seem that not all bishops have done this, since the 1993 *Directory for Ecumenism* strongly recommends that diocesan bishops, taking into account any norms which may have been established for this matter by the episcopal conference, establish such general norms for judging situations of grave and pressing need (n. 130). The *Directory* itself, with regard to the administration of the Eucharist to the non-Catholic party when an interchurch marriage takes place during the Eucharistic liturgy, says that one applies the general norms "taking into account the particular situation of the reception of the sacrament of Christian marriage by the two baptized Christians" (n. 159). This would suggest that here one could envisage the force of "grave necessity" being considerably mitigated.

There are some further canonical points. Concelebration with ministers of other faiths is forbidden (CIC 908). Exceptionally and for a just cause the local bishop may allow a member of another Church to be a reader at Mass (1993 *Directory* 133) but not to preach the homily, which is reserved in Church law to a deacon or priest (*Directory* 134; see CIC 767; CCEO 614 § 4). Here we have some further institutional recognition to the unity which already exists between Christians: we share the one Scriptures. The issue of intercommunion is briefly treated in the new *Catechism* (nn. 1399–1401).

Interest in the question of Intercommunion was undoubtedly greater among Protestants from the 1950s to 1970s.[7] Most recent literature is taken up with the Orthodox and Catholic Churches. In recent years their official position has been explained, gently probed, not to say challenged.[8] Some hierarchies, notably the Swiss and French, have made some further tentative steps along the path approved by Vatican documents;[9] these have not always been well received.[10]

The position of Orthodox Churches with regard to intercommunion is more strict than the Roman norms;[11] they generally refuse to use economy (q.v.) to admit Catholics to communion, even in those cases in which Catholics would admit Orthodox.

The main arguments for greater openness to at least occasional intercommunion can be summarized as follows: there is substantial faith agreement based on the ancient creeds among many of the Churches; baptism should lead to Eucharist and to unity; there is significant communion and fellowship among several Churches; there is need for sensitivity especially in ecumenical gatherings, and most particularly in the situation of interchurch marriages; marriage between a Catholic and another Christian is truly a sacramental *communicatio in sacris,* already allowed under the 1917 canon law (cc. 1060–1064);[12] the inclusion, however heavily qualified, of spiritual advantage suggesting *(vera spiritualis utilitas id suadet)* that Catholic individuals receive sacraments outside their Church (CIC 844 § 2) would seem to provide some opening for further development.

A further question arises from the very notion of unity of faith. In ecumenical circles it is now being questioned whether complete accord on every doctrinal issue is necessary for institutional unity (v. ECU- MENISM, UNION). It goes without saying that other Christians are generally in good faith; this was accepted at Vatican II to the extent that a statement to the effect was considered unnecessary.[13] The teaching of St. Thomas Aquinas where he considers the situation of those who do not know some doctrines of the faith but have implicit faith,[14] could fruitfully be investigated. People, with very erroneous positions on matters of faith, do in fact receive the Eucharist in the Catholic Church. Moreover, a level of existential faith, considered as commitment to Jesus as Lord, can be expressed and shared by Catholics and other Christians on a deeper level than between Catholics themselves. The position of interchurch families[15] can also be viewed in this perspective.

While one may be sympathetic to these arguments, the statement by A. Dulles more than a decade ago still challenges: "To violate the known discipline of one's own church, it would seem, is rarely a source of edification or of spiritual blessings."[16] As in many other issues in ecclesiology, it will be the sense of the faith (q.v.) guided indeed by the magisterium, rather than a priori legislation, that will bring about change, if this truly be the will of the Spirit.

[1]T. Sartory, *The Oecumenical Movement and the Unity of the Church* (Oxford: Blackwell, 1963) 52–53. [2]O.S. Tomkins, ed., *The Third World Conference on Faith and Order* (London: SCM, 1953) 52. [3]L. Vischer, ed., *A Documentary History of Faith and Order 1927–1963* (St. Louis: Bethany, 1963) 118–119/Bell, Documents 283. [4]G. Wainwright, "Intercommunion," DictEcum Mov 518–520. [5]CathIntern 4 (1993) 351–399. [6]AAS 59 (1967) 574–592/Flannery 1:483-501; *Dans ces derniers temps*—AAS 62 (1970) 184–188/Flannery 1:502-507; In quibus rerum circumstantiis—AAS 64 (1972) 518–525/Flannery 1:554-559; *Dopo le publicazione*—AAS 65 (1973) 616–619/Flannery 1:560-563. [7]"Beyond Intercommunion: On the Way to Communion in Eucharist," Faith and Order: Louvain 1971 (Geneva: WCC, 1971); D. Baillie and J. Marsh, eds., *Intercommunion* (London: SCM, 1952); L. Hodgeson, *Church and Sacraments in a Divided Christendom* (London: SPCK, 1959); P.S. Kaufman, "Intercommunion and Union," JEcuSt 22 (1985) 594–603; [8]AA.VV. *L' Eucharistie* (Paris: Mame, 1970); AA.VV. *Vers l'intercommunion* (Paris: Mame, 1970); V.M. Borovoy and J. Pronk, "Taking Steps towards Unity. Life in Unity. Bread for All," EcuR 36(1984) 10–15; M. Brogi, "Ulteriori possibilità di *communicatio in sacris,*" Antonian 60 (1985) 455–471; F. Coccopalmerio, "La 'Communicatio in Sacris' comme problème de communion ecclésiale," AnnéeC 25 (1981) 201–229; T. Goffi, "'Communicatio in sacris' vissuta in modo non confessionale ma ecumenica," StEcum 6 (1988) 325–331; A. Hastings, "Intercommunion Today," OneChr 14 (1978) 312–317; R. Girault, "Les problèmes d' 'intercommunion' aujourd'hui: Une réflexion catholique à la lumière de l'histoire récente," EspVie 97 (1987) 465–479, 481–496, 497–501; S. Manna, "Riconoscimento dei sacramenti delle altre Chiese da parte della Chiesa cattolico-romano," Nicol 13 (1986) 29–54; A. Nicolas, "La cène du Seigneur et la vie oecuménique," Istina 29 (1984) 152–168; D. Salachas, "La professione di fede non piena impedisce la comune celebrazione eucaristica: Quali i limiti?," Nicol 10 (1982) 307–332; A. Stacpoole, "Intent or Intercommunion," AmplefJ 83 (1978) 2:42-56; J. Willebrands, "Vingt années de Secrétariat pour l'unité," Irén 54 (1981) 5–23 esp. 17–19. [9]DocCath 1849 (1983) 368–369; "Eucharistic Hospitality: Note from the Swiss Catholic Episcopal Conference," OneChr 23 (1987) 280–283. [10]E.g., B. Franck, "Remarques au sujet de la note épiscopale concernant l'hospitalité eucharistique avec les Églises issues de la Réforme," RDroitC 35 (1985) 156–171. [11]E. Timiadis, "Problèmes liés à l'intercommunion entre nos deux Églises," Nicol 9 (1981) 263–273. [12]E. Lanne, "'La communicatio in sacris' du point de vue catholique-romain," Kanon 8 (1987) 135–149. [13]ActsSyn 3/2:335-336. [14]ST 2–2ae, q.2, aa. 5–6. [15]"Sharing Eucharistic Communion in the Context of an Interchurch Family. Association of Interchurch Families Survey," OneChr 19 (1983) 42–87; P. Devine, "Eucharistic Hospitality and Interchurch Families," IrTQ 47 (1980) 133–145. [16]"Eucharistic Sharing as an Ecumenical Problem," in *The Resilient Church: The Necessity and Limits of Adaptation* (Dublin: Gill and Macmillan, 1978) 153–171 at 171.

# INTERNATIONAL THEOLOGICAL COMMISSION

At the first Synod of Bishops (1969) there was a proposal to establish a commission of eminent theologians of various schools in various parts of the world "for the purpose of offering effective assistance to the Holy See, and in particular the Congregation for the Doctrine of the Faith, especially in doctrinal questions of greater moment." At the same time it was suggested that episcopal conferences, having consulted universities and theological faculties in their area, should suggest theologians for membership.[1] The intention of the synod members would seem to be clear: to get a wider spectrum of theological opinion than that normally available to the Roman Congregations from among theologians, mostly resident in Rome.

In April 1969 Pope Paul VI announced the establishment of the International Theological Commission (ITC) and approved provisional statutes for the new body.[2] The first meeting took place in October 1969, and henceforth on an annual basis. From the beginning there was a tension in the relations between the ITC and the Congregation for the Doctrine of the Faith (CDF). Cardinal Franjo Seper refused to relinquish control over doctrinal matters. By 1974 the ITC was revamped: only thirteen of its original thirty members were retained. K. Rahner resigned, regarding it as an impotent group not seriously consulted on major issues affecting the CDF.

In 1982 John Paul II gave definitive statutes to the Commission,[3] altering substantially the original project envisaged by the bishops at the 1967 Synod, including perhaps the initial vision of Paul VI,[4] though by 1974 even he had acquiesced in its having a changed role. From 1982 instead of a Commission advisory to the Holy See, and complementing or rather countering the exclusive influence of the theologians normally consulted by the CDF, it now became thoroughly subordinate to this Congregation. The President is the Cardinal Prefect of the CDF; its members are selected by him for approval by the pope. Its documents are submitted to the pope and can be published only if no difficulties are voiced by the Holy See, which in practice means the CDF. One might have thought that the ITC would have been consulted on major controversial issues such as the admission of women to priestly ministry (v. WOMEN, ORDINATION), but this does not seem to have happened.[5]

The earlier documents of the ITC have been collected,[6] and they are published on appearance by various theological journals.[7] For ecclesiology several studies of the ITC are significant: "The Priestly Ministry" (1970), "Theological Pluralism" (1972), "Theses on the Relationship between the Ecclesiastical Magisterium and Theology" (1975), "Select Themes of Ecclesiology on the Occasion of the Eighth Anniversary of the Closing of the Second Vatican Council" (1984), "Faith and Inculturation" (1988), "Interpretation and Dogma" (1990), "Some Questions on Eschatology" (1991). The theology of the Commission reflects several elements of the tasks of theologians (q.v.): it faithfully interprets the magisterium; it draws out implications from this teaching; but there are indications of some more creative theologizing, even though this is not the most marked characteristic of the Commission's studies to date. The high point of its existence to now was probably its theses on ministry, largely the work of Hans Urs von Balthasar (q.v.), which had some influence on the 1971 Synod and the

CDF document *Mysterium Ecclesiae*[8] in the matter of the historical conditioning of dogmas.

[1]G. Caprile, *Il Sinodo dei Vescovi: Prima Assemblea Generale* (Rome, 1968) 234. See F.A. Sullivan, *Magisterium: Teaching Authority in the Catholic Church* (Dublin: Gill and Macmillan, 1983) 174–176.  [2]AAS 61 (1969) 431–432; 540–541.  [3]Mp. *Tredecim anni iam*—AAS 74 (1982) 1201–1205.  [4]See P. Delhaye, "Paul VI et la Commission théologique internationale," RTLv 9 (1978) 417–423.  [5]K. Rahner, "The Congregation of the Faith and the Commission of Theologians," ThInvest 14:98-115; Sullivan (n. 1) 175–176 with n. 8.  [6]M. Sharkey, ed., *International Theological Commission: Texts and Documents 1969–1985* (San Francisco: Ignatius, 1989).  [7]E.g., Greg., EspVie, IrTQ (some).  [8]AAS 65 (1973) 396–408—Flannery 2:428-440.

## INVESTITURE CONTROVERSY

There was controversy in the late 11th and 12th centuries about the roles of the emperor and of princes in the creation of abbots and bishops.[1] The abbot or bishop-elect received the ring and staff from the emperor and prince, and he did homage to the secular leader before being consecrated and blessed as abbot or bishop. At the heart of the problem was the role of the secular authority in the appointment of the Church dignitary. Lay investiture was first condemned by Nicholas II (1058–1061) in 1059, and frequently by succeeding popes. Various compromises were effected in different countries until the matter was finally settled at the Concordat of Worms (1122) at a meeting of Callistus II (1119–1124) and the emperor Henry V. The issues at stake had been clarified by Guido of Ferrara (1086) and still further by Ives of Chartres: spiritual matters *(spiritualia)* were the domain of the Church; temporal matters *(temporalia)* were of the secular power but both were implicated in the office of bishop or abbot. The emperor gave up the right to investiture of ring and staff (symbols of ecclesiastical office) and conceded canonical election and free consecration. The pope conceded to the emperor the right to be present at German elections, and to give the scepter (symbol of such secular power or dominion as was to be exercised by the bishop) before the consecration.[2]

The lay investiture controversy was a step in the gradual unweaving of the relation between Church (bishops, clergy, and monks) and state (princes and laity) in the Middle Ages, one which would take some centuries more to complete.[3]

[1]J. Gaudemet, "Investiture Struggle," NCE 7; 600-604; I.S. Robinson, *Authority and Resistance in the Investiture Controversy: The Polemical Literature of the Late Eleventh Century* (New York: Manchester UP—Holmes and Meier, 1978).  [2]Text S.Z. Ehler and J.B. Morall, eds., *Church and State Through the Centuries* (Westminster, Md., 1954) 48–49; Bettenson 111–112. Cf. A. Brent, "The Investiture Controversy: An Issue in Sacramental Theology," ETL 63 (1987) 59–89.  [3]Congar, Augustin 118–122.

## IRENAEUS, St. (ca. 130–200)

Born in Asia Minor about 130, Irenaeus tells us that he listened as a young man to Polycarp (q.v.), a disciple of the apostle John. Irenaeus traveled to Rome, and later to Lyons, where he became bishop. He is thus a witness to the tradition of three major, widely separated, Churches. He died about 200 C.E.; the evidence for martyrdom is late and not compelling.

Two important works survive: his *Adversus haereses* ("The Unmasking and Refutation of False Gnosis")[1] and *The Demonstration of the Apostolic Preaching,* rediscovered only in 1904.[2] Like many early Christian writers, Irenaeus wrote mainly to defend Christianity against the heresies of the period. It is not, therefore, orderly or systematic. As his adversaries were mainly Gnostic (v. GNOSTICISM), we find in Irenaeus important assertions about God, creation, redemption, revelation, anthropology.[3] His doctrine of recapitulation *(anakephalaiôsis)* is significant for soteriology and Mariology: every false step taken by humankind at the beginning was reversed in the redemption, and so we have Christ-Adam/Mary-Eve parallels.[4] He was also the first writer to ponder extensively the question of orthodoxy and heresy.[5] But though his immediate aim was to counter heresy, he unfolded a profound theological vision of the whole mystery of God and of the world.[6]

The importance of Irenaeus for ecclesiology is exceptional. His texts are not easy to interpret. We have a complete version of the *Adversus haereses* only in Latin, but when it can be compared with passages of the original Greek, it proves to be a quite slavish translation. In his conflict with the Gnostics he had to deal with their claim to possess secret knowledge and their theory of emanations; his response was to stress the catholicity of the Church and the solidity of its tradition. In doing so he left in his writings an early witness to some critical ecclesiological themes.[7]

Briefly, in his *Adversus haereses* Irenaeus argued against the Gnostics that truth is to be found in the united witness of the Churches[8] to which the apostles committed the teaching they received. The successors of the apostles can be enumerated as the bishops in all places (v. APOSTOLIC SUCCESSION).[9] These bishops have received a certain charism of truth.[10] Instead of going through the laborious process of investigating each Church, he singled out the greatest of the Churches, the one founded by the Apostles Peter and Paul.[11] He then makes a most important statement for which the original Greek is missing and the meaning is not one hundred per cent certain: "For with this Church, because of its more eminent origin *(propter potentiorem principalitatem)* every Church that is, the faithful everywhere, must agree *(necesse est . . . convenire),* because in this Church the apostolic tradition has always been preserved by those from everywhere."[12] This translation takes the first part to allude to the founding of Rome on Peter and Paul, to which Irenaeus refers in the context; the second part to point to the cosmopolitan character of the Roman Church. At the very least Irenaeus is ascribing some kind of preeminence to the Roman Church in the matter of leadership and doctrine (v. PAPAL PRIMACY). He also testifies to the hierarchical structure of the Church: each place has a single bishop and presbyters.[13]

The importance of Irenaeus' witness lies in his antiquity and in his knowledge of three Churches: Asia Minor, Rome, and Gaul. By his time the Church showed the key elements of institution which still characterize it today.

[1]Texts PG 7:437-1224/Books: 1—SC 263–264; 2—293–294; 3—210–211; 4—100 (2 vols.); 5—SC 152–153/ANL 5:1–480; 9:187. H.U. von Balthasar, ed. and introd., *The Scandal of the Incarnation: Irenaeus Against the Heresies* (San Francisco, Ignatius, 1990). [2]SC 62/PO 12:655-802 with English and French trans./ACW 16/J.A. Robinson, *St. Irenaeus, The Demonstration of the Apostolic Preaching Translated from the Armenian* (London, 1920).   [3]M.A. Donovan, "Irenaeus in Recent Scholarship," SecC 4 (1984) 219–241; A. Orbe, "Irenaeus," EncycEarCh 1:413-416.   [4]*Adv. haer.* 3:22, 4—SC 211:438-444; 5:19, 1—SC 153:248-250.   [5]A. Benoit, "Irénée et l'hérésie: Les conceptions hérésiologiques de l'évêque de Lyon," AugR 20 (1980) 55–67; Y. de Andía, "L'hérésie et sa réfutation selon Irénée de Lyon," AugR 25 (1985) 609–644; E. Peretto, "Criteri di ortodossia et di eresia nella Epideixis di Ireneo," AugR 25 (1985) 645–666.   [6]H.U. von Balthasar, *The Glory of the Lord: A Theological Aesthetics. II—Studies in Theological Style: Clerical Styles* (San Francisco: Ignatius—New York: Crossroad—Edinburgh: Clark, 1984) 31–94.   [7]G. Bardy, *La théologie de l'Église de saint Clément de Rome à saint Irénée* (Paris, 1945) 167–169, 184–198, 204–210; P. Batiffol, *L'Église naissante et le catholicisme* (Paris, [2]1902, repr. Paris: Cerf, 1971) 195–276—Eng. trans. *Primitive Catholicism* (1911); Y. de Andia, "Irénée, théologien de l'unité," NRT 109 (1987) 31–48; R. Kereszty, "The Unity of the Church in the Theology of Irenaeus," SecC 4 (1985) 202–218; D. Papandreou, "L'ecclésiologie irénique d'Irénée de Lyon," *La foi et la gnose hier et aujourd'hui: Irénée de Lyon.* Cahiers de l'Institut Catholique de Lyon 15 (Paris: Soc. d'Éd. Operex, 1985) 105–116.   [8]*Adv. haer.* 1:10, 1–2—SC 264:158-160; M. Jourjon, "La tradition apostolique chez saint Irénée," AnnéeCan 23 (1979) 193–202.   [9]*Adv. haer.* 3:3, 1–4—SC 211:30.   [10]J.D. Quinn, "Charisma vertitatis certum: Irenaeus, Adversus haereses 4, 26, 2," TS 39 (1978) 520–525.   [11]*Adv. haer.* 3:3, 2–3—SC 211:32-38.   [12]Another trans. in Patrology 1:302-303; see D.J. Ungar, "St. Irenaeus and the Roman Primacy," TS 13 (1952) 389–405.   [13]*Adv. haer.* 4:26, 2—SC 100:718; see M.A. Donovan, "Insights on Ministry: Irenaeus," TorontoJT 2 (1986) 79–93; W.C. van Unnik, "The Authority of the Presbyters in Irenaeus' Work," in J. Jervell, ed., *God's Christ and His People* (Oslo: UP, 1977) 248–260.

## ISLAM

Islam[1] appeared in Arabia at the beginning of the 7th century in a pagan Arab environment which was in contact with small groups of Jews and Christians. It took its origin from the revelations which Muhammad (ca. 570–632) claimed to have received, beginning from about 610 C.E., and which are to be found in the *Qur'an.* It quickly spread in the Near East and in succeeding centuries to North and East Africa, and what are now Pakistan, Bangladesh, Indonesia. Immigration has led to notable Muslim/Moslem minorities in many European countries.

There are two major divisions in Islam, based to an extent on political considerations, and notably on who can be caliph or leader of the Muslim community: the Sunnites/Sunnis (about 90% of Muslims), who hold that the command must come from the Quraysh tribe of Mohammad; the Shiites (about 10% of Muslims), for whom only a descendant of the Prophet can be invested with supreme command. The former stress the role of the community in interpreting the *Qur'an;* the latter restrict this to the Imâms, who are the sole interpreters of the Prophet's thought.

The main doctrines are to be found in the *Qur'an* 4:6 and 2:177. They are parallel to Jewish and Christian beliefs. First, belief in God, the omnipotent creator, infinitely good and merciful, who punishes severely those who oppose him. The devout Muslim knows ninety-nine names for God, which are invoked according to circumstances. Creation is celebrated as a great act revealing the mercy of God. Second, there is a lively belief in angels; each Muslim believes in two personal guardian angels. Third, the sacred book of the *Qur'an* contains all that is really necessary to know, even though some OT books are venerated in theory but generally ignored in practice. Fourth, there are the prophets, including Moses, David, Jesus, who were sent only to the children of Israel, and the greatest—Muhammad, sent to all humanity. These come after the book, for the *Qur'an* is conceived as preexisting and only later as having been dictated to Muhammad. Fifth, there is a strong belief in the last things—resurrection, judgment, heaven, and hell. Sixth, Islamic tradition insists on the divine decree: everything has been decided by God and one must entrust oneself to God's providence. Christianity is seen as opposed to the unity of God.

Muslim law is enshrined in the "Five Pillars of Islam." These are a path to holiness (v. HOLY).[2] The first, "There is no god but Allah and Muhammad is his prophet," is a statement of uncompromising monotheism. The other pillars are ritual prayer, the *zakat* social and charitable tax, the month-long fast of Ramadan, and the *hajj* or once-in-a-lifetime pilgrimage to Mecca. Islam is more than a religion: it is a social and political system embracing all aspects of the believers' lives.

From the Middle Ages, though not at the beginning, Islam was hostile to Christianity; the antipathy was indeed mutual.[3] With Vatican II there was a new openness in the official position of the Church,[4] one anticipated by more enlightened missionaries such as the White Fathers (Missionaries of Africa). In the submissions of the various hierarchies preparatory to Vatican II, there were few references to Islam. Some of these were negative: a condemnation of the errors of Islam; the difficulties for missionaries raised by the Muslim religion and its peoples. Some were positive: a few noted valuable features of Islam. These submissions were not accepted into the document on the missions, *Ad gentes,* which considered other religions only generically. Attempts in the first sessions of the council to make a statement about Jews were countered by requests that the council also refer to Islam, and indeed other religions. In 1964 Pope Paul VI set up a Secretariat for Non-Christians.[5]

The first reference to Islam inserted into the Constitution on the Church was judged mainly by Eastern bishops to be unsatisfactory. The finally approved version reads: "But the plan of salvation also embraces those who acknowledge the Creator, and among these the Muslims are first; they profess to hold the faith of Abraham and along with us they worship the one merciful God who will judge humanity on the last day" (LG 16). There was much discussion of the Declaration on Non-Christian Religions[6] before it was finally approved in October 1965: "The Church also looks upon Muslims with respect. They worship the one God living and subsistent, merciful and almighty, creator of heaven and earth, who has spoken to humanity, and to whose decrees, even the hidden ones, they seek to submit themselves wholeheartedly, just as Abraham, to whom the Islamic faith readily relates itself, submitted to God. They venerate Jesus as a prophet, even though they do not acknowledge him as God, and they honor the virgin mother Mary and even sometimes devoutly call upon her. Furthermore they await the day of judgment when God will requite all people brought back to life. Hence they have regard for the moral life and worship God especially in prayer, almsgiving, and fasting. Although considerable dissensions and enmities between Christians and Muslims may have arisen in the course of the centuries, this synod urges all parties that, forgetting past things, they train themselves towards sincere mutual understanding and together maintain social justice and moral values as well as peace and freedom for all people" (NA 3). These two texts represent the first major positive statements on Islam by the magisterium: they acknowledge the truly religious values of Islamic faith; they consider Muslims not as infidels but as believers; they see Christians and Muslims united in a monotheistic faith in the one God; they see a community of riches between the Church and the followers of the Prophet; dialogue is sought.[7] In succeeding decades the magisterium has continued to speak positively about Islam,[8] notably in the two papal addresses at Casablanca (1985).[9]

Among Catholic Islamologists the question of the acceptance of the *Qur'an* as revelation arises. Some reject the idea on the basis of contradictions between it and the Christian Scriptures. Others see in it genuine revelation with distortions arising from its human reception; they point out that the conflict between the *Qur'an* and authentic Christian belief is not much greater in some ways than between the OT and NT.[10]

The *Qur'an* is traditionally interpreted by Muslims in three main ways: *tafsir,* the preferred method of the Sunnites/Sunnis, holding tightly to the letter of the text; *ta'wil,* favored by Shiite Muslims, which goes past the letter to an inner, allegorical or applied meaning; *istinbat,* followed by the Sufis but rejected by other Muslims, seeks a mystical, symbolic significance of the text.

Since Vatican II there has been a growth of dialogue (q.v.) with Muslims (v. NON-CHRISTIAN RELIGIONS).[11] It has several inherent difficulties: Muslims do not favor, and can even resent, the use of scientific historical-critical method applied to the *Qur'an* and other sacred books by Orientalists, now usually called Islamologists;[12] though there are many experts in Islam in the Christian Churches, there are few, if any, real experts in Christianity among Islamic scholars, who often repeat stereotypes derived from polemic writings.[13] Again, whereas the Pontifical Council for Interreligious Dialogue and the WCC are official bodies of the Christian Churches, there are no corresponding official organs in Islam, so that dialogue is with university personnel, political bodies, heads of state, or private individuals. Furthermore, along with the pluralism of Christian dialogue partners there is a wide range of Islamic opinion—liberals, fundamentalists, laicists, integralists, practicing believers, and mystics. It may be better to avoid the expression "wider ecumenism" about such dialogue: it is not modeled on the dialogue between Catholics, Orthodox, and Protestants which is aimed at unity between them. Muslims and Christians coming together do not envisage unity, but seek common truths especially about God, humanity, social issues, and peace (see NA 3).[14]

One of the issues that surfaces in dialogue is the mission of Christians, much resented by Muslims. It would have to be said though that direct evangelization of Muslims has few dramatic results, the main mission task being a silent witness of love in the midst of Islam (AG 10–11).[15]

Another significant issue for dialogue is that of spirituality and holiness (v. HOLY).[16] Most explicit on mysticism are the Sufis (from Arabic *suf,* "wool," indicating their garment). The golden age of mysticism was 750–950, though some important figures like Al-Ghazali (1057–1111) and Ibn Arabi (1165–1240) come later. Sufism is an ascetical movement based on mysti-cal insights into the love of God and union with him. Sufism has influenced popular piety in Islam, though it has not been widely accepted by mainstream Islam.

Though the rise of Islamic fundamentalism (q.v.)[17] has posed new difficulties in the way of dialogue or even peaceful co-existence between Christians and Muslims, work for respectful relations between the two faiths, which together make up half of humanity, is crucial for the well-being of the Church in many countries in Asia, Africa, and the Middle East. And in true dialogue both parties are enriched; the greatest value of dialogue for the Church in an age that dislikes commitment and absolutes may well be Islam's uncompromising witness to unnegotiable values both moral and theological.

---

[1]K. Cragg, *The Call of the Minaret* (Maryknoll: Orbis, 1985—London: Collins, [2]1986); D. Ede et al., *Guide to Islam* (Boston: Hall, 1983); J.L. Esposito, *Islam: The Straight Path* (Oxford: UP, 1989); H.A.R. Gibb, *Shorter Encyclopedia of Islam* (Leiden: Brill, [3]1991); P.M. Holt et al., eds., *The Cambridge History of Islam.* 4 vols. (Cambridge: UP, 1970); J. Jonier, *How to Understand Islam* (London: SCM, 1989); T. Michel, "A Short Islamic Bibliography for Seminary Libraries," AustralCR 64 (1987) 69–72; G.J. Roper, *Index Islamicus: A Bibliography of Books and Articles on the Muslim World 1981–1985.* 2 vols. (London: Mansell, 1991); P. Shinar, *Essai de bibliographie sélective et annotée sur l'Islam* (Paris: CNRS, 1983); *Encyclopédie de l'Islam.* Nouvelle edition (Leiden: Brill, 1960– ). [2]R. Caspar, "Quelques types de sainteté en Islam," StMiss 35 (1986) 123–159; K. Cragg, *The Call of the Minaret* (Maryknoll: Orbis, [2]1985—London: Collins, [2]1986) 95–126. 137–141; idem, "Sainthood and Spirituality in Islam," StMiss 35 (1986) 179–198. [3]J.-M. Gaudeul, *Encounters and Clashes: Islam and Christianity in History.* 2 vols. (Rome: Pont. Instit. Arabic and Islamic Studies, 1984); S. Ghrab, "Islam and Christianity: From Opposition to Dialogue," IslamChr 13 (1987) 99–111. [4]J. Farrugia, *Vatican II and the Muslims: The Church's Consideration of Islam in Vatican II and Its Resonance in Subsequent Christian Muslim Relations.* Diss. exc. (Rome: Gregorian UP, 1987); idem, "The Genesis of the Conciliar Statements Regarding the Muslims," MelitaT 40 (1989) 1–26; idem, "The Evolution of the Conciliar Texts Regarding the Muslims," MelitaT 41 (1991) 115–139. [5]AAS 56 (1964) 432–433. [6]See Ferrugia, op. cit. (n. 4); R. Casper, "La religion musulamane: Élaboration et commentaire des textes de la Déclaration," in A.M. Henry, ed., *Les relations de l'Église avec les religions non chrétiennes.* US 61 (Paris 1966) 201–236; idem, "Islam According to Vatican II: On the Tenth Anniversary of 'Nostra aetate'," Encounter 21 (1976) 1–7; idem, "Le Concile et Islam," Études 324 (1966) 114–126; A. Roest Crollius, "Vatican II et le religioni non christiane," RasT 8 (1967) 65–74. [7]Ferrugia (n. 4) Vatican II 67–76; M. Zago, *La "Nostra aetate" e il dialogo interreligioso a vent'anni dal Concilio* (Grottaferrato: Piemme, 1986). [8]T. Michel, "Islamo-Christian Dialogue: Reflections on the Recent Teachings of the Church," Bulletin 20 (1985) 172–193; M. Zago, "Le magistère sur le Dialogue Islamo-Chrétien," Bulletin 21 (1986) 171–181. [9]Bulletin 20 (1985) 237–257. [10]R. Caspar, "Une rencontre avec l'Islam," Spiritus 122 (32) 15–25 at 22; see K. Rahner, "Oneness and Threefoldness of God in Discussion with Islam," ThInvest 18:105-121; N. Robinson, *Christ in Islam and Christianity: Representations of Jesus in the Qur'an and the Classical Muslim Commentaries* (Basingstoke UK: Macmillan, 1991). [11]See journals: *Bulletin, Islamochristiana, Islam and Christian-Muslim Relations;* A. Bouhdiba, "L'avenir du dialogue islamo-chrétien,"

IslamChr 15 (1989) 87–93; M. Borrmans, *Orientations pour un dialogue entre Chrétiens et Musulmans* (Paris: Cerf, 1981—Paulist English, 1989); idem, "La porte etroit du dialogue islamo-chrétien," RAfrT 8/15 (1984) 47–68; idem, "Difficulties of the Dialogue Between Christians and Muslims," JDhara 18 (1988) 212–218; S.E. Brown, ed., *Meeting in Faith: Twenty Years of Christian-Muslim Conversations Sponsored by the World Council of Churches* (Geneva: WCC, 1989); M.L. Fitzgerald, "Twenty-five Years of Dialogue: The Pontifical Council for Interreligious Dialogue," IslamChr 15 (1989) 109–120; idem, "25 Years of Christian Muslim Dialogue: A Personal Journey," PrOrChr 40 (1990) 258–271; F. Gonzáles, "¿Es posible un diálogo con el Islam?," RazFe 223 (1991) 518–528; C. Kimball, *Striving Together: A Way forward in Christian-Muslim Relations* (Maryknoll: Orbis, 1991); T. Michel, "The Theological Situation in Muslim-Christian Dialogue," JDhara 18 (1988) 157–166; A. Roest Crollius, "The Church Looks at Muslims," in Latourelle, Vatican II, 3:324-334; J. Renard, "Christian-Muslim Dialogue: A Review of Six Post-Vatican II Church-related Documents," JEcuS 23 (1986) 69–89.   [12]W. Montgomery Watts, "The Study of Islam by Orientalists," IslamChr 14 (1988) 201–210. [13]M. Ayoub, "Muslim Views of Christianity: Some Modern Examples," IslamChr 10 (1984) 49–70.   [14]M. Borrmans, "The Muslim-Christian Dialogue of the Past Ten Years," ProMundVit Bulletin 74 (1978) 46; T. Michel, "Christian-Muslim Dialogue in a Changing World," TDig 39 (1992) 303–320.   [15]D.A. Kerr, "Christian Witness in Relation to Muslim Neighbors," IslamChr 10 (1984) 1–30.   [16]"Holiness in Islam and Christianity," IslamChr 11 (1985); K. Cragg, "Sainthood and Spirituality in Islam," StMiss 35 (1986) 179–198; C. Gillot, "Sainteté et mystique en Islam," VieSp 143 (1989) 269–281; R. Gramlich, "Nur Gott allein: Ein Wesenzug islamischer Mystik," GeistL 62 (1989) 459–469; R.A. Nicholson, *Studies in Islamic Mysticism* (Cambridge: UP, 1921, 1967); F.J. Peirone and G. Rizzardi, *La spiritualità islamica—La spiritualità non christiana.* Storia e testi 5 (Rome: Ed. Studium, 1986); A. Schimmel, *Mystical Dimensions of Islam* (Chapel Hill, Univ. North Carolina, 1975); H. Sanson, *Dialogue intérieur avec l'Islam.* Religions en dialogue (Paris: Centurion, 1990).   [17]D. Hiro, *Islamic Fundamentalism* (London: Paladin, 1988); J.P. Rajashekar, "Islamic Fundamantalism: Reviewing a Stereotype," EcuR 41 (1989) 64–72; W. Shepherd, "What Is 'Islamic Fundamentalism'?," StRel 17 (1988) 5–26; W. Montgomery Watt, *Islamic Fundamentalism and Modernity* (London—New York: Routledge, 1988); idem, "Islamic Fundamentalism," StMiss 41 (1992) 241–252.

## IUS DIVINUM

The notion of *ius divinum* ("divine law") is rather ambiguous and unclear. At one level it can be useful to distinguish between human and divine law; one may also wish to distinguish natural law and divine positive law. But in the history of the term, at least from the Middle Ages, *ius divinum* is used much more about institutions established by God than about divine law.[1]

In teaching about its institutions and its sacraments, the Catholic Church often appeals to *ius divinum* in support of its positions. The fact that Protestants do not generally accept this approach certainly suggests that the issue is complicated and may not be solvable merely at the level of mutually agreed rational arguments.[2]

The problem arises mainly from a situation in which several possibilities appear to exist, of which afterwards one becomes normative. The Catholic position

on some of these, e.g., the threefold order of bishop, priest, and deacon, is that they are irreversible.

Though Vatican II never used the words *ius divinum,* it surely used equivalent expressions: on the Church "lies the duty by divine command *(mandato divino)* . . . of preaching the gospel to all humanity" (DH 13; see CD 2); "the Roman Pontiff, as successor of Peter . . . has from divine institution *(ex divina institutione)* supreme, full, immediate and universal power for the care of souls" (CD 2 from Vatican I[3]); "by divine institution *(ex divina institutione)* the bishops have succeeded to the place of the apostles" (LG 20); "as members of the episcopal college . . . individual bishops through the institution and command of Christ *(ex Christi institutione et praecepto)* are bound to be concerned with the whole Church" (LG 23); "Holy Church, by divine institution *(ex divina institutione),* is ordered and directed with wonderful variety" (LG 32). The council delicately shades its assertions about the historically difficult origin of ministry: Christ established that the apostles and their successors the bishops would share in his mission, and these latter handed on the ministry in varying degrees to others, "in this way the divinely instituted hierarchical ministry *(ministerium ecclesiasticum divinitus institutum)* is exercised in different orders by those who from ancient times have been called bishops, priests and deacons" (LG 28).

We leave aside the ahistorical position found in the 1917 *Code of Canon Law* and in manual theology before Vatican II: whatever is essential to the Church must have come from apostolic times, if not from Christ himself. There are too many lacunae in the history of the sacraments and of institutions for this view to be comfortably held today. The medieval discussions about the divine origin of the cardinalate and of parish priests is a warning about where a subjective view of what is essential to the Church may lead us.

A moderate view shared by some Lutherans, such as E. Schlink, sees four essential elements as belonging to the Church: the mission of preaching, baptism, the Eucharist, the power of binding and loosing.[4] However, the structures by which these essential elements are administered derive from human law; Lutherans speak of such structures as *adiaphora* (q.v.), i.e, "indifferent things"). They are not irreversible.

K. Rahner espouses a more developmental position.[5] He holds that during the primitive or apostolic age of the Church, human decisions about Church structure were made under the guidance of the Spirit, which can be interpreted as irreversible expressions of the divine will. C.J. Peter is more ready to assert actual irreversibility, and suggests an analogy with the development of the creeds in the early councils.[6]

There are other views, like that of the early E. Schillebeeckx (q.v.), which may grant that a genuine development has taken place, but would deny its irreversibility.[7] Such views are sometimes called "functionalist."[8]

A. Dulles attempts both to expose the current positions, and to see a way out of the impasse of *ius divinum*.[9] While he agrees that the terminology is not very helpful,[10] he insists that the reality behind it must be retained. He lays down as the essentials of the Church its character of being one, holy, catholic, and apostolic. He envisages four concentric circles in which matters will appear in their relation to what is essential in the Church, viz., being "a lasting incarnation of God's redeeming love for all humankind as originally signified and concretized in Jesus Christ." In the first circle we have the essentials noted above agreed to by the Lutherans. These are clear in the will of Christ. The second circle includes elements which have a clear connection with biblical revelation, e.g., the other four sacraments, papacy, and episcopacy. The third circle are reversible institutions which were willed by God for a time. There could be an institution which once expressed God's will, but in a later age, in a different culture, could be considered harmful. Some would place the Latin law of clerical celibacy (q.v.) in this category. A fourth circle takes in matters solely related to ecclesiastical law, where some choices are made among many other legitimate ones. These last are clearly reversible, e.g., norms for papal elections, which have been modified several times in this century.

The ecumenical convergence on *ius divinum* about the primacy found in the Anglican-Roman Catholic International Commission (ARCIC) *Final Report*[11] (v. ANGLICAN ECUMENISM) was found to be inadequate in the 1992 Vatican response which sought a more literal adherence to Vatican I.[12] The response would seem to reflect a position that only the past formulations of Catholic doctrines can assure their secure transmission.[13] It renders the ongoing study of ius divinum all the more urgent in the contemporary Church, and not only for its ecumenical significance.

[1]Y. Congar, "Jus divinum," RDroitC 28/2 (1978) 108–122; M.A. Fahey, "Continuity in the Church amid Structural Changes," TS 35 (1974) 315–440.   [2]K. Rahner, "Reflection on the Concept of 'Ius divinum' in Catholic Thought," ThInvest 5:219-243.   [3]See DS 3064/ND 830.   [4]See A. Dulles, "Ius divinum as an Ecumenical Problem," TS 38 (1977) 681–708 = *A Church to Believe In: Discipleship and the Dynamics of Freedom* (New York: Crossroad, 1983) 80–102 at 87–88; G.A. Lindbeck, "Papacy and *Ius divinum*: A Lutheran View," in P.C. Empie and T.A. Murphy, *Papal Primacy and the Universal Church*. Lutherans and Roman Catholics in Dialogue 5 (Minneapolis: Augsburg, 1974) 193–208.   [5]Art. cit. (n. 2).   [6]"Dimensions of *Jus divinum* in Roman Catholic Theology," TS 34 (1973) 227–250.   [7]Cf. E. Schillebeeckx, "The Catholic Understanding of Office in the Church," TS 30 (1969) 567–587.   [8]Lindbeck (n. 4) 203–207; Dulles (n. 4) 92.   [9]Art. cit. (n. 4). See also T.I. Jiménez Urresti, "El 'jus divinum': noción, grados y lógica de su estudio," Salm 3 (1992) 35–77.   [10]See P. Fransen, "Criticism of Some Basic Theological Notions in Matters of Church Authority," JEcuSt 19 (1982) 48–74 at 59–68; H. Wagner, "Zur Problematik des 'ius divinum'," TrierTZ 88 (1979) 132–144.   [11]"Authority in the Church I," n. 24b; "Elucidations," n. 8; and "Authority in the Church II," n. 11 (London: SPCK—CTS, 1982), 64–65, 76–77, 86. See A. van der Helm, "Le droit divin dans une perspective oecuménique," PraxJurRel 3 (1986) 225–231.   [12]DS 3058/ND 824—CathIntern 3 (1992) 128.   [13]See F.A. Sullivan, "The Vatican Response to ARCIC—I," OneChr 28 (1992) 223–231 = Greg 73 (1992) 489–498.

# J

## JEDIN, Hubert (1900–1980)

Hubert Jedin is arguably the most important Catholic Church historian of the 20th century, though not perhaps sufficiently appreciated in the English–speaking world.[1] After studies in various German universities, he spent four years perfecting his professionalism working in the secret archives of the Vatican. From the time of his doctoral thesis on Johannes Cochlaeus (1479–1552) he showed his interest in the 15th and 16th centuries. He brought a new standard of accuracy, objectivity, and empathy into Reformation studies. His great work was his history of the Council of Trent, in five volumes, only the first two of which have been translated into English, though all are in Italian.[2]

Not less monumental was his edition of the speeches, diaries, and letters relating to the Council of Trent.[3] His best-known work in English is the ten-volume history of the Church which he edited—J.P. Dolan being the editor of the English edition.[4] His view of Church history is to be found in the first volume of this series.[5] He sees Church history as an ecclesiastical discipline which, while demanding the highest critical standards, is also, and ultimately, an exposition of salvation history.[6]

---

[1]Bibliog. by R. Samulski, in E. Iserloh and K. Repgen eds., *Reformata reformanda*. FS H. Jedin (Münster en W.: Aschendorff, 1965) 2:655-715 supplemented "Bibliographie Hubert Jedin 1965–1976," AHC 8 (1976) 612–637. [2]*Geschichte des Konzils von Trient.* 5 vols. (Freiburg, 1949–1975)—Eng. trans. *A History of the Council of Trent.* 2 vols. (London, 1957, 1961)—Italian trans. *Storia del Concilio di Trento.* 4 vols. in 5 tomes (Brescia, [2]1973–1981). [3]*Tridentinum. Diariorum, actorum, epistolarum, tratatuum, nova collectio* (Freiburg, 1901– ). [4]*History of the Church.* 10 vols. (New York: Crossroad—London: Burns & Oates, 1980–1981)—German, in 8 vols. [5]"General Introduction to Church History," Jedin-Dolan 1:1-47. [6]J.P. Dolan, in Jedin-Dolan 10:xv-xvi; G. Alberigo, "Hubert Jedin," CrNSt 1 (1980) 273–278.

## JERUSALEM—ZION

In a political master-stroke, King David chose a formerly Jebusite neutral city as his royal residence when, in 1000 B.C.E., he became conjointly king of Israel and Judah; Jerusalem[1] is just south of the border between the two regions. By the transfer of the ark of the covenant, the city obtained a religious significance it was not to lose. The building of the first temple, by Solomon, enhanced its symbolism: it was the place where God dwelt and was worshiped (V. TEMPLE). Zion/Sion may originally have been a refugee camp north of the Temple, facing Assyria.[2]

Zion, and the associated "Daughter of Zion" soon became a sacral name for Jerusalem, often interchangeable with it; it was also used in preference to "Jerusalem" in messianic contexts (Isa 60:14). Four motifs emerge which are found in germinal form in Ps 68: the divine mountain (15-16); the conquest of chaos (21-23); the defeat of the nations (11-14); the pilgrimage of the nations (30-32).

By the time of the NT the concept of Zion as the mother of many nations had become firmly established (see Isa 54:1 cited in Gal 4:26). Luke records the messianic expectations of Simeon and Anna as the "consolation of Israel" and the "redemption of Jerusalem" (2:25-38).

Though the public ministry of Jesus was mostly in Galilee, its true center was Jerusalem. Luke's Gospel is a massive *inclusio* of Jerusalem: its temple is at the beginning and the end (1:8–24:53). He describes a preliminary mission in Galilee followed by a journey to Jerusalem (9:51), carefully punctuated by references to the city (9:53; 10:1 . . .).[3]

The apostles are to remain in Jerusalem after Jesus' departure (Luke 24:49; Acts 1:4), from whence their mission will begin (Luke 24:47; Acts 1:8) after they are baptized with the Holy Spirit (Acts 1:5). For several decades Jerusalem retained its importance as the Mother Church, at least up to the stage represented by Acts 15 (ca. 49 C.E.). Paul, who visited Jerusalem for some authentication of his ministry (Gal 2:1-2, 6–9), saw his preaching as coming from Jerusalem (*apo Ierousalêm*—Rom 15:19).

Already in the early Letter to the Galatians there is a spiritual/heavenly Jerusalem of freedom which is contrasted with the material city marked by slavery (4:21-31). In Hebrews, Mount Zion, the heavenly Jerusalem, is not only the goal of the pilgrim people (13:14) but is already somehow attained (12:22-24). In Revelation the new Jerusalem is presented as an eschatological hope (3:12; 21:2, 10; 22:1-5).

Apart from an incidental reference in the *Letter of Barnabas,* where Zion is given a Christological sense (6:2), and one in the *First Letter of Clement,* in an exhortatory context (41:2), we have to wait for Origen (q.v.) for significant development of the theme of Jerusalem/Zion. The true Jerusalem is now the Church built up of living stones.[4] It becomes a major theme in St. Ambrose.[5] Augustine interprets Jerusalem sometimes as earthly, sometimes as heavenly, sometimes as both.[6] In time various allegorical interpretations were given, some ecclesiological, some spiritual.[7] In the present liturgy the future perfection of the Church is described as "the heavenly city of Jerusalem."[8]

The theme of Jerusalem appears several times in Vatican II, without any very significant accent: the example of the primitive Church of Jerusalem (PO 21); it did not know the time of its visitation (NA 4; see Luke 19:44); the liturgy anticipates the celebration of the Holy City of Jerusalem, towards which the Church is on pilgrimage (SC 8); the heavenly city (LG 51).

In medieval times the crusades (q.v.) saw as their special aim the freedom of Jerusalem. In modern times it remains a city with particular religious significance for Jews, Christians, and Muslims.

---

[1]G. Fohrer and E. Lohr, "Siôn, Ierousalêm etc.," TDNT 7:292-338. [2]H. Cazelles, "Fille de Sion et théologie mariale dans la Bible," ÉtMar 21 (1964) 51–71. [3]W.C. Robinson, "The Theological Context for Interpreting Luke's Travel Narrative (9:51ff)," JBL 79 (1960) 20–31. [4]*Hom. in Jer.* 9:2—PG 13:349-351. [5]É. Lamirande, "Le thème de la Jérusalem céleste chez saint Ambroise," RevÉtAug 29 (1983) 209–232; idem, "Jerusalem Céleste," DSpir 8:944-958. [6]*De civ. Dei* 17:3 CCL 48:553-554; see É. Lamirande, *L'Église céleste selon saint Augustin* (Paris, 1963). [7]F. Cocchini, "Jerusalem," EncycEarCh 1:433. [8]Preface of the Dedication of a Church.

## JEWS, THE CHURCH AND THE

The history of the Church in relationship to the Jews[1] is not a glorious one. But it is not such an unrelieved dark picture as some Jewish historians would suggest.

Within the NT period, and immediately subsequent to it, there were problems between Church and synagogue; in particular there was tension with nascent Christianity about the attitude to Judaic prescriptions (v. NEW TESTAMENT ECCLESIOLOGY).[2] The continuance of the Jewish religion after the NT time was a stumbling block for some writers in the patristic period. Some of the Fathers evolved the notion of Jewish servitude *(servitus Iudaeorum)* based on Gen 25:23: like Esau, the Jewish people forfeited its inheritance and must serve the younger Christian people prefigured in Isaac. Originally this servitude was seen in spiritual terms, but in time it became legal and operative in social and political areas.

"Anti-Semitism" as a word was coined by Wilhelm Marr in 1829; the reality, however, was present in the Middle Ages.[3] One should distinguish between anti-Judaism among Christians on religious grounds (e.g., that the Jews are all guilty of rejecting and crucifying Christ) and anti-Semitism on racial grounds (contempt or hatred for the Jews as a people), which was common enough prior to the advent of Christianity, and of which many Christians no doubt have been guilty. The fact that Hitler persecuted Jews who had become Christian, like Bl. Edith Stein, shows that his was a racial anti-Semitism, as indeed was the Holocaust.

In the Middle Ages we find persecution of the Jews in connection with the Crusades: they were seen as "enemies of Christ" to be liquidated before the armies moved on to the Holy Land.[4] At the same time some bishops, emperors, and popes protected them. But this protection was often in return for a tax to be paid by the Jews. Protection of Jews became a source of revenue for Christian rulers and bishops. From the 13th century we find pogroms in various parts of Europe, usually on the pretext that Jews had desecrated the Sacred Host and committed ritual murder of children. The Black Death (1348–1349) was attributed to the poisoning of wells by Jews. The Fourth Lateran Council (1215—q.v.) promulgated four canons against Jews which were more extensive than those of Lateran III (q.v.):[5] they were forbidden to practice usury; they had to wear a special dress; they were prevented from holding public office; upon conversion to Christianity, they could not maintain their old rite.[6] It can be argued that these prescriptions were pastoral measures to protect simple people who would not understand that the Jews were of a different religion.[7] In its 19th session (7 Sept. 1434) the Council of Basle (q.v.) passed some very restrictive legislation against Jews and infidels (Muslims?): they were compelled to listen to sermons several times a year; Christians could not be their servants; most social intercourse with Jews was forbidden, and they were barred from public office and from academic degrees; they were to wear a distinguishing garment, and were to live physically apart from

Christians; on their conversion, however, their property was safeguarded.[8] Otherwise their property was in many places routinely confiscated, and they were not allowed to trade, so that money-lending was one of the few occupations open to them. Forced baptisms were frequent; this was often through moral pressure, as in Spain, when they were given the choice between baptism and exile. The expulsion of Jews from whole cities and states became common in the 15th century, e.g., Freibourg (1401 and 1424), Trier (1418), Spain (1492). Yet during that period several popes gave them their protection, and renewed the bull *Sicut Iudaeis,* which assured them of religious freedom and forbade compulsory baptism.[9] But one can say that at best Jews were tolerated. There were two main grounds in medieval times for what was anti-Judaism rather than anti-Semitism: Jews were considered to be in bad faith since they did not accept Christianity; they were perceived as guilty of deicide, and the self-imposed curse of Matt 27:25 was seen as still operative. Jews converting to Christianity were objects of the Inquisition's (q.v.) invigilation; in many cases they were suspected of continuing Jewish practices, which for the Inquisition was a sign of heresy or apostasy—the Inquisition has no jurisdiction over the unbaptized.

Medieval ideas were carried forward to the Reformation, e.g., in Luther.[10] Anti-Judaism combined with some anti-Semitism continued right down to the 19th and 20th centuries. The Church's attitude has been described by the Jewish historian Jules Isaac—not without some justice—as *l'enseignement du mépris,* i.e., the teaching of contempt. Anti-Semitism culminated in the Holocaust (Hebrew *Shoah* = catastrophe) of 1938–1945, when six million Jews were exterminated by the Nazis.

Vatican II spoke very positively about Jews in its Constitution on the Church (LG 16): "In the first place, there is that people from whom Christ was born according to the flesh (see Rom 9:4-5), a people according to their election most dear because of their ancestors: for God never goes back on his gifts and his calling (see Rom 11:28-29)." The council also proposed a statement on Jews as part of the decree on ecumenism. Fears of bishops from Islamic countries led to some compromise in the finally approved text which is to be found in the Declaration on Non-Christian Religions *(Nostra aetate).* Its fifteen sentences indicate an irreversible turning point in the Catholic perception of Judaism: it recalls common roots in the covenant; God's gift and call to them is without regret; the death of Jesus cannot be ascribed indiscriminately to all Jews living at the time or to those who came after; Scripture does not support the idea that the Jews were accursed; finally, the Church "deplores feelings of hatred, persecutions and demon-

strations of anti-Semitism directed against the Jews at whatever time and by whomsoever" (NA 4).[11]

In the period immediately before and after Vatican II, there have been important statements and meetings involving the Churches and the Jews.[12] Dialogue is ongoing.[13] In the Catholic Church the Commission for Religious Relations with the Jews was set up in 1974. It produced two important documents: *Guidelines and Suggestions for Implementing the Conciliar Declaration "Nostra aetate" (No. 4)*—1974 (G.) and *Notes on the Correct Way to Present Jews and Judaism in Preaching and Catechesis in the Roman Catholic Church*—1985 (N.).[14]

These two documents (G. and N.) deal with most of the key issues and give positions which build on, and advance, Vatican II even if they do not fully satisfy Jewish critics.[15] The documents call for dialogue: "Dialogue presupposes that each side wishes to know the other, and wishes to increase and deepen a knowledge of the other" (G. I; N. VI:27). The Old Testament retains its own perpetual value (G. II; N. II:3); typology is a way of understanding the relation between the two covenants, but it is limited and not the only way (N. II:1-11). God speaks in the old and new Covenants. In particular the OT must not be seen as constituting a religion only of justice, fear, and legalism, with no appeal to love of God and neighbor (G. III). The Jewishness of Jesus[16] must be stressed (G. III; N. III:12-15). The NT picture of the Pharisees is not completely negative, and it is significant that they are not mentioned in connection with the Passion (N. III:16-19). The history of Judaism did not end with the destruction of Jerusalem "but rather went on to develop a religious tradition. And although we believe that the importance and meaning of that tradition were deeply affected by the coming of Christ, it is still nonetheless rich in religious values" (G. III; N. I:3). Both Jews and Christians have eschatological expectations (G. III). Christians are seen as grafted onto the earlier Covenant (G. conclusion). Some other important points are made in both documents. There is a danger from anti-Semitism "which is always ready to reappear under different guises" (N. I:8; G. preamble). In particular, the term "the Jews" in the NT often means "leaders of the Jews" or "adversaries of Jesus" (G. II, note; N. IV:21).[17] With reference to the State of Israel, "Christians are invited to understand this religious attachment which finds its roots in biblical tradition, without however making their own any particular religious interpretation of this relationship" (N. 25). We must see the continuance of the independent faith community of Judaism as "accompanied by continuous spiritual fecundity, in the rabbinical period, in the Middle Ages, and in modern times" (N. VI:25). The *Notes,* however, state that "Church and Judaism cannot then be seen as two parallel ways of salvation and the Church must witness to Christ as the Redeemer" (N. 1:7). The key theological issue remains that of understanding the meaning of Judaism.[18] Of special significance must be the tortured reflection of Paul in Romans 9–11.[19] Much further study has to be done on the notion of covenant, and in particular whether we ought to speak of one covenant or more.[20] It must be admitted, however, that the notion of covenant does not have an equal resonance in Jewish theology compared with Christian thought.

In dialogue with Jews, Catholics need to be sensitive to the deep Jewish feelings about the Holocaust, which is seen by many Jews as an instance of the Churches having lost moral credibility (v. PIUS XII). The Holocaust questions Jewish faith at its deepest level.[21] It raises questions for Christian theologians too,[22] especially in the areas of Christology and salvation history. Second, while avoiding biblical fundamentalism, Christians must try to understand the Jewish attachment to the State of Israel, which for many is a religious matter and linked with fears from the past, notably the Holocaust and earlier anti-Semitism. Finally, though some would suggest that much further advance in dialogue is unlikely, a more open approach would suggest that true dialogue with Judaism is yet in its early stages. Three areas, as yet rather peripheral in the dialogue, may become more significant in the years ahead: liberation,[23] and spirituality;[24] the Messianic or "Christian Jews" movement.[25] In all dialogue it must be remembered that modern Judaism is a very complex reality, with subtle differences not adequately covered by the usual categories of Orthodox, Conservative, and Reform; the emergence of a secular Judaism is a further complicating factor.[26]

[1]P. Johnson, *A History of the Jews* (London: Weidenfeld & Nicholson, 1987); W.D. Davies and L. Finkelstein, *The Cambridge History of Judaism*. 4 vols. (Cambridge: UP, 1984); H. Küng, *Judaism* (London: SCM, 1992); J. Kaplan, ed., *International Bibliography of Jewish History and Thought* (Jerusalem: Hebrew University, 1984); J. Limburg, *Judaism: An Introduction for Christians* (Minneapolis: Augsburg, 1987); J. Neusner, *Torah through the Ages: A Short History of Judaism* (London: SCM—Philadelphia: Trinity, 1990); E.D. Starkey, *Judaism and Christianity: A Guide to the Reference Literature. Reference Sources in the Humanities* (Englewood, Colo.: Libraries Unlimited, 1991); cf. Conc 8/10 (1976); JES 14 (1977) 522–672; 25 (1988) 22–73; LumièreV 38/196 (1990) 2–137; GkOrTR 22 (1977) 6–113. [2]*Anti-Judaism in Early Christianity.* Vol. 1 ed. P. Richardson and D. Granskou; Vol. 2 ed. S.G. Wilson. Studies in Christianity and Early Judaism 2 (Waterloo, Ont.: Laurier UP, 1986)—cf. Bijd 49 (1988) 426–434. See D.R. Bourquin, *A First Century Palestinian Judaism: A Bibliography of Works in English.* Studies in Judaica and the Holocaust 8 (San Bernardino Calif.: Borgo, 1990). [3]E. Iserloh, in Jedin-Dolan 4:603-613; G.I. Langmuir, *Toward a Definition of Antisemitism* (Berkeley: University of California, 1991); B. Litvinoff, *The Burning Bush: Anti-Semitism and World History* (London: Collins, 1988); J.E. Monti, *Who Do You Say that I Am? The Christian Understanding of Christ and Antisemitism* (Ramsey: Paulist, 1984); M. Saperstein, *Moments of Crisis in Jewish-*

*Christian Relations* (London: SCM—Philadelphia: Trinity, 1989). Radical but influential is R. Ruether, *Faith and Fratricide* (New York: Seabury—Crossroad, 1979). Cf. J. Katz, "L'antisémitisme: un point de vue juif," Istina 36(1991) 231–236 with J. Dujardin, "L'antisémitisme: un point de vue chrétien," ibid., 237–250. [4]B. Blumenkranz, "Relations Between Jews and Christians in the Eleventh Century," Conc 130 (1979) 40–48. [5]Can. 26—Tanner 1:223-224. [6]Can. 67–70—Tanner 1:265-267. [7]H. Wolter, in Jedin-Dolan 4:172. [8]Tanner 1:483-485. [9]S. Simonsohn, *The Apostolic See and the Jews: Documents 492–1404.* Studies and Texts 94 (Toronto: Pont. Institute Medieval Studies, 1988). [10]G. Rupp, "Martin Luther and the Jews," NedTTs 31 (1977) 121–135; H.O. Oberman, "Luthers Beziehungen zu den Juden: Ahnen und Geahndete," in H. Junghams, ed., *Leben und Werk Martin Luthers.* 2 vols. (Göttingen: Vanderhoek & Ruprecht, 1981) 1:519-530; 2:894-904. See J.H. Robinson, *John Calvin and the Jews.* American University Studies VII/123 (New York-Bern: Lang, 1992). [11]A. Bea, *The Church and the Jewish People: A Commentary on the 2nd Vatican Council's Declaration on the Relation of the Church to Non-Christian Religions* (London: Chapman, 1966). [12]*The Theology of the Churches and the Jewish People: Statements by the World Council of Churches and Its Member Churches* (Geneva: WCC, 1988); H. Croner, ed., *Stepping Stones to Further Jewish-Christian Relations.* Stimulus Books (Mahwah: Paulist, 1977); idem, *More Stepping Stones to Jewish-Christian Relations.* Stimulus Books (New York: Paulist, 1985); E.J. Fisher et al., eds., *Twenty Years of Jewish-Catholic Relations* (New York—Mahwah: Paulist, 1986); L. Klenicki and G. Wigoder, eds., *A Dictionary of the Jewish-Christian Dialogue.* Stimulus Books (New York: Paulist, 1984); M. Shermis, *Jewish-Christian Relations: An Annotated Bibliography and Resource Guide* (Bloomington, Ind.: Indianapolis UP, 1988); G. Wigoder, *Jewish-Christian Relations Since the Second World War* (Manchester: UP, 1988). [13]N. Ben Chorin, "'Nostra aetate' venticinque anni dopo: Valutazione ebraica," Ambros 67 (1991) 529–542 with P.F. Fumagalli, "Valutazione cattolica," ibid., 543–550; M. Braybrooke, *Time to Meet: Towards a Deeper Relationship Between Jews and Christians* (London: SCM—Philadelphia: Trinity, 1990); E.J. Fisher, "Catholics and Jews: Face to Face," Pacifica 4 (1991) 62–75; S.M. Katunarich, "A proposto del dialogo tra ebrei e christiani," CivCatt 138 (1987) 4:249-259; N. Lohfink, *The Covenant Never Revoked: Biblical Reflections on Christian Jewish Dialogue* (New York—Mahwah: Paulist, 1991); D. Novak, *Jewish-Christian Dialogue: A Jewish Justification* (Oxford: UP, 1990); G. Riegner, "Commemoration of the Twenty-fifth Anniversary of *Nostra aetate*: Rome 5 Dec. 1990," ChristJewRel 24 (1991) 36–45; N. Solomon, "The Context of the Jewish-Christian Dialogue," ChristJewRel 24 (1991) 54–75. [14]*Fifteen Years of Catholic-Jewish Dialogue 1970–1985* (Vatican, 1988) 293–298, 306–314. See F. Mussner, "Catholic-Jewish Dialogue Since 1945: Survey and Observations," *Immanuel* 24–25 (1990) 280–291; J. Neusner, "There Has Never Been a Judeo-Christian Dialogue—But There Can Be One," CrossC 42 (1992–1993) 3–24. [15]L. Klenicki, ed., *Towards a Theological Encounter: Jewish Understandings of Christianity.* Stimulus Books (Mahwah: Paulist, 1991); J.T. Pawlikowski, *What Are They Saying About Christian-Jewish Relations?* (New York—Ramsey: Paulist, 1980); idem, *Christ in the Light of the Christian-Jewish Dialogue.* Stimulus Books (New York—Ramsey, 1982). [16]J.P. Meier, *A Marginal Jew: Rethinking the Historical Jesus. Vol. 1—The Roots of the Problem and the Person.* The Anchor Bible Reference Library (Garden City, N.Y.: Doubleday, 1991). [17]M.J. Cook, "The Gospel of John and the Jews," RExp 84 (1987) 259–272; T.M. Dowell, "Jews and Christians in Conflict: Why the Fourth Gospel Changed the Synoptic Tradition," LouvSt 15 (1990) 19–37; P.F. Kaufman, "Anti-Semitism in the New Testament: The Witness of the Beloved Disciple," Worship 63 (1989) 386–401; F. Mussner, "Die Juden im Neuen Testament," BLtg 55 (1982) 4–14;

W. Pratscher, "Die Juden im Johannesevangelium," Bltg 59 (1986) 177–185; A. Vanhoye, "Les juifs selon les Actes des Apôtres et les épîtres du Nouveau Testament," Bib 72 (1991) 70–89; U.C. von Wahlde, "The Johannine 'Jews': A Critical Survey," NTS 28 (1982) 33–60. [18]E. Bianchi, "Israele e la chiesa," CrNSt 10 (1989) 77–106; K. Hruby, "L'aspetto teologico del giudaismo attuale," Communio 10 (1973) [600–611] 33–44; M. Remaud, "Réflexions sur la permanence d'Israël," NRT 97 (1977) 507–517. [19]See commentaries and M.A. Getty, "Paul and the Salvation of Israel: A Perspective on Romans 9–11," CBQ 50 (1988) 456–469; S. Lyonnet, *Le rôle d'Israel dans l'histoire du salut selon Rom 9–11.* Analecta biblica 120 (Rome: Biblicum, 1977). B.W. Longenecker, "Different Answers to Different Situations: Israel, the Gentiles and Salvation History in Romans 9–11," JStNT J. Radermakers and J.-P. Sonnet, "Israël et L'Église," NRT 107 (1985) 675–697; G.S. Worgul, "Romans 9–11 and Ecclesiology," BibTB 7 (1977) 99–109. [20]G. D'Costa, "One Covenant or Many Covenants? Towards a Theology of Christian-Jewish Relations," JES 27 (1991) 441–452. [21]E.Z. Charry, "Jewish Holocaust Theology: An Assessment," JES 18 (1981) 128–139; D. Cohn-Sherbok, *Holocaust Theology* (London: Marshall Pickering, 1990—San Francisco: Harper, 1991); E. Fleischner, "A Select Annotated Bibliography on the Holocaust," Horizons 4 (1977) 61–84; J.M. Grondelski, "What is the Holocaust?," NBlackfr 72 (1991) 482–488; S.T. Katz, *Post-Holocaust Dialogues: Critical Studies in Modern Jewish Thought* (New York: UP, 1983); M. Oppenheim, "Can We Still Stay with Him: Two Jewish Theologians Confront the Holocaust," StRel 16 (1987) 405–419; R. Rubinstein and J. Roth, *Approaches to Auschwitz* (London: SCM, 1988); G. Wigoder, "La pensée juive après l'Holocauste," Istina 36 (1991) 274–290. [22]H.J. Carjas, *Shadows of Auschwitz: A Critical Response to the Holocaust* (New York: Crossroad, 1991). C. De Celles, "The Importance of Dialoguing with the Holocaust," AmBenR 33 (1982) 75–101; E. Fleischner, ed., *Auschwitz: Beginning of a New Era?* (New York: Ktav, 1977); eadem, "A Select Annotated Bibliography on the Holocaust," Horizons 4 (1977) 61–84; R.S. Gottlieb, ed., *Thinking the Unthinkable: Meanings of the Holocaust* (Mahwah: Paulist, 1990); I. Wollaston, "Bibliography: Christian Responses to the Holocaust," ModChm 30 (1988–1989) 34–39. [23]D. Cohn-Sherbok, "Judaism and Liberation Theology," ModT 3 (1986) 1–19 = TDig 34 (1987) 127–131; M.H. Ellis, *Toward a Jewish Theology of Liberation* (Maryknoll: Orbis, 1987). [24]D.R. Blumenthal, *God at the Center: Meditations on Jewish Spirituality* (San Francisco, Harper & Row, 1988); T. Zahavy, *Studies in Jewish Prayers.* Studies in Judaism (Lanham, Md.—New York—London: UP of America, 1990); G. Zananiri, "Spiritual Semitism," NBlackfr 72 (1991) 508–517. [25]F. Rossi de Gasperis, "Un nuovo giudeo-cristianesimo e la sua possibile rilevanza ecclesiale," CrNSt 12 (1991) 119–162. [26]E.B. Borowitz, "The Postsecular Situation of Jewish Theology," TS 31 (1970) 460–475.

## JOACHIM OF FIORE/FLORA (ca. 1132–1202)

Little accurate information about Joachim is available, though there are many legends.[1] After a conversion experience he entered the Cistercian Order and was appointed abbot against his will. He resigned a few years later and subsequently founded a monastery of his own at Fiore in Calabria. Before he died he asked his disciples to seek approval for his works and to abide by the decision of the Church.

Joachim opposed the Trinitarian theology of Peter Lombard, taking a more Eastern line. His apocalyptic works treat of three ages of history corresponding to the three divine Persons, variously described, e.g.: the age of the laity in the OT *(ordo conjugatorum),* or the age of the Father; the age of the clergy *(ordo clericorum),* from the time of Jesus; the age of monks or contemplatives *(ordo monachorum/contemplantium),* which was expected after forty-two generations, and would be the age of the Spirit, beginning about 1260. This last age would initiate the time of the *Ecclesia spiritualis,* when religious orders would encompass the world. In succeeding centuries extremist groups saw themselves as this "spiritual Church."

Some of Joachim's Trinitarian positions were condemned by the Fourth Lateran Council (q.v.).[2] There has been some reinterpretation and rehabilitation of Joachim in the substantial modern studies devoted to him.[3]

---

[1]Main works OxDCC 740. [2]Tanner 1:231-233/DS 803–807/ND 317–320. [3]E. Benz, "Joachim-Studien," ZKG 50 (1931) 24–111; 51 (1932) 415–455; 53 (1934) 52–116; M.W. Bloomfield, "Joachim of Flora: A Critical Study," Trad 13 (1957) 259–311; idem, "Recent Scholarship on Joachim of Fiore and his Influence," in A. Williams, ed., *Prophecy and Millenarism.* FS Marjorie Reeves (Harlow UK: Longmans, 1980); Congar, Augustin 209–214; idem, *I Believe in the Holy Spirit.* 3 vols. (New York: Seabury—London: Chapman, 1983) 1:126-137; A. Crocco, *Gioacchino da Fiore* (Naples, 1960); H. de Lubac, *Exégèse médiévale.* Théologie 42 (Paris: Aubier, 1961) 2/1:437-558; G. di Napoli, "La teologia trinitaria di Gioacchino da Fiore," Divinitas 23 (1979) 281–312; idem, "L'ecclesiologia di Gioacchino da Fiore," DoctCom 32 (1979) 302–326; H. Grundmann, *Neue Forschungen über Joachim von Fiore* (Marburg, 1950); B. Hirsch-Reich, "Eine Bibliographie über Joachim von Fiore und dessen Nachwirkung (= F. Rosso *Bibliografia Gioachimita* [Florence, 1954])," RechTAncMéd 24 (1957) 27–44; B. McGinn, *The Calabrian Abbot: Joachim of Fiore in the History of Western Thought* (New York: Macmillan, 1985). M.E. Reeves, *The Influence of Prophecy in the Later Middle Ages: A Study in Joachimism* (Oxford, 1969).

## JOHN XXIII, Pope (1958–1963)

Angelo Giuseppe Roncalli was born of poor farming parents in 1881 near Bergamo in Sotto il Monte.[1] After doctoral studies in Rome, he became secretary of the bishop of Bergamo and lectured in Church history in the seminary there. Pius XI, who as Achille Ratti had been a friend and fellow historian, brought him into the diplomatic service first in 1925 as apostolic visitor and later apostolic delegate to Bulgaria. From 1934 Roncalli held the same office for Turkey and Greece. He enjoyed friendly relations with both politicians and Orthodox leaders. He was transferred as nuncio to Paris in 1944, and again showed himself an able diplomat during complex negotiations in postwar France. He was Vatican permanent observer at the United Nations Educational, Scientific, and Cultural Organization (UNESCO) from 1952. He became cardinal and patriarch of Venice in 1953, where he was notable for his amicability and pastoral vigor.

He also completed there his five-volume work on St. Charles Borromeo, whom he had begun to study while in Bergamo.[2] Throughout his life he kept an occasional spiritual diary, later published posthumously, which is indispensable for any account of his inner life and vision of the Church.[3]

When nearly seventy-seven he was elected pope (1958). People saw him as an interim, caretaker pope; he would prove immediately to be nothing of the sort. In just over a year he had announced three notable projects: a Roman synod, an ecumenical council, and the revision of canon law.

He gave as an aim to Vatican II (q.v.) the much debated word *aggiornamento,* which has as a basic meaning "bringing up to date," but which for him had also the idea of inner renewal of the Church. In the preparations for the council he was continually frustrated by some conservatives who either did not want a council or wanted one according to their ideas. Gradually, with much diplomacy and great firmness, he succeeded in inaugurating the council on 11 October 1962. In his opening address, the much cited *Gaudet Mater Ecclesia,*[4] he made it clear that he did not want anathemas or condemnations or the prophets of doom, but renewal. He noted carefully that "one thing is the deposit of faith, that is, the truths which are contained in our revered doctrine; another is the form in which these are enunciated." The Latin text seems to have added to the pope's Italian, "retaining however the same meaning and significance *(eodem tamen sensu eademque sententia).*" He wished the council to further Christian unity. Though historians may vary in their interpretation of his moderate guidance of the first session of the council, it seems defensible to hold that he allowed it to find its own feet and to let its tensions emerge without seeking to control it. The council found its direction only in the second session (1963). But John XXIII was not alive to see it.

His main papal teaching consisted of five minor and three major encyclicals: *Ad Petri Cathedram,* an appeal for unity and peace, in which he used the celebrated phrase "separated brethren";[5] *Mater et magistra,* an updating and underscoring of the social teaching of Leo XIII and Pius IX,[6] and *Pacem in terris,* addressed to all humanity on human rights and peace, and marking a more open approach of the Vatican to the Eastern Bloc, the countries of Eastern Europe then under communist control.[7]

Much study remains to be done on the life, spirituality, and writings of John XXIII, especially of the years preceding his pontificate; a concordance of all his works will greatly assist scholars.[8]

The pontificate of John XXIII was marked not only by his obvious achievements noted above, but by a new style of papacy, characterized by a human warmth and jovial good humor, which was appreciated by all Christians and by people of other faiths, or none. The cause for his beatification opened at the earliest possible date after his death on 3 June 1963.

[1]A. and G. Alberigo, *Profezia nella fedeltà* (Brescia: Queriniana, 1978); G. Alberigo, ed., *Giovanni XXIII transizione del papato e della Chiesa* (Rome: Borla, 1988); L. Algisi, *John the Twenty-Third* (London and Westminster, Md., 1963); R. Bonnot, *Pope John XXIII: An Astute Pastoral Leader* (New York: Alba House, 1979); J. Grootaers, *I protagonisti del Vaticano II* (Milan: San Paolo, 1994) 11–47; P. Hebblethwaite, *John XXIII: Pope of the Council* (London: Chapman, 1984) but cf. critique A. Melloni, "Pope John XXIII: Open Questions for a Biography," CHRev 72 (1986) 51–67; E.E. Hales, *Pope John and His Revolution* (London and Garden City, N.Y., 1965). [2]*Gli atti della visita apostolica di San Carolo Borromeo a Bergamo (1575).* 2 vols in 5 tomes (Florence: Olschki, 1936–1957). [3]*Journal of a Soul: Pope John XXIII* (London: Chapman, revised ed. 1980); critical ed. A. Melloni, Bologna: Istituto per le Scienze Religiose, 1987). [4]ActaSyn 1/1:172. For drafts and questions of authenticity, see G. Alberigo and A. Melloni, "L'allocuzione *Gaudet Mater Ecclesia* (11 ottobre 1962)," in AA.VV. *Fede tradizione profezia: Studi su Giovanni XXIII e sul Vaticano II* (Brescia: Paideia, 1984) 187–283; F.A. Sullivan, Tablet 246/7904 (1 Feb. 1992) 139–140; cf. P. Hebblethwaite, "Le discours de Jean XXIII à l'ouverture de Vatican II," RechSR 71 (1983) 203–212. [5]29 June 1959—AAS 51 (1959) 497–531/Carlen 5:5-20. [6]15 May 1961—AAS 53 (1961) 401–464/Carlen 5:59-90. [7]11 April 1963—AAS 55 (1963) 257–304/Carlen 5:107-129. [8]Istituto di Scienze Religiose, Bologna; A. Melloni, "Corcordanza degli scritti di A.G. Roncalli/Giovanni XXIII," CrNSt 7 (1986) 353–360.

## JOHN PAUL I, Pope (1978)

Albino Luciani was born in a village near Belluno, Italy, in 1912.[1] His studies in Rome led to a doctorate (Gregorian University) on the theme of A. Rosmini (q.v.). He had a special interest in catechetics and had remarkable journalistic gifts. He became the patriarch of Venice in 1969, where his pastoral ministry was characterized both by support for ecumenism and anti-communism. His election to the papacy on 26 August 1978, at only the third ballot, indicated that the conclave wanted somebody of a different style to the curial Paul VI (q.v.). He died on 29 September, just thirty-three days after his election. Rumors about his having been murdered circulated for a time but can be completely discounted.[2]

One can only guess what sort of pope he might have been.[3] His choice of name indicated that he wanted to be in continuity with both John XXIII and Paul VI. One noticeable innovation was his installation as pope: he dispensed with a coronation, and was simply invested with a pallium as a sign of pastoral office. The choice of Luciani as a pope in a new mold paved the way for the election of a still more innovative successor, a Pole, Pope John Paul II (q.v.).

[1]P. Hebblethwaithe, *The Year of the Three Popes* (London: Collins, 1978). [2]J. Cornwell, *A Thief in the Night: The Mysterious Death of John Paul I* (London:Viking, 1989). [3]*See In memoriam tributes,* e.g., EspVie 88 (1978) 657–659; Bib 59 (1978) 462; ETL 54 (1978) 394–397; Greg 59 (1978) 659–600.

## JOHN PAUL II, Pope (1978– )

The first non-Italian pope since the Dutchman Hadrian VI (1522-1523), and the first Slav ever to hold the office, Karol Wojtyla was born near Krakow in 1920.[1] A student of Polish literature in the Jagiellonian University from 1938, he worked as a laborer during the German occupation, but from 1942 secretly studied for the priesthood. He was ordained in 1946, the same year that his first volume of poetry, *Song of the Hidden God,* was published. At the Angelicum University in Rome, he obtained a doctorate for a thesis on St. John of the Cross. Returning to Poland he studied philosophy, especially Buber and Marcel, and also Max Scheler, on whom he wrote a thesis. He lectured in ethics even after he became auxiliary bishop of Ombi in 1958. He became archbishop of Krakow in 1963 and cardinal in 1967. He took an active part in Vatican II both in the *aula* and in commissions. In Poland, among other works, he wrote a book on sexuality[2] and a volume on Vatican II, written to mediate the council to his diocese.[3]

In 1978 Karol Wojtyla was elected pope after the brief pontificate of John Paul I (q.v.). His choice of name was an indication of his desire for continuity with the Vatican II Church. It is notoriously difficult to evaluate a current papacy.[4] In the case of John Paul II, the problem is exacerbated by the enormous number of his speeches and writings since 1978;[5] there are over fifteen major documents, such as encyclicals and post-synodal exhortations. Full control of all of his teaching is probably beyond the ability of anyone who has not the leisure afforded writers of theses, and we do not yet have sufficient monographs. A few short, general paragraphs on matters relating to ecclesiology is all that is possible at this stage.

There is first of all the ecclesiological significance of his many journeys to all continents, and sometimes return visits to a country or area. These were almost sixty by 1994, and each has lasted from a few to about ten days. The enormous preparation for these visits, including learning from phonetics to speak to people in their own language, has surely taken from the time necessary to have proper supervision of the Vatican Curia (q.v.). But the Church must respect his pastoral decision to take the papacy to the world, and learn to live with whatever negative consequences result. In these visits his teaching tends to emphasize morality, especially the Church's teaching on divorce, contraception, and abortion. He speaks bluntly on human rights even in the very places in which there are abuses. He often refers to Vatican II, and seeks the implementation of what he sees as its message. Most notably in the public addresses and in all of his dialogue with bishops—in their own countries and during their *ad limina* visits to Rome—he calls for obedience to the magisterium (q.v.).

Second, his magisterium shows a deep conviction that the Church has a message for contemporary society. He stresses both the moral teaching of which the Church is a privileged guardian,[6] and issues of human rights, justice, peace; especially notable is the social encyclical *Sollicitudo rei socialis* (1987) on the twentieth anniversary of Paul VI's *Populorum progressio.*[7] He also is forthright on the need for humankind to have a spiritual dimension to life in worship and faith.

Third, though often different in language and style from previous popes, he is very much in the tradition of the previous magisterium. When he speaks on the council, he sometimes gives the impression of praising in particular those matters in which the council shows continuity with the past, rather than areas where the council was truly innovative.

Fourth, there are distinctive features in his presentation of Catholic faith and morals. His approach is often to begin with human experience, and is strongly personalist.[8] His own deep piety shows clearly in most of his utterances; his Marian devotion is well known. Of significance to ecclesiology is the Trinitarian dimension of his teaching, witnessed in his trilogy:[9] *Redemptor hominis* (1979—Christ), *Dives in misericordia* (1980—the Father), and *Dominum et Vivificantem* (1986—the Holy Spirit). He has given important teaching of laity (q.v.), women (q.v.), evangelization (q.v.), morality,[10] and most recently on ecumenism, with the encyclical *Ut unum sint* (1995).

Fifth, he has ensured that the new *Codes of Canon Law* for the Latin and Eastern Churches were brought to completion. He sponsored yet another reform of the Roman Curia (q.v.) in *Pastor bonus.*[11] He saw the completion of the new *Catechism of the Catholic Church,* desired by the 1985 synod of bishops.

Sixth, one should note the encouragement he has given to certain movements (q.v.), mostly of renewal in the Church. These, along with the secular institute Opus Dei (q.v.), are marked by their strong loyalty to the papacy.

Seventh, there has been a notable increase in the number of beatifications and canonizations of saints (q.v.) during this pontificate. The number of models of sanctity being proposed other than European Latin ones is striking, though these continue to be numerous. Along with this, he promotes popular religiosity (q.v.), especially Marian, in exhortations and visits to shrines.

Eighth, one can look at the Roman Curia, over which he presides, and to which he presumably gives direction: it has been rather slow to take advantage of the ecumenical vision of Vatican II; it has been harsh with dissenting theologians and bishops; it has with some notable exceptions chosen safe rather than inspiring men for bishops; it does not seem to have given much leadership in the area of inculturation (q.v.); it put a brake on dispensations from the priestly state for the first ten years of his pontificate; it gives an impression of fear and caution which reminds one of pontificates before that of John XXIII; many important documents from the various dicasteries seem to speak with a forked tongue, partly open and expansive, and partly defensive. The emphasis on communion (q.v.) in curial documents as a key to Vatican II is notable, but the notion is open to various interpretations, some more than others in harmony with the documents and spirit of the council.

Ninth, he has shown himself very concerned with ecumenism. From the 1990s his interest is more notably with Eastern Churches, particularly the Oriental Orthodox.

Future historians will evaluate the extent of his contribution to political changes in Eastern Europe in the late 1980s, especially in his native Poland.

Perhaps the most serious danger during this pontificate is the alienation and anger expressed at so many levels throughout the Church. Questions like priestly celibacy (q.v.), contraception, and, indeed, the ordination of women will still be around in the foreseeable future. There is an ominous anti-Romanism, which H.Urs von Balthasar (q.v.) has clearly articulated. The problems facing the Church as it approaches the third millennium are not of the pope's making; neither are they susceptible to a merely papal resolution. Fascinating insights into his theology and spirituality on these and a wide variety of topics emerge in his recently published collection of interviews.[12] Though we have all the advantages of a peripatetic pope, the solutions lie mostly at the level of local Churches, with of course papal guidance. One can make the mistake of expecting too much from one person, even from a pope as gifted and energetic as John Paul II.

[1]OxDictPopes 326-328; G. Blazynski, *Pope John Paul II: A Man from Krakow* (London: Sphere Books—Weidenfeld & Nicolson, 1979); M. Craig, *Man from a Far Country: A Portrait of John Paul II* (London: Hodder and Stoughton, 1979); P. Hebblethwaite, *Introducing John Paul II* (London: Collins Fount, 1982); A. Frossard in conversation with John Paul II, *Be Not Afraid!* (London: Bodley Head, 1984); M. Walsh, *John Paul II* (London: Harper Collins Publishers, 1994). [2]*Love and Responsibility* (Polish 1960, Eng. trans. 1981). [3]*Sources of Renewal: The Implementation of Vatican II* (Polish 1972; San Francisco: Harper & Row—London: Collins, 1980). [4]G. Alberigo, "Jean-Paul II: Dix ans de pontificat," Études 368/5 (1988) 669-682. [5]C. Semeraro, "Wojtyliensia: Contributo per una rassegna bibliografica sistematica sul pontificato di Giovanni Paolo II," Sales 44 (1982) 349-383. [6]R. Modras, "The Moral Philosophy of Pope John Paul II," TS 41 (1980) 683-697. [7]AAS 80 (1988) 513-586. See R. Preston, "Twenty Years After *Populorum Progressio:* An Appraisal of Pope John Paul's Commemorative Encyclical," Theology 92 (1989) 519-525. [8]J. Hellman, "John Paul II and the Personalist Movement," CrossC 30 (1980-81) 409-419; J.L. Llanes, "Antropocentrismo y teocentrismo en la enseñanza de Juan Pablo II," ScriptTPamp 20 (1988) 643-665; J.W. Gakowski, "The Place of Thomism in the Anthropology of K. Wojtyla," Ang 66 (1988) 181-194. [9]Ngindu Mushete, "La vision de l'Église dans *Redemptor hominis*," RAfrT 3 (1979) 231-236; C.M. Martini, "Il disegno delle tre grandi encicliche nel pontificato di Giovanni Paolo II," CivCatt 139 (1988) 4:114-127; J.R. Villar, "El magisterio de la Iglesia en la trilogía trinitaria de Juan Pablo II," ScriptTPamp 20 (1988) 727-743; A. Aranda, "Revelación trinitaria y misión de la Iglesia," ibid., 439-456. [10]Encyc. *Veritatis splendor*—AAS 85 (1993) 1134-1228. [11]AAS 80 (1988) 841-934. [12]John Paul II, *Crossing the Threshold of Hope* (London: Cape, 1994)—V. Messori, ed.

## JOSEPH, St.

Joseph[1] is presented in the NT as the husband of the Virgin Mary (Matt 1–2; Luke 1–2). His cult was slow to develop in the Western Church, probably because of rather flamboyant apocryphal literature such as *The History of Joseph the Carpenter* (4th–7th centuries). His feast was introduced into the Roman calendar in 1479. In 1729 Benedict XIII inserted his name into the Litany of the Saints. St. Joseph was declared "Patron of the Universal Church" by Pius IX in 1870. John XXIII entered his name into the Roman Canon (Eucharistic Prayer I) in 1962. There are two current liturgical celebrations: 19 March, a solemnity; 1 May, "St. Joseph the Worker," introduced by Pius XII in 1955 to counter civil celebrations of Worker's Day, especially in communist countries—it is now an optional memorial. His feast in the East is the Sunday after Christmas.

On the centenary of an encyclical on St. Joseph by Leo XIII,[2] Pope John Paul II in 1989 wrote a short apostolic exhortation "On the Person and Mission of Saint Joseph in the Life of Christ and of the Church."[3] In it he emphasized the genuine nature of the true marriage of Mary and Joseph and the reality of his being a husband, and spoke as well of his role in the Church.

[1]O'Carroll, Theotokos 206–209; F.L. Filas, NCE 7:1106-1113; OxDCC 757–758; L.J. Suenens, *Dear Saint Joseph* (Brussels: Ertvelde, 1994). [2]*Quamquam pluries*—ASS 22:65-69/Carlen 2:207-210. [3]*Redemptoris custos* (15 Aug. 1989)—AAS 82 (1990) 5–34.

## JOSEPHINISM

Called after Joseph II, emperor 1765–1790, Josephinism[1] took up, extended, and put into practice ideas of Febronius (v. FEBRONIANISM). The state was considered sovereign and the Church was to be subject to it. The main purpose of the Church was to serve the state: the state had the right to regulate ecclesiastical affairs, to reform abuses irrespective of Rome, to permit or not the publication of any papal statement, to acquire Church property, to control ecclesiastical studies, to disband what was of no use to the state, e.g., contemplative orders. An edict of toleration was issued in 1781, which granted all religious bodies the right to practice their beliefs without obstruction. Josephinist ideas continued to be operative in areas under Austrian control until Josephinism was abandoned by the young emperor Francis Joseph I in 1850. But its consequences continued much longer in various Church-State situations.

[1]Congar, Augustin 410–411; J. Felderer, "Der Kirchenbegriff in den Flugschriften des josephinischen Jahrzents," ZKT 75 (1953) 257–330; M.C. Goodwin, *The Papal Conflict with Josephinism* (New York, 1938); F. Maas, NCE 7:1118-1119; idem, *Der Josephinismus: Quellen zu seiner Geschichte in Österreich.* 5 vols. (Vienna—Munich, 1951–1961); H. Raab, in Jedin-Dolan 6:472-482.

## JOURNET, Cardinal Charles (1891–1975)

Charles Journet is perhaps best known for his unfinished large-scale work, *L'Église du Verbe Incarné.*[1] But in the 1930s he had already begun to consider the political implications of theology and Christianity; like the young Y. Congar (q.v.) at the time, he saw the need for the incarnation of Catholic faith in society;[2] his criticisms of Nazi atrocities were particularly striking.

Journet taught theology at Fribourg for many years, writing on a wide variety of theological topics. His work was greatly admired by Paul VI, who made him cardinal.[3] He was a representative of neo-Thomism. Despite remaining within its confines, and largely within the notion of the Church as perfect society (q.v.), he nevertheless wrote a work on the Church that was truly a dogmatic theology.[4]

He used the scholastic understanding of causality but developed a profoundly Trinitarian view of the Church. In his introduction to what would finally be a trilogy, he sets out his aim for four books. The first would deal with the efficient causality of the Church: its sacramental life and jurisdiction through the apostolic hierarchy.[5] The second was to study the nature of the Church in the image of Christ and humankind, consisting of a formal cause or spiritual element with a visible material cause; Christ was clearly the Church's exemplary cause; the uncreated formal cause of the Church was its soul, the Holy Spirit giving a created soul or Christified grace or love.[6] The third book was to treat the final cause of the Church which was ultimately the Divine Good, immanent, however, in the Church in its holiness. The final volume was to show how the Church emerged from Christ until its final glory.

Even though his work, for all its clarity and precision, is difficult to read in the post-Vatican II climate, its historical importance cannot be ignored. Journet was one of the theologians who made possible the council's achievement of presenting a truly theological vision of the Church, one which incomparably transcended the juridical and apologetic approach of the manuals. The manuals had little pneumatology, and they certainly did not, like Journet, speak of Mary as the heart of the Church.

[1]3 vols. (Paris: Desclée de Brouwer, 1941/[2]1952, 1962, 1969), abbreviated as *Théologie de l'Église.* Textes et études théologiques 10 (Paris: Desclée de Brouwer, [2]1958). Eng. trans. *The Church of the Word Incarnate: An Essay in Speculative Theology.* Vol. 1 (London: Sheed & Ward, 1954). [2]*La juridiction de l'Église dans la cité* (Paris, 1931); M.-A. Cabanne, "Charles Journet, un théologien qui s'engage dans la foi," NVet 60 (1985) 81–97. [3]J.P. Torell, "Paul VI et le Cardinal Journet. Aux sources d'une ecclésiologie," NVet 61 (1986) 161–174. [4]Congar, Augustin 464–465; see B. Mondin, *Le nuove ecclesiologie: Un'immagine attuale della chiesa* (Rome: Paoline, 1980) 28–44. [5]T.F. O'Meara, "The Teaching Office of Bishops in the Ecclesiology of Charles Journet," Jurist 49 (1989) 23–47; E. Lemière, "'Les grandeurs de hiérarchie au service des grandeurs de sainteté': Aux sources d'un principe ecclésiologique du cardinal Journet," NVet 66 (1991/94) 66–79; idem, "La hiérarchie de l'amour: En relisant l'ecclésiologie de Charles Journet," NVet 67 (1992) 193–201. [6] C. Morerod, "Le Saint-Esprit dans l'ecclésiologie de Charles Journet," NVet 66 (1991/94) 53–65.

## JURISDICTION

Jurisdiction is a term coming from classical Roman law, referring to a specific judicial authority of the praetor over civil trials. It came into Church usage at about the time of Gregory the Great (q.v.). In the Middle Ages it was used to distinguish an authority of the Church from its power of order and from the administration of temporal goods. Always a rather fluid concept,[1] jurisdiction gradually took on the meaning of the general governing power of the Church, though in the 19th century it was for a time contradistinguished from the power of magisterium.

In the 1917 canon law, jurisdiction was also called the power of governing, and it operated in the external forum and the internal forum or conscience, as well as in sacramental and non-sacramental areas (CIC 196; cf. 103 § 3). It was deemed "ordinary" when annexed to an office, "delegated" when committed to a person. The power of making laws or imposing precepts or penalties belonged to jurisdiction (CIC 2220 § 1). In practice the most common concern was about the jurisdiction necessary for the minister of the sacrament of penance (1917 law CIC 872–883), which was a power additional to priesthood, having to be sought from the ordinary (in a diocese a bishop, in clerical orders a provincial or higher superior).

Vatican I six times used the word "jurisdiction," and equivalents six more times in the crucial constitution *Pastor aeternus,* where the pope, like Peter, is declared to have jurisdiction over the whole Church.[2] Indeed the supreme apostolic authority includes the power of teaching, as the definition on infallibility shows.[3] It is urgent for ecumenical discussions to get behind the word "jurisdiction" to the core of the council's teaching.[4]

Pius XII went further in declaring that bishops receive their jurisdiction from the pope;[5] this position was reversed by Vatican II (LG 21). The concept of jurisdiction fits more comfortably with a view of the

Church as a perfect society (q.v.); it includes legislative, executive, and juridical (also penal) power.[6]

Vatican II used the word "jurisdiction" very sparingly, and not in doctrinally significant ways; it was deliberately dropped from the penultimate drafts of LG 28.[7] It is found, for example, in the section dealing with the general obligation of bishops to care for the whole Church (LG 23), in relation to the area in which pontificals can be appropriately worn (SC 130), and in the *Nota praevia* of LG chapter 3. The council is not altogether clear on the sharing by lay people in the sacred powers of the Church.[8]

The new *Code of Canon Law* uses the word "jurisdiction" only five times.[9] It employs instead *potestas regiminis* (power of governing [v. AUTHORITY]—CIC 129): "§ 1. In accord with the prescriptions of law, those who have received sacred orders are capable of the power of governance, which exists in the Church by divine institution and is also called the power of jurisdiction. § 2. Lay members of the Christian faithful can cooperate in the exercise of this power in accord with the norm of law." This last sentence is deliberately ambiguous: it may be interpreted as saying that the laity do, or do not, have the capacity for jurisdiction. In the former case it would be stating that the laity really have jurisdiction "when they cooperate"; in the latter case it would be asserting that jurisdiction comes only with the sacrament of orders. Elsewhere it states: "Only clerics can obtain those offices for whose exercise there is required the power of orders or the power of ecclesiastical governance" (CIC 274 § 1). This canon does not resolve the ambiguity.[10] The fact that laity can act as a judge might argue to some sharing in governance or jurisdiction.[11]

The ambiguity of the *Code,* here and elsewhere, ultimately arises from two different ecclesiologies operating in the law. There are many canons that fit in best with the view of the Church as perfect society (q.v.), which some people claim to find in LG 8, par. 1. Other canons seem to rest on an understanding of the Church in terms of communion, and the use, not always thorough, of the triple office of priest, prophet, and king (q.v.), which is central in the ecclesiology of the council.[12]

For the sacrament of penance or reconciliation (q.v.), the new law avoids the word "jurisdiction" of the 1917 *Code.* Instead it uses the word "faculty" (CIC 966–976).

In general it may be said that the current law and Church practice prefers the term "sacred power" *(potestas sacra),* but the wide content given to this term makes it difficult at several points to grasp the theoretical or ecclesiological underpinning of particular canons.

[1]G. Alberigo, "La juridiction: Remarques sur un terme ambigu," Irén 49 (1976) 167–180; see W. Aymans, "Oberhirtliche Gewalt,"

ArcKK 157/1 (1988) 3–38; J. Gaudemet, "Pouvoir d'ordre et de juridiction: Quelques repères historiques," AnnéeCan 39 (1985–1986) 83–98.    [2]Tanner 2:812, 814/DS 3053, 3064/ND 819, 830.    [3]Tanner 2:816/DS 3074/ND 839.    [4]See J.M.R. Tillard, *The Bishop of Rome. Theology and Life* 5 (Wilmington: Glazier—London: SPCK, 1983) 142–150.    [5]*Mystici corporis*—AAS 35 (1943) 211–212/Carlen 4:45/DS 3804.    [6]Alberigo (n. 1) 174; B. Gangoiti, "I termini ed it concetti di 'auctoritas, potestas, iurisdictio' in diritto canonico," Apoll 51 (1978) 562–576; R. Torfs, "Auctoritas—potestas—jurisdictio—facultas—officium—munus: A Conceptual Analysis," Conc 197 (1988) 63–73; G. Ghirlanda, "De natura, origine et exercitio potestatis regiminis iuxta novum Codicem," Periodica 74 (1985) 109–164.    [7]Alberigo-Magistretti 151.    [8]E. Kilmartin, "Lay Participation in the Apostolate of the Hierarchy," Jurist 41 (1981) 343–370.    [9]CIC 129, 1417 § 2, 1469 § 1 (twice), 1512 § 1.    [10]J.E. Lynch in Coriden CIC 202–204; A. Celeghin, "Sacra potestas: Quaestio post Conciliaris," Periodica 74 (1985) 165–225; J.H. Provost, "The Participation of the Laity in the Governance of the Church," StCan 11 (1983) 417–448.    [11]J.B. Beyer, "Iudex laicus vir vel mulier," Periodica 75 (1986) 29–60; cf. F.J. Urrutia, "Delegation of the Executive Power of Governance," StCan 19 (1985) 339–355.    [12]E. Corecco, "Aspects of the Reception of Vatican II in the Code of Canon Law," in G. Alberigo et al., eds., *The Reception of Vatican II* (Washington, D.C.: The Catholic University of America—Tunbridge Wells UK: Burns & Oates, 1987) 249–296.

## JUSTIN, St. (ca. 100–165)

Born in Palestine around 100 C.E., Justin was a son of Greek parents. He joined various schools of philosophy before becoming a Christian ca. 130. He went to Rome about 150 and held many disputations with Jews, pagans, and heretics. He had two concerns: the rise of persecution and the opportunities for the spread of the gospel. He belonged to the group of Apologetic Fathers (Greek *apologia* = "defense"). Commonly regarded as the first Christian philosopher, he sought to convince others of the truth which he himself had found in Christ and the Scriptures, and to defend Christianity from intellectual attack and its members from persecution. He died as a martyr, refusing to sacrifice to idols (165 C.E.).

Three works of Justin have come down to us: two *Apologies,* the second being probably an appendix or addition to the first—both were addressed to the emperor Antoninus Pius (138–161); the *Dialogue with Trypho,* a Jew.[1] These are very significant early witnesses for the history of theology. Some of the crucial areas are: creation; the relation of OT and NT; Christology; redemption through the Logos, incarnate through the Virgin Mary; millenarianism (q.v.); credal formulae;[2] emerging Trinitarian theology; relationship of philosophy with Christianity. There is a secondary bibliography on these and other aspects of his thought.[3]

From the point of view of ecclesiology, several themes are very important. Justin seems to indicate a primitive catechumenate (q.v.), and he describes in detail the rites of baptism and Eucharist—something that later on would have been forbidden in many places by the *disciplina arcani* (q.v.).[4] Though he notes that someone presides at the Eucharist, he does not give further information about that person, probably because such a matter would not concern the emperor whom he is addressing. Given the context in which he wrote, his silence about *presbuteroi/episkopoi* cannot be an argument against other clear evidence (v. MINISTRY, APOSTOLIC, APOSTOLIC SUCCESSION). In discussions with Trypho, he indicates the sacrificial character of the Eucharist, alluding to Mal 1:11.[5] Sunday is a holy day because both creation and resurrection took place on that day. On that day people come together to celebrate the Eucharist; alms are collected for widows (q.v.) and those in need.[6]

Justin is at pains to show throughout his *Apologies* that Christians are good citizens, that there is no inherent conflict between Church and State. Perhaps his most profound contribution to ecclesiology lies in his vision of the Logos bringing together the whole history of humanity; Christianity is for Justin a universal religion in which everything has its ultimate meaning through Christ; it fulfills all the promises of the OT.[7]

[1]Texts: G. Krüger, *Die Apologien* (Freiburg im Br., repr. 1968)/ANF 1:159-270/FC 6; *I Apology*—LCC 1:225-289. See S. Denning-Bolle, "Christian Dialogue and Apologetics: The Case of Justin Martyr Seen in Historical Context," BJRyL 69 (1986–1987) 492–510; C. Munier, "A propos des Apologies de Justin," RevSR 61 (1987) 177–186; idem, "La méthode apologétique de Justin le martyr," RevSR 62 (1988) 90–100, 227–239; J. Nilson, "To Whom Is Justin's *Dialogue with Trypho* Addressed?," TS 38 (1977) 538–546. [2]J.N.D. Kelly, *Early Christian Creeds* (London: Longmans, [3]1972) 70–76. [3]A. Davids, *Justinus philosophus et martyr: Bibliographie 1923–1973* (Nijmegen: Katholieke Universiteit, Faculteit der Godgeleerdheid, 1983); R.J. De Simone, "Justin," in EncycEarCh 1:462-464; Patrology 1:196-219. [4]*1 Apol.* 61–67. [5]*Dial.* 41:117; see *1 Apol.*13. [6]*1 Apol.* 67. [7]*1 Apol.* 23, 46; *2 Apol.* 10; *Dial.* passim.

# K

## KENÔSIS OF THE CHURCH

The Greek *kenos* (empty)[1] is used in the NT in a variety of texts, at times without serious theological implications. In the verbal form its most crucial usage is Phil 2:7, where we read that Christ Jesus emptied himself *(ekenôsen)* from being in the form of God (2:5). It does not mean that Jesus abandoned his divine nature, but that he assumed all the limitations of humanity and, except for the transfiguration, left his glory hidden until after the resurrection. The Fathers did not have a common theory of *kenôsis,* but they agreed that it did not affect the Chalcedon doctrine of Christ having inseparably a divine and a human nature.[2]

The notion of *kenôsis* has in the 20th century featured more widely in theology, especially soteriology,[3] and it is occasionally found in ecclesiology.[4]

Though a few authors in patristic times speak of a preexistence of the Church,[5] it is hard to see how *kenôsis* in the strict sense of the word can be applied to the Church. This would entail the Church as preexisting and then becoming emptied by coming on earth, or through a fall from some previous glory. One can, however, say that the Church must imitate its Lord who emptied himself for us. This involves an analogical (technically "improper") use of *kenôsis* applied to the Church. In practice it means that the Church must take the form of a servant (see Matt 20:24-28; John 13:15-17) and become poor (q.v.). The highest model for the self-emptying of the Church is the Marian declaration of slavery and obedience (Luke 1:38).[6]

[1]P. Henry, "Kénose," SuppDictBib 5:7-161; A. Oepke, "Kenos etc," TDNT 3:659-662. [2]Henry (n. 1) 56–136. [3]Y. Congar and G. Jacquemet, "Kénose," Catholicisme 6:1399-1404; K. Sereschnikoff, "Die Kenosis-Lehre Sergej Bulgakovs," Kyrios 4 (1939/40) 142–150; P. Schoonenberg, "Kenosis," Conc 1/2 (1966) 27–36. [4]H.U. von Balthasar, "Kénose (de l'Église)," DSpir 8:1706–1712; cf. R. Adolfs, *The Grave of God: Has the Church a Future?* Compass Books (London: Burns & Oates, 1967). [5]E.g., Pseudo-Clement, *Letter* 2:14, 1–3; Hermas, *Vision* 1:2; 2:4, 1. [6]Von Balthasar (n. 4) 1710–1711.

## KHOMIAKOV, Aleksei (1804–1860)

The lay theologian and polymath Aleksei Khomiakov (Chomjakov, Khomyakov, Xomiakov) stands at the head of an indigenous Russian tradition in theology.[1] His philosophical positions in reaction to, but not uninfluenced by, German idealism,[2] color his theological insights. Though he is not systematic in either his philosophy or his theology, several ideas recur and are basic to his thought. True knowledge is not exterior but interior, involving not only reason but free will and faith. In history he distinguishes *kushitism* (necessity or exteriority) and *iranism* (interiority, freedom). Indeed, full knowledge can only be attained by the participation of all human faculties (reason, will, faith) and only by living in a community of love. A lifelong Slavophile, he saw the Russian Orthodox Church as the true and ideal Church: the Latin Church had only exterior truth, and the Protestant Churches had only freedom. His stance in ecclesiology is anti-Roman:[3] by the "sin" of the addition of the *Filioque* (q.v.), it is left only with externals which do not lead to full truth.

The Church is the creation of the Holy Trinity and bears the marks of its divine origins. Khomiakov's Christology develops from a very ahistorical Christ to a deeper sense of the divine missions.[4] He views the Church at three levels: a) as the grace of God, in which sense the Church is a purely interior reality bearing within it the active presence of Christ and the Spirit; b) as visible, principally in its sacraments, but visible only to the eyes of faith—these two levels belonging in fact only to the Orthodox Church, especially the Russian one; c) a sociological reality—such as the Latin Church.[5] There is some similarity in his thought with that of J.A. Möhler (q.v.), and it has been suggested that Khomiakov was directly influenced by him.[6]

Khomiakov's continuing importance is his development of two themes: reception (q.v.) and *sobornost'* (q.v.). For him it is the reception of teaching by the whole Church at local level that is the cause of the truth of the teaching or the ecumenicity of a council. (Catholic theologians would use the word "guarantee" rather than "cause.") *Sobornost'* is a difficult idea to translate. It is based on Khomiakov's idealized view of the Russian commune *(obshchina)* and means the fundamental link between truth and mutual love in the Church. The mutual love of Christians is at the heart of the Church's mystery, and is in turn the guarantee of its truth.[7] But he seriously downplays any role for an episcopal magisterium, an issue for which he has been criticized by theologians of both East and West.[8] In addition to those who are in some sense his disciples, the influence of Khomiakov in Orthodoxy remains very great.[9] It is still somewhat valid to say, "Orthodoxy today is faced with the question: for or against Khomiakov?."[10] Through Eastern theologians his insights are being taken over and modified by Western theologians.

[1]P.P. O'Leary, *The Triune Church: A Study in the Ecclesiology of A.S. Xomjakov* (Dublin: Dominican Publications—Freiburg, Switz.: UP 1982) 15, 22; P. Baron, *Un théologien laïc orthodoxe au XIXe siècle.* OrChrAn 127 (Rome: Istit. Orientale, 1940); G.A. Maloney, *A History of Orthodox Theology Since 1453* (Belmont, Mass.: Nordland, 1976) 57–61; N.V. Riasanovsky, "A.S. Khomiakov's Religious Thought," SVlad 23 (1979) 87–100; J.S. Romanides, "Orthodox Ecclesiology According to Alexis Khomyakov," GrOrTR 2 (1956) 57–73; E.C. Suttner, *Offenbarung, Gnade und Kirche bei A.S. Chomjakov* (Würzburg, 1967); N. Zernov, *Three Russian Prophets: Khomiakov, Dostoevsky, Soloviev* (London, 1944). [2]O'Leary (n. 1) 24–44; G. Cioffari, "A.S. Chomjakov e l'itinerario filosofico della *Sobornost,*" Nicol 6 (1978) 87–129; B. Schultze, "Vertiefte Chomjakov-Forschung: Ekklesiologie, Dialektik, Soteriologie, Gemeinschaftsmystik," OrChrPer 34 (1968) 360–411 at 364–382. [3]See collected essays *L'Église latine et Protestantisme au point de vue de l'Église d'Orient* (Lausanne et Vevey, 1892). His other important work on the Church *Tserkov' odna,* is in Italian trans. in L. Peano, *La chiesa nel pensiero russo slavofilo* (Brescia: Morcelliana, 1964) 123–147. P. Plank, "Paralipomena zur Ekklesiologie A.S. Chomjakovs," OstKSt 29 (1980) 3–29. [4]O'Leary (n. 1) 63–72. [5]Ibid., 156; cf. 80–82, 104–105. [6]S. Bolshakoff, *The Doctrine of the Unity of the Church in the Works of Khomyakov and Moehler* (London, 1946) 216, cited R.E. Asher, "The Ecclesiology of Alexis Khomyakov," AmBenR 40 (1989) 204–219 at 216. [7]Ibid., 89–90. [8]O'Leary (n. 1) 114–124; A. Schmemann, "The Idea of Primacy in Orthodox Ecclesiology," SVlad 4/2–3 (1960) 49–75 at 53; idem, "The Church is Hierarchical," SVlad 3/4 (1959) 36–41, 61 [9]J. van Rossum, "A.S. Khomiakov and Orthodox Ecclesiology," SVald 35 (1991) 67–82; cf. KerkT 40 (1989) 19–32. [10]B. Schultze, "Chomjakow und das Halbjahrtausend Jubilaum des Einigungskonzils von Florenz," OrChrPer 4 (1938) 473–476 at 490.

# KINGDOM OF GOD

Many exegetes prefer to speak of the reign of God[1] as a more dynamic translation of *basileia* and its linguistic substrata. But there are also some advantages in returning to the use of kingdom; the four most recent translations of the NT have done so.[2] The question of nomenclature alerts us to the complex problems of the notion which are present even in its NT evolution: Jesus preached the kingdom; the earliest books of the NT are relatively silent on kingdom; a few decades later it is central in the Synoptic Gospels; the notion of kingdom is not dominant in the last books of the NT.

The earliest recorded preaching of Jesus[3] is in terms of the kingdom: "The time is fulfilled, and the kingdom of God is close at hand. Repent, and believe the gospel" (Mark 1:15). Here, two parallel indicative statements clarify one another (time/kingdom), as do two parallel imperatives (repent/believe). This teaching of Jesus is in continuation with that of John the Baptist (Matt 3:2). More significantly Jesus can declare the imminence of the kingdom without having to explain it to his audience. The idea of God being king or reigning is clear in the OT: he is majestic in saving his people at the Exodus (Exod 15:11-13); the throne of the human king represents the royal throne of the Lord over Israel (1 Chr 28:4-5); more than this, God is king over the earth (Pss 29; 74:12-17); the pious Israelite could come to God in simple trust (Pss 5:2; 44:4); God is a cosmic king but also a reliable help to the people (Ps 145). In time it will be asserted more emphatically that the Lord is king over all peoples, so that two ideas coalesce: God protects the people and he has also a universal rule (Jer 10:7; Zech 14:9; Mal 1:11, 14).[4] In the temple, God is proclaimed king in the praises of his people so that the human king can expect blessings from the universal king (Pss 2; 18; 21; 45; 72; 101; 110; 144:1-11).

At the time of Jesus there were three preponderant ideas about the kingdom of God. First there was a nationalistic political view that saw God's reign as within history: Israel would be free from oppression—it is the view of Jesus' disciples (Luke 24:21; Acts 1:6). The covenant God (Deut 29:9-12) will do a new thing for his people (Isa 43:19): new heart (Ezek 36:24-28), new creation (Isa 26:19; Ezek 37), new people (Isa 2:1-5; 19:16-25). So the people are to live in hope. Second, there was an apocalyptic expectancy in which the kingdom is beyond history. Some dualism was involved here: from a world subjected to evil (Gen 3–10), the Jews looked forward to a totally transformed universe.[5] Third, we find an ethical understanding of the kingdom in which it is already present: "to take upon oneself the yoke of the kingdom" by fidelity to the *Shema* (Deut 6:4-5) is to submit to God's will and to the kingdom.[6]

The political view was to be found also in the second and third ideas of the kingdom above, so that this was a powerful and unifying idea at the time of Jesus,[7] and in the rabbinic Targums, some of which are contemporary with or predate the Incarnation.[8]

Matthew generally uses the expression "kingdom of heaven" to avoid the divine name, and also for an eschatological sense not found when he uses "kingdom of God."[9] When it comes to grasping what Jesus himself meant in his preaching of the kingdom of God, there is some growing scholarly consensus about only a few key points: the kingdom is not merely the society characterized by trust and love as held by A. Ritschl[10] and the American Social Gospel theologians; it is not something that Jesus expected in the near future or soon after his death, e.g., J. Weiss,[11] A. Schweitzer;[12] it is not the realized eschatology of C.H. Dodd—the kingdom has already come in its fullness in Jesus and one can only make a decision for or against.[13] Each of these views oversimplifies a complex reality. In the teaching of Jesus the kingdom is eschatological and apocalyptic (Matt 25:31-46). There is a conflict between the rule of God and the rule of Satan (Mark 1:16–3:12), but victory is assured through the paschal mystery (Luke 11:12-22; cf. Col 2:14-15). Again, the kingdom is a gift of God:[14] we may pray for it as in the Our Father (Matt 6:10);[15] we must remain in readiness (Matt 24:36–25:13), but it is to be received as a gift (Luke 12:31-32). Further, though Jesus cannot be shown to be a revolutionary,[16] his kingdom teaching gives norms not only for individual but also for political morality. The Sermon on the Mount is not a new Pharisaic law, an impossible ideal, or an interim short-term ethic (because the kingdom will soon arrive), but it is the life that people will want to live if they have allowed the kingdom fully into their hearts.[17] Moreover, in Jesus' teaching, the kingdom is an offer of salvation to all: it is good news (Mark 1:15); it is a time of rejoicing (Matt 9:14-17); the nations are to share in it (Matt 8:11; 21:43).[18] Finally, and above all, the kingdom is a challenge: before the proclamation of Jesus, as of that of John the Baptist, people are invited to repent. This repentance involves both a turning away from sin, and an openness to God's saving will:[19] in synoptic terms it is discipleship; in Johannine language it is to believe in Jesus—it is in the person and in the mission of Jesus that the kingdom is encountered.

There is increasing scholarly agreement that an adequate description of the kingdom as preached by Jesus will involve an *already* and a *not yet,* though authors will vary in the emphasis given to each member of the dialectic. The kingdom is already present (Luke 11:20; 17:21; Matt 12:28). It can be experienced in the signs given in the ministry of Jesus: healing, exorcism, the forgiveness of sins.[20] It has an unobtrusive beginning but will grow in significance, as in the parables of growth—the sower (Mark 4:3-9 par), the seed growing by itself (Mark 4:26-29), the mustard seed and the leaven (Luke 13:18-21 par).[21] It is coming soon (Matt 4:17; Mark 9:1; Luke 21:31-32). Jesus also speaks about a coming of the kingdom at some indefinite future date (Matt 24:36; Acts 1:6-7; Mark 13:32; Luke 22:18), when the apostles will reign (Luke 22:30): the kingdom is then "not yet." The tension between *already* and *not yet* must not be avoided.[22] The future of the kingdom is already influencing the present and giving it meaning.[23] Finally, the kingdom is of surpassing worth, as the parables of the pearl and the hidden treasure indicate (Matt 13:44-46).

In the rest of the NT it is important to note the vision of Acts. Luke's second work is a description of the spread of the Church in the power of the Spirit, but it is written as a massive *inclusio* (indicating unity) about the kingdom (Acts 1:3 with 28:31). Moreover, the activity of Philip and Paul is described in terms of proclaiming the kingdom (Acts 8:12; 19:8; 20:25; 28:23. 31). Luke also speaks about the many trials involved in entering the kingdom of God, in a passage in which it is not possible to discern whether it is the present manifestation or the eschatological perfection that is involved (Acts 14:22). The Pauline references to the kingdom are a significant protection against oversimplifying the notion.[24] There are certain categories of sin that involve exclusion from the (future) kingdom (1 Cor 6:9-10; Gal 5:21; Eph 5:5; cf. 1 Cor 15:24). The text of 1 Cor 15:24-25 refers to the parousia, and should not be interpreted in a chiliastic way (v. MILLENARIANISM).[25] We have already been transferred into the kingdom of the Son (Col 1:13). We are called into the kingdom (1 Thess 2:12), a kingdom which is future (2 Thess 1:5; 2 Tim 4:1, 18). There are fellow-workers for the kingdom (*eis tên basileian*—Col 4:11). Moreover the Pauline writings give two descriptions of the kingdom: "the kingdom of God does not consist in talk but in power" (*en dunamei*—1 Cor 4:20); "the kingdom of God does not mean food and drink but righteousness and peace and joy in the Holy Spirit" (Rom 14:17). Though the Pauline corpus does not use the term "kingdom" with frequency, the occurrences of the notion retain the tension of *already* and *not yet* that is present in the preaching of Jesus; the Pauline word "mystery" found in the Synoptics is moreover a pointer to the reality of the kingdom (Mark 4:11).[26]

In the Johannine literature, references to the kingdom are sparse: rebirth in water and Spirit are necessary to enter the kingdom (John 3:3, 5); Jesus' kingdom is not of this world (John 18:36). The remaining NT texts concern the kingdom which we enter on earth (Heb 12:28; Rev 1:9), or to which we are heirs to (Jas 2:5), or which is eschatological (Rev 12:10).

Texts in the Apostolic Fathers (q.v.) are of several kinds: they repeat Paul's exclusion texts relying on 1 Cor 6:9-10;[27] Clement speaks of the kingdom that is to come;[28] several texts are clearly eschatological, speaking of the heavenly or everlasting kingdom;[29] watching for the signs of the kingdom appears only once,[30] as does the idea of entering it.[31] Apart from these references, we only have the *Didachê* (q.v.) in the apostolic or sub-apostolic period: it gives the text for the Our Father, and speaks of the Church being gathered into the kingdom (9:4; 10:5). In the Apologetic Fathers we find the kingdom only in Athenagoras and in Justin.[32]

In succeeding centuries the notion of the kingdom of God was spiritualized in some of the Greek Fathers. In the West it took on political overtones from the time of Charlemagne, and later was at the basis of theocratic visions of the Church and of the world. At the time of the Reformation the notion was again spiritualized. After the Enlightenment there arose various Utopian constructs which influenced both German pietism and Catholic as well as Protestant ecclesiology.[33]

In modern times the kingdom has become an important theological theme, or indeed a symbol. At Vatican II over 240 council members requested that there be an explicit treatment of the theme of kingdom because: it is frequent in Scripture; it manifests at once the visible and spiritual nature of the society of the Church; it also shows forth its historical and eschatological aspect.[34] The article in response to these demands is in two parts: the institution of the kingdom is shown in the words, miracles, and especially in the person of Christ (LG 5); the second paragraph states that having received the Holy Spirit, the Church is given "the mission of announcing and establishing *(annuntiandi . . . instaurandi)* in every people the kingdom of Christ and of God, and of being on earth the seed and beginning of the kingdom" (LG 5). The ideas in this article are found with some development elsewhere in the council's texts. The kingdom of Christ is not of this world, therefore the Church, in introducing *(inducens)* the kingdom, does not take away the temporal goods of any people (LG 13). The kingdom to which the People of God belong is not earthly but heavenly (LG 13). Eschatological expectation should give increased commitment in the present world: "Therefore, although we must carefully distinguish earthly progress from an increase in the kingdom of Christ, such progress is of vital concern for the kingdom of God, in so far as it can better order human society" (GS 39). "To carry out the will of the Father Christ inaugurated the kingdom of heaven on earth and revealed the mystery to us. . . . The Church, or the kingdom of Christ already present in mystery *(Ecclesia seu regnum Christi iam praesens in mysterio),* visibly grows in the world by the power of God" (LG 3; cf. GS 39—"on earth the kingdom is already present in mystery *(regnum iam in mysterio adest)*. The Christian family "proclaims aloud the present power *(praesentes virtutes)* of the kingdom of God, as well as hope of the blessed life" (LG 35). In those more transformed into Christ, God gives us a sign of his kingdom (cf. LG 50). Christians "united in Christ are directed by the Holy Spirit in their pilgrimage to the kingdom of the Father" (GS 1). The pursuit of perfect charity by the evangelical counsels is an outstanding sign of the kingdom of heaven (cf. PC 1). Religious are to combine contemplation and apostolic love "by which they endeavor to be associated with the work of redemption and to spread the kingdom *(dilatare . . . regnum)"*—PC 5). The religious state proclaims the glory of the heavenly kingdom and shows the kingdom of God to be elevated above all earthly things (LG 44). The lack of holiness in members of the Church results in the fact that "the growth of the kingdom of God is retarded" (UR 4). The Catholic school prepares pupils "to work for the extension of the kingdom of God *(servitium pro regno Dei dilatando)"*—GE 8. Christ gave birth to the Church in announcing the coming of the kingdom of God (LG 3). "While it helps the world and receives much from the world, the Church has only one goal, namely, the coming of God's kingdom and the accomplishment of salvation for the whole human race" (GS 45).

There is a certain overall lack of clarity in some of these points due to two factors: the council did not wish to canonize any of the various theologies of the kingdom; the theology of the kingdom was at the time of the council only imperfectly developed. Nonetheless, we can notice continuity in the presentation of the kingdom as being *already* and *not yet.* Furthermore, the council does not absolutely identify Church and kingdom, preferring to speak of the Church as the kingdom mysteriously present. An important development is the notion, not fully clarified, of the Church contributing to the growth of the kingdom. Some theologians, like H. Küng, stress so much the fact that the kingdom is of God that they are slow to allow the Church any real contribution to the kingdom apart from proclaiming or announcing it.[35] Others will speak of the Church as both sign and instrument of the kingdom of God.[36] This latter approach is very much to the fore in various liberation theologies (q.v.).[37] The Church is a preparation for the kingdom, but it is not the only one: other religions, Judaism in particular, are also its preparation.[38]

Though we must not identify the Church with the kingdom, it is no less an error to weaken or destroy the relationship of the Church to the future kingdom of God. We need also take up the indication of LG 5 and see the kingdom as the area of the work of the Holy Spirit. The orientation of the Church is most beautifully expressed in the Eucharist: there is the *already,* for the power of Christ in the Spirit is present for the community; but the Eucharist reminds us that *not yet* are we able to partake of its eschatological fullness (Mark 14:25).[39] Reflection on the kingdom is always in danger of ignoring or giving insufficient attention to one or other of the vital elements in this complex symbol.[40]

[1]M.I. Boucher, *The Parables*. NTMess 7 (Wilmington: Glazier—Dublin: Veritas, 1981); P. Hünermann, "Reign of God," SM 5:233-240; R. Schnackenburg, *God's Rule and Kingdom* (London-New York, 1963); D. Senior, 'Reign of God,' NDT 851–861. But cf. K.H. Schelkle, *Theology of the New Testament*. Vol. 4—*The Rule of God: Church—Eschatology* (Collegeville: The Liturgical Press, 1978). [2]RNAB, NJB, REB, NRSV. Cf. H. Kleinknecht et al., "Basileia," TDNT 1:564-593. [3]J. Schlosser, *Le règne de Dieu dans les dites de Jésus*. Études bibliques. 2 vols. (Paris: Gabalda, 1980); R.A. "El mensaje de Jesús y los ideales del Reino de Dios," Lumen 38 (1989) 449–473. [4]R. Schnackenburg, "Kingdom of God," in Bauer 2:455-470 at 457; cf. M.J. Selmen, "The Kingdom of God in the Old Testament," TyndB 40 (1989) 161–183. [5]A. Yarbro Collins, "Eschatology and Apocalypticism," NJBC 81:27–42. [6]S. Schechter, *Aspects of Rabbinic Theology* (New York, 1961) 65–78. [7]Schnackenburg (n. 1) 41–74. [8]B.C. Chilton, "Regnum Dei Deus Est," ScotJT 31 (1978) 261–270. [9]M. Pamment, "The Kingdom of Heaven According to the First Gospel," NTS 27 (1981) 211–232. [10]D.L. Deegan, "Albrecht Ritschl on the Historical Jesus," ScotJT 15 (1962) 133–150; idem, "The Ritschlian School, the Essence of Christianity and Karl Barth," ScotJT 16 (1963) 390–414; OxDCC 1189. [11]*Jesus' Proclamation of the Kingdom* (1892), trans. and introd. R.H. Hiers and D.L. Holland (London: SCM, 1971) = *Die Predigt Jesu vom Reiche Gottes* ([2]1902); R. Schäfer, "Das Reich Gottes bei Albrecht Ritschl und Johannes Weiss," ZTK 61 (1964) 68–88. [12]*The Kingdom of God and Primitive Christiantiy* (posthumously—1967, London: Black, 1968). [13]*The Parables of the Kingdom* (New York, 1961). [14]H. Küng, *The Church* (London: Search Press, 1968, 1973) 98–99. [15]R. Brown, "The Pater Noster as an Eschatological Prayer," in *New Testament Essays* (Milwaukee, 1965) 293–321 = TS 22 (1961) 175–208; J. Jeremias, *The Lord's Prayer* (Philadelphia, 1966). [16]Cf. G. Theisen, *The First Followers of Jesus* (London: SCM, 1978); idem, *Sociology of Early Palestinian Christianity* (Philadelphia: Fortress, 1978). [17]R. Schnackenburg, *The Moral Teaching of the New Testament* (London: Burns & Oates, 1975 from German [2]1962) 73–88. [18]J. Jeremias, *Jesus' Promise to the Nations* (London, 1967) 55–73; A. Feuillet, "Le caractère purement religieux et universel du Règne de Dieu d'après les evangiles synoptiques," Divinitas 22 (1978) 153–175; A. Kallikuzhuppil, "The Church and the Kingdom of God in the Synoptic Gospels: A Comparative and Synthetic Study," JDhara 15 (1985–1986) 85–93. [19]J. Giblet and P. Grelot, "Repentance and Conversion," DBT 486–490. [20]N. Perrin, *The Kingdom of God in the Teaching of Jesus* (London: SCM, 1965) 154–206. [21]Boucher (n. 1) 67–76; B.B. Scott, "Parables of Growth Revisited: Notes on the Current State of Parable Research," BibTB 11 (1981) 3–9. [22]J.M. McDermott, "Jesus and the Kingdom of God in the Synoptics, Paul and John," EglT 19 (1988) 69–91. [23]See W. Pannenberg, *Theology of the Kingdom of God* (Philadelphia: Westminster, 1985) 62–63. [24]A. Salas, "Teología del reino en el pensamiento paulino," CiuD 193 (1980) 3–18. [25]C.E. Hill, "Paul's Understanding of Christ's Kingdom in 1 Corinthians 15:20-28," NT 30 (1988) 297–320. [26]R. Hill, "Synoptic 'Basileia' and Pauline 'Mysterion,'" EstBib 47 (1987) 309–324. [27]*Ignatius Eph.* 16:1; *Philadel.* 2:3; Polycarp, *Letter* 5:3. [28]*1 Letter* 42. [29]Clement *1 Letter* 66; Ps-Clem. *2 Letter* 5:5; 9:6; 11:7; 12:2; *Martyrdom of Polycarp* 20:2; 22:3; 23:5; *Letter to Diognetus* 10:2. [30]Ps-Clement, *2 Letter* 12:6. [31]*Letter to Diognetus* 9:1. [32]E. Dal Covolo, "Il regno di Dio in alcune testimonianze del secondo secolo," RivBib 27 (1979) 313–324. [33]P. Hünermann (n. 1) 238–240. [34]Commentary of Doctrinal Commission (July 1964)—ActaSyn 3/1:173—Alberigo-Magistretti 438. [35]Op. cit. (n. 13 ) 88–104. [36]R.P. McBrien, *Catholicism*. Study Edition (London: Search, 1984) 585; cf. D. Lane, *Christ at the Centre* (Dublin: Veritas, 1990) 11–52; J.P. Mackey, *Modern Theology: A Sense of Direction* (Oxford: UP, 1987) 113–119. [37]See J. Richard, "Le royaume de Dieu dans la théologie contemporaine," LavalTP 38 (1982) 153–171. [38]B. Lauret, ed., *Conversations with Yves Congar* (London: SCM, 1988) 19–20; S.J. Samartha, "The Kingdom of God in a Religiously Plural World," EcuR 32 (1980) 152–165. [39]R. Schnackenburg, *The Church in the New Testament* (London: Burns & Oates, 1974) 187–193. [40]D. Senior (n. 1) 861; W. Willis, ed., *The Kingdom of God in 20th-Century Interpretation* (Peabody: Hendrickson, 1987).

## KNOX, John (ca. 1513–1572)

The Scottish Reformer John Knox was born ca. 1513 at Haddington. He received some orders, perhaps even priesthood, and became a lawyer in his native town. Sometime after 1544 he embraced the Reformation.[1] He was captured by French galleys and taken prisoner to France, but was released in 1549 and returned to England where he was chaplain to Edward VI. He collaborated in the writing of the *Second Prayer Book*. When Mary ascended the throne, he fled to Geneva, where he met Calvin (q.v.), but returned to Scotland two years later (1555).

His vision was narrowly scriptural in a most literal sense; moreover, he was more at home in the OT than in the NT. In his active preaching, two themes emerged with special prominence: his undying hatred of the Mass, which he considered to be idolatrous; his intolerance of having a woman as queen, due to his conviction that God had ordained a secondary place for women, and therefore government by women was for him counter to the divine ordinance and natural order.

A Church leader rather than a theologian,[2] Knox organized the reformed Church in Scotland along mainly Calvinist lines in the first *Book of Discipline* (1560). He was probably the main author of the first Scottish Confession (1560).[3] In two articles (16 and 18) the *Confession* deals with the Church: it has existed from the beginning, consisting of those chosen by God and having faith in Christ; it is necessary for salvation; its members are known only to God. The true Church is known where there is true preaching of the Word, the right administration of the sacraments, and ecclesiastical discipline rightly ministered according to God's Word. Though he seems to hold that Abel, Isaac, and holy persons of the OT belonged to the Church, he does not make clear how they had saving faith in Christ. The true Church is "the immaculate spouse of Christ" (art. 18).

Knox's best-known writing was his *History of the Reformation in Scotland*.[4] To him more than anybody else is due the fact that the Church of Scotland is Presbyterian and Calvinist.

[1]E. Iserloh, in Jedin-Dolan 5:410-419; Schaff, Creeds 1:673-680. [2]*Works.* 6 vols. (Edinburgh 1846–1864 and 1895); R.G. Kyle, "John Knox: The Main Themes of his Thought," PrincSemB 4 (1983) 101–112. [3]Schaff, Creeds 1:681, n. 2; text 3:437-479. [4]2 vols. (London, 1949).

## KÜNG, Hans (1928– )

Hans Küng was born near Lucerne, Switzerland, in 1928.[1] He obtained a license in theology from the Gregorian University in Rome, and studied also in Germany and France. His first major book was a doctoral thesis (1957) which sought to show that there was no conflict between the Council of Trent (q.v.) and the theology of K. Barth (q.v.) on justification.[2]

When Vatican II was announced, he hastily wrote a popular, flawed but very influential book, *The Council, Reform and Reunion,*[3] which alerted many people to the possibilities of a council. It can be argued that it was a most important contribution to the Church at the time. During the council, at which he was a *peritus,* he was summoned by the Holy Office in connection with his book on the structures of the Church.[4] He was treated leniently and was merely told to adhere more closely to Church teaching.

A meeting with E. Käsemann led to intensive scriptural studies, a fruit of which can be seen in his large book *The Church.*[5] But it was his questioning, indeed rejection, of infallibility (q.v.) that brought him most attention. *Infallible? An Enquiry*[6] had supporters[7] and critics, most notably K. Rahner.[8] Historians in particular have been critical about this as well as other works, notably *Structures of the Church.* Some of his critics have entered into constructive dialogue with him, pointing out philosophical weaknesses as well problems with his method, which is overly restricted to the historical-critical and in Scripture tends to see a canon within the canon.[9] The book on infallibility provoked hostile reaction in Rome, and led to his losing his title as a Catholic theologian;[10] he retained his university post in the Ecumenical Institute at Tübingen. He remains a Catholic priest[11] and has continued to write extensively, his recent interest turning also to dialogue with world religions.[12] He retired from teaching in 1996.

His work has obvious strong points: he writes with clarity, with a passion for restating revelation for contemporary society; he writes on the burning issues of the time; he provokes others to reexamine issues that he rather abrasively tackles. But he seems affectively alienated from the official Church, and his work displays an asperity and a tendentiousness that ill serves his cause.

[1]J.J. Bacik, *Contemporary Theologians* (Cork, Ireland: Mercier, 1992) 79–90; H. Häring and K.-J. Kuschel, eds., *Hans Küng: His Work and His Way* (Garden City, N.Y.: Image, 1979); W.G. Jeanrond, "Hans Küng," in D.F. Ford, ed., *The Modern Theologians: An Introduction to Christian Theology in the Twentieth Century.* 2 vols. (Oxford: Blackwell, 1989) 1:164-180; J. Kiwiet, *Hans Küng.* Makers of the Modern Theological Mind (Waco, Tex.: Word Books, 1985); R. Nowell, *A Passion for Truth: Hans Küng—A Biography* (New York: Crossroad, 1981). [2]*Justification: The Doctrine of Karl Barth* (New York: Nelson, 1964). [3]New York: Sheed & Ward, 1961. [4]*Structures of the Church* (New York: Nelson, 1964). [5]New York: Sheed & Ward, 1967. [6]New York: Doubleday, 1971. [7]Cf. J.J. Kirwin, ed., *The Infallibility Debate* (New York: Paulist, 1971); H. Küng, ed., *Fehlbar? Eine Bilanz* (Zürich: Benzinger, 1973). [8]K. Rahner, ed., *Zum Problem Unfehlbarkeit* (Freiburg: Herder, 1971); see C.J. Peter, "A Rahner-Küng Debate and Ecumenical Possibilities," in P.C. Empie, T.A. Murphy et al., eds., *Teaching Authority and Infallibility in the Church.* Lutherans and Catholics in Dialogue 6 (Minneapolis: Augsburg, 1978) 159–168. [9]P. Chirico, "Hans Küng's Christology: An Evaluation of Its Perspectives," TS 40 (1979) 256–272; idem, "Infallibility: Rapprochement Between Küng and the Official Church?," TS 42 (1981) 529–560. See C.M. LaCugna, "The Function of Tradition in the Theological Method of Hans Küng," LouvSt8 (1980–1981) 382–402; F.A. Sullivan, *Magisterium: Teaching Authority in the Catholic Church* (Dublin: Gill and Macmillan—New York: Paulist, 1983) esp. 37–41, 44–46, 96–98. [10]The Küng Dialogue (Washington, D.C.: U.S. Catholic Conference, 1980); L. Swidler, ed., *Küng in Conflict* (Garden City, N.Y.: Doubleday, 1981). [11]"Why I Remain a Catholic," JEcuSt 17 (1980) 141–147. [12]E.g., *On Being a Christian* (Garden City, N.Y.: Doubleday, 1976). *Does God Exist? An Answer for Today* (Garden City, N.Y.: Doubleday, 1980); *Theology for the Third Millennium: An Ecumenical View* (Garden City, N.Y.: Doubleday, 1988); *Judaism* (London: SCM, 1992); *Global Responsibility: In Search of a New World Ethic* (London: SCM, 1991).

# L

## LAITY

In 1906 Pope St. Pius X wrote: "In the hierarchy alone reside the power and authority necessary to move and direct all the members of the society to its end. As to the many, they have no other right than to let themselves be guided and so follow their pastors in docility."[1] Pope John Paul II observed in 1988: "The lay faithful participate in the life of the Church not only in exercising their tasks and charisms but also in many other ways. Such participation finds its first and necessary expression in the life of the particular Church, in the diocese . . ." (CL 25). Between these two statements there was: 1) a profound pastoral, theological (especially Y. Congar[2]), and historical exploration of the role of the laity; 2) Vatican II; 3) the 1983 *Code of Canon Law;* 4) the 1987 Synod of Bishops. A key to understanding the changes in the 20th century is the shift from a highly institutional view of the Church—for which Congar coined the word "hierarchology"[3]—and the ecclesiologies which emerged before, during, and after Vatican II (q.v.). The literature on the laity since Vatican II is enormous,[4] with many journals devoting an entire issue to the topic at the time of the 1987 Synod.[5]

There was little direct participation of the laity in the preparatory stages of Vatican II. In the second session thirteen laity were nominated as auditors—a number which would later rise to fifty-two, including ten female religious, one married couple, twenty-eight laymen, and twelve laywomen. They took an active part in the preparation of the decree AA (on the Laity) and of the constitution GS, in particular its second part.[6] The council left an important body of texts about the laity (LG chs. 2 and 4; AA, GS, AG), which, along with the statements of Medellín and Puebla and the new *Code,* would be the foundation for serious reflection in the following decades.

An understanding of the laity today is helped by recent historical studies, particularly of the early period.[7] Broadly speaking one can say that the main tension in the first three centuries was between the Church and the world; after Constantine, the tension between clergy and laity became prominent. In secular Greek *laos* meant those who were governed or subjected to taxes. The word "lay" *(laikos)* does not appear in LXX or NT.[8] Rather we find words like "believers, elect, chosen, saints, brethren." Its first appearance is in the Letter of Clement: "the layman is bound by the ordinances of the laity" *(ho laikos anthrôpos tois laikois prostragmasin dedetai),*[9] an enigmatic saying: some take it as giving the origin of the Christian layman;[10] others hold that it refers to one who is like a Jew not accepting Christian ways and thus, bereft of true wisdom, has therefore the obligation only to obey.[11] The word does not occur at all in Justin or Irenaeus, but when we find it in Clement of Alexandria, it is approaching our modern usage. In two cases the word means what is vulgar or unbelieving,[12] but the third usage is in the context of Encratite positions on marriage: the man of one wife, be he priest, deacon, or lay, will be saved through engendering children.[13] The laity are distinguished from priests and deacons but not as yet opposed to them. Tertullian shows a clear dichotomy between cleric and layman. He allows that the laity can baptize, though they should be extremely discreet in respecting the rights of the bishop.[14] But he held, especially in his Montanist phase, that the distinction between clergy and laity arose by decision of the Church, and that the clergy therefore come from the laity. In other respects his later views were quite radical in their emphasis on, and in the conclusions he drew from, the priesthood of all Christians.[15] At the time of Origen it appears that the distinction of functions of laity and clergy was becoming hardened: widely respected as a teacher and still a layman, he was invited by the local bishops to preach during his journey to Caesarea and Jerusalem. His own bishop, Demetrius, objected strongly to a layman preaching in the presence of bishops. (Origen was later ordained a priest.) It is thus that at least by the generation of 180–230 the definitive differentiation of clergy and laity took place. Initially the difference between laity and clergy was on the basis of liturgy (v. APOSTOLIC TRADITION and MINISTRY), but gradually two different states arose in both East and West.[16] The liturgical and canonical legislation of the 3rd and following centuries (v. APOSTOLIC COLLECTIONS OR PSEUDEPIGRAPHA) set down clearly the more passive role of laity, except—on the model of the support of the Levites in the OT[17]—for their active duty of contributing money for the support of the clergy and of those poor assisted by the bishop. The *Apostolic Constitutions* (q.v.) in legislation from the 3rd and 4th centuries clearly assigns the place of the laity and their states in life;[18] Moreover, they have the responsibility of avoiding scandal and of expanding the Church through helping in the conversion of sinners.[19] The language about laity would still seem to be in the process of evolution.[20] It was probably because women, as young virgins, wives, or widows, would not have had independent means to undertake this ever more important and almost single lay ministry of support, that they are almost never referred to as laity.[21]

While in one way we see a restriction of the ministry of the laity, there was for example in Africa a wide consultation of the laity in Church matters attested in St. Cyprian (q.v.).[22] They were consulted about the *lapsi* (v. RECONCILIATION, SACRAMENT OF), about the election of bishops,[23] though we do not always know who precisely were consulted or how—in some cases the laity chose from a short list; in others they accepted the candidate proposed.[24] Cyprian held as a principle not to act without consultation, even though he overruled the people at times.[25] The laity were to support the clergy, who were to be dedicated to the service of the altar and to prayer.[26] The *Apostolic Tradition* (q.v.) attests to the consultation of the laity at Rome in the case of the appointment of bishops.

From the 5th century the division of clergy/laity was all but complete, with the presbyters tending to subsume all the previous ministries except for the crucial lay ministry of financial support; some of the offices from earlier centuries did, however, continue for a time in various particular churches.[27] When monasticism arose, the laity were at the bottom rank: clergy, monks, and lastly laity. In subsequent theology and law the laity tended to be described or defined as those who are not clergy or religious. The definition found in the canonist Gratian (d. ca. 1159) is famous: "There are two kinds of Christians, clerics and lay people."[28]

There would be little change for about 1000 years. The struggle of Gregory VII (1073–1085—q.v.) and his successors against lay investiture furthered the distinction between clergy and laity. There was a frontier between them, but the Church itself in liturgy and in the better medieval theologians was seen as a gathering of the faithful, a communion, God's people. The emphasis on the hierarchical clergy would, however, provoke a reaction in the various lay movements of the Middle Ages, and in such orthodox and heterodox authors as Huss, Wycliffe, Dante, Marsilius of Padua (d. 1342).

The Reformers insisted on the scriptural doctrine of the priesthood of all believers as one way of deemphasizing the hierarchy, but this led to a still clearer insistence on the hierarchical structure in the Church by the Council of Trent. The official or dominant ecclesiology of the "perfect society" (q.v.) and also "unequal" society left little room for a positive appreciation of the laity before Vatican II.

In the 20th century we had not only scholarly work, but the rise of secular institutes, Catholic Action, and a new emphasis on the apostolate (q.v.) of the laity. In 1946 Pius XII stated to the College of Cardinals that the laity "are the Church."[29] At the second World Congress on the Lay Apostolate (1957; the first was 1951; the third would be 1967), Pius XII spoke of "consecration of the world" as a prime activity of the laity. The phrase would be used once only at Vatican II (LG 34), the council preferring equivalent phrases such as "directing temporal things according to God's will" (LG 31), "spread the kingdom of Christ" (AA 2). But an extensive literature grew up around the idea.[30] Before the council the "consecration of the world" was often seen as an action in collaboration with, or on behalf of, the hierarchy; but afterwards several addresses of Pope Paul VI speak of consecration of the world as a specific task in the laity's mission.[31]

At the opening of Vatican II there had been much study but not yet a mature theology of the laity on which the council could build.[32] In its crucial Constitution on the Church, the decision to speak about the whole People of God (ch. 2) before dealing with the hierarchy (ch. 3) and the laity (ch. 4), is perhaps the most significant act of the council with regard to the laity. It also made a determined effort at describing the laity in positive terms: "Under the title of laity are here understood all Christ's faithful, except those in sacred orders or are members of a religious state that is recognized by the church; that is to say, the faithful who, since they have been incorporated into Christ by baptism, constitute the people of God and, in their own way made sharers in Christ's priestly, prophetic, and royal office, play their own part in the mission of the whole Christian people in the church and in the world" (LG 31).[33] This description of the laity is not without problems, and there have been several attempts to develop its implications or to reformulate it from a theological or juridical point of view.[34]

The council adds in LG 31: "The laity have their own special character (indoles saecularis propria et peculiaris) which is secular." However, propria and peculiaris are to be considered as stable elements, and not what is specific only to the laity. It is allowed that clergy and religious may engage in secular matters, but the council seeks to clarify what the secular character of the laity is: "It is the special vocation of the laity to seek the kingdom of God by engaging in temporal affairs and ordering these in accordance with God's will" (LG 31; cf. GS 43). This idea is further developed as the document shows how the laity share in the priestly (LG 34), prophetic (LG 35), and kingly (LG 36) office of Christ (v. PRIEST, PROPHET, KING). But the fundamental way of being Church is as a member of the faithful, as layperson. Other specifications are added (sacred orders, religious profession). We do not so much need a theology of the laity as a theology of the Christian faithful.

A key notion is the statement: "The apostolate of the laity is a sharing in the church's mission of salvation (ipsius salvificae missionis ecclesiae), and everyone is commissioned to this apostolate by the Lord himself through baptism and confirmation" (LG 33; cf. AA 3). Here we have an advance on the narrow views of the apostolate (q.v.) sometimes espoused by Catholic Action: the laity have their apostolate rooted in the sacraments received, so that they "have the special vocation to make the church present and active in those places and circumstances where only through them can it become the salt of the earth" (LG 33). The notion of being a leaven in the world is found both in LG 31 and AA 2; this latter passage also speaks of the laity sharing in the priestly, prophetic, and kingly office of Christ. The council is clearly aware of the dual position and apostolate of the laity in the Church and in the world (LG 36; AA 5–6; GS 43 . . .).[35] It is not so clear what is included in the words "mission of salvation" in LG 33. But in some sense we can see AA as a decree that looks back to LG and forward to GS. There is a special urgency about transforming the temporal order: it "needs to be established in such a way that, while its own laws are respected, it is brought into conformity, beyond these, to the principles of the Christian life and adapted to the various circumstances of time and place and of different peoples" (AA 7). And again, "The apostolate of our social environment—that is the endeavor to inform with the Christian spirit the minds, customs, laws, and community structures in which each of us lives—is a duty and task for the laity and cannot be carried out by others" (AA 13). The apostolate of the laity is operative within every aspect of life; it can take many forms (AA 9–22; EN 70–74) and will

relate in various ways with the hierarchy (AA 23–26). As the council progressed, there was an extension in the understanding of ministry (q.v.), though the new Code would appear more restrictive.[36] But it is clear that the lack of a cohesive theology linking Church, kingdom, and world has left in the council's statements some matters that are insufficiently developed, especially the very notion of the "secular."[37] In the postsynodal apostolic exhortation, Christifideles laici (1988)[38] we find a further clarification: "The term secular must be understood in light of the act of God the creator and redeemer who has handed over the world to women and men, so that they may participate in the work of creation, free creation from the influence of sin and sanctify themselves in marriage or the celibate life, in a family, in a profession and in the various activities of society. The lay faithful's position in the Church, then, comes to be fundamentally defined by their newness in Christian life and distinguished by their secular character" (CL 15 emphasis of original).

The authors of the Code of Canon Law made many attempts at defining "laity," and sought to avoid a merely negative definition as in the 1917 Code. In the end it did not give a definition of the laity, and instead focussed on the notion of the Christian faithful, some of whose members are clerics and some lay.[39] The Code takes the description of the laity in LG 31 above and, modifying it slightly, applies it to the Christian faithful, viz., to all the people of God, hierarchy and laity (CIC 204; cf. also 96). Though laity will remain a canonical term, it would seem better to focus on Christian faithful (Christifideles).[40] But the key notions of priestly, prophetic,[41] and kingly offices (CIC 204 § 1—q.v.) are not convincingly carried through in the later parts of the Code.[42] The Code describes two positions within the People of God by divine institution: sacred ministers and other Christian faithful—the former are called clerics in law, the latter laity. The same canon notes that those who are consecrated to God in a special way and make profession in a form recognized and sanctioned by the Church can be either clerics or laity (CIC 207).

A highly significant statement in the Code is taken from LG 32, and after a long, complex gestation, appears as an assertion of the radical equality of all the Christian faithful based on their baptism: "In virtue of their rebirth in Christ there exists among all the Christian faithful a true equality with regard to dignity and the activity whereby all cooperate in the building up of the Body of Christ in accord with each one's condition and function" (CIC 208).[43] This is an aspect of the Church's social and theological life which neither laity nor pastors have yet sufficiently grasped. The pastors are "brothers in Christ" of the laity (LG 37), and indeed bishops and priests regularly address their people as "brethren" or more properly "brothers and sisters." But from the side of the laity there has not yet sufficiently emerged that sense of sisterhood and brotherhood towards the pastors whom they are told in the very same article of *Lumen gentium* they must revere and obey.

Another very important feature of the 1983 *Code* is that for the first time in Church law there is quite a comprehensive listing of rights and duties for various groups in the Church. Affecting the laity there are the rights and duties of all the Christian faithful, viz., clergy and laity (CIC 208–223), and a special supplementary series of rights and duties of the lay faithful (CIC 224–231).[44] It can be argued that these canons do not so much grant rights as acknowledge the rights and duties consequent on being a Christian.[45] For all the Christian faithful it states: the basic equality of all, the universal call to holiness and to the mission of the Church (CIC 208–211); obedience to hierarchy with a right to petition and express one's opinion to them (CIC 212); rights to the spiritual goods of the Church, to worship according to one's rite (q.v.), and to have a spirituality in conformity with Church teaching (CIC 213–214); rights to association (q.v.) and assembly, to education, and to freedom of research and enquiry in sacred studies, with due deference to the magisterium (CIC 215–218); personal rights—freedom from coercion in choosing state in life, good name, privacy, vindication of rights, due process, and a restriction of legal penalties so that they accord with law (CIC 219–221); social duties—support for the Church, promotion of justice, aid for the poor, respect for the common good, limitation of rights for the sake of the common good (CIC 222–223). In addition (CIC 224–231) there are seven obligations and rights and six capacities particular to the lay faithful: obligations and rights—sharing in the mission of the Church, the vocation of married persons, duties of parents, Christian education, higher theological education, just wage and benefits when employed in Church service; capacities—to study and obtain degrees in theology and teach it, to be ministers in liturgy in various ways, to be consultants. These lists are basic rights and duties; other more particular ones are to be found elsewhere in the *Code*. A surprising omission, however, is the right and duty of the laity to exercise their charisms (q.v.) in the Church—a point strongly made in Vatican II (AA 3; PO 9; cf. LG 12), indeed a discernment of the charisms of the laity is always a pressing ecclesial task.[46] A possible weakness in the exercise of these important rights is practical ignorance of the various forms of recourse open to members of the Church who believe that their rights have been infringed. The right of vindicating and defending rights is stated (CIC 221), and there are structures in this regard, unknown to most members of the Church: judicial procedure for vindication of rights (CIC 1400–1670), procedure for recourse against administrative acts (CIC 1732–1739), and norms allowing for conciliation and arbitration (CIC 1733).[47]

While it is clear that the *Code* envisages that lay persons can hold offices involving jurisdiction (q.v.) in the Church, it is not so clear that they can be bearers of power *(potestas)*. There are two schools of thought about this latter point,[48] the so-called "German School," which is negative, and the "Roman School," which is positive in asserting the possibility of laity having ecclesiastical power;[49] a touchstone for each school is the interpretation of CIC 274 § 1 and 1421 § 1. It is clear that the *Code* was unwilling to determine juridically a point still unclear in ecclesiology.[50]

Those who are concerned with the difficult and sensitive area of the danger of clericalizing the laity would seem to fall into several groups: some would wish to keep the laity well apart from areas thought to belong to the clerical domain; others would wish to focus the attention of the laity on the need to inculturate the gospel in the world; others again, perhaps, are concerned to keep women from thinking that they could be called to ordained ministry.[51] The problem of clericalization can easily arise when the laity are seen to be acting on behalf of, or under a narrow supervision by, the clergy rather than in virtue of their state resulting from baptism and confirmation (cf. CL 23). They share in the priestly, prophetic, and kingly office of Christ, and should only occasionally be seen as sharing or collaborating with the hierarchy in its exercise of this triple function.[52]

There have been enormous developments in the understanding of, and participation in, the liturgy by the laity.[53] The liturgy is primarily an activity of the whole People of God, that is, of all the faithful both laity and clergy, each according to their state. The liturgy is the high point of the Church's life, but it does not exhaust the Church's mission (SC 9). What determines a person's juridical place in the Church is not so much the function he or she fulfills but rather the sacraments they have received (baptism, confirmation, marriage, orders) and their consecration or not by the evangelical counsels.[54] The encyclical of Pius XII, *Mediator Dei,* as well as Vatican II, prepared the way for the present canonical dispositions with regard to the laity in liturgy: "The rest of the faithful by active participation in celebrations of the liturgy especially in the Eucharist in their own way also have their own part in the office of sanctification" (CIC 835 § 4); "Liturgical actions are not private actions but celebrations of the Church itself. . . . Liturgical actions, to the extent that by their proper nature they involve a common celebration, are to be celebrated where possible with the presence and active participation of the Christian faithful" (CIC 837). Furthermore, the laity can administer 19 sacramentals (q.v.) or blessings (CIC 1168)) in the revised Roman Ritual.[55]

An important new development in theology is the growing number of laymen and laywomen, as well as non-ordained religious, who are professionally engaged as theologians (q.v.). This return to an ancient situation[56] can only enrich the Church with new insights into the Scriptures and theology and deepen our understanding of the Church itself.

A dimension of growing significance in regard to laity is ecumenism. It challenges the Catholic Church in two ways: other Churches will certainly look to its treatment of laity before any thought of reunion; the Catholic Church, while retaining its hierarchical structure, can learn a lot from the spirit, and often the practices, of other Churches in the role they assign to the laity.[57]

An area which is in need of much attention is that of the spirituality of the laity (AA 4; cf. LG 11, 41; CL 16–17).[58] Many, though by no means all, of the great spiritual writers were clerics or religious: the Church needs reflection on lay spirituality, so that all states—single (temporary or permanent), married, widowed—may find their own particular conformation to Christ and way of living under the guidance of the Holy Spirit based on the sacraments of baptism and confirmation. The universal call to holiness of LG chapter 5 is a major challenge to the Church.

Finally, one should note the developments within the Vatican with regard to the laity.[59] Vatican II expressed a desire that there be a secretariat in service of the apostolate of the laity (AA 26). Pope Paul VI set up *ad experimentum* the Council for the Laity in his *"motu proprio" Catholicam Christi Ecclesiam* in 1967.[60] Though in obtaining its formal structure in 1976 with *Apostolatus peragendi*,[61] the body became The Pontifical Council for the Laity and was greatly strengthened; it has been argued that it has since become more clericalized and less flexible in the service of the laity.[62]

[1]Encyc. *Vehementer nos,* ASS 39 (1906) 8–9. [2]See his classic *Jalons pour une théologie du laicat* (1953), Eng. trans. *Lay People in the Church* (London, 1957), and his "My Pathfindings in the Theology of Laity and Ministry," Jurist 32 (1972) 169–188. [3]"My Pathfindings," (n. 2) 170. [4]L. Doohan, *The Laity: A Bibliography* (Wilmington: Glazier, 1987); R. Goldie, "Lay, Laity, Laicity: A Bibliographical Survey of Three Decades," *The Laity Today* 26 (1979) 107–143 = "Laici, laicato e laicità: bilancio di trent'anni di bibliografia," RasT 22 (1981) 295–305, 386–394, 445–460; A Sola et al., ed., *Il laicato: Rassegna bibliografia in lingua italiana, tedesca e francese* (Vatican, 1987). [5]E.g., Greg 68 (1987); LumièreV 36/152 (1987); Jurist 47 (1987) 1–245. [6]R. Goldie, "La participation des laïcs aux travaux du Concile Vatican II," RevSR 62 (1988) 54–73. [7]P.F. Bradshaw, "Modèles de ministère: Le rôle des laïcs dans la liturgie," MaisD 154 (1983) 127–150; A. Faivre, "The Laity in the First Centuries: Issues Revealed by Historical Research," LumVit (English) 42 (1987) 129–139; idem, infra (n.

11); J. Gaudemet, "Les laïcs dans les premiers siècles de l'Église," Communio (French) 12/1 (1987) 61–75; V. Grossi, "Per una rilettura del 'laico' nelle fonti christiane antiche," Later 53 (1987) 281–293; L. Longobardo, "Il laicato nella chiesa antica," Asp 34 (1987) 131–143; J. Tracy Ellis, "The Catholic Laity: A View from History," AmBenR 37 (1986) 256–268. [8]I. de la Potterie, "L'origine et le sens primitif du mot 'laïc,'" in I. de la Potterie and S. Lyonnet, *La vie selon l'Esprit.* US 55 (Paris: Cerf, 1965) 13–29, with corrections to his article NRT 80 (1959) 840–853; V. Liberti, ed., *I laici nel popolo di Dio: Esegesi biblica.* Studio biblico teologico aquilano (Rome: Ed. Dehoniane, 1990). [9]*Letter* 40:5—SC 167:166. [10]Thus M. Jourjon, "Les premiers emplois du mot laïc dans la littérature patristique," LumièreV 12 (1969) 37–42, esp. 38. [11]E.g., C. A. Faivre, "Naissance d'un laïcat chrétien: Les enjeux d'un mot," FreibZ 33 (1986) 391–429 at 393–403, modifying somewhat his view in *Les laïcs aux origines de l'Église* (Paris: Centurion, 1984) 31–40; G.H. Williams, "The Role of the Layman in the Ancient Church," EcuR 10 (1958) 225–248. [12]*Stromata* 5:6, 33, 2—SC 278:78-81; *Paidagôgos* 2:10, 93, 2—SC 108:178–180. [13]*Stromata* 3:12—PG 8:1177-1192. [14]*De baptismo* 17:1-2—CCL 1:291. [15]*De exhortatione castitatis* 7:3—CCL 2:1024–1025; cf. P. Mattei, "'Habere ius sacerdotis.' Sacerdoce et laïcat au témoignage de Tertullian *De exhortatione castitatis et De monogamia*," RevSR 59 (1985) 200–221. [16]A. Faivre, "Clerc/laïc: histoire d'une frontière," RevSR 57 (1983) 195–200. [17]Faivre, "Naissance . . ." (n. 11) 423–428. [18]*Apostolic Constitutions* 2:57, 12—SC 320:314; 8:13, 14—SC 336: 208–210. [19]Ibid., 2:56, 4—SC 320:310. [20]M. Metzger, SC 329: 43 with n. 1. [21]Faivre, *Les laïcs* (n. 11) 130–131. [22]*Epist.* 14:4—CSEL 3/2:512; cf. Faivre, *Les laïcs . . .* (n. 11) 135–159. [23]*Epist.* 59:6, 1; 43:4; 55:8, 4—CSEL 3/2:673; 593; 629–630. [24]*Epist.* 67:2-4—CSEL 3/2:736-738; cf. Eusebius, *Hist. eccl.* 6:29. [25]Cp. *Epist.* 16 with *Epist.* 17—CSEL 3/2:517-523. [26]*Epist.* 1:1—CSEL 3/2:465-466. [27]A. Faivre, *Naissance d'une hiérarchie.* Théologie historique 40 (Paris: Beauchesne, 1977); J. Gaudemet, "Les laïcs dans les premiers siècles de l'Église," Communio 12/1 (1987) 61–75. Cf. *Decretum Magistri Gratiani* 2 pars, causa 12, q.1, cap. 6, in A. Friedberg, ed., *Corpus iuris canonici,* pars prior (Leipzig, 1879) 678. [28]*Concord. discord. can.*—causa 12, q.1 c.7—PL 187:884. [29]DocCath 43 (1946) 176. [30]E.g., M.-D. Chenu, "Consecratio mundi," NRT 86 (1964) 608–616; G. Lazzati, *La "consecratio Mundi" e i laici* (Rome: UCCIM, 1960); K. Rahner, "The Consecration of the Layman to the Care of Souls," ThInvest 3:263-276. [31]Address to 3rd World Council on Laity (15 Oct. 1967) in AAS 59 (1967) 1040–1048 at 1046; general audience, 23 April 1969—DocCath 66 (1969) 502–503. [32]A. Oberti, "Théologie du laïcat," VieCons 58 (1956) 67–80. [33]See commentaries and L. Moreira Neves, "I laici cristiani: essere e agire alla luce del Concilio Ecumenico Vaticano II," Ang 64 (1987) 547–561; M. Semeraro, "Il cristiano laico nel testo conciliare di *Lumen gentium* 30–31," Later 56 (1990) 143–181. [34]ActaSyn 3/3: 62—Alberigo-Magistretti 468; P.A. Bonnet, "De laicorum notione adumbratio," Periodica 74 (1985) 227–271; G. Magnani, "Does the So-called Theology of the Laity Possess a Theological Status?" in Latourelle, Vatican II 1:568-633; K.B. Osborne, "The Meaning of Lay, Laity and Lay Ministry in the Christian Theology of the Church," Antonian 63 (1988) 227–258. E. Schillebeeckx, "The Typological Definition of the Christian Layman According to Vatican II," in *The Mission of the Church* (New York: Seabury, 1973) 90–117. [35]M.D. Place, "'In the Manner of a Leaven': The Lay Mission to the Secular World," Jurist 47 (1987) 86–102; J.H. Nicolas, "Les laïcs et l'annonce de la parole de Dieu," NRT 93 (1971) 821–848; F. Sabogal Viana, "La misión de los fieles cristianos laicos," TXav 39 (1989) 293–304; G. Thils, "Les fidèles laïcs: leur sécularité, leur ecclésialité," NRT 109 (1987) 182–207. [36]E. Rinere, "Conciliar and Canonical Applications of Ministry to the Laity," Jurist 47 (1987) 204–227 at 219–220,

226–227; J. Herranz, "The Juridical Status of the Laity: the Contribution of the Conciliar Documents and the 1983 Code of Canon Law," Communicationes 17 (1985) 287–315 at 307–312 = (French) StCan 19 (1985) 229–257 at 249–257; Antón 2:1028. [37]G. Chantraine, *Les laïcs, chrétiens dans le monde* (Paris: Fayard, 1987); B. Forte, *Laicato e laicità: Saggi ecclesiologici* (Goboa: Marietti, 1986); J.L. Illanes, "La discusión teológica sobre la noción de laico," ScripTPamp 22 (1990) 771–789; G.M. Keightley, "Laity," NDictT 558–564 at 563; J.A. Komonchak, "Clergy, Laity and the Church's Mission in the World," Jurist 41 (1981) 422–447; M.D. Place, art. cit. (n. 35) 93–97; G. Thils (n. 35). [38]Apost. Exhortation, *Christifideles laici* AAS 81 (1989) 393–521—"On the Vocation and Mission of the Lay Faithful in the Church and in the World"; cf. P. Delhaye, "Les grandes leçons du Synode de 1987: Guide de lecture de l'Exhortation Apostolique Post-Synodale *Christifideles laïci,*" EspVie 99 (1989) 321–336, 417–432; H.J. Görtz, "Das kirchliche Handeln des Laien: 'Christifideles laici' im Kontext der 'Communio-Ekklesiologie' von 'Lumen gentium,'" TPh 66 (1991) 177–191; R. Lanzetti, "L'indole secolare propria dei fedeli laici secondo l'Esortazione Apostolica 'Christifideles laici,'" AnnalT 3 (1989) 35–51; J.M. Ochoa, "La exhortación apostólica '*Christifideles laici*': Riqueza y cuestión pendiente," Lumen 38 (1989) 353–381; T. Rincon-Perez, "La participación de los fieles en la función santificadora de la Iglesia (Reflexiones canónicas a la luz de la exh. apost. '*Christifideles laici,*'" IusCan 39 (1089) 617–662; J. Thomas, "L'exhortation *Les laïcs fidèles du Christ*: Plaidoyer pour l'engagement temporel," Études 370 (1989) 689–692. [39] F. Coccopalmerio, "De conceptibus *christifideles* et *laici* in Codice iuris canonici," Periodica 77 (1988) 381–424; Herranz (n. 36) 292–300; J. Komonchak, "The Status of the Faithful in the Revised Code of Canon Law," Conc 147(1981) 37–44 (pre-code); G. Thils, *Laïcs dans le nouveau Code et au IIe concile du Vatican.* Cahiers de la Revue théologique de Louvain 10 (Louvain-la-Neuve: Faculté de Théologie, 1983). [40]A. Prew-Winters, "Who Is a Lay Person?," Jurist 47 (1987) 51–70 at 70. [41]N. Weis, *Das prophetische Amt der Laien in der Kirche.* Analacta Gregoriana 225 (Rome: Gregorian UP, 1981). [42]F.R. McManus, "Laity in Church Law: New Code, New Focus," Jurist 47 (1987) 11–31; E. Corecco, "Aspects of the Reception of Vatican II in the Code of Canon Law," in G. Alberigo et al., eds., *The Reception of Vatican II* (Washington, D.C.: Catholic UP—Tunbridge Wells UK: Burns & Oates, 1987) 269–273; F.L. Morrissey, "The Laity in the New Code of Canon Law," StCan 17 (1983) 135–148, more positive 141–147. [43]S. Holland, "Equality, Dignity and Rights of the Laity," Jurist 47 (1987) 103–128. [44]J.H. Provost in Coriden CIC 119–173. Also, most journals of canon law commented on these articles, e.g., G. Daquattro, "Lo statuto giuridico dei 'Christifideles' nel ordinamento di diritto canonico," Apoll 59 (1986) 77–114; *El laicado en la Iglesia.* XXI Semana española de derecho canónico. Bibliotheca salmanticensis—Estudios 124 (Salamanca: UP, 1989). [45]R.J. Castillo Lara, "Some General Reflections on the Rights and Duties of the Christian Faithful," StCan 20 (1986) 7–32. [46]G. Rambaldi, "Carismi e laicato nella Chiesa: Teologia dei carismi, comunione e corresponsabilità dei laici nella Chiesa," Greg 68 (1987) 57–101; B. Forte, "Comunione, missione e laicità. Riflessioni teologiche e pastorale in vista del Sinodo sui laici," Asp 34 (1987) 144–158; W.J. Rademacher, *Lay Ministry: A Theological, Spiritual and Pastoral Handbook* (New York: Crossroad, 1991). [47]J.B. Beal, "Protecting the Rights of Lay Catholics," Jurist 47 (1987) 129–164. [48]J.H. Provost, "The Participation of the Laity in the Governance of the Church," StCan 17 (1983) 417–448 at 422–432; cf. M.E. Olmos Ortega, "La participación de los laicos en los órganos de la Iglesia (con especial referencia a la mujer," REspDerCan 46 (1989) 89–114. [49]See P. Ciprotti, "I laici nel nuovo Codice," Apoll 56 (1983) 442–453; J.H. Provost (n. 44); J.M. Huels, "Another Look at Lay Jurisdiction," Jurist 41 (1981) 59–80, commenting on J.J. Cuneo, "The Power of

Jurisdiction: Empowerment for Church Functioning and Mission Distinct from the Power of Orders," Jurist 39 (1979) 183–219. [50]E. McDonough, "Laity and Inner Working of the Church," Jurist 47 (1987) 228–245 at 231–237 and n. 18; A. Celeghin, "Sacra potestas: Quaestio post conciliaris," Periodica 74 (1985) 165–225. [51]G. Thils, "Ne pas 'cléricaliser les laïcs'," RTLv 18 (1987) 484–486. [52]See e.g., G. Della Torre, "La collaborazione dei laici alle funzioni sacerdotale profetica e regale dei ministri sacri," MonEccl 109 (1984) 140–165; J.J. Koury, "The Limits of Collaboration: The New Legal Language for the Laity," StCan 26 (1992) 415–436. [53]P.-M. Gy, "Les fonctions des laïcs dans la liturgie," Notitiae 20 (1984) 796–805; J. Manzanares, "Les laïcs et la vie liturgique," AnnéeCan 29 (1985–1986) 123–140. [54]E. Corecco, "I laici nel nuovo codice di diritto canonico," ScuolC 112 (1984) 201; K. Rahner, "The Sacramental Basis for the Role of the Layman in the Church," ThInvest 8:51-74. [55]*Rituale Romanum. De benedictionibus* (Vatican, 1984). [56]A. Faivre, "Théologiens 'laïcs' et laïcs théologiens," Irén 60 (1987) 193–217; 350–377. [57]P.F. Bradshaw, "Modèles de ministère: Le rôle des laïcs dans la liturgie," MaisD 154 (1983) 127–150 at 139–147; D.C. Ford, "The Interrelationship of Clergy and Laity Within the Church According to St. John Chrysostom," SVlad 36 (1992) 329–353. Cf. N. Afanassieff, "The Ministry of the Laity in the Church," EcuR 10 (1957–1958) 255–263; F. Frost, "Les laïcs dans l'Anglicanisme," MélSR 43 (1987) 145–155 = AnnéeCan 29 (1985–1986) 183–192; A. Ismail, "Laity in BEM: A Theological and Educational Critique," EcuR 41 (1989) 73–77; A. Kowalchuk, "The Participation of the Laity in the Church," PatByzR 3 (1984) 113–121; S.C. Neil and H.-R. Weber, eds., *The Layman in Christian History* (London, 1963); D. Salachas, "I fedeli nel diritto delle Chiese orientali cattoliche," Apoll 62 (1989) 633–640; F.H. Thompsett, "The Laity," in S. Sykes and J. Booty, *The Study of Anglicanism* (London: SCM—Philadelphia: Fortress, 1988) 245–260; T. Valdman, "Il laicato nella Chiesa Orthodossa," StEcum 6 (1988) 105–114. [58]AA.VV., *Dizionario di spiritualità dei laici* (Milan, Ed. O.R., 1981); A. Alvarez-Suárez, "Hacia una 'espiritualidad laical' desde la doctrina eclesial," Burgense 30 (1989) 219–224; H.U. von Balthasar, *The Christian State of Life* (San Francisco, Ignatius, 1983 from German 1977); A. Barruffo, "Laico," NDizSpir 810–828; R. Berzosa Martínez, "Bases teológico-eclesiológicas de una espiritualidad laical," Burgense 30 (1989) 203–218; P. Brugnoli, *La spiritualità dei laici* (Brescia: Morcelliana, 1967); G. Chantraine, "Le laïc à l'intérieur des missions divines," NRT 109 (1987) 362–381; Y. Congar, "Laïc et laïcat," DSpir 9:79-103; P. Coughlan, *The Hour of the Laity: Their Expanding Role—Exploring Christifideles Laici* (Newtown, N.S.W.—Philadelphia, 1989) 36–38; L. Doohan, "The Spiritual Life of the Laity," in L. Doohan, ed., *John Paul and the Laity* (New York: Le Jacq, 1984) 69–98; Doohan, Laity 115–122 for bibliog.; idem, *The Lay-Centred Church: Theology and Spirituality* (London: Chapman, 1988); E. Dreyer, "A Spirituality for the Laity: Yes or No?," SpToday38 (1986) 197–208; K.J. Egan, "The Call of the Laity to a Spirituality of Discipleship," Jurist 47(1987) 71–85; D. Orsuto, in E.G. de Cea, ed., "Spiritualità dei laici," in *Compendio di teologia spirituale.* FS J. Aumann (Rome: PUST, 1992) 305–329; G. Thils, *Les laïcs et l'enjeu des temps "post-modernes"* (Louvain-la Neuve: Faculté de Théologie, 1988) 90–117; A. Vauchez, "La sainteté du laïc dans l'occident médiéval: naissance et évolution d'un modèle hagiographique (XIIe—début XIIIe siècle)," ProbHistChrist 19 (1989) 57–66; WaySupp 6 (1987) 1–80. [59]S. Berlingò, "Il pontificio Consiglio per i laici," in P. A. Bonnet and C. Gullo, eds., *La curia romana nella Cost. Ap. "Pastor bonus."* Studi giuridici 21 (Vatican, 1990) 443–453. [60]6.1.1967—AAS 59 (1867) 25–28. [61]10.12.1976—AAS 68 (1976) 696–700. [62]P. Monnot, "Les laïcs et 'le pouvoir de gouvernement' au sein de la Curie romaine," PraxJurRel 3 (1986) 173–184.

## LAMBETH QUADRILATERAL

See ANGLICAN COMMUNION, ECUMENISM

## LATERAN I, Council of (1123)

Lateran I (March 1123) was the first of the so-called seven papal councils (v. COUNCILS) of the Middle Ages.[1] It was summoned by Callistus II (1119–1124). It ratified the Concordat of Worms (1122), which put an end to the investiture controversy (q.v.), even though there were those at the council who thought that the pope had conceded too much.

The commonly accepted twenty-two canons[2] promulgated at the council did not add much new; they were in line with the reforms of the time (cc. 7, 21). The following are some of the more significant enactments: the attempt to strengthen the position of bishops (c. 4), especially vis-à-vis the ever-growing number of monks whose pastoral activities were to be curtailed (c. 16); the effort to ensure lawful episcopal elections and consecration (c. 3); the juridical description of crusaders and the protection of their property in their absence (c. 10). The council secured a measure of peace for the Church. Noteworthy, too, is the interest in secular affairs on the part of the Roman Church through this council: it reenacted previous legislation of the popes about the 11th-century truce of God (q.v.) on arson and on public highways (c. 15).[3]

The decrees of this traditionally called ninth ecumenical council were received by a number of local synods in years up to 1130.

[1]R. Foreville, *Latran I, II, III et Latran IV.* Histoire des conciles 6 (Paris: Ed. l'Orante, 1965); G. Franzen, "L'ecclésiologie des conciles médiévaux," in O. Rousseau, ed., *Le concile et les conciles* (Chevetogne, 1960) 125–141.   [2]Tanner 187–189 with canons 190–194.   [3]R. Kemp, in Jedin-Dolan 3:436-445.

## LATERAN II, Council of (1139)

Traditionally called the tenth ecumenical council, Lateran II[1] was also the second of the medieval papal councils (v. COUNCILS). It was summoned by Innocent II (1130–1143). His election was irregular and clandestine, and opposition to it gave rise to a rival anti-pope, Anacletus II (1130–1138).[2] Though Anacletus had died, and his successor, anti-pope Victor IV, had resigned after only a few months, Innocent wanted a council to settle all the problems which had arisen out of the schism. The council declared all acts, decisions, consecrations, and ordinations of the anti-pope null and void (c. 30).

Many of its thirty canons[3] are taken from earlier councils and synods, and are, moreover, incorporated into the collection of Gratian (v. LAW OF THE CHURCH). The following emerge in the canons: the growing in-

fluence of the papacy in the more secular aspects of Christendom (cc. 11, 12, 14, 15, 18, 19, 29; v. LATERAN I); the improvement of the quality of bishops and clergy (cc. 4, 16, 28); the growing importance of monasticism and religious life reflected in various norms (cc. 7, 8, 9, 26, 27); the prohibitions of simony (cc. 1, 2, 24),[4] and concubinage (c. 6); the clarification of legal norms, e.g., excommunications (c. 3), marriage (c. 17); the protection of consecrated persons and sacraments (cc. 15, 22, 23).[5] Its general concern with reform led to this council being called "The Epilogue of the Gregorian Age" (v. GREGORY VII).[6]

[1]R. Foreville, *Latran I, II, III et IV.* Histoire des conciles 6 (Paris: Ed. l'Orante, 1965); A. Melloni, in Alberigo, Concili 191–194; H. Wolter, in Jedin-Dolan 4:10.   [2]H. Bloch, "The Schism of Anacletus and the Glanfeuil Forgeries of Peter the Deacon," Trad 8 (1952) 159–264.   [3]Tanner 1:197-203.   [4]DS 715.   [5]DS 717–718.   [6]A. Fliche, in Fliche-Martin 10/1: 178.

## LATERAN III, Council of (1179)

Enumerated traditionally as the 11th ecumenical council, Lateran III[1] was summoned by Alexander III (1159–1181) after he made peace in 1177 with the emperor Frederick Barbarossa, who had sided with three anti-popes, Victor IV (1159–1164), Paschal III (1164–1168), Callistus III (1168–1178).[2]

Better attended than the two previous councils, with impressive representation from many parts of Europe, this council has in the past been called *the* Lateran Council. Its character and self-awareness is indicated in the convocation letter of Pope Alexander in 1178, "so that according to the custom of the ancient fathers, the good should be sought and confirmed by many, and that with the cooperation of the grace of the Holy Spirit, by the efforts of all, there should be carried out what was required for the correction of abuses and the establishment of what was pleasing to God."[3]

The acts of the council are no longer extant, and the MS tradition of its canons is still not fully clear.[4] Many of these twenty-seven canons[5] found their place in compilations of canon law (v. LAW OF THE CHURCH). The first canon, its most important, and one still obtaining, is the requirement of a two-thirds majority in papal elections; it also states the principle that no recourse can be made to a higher authority than the Church of Rome (c. 1). Other notable matters decreed by the council include: the invalidity of the ordinances of the three recent anti-popes (c. 2); the qualities and behavior required of bishops and other clerics (cc. 3, 4, 12, 15, 16); restrictions on excommunications and appeals (c. 6); simony (c. 7); norms reflecting the growing importance of monks, Templars, and religious (cc. 9, 10); the recurring problem of concubinage (c. 11); multiple benefices (cc. 13, 14); provision of free education for poor children at cathedral churches (c. 18); inordinate taxation on churches prohibited (c. 19); civil and moral matters falling under the council's scope (cc. 20, 22); pastoral and compassionate legislation for lepers (c. 23); prohibition of arms-dealing with Saracens (c. 24); norms against usury (c. 25); restrictions placed on Jews and Saracens, and their evidence not being accepted against a Christian's (c. 26); legislation against heretics with some crusader privileges awarded to those who campaign against heresy (c. 27).

While the pope received the Albigensians (q.v.) sympathetically, permission for them to preach was not, however, given by the council, but left to the discretion of the local bishop; soon there would be an acute problem with Albigensian heretics.

Like the other medieval papal councils, Lateran III displayed an eagerness for reform, one not, however, translated into practice, as succeeding councils would show.

---

[1]R. Foreville, *Latran I, II, III et Latran IV.* Histoire des conciles 6 (Paris: Ed. l'Orante, 1965); J. Longère, ed., *Le troisième concile de Latran (1179): Sa place dans l'histoire* (Paris: Études Augustiniennes, 1982); A. Melloni, in Alberigo, Concili 195–200; H. Wolter, in Jedin-Dolan 4:63-66. [2]OxDPopes 176–180. [3]PL 200:1184, trans. Tanner 1:205. [4]Tanner 1:206-210; S. Kuttner, "Brief Note Concerning the Canons of the Third Lateran Council," Trad 13 (1957) 505–506. [5]Text, Tanner 1:211-225.

## LATERAN IV, Council of (1215)

Commonly considered the twelfth ecumenical council, Lateran IV[1] was the most important of the medieval councils of the Latin Church. Its purpose was laid down by Innocent III (1198-1216) in the letter of convocation: ". . . to eradicate vices and to plant virtues, to correct faults and reform morals, to remove heresies and to strengthen faith, to settle discord and establish peace, to get rid of oppression and to foster liberty, to induce princes and Christian people to come to the aid and succor of the holy Land."[2] One of the greatest popes of the Middle Ages, and an accomplished canonist, Innocent III (q.v.)[3] was embroiled in politics for most of his reign, but he was, above all, concerned with the crusade, the extirpation of heresy, and reform. He gave two years notice of the council and expected all residential bishops to attend. He also encouraged them to submit issues for the council; over 400 bishops and 800 abbots and superiors of chapters were present. The intervening period was well used to draw up lists of matters needing attention, which were embodied in the seventy-one constitutions of the council. There was some discussion at the council, but the substance had been mostly prepared in the previous two years and was based on the huge canonical output of the pope. Much of the material, moreover, was new in form or content.

The first constitution[4] is largely a new profession of faith, with some basis in the 1210 profession of faith imposed on Bernard Primus. Directed against the Albigensians and Cathars, it is strongly Trinitarian and sacramental: it sets out the faith about baptism, penance, official priesthood, and matrimony; it proposes the orthodox doctrine of the Eucharist, using for the first time in conciliar teaching the word coined by early scholastics, *transsubstantiatis*. The 2nd constitution[5] against errors of Joachim of Fiores (q.v.) is complementary, dealing mostly with Trinitarian doctrine. A condemnation of, and measures against, all heresy is found in the 3rd constitution;[6] an episcopal inquisition (q.v.) already operative in some places is extended to the whole Church.

It would seem as though Innocent believed that union with the Greeks would be assured by establishing the Latin Empire. Constitution 4 is unsympathetic to the Greeks and the following one sees the patriarchs (q.v.) through Latin eyes. Decrees about diversity of rites (9th) and celibacy (14th) are more open to the situation of the Greeks.

The remaining constitutions[7] are wide-ranging: Church discipline (6–13), the reform of clerical morals (14–22), administration of benefices (23–32), taxes (33–34), canonical suits (35–49), matrimony (50–52), tithes (53–61), simony (63–66), and Jews (67–70). Some of the most significant are: the provision of preachers (c. 10); yearly confession and Easter Communion with very strict obligation of the seal, or secrecy, of confession (c. 21); general chapters, which had proved effective in the Cistercian Order, now recommended for other monks (c. 12); prohibition of new religious orders (c. 13); the distinction between ecclesiastical and secular courts (c. 42); exemption of clerics from taxes (c. 46); limitation of marriage impediments and prohibition of clandestine marriages (cc. 51, 52).

The final constitution deals in great detail with the crusade (q.v.) proposed for 1 June 1217.[8] But before it could take place, Innocent III had died, and the crusade was ineffectual. Lateran IV proved to be rather unproductive in its political decisions but very significant for its law. Fifty-nine of its constitutions were incorporated into *Liber extra,* the law book of Gregory IX (1227–1241), and no council apart from Trent had more norms evidenced in the 1917 *Code.*

---

[1]A. García y García, ed., *Constitutiones concilii quarti laterensis una cum commentariis glossatorum* (Vatican, 1981), cf. J.M. Soto Rábanos, RET 41 (1981) 259-265; R. Foreville, *Latran I, II, III et Latran IV.* Histoire des conciles (Paris: Ed. l'Orante, 1965); G. Franzen, "L'ecclésiologie des conciles médiévaux," in O. Rousseau, ed., *Le concile et les conciles* (Chevetogne, 1960) 125-141; M. Maccarone, "Il IV concilio lateranense," Divinitas 5 (1961) 270-298; A. Melloni, in Alberigo, Concili 200-204; H. Wolter, in Jedin-Dolan 4:166-172. [2]PL 216:824—Tanner 1:227. [3]A. Fliche, "Innocent III et la réforme de l'église," RHE 44 (1949) 144-152; H.

Tillmann, *Innocent III* (Bonn, 1954—Amsterdam 1980); OxDPopes 186-188.  [4]Tanner 1:230-231/DS 800-802/ND 19-21.  [5]Tanner 1:231-233/DS 803-807/ND 317-320.  [6]Tanner 1:233-235.  [7]Tanner 1:236-267.  [8]Tanner 1:267-271; T.C. Van Cleve, "The Fifth Crusade," in K.M. Setton, ed., *A History of the Crusades*. Vol. 2 (Philadelphia, 1962) 377-428.

## LATERAN V, Council of (1512–1517)

When threatened with deposition by the rebel Synod of Pisa (1511), the energetic and military Pope Julius II (1503–1513) summoned Lateran V to meet in Rome (1512).[1] Its five sessions during his lifetime were mostly concerned with condemning the Pisan council and the Pragmatic Sanction (q.v.).[2]

Under his successor, Leo X (1513–1521), the council resumed on 27 April 1513 (6th session). From that time until the final 12th session (16 March 1517), there were important decisions on reform, especially at the 9th session, which was concerned with the curia and the cardinals. But these were mainly on paper, the pope fearing a too radical reform of head and members—from papacy down—in the Church.

There were some decisions on doctrinal matters: a system for the censorship of books (q.v.) was established;[3] the immortality of the human soul and the subservience of philosophy to theology were decreed.[4] There was an important decree on preaching (q.v.), which also denounced sermons on the imminence of the last days.[5] The council was, however, also directed against overzealous reformers who criticized the ecclesiastical hierarchy and the clergy.

In ending the Pragmatic Sanction (q.v.),[6] the council gave in excessively to the king of France, allowing him the nomination of bishops and the majority of abbots; in time this would lead to even greater abuses than the ones it sought to cure.

Lateran V finished just six months before the entry of Luther upon the scene. Its reforms were never carried through with any energy.[7] Its most enduring achievement was to see the end of conciliarism (q.v.).

[1]O. de la Brosse et al., *Latran V et Trent*. Histoire des conciles 10 (Paris: Ed. l'Orante, 1975); K.A. Fink, in Jedin-Dolan 4:558-562; H. Jedin, *A History of the Council of Trent* (London, 1957) 1:117-138; N. Minnich, "Concepts of Reform Proposed at the Fifth Lateran Council," ArHPont 7 (1969) 163–251; M. Venard, in Alberigo, Concili 323-329.  [2]Tanner 1:595-603.  [3]Tanner 1:632-633.  [4]Tanner 1:605-606.  [5]Tanner 1:634-638.  [6]Tanner 1:638-645.  [7]R. Shoeck, "The Fifth Lateran Council: Its Partial Successes and Its Larger Failures," in G. Lytle, ed., *Reform and Authority in the Medieval and Reformation Church* (Washington, D.C.: The Catholic University of America Press, 1981) 127–142.

## LAW OF THE CHURCH

The Israelites were immensely proud of the fact that their God had given them a law (Deut 4:5-7; 26:16-19).

The earliest codification of Hebrew law (Exod 20:1-17; 22:20-23:19; 34:11-26) dates from the 12th–11th centuries B.C.E., but it would be the 5th century before the Pentateuch was finally completed. Though the Israelites celebrated the Law (Ps 119), they were not particularly good at observing it; they were given a line of prophecy which spoke of a new law written on the heart of the people (Jer 31:33) and of a new spirit with which to keep the law (Ezek 36:26-27). By the time of Jesus, the Torah (instruction or law) comprised 613 precepts (248 positive, 365 negative). Though "Christ is the end of the law" (Rom 10:4), he did not come to abolish it but to bring it to perfection (Matt 5:17-19). The moral norms of the law remained in force; the ceremonial ones were not binding on Christians.

The attitude of Paul to the law is of great importance for an understanding of the NT and also of the jurisprudence of the Church at every age. Paul as a Pharisee was in a position to appreciate the Torah, which Jews continued to consider a gift rather than a burden. His perspective on the law was that of the death and resurrection of Jesus, and we can draw out four lines in his teaching: the law was powerless to achieve the saving justice that God offered through Jesus (cf. Rom 3:20; Gal 2:21; 5:4); the command of love fulfilled the law (Gal 5:13-14; Rom 13:8b-10); the end of the law is Christ who brought the law to fulfillment but put an end to it as a closed religious system (1 Cor 9:21; Rom 10:4); the Spirit frees us from the law of sin and death (1 Cor 3:14b-18), animating us from within (Gal 5:18; Rom 8:4-14). In the Judaizing conflict, Paul was on the side of freedom for the pagan converts.[1]

The roots of Church law are to be found in the NT itself. In an eminent position is the divine and natural law, which is reiterated many times by Jesus and by the early Church (e.g., Matt 19:18-19; Gal 5:19-21). But we find Paul legislating for the confusion at Corinth (1 Cor 14:27-30). Another example is the apostolic meeting in Jerusalem (Acts 15). These are instances of what was to become a pattern in Church law: a problem arises; an answer is sought in the Scriptures and Tradition, and then promulgated with divine authority; if there are no such mandatory norms, then the Church uses reason to provide a wise decision from various possible courses of action. This eventual decision is aimed at establishing order where there was a problem or disarray.

Very soon there were collections of such decisions, or norms brought together for a particular Church; some can perhaps be found in the *Apostolic Tradition* (q.v.), but many more in the later Apostolic Collections (q.v.). Provincial and more universal councils also passed decrees, as did popes from the end of the 4th century. Decrees and statements of influential bishops ("canonical letters") also formed part of the emerging tradition of law.[2] This growing tradition of law was seen as an aberration by R. Sohm. For him the Church was wholly spiritual and law was wholly secular. Hence the development of canon law, which he saw as an example of "Catholicism" (v. CATHOLICISM, EARLY), an abandonment of the primitive ideal of a fundamentally charismatic Church.[3]

The Christianization of the Germanic peoples raised new problems, which in turn gave rise to new legislation. The more generous use of the sacrament of reconciliation led to the writing of penitentials or manuals for priests dealing with various kinds of sin. The Carolingian reforms relied heavily on laws and were the occasion for various collections.[4] Collections of laws and decrees had been made from the 6th century, notable among them the 9th-century *False Decretals* (q.v.) ascribed to Isidore (d. 636), which contained some genuine canons of councils and letters of popes along with many forgeries. The Gregorian reform (v. GREGORY VII) was the occasion of other collections.[5] In the 12th century, some time after 1139, Gratian (q.v.), the father of canon law, drew up his great collection of decrees, the *Decretum Gratiani* or *Concordantia discordantium canonum.*[6] Gratian sought by faith and especially by reason to harmonize where possible the discordant canons. His work was to be the textbook of canon law for centuries, and it later became the first part of the *Corpus iuris canonici* (Body of Canon Law). This last was the chief collection of canon law in the Church, and it comprised, in addition to the *Decretum,* various further collections up to the 15th century. The name *Corpus iuris canonici* did not come into use until after the bull *Cum pro munere* of Gregory XIII (1580). After this there was the Council of Trent and still more decrees of popes and Roman offices until Vatican I sought a compilation of all this, sometimes contradictory, material. In 1904 Pius X initiated the codification, which was mainly the work of Cardinal Pietro Gasparri. Finished in 1917, it was the first complete code of Church law. Its 2,414 canons were the most radical revision of Church law ever accomplished. Deeply rooted in the past, its apparatus of sources contained over 25,000 citations of earlier texts. It was divided into five books: General Norms, Persons, Things, Procedures, and Penalties. The ecclesiology behind this 1917 *Code of Canon Law* was that of the "perfect society" (q.v.); it was very institutional and hierarchical. But while it provided order in the Church, it did not prove a blockage in the many renewal movements (q.v.) which paved the way for Vatican II. The *Code* was, however, solely for the Latin Church. The Eastern Churches had only collections of ancient canons, the traditions of their Churches, and more modern decrees to guide them.

In 1959 Pope John XXIII announced simultaneously his intention to call an ecumenical council and initiate a revision of canon law. Though a commission was appointed in 1963, it was clear that work on the revision of law would have to await the conclusion of the council. Paul VI inaugurated the work of the Pontifical Commission in November 1965. In time there would be three stages in the revision of Church law: the *Code of Canon Law (Codex iuris canonici)* for the Latin Church (1983); *Pastor bonus,* the reform of the Curia (1988—v. VATICAN); the *Code of the Canons of the Oriental Churches (Codex canonum ecclesiarum orientalium*—1991).

In the drafting of the Code for the Latin Church, ten principles were adopted to guide its work; these were submitted to the 1967 Synod of Bishops (q.v.). Their intention was to ensure that it would be both a juridical document and one in harmony with the principles and themes of Vatican II. From 1972, drafts of various sections were widely circulated to the worldwide episcopate, pontifical universities, and other groups. A contentious issue from the beginning was the question of incorporating a *Lex Ecclesiae Fundamentalis,* that is, a fundamental law or constitution, for the whole Church (and not just the Latin Rite).[7] At a very late stage it was judged that it was not opportune to produce such a document, and eventually about half of its canons were inserted into the new *Code,* mainly as rights and duties of the Catholic faithful and of the laity (CIC 208–231). The work was completed in 1981, but Pope John Paul II studied the text for a year with the help of a small group of canonists. It was promulgated on 25 January 1983, twenty-four years to the day after John XXIII had announced the revision.

The 1,752 canons of the *Code* touch almost every facet of Church life from its hierarchical structure to personal spirituality, from internal governance to the mission of justice and peace.[8] The structure of the *Code* reflects the ecclesiology of Vatican II: Bk 1—General Norms; Bk 2—The People of God; Bk 3—The Teaching Office of the Church; Bk 4—the Sanctifying Office; Bk 5—Temporal Goods; Bks 6 and 7—Sanctions and Procedures. This organization of the *Code* depends on the key canon 204: "The Christian faithful are those who, inasmuch as they have been incorporated in Christ through baptism, have been constituted as the People of God; for this reason, since they have become sharers in Christ's priestly, prophetic, and royal office in their own manner, they are called to exercise the mission which God has entrusted to the Church to fulfill in the world, in accord with the condition of each one." This text which is a reworking of Vatican II, LG 31, has been seen by some, such as Cardinal J. Hamer, as the key to understanding the entire *Code* when taken alongside with canon 205: "Those baptized are fully in communion with the Catholic Church on this earth who are joined with Christ in its visible structure by the bonds of profession of faith, of the sacraments and of ecclesiastical governance."[9]

The *Code* reflects the sacramental status of each one, especially through baptism, confirmation, and orders. It is not a purely juridic document but a theological one. Indeed what distinguishes it from civil law—both European and Anglo-Saxon—is its establishment of theological principles, rather than the detail which we expect in statutory enactments, common law, judicial precedents, or administrative law. The relatively small number of Church laws, the comparative ease with which necessary dispensations can be obtained (CIC 85–93), the inflexible nature of the main principles involved, these and other factors point to canon law as a legal culture quite removed from that of civil jurisprudence.[10]

J.A. Alesandro gives nine beneficial developments to be found in the revised *Code:* the Church as the People of God and the threefold sharing in the office of Christ as priest, prophet, and king (q.v.); fundamental equality of all members of the Church; enhanced role of laity; the emphasis on persons rather than juridic functions; subsidiarity; the particular church as "portion of the People of God" (v. LOCAL CHURCH); consultation at all levels; accountability with regard to temporalities; pastoral care and flexibility in the realization of the Church's fundamental mission.[11] Nevertheless, in the new *Code* there is some evidence of a return to a more juridic picture of the Church than that proposed by Vatican II (v. PEOPLE OF GOD).[12] One must on the other hand also note the Trinitarian references and the theology of the Church as sacrament, which are welcome elements.[13]

The idea of codifying the laws of the Eastern Churches can be found from the 18th century, and it was enunciated at Vatican I. Practical steps were taken by Pius XI in 1927 when he established a commission for the purpose. It was to be a long process, being completed only in 1991.[14] An early idea was to seek to have one law only for both the Latin and Eastern Churches, but Pius XI rejected this proposal in 1930. Pius XII promulgated four parts of the new *Code* between 1949–1957.[15] John XXIII was reluctant to promulgate the remaining parts, preferring to leave it to the council. It was clear at the council that the same ecclesiology and world-view imbued both the 1917 Latin *Code* and the promulgated and proposed parts of the oriental *Code*, and all needed revision.

It was not until June 1972 that Paul VI set up a Commission for the revision of the oriental *Code*. Some feared Latinization, a charge which could be leveled at some of the elements of the parts already prepared or promulgated. There was also a fear for the canonical traditions of the East.[16] Paul VI in 1974 fixed the reform to a double principle: renewal and fidelity in the bond of unity; fidelity to genuine oriental traditions and to the spirit and directives of Vatican II.[17]

In October 1991 Pope John Paul II promulgated the new *Code*. In accord with the Eastern mentality, it is called the *Code of Canons of the Oriental Churches:* "canons" is a term consecrated by tradition; there is not an Eastern Church, but Eastern Churches. The structure is different from the Latin *Code,* being composed not of chapters but of 30 Titles. As the general law for the Eastern Churches, it allows liberty in many ways for each Church to make particular laws.[18]

The current law of the Eastern Orthodox Churches is found in the collection *The Pêdalion/Timone* published by two monks of Mount Athos, Agapios and Nicodimos, in 1800.[19] It comprises *The Canons of the Apostles,* the canons of the first seven councils, of local synods, and of the Holy Fathers.

In the whole period from Gratian to Vatican II, law and theology tended to drift apart rather than be in healthy tension. In the great scholastics, law was truly a second handmaid of theology. Indeed, St. Thomas Aquinas held that law was intimately related to, and in the last analysis a servant of, the Church's sacramental life.[20] But theology and canon law after Gratian became independent disciplines with their own methodology.[21] The lack of interdependence was a weakness both for law and for theology (v. THEOLOGICAL SOURCES)

In the 1983 *Code* there was an attempt to incorporate the theology of Vatican II according to principles enunciated by Paul VI.[22] In promulgating the new law Pope John Paul II stated: "It appears sufficiently clear that the *Code* is in no way intended as a substitute for faith, grace, charisms, and especially charity in the life of the Church and of the faithful. On the contrary, its purpose is rather to create such an order in the ecclesial society that, while assigning the primacy to love, grace, and charisms, it at the same time renders their organic development easier in the life of the ecclesial community and the individual persons who belong to it." The pope also noted: "Indeed, in a certain sense this new *Code* could be understood as a great effort to translate this conciliar doctrine into *canonical* language."[23] In this it was only partially successful.[24] It is implied perhaps by the Apostolic Constitution promulgating the *Code* that the key to its interpretation should be the council, in preference to any other norms.[25]

In the light of this principle applied to both Latin and Eastern *Codes,* it is disappointing not to find any canonical treatment or encouragement of charism (q.v.) which featured so strongly in Vatican II (LG 12; PO 9; AA 3). A Protestant may welcome its greater openness to ecumenism, its advance on matters of the laity, even while finding the section on inter-Church marriages not very helpful.[26]

The Latin and Eastern *Codes,* and the reform of the Curia are the final documents of Vatican II. They are indeed in a different, juridical language, one which is not easy to understand, and which may repel by its very abstractness and succinctness. But these legal documents repay study, for they will continue to influence the life of the Church in the foreseeable future.[27]

[1]P. de Surgy, "Paul et la Torah: Paul et la régulation des prèmieres communautés chrétiennes," AnnéeCan 21 (1977) 111-128; D. Ryan, "Law in the Church: The Vision of Scripture," StCan 17 (1983) 5-27; R. Schnackenburg, *The Moral Teaching of the New Testament* (London, 1962) 56-81. [2]J. A. Alesandro, in Coriden, CIC 1-22; P. Erdö, "Quid significat 'lex' in iure canonico antiquitatis (saecula III-VII)," Periodica 76 (1987) 381-412; J. Gaudemet, "Théologie et droit canonique: Les leçons de l'histoire," RDroitC 39 (1989) 3-13; C. van de Wiel, *History of Canon Law.* Theological and Pastoral Monographs 5 (Leuven: Peeters, 1991). [3]Y. Congar, "Rudolf Sohm nous interroge encore," RSPT 57 (1973) 263-294. [4]P. Erdö, *Introductio in historiam scientiae canonicae: Praenotanda ad Codicem* (Rome: Gregorian UP, 1990). [5]F. Kempf, in Jedin-Dolan 3:426-436. [6]H. Wolter, in Jedin-Dolan 4:93-95, 224-233. [7]G. Alberigo, "Notes sur un nouveau projet de Loi Fondamentale de l'Église," RSPT 62 (1978) 505-522; E. Corecco et al eds., *Les droits fondamentaux du chrétien dans l'Église et dans la société* (Freibourg, Switz.: UP—Freiburg im Br.: Herder, 1981); C. Corral Salvador, "La receptión de la proyectada 'Ley fundamental de la Iglesia' en el Nuevo Código de derecho canónico," EstE 58 (1983) 137-161; E. Lanne, "Réflexions sur une éventuelle loi fondamentale de l'Église," Irén 52 (163-199). [8]Alesandro (n. 2) 8; idem, "The Revision of the Code of Canon Law: A Background Study," StCan 24 (1990) 91-146; F. D'Ostilo, "L'opera di revisione del Codex Iuris Canonici della Chiesa latina," Apoll 55 (1982) 308-369; J. Fox, "A General Synthesis of the Work of the Pontifical Commission for the Revision of the Code of Canon Law," Jurist 48 (1988) 800-848; Conc 170 (1983). [9]OssRomano 26 Jan. 1983, cited J. Herranz, "The Juridical Status of the Laity: The Contribution of the Conciliar Documents and the 1983 Code of Canon Law," Communicationes 17 (1985) 287-315 at 295 = StCan in French 19 (1985) 229-257 at 237, n. 24. See J. Milet, "Les soubassements philosophiques du nouveau Code de Droit Canonique," AnnéeCan 28 (1984) 67-82; H. Müller, "Utrum 'communio' sit principium formale-canonicum novae codificationis iuris canonici Ecclesiae latinae," Periodica 74 (1985) 85-108. [10]Alesandro (n. 2) 11-14; M. Lejeune, "Le droit canonique: règle de droit ou règle d'Église?," StCan 23 (1989) 27-38. See E. Corecco, *Théologie et droit canonique: Écrits pour une nouvelle théorie générale du droit canonique.* Studia friburgensia n.s. 68 (Fribourg: UP, 1990). [11]Alesandro (n. 2) 21. [12]T. Green, "The Use of Vatican II Texts in the Draft *De Populo Dei,*" Conc 147 (1981) 45-53; idem, "Critical Reflections on the Schema on the People of God," StCan 14 (1980) 235-322; H. Rikhof, "The Ecclesiologies of *Lumen gentium,* the *Lex Ecclesiae Fundamentalis* and the Draft Code," Conc 147 (1981) 54-63. [13]J.J. Herrera Aceves, "Eclesiología conciliar y nuevo Código de derecho canónico," EfMex 1/3 (1983) 21-50; see J. Beyer, "Le nouveau Code de Droit Canonique," NRT 106 (1984) 360-382, 566-583; P. Bianchi, "Elementa ecclesiologica in constitutione conciliare *Lumen gentium* cap. 1 et natura iuris canonici," Periodica 72 (1983) 13-51; A. Gómez-López, "Pablo VI: El Derecho Canónico en mistero de la Iglesia," EstFranc 85 (1984) 111-148; S. Pinckaers, "L'Église dans la loi nouvelle: Esprit et institution," NVet 62 (1987) 246-262; G. Thils, "La révision du droit canonique et les problèmes ecclésiologiques qu'elle recontre," RTLv 9 (1978) 329-341. [14]AAS 82 (1990) 1045-1363—*Code of Canons of the Eastern Churches. Latin-English Edition* (Washington, D.C.: Canon Law Society of America, 1992). See O. Bucci, "Il Codice di diritto canonico orientale nella storia della Chiesa," Apoll 55 (1982) 370-448; C. Gallagher, ed., *The Code of Canons of the Oriental Churches: An Introduction* (Rome: Mar Thoma Yogam/St. Thomas Christian Fellowship, 1991); J. Madey, "Das zweite vatikanische Konzil und die Revision des Ostkirchenrechts," Catholica 32 (1978) 188-211; R. Metz, "Quel est le droit pour les Églises orientales unies à Rome," AnnéeCan 30 (1987) 393-409; G. Nedungatt, "The Title of the New Oriental Code," StCan 25 (1991) 465-476. [15]*Crebrae allatae*—AAS 41 (1949) 89-119; *Sollicitudinem nostram*—AAS 42 (1950) 5-120; *Postquam apostolicis litteris*—AAS 44 (1952) 65-152; *Cleri sanctitati*—AAS 49 (1957) 433-603. See V.J. Pospishil, "Oriental Codes," NCE 10:763-767; M.M. Wojnar, "The Code of Oriental Canon Law: *De ritibus orientalibus and De personis,*" Jurist 19 (1959) 212-245, 277-299, 413-464. [16]E. Lanne, "La révision du Droit canonique orientale et le retour aux traditions authentiques de l'Orient," Irén 54 (1981) 485-497. [17]AAS 66 (1974) 246. [18]Apost. Constit. *Sacri canones* (18 Oct. 1991)—*Code of Canon,*[5] (n. 14) pp. xi-xix. See M. Brogi, "Il nuovo Codice orientale e la Chiesa latina," Antonian 66 (1991) 455-468; idem, "Aperture ecumeniche del Codex canonum ecclesiarum orientalium," ibid., 455-468; G. Caprile, "Il nuovo Codice dei canoni delle chiese orientali," CivCatt 142 (1991) 1:171-177; E. Eid, "La révision du Code de droit canonique oriental: histoire et principes," AnnéeCan 33 (1990) 11-27; R. Metz, "Rome et les Églises orientales: Le 'Code des canons' des Églises orientales," Études 375 (1991) 683-691; G. Nedungatt, "The Title of the New Oriental Code," StCan 25 (1991) 465-476; idem, "Glossary of the Main Terms Used in the Code of Canons of the Eastern Churches," Jurist 51 (1991) 451-459; D. Salachas, "Ecclesia universa et Ecclesia sui iuris nel Codice latino e nel Codice dei Canoni della Chiese Orintali," Apoll 65 (1991) 65-76. [19]Reprint. Athens, 1970. [20]M. Useros Carretero, *"Statuta Ecclesiae" y "Sacramenta Ecclesiae" en la eclesiología de St. Tomás.* Analecta Gregoriana 119 (Rome: Gregorian UP, 1962). Cf. P.A. Bonnet, "Eucharistia et ius," Periodica 66 (1977) 583-616; P.M. Garín, "Hacia una teología del derecho canónico," EstE 56 (1981) 1433-1450; M. Wijlens, *Theology and Canon Law: The Theories of Klaus Morsdorf and Eugenio Correco* (London: University Press of America, 1992). [21]R. Foreville, "Le recours aux sources scripturaires: A quel moment de l'histoire l'Écriture a-t-elle cessé d'être source directe du droit de l'Église?," AnnéeCan 21 (1977) 49-55; C. Munier, "L'autorité de l'Église dans le système des sources du droit médiéval," IusCan 16 (1976) 39-60; D. Shanahan, "Legislating for the People of God: The Lessons from History," StCan 17 (1983) 29-45. [22]Address to Canon Law Congress, "The Juridical Structure of the Church as Protection of Spiritual Order," OssRomanoEnglish (4 Oct. 1973) 2. [23]Apost. Constit. *Sacrae disciplinae leges* (1983); Cf. M. López, "Naturaleza teológico de la ciencia del derecho canónico," EfMex 3/9 (1985) 88-103; L. Örsy, "Integrated Interpretation or, The Role of Theology in the Interpretation of Canon Law," StCan 22 (1988) 245-264; R. Sublon, "Théologie et loi," RDroitC 39 (1989) 15-30. [24]E.Corecco, "Aspects of the Reception of Vatican II in the Code of Canon Law," in G. Alberigo et al., eds., *The Reception of Vatican II* (Tunbridge Wells UK: Burns & Oates—Washington, D.C.: The Catholic University of America Press, 1987) 249-296. [25]Ibid., 295-296. [26]R. Voeltzel, "Une lecture protestante du nouveau Code de droit canonique," RHPR 66 (1986) 109-121; J.R. Wright, "The 1983 Code of Canon Law: An Anglican Evaluation," Jurist 46 (1986) 394-418; cf. L. Vischer, "Church Law and the Ecumenical Movement," Jurist 37 (1977) 1-13. [27]J. Beyer, "Studium Codicis, Schola Concilii," Seminarium 34 (1983) 455-471—in French; G. Thils, "Le nouveau Code de droit canonique et l'ecclésiologie de Vatican II," RTLv 14 (1983) 289-301. For sources, see X. Ochoa, ed., *Leges Ecclesiae,* six vols., 1917-1984 (Rome: Instit. Iuridicum Claretianum, 1966-1987); D.A. Gutiérrez, ed., vol. 7, 1983-1992 (ibid., 1994).

## LECTORS

See READERS

## LEFEBVRE, Archbishop Marcel (1906–1991)

Formerly an African missionary bishop of Dakar and Tulle, Marcel Lefebvre belonged to the more conservative wing at Vatican II (q.v.), though he signed most of its documents. From early on he was an opponent of liturgical reform, charging that "the principal director (Bugnini q.v.) of liturgical reform at the Vatican was a Freemason."[1] He became the leader of opposition to the conciliar liturgical renewal and to the council itself. He was a founder of the Fraternity of Pius X and the seminary at Écône. The quasi-official organ of the movement was *Lettre aux amis.*

His Profession of Faith (1974) summarizes his views: ". . . we refuse and always have refused to follow the Rome of neo-modernist and neo-Protestant tendencies which clearly manifested themselves in the Second Vatican Council and after the Council in all the reforms which issued from it. . . . The *lex orandi* cannot be profoundly modified without also modifying the *lex credendi.* To the new Mass correspond a new Catechism, new priesthood, new seminaries, new universities, a Charismatic Pentecostal Church—all things that are opposed to orthodoxy and the magisterium as they have always been. This reform, the fruit of liberalism and modernism, is completely and utterly poisoned; it starts from heresy and ends with heresy, even if not all its acts are formally heretical. It is accordingly impossible for any aware and faithful Catholic to adopt this reform and to submit to it in any way whatsoever."[2]

A Vatican visitation of Écône in 1975 provoked by the Profession of Faith recommended the dissolution of the Fraternity, the closing of the seminary, and a prohibition against any support for the work of the archbishop by clergy or laity. Lefebvre met Paul VI in 1976 but did not change his views. He was suspended from priestly ministry in that year for defying a Vatican order not to ordain priests. In 1988, despite an exchange of letters and attempts at reconciliation on the part of the Congregation of the Doctrine of the Faith,[3] he proceeded to ordain four of his priests as bishops. He was immediately excommunicated. Some would call into question not only the licitness, but also the validity, of such a schismatic consecration.[4]

Though extreme views on the right (and the left) are a constant feature of the Church's history, they are always a challenge to the unity and catholicity in the communion (q.v.) of the Church.[5]

[1]A. Bugnini, *The Reform of the Liturgy 1948–1975* (Collegeville: The Liturgical Press, 1990) 91, n. 36. [2]Text, in Y. Congar, *Challenge to the Church: The Case of Archbishop Lefebvre* (London: Collins—Dublin: Veritas, 1976) 77–78. [3]Origins 18 (1988) 97–101. [4]E.g., G. Mucci, "Mons. Lefebvre e la consacrazione episcopale," Sap 42 (1989) 65–70; Congar (n. 2) 22; cf. J.M.R. Tillard, "Sacrements et communion ecclésiale: Le cas de Lambeth et d'Écône," NRT 111 (1989) 641–663; M. Zalba, "Num Ecclesia habeat potestatem invalidandi ritum sacramentalem ordinis ab episcopis exclusis peractum," Periodica 78 (1989) 187–242. [5]B. de Margerie, *Écône: comment dénouer la tragédie: Réflexions théologiques et pastorales* (Paris: Téqui, 1988); cf. A. Fischer, "Lefebvrism—Jansenism Revisited," NBlackfr 71 (1990) 274–286; H. O'Leary, "The Lefebvre Movement: A Catholic Manifestation of Fundamentalism," AustralCR 67 (1990) 401–412.

## LEO I—Pope St. LEO THE GREAT (440–461)

Little is known about the youth of Leo,[1] except that as a deacon he strongly opposed Pelagianism. He was born probably in the late 4th century. He clearly had a fine classical education, which is obvious in his terse and harmonious Latin style. He became pope in 440, and his papacy is noted for two features: his defense of orthodox Christology and his assertions of papal power. What he called the "Robber Council" *(Latrocinium)*[2] at Ephesus in 449 acquitted Eutyches of heresy in his doctrine of only one nature in Christ, deposed the orthodox Flavian, and insulted the papal legates who had brought Leo's *Tome (Epistola dogmatica).* He agreed to the summoning of the Council of Chalcedon (451—q.v.), where his *Tome* was greeted as the voice of Peter. He was not, however, pleased with the 28th canon of that council, which elevated Constantinople to a patriarchal see equal to Rome, since both were imperial cities.[3] Initially he resisted approving this canon, appealing to the Ephesus canon, drawn up before Constantinople became an imperial city,[4] on the grounds that he was defending Antioch and Alexandria, both of which were considered to be Petrine sees.[5]

Leo developed the theory and practice of papal power, but in line with his predecessor Celestine I (422–432): Peter still presides in the see of Rome and speaks through it.[6] Leo reminded his vicar in Thessalonica that the latter did not possess a plenitude of power.[7] There is some universal primacy: "Peter rules all whom Christ also ruled originally";[8] a key notion of the Petrine ministry is to ensure *firmitas,* and thus local or regional decisions should be forwarded to Rome for confirmation;[9] novelty was eschewed—Leo did not so much want to begin new things as to renew the old; decisions of earlier approved councils and of popes were irreversible.[10] Leo encouraged the holding of synods at Rome and elsewhere; indeed, these were a key element in his view of, and use of, papal authority.[11] With regard to titles, he seldom called Christ the Supreme Pontiff,[12] but he saw Christ and Peter being present and active in the power and care *(potestas—sollicitudo)* of the bishop of Rome.[13] Contrary to widely held views, Leo does not seem to have used the title *Pontifex maximus* as a papal one, a title used in late medieval times.[14]

Leo's ecclesiology is much broader than his well-known positions on the papacy. Though he is in the line of the ecclesiology of the Latin Fathers, notably Augustine, he was also open to a more Alexandrian theology espoused by Hilary.[15] In his Christmas, Paschal, and Pentecost sermons he drew out the ecclesiological implications of these mysteries:[16] "Christmas is the origin of the Christian people, and the birthday of the head is the birthday of the body";[17] in the Incarnation humanity is reformed;[18] with the Ascension "what was visible has now passed into the sacraments";[19] this change is due to the Spirit at Pentecost who causes the Church to be born visibly;[20] the Spirit unveils a Church already existing in Christ, and the apostles see themselves as its members.[21] In the sermons preached yearly on 29 September, the anniversary of his episcopal ordination, he draws out the implications of ministry and the People of God, especially the priestly character of all the members of the Church.[22]

The ecclesiology of Leo is at its basis Trinitarian: he sees the Church as the visible sacrament of the Trinity,[23] and from this arises the injunction: let us imitate what we want to celebrate (*quod celebrare optamus imitemur*).[24] In this Trinitarian context G. Hudon points out that the titles given to the Church by Leo assume a profound meaning: holy Church, Church of God, universal Church, Church of the faithful people, Body of Christ, Body of the Church, body of Christian unity, body of catholic communion, joining of the Body of Christ, joining of catholic companionship, holy city, city of God, eternal temple, sacred building, paradise of the Church, house of God, Spouse of the Word, family of God, building of the eternal temple, camp of the Lord, virgin Church, spouse of the one man Christ.[25]

[1]OxDPopes 43–45; K. Baus, in Jedin-Dolan 2:264-269.    [2]*Epist.* 95 to Empress Pulcheria—PL 54:943.    [3]Tanner 1:99-100.    [4]Canon 6—ibid., 1:8-9.    [5]R.B. Eno, *The Rise of the Papacy.* Theology and Life 32 (Wilmington: Glazier, 1990) 110, 112–113.    [6]*Serm.* 5:4— PL 54:154-155; *Epist.* 25:2—PL 54:741-743; *Serm.* 2:2; 3:3; and 4—PL 54:143-144, 146, 148-152.    [7]*Epist.* 14:1—PL 54:668-671. [8]*Serm.* 4:2—PL 54:150.    [9]*Epist.* 12:13—PL 54:656.    [10]Eno (n. 4) 110–115; P.McShane, "Leo the Great, Guardian of Doctrine and Discipline," EgIT 14 (1983) 9–24.    [11]H.J.Sieben, "Episcopal Conferences in the Light of Particular Councils During the First Millennium," Jurist 48 (1988) 30–56.    [12]*Serm.* 5:3—PL 54:154. [13]P.A. McShane, *La romanitas et le Pape Léon le Grand.* Théologie 24 (Paris-Tournai: Desclée—Montreal: Bellarmin, 1979) 136–232; P. Studer, "Leo der Grosse und der Primat des römischen Bischofs," in J. Brantschen and P. Selvatico, eds., *Unterwegs zur Einheit.* FS H. Sturnimann (Fribourg: UP, 1980) 617–630; W. Ullmann, "Leo I and the Theme of Papal Primacy," JRelSt 11 (1960) 25–51;    [14]Y. Congar, "Titres donnés au pape," Conc (French) 108 (1975) 55–65 at 62–63.    [15]P.-T. Camelot, "Les sens de l'Église chez les Pères Latins," NRT 83 (1961) 367–381.    [16]G. Hudon, "L'Église dans la pensée de saint Léon," EgIT 14 (1983) 305–336; idem, "Le concept d'‘assumptio' dans l'ecclésiologie de Léon le Grand," StPatr 18/1 (1989) 155–169.    [17]*Serm.* 26:2—PL 54:213.    [18]*Serm.* 27:6—PL 54:220-221.    [19]*Serm.* 74:2—PL 54:398.    [20]*Serm.* 76:3—PL 54: 405-406.    [21]Hudon (n. 17) 325.    [22]*Serm.* 2:2 and 4:1—PL 54:143-144, 148–149.    [23]Hudon (n. 16) 334.    [24]*Serm.* 50:3—PL 54:307-308.    [25]Art. cit. (n. 16) 334–335.

## LEO XIII, Pope (1878–1903)

Vincenzo Gioacchino Pecci was born south of Rome in 1810. Soon after his ordination he entered the papal service and was a papal diplomat in several countries before becoming bishop of Perugia (1846–1878) and cardinal, in 1853. Already as bishop he began to seek a *rapprochement* with contemporary culture. His election when he was in frail health and aged sixty-eight seemed to indicate an interim papacy, but he was to be a most accomplished pope during a very long reign (1878–1903).[1]

In his encyclical *Divinum illud* on the Holy Spirit (1897) he reflected on the twin aims of his pontificate: "The restoration . . . of the principles of the Christian life in civil and domestic society (and the promotion) of Christian unity."[2] He was certainly too modest, for his wide magisterium included eighty-six encyclicals, though some of them would today be given a different classification.[3]

He promoted Church-State relations in many countries though he had little success with France or his native Italy. He fostered the study of St. Thomas Aquinas with the encyclical *Aeterni Patris* (q.v.) and gave his name to the Leonine Commission which was charged with the production of a critical edition of St. Thomas Aquinas (begun 1882 and still not nearing completion). He opened the Vatican archives to scholars of any creed (1883). With *Providentissimus Deus* (1893),[4] he gave some limited encouragement to modern biblical research. His best known work is the foundation of modern Catholic social teaching, *Rerum novarum* (1891).[5] In it he endorsed private property but spoke also about workers' rights, trade unions, the just wage.

Even though modern ecumenism (q.v.) was not yet born, Leo was deeply concerned with Christian unity and was apparently the first pope to speak of separated brothers. In the encyclical *Praeclara* (1884)[6] he sought the return of the Orthodox and Protestants to Rome. Two years later he rejected a federal solution to the problem of disunity in an encyclical, *Satis cognitum,* which laid heavy stress on the magisterium (q.v.), the papacy (v. PAPAL PRIMACY) and bishops (q.v.).[7]

Leo XIII had a special concern for England: he sought its conversion in several ways: he wrote a letter to the English hierarchy;[8] he made J.H. Newman (q.v.) a cardinal (1879); he set up a commission to investigate Anglican Orders (q.v.), but in the end pronounced them invalid.[9]

Other significant documents include his encyclical on the Holy Spirit, *Divinum illud munus*,[10] as well as a rich corpus of ten encyclicals on the Virgin Mary.[11] One of the most interesting of the latter is *Adjutricem populi* (1895), in which he acknowledges the Eastern contribution to Mariology and invokes Mary's intercession on behalf of Christian unity.[12]

Towards the end of his reign Leo became more cautious and severe in his attitudes: he set up the Biblical Commission (1902); he published new norms for censorship (1897) and a new *Index* (1900). He was drawn into the controversy about "Americanism" in a letter to Cardinal Gibbons (1899).[13] The term and theory arose in ultraconservative French circles, which took issue with a translation of the biography of the founder of the Paulists, Isaac Hecker (1819–1888). They accused Hecker and other American Catholics of watering down Catholic doctrine in order to facilitate conversions and Church unity, and of substituting American values like democracy and pragmatism for more traditional ones. "Americanism" was largely a phantom heresy, and there is little evidence that many significant Americans actually held the views condemned.[14]

Leo XIII vigorously encouraged the expansion of Church structures outside Europe: 248 sees, 48 vicariates/prefectures and 2 patriarchates.

[1]OxDPopes 311–313; O. Köhler, in Jedin-Dolan 9:3–10, bibliog. 587–589; J. Schmidlin, *Papstgeschichte der neuesten Zeit*. 4 vols. (Munich, 1933–1939) 2:231–589; L.P. Wallace, *Leo XIII* (Durham, N.C., 1966); cf. E.T. Gargan, ed., *Leo XIII and the Modern World* (New York, 1961).   [2]ASS 29 (1896–1897) 644–645/Carlen 2:409–410.   [3]English text, Carlen 2:5–518.   [4]ASS 26 (1893–1894) 269–292/Carlen 2:325–338.   [5]ASS 23 (1890–1891) 641–670/Carlen 2:241–261; see G. Antonazzi, critical ed. (Rome, 1957); O. Köhler, in Jedin-Dolan 9:195–209 with bibliog., 599–602.   [6]*Praeclara*—ASS 26 (1893–1894) 705–717.   [7]*Satis cognitum*—ASS 28 (1895–1896) 708–739/Carlen 2:387–404.   [8]*Amantissimae voluntatis* (14 April 1895)—ASS 27 (1894–1895) 583–593.   [9]*Apostolicae curae*—ASS 29 (1896–1897) 193–203.   [10]ASS 29 (1896–1897) 644–658/Carlen 2:409–492. See Antón 2:480–492.   [11]List G.M. Roschini, *Maria santissima nella storia della salvezza*. 4 vols. (Isola del Liri: Ed. Pisani, 1969) 1:263; see J. Bittremieux, *Doctrina mariana Leonis XIII* (Bruges, 1928).   [12]ASS 28 (1895–1896) 129–136/Carlen 2:375–385.   [13]*Testem benevolentiae*—ASS 31 (1898–1899) 470–479/in part DS 3340–3346/ND 2015–2018.   [14]O. Köhler, in Jedin-Dolan 9:331–334; T.T. McAvoy, *The Great Crisis in American Catholic History 1895–1900* (Chicago: Regnery, 1957).

## LIBERAL PROTESTANTISM

The word "liberal," in general use since the early 19th century, has many meanings. It can be taken to imply an openness to new ideas, to freedom, and to progress. But the form which such openness takes varies in each movement which is styled liberal. In the 19th century there were Catholic liberals who were basically orthodox, but favored political democracy and Church reform.

In ecclesiology Protestant liberalism indicates a set of views which are strongly anti-dogmatic and anti-institutional;[1] it sought a reconstruction of Christian origins and faith in terms that today would be judged as excessively humanist. The origins of Liberal Protestantism can be traced to the Enlightenment and especially to F. Schleiermacher (1768–1834), in particular to his emphasis on religious feeling as absolute dependence *(schlecthin abhängig)* and to his primacy of the experience of Jesus.[2] Later, A. Harnack (1851–1930) would see Catholicism arising out of the struggle with Gnosticism, and as having four characteristics: traditionalism, orthodoxy, ritualism, and monasticism, with a fifth in the West, viz., legalism.[3] R. Sohm (1841–1917) saw all law, and not just legalism, as irreconcilable with a Church that is a spiritual community. A. Dulles notes: "In summary, Catholicism as viewed by liberal Protestants is preeminently the religion of dogma and law, tradition and hierarchy, sacrament and monasticism. These institutional elements, it is alleged, are foreign to the religion of Jesus."[4] By the First World War, Liberal Protestantism was on the wane, and was decisively rejected in the neo-orthodoxy of K. Barth (q.v.).

[1]B.M.G. Reardon, *Liberal Protestantism* (Cambridge: UP, 1968).   [2]K.W. Clements, *Friedrich Schleiermacher: Pioneer of Modern Theology*. The Making of Modern Theology 1 (London—San Francisco: Collins, 1987).   [3]*What Is Christianity?* (New York: Harper, 1957) 207–268.   [4]*The Catholicity of the Church* (Oxford: Clarendon, 1985) 108.

## LIBERATION THEOLOGIES AND ECCLESIOLOGY

In the past two decades there has been an enormous bibliography in the area of liberation. Its main lines are clear,[1] though we have to understand that we are dealing with theologies of liberation, with significant variations from author to author, from country to country, from culture to culture. This article concentrates on liberation theologies and ecclesiology.

Authors give various dates for the origins of liberation theology. Some will place it in the years immediately preceding 1965, when there were some indicators of liberation in the then current language of development and progress. The idea of countries and peoples being in a state of privative dependence began to emerge. The father of liberation theology is usually reckoned to be G. Gutiérrez (q.v.), though some of its themes can be traced to J. Ellul,[2] and to the educational work of P. Freire.[3] Some will go even further back to the conversion of Bartolomé de las Casas in 1514, whom Gutiérrez himself numbers among the "fathers" of liberation theology.[4] Even though Latin American theologians are often at pains to distance or dissociate themselves from European theology, the political theology of J.B. Metz (q.v.) and J. Moltmann (q.v.) was not without influence, especially since many of the liberation theologians studied in Europe. A significant lecture by G. Gutiérrez[5] in the months before Medellín gives a good indication of the position of liberation theology before that historic meeting of the Episcopal Conference of Latin America (CELAM) in 1968. Medellín stated that solidarity with the poor was to be a characteristic of the Church in Latin America.[6] Though the conference did not use the technical term "liberation theology," it spoke frequently of "liberation." L. Boff (q.v.) has described Medellín as a creative reception of Vatican II.[7] In the years before the next CELAM conference (Puebla 1979) there was an explosion of creative writing and reflection on the theme of liberation. Some will divide the period into two phases: the formative phase (1968–1975) and the systematizing phase (from 1976).[8] It is important to realize that liberation theology is rapidly evolving, and the picture given by books a decade ago may not be an accurate reflection of the present; moreover, there can be quite a time-lag between the original publication of a book and its appearance in an English translation.

The method[9] of liberation theology in its common Latin American form begins with reality, which it analyzes as a state of deprivation and above all of dependence instead of God-willed freedom. It gives first place to *praxis,* which must be carefully understood. It refers above all to the action of the oppressed people themselves towards their own liberation. Whereas practice is just action, *praxis* is an orientation-towards-theory; *praxis* precedes and leads to theological theory, and theology arises from, and is in fact, critical reflection on *praxis,* especially in the light of the Scriptures. The Scriptures themselves are studied not so much with the tools of exegesis but from within the human situation in which they are read;[10] there is a "hermeneutical circle," which does not study the sources of revelation in the abstract but from a specific situation.[11] While the earlier works on liberation theology emphasized the Exodus-Sinai tradition and the OT prophets, later studies focus much more on the NT, especially the kingdom (q.v.) paradigm.[12] The favored texts now are Luke 4:18-19 and Matt 25, though Pauline texts are at present also coming to the fore.

Up to nine currents have been detected in the theologies of liberation: first, spiritual/pastoral (commitment on the basis of the gospel—Cardinals P.E. Arns and H. Camara, J.L. Segundo, and the Basic Christian Communities—q.v.); second, methodological (systematic attempts to undertake interdisciplinary theology—I. Ellacuria, L. and C. Boff); third, sociological (analysis of situation as necessary presupposition for theology—H. Assmann); fourth, historical (reinter-

pretation of Latin American history in the light of Marxist analysis—E. Dussel); fifth, political (a political praxis for all, priests and religious as well as laity—G. Arroyo); sixth, ecclesiological/popular (the base community as expressing the people of God with attempt to integrate religiosity, cultures—L. Boff, S. Galilea); seventh, Christological (study of Jesus as liberator—J. Sobrino, L. Boff); eighth, pedagogical (liberating education—P. Freire, I. Illich); ninth, self-criticism (certain themes of liberation theology accepted with caution—B. Kloppenburg, J. Comblin).[13] Others might add those who write on revolutionary violence (J. Comblin), though liberation theologians stand clear of violence. J.L. Segundo prefers to speak of two forms of theology which coexist in Latin America. The first, which was a study of the conditions of the poor, and how the Church could help them, originated in university circles in the 1960s. The second was the involvement of the poor in their own liberation; reality and the Church are at this stage viewed from the perspective of the poor.[14]

There is a clear distinction between European ecclesiology and Latin American liberation ecclesiology: the former seeks to understand the reality of the Church, using up-to-date tools of exegesis, patristics, tradition, the legacy of Vatican II, and reading the signs of the times, and so forth; the latter seeks to change the Church by reforming it from the perspective of the poor.[15]

One of the key insights of Latin American liberation theology is its sharp perception of the historical and social location of faith, the perception that faith is always embodied in a particular social context.[16] Along with that, there is the issue of salvation: the liberation theologian is not satisfied with personal eschatological expectation but demands that the good news be seen to be operative in our world also:[17] the history of salvation yields to the salvation of history.[18] Salvation "embraces every aspect of humanity: body and spirit, individual and society, person and cosmos, time and eternity."[19] The Boff brothers state that salvation has to do with "the eschatological condition of the human being'"and therefore with the deeper dimension of the person than with economic, political, and social integrity, though not excluding these.[20] The underlying issues were addressed by the International Theological Commission from 1974 to 1977. Its final document, *Human Promotion and Christian Salvation* praised the concern for the poor but was cautious on the issue of salvation, stressing the need to maintain the correct relationship between salvation which comes from God and human development, which is the work of men and women.[21]

The second meeting of the Conference of Latin American Bishops (CELAM) at Puebla (1979) was more confrontational in that many of the participants (and the organizers) interpreted quite differently the road which had been traveled from the CELAM Medellín a decade earlier.[22] A significant limitation of Puebla was the deliberate exclusion of liberation theologians who had, at most, indirect influence only on the final text. The prolix Final Document shows two unreconciled theologies: one a traditional conservative Christology and ecclesiology, the other arising from the questions and the situation in which liberation theology was thriving, viz., in the midst of the poor. Nonetheless the adoption of a preferential option for the poor in its Final Report[23] was a major development for the whole Latin American Church.

In 1984 and 1986 two documents were issued by the Congregation for the Doctrine of the Faith (CDF): *Instruction on Certain Aspects of the "Theology of Liberation"* and *Instruction on Christian Liberation and Freedom.* The first was mainly negative, with a heavy emphasis on the danger of Marxism; the second was much more positive.[24] It was the intention of the Congregation that both documents be read together. Commentators were quick to realize that even the first, more negative, document by its very publication gave an ecclesial status to the theology of liberation. Since it envisaged no one particular liberation theologian but examined trends, it is open to more positive interpretations than it has often received. On the key issue of Marxism some clarification must be made. Liberation theologians have usually distinguished three different functions of Marxism: as a scientific analysis of society; as a political project for society; as a world-view. They claim to use only the first of these. But its conclusions can be arrived at without necessarily any recourse to Marx.[25] W.R. Barr notes that "the use of Marxist analysis in liberation theology seems to function more as an instrument of critique than as a prescription for achieving the needed transformation of society." He further observes that the use of Marxist analysis certainly does not involve adherence to Marxist political parties or movement. Furthermore, liberationists point out the narrowness of classical Marxism, which does not take account of moral, mystical, and eschatological dimensions of human endeavor.[26] Others will argue that only a selective use of Marxism is itself a reason for failure in liberation theologies.[27] There is a truth in Latin American theologies of liberation: the necessity of the application of the principles of the gospel to society especially in the realm of justice. But the CDF is afraid that any use of Marxism will run the risk of adopting the whole Marxist view of society and of its betterment.

The influence of Marxism has turned some theologians towards a presentation of a political Christ, of a Church involved in class struggle, and in the revolu-tionary process. Closely connected then with ecclesiology is the Christology of liberation theologians. The Christology espoused by some liberation theologians stresses Jesus' relationship with the Zealots, his attitude towards the rich and powerful, and his death at the hands of political authority. All of these themes do not exhaust the picture of Jesus and can seriously compromise the central kingdom message of Jesus and his assertions that his kingdom is not of this world (John 18:36; cf. John 6:15; Mark 12:17). There is nonetheless a broad consensus that Jesus concentrated his ministry among the poor and proclaimed the kingdom as a radical transformation not only of personal but also of social existence. Such Christologies arise not from academic studies but from the attempt to understand the meaning of Jesus Christ today in the struggles and suffering of the poor.[28]

The Basic Christian Communities (q.v.) are a significant feature in Latin American ecclesiology. In this context "basic" indicates both what is at the bottom of the socio-economic pyramid, and also what is primarily lay. Both the theoreticians and the pastorally involved see the Basic Christian Communities as a new way of being Church.[29] There is some danger of excessively playing down the hierarchical structure of the Church. After some earlier hesitation, Pope Paul VI spoke with guarded enthusiasm about such communities in his great exhortation *Evangelization in the Modern World.*[30] The theme was given extensive treatment at Puebla.

The issue of popular religiosity (q.v.) is ambivalent. Popular is to be taken in its Spanish sense as "of the people." In the beginning, liberation theologians tended to see as insignificant, or even negative, the popular religion of the people, with their fiestas and other manifestations. Now there is a greater openness to see these manifestations as part of the culture and authentic expression of the faith of the little ones of society.[31] But it has dangers of being a peripheral element in the life of the Church, and of containing erroneous or unhealthy elements. But in the above mentioned exhortation, Paul VI saw their possibilities both for evangelization and for a full living of the Christian vocation.[32] Popular religion has also been taken as seeing a Church of the people parallel to, or even excluding, the institutional Church. Hence the post-synodal exhortation on the laity of Pope John Paul II lays down criteria for the ecclesiality of groups.[33]

Since a 1975 conference in Detroit, there has been a widening of the range of liberation theology: Latin American liberation began to be associated with black theology (q.v.)[34] and feminist theology (v. FEMINISM);[35] an incipient liberation theology for homosexuals is also found.[36] With the foundation of The Ecumenical Association of Third World Theologians, liberation theology began to spread into Africa,[37] India,[38] Asia,[39] and the Third World generally.[40] A Jewish liberation theology is also developing.[41] In places like Europe and North America a distinctive liberation theology must be sought, which will not be a simple displacement of models from other countries; the work of E. Schillebeeckx (q.v.) and R. Haight are examples of beginnings of this process.[42] In Protestant Churches the reception of liberation varies and reflects much of the diversity in the Catholic Church.[43] Furthermore, the insights of liberation theology inevitably raise the question of the need for liberation in some areas within the Church[44] (v. HUMAN RIGHTS).

The documents of the CDF insist on an integral liberation, so that F.A. Sullivan, drawing on them and on documents of Vatican II and other magisterial pronouncements, can rightly call the Church the "Sacrament of Integral Salvation."[45] What we have to seek is liberation from all oppressive forces, the greatest of which are sin and death. Jesus brings liberation (John 8:33-35) by giving his life for the many (Mark 10:45; 20:28). His kingdom is to be characterized by love (John 13:34; 15:12), the new foundation of a loving and caring society (v. BROTHERS AND SISTERS). The gospel does not lay down regulations regarding the duties of justice; it makes no insistent appeal to an oppressed group, nor does it present the Messiah as the righteous judge. In Jesus' manner of speaking, justice preserves its biblical meaning of fidelity to the law.[46] Orthodox theology would lean towards the view of integral liberation.[47]

If theologies of liberation are to fulfil their promise and hope, they will have to be supported by a deepened spirituality. From quite early on, essays on spirituality began to appear,[48] but as these were not quickly translated, the charge was made that liberation theology was bereft of a spirituality. Another weakness has been pneumatology (q.v.) and theological reflection on charism (q.v.), for there are many ways of being committed to authentic liberation according to the personal gifting of the Holy Spirit. This lacuna is now being remedied.[49] A serious weakness is the absence of a strong philosophical foundation in liberation theology—one of the reasons for its dalliance with Marxism and explaining Cardinal J. Ratzinger's criticism of philosophical irrationality, even though this latter is perhaps over-harshly stated.[50]

Liberation theology will also have to be more open to hostile[51] and sympathetic attempts at criticism;[52] there is much to be learned by all in the story of L. Boff (q.v.). There is a danger that liberation theology's primary emphasis on *praxis* may lead it to reject the contribution that the Church's tradition as well as the Bible can helpfully bring on its findings. Moreover, there is a certain tendency to romanticize the poor so

that they are seen almost as infallible guides to the positions the Church must adopt in order to be faithful to Christ. Above all, liberation theology must be open to the *Catholica;*[53] otherwise it risks becoming peripheral both to the Church and the world.

Many liberation theologians look to Mary's *Magnificat* as a song of liberation. The second CDF document echoes this theme but goes deeper in seeing Mary as "the perfect image of freedom, and of the liberation of humanity and of the universe."[54]

[1]Bibliog. J.J. Alemany and J.L. Barbero, "Teología de la liberación: Bibliografía de revistas 1970–1988," MiscCom 46 (1988) 489–584. See L. Boff and C. Boff, *Introducing Liberation Theology* (London: Burns & Oates—Maryknoll: Orbis, 1987); D. Carroll, *What Is Liberation Theology?* (Dublin—Cork, Mercier, 1986); I. Ellacuría and J. Sobrino, eds., *Mysterium liberationis: Conceptos fundamentales de la teología de la liberación.* 2 vols. (Madrid: Ed. Trotta, 1990); M.H. Ellis and O. Maduro, eds., *The Future of Liberation Theology.* FS G. Gutiérrez (Maryknoll: Orbis, 1989); D.W. Ferm, *Profiles in Liberation: 36 Portraits of Third World Theologians* (Mystic: 23rd Publications, 1988); R. Gibellini, *The Liberation Theology Debate* (London: SCM, 1987); R. Haight, *An Alternative Vision: An Interpretation of Liberation Theology* (Mahwah: Paulist, 1985); idem, "Liberation Theology," NDictT 570–576; A.F. Mc Govern, *Liberation Theology and Its Critics: Toward an Assessment* (Maryknoll: Orbis, 1989); R. Marlé, *Introduction à la théologie de la libération* (Paris: Desclée de Brouwer, 1988); C. Ménard, "L'ecclésiologie des théologiens de la libération: Contexte générale et analyse de quelques questions ecclésiologiques discutées par Leonardo Boff," EglT 19 (1988) 349–372; J.B. Metz, ed., *Die Theologie der Befreiung: Hoffnung oder Gefahr für die Kirche* (Düsseldorf: Patmos, 1986).   [2]G. Gutiérrez, "Notes for a Theology of Liberation," TS 31 (1970) 243–261; T. Hanks, "The Original 'Liberation Theologian,'" CrossC 35 (1985–1986) 17–31.   [3]Cf. D.E. Collins, *Paulo Freire: His Life, Works and Thought* (New York: Paulist, 1977); P. Freire, *Pedagogy of the Oppressed* (New York: Herder & Herder, 1970—Brazil 1967).   [4]M. Sievernich, "'Liberation Theology' in Intercultural Dialogue," TDig 34 (1987) 117–121 at 118.   [5]"Toward a Theology of Liberation," in A.T. Hennelly, ed., *Liberation Theology: A Documentary History* (Maryknoll: Orbis, 1990) 62–76.   [6]Ibid., 114–119.   [7]"Eine kreative Rezeption des II. Vatikanums aus der Sicht der Armen: Die Theologie der Befreiung," TJb 1987, 167–188. Cf. S. Galilea, "Latin America in the Medellín and Puebla Conferences: An Example of Selective and Creative Reception of Vatican II," in G. Alberigo et al., eds., *The Reception of Vatican II* (Washington, D.C.: The Catholic University of America—Tunbridge Wells UK: Burns & Oates, 1987) 59–73; A. Gonzales Montes, "Sobre la teología de la liberación," Carthag 1 (1985) 95–119 at 101–102.   [8]E.g., Gibellini (n. 1) 2.   [9]R. Haight (n. 1) 43–63. Cf. A.Alvarez-Suárez, "Repensamiento teológico de la 'teología de la liberación,'" Teres 40 (1989) 23–43; J. Andrés Vela, "Elementos metodológicos en la teología de la liberación," TXav 38 (1988) 105–133; M.C. Bingemer, "Solidariedade ou conflito—Possibilidades de diálogo entre a doutrina social da igreja e a teologia de libertação," REBras 50 (1990) 844–957; C. Boff, *Theology and Praxis: Epistemological Foundations* (Maryknoll: Orbis, 1987—Brazil 1978); G. Colombo, "La teologia della liberazione: La questione del metodo," Teologia 12 (1982) 167–196, 264–282; Gibellini (n. 1) 1–19; idem, "Origine e metodo della teologia della liberazione," RasT 26 (1985) 302–324; R. García-Mateo, "Die Methode der Theologie der Befreiung: Zur Überwindung des Erfahrungsdefizits in der Theologie," StimZ 204 (1986) 386–396; A.T. Hennelly, *Theology for a Liberating Church: The New Praxis of*

*Freedom* (Washington, D.C.: Georgetown UP, 1989); J.G. O'Donnell, "The Problem of Methodology in Liberation Theology," LouvSt 8 (1980–1981) 258–264; R. Sánchez Chamoso, "La recuperación de la ortopraxis y sus causas explicativas," CiTom 71 (1980) 481–518; M.T. Vizcaya, "El método en la teología de la liberación," CiTom 114 (1987) 521–546.  [10]C. Mesters, "The Use of the Bible in Christian Communities of Common People," in Hennelly (n. 5) 14–28, or in S. Torres and J. Eagleson, eds., *The Challenge of Basic Christian Communities* (Maryknoll: Orbis, 1971) 197–210. Cf. S. Croatto, "Biblical Hermeneutics in the Theology of the Oppressed," VYoti 46 (1982) 54–69; R. Duarte, "Reflexión bíblica sobre la teología de la liberación," EfMex 6/17 (1988) 249–258; A. Rizzi, "Elementi di una teologia della liberazione per l'Occidente," RasT 28 (1987) 556–577; 29 (1988) 63–77.  [11]J.L. Segundo, *The Liberation of Theology* (Maryknoll: Orbis, 1975).  [12]J.E. Emmette Weir, "Liberation Theology Comes of Age," ExpTim 98 (1986–1987) 3–9; cf. G.V. Pixley, *On Exodus: A Liberation Perspective* (Maryknoll: Orbis, 1987–1983 Spanish).  [13]Cf. J. Mitterhöfer, "Theologie der Befreiung: Ein Zwischen-bericht," TPQ 133 (1085) 333–342 = TDig 34 (1987) 15–18; A. Alcalá, *Théologie de la libération: Histoire, courants, critique* (Paris: Centurion, 1986) 31.  [14]"Les deux théologies de la libération en Amérique latine," Études 361/3 (1984) 149–161; I. Berten, "Les pauvres à l'étroit dans l'ecclésiologie romaine," LumièreV 35/177 (June 1986) 75–89 = TDig 34 (1987) 154–158.  [15]A. Quiroz Magaña, *Eclesiología en la teología de la liberación* (Salamanca: Sigueme, 1983). Cf. F. Martínez Diez, *Teología Latinoamericana y teología europea: El debate en torno a la liberación* (Madrid, Ed. Paulinas, 1989); C. Ménard, "L'ecclésiologie des théologiens de la libération: Contexte général et analyse de quelques questions ecclésiologiques discutées par Leonardo Boff," EglT 19 (1988) 349–372.  [16]W.R. Barr, "Debated Issues in Liberation Theology," TTod 43 (1986–1987) 511–523 at 517.  [17]Haight (n. 1) 121–161.  [18]E. McDonagh, "Liberation and New Creation: A Theological Conversation," IrTQ 53 (1987) 258–266 at 261.  [19]G. Gutiérrez, *A Theology of Liberation* (Maryknoll: Orbis, 1973) 151–152.  [20]L. and C. Boff, *Salvation and Liberation* (Maryknoll: Orbis, 1984) 56–60.  [21]Text, Hennelly (n. 5) 205–219/DocCath 74 (1977) 761–768; cf. R. Page, "Human Liberation and Divine Transcendence," Theology 85 (1982) 180–190; T.H. Sanks, "Liberation Theology and the Social Gospel," TS 41 (1980) 668–682.  [22]J. Eagleson and P. Sharper, eds., *Puebla and Beyond: Documentation and Commentary* (Maryknoll: Orbis, 1979). Cf. J.B. Chethimattam, "The Achievement and Significance of Puebla," JDhara 10 (1980) 184–199; M. Schooyans, "La conférence de Puebla: Un risque, un espoir," NRT 100 (1979) 641–675. Cf. G. Cardona Grisales, "Medellín: un camino de fe eclesial concreta," Txav 38 (1988) 327–340.  [23]Eagleson and Sharper (n. 22) 264–267; *Puebla. Official English Edition* (Washington, D.C.: National Conference of Bishops, 1979—Slough UK: St. Paul—London: CIIR, 1980) 178–181; cf. L. Boff, "Eine kreative Rezeption des II. Vatikanums aus der Sicht der Armen: Die Theologie der Befreiung," TJb 1987: 167–188; E. Dussel, "Analysis of the Final Document of Puebla: the Relationship Between Economics and Christian Ethics," Conc 140 (1980) 101–110; R. Muñoz, *La Iglesia en el pueblo. Hacia una eclesiología latinoamericana* (Lima: CEP, 1983).  [24]R. Haight (n. 1) 257–268; J.Y. Calvez, "La théologie de la libération critiquée et accueillie," NRT 108 (1986) 845–859; C. Illickamury, "Roman Document on the Theology of Liberation—A Theological Appraisal," JDhara 15 (1985) 431–453; R. Lafontaine, "La liberté religieuse et la libération: Réflexions sur l'Instruction romaine," NRT 110 (1988) 181–211; A.K. Min, "The Vatican, Marxism, and Liberation Theology," CrossC 34 (1984–1985) 439–455; M. Novak, *Will It Liberate? Questions About Liberation Theology* (New York: Paulist, 1986) 218–229; L. Múnera Ruiz, "La Congregación para la Doctrina de la Fe y su concepto sobre el Marxismo," TXav 34 (1984) 439–452; G. Thils, "La portée de l'Instruction sur la 'théologie de la

libération,'" RTLv 15 (1984) 458–461; M. Parinthiricka, "Roman Document on the Theology of Liberation—A Pastoral Assessment," JDhara 15 (1985) 454–473; M. Toso, "Riflessioni in margine all 'Istruzione su alcuni aspetti della teologia della liberazione,'" Sales 47 (1985), 843–853. Cf. C.I. Gonzalez, "La teología de la liberación a la luz del magisterio de Juan Pablo II en América Latina," Greg 67 (1986) 5–46; G.V. Lobo, "Rome Accepts Liberation Theology," VYoti 50 (1986) 519–530; A.F. McGovern, "Marxism, Liberation Theology and John Paul II," TDig 32 (1985) 103–107; F.A. Pastor, "Ortopraxis y orthodoxia: El debate teológico sobre Iglesia y liberación en la perspectiva del Magisterio eclesial," Greg 70 (1989) 689–739.  [25]G. Hunsinger, "Karl Barth and Liberation Theology," JRel 63 (1983) 247–263; G. Cittier, "La théologie de la libération et le marxisme. Le piège de la double fidélité," NVet 60 (1985) 66–73.  [26]W.R. Barr (n. 16) 517 and 518; cf. K. Aman, "Marxism(s) in Liberation Theology," CrossC 34 (1984–1985) 427–438; J. Thrower, "Marxism: the Liberation of Theology or a Theology of Liberation," Theology 87 (1984) 420–426.  [27]E.g., A. Kee, *Marx and the Failure of Liberation Theology* (London: SCM—Philadelphia: Trinity Press International, 1990).  [28]Cf. J.M. Bonino, ed., *Faces of Jesus: Latin American Christologies* (Maryknoll: Orbis, 1984); J. Galot, "Jesús, liberador de la humanidad," Burgense 21 (1980) 535–548; B. McNeil, "Liberation Theology and the Imitation of Christ," Ang 59 (1982) 153–161.  [29]L. Boff, *Ecclesiogenesis: The Base Communities Reinvent the Church* (London: Collins, 1986 from Portuguese 1977); A.F. McGovern (n. 1) 197–226 and works cited nn. 1, 9, and 10.  [30]*Evangelii nuntiandi* (1975) n. 58—Flannery 2:738–740. Cf. John Paul II, *Christifideles laici* "The Vocation of the Lay Faithful." (Vatican Press—Dublin: Veritas, 1988) nn. 29–30; J. Espeja, "Teología y comunidad. El diálogo con la teología de la liberación," CiTom 112 (1985) 365–384.  [31]J. Equiza, "Teología de la liberación y religiosidad," Lumen 36 (1987) 53–91.  [32]*Evangelii nuntiandi* 48—Flannery 2:731-732.  [33]*Christifideles laici* (1988) n. 30 (Vatican Press—Dublin: Veritas, 1988) 82–85.  [34]G.H. Anderson and T.F. Stransky, eds., *Liberation Theologies*. Mission Trends 4 (New York: Paulist—Grand Rapids: Eerdmans, 1979) 113–172; J.H. Cone, "Black Theology: Its Origin, Method and Relation to Third World Theologies," in W.K. Tabb, ed., *Churches in Struggle: Liberation Theologies and Social Change in North America* (New York: Monthly Review Press, 1986) 32–45; H. Wayne House, "An Investigation of Black Liberation Theology," BiblSac 139 (1982) 159–176.  [35]A. Alcalá, "The Challenge of Women's Liberation to Theology and Church Reform," Conc 184 (1980) 95–101; G.H. Anderson and T.F. Stransky (n. 34) 175–243; M.I. Buckley, "Feminist Perspectives on a Faith that Liberates," ChicSt 19 (1980) 129–143; E. Schüssler Fiorenza, "Feminist Theology as Critical Theology," in Tabb (n. 34) 46–66 = TS 36 (1975) 605–626; S. Welch, *Communities of Resistance and Solidarity: A Feminist Theology of Liberation* (Maryknoll: Orbis, 1985).  [36]M. Macourt, *Towards a Theology of Gay Liberation* (London: SCM, 1977).  [37]*Libération en Jésus Christ*. Actes de la 12e semaine théologique de Kinshasa (Kinshasa: Faculté de Théol. Cath. 1980); J.W. de Gruchy, *Liberating Reformed Theology: A South African Contribution to the Ecumenical Debate* (Grand Rapids: Eerdmans, 1991); C. Mbuka, "Mission et libération: Approche théologique," BTAfr 6 (1984) 309–317; C.B. Okolo, "Liberation Theology and African Church," BTAfr 4 (1982) 173–187; Olubayo Obijole, "South African Liberation Theologies of Boesek and Tutu—A Critical Evaluation," AfTQ 16 (1987) 201–215.  [38]Indian Theological Association, "Towards an Indian Theology of Liberation," JDhara 16 (1986) 185–200; Y. Ambroise, "Theology of Liberation: Its Emergence, Persistence and Its Future in the Indian Context from a Sociological Perspective," IndTS 24 (1987) 103–142; S. Arulsamy, "Liberation Theology in India," IndTS 22 (1985) 266–288; F.X. D'Sa, "Karma: Work for Liberation and Means of Bondage: Towards a Theology of Work," JDhara 13 (1983) 196–212; I. Jesudasan, *Ghandian Theology of Liberation* (Anand: Guyarat

Sahitya Prakash, 1987; abridged ed. Maryknoll: Orbis, 1984, 1986).
[39]S. Arokiasamy and G. Gispert-Sauch, eds., *Liberation in Asia: Theological Perspectives.* Jesuit Theological Forum, Reflections 1 (Delhi: Vidyajyoti—Anand: Guyarat Sahitya Prakash, 1987); A. Pieris, *An Asian Theology of Liberation* (Maryknoll: Orbis, 1988); idem, "Towards an Asian Theology of Liberation: Some Religio-Cultural Guidelines," ZMissRW 63 (1979) 161–182 = VYoti 43 (1979) 261–284; idem, "A Theology of Liberation in Asian Churches?," Month 19 (1986) 231–239 = VYoti 50 (1986) 330–351. Cf. J.C. England, *Living Theology in Asia* (London: SCM, 1981).
[40]G.H. Anderson and T.F. Stransky, *Liberation Theologies.* Mission Trends 4 (New York: Paulist—Grand Rapids: Eerdmans, 1979); V. Fabella and S. Torres, eds., *Irruption of the Third World: Challenge to Theology* (Maryknoll: Orbis, 1983); D.W. Ferm, *Third World Liberation Theologies: An Introductory Survey* (Maryknoll: Orbis, 1986); idem, *Third World Liberation Theologies: A Reader* (Maryknoll: Orbis, 1986); idem, "Third World Liberation Theology: What's It All About?," IrTQ 51 (1985) 309–318. [41]D. Cohn-Sherbok, "Judaism and the Theology of Liberation," ModT 3 (1986) 1–19 = TDig 34 (1987) 127–131; M.H. Ellis, *Towards a Jewish Theology of Liberation* (Maryknoll: Orbis, 1987); idem, "Notes Toward a Jewish Theology of Liberation" in Tabb (n. 34) 67–84.
[42]Haight (n. 1); B. Mahan and L.D. Richesin, eds., *The Challenge of Liberation Theology: A First World Response* (Maryknoll: Orbis, 1981); A. Rizzi, "Elementi di una teologia della liberazione per l'Occidente," RasT 28 (1987) 557–577; 29 (1988) 63–77. [43]J.G.H. Hoffmann, "La théologie de la libération: Facteur de déstabilisation de la foi," RRéf 37 (1986) 87–97; K. Raiser, "Für und wider die Befreiungstheologie," ZEvEthik 29 (1985) 138–146; L.A. Rutschman, "Latin American Liberation Theology and Radical Anabaptism," JEcuSt 19 (1982) 38–56; P. Wells, 'Le Conseil Oecuménique des Églises et la libération,' RRéf 37 (1986) 72–86.
[44]F.J. Laishley, "Repression and Liberation in the Church," HeythJ 29 (1988) 157–174, 329–342, 450–460. [45]*The Church We Believe In: One, Holy, Catholic and Apostolic* (Dublin: Gill and Macmillan—Mahwah: Paulist, 1988) 132–151. Cf. J. Alfaro, *Christian Hope and the Liberation of Man* (Rome and Sydney: Dwyer, 1978); H. Urs von Balthasar, "Consideraciones historico-salvificas sobre la teologia de la liberación," Salm 24 (1977) 511–524—NRT 99 (1977) 518–531; L. Boff, *The Lord's Prayer: The Prayer of Integral Liberation* (Melbourne: Dove—Maryknoll: Orbis, 1983); J. Esquerda Bifet, "La missione liberatrice della Chiesa nell'evangelizzazione dei popoli," EuntDoc 39 (1986) 247–252; E. McDonagh, "Liberation and New Creation: A Theological Conversation," IrTQ 53 (1987) 258–266. [46]A. Descamps, "Justice," DBT 281–286 at 283 [47]J. Allen, "An Orthodox Perspective of Liberation," GrOrTR 26 (1981) 71–80; O. Clément, "Orthodox Reflections on 'Liberation Theology'," SVlad 29 (1985) 63–72. [48]D.W. Buggert, "Liberation Theology: Praxis and Contemplation," Carmelus 34 (1987) 3–58; J. Espeja, "Liberación y espiritualidad en América latina," CiTom 111 (1984) 87–122; V. Fabekka et al., eds., *Asian Christian Spirituality: Reclaiming Traditions* (Maryknoll: Orbis, 1992); S. Galilea, "The Spirituality of Liberation," Way 25 (1985) 186–194; idem, *Spirituality of Hope* (Maryknoll: Orbis, 1989); idem, *The Future of Our Past* (Notre Dame: Ave Maria, 1985); G. Gutiérrez, *We Drink from Our Own Wells* (Maryknoll: Orbis—London: SCM, 1984); Haight (n. 1) 233–256; R.P. Hardy, "Liberation Theology and Saint John of the Cross: A Meeting," EglT 20 (1989) 259–282; M. O'Neill, *God Hears the Cry of the Poor: The Emerging Spirituality in Christian Communities in Peru (1965–1986).* Diss. (Rome: Gregorian, 1990); J. Sobrino, *Spirituality of Liberation. Toward Political Wholeness* (Maryknoll: Orbis, 1988); P.G. van Breemen, "Spirituality of Liberation," RRel 49 (1990) 825–836. [49]E.g., J. Comblin, *The Holy Spirit and Liberation.* Liberation and Theology 4 (Maryknoll: Orbis—Tunbridge Wells UK: Burns & Oates, 1989). [50]*Politik und Erlösung: Zum Verhältnis von Glaube, Rationalität und Irrationalem*

*in der sogennanten Theologie der Befreiung.* Rheinisch-Westfälische Akademie der Wissenschaften Vorträge G 279 (Opladen: Westdeutscher Verlag, 1986) see 20. [51]M. Novak, *Will It Liberate? Questions About Liberation Theology* (New York—Mahwah: Paulist, 1986). [52]G. Márkus, "What Future for Liberation Theology?," NBlackfr 72 (1991) 441–450; A. Nicols, "The Rise and Fall of Liberation Theology: An Evaluative Chronicle," NBlackfr 72 (1991) 408–423; A. Peter, "Versuch einer systematischen Bilanz der Theologie der Befreiung," FreibZ 39 (1992) 424–448; Conc 199 (1988). [53]H.U. von Balthasar, "Considérations sur l'histoire du salut: à propos de la théologie de la libération," NRT 99 (1977) 518–531 = Salm 24 (1977) 511–524. [54]N. 97. Cf. B. de Margerie, "Mary in Latin American Liberation Theology," MarSt 38 (1987) 47–62; S. Galilea, *Following Jesus* (Maryknoll: Orbis, 1981) 110–119; J. Galot, "Maria e la liberazione dell'umanità," CivCatt 131 (1980) 2:218-230; J.J. Herrera Aceves, "El Magnificat, canto de la liberación," EfMex 6/18 (1988) 367–390. See CELAM, Santo Domingo (1992) nn. 27, 34, 74, 123, 157, 243.

## LIBERIUS, Pope (352–366)

A Roman, Liberius[1] was elected pope at the time when the pro-Arians were strong in the East and favored by the emperor Constantius II (337–361); the emperor sought to have the champion of Nicene (q.v.) orthodoxy, Athanasius of Alexandria, anathematized also in the West. As Western bishops increasingly gave way, Liberius endeavored to have a council on the grounds that the Nicene faith and not just the deposition of Athanasius was at stake. After the Council of Milan (355), at which all but three bishops condemned Athanasius, Liberius was exiled to Thrace, where he came under great pressure to acquiesce to Athanasius' excommunication. Eventually he did so and accepted the ambiguous Creed of Sirmium, one which omitted the Nicene *homoousios* ("one in being [with the Father]"); it seems clear though that this creed ignored rather than denied the Nicene *homoousios.*

On his return to Rome after the death of the emperor, Liberius became once again a strong advocate of Nicene faith. The picture we get of Liberius is of a weak pope, who temporarily capitulated into signing an ambiguous formula but sought to undo the damage he caused when he was free from intimidation. His case was never seen as that of a pope, or the Roman Church, leading the universal Church into error; it is not a serious argument against papal infallibility (q.v.).

[1]OxDPopes 30–31; É. Amann, "Liberius," DTC 9:631-659; K. Baus, in Jedin-Dolan 3:41-48, 61–63, 248–250.

## LIMBO

The issue of Limbo (Latin *limbus,* fringe) arose in the context of the fate of unbaptized infants. Scripture and Tradition speak of the necessity of baptism (q.v.) for salvation. In the case of adults, grace-assisted acts of love have long been seen to supply for baptism in the case of those ignorant of it or incapable of receiving it. Babies have no such possibility of an act of supernatural charity. Augustine at first thought that such babies might come to some sort of middle state between beatitude and damnation.[1] Later, in the deepening polemic against the Pelagians, he concluded that they went indeed to hell,[2] but to suffer the mildest of punishment along with exclusion from the vision of God.

In the Middle Ages it was commonly thought that unbaptized infants were excluded from the beatific vision. In the patristic age, as well as among the scholastics, there was some teaching on the *limbus patrum,* the state of the OT "fathers" as they awaited Christ's redemption. Gradually, by analogy, theologians began to speak of the *limbus puerorum,* the Limbo of children who were deprived of the beatific vision because of their lack of baptism. They were thus on the "fringe" of hell but not in hell, and suffered none of its pains.

At Trent (q.v.) there was some discussion of the state of the unbaptized, but no statement on the matter was issued. The first statement by the magisterium about Limbo needs careful exegesis. By the 18th century many Catholic theologians understood Limbo as a state of purely natural happiness for those who through no fault of their own were deprived of the beatific vision.

The Jansenist Synod of Pistoia (1786—q.v.) declared that such a position was heretical. It was that extreme position that Pius VI condemned as "false, temerarious, and damaging to Catholic [theological] schools."[3] The pope did not explicitly teach about Limbo, but he clearly allowed that it was a permissible theological position.

In the 1940s and 50s there was a great deal of writing by theologians on the fate of unbaptized infants.[4] They sought to protect and harmonize two truths: the necessity of baptism and God's universal will to save all. There is consensus today that unbaptized infants are saved, but there is no agreed theological explanation as to how their salvation is effected. Limbo is no longer taught; it is not found in the new *Catechism of the Catholic Church.* It never was a dogma of the Church but a theological opinion which on a few occasions was used by the magisterium.

The pastoral issue remains for mothers and others concerned with babies dying without baptism. Theology does not have a convincing and healing answer which will always convince those anxious about the matter. The best pastoral approach would seem to be a forceful assertion that God loves the babies much more than their parents do, and that such children are safe in his loving care.

[1]*De lib. arbit.* 3:66—PL 32:1302.  [2]*Serm.* 294:2, 2—PL 38:1336; *De anima et eius orig.* 1:9, 11; 4:11, 16—PL 44:481, 533.  [3]*Const. Auctorem fidei* (1794)—DS 2626.  [4]W. van Roo, "Infants Dying Without Baptism: A Survey of Recent Literature and Determination of the State of the Question," Greg 35 (1954) 406–473.

# LITURGY

The term "liturgy" is derived from the Greek *leitourgia* from *ergon* (work) and *leïtos* (public), which described a public service, especially one rendered by private citizens at their own expense. In addition to its religious meaning, it had in ancient Greece a secular one of public works. In the NT it is used of various kinds of service, especially sacred (Luke 1:23; Heb 8:6). In religions, generally, liturgy is a system or set of rituals that is prescribed for public or corporate performance. It is corporate rather than private, systematic rather than completely spontaneous, generally related in some way to time—past, present, or essentially timeless—with a strong ability to unify or coordinate the experiences of a people.[1]

Right within the NT period, we find the followers of Jesus gathering for worship:[2] at first still within the temple (Acts 2:46; 3:1) or with Jews (Acts 16:13,16); soon independently in the breaking of bread (Acts 2:42; 20:7,11) from an early time called the Lord's Supper (1 Cor 11:20-33). By the time of the *Didachê* (ca. 95—q.v.) and Justin (ca. 160—q.v.), the central liturgy of the Christians was clear. It consisted of Scripture readings, teaching, prayers, and the Eucharist. The *Apostolic Tradition* (q.v.) from the early 3rd century was an attempt to order liturgy according to an earlier format, probably of the late 2nd century.

But early Christian worship was not confined to the Eucharist. The primitive Church took over the Jewish custom of frequent daily prayer (Ps 119:164). Again in the *Apostolic Tradition* we find an account of a communal evening prayer when the deacon brought in the lamp, the bishop gave a solemn thanksgiving on the theme of light, children and virgins sang psalms, and all the community sang those psalms containing Alleluia (26/26:18-32). A communal morning instruction was also found. There were also times of prayer at the third, sixth, ninth hours, going to bed, and at midnight (41/36).[3] The prayer at the third, sixth, and ninth hours are aligned to the Marcan passion account (Mark 15:25, 33, 34): the first and last were prayers of praise; the prayer at the sixth hour was apparently to represent Christ's cry on the cross. The prayer at midnight celebrated God's praise along with all creation. There is reference, too, to prayer at cock crow: later tradition would identify this with either the midnight prayer, or the morning one.

From the 6th century and earlier (v. APOSTOLIC CONSTITUTIONS), there were in the various Churches major collections of liturgical texts for the sacraments, Eucharistic liturgy, and for the Liturgy of the Hours. In turn these collections led to standardization, which included the suppression of many local rites or liturgies. By the 12th century the liturgy was more or less uniform in the Latin Church, with some exceptions, like the Church of Milan; there was also a tendency to uniformity within each of the Eastern Churches, though they differed from one another. The liturgy was in hieratic languages: Latin in the West; ancient tongues in the East, though there some vernaculars did emerge.

In the Middle Ages as represented by Thomas Aquinas (q.v.), there was a harmony between ecclesiology and liturgy. The Church was seen primarily in the same terms as that of the Roman Canon (Eucharist Prayer I): it is the gathering of the people *(congregatio)* in communion and in a worship that unites the whole Church on earth with the heavenly Church in glory; it celebrates the paschal mystery and seeks its fruits; it remembers the dead; it is consciously a worship of sinners who hope for mercy; it seeks help and protection in its task in the world.

With the Reformation there was a pressure to drop Latin in favor of the vernacular; it was resisted, even though the Reformers all chose to celebrate liturgy in the language of the people, and they made special efforts to translate the Bible. In the Latin Church uniformity prevailed more and more.

As with all movements, different dates can be given for their origins; it is convenient and not inappropriate to indicate as the origin of the liturgical movement the work of the Benedictine Dom Prosper Louis Paschal Guéranger (1805–1875). He acquired the priory of Solesmes in 1832 and became its abbot. He wrote extensively on the liturgy and promoted Gregorian chant.[4]

In the 19th and 20th centuries the liturgical movement[5] had a number of high points. Ancient liturgical texts were edited. Various monasteries like Maredsous, Solesmes, Mont César, St. John's Abbey, Collegeville, became centers of research and publication. Other centers developed, such as the Institut Supérieur de Liturgie Paris (1947), Trier (1947), Maria Laach (1948). The speculative thought of Odo Casel (1886–1948—q.v.) proved to be highly influential, even if not at all points followed. Journals, congresses, and seminars multiplied, covering all aspects of liturgy: theology, history, art, and music. A distinctive feature of the movement was its pastoral focus; a leader like J.A. Jungmann, author of one of the most influential books of the pre-Vatican II period,[6] was also deeply involved in catechetics. Liturgy also attracted the attention of systematic theologians like K. Rahner before the council and subsequent to it.[7]

In the 20th century there was also steady encouragement of liturgical renewal from the popes, beginning with Pius X (q.v.)[8] on chant,[9] on the Divine Office,[10] on daily Communion,[11] on lowering the age of First Communion.[12] Under Pius XI (q.v.) the movement continued to have support, as with the decrees on the "Dialogue Mass" (1922), on vestments (1925), and on chant (1928).[13] The great 20th century document of the papal magisterium on liturgy was an encyclical, *Mediator Dei,* of Pius XII (q.v.) in 1947.[14] It encouraged active participation of the people in liturgy, a notion that was already present in Pius X's first liturgical document in music. Pius XII also sanctioned the radical revision of the Holy Week Liturgy in 1955 (initiated on a trial basis in selected places in 1951).

By the time of the opening of Vatican II (q.v.), the liturgical movement was mature, and it had both assured historical and scientific findings as well as positive pastoral experiences in monasteries and at the parish level, especially in Germany and France. The Liturgy Constitution was debated in the first session from 22 October to 14 November 1962. Already the tensions that would mark the whole council were in evidence, especially on the issue of vernacular liturgy and the nature of the revision of the liturgical books. The document was revised the following spring, and decisively approved on 22 November 1963. The final document, *Sacrosanctum concilium* (SC), was to put an end to the idea of liturgy as being mainly concerned with rubrics, and opened the way for comprehensive renewal. By January 1964 Paul VI had established a Consilium (full title "Commission for the Implementation of the Constitution on the Liturgy"), which immediately set to work.[15] Its chief architect was A. Bugnini (q.v.).[16] Its journal was *Notitiae,*[17] an indispensable tool for a grasp of the evolution of the new texts and their meaning. The brief given by SC included the simplification of the rites and the possibility of variation (SC 34–39). The approach of the Consilium was interdisciplinary and experimental; various modified rites were tried out in selected places before a definitive text was issued. A notable feature of all the revised texts is the *General Instruction* (GI) which precedes each one; it gives not only practical matters of celebration but a short, yet profound, theology of the rite in question. The revision of the rites is due in large part to the enthusiasm and commitment of Paul VI and to Bugnini, who enjoyed the pope's trust at least until 1975.

From our point of view, ecclesiology, Vatican II's Constitution on the Liturgy (SC), and the subsequent reforms are of enormous significance.[18] The council did not define liturgy, but there are as many definitions or descriptions as there are liturgists. The preconciliar description by H. Urs von Balthasar has theological and spiritual depth: "Liturgy is the Church's sacred service or prayer in the presence of God. Here, in an ultimate, pure selflessness, it seeks for nothing but God's glorification through worship, praise and thanksgiving."[19] The liturgy is central in the Church's life, but it must be preceded by proclamation (SC 9):

"The liturgy is, all the same, the high point towards which the activity of the Church is directed, and, simultaneously, the source from which all its power flows out" (SC 10). The liturgy, especially the Eucharist, becomes "the chief means through which believers are expressing in their lives and demonstrating to others the mystery which is Christ, and the sort of entity the true Church really is" (SC 2). Later the council will state that the Eucharistic sacrifice is "the source and culmination of the whole Christian life" (LG 11). The Church "very much wants all believers to take a full, conscious and active part in liturgical celebration. . . . This full and active sharing on the part of the whole people is of paramount concern in the process of renewing the liturgy and helping it to grow" (SC 14).[20] The council develops with new clarity the presence of Christ: in the Mass in the person of the minister, in the Eucharistic species, in the sacraments, in the Word read in Church, in the Church praying (SC 7).[21] Even though the liturgy is not the only activity of the Church (SC 9), as an act of Christ the priest and of his Body, nothing else is of such preeminence or efficacy (SC 7). A weakness of the Constitution on the Liturgy arises from the fact that it was an early text of the council and did not have the advantage of the ecclesiology which developed in LG, UR, DV, and GS. It is not strong on the notion of the common priesthood (LG 10) or the trilogy of priest-prophet-king (q.v.); it is also deficient in pneumatology (q.v.). However, it can be argued that the dynamic which developed in the production of its text, and the liturgy constitution itself, paved the way for later conciliar documents.

A sleeper in the Constitution was the existence of the scarcely striking articles on Scripture (SC 24; 35/1; 51). However, in the revision of all the rites they would arise to assume great importance; the use of Scripture has become central for all liturgical acts, even though it is still too early to expect a deep biblical culture to have emerged in the Church as a whole.

Many of the revised texts are based on ancient liturgies, e.g., the second and fourth Eucharist Prayers; others are new compositions, e.g., the third Eucharist Prayer. Though the ecclesiology of each liturgical rite can have subtle variants, one can say that the basic view of the Church is that of communion. It is vertical in being worship and a source of grace; it is horizontal in demanding concrete commitments in the lives of the worshiper and of the community. One can, however, regret the subsequent lack of attention to the essential eschatological dimension of liturgy (see SC 8). The revised texts, though strongly Christological, have also a heightened pneumatology;[22] many have an *epiclêsis* (q.v.) or otherwise refer to the Spirit active in the liturgy being celebrated. The revision of the liturgical books has transcended the council's vision of liturgy;

the early revision of the Eucharistic liturgy is notably more cautious than some of the later, more creative, liturgies, such as the Rite for Christian Initiation of Adults, the liturgy for the sick, and funerals.

In the thirty years since the council there has been an enormous explosion of liturgical publications. The theology of liturgy itself is developing in a significant way,[23] especially through the influence of Eastern Christianity.[24]

There are innumerable works on art and architecture, pastoral aids, catechetics, music, homiletic materials (v. PREACHING).[25] Of particular importance, with an extensive literature, is the area of symbolism.[26] Not only the specialist liturgical journals but nearly all theological reviews regularly carry liturgical studies. There are also many significant historical and retrospective studies of the Constitution on the Liturgy and the subsequent renewal.[27] The results of the liturgical reforms are somewhat patchy. In places there is liturgy which is very much alive and marked by very active participation; elsewhere, though reformed texts are in use, there is little life. Much depends on the outlook and energy of local pastors, who either empower the laity or fail to realize the potential of the community.

There are two important tasks that despite some important achievements are still at an initial stage. First, there is need for the development of a deep liturgical spirituality that will enable people to insert the whole of their lives and concerns into their liturgy.[28] Liturgy which inspires a sense of mystery already opens people up to the transcendent in daily life,[29] while each celebration and the liturgical year[30] opens out into eschatological tension as well as joining in the liturgy of the heavenly Jerusalem;[31] at its heart, as Maximus the Confessor (q.v.) has already taught, liturgy is also cosmic.[32]

Second, we still await any profound inculturation (q.v.) of the liturgy for each people, a process that is as yet mostly superficial, since to all intents we still have a basically Latin liturgy translated into different languages.[33]

A separate area of the ecclesiology of liturgy is to be found in liberation theologies (q.v.)[34] and in the Basic Christian Communities (q.v.), in which liturgy must have a special place. There is a further need for works that develop the social and missionary implications of liturgical celebration.[35]

The study of the ecclesiology of liturgy though extensive is still at an early stage.[36] Even an individual liturgical book can yield rich findings.[37] There is also a growing awareness of liturgy as a *locus theologicus* or source for sacramental theology[38] and indeed for all theology (v. THEOLOGICAL SOURCES).

There is ongoing renewal of liturgy in various non-Roman Catholic Churches,[39] but as yet liturgy has not been central to ecumenical discussions except for the Lima Faith and Order document, *Baptism, Eucharist, and ministry*.[40] Foundational work on comparison and evaluation of liturgical texts has, however, been proceeding for many years.[4]

[1]T.W. Jennings, "Liturgy," EncycRel 8:580-583. [2]R.P. Martins, "Patterns of Worship in New Testament Churches," JStNT 37 (1989) 59–85. [3]L.E. Phillips, "Daily Prayer in the *Apostolic Tradition* of Hippolytus,' JTS 40 (1989) 389–400; see further P.F. Bradshaw, *Daily Prayer in the Early Church* (London: SPCK, 1981); J.D. Crichton, *Christian Celebration: The Prayer of the Church* (London: Chapman, 1976); I.H. Dalmais, "Origine et constitution de l'office," MaisD 21 (1950) 21–39; B. Fischer, "La prière ecclésiale et familiale dans le christianisme ancien," MaisD 116 (1973) 41–58; A.G. Martimort in A.G. Martimort, ed., *The Church at Prayer.* 4 vols. (Collegeville: The Liturgical Press—London: Chapman, 1983–1986) 4:151-275; G.M. Oury, "Office divin en occident," DSpir 11:685-707; R. Taft, *The Liturgy of the Hours in East and West* (Collegeville: The Liturgical Press, 1986). [4][P. Delatte], *Dom Guéranger.* 2 vols. (Paris, 1909); writings: F. Cabrol, *Bibliographie des bénédictins de la congrégation de France* (Solesmes, 1889) 3–33; A. Schilson, "Rinnovamento dello spirito della restaurazione: Uno sguardo all'origine del movimento liturgico in Prosper Guéranger," CrNSt 12 (1991) 569–602. [5]A. Adam, *Foundations of Liturgy: An Introduction to Its History and Practice* (Collegeville: The Liturgical Press—Pueblo, 1992); V.G. Funk, "Liturgical Movement (1830–1969), The,"NDictSacWorship 695–715; P. Jounel, "The History of the Liturgy," in A.G. Martimort (n. 3) 1:19-84; H.A.J. Wegman, *Christian Worship in East and West: A Study Guide to Liturgical History* (New York: Pueblo, 1985); A. Verheul, *Introducing the Liturgy* (Wheathampstead UK: Clark, 1972). [6]*The Mass of the Roman Rite.* Revised and abridged C.K. Riepe (London: Burns & Oates, 1959). [7]K. Rahner, "The Presence of the Lord in the Christian Community at Worship," ThInvest 10:71-83; idem, "On the Theology of Worship," ThInvest 19:141-150; cf. M. Skelly, "The Liturgy of the World and the Liturgy of the Church. Karl Rahner's Idea of Worship," Worship 63 (1989) 112–132. [8]R. Aubert, in Jedin-Dolan 9:403-412. [9]Mp. *Inter plurimas pastoralis officii = Tra le sollecitudini* ASS 36 (1903–1904) 329–332 and 387–395. [10]*Divino afflatu*—AAS 3 (1911) 631–636. [11]*Sacra tridentina synodus* (1905)—*Actes Pie X* 2:254-260. [12]S. Cong. Sac., *Quam singulari* (1910)—AAS 2 (1910) 577–583. [13]AAS 14 (1922) 505; 18 (1926) 58–59; 21 (1929) 33–41. [14]*Mediator Dei*—AAS 39 (1947) 521–595/Carlen 4:119-154. [15]Mp. *Sacram liturgiam*—AAS 56 (1964) 139–144, on which see A. Bugnini, *The Reform of the Liturgy (1948–1975)* (Collegeville: The Liturgical Press, 1990) 54–59; Paul VI, Address *Haud mediocre*—AAS 56 (1964) 993–996. [16]Ibid., Bugnini. [17]1 (1965)—; see also DOL. [18]W. Baraúna, ed., *The Liturgy of Vatican II.* 2 vols. (Chicago: Franciscan Herald, 1966); J.-P. Jossua and Y. Congar, *La liturgie après Vatican II.* US 66 (Paris, 1967); P. Jounel, Genèse et théologie de la Constitution 'Sacrosanctum concilium,'" HoTheol 1 (1983) 349–366; I. Oñatibia, "La eclesiología de la 'Sacrosanctum concilium,'" in Congregation for Divine Worship, *Constituzione liturgica Sacrosanctum concilium studi.* Bibliotheca "Ephemerides liturgicae" subsidia 38 (Rome: CLV—Ed. Liturgiche, 1986) 171–182. [19]*Prayer* (San Francisco, 1986) 108 = (New York: Paulist "Deus Books," 1961) 88. [20]J.M. Huels, "Participation by the Faithful in the Liturgy," Jurist 48 (1988) 608–637. [21]B. Bürki, "Le Christ dans la liturgie, d'après l'article 7 de la Constitution Sacrosanctum concilium de Vatican II," QLtg 64 (1983) 195–212; P. Parré, "Présence réele et modes de présence du Christ," QLtg 69 (1988) 163–183. [22]L. Leijssen, "L'Esprit Saint et la liturgie," Qltg 67 (1986) 81–86; F. Mancini, "Lo Spirito Santo e il dinamismo della liturgia nella vita della chiesa e del credente,"

VitaMonast 43/176 (1989) 33–47. [23]J. Hermans, "L'étude de la liturgie comme discipline théologique: Problèmes et méthodes," RTLv 18 (1987) 337–360; K.W. Irwin, *Liturgical Theology: A Primer.* American Essays in Liturgy (Collegeville: The Liturgical Press, 1990); E.J. Kilmartin, *Christian Liturgy: Theology and Practice.* Vol. 1 (Kansas: Sheed & Ward, 1988); C. Jones, G. Wainwright, and E. Yarnold, eds., *The Study of Liturgy* (London: SPCK, [2]1980); A. Kavanagh, *On Liturgical Theology* (New York: Pueblo, 1984); K. Richter, ed., *Liturgie—ein vergessenes Thema der Theologie.* QDisput 107 (Freiburg-Basle-Vienna: Herder, 1986); C. Vagaggini, *Theological Dimensions of the Liturgy: A General Treatise on the Theology of the Liturgy* (Collegeville: The Liturgical Press, 1976, from 4th Italian ed.); Conc 162 (1983); Worship 80 (1983) 7–134. [24]M. Arranz, "La liturgia orientale," Seminarium 27 (1987) 240–250; A. Kallis, "Theologie als Doxologie: Der Stellenwert der Liturgie in der orthodoxen Kirche und Theologie," ThJb 1988:137–144; A. Schmemann, *Introduction to Liturgical Theology* (New York: St. Vladimir's Seminary Press, 1975); C.N. Tsirpanlis, "The Structure of the Church in the Liturgical Tradition of the First Three Centuries," PatByzR 1 (1982) 44–62. [25]See articles in NDictSacWorship. [26]E.g., D.N. Power, *Unsearchable Riches: The Symbolic Nature of Liturgy* (New York: Pueblo, 1984); S. Happel, "Symbol," NDictSacWorship 1237–1245. [27]John Paul II, *Quinto iam lustro*—AAS 81 (1989) 897–918, on which see P. Rouillard in EspVie 99 (1989) 401–409; T. Berger, "Sacrosanctum Concilium in the 1980s: The Literature Between the Two Anniversaries (1983–1988)," StLtg 19 (1989) 218–222; B. Botte, "Vatican II et le renouveau liturgique," QLtg 62 (1981) 113–134; M. Collins, *Contemplative Participation: "Sacrosanctum Concilium" Twenty-five Years Later* (Collegeville: The Liturgical Press, 1990); B. Fischer, "A los veinticinco años de la constitución de la liturgia: La recepción de sus principios fundamentales," Phase 170 (1989) 89–103; P. Gleeson, "Vatican II Twenty Years On: The Liturgy," DoctLife 33 (1983) 523–528; K.W. Irwin, "The Constitution on the Liturgy *Sacrosanctum concilium*, 4 December 1963," in T.E. O'Connell, ed., *Vatican II and Its Documents: An American Reappraisal.* Theology and Life 15 (Wilmington: Glazier, 1986); B. Kleinheyer, "*Sacrosanctum concilium*: Eine Relecture der Liturgiekonstitution," LtgJb 38 (1988) 4–29; A.G. Martimort, "La réforme liturgique de Vatican II," QuatreF 21–22 (1985) 81–94; idem, "La constitution sur la liturgie de Vatican II," MaisD 157 (1984) (33–52)—BLitE 85 (1984) 60–74. [28]P.E. Fink, "Liturgy and Spirituality: A Timely Intersection," in E. Bernstein, ed., *Liturgy and Spirituality in Context* (Collegeville: The Liturgical Press, 1990) 47–61; B. Neunhauser, "Spiritualità liturgica," NDizLit 1419–1442; S.S. Madigan, *Liturgy, Source of Spirituality* (Washington, D.C.: Pastoral Press, 1989); idem, "Spirituality, Liturgical," NDictSacWorship 1224–1231; A.M. Triacca, "Per una definizione di 'spiritualità christiana' dall'ambito liturgico," Notitiae 25 (1989) 277–288. [29]P. Visentin, "La liturgia rinnovata e il 'senso del mistero,'" RivLtg 74 (1987) 305–320. [30]See works (n. 22); RivLtg 75 (1988) 473–553. [31]W. Rordorf, "Liturgie et eschatologie," EphLtg 94 (1980) 385–395; A. Schmemann, "Liturgy and Eschatology," Sobornost 7/1 (1985) 6–14; A.M. Triacca and A. Pistoia, eds., *Eschatologie et liturgie.* Conférences Saint Serge 31. Bibliotheca "Ephemerides liturgicae" subsidia 35 (Rome: CLV—Ed. Liturgiche, 1985). [32]A.A. Häussling, "Kosmische Dimension und gesellschaftliche Wirklichkeit: Zu einem Erfahrungswandel in der Liturgie," ArLtgW 25 (1983) 1–8. [33]M. Amaladoss, "The Liturgy: Twenty Years after Vatican II," VYoti 47 (1983) 231–240. [34]CELAM, *Puebla Document* (Slough UK: St. Paul—London: CIIR, 1980) nn. 896–909, 916–934, 938–951; J.H. McKenna, "Liturgy: Towards Liberation or Oppression," Worship 56 (1982) 291–308. [35]D. Borobio, "Leitourgia y diakonia: La liturgia como expresión y realización de las cuarto dimensiones de la misión," Salm 36 (1989) 135–155; C.F. Jegen, "Worship and Mission,"

Jurist 39 (1979) 88–118; M. Hellwig, *The Eucharist and the Hunger of the World*. Deus Books (New York: Paulist, 1976). C. Kiesling, "Liturgy and Social Justice," Worship 51 (1977) 249–267; R. Mouret, "L'Église que nous construisons," ComLtg 62 (1980) 199–207. [36]C. Braga, "Il valore ecclesiale della norma liturgica," Ambrosius 65 (1989) 356–373; P.-M. Gy, "Tradition vivante: Réforme liturgique et identité ecclésiale," MaisD 178 (1989) 93–106; A. Kavanagh, "Liturgy and Ecclesial Consciousness: A Dialectic of Change," StLtg 15 (1982–1983) 2–17; K. McDonnell, "Themes in Ecclesiology and Liturgy from Vatican II," Worship 41 (1967) 66–84; C. Pottie and D. Lebrun, "La doctrine de *l'Ecclesia*, sujet intégrale de la célébration dans les livres liturgiques depuis Vatican II," MaisD 176 (1989) 117–132; R.F. Quilotti, *Aspetti dell'ecclesiologia del "Missale Romanum": Vocabolario e teologia della Chiesa nell'eucologia delle messe "Pro sancta Ecclesia e della dedicazione*. Diss. exc. (Bologna—Rome: St. Anselmo, 1990); idem, "L'ecclesiologia del Messale Romano," SacDoct 32 (1987) 564–589, 621–664; G. Rapisarda, "L'ecclesiologia nella Constituzione liturgica del Vaticano II," Synaxis 2 (1984) 44–63; A.M. Triacca and A. Pistoia, eds., *L'Église dans la liturgie*. Conférences Saint-Serge 26. Bibliotheca "Ephemerides liturgicae" subsidia 18 (Rome: CLV, 1980); R.M. Valabek, "The Liturgy: Expression and Celebration of the Faith," Carmelus 27 (1980) 191–222. [37]E.g., J. Pierce, "A Study of the Ecclesiology of the Missal of Troyes (1736)," EcOr 6 (1989) 33–68. [38]A. Houssiau, "La redécouverte de la liturgie par la théologie sacramentaire (1950–1980)," MaisD 149 (1982) 27–55. M.M. Kelleher, "Liturgy as a Source for Sacramental Theology," Qltg 72 (1991) 25–42; T. Maag-Ewerd, "Die Liturgie in der Theologie," LtgJB 38 (1988) 173–196; D. Power, "Cult to Culture: The Liturgical Foundation of Theology," Worship 54 (1980) 482–494; K. Richter (n. 23); R. Taft, "Liturgy as Theology," Worship 56 (1982) 113–117. [39]"The Identity of the Church and the Nature and Function of Worship: Report to the LWF Commission on Studies, 1979," StLtg (1980–1981) 65–70. See *The Study of Liturgy* (n. 23); Adam (n. 4) 93–100; T. Berger, "*Sacrosanctum concilium* and 'Worship and the Oneness of Christ's Church.' Twenty-five Years Later," Worship 62 (1981) 299–311; K. Schlemmer, ed., *Gemeinsame Liturgie in getrennten Kirchen?*, QDisput 132 (Freiburg-Basel-Vienna, 1991); S. Sykes and J. Booty, eds., *The Study of Anglicanism* (London: SPCK—Philadelphia: Fortress, 1988); J.M.R. Tillard, "Liturgical Reform and Christian Unity," OnChr 19 (1983) 227–249; [40]Faith and Order Paper 111 (Geneva: WCC, 1982). [41]E.g., J.M. Barkley, *The Worship of the Reformed Church*. Ecumenical Studies in Worship 15 (London: Lutterworth—Richmond, Va.: John Knox, 1966); R.C.D. Jasper and G.J. Cuming, *Prayers of the Eucharist: Early and Reformed* (New York: Pueblo, [3]1987).

## LOCAL CHURCH

One of the most significant themes to emerge from Vatican II was that of the local Church. The relation of the local Church to the universal Church is a problem which has concerned ecclesiology, especially after the council. Before examining this issue and the recent guidance offered by the Congregation for the Doctrine of the Faith (CDF), we need to look at the historical emergence of the notion of the local Church and its relation to the Church universal, from the NT to the complex teaching of Vatican II. One can anticipate the findings of the survey by saying that the Church is always considered both as local and as universal, with occasional tensions between the two truths.

Particularly from the Pauline letters we get the idea that the Church had different local manifestations.[1] The diaspora domestic synagogues may well have provided an early model for the primitive Church (v. NEW TESTAMENT ECCLESIOLOGIES). The Church is said to pertain to the local people and is qualified as "in God the Father and the Lord Jesus Christ" (1 Thess 1:1). The two Corinthian letters focus on the Church existing in the city, and describe it as "the Church of God" (1 Cor 1:2; 2 Cor 1:1). The Letter to the Galatians indicates that there is more than one Church in the area: "to the Churches of Galatia" (1:2; cf. 1 Cor 16:1). Philemon addresses three persons "and the church of God in your house" (Phlm 1).[2] Other indubitable letters of Paul speak of "God's beloved in Rome" (Rom 1:7) and "the saints of God who are in Philippi" (Phil 1:1). Elsewhere Paul speaks of "the Churches of Asia" (1 Cor 16:19) and "in every Church" (1 Cor 4:17; cf. 11:16), as well as when they "come together as a church" (*en ekklêsia*—1 Cor 11:18). The earlier letters envisage the local Church gathered as a community; the later Pauline letters point to a universal Church (cf. Eph 3:10). The Lucan picture is of groups coming together to form a Church (Acts 2:42-47; 4:32:37; 5:12-14) characterized by faith, *koinônia* (v. COMMUNION), worship, mutual love, and moving out in deeds of witnessing and of power. There were groups of believers also in Samaria (Acts 8:1-13) and Antioch[3] (Acts 11:20-29; 13:1-3), over which the Jerusalem Church exercised some supervision, ministry, or encouragement. Further, Luke refers to Paul appointing elders (*presbuteroi*) for every Church he founded (Acts 14:20-23). The Pastoral Epistles also envisage the appointment of leaders for the Church in various places (v. APOSTOLIC SUCCESSION). The Johannine picture is enigmatic[4] (v. NEW TESTAMENT ECCLESIOLOGIES): surely significant is the self-awareness of the author and his community, with the twenty-nine uses of "we" in his Gospel.

The unity of the Church and its upbuilding in each place is the work of the Holy Spirit (v. PNEUMATOLOGY), who works through ministers and the charisms (q.v.) he gives for the good of the Church. There is also great insistence on a unity of faith (v. TEACHING). In 1 Cor 10:17 the Eucharist is the bond of unity (cf. 1 Cor 11:20, 34).

Immediately after the NT period we find in the letters of Ignatius (q.v.) Churches in cities presided over by a single bishop with presbyters and deacons. The *Didachê* (q.v.) is clearly descriptive of a local Church with its ordinances both moral and liturgical. From the time of Irenaeus (q.v.) it is clear that the Ignatian model of Church order was to be found everywhere. In time the Church of Rome would become the touchstone for both unity and orthodoxy (v. PETRINE MINISTRY). As the Church expanded beyond the larger cities and towns, the parish (q.v.) structure began to emerge. Originally parish (Greek *paroikia* = a district) could mean diocese, but from late the 4th century it came to mean a subdivision of the diocese over which the bishop placed a resident priest. In the patristic period there was great autonomy in each diocese, but the notion of the universal Church was kept to the fore through councils and the exchange of correspondence, theological treatises, and by traveling.[5] It is also important to note that a person excommunicated in one local Church was not admitted to communion in any other Church.

In the Middle Ages we find intuitions in St. Thomas (q.v.) which point not only to the universal Church (congregation of the faithful) but to local congregations each having its own head.[6] In the whole medieval period[7] there was a preponderant, but by no means exclusive, emphasis on the parish. There were also the churches of religious, especially of the friars noted for their preaching, as well as other places of pilgrimage and devotion. There were confraternities, third orders, various spiritual movements, and lay associations which were very local in character, even if feeding into a wider group like a religious order. At the same time the centralization of Rome begun in the 11th century continued, with the papacy and the emperor both having universalist functions. The major religious orders and the great universities were symbolic of the universal character of the Church.

At the time of the Reformation the picture at the parish level was quite distressing. The reform of Trent reaffirmed the structure of parish and diocese.[8] It sought to improve the education, morals, and pastoral ministry of diocesan priests. On the whole it would perhaps be true to say that the various Protestant Churches had (and in many places still have) a greater sense of community at the local level than the Catholic parish. Meanwhile the Counter-Reformation engaged in strong centralization, with an insistence on uniformity through the publication of a catechism (q.v.), liturgical books, and the Vulgate Bible.

In the 18th century various movements like Gallicanism (q.v.) and Josephinism (q.v.) were an expression of the desire of secular rulers or bishops to weaken the hold of Rome over the Churches in their country. The French Revolution disoriented the relationship between local and universal Church, and in time would lead to still greater centralization at Vatican I (q.v.). It was only under Pius VII (1800–1823) that the pope took over the appointment of French bishops. Unity by then was to an extent corrupted into uniformity, a process heightened by the publication in 1917 of the first ever *Code of Canon Law* for the whole Western Church.

There are not only theological issues to be considered but also sociological ones. At the local level the Church failed to find a suitable pastoral approach in the increasing urbanization of the 19th and 20th centuries. In the Middle Ages and right up to the 19th century the "normal" parish in rural areas might have been only about 40 to 80 families. With industrialization and missionary expansion, one can find 20th century parishes numbering 100,000 persons; these can only be anonymous and very institutional.[9]

In the preliminary documentation for Vatican II there was much interest in the parish, an emphasis which is less conspicuous in the council's later documents. When we come to its documents we find a variety of terminology, at times of uncertain significance (v. PARTICULAR CHURCHES). In the council's first Constitution we have a picture of the local Church: "the Church is displayed with special clarity (*praecipuam manifestationem*—'a primary manifestation') when the holy people of God, all of them, are actively and fully sharing in the same liturgical celebrations—especially when it is the same Eucharist—sharing one prayer at one altar, at which the bishop is presiding, surrounded by his presbyterate and his ministers" (SC 41, with footnote references to Ignatius of Antioch). The liturgy constitution goes on to say that of all assemblies of believers the parishes "in some way exhibit the visible Church set up throughout the nations of the world" (SC 42). In the Decree on Bishops there is some careful use of language: the diocese is described as "a particular Church" (*ecclesia particularis* CD 28; cf. 3, 6); the parish is a specific part *(pars determinata)* of the diocese (CD 30) and is referred to as a community (CD 30); parish priests are really to feel that they are members of the diocese and of the whole universal Church (CD 30); there is a distinction between the universal and individual Churches (*singularum ecclesiarum*—CD 2); bishops have responsibility for particular Churches which are parts of the one Church CD 6); bishops have a care for all of the Church (*universae ecclesiae*—CD 5); "a diocese is a section of the people of God *(Populi Dei portio)* whose pastoral care is entrusted to a bishop in cooperation with his priests" (CD 11; cf. AG 19–22); bishops are to sanctify the "Churches entrusted to them" *(ecclesias sibi concreditas);* finally, in CD 36 the words "particular" *(pecularibus),* "individual" *(singularum),* and "different" *(variis)* Churches are used about dioceses.

The word "local" applied to a patriarchate or diocese is found in UR 14; LG 23, 26; AG 19, 27; and PO 6. The word "particular" means rite in some cases (LG 13, 23; OE 2) There are other key texts in Vatican II, such as LG 26, devoted to the sanctifying office of the bishop.[10] It begins with a statement that the Eucharist is the source of the Church's life and growth, and continues: "This Church of Christ is truly present in all lawful congregations of the faithful which, united to their shepherd, are themselves called churches in the New Testament . . . In these communities, although frequently small and poor, or dispersed, Christ is present by whose power the one, holy catholic and apostolic Church is gathered together" (LG 26; cf. CD 11). The Eucharist is the "source and culmination *(fontem et culmen)* of the whole Christian life" (LG 11; cf. SC 10): St. Augustine notes that if the Church alone makes the Eucharist, it is also true that the Eucharist makes the Church.[11] The Eucharist brings about the emergence of the Church in a determined place.[12] LG 23 deals with the relations between the particular and the universal Church: collegial unity can be seen in the mutual relations of individual bishops with particular Churches and with the universal Church; "The individual bishops, however, are the visible principle and foundation of unity in their own particular churches, formed in the likeness of the universal Church"; bishops have pastoral authority over the particular Churches committed to them, but not over the universal Church, though they must show care for it; grouping of dioceses, such as patriarchates, have arisen; "This variety of local churches, in harmony among themselves, demonstrates with greater clarity the catholicity of the undivided Church" (LG 23).

Despite the fluid vocabulary of Vatican II about local/particular churches/dioceses, the main theological underpinning of their relation to the universal Church is in the lapidary "in and from *(in quibus et ex quibus)* these particular Churches there exists the one unique catholic Church" (LG 23): if only the *in quibus* is considered, the universal Church would degenerate into particular Churches and would remain only an abstraction; if one takes merely the *ex quibus,* then one would get a purely sociological picture of the Church. Both elements must be maintained in view of the communion (q.v.) of the Church. The apostolic succession (q.v.) secures vertical communion, so that the bishops share in the identity of the Church of the apostles—an identity across time. There must also be a horizontal communion which will guarantee the identity of the local Church with all the other local Churches here and now dispersed throughout the world—an identity across space.[13]

In the council it would seem that the term "local Church" *(ecclesia localis)* is used more about an area, than the other words above, which are more concerned with theological and spiritual traditions and with government.[14] The bonds between the diocese and the universal Church are seen as those of hierarchical communion.

In the period after the council there were many developments.[15] Episcopal conferences (q.v. and cf. CD 37–39) began to be more active. But a certain distrust of this mainly 20th-century institution would indicate that the practical and psychological problems of the relation of the local to universal Church have not yet been solved. In Latin America the Basic Christian Communities (q.v.)[16] began to be another expression of local Church. The synods (q.v.), which were intended to be a place for the interaction of the Churches dispersed throughout the world, and with its Roman center, may not have yielded yet their full potential.

In the revision of the *Code of Canon Law* there was an attempt to recapture the spirit of Vatican II's sense of the diocese being a particular Church (CIC 368–374),[17] though some would express disappointment with the final text.[18] Following on Vatican II, the *Code* has made provision for many expressions of collegiality and identity for the Church at the diocesan level; many ordinaries have not taken these up with anything like enthusiasm (v. SYNODS AND COUNCILS and BISHOPS).

In the East the idea of local church is very developed. The principle of "one bishop, one city" is generally upheld.[19] The emphasis on the Eucharist in Orthodox ecclesiology makes for a deep sense of the universal, the celestial Church being made locally manifest in what is a cosmic liturgy.[20]

Ongoing reflection on the local Church is at various levels. There are practical issues between Churches and with the Holy See. Theology needs strong confident local Churches if it is to be relevant for our times.[21] There is the all-important question of indigenization and inculturation (q.v.).[22] There must be adequate expression of different cultures within the one unity of faith.[23] Only within a broad ecclesiology of communion (q.v.) will it be possible to live in a local Church but with spiritual and other bonds with other Churches, and especially with the Roman See. All that is needed for salvation is present in each local Church, but no local Church may be isolated from the others. People *know about* the universal Church; they *experience* the local one. At the ecumenical level we need to emphasize those bonds that already exist and, through grace, create others.[24] Crucial to the development of the local Church is the bishop, bound to his Church as to a spouse.[25] He is the chief symbol of the unity of the local Church in itself and with other Churches, as well as of its power to make holy its members.[26]

The 1992 letter to bishops from the CDF on "Some Aspects of the Church as Communion"[27] gives much attention to the tension between universal and local Church (nn. 9–14). It is somewhat unusual in seeking to settle matters being freely discussed by theologians (n. 2). It insists on the primacy of the universal Church, which "in its essential mystery, is a reality ontologically and temporally prior to every individual particular Church" (n. 9). While the argumentation of the letter is not always easy to follow, it does serve as a warning against dissociating the local Church from the universal Church, a point which the letter notes was previously made by Paul VI in his apostolic exhortation on evangelization.[28]

Finally, this article has used the Vatican II terminology and its statements on the local Church. There is also a need to see "local" as being wider than a diocese and embracing a country, a race, a homogeneous people, a broadly consistent linguistic and cultural area. It is surely one of the triumphs of Latin American liberation theology (q.v.) to have found a way of compatible working and listening in a huge subcontinent, all the time respecting sectional differences. The local Church issue is one that concerns the very catholicity (v. CATHOLIC) of the Church, its unity in diversity.[29]

[1]R.F. Collins, "Aperçus sur quelques Églises locales à l'époque du Nouveau Testament," MaisD 165 (1986) 7–47; B. Maggioni, "Alcune comunità cristiane del Nuovo Testamento: Coscienza di sé, tensioni e comunione," ScuolC 113 (1985) 404–431. [2]V. Branick, *The House Church in the Writings of Paul.* Zacchaeus Studies (Wilmington: Glazier, 1989). [3]P. Grech, "Gerusalemme ed Antiochia: Il ruolo di due chiese nella soluzione di un problema teologico," Later 50 (1984) 77–85. [4]R.E. Brown, *The Community of the Beloved Disciple* (New York: Paulist, 1979—London Chapman, 1983). [5]G. Galeota and A. Mancia, "La chiesa locale nei padri e nei primi concili," Asp 35 (1988) 195–214 = TDig 36 (1989) 243–245. [6]Y. Congar, "Vision de l'Église chez Thomas d'Aquin," RSPT 62 (1978) 523–541 at 536 and n. 82 referring to *In 4 Sent.* d.20, q.1, a.4, sol.1; *De pot.* q.5, a.6 ad 3. [7]G. Alberigo, "The Local Church in the West (1500–1945)," HeythJ 28 (1987) 125–143 = MaisD 165 (1986) 49–71. [8]Session 21—Tanner 2:729-732. [9]J. Kerkhofs, "L'Église locale de Vatican II jusqu'à nos jours," MaisD 165 (1986) 73–100 at 96. [10]A. Tourneux, "L'évêque, l'Eucharistie et l'Église locale dans *Lumen gentium,* 26," ETL 64 (1988) 106–141; H. de Lubac, "Particular Churches in the Universal Church," in *The Motherhood of the Church* (San Francisco: Ignatius, 1982) 169–335. [11]*Contra Faustum* 12:20—PL 42:265 a text quoted in earlier conciliar drafts. [12] See J.M.R. Tillard, *The Bishop of Rome.* Theology and Life 5 (Wilmington: Glazier, 1983) 150–151; L. Martinez Sistach, "La eucaristia, manifestación principal de la Iglesia locale: Referencia a la Iglesia particular," Phase 170 (1969) 105–121. [13]Tillard, ibid., 152–153. [14]G. Ghirlanda, "De definitione Ecclesiae universalis, particularis, localis iuxta Concilium Vaticanum secundum," Periodica 71 (1982) 605–636 at 617; cf. G. Galeota, "La teologia della chiesa locale nell'ottica del concilio Vaticano II," Asp 37 (1990) 145–165, 267–277. [15]J.A. Komonchak, "The Local Church," ChicSt 28 (1989) 320–334; G. Routhier, "'Église locale' ou 'Église particulière': querelle sémantique ou option théologique," StCan 25 (1991) 277–334. [16]H. Teissier, "Pour que croissent de vraies communautés chrétiennes de base," MaisD 165 (1986) 117–134. [17]T.J. Green, in Coriden, CIC 313–319; B. David, "L'Église particulière ou diocèse," EspVie 96 (1986) 481–486; J. Duval, "Église particulière et communion: Le canon 369," AnnéeCan 30 (1987) 51–59; G. Routier, "'Église locale' ou 'Église particulière': querelle sémantique ou option théologique," StCan 25 (1991) 277–334. [18]E.g., R.J. Austin, "The Particular Church and the Universal Church in the 1983 *Code of Canon Law,*" StCan 22 (1988) 339–357. [19]J. Rinne, "One Bishop—One City," Kan 7 (1985) 91–109. [20]G. Ferrari, "Il ministero del Vescovo che presiede l'eucaristia celebrata nella Chiesa locale (Punto di vista orientale)," Nicol 10 (1982) 273–287; G. Galeota and A. Mancia, "La Chiesa locale nel Nuovo Testamento alla luce dei principi costitutivi dell'ecclesiologia ortodossa," Asp 34 (1987) 363–374; iidem, "La Chiesa locale nell'ecclesiologia ortodossa contemporanea," Asp 34 (1987) 267–283; E. Timiadis, "The Physiognomy of a Local Church," GkOrTR 33 (1988) 417–443. [21]M. Löhrer, "Chiesa locale e teologia," Later 50 (1984) 1–17; J.M.R. Tillard, "Rome dans la communion des Églises locales," Nicol 18 (1991) 157–189. [22]M. Hebga, "The Particular Church and the Universal Church: Sociological and Ecclesiological Considerations," IndTS 17 (1980) 47–63; G. Locatelli, "Il significato della chiesa locale," Ambros 68 (1992) 148–157; G. Routhier, "La synodalité de l'Église locale," StCan 26 (1992) 111–161; G. Vodopivec, "La teologia e le chiese locali in diverse aree culturali," Later 50 (1984) 38–76; J.M. Waliggo et al., *Inculturation: Its Meaning and Urgency* (Kampala: St. Paul, 1986). [23]J.M.R. Tillard, "L'universel et le local: Réflexion sur Église universelle et Églises locales," Irén 60 (1987) 483–494; 61 (1988) 28–40. [24]J.M.R. Tillard, "Le local et l'universel dans l'Église de Dieu," PrOrChr 37 (1987) 225–235. [25]J. Gaudemet, "Le symbolisme du mariage entre l'évêque et son Église et ses conséquences juridiques," Kan 7 (1985) 110–123. [26]A. Rose, "La signification de la messe chrismale," QLtg 69 (1988) 26–66. [27]CathIntern 3 (1992) 761–767. [28]*Evangelii nuntiandi,* n. 64—AAS 68 (1976) 54–55/Flannery 2:743. [29]E. Lanne, "The Local Church: Its Catholicity and Apostolicity," OneChr 6 (1970) 288–313.

## LOCI THEOLOGICI

See THEOLOGICAL SOURCES

## LOVE FOR THE CHURCH

Love of the Church is a traditional value in Christian spirituality, though not so much emphasized in recent ecclesiology. Its basis is Christ's own love for the Church for which "he gave himself up" and which he nourishes and cares for; indeed the relationship of Christ and the Church is the foundation mystery for married love (Eph 5:25, 27, 32). In fact the extensive teaching of the NT about loving the brothers and sisters is implicitly a command to love the Church's members (e.g., 1 John 2:10-11; 3:11-18). It goes without saying that Christians are to love Christ, the head of the Church (v. BODY).

Nonetheless, love for the Church is often problematic. There are of course many reasons: sin and failure make love difficult; ill-timed or badly presented magisterial teaching can give rise to anger or rejection; Church teaching, especially on moral issues, seems intrusive to some, and destructive of their freedom; institutions (q.v.) can seem oppressive and perhaps not only unloving but for some unlovable; the bureaucracy of the Church—much of it necessary—is felt by some to be cold and indifferent. The sense of patriarchy perceived in the Church makes for serious difficulties for some, indeed many, women (v. FEMINISM AND THE CHURCH).

But we have to love the real Church, its concrete institutions, the communion of believers—hierarchical and lay—who are sinners being continually saved. There is always the danger of trying to love an abstract

Church rather than the existing body of sinful believers, with the pope as its center of unity, Mary as its Mother, and Christ as its Head.

The Church is holy, and the Church is also in some sense sinful (v. HOLY). But H. Küng rightly noted that "we cannot assume that everything in the Church which is imperfect, erroneous, or misguided should simply be regarded as sinful. . . . There is much we can find in the Church and its history which cannot be laid at the door of any particular person."[1] Along with the beauty of the Church seen in its members and in its institutions, there is also ambiguity and failure in both of these. The flaws in the Church give rise to anger and distrust, which some people find difficult to overcome. Though there is an English saying that "love is blind," in our context it is perhaps more true to say that only love can see properly. The goodness and beauty of the Church in its members and institutions can be seen only through love, often a love that has to be marked by understanding and compassion, by a love illumined by faith.

From the tradition of ecclesiology there are several themes that can point to love of the Church: bride, mother (q.v.), queen (q.v.), Body of Christ (q.v.), People of God (q.v.) and Temple (q.v.), martyr (q.v.). Major teachers of the faith have insisted on love of the Church. One could take two examples, one ancient and one modern. St. Augustine stated: "We have the Holy Spirit if we love the Church: we love the Church if we remain in her unity and charity."[2] Pius XII concluded his encyclical *Mystici Corporis* with a long section on loving the Church.[3]

The late 20th century has given us some forthright examples of love of the Church. For example, in the 1950s Y. Congar (q.v.) and H. de Lubac (q.v.), among others, suffered much persecution and harassment from Church authorities after the encyclical *Humani generis* (1950—v. PIUS XII). Afterwards, the former wrote a book entitled *The Church Which I Love*.[4] The latter developed powerfully both the idea of motherhood and that of the splendor of the Church;[5] in an interview some time before his death, De Lubac remarked: "It is not enough that we learn to suffer for the Church; we must also learn to suffer from the Church." A. Bugnini (q.v.) encountered much opposition to the liturgical reforms which he steered so masterfully, and was eventually consigned to semi-exile in Iran. Before he died he said of himself, "I have served the Church, I have loved the Church, I have suffered for the Church."[6] In his *Thoughts of Death,* Paul VI exclaimed, "I could say that I have always loved the Church . . . and it seems to me that I have lived for her, not for anything else."[7] John XXIII expressed similar ideas in recalling the day of his priestly ordination.[8]

The problems of dissent (q.v.), and the need of appropriate criticism of the Church from within it, all raise the question of love of the Church. Where love is not explicit and obvious, negative expressions about the Church, even if apparently necessary in themselves, will not bear fruit. Finally, the obligation to love the Church is specified by law in the case of neophytes (CIC 789).

---

[1]*The Church* (London: Search, 1968) 320, see 319–330.    [2]*Tract. in Ioan.* 32:8—PL 35: 1646, cited by John Paul II, *Augustinum hipponensem*—AAS 79 (1987) 156 at note 157; cf. *Tract. in Ioan.* 32:8—CCL 36:304.    [3]AAS 35 (1943) 237–248/Carlen 4:56-61. [4]Denville, N.J.: Dimension, 1969.    [5]*The Splendor of the Church* (San Francisco: Ignatius, 1986—French 1953); *The Motherhood of the Church* (San Francisco: Ignatius, 1982—French 1971).    [6]Recorded by G. Pasqualetti, in A. Bugnini, *The Reform of the Liturgy (1948–1975)* (Collegeville: The Liturgical Press, 1990) xxii. [7]Cited C. Martini, *Some Years After: Reflections on the Ministry of the Priest.* Cathedral Series 5 (Dublin: Veritas, 1991) 78–79. [8]*Journal of a Soul* (London: Chapman, 1964) 160.

## LUCIFERIANS

The Luciferians were a schismatic sect named after its founder, or perhaps leading protagonist, Lucifer of Cagliari (d. 370).[1] They originated in a rejection of the pro-Arian policy of the emperor Constantius II at the provincial council of Milan (354). Later they refused communion with reconciled Arians, or even with those who accepted the latter. They sought complete purity of faith, and saw themselves as the only faithful remnant.

---

[1]Patrology 4:64-69; works PL 13:767-1049; PLS 1:351-352.

## LUMEN GENTIUM, Vatican II: Constitution on the Church

The Constitution *Lumen gentium* ("Light of peoples" = Christ) is the most important document of Vatican II (q.v.). Indeed, one of the four aims given to the council when it was reconvened by Paul VI was to develop a fuller definition of the Church.[1] The document was to have a long and tortuous evolution before its final promulgation on 21 November 1964.[2] The first draft on the Church from the Preparatory Commission, *Aeternus Unigeniti Pater,* was in the tradition from Bellarmine (q.v.) and of the papal magisterium of the previous decades. This text viewed the Church as a "perfect society" (q.v.) and stressed its hierarchical structure.[3] It was largely rejected by the council members; Bishop De Smedt of Bruges called it too triumphalistic, clerical, and juridical; Cardinal Montini criticized it as lacking a proper doctrine of the relation of Christ to the Church. Its eleven chapters were returned for redrafting. The next draft, called *Lumen gentium,* was introduced at the second session on 30 September 1963, and it consisted of four chapters: the Church as mystery; its hierarchical structure; the People of God and the laity;

holiness of the Church. Cardinals Frings and Suenens suggested that the second and third chapters be reversed; Frings also proposed that a chapter be added on the eschatological character of the Church, and that the text on the Mother of God be incorporated in the constitution. After a debate of one month, voting showed a majority agreement on some thorny questions: the sacramentality of episcopal ordination, the College of Bishops (v. BISHOPS, COLLEGIALITY), the permanent diaconate (v. DEACONS), and the inclusion of the text on the Blessed Virgin. Further emendations were made while the council was in recess, and the final draft was debated, modified, and finally approved during the third session of the council. It was promulgated on 21 November 1964, but with an explanatory note *(Nota explicativa praevia)* to protect from misinterpretation the notion of episcopal collegiality.

Despite its slow evolution, the constitution has a fine unity. The opening chapter, "The Mystery of the Church," shows the eternal divine and Trinitarian plan being worked out in the Church. The second chapter, "The People of God," speaks of the whole Church without differentiation, based on function or state: God is shown to have a plan for the whole people; the common priesthood (q.v.) is shared by all (LG 10) and exercised in the sacraments (LG 11); the whole people is related in diverging degrees to members of the Catholic Church who are fully incorporated into it (LG 15), to others—Christians (LG 16), non-Christians (LG 17). The third chapter deals with the hierarchy. The earlier work of the First Vatican Council, which spoke only of the pope is now complemented by an extensive treatment of the episcopal college. Chapter 4, "The Laity," shows their special calling through their sharing in the priestly, prophetic, and kingly office of Christ. The next chapter returns to the whole Church, for all are called to holiness. There follows a short sixth chapter on the particular role of religious in the Church. The seventh chapter is again about the universal Church on its eschatological pilgrimage. The final chapter, the eighth, is called, "The Blessed Virgin Mary, Mother of God, in the Mystery of Christ and of the Church." It has two main parts: it shows Mary's relationship to Christ and to the Church.

Despite the fine structure of the Constitution, the chapter arrangement already being a statement on the nature and destiny of the Church, it would not be true to say that this document gives us the ecclesiology of Vatican II. There are more than one, even more than two,[4] ecclesiologies operating in the council (v. VATICAN II). The constitution is a key for the interpretation of the other texts of the council, and it, in turn, must be interpreted with their help.

---

[1]Discourse at opening of 2nd session, 29.10.63—AAS 55 (1963) 841–859 at 847-858/ActaSyn 2/1:183-199 at 187–199.  [2]H.

Jedin, "The Second Vatican Council," in Jedin-Dolan 10:96-151, and standard commentaries, especially Msgr. Philips, *L'Église et son mystère: Histoire, textes et commentaire de la Constitution "Lumen gentium."* 2 vols. (Paris: Desclée, 1967) 1:13-68; Baraúna-Congar I-III; J. Linnan, "Dogmatic Constitution on the Church, *Lumen gentium* (21 Nov. 1964) and Decree on the Pastoral Office of the Bishops in the Church, *Christus dominus* (28 Oct. 1965)," in T.E. O'Connell, ed., *Vatican II and Its Documents: An American Reappraisal.* Theology and Life 15 (Wilmington: Glazier, 1986) 39–61; On development of the drafts see Alberigo-Magistretti. [3]Y. Congar, "Situation ecclésiologique au moment de 'Ecclesiam suam' et passage à une Église dans l'itinéraire des hommes," in *Le Concile de Vatican II: Son Église—Peuple de Dieu et Corps du Christ.* Théologie historique 71 (Paris: Beauchesne, 1984) 7–32. [4]A. Acerbi, *Due ecclesiologie: Ecclesiologia giurdica ed ecclesiologia di comunione nella "Lumen gentium"* (Bologna: Ed. Dehoniane, 1975).

## LUTHER, Martin (1483–1546)

Martin Luther was born in Saxony in 1483. He studied law at Eisenach and at Erfurt universities (1501–1505). He entered the Augustinian hermits in 1505 and was ordained in 1507. The following year he was sent to the newly founded university of Wittenberg to lecture and engage in further studies. In 1512 he became a doctor of theology and professor of Scripture, a post he held, with interruptions, until his death in 1546.

Catholic historians of the past demonized Luther. Particularly significant for the 20th-century Catholic understanding of Luther were the hostile studies by H. Denifle (1904) and H. Grisar's six volumes (1913–1917, with a one-volume summary 1926). An essay by S. Merkle in 1929[1] was to be the beginning of a more open and sympathetic understanding of Luther, which was to come to fruition in the great work by J. Lortz.[2] Serious Catholic studies on Luther followed; while not uncritical, they have sought to be fair to Luther and to his work as the leader of the German reform.[3]

Studies on Luther continue to multiply,[4] due in no small part to his own huge output[5] and to the complexity both of his own personality and of the reform he engendered.[6] The fifth centenary of his birth gave rise to a number of significant collected studies[7] and biographies.[8]

There are clearly two circumstances that changed the friar Luther to Luther the reformer. One was his own internal spiritual struggles contemporaneous with his lecturing on the psalms (1513–1515) and Romans (1515–1516). At some time during that period, or before 1518, he had the famous "tower experience," in which he understood clearly that faith alone justifies. The other was the state of the Church, which was symbolized in the indulgences scandal which Luther met in the preaching of J. Tetzel in 1517. It now seems clear that theses were not posted on the door of the Church at Wittenberg, an event recorded by Melanchthon (q.v.) only after Luther's death.[9] Luther observed the normal channels of sending his views (theses) to bishops, and only after failing to get a response, spread them more widely in the academic community. Gradually Luther's positions hardened on a whole variety of issues in need of reform.

By 1520, after both an investigation by his order (1518) and a disputation with J. Eck (1519), his own break with the medieval Church was complete, especially through the publication of his *Babylonian Captivity of the Church* in that year. His excommunication followed in 1521. In brief it can be said that Luther rejected priestly mediations in favor of a personal saving encounter through faith with God, who had released him from his own spiritual torments. Moreover, his experience of Church politics did not give him much trust in institutions, above all in the papacy. For him, the only objective norm capable of effecting reform was the Word of God; Luther's position on Scripture alone (*scriptura sola*) progressively developed as more and more issues emerged. At its root the Reformation ended up by being a denial of development (q.v.): what had emerged in the Church after the NT, especially in medieval times, was gradually rejected.

In coming to an understanding of Luther's view of the Church, we have to remember that though he continually spoke about it, he never advanced a coherent ecclesiology[10] but rather responded to practical difficulties as they arose. He never wanted to found a new Church but to reform the true Church.[11] When his attempts at reform were spurned and he was excommunicated, he concluded that it was not the authentic Church, Christ's, which had done so.[12] Further, as the *Articles of Schmalkalden,* written by Luther in 1536, clearly show, he did have what we would might today call a "hierarchy of truths" in his emerging reform program: there were uncontroverted issues such as Trinity, Christology; there were issues on which he would not compromise, like his views on atonement and justification, and his conviction that the Mass and papacy were not divine institutions; there were issues that could be discussed with scholars, such as sin, penance, confession, religious vows, etc.[13] Moreover, he was fighting on many fronts. He was opposed not only to the Roman Church but also to the various spiritual movements that had sprung up, like the Anabaptists (from 1525—q.v.), Mennonites (from 1536), the *Schwärmer* fanatics, as well as other reformers, for example Zwingli's (q.v.) views on the Eucharist.

Central to his ecclesiology[14] at all times was the preached Word. From it he expected that institutions and structures would emerge in congregations, that a moral transformation of Christians would occur, that the sacraments, particularly of baptism and the Lord's Supper, would be worthily celebrated. He strongly supported the priesthood of the laity. From this he de-

nied a special ministerial sacrament but did insist that people be called by the community to administer Word and sacrament on its behalf. This represented his views about 1520–1523; later he was more insistent on Church order, even holding a role for bishops and ordained ministers, without however conceding that orders was a sacrament.[15]

Luther strongly held the communion of saints.[16] He tended to avoid the word "Church," which he wrongly deduced from the word "curia," preferring to speak of the Christian people or using other synonyms.[17] In 1539, in his work *On the Councils and the Church,* Luther stated the overall characteristics of the Holy Christian People in seven main marks or notes (q.v.) of the Church: the holy Word of God; the sacrament of baptism; the holy sacrament of the altar; the office of the keys (confession and absolution); the calling or consecration of ministers; prayer, praise, and worship of God; the Cross, for persecution is inevitable.[18]

Two years later, in *Against Hanswurst,* his marks of the Church were still more elaborate: baptism; the Lord's Supper; the office of the keys; the office of preaching the Word of God; the Apostles' Creed; the Lord's Prayer; respect for secular government; praise of marriage as created by, and acceptable to, God; suffering of the true Church; willingness to suffer persecution without seeking revenge.[19] Luther saw himself more as an evangelistic preacher of God's mercy than a reformer. He did indeed seek reform, but it was a religious, theological, and pastoral one, and not concerned with mere externals, which he dismissed as trivia.[20]

There is a continual problem with Luther's assertions that the true Church is spiritual: a hidden reality of pure faith rooted in the gospel and practiced without, or behind, visible signs. He does not seem to be setting up two Churches in opposition, a spiritual and an external or physical one *(leiblich).* N.A. Nissiotis is perhaps right in saying that for Luther the Word was more than Scripture or preaching but included a Christology and a pneumatology in which God is active and the human largely passive. This would affect our understanding of his often repeated dictum that the Church is where the gospel is purely preached and the sacraments are administered. But the emphasis is on Word more than sacrament: "The one eternal and unmistakable mark of the Church is, and always has been, the Word."[21]

Thus in the *Short Catechism,* in explaining the third part of the Creed, "On Sanctification," he states that we cannot by our own power approach God: "The Holy Spirit called me by the Gospel, illumined me by his gifts, sanctified and conserved me in right faith, just as he is accustomed to call, to gather, to illuminate and to sanctify the whole Church *(totam ecclesiam/die ganze Christenheit auf Erden),* and to conserve it in Jesus Christ through the right faith."[22]

A very problematic area of Luther research is his doctrine of the two kingdoms, described by E. Iserloh as "a maze."[23] Luther himself did not use the term, which appeared only in 1922 to cover a number of issues involving the secular and the sacred, and hence much wider than civil and ecclesiastical powers. Luther would seem to have proposed independence rather than autonomy of the realm of the secular; secular government is necessary because of human sin. The secular and the sacred are both under God, who acts in a hidden way in secular government. Secular government exists primarily to ensure an area for the proclamation of the Word and the administration of the sacraments.

The Lutheran Churches (q.v.) have retained from their origin in Luther a seriousness about doctrine and moral behavior. The Lutheran stress on individual conversion that must be lived out within a community of Church and world is a valuable emphasis in the ecumenical movement, which itself experiences the tension between the secular and the sacred, between the horizontal and the vertical. The understanding of the Church as sacrament, if duly clarified, might focus a common understanding between Catholics and Lutherans.[24] Catholics in particular can no longer be content with parodies of Luther; they have to recognize him as a major theologian and a spiritual writer of great power.[25] The scandal of the Reformation divisions in the Church arose from a double cause: the refusal of the official Church to listen to Luther; the failure of Luther truly to engage in a meaningful dialogue—since dialogue is scarcely possible in an atmosphere of polemics or for one so passionate as the young Luther.

[1]"Gutes an Luther und Übles an seinen Tadlern," in A. von Martin, ed., *Luther in ökumenischer Sicht* (Stuttgart, 1929) 9–19.  [2]*History of the Reformation in Germany.* 2 vols. (New York, 1968 from German 1939–1940) 1:428-488.  [3]See J. Wicks, *Luther and His Spiritual Legacy.* Theology and Life 7 (Wilmington: Glazier—Dublin: Dominican, 1983) ch. 1—"Images of Luther" 11–34; idem, "L'orizzonte dell'incontro cattolico con Lutero," Asp 30 (1983) 341–350; idem, "Martin Luther Through Catholic Eyes," ChicSt 8 (1969) 275–285; W. Brandmüller, "Die Reformation Martin Luthers in katholischer Sicht," MüTZ 35 (1984) 32–46; J. Brosseder, "Das heutige katholische Lutherbild," UnaSan 37 (1982) 281–292; H. Jedin, "Luther: A New View," ChicSt 5 (1966) 53–63; A. Klein, "La recezione cattolica di Martin Lutero," Asp 30 (1983) 351–362; L. Spitz, "Current Accents in Luther Studies 1960–1967," TS 28 (1967) 549–573.  [4]See annual bibliog. in *Lutherjahrbuch.*  [5]German critical edition "Weimar Ausgabe (WA)," *Martin Luthers Werke, Kritische Ausgabe.* 57 vols. from 1883, with vol. 58 beginning index; Eng. trans. J. Pelikan et al., eds., *Luther's Works.* vols. 1–30 (St. Louis: Concordia), vols. 31–54 (Philadelphia: Fortress), vol. 55 "Index," ed. J.W. Lundeen (Philadelphia: Fortress, 1986).  [6]E. Iserloh, in Jedin-Dolan 5:3-104; 144–156; 213–224.  [7]Bibliog., K. Hagen and F. Posset, *Annotated Bibliography of Luther Studies 1977–1983.* Sixteenth Century Bibliography 24 (St. Louis: Center for Reformation Research, 1985); J.J. Alemany, "Panorama bibli-ográfico del centenario luterano," MiscCom 42 (1984) 79–101; M. Cassese, "Lutero nel 5° centenario della nascita," RasT 24 (1983) 51–63; J.F. Gilmont, "Le cinquième centenaire de la naissance de Luther: Bilan des publications en français," RTLv 15 (1984) 207–255; L. Lago, "Boletín bibliográfico sobre Lutero," CiTom 110 (1983) 606–618; "Lutherbibliographie 1984," LuthJb 51 (1984) 109–200; D.K. McKim, "Recent Lutheran Studies," TS 48 (1987) 499–504; Studies: AA.VV. *Luther et la réforme allemande dans une perspective oecuménique.* Les études théologiques de Chambésy 3 (Chambésy—Geneva: Ed. du Centre Orthodoxe du Patriarchat oecuménique, 1983); J. Becker, ed., *Luthers bleibende Bedeutung* (Husum: Husum Druck-und Verlag, 1983); H.R. Boudin and A. Houssiau, eds., *Luther aujourd'hui par les professeurs de théologie protestante et de la faculté de théologie de l'Université Catholique.* Cahiers de la *Revue théologique de Louvain* 11 (Louvain-la-Neuve: Publications de la Faculté de Théologie, 1983); P.N. Brooks, *Seven-Headed Luther: Essays in Commemoration of a Quincentenary 1483–1983* (Oxford: Clarendon, 1983); H. Junghans, ed., *Leben und Werk Martin Luthers von 1526 bis 1546. Festgabe zu seinem Geburtstag.* 2 vols. (Göttingen: Vandenhoeck & Ruprecht, 1981); G. Yule, ed., *Luther: Theologian for Catholics and Protestants* (Edinburgh: Clark, 1985); Communio (Paris) 12 (1983).  [8]J. Atkinson, *Martin Luther: Prophet to the Catholic Church* (Exeter: Paternoster—Grand Rapids, Mich.: Eerdmans, 1983); H. Diwald, *Luther: Eine Biographie* (Bergisch Gladbach: Lübbe, 1982); J. Rogge, *Martin Luther: Sein Leben, seine Zeit, seine Wirkungen. Eine Bildbibliographie* (Gütersloh: Mohn, 1982). On older biographies see Wicks (n.3) 158–160.  [9]E. Iserloh, *The Theses Were Not Posted: Luther Between Reform and Reformation* (Boston, 1968); idem, Jedin-Dolan 5:47-48.  [10]Congar, Augustin 352–358; M. Beyer, "Luthers Ekklesiologie," in Junghams (n. 7) 1:93-117; 2:755-765; O.H. Pesch, "Luther und die Kirche," LuthJb 52 (1985) 113–139.  [11]Y. Congar, *Martin Luther: Sa vie, sa foi, sa réforme: Études de théologie historique.* Cogitatio fidei 119 (Paris: Cerf, 1983) 59–79; idem, "Comment Luther devint Luther," LumiereV 158/31 (1982) 77–86; J. Pelikan, *Obedient Rebels: Catholic Substance and Protestant Principle in Luther's Reformation* (London, 1964).  [12]Congar (n. 11) 59.  [13]Bekenntnisschriften 414–468, see 416.  [14]Iserloh, in Jedin-Dolan 5:213-225; S. Folgado Flórez, "'La comunidad de los creyentes': Iglesia de Lutero," CiuD 196 (1983) 409–434; G.W. Forell, "Luther's Ecclesiology and the Unity of the Church," in *Luther et la réforme allemande* (n. 7) 447–454; M. Lienhard, *L'évangile et l'église chez Luther.* Théologie et sciences religieuses. Cogitatio fidei 153 (Paris: Cerf, 1989); N.A. Nissiotis, "Is There a Church Ontology in Martin Luther's Ecclesiology?," ibid., 403–426; B. Lohse, *Martin Luther: An Introduction to His Life and Work* (Philadelphia: Fortress, 1986—Edinburgh: Clark, 1987—German 1980) 174–186. See P.O.L. Avis, "The True Church in Reformation Theology," ScotJT 30 (1977) 319–343.  [15]Lohse (n. 14) 182–186.  [16]V. Vajta, "Die Kirche als geistlich-sakramentale Communio mit Christus und seinen Heiligen bei Luther," LuthJb 51(1984) 10–62.  [17]*Large Catechism*—"Third Article of Creed"—Bekenntnisschriften 655–656.  [18]H. Kunst, *Die Kirche bei Luther* (Stuttgart: Evangelisches Verlag, 1971) 148–164, cited Nissiotis (n. 14) 411; Lohse (n. 14) 181.  [19]Lohse (n. 14) 181.  [20]J.E. Vercruysse, "Luther as Reformer Within Christendom," StMiss 34 (1985) 351–371.  [21]WA 25:97 cited Lohse (n. 14) 181.  [22]Bekenntnisschriften 512; cf. S. Cavallotto, "Il 'credo ecclesiam.' Dalla *professione di fede* di Lutero (1527/'28) agli articoli di Schwabach (1529)," Asp 30 (1983) 383–415.  [23]Iserloh, in Jedin-Dolan 5:217-220 at 217; Lohse (n. 14) 186–193.  [24]A. Birmelé, "La sacramentalité de l'Église et la tradition luthérienne," Irén 59 (1986) 482–507.  [25]Wicks (n. 3).

## LUTHERAN CHURCHES

The symbolic gesture, doubtless apocryphal, by Martin Luther (1483–1546—q.v.) of affixing 95 theses to the church door in Wittenberg in 1517 marked a movement of reform which spread throughout Germany. The Peace of Augsburg (1555) gave toleration to Lutherans on a territorial basis according to the principle *cuius princeps eius religio* (the religion of the ruler decides the religion of the subjects). By that time Lutheranism had already spread to Eastern Europe and northwards to Scandinavia; it would later be worldwide. From an early date Luther and his followers began to supply confessional statements which became normative in Lutheran Churches:[1] Luther's *Short Catechism* (1529),[2] the *Longer Catechism* (1529),[3] the *Augsburg Confession* (1530—q.v.),[4] the *Articles of Schmalkalden* (1537),[5] the *Formula of Concord* (1577),[6] combined in the *Book of Concord* (1580).

Lutheranism also held the three ancient creeds (q.v.): *Apostles', Nicene,* and *Athanasian.* The main Lutheran doctrines are in four areas: justification ("faith alone"), forgiveness ("grace alone"), authority ("Scripture alone") and soteriology ("Christ alone"). On the Church, the *Augsburg Confession* states: "The one holy Church is to continue forever. But the Church is the congregation of saints, in which the Gospel is rightly preached and the Sacraments rightly administered. And unto the true unity of the Church, it is sufficient to agree concerning the doctrine of the Gospel and the administration of the sacraments" (art. 7). Lutheran worship stresses the Liturgy of the Word, especially the sermon, and the Lord's Supper. Government of the Church is by synods of clergy and laity.

In the 19th and 20th centuries there were unions and mergers of Lutheran Churches in various countries.[7] The Lutheran World Federation (LWF—1947) had 105 member Churches by 1990, when it adopted a new constitution including the declaration, "The LWF is a communion of Churches which confess the Triune God, agree in the proclamation of the word of God and are united in pulpit and altar fellowship."[8] The LWF has sponsored important international dialogues with Anglicans (q.v.) and Baptists (q.v.).

Dialogue with the Methodists took place 1977–1984, leading to the recommendation that steps be taken to declare and establish full fellowship of word and sacrament.[9]

There were some 16th-century contacts between Lutherans and Orthodox, and in the 20th century various regional discussions. International meetings were agreed upon in 1976–1977, and five meetings took place from 1981–1989,[10] studying under various headings "Participation in the Mystery of the Church."[11] The next stage is study of "Authority in, and of, the Church."[12]

Discussion with Reformed Churches has been taking place in various countries since the 16th century. The European Leuenberg talks began in 1969 and were centered on the *Augsburg Confession* art. 7 above. It proposed full fellowship in Eucharistic and pulpit sharing. A further dialogue in 1981 proposed that some urgent action be taken on fellowship, but its report, *An Invitation to Action,* proved controversial especially in the U.S.[13] In 1985 dialogue on this became worldwide, with *Toward Church Fellowship.*[14]

Dialogue with the Roman Catholic Church has been intensive both internationally and locally.[15] One of the earliest world dialogues undertaken by the newly formed Vatican Secretariat for Promoting Christian Unity was with the LWF in 1967. This has given rise to a number of significant reports beginning with the general "Malta Report" (1972),[16] followed by "Eucharist" (1978),[17] "Ways to Community" (1980),[18] "All Under One Christ" (1980),[19] "The Ministry in the Church" (1981),[20] "Facing Unity" (1985),[21] and "Church and Justification" (1994).[22] Further dialogues on ecclesiology began in 1986. There are several conversations at the national level between Lutherans and Roman Catholics, e.g., Australia, Canada, Germany, India, Japan, Norway, and Sweden. A very significant series of dialogues[23] has taken place in the U.S.: Nicene Creed (1965), Baptism (1966), Eucharist (1967, 1970), Papal Primacy (1973) and Infallibility (1978), Justification (1983), The One Mediator, the Saints and Mary (1992). Studies were also commissioned on *Peter in the New Testament* (1973),[24] *Mary in the New Testament* (1978),[25] *Righteousness in the New Testament* (1982).[26]

A major ecumenical dialogue is the ongoing trilateral one between the Lutheran, Reformed, and Roman Catholic Churches; a significant outcome has been its document on interfaith marriages (1976—v. MARRIAGE, INTERFAITH).[27]

Vatican II theology, especially on sacramentality, provides many possibilities for dialogue with Lutherans.[28] From the beginning Lutheranism[29] has emphasized theological studies and has been to the fore in scientific advances in all areas of biblical study. The specific contribution of Lutheranism to ecumenism is especially its emphasis on the Word of God, its theological depth, its stress on faith and justification, its focus on the Lord's Supper, and its theology of the Cross.[30]

[1]Schaff, Creeds 1:211-353; E. Schlink, *Theology of Lutheran Confessions* (Philadelphia: Mühlenberg, 1961); T.G. Tappert, *The Confessions of the Evangelical Lutheran Church* (Philadelphia: Mühlenberg, 1959); V. Vajta and H. Weissgerber eds., *The Church and the Confessions: The Role of the Confessions in the Life and Doctrine of the Lutheran Churches* (Philadelphia: Fortress, 1963). [2]Schaff, Creeds 3:74–92/Bekenntnisschriften 501–527. [3]Bekenntnisschriften 545–733. [4]Schaff, Creeds 3:3–73/Bekenntnisschrif-

ten 31–137.  [5]Bekenntnisschriften 407–468.  [6]Schaff, Creeds 3:93-180/Bekenntnisschriften 739–1100.  [7]A. R. Wentz, *The Lutheran Churches of the World* (Geneva: LWF, 1952).  [8]N.A. Hjejm, "Lutheran World Fellowship" in DictEcumMov 640–641.  [9]*The Church: A Community of Grace* (Geneva: LWF—Lake Junaluska: WMC, 1984); Irén 59 (1986) 536.  [10]J. Travis, "Orthodox-Lutheran Relations: Their Historical Beginnings," GkOrTR 29 (1984) 303–325.  [11]T. Nickolau, "Der offizielle orthodoxlutherische Dialog: Geschichtlicher Überblick und gemeinsame Texte," OrthFor 4 (1990) 83–99; E. Schlink, "Changes in Protestant Thinking About the Eastern Church," Ecu 10 (1957–1958) 386–400.  [12]D.F. Martensen, "Lutheran-Orthodox Dialogue," DictEcumMov 635–636.  [13]J.E. Andrews and J.A. Burgess, eds., *An Invitation to Action* (Philadelphia: Fortress, 1984).  [14]Geneva: LWF—WARC, 1989; P.R. Fries, "Lutheran—Reformed Dialogue," DictEcumMov 636–638.  [15]H. Meyer, "Roman Catholic/Lutheran Dialogue," OneChr 22 (1986) 146–168; M. Root, "Lutheran—Roman Catholic Dialogue," DictEcumMov 638–640; D. Salado, "III Congreso Luterano-Católico (Salamanca, 26–30 de septiembre de 1983)," CiTom 110 (1983) 593–602; J. Wicks, "Ecclesiological Issues in the Lutheran-Catholic Dialogue (1965–1985)," in Latourelle, Vatican II 2:305-346.  [16]H. Meyer and L. Vischer, *Growth in Agreement.* Ecumenical Documents 2—Faith and Order Paper 109 (New York: Paulist—Geneva: WCC, 1984) 168–189.  [17]Ibid., 190–214.  [18]Ibid., 215–240.  [19]Ibid., 241–247.  [20]Ibid., 248–275.  [21]DocCath 84 (1987) 294–321; H. Legrand and H. Meyer, eds., *Face à l'unité: L'ensemble des textes adoptés* (1972–1985)—(Paris: Cerf, 1986).  [22] "Church and Justification: Understanding the Church in the Light of the Doctrine of Justification," CathInter 6 (1995) 329–347.  [23]Texts publ. Augsburg, Minneapolis; J.A. Burgess and J. Gros, *Building Unity.* Ecumenical Documents 4 (New York—Mahwah: Paulist, 1989) 83–290; J. Reumann, "A Quarter Century of Lutheran-Roman Catholic Dialogue in the United States," OneChr 27 (1991) 185–191;  [24]R.E. Brown et al., eds. (Minneapolis: Augsburg—New York: Paulist, 1973).  [25]R.E. Brown et al., eds. (Philadelphia: Fortress—New York: Paulist, 1978).  [26]J. Reumann et al. (Philadelphia: Fortress—New York: Paulist, 1982).  [27]Mayer and Vischer (n. 16) 277–306.  [28]A. Birmelé, "La sacramentalité de l'Église et la tradition luthérienne," Irén 59 (1986) 482–507.  [29]Bibliog. annual *Lutherjahrbuch* (Göttingen: Vandenhoeck & Ruprecht).  [30]J.E. Vercruysse, "Luther's Theology of the Cross: Its Relevance for Ecumenism," BullCentUn 35 (1989) 2–11.

## LYONS I, Council of (1245)

Relations between the papacy and the empire were very strained from the time of the coronation of Frederick II in 1220. Honorius III (1216–1227) and the emperor were in conflict over a promise to undertake a crusade; later Gregory IX (1227–1241) opposed the emperor's attempts at hegemony, especially in Italy. In 1240 Gregory attempted to call a council, but the emperor prevented it from meeting. His successor, Innocent IV (1243–1254), escaped to Lyons and called a council which met there in 1245.[1] It would be regarded as the 13th ecumenical council. Its aim emerged in Innocent's opening address, in which he described the five wounds of the Church: the corrupt state of faith and morals; the capture of Jerusalem and the situation in the Holy Land; the Eastern Schism; the threat of the Mongols or Tartars; the conflict with the emperor Frederick. It was the last of

these which was most prominent in the pope's mind and surfaced in each of the council's sessions.

Though ably defended by his representative, Thaddaeus of Suessa, who among other things attacked the ecumenicity of the council, the emperor Frederick was not to escape condemnation. Because of four crimes —perjury, breach of peace, sacrilege in imprisoning prelates, and suspicion of heresy—he was deposed as Roman Emperor, King of Germany and of Sicily; he was stripped of all honors, and his subjects were released from their oath of loyalty.[2] This was an exercise of the *Dictatus papae* (q.v.) of Gregory VII: the power to depose an emperor (prop. 12); the faculty of releasing people from fealty to unjust ruler (prop. 27).

The textual history of the conciliar constitutions is complex and not fully clear on all points.[3] Constitutions were enacted on some legal points: rescripts (cc. 1–3), elections and judicial processes (cc. 4–17); homicide and the employment of assassins (c. 18), excommunications (cc. 19–22).[4] These were sent to the universities in August 1245, after the final session of the council (17 July). Another set of constitutions was published in the following year.[5] These would seem to be the ones dealing with usury (c. II/1), help for the empire of Constantinople (c. II/2–3), the Tartars (c. II/4), the crusade (c. II/5).

The fruits of the council were mixed. Frederick continued his struggle against the papacy until he died in 1250; the male line of his Hohenstaufen dynasty came to an end in 1268. Most of the constitutions associated with the council were incorporated in 1298 into the canonical collection *Liber sextus,* and were later commented on in the legal schools. But the council, unlike the other medieval papal councils, did not produce canons dealing with heresy and reform of the Church. The impetus of the Gregorian reform movement (v. GREGORY VII) seems by then to have become enfeebled.

[1]A. Melloni in Alberigo, Concili 204–207; H. Wolter, in Jedin-Dolan 4:195-198; H. Wolter and H. Holstein, *Lyon I et Lyon II.* Histoire des conciles 7 (Paris: Ed. l'Orante, 1966).  [2]Bull of Deposition—Tanner 1:278-283.  [3]Tanner 1:274-276.  [4]Tanner 1:274-275.  [5]Tanner 1:293-301.

## LYONS II, Council of (1274)

For centuries the Second Council of Lyons (1274) was regarded as ecumenical (14th): it was convoked, directed, and approved by the pope.[1] It has never been accepted as ecumenical by the Orthodox because all the patriarchs were not present, and its decrees lacked reception (q.v.) in the East. Recently there is found a distinction between the "great councils" of the first millennium and the Western councils; Paul VI, on the seventh centenary in 1974 of Lyons II, would seem to have followed this line. Moreover, in the later Middle

Ages and early modern times, the Council of Florence (q.v.) was often called the eighth ecumenical council.

The primary aim of Gregory X (1271–1276)[2] was support for the Holy Land (v. CRUSADES). The first period of the council (May 1274) was entirely devoted to this. Gregory sought and obtained six years of tithing of all ecclesiastical revenues.[3]

The second end was reunion with the Greeks. Though 1054, with its excommunications, was a turning point in the progressive alienation of East and West, it was the sack of Constantinople during the 4th crusade (1204) that finally confirmed the rupture. Nonetheless, in the 13th century there were attempts at dialogue and reunion.[4] The arrival of the unscrupulous Michael Palaeologus on the imperial throne in 1258[5] led to an increase in such efforts: he offered union in exchange for peace. The popes, from Urban IV (1261–1264) to Gregory X, all insisted that union must precede peace. Already in 1267 Clement IV (1265–1268) had sent a letter to Michael, containing a profession of faith about the Trinity and the Roman primacy. The latter requested through the papal legates that the Greek creed as well as canonical and liturgical traditions would remain untouched. The official act of union took place at Constantinople in February 1274; in the 4th session of the council (6 July 1274), Gregory announced the submission of the East.[6] It was not to outlive its protagonists, the emperor (d. 1282) and the pope (d. 1276). The reasons for the failure are complex: the pope sought an extension of his authority, while the emperor wanted political stability; there was an unbridged ecclesial distance between East and West; Lyons II was neither a council marked by debate nor a meeting of minds; the profession of faith imposed on the East by the emperor and pope was in a scholastic mold;[7] above all, there was no serious attempt to take into account the position of the patriarchs of the East, who since Lateran IV (1215—q.v.) had been treated more or less as if they were Latins.[8]

With regard to the third aim of the council—reform—there was a reading of twelve constitutions on 4 June; other reform documents came at the end of, or after, the council. A main reform, *Ubi periculum,* concerned papal conclaves.[9] Its provisions, frequently revised, were to be largely observed right up to modern times. Other decrees concerned the approval of some orders, notably the Franciscans and Dominicans, and the suppression of recent foundations.[10]

At the final session (17 July) the dogmatic constitution on the procession of the Holy Spirit, *Fideli ac devota,* was promulgated, though its final form is postconciliar.[11]

The council had little long-term effect: the union with the Greeks was short-lived; the crusade never got under way; the disciplinary decrees fell far short of the needed reform "in head and members."

---

[1]J. Gill, *Byzantium and the Papacy 1198–1400* (New Brunswick: Rutgers UP, 1979) 120–141; Jedin, Councils 87–94; U. Proch in Alberigo, Concili 285–299; H. Wolter, in Jedin-Dolan 4:203-207; H. Wolter and H. Holstein, *Lyon I et Lyon II.* Histoire des conciles 7 (Paris: Ed. l'Orante, 1966). [2]L. Gatto, *Il pontificato di Gregorio X (1271–1276)* (Rome, 1959). [3]Tanner 1:310. [4]D. Nicol, "The Greeks and the Union of the Churches: The Preliminaries to the Second Council of Lyons 1261–1274," in *Medieval Studies Presented to Aubrey Gwynn* (Dublin, 1961) 454–480. [5]D.J. Geanakoplos, *Emperor Michael Palaeologus and the West: A Study in Byzantine-Latin Relations* (Cambridge, Mass., 1959). [6]M. Villain, "La question de l'union des Églises entre Grecs et Latins depuis le concile de Lyon jusqu'à celui de Florence," RHE 17 (1921) 260–305; 515–532; 18 (1922) 20–60; J. Gill, *Church Union: Rome and Byzantium* (London: Variorum Reprints, 1979). [7]DS 851–861/ND 22–29. [8]Constit. 5—Tanner 1:236. [9]Tanner 1:314-318. [10]Tanner 1:326-327. See R.W. Emery, "The Second Council of Lyons and the Mendicant Orders," CHRev 39 (1954) 257–271. [11]Tanner 1:314/DS 850/ND 321.

# M

## MAGISTERIUM

There exist controverted issues and an abundant literature on every aspect of the magisterium, or teaching authority, especially its scriptural foundations,[1] history, and contemporary concerns,[2] including councils (q.v.), infallibility (q.v.), theologians (q.v.), dissent (q.v.).

Within the NT itself there are several words that bear on the origins of teaching with authority, such as *didaskô* (teach), *kêrussô* (proclaim or herald), *euaggelizomai* (bring good news), and their cognates,[3] to which could be added *katêcheô* (teach by word of mouth—Gal 6:6), *paradosis* (tradition—1 Cor 11:2), *paideuô* (teach/educate—Titus 2:12).[4] We have to bear in mind, too, that an awareness of having received the Holy Spirit underlies the NT communities' understanding of teachers and teaching.[5] Since the time of C.H. Dodd,[6] exegetes have frequently distinguished between preaching and teaching *(kêrugma/ didachê),*[7] but the difference should not be unduly forced as the Good News includes both.[8]

Paul rarely describes himself as a teacher (but see 1 Cor 4:17), preferring the title "apostle" (q.v.). He insists on the "truth of the gospel" (Gal 2:5, 14) and on teaching received (Rom 16:17) as normative. He knows of teachers (1 Cor 12:28) and of those who teach (Rom 12:7), but exegetes do not agree on how these are distinguished from prophets (q.v.), who are placed before them in the Pauline lists (1 Cor 12:28; Rom 12:6-7; cf. Eph 4:11).

Several letters have catechetical or hymn formulae which exegetes see as examples of earlier traditions (e.g., 1 Cor 11:2 with 11:23-25; 15:3-7; Phil 2:5-11; cf. 2 Tim 2:11-13). In other Pauline letters we find reference to traditions *(paradoseis)* that must be retained (2 Thess 2:15), and to the mystery of Christ which is taught (Col 1:25-28; cf. Eph 4:21). In the Pastoral Letters the term "teaching" *(didaskalia)* is very common (15 occurrences out of a total of 21 in the NT), and the author "Paul" is described as herald *(kêrux),* apostle, and teacher (2 Tim 1:11; cf. 3:10). There is great concern for sound teaching, and Timothy and Titus have a function in its regard (1 Tim 4:11, 13, 16; 2 Tim 3:16; 4:2; Titus 2:7), as do the leaders of the community (1 Tim 3:2; Titus 1:9)—all this being a work of the Spirit.[9] J.A. Fitzmyer notes: "Moreover there emerges in these letters the implication of a succession of doctrine, allegedly from Paul to Timothy and Titus, and from them to the *episkopoi.*"[10]

The position of the Synoptic Gospels on teaching is complex.[11] Jesus is clearly seen as the Teacher with a message of good news which included not only teaching but also his miracles (cf. Mark 1:14-15, 27). We can see all three Gospels as aiming to do what Luke did for Theophilus: show the sound basis for what was being taught in the Churches (cf. Luke 1:4). Again, the conclusion of Matthew shows a promise of the risen Lord to be with his eleven disciples as they go forth to teach all he had commanded them (Matt 28:18-20), which is a further indication of continuity between the teaching of Jesus in his public ministry and the later proclamation of the Church. But we do not have enough evidence to understand the situation in Matthew's community which led to a prohibition about titles, especially "rabbi," since there was only one teacher *(didaskalos*—23:8-10).

In Acts 1:1, Luke sums up the Gospel as an account of "all that Jesus began to do and teach." His second volume is concerned with showing the spread of the Church through the preaching and teaching of the apostles and Paul. One of the four main characteristics of the early community is precisely a dedication to the teaching *(didachê)* of the apostles (2:42). There is some indication of an official position enjoyed by the "prophets and teachers" at Antioch (13:1). It is not clear how preaching might be distinct from teaching in Acts; both could be said to be "ministry of the word" (6:4). In the Letter of James, which may date from about the time of Acts, we find a warning against wanting to be a teacher, and about the danger of making mistakes (Jas 3:1-2); the teacher seems to have some official position.

The Johannine writings point to Jesus as Teacher (John 1:38; 11:28; 13:13-14), and he is several times described as teaching (e.g., John 6:59). But here his teaching is what he receives from the Father (John 7:16-17; 8:28). The disciples in turn will teach the message of Jesus under the Spirit's guidance (John 14:26; 16:13). But there are also indications of a charism of truth which should protect the community from false teachers (1 John 2:26-27), though the apparent absence of official teachers probably led to the collapse of the Johannine community.[12]

As in other areas, e.g., ministry (q.v.), we find a pluralism about teaching in the NT, but with some tendency in the later books (apart from Johannine writings) to stress the function of teaching by officials. After the NT period the function of teaching was largely taken over by bishops (q.v.), a development perhaps hinted at in Eph 4:11, where pastors and teachers are joined with the one Greek definite article *(tous)*.[13] Non-ordained teachers like Justin (q.v.), priests like Origen (q.v.) and Jerome, and deacons like Ephrem will later still be acknowledged as teachers in the Church. But we have to recognize that the universal acceptance by the Churches in the 3rd and later centuries of bishops being authoritative teachers as an element pertaining to the very norm of the Church's faith, constitutes an apodictic argument for the fact that this development is by divine providence or *iure divino* (q.v.).[14] This evolution was aided by the problem of heresy or unorthodox teaching which led to the question "Where is the truth to be found?"[15] The answer would be in the apostolic Churches, and in the witness of their bishops.

When we come to examine the use of the term "magisterium," we find a complicated development.[16] *Magister* described a leader in any situation, and *magisterium* was used of leadership positions. Up to the Middle Ages it was used of various exercises of authority in the Church, only one of which was teaching. In the scholastic period, St. Thomas Aquinas is witness to a distinction between the pastoral teaching office *(magisterium cathedrae pastoralis)* and the teaching office of the master of theology *(magisterium cathedrae magistralis)*.[17] In addition to signifying the exercise of teaching authority, the word magisterium was also used from the time of Cyprian for what was taught.[18] But it was only in the 1820s, at first among German canonists, that the word magisterium took on widely its modern meaning, namely, of the hierarchical body which has the authority to teach. From 1835 the word entered papal documents with that meaning, and soon became general.[19] In the early centuries the authority which led to a teaching being accepted as binding came from the truth of the teaching and its objective conformity with apostolic faith; now authority was seen to flow from the office of the one who taught that "to gauge the truth of a proposition you looked first of all at who said it, not, as in the days of Leo the Great, at what was said."[20] In Vatican I (q.v.) we find the word with the sense of office and of the activity of teaching as well as the distinction between "solemn judgment and ordinary and universal magisterium."[21] The idea of "the magisterium" to indicate at once the function or the hierarchical activity of teaching and the body of pastors who are responsible for it is common in Pius XII,[22] and later in Paul VI.[23] A further point in the last two centuries is the appearance of the duo "Scripture and Magisterium," where earlier theology would think of "Scripture and Tradition" (v. TRADITION).

The response to the magisterium varies, depending on whether it is infallible (q.v.) or non-infallible: to the former the response must be an irrevocable act of faith; it cannot be unconditional to the latter. J.R. Dione has shown that previous Church teaching was reversed by Vatican II on such issues as the position of non-Christian religions, Church/State relations, religious freedom (q.v.), Church membership.[24] History shows that there has been erroneous teaching by the magisterium,[25] and teaching which at a later stage no longer has binding force, e.g., *Mortalium animos* of Pius XI, reformed by the Decree on Ecumenism of Vatican II.[26]

It would be foolish to the extreme to rely only on infallible teaching and neglect all non-infallible statements of the magisterium: much of the life of the Church, e.g., in liturgy, papal teaching, and canon law, is sustained and enriched by documents which do not fall into the narrow category of infallible teaching. An important statement on non-infallible teaching by the German hierarchy in 1967 points out that provisional guidance on doctrinal and moral issues is both valuable and necessary;[27] fallible authority in the Church as a rule is true through the help of the Holy Spirit, and has only in a few cases been erroneous.[28] A significant instance of non-infallible magisterium is the authoritative teaching of the bishop in his own diocese (LG 25).

A difficulty arises in the understanding of the Latin word *authenticus* and its cognates. It is usually translated as "authentic." But F.A. Sullivan has shown that the correct translation must be "authoritative." In DV 10 we read that the task of interpreting the word of God *authentice* belongs only to the magisterium.

Since clearly many exegetes accurately and truly interpret the Bible, *authentice* cannot here mean "authentic" in the sense of "true" or "genuine," but must signify an authoritative interpretation.[29] A true interpretation by exegetes and theologians demands assent only by virtue of the arguments adduced; an *authoritative* interpretation calls for assent from its origin in the magisterium.

Vatican II indicates in the context of non-infallible papal teaching the response that is demanded: it is by religious submission of the will and the mind (*religiosum voluntatis et intellectus obsequium*—LG 25). It is not accurate, as some have done,[30] to explain the response as "due respect."[31] The interpretation of Sullivan seems judicious: "One could sum up what the free will is called upon to do, by saying that I am obliged to renounce any attitude of *obstinacy* in my own opinion, and to adopt an attitude of *docility* toward the teaching of the pope." Obstinacy would refer to having one's mind closed, to refusing to give the official teaching a fair hearing. Docility calls for an open attitude towards the teaching, "doing one's best to appreciate the reasons in its favor so as to convince oneself of its truth, and thus facilitate one's intellectual assent to it."[32]

The text of Vatican II indicates some criteria for knowing the mind and will of the pope in order to adhere sincerely to his judgments. Such are the character of the document, the frequent repetition of the same doctrine and the pope's manner of speaking (LG 25). But the matter is complicated by the fact that magisterium means more than papal teaching, and other bodies in the Church can make peremptory demands for the acceptance of their statements. L. Örsy makes a list of non-infallible magisterial organs, which he does not claim to be exhaustive: non-infallible pronouncement by the pope (can be the proclamation of truth; can be an evolving theological opinion); declaration by an office of the Holy See, approved *specifically* by the pope (he made it his own); declaration by an office, with routine approval (by which the pope does not lend his authority to the core of the teaching, hence its critical assessment is warranted); a great variety of pronouncements which may come from episcopal synods, conferences, or individual bishops (all to be weighed and measured according to their content and circumstances).[33] Something of the docility demanded before papal teaching is appropriate for these kinds of utterances: one should approach them positively, wishing to learn and to be convinced. But one cannot be bound to regard them all as equal, and a hermeneutic for such documents is very necessary (v. DISSENT).

It should be noted that at Vatican II the Doctrinal Commission, in presenting LG 25, did deal with the possibility of dissent (q.v.), stating that approved theological authors should be followed in such instances.[34]

At the time of the Reformation great emphasis was placed by Protestants on the principle of "Scripture alone," and teaching authority was downplayed. In recent years among Lutherans,[35] Reformed,[36] and Anglicans,[37] there is growing awareness about some place for teaching authority.

Apart from the issue of dissent, there are several practical and theological issues regarding the magisterium of considerable significance for the life of the Church. The magisterium has a double function: to proclaim truth; to condemn error. At a particular time either one or other may dominate.[38] The relation of magisterium to history, to tradition, and to Scripture as its ultimate norm, must always be kept clear.[39] The magisterium is not the only source of truth in the Church: the *sensus fidelium* (v. SENSE OF THE FAITH) will always be a significant witness to truth (LG 12, 35).[40] Those who teach with authority must not rely solely on the juridical power they possess; they have an obligation to so present the truth with clear and convincing arguments that the faithful to whom the teaching is addressed may be helped to assent to it.[41] In this regard a consideration of recent history is important. Prior to Vatican II papal teaching was presented in a Roman style, embodying a Roman kind of theologizing. The council found a new, vivid language, which is at once biblical, patristic, traditional, and transcultural, to present its teaching. After the bishops had dispersed at the end of the council, Vatican teaching was again in danger of reverting to an earlier form. It has tended to present only one of several possible theologies, and in a language which often obfuscates the message being communicated. The solution partly lies with episcopal conferences and theologians, who must translate such teaching for local situations. Wide consultation in both the composition and editing of the more important documents is also necessary.

In the relationship between the magisterium and theologians (q.v.) a problem can arise if a text of Pius XII in *Humani generis* is not handled with care: in it he stated that the magisterium "must be for every theologian a/the proximate and universal norm of truth."[42] If applied too rigidly, this norm could easily lead to the stultifying of creative interaction between the magisterium and theology; at times this interaction can lead to corrections in what may have been inadequately, or even incorrectly, taught by authoritative teachers (v. DISSENT). Moreover, the magisterium is not a universal norm of truth in the usual meaning of the word "universal." There are many other normative sources for theology, above all Scripture, liturgy, and the Fathers (v. SOURCES OF THEOLOGY). It is essential that theologians always remain in dialogue with the magisterium, even if that may at times demand a critique which is at once respectful and honest.[43] There is a sense in which the theologian is a servant of the magisterium, interpreting its teaching and developing it. But the theologian is even more a servant of revelation and tradition, reinterpreting creatively the Christian message in a particular culture and time.[44] The tendency of some writers to speak of a magisterium of theologians is to be resisted.[45] There is not a parallel magisterium. The pope and bishops have authority to teach in the name of Christ arising from their special sharing in his prophetic office (cf. LG 25); the only authority that theologians have is from learning and special competence.

The *Code* devotes its third book to "The Teaching Office of the Church" (CIC 747–833).[46] This subject is also treated at length in the *Code* of the Eastern Churches.[47] Though Latin law deals with the magisterium in a number of important articles (CIC 748–756), it also lays down norms about catechetical instruction (CIC 773–780), the missionary or evangelistic task of the Church (CIC 780–792), Catholic education at all levels (CIC 793–821). Compared with the 1917 *Code,* the 1983 *Code* gives an important role to laity in the Church's teaching office, even if they, like priests, do not share in the official magisterium. But it has been argued that the law does not fully reflect the riches of Vatican II.[48]

A final practical difficulty arises from the sheer volume of papal teaching, especially from the time of Pius XII. Pope John Paul II issued almost twenty major documents in the period 1979–1995, in addition to the new *Code* and the *Catechism.* There are so many statements, many of them inherently important ones such as encyclicals and apostolic exhortations, that they cannot all be assimilated, and so they are not received (v. RECEPTION) and made fruitful in the life of the Church.

[1]E.g., J.A. Fitzmyer, "The Office of Teaching in the Christian Church According to the New Testament," in P.C. Empie, T.A. Murphy, and J.A. Burgess, *Teaching Authority and Infallibility in the Church.* Lutherans and Roman Catholics in Dialogue VI (Minneapolis: Augsburg, 1978) 185–212, 328–335; J. Reumann, "Teaching Office in the New Testament? A Response to Professor Fitzmyer's Essay," ibid., 213–231, 336–342.   [2]See essays in C.E. Curran and R.A. McCormick, eds., *The Magisterium and Morality.* Readings in Moral Theology 3 (New York—Ramsey: Paulist, 1982. L. Örsy, *The Church: Learning and Teaching* (Wilmington: Glazier—Dublin: Dominican—Leominster UK: Fowler Wright, 1987); F.A. Sullivan, *Magisterium: Teaching Authority in the Catholic Church* (Dublin: Gill and Macmillan—Mahwah, N.Y.: Paulist, 1983.)   [3]Fitzmyer (n. 1); K.H. Rengstorf, "Didaskô," TDNT 2:138-148; G. Friedrich, "Kêrux etc." TDNT 3:683-714; "Euaggelizomai," TDNT 2:717-721.   [4]Reumann (n. 1) 216, 336 n. 3; H.W. Beyer, "Katêcheô," TDNT 3:638-640; F. Büchsel, "Paradosis," TDNT 2:172-173; G. Bertram, "Paideuô," TDNT 5:619-625.   [5]Reumann (n. 1) 217.   [6]*The Apostolic Preaching and Its Developments* (London, 1936); *Gospel and Law: The Relation of Faith and Ethics in Early Christianity* (New York, 1951).

[7]Fitzmyer (n. 1) passim; G. Friedrich, "Kêrugma," TDNT 3:714-717; K.H. Rengstorf, "Didachê," TDNT 2:163-165.   [8]Reumann (n. 1) 217–221; idem, *Jesus in the Church's Gospels* (Philadelphia: Fortress, 1968) 30–36.   [9]J.D. Quinn, "On the Terminology for Faith, Truth, Teaching and the Spirit in the Pastoral Epistles: A Summary," in Empie et al. (n. 1) 232–237.   [10]Art. cit. (n. 1) 207.   [11]See Fitzmyer (n. 1) 197–202; Reumann (n. 1) 228.   [12]R.E. Brown, *The Churches the Apostles Left Behind* (New York—Ramsey: Paulist, 1984) 102–123, esp. 121–123.   [13]Fitzmyer (n. 1) 196 following K.H. Rengstorf, TDNT 2:149.   [14]Sullivan (n. 2) 49–51; J.K. Coyle, "The Exercise of Teaching in the Post Apostolic Church," EglT 15 (1984) 23–43.   [15]A. Faivre, "'Où est la vérité?': Déplacements et enjeux d'une question," LumièreV 35/180 (1986) 5–16.   [16]Y. Congar, "A Semantic History of the Term 'Magisterium,'" in Curran et al. (n. 2) 297–313 = RSPT 60 (1976) 85–98.   [17]*Quodl.* 3, q.4, a.1 (9); cf. *In 4 Sent.* d.19, q.2, a.2, qa 2 ad 4.   [18]Congar (n. 16) 304.   [19]DS 2739, 2875.   [20]J.M.R. Tillard, *The Bishop of Rome.* Theology and Life 5 (Wilmington: Glazier, 1983) 171.   [21]Tanner 2:807, 815/DS 3011, 3065/ND 121, 831.   [22]E.g., Ency. *Humani generis* (1950) AAS 42 (1950) 567–568, 571, 575–576—Carlen 4:178-182/DS 3884–3886, 3892, 3896/ND 858–859/ND 858–859.   [23]Congar (n. 16) 308–309.   [24]*The Papacy and the Church: A Study of Praxis and Reception in Ecumenical Perspective* (New York: Philosophical Library, 1987); cf. L. Örsy, "Magisterium: Assent and Dissent," TS 68 (1987) 473–498; T.P. Rausch, "Talking Back to Rome? J.R. Dione on Papal Magisterium and the Church," OneChr 24 (1988) 180–189.   [25]Examples in K. Rahner, "The Dispute Concerning the Teaching Office of the Church," in Curran et al. (n. 2) 113–128 at 123–124 = ThInvest 14:85-97 at 92–93.   [26]See Sullivan (n. 2) 157 for other examples.   [27]Text in C.E. Curran and R.A. McCormick, eds., *Dissent in the Church.* Readings in Moral Theology 6 (New York-Mahwah: Paulist, 1988) 129–132; K. Rahner, "Magisterium," SM 3:356-357. See important commentaries by Sullivan (n. 2) 157–158 and K. Rahner, art. cit. (n. 25); J. Fuchs, "The Magisterium and Moral Theology," TDig 38 (1991) 103–107.   [28]See B. Schuller, "Remarks on the Authentic Teaching of the Magisterium of the Church," in Curran et al. (n. 2) 14–33.   [29]Op. cit. (n. 2) 26–28.   [30]E.g., B.C. Butler, "Infallible; Authenticum: Assensus: Obsequium: Christian Teaching Authority and the Christian's Response," DoctLife 32 (1981) 77–89.   [31]Sullivan (n. 2) 159–161.   [32]Ibid., 164 (author's italics); idem, "The Response Due to the Non-Definitive Exercise of Magisterium (canon 752)," StCan 23 (1989) 267–283; L. Janssens, "The Non-infallible Magisterium and Theologians," LouvSt 14 (1989) 195–259. See M. Heim, "Obsequium religiosum intellectus et voluntatis," MüTZ 42 (1991) 358–370.   [33]Op. cit. (n. 2) 53.   [34]ActSyn 3/8:88—Alberigo-Magistretti 532; cf. J.A. Komonchak, "Ordinary Papal Magisterium and Religious Assent," in Curran et al. (n. 2) 67–90; L. Örsy, "Magisterium: Assent and Dissent," TS 48 (1987) 473–498.   [35]E.W. Gritsch, "Lutheran Teaching Authority: Historical Dimensions and Ecumenical Implications," LuthQ 25 (1973) 381–394 = TDig 22 (1974) 222–225; P.C. Empie et al. (n. 1).   [36]J.-P. Monserrat, "La doctrine des Églises Réformées sur ce qu'elles refusent d'appeler magistère," LumièreV 35/180 (1986) 55–64.   [37]S. Sykes and J. Booty, eds., *The Study of Anglicanism* (London: SPCK—Philadelphia: Fortress, 1988); ARCIC *The Final Report* (London: CTS—SPCK, 1982).   [38]See G. Alberigo, "Du bâton à la miséricorde: Le magistère catholique de 1830 à 1980," LumièreV 35/180 (1986) 17–36 = CrNSt 2 (1981) 487–521.   [39]C. Wackenheim, "Le magistère en ses connexions avec l'écriture, la tradition et la théologie," LumièreV 35/180 (1986) 95–107; C. Duquoc, "Magistère et historicitè," ibid., 83–94.   [40]"The Teaching Authority of Believers," Conc 180 (1985) 1–91.   [41]Sullivan (n. 2) 165–166.   [42]Ency. *Humani generis* (1950)—AAS 42 (1950) 567/Carlen 4:178/DS

3884.    [43]F.A. Sullivan, "Magisterium and Theology," CTSAP 43 (1988) 65–75 (response R.P. McBrien 76–79); J. Fuchs, "The Magisterium and Moral Theology," TDig 38 (1991) 103–107; J. Losada Espinosa, "Teología y magisterio de la Iglesia," RET 49 (1989) 209–239; K. Rahner, "Theology and the Church's Teaching Authority after the Council," ThInvest 9:83-100; idem, "The Teaching Office of the Church in the Present Day Crisis of Authority," ThInvest 12:3-30; idem, "The Dispute Concerning the Church's Teaching Office," ThInvest 14:86-97; "Mysterium Ecclesiae," ThInvest 17:139-155; idem, "Magisterium and Theology," ThInvest 18:54-73; idem, "On Bad Arguments in Moral Theology," ThInvest 18:74-85; J. Stern, "Le magistère et les théologiens," Seminarium 29 (1989) 399–420.    [44]J. Hoffman, "Theology and the Magisterium: A 'Model' Deriving from Vatican I," CleR 68 (1983) 3–17.    [45]Sullivan (n. 2) 28–29.    [46]J.A. Coriden in Coriden, CIC 543–589; J.I. Arrieta, "The Active Subject of the Church's Teaching Office (Canons 747–748)," StCan 23 (1989) 243–256; L.J. Crowley, "The Teaching Power and Mission of the Church," StCan 9 (1975) 215–234; V. de Paolis, "La funzione di insegnamento nel Codice di diritto canonico," Seminarium 29 (1989) 446–462; C.J. Errázuriz, "La dimensione giuridica del 'munus docendi' nella chiesa," IusEc 1 (1989) 177–193; D. le Tourneau, "La prédication de la parole de Dieu et la participation des laïcs au *munus docendi:* fondements conciliaires et codification," IusEc 2 (1990) 101–125; G. Nedungatt, "Magisterio ecclesiastico nei due Codici," Apoll 65 (1992) 313–328; L. Schick, "La fonction d'enseignement de l'Église dans le Code de droit canonique," NRT 108 (1986) 374–387; N. Weis, "Quaedam de laicorum prophetico munere in Ecclesia iuxta Concilium Vaticanum II," Periodica 70 (1981) 429–448.    [47]CCEO Title XV, "The Ecclesiastical Magisterium" cc. 595–666; G. Nedungatt, "The Teaching Function of the Church in Oriental Canon Law," StCan 23 (1989) 39–60.    [48]E. Corecco, "Aspects of the Reception of Vatican II in the Code of Canon Law," in G. Alberigo et al. eds., *The Reception of Vatican II* (Washington, D.C.: The Catholic University of America Press—Tunbridge Wells UK: Burns & Oates, 1987) 247–296 at 267.

## MALINES CONVERSATIONS

A group of Anglican and Roman Catholic theologians met at Malines from 1921–1925 under the presidency of Cardinal D.J. Mercier. The meetings, though unofficial, had ecclesiastical approval. The initiative came from Lord Halifax (1839–1934), who had earlier started theological discussions in Rome (1894–1896) which terminated with *Apostolicae curae* (v. ANGLICAN ORDERS). Notable on the Anglican side were J.A. Robinson, W.H. Frere, C. Gore and, from the RCC, J.E. van Roey, F. Portal, and P. Battifol. There were several areas of agreement: the pope has a primacy of honor; the Body and Blood of Christ are really taken in the Eucharist; the Mass is a true sacrifice but in a mystical manner; the episcopacy is of divine law.[1]

The more Protestant wing of the Anglican Communion (q.v.) distrusted the talks, while on the Roman side the encyclical *Mortalium animos* (1928) (v. ECUMENISM, RCC) proved a death-knell for such endeavors. The conversations did, however, underscore for Roman Catholic theologians the Catholic side of Anglicanism, and they furthered mutual respect and interest between the two communions; an example might be the special position of the Anglican Communion acknowledged by Vatican II (UR 13).

[1]*The Conversations at Malines 1921–1925. Les conversations de Malines 1921–1925* (Oxford: UP, 1927); Second Viscount Halifax, ed., *The Conversations at Malines* (London, 1930); J. de Bivort de la Saudée, *Anglicans et catholiques*. 2 vols. (Brussels, 1949); W.H. Frere, *Recollections of Malines* (London, 1935); H.R.T. Brandreth, HistEcumMov 1:298-300.

## MARRIAGE AND THE CHURCH

Marriage as a human institution is found in almost all cultures.[1] It was regarded as God-created in the OT (Gen 1:28; 2:24), a view reiterated by Jesus in the NT (Matt 19:4-6). The marriage relationship of husband and wife became an image of God's covenant relationship with God's people (Hos 1–3; Isa 54:4-8), a covenant often broken by the people, though the love of God, the spouse (q.v.), remains faithful (Jer 2:2, 20; Ezek 16; Isa 61:10; 62:4-5). This spousal image is carried into the NT, where married couples are to mirror the relationship of Christ and his Church (Eph 5:22-32).[2]

Jesus reestablished the original intentions of God with regard to marriage (Matt 19:4-9).[3] Despite its exaltation of virginity (Matt 19:11-12; 1 Cor 7:8, 25-28), marriage, love, and family were highly regarded by the NT (1 Cor 7:1-7; Col 3:18-21; Heb 13:4).[4] The various "household codes" show the lofty values espoused (1 Pet 2:18-3:7; Col 3:18-4:1; Eph 5:22-6:9), but some elements are culturally conditioned and need careful interpretation. Adultery, even in the heart (Matt 5:27-28), is regularly condemned (1 Cor 6:9; Rom 13:9). There is no single interpretation of 1 Tim 3:2, which commands the assent of all exegetes;[5] the text has implications for ministry, especially married deacons.

Throughout its history the Church has shown in many ways its concern for marriage, a concern expressed in legislation and teaching. Though there is a consistent preference for virginity over marriage in many of the Fathers, the Church was never contaminated by any of the sects like the Marcionites, or various encratites, who despised or rejected marriage. It must be admitted, however, that several of the Fathers, including major figures like Augustine and Origen, would seem to have had reservations about the full or integral moral goodness of marital intercourse; but the evidence is sparse and requires delicate evaluation.[6] Many of the Fathers were also disapproving of remarriage after the death of a spouse (v. WIDOWS); they were quite hostile towards marriages between a member of the Church and a non-Christian.

The recognition of the sacramentality of marriage was slow.[7] Augustine seized on the word *"sacramentum"* in Eph 5:32; the Greeks reading there *"mystêrion"* thought more of the divine plan. It would take some centuries before marriage had a rite universally celebrated within the Church,[8] even though there are perhaps traces of nuptial blessings as early as Tertullian (q.v.).[9] The late 4th-century *Apostolic Constitutions* (q.v.) place great emphasis on the holiness of marriage and severely condemns anything to the contrary.[10] Repudiation of one's wife is forbidden except in the case of loose-living and adultery; a repudiated wife could not be married.[11]

The first medieval council to support Christian marriage was Lateran II (q.v.),[12] matter taken up by Innocent III in the profession of faith demanded from the Waldensians (1208).[13] Marriage would seem to have been called a sacrament for the first time in a magisterial statement at a local council at Verona (1184).[14] From Lyons II (q.v.) it is numbered among the seven sacraments,[15] teaching repeated at Florence and Trent.[16] The essentials for Christian marriage were disputed in the Middle Ages; it was under Alexander III (1159–1181) that it was settled that consent gives rise to true Christian marriage, with indissolubility following on subsequent consummation by sexual intercourse *(ratum et consummatum)*.[17]

The Reformers rejected the complex canonical legislation that had arisen since the Middle Ages, but held marriage in high honor, even though they generally felt it belonged to the secular rather than the sacramental sphere. Trent developed a substantial teaching against the perceived errors of the reformers,[18] as well as laying down reforms, chiefly about secret or clandestine marriages, the necessity of consent being exchanged before the parish priest, impediments, and abuses.[19]

In the 20th century there were various statements on marriage: Pius XI—*Casti connubii* (1930)[20] and many references in the addresses of Pius XII.[21] Vatican II presented a rich theology and spirituality of marriage:[22] it called for a revision of the rite (SC 77–78); it saw marriage as a sacramental exercise of the common priesthood (LG 11); it taught that marriage was a significant exercise of the prophetic office of the baptized (LG 35), and spoke of the call to holiness within the sacrament (LG 41).[23] Aware of the current threats to marriage, the council spoke of the true meaning of marriage in the Pastoral Constitution (GS 47–52).[24]

After the council there was significant positive teaching about marriage, often overlooked, in the encyclical on the regulation of births,[25] and in the post-synodal apostolic exhortation "The Christian Family in the Modern World."[26] This last document, along with the Vatican II teaching, provided the basis for the canons on marriage in the revised *Code of Canon Law.*[27] The power over Christian marriage in the Church is extensive. By the Petrine (q.v.) and Pauline (q.v.) privileges, it can set aside marriages where non-Christians and

Catholics are involved. The only marriage that is regarded as utterly indissoluble in the Roman Catholic Church is a marriage between Christians which is *ratum et consummatum* (CIC 1141); annulment is not a dissolution of a marriage but merely an official statement that a true marriage did not exist in the first place (CIC 1671–1691). The grounds for such a declaration have been significantly widened in this century.[28] The Catholic Church claims the right to regulate the celebration of marriage (CIC 1108–1123) and to establish impediments, some of which may be of natural law; others arise from Church law (CIC 1073–1094).

There is a very serious problem in the Church today with regard to marriage. Notwithstanding excellent pastoral studies and the present availability of the insights of psychology, two crises are identified by H. Vorgrimler: "the increasing inability of couples to sustain successful relationships, and the rapid decline of the authority of the Catholic Church."[29] The Church's response has been a firm, to some a harsh, insistence on moral principles about marriage, combined with much emphasis on the catechetical preparation and pastoral care of the couples before marriage (CIC 1063). There is a particular pastoral problem for those who have entered into second relationships after civil divorce or separation: are they to be denied the sacraments? Contrary to a widespread and mistaken opinion, the Orthodox Church[30] in principle does not allow divorce and remarriage in some wide interpretation of Matt 19:9. Rather it invokes compassion and economy (q.v.) for those whose marriages have broken down. Some authors suggest that this Orthodox pastoral approach be more closely studied by Catholics.[31] The present attitude of the Catholic Church is one of pastoral care but a refusal of admission to the Eucharist, and reception of the sacrament of penance only for those who are prepared to undertake complete continence.[32]

One of the important insights of feminism (q.v.) in the Church has been a much more holistic view of marriage, and of the mutual responsibilities of both partners.[33] These intuitions need to be combined with a spirituality of marriage appropriate to each particular culture.[34]

The theology of marriage is not yet highly developed;[35] the ecclesial dimension of the sacrament is very important.[36] A deepened understanding of marriage will in turn allow a fuller penetration into the mystery of the Church as spouse (q.v.).[37] It is the domestic Church (LG 11; AA 11) in which the faith is proclaimed, handed on, and lived out under the shadow of the Cross. The relationship between marriage and the Eucharist is particularly significant.[38]

The fact that the ministers of the sacrament[39] are the contracting couple, and hence each acting *in persona*

*Christi* and as his instruments of grace for the other, has important implications for general sacramental theory in the Church, and for its whole theology of ministry. The Catholic Church is striking, but not completely alone, in its rigorous defense of sexual and marital ethics; there are immense problems for the credibility of its magisterium (q.v.) and for its mission in the world to state a clear "no" to a liberal agenda in these areas. The sacrament of marriage is complemented by confirmation (q.v.) in providing couples with the strength to bear witness to the possibility of enduring Christian marriage, which today may be even more difficult to live successfully than celibacy.

[1]E. Turner and P.R. Frese, "Marriage," EncycRel 9:218-222. [2]J. Sampley, *And the Two Shall Become One Flesh: A Study of Traditions in Eph 5:21-33* (Cambridge: UP, 1971). [3]Cf. C. Marucci, *Parole di Gesù sul divorzio: Richerche scritturistiche previe ad un ripensamento teologico, canonistico e pastorale della dottrina cattolica dell'indissolubilità del matrimonio.* Aloisiana 16 (Brescia: Morcelliana—Rome: Gregorian UP, 1982). [4]P. Benoit, "Le mariage chrétien selon saint Paul," in *Exégèse et théologie.* 4 vols. Cogitatio Fidei (Paris: Cerf, 1961–1982) 4:263-290—CleR 65 (1980) 309–321; W. Rordorf, "Marriage in the New Testament and the Early Church," JEH 20 (1969) 193–210. [5]E. Grasscock, "'The Husband of One Wife' Requirement in 1 Timothy 3:2," BiblSac 140 (1983) 244–258. [6]H. Crouzel, "Marriage" in EncycEarCh 528. [7]R. Béraudy, "Le mariage des chrétiens: Étude historique," NRT 104 (1982) 50–69; W. Kasper, *Theology of Marriage* (New York: Seabury, 1980); T. Mackin, trilogy—*What is Marriage?; Divorce and Remarriage; The Marital Sacrament* (New York: Paulist, 1982–1990). [8]K. Stevenson, *Nuptial Blessing: A Study of Christian Marriage Rites.* Alcuin Club Collections 64 (London: SPCK, 1982); D.M. Patras, "The Liturgical Theology," Diak (USA) 16 (1981) 225–237. [9]*Ad uxorem* 2:8, 6—PL 1:1291-1292/ACW 13:27. [10]6:28-29—SC 329:382-388. [11]6:14, 4—SC 320:329:340; 1:1, 4 and 1:3—SC 320:104, 110–114; 7:2, 9—SC 336:28-30; 8:47, 48—SC 336:290. [12]Can. 23—Tanner 1:202/DS 718. [13]DS 794/ND 1802. [14]DS 761. [15]DS 860/ND 28. [16]Tanner 1:550/DS 1327/ND 1803 and Tanner 2:754/DS 1801/ND 1808; see G. Baldanza, "La grazia sacramentale matrimoniale al Concilio di Trento," EphLtg 97 (1983) 89–140. [17]Cf. L.G. Wrenn, "Refining the Essence of Marriage," Jurist 46 (1986) 532–551; I. Gramunt, "The Essence of Marriage and the Code of Canon Law," StCan 25 (1991) 365–383. [18]Tanner 2:753–755/DS 1797–1812/ND 1804–1819. [19]Sess. 24 on reform—Tanner 2:755-759. [20]AAS 22 (1930) 539–592, 604/Carlen 3:391-414. [21]P. Barberi and D. Tettamanzi, eds., *Matrimonio e famiglia nel magistero della chiesa* (Milan: Vita e Pensiero, 1986). [22]A.P. D'Souza, "Marriage According to the Second Vatican Council," IndTS 17 (1980) 365–387. [23]G.T. della Mura, "Considerazioni sullo 'status' coniugale nella costituzione conciliare 'Lumen gentium,'" MonEccl 106 (1981) 480–488. [24]Helpful for interpretation J.A. Selling, "Re-Reading *Gaudium et spes* on Marriage and the Family," LouvSt 8 (1980–1981) 82–94. [25]*Humanae vitae*—AAS 60 (1968) 481–503/Flannery 2:397-416; L. Ciccone, "Paolo VI e il decennio della 'Humanae vitae,'" DivThom 83 (1980) 24–48. [26]*Familiaris consortio*—AAS 74 (1983) 81–191/Flannery 2:815-898. [27]Mainly CIC 1055-1165; see T.P. Doyle in Coriden, CIC 737–833; for East see CCEO 776–866; J. Joyce, "The New Code and Marriage," CleR 68 (1983) 367–370; A. Mendonça, "The Theological and Juridical Aspects of Marriage," StCan 22 (1988) 265–304; U. Navarrete, "Ius matrimoniale latinum et orientale: Collatio Codicem latinum inter et orientalem," Periodica 80 (1991) 609–639. [28]P. Ciprotti, "Nullité et dissolution du mariage: Aspects anciens et récents," AnnéeCan 32 (1989) 179–195; L. de Naurois, "Le problème de la dissolution du mariage: Réflexions d'un juriste," NRT 93 (1971) 50–77; R. Vaillancourt, "Théologie de l'indissolubilité du mariage dans l'Église catholique romaine," StCan 21 (1987) 261–264; J. Vernay, "Les dissolutions du lien matrimonial en droit canonique," AnnéeCan 32 (1989) 139–158; W.J.S. Wamboldt, "Canon Law on Indissolubility of Marriage in the Roman Catholic Church," StCan 21 (1987) 265–270. [29]*Sacramental Theology* (Collegeville: The Liturgical Press, 1992 from German [3]1992) 285. See M.D. Place and S.L. Maletta Jr., "Marital Failure: The Church's Response," ChicSt 31 (1992) 271–281. [30]P. L'Huillier, "L'indissolubilité du mariage dans le droit et la pratique orthodoxe," StCan 21 (1987) 239–260. See P. Evdokimov, *Le sacrament de l'amour* (Paris: Epi, 1968) = *The Sacrament of Love* (Crestwood, N.Y.: St. Vladimir's Seminary Press, 1985); K. Ware, "The Sacrament of Love: The Orthodox Understanding of Marriage and Its Breakdown," DowR 109 (1991) 79–93. [31]M. Huftier, "Les divorcés remariés: La Pénitence et l'Eucharistie," EspVie 99 (1989) 385–391. [32]John Paul II, *Familiaris consortio* (The Christian Family in the Modern World 1981) n. 84. [33]D.L. Carmody, *Caring for Marriage: Feminist and Biblical Reflections* (New York-Mahwah: Paulist, 1985). [34]H.U. von Balthasar, *The Christian State of Life* (San Francisco: Ignatius, 1983) 224–249; M.G. Lawler, "The Mutual Love and Personal Faith of the Spouses as the Matrix of the Sacrament of Marriage," Worship 65 (1991) 339; C. and W. Roberts, *Partners in Intimacy: Living Christian Marriage Today* (New York: Paulist, 1988); D.M. Thomas, "Marriage" in NDictCSpir 624–631. [35]J. Chryssavgis, "The Sacrament of Marriage: An Orthodox Perspective," StLtg 19 (1989) 17–27; T. Doyle, "The Theology of Marriage: Where Are We Today?," StCan 19 (1985) 81–98; P. Eliot, *What God Has Joined Together: The Sacramentality of Marriage* (New York: Alba, 1990); P. Gaalaas, "In What Sense Can Marriage Be Called a Sacrament?," LouvSt 8 (1980–1981) 403–409; I. Gramunt, "The Essence of Marriage and the *Code of Canon Law,*" StCan 25 (1991) 365–383; G. Martínez, "Marriage as Sacramental Mystery," EglT 22 (1991) 67–84; J.J. O'Donnell, "H.U. von Balthasar sulla teologia del matrimonio," CivCatt 139 (1988) 3:483-488; K. Rahner, "Marriage as a Sacrament," ThInvest 10:199-221; W.P. Roberts, ed., *Commitment to Partnership: Explorations of the Theology of Marriage* (New York: Paulist, 1987); E. Schillebeeckx, *Marriage: Secular Reality and Saving Mystery* (New York, 1965); D.M. Thomas, *Christian Marriage: A Journey Together* (Wilmington: Glazier, 1983); Conc 55 (1970). [36]S. Folgado Flórez, "Eclesiología y sacramentalidad del matrimonio cristiano," CiudD 193 (1980) 223–257; A. Brien, "Couple et corps ecclésial," RDroitC 31 (1981) 58–65; R. Mehl, "Le couple dans la communauté ecclésiale," ibid., 66–76; E. Melia, "Le couple chrétien ou la conception chrétienne du couple: Un point de vue orthodoxe," ibid., 77–85; C. Wackenheim, "Le couple dans la communauté ecclésiale: Point de vue catholique," 86–94. [37]John Paul II, Apost. Exhort. *Mulieris dignitatem* 23—AAS 80 (1988) 1708–1710. [38]F. Marinelli, "Matrimonio ed Eucaristia," Later 56 (1990) 117–142. [39]F.R. McManus, "The Ministers of the Sacrament of Marriage in Western Tradition," StCan 20 (1986) 85–104.

## MARRIAGE, INTERCHURCH (MIXED)

Marriages between people of different Christian confessions were formerly called "mixed marriages"—the term retained in the Catholic *Code of Canon Law* (1983—CIC 1124–1129). The expression "ecumenical marriages" or "interchurch marriages" is nowadays more generally favored, at least in English.[1] Some early councils legislated against marriages with heretics, e.g., Chalcedon (q.v.), "unless of course the person to be married to the orthodox party promises to convert to the orthodox faith."[2] This remained the situation for many centuries. During the Middle Ages marriages with heretics were forbidden but were regarded as valid in virtue of the baptism of both parties.[3]

By the 18th century there were papal dispensations and, soon after, episcopal ones allowing marriage with other Christians but with promises demanded about freedom of Catholic parties to practice their faith and to bring up the children in the Catholic faith. The 1917 canon law "severely prohibited" mixed marriages but allowed dispensations under stringent conditions (CIC 1060–1065). The reason for such strict legislation was the belief that such marriages posed a threat to the continued practice of the faith by the Catholic party and to the baptism and Catholic upbringing of any children arising from the union.

Vatican II engaged in a positive evaluation of other Churches (UR 3 . . .). There was a brief discussion of mixed marriages at the council, but the matter was left to the pope to establish norms. The first document from the S. Cong. for the Doctrine of the Faith in 1966 both reflected a less negative view of interchurch marriages, and at the same time retained some of the strict provisions of the 1917 *Code*.[4] Four years later the mp. of Paul VI, *Matrimonia mixta*,[5] proved to be much more open: it showed pastoral concern for interchurch marriages; it sought to involve the minister of the other Church in such care; ecclesiastical penalties arising from the 1917 law were abrogated retrospectively. This document provided the general basis for the legislation of the 1983 *Code*.[6] There we find both a prohibition and a definition of interchurch marriages: "Without the express permission of the competent authority, marriage is forbidden between two baptized persons, one of whom was baptized in the Catholic Church or received into it after baptism and has not left it by formal act, and the other of whom is a member of a Church or ecclesiastical community which is not in full communion with the Catholic Church" (CIC 1124). The bishop can give a dispensation under conditions (CIC 1125). The non-Roman Catholic is no longer required to make promises; instead he or she is to be made aware that the Catholic "makes a sincere promise to do all in his or her power to have *(praestet se omnia pro viribus facturam esse)* all the children baptized and brought up in the Catholic Church" (CIC 1125 § 1). The interpretation of this commitment of the Catholic is difficult; "it does not mean an absolute promise at the risk of jeopardizing the marriage itself."[7] The local conference of bishops is to draw up norms with regard to promises and declarations; one should take cognizance of these in one's own country or area. A long canon is devoted to the canonical form; dispensations may be granted in serious cases according to the norms of the episcopal conference (CIC 1127).[8] Truly double ceremonies are forbidden, viz., a repetition of the exchange of consent (CIC 1127 § 3); readings, prayers, exhortations, or blessings by priests or ministers of both Churches are not excluded;[9] local norms on the matter should be observed.

The question of pastoral care of those in interchurch marriages is crucial. There is no fully satisfactory solution to the problems that arise when both contracting partners in the union are deeply committed to their respective Churches. The marriage itself represents in miniature the divided state of Christendom. Pope John Paul II stated in the post-synodal apostolic exhortation on "Christian Family in the Modern World" that "marriages between Catholics and other baptized persons have their own particular nature, but they contain numerous elements that could well be made use of and developed, both for their intrinsic value and for the contribution they can make to the ecumenical movement. This is particularly true when both parties are faithful to their religious duties."[10] There is a growing literature on such positive aspects of interchurch marriages and their pastoral care.[11]

There are also ecumenical initiatives taken by the marriage partners themselves, some of which, though sincerely meant, are not in accordance with Church discipline. There have been a number of documents from ecumenical dialogues on the issue of interchurch marriages,[12] guidelines agreed between Churches,[13] as well as journals specially devoted to the matter.[14]

[1]R. Beaupère, "Marriage, Mixed," DictEcumMov 654–658.  [2]Can. 14—Tanner 1:94.  [3]St. Thomas Aquinas, *Supp.* q.59, a.1 ad 5. [4]*Matrimonii sacramentum*—AAS 58(1966) 235–239/Flannery 1:474-478.  [5]AAS 62 (1970) 257–263/Flannery 1:508-514.  [6]See T.P. Doyle in Coriden, CIC 800–806.  [7]Ibid., 803.  [8]Ibid., 804–806.  [9]J. Bernhard, "Les mariages entre chrétiens de confession différente," AnnéeCan 30 (1987) 367–391 at 381.  [10]*Familiaris consortio* n. 78—AAS 74 (1982) 178–180/Flannery 2:883-885. [11]S. Butler, "Interchurch Marriage: Problems and Prospects," ChicSt 19 (1980) 209–223; A. Heron, *Two Churches, One Love: Interchurch Marriage Between Protestants and Roman Catholics* (Dublin: APCK, 1977); M. Hurley, ed., *Beyond Tolerance: The Challenge of Mixed Marriages* (London: Chapman, 1975); B. Lennon, "Interchurch Marriages: Torn Between Divided Churches," Furrow 31 (1981) 309–321; G.V. Lobo, "Pastoral Dimensions of Mixed Marriage," VYoti 44 (1980) 302–312; T. Lull, "Ecumenical Marriages: Pastoral Problem or Opportunity," JEcuSt 16 (1979) 643–650; E. Sunderland, "The Pastoral care of Ecumenical Marriages—The Episcopal Perspective," JEcuSt 16 (1979) 619–628; D. Thompson, "Interchurch Marriages: Support and Catechesis," OneChr 26 (1990) 215–225; cf. R.G. Stephanopoulos, "Marriage and Family in Ecumenical Perspective," SVlad 25 (1981) 21–34. [12]E.g., Roman-Catholic and Lutheran (1976) in *Growth in Agreement*. Faith and Order Paper 108. Ecumenical Documents 2 (New York: Paulist—Geneva: WCC, 1984) 278–306; Anglican-Roman Catholic (1976) in *Called to Full Unity: Documents on*

*Anglican-Roman Catholic Relations 1966–1983·* (Washington, D.C.: U.S. Catholic Conference, 1986) 99–131. Cf. E. de Bhaldraithe, "Mixed Marriages in the New Code: Can We Now Implement the Anglican-Roman Catholic Recommendations?," Jurist 46 (1986) 419–451.   [13]E.g., *Pastoral Guidelines for Interchurch Marriages Between Anglicans and Roman Catholics in Canada* (Ottawa: Public. Canadian Conf. Cath. Bishops, 1987); "Southern Baptist—Roman Catholic Interchurch Marriage Guidelines Recommended for the Archdiocese of Louisville and the Long Run Baptist Association," Midstream 29 (1990) 303–312.   [14]E.g., *Foyers mixtes* (Lyons, 1968– ); *Interchurch Families* (London, 1979– ); *The Ark* (Louisville, Ky., 1989– ).

## MARRIAGE, INTERFAITH

Though some of the most illustrious figures of the OT married women outside Israelite faith, e.g., Joseph, Moses, David, Solomon, nonetheless, later teaching and practice would be very negative towards such marriages for fear of compromising the faith (see Deut 7:3-4; Ezra 9–10; Neh 13:23-29; Mal 2:10). In the NT Paul advised against these marriages (1 Cor 7:39), but counseled people to remain within them if possible when they had already been contracted (see 1 Cor 7:12-16 and PAULINE PRIVILEGE).

In the patristic period the Church was extremely negative towards marriages outside the faith. The Council of Chalcedon (q.v.) prohibited such marriages "unless of course the person who is to be married to the orthodox party promises to convert to the orthodox faith."[1] This became the norm for the Church for many centuries. Interfaith marriage is technically called "disparity of cult" in canon law; it was formalized as a diriment, viz., invalidating, marriage impediment in the 1917 canon law (CIC 1070–1071 with 1060–1064). The 1983 law reiterated the impediment (CIC 1086 with 1125–1126). The same obligations with regard to practice of the faith and the upbringing of children applies as in the case of interchurch marriages (v. MARRIAGES, INTERCHURCH).

The attitudes of the various religions to marriages entered into with members of another faith vary; none could be said to be positive.[2] The problems encountered in interfaith marriages include not only those also found in interchurch marriages, especially relating to the upbringing of the children in religious belief, but also deep cultural differences, and, in places, polygamy. As such marriages are increasing in number, the need for special pastoral care is also growing.[3]

[1]Canon 14—Tanner 1:94.   [2]S.W. Ariarajah, "Marriage, Interfaith," DictEcumMov 652–654.   [3]Cf. C. Lamb, *Mixed-Faith Marriage: A Case for Care* (London: BCC, 1982).

## MARTYR

The word martyr *(marturion)* originally meant "witness" or "testimony." Its modern meaning can be de-tected in the later NT writings (Rev 6:9; 17:6; 20:4).[1] The reality is earlier, as we can see in the cases of Stephen, whose witness cost him his life (Acts 7:56-60), and of James (Acts 12:2). The martyrdom of Peter and Paul in Rome by about 67 C.E. is not attested in the NT, though there is an allusion to Peter's death (John 21:18-19).[2]

Towards 110 C.E. Ignatius of Antioch (q.v.) is writing to the Romans to beg them not to interfere with his martyrdom. Already in this text there is a mystical approach to the cruel and violent death of the true witness: "Pray leave me to be a meal for the beasts, for it is they who can provide my way to God. I am his wheat, ground fine by the lions' teeth to be made purest bread for Christ. Better still, incite the creatures to become a sepulcher for me . . . then I shall be truly Jesus Christ's disciple."[3] It is love that is the key motivation of the martyr.

Martyrdom in the Roman Empire was sporadic until the so-called "Edict" of Constantine (q.v.); it depended on the attitude of the emperor or the whims of local Roman officials. Persecution could then break out at any time or in any place. The point at issue at the trials of martyrs was more often their refusal to take part in the official pagan cult of the empire or emperor, rather than the proscription of the Christian religion as such (v. PERSECUTION).[4]

The age of the martyrs gave rise to a new genus of Christian writings, i.e., exhortations to martyrdom. Writers gave encouragement to those being persecuted to strengthen their resolve.[5] A spirituality of martyrdom also arose.[6]

The records of the better-known martyrs are found in three kinds of document.[7] First, there are the *Acta,* the official proceedings in court comprising the questioning of the accused, their answers, and the sentence.[8] Second, there are the *Passiones,* or *Martyria,* namely, eyewitness or contemporary accounts of the martyrdom.[9] Third, there are edifying legends written afterwards; they have little historical value, but they often contain a significant implicit theology and spirituality of martyrdom.

Reflection on martyrdom proceeds in various directions. In a typically obscure passage, it would seem that Hermas (q.v.) asserted the right of martyrs to sit on the presbyteral bench, at least in the heavenly Church.[10] Another quasi-technical expression is found in Eusebius: Christians are said to be admitted to the ranks of the martyrs *(klêron tôn marturôn).*[11] Soon after 250 C.E. we find martyrs asking for favorable treatment of those who had fallen away *(lapsi)* in a letter called a *"libellus."*[12] Though accepted in principle, the giving of the martyr's letter would in time cause disorder, especially at Carthage (v. RECONCILIATION, SACRAMENT OF and CONFESSORS).

The cult of the martyrs was the first evidence of the veneration of the saints (q.v.). Mass was celebrated at the place of their burial or death on their "birthday" *(dies natalis),* the day on which they entered into glory.[13] St. Augustine represents the widespread conviction of the Church in the patristic period: "the Church does not pray for martyrs, but rather it commends itself to their prayers."[14]

There was some ongoing theologizing about martyrdom in the Fathers. Eusebius recalled that the Spirit is present to the martyrs.[15] Christian martyrdom was for Irenaeus a proof that the Spirit of the prophets rests on the Church.[16] As Catholic and as Montanist, Tertullian stated that Christ himself dwells and suffers in the martyrs, and the Holy Spirit trains them for combat.[17] Martyrdom requires the gift of biblical boldness (q.v.).[18]

From early centuries, martyrdom was considered to have the same effects as baptism: catechumens who died for their faith were venerated as martyrs, as they had received the "baptism of blood."[19] Those martyred for the name of Christ had a real commitment to him, one which is found ritually in baptism. In patristic times we also find "white" martyrdom, namely, the ascetic life, and in the Celtic Church "green" martyrdom, that is, suppression of the passions and ceaseless penance.

In the scholastic period there is some sharpening of the theology of martyrdom. The teaching of St. Thomas Aquinas is succinct:[20] martyrdom involves standing firm in truth and is thus a virtuous act; the act of martyrdom is a refusal to abandon faith or justice; its highest motive is love, and it is the supreme manifestation of love; death belongs to the perfection of martyrdom; the martyr may be witnessing to faith directly, or by actions which implicitly involve faith, as in the case of John the Baptist, who died because he condemned adultery; unless it is related to God, patriotism is not a cause of martyrdom.

Prospero Lambertini, the future Benedict XIV (1740–1758), clarified the matter of martyrdom, as he had done in so many matters concerning the saints (q.v.): "martyrdom is a voluntary suffering or endurance of death for the sake of faith in Christ or of another act of virtue related to God *(voluntariam mortis perpessionem seu tolerantiam propter fidem Christi, vel alium virtutis actum in Deum relatum).*[21]

Central to a theology of martyrdom is the fact of freedom: the martyr is one who does not have to die but chooses death for the faith, or acts for the faith and God in such a way that death results.[22] There is some ambiguity about people putting themselves forward for martyrdom.[23] Though there are many examples of coming forward for death in a voluntary, explicit witness for the faith, the tradition also states strongly that in case of persecution one can, and perhaps should, flee (cf. Matt 10:23; Acts 9:25). Many of the great martyrs, like Polycarp and Cyprian, first escaped, and then confessed their faith when apprehended. Except where a great charism has been given, it would probably be presumptuous to offer oneself for martyrdom; who can guarantee that they will stand firm to the end? Martyrdom is ultimately a gift of the Spirit.

Martyrdom belongs to the inner life of the Church: the martyr comes forth from the community of the Church and, in the name of the Church, witnesses by word or action, thus calling on all members of the Church to persevere in fidelity.[24]

Vatican II made several notable statements about martyrs and martyrdom: the martyrs are commemorated in the liturgy (SC 104), in which they join (SC 50); they are striking witnesses to the faith of the Church (GS 21) and bear the supreme witness of love (LG 42); missionary spirituality includes a readiness to shed one's blood for the gospel (AG 24; cf. DH 14); civil powers have at times to be resisted even to the point of martyrdom (DH 11). Before Vatican II theologians were slow to recognize genuine martyrdom outside the Catholic Church: it was felt that the witness of other Christians lacked the integrity of full Catholic truth. An early draft of *Lumen gentium* spoke of martyrdom among other Christians, but since the meaning of martyrdom was not unanimous among theologians, the phrase "to the shedding of their blood" was chosen instead (LG 15).[25] Since the council there has been less hesitation in ascribing true martyrdom to many non-Catholic Christians. Significant in this respect was the lighting of seven candles at Canterbury (29 May 1982) by the pope and the archbishop of Canterbury in honor of Maximilian Kolbe, Dietrich Bonhoeffer, Janani Luwum, Maria Skobtsova, Martin Luther King, Oscar Romero, and "the unknown martyrs of our time." Though they stop short of veneration of martyrs in the sense of asking for their intercession, Protestants are more open to holding martyrs in a place of honor,[26] and in this way are rediscovering some Reformation roots.[27]

In the 20th century we have a new age of martyrs and much theological reflection on the theme.[28] Martyrs are to be found especially in the Churches of Eastern Europe prior to 1989[29] and everywhere in Latin America,[30] as well as in many countries in Africa and Asia, particularly China. There may be fewer than twenty Churches in the world in which there have not been martyrs in the 20th century.[31] Martyrs are to be found in all of the Churches, and they provide a new, radical bond of unity among the Christian people. There has often been a difficulty in discerning true martyrdom when other, e.g., political, motives are also involved in the death of the persons.

Especially in Latin America we see people dying violently not always explicitly for a tenet of the faith but rather for their commitment to human rights; but the actions leading up to their death are founded on the ineluctable datum of revelation about human dignity and about the inalienable rights of the human person. Some 20th-century figures give evidence of a wider interpretation of martyrdom. The canonization in 1950 of St. Maria Goretti (1890–1902) was at the time stated to have been that of a martyr in that it was seen to have chosen death rather than unchastity. Bl. Titus Brandsma (1881–1942) was beatified as a martyr after his death at the Dachau concentration camp; he had been arrested because, as representative of the Dutch hierarchy and on their instructions, he opposed Nazi propaganda in the Catholic press and refused to countenance the expulsion of Jewish children from Catholic schools. St. Maximilian Kolbe (1894–1941) substituted himself for another prisoner at Auschwitz; he was beatified as a confessor (q.v.), but John Paul II, ignoring the contrary advice of his cardinals, canonized him as a martyr (1982). At all times the Church has known that it has been made fruitful and built up by the supreme witness of the martyrs.

No exact number of the martyrs can be made: scholars range from 10,000 to 100,000 for the martyrs in the early centuries—as many more may be found in the succeeding centuries. Only a small fraction of the actual martyrs are recorded in the liturgical book registering them, the *Martyrology,* the first examples of which date from patristic times.

[1]B. Reicke, "The Inauguration of Catholic Martyrdom According to St. John the Divine," AugR 20 (1980) 275–283. [2]W.R. Farmer and R. Kereszty, *Peter and Paul in the Church of Rome: The Ecumenical Potential of a Forgotten Perspective* (New York-Mahwah: Paulist, 1990). [3]*Ad Rom.* 4:1-2. [4]K. Baus, in Jedin-Dolan 1:217-228, 292–295, 367–388; B. Kreigbaum, "La persécution dans l'Église primitive: Réflexions sur un thème éternellement actuel," Communio—Paris 12/2(1987) 18–31; W.H.C. Frend, *Martyrdom and Persecution in the Early Church* (Oxford, 1965); C. Saulnier, "La persécution des chrétiens et la théologie du pouvoir à Rome (Ier—IVe s.)," RevSR 58 (1984) 251–279. [5]Cyprian, *Ad Fortunatum de exhortatione martyrii*—PL 4:654-676/ANF 5:496-507; Origen, *Exhortatio ad martyrium*—ACW 19/*Origen.* Classics of Western Spirituality (New York: Paulist, 1979) 41–79; Tertullian, *Ad martyras* ANL 2:1-7/ANF 3:693-696; cf. R. Braun, "Dossier sur l'*Ad martyras* de Tertullian," RevÉtAug 26 (1980) 3–17; C. Moreschini, "Aspetti della dottrina del martirio in Tertulliano," Compest 35 (1990) 55–70. [6]J. Janssens, "Martirio ed esperienza spirituale nella chiesa antica," RasT 29 (1988) 361–381. [7]Patrology 1:176-185. [8]E.g., H. Musurillo, trans. and ed., *The Acts of the Christian Martyrs.* Oxford Early Christian Texts (Oxford: Clarendon, 1972). [9]E.g., *The Martyrdom of Polycarp* (ca. 155)—many trans. e.g., LCC 1:149-158. [10]*Vis.* 3:1, 8. [11]Eusebius, *Hist. eccl.* 5:1, 10, 26, 48 . . . [12]Eusebius, *Hist. eccl.* 6:42, 5f. [13]A. Amore, "Culto e canonizzazione dei santi nell'antichità cristiana," Antonian 52 (1977) 38–80 esp. 39–49; H. Delhaye, *Les origines du culte des martyrs* (Paris-Brussels, [2]1933); B. de Gaiffier, "Réflexions sur les origines du culte des martyrs," MaisD 52 (1957) 19–43; J.A. Jungmann, *The Early Liturgy to the Time of Gregory the Great* (Notre Dame: UP, 1959) 175–187; W. Rordorf, "Aux origines du culte des martyrs," Irén 46 (1972) 315–331; O. Pasquato, "Religiosità popolare e culto ai martiri, in particolare a Costantinople nei secc. IV–V, tra paganesimo, eresia e ortodossia," AugR 21 (1981) 207–242; C. Vogel, "Prière or intercession? Une ambiguité dans le culte paléochretien des martyrs," in *Communio Sanctorum.* FS J.J. von Allmen (Geneva: Labor et Fides, 1982) 284–290. [14]*Serm.* 284:5—PL 38:1291. [15]*Hist. eccl.* 5:1, 10; cf. 5:1, 34. [16]*Adv. haer.* 4:33, 9; R. Tremblay, "Le martyr selon Saint Irenée de Lyon," StMor 16 (1978) 167–189. [17]*Ad mart.* 1:3; *De fuga* 8, 10, 14; *De pud.* 22. [18]C. Noce, "La parrhesia terrestre del martire," EuntDoc 39 (1986) 321–340. [19]A. Quacquarelli, "Il battesimo di sangue," VetChr 25 (1988) 289–302; St Thomas ST 3a, q.66, aa.11–12. [20]ST 2–2ae, q.124. [21]*De servorum Dei beatificatione et beatorum canonizazione* (Rome, 1748) 3:2, 1. [22]K. Rahner, "On Martyrdom," in *On the Theology of Death.* QDisput 2 (Freiburg: Herder—Edinburgh: Nelson, 1961) 89–127. [23]J. Janssens, "Il cristiano di fronte al martirio imminente: Testimonianze e dottrina nella chiesa antica," Greg 66 (1985) 405–427; D. Wendebourg, "Das Martyrium in der Alten Kirche als ethisches Problem," ZkG 98 (1987) 295–320. [24]M. Pellegrino, "Les sens ecclesial du martyre," RevSR 35 (1961) 151–175. [25]ActSyn 3/6:100/Alberigo-Magistretti 510. [26]See Lutherans and Catholics in Dialogue VIII, *The One Mediator, the Saints and Mary* (1990). [27]Calvin, *Institutes of Religion* 1:8, 13; 3:5, 3—LCC 20:92, 672–673; Cf. D. Fischer, "La notion du martyr dans la théologie de Luther," ETR 57 (1982) 501–518. [28]Conc 163 (1983); D. Dewar, *All for Christ: Some Twentieth Century Martyrs* (Oxford-New York: Oxford UP, 1980); B. Gherardini, "Il martirio nella moderna prospettiva teologica," Divinitas 26 (1982) 19–35; C.I. González, "Meditación sobre el martirio," TXav 40 (1990) 223–237. [29]F. Rouleau, "La persécution religieuse en U.R.S.S. et sa 'dialectique,'" Communio—Paris 12/2 (1987) 51–61. [30]R. García-Ramírez, "El martirio en la iglesia latino-americano," EstFranc 84 (1983) 143–171; J. Sobrino, *Liberación con Espiritu. Apuntes para una nueva espiritualidad.* Presencia teologica 13 (Santander: Sal Terrae, 1985) 109–125. [31]See individual countries in Jedin-Dolan, vol. 10.

## MARY AND THE CHURCH

The 19th and 20th centuries were a time of great devotion and scholarship about Mary. Each had its climax: the proclamation of the dogma of the Immaculate Conception (1848),[1] and of the Assumption (1950).[2] In the interim between the two definitions, the "Marian movement" arose. This movement was marked by an enormous number of publications about Mary, both devotional and scientific, by congresses, pilgrimages, devotions, and feasts.[3]

Despite all this activity, the study of Mary became divorced from the mainstream of theology, and Mariology developed (the word was coined in the 17th century). Mariology became the realm of specialists, with very few of the great theologians writing significantly about Mary. There were, however, some exceptions, e.g., M. Scheeben, J.H. Newman, K. Rahner. In their closed discipline, Mariologists, who were frequently controversialists, were classed as "maximalist" and "minimalist." The former desired more feasts, new definitions, more devotions; they were very interested in apparitions and were somewhat less than critical in their use of the Scripture and patristic writings. The latter tended to want to develop existing doctrines and feasts, to be more stringent in their use of Scripture and patristic writings, and on the whole to be more ecumenically sensitive, with less interest in apparitions. This unfruitful and often acrimonious division was transcended around the time of the Lourdes Mariological Congress (1958) by the recognition of two different emphases in writing: a Christotypical one, in which all of the mysteries were seen more in relation to Christ; an ecclesiotypical one in which the Marian dogmas were primarily seen in their relation to the Church.[4]

In the 1950s there began to be some important writing on Mary in the context of ecclesiology:[5] she was seen as the heart of the Church by C. Journet (q.v.); various theologians began to explore the analogy between Mary and the Church, and especially to compare her maternity with the Church's.

In the submission to the antepreparatory commission of Vatican II (q.v.) there were nearly six hundred future members of the council who wanted a Marian pronouncement; the largest number of requests for anything in the council was 382, and this was for a statement on Mary's mediation (the next highest was 320 seeking one on communism); indeed, 266 requested a dogmatic definition on mediation.[6]

A document or schema, *Mary the Mother of God and Mother of Men,* was prepared before the council but not discussed at the first session.[7] It was traditional and manualistic, with 117 references to papal magisterium, 57 to Scripture, and 30 to the Fathers of the Church. At the beginning of the second session, several members requested that the subject of Mary be treated in the document on the Church. Eventually, on 24 October 1963, the two positions were argued by Cardinal F. Koenig of Vienna, who favored inclusion, and Cardinal R. Santos of Manila, who wanted a separate text. Five days later, by the narrowest vote of the whole council (1114 to 1074), it was decided that the document on Mary would be included in the Constitution on the Church.

When it came to writing the text of what would be chapter 8 of LG, there was great difficulty. It was necessary to produce a text that would obtain a consensus of the council, which had just voted so narrowly about the place of Mary in the council's texts, and thus implicitly about the way Mary should be seen in the Church today. The theological positions that were mature were those of the 1958 Lourdes Congress.

The text we have in LG chapter 8 does not really get beyond these theological reflections from 1958; indeed one can see the two positions being placed rather in parallel fashion, though with some overlapping: LG 55–59 is mainly Christological and LG 60–65 is mainly ecclesiological. The postconciliar liturgical texts in the main also situate the two insights in paral-

lel, as the prefaces for the feasts of the Immaculate Conception and the Assumption clearly show.

With some exceptions, like the commentaries by G. Philips[8] and K. Balić,[9] who were the main authors of LG chapter 8, all the early ones, despite their many merits, suffer from the fact that their authors did not have access to the *Acts* of the council.[10] The second generation commentaries have this rich source material and give a better understanding both of the genesis and the meaning of the text.[11]

The vexed question of Mary's mediation was subtly treated in the text of LG 62. There was a clear assertion of the unique mediation of Christ (LG 60); Mary was stated to be the companion of Christ in his life and is hence our spiritual mother (LG 61). She continues that role: "Therefore in the Church the blessed Virgin is invoked by the titles of advocate, benefactress, helper and mediatrix" (LG 62). The same article goes on to suggest an explanation of these titles in terms of participation, and adds: "This subordinate role of Mary the Church does not hesitate to profess."

The ecclesiological aspects of Mary's role are developed most fully in LG 60–69: maternal (60–61), associate and handmaid of the redeemer (61), intercessor (62), type and model of the Church (63–65), model of the apostolate of the Church (65). Two important articles are added on devotion to Mary in the Church (66–67). The chapter ends with Mary as an image of the Church in its perfection and refers to the devotion which some other Christians have to her (68–69). The Church constitution was not the only Vatican II document to speak of Mary: she is mentioned in twelve of its sixteen documents. After the council there was a marked decline of interest in Mary, which cannot fairly be blamed on the council.[12]

At the end of the third session of Vatican II, Paul VI proclaimed Mary as Mother of the Church. The title had been considered by the Theological Commission of the council and rejected, probably because it was liable to be misunderstood: it might seem to place Mary outside the Church instead of within it. At the time and since, there has been discussion about why Paul VI took this initiative. While it is possible that he saw in it an opportunity of assuaging the more conservative wing and especially those who had voted for a special document, the more likely explanation seems to be that the pope esteemed the title.[13] Since the council, the title "Mother of the Church" has been investigated by theologians:[14] it is not an early title of Mary, being first attested about the 9th century; it is found, if infrequently, in the Middle Ages and afterwards; it harmonizes with the Catholic belief that Mary is our mother; it explicates what is already in LG chapter 8.

There is, however, a strong patristic tradition about Mary and the Church: she is its type;[15] the beauty of the Virgin and of the Church are seen together;[16] Mary and the Church are both virgins[17] and mothers;[18] Christ born of Mary espouses the Church;[19] it was greater for Mary to be Christ's disciple than to be his mother;[20] Mary is a supereminent member of the Church.[21]

If Vatican II was concerned with the Christ-Church typology, important papal documents made further developments:[22] Paul VI in 1974, by emphasizing liturgy, Scripture, ecumenism, and anthropology;[23] John Paul II, in 1987, by re-presenting the Marian teaching of Vatican II within a spirituality in which maternal mediation occupied an important place.[24]

After Vatican II there have been rich explorations into the relationship of Mary and the Church, none more than H. U. von Balthasar's (q.v.). Though he has seldom written extensively on Mary except at a popular level,[25] his Marian ecclesial insights are among the richest of this century; indeed, the figure of Mary is central to his theological work. He sees two poles of the Church: the Petrine (institutional) and the Marian (obedient and receptive). The former exists solely to serve the latter. Only in Mary does the Church take on her true form, which is the form of Christ; the experiences of Mary on earth are to be shared by the Church through grace. These insights were mature by the first volume of his trilogy (1961).[26] About the same time he developed them in presenting Mary as being at the heart of all spirituality in the Church.[27]

In much recent writing on Mariology, ecclesiology is seldom absent,[28] and much work of high quality is being produced,[29] especially on Mary and the Holy Spirit,[30] a theme insufficiently emphasized in Vatican II.[31] More and more we find writing on Mary in liberation theology (q.v.) with an emphasis, but not an exclusive one, on the *Magnificat*.[32]

Feminist theologians (v. FEMINISM) vary enormously in their attitude to Mary.[33] Some resent what they see as a use of Mary by the patriarchal Church to keep women in subjection;[34] others are seeking to develop an understanding of Mary from a feminist perspective.[35] The whole Church needs the contribution of women to deepen its grasp of the person and role of Mary in salvation history and in the Church.

The question of Mary is also significant in ecumenism:[36] the Catholic dogmas are not accepted by most Protestants; the Orthodox refuse the Immaculate Conception. The Anglican-Roman Catholic International Commission (ARCIC, v. ANGLICANISM AND ECUMENISM) has shown some opening towards a common understanding.[37] The Lutheran-Roman Catholic study on Mary in the Scriptures is somewhat limited through the strict exegetical methodology used; it did, however, reach, nonetheless, a consensus at a certain level.[38] A later study from the same Churches seems rather restricted in the amount of genuine agreement achieved on the crucial and divisive issues.[39] There is much more openness in the ecumenical statements published on the occasion of the international Mariological congresses,[40] in the scholarly publications of the Ecumenical Society of the Blessed Virgin Mary and of its members.[41] The Old Catholic—Orthodox conversations (1977) produced a notable statement on Mary, far in advance of anything agreed by Churches of the West.[42]

Luxuriant as it may appear, Catholic Mariology seems to pale before the profound intuitions and rhapsodic lyricism of the Christian East in its Marian theology and liturgy. The key to this rich Mariology lies in the fact that Mary is the prime example of that divinization which is at the heart of Eastern soteriology and spirituality.[43] The Orthodox worshiper can never forget her presence in the liturgy and in the Church: the iconostasis presents and celebrates her as Theotokos—Mother of God, as Deesis, intercessor for the whole Church, and as the Hodegitria, the one who points the way to Jesus.

It is perhaps above all in liturgy that Mary is best seen in the Church as its Mother, model, and intercessor. Before the often testy debates at Vatican II about where to locate its main statement on Mary, the Constitution on the Liturgy produced perhaps the council's most succinct and profound ecclesiological statement about her: "While it celebrates this annual round of the events of Christ's sacramental life and work, holy Church gives honor to Mary the Mother of God, with a quite special love. She is inseparably linked to the saving work of her Son; in her, the Church admires and holds up the outstanding result of the redemption, and joyfully contemplates what is, as it were, a totally undistorted picture of its desires and hopes for itself as a whole" (SC 103).

[1]DS 2803–2804/ND 709.   [2]DS 3902–3903/ND 713–715.   [3]R. Laurentin, *Mary's Place in the Church* (London, 1965) 29–52. [4]Laurentin (n. 3) 53–81; M. O'Carroll, Theotokos 100–101; C. Pozo, *Maria en la obra de la salvación* (Madrid: BAC, 1974) 20–64. [5]Antó 2:558.   [6]M. O'Carroll, Theotokos 352.   [7]ActaSyn 1:4/92–97 notes 98–121. Eng. trans. MarSt 37 (1986) 199–211; see G.M. Besutti, *Lo schema mariano del Concilio Vaticano II: Documentazione e note di cronica* (Rome: Marianum—Desclée, 1966). [8]*L'Église et son mystère au IIe Concile du Vatican: Histoire, texts et commentaire de la constitution Lumen gentium.* 2 vols. (Paris: Desclée, 1968) 2:207-289   [9]"El capítulo VIII de la constitución 'Lumen gentium' comparado con el primer esquema de la Virgen Madre de la Iglesia," EstMar 27/1 (1966) 133–183.   [10]E.g., D. Flanagan, in K. McNamara, ed., *Vatican II: The Constitution on the Church—A Theological and Pastoral Commentary* (London: Chapman, 1968—Dublin: Veritas, 1983) 317–356; G. Baraúna, "La très sainte Vierge au service de l'économie du salut," in Baraúna-Congar 2:1219-1241; J. Galot, "Marie, type et modèle de l'Église," ibid., 2:1243-1259.   [11]E.g., F.M. Jelly, J.T. O'Connor, C.W. Neumann, and G.F. Kirwin, in MarSt 37 (1986) 43–164, with appendices 197–265.   [12]S. de Fiores, *Maria nella teologia contemporanea*

(Rome: Centro "Mater Ecclesiae," ²1987) 123–136.   ¹³ActaSyn 3/8:915-918.   ¹⁴Bibliog., A. Rivera, "Bibliografía sobre María, Madre de la Iglesia," EphMar 32 (1981) 265–271. See R. Casanovas Cortés, "El título 'Madre de la Iglesia' en los textos y en las Actas del concilio Vaticano II," EphMar 32 (1982) 237–264; S. De Fiores (n. 12) 171–175; D. Fernández, "Orígenes históricos de la expressión 'Mater Ecclesiae,'" EphMar 32 (1982) 189–200; J. Galot, "Mère de l'Église," NRT 86 (1964) 1163–1185; idem, "Théologie du titre 'Mère de l'Église,'" EphMar 32 (1982) 159–173; G.W. Shea, "Pope Paul VI and the 'Mother of the Church,'" MarSt 16 (1965) 21–28.   ¹⁵Ambrose, Expos. in Luc. 2:1, 7—PL 15:1555; Augustine, Serm. Denis 25:8—PL 46:938; Peter Chrysologus, De nativ. Domini—PLS 3:181; Quodvultus, De sym. 1:1—PL 40:661; Isidore, Alleg. s.script. 139—PL 83:117.   ¹⁶Ambrose, De institut. virg. 14:88-89—PL 16:326.   ¹⁷Augustine, De sancta virginitate 2:2; 6:6—PL 40:397, 399; Serm. 191: 2, 3—PL 38:1010-1011; Enchirid. 34:10—PL 40:429; Quodvultus, De sym. 4:4—PL 40:655-656; Apponius (5th cent.), In cant. cant. 7—PLS 1:913; Coll. Eusebii gall (5th cent.), Serm. de Trin. 33—PLS 3:631.   ¹⁸Augustine, De sancta virginitate 5:5; 6:6—PL 40:399; Serm. 195:2—PL 38:1018; Leo the Great, Serm. 29[28]:1—PL 54:227; Caesarius Arles, Hom. 3—PL 67:1048.   ¹⁹Augustine, Serm. 264:4—PL 38:1215; Gregory the Great, Hom. 38:3—PL 76:1283.   ²⁰Augustine, Serm. Denis 25:4 and 7—PL 46:935, 937.   ²¹Augustine, Serm. Denis 7—PL 46:938.   ²²E. Llamas Martínez, "La mariología en el Magisterio postconciliar. Mariología y Magisterio," EphMar 36 (1986) 221–258.   ²³Marialis cultus ("To Honor Mary")—AAS 66 (1974) 113–168.   ²⁴Redemptoris Mater ("The Blessed Virgin Mary in the Life of the Pilgrim Church")—AAS 79 (1987) 361–433.   ²⁵But see "Die marianische Prägung der Kirche," in W. Beinert, ed., Maria heute ehren (Freiburg: Herder, 1977) 263–279; "The Marian Principle," in Elucidations (London: SPCK, 1975) 64–72. See De Fiores (n. 12) 351–370; J.L. Heft, "Marian Themes in the Writings of Hans Urs von Balthasar," MarSt 31 (1980) 40–65; W. Smith, "Mary in the Theology of Hans Urs von Balthasar," in A. Stacpoole, ed., Mary and the Churches (Dublin: Columba, 1987) 142–148.   ²⁶The Glory of the Lord: A Theological Aesthetics. Vol. 1—Seeing the Form (Edinburgh: Clark, 1984) 338–343, 362–364, 421–422, 562–565, 599.   ²⁷Essays in Theology 2 (New York: Herder & Herder, 1965) 87–108 = Verbum Caro. Skizzen zur Theologie 1/2 (Einsiedln: Joannes, 1960).   ²⁸De Fiores (n. 12) 159–174.   ²⁹F.M. Jelly, "Characteristics of Contemporary Mariology," ChicSt 27 (1988) 63–79; see R. Cantalamessa, Mary Mirror of the Church (Collegeville: The Liturgical Press, 1992); B. Gherardini, "Chiesa," NDizMar 350–368; J. Paredes, Mary and the Kingdom of God: A Synthesis of Mariology (Slough UK: St. Paul, 1991).   ³⁰De Fiores (n. 12) 256–287.   ³¹X. Pikaza, "María y el Espíritu Santo (Hech 1, 14): Apuntes para una mariología pneumatológico," EstTrin 15 (1981) 3–82.   ³²J.J. Herrera Aceves, "El Magníficat, canto de liberación," EfemMex 6 (1988) 365–390; B. de Margerie, "Mary in Latin American Liberation Theologies," in Kecharitômenê. FS R. Laurentin (Paris: Desclée, 1990) 365–376 = MarSt 38 (1987) 47–62; N. Zevallos, "María y la experiencia del pueblo," Paginas 5 (1980) 8–12.   ³³W. Beinert, "Maria und die Frauenfrage," StimZ 201 (1983) 31–44; E.A. Johnson, "Mary and the Female Face of God," TS 50 (1989) 500–526; J. Massingberd Ford, "Our Lady and the Ministry of Women in the Church," MarSt 23 (1972) 79–112; M. Pintos and J.J. Tamayo, "María en perspectiva feminista," EphMar 41 (1991) 107–123; cf. K. Rahner, "Mary and the Christian Image of Woman," ThInvest 19:211-217.   ³⁴E.g., M. Warner, Alone of All Her Sex (New York: Knopf, 1976); see E.R. Carroll MarSt29 (1978) 122–123 for reviews.   ³⁵I. Gebara and M. Bingemer, Mary Mother of God, Mother of the Poor. Theology and Liberation Series (Maryknoll: Orbis, 1989); C.F. Jegen, ed., Mary According to Women (Kansas City, Mo.: Leaven, 1985); C. Halkes, "Mary and

Women," Conc 168 (1983) 66–73; R.R. Ruether, Mary—The Feminine Face of the Church (Philadelphia: Westminster, 1977).   ³⁶Conc 168 (1983); C. O'Donnell, "Mary and Ecumenism: Paths Ahead," in O. Rafferty, ed., Reconciliation. FS M. Hurley (Dublin: Columba, 1993) 80–97.   ³⁷"Authority in the Church II," n. 30 in The Final Report (London: SPCK—CTS, 1982) 95–96, with n. 6.   ³⁸R.E. Brown et al., eds., Mary in the New Testament (Philadelphia: Fortress—London: Chapman, 1978).   ³⁹H.G. Anderson et al., eds., The One Mediator, the Saints and Mary: Lutherans and Catholics in Dialogue 8 (Minneapolis: Augsburg, 1992).   ⁴⁰Texts: StEcum 5 (1987) 529–543; see E.R. Carroll, "Ecumenical Roundtables at International Mariological Congresses," in Mater fidei et fidelium. Marian Library Studies 17–23 (Dayton: UP, 1991) 292–305.   ⁴¹Pamphlets and three books, A. Stacpoole, ed. Mary's Place in Christian Dialogue (Slough UK: St. Paul, 1982); Mary and the Churches (Dublin: Columba, 1987); Mary in Doctrine and Devotion (Dublin: Columba, 1990).   ⁴²H. Meyer and L. Vischer, eds., Growth in Agreement. Ecumenical Documents 2. Faith and Order Paper 108 (New York: Paulist—Geneva: WCC, 1984) 399–401.   ⁴³M. O'Carroll, Theotokos 275–276 and related arts.; T. Špidlík, The Spirituality of the Christian East. Cistercian Studies 79 (Kalamazoo, Mich.: Cistercian Publications, 1986) 158–159; P.N. Trembelas, Dogmatique de l'Église orthodoxe catholique. 3 vols. (Paris—Chevetogne, 1966–1968) 2:222-234.

## MAXIMUS THE CONFESSOR (ca. 580–662)

We know little about Maximus before he became a monk about 614, probably after being a secretary at the court of the emperor Heraclius (575–641).[1] Perhaps the finest theologian of his day, he was an unrelenting opponent of Monothelitism, the heresy which denied a human will in Christ. He suffered much for the faith, being known as the "confessor" (q.v.); afterwards he died in exile.

He was one of the most influential mystical writers of the East. He is steadily becoming better known in the West, especially through H. U. von Balthasar,[2] studies coming from the Pontifical Oriental Institute in Rome,[3] and others in France, Germany, and the United States during the past fifty years.[4]

He was a prolific writer, but not many of his works are in critical editions or translations.[5] His theology was often occasioned by practical situations, such as heresy, or requests for guidance. It is suffused by his mystical vision of the Incarnate Word. Central to all his work is the Greek theme of the divinization of the person by grace (cf. 2 Pet 1:4). In the history of theology he was a key interpreter of the Pseudo-Dionysius (v. DIONYSIUS, PSEUDO), showing him to be an orthodox representative of Neo-Platonism in Christian theology.

Ecclesiology is found throughout his works, but especially in the Mystagogy,[6] a symbolic commentary on the liturgy modeled on Pseudo-Dionysius but developing the latter. He begins the main part of the work by seeing the Church as an image: it is an image of God "since it has the same activity as he does by imitation and in figure. . . . The holy Church will be shown to be working for us the same effects as God. . . . All are born into the Church and through it are reborn and recreated in the Spirit."[7] The Church is also a figure and image of the entire world, of the sensible world, of the human person, and of the soul.[8] The liturgy is the entrance into the mystery which encompasses also the liturgy of the angels and the saints,[9] it is a sharing of a liturgy that will perdure to all eternity.[10]

Through his powerful theology of icon, Maximus unifies time and eternity, the Church on earth and in heaven, the Church and the world, the Church and the individual. It is through Maximus and his mentor, the Pseudo-Dionysius (q.v.), that we perhaps best approach the Church, concretized in, and understood through, liturgy—its highest work.

[1]R. Devréesse, "La Vie de S. Maxime le Confesseur et ses recensions," AnBoll 46 (1928) 5–49; cf. on a hostile biography S. Brock, "An Early Syriac Life of Maximus the Confessor," AnBoll 91 (1973) 299–346. [2]Komische Liturgie. Das Weltbild Maximus des Bekenners (Einsiedeln, [2]1961). [3]E.g., I. Hausherr, Philautie: De la tendresse pour soi à la charité, selon Saint Maxime le Confesseur. OrChrAn 137(Rome, 1952). [4]Bibliog., A. Ceresa-Gasltaldo, "Maximus Confessor," EncycEarCh 1:547-548; F. Heinzer and C. Schönborn, eds., Maximus Confessor. Actes du Symposium sur Maxime le Confesseur 2–5 septembre 1980 (Fribourg: Ed. Universitaires, 1982); L. Thunburg, The Vision of St. Maximus the Confessor (Crestwood, N.Y.: St. Vladimir's Seminary Press, ca. 1985. [5]PG 90–91; CSSG 10; ACW 21 = SC 9. [6]Maximus the Confessor. The Classics of Western Spirituality (New York: Paulist, 1985) 183–225; J. Auxentios-Thornton, "Three Byzantine Commentaries on the Divine Liturgy: A Comparative Treatment (Dionysius, Maximus, Germanus)," GkOrTR 32 (1987) 285–308; G.C. Berthold, "The Church as Mysterion: Diversity and Unity According to Maximus Confessor," PatByzR 6 (1987) 20–29; G. Dion Dragas, "The Church in St. Maximus' Mystagogy," IrTQ 53 (1987) 113–129; I.H. Dalmais, "L'Église icône du mystère": La Mystagogia de S. Maxime le Confesseur, une ecclésiologie liturgique," in A.M. Triacca and A. Pistoia, eds., L'Église dans la liturgie. Bibliotheca Ephemerides liturgicae. Subsidia 18 (Rome: Ed. Liturgiche, 1980) 107–117; A. Riou, Le monde et l'Église selon Maxime le Confesseur. Théologie historique 22 (Paris: Beauchesne, 1973); V.M. Zhikov, "The Mystagogia of Maximus the Confessor and the Development of the Byzantine Theory of the Image," SVlad 31 (1987) 349–376. [7]Ch. 1—Maximus the Confessor (n. 6) 186–187. [8]Chs. 2–5—ibid., 188–195. [9]Chs. 21, 23—ibid., 203–205. [10]Ch. 18—ibid., 202. See further A. Nicols, Byzantine Gospel: Maximus the Confessor in Recent Scholarship (Edinburgh: Clark, 1993).

## MELANCHTHON, Philip (1497–1560)

The Reformer Philip Melanchthon was born in the Palatinate in 1497.[1] Already at a very early age he was an outstanding humanist scholar. He taught at the University of Wittenberg, where his antipathy to the scholastics ("the Sophists") soon became apparent, and where he fell under the spell of Martin Luther. His first major, best-known, and often revised work, Loci communes (1521),[2] is a defense of Lutheran positions and the first dogmatic treatise of the Reformation. It was meant to be a guide to accompany the study of

Scripture. It would prove very influential in being one of the classics of Lutheran theology. Luther himself said that "next to Holy Scripture there is no better book."[3]

He was mainly responsible for the Augsburg Confession (q.v.), which shows his ecclesiology to be basically a Reformation one.[4] Subsequently, his Apologia for the Confession was widely adopted. His was one of the more conciliatory spirits of the Reformation period: in 1537 he signed the Schmalkaldic Articles with the reservation that he would accept a revised and reformed papacy;[5] at one stage he stated that he would not be totally adverse to attending the future council (Trent).[6]

[1]C.L. Manschreck, Melanchthon: The Quiet Reformer (New York, 1958); W. Maurer, Der junge Melanchthon. 2 vols. (Göttingen, 1967–1969); R. Stupperich, Melanchthon (Berlin, 1960—Philadelphia, 1965); E. Iserloh, in Jedin-Dolan 5:97-104, 253–265. [2]LCC 19:18-152. [3]Table Talk 5:5511 in Luther's Works (Philadelphia: Fortress, 1967) 54:440. [4]Antón 1:586-620. [5]Bekenntnisschriften 463–464. [6]E. Iserloh, in Jedin-Dolan 5:270-272.

## MEMBERSHIP OF THE CHURCH

The NT position on membership of the Church is not simple. In some cases people enter the community after preaching and belief and baptism (Acts 2:41); in other cases there is preaching, baptism, and a laying on of hands (Acts 8:2-25; 19:1-6); in at least one other case there is a previous gift of the Spirit before baptism (Acts 10:44-48), which would later be mirrored in the Syriac ordering of initiation rites.[1] In the early Church, membership was synonymous with communion (q.v.), which embraced reception of the Eucharist (v. EUCHARIST AND THE CHURCH).[2]

Vatican II avoided the term "member" of the Church; nonetheless, a knowledge of the notion's prehistory is necessary to understand both the Council's developed teaching and the axiom "outside the Church there is no salvation" (q.v.). The tradition expressed in the Fathers, theologians, and in the magisterium is unanimous in asserting that entry to the Church is only by baptism. Furthermore, profession of faith is demanded, so that formal heretics and schismatics are excluded from the Church. It has been controverted whether occult heretics are members or not; the majority of manualists following Bellarmine (q.v.) allow that they are members, since they are still visibly associated with the visible Church.[3]

Pius XII (q.v.) in the encyclical Mystici Corporis (q.v.) made three main contributions to the question: he asserted that "the Holy, Catholic, Apostolic, Roman Church," which is the "true Church of Christ," is rightly defined and described (definiendam describendamque) by the term "the mystical Body of Jesus Christ";[4] he stated that "only those are to be accounted really (reapse) members of the Church who have been regenerated in the waters of baptism and profess the true faith, and have not unhappily cut themselves off from the structure of the Body, or for very grave crimes have been severed by legitimate authority";[5] he allowed that others could be ordered to the Church "by some unconscious yearning or desire (inconscio quodam desiderio ac voto)."[6] A few years later he reiterated this teaching in the encyclical Humani generis, when he complained that some theologians "imagine that they are not bound to it" (that the Mystical Body of Christ and the Catholic Church in communion with Rome are one and the same thing).[7] In the years before Vatican II, theologians endeavored to understand the implications of the teaching of Pius XII, and more significantly sought to test the exclusive identification of the Roman Catholic Church with the Mystical Body, for example, K. Rahner, by speaking about strata of membership and by exploring the implications of sacramentality, as did P. Gribomont; Congar, by observing that the Church has wider meanings than that of the Church militant; A. Liégé, by admitting a belonging to the invisible Church; A. Chevasse, by interpreting reapse as "effective" members.[8]

Vatican II did not follow Pius XII in treating of the members of the Church but spoke instead of "incorporation" and being "ordered to" the Church in various degrees. LG 14 states: "Fully incorporated into the Church are those who, possessing the Spirit of Christ, accept all the means of salvation given to the Church together with her entire organization, and who—by the bonds constituted by the profession of faith, the sacraments, and ecclesiastical government and communion—are joined in the visible structure of the Church of Christ, who rules her through the Supreme Pontiff and the bishops" (cf. OE 2). We know from the explanatory document supplied to the council members that the phrase "having the Spirit of Christ" means that sinners are not fully incorporated into the Church.[9] Full incorporation therefore means that in addition to the triple bond (found in apologetics as far back as Bellarmine[10]), the state of grace is needed; those in serious sin are not fully incorporated. But the notion of incomplete incorporation is not followed through when the constitution treats of other Christians with whom the Church knows itself "to be joined in many ways" (plures ob rationes coniunctam—LG 15). Others are ordered (ordinantur) to the People of God (LG 16). But the Decree on Ecumenism speaks of imperfect communion (v. COMMUNION) of other Christians with the Catholic Church ("in quadam . . . communione, etsi non perfecta"—UR 3), and of their being separated from full communion (UR 4). Although the council several times speaks of entry to the Church being through baptism (LG 7, 11,

14, 21; AA 3; AG 6, 15; PO 5), it avoids saying that baptism alone gives complete incorporation into the Church but speaks about gradual communion or, as in UR 22, about incorporation into Christ.[11] Indeed, the language of SC 69 suggests a significant difference, for one rite is to show that babies are already received into the Church, while the rite for Christians coming to the Catholic Church is to show that they are being admitted to the communion of the Church (eos in Ecclesiae communionem admitti). The meaning of the council is made clearer if we see the baptism of an adult not only as a sign and cause of grace but also a sacrament of faith and a seal of faith. Thus one baptized in another Church is truly baptized but is not incorporated into the Church in the fullest possible sense of the word, which in addition to grace would involve the acceptance of the triple bond of faith, sacramental life, and ecclesiastical government. Such a baptism does not therefore completely express the faith of the Church, and therefore we speak of such an adult having a real but incomplete communion with the Church (cf. UR 3).

Catechumens (v. CATECHUMENATE) are already joined to the Church through their intention to join it: "with love and solicitude the Church already embraces them as her own" (LG 14).

The Code of Canon Law in canon 205 follows not the tradition of Vatican II but rather the juridical model of the 1917 Code: "By baptism one is incorporated into the Church of Christ and is constituted a person in it with duties and rights which are proper to Christians, in keeping with their condition, to the extent that they are in ecclesiastical communion and unless a legitimately issued sanction stands in the way." Probably the juridic and public nature of canon law is the reason why a condition of Vatican II (LG 14—grace/"having the Holy Spirit") does not feature here.[12] The norm of CIC 96 states a dual effect of baptism: it incorporates a human being into the Church of Christ; it bestows personhood on him or her—in the classical meaning of personhood, viz., a subject of rights and duties.[13] This canon has to be read in conjunction with CIC 11, which states the exemption of non-Catholic Christians from Church law; with CIC 205, which states the necessity of the triple bond of profession of faith, sacraments, and ecclesiastical governance for communion (q.v.); with CIC 204 § 2, which states that the Church subsists (q.v.) in the Catholic Church (v. PEOPLE OF GOD); with CIC 751 on heresy (q.v.) and schism (q.v.), and with CIC 1331 on excommunication (q.v.).

A serious and unresolved problem remains with CIC 96 quoted above. There is no canonical provision for those who have been baptized into the Catholic Church as infants but—perhaps through no fault of their own—have never been truly in ecclesiastical communion.

They cannot be said to have left such communion since they have never really accepted it. Yet they may consider themselves as Catholics when requesting a sacrament such as marriage; "canon law has not been able to work out satisfactory practical norms regarding the situation (rights and duties) of such baptized non-believers."[14]

A most difficult problem is that of the frontiers of the Church:[15] we can with some ease point to where the Church is; we cannot so simply declare who is excluded from the Church (v. NON-CHRISTIAN). One can be a member of the Church either *in re* (in fact) or *in voto* (by [implicit] desire). Anyone who is baptized and has not formally renounced membership in the Christian community is a member *in re*. (Of course, a person who is a member *in re* of the Church by baptism can be in a state of full or less than full communion with the Catholic Church.) Anyone who is in the state of grace is a member of the Church *in voto*. But members *in voto* are not actually members, and since the Church on earth is visible, its actual frontiers include only the baptized. Those who die as members *in voto* of the earthly Church will be actual members of the eschatological Church, the "Church from Abel," (v. ABEL, CHURCH FROM), which consists of all and only the just. Membership of the Church is an issue that belongs to eschatology and ultimately to the mystery of the divine will of incorporating all in Christ.

The post-Vatican II period, sometimes called the "post-Christian era," has seen a hemorrhage in the Church's membership. While the many causes for this must be sought through interdisciplinary studies (history, sociology, culture, psychology, etc.), one can with some confidence point to people, especially the young, as failing to have their expectations of belonging answered in the Church community. Belonging to a religious group, here the Church, has several characteristics:[16] there is a minimum of interaction needed, which varies from nominal adherence to full participation; the values and norms of the group have to be seen as relevant; people feel the need to be accepted and recognized in and by the group; they have to move further to identification with the group, which supposes an interiorization of its aims and values. Large parishes of themselves, especially in urban areas, simply do not provide an environment in which people will have a sense of fully belonging. Among the answers in the contemporary Church are Basic Christian Communities (q.v.) and associations (q.v.).

[1]T.W. Manson, "Entry into Membership of the Early Church," JTS 48(1947) 25–33. [2]H.-M. Legrand, "Communion ecclésiale et Eucharistie aux premiers siècles," AnnéeCan 25 (1981) 125–148. [3]K. Rahner, "Membership of the Church According to the Teaching of Pius XII's Encyclical *Mystici Corporis Christi*," ThInvest 2:1-88 at 13–14; Salaverri De Ecclesia 835–854. [4]AAS 35 (1943) 199/Carlen 4:39-40/ND 847. [5]AAS 35 (1943) 202/Carlen 4:41/DS 3802/ND 849. [6]AAS 35 (1943) 243/Carlen 4:58/DS 3821. [7]AAS 42 (1950) 571/Carlen 4:179. [8]Rahner (n. 2); Y. Congar, "Hors de l'Église, pas de salut," *Sainte Église. Études et approches ecclésiologiques.* US 41 (Paris, 1963) 416–432; P. Gribomont, "Du sacrement de l'Église et ses réalisations imparfaites," Irén 22 (1949) 345–367; C. Liégé, "L'appartenance à l'Église et l'encyclique *Mystici Corporis Christi,*" RSPT 32 (1948) 351–357; V. Morel, "Le Corps mystique du Christ et l'Église catholique romaine," NRT 70 (1948) 703–726; A. Chevasse, "Ordonnés au Corps mystique," ibid., 690–702; Antón 2:641-644, 648, 651; O. Semmelroth, "Kirche," LTK 3:784-787. Cf. ABEL, CHURCH FROM and C.E. O'Neill, "Members of the Church: Mystici corporis and St. Thomas," AmER 148 (1963) 113–128, 167–184. [9]ActaSyn 3/1:203—Alberigo-Magistretti 446. [10]*De controversiis* 2:3, "De ecclesia militante," ch. 2. [11]K.J. Becker, "The Teaching of Vatican II on Baptism: A Stimulus for Theology," in Latourelle, Vatican II, 2:47-99. [12]E. Corecco, "Aspects of the Reception of Vatican II in the Code of Canon Law," in G. Alberigo et al., eds., *The Reception of Vatican II* (Washington, D.C.: Catholic UP—Tunbridge Wells, 1987) 276. [13]E. Kneal, in Coriden CIC 70–71; M. Hughes, "The Juridical Nature of Joining the Catholic Church," StCan 8 (1974) 45–74, 379–431. [14]L. Örsy in Coriden CIC 31. [15]P. Meinhold, ed., *Das Problem der Kirchengliedschaft.* Wege der Forschung 534 (Darmstadt: Wissenschaftliche Buchgesellschaft, 1979); H. U. von Balthasar, "Frontiers of the Church," TDig 22 (1974) 239–241; E. Clapsis, "The Boundaries of the Church: An Orthodox Debate," GrOrTR 35 (1990) 113–127; G. Dejaifve, "L'appartenance à l'Église du concile de Florence à Vatican II," NRT 99 (1977) 21–50; Y. Spiteris, "L'appartenza all Chiesa secondo la teologia greco-ortodossa," EuntDoc 45 (1992) 429–440. [16]H. Carrier, "Appartenance religieuse," in P. Poupard, ed., *Dictionnaire des religions* (Paris: PUF, 1984) 87–90.

## MENNONITES

See ANABAPTISTS

## METHODISM

John Wesley (1703–1791 q.v.) traced the origins of Methodism to the "Holy Club" of spiritually committed people at Oxford, of which he and his brother Charles were members. John later became its leader. "Methodism" was originally a pejorative term used in relation to the club, but Wesley himself understood it as a methodical pursuit of biblical holiness within the Church of England.

John and Charles Wesley went as missionaries to the U.S. in 1736, and on their return both received a second conversion in 1738. After that, John began open-air preaching to those who would never have entered a church, much less have been members of the Established Church of the time. It was a preaching about Christ and the Trinity, and a joyful message of salvation (against Calvinist predestination). The need to provide for ministers led John Wesley, who was a priest, to "set apart" or ordain Thomas Cole (d. 1814) as superintendent in America with authority to establish an independent Church (1784). The term "superintendent" in the U.S. gave way to "bishop" in 1787, but this latter term was not used in England.

John Wesley, at the outset, never intended to found a Church but to inspire and organize a movement of Church renewal; he died as a member of the Church of England. His society later became a separate Church. There were to be several schisms both in England and in the U.S. in the 19th century, during which this Church lost the profound sacramentalism of the Wesley brothers and became more aligned with non-conformist positions. The Ecumenical Methodist Conference (1881) was the beginning of the healing of divisions. At the 8th Conference (1951) the name World Methodist Council (WMC) was adopted. The WMC meets every five years.[1]

From its beginnings, the four "ours" encapsulated the Methodist ethos: "our doctrines"—justification by faith, assurance, and new birth; "our hymns"—mainly the immense treasury of magnificent hymns by Charles Wesley; "our literature"—tracts and the sermons of John Wesley; "our discipline"—mainly the structures of Methodism. Though the word is not used, the structure of Methodism is generally collegial; however, in the U.S. there are bishops. Methodism is organized in societies, circuits, and annual conferences. There is much lay involvement in ministry; the ordained ministry is open to women.

An evangelical Methodist affirmation sees the Church as being authentic "wherever the pure Word of God is preached and taught, wherever the Sacraments of Baptism and Holy Communion are celebrated in obedience to Christ's command; wherever the gifts of the Holy Spirit upbuild the body and bring spiritual growth; wherever the Spirit of God creates a loving, caring fellowship, and a faithfulness in witness and service to the world; and wherever discipline is administered with love under the guidance of the Word of God. The Church, as the Bride of Christ, will ultimately be joined with her Lord in triumphant glory."[2] This affirmation also includes typical Wesleyan themes of the love of Jesus in the Spirit, sanctification, and social commitment.[3]

For his time John Wesley himself was remarkably free from religious prejudice.[4] Methodists have been to the fore in ecumenical endeavors.[5] There has been a unique relationship with the Anglican Communion (q.v.). In the Churches of South (1947) and North India (1970), Methodists and Anglicans have reached union. In England there were two attempts to unite the two Churches (1969 and 1972), both failing on the issue of how Methodism would "take episcopacy into its system." In 1988 the Lambeth Conference stated that it wished to begin dialogue with the World Methodist Council; the latter agreed in 1989.

At present there are a significant number of other dialogues taking place. The Lutheran World Federation and the WMC conducted bilateral conversations from 1977–1984.[6] With U.S. Lutherans there has been study of episcopacy and baptism.[7] It was agreed in 1990 that meetings with the Orthodox should take place; these began in 1992. Dialogue with Reformed Churches has shown a substantial degree of agreement which, in some places, has led to union at local levels.[8]

From 1967 there has been dialogue between the WMC and the Roman Catholic Church. The joint commission reported on a wide range of topics to the WMC meetings in Denver (1971)[9] and Dublin (1976);[10] For the Honolulu meeting (1981) there was *Towards an Agreed Statement on the Holy Spirit;*[11] for Nairobi (1986), *Towards a Statement on the Church;*[12] and for Singapore (1991), *The Apostolic Tradition.*[13]

All of these dialogues are characterized by a particular emphasis on holiness and on fellowship *(koinô-nia),* which are a special Methodist gift in the ecumenical movement.

---

[1]R.E. Davies, *Methodism* (London: Epworth, [2]1985); R.E. Davies, A.R. George, and G. Rupp, *A History of the Methodist Church in Great Britain.* 4 vols. (London: Epworth, 1965–1988); N.B. Harmon, *Understanding the Methodist Church* (Nashville: Methodist, 1955); E.S. Bucke, ed., *The History of American Methodism.* 3 vols. (New York: Abingdon, 1964).    [2]"The Junaluska Affirmation (1975)," in P.A. Mickey, *Essentials of Wesleyan Theology: A Contemporary Affirmation* (Grand Rapids: Zondervan, 1980) 19.    [3]J. Munsey Turner, "John Wesley—People's Theologian," OneChr 14 (1978) 328–339; G.S. Wakefield, "La littérature du Désert chez John Wesley," Irén 51 (1978) 155–170, 295.    [4]M. Hurley, ed., *John Wesley's Letter to a Roman Catholic* (London: Chapman, 1968).    [5]G. Wainwright, "Methodism's Ecclesial Location and Ecumenical Vocation," OneChr 19 (1983) 104–134.    [6]*The Church: A Community of Grace 1979–1984* (Geneva: LWF—Lake Junaluska: Methodist Council, 1984)    [7]J. Burgess, "The Lutheran-United Methodist Statement on Episcopacy," EcuTrends 18 (1989) 163–165; B.A. Nitschke, "By Water and the Spirit—A United Methodist Understanding of Baptism: A Lutheran Response," EcuTrends 22 (1993) 3–7.    [8]*Reformed and Methodists in Dialogue: Report of the Reformed/Methodist Conversations in 1985 and 1987* (Geneva: World Alliance of Reformed Churches, 1988).    [9]H. Meyer and L. Vischer, eds., *Growth in Agreement.* Ecumenical Documents 2 (New York: Paulist—Geneva: WCC, 1984) 308–339    [10]Ibid., 340–366.    [11]Ibid., 367–387.    [12]OneChr 22 (1986) 241–259; K. McDonald, "Catholic-Anglican and Catholic-Methodist Relations," OneChr 24 (1988) 63–71 at 69–71; J.M.R. Tillard, "Commentary on 'Towards a Statement on the Church,'" OneChr 22 (1986) 259–266; D. Cartier, "Catholic, Methodists and Reception," OneChr 28 (1992) 232–237.    [13]CathInter3/3 (1992) 106–120; J. Wicks and A.R. George, "Commentary and Assessment of 'The Apostolic Tradition,'" OneChr 28 (1992) 74–81 and 82–86.

## METZ, Johann Baptist (1928–)

Johann Baptist Metz was born in Bavaria in 1928. A student of Karl Rahner (q.v.), he has persistently pursued a fundamental theology in response to the Enlightenment's critique of religion in the name of human autonomy, freedom, and subjectivity.[1] His response has been a "political theology," gradually worked out over several decades.[2]

For Metz, history and religion are related, and an authentic praxis is necessary for the fullness of Christian life, something missing both in transcendental theology and in various manifestations of bourgeois religiosity. He has profoundly influenced liberation theologies (q.v.) and in turn been influenced by them. He turns from both consumerism and evolutionary thought, proposing instead an apocalyptic eschatology which takes seriously both evil and history. His radical critiques of contemporary Church life and ecclesiology make him a challenging but uncomfortable figure, as witnessed by the ecclesiastical opposition to his securing an appointment to the Catholic faculty of theology at the University of Munich prior to his appointment at Münster. His questioning cannot, however, be ignored in an ecclesiology which seeks to be truly contemporary.[3]

---

[1]F. Schüssler Fiorenza, "Fundamental Theology and the Enlightenment," JRel 6 (1982) 289–298.  [2]Bibliog., E. Schillebeeckx, ed., *Mystik und Politik: Theologie im Ringen um Geschichte und Gesellschaft*. FS J.B. Metz (Mainz: Matthias-Grünewald, 1988) 407–411. See in English his *Theology of the World* (London, 1969); *Faith in History and Society: Towards a Practical Fundamental Theology* (New York: Seabury-London: Burns & Oates, 1980); *The Emergent Church: The Future of Christianity in a Post-Bourgeois World* (New York: Crossroad-London: SCM, 1981).  [3]A. Alvarez-Suárez, "La iglesia y su misión crítica en el pensamiento de Juan Bautista Metz," Burgense 19 (1978) 131–156.

## MEYENDORFF, John (1926–1992)

John Meyendorff was born in Neuilly-sur-Seine in France in 1926. He studied theology at St. Sergius, the Orthodox Theological Institute, and at the Sorbonne. After his ordination he joined the faculty of St. Vladimir's Seminary, Crestwood, New York.

His scholarly work began with a study of the Byzantine spiritual author St. Gregory Palamas (d. 1359).[1] He wrote on a wide variety of subjects[2] and was very actively involved with ecumenism for many years, especially with the World Council of Churches (v. ECUMENISM). Though at times critical of the Roman Catholic Church, Meyendorff was one of a second generation of scholars who have mediated Christian Eastern thought to the West. In his ecclesiology we can recognize a common heritage, elements of which may have been better preserved in Orthodoxy, especially the integration of spirituality and doctrine, which is such a feature of our sister Church.

---

[1]*Grégoire Palamas, Triades pour la défense des saints hésychastes.* Ed. and trans. J. Meyendorff. 2 vols. (Louvain, 1959, [2]1974); *St. Gregory and Orthodox Spirituality* (New York, 1974—French 1959); *A Study of Gregory Palamas* (London, 1964—French 1959), updated in "Palamas (Grégoire)," DSpir 12:81-107.  [2]E.g., *Catholicity and the Church* (Crestwood, N.Y.: St. Vladimir's Seminary Press, 1983); *Byzantine Theology. Historical Trends and Doctrinal Themes* (London—Oxford: Mowbrays—New York: Fordham UP, 1974); *Christ in Eastern Christian Thought* (Crestwood, N.Y.: St. Vladimir's Seminary Press, 1975—French 1969); *Witness to the World* (Crestwood, N.Y.: St. Vladimir's Seminary Press, 1987)—a varied collection of short essays. See "Protopresbyter John Meyendorff: In Memoriam," SVlad 36 (1992) 180-182.

## MILLENARIANISM—MILLENARISM—MILLENNIALISM

The belief in a millennium,[1] a thousand years of blessedness, was found in pre-Christian Jewish apocalyptic writing. The term "chiliasm" (Greek *chilias* = a thousand) is also used. It is found in two forms: some hold a thousand years of blessedness after the second coming of Christ; others look to a millennium of blessedness and righteousness preceding the parousia. A key biblical text is Rev 20:4 which should, however, be interpreted within the total symbolism of the book. Irenaeus (q.v.) would seem to have held a literal interpretation.[2] Augustine (q.v.), while recanting on earlier views, spiritualized the notion[3] and rejected the crude form found in the *Apocalypse of Paul*.[4] Even Jerome (q.v.), who does not accept millenarianism, will not condemn it, "for many martyrs and ecclesiastics have said such things."[5] Although millenarianism was not to be found in Catholic theology after Augustine, it would continually reappear in the sects and non-orthodox circles and is still to be found in some present-day sects and fundamentalists.

---

[1]Bibliog., R. Keuhner and J.P. Dolan, "Millenarianism," NCE 9:852-854; "Millenarianism," OxDCC 916; M. Simonetti, "Millenarism," EncycEarCh 1:560. See L.I. Sweet, "Millennialism in America: Recent Studies," TS 40 (1979) 510-531. See N. Cohn, *The Pursuit of the Millennium* (London, [2]1969).  [2]*Adv. haer.* 5:33-36, esp. 35, 1—SC 405-466, esp. 436–442.  [3]G. Bonner, "Augustine and Millenarianism," in R. Williams, ed., *The Making of Orthodoxy*. FS H. Chadwick (Cambridge: UP, 1989) 234-254.  [4]*Tr. in Ioan.* 98:8—PL 35:1884-1885/CCL 36:581; see Bonner (n. 3) 241.  [5]*Comm. in Ierem.* 19:10—PL 24:833.

## MINISTRY

In the past two decades there has been very extensive writing on ministry.[1] A treatment of ministry will inevitably overlap with matter in other questions, all of which are complementary, in a search for the understanding of ministry. This article deals with the NT evidence, before going on to look at the issue of ministry and laity. The articles on "Apostles," "Bishops," "Charism," "Laity," and "Priests, Ministerial," with their accompanying notes and bibliographies, should be read in conjunction with what follows.

In the NT we find various kinds of ministry and different kinds of structure throughout the diverse books, which were written over a period of about 50 years.[2] Two main questions arise: What were the officials called? What was their function? As the most complete record is found in the Pauline corpus, we take this as our basis, noting other usages in passing. The Greek terms *episkopos* (overseer) and *presbuteros* (elder) are used to avoid overhasty identification of these officials with bishops and priests in a later phase of development.

In the Pauline Churches we find several words indicating authority and ministry: *episkopos* (Phil 1:1; cf. Acts 20:28), *diakonos* (Rom 16:1; 1 Cor 3:5; Phil 1:1), *presbutês* (old man—Phlm 9), and *sunergos* (fellow-worker—Rom 16:3; 1 Cor 3:9; 2 Cor 1:24; 8:23; Phil 2:25; 4:3; Phlm vv. 1, 24), as well as *apostolos* (v. APOSTLES). (In the indubitably authentic letters of Paul we do not find *presbuteros*.) The greetings of several letters have the names of Timothy and Sosthenes (cf. 1 Thess 1:1; 1 Cor 1:1; 2 Cor 1:1; Phlm 1; see also Col 1:1), who are described as "brother." Paul states that they preached with him (Silvanus and Timothy—2 Cor 1:19). We see that they are given missions by Paul in the Churches he founded (Timothy to Thessalonica—1 Thess 3:2, to Corinth—1 Cor 4:17; 16:10; and to Philippi—Phil 2:19-24; Titus in Corinth—2 Cor 2:13; 7:6-16; 12:18). Silas (probably Silvanus) is the companion of Paul in Acts (cc. 15–18), along with Timothy. We thus get the idea of a team ministry, but with Paul very much the leader. In addition in the very first NT writing from about 51 C.E., there are unnamed people described as "those who labor among you and have charge of you in the Lord and admonish you"; they are to be respected and loved because of their work (1 Thess 5:12-13).

The names indicating ministry are of two kinds: official and charismatic. In Phil 1:1 we find the *episkopoi* and *diakonoi* addressed. We also find in Ephesus, a Church evangelized by Paul, *episkopoi* and *presbuteroi* used apparently interchangeably (Acts 20:17, 28); the former tends to reflect a Greek culture and the latter a more Jewish one, though in the light of the Dead Sea Scrolls this distinction should not be unduly emphasized.[3]

Among the most important documents for an appreciation of NT ministry, and indeed for the transition from the situation of the Church in the 30s to the 60s C.E. to the structures found in the Churches visited by Ignatius ca. 110 C.E., are the deutero-Pauline letters to Timothy and to Titus, which can, with some reasonable probability, be dated in the 90s. Their central concern is with good order in the household of God, which is the Church. The situations being confronted are basically two: immorality and false doctrine. Timothy and Titus each appear as a disciple, a true or beloved child of Paul (1 Tim 1:2; 2 Tim 1:2; Titus 1:3), and thus legitimate ministers. Timothy is not called either *episkopos* or *presbuteros* even though hands were laid

on him by both Paul (2 Tim 1:6) and by the *presbuteroi* (1 Tim 4:14). Paul himself is depicted as nearing the end of his life and making provision for the Churches through the ministry of Timothy and Titus and those whom they would appoint as either *episkopoi* or *presbuteroi*. He himself is called an apostle of Jesus Christ in the opening verse of each letter, as well as herald, apostle, and teacher (2 Tim 1:11). Instruction in, and transmission of, true doctrine is clearly at the heart of these letters; it is the deposit (*parathêkê*—1 Tim 6:20; 2 Tim 1:12, 14), the gospel (2 Tim 1:11; 2:8), teaching (*didaskalia* = 1 Tim 1:10; 4:6 . . .). E. Schillebeeckx is right to indicate that apostolic tradition is central to the Pastoral Letters and that the charism of the Spirit helps to ensure that this pledge is preserved and proclaimed, but he might have stressed somewhat more the undoubted authority that is ascribed to Timothy and to Titus as well as to those whom they place as leaders in the community.[4] These leaders are called *episkopos* (1 Tim 3:2; Titus 1:7), *presbuteros* (1 Tim 5:17, 19; Titus 1:5), and *diakonos* (1 Tim 3:8, 12). Their functions are not clearly specified except for the fact that they are to teach and to exercise authority. They are to be tested—by whom it is not clear (1 Tim 3:10); hands are not to be imposed lightly (1 Tim 5:22). It is implied that there are several *presbuteroi* in a place; it is not clear, however, if there is only one or several *episkopoi* (cf. Phil 1:1, which has several). At one time it would seem that the *presbuteroi* were in charge of the local Church: Paul is described as appointing them in every Church (Acts 14:23) even though the Pastorals indicate that there were Churches without them (Titus 1:5). In the second part of Acts the leading figures in Jerusalem become James and the *presbuteroi* rather than the apostles (21:18; cf. 16:4, where the apostles and *presbuteroi* are an authority). Again, the position of the *presbuteroi* is clearly established in the letter of James, which may date before 70 C.E. (Jas 5:14) and 1 Peter, which may be somewhat earlier (1 Pet 5:1, 5). The use of *presbuteros* by the author of John 2 and 3 is difficult to evaluate; it is hardly parallel to the usage elsewhere in the NT (see 2 John 1; 3 John 1).

Officials are to be chosen with care both for moral probity and doctrinal orthodoxy (1 Tim 3:1-10; Titus 1:5-9). There is no clear reference to their enjoying charisms for their work, unlike Timothy (1 Tim 1:18; 4:18; 1 Tim 1:6-7, 14) and Paul (2 Tim 4:17), who are said to have been gifted in various ways. The picture here contrasts strongly with earlier NT writings, which appear to conflate somewhat charism and office (1 Cor 12:28-30; Rom 12:6-8; Eph 4:11) with apostles, prophets, and teachers or evangelists in the first three positions (except Rom—prophecy, *diakonia,* and teacher). In these lists, as A.M. Meeks observes, "the curious mixture of nouns or participles designating persons and abstract nouns denoting activities draws attention to the functions themselves rather than to the status of those who exercise them."[5] It would also indicate a fluid situation, in which charism and office are not yet very distinct. Detailed explanation of these terms and of the difference between them[6] remains very much at the level of hypothesis.

The style in which ministry is to be exercised is characterized above all by the words indicating service or slavery.[7] *Diakonia* indicated the activity of a slave, especially serving at table; as Jesus took on the form of a slave (see Phil 2:7), *diakonia* was applied to his life and ministry; it became the Christian word for lowly service in love of the neighbor; it was the word associated with various ways of caring for the community. The Gentiles lord it over their subjects, but Jesus warned, "But it is not so among you" (Mark 10:43; cf. Matt 23:11-12); "Whoever wishes to be great among you must be your servant *(diakonos),* and whoever wishes to be first among you must be your slave *(doulos—*Matt 20:26-27). Gifts are given "to equip the saints for the work of ministry, for building up the body of Christ" (Eph 4:12). An important NT theme is that of the ministry of reconciliation (2 Cor 5:18); indeed the central part of 2 Corinthians can be seen as an extended reflection on ministry (2:12–6:13), carried out in weakness (2 Cor 12:7-10).[8]

In the light of clear indications in Ignatius of Antioch (q.v.), and perhaps in the *Didachê* (q.v.), it is important to note that nowhere in the NT do we find any association between the celebration of the Eucharist and any particular ministry; the Last Supper's "Do this in remembrance of me" (1 Cor 11:25; cf. Luke 22:19, not in all MSS) can hardly have been restricted only to the college of apostles. Finally, there is a clear indication that ministers should be sustained financially (1 Tim 5:17-18; cf. Luke 10:7), even though Paul himself made a point of supporting himself (1 Cor 9:6, 18; 2 Cor 11:7). This consideration of NT ministries is important also for the history and theology of apostolicity (v. APOSTOLIC and APOSTOLIC SUCCESSION).

In the first centuries there was a flowering of ministries in the Church. These were gradually to fade and be coalesced into ordained ministry. The causes for the change are multiple: women's ministries gradually disappeared (v. WIDOWS, DEACONESS, VIRGINS); monastic life arose as a possibility for those who wished to be involved deeply in the life of the Church; the ordained priest and bishop were seen as containing all the lesser ministries, so that the latter's autonomy and scope gradually disappeared.[9] There is another, slightly different way of reading the evidence of the early centuries: in the NT period it was difficult to distinguish charism and office; office then predominated; then office became a state of life; finally the gulf between clergy and laity grew, and the ministries were subsumed into the sacrament of orders.[10]

Before Vatican II, "ministry" had a narrow meaning almost exclusively confined to the activity of the ordained. Characteristic of its use for the function of the ordained is the passage in LG 28 which links ministry to apostolic succession: "Christ, whom the Father sanctified and sent into the world, has through his apostles made their successors, the bishops, sharers in his consecration and mission; and these have legitimately handed on the office of their ministry in varying degrees to various subjects in the church. In this way the divinely instituted ecclesiastical ministry is exercised in different orders by those who right from ancient times have been called bishops, priests and deacons." The council continually developed the idea of ministry, and moved from this view of ministry to one which embraced the various functions of the laity. The words "minister" or "ministry" occur about 200 times in its documents. Our immediate interest is in the 19 usages about lay activity.[11]

In the Liturgy Constitution, laity have various ministries in the Church's liturgical life (SC 29, 35, 112, 122). The Decree on Bishops stresses that priests and laity working in the diocesan curia are "assistants in the pastoral ministry of the bishop" (CD 27). The Declaration on Education describes teaching in Catholic schools as ministry and apostolate (GE 8), teaching the faith in non-Catholic schools as ministry (GE 7) but other activities in these schools as apostolic action (GE 7 with n. 23). In the Decree on the Apostolate of the Laity, an evangelization by priests in which the laity share is described as a "ministry of word and sacrament" (AA 6). It is later explained as involving the witness of life and verbal proclamation of Christ both outside and within the Church. The laity's sharing in the works of associations to do with the apostolate is also described as ministry (AA 22). More developed still is the Decree on Missionary Activity: lay catechists have a ministry (AG 15, 17); Catholic Action (v. APOSTOLATE) is a ministry (AG 15); there are ministries of service by non-ordained (AG 16); finally, missionaries are called ministers (AG 23, 24, 26). In all these texts there is an element of ambiguity about the basis of the ministry: in some, at least, ministry is seen as a sharing in the ministry or works of the ordained; in others, it arises from the common priesthood (LG 10). But in its final document the council applied the word "ministry" to ordinary activities of human life: earthly service (GS 38); safeguarding life (GS 51); service of security and liberty by soldiers (GS 79).

Between Vatican II and the *Code,* there were from Paul VI significant developments about ministry, mostly liturgical.[12] In his apostolic letter *Ministeria quaedam* (1972)[13] he abolished tonsure, the minor orders of porter and exorcist, and subdiaconate. He laid down that in place of "minor orders" the word "ministries" was to be used; people were to be "instituted," not "ordained" into these. He decreed that these were no longer merely steps towards priesthood, but that they could be received by laymen. Moreover, bishops conferences may ask for the establishment of other ministries in their area, and the pope gave the examples of porter, exorcist, catechist, and many others. On the same day, he legislated for the diaconate in a *motu proprio*.[14] On the journey to ministerial priesthood it is diaconate that admits to the clerical state. But there is also the possibility of a person entering the permanent diaconate with no intention of proceeding to further orders (v. DEACONS). Pope Paul also allowed the introduction of extraordinary ministers of the Eucharist.[15] The pope saw these not as accidental but as part of a broader understanding of lay ministry in the Church, a theme to which he would return in the apostolic exhortation on evangelization.[16]

On the juridical and organizational level there is a triple category of ministry: ministries recognized by the Church, or *de facto* ministries; ministers instituted by a liturgical act, which at the moment are acolyte and lector; ministries conferred by ordination, viz., deacon, priest, bishop.[17]

Canon law restricts the formal institution of the ministries of acolyte and reader to men only (CIC 230), but other liturgical ministries of the word, including preaching and catechesis can, in the absence of priests, be committed to laity, men or women, by the hierarchy (CIC 230). Ministry of the Word appears again in canon 759, but it is restricted compared with the conciliar position in AA. Canons 910 and 943 allow laity to be extraordinary ministers of the Eucharist. But this can be seen as a sharing in the hierarchical ministry rather than a ministry that arises from baptism and confirmation. It is not clear if the same can be said for canons 1481, 1502, and 1643, which allow laity to serve on tribunals as procurator, advocate, or judge (v. JURISDICTION).

For the *Code,* the word "apostolate" (q.v.) covers all aspects of the Church's mission, and is used where Vatican II often used "ministry." Also to be noted is that the word "service" is only once applied to the laity (CIC 231 § 1); on all other occasions it refers to the hierarchical offices of teaching, governing, and sanctifying, whereas it is used about various levels of activity in the council.[18] Canon law uses three words: "ministry" *(ministerium),* "task" *(munus),* and "office" *(officium).* Though similar, they are not interchangeable.[19] "Ministry," used 70 times, means the act of ministering in 57 instances; 7 times it signifies a work that is under

obligation; other meanings are the liturgical ministries of acolyte, etc. "Task" is used 189 times, usually in the sense of a complexity of duties and rights; *munus* is often translated in English as "office," especially in the titles of Books Three and Four—"The Teaching/ Sanctifying Office in the Church." "Office" is found 270 times: in 70 places it carries a sense of obligation; the principal usage is for a grade or dignity, that is, a specific task which has its obligations and rights (see CIC 145 § 1).

The post-synodal apostolic exhortation, *Christifideles laici* (CL), finally gave a clarity to the issue of ministry by explicitly stating that some ministries come from the sacrament of orders, while others find their foundation in the sacraments of baptism and confirmation and have a specific lay character. The exhortation also uses together the terms "ministries, offices, and roles," which seems to indicate an evolving situation for the study of which a new commission was to be established.(CL 21–23). There are two tendencies in the theologians and canonists: one is to extend the use of the word "ministry"; the other is to somewhat restrict its usage. Some of those holding the latter view would agree with Cardinal Rossi that "a certain corruption of the adjective ministerial was reached up to the point of including every responsibility assumed by the laity."[20]

There are some who will tend to confine the word "ministry" to activities publicly acknowledged in the Church, for instance, by liturgical deputation. Thus T.F. O'Meara gives six characteristics: "Ministry is: (1) doing something; (2) for the advent of the kingdom; (3) in public; (4) on behalf of a Christian community; (5) which is a gift received in faith, baptism, and ordination; and (6) which is an activity with its own limits and identity within a diversity of ministerial action."[21] But though such determinants do indeed specify ministry, one could argue that there is a ministry involved when somebody with a charism for helping the bereaved quietly uses this gift in a parish or neighborhood. Though it is probably wise not to overuse the term "ministry," it can be argued that in a wide sense what specifies ministry in the Church is the bestowal of charism by the Spirit and its regular use by the recipient. One can agree with G.H. Tavard that four functions of ministry have a special importance: mediation, proclamation, service, and education.[22]

In the past decades, four levels of ministry emerged: that of the baptized, who exercise a general, unspecified ministry; that of volunteers, who make a specific commitment to the exercise of ecclesial ministry; that of professionals, whose commitment is still more specific and of lasting duration; that of those "installed" in ministry, for whom the community itself makes a type of commitment.[23]

It is important also to distinguish mission and ministry: mission belongs to the nature of the Church (AG 2) and is primarily *ad extra* or outward; ministry is *ad intra,* inward in building up the communion of the Church. The pastoral options about ministry adopted in a particular Church will betray an ecclesiology.[24] The implicit theology of CL is predominantly a communion one (q.v.).

In the whole area of ministry there is a need to avoid the clericalization of the laity. One may instinctively sense clericalization, though it is hard to define. The most obvious danger arises when a ministry is seen to be done on behalf of the clergy or delegated by a priest, or at times in place of one. The rooting of ministry firmly in baptism and confirmation is the best protection against the omnipresent danger of clericalism, to be found as much among the laity as in the clergy.

One can sense that despite the major advances since Vatican II, we are still at the beginning of a new theology and pastorale of ministry. The theology of lay ministry will not be clarified unless the theology of ministerial priesthood is deepened; yet the ongoing work on lay ministry is perhaps the best contribution to a deepened understanding of ministerial priesthood. Both must proceed simultaneously.[25] And with a theology of ministry there is need also for a spirituality of ministries in the Church.[26]

---

[1]P. Bernier, *Ministry in the Church: A Historical and Pastoral Approach* (Mystic, Conn.: Twenty-third Publications, 1992); M. Collins, "The Public Language of Ministry," Jurist 41 (1981) 261–294; B. Cooke, *Ministry to Word and Sacrament: History and Theology* (Philadelphia: Fortress, 1975)—cf. TS 38 (1977) 547–554 (E.J. Kilmartin); M.G. Lawler, *A Theology of Ministry* (Kansas City, Mo.: Sheed & Ward, 1990); M.V. Leroy, "Le ministère et les ministères dans l'Église," RThom 75 (1975) 625–654; L. Sartori, ed., *I ministeri ecclesiali oggi* (Rome: Borla, 1977); G.H. Tavard, *A Theology of Ministry.* Theology and Life 6 (Wilmington: Glazier, 1983); L.B. Terrien, "Theology of Ministry: A Review of Recent Literature," LouvSt 9 (1982–1983) 154–175; Conc 133 (1980); Jurist 41 (1981). [2]Conc 4/8 (1972); J.T. Forestell, *As Ministers of Christ: The Christological Dimension of Ministry in the New Testament* (New York-Mahwah: Paulist, 1991); K. Giles, *Patterns of Ministry Among the First Christians* (Melbourne: Collins Dove, 1989); J. Murphy-O'Connor, "Christ and Ministry," Pacifica 4 (1991) 121–136; J.F. O'Grady, *Disciples and Leaders: The Origins of Christian Ministry in the New Testament* (New York-Mahwah: Paulist, 1991); E. Nardoni, "Ministries in the New Testament," StCan 11 (1977) 5–36; J. Onaiyekan, "Ministries in the Acts of the Apostles," RAfrT 13/25 (1990) 41–57; R. Schnackenburg, *The Church in the New Testament* (London: Burns & Oates, 1974) 22–35; J.M.R. Tillard, "The Apostolic Foundations of Christian Ministry," Worship 63 (1989) 290–300 = OneChr 25 (1989) 14–22. [3]R.E. Brown, *The Churches the Apostles Left Behind* (New York: Paulist, 1984) 33; J.N. Collins, *Diakonia: Reinterpreting the Ancient Sources* (New York: Oxford UP, 1990); W.A. Meeks, *The First Urban Christians: The Social World of the Apostle Paul* (New Haven: Yale, 1983) 79–80. [4]*The Church with a Human Face: A New and Expanded Theology of Ministry* (London: SCM, 1985) 99–103; idem, "The Changing Meaning of Ministry: The Social Context of Historical Shifts in the Church," CrossC 33 (1983–1984) 432–454; 34 (1984–1985) 65–82. [5]Op. cit. (n. 3) 135. [6]E.g., H. Küng, *The Church* (London: Search, 1968) 394–402. [7]H.W. Beyer, "Diakoneô etc." TDNT 2:81-93; K.H. Rengstorf, "Doulos etc." TDNT 2:261-280; J. N. Collins, "Once More on Ministry: Forcing a Turnover in the Linguistic Field," OneChr 27 (1991) 234–245; L. Swain, "Service and Ministry in the New Testament," CleR 55 (1970) 342–350. [8]M. Neumann, "Ministry, Weakness and Spirit in II Corinthians," CleR 59 (1974) 647–660. [9]A. Cunningham, "Church People as Missionary: A Ministerial Church," Jurist 39 (1979) 152–182 at 163–167. [10]P.F. Bradshaw, "Modèles de ministère: le rôle des laïcs dans la liturgie," MaisD 154 (1983) 127–150; cf. A. Brent, "Pseudonymity and Charisma in the Ministry of the Early Church," AugR 27 (1987) 347–376; J.T. Lienhard, *Ministry.* MessF 8 (Wilmington: Glazier, 1984). [11]E. Rinere, "Conciliar and Canonical Applications of 'Ministry' to the Laity," Jurist 47 (1987) 204–227. [12]D.N. Power, *Gifts that Differ: Lay Ministries Established and Unestablished.* Studies in the Reformed Rites of the Catholic Church 8 (New York: Pueblo, 1980). [13]AAS 64 (1972) 529–534/Eng. trans. *The Rites of the Catholic Church.* 2 vols. (Collegeville: The Liturgical Press, study edition, 1988–1991) 2:6-11. [14]*Ad pascendum* AAS 64 (1972) 534–540/*The Rites* (n. 13) 2:31-38. Cf. *Sacrum diaconatus ordinem* on the restoration of the permanent diaconate, AAS 59 (1967) 657–697. [15]S. Cong. Divine Worship, Instruction, *Immensae caritatis*—AAS 65 (1973) 264–271. [16]*Evangelii nuntiandi* (1975)—Flannery 2:711-761, esp. n. 73. [17]G. dalla Torre, "La collaborazione dei laici alle funzioni sacerdotale, profetica e regale dei ministri sacri," MonEccl 109 (1984) 140–165 at 152, n. 25. [18]Rinere (n. 11) 225–226; J.H. Provost, "Ministry: Reflections on Some Canonical Issues," HeythJ 29 (1988) 285–299. [19]P. Erdö, "Ministerium, munus et officium in Codice iuris canonici," Periodica 78 (1989) 411–436. [20]"La figura del laico nel Concilio Vaticano II," MonEccl 107 (1982) 476–490 at 481. [21]"Ministry," NDictTheol 659–660; cf. idem, *Theology of Ministry* (New York-Ramsey: Paulist, 1983). [22]Op. cit. (n. 1). [23]Cunningham (n. 9) 167, following B. Griffin. See P. Jounel, "Les ministères non-ordonnés dans l'Église," MaisD 149 (1982) 91–109; J.A. Komonchak, "'Non-ordained' and 'Ordained' Ministries in the Local Church," Conc 133 (1980) 44–50. [24]J.J. Shea, "Notes Toward a Theology of Ministry," ChicSt 17 (1978) 317–330; R. McBrien, "Church and Ministry: The Achievement of Yves Congar," TDig 32 (1985) 203–211. [25]W.J. Rademacher, *Lay Ministry: A Theological, Spiritual and Pastoral Handbook* (Slough UK: St. Paul, 1991); J.E. Linnan, "Ministry since Vatican II: A Time of Change and Growth," NewTR 3/1 (1990) 33–45. [26]C. Clarke, "A Spirituality of Ministerial Action," ChicSt 29 (1990) 153–164; P. Scabini, "Ministeri 'laicali.' Aspetti teologico-pastorali e spirituali," Iater 53 (1987) 256–267.

## MISSION

Though some writers following M. Hengel speak of Christ as the original or founding missionary *(Urmissionar),* and most see mission as rooted in the incarnation and in the Trinitarian missions (AG 2–4),[1] the use of the word "mission" to designate the proclamation of the faith is not ancient; it would seem to have first appeared in a letter of the second Jesuit general J. Laynez (1558).[2]

The changing vocabulary about what was once called "missions" is indicative of profound changes of understanding, and more probably also of an interim situation in the Church:[3] now missions have become "young Churches"; missions have become the singular "mission," often replaced with the word "evangelization" (q.v.); the notion of "development" (q.v.) has given way to "liberation" (q.v.); "adaptation" has ceded to "indigenization/acculturation/contextualization" and finally to "inculturation" (q.v.).[4]

But the modern shift is just one of many that have occurred since NT times.[5] An important but ambiguous feature about missions since the late 15th century has been the association of colonization with the spread of the gospel in many parts of the world; even in earlier centuries mission activity had been aligned with secular powers. The alliance had indeed many negative features; it was not without positive elements, too, especially in the area of education and health care. This early worldwide missionary expansion was often undergirded by an inadequate theology, especially about how salvation is related to actual membership of the Church (v. OUTSIDE THE CHURCH).

Missiology, or theology of missions, became a distinctive discipline in the late 19th century. The first Protestant chair of missiology was held by G. Warneck (1896); the first Catholic chair was at Münster (1914), occupied by J. Schmidlin, who may be considered the founder of Catholic missiology, though a missiological journal had begun a few years earlier.[6] In the period between the 20th-century world wars, the notion of "planting the Church" was espoused by, among others, P. Charles. It lay behind a great missionary élan represented by five major encyclicals (1919–1959).[7] Meanwhile, during World War II the term "mission" was also being applied to established Churches, to their chagrin.[8] But the idea of mission was often so widened that there was a risk of its losing any very specific meaning.

At Vatican II there was much talk about mission, a topic which features in many of the promulgated texts.[9] An early schema on the missions was criticized and then reduced to a few summary points. Despite the fact that Paul VI personally recommended their adoption in the *aula* on 6 November 1964, this draft was decisively rejected by missionary bishops, notably the Irish Carmelite Donal Lamont from Rhodesia (Zimbabwe). A new decree emerged, largely the work of the Divine Word General J. Schütte; it was discussed from 7 to 12 October 1965 and approved 7 December as *Ad gentes* (AG).[10]

The *Decree on the Missionary Activity of the Church* consists of six chapters: Doctrinal Principles, Missionary Work, Particular Churches, Missionaries, The Organization of Missionary Activity, and Cooperation. The first is extremely rich and dense: AG 2–4, paralleled with LG 2–4 in giving the Trinitarian missions as the grounds for ecclesial mission; it is also an extended commentary on LG 17; it gives the basis for mission in both Scripture[11] and in tradition. The fifth article takes up the controverted question of the nature of mission. "The mission of the Church, therefore, is fulfilled through an activity by which, obedient to the command of Christ and moved by the grace and charity of the Holy Spirit, it makes itself fully present to all people and nations, so that by the example of its life and by preaching, by the sacraments and other means of grace, it may lead them to the faith, to the freedom and peace of Christ. Its goal is to open to them a free and reliable way to full sharing in the mystery of Christ" (AG 5). Mission is characterized more by peoples than by places. But the Decree does recognize certain places designated by the Holy See, in which "the true goal . . . is evangelization and the establishing of the Church among peoples and groups where it has not taken root" (AG 6). The document tends to speak of the "mission" of the whole Church and of "missions and missionary activity" for work among those who are not Christian.

Before dealing with missionary work (ch. 2), two articles (AG 11–12) were added at a late stage, which speak of the witness of life, dialogue, and presence in love as a preamble to mission more properly called "catechumenal"; these were at the request of the bishops of North Africa who, working among Moslems, had few catechumens. Far from adopting the vision of the 1917 *Code of Canon Law* in which missions were the responsibility of the Holy See (can. 1350 § 2), the Decree spelled out the fact that mission is the responsibility of the whole Church (AG 6), that mission arose from the very nature of the Church (*intime ex ipsa natura ecclesiae profluere*—AG 6), and that the whole college of bishops had a responsibility for the Church's mission (AG 6; cf. LG 22–23).

The other chapters, except perhaps for the passage on particular Churches (AG 19–22), were of immediate concern mostly at the time of the council; events would soon sharpen the relevance of some passages; others decreased in immediacy. The events which led to newer approaches were numerous: decolonization; development (q.v.); the call for justice sounded at the 1971 Synod of Bishops;[12] liberation especially at Medellín (1968) and Puebla (1979—v. LIBERATION THEOLOGIES); the hugely influential apostolic exhortation of Paul VI on evangelization (EN),[13] the tension between what is religious and what is secular;[14] the decline of religious and clerical vocations with a concomitant development of lay missionaries.[15] Even though missionaries from early modern times brought education, health, and social care along with their proclamation of the gospel, there emerged a new sense in which the Church had to be concerned with human development, understood especially as the liberation of those oppressed by injustice. Hence grass-roots, basic Christian communities (q.v.) in places became more significant than the missionary from abroad, because they arose from the people's own experience and they were led by their own pastoral agents. Though Vatican II spoke of adaptation, it was now realized that a deeper insertion was needed, now called "inculturation," a neologism dating from about 1959,[16] but only becoming predominant in the 1980s. Indeed as early as 1659 missionaries were warned by Rome not to transport Spain, Italy, or France to the Far East.[17] Catholic missionaries always tried to learn the languages of the place and the customs of the peoples; but the attempt was often superficial, and not always with a positive approach that would enable hidden values to be detected. The full implications of a Vatican II statement was being grasped only in the 1980s: "The results of its [the Church's missionary] activity is that the good seed that is found in people's hearts and minds, or in their particular rites and cultures, is not only saved from destruction but is made whole, raised up and brought to completion to the glory of God, the confusion of the devil and the happiness of humanity" (LG 17; see EN 20).[18]

The insight of AG about the missionary character of the Church became more explicit in subsequent documents: "Evangelization is the special grace and vocation of the Church. . . . Evangelization is inherent in the very nature of the Church" (EN 14–15); and in John Paul II's mission encyclical, "The mission *Ad gentes* is incumbent on the entire People of God."[19] An innovation of the 1983 *Code of Canon Law* was a new title, "Missionary Activity of the Church," which drew on these documents, insisting on the missionary responsibility of the whole Church (CIC 781–792).[20]

In the post-Vatican II Church, critical objections arose about mission.[21] They can be resumed in a few questions: Cannot people be saved without the Christian message? Should we impose a Christian identity on people who have their own rich cultures? Are we not imposing our religion unnecessarily on others? Some of these issues are treated elsewhere (v. NON-CHRISTIAN RELIGIONS); some belong to the rather recent theological discipline of missiology.[22] Ultimately the justification of mission is the command of Christ (Matt 20:18-20; Acts 1:8) and the divine will that all should have fullness of life in him (see John 10:10).

The pluralism evident in very many areas of Church life is also to be found in its mission[23] and in the theology of mission.[24] It would seem helpful not to identify ministry and mission: the latter pertains to the essence of the Church, the former is one of the Church's activities, though indispensable for mission.[25] Evangelization, too, is wider than mission, though constituent of it.[26]

Each area has its own story of mission and its own contemporary concerns:[27] Africa, marked especially with problems of inculturation, is not one entity, however, but a multiplicity of cultures;[28] Asia is in three-fold dialogue with cultures, religions, and the poor;[29] Latin America is developing liberation theologies (q.v.); Oceania is linked both with Asian concerns and with liberation.

When we come to read the missionary encyclical of John Paul II (RM),[30] we have to see how these issues raised in modern missiology are addressed. It is throughout an endorsement of the continued validity of missionary activity, which is a matter for the whole Church. It focuses on Christ the Redeemer and on salvation (RM 4–11). But following many modern writers, its primary emphasis is not so much on the Church as on the kingdom (RM 12–19) which the Church serves (RM 20). It markedly develops AG 4 in a chapter on "The Holy Spirit, the Principal Agent of Mission" (RM 21–30).[31] The encyclical reiterates the value and place of the mission *ad gentes* (RM 31–40), even while it distinguishes it from mature Christian communities needing pastoral care, and from communities that have lost a living sense of the faith and need "new evangelization" or "re-evangelization" (RM 33). Witnessing, evangelization, inculturation, the formation of local Churches, dialogue, and charity are the paths of mission (ch. 5—RM 41–60). The pope stresses dialogue (RM 55–57—q.v.) as part of the Church's evangelizing mission (RM 55), but is not a tactic (RM 56) nor a substitute for the mission *ad gentes*: "These two elements must maintain both their intimate connection and their distinctiveness; therefore they should not be confused, manipulated or regarded as identical, as though they were interchangeable" (RM 55).[32] The agents of mission are then treated (ch. 6): they are those of AG 23–27 and EN 59–73, but there is a very strong emphasis on the laity, who are missionaries by baptism (RM 71–73). A chapter about cooperation follows, for the whole Church must be involved in missionary activity (RM 77–86). A very significant chapter, "Missionary Spirituality," concludes the encyclical (RM 87–91);[33] with the secularization of much former missionary activity, this chapter can give a new focus and impetus, especially to those most directly in missionary activity. The most important evaluation of the encyclical will depend mostly on active missionaries who with their people will receive it or not (v. RECEPTION). However, it is also addressed to the whole Church *ad intra* and *ad extra* for its reception. This encyclical is certainly written with greater clarity than others; it carries forward the teaching of Vatican II and Paul VI; it is a strong affirmation of, and a clear teaching on, the relevance of the Church's mission and missions in our time; however, despite avowals to the contrary, it appears somewhat fearful of, or diffident about, inculturation (RM 52),[34] which is surely one of the most important problems facing mission today, one pertinent for every single country of the world.

In the past the Churches of the East have not been perceived in the West as being very concerned with mission outside the Greek and Slav cultures. This judgment is not altogether fair, and there is, moreover, increasingly significant Orthodox missionary reflection.[35]

In ecumenical discussions the term often preferred by Protestants is "evangelism,"[36] though "mission" is becoming more frequent. It must be remembered that the modern ecumenical movement grew out of the scandal of divisions in missionary countries (Edinburgh Conference, 1910—v. ECUMENICAL MOVEMENT). Especially since the International Missionary Conference became part of it in 1961, the World Council of Churches has been determinedly supportive of mission or evangelism,[37] with the Melbourne conference on mission and evangelism (1980) being quite important.[38] The WCC has cooperated with the Catholic Church both in condemning proselytizing (q.v.) in common study and documents.[39] It would seem appropriate that future Catholic documents on ecumenism should speak more about mission, and documents on mission should deal more explicitly with ecumenism[40] and interfaith relations.

[1]J. Mitterhöfer, "Der Missionsbegriff: Werden und Wandel," ThJb 1987: 422-436, citing M. Hengel, "Die Ursprünge der christlichen Mission," NTS 18 (1971–1972) 15–38; T. Kramm, "Das Heil der Welt. Überlegungen zum Ausgangspunkt einer Theologie der Mission," ZMissRW 62 (1978) 161–168. [2]M. Kratz, "Changes in the Understanding of Mission," TDig 34 (1987) 9–14 at 9. [3]See annual Bibliografia missionaria (Rome: Urbaniana UP); IntRMiss; Evangelisation and Mission: Évangélisation et Mission. International Bibliography 1975–1982. RIC Supplément 74–77 (Strasbourg: Cerdic 1982); A.F. Walls, "A Bibliography on Mission Studies," InterRMiss 81 (1992) 139–167, 329–353, 495–518, 623–649. [4]P. Tihon, "Des missions à la mission," NRT 107 (1985) 520–536, 698–721; P. Flanagan, ed., A New Missionary Era (Maryknoll: Orbis, 1982). [5] D.J. Bosch, Transforming Mission: Paradigm Shifts in Theology of Mission. American Society of Missiology 16 (Maryknoll: Orbis, 1990); A. Glasser and D. McGavran, Contemporary Theologies of Mission (Grand Rapids, Mich.: Eerdmans 1983); for earlier views see A. Shorter, Theology of Mission. Theology Today 37 (Cork: Mercier, 1972); K.S. Latourette, A History of the Expansion of Christianity. 7 vols. (New York, 1937–1945); J. López-Gay, Storia delle missioni (Rome: Gregorian UP, 1987). [6]Zeitschrift für Missionswissenschaft (1911). [7]Pius XI, Rerum Ecclesiae AAS 18 (1926) 65–83/Carlen 3:281-291; Pius XII, Evangelii praecones—AAS 43 (1951) 497–528/Carlen 4:189-202 and Fidei donum—AAS 49 (1957) 225–248/Carlen 4:321-332; John XXIII, Princeps pastorum—AAS 51 (1959) 833–864/Carlen 5:39-42. See T. Burke, ed., Four Great Missionary Encyclicals (New York, 1957). Benedict XV, Apost. Lit. Maximum illud—AAS 11 (1919) 440–445. [8]H. Godin, with Y. Daniel, La France pays de mission?, Rencontres 12 (Paris: Cerf, 1943)—Eng. trans. in M. Ward, France Pagan? The Mission of Abbé Godin (London, 1949) 65–191; G. Michonneau, Paroisse, communauté missionnaire. Rencontres 21–22 (Paris: Cerf, 1945). [9]J. Ratzinger, "La mission d'après les autres textes conciliaires," in J. Schütte, ed.,

L'activité missionnaire de l'Église: Décret "Ad gentes." US 67 (Paris: Cerf, 1967) 121–147. [10]W. Henkel, "Bibliografia sul Decreto De activitate missionali ecclesiae: 'Ad gentes' (1975–1985)," EuntDoc 39 (1986) 263–274. [11]S. di Giorgi, "La vocazione missionaria nel Nuovo Testamento," EuntDoc 30 (1977) 165–190; G. Ghiberti, "Il problema biblico della missione," RivBib 36 (1988) 259–265 (a survey); A.J. Gittens, "Call and Response: Missionary Considerations," LouvSt 10 (1984–1985) 264–285; K. Kertlege, Mission im neuen Testament. QDisput. 93 (Freiburg-Basel-Vienna: Herder, 1982); J. Matthey, "La mission de l'église au temps des apôtres et au temps de Luc," LumièreV 30/153–154 (1981) 61–71; D. Senior and C. Stuhlmueller, The Biblical Foundations for Mission (Maryknoll: Orbis, 1983, 1989); P. Sessolo, "Strategia e metodo nell'opera missionaria di san Paolo," EuntDoc 35 (1982) 225–232. [12]Flannery 2:695-710; J.A. Coleman, "The Mission of the Church and Action on Behalf of Justice," Jurist 39 (1979) 119–151. [13]Evangelii nuntiandi—AAS 68 (1976) 1–96/Flannery 2:711-761; see A.H. Anderson and T.F. Stransky, eds., Evangelization. Mission Trends 2 (New York: Paulist—Grand Rapids Mich.: Eerdmans, 1975); D. Bohr, "Evangelization: The Essential and Primary Mission of the Church," Jurist 39 (1979) 40–87. [14]R. Haight, "The 'Established' Church as Mission: The Relation of the Church to the Modern World," Jurist 39 (1979) 4–39; F. Noriega, "Misión religiosa de la Iglesia y realización del orden temporal según documentos del Concilio Vaticano II," EfMex 2/6 (1984) 114–139. [15]Doohan, Laity 77–82; F. Santovito, "Il laicato nella chiesa missionaria: Prospettiva ecumenica," Nicol 13 (1986) 141–152. [16]B. Chenu, "Glissements progressifs d'un agir missionaire," LumVit 33 (1984) 69. [17]Cong. Propaganda Fidei Instruction, cited J. Masson, "La mission à la lumière de l'Incarnation," NRT 98 (1976) 865–887 at 880, n. 24. [18]Tihon (n. 4) 712–717; R.C. Neville, "Missions on an Ecumenical Globe," JDhara 13 (1983) 335–342. [19]Redemptoris missio—AAS 83 (1991) 249–340/CathIntern 2 (1991) 252–292—art. 71; see art. 77. See R.D. Haight, "Mission: The Symbol for Understanding the Church Today," TS 37 (1976) 620–649 with response R.T. Sears 649–651. [20]J.A. Coriden, in Coriden, CIC 559–564 with bibliog. 588; A. Reuter, "The Missions in the New Code of Canon Law," Bibliog MissSupp 46 (1982) 361–370; idem, "The Missionary Activity of the Church (Canons 781–792)," StCan 23 (1989) 387–407; E. Saste Santos, "Perspectivas de derecho misionero después de Código de 1983," EuntDoc 36 (1983) 295–310; I. Ting Pong Lee, "De actione Ecclesiae missionali in Novo Codice iuris canonici," ComRelM 64 (1983) 97–106. [21]J. Neuner, "Why Missions?," IndTS 17 (1980) 15–33; J. López-Gay, "Ecclesiology in the Missiological Thinking of the Post-Conciliar Years," BibliogMissSupp 46 (1982) 370–381. [22]A. Seumois, "Organizzazione della missiologia secondo le nuove prospettive della sistematizzazione teologica," EuntDoc 36 (1983) 3–18. [23]M. Amaladoss, Making All Things New: Dialogue, Pluralism and Evangelization in Asia (Maryknoll: Orbis, 1990); J.P. Brennan, Christian Mission in a Pluralistic World (Slough UK: St. Paul, 1990). [24]W. Jenkinson and H. O'Sullivan eds., Trends in Mission: Towards the Third Millennium. Essays in Celebration of Twenty-Five Years of SEDOS (Maryknoll: Orbis, 1991); K. Müller, Mission Theology: An Introduction. Studia Instituti Missiologici SVD 39 (Netteral Germany: Steyler, 1987); A. Seumois, Théologie missionaire. 4 vols. (Rome: Urbaniana UP, 1980–1983). [25]A. Cunningham, "Church People as Missionary: A Missionary Church," Jurist 39 (1979) 152–182. [26]See Haight (n. 14) 12 with n. 20. [27]See Jedin-Dolan, vol. 10 for each country. [28]R. Hickey, ed., Modern Missionary Documents and Africa (Dublin: Dominican, 1982); A. Hastings, African Christianity: An Essay in Interpretation (London: Chapman, 1976); A.N. Mushete, La teologia africana in cammino (Bologna: EDB, 1988); E.S. Utuk, "An Analysis of John Mbiti's Missiology," AfTJ 15 (1986) 3–15. [29]M. Amaladoss, "The

Challenges of Mission Today," in Jenkinson and O'Sullivan (n. 24) 359–397 esp. developing Asian Bishops' Conferences, "Evangelization in Modern Day Asia" no. 12, in *For All the Peoples of Asia* (Manila: IMC, 1984) 29. [30]N. 19; see index by F.J. Urrutia, Periodica 80 (1991) 641–659; D. Colombo, "Fundamenti teologici e identità della *missio ad gentes* nella *Redemtio missio*," EuntDoc 44 (1991) 203–223; P. Tihon, "Retour aux missions? Une lecture de l'encyclique 'Redemptoris missio'," NRT 114 (1992) 69–86; H. Waldenfels, "Zur Ekklesiologie der Enzyklika 'Redemptoris missio,'" ZMissRW 75 (1991) 176–190. [31]J. López Gay, *Lo Spirito Santo e la missione*. Notes for Students (Rome: Gregorian UP, 1989)—excellent bibliog. [32]J. Saraiva Martins, "Missione e dialogo," EuntDoc 38 (1985) 37–59. [33]T. Clements, *Missionary Spirituality: For the Praise of his Glory*. Living Flame 31 (Dublin: Carmelite Center for Spirituality, 1987); J. Esquerda Bifet, "Cooperazione e spiritualità missionaria nella Redemptoris missio," EuntDoc 44 (1991) 287–299; H. Hegkeren, "Spirituality for Mission on Six Continents: Signs of the Spirit Today," InterRMiss 70 (1981) 267–275. [34]But see encyc. on Cyril and Methodius, *Slavorum apostoli*—AAS (1985) 779–813. [35]Bishop Anastasios, "Remembering Some Basic Facts in Today's Mission," InterRMiss 77 (1988) 4–11; I. Bria, ed., *Martyria/Mission: The Witness of the Orthodox Churches Today* (Geneva: WCC, 1980); I. Bria, ed., *Go Forth in Peace: Orthodox Perspectives on Mission*. WCC Mission Series (Geneva: WCC, 1986); J. Meyendorff, "An Orthodox View on Mission and Integration," InterRMiss 70 (1981) 256–258; J.J. Stamoulis, "The Imperative of Mission in Orthodox Theology," GkOrTR 33 (1988) 63–80; A. Veronis, "Orthodox Concepts of Evangelism and Mission," GkOrTR 27 (1982) 44–57. [36]E. Castro, "Evangelism," DictEcumMov 396–400; S. Sykes, "An Anglican Theology of Evangelism," Theology 94 (1991) 405–414. [37]*Mission and Evangelism: An Ecumenical Affirmation* (Geneva: WCC, 1982); R.C. Bassham, *Mission Theology 1948–1975: Years of Worldwide Creative Tension—Ecumenical, Evangelical and Roman Catholic* (Pasadena, Cal.: William Carey Library, 1979); E. Castro, *Freedom in Mission: The Perspective of the Kingdom of God: An Ecumenical Enquiry* (Geneva: WCC, 1985). [38]*Your Kingdom Come: Mission Perspectives*. Report on World Conference on Mission and Evangelism Melbourne, 12–25 May 1980 (Geneva: WCC, 1980). [39]Joint Working Group, *Common Witness* (Geneva: WCC, 1982). [40]*Report of the Evangelical-Roman Catholic Dialogue on Mission, 1977–1984* (Pontifical Commission for the Promotion of the Unity of Christians *Information Service* 60 [1986] 71–97—Exeter UK: Paternoster Press—Grand Rapids, Mich.: Eerdmans, 1986); K. Bridston, "The Future of Mission as Ecumenical Activity," GkOrTR 16 (1981) 325–331; L. Newbigen, "The Missionary Dimension of the Ecumenical Movement," InterRMiss 70 (1981) 240–246.

## MODELS

In a very influential book, A. Dulles (q.v.) proposed models of the Church which would both explain and explore something of the meaning of the mystery of the Church. Models serve to synthesize and to lead to new insights.[1] Dulles states that when an image (q.v.) "is employed reflectively and critically to deepen one's theoretical understanding of a reality, it becomes what is today called a 'model.'"[2]

A model rises to the status of a paradigm when it has proved successful in solving a great variety of problems and is expected to be an appropriate tool for unravelling anomalies as yet unsolved. The paradigm of the perfect society (q.v.) has given way to a variety of others, which has naturally led to polarization and mutual incomprehension in the Church.[3]

Dulles presented five models of the Church: institution—as a structure continuing the ministry of Christ not in a mere sociological sense; mystical communion—incorporating Body of Christ (q.v.) and People of God (q.v.); sacrament—as visible and effective sign of saving grace; herald—proclaiming the message of the kingdom and challenging a response; servant—as alert to the needs of the world. Though he stated that each model was limited and needed to be complemented by others, he showed in the first edition of the book a preference for the sacramental model, even hinting at the possibility of using that model as the basis for a systematic ecclesiology (q.v.).[4] In the second edition he proposed a new model, the community of disciples engaged in worship and mission.[5]

The notion of model was taken up and applied to other areas of theology,[6] and other models have been proposed for ecclesiology. V. Codina studied the preconciliar notion of the kingdom of God on earth or perfect society; Vatican II communion and sacrament; Medellín-Puebla Church of the poor and the historical sacrament of liberation;[7] G. Segalla sees seven NT models in four categories. First he describes two models of polarity—the house/temple of God pointing to God's presence in the Church, and heavenly Jerusalem/mother indicating its divine origin and eschatological end. Second, he gives three models of belonging—the Church belongs to Christ as spouse, people, and body. Third, he delineates a multiple model of agricultural images—vine, olive, and field indicate God's care for the Church and the need for bearing fruit or fidelity. Fourth, he portrays the pastoral model indicating the continuance of the mission of Jesus—he is chief shepherd who commits the flock to the care of others, such as apostles who must seek out the lost. In all of these models there is an emphasis on unity expressed in differing cultural and religious experiences of the Christian community.[8] T.F. O'Meara shows five distinct philosophical frameworks or models to be operative in ecclesiologies today: Neo-Platonic, Aristotelian, nominalist, idealist, phenomenological-historical.[9]

It could be argued that their tendency to remain at the level of phenomenology militates against models being an ultimate basis for a systematic account of ecclesiology. Dulles' own later exposition of the community of disciples might be said to have passed somewhat beyond model towards being just such a basis.

[1]A. Dulles, *Models of the Church: A Critical Assessment of the Church in All its Aspects* (Dublin: Gill and Macmillan, [1]1974, [2]1987) 24–25. [2]Ibid., 23. [3]Ibid., 29, 32. [4]Ibid., 197–199, 206. [5]Ibid., 207–226. [6]E.g., A. Dulles, *Models of Revelation* (Garden City, N.Y.: Doubleday—Dublin: Gill and Macmillan, 1983); S.

McFague, *Models of God: Theology for an Ecological, Nuclear Age* (Philadelphia: Fortress, 1987); J.F. O'Grady, *Models of Jesus* (New York: Doubleday, 1981).    [7]"Tres modelos de eclesiología," EstE 58 (1983) 55–88.    [8]"L'unità della Chiesa e la varietà dei suoi modelli nel Nuovo Testamento," in Commission Biblique Pontificale, *Unité et diversité dans l'Église* (Vatican, 1989) 297–311. [9]"Philosophical Models in Ecclesiology," TS 39 (1978) 3–21.

## MODERNISM

Modernism was a crisis in the Catholic Church at the beginning of the 20th century. There is extensive contemporary writing, with some revisionism.[1] The roots of modernism lay in the previous century, when there was a general diffuse movement in the Church seeking reform and adaptation to modern conditions. From the mid–1890s to the death of Pius X (q.v.), one can detect three major groupings. There was an intransigent, mainly neo-scholastic, group on the right, which refused any adaptation or change. There was a left-of-center group, which recognized the need for change and adaptation, but which refused to accept all the novelties, some of which it judged as good, some bad. A third group was the extreme left, which in the name of science, reason, and modernity was prepared to jettison Church tradition and magisterium. Only this third group were true modernists, though the conservative right often stigmatized as modernist those who belonged to the second, centrist group, like M.J. Lagrange (1855–1938), M. Blondel (1861–1949), L. Duchesne (1843–1922).

There were three main centers of modernism. In France[2] the main protagonist was A. Loisy (1857–1940)[3] who, in reply to the liberal Protestant A. Harnack (1851–1940), used critical method to reformulate the study of Christian origins in a small work on the gospel and the Church[4] which was followed by other works, especially his commentary on the Synoptic Gospels (1907–1908). Though critical scholarship was indeed necessary, many otherwise sympathetic readers would not agree with his radical autonomy from ecclesiastical teaching and his attack on the basic concept of orthodoxy. He was later to lose both his Christian and theistic faith. Other major French figures included: L. Laberthonnière (1860–1932)[5] whose "moral dogmatism," or perhaps better—"affirmation," was in direct opposition to what he perceived as Thomistic intellectualism; É. LeRoy (1870–1954)[6] stressed the intuitive rather than intellectual element in dogma, which negatively only prevented error, and positively led to proper religious attitudes.

In Italy[7] modernism took on a particular visage which was more populist than in France: some attempted to bring ecclesiastical studies up to date, while seeking to remain within the Church, though some, like its leader E. Buonaiuti (1881–1946), were later excommunicated; others, more extreme, sought to lay the foundations of true Christian democracy, e.g., R. Murri (1870–1944), who appealed for a return to the ideals of the gospel but came into conflict with the hierarchy when he moved into the area of philosophical and theological modernism; a third group, opposed to the excesses of the second, sought to reconcile the Church with the modern world, e.g., A. Fogazzaro (1842–1911).

In England, where Catholicism was the faith of a minority, and intellectual life was not well established, there were two chief figures with modernist views. G. Tyrrell (1861–1909),[8] at first a devotional writer, stressed the non-intellectual and experiential aspects of religion, and later moved into increasingly sharp denunciation of scholastic positions on revelation and theology. The other key English figure was Baron F. von Hügel (1852–1925).[9] His cosmopolitan outlook and contacts, his wide European culture, his learning in biblical scholarship and theology, and his sensitivity meant that he not only grasped the crucial positive points the modernists were making, but he was able to stand back, refusing the ultimate step so many of his friends and admirers felt compelled to take outside the limits of orthodoxy. For many modernists he was an inspiration, friend, and perceptive critic.

Contemporaneously in England, there was an Anglican modernism, with its origins in Latitudinarian and Broad Church positions (v. ANGLICAN COMMUNION). It shared some views with Liberal Protestantism (q.v.) and had four main focuses: The Modern Churchman's Union (from 1898); the journal *The Modern Churchman* (from 1911); the Modern Churchman conferences (from 1914), and the seminary at Ripon Hall (from 1897, moving to Oxford 1919). This modernism was most influential between the world wars, becoming eclipsed by biblical theologians from the 1950s and the new radicalism.[10]

The era of modernism can be understood as a clash of cultures. Writers vary in determining where the key to modernism lies. Its scientific tools were basically biblical and historical criticism; its philosophical positions were usually developments—authentic or otherwise—of M. Blondel (1861–1949), with the question of immanence and transcendence either explicit or implicit in its theologico-philosophical positions.[11]

The reaction of Church authorities took a few years to emerge; when it did it might not unfairly be said to have been a combination of panic and excess. Books of modernists were put on the Index (q.v.) from 1903. In 1907 the Holy Office produced a condemnation of sixty-five propositions characteristic of biblical and theological Modernism.[12]

Within three months Pius X (q.v.) issued the encyclical *Pascendi.*[13] Apart from an introduction and concluding pastoral strategies such as an insistence on

Thomism, this attempt to synthesize Modernism is now known to have been the work of P.J. Lemius (1860–1923).[14] It signaled out agnosticism, immanentism, personal religious experience—especially arising from the subconscious—as well as biblical criticism and subjective apologetics as the crucial roots of the modernist system, which really existed as a unified or coherent system only in the encyclical itself. The Index and the Biblical Commission became increasingly active. Pius X, fearing cryptomodernism in 1910, imposed a profession of faith, known as the "Antimodernist Oath," which was finally dropped in 1967.[15] The credal statement did not add anything to the previous magisterium of the pope, but for decades it was used as a yardstick for orthodoxy.

In his last years, Pius X undoubtedly presided over a lamentable witch-hunt carried out by integralists (v. INTEGRALISM); one of the first acts of Benedict XV was an appeal for peace and charity.[16] The official reaction to modernism had a debilitating effect on Catholic theology and exegesis for a long time, though some works of quality and new journals began to emerge even before the death of Pius X.[17]

With G. Daly, one must avoid oversimplifications such as "Modernism proposed wrong solutions to many problems it had grasped aright."[18] It remains true, however, that the issues of those times have a certain perennial quality:[19] religious persons are not pure intellect but must seek a more integral grasp of reality than intellect alone can furnish. But an incarnate Christianity must still have norms of belief and practice if it is not to vanish into an unfleshed chimera.[20] Moreover, in every age the Church must engage each manifestation of modernity in dialogue; failure to do so risks irrelevance.

Modernism has since been used as an abusive term by those of very conservative bent. In the "New Theology" period of 1950s (v. PIUS XII), some in the Church feared a recrudescence of modernism. Even in the post-Vatican II period, Modernism is a charge that one hears made against theologians. As such, it is largely meaningless, though undoubtedly damaging; it is best to use the term only about the period from about 1895 to 1914, one in which neither the extreme left nor the champions of orthodoxy emerged with much distinction. It is not without interest that at the time of the canonization of Pius X, the then reigning pope, Pius XII, restricted investigation to the personal virtue of the earlier pope, and did not allow examination of his rather ambivalent exercise of the papal office.

[1]R. Aubert, "Recent Publications on the Modernist Movement," Conc [17] 7 (1966) 47-55; P. Olivier, "Travaux récents sur les modernistes et les modernismes," RechSR 70 (1982) 237-268; idem, "Les modernismes et les modernistes," RechSR 74 (1986) 397-440; R. Aubert, in Jedin-Dolan 9:420-480 bibliog. 616-620; idem, "Modernisme" in Catholicisme 9:448-455; G. Daly, Transcendence

and Immanence: A Study in Catholic Modernism and Integralism (Oxford: Clarendon, 1980); L. da Veiga Coutinho, Tradition et histoire dans la controverse moderniste (1898-1910). AnGreg 73 (Rome: Gregorian UP, 1954); L.R. Kurtz, The Politics of Heresy: The Modernist Heresy in Roman Catholicism (Berkeley: Calif. UP, 1986); É. Poulat, Histoire, dogme et critique dans la crise moderniste (Paris—Tournai, 1962); C. Tresmontant, La crise moderniste (Paris: Seuil, 1979); Still useful, J. Rivière, Le Modernisme dans l'Église: Étude d'histoire religieuse contemporaine (Paris, 1929); A.R. Vidler, The Modernist Movement in the Roman Church (Cambridge UK, 1934). Unsympathetic, P.G. Rossi, "Il modernismo," Renovatio 25 (1990) 193-228, 377-416.    [2]Aubert, in Jedin-Dolan 9:431-441; R.D. Haight, "The Unfolding of Modernism in France: Blondel, Laberthonnière, LeRoy," TS 35 (1974) 632-666; M.F. Reardon, "Science and Religious Modernism: The New Apologetic in France, 1890-1913," JRel 57 (1977) 48-63.    [3]Daly (n. 1) 51-68; N. Provencher, "The Origin and Development of Alfred Loisy's Modernism," ScEsp 32 (1980) 317-330.    [4]L'Évangile et l'Église (Paris 1902).    [5]Daly (n. 1) 91-116.    [6]Daly (n. 1) 109-115.    [7]Aubert, in Jedin-Dolan 9:448-455; P. Scoppola, Crisi modernista e rinnovamento cattolico (Bologna, [2]1969).    [8]Daly (n. 1) 140-164; see J.C. Livingston, ed., George Tyrrell. Tradition and the Critical Spirit: Catholic Modernist Writings. Fortress Texts in Modern Theology (Minneapolis: Fortress, 1991) esp. introduction ix-xxxv; N. Sagovsky, "On God's Side?" A Life of George Tyrrell (Oxford: Clarendon, 1990); Daly (n.) 140-164; T. Foudy, "George Tyrrell and Modernism," IrTQ 49 (1982) 1-18; J.D. Root, "English Catholic Modernism and Science: The Case of George Tyrrell," HeythJ 18 (1977) 271-288.    [9]Daly (n. 1) 117-139; J.J. Kelly, "The Modernist Crisis: Von Hügel and Blondel," ETL 55 (1979) 297-330; W.J. Schoenl, "Von Hügel after the Modernist Crisis," CleR 63 (1978) 211-219; P.J. Sheery, "Von Hügel's Retrospective View of Modernism," HeythJ 28 (1987) 179-191.    [10]See A.M.G. Stephenson, The Rise and Decline of English Modernism (London: SPCK, 1984) with rev. S. Gilbey HeythJ 29 (1988) 261-262.    [11]Daly (n. 1) passim.    [12]Lamentabili—DS 3401-3466/in part ND 228, 650, 846.    [13]ASS 40 (1907) 593-650/Carlen 3:71-97/in part DS 3475-3500.    [14]Daly (n. 1) 179-187, 195-198 and esp. 232-234 complementing the work of J. Rivière.    [15]AAS 2 (1910) 669-672/DS 3537-3550/ND 143.    [16]Ad beatissimi—ASS 6 (1914) 565–581/Carlen 3:143-151/in part DS 3625-3626.    [17]Aubert, in Jedin-Dolan 9:465-467.    [18]Daly (n. 1) 2-3.    [19]Cf. A. Boland, La crise moderniste hier et aujourd'hui: Un parcours spirituel. Le point théologique 35 (Paris: Beauchesne, 1980).    [20]É. Poulat, "La crise du modernisme dans l'Église catholique: Prolégomènes à une réflexion sur l'orthodoxie," Supp 165 (1988) 57-74.

## MÖHLER, Johann Adam (1796–1838)

J.A. Möhler is recognized as one of the founders of modern ecclesiology.[1] In his youth he traveled around the German universities on an intellectual pilgrimage which he always claimed was of immense benefit to him. His first foray into ecclesiology was in his Tübingen lectures on canon law (1823–1825).[2] There, he drew on Enlightenment ideas of sociology and the individual. The approach is an "outer-inner" dialectic. The outer forms make possible the inner effects of religion. We can see here, too, the concern with the visibility of the Church, so important to those of the Bellarmine (q.v.) apologetic tradition. The consequence of this kind of ecclesiology is an excessive concern with the hierarchical structures, though Möhler was

critical of overly institutional views. It also overempha-
sized the human dimension of the Church. Two
Tübingen theologians were to influence him greatly:
his teacher, J.S. Drey (1777–1853), gave him a sense of
the development of the divine plan throughout history;
from J.M. Sailer (1751–1832) he received a perception
of the Body of Christ, not untinged with German romanticism but still profoundly a sense of Spirit-filled
members of Christ. In his first major published work,
*Die Einheit*, he saw the Holy Spirit building up the
Church as community.[3] What is external is being built
up from the internal life of individuals who make up the
community. The externals in the Church are an expression of, and live only as, an expression of interior belief
and working of the Holy Spirit. It is the Spirit who unifies believers and is the Church's continual life-giving
principle. *Die Einheit* has three shifts of direction: from
the individual to the communal—the Spirit overcomes
all individual barriers in the Church; from a homogeneous to a diversified notion of the Church—the diversity of each individual is held in tension in the living
organism of the Church; from the static to the dynamic—the Church is a historical community given life
by the Spirit.[4] Möhler became unhappy with this presentation and refused to re-edit the book.

Though arguably *Die Einheit* is a more profound intuition of the Church and more influential, in *Symbolism,* Möhler's best-known work, he distanced himself
from some of its emphases: an over-subjective view of
the Church; a rather too exclusive stress on the Holy
Spirit, which did not allow sufficiently for his transcendence or for the role of human freedom; a weak
presentation of the Christological dimension of the
Church.[5] His Christological reflections[6] bore fruit in a
widened ecclesiology with its famous text: "Thus, the
visible Church, from the point of view here taken, is
the Son of God himself, everlastingly manifesting
himself among men in a human form, perpetually ren-
ovated, and eternally young—the permanent incarnation of the same, as in Holy Writ, even the faithful are
called 'the body of Christ.' Hence it is evident that the
Church, though composed of men, is yet not purely
human."[7] The fact that Möhler is proposing an analogy rather than an identification between Christ and
the Church is clear from an earlier passage which
summarizes something of traditional ecclesiology in a
Christological context: "By the Church on earth,
Catholics understand the visible community of believers, founded by Christ, in which, by means of an enduring apostleship, established by him, and appointed
to conduct all nations, in the course of ages back to
God, the works wrought by him during his earthly
life, for the redemption and sanctification of mankind,
are, under the guidance of his spirit, continued to the
end of the world."[8] This latter text also retains something of Möhler's sense of the Church being in history
yet in constant contact with its beginning.

It is surely significant that Möhler was moved by
what we today would call an ecumenical intent in this
his third major reflection on the Church. His exposition
of the differences between Catholics and Protestants is
rarely presented as contradictions but rather as oppositions that need to be resolved in a higher unity.[9] With
the neo-scholastic revival, the works of Möhler were
largely ignored until, through the labors of his editor
J.R. Geiselmann and others, like Y. Congar, they were
to influence 20th-century ecclesiology profoundly.
Möhler's theology was a constant search, and though
we have three states of his ecclesiological reflections, a
final synthesis of his work was prevented by his death
even as he was revising *Symbolism*.[10] Möhler's contribution to theology is more than ecclesiology,[11] but it is
in this area that his influence has been most felt: he
paved a way for a truly theological study of the Church
which, with its Trinitarian dimension, was incalculably
richer than the more polemic and apologetic ecclesiology of previous and following generations.

[1]Y. Congar, "Sur l'évolution et l'interprétation de la pensée de
Moehler," RSPT 27 (1938) 205–212; Congar, *Augustin* 419–423;
G.G. Gilmore, "J.A. Möhler on Doctrinal Development," HeythJ 19
(1978) 383–398; P. Riga, "The Ecclesiology of Johann Adam
Möhler," TS 22 (1961) 563–587; P. Rosato, "Between Christocentri-
cism and Pneumatocentricism: An Interpretation of Johann Adam
Möhler's Ecclesiology," HeythJ 19 (1978) 46–70; P.-W. Scheele,
"Johann Adam Möhler," in H. Fries and G. Schwaiger, eds.,
*Katholische Theologen Deutschlands im 19. Jahrhundert.* 3 vols.
(Munich: Kösel, 1975) 2:70-98; H. Wagner, "Johann Adam Möhler,"
in H. Fries and G. Kretschmar, eds., *Klassiker der Theologie.* 2 vols.
(Munich: Beck, 1983) 2:111-126. [2]Rosato (n. 1) 48–52. [3]*Die
Einheit in der Kirche oder das Prinzip der Katholizismus dargestellt
im Geiste der Kirchenväter der drei ersten Jahrhunderte,* J.R.
Geiselmann, ed. (Darmstadt—Cologne, 1957); French trans. US 2
(Paris, 1938). Cf. N. Bux, "L'unità cattolica del popolo di Dio nel pen-
siero di Johann Adam Möhler," Nocol 16 (1989) 185–201. [4]Cf.
Rosato (n. 1) 57–58; A. Houssiau, "Images diverses de l'unité de
l'Église," RTLv 10 (1979) 131–158 at 146–158; W. van Roo,
"Möhler's Earlier Symbolism," Greg 72 (1991) 129–138; H. Wagner,
*Die eine Kirche und die vielen Kirchen: Ekklesiologie und Symbolik
beim jungen Möhler* (Munich—Paderborn—Vienna: Schöningh,
1977). [5]*Symbolik oder Darstellung der dogmatischen Gegensätzen
der Katholiken und Protestanten nach ihren öffentlichen Bekennt-
nisschhriften*—Eng. trans. J.B. Robertson, *Symbolism or Exposition
of the Doctrinal Differences between Catholics and Protestants as
Evidenced by Their Symbolical Writings* (London, [5]1906). [6]J.R.
Geiselmann, "Der Einfluss der Christologie des Konzils von
Chalkedon auf die Theologie Johann Adam Möhlers," in A.
Grillmeier et al., *Das Konzil von Chalkedon.* 3 vols. (Würzburg, 1954)
3:341-420. [7]*Symbolik* (n. 5) 1:389; *Symbolism* 259. [8]*Symbolism*
258. [9]L. Meulenberg, "J.A. Möhler et le problème du pluralisme
dans l'Église," in M. Fois et al. eds., *Dalla chiesa antica alla chiesa
moderna.* Miscellenea historiae pontificae 50 (Rome: Gregorian UP,
1983) 405–425; R. Blasquez, "El ministero eclesial en J.A. Möhler,"
Salm 32 (1986) 303–331; B.D. Dupuy, "Schisme et primauté chez
J.A. Möhler," in AA.VV. *L'ecclésiologie au XIXe siècle.* US 34 (Paris,
1960) 197–231 = RevSR 34 (1960) 197–231; H. Petri, "Katholizität

in der Sicht Johann Adam Möhlers und ihre Bedeutung für den ökumenischen Dialog," Catholica 42 (1988) 92–107. ¹⁰J.R. Geiselmann, "Les variations de la définition de l'Église chez Joh. Adam Möhler particulièrement en ce qui concerne les relations entre l'Episcopat et le Primat" in AA.VV. L'ecclésiologie au XIXe siècle. US 34 (Paris, 1960) 141–195. ¹¹G.L. Müller, "Die Suche J.A. Möhlers nach der Einheit von geschichtlicher und theologischer Vernunft," MüTZ 38 (1988) 195–206; P. Stockmeier, "Johann Adam Möhler und der Aufbruch der wissenschaftlichen Kirchengeschichtsschreibung," MüTZ 38 (1987) 181–194. See (n. 3) Unity in the Church (Washington, D.C.: Catholic UP, 1995).

## MOLTMANN, Jürgen (1926– )

Jürgen Moltmann was born in 1926 in Hamburg. He was forced to enter military service in 1944 and was a prisoner of war 1945–1948. In 1967, after studies in Göttingen, he became professor in Tübingen. He was much influenced by the works of D. Bonhoeffer (q.v.) and the Jewish Marxist philosopher Ernst Bloch; his first major work on hope can be seen as an attempt to parallel in theology Bloch's philosophy of hope.

Moltmann's extensive work[1] to date can be considered to have two parts; his early trilogy on hope, Christ, and the Church;[2] his later works moving towards a "dogmatics," which he called a series of "contributions" to theological discussion.[3]

Central to Moltmann's work is his apprehension of Cross and Resurrection leading to an eschatological vision of present and future as he tries to make Christian faith relevant for modern society. He has greatly influenced liberation theology (q.v.), even though the liberationists at times see his eschatology as too other-worldly. On the other hand they welcome his commitment to the poor and his demand that the Church take up a critical stance in, and more especially against, society which oppresses the marginalized.[4] Moltmann describes his ecclesiology as being both "messianic" and "relational." It is strongly Trinitarian: the Spirit operates between the first and second coming of Christ to establish a community of committed fellowship in a messianic people. From a Catholic point of view there is insufficient emphasis on the role of ministry (q.v.) and some lack of clarity about the position of the Church vis-a-vis both the world and other religions. Deeply intuitive rather than rigorously rational, Moltmann's theology is highly influential even for those who do not follow him on every point; he continually raises important questions for ecclesiology and indeed for all of theology.

¹D. Ising et al., Bibliographie Jürgen Moltmann (Munich: Kaiser, 1987); R. Bauckham, ModChm 28/12 (1985–1986) 55–60. See "Jürgen Moltmann," in D.F. Ford, ed., The Modern Theologians: An Introduction to Christian Theology in the Twentieth Century. 2 vols. (Oxford: Blackwell, 1989) 1:293-310. ²Theology of Hope (New York: Harper & Row, 1967); The Crucified God (New York: Harper & Row, 1974); The Church in the Power of the Spirit (London: SCM, 1977). See F. Herzog, ed., The Future of Hope: Theology and Eschatology (New York: Herder & Herder, 1970). ³The Trinity and the Kingdom of God (London: SCM, 1981); God in Creation (London: SCM, 1985). See R. Bauckham, Moltmann: Messianic Theology in the Making (Basingstoke UK: Marshall Pickering, 1987); C. Morse, The Logic of Promise in Moltmann's Theology (Philadelphia: Fortress, 1979). ⁴Cf. M.R. Tripole, "A Church for the Poor and the World: At Issue with Moltmann's Ecclesiology," TS 42 (1981) 645–659.

## MONTANISM

Montanus appeared in Phrygia 155–160 C.E., claiming to be the mouthpiece of the Holy Spirit. Along with two prophetesses, Prisc(ill)a and Maximilla, Montanus claimed to be the voice of Christ and of the Spirit. His doctrines[1] spread because of a certain cooling of spiritual fervor after the 1st century. Montanism extended through Asia Minor, Gaul, and North Africa. The main Montanist writings have been destroyed, and we know it only from fragments, from the admittedly biased accounts of its adversaries,[2] and from the writings of Tertullian (q.v.), its most illustrious convert (207 C.E.); given Tertullian's strong personality and independent spirit, he may not always give an objective picture of the movement.

Montanists were characterized by extreme rigorism, enthusiasm, ecstatic prophecy, and glossolalia. They claimed the authority of the Holy Spirit for their actions and rejected all hierarchy. An apocalyptic movement, they expected an imminent end of the world. They held that only the saints (pneumatici) formed the true Church, and so only they could truly baptize. The fact that otherwise they did not hold heterodox doctrines made it difficult for Church leaders to combat the Montanists;[3] it was a matter of discernment of spirits rather than a straightforward examination of their orthodoxy.[4] Though mentioned in lists of heresies for many centuries, Montanism died away rather soon in most places, though we hear of small splinter groups in places up to the 9th century. The reaction against Montanism led to the first episcopal synods (q.v.), which met in Asia Minor.

The experience of Montanism is usually given as a (main) reason for the decline of charisms (q.v.), especially prophecy, in the early Church: charism could be a threat to the institutions of the Church, and it was henceforth played down, or at least the expectation of charism being widely given in the Church was not encouraged.

¹B. Aland, "Montanus—Montanism," EncycEarCh 1:570-571 with bibliog.; T.D. Barnes, "The Chronology of Montanism," JTS 21 (1971) 403–408; K. Baus, in Jedin-Dolan 1:199-205; F. Blanchetière, "Le Montanisme originel," RevSR 52 (1978) 118–134; 53 (1979) 1–22; W.H.C Frend, "Montanism: Research and Problems," RivStorLettRel 30 (1984) 521–537; idem, "Montanism: A Movement of Prophecy and Religious Identity in the Early Church," BJRyL 70/3 (1988) 25–34; R. Heine, The Montanist Oracles and

*Testimonies*. American Patristic Series 14 (Macon, Ga.: Mercer—Leuven: Peeters, 1989).    [2]Eusebius, *Hist. eccl* 5:18.    [3]Aland (n. 1) 570.    [4]Eusebius, *Hist. eccl.* 5:16.

## MOTHER, Church as

In the NT we find some texts that point to the maternal dimension of life in the Christian community. The Church recalled the saying of Jesus, who likened himself to a hen gathering and protecting her chickens: it is Jerusalem that he apostrophized (Matt 23:37), Jerusalem who was to be the universal mother of peoples (Isa 66:10-23). Early Christian reflection looked to the new Jerusalem, the true Jerusalem on high, who is our mother (Gal 4:26, 31). Both spousal and maternal features of the Church appear in the Pauline writings (2 Cor 11:2; Gal 4:19; Eph 5:24-33; 1 Thess 2:7-9), as well as in the Johannine corpus (2 John 1, 4, 13; Rev 12).[1]

The earlier Christian writers take up and develop the notion of the Church as a maternal figure, e.g., Hermas (q.v.).[2] It is highly evolved by Origen (q.v.) in the East.[3] But it was perhaps the African Church which most popularized the notion of the Church as Mother,[4] even adding the word to the Creed: "I believe in holy mother Church."[5] Cyprian (q.v.) keeps insisting on it: "You cannot have God for your Father if you do not have the Church as your mother,"[6] an idea found earlier in Origen,[7] and subsequently taken up by Augustine (q.v.). Optatus of Milevis, writing about 365, has phrases of Augustinian flavor: "One mother the Church brought us to birth, one God the Father welcomed (*excepit*) us."[8] It would appear that the first extensive use of the concept was Tertullian (q.v.), who spoke of *Domina mater ecclesia* (lady and mother), which includes the idea of reverence and love.[9] It is found developed in Ambrose: the Church is a virgin and fruitful mother.[10] His contemporary, Zeno of Verona, spoke eloquently of the Church as engendering mother to be loved and obeyed.[11]

The most substantial development of the theme was probably that of Augustine (q.v.),[12] who exploited the full range of maternal functions and symbols: "The Church is most truly mother of Christians"[13]; she is a chaste mother[14]; "To the Church as to Mary belong perpetual integrity and incorrupt fecundity,"[15] a theme common in his Christmas homilies; the Church nourishes as a mother,[16]—"because you are given milk give praise, because you are supported give praise, because you are nourished advance in wisdom and age"[17]; "The Church is a mother with two breasts, the Old and the New Testament, to suckle with the milk of all the sacraments"[18]; the Church feeds on the bread of heaven and so can give milk to its children;[19] the Church is the Mother of love;[20] she is the teacher;[21] she is a virgin—"The whole Church is called by the one name, vir-

gin"[22]; "The Church is a wife, but is a virgin through faith, hope and love";[23] she is a spouse—"The whole Church is the spouse of Christ, whose principle and first-fruits is the flesh of Christ, the spouse is joined to the Spouse in the flesh";[24] the Church is a sorrowful mother because of sin,[25] tribulation,[26] schism, and heresy;[27] she has a mixed progeny of good and bad children stretching back through the OT.[28]

It is clear that Augustine regards the whole Church, and not merely the hierarchy, as mother: the whole Church is mother and the whole Church is virgin;[29] "The whole Church binds and looses sin," for all labor for the conversion of the sinner.[30] St. Augustine frequently expresses the need to honor, love, respect the Church—"Let us love God our God, let us love his Church, the former as Father, the latter as mother."[31] Finally Augustine recognizes the heavenly Church as mother: "We know another Mother, the heavenly Jerusalem, which is holy Church, part of which is on pilgrimage on earth,"[32] The Church below tends to heaven."[33]

After Augustine, the theme of Church as mother became commonplace in patristic thought, appearing in the Carolingian,[34] and in the scholastic periods, e.g., St. Thomas Aquinas.[35] In the medieval reunion councils and papal statements, the term "returning to mother Church" was found in connection with the Roman See.[36] The reformers and modern Protestants[37] retained the epithet "Mother" but without giving it much emphasis, e.g., Calvin,[38] Luther.[39] It was often associated with the idea of spouse (q.v.).

In Vatican II we can distinguish broadly two kinds of texts: those in which "Mother" appears only as a name for the Church, e.g., SC 4, 60, 122, IM 2, GE preface and 3, DV 11, 19; those which show some theological reflection on the Church's motherhood. The latter forms a rich and complex series: LG 6 develops the twin notions of spouse and mother but with emphasis more on spouse; PO 6 states that "the ecclesial community exercises a truly motherly function in leading souls to Christ by its charity, its prayer, its example and its penitential works;" LG 14 notes that "with love and solicitude mother Church already embraces (catechumens) as her own"; LG speaks of the goal of Christian unity and adds, "Mother Church never ceases to pray, hope and work that this may be achieved, and she exhorts her children to purification and renewal so that the sign of Christ may shine more brightly over the face of the Church"—an idea which GS 43 repeats; CD 13 asserts that bishops in teaching should proclaim the maternal solicitude of the Church for all whether they be Catholics or not; LG 41 affirms that married people by their lives of love "build up the fraternity of charity, and they stand as witnesses and cooperators of the fruitfulness of mother Church"; LG 42 speaking about the evangelical counsels states that "mother Church rejoices that she has within her many men and women who pursue the Savior's self-emptying . . ."; LG 64 is the most dense text about the Church as mother, virgin, and spouse so that "imitating the mother of the Lord, and by the power of the Holy Spirit, she keeps intact faith, firm hope and sincere charity."

Theological reflection on the Church's motherhood needs to keep in mind, as Augustine and the whole tradition stated, that it is the *whole* Church and not its pastors that are the Mother. It should proceed from the main double aspect of motherhood: first, giving life; secondly, sustaining life and educating. It will emphasize the care and the love of Mother Church and will also stress the obligation of all to show love (q.v.) for the Church. There would seem to be a need to deepen our appreciation of the full implications of Mark 3:35par.: those who do the will of the Father are Mother to Jesus. By such obedience they bring Jesus to be born and present where his influence did not previously penetrate. Finally, an emphasis on the motherhood of the Church should encourage people to take their role in caring for the Church—their mother, and also to share in her motherhood. It is perhaps paradoxical that many of those who use the term "Mother Church" are people who have a strongly institutional perception of the Church. One might be led to expect that the rich warmth of the Mother image would soften any harsh institutional or juridical views, as in the moving meditation on the Church by H. De Lubac (q.v.), pondering how a *homo ecclesiasticus,* or loyal Church person, should think and act.[40]

[1]G. Baril, *Feminine Face of the People of God: Biblical Symbols of the Church as Bride and Mother* (Slough UK: St. Paul, 1991); H. de Lubac, *The Motherhood of the Church* (San Francisco: Ignatius, 1982) 39–46. [2]*Vision* 3:17, 9—SC 53bis:123-124. [3]De Lubac (n. 1) 52 quoting K. Delahaye, *Ecclesia Mater chez les Pères des trois premiers siècles* (Paris: Cerf, 1964) 120. [4]V. Capánaga, "La Iglesia en la espiritualidad de S. Agustín," in AA.VV., *Mysterium ecclesiae in conscientia sanctorum* (Rome: Teresianum, 1967) 88–133 at 98 = EphCarm 17 (1966) 88–133; E. Lanne, "Église soeur et Église mère dans le vocabulaire de l'Église ancienne," in B. Bobrinskoy et al. eds., *Communio sanctorum.* FS J.J. Allmen (Geneva: Labor et fides, 1982) 86–97; J.C. Plumpe, *Mater Ecclesia: An Inquiry into the Concept of the Church as Mother in Early Christianity* (Washington, D.C., 1943) 104. [5]Delahaye (n. 3) 98, 108. [6]*De catholicae ecclesiae unitate*—PL 4:502; *Epist.* 46—FC 118; see J. Ratzinger, *Volk und Haus Gottes in Augustins Lehre von der Kirche.* Münchener theologische Studien 2/7 (Munich, 1954) 87–89. [7]*In Lev. hom.* 11:3—PG 12:534. [8]*De schis. donatist.* 4:5—PL 11:1033; cf. also 1:11; 2:10; 2:15—PL 11:906, 963, 967. [9]*Ad Martyr.* 1—PL 1:619; *De bapt.* 20—PL 1:1224; *De carne Christi* 17—PL 1:781; *De pudicitia* 5:14—PL 2:989; *De oratione* 2—PL 1:1154; *De poenitentia* 10—PL 1254; see J. Quasten, Patrology 2:330-331. [10]*De virginibus* 1:6—PL 16:208; *In Luc. hom.* 2:57—PL 15:1655. [11]*Tract.* 30—PL 11:476; 32—PL 11:477-478; 33—PL 11:479; 42—PL 492; 54—PL 11:510. [12]Capánaga (n. 4) 99–124; R. Palmero-Ramos,

*"Ecclesia mater," en san Augustín. Teología de la imagen en los escritos antidonatistas* (Madrid: Ed. Cristiandad, 1970). [13]*De mor. eccl. cath.* 1:30, 62–63—PL 32:1336. [14]*Serm.* 223:1—PL 38:1092. [15]*Serm.* 195:2—PL 38:1018. [16]*De quantitate animae* 33:76—PL 32:1077. [17]*Serm.* 216:7-8—PL 38:1080-1081. [18]*In Ioan. ep.* 3:1—PL 35:1998. Cf. *In Jer. tr.* 12:2—PL 35: 1484, 1486. [19]*Enarr. in Ps.* 33:1, 6—PL 36:303; cf. 38:3—PL 36:415. [20]Capá-naga (n. 4) 104–110. [21]*Serm.* 216:7-8—PL 38:1080-1081. [22]*Serm.* 93:3—PL 38:575. [23]*De bono viduit.* 10:13—PL 40:438; cf. *Serm.* 288:4—PL 38:1005. [24]*In Ioan. ep.* 2:2—PL 35:1990; *Serm.* 265:5—PL 38:1221; 341:12—PL 38:1500. [25]Capánaga (n. 4) 115–118. [26]*Enarr. in Ps.* 37:9—PL 36:401; 29:1, 8—PL 36:221; *Serm.* 47:17—PL 38:305; *Epist.* 55:6, 10—PL 33:209. [27]*Epist.* 33—PL 33:130-131; 34—PL 33:132-133; *Serm.* 47:16—PL 38:304; 265:6—PL 38:1221; 360—PL 38:1598-1599; cf. *De cantico novo* 10—PL 40:686. [28]*De bapt.* 1:16, 25—CSEL 51:169. [29]Capánaga (n. 4) 118; see *Epist.* 98:5—PL 33:362; *De sancta virg.* 5—PL 40:399. [30]*Tr. in Jer.* 124:7—PL 35:1976. [31]*Enarr. in Ps.* 88:13—PL 37:1140; cf. *Serm.* 213:7—PL 38:1063; 344:2—PL 39:1512. [32]*Enarr. in Ps.* 26:2—PL 36:208; cf. 149:5—PL 37:1952. [33]*Enarr. in Ps.* 30:10—PL 36:223. [34]Y. Congar, *L'ecclésiologie du haut moyen âge* (Paris, 1968) 77–81. [35]*In Eph.* 5, lect. 8 (264–267); *In Gal.* 4 lect. 8 (263–267). [36]Lateran IV—DS 810/Tanner 1:236; cf. Lyons II—Tanner 1:309 See Y. Congar, "Romanité et catholicité: Histoire de la conjonction changeante de deux dimensions de l'Église," RSPT 71 (1987) 161–190, at 169–70. [37]R. Mumm, "Die Kirche als Braut und Mutter nach dem evangelischen Bekenntnis," in W. Baier et al. eds., *Weisheit Gottes—Weisheit der Welt.* 2 vols. FS J. Ratzinger (St. Ottilien: EOS, 1987) 2:1087-1108. [38]*Institutes of the Christian Religion* 4:1-4—LCC 21:1011-1016. [39]*Large Catechism* 3:42—Bekennt-nisschriften 655. [40]"Ecclesia Mater," in *The Splendor of the Church,* ch. 7 (San Francisco: Ignatius, 1986) 237–278.

## MOVEMENTS, ECCLESIAL

Since Vatican II there have been a number of renewal movements[1] within the Church that share certain characteristics. They are called "movements" because they are groups of persons, originally spontaneous, usually under the direction of a charismatic leader or leaders, exhorting them to a particular spiritual or apostolic experience and often to a global view of reality. They are "ecclesial" because they see themselves as being in the Church, even as "being Church," and as serving the reign of God under, or at least with the tacit approval of, the pastors of the Church. They are "contemporary" because they are usually recently founded, or are a radical refoundation of an earlier movement. They are mostly of Latin European origin.

The discernment of such movements is delicate because their basic program, or guiding insight, is truly Christian. Pope John Paul II has generally been positive towards such groups. In the post-synodal Exhortation on the Laity, he notes with approval their fruits, and stresses the freedom given in Church law for people to come together for charitable and religious purposes.[2]

However, some of the modern ecclesial movements have provoked quite negative reactions on the part of bishops and pastors. They are difficult to typify: each enshrines a particular Christian insight with varying cultural features, objectives, methods, aims, and relationships to other members of the Church. As movements they develop, so that evaluations may have to be modified from time to time. One also has to distinguish between the aims of a movement and the sometimes incomplete, frail, or ambiguous realization of its ideals.[3]

In evaluating them, one must also take account of local manifestations: a movement may be quite sound in one country but show some negative factors in another. An objective and balanced discernment is often difficult.[4] One can, however, outline in a general way both the values and the deviations that are possible, and which are actually found at least in places in some of the movements.

Current ecclesial movements have many positive features. They tend to be centered on conversion, even if some seem to see themselves as *the* way rather than *a* way of being Christian. They are community forming with a strong sense of identity, though often with a perceived sense of being misunderstood or rejected by others who have not seen the light or who do not share their vision. They are within the Church, and as such are to be distinguished from New Age and cults (v. MOVEMENTS, NON-CHRISTIAN), even though they may bear some superficial resemblance to the latter. Since they insist on generous dedication to Christ, they often draw very committed laity, priests, and religious to their membership. The evident fruits of conversion, holiness, and fidelity to some important teaching of the recent magisterium have led to their winning wide acceptance in the Church, even in its higher echelons, for instance, at the synods of bishops and commendatory papal statements.

But there are also negative features. Their reading of the Scriptures is often partial, even fundamentalist, and they can lack a real sense of the true catholicity of the Church. They sometimes do not respect the other, quite different, charisms found in the Church; their vision of the Church and of the world may be inadequate. They may prove divisive in a diocese, in a parish, in families, in a religious congregation.[5] Confident that they have a light not shared by others, they are frequently not open to criticism from outside, and so one finds a closed group mutually affirming and discerning itself. They are also exposed to the danger of overestimating immediacy in religious experience.

There are so many groups that only a few which have extended far beyond Southern Europe can be treated here. To be found in separate articles are Basic Christian Communities (q.v.) and Charismatic Renewal (q.v.), which though not without negative features of their own, have escaped the main dangers of these other movements by their basic openness to others and their lack of strong bonding within the membership. The controversial Opus Dei (q.v.) is also treated elsewhere, for though it shares some of the characteristics of the movements, it is a secular institute, erected as a personal prelature (q.v.) in the Church. Some movements have the status of associations (q.v.).

One of the early modern movements is the *Christian Cursillo,* which originated in Catholic Action (v. APOSTOLATE) youth circles in Majorca (Spain) about 1949. One of its early leaders was Bishop Juan Hervás y Benet. The cursillo (Spanish "small course") is a three-day seminar which is strongly evangelistic, leading to a recommitment to Christian ideals, especially one's baptism. It is preceded by a precursillo, which seeks out prospective invitees. Those who have done this meet weekly on a transparochial basis in groups of 4 to 7 persons (*ultreya*) for support and deepening of commitment; these groups are for prayer, study, Scripture reflection, and Christian friendship. They should lead to further evangelization in the world. The Cursillo was given St. Paul as its patron by Paul VI in 1963.[6]

The *Focolare* (Italian "hearth/fireplace") movement, whose official title is *Opera di Maria* ("The Work of Mary"), was founded by Chiara Lubich in Trent (northern Italy) in 1943.[7] She was inspired and assisted by the historian I. Giordani.[8] After a profound searching for God's will for herself, she was led by various scriptural texts, Matt 7:21, John 15:12-13, especially John 17:21—"may they be one in us, that the world may know that you have sent me"—and Matt 18:20—"Where two or three are gathered in my name, I am there among them." Various people gathered around her even during the wartime bombardment of Trent. From the beginning, the aim was a total self-gift to God. Central to the Focolare vision is "Jesus crucified and abandoned." At first it was a movement of single lay people who, living in communities with vows of chastity, poverty, and obedience, are still its heart. The movement later included married persons, priests, and religious affiliated to it to varying degrees and living according to the spiritual ideals of the movement. The second generation, "The Gen" began in 1966, a youth movement with various outgrowths in different countries. From 1968 there were ecumenical groupings. Approval of the movement was slow: Pius XII gave private encouragement to its founder in 1953; John XXIII approved it in 1962; in 1978 it came under the Pontifical Council of the Laity.

The *Neo-Catechumenate* movement arose in a Madrid slum through Kiko Argüello in 1964.[9] Kiko, a painter, living poorly with his Bible, crucifix, and guitar, found that people gathered around him, with whom he shared the good news about Jesus. Gradually a community formed from among the poor. In time the groups saw themselves as following "The Way," a journey which is an authentic expression of Christian life.

The movement (a term resisted by its adherents) spread, until by 1972 it had developed a program of evangelization and commitment. A team generally approaches the bishop for permission to catechize or evangelize in the diocese. Association with "The Way" takes a period of "catechumenate" lasting two or more years and consisting of the following stages: announcement of kerygma, precatechumenate, catechumenate, election, renewal of baptismal promises. People then join a community which meets weekly for Scripture reading and reflection and, on Saturday evening, for a Eucharistic celebration. The Neo-Catechumenate tends not to take seriously RCIA programs in the parish or diocese; theirs, they think, is the authentic awakening to faith. Though the commitment of its members is obvious, there is evidence of negative evaluations on the part of bishops and priests, who find the Neo-Catechumenate seeming to set up parallel structures in the parish or diocese, and too closed or elitist. Nevertheless, the Neo-Catechumenical Way has been given impressive affirmation by Popes Paul VI and John Paul II.[10]

A youth movement, *Gioventù Studentesca* ("Student Youth"), founded by Don Luigi Giussani in the 1950s, became *Communion and Liberation* at the time of the student rebellions in 1968.[11] By the 1970s it had attracted a good number of former radicals into its membership. In Italian politics it judged the Christian Democrat party to be being largely bankrupt as a Christian organization, having become too secular and infected with *laicismo* (an Italian approximation of secular humanism). *Communion and Liberation* emphasizes commitment to the moral teaching of the Church; it is quite papalist and often critical of local hierarchies. It has a triple focus: culture, charitable works, and mission. Its basis is a conversion to Christ, from which these commitments follow. The movement naturally rejects the accusations made against it of being authoritarian, ideological, integralist, and of having a greater practical emphasis on the magisterium than on the Scriptures. But these charges and its occasionally confrontational style give rise to opposition on the part of some bishops and pastors despite the evident favor the movement enjoys at the highest level in the Church.

There are also innumerable movements which have a more specific focus, e.g., the *L'Arche* (Ark) communities for the handicapped founded by Jean Vanier (1964), the *Legion of Mary,* a lay apostolic movement founded in Dublin by Frank Duff (1921), *Marriage Encounter,* founded in Spain by Gabriel Calvo in the early 1960s, soon moving to U.S.; these three are international. Some of the other movements are found in several countries or are worldwide; others are in only one or a few places.

Given the diversity of movements, it is not possible to make a specific evaluation. In general one must acknowledge that they are a powerful work of the Spirit in this age; each has one or several notable charisms. But being human, they can have distortions or deviations. They need pastoral care by bishops and delegated priests or laity to ensure that they remain within the wider communion (q.v.) of the Church and its mission, and that they remain healthy from both a psychological and a spiritual point of view. Movements found in several countries must also take heed of the demands of inculturation (q.v.): the structures appropriate for one country may not suit another.

One can only take a negative view of some extreme right-wing movements in the Church which reject Vatican II and see Pius XII (q.v.) as the last authentic pope. Such are the movements gathered around the late Archbishop Lefebvre (q.v.) and the group publishing the *Courrier de Rome—Si si no no,* which consistently vilifies Paul VI (q.v.). Their ideal popes are Pius X (q.v.), for his condemnation of Modernism (q.v.), and Pius XII (q.v.), for his encyclical *Humani generis* against the "New Theology" which he perceived as a recrudescence of Modernistic tendencies.

Finally, one should note that there are renewal movements also in the Protestant Churches,[12] some of which are very hostile to Catholicism.

[1]J. Beyer, "I 'Movimenti ecclesiali,'" VitaCons 23 (1987) 143–156; M. Camisasca and M. Vitali, *I movimenti nella Chiesa negli anni '80.* Atti del 1o Convegno Internazionale Roma 23–27 settembre 1981 (Milan: Jaca, 1981); P. Coda, "I movimenti ecclesiali: Una lettura ecclesiologica," Later 57 (1991) 129–144; P.J. Cordes, "Nouveaux mouvements spirituels dans l'Église," NRT 109 (1987) 49–65; C. Dagens, "Les mouvements spirituels contemporains: Jalons pour un discernement," NRT 106 (1984) 885–899; A. Favale et al, *Movimenti ecclesiali contemporanei: Dimensioni storiche teologico-spirituali ed apostoliche* (Rome: LAS, [4]1991); J. Palard, "D'un christianisme de position à un christianisme de mouvement(s)," NRT 102 (1980) 853–878; The Tablet (London) 5 arts.—20 Feb. to 19 March 1988. [2]*Christifideles laici* (1988) n. 29 and citing CIC 215.   [3]A. Favale (n. 1) 18–19; B. Secondin, *Segni di profezia nella Chiesa. Comunità Gruppi Movimenti* (Milan: Ed. OR, 1987) 36–51; idem, *I nuovi protagonisti: Movimenti, associazioni, gruppi nella Chiesa* (Milan: Paoline, 1991).   [4]C. Dagens, "Les mouvements spirituels contemporains: Jalons pour un discernment," NRT 106 (1984) 885–899. [5]G.A. Arbuckle, "Is the Neo-Catechumenate Way Compatible with Religious Life," RelLifeR 33 (1994) 2–7.   [6]*Viget salubriter*—AAS 56 (1964) 524–525.   [7]AA.VV. *Il movimento dei Focolari* (Rome: Città Nuova, [3]1977); F. Zambonini, *Chiara Lubich: A Life for Unity* (London: New City, 1992). See works by C. Lubich: *Why Have You Forsaken Me? The Key to Unity* (London: New City, 1985); *Servants of All* (London: New City, 1979); *Charity* (London: New City, 1981). [8]*Diary of Fire* (London: New City, 1981).   [9]R. Blázquez, *Neo-Catechumenal Communities: A Theological Discernment* (Slough UK: St. Paul, 1988)—positive; J.C. Buckley, "The Neo-Catechumenate," PrPeople 2/5 (1988) 175–186—negative.   [10]*The Neo-Catechumenal Way in the Discourses of Paul VI and John Paul II* (Rome: Neo-Catechumenal Center, 1987).   [11]F. Perrenchio in Favale (n. 3) 393–424; H. Portelli, "Le mouvement 'Communion et Libération,'" Études 368/6 (1988) 833–840.   [12]U. Gastaldi, "Alcuni caratteri dei movimenti di risveglio nel mondo protestante," StEcum 5 (1987) 75–101.

## MOVEMENTS, NON-CHRISTIAN AND NEW AGE

The term "New Religious Movements" (NRM) covers a bewildering variety of groups. There are four main typologies: some have clear roots in biblical Christianity and in mainline Churches; others have their origin in the great Eastern religions, most notably, but not exclusively, Buddhism and Hinduism, and may, as well, adopt elements from Christianity in a syncretist way; a third group of sects comprises those based on a distortion of the genuine idea of religion, and represent a return to paganism; finally, there are sects of a gnostic nature, that is, purveying secret or hidden knowledge (Greek *gnôsis* = "knowledge"). With regard to the Church, we can again distinguish four doctrinal positions of the NRM: those which reject the Church; those that reject Christ; those which reject God but may maintain a generic sense of "religion;" those that reject the role of religion but maintain some sense of the "sacred," if only to manipulate others.[1]

The New Age[2] is the most important of the NRM, but it is extremely difficult to pin down or identify. It began in the USA; in Europe it is to be found mainly in English–and German[3]-speaking countries, with gradual penetration into France.[4] It is not highly organized like an association, sect, or church. It is more an ideology of varying elements coalescing around some central ideas which many, though not all, who are touched by New Age ideas will espouse. As a working definition the New Age movement has been described as a coalition of various networking organizations that a) believe in a new world religion, b) are working for a new world order, and c) expect a New Age Christ. Not all of those touched by the New Age will necessarily hold these aims in an explicit way, but they are present in the networking of conferences, phone calls, travel, books, phantom organizations, papers and magazines, circulated photocopies, lectures, workshops and seminars, grapevine, tapes, and newsletters.[5] However, in New Age we are not necessarily thinking of a tightly organized group or society. The New Age tends to be more a network of groups of like-minded people who share some common ground.

There have not been any major Church statements on the New Age at a universal level.[6] But there are three studies on cults, or more accurately on NRM, which can help us in forming a Catholic response to them and to New Age thinking and practices.[7] One cannot say that New Age manifestations are always the same as those found in cults, sects, or NRM, though there are significant resemblances. Rather both the New Age and the NRM (sects and cults) have all pierced through weak points in the Church's armor and have drawn people away from central tenets of Catholic faith and life. Though the New Age and other NRM can differ, the challenges they pose to the Church are very similar. Moreover, the pastoral strategies that will counter one will be helpful also against the other.

The New Age tends to use such language as a "spirit," a "hope," an "agenda," and look to personal and social transformation that will give individuals or humanity a fresh start in a new age, often referred to as the Age of Aquarius (the Water Carrier of astrology) which will be marked by love, light, and a satisfying of the deep spiritual thirst of humankind. At the heart of much New Age thinking is secular humanism and something akin to such modern psychologists as Carl Rogers. There is a perception that people are basically good. It is further held that they may do as they please so long as they do not obviously harm another. Many will insist that each person is a god. Also fundamental is a belief in the spiritual dimension of people and the universe: there is a "spirit realm" in which all do or can share; the New Age stresses people reaching their maximum potential. Hence we find deliberate altering of states of consciousness, interest in psychic experience, Silva Mind Control, TM, the Forum (EST), the mediation of spirits of a past age or of beings from another planet or galaxy. Common is a doctrine of reincarnation[8] which removes guilt and personal responsibility for wrong-doing, since everything can be blamed on a person's karma, the inevitable state in which one does, or will, find oneself in a particular reincarnation. We find New Age ideas also in the way in which some people think about holistic health and alternative medicine, as well as ecology. One also encounters in New Age traditional occult practices, witchcraft, wicca, astrology, druidism, belief in the power of crystals, fertility cults. Various forms of Satanism can also be found. The latent philosophy of many glossy magazines for men and women is often a New Age one. Music with built-in subliminal suggestions can reflect many New Age ideas, especially some hard rock and heavy metal; there is also music that is specifically New Age, for instance, what helps or accompanies altered states of consciousness.

When we begin to think of the Church's attitude to New Age ideas and practices, we are faced with what at times is a very delicate process of discernment. Some of the ideas just mentioned are obviously wrong. But some ideas taken up by New Age people are good and by no means obviously false or evil. For instance, one can seek alternative medicine which is soundly based and not tied to an anti-Christian world vision. We can easily accept holistic views of health—a person-centered rather than disease-centered approach. But when we encounter language like "the healing depths of one's soul," etc., we may be on the edge of New Age. Again, one can use yoga for relaxation without taking on board a yogic philosophy of human nature and of the world. K. Hoyt has identified ten areas in which Christians might agree with New Age: an emphasis on cooperation rather than on personal competition; the desire to protect the environment; the interest in creativity; the cause of peace in the world; the call for radical human transformation—in practice, however, the Christian and the New Age understanding of the transformation needed differs enormously; the emphasis on proper care of our bodies; the support for human potential and a positive self-image; the fact of the global village with multiple interdependency; the desire for a nontoxic environment; the use of networking—indeed the Christian Church has by far the most elaborate network, even though its potential for multiple contacts is not fully exploited.[9]

Discernment is therefore very necessary. At a risk of some oversimplification, one can say that whereas the philosophy of the New Age is ambiguous, its theology is false. Language which sounds very Christian may have an entirely different meaning in a New Age setting. The Christian believes that we are made in the image and likeness of God (see Gen 1:26) and that God dwells in one who is graced (see John 14:23; 1 Cor 6:19). But this Christian teaching never overlooks the transcendence of the omnipotent God who, though dwelling with us by grace, still remains always the wholly Other. New Age thinking speaks about human nature being divine in a way that is totally unacceptable to Christians. The discernment required is not easy but nonetheless is very necessary for our time in accordance with the word of Paul: "Test everything; hold fast to what is good; abstain from every form of evil" (1 Thess 5:21-22).

Christians in the evangelical tradition are vehemently opposed to the New Age;[10] some see it as a manifestation of the Anti-Christ. But they risk rejecting as belonging to New Age things that are not incompatible with Christianity, for example, the useful, if limited, psychological classification of personality found in the Enneagram or Myers-Briggs typology, or a discreet use of Jungian psychology.[11]

We can develop a response to the New Age in several stages. First, we can show the ways in which it is profoundly opposed to Christianity. Second, we can indicate those areas of human needs which some people feel are being answered by the New Age. Third, we can point to some necessary pastoral strategies to counter the New Age influences which are everywhere surrounding us.

The most profound objection to New Age thinking involves the Christian doctrine about salvation and about Christ. At the most profound level, New Age thinking offers "salvation." We all know the most fundamental problems of humanity: deprivation, a welter of anxieties, sin, guilt, failure, suffering, evil, death, the after-life (GS 9–10). New Age thinking and practices offer a way through these difficulties and propose a "salvation" which is either purely human or humanistic, or else comes from a power other than that of the Father of our Lord Jesus Christ. In this offer of "salvation" we find the ancient heresy of Pelagianism (people can save themselves). For New Age, what is needed is not reconciliation with God through Jesus Christ but rather knowledge or *gnosis* of the divine splendor of men and women. The description Neo-Gnostic is often aptly applied to the New Age. Allied to this humanistic reductionism there is a denial of God or a false view of the Creator which is either monistic (all is a single reality) or pantheistic (all is God).

Still looking at the deepest objections to New Age thinking, we find views about Christ which are not acceptable to believers. New Age thinkers like David Spangler,[12] distinguish between Jesus and Christ. Jesus was a human being at the beginning of our era. "Christ" on the other hand is a universal spirit who has dwelt in great religious leaders, including Buddha, Jesus, and other gurus. Such views strike at the heart of the Christian religion in which Jesus is proclaimed as God and man, and has been established as Lord (1 Cor 12:3) through the resurrection which followed his atoning death (Rom 1:4).

Second, the question that must be asked about both the cults and the New Age is surely why people are drawn to these movements from the various Churches, including the Catholic Church. J. Saliba noted about a decade ago that while some cults had peaked and were declining, "it is unlikely that the cultic phenomenon as a whole will pass away, if for no other reason than that the social, cultural, and religious factors contributing to their rise are still with us."[13] A similar conclusion is called for in the case of the New Age. We need then to look at these factors to understand why members of the Church have been vulnerable to cults and the NRMs. First of all, people can feel lost in a time of cultural change, and search for meaning. Second, people feel a void in the religion in which they find themselves: it does not seem to answer profound needs that they experience. Third, the answers which the Church proposes to deep human problems do not seem relevant or helpful. Fourth, the Church is perceived as being too institutionalized and impersonal so that people do not have a sense of belonging or involvement. Fifth, the Church does not seem sufficiently to stress human promotion or emotional fulfillment. Sixth, the Church has failed to present to the faithful its rich tradition of prayer and mystical experience. Seventh, the Church's insistence on sin and on moral behavior seems to be a heavy burden or an infringement on people's "right to be healthy, happy, holy"—the 3HO credo (3H Organization Foundation). Finally, there is the human desire for transcendence, for knowledge, for vision.

Catholics would hope that the Church can provide answers to these deep desires of the human heart so that recourse to NRM and to the New Age would not be necessary. But at the outset one would have to say that the Church which people experience is very often a Church badly in need of renewal, a local Church which is not living out the fullness of the gifts given by its Lord through the Spirit. People know about the universal Church, but this is largely intellectual perception; they experience the Church at parish and local levels.

Bishop Juan Hervas of Cuidad Real in Spain, one of the founders of the Cursillo Movement (v. MOVEMENTS, ECCLESIAL) in the late 1940s, spoke of "the minimalist corruption of Christianity." It was his contention that people are being offered a seriously corrupt Christianity because it has been diminished in the range of its message and in the power of its Good News. Too often people still encounter a form of Christianity that is more or less exhausted by the injunction to keep the commandments, love your neighbor, and attend Sunday Mass. Such a Catholicism is corrupt in presenting a severely deficient vision for people's lives in the modern age; it is a very impaired notion of the Good News. The Church needs to offer the full gospel and not short-change people with the minimum. It must offer a pertinent spirituality, the full riches offered by Christ through his Church. It is clear that people are not satisfied by what the Church appears to be offering: they go to religions of the East, to cults, to sects, to the New Age movement to seek what will satisfy their deepest desires. Yet lying often forgotten is the Church's great mystical tradition, its centuries-old wisdom about spirituality and religious experience. We appeal to the head without the heart at our peril. But too often the Christianity people meet is over-intellectual and moralistic: it fails to attract the whole person and to fulfill the deepest needs of young people and old alike.

With regard to NRM there are other pastoral problems. There are several danger signs about groups which pastors and parents should note: a movement begins to cut itself off socially or geographically; the convert becomes increasingly dependent on the movement for definitions about, and testing of, reality; sharp boundaries are drawn between "them/us," Satanic and Godly, good and bad; important decisions in the recruits' lives are made by others; leaders claim divine authority for their actions and commands; excessively singleminded or oversimplified goals for life are proposed. Furthermore there is usually either "love bombing"—showering attention on recruits—or a playing on their guilt feelings. It is thus difficult for people to leave a cult or NRM, and the Churches often do not have much to offer for those who seek immediacy of religious experience and a deep sense of fellowship. It is not usually helpful to posit brainwashing, thus absolving people from any kind of personal responsibility. Nevertheless, those leaving NRM or cults may need counseling and/or psychological and spiritual healing.

Ultimately the NRMs are a challenge to the Churches[14] for profound renewal, for building community, and for preaching the joy and ultimate meaning that are to be found in both Cross and Resurrection.

[1]Card. F. Arinze, Address to consistory (4–7 April 1991), "Pastoral Responses to the Challenge of Sects," CathIntern 2 (1991) 605–611 at 606–607; see M. Tierney, *The New Elect: The Church and New Religious Groups* (Dublin: Veritas, 1985); F. Lovsky, "The Church and the Sects," OneChr 27 (1991) 222–233. [2]Excellent are R. Chandler, *Understanding the New Age* (Milton Keynes, 1988), T. Peters, *The Cosmic Self: A Penetrating Look at Today's New Age Movements* (San Francisco: Harper, 1991) and A. Nichols, "The New Age Movement," Month 253/1491 (1992) 84–89. See, too, J.J. LeBar et al., *Cults, Sects and the New Age* (Huntington: Our Sunday Visitor, 1989). [3]K. Hollmann, "New Age Bewegung und christliche Spiritualität," TGl 77 (1987) 474–482; M. Kehl, "Die Heilsverheißung des New Age: Eine theologische Auseindersetzung," GeistL 62 (1989) 4–18; H.J. Türk, "New Age und christlicher Glaube," StimZ 202 (1988) 664–678. [4]J. Vernette, "Le 'Nouvel-Âge'," NRT 111 (1989) 879–894. [5]N.L. Geisler, "The New Age Movement," BiblSac 144 (1987) 79–104 at 82; cf. M. Ferguson, *The Aquarian Conspiracy* (Los Angeles: Torcher, 1980) 62–63. [6]But see G. Card Danneels, *Christ or Aquarius?* (Dublin: Veritas, 1992). [7]Vatican Report, 4 May 1986, from Secretariats for Promoting Christian Unity, for Non-Christians and for Non-Believers and the Pontifical Council for Culture, Origins 16 (22 May 1986) 3–10; Addresses by six cardinals at the special consistory 4–7 April 1991, CathIntern 2 (1991) 605–618; A.R. Brockway and J.P. Rajashekar, *New Religious Movements and the Churches*. Report and Papers of a Consultation Sponsored by the Lutheran World Federation and the World Council of Churches, September 1986 (Geneva: WCC, 1987). See J.A. Saliba, "Vatican Response to New Religious Movements," TS 53 (1992) 3–39; idem, "The Christian Church and the New Religious Movements: Towards Theological Understanding," TS 43 (1982) 468–485. [8]J. Vernette, "La réincarnation: Une croyance ancienne, reprendue et séduisante," EspVie 98 (1988) 655–662, 667–683, 694–700. [9]Introduction to *The New Age Rage*, cited in Chandler (n. 2) 222–223. [10]Thus R.N. Baer, *Inside the New Age Nightmare* (Layfayette La.: Huntington, 1989); D.R. Groothus, *Unmasking the New Age* (Downers Grove, Ill.—Leicester UK: InterVarsity Press, 1986, 1991). [11]Thus the Jesuit M. Pacwa, *Catholics and the New Age: How Good People Are Being Drawn into Jungian Psychology, the Enneagram and the Age of Aquarius* (Ann Arbor, Mich.: Servant, 1992). [12]R.C. Rhodes, "The New Age Christology of David Spangler," BiblSac 144 (1987) 402–418; A. Romarheim, "The Aquarian Christ," BJRyL 70 (1988) 197–207; J. Vernette, "'Jésus' dans la nouvelle religiosité," EspVie 99 (1989) 97–109. [13]Art. cit. (n. 7) 485. [14]J. Drane, *What Is the New Age Saying to the Church?* (London: Marshall Pickering/HarperCollinsReligious, 1991); J. Finnegan, "Cults, Sects and Spiritual Movements: The Challenge to the Church," Fur 32 (1981) 772–783; J. Vernette, "Le foisonnement des sectes: Question posé à la pastorale," NRT 103 (1981) 641–663 and n. 7 above.

## MURATORIAN FRAGMENT

Discovered by L.A. Muratori in the mid-18th century, the Muratorian Fragment, written in very poor Latin but probably based on a Greek text of the 2nd century, gives the earliest canon or list of authentic Scriptures. It mentions Hermas (q.v.) only to exclude him from the canon along with other texts mainly of Gnostic or Montanist tendency. It begins with what must have been an account of Mark and goes on to mention what it calls the 3rd and 4th Gospels, Luke and John. It gives all the other NT books except Hebrews, James, 1 and 2 Peter.[1]

---

[1]Text Rouët de Journel 268; Bettenson, Documents 28–19; see M.-J. Lagrange, "Le Canon d'Hippolyte et le fragment de Muratori," RB 42 (1933) 161–186; OxDCC 950.

## MURRAY, John Courtney (1904–1967)

Born in New York, where he died in 1967, the Jesuit John Courtney Murray is best known for his writings on Church-State relations. He began writing on this topic as well as on ecumenical issues in the fledgling *Theological Studies* (from 1943), of which he was an editor. Against conservative opposition, he proposed a pluralist system of Church-State relations. Urged by his Roman superiors not to write on the topic in the 1950s, he turned his attention to systematic theology, which he taught at Woodstock,[1]

He continued to reflect on the situation of the Church in the U.S., publishing a collection of essays in 1960.[2] During Vatican II he published an important study on religious freedom.[3] A *peritus* at Vatican II from the second session, he had a major input into the document on Religious Freedom (DH, v. FREEDOM, RELIGIOUS), which reflects much of what he had earlier written.[4] After the council he wrote over a dozen articles explaining its teaching on religious freedom and on Church-State issues.[5]

---

[1]*The Problem of God* (New Haven—London, Yale UP, 1964). [2]*We Hold These Truths. Catholic Reflections on the American Proposition* (New York, 1960). [3]*The Problem of Religious Freedom* (London—Dublin, 1965), see TS 25 (1964) 503–573. [4]R.O. McEvoy, *John Courtney Murray's Thought on Religious Liberty in Its Final Phase.* Diss. Abs. (Rome: Alfonsiana, 1973). See D. Hollenbach, ed., "Theology and Philosophy in Public: A Symposium on John Courtney Murray's Unfinished Agenda," TS 40 (1979) 600–717; R. Hunt and K.L. Grasso, eds., *John Courtney Murray and the American Civil Conversation* (Grand Rapids, Mich.: Eerdmans, 1992); cf. M.J. Schuck, "John Courtney Murray's Problematic Interpretations of Leo XIII and the American Founders," Thom 55 (1991) 595–612. [5]E.g., "The Declaration on Religious Freedom," Conc 5 (May 1966) 3–10; "The Issue of Church and State at Vatican II," TS 27 (1966) 580–606.

## MYSTICI CORPORIS, The Encyclical

The encyclical of Pius XII on the Mystical Body (1943)[1] was a major ecclesiological statement by the magisterium, one which prepared the way for the Constitution on the Church of Vatican II, even though LG did not follow all the positions of the earlier document. It is a comprehensive statement on the doctrine of the Body of Christ, which had been gaining appreciation in the previous decades (cf. BODY OF CHRIST). In the opening paragraphs the pope indicated a twofold motivation for writing the encyclical: the value and sublimity of the doctrine; several dangerous errors that had appeared. On the errors, to which he returns several times in the course of the document, Pius XII noted: "On the one hand the error of *rationalism* persists, rejecting as absurd anything which transcends the powers of the human mind, side by side with the kindred false doctrine of naturalism which in the Church of Christ sees nothing, and refuses to see anything, apart from purely juridical and social ties. On the other hand there is the insidious growth of a false *mysticism* which, with its attempts to obliterate the inviolable frontiers between things created and their Creator, falsifies the Sacred Scriptures."[2] He also noted the danger of quietism associated with this latter error.[3]

The doctrinal exposition of the encyclical is outlined in stages: the Church is a body; the Church is the Body of Christ; Christ is the Head of the Body; the Church is the Mystical Body. The second part outlines the union of the faithful in and with Christ. The perspective within which the Pauline doctrine is viewed is an institutional model of the Church in which the Church is a "perfect society" (q.v.): "The true meaning of the word 'mystical' therefore reminds us that the Church, which must be held to be a perfect society in its own order, does not consist merely of social and juridical elements nor rest solely on such grounds. . . . That which raises the Christian society to a level utterly surpassing any order of nature is the Spirit of our Redeemer, the source of all graces, gifts, and miraculous powers, perennially and intimately pervading the Church and acting in her."[4] The equation of the Roman Catholic Church with the Mystical Body[5] and the description of the Body's membership[6] (v. MEMBERSHIP OF THE CHURCH) were not followed exactly by Vatican II. As he was a principal author, the notes of S. Tromp (q.v.) on the encyclical and his volumes on the Body of Christ are of particular value for its interpretation.[7]

---

[1]AAS 35 (1943) 193–248/Carlen 4:37-62 with extensive bibliog. [2]AAS 35 (1943) 197, 211, 223, 234/Carlen 4:39, 45, 49–50, 54/DS 3816–3817. [3]Ibid.—AAS 234/Carlen 54. [4]Ibid.—AAS 222–233/Carlen 49–50. [5]Ibid—AAS 199/Carlen 39–40. [6]Ibid.—AAS 202/Carlen 41/DS 3802/ND 849. [7]*Litterae encyclicae: Pius Papa XII De mystico Iesu Christi Corpore.* Textus et Documenta, series theologica 26 (Rome: Gregorian University, 1948); idem, *Corpus Christi quod est Ecclesia.* 4 vols. (Rome 1937–1962).

# N

## NEW AGE

See MOVEMENTS, NON-CHRISTIAN AND NEW AGE

## NEW TESTAMENT ECCLESIOLOGIES

The Church as the community of the disciples of the risen Lord existed of course before the NT came to be written. But we can glean much information about the life of the primitive Church (q.v.) and of local Churches (q.v.) by close study of the various books of the NT.[1]

But if by ecclesiology we mean some unified understanding of the Church, then there is wide agreement among Catholic,[2] Protestant,[3] and Orthodox[4] scholars that there is no single NT ecclesiology. Modern authors of NT biblical theologies will have a section on the Church, often conditioned by their overall perspective of the NT. No book or author of the NT gives a complete ecclesiology, one which would include a unified vision of the Church and a statement of how its various aspects interrelate. Instead we have partial affirmations which have to be interpreted within the scope of the particular NT book and within the total NT message about the person and mission of Christ. We do not always have detailed information about the ways in which the books of the NT are each occasioned by a set of problems, or are at least an attempt to present to a specific group some aspect of the mystery of Christ. Questions about the Church will thus have a greater centrality in some books than in others. The community of believers existed prior to any reflection on their structuring or detailed consideration of their self-understanding. Finally, we need to note that during the NT period, i.e., up to the end of the 1st century, there was both development and pluralism in the various local Churches.

What follows is a brief chronological account of the NT writings; from the enormous amount of scholarly writing on the topic, it seeks to give an outline of positions that carry reasonably wide support, together with more recent bibliography. The standard commentaries are not usually noted. Indications about the life, attitudes, and problems in the various Churches are all important gleanings for an understanding of the Church in the NT. It will be obvious that many of these concerns of the NT Church retain a relevance for today, either as questions which are still pertinent or as permanently valid insights into the mystery of the Church.

We begin with St Paul.[5] His first work and the earliest NT book is 1 Thessalonians (50 C.E.).[6] The gospel has been preached to them, and they have received it in faith, hope, and love (1:2-3; 3:6-7); they are to continue to live in holiness (4:1-12; 5:14-18). The delay of the parousia (q.v.) is already causing some concern, and their response must be watchfulness (4:14–5:11). The community is bearing witness (1:8). There are leaders of some kind (5:12). There would seem already to be some problems arising from the charisms (q.v.) of the Holy Spirit—hence the call for discernment and for the acceptance of genuine gifts (5:19-22). Charism would also seem to be implied in the power with which the gospel has been proclaimed (2:5, 13). Finally, there is some indication of opposition from the Jews (2:14; cf. 1:6; 3:2-4).

If 2 Thessalonians is written by Paul, it could be dated about 51 C.E., but many scholars regard it as pseudonymous and place it some decades later.[7] Many of the same themes appear but with some deepening: life in faith, hope, love (1:2-3; 3:16); persecution (1:4-7); the delay in the parousia (2:1-12). There is a strong emphasis on fidelity to the apostolic preaching and tradition (2:13-15; 3:6, 13-14). The central proclamation of the risen Lord is implied in both letters.

The letters to the Corinthians can be dated about 57 C.E.[8] The Church at Corinth was composed mostly of Gentile converts, most of them probably of a lower social class (1 Cor 1:26-28). Coming straight from his failure in Athens, Paul's preaching in the power of the Spirit is focused on the cross of Jesus (cf. Acts 17:16-18:1 with 1 Cor 2:1-5). Richly endowed with charismatic gifts (1 Cor 1:4-7), the community is beset with problems: divisions (1 Cor 1:4-7), deviant sexual morality (5:1-13; 6:12-20), abuses in worship—especially at the Lord's Supper (1 Cor 11), disorder in the use of charisms (1 Cor 12; 14), confusion about the resurrection (1 Cor 15; 16), and the rejection by some of Paul's own apostolic authority (1 Cor 9; 2 Cor 10-12).

In dealing with these problems of an immature Church (1 Cor 3:1-3), Paul develops at length several ecclesiological themes: the unifying and empowering role of the Holy Spirit (1 Cor 2; 12:3-11); the local community as the Body of Christ (1 Cor 12:12-27; 10:16-17; cf. 6:15-20); the authority to regulate charisms (1 Cor 14); the centrality of both Eucharist (1 Cor 11:23-26) and the resurrection of Christ (1 Cor 15:3-19) in the faith and life of the Church; the characteristics of Christian ministry (q.v.)—commended by the Spirit (2 Cor 3:1-6), splendor (3:7-18), honesty (4:1-6), trials (4:7-10; 6:1-12), reconciliation (5:11-21). Furthermore, the collection for the famine-struck Church at Jerusalem shows both the value of practical charity and the need Paul felt of forging deeper bonds with the Mother Church (1 Cor 16:1-4; 2 Cor 8:1-9:15; cf. Acts 11:27-30; 24:17; Rom 15:25-31).

The abundance of charisms at Corinth and the absence of any authority figures apart from Paul and his associates have led some to favor as being more authentic the Corinthian model of Church order. The injunction to be submissive to the household of Stephanus (1 Cor 16:15-16) is often overlooked. It is, however, undoubtedly true that Catholic practice and ecclesiology in the past has esteemed the Pastoral Epistle model more highly than the Corinthian one.[9]

The letters to the Galatians and Romans belong to the same period, about 57-58 C.E.[10] In both, a dominant consideration is the relation of the Church to Judaism and to the OT. In Gal 2:1-10 we have Paul's account of the discussions at Jerusalem, one which does not harmonize in every detail with Acts 15:1-35 (v. PRIMITIVE CHURCH).[11] In this letter the most important theme is the role of the law and that of faith (2:11–5:6), one developed further in Rom 4 and 7. This latter also ponders profoundly the relation between the Israel of the OT and the Israel constituted by the followers of Jesus (Rom 9–11). Important ecclesiological themes are: the radical equality of all the baptized (Gal 3:29; cf. Rom

8:14-17); the importance of charisms—presumed to be known in a Church that Paul had not visited (Rom 12:6-8); the living tradition handed on (Gal 1:8, 11; Rom 1:1-5); living en Christô crucified and risen (Gal 2:19-20; Rom 6:1-11); obedience to secular authority (Rom 13:1-7). As in other Pauline letters, the concluding chapters deal with moral exhortation;[12] unity and charity are again important topics (Rom 12:4-5, 9-21; 16:17; Gal 5:15; 6:2, 10). Neither letter gives much information about any leadership structures in Galatia or Rome. In Romans, however, Paul calls himself an apostle (Rom 1:1). This title is given also to Andronicus and Junia—the latter probably a woman (Rom 16:7). Some of the charisms in Rom 12:6-8 might indicate offices as well as gifts. Various people in Rom 16 are described as working for the gospel, while Phoebe, a woman, is described as diakonos (Rom 16:1, v. DEACONESS—WOMEN DEACONS), which may refer either to an office (cf. 1 Tim 3:8) or more generally to serving (cf. 2 Cor 11:23).

Though the unity of Philippians has been questioned,[13] its authorship by Paul is less frequently challenged. The letter is intensely personal in style and is largely exhortation to deepen koinônia (v. COMMUNION) and to rejoice.[14] It contains some hints about church leadership: it is addressed to the holy ones (hagioi) with their bishops and deacons (sun episkopois kai diakonois—1:1); both Timothy and Epaphroditus are to be well received (2:19-30). It is not possible to come to any sure conclusion about the leadership structures of 53–63 C.E., the decade during which Paul wrote the letter(s).[15]

The brief Letter to Philemon concerning the runaway slave Onesimus is probably dated 62–63 C.E. It is usually studied for position on slavery, which Paul only mentions in one other place (1 Cor 7:17-24). But it has some notable ecclesiological purport: the Church meets in the house of Philemon (v. 2); faith is to be shared (v. 6); Paul asserts his right to command Philemon, though he does not exercise it (vv. 8-9, 21); Onesimus is a "brother" to Philemon: the slave transformed in Christ is himself an offer of freedom to his master;[16] for though he appears to leave the matter entirely to the goodwill of Philemon, Paul in fact places him in a dilemma which involves compromising either the Christian teaching of love and the equality of all or the social standards of the time.[17]

After dealing with the indisputably authentic letters of Paul, we can now turn to the Synoptic Gospels, the first of which is Mark, variously dated but more often 65–75 C.E. From the point of view of ecclesiology, Mark's Gospel is especially significant for three themes. First, Jesus' preaching and ministry are summarized at the beginning and throughout in terms of the kingdom (q.v.): "The time is fulfilled, and the kingdom of God has come near; repent and believe in the good news" (1:15). Second, "Mark describes Jesus as constituting a new and radical family for which he is the model" (cf. 3:31-35; 10:29-30).[18] It is, therefore, discipleship that is the main ideal placed before the Christian community, though the response varies greatly.[19] Third, the Twelve (v. APOSTLES) have as their primary function to be with Jesus and to carry out his mission (3:14-15). Three of them, Peter, James, and John (sometimes with Andrew), are the recipients of special revelation about Jesus (cf. 1:29; 5:37; 9:2-8; 13:3; 14:32-42).[20]

We can date the Gospel of Matthew about a decade after Mark's. Its audience was a Jewish-Christian community, possibly at Antioch.[21] Its sources are Mark's Gospel, Q—a tradition known also to Luke—and material which is proper to Matthew. These traditions probably intermingled quite freely before the composition of the Gospel.[22] Matthew is concerned to bring forth "new things and old" (cf. 13:52), to retain both the old and the new wineskins (cf. 9:17). His Gospel has many important points for ecclesiology:[23] it has a vision of salvation history which embraces three stages—OT, the time of fulfillment in Jesus, and the universal mission of the Church; it accounts for the displacement of Israelites by the Gentiles (21:43); there is consequently a lot of interest in the role of the Torah for the Christian community;[24] the nexus between Christ, the Church, and morality has been called the specific characteristic of this Gospel; Matthew is the only evangelist to use the word Church, on each occasion in the context of authority (Matt 16:18; 18:17), and he also edits Markan material to heighten its ecclesial significance (e.g., the power to forgive sins given to men—9:8); he knows of charismatic figures, but the warning that the bearing of charism does not necessarily lead to salvation (7:21-23) may indicate some tension concerning charism, hence the need for discernment (7:15-20);[25] as in Mark the proclamation of the kingdom is to the fore, but there are major discourses about the community absent from Mark (chs. 5–7; 10; 18); there is an important stress on brother-sisterhood (e.g., 23:8; 25:40)[26] among all who have the one heavenly Father; finally, the story of Jesus' ministry could not be told without an emphasis on the role of Peter (q.v.),[27] which would suggest that the Matthean picture of this apostle coheres with the experience and memory of the evangelist's audience. There is little direct teaching about leadership in the community except for warnings against aping the rabbis and Pharisees (23:1-12).

The Gospel of Luke and the Book of Acts may be taken together, as they clearly have a common vision arising from their one author.[28] Both books were written about the time of Matthew, that is, probably in the 80s. Luke unfolds six stages of the Church's emergence: the OT; the ministry of John the Baptist; the community of disciples formed around Jesus during his public life, with the apostles and a mission to Israel having some importance; the appearances of the risen Lord; Pentecost, which leads on to preaching to Israel with signs and wonders; the proclamation of the word with boldness (q.v.); the admission of the pagans to the Church.[29] Foreshadowed in the Gospel, the Holy Spirit dominates the story of Acts as it guides the nascent Church and sustains it despite persecutions and a series of crises and challenges: the problem of the Hellenists (Acts 6); the need for an identity other than as a sect within Judaism (Stephen); the entry of the pagans (Cornelius); the missionary thrust of the infant Church of Antioch; the relationship between the Torah and Christian freedom (Jerusalem meeting).[30] Above all, Luke gives idealized pictures of the early community (Acts 2:42-47; 4:23-37; 5:12-16),[31] which have been a constant inspiration for groups within the Church ever since. But all is not easy, though Luke strives to put a peaceful gloss on serious difficulties, especially the relationship of Jewish Christians and Hellenist ones (v. PRIMITIVE CHURCH). The question of leadership is a complex one: Peter is the key figure in the early chapters of Acts, but later he seems to give way to James; the apostles have an important role at the beginning (Acts 1:15-26), but one which lessens as the story of Acts progresses; there would seem to be a "twelve" authority structure for the Jewish Christians and a somehow subordinate "seven" structure for the Hellenists (see Acts 6–8, where the seven do not confine their services to ministering at tables—Acts 6:1-3); Paul sends for the elders of the Church (tous presbuterous tês ekklêsias) of Ephesus (Acts 20:17)—the same are episkopoi who have charge of the flock committed to them by the Spirit (Acts 20:28). Paul and Barnabas are pictured as appointing elders (presbuteroi) in every place (Acts 14:23).

The letters to the Ephesians and Colossians are difficult to date: the many scholars who call them Deutero-Pauline would suggest some time in the 80s, others would argue a Pauline authorship and place them in the 60s.[32] Even if they are not actually dictated by Paul, these letters are from the Pauline school. Here we are in the presence of a profound ecclesiology, not in terms of the Church's institutions but of its meaning. The following are important elements: the emphasis is not now on the local church (q.v.), but on a universal or cosmic Church which is the Body of Christ (q.v.); the Church is holy as this Body (Eph 1:22-23; 5:32); in Christ there is dwelling a fullness (plêrôma—Col 2:9; Eph 1:23); the Church reaches into the heavenly places (Eph 3:9-10; Col 1:15-20). But the stress on the beauty of the Church does not obscure the need for moral behavior based on the gifts received (Eph 4–6; Col 3–4). Charismatic gifts, or offices, are given for upbuilding (Eph 4:11-12). On the whole the ecclesiology of Ephesians is more developed than that of Colossians.

The Pastoral Letters, 1 and 2 Timothy, Titus, are now generally felt not to have been written by Paul, though there is much Pauline theology in them. A date sometime after 95 C.E. seems plausible.[33] The situation is very much changed from the previous decades. The problem facing the Churches for which the letters were written was to preserve integrity in a transitional situation. The means sought was authority figures, overseers (episkopoi), elders (presbuteroi), and ministers (diakonoi), who in each place would have a care above all for sound teaching (Titus 1:9-2:1; 1 Tim 4:1-11; cf. 2 Tim 1:14). The presbyter-bishops were to rule the local Churches like a father taking responsibility for a home, hence the qualities needed (Titus 1:5-11; 1 Tim 3:2-7). It is easy to see why it is above all from the structured Churches of the Pastoral Epistles that the constitution of the Church in the early 2nd century (as in Ignatius of Antioch—q.v.) came about. For some Protestant scholars these characteristics, especially the institutional norms, are seen as signs of "Early Catholicism" (v. CATHOLICISM, EARLY).

With regard to the Gospel of John,[34] which can be dated about 95 C.E., F. Schüssler Fiorenza aptly notes: "To search John's Gospel for a concretization of the relation between Jesus and the Church is to enter a battleground already strewn with the corpses of fallen hypotheses."[35] One can say that there is only an implicit ecclesiology in John: what is central is a relationship to Jesus as his disciple: one is challenged to take the side of the unbelieving Jews or to be with Jesus which is to be in the sheepfold (ch. 10), to belong to the vine (15:1-11). The synagogue and the Johannine community are alienated.[36] The great I AM statements are but some of the indications that judgment is already present and will be exercised in Jesus' name by the Spirit (16:7-10). While clearly dominant roles are assigned to Peter and to the Beloved Disciple, the message is clear: "All Christians are disciples and among them greatness is determined by a loving relation to Jesus, not by function or office."[37] Peter has to learn that the condition for authority must be love (cf. 21:15-17 with 10:1-18). It is the high Christology of John that allows him to go to the heart of what the Church is about: love for Jesus, love for others (15:9-17).[38]

R.E. Brown remarks that Johannine ecclesiology is the most attractive and exciting in the NT, and is also the least stable.[39] We have to turn to the Letters of John from the same tradition as the Gospel to complete the picture.[40] One of the most significant elements in the Gospel of John is the coming of the Paraclete who would be Jesus' ongoing presence in the believer for all times; the Spirit, moreover, is the Teacher (14:15-17, 26; 16:13-14). R.E. Brown, who places the letters within a decade of the Gospel, notes evidence of internal dissension within the community: the humanity of Jesus is neglected (1 John 4:2; 2 John 7); the only sin is a refusal to believe in Jesus (1 John 1:8, 10); love seems confined to the true brethren (1 John 2:7-11; 4:21; 2 John 4–6); guidance of individuals by the Holy Spirit requires not only discernment (1 John 2:27; 4:1-6) but also some external authority.[41] Johannine ecclesiology, like others in the NT, is not sufficiently whole to survive in its pure state.

J. Casey notes that "very little agreement exists concerning most points of Hebrews."[42] It was written before 95 C.E., probably to a group of Jewish Christians who pined for the splendor of the OT rites. But there is a radical displacement: there is only one tabernacle, which is in heaven (8:1-2; 9:24); the old covenant is nullified by the new (8:13); the Church is the wandering people of God (3:7–4:11); the law and priesthood have been transformed (7:12); the cult of the Church is not external sacrifice but the worship of Christ, the eternal High Priest (chs. 3–10). There is a realized eschatology: already we are in union with the heavenly mediator whose blood has cleansed us from sin (9:12-15; 10:10, 14), and we enter the sanctuary through him (10:19-22). From this doctrinal exposition clear imperatives emerge: faith, perseverance, and endurance (chs. 11–13). Though the language, theological concerns, and images differ, the ecclesiology of Hebrews resembles more that of Ephesians and Revelation than any other NT work.

Sometime between the 70s and the 90s is suggested for 1 Peter,[43] though some scholars date it in the 60s.[44] The readers seem to be undergoing hardship, if not by actual persecution, at least by social and religious trials (4:12-14), so that they are aliens (1:1; 2:11). The letter, which has a strong baptismal character, is an appeal to stand firm; Exodus motifs are put before them (chs. 1–2); they are to think of their dignity as God's people (2:4-10, which takes over the promises and titles of the OT); in a hostile environment they are to be careful not to give offense (2:11–3:7; 4:4, 14-18) but rather to give witness to the world (2:9).[45] The Churches have a structure similar to the pastorals, i.e., with elders (presbuteroi—5:1, 5). Authority is to be exercised as in Mark 10:42 by not being domineering (katakurieuontes—5:3). The letter is also characterized by emphasis on belonging despite the "time of exile" (1:17).

One of the last of the NT books to be written was 2 Peter.[46] Like the Letter of Jude, with which it has several affinities, the main concern is with false teachers (2:1-2; cf. Jude 5–19) and with those who deceive the community through immoral living (2:10-22; cf. Jude

4, 18-19). The recipients are warned to be steadfast in the apostolic teaching they have received (1:12-19; 3:2; cf. Jude 3). By the composition of these two letters it is clear that the Church has some accepted body of teaching which is normative.

The Letter of James is to be dated before 95 C.E.[47] Its significance for ecclesiology lies mainly in its moral exhortations, which resemble the wisdom literature of the OT. We get the picture of the Church committed to living in the world and having to fight against the sins and the unacceptable values of its environment. An important feature of the work is its sense of continuity with the OT, in which it is quite unlike Hebrews.

Finally, there is the difficult Book of Revelation,[48] from about 90–95 C.E. It is an apocalypse, that is, a work of visions and symbols with a message to those suffering persecution and distress. The situation of the Church is difficult because of the increasing hostility of the Roman Empire, and the struggle on earth of the Church reflects the cosmic struggle between good and evil. Y.A. Collins has argued that the unity of the work can be seen in a recurring triple theme of persecution, judgment, and triumph.[49] Another key idea is that of bearing witness.[50] The letters to the seven Churches (chs. 2–3)[51] indicate their problems and failures: reduced love (2:4); following false leaders and teachers (2:6, 14–15, 20); compromise (3:20); falling away (3:3); complacency (3:15-18). They are called upon to be faithful (2:10, 23; 3:9-10), to repent (3:3, 18-20), to endure (2:3, 17), and each is offered divine gifts if it perseveres. The Book of Revelation is always contemporary, not for the themes emphasized by the millenarianisms (q.v.) of yesterday and today but for its permanent challenge to Christians living in the world to hold fast to the lordship of Jesus (13:8), supported by the promise of the ultimate victory already being celebrated by those who have remained faithful. Like Ephesians and Hebrews, the teaching of Revelation invites us to consider the Church in glory as an encouragement for the Church still struggling.

It is clear that each of the various NT books has an emphasis on particular aspects of the mystery of the Church. The NT authors also show different models (q.v.) for understanding the Church and Christ-event. The task for ecclesiology is to be as comprehensive as possible in bringing out all the relevant teaching of the NT books and applying it to the contemporary local and universal Church.

[1]R.E. Brown, *The Churches the Apostles Left Behind* (Ramsey: Paulist, 1984); R. Morgan, "The One Fellowship of Churches in the New Testament," Conc 144 (1981) 27–33; K.H. Schelke, *Theology of the New Testament. 4.—The Rule of God: Church—Eschatology* (Collegeville: The Liturgical Press, 1974); V. Warnach, "Church," Bauer 1:101-116; cf. J.P. Meier, *The Mission of Christ and His Church.* Good News Studies 30 (Wilmington: Glazier, 1990); K.

Rahner, "Theology in the New Testament," ThInvest 5:23-41.   [2]A. Antón, *La Iglesia de Cristo: El Israel de la Vieja y la Nueva Alianza.* BAC Maior 15 (Madrid: La Editorial Católica, 1977) 307–309; R.E. Brown, "The Unity and Diversity in New Testament Ecclesiology," in *New Testament Essays* (London: Chapman, 1965) 36–47; Commission Biblique Pontificale, *Unité et diversité dans l'Église* (Vatican, 1989); P. Grech, "Unità e diversità nel Nuovo testamento: Lo stato della questione," RivBib 30 (1982) 291–299; T.P. Rausch, "Unity and Diversity in New Testament Ecclesiology: Twenty-five Years after Käsemann and Brown," IrTQ 54 (1988) 131–139.   [3]M.A. Chevallier, "L'unité plurielle de l'Église d'après le Nouveau Testament," RHPR 66 (1986) 3–20; A.J.M. Wedderburn, "A New Testament Church Today?," ScotJT 31 (1978) 517–532.   [4]V. Kesich, "Unity and Diversity in New Testament Ecclesiology," SVlad 19 (1975) 109–127.   [5]V.P. Branick, *The House Church in the Writings of Paul.* Zacchaeus Studies: New Testament (Wilmington: Glazier, 1989); H. Doohan, *Paul's Vision of Church.* Good News Studies 32 (Wilmington: Glazier, 1989); W.A. Meeks, *The First Urban Christians: The Social World of the Apostle Paul* (New Haven: Yale UP, 1983).   [6]R.F. Collins, "The Church of the Thessalonians," LouvSt 5 (1974–1975) 336–349; idem, "1 Thess and the Liturgy of the Early Church," BibTB 10 (1980) 51–64; E.F. Harrison, *The Apostolic Church* (Grand Rapids: Eerdmans, 1985) 195–201; A.J. Malherbe, "'Pastoral Care' in the Thessalonican Church (1 Th 5:14-15)," NTS 36 (1990) 375–391.   [7]For views, see J.A. Bailey, "Who Wrote II Thessalonians?," NTS 25 (1979) 131–145.   [8]S. Cipriani, "La comunità di Corinto come 'stimolo' alla riflessione teologica di S. Paolo," Later 50 (1984) 86–100; F.J. Cwiekowski, *The Beginnings of the Church* (Mahwah: Paulist— Dublin: Gill and Macmillan, 1988) 107–111; T. Engberg-Pedersen, "The Gospel and Social Practice According to 1 Corinthians," NTS 33 (1987) 557–584; Harrison, (n. 6) 199–207; N. Koulomzine, "L'unité de l'Église selon 1 Cor," Nicol 9 (1981) 275–282; J. Murphy-O'Connor, *St. Paul's Corinth.* Good News Studies 6 (Wilmington: Glazier, 1983); idem, *The Theology of the Second Letter to the Corinthians* (Cambridge: UP, 1991); A.C. Thiselton, "Realized Eschatology at Corinth," NTS 24 (1978) 510–526; L.L. Welborn, "On the Discord in Corinth: 1 Corinthians 1–4 and Ancient Politics," JBL 106 (1987) 85–111.   [9]Cf. H. Küng, *The Church* (London: Search Press, 1971) 179–203; M.Y. McDonald, *The Pauline Churches: A Socio-historical Study of Institutionalism in the Pauline and Deutero-Pauline Writings.* Soc. NT Studies 60 (Cambridge: UP, 1988).   [10]R.E. Brown, in R.E. Brown and J.P. Meier, *Antioch and Rome: New Testament Cradles of Catholic Christianity* (London: Chapman—Mahwah: Paulist, 1983) 105–127; Harrison (n. 6) 219–228; J. Lambrecht, "Unity and Diversity in Gal 1–2," in Commission Bibl. Pont. (n. 2) 127–142.   [11]See J.P. Meier, in Brown and Meier (n. 10) 36–44; P.J. Achtemeier, "An Elusive Unity: Paul, Acts, and the Early Church," CBQ 48 (1986) 1–26; T.D. Gordon, "The Problem at Galatia," Interp 41 (1987) 32–43.   [12]F. Vouga, "L'Épître aux Romains comme document ecclésiologique (Rom 12–15)," ETR 61 (1986) 485–495; M. Mullins, *Called to be Saints: Christian Living in First Century Rome* (Dublin: Veritas, 1991).   [13]See J.A. Fitzmyer, JBC 2:248; B. Byrne, NJBC 791–792.   [14]Harrison, (n. 6) 190–195; A. di Marco, "Koinonia—communio: Flp 2,1," Laur 21 (1986) 376–403; C.L. Mearns, "The Identity of Paul's Opponents at Philippi," NTS 33 (1987) 194–204.   [15]See Cwiekowski (n. 8) 106–107.   [16]See J.-F. Collange, *L'épître de saint Paul à Philémon* (Geneva: Labor et Fides, 1987).   [17]M.A. Getty, *Philippians and Philemon.* NTMess 14 (Wilmington: Glazier—Dublin: Veritas, 1980) 78–79; D.M. Derrett, "The Functions of the Epistle to Philemon," ZNW 79 (1988) 63–91; S.C. Winter, "Paul's Letter to Philemon," NTS 33 (1987) 1–15.   [18]F. Schüssler Fiorenza, *Foundational Theology: Jesus and the Church* (New York: Crossroad, 1985) 134; G.

Dautzenberg, "Mark and Early Christian Theology," TDig 26 (1978) 28–29 (= Kair 18 [1976] 281–291). [19]P.J. Achtemeier, "'And He Followed Him': Miracles and Discipleship in Mark 1:46-52," Semeia 11 (1978) 115–146; E. Best, "The Role of the Disciples in Mark," NTS 23 (1976–1977) 377–401; idem, *Disciples and Discipleship: Studies in the Gospel of Mark* (Edinburgh: Clark, 1986); idem, *Following Jesus: Discipleship in the Gospel of Mark*. JSNT Supplement 4 (Sheffield: JSOT Press, 1981); C.C. Black, *The Disciples According to Mark: Markan Redaction in Current Debate*. JSNT Supp. series 27 (Sheffield: JSOT Press, 1989); F.J. Maloney, "The Vocation of the Disciples in the Gospel of Luke," Sales 43 (1981) 487–515; D. Rhodes, "Losing Life for Others in the Face of Death: Mark's Standards of Judgment," Inter 47 (1993) 358–369; A. Rodríguez Carmona, "La Iglesia en Marcos," EstE 63 (1988) 129–163; A. Stock, *Call to Discipleship: A Literary Study of St. Mark's Gospel*. Good News Studies 1 (Wilmington: Glazier, 1982); E. Struthers Malbon, "Fallible Followers: Women and Men in the Gospel of Mark," Semeia 28 (1983) 29–48; eadem., "Disciples/Crowds/Whoever: Markan Characters and Readers," NT 28 (1986) 104–130; D.M. Sweetland, *Our Journey with Jesus: Discipleship According to Mark*. Good News Studies 22 (Wilmington: Glazier, 1987). [20]See Schüssler Fiorenza (n. 18) 136–137. [21]D.I. Balch, ed., *Social History of the Matthean Community: Cross Disciplinary Approaches* (Minneapolis: Fortress, 1991); P. Bolognesi, "Matteo 18, 20 e la dottrina della Chiesa," BibbiaOr 29 (1987) 171–177; R.E. Brown and J.P. Meier (n. 11) 45–72; Cwiekowski (n. 8) 154–159; B.R. Doyle, "Matthew's Intention as Discerned by His Structure," RB 95 (1988) 34–54; V. Fusco, "Il 'vissuto' della Chiesa in Matteo—Appunti metodologici con esemplificazione da Mt 7, 15-23," Asp 27 (1980) 3–26; D.J. Harrington, "Matthean Studies since Joachim Rohde," in *Light of All Nations*. Good News Studies 3 (Wilmington: Glazier—Dublin: Veritas, 1982) 93–109 = HeythJ 16 (1975) 375–388; J.D. Kingsbury, "The Word *akolouthein* ('to follow') an Index of Matthew's View of His Community," JBL 97 (1978) 56–73; E.A.LaVerdiere and W.G. Thompson, "New Testament Communities in Transition: A Study of Matthew and Luke," TS 37 (1976) 568–597 esp. 571–582 (by Thompson); J.P. Meier, *The Vision of Matthew: Christ, Church and Morality in the First Gospel* (New York: Paulist, 1979); idem (n. 11) 45–72; J. Roloff, "Das Kirchenverständnis des Matthäus im Spiegel seiner Gleichnisse," NTS 38 (1992) 337–356; R. Schnackenburg, *The Church in the New Testament* (London: Burns & Oates, 1965) 69–77; D. Senior, *What Are They Saying About Matthew?* (Ramsey: Paulist, 1983); M.J. Wilkins, *The Concept of Disciple in Matthew's Gospel as Reflected in the Term "Mathêtês."* Supplements to the NT 59 (Leiden: Brill, 1988). [22]Meier, in Brown-Meier (n. 10) 55–57. [23]Ibid., 59–72. [24]P. Beauchamp, "L'Évangile de Matthieu et l'héritage d'Israel," RechSR 76 (1988) 5–38; J.D. Kingsbury, "The Developing Conflict Between Jesus and the Jewish Leaders in Matthew's Gospel: A Literary Critical Study," CBQ 49 (1987) 57–73; Schnackenburg (n. 21) 71–72. [25]Cf. E. Schweiger, "Observance of the Law and Charismatic Activity in Matthew," NTS 16 (1969–1970) 213–230; D. Hill, "False Prophets and Charismatics: Structure and Interpretation in Mt 7:15-23," Bib 57 (1976) 327–348. [26]R. Hoet, *"Omnes autem fratres estis": Étude du concept ecclésiologique des "frères" selon Mt. 23:8-12*. AnGreg 232 (Rome: Gregorian UP, 1982). [27]Schüssler Fiorenza (n. 18) 140–147; J.A. Burgess, *A History of the Exegesis of Matthew 16:17-19 from 1781–1965* (Ann Arbor: Edwards, 1976); R.E. Brown et al, *Peter in the New Testament* (Minneapolis: Augsburg—London: Chapman, 1973) 75–107. [28]Cf. Schnackenburg (n. 21) 62–68; R.E. Brown (n. 1) 61–74; P. Diaman Akunonu, "The Church and Churches in the Acts of the Apostles," RAfrT 13 (1989) 17–30; J. Dupont, *Teologia della Chiesa negli Atti degli Apostoli*. Studi biblici 10 (Bologna: Dehoniane, 1984); J.A.

Fitzmyer, "The Designations of Christians in Acts and Their Significance," Commission Bibl. Pont. (n. 2) 223–236; P. Jovino, "L'Église communauté des saints dans *les Actes des apôtres* et dans les épîtres aux Thessaloniciens," RivBib 16 (1968) 495–526; LaVerdiere and Thompson (n. 21) esp. 582–593 (by LaVerdiere); W.E. Mills, *A Bibliography of the Periodical Literature on the Acts of the Apostles (1962–1984)*. Supplement to *Novum Testamentum* 58 (Leiden: Brill, 1986); L. Monsengwo Pasinya, "Unité et diversité dans les Actes des Apôtres: Le problème des groupes culturels," in Commission Bibl. Pont. (n. 2) 199–208; R.F. O'Toole, *The Unity of Luke's Theology: An Analysis of Luke-Acts* (Wilmington: Glazier, 1984); J. Pathrapankal, "The Church in the Acts of the Apostles: A Model for Our Times," TDig 34 (1987) 19–24 = ZMissRW 70 (1986) 275–287; M.A. Powell, *What Are They Saying About Luke?* (New York—Mahwah: Paulist, 1989). [29]D.C. Allison Jr., "Was There a 'Lukan Community'?," IrBSt 10 (1988) 62–70; F.F. Bruce, "Paul's Apologetic and the Purpose of Acts," BJRyL 69 (1986–1987) 379–393; K.N. Giles, "The Church in the Gospel of Luke," ScotJT 34 (1981) 121–146; J.A. Jauregui, "Israel y la Iglesia en la teología de Luca," EstE 61 (1986) 129–149; B. Papa, "Lo sfondo ecclesiale dell'opera lucana," Asp 27 (1980) 27–40; Schüssler Fiorenza, op. cit. (n. 18) 137–138. [30]C.K. Barrett, "The Apostolic Decree of Acts 15:29," AustralBR 35 (1987) 50–59; G. Betori, "Lo Spirito e l'annuncio della parola negli Atti degli Apostoli," RivBib 35 (1987) 399–441; M.-É. Boismard, "Le 'Concile' de Jérusalem (Act 15:1-33): Essai de critique Littéraire," ETL 64 (1988) 433–440; M. Carrez, "Les principes de l'unité et de la cohésion ecclésiale d'après Luc (livre des Actes): 'Koinonia' et organisation institutionnelle," AnnéeCan 21 (1977) 141–152; L. Legrand, "The Structure of Acts 2: The Integral Dimensions of the Charismatic Movement According to Luke," IndTSt 19 (1982) 193–209; R. Michaels, "The Model of Church in the First Christian Community of Jerusalem. Ideal and Reality," LouvSt 10 (1984–1985) 303–323. [31]P.C. Bori, *Chiesa primitiva: L'Immagine della comunità delle origini, Atti 2, 42-47; 4, 32-37 nella storia della chiesa antica* (Brescia: Paideia, 1974); idem, "La référence à la communauté de Jérusalem dans les sources chrétiennes orientales at occidentales jusqu'au Ve siècle," Istina 19 (1974) 31–48; L. Cerfaux, *La communauté apostolique. Témoins de Dieu* (Paris, 1956); P.S. Esler, *Community and Gospel in Luke-Acts: The Social and Political Motivations of Lucan Theology*. Society for NT Monographs 57 (Cambridge: UP, 1987); D.J. Harrington, *God's People in Christ. Overtures to Biblical Theology* (Philadelphia: Fortress, 1980) 33–44; Harrison (n. 6) 176–183. R. Michiels, "The 'Model of Church' in the First Christian Community of Jerusalem: Ideal and Reality," LouvSt 10 (1984–1985) 303–323; F. Montagnini, "La comunità primitiva come luogo culturale. Nota ad At 2, 42-46," RivBib 35 (1987) 477–484. [32]L. Swain, *Ephesians*. NTMess 13, and P.V. Rogers, *Colossians*. NTMess 15 (Wilmington: Glazier—Dublin: Veritas, 1980); Cwiekowski (n. 8) 137–140; Brown (n. 1) 47–60; K. Usami, *Somatic Comprehension of Unity: The Church in Ephesus*. Analecta biblica 101 (Rome: Biblical Institute, 1983); J. Gnilka, *Der Epheserbrief* (Freiburg: Herder, 1971) 99–111; idem, "Das Kirchenmodell des Epheserbriefes," in Commission Bibl. Pont. (n. 2) 157–174; Harrington (n. 31) 67–74; Harrison (n. 6) 216–219; L. Cerfaux, *The Church in the Theology of St. Paul* (New York: Herder & Herder—Edinburgh/London: Nelson, 1959 from French ed. 1947) 290–356. [33]Brown (n. 1) 47–60; P. Rogers, *The Few in Charge of the Many: The Model of Ministerial Authority in the Pastoral Epistles as a Positive Norm for the Church* (Rome: Gregorian University, 1977). [34]R.E. Brown, *The Community of the Beloved Disciple* (New York: Paulist—London: Chapman, 1983); idem, *The Gospel According to John*. Anchor Bible 29, 29A (Garden City, N.Y.: Doubleday, 1966, 1970—London: Chapman, 1971); idem, *The Churches the Apostles*

*Left Behind* (n. 1) 102–123; P. Benoit, "L'unité de la communion ecclésiale dans l'Esprit selon le quatrième Évangile," in Commission Bibl. Pont. (n. 2) 265–283; Schüssler Fiorenza (n. 18) 147–154; J.F. O'Grady, "Johannine Ecclesiology: A Critical Evaluation," BibTB 7 (1977) 36–44; U. Schnelle, "Johanneische Ekklesiologie," NTS 37 (1991) 37–50. [35]Op. cit. (n. 18) 149. [36]Brown (n. 1) 104. [37]Brown (n. 1) 93; cf. idem, "Crucial Questions in Johannine Theology," in *The Gospel According to John* (n. 36) 1:cv-cxi with bibliog. cxxvii; M.-A. Chevalier, "La fondation de 'l'Église' dans la quatrième évangile," ETR 58 (1983) 343–354; S.A. Panimolle, *L'evangelista Giovanni: Pensiere e opera letteraria di quatto evangelista* (Rome: Ed. Borla, 1985) 205–269; F.A. Pastor, "Comunidad y ministerio en el evangelio joaneo," EstE 50 (1975) 323–356; S.S. Smalley, "John's Revelation and John's Community," BJRyL 69 (1986–1987) 549–571. [38]Brown (n. 1) 97–98; J.F. O'Grady, "The Good Shepherd and the Vine and the Branches," BibTB 8 (1978) 86–89. [39]Op. cit. (n. 1) 123. [40]R.E. Brown, *The Epistles of John.* Anchor Bible 30 (Garden City, N.Y.: Doubleday, 1982—London: Chapman, 1983); C.C. Black II, "The Johannine Epistles and the Question of Early Catholicism," NT 28 (1986) 131–138. [41]Brown, op. cit. (n. 1) 122–123. [42]*Hebrews.* NTMess 18 (Wilmington: Glazier—Dublin: Veritas, 1980) xi; M.M. Bourke, "The Epistle to the Hebrews," JBC 2:381-405; Cwiekowski, op. cit. (n. 8) 176–179; R.E. Brown, in Brown and Meier (n. 10) 139–158; Schnackenburg (n. 20) 89–94; Harrington (n. 30). [43]D. Senior, *1 and 2 Peter.* NTMess 20 (Wilmington: Glazier—Dublin: Veritas, 1980); Brown (n. 1) 75–83; Schnackenburg (n. 20) 85–89; Cwiekowski (n. 8) 173–176; J.H. Elliott, *A Home for the Homeless: A Sociological Exegesis of 1 Peter—Its Situation and Strategy* (London: SCM, 1982); Harrington (n. 31) 81–85. [44]B. Reicke, *The Epistles of James, Peter, and Jude.* Anchor Bible 37 (Garden City, N.Y.: Doubleday, 1964) 71–73 (with caution). [45]J.H. Elliott, *The Elect and the Holy. An Exegetical Examination of 1 Peter 2:4-10 and the Phrase Basileion Hierateuma* (Leiden: Brill, 1966); E. Bosetti, *Il pastore, Cristo e la Chiesa nella prima lettera di Pietro.* Supplementi alla Rivista biblica 21 (Bologna: Dehoniane, 1990). [46]Cf. Senior (n. 43) 99–101; Reicke (n. 44) 143–145. [47]R. Kugelman, *James and Jude.* NTMess 19 (Wilmington: Glazier—Dublin: Veritas, 1980); Reicke (n. 44) xv–xvi, 5–6. [48]Cf. A.Y. Collins, *The Apocalypse.* NTMess 22 (Wilmington: Glazier—Dublin: Veritas, 1979); F. Contreras Molina, "Las cartas a las siete iglesias," EstBib 46 (1988) 141–172; Cwiekowski (n. 8) 186–190; W.J. Harrington, *Revelation.* Sacra Pagina 16 (Collegeville: Glazier—The Liturgical Press, 1993); A. Jankowski, "De Ecclesia multiformi et una secundum Apocalypsim Joannis," in Commission Bibl. Pont. (n. 2) 285–296; X. Léon-Dufour, "Bulletin d'exégèse du Nouveau Testament: Autour de l'Apocalypse de Jean," RSR 71 (1983) 309–336; C.R. Smith, "The Portrayal of the Church as the New Israel in the Names and Order of the Tribes in Revelation 7,5-8," JStNT 39 (1990) 111–118. [49]Op. cit. (n. 47) xii–xiii and passim. [50]P. Poucouta, "La mission prophétique de l'Église dans l'Apocalypse johannique," NRT 110 (1988) 38–57; K.A. Strand, "The Two Witnesses of Rev 11:3-12," AndrUnS 19 (1981) 377–392. [51]C.J. Hemer, *The Letters to the Seven Churches in Their Social Setting* (Sheffield: JSOT, 1986); C. Trevett, "The Other Letters to the Churches of Asia: Apocalypse and Ignatius of Antioch," JStNT 37 (1989) 117–135.

## NEWMAN, John Henry (1801–1890)

An understanding of J.H. Newman's life[1] is essential for grasping the 19th-century history of both Anglicanism (v. ANGLICAN COMMUNION) and the Roman Catholic Church in England. Newman was brought up as an Anglican in the evangelical tradition, and he was educated at Oxford, where he became a fellow (1822). Ordained a priest, he was Vicar of St. Mary's, Oxford. From about 1834 he became associated with, and in time the guiding spirit of, the Oxford Movement (q.v.), which brought alive the High Church ideals of the 17th century. The movement authored popular expositions of its ideals in the "Tracts for the Times" (1833–1841), twenty-four of which Newman wrote. During that time Newman embarked on a deep study of the Fathers (q.v.), which resulted in *The Arians of the Fourth Century* (1833). In the volumes of the *Via Media* (1837–1838)[2] he advocated the view that the Church of England was an intermediate position between modern Romanism and Modern Protestantism (dissent). P. Avis, who remarks that the *Prophetical Office* still remains a valuable exposition of the Anglican position, also asserts that Newman's gift of historical empathy had one major blind spot—the Reformation.[3]

From 1839 he began to have some doubts about the claims of the Church of England, and in 1845 he was received into the Catholic Church, but not before he caused a major stir with Tract 90, which interpreted the *Thirty-nine Articles* (v. ANGLICAN COMMUNION) in a way favorable to the Council of Trent (1841). He was ordained a Catholic priest in 1847 and from 1854–1858 was Rector of the ill-judged and poorly supported Catholic University in Dublin.[4] He established the Oratory in Birmingham in 1849 and continued to engage in controversial writings. In 1879 he was made cardinal by Leo XIII. Around the centenary of his death (1890) several significant studies touching his ecclesiology appeared.[5]

His intellectual and spiritual odyssey was remarkable, and can be seen to have had several turning points. His autobiographical *Apologia Pro Vita Sua* (1864) helps us to chart his journey.[6] He had abandoned the evangelical mode of Anglicanism even before he became involved in the Tractarian Movement. He was, as a result, more open to the Catholic side of Christianity. His study of early Church history brought home to him uncomfortable parallels with 19th-century England: he saw himself as Monophysite and Donatist, with the Roman Church having preserved the truth. A phrase of Augustine (q.v.) indicating security to rest in universality *(Securus judicat orbis terrarum)* led to an intellectual conversion that destroyed for him the *Via Media.* The *Essay on the Development of Christian Doctrine* begun in 1844 carried him through to affiliation with Rome. He developed his ideas on education in his *Idea of a University* (1853). A sentence he wrote in the *Rambler* magazine was bitterly attacked: "In the preparation of a dogmatic definition, the faithful are consulted, as lately in the instance of the Immaculate Conception." His response was the essay *On Consulting* the *Faithful in Matters of Doctrine* (1859).[7] *The Grammar of Assent* (1870) dealt with faith and religious certitude. His most complete ecclesiology is found in the Preface to the 3rd edition (1877) of the *Lectures on the Prophetical Office of the Church*.[8] It has a developed idea of the priestly, prophetic, and kingly office of the Church (q.v.).[9] It seeks to deal sympathetically with what appear to be the flaws and failures of the Church,[10] and shows Newman's historical sense at fine pitch. Remarkable, too, in this mature reflection is his pastoral sense of what may be expedient for the Church to do or say at a particular time. But it is not possible to find in one work an exposition of Newman's ecclesiology: he was a controversialist engaged in a three-pronged defense against Protestant extremes, Roman excesses, and liberalism.[11] Thus he reflected and wrote much on infallibility, both for private circulation and for publication, when it was a burning issue (1865–1874). During this time his own finely crafted view became clarified.[12]

In many other ways Newman was to anticipate modern theological concerns,[13] not least the theology of the laity, the *consensus fidelium* (v. SENSE OF THE FAITH), the nature of theology,[14] the theological grounding of doctrinal development,[15] and the notion of communion (q.v.).[16] His theological creativity was allied to personal holiness, and his cause of beatification has reached the stage of his being called Venerable.

[1]S. Gilley, *Newman and His Age* (London: Darton, Longman & Todd, 1990); I. Ker, *John Henry Newman: A Biography* (New York—Oxford: UP, 1988); B. Martin, *John Henry Newman: His Life and Work* (London: Chapman—Mowbray, 1990); H. Fries, "John Henry Newman," KlassTheol 2:151-173.    [2]*The Via Media of the Anglican Church* (London, 1891).    [3]P. Avis, *Anglicanism and the Christian Church: Theological Resources in Historical Perspective* (Edinburgh: Clark, 1989) 219.    [4]L. McRedmond, *Thrown Among Strangers: John Henry Newman in Ireland* (Dublin: Veritas, 1990).    [5]See following notes and A. Dulles, "From Image to Truth: Newman on Revelation and Faith," TS 51 (1990) 252-267; idem, "Newman, Conversion and Ecumenism," ibid., 717–731; F. Gonzáles Fernández, "John Henry Newman: Sua incidenza nella vita della Chiesa," EuntDoc 43 (1990) 477-522; G. Magill, "Newman's Personal Reasoning: The Inspiration of the Early Church," IrTQ 52 (1992) 305-313; H. Imbrechts, "Les laïcs dans l'Église selon J.H. Newman," RAfrT 15 (1991) 79–92; I. Ker and A.G. Hill, eds., *Newman After a Hundred Years* (Oxford: Clarendon, 1990); M.R. O'Connell, "Newman: the Victorian Intellectual as Pastor," TS 46 (1985) 320-344; J. Stern, "La Chiesa, il magistero e i teologi secondo J.H. Newman," EuntDoc 43 (1990) 457-476.    [6]*Apologia pro vita sua*. Oxford English Texts. Ed. M.J. Svaglic (Oxford: Clarendon, 1967); V.F. Blehl, *John Henry Newman: A Bibliographical Catalogue of His Writings* (Charlottesville: Virginia UP, 1978); J. Artz, "Newman Bibliographie," in H. Fries et al., eds., *Newman Studien* (Heroldsberg bei Nürnberg: Glock u. Lutz, 1980) 216-247; J.T. Ford, "Newman Studies: Recent Resources and Research," Thom 46 (1982) 283-306.    [7]Ed. J. Coulson (London, 1961).    [8]*Via Media* (n. 2); AA.VV. *John Henry Newman: Theologian and Cardinal* (Brescia: Paideia—Rome: Urbaniana UP, 1981); C.S. Dessain, "Cardinal Newman Considered as a Prophet," Conc 7/4—37 (1968) 41–50; J. Miller, "Newman's Dialogical

Vision of the Church," LouvSt 8 (1980–1981) 318–331; E.J. Miller, *John Henry Newman on the Idea of the Church* (Shepherdstown, W.Va.: Patmos, 1987); N. Schiffers, *Die Einheit der Kirche nach Newman* (Dusseldorf, 1956).    [9]K.D. Bucher, "Newman on the Functions of the Church: A Prophetic Voice for Today," LouvSt 7 (1978–1979) 15–23; M.T. Yakaitis, *The Office of Priest, Prophet and King in the Thought of John Henry Newman*. Diss. (Rome: Gregorian, 1990).    [10]J. Gaffney, "Newman's Criticism of the Church: Lessons and Object Lessons" HeythJ 29 (1988) 1–20.    [11]T. Norris, "Cardinal Newman and the Liberals: The Strategy and the Struggle," IrTQ 53 (1987) 1–16; cf. R. Boudens, "Newman and the Roman Authorities," LouvSt 15 (1990) 301–317.    [12]A. Dulles, "Newman on Infallibility," TS 51 (1990) 434–449; J.D. Holmes, ed., *The Theological Papers of John Henry Newman on Biblical Inspiration and Infallibility* (Oxford: Clarendon, 1979); P. Misner, *Papacy and Development: Newman and the Primacy of the Pope* (Leiden: Brill, 1976); J. Stern, "L'infaillibilité de l'Église dans la pensée de J.H. Newman," RechSR 61 (1973) 161–185; F.A. Sullivan, "Newman on Infallibility," in I. Ker and A.G. Hill, eds., (n. 5) 419–446.    [13]L. Bouyer, "Actualité de Newman," Communio 13/3 (May–June 1987) 115–122; idem, *Newman's Vision of Faith* (San Francisco: Ignatius, 1986).    [14]K.D. Bucher, "Newman on the Theologian in the Church: Some Kindly Light on a Contemporary Problem," LouvSt 8 (1980–1981) 307–317; T. Merrigan, "Newman on the Practice of Theology," LouvSt 14 (1989) 260–284; J. Stern, "La Chiesa, il magistero e i teologi secondo J.H. Newman," EuntDoc 43 (1990) 457–476 cf. Seminarium 29 (1990) 383–398 (French).    [15]P. Misner, "Newman's Conception of Revelation and the Development of Doctrine," HeythJ 11 (1970) 32–47; N. Lash, *Newman on Development* (Shepherdstown, W.Va.: Patmos, 1975); T. O'Loughlin, "Newman, Vincent of Lerins and Development," IrTQ 57 (1991) 147–166.    [16]J. Tolhurst, *The Church . . . A Communion in the Preaching and Thought of John Henry Newman* (Leominster UK: Fowler Wright, 1988); J. Stern, "La communion universelle comme lieu théologique de Vatican I selon J.H. Newman: Securus judicat orbis terrarum," NRT 99 (1977) 171–188.

## NICAEA I, Council of (325)

The First Ecumenical Council of Nicaea (325) has been known as "The Synod of the 318 Fathers" (cf. Gen 14:14), though its actual numbers were 200–250. It was summoned by the emperor Constantine, who had in mind the unity and peace of the empire rather than theological decisions. The majority of the council's members were Eastern bishops, with only about seven from the West, including two priests who represented the pope. The decisions of the council were both doctrinal and canonical.

Lacking the acts of the council, we cannot be sure of its evolution.[1] Doctrinally, the most important issue was Arianism. Arius had already been condemned by his own bishop, Alexander of Alexandria (ca. 320), for his assertion that the Son was a creature *(ktisma* or *poiêma)*. Eusebius of Caesarea presented a creed from his Church, probably a baptismal creed from Jerusalem, which may have provided the basis for the creed adopted by the council. Four key phrases were added to exclude Arian tenets. The Son was said to be: of the essence/substance of the Father *(ek tês ousias tou patros);* he is true God of true God *(theon alêthinon ek theou alêthinou);* generated not created *(gennêthenta ou poiêthenta);* consubstantial with the Father *(homoousion tô patri).* This final phrase was the clearest denial of the Arian position—the Son shared and participated in the same being of the Father.[2] But the word would later be controverted: it could be taken in a material sense; it might have a modalist meaning; some would hold that it was condemned in Paul of Samosata; it was not biblical. But given the Arian meaning ascribed to Scripture, it was not possible to confine doctrinal statements to biblical language.

Along with its profession of faith the council added anathemas against various positions: "Those who say 'there once was when he was not,' and 'before he was begotten he was not,' and that he came to be from things that were not, or from another hypostasis or substance, affirming that the Son of God is subject to change or alteration."[3]

The council approved twenty canons,[4] which can also be seen as enshrining Constantine's desire for order and peace in the empire. One series of canons envisages Church order: the election of a new bishop is a matter for the province (c. 4); an election without the consent of the metropolitan is not valid (c. 6); provincial councils are to be held biannually (c. 5); the bishop of Alexandria is to have authority in the region of Egypt, Libya, and Pentapolis—Rome has a similar but undefined position, with Antioch having some lesser prerogatives (c. 6);[5] Jerusalem is to have a position of honor (c. 7). On the clergy, it legislated for various cases concerning eunuchs (c. 1). Other canons made the following stipulations: movement from one diocese to another was forbidden (cc. 15–16); one could be ordained without the consent of one's own bishop (c. 16); the cohabitation of clergy and women was regulated (c. 3); rapid promotion to the clerical state after baptism was forbidden (c. 2); the *lapsi* (v. RECONCILIATION, SACRAMENT OF) were considered in two canons (cc. 9, 10); clerics were not to engage in usury (c. 17); deacons were to keep their place with respect to bishops and priests at liturgical functions (c. 18); a not totally clear canon seemed to regard deaconesses as laity (c. 19). Four canons treated public penance (cc. 11–14):[6] the *lapsi* in a custom peculiar perhaps to Asia Minor are received back in three steps—some years of penance as listeners, with those prostrate, with those who pray. The important canon 13 decreed that the dying are not to be refused the Eucharist. The other canons concern the Cathars or Novatians (c. 8), and the Paulinists or followers of Paul of Samosata (c. 19), liturgical norms and genuflections (c. 20). The council also sent a letter to the Egyptians dealing with the Meletian schism and the date of Easter.[7]

At Nicaea we have for the first time canonical legislation envisaging the whole Church, unlike the canons of earlier provincial synods; thus the isolation of local Churches and their bishops is countered. The council established the orthodox faith against the Arians. But more councils would be required to finalize the Trinitarian and Christological issues first defined in 325.

---

[1]K. Baus, in Jedin-Dolan 2:22-29; Davis, Councils, 33–80; A. de Halleux, "La réception du symbole oecuménique, de Nicée à Chalcédoine," ETL 61 (1975) 5–47; J.N.D. Kelly, *Early Christian Creeds* (London: Longman, [3]1972) 205–262; I. Ortiz de Urbina, *Nicée et Constantinople.* Histoire des conciles 1 (Paris: Ed. de l'Orante, 1963); L. Perrone in Alberigo, Concili 13–45. Text of Council Mansi 2:635-1082 (some spurious)/Tanner 1:5-19.   [2]L. Bouyer, "Omoousios: Sa signification historique dans le symbole de la foi," RSPT 32 (1941–1942) 52–62; J. Lebon, "Le sort du consubstantiel nicéen," RHE 47 (1952) 485–529; 48 (1953) 632–682; B.J.F. Lonergan, *The Road to Nicea: The Dialectical Development of Trinitarian Theology* (London: Darton, Longman & Todd, 1976).   [3]Tanner 1:5/DS 125–126/ND 7–8.   [4]Tanner 1:6-16. P. l'Huillier, "Ecclesiology in the Canons of the First Nicene Council," SVlad 27 (1983) 119–131; W. de Vries, *Orient et occident: Les structures ecclésiales vues dans l'histoire des sept premiers conciles oecuméniques* (Paris: Cerf, 1974) 13–42.   [5]H. Chadwick, "Faith and Order at the Council of Nicea: A Note on the Background of the Sixth Canon," HarvTR 53 (1960) 171–195.   [6]P. Galtier, "Les canons pénitentiels de Nicée," Greg 29 (1948) 288–294.   [7]Tanner 1:16-19.

## NICAEA II, Council of (787)

From the 4th century, Christian art began to flourish in places of worship even though reservations were continually expressed. Representations of the sacred gradually began to appear. By the 8th century there were abuses which provoked reactions. There was also an influence from Judaism and Islam, both of which prohibited sacred images.[1]

The emperor Leo III (717–741) published in 726 C.E. an exhortation which encouraged people to get rid of images. Iconoclasm (*icon* = image, *klaein* = to break), strictly so called, began when the emperor published an edict against all images in 730. Persecution of those who venerated images followed, but they would find support from the Syrian monk St. John Damascene (ca. 675–ca. 749) who developed a theology of icons.[2] Leo's son, the emperor Constantine V (741–775), called in 753 a council which met at Hieria in the following year.[3] The 338 fathers considered themselves an ecumenical council. But there was no papal representation, and the council was not received afterwards as ecumenical. Its synodal decree, *Horos,* condemned images, asserting that the only true image of Christ was the Eucharist. Fresh persecutions followed, which became a generalized campaign against monks who with the common people supported the use of icons.

The empress Irene, in the stead of her minor son Constantine VI, ensured in 784 the appointment as patriarch of Constantinople a layman, Tarasius, who was favorable to icons. Pope Hadrian I (772–795) agreed to overtures from the East about a general council, which met in Constantinople in 786. Interference by icono-clast armed troops forced its transfer to Nicaea, where it undertook its work the following year. At maximum there were 335 bishops at this, the Seventh Ecumenical Council.[4]

The council proceeded in a leisurely way without any great theological depth. It refuted the *Horos* of Hieria point by point.[5] The decree condemning iconoclasm was passed in its seventh session,[6] and in its final session twenty-two canons.[7] These continued in the tradition of the Council of Trullo (q.v.), and dealt with matters such as law (c. 1), the activity of bishops (cc. 2–4, 11, 12), simony (c. 4), clergy (cc. 10, 15, 16), monks (cc. 18–22).

This last council of the undivided Church was the beginning of the end of iconoclasm, though it would be over fifty years before iconoclasm was finally defeated in the East at the Synod of Constantinople in 843.[8] A corrupt translation of the acts of Nicaea II led to the rejection of the council in the Frankish kingdom well into the next century.

The issues at Nicaea II were not peripheral but were at the heart of orthodox Christology. It is the truth of Chalcedon (q.v.) of the Son becoming flesh in a single person but in two natures that allows the Incarnate Word to be represented by an image, and worshiped with its assistance. Adoration belongs only to God, but images are venerated with the honor going to the person depicted, and ultimately to God.

Since Nicaea II, Eastern Christianity has taken icons very seriously. In the latter part of the 20th century there is also interest in icons on the part of Catholics. In Eastern liturgy the screen of icons (iconostasis) is felt to be part of the liturgy rather than a distraction; this is in marked contrast to the *Roman Missal,* which warns against images taking attention away from the liturgy.[9] The screen depicts Christ, Mary, and John the Baptist in prominent places; other higher rows include notable saints and apostles, the twelve (major) feasts of Orthodoxy, the patriarchs, prophets, and angels. Norms have been handed down for the painting of icons; the shapes and colors form a complex theological statement. Icons are symbolic rather than realistic in their expression. They are sacramental in being a meeting place between the worshiper and the holy person; it is more important to be seen by the saint than to gaze on the image. There is a huge bibliography on icons in this century, especially from Eastern writers[10] but also from an ecumenical perspective in which the traditional Protestant reserve towards, not to say antipathy to, sacred images is being reassessed.[11]

---

[1]N.H. Baynes, "The Icons before Iconoclasm," HarvTR 44 (1951) 93–106; Davis, Councils 290–300; E. Ewig, in Jedin-Dolan 3:26-32; G. Ladner, "Origin and Significance of the Byzantine Iconoclastic Controversy," MedSt 2 (1940) 127–149; J. Meyendorff, *Christ in Eastern Christian Thought* (Crestwood, N.Y.: St. Vladimir's Seminary Press, 1975) 173–192. [2]*Pro sacris imaginibus III orat.*—PG 94:1227-1420; Trans. D. Anderson, *On the Divine Images* (Crestwood, N.Y.: St. Vladimir's Seminary Press, 1980). [3]F. Boespflug and N. Lossky, eds., *Nicée II* (Paris: Cerf, 1987); D.H. Sahas, *Icon and Logos* (Toronto: UP, 1986). [4]N. Chifar, *Das VII. Ökumenische Konzil von Nikaia: Das letze Konzil der ungeteilten Kirche.* Oikonomia: Quellen und Studien zur ortodoxen Theologie 32 (Erlangen: Lehrst. f. Geschicht, 1993); E. Ewig, in Jedin-Dolan 3:34-36; Davis, Councils 308–311; G. Dumeige, *Nicée II.* Histoire des conciles 4 (Paris: Ed. l'Orante, 1978); W. de Vries, *Orient et occident: Les structures ecclésiales vues dans l'histoire des sept premiers conciles oecuméniques* (Paris: Cerf, 1974) 221–244; P.A. Yannopoulos in Alberigo, Concili 145–154. [5]Mansi 13:204-364. [6]Tanner 1:133-138. [7]Tanner 1:138-156. [8]Ewig (n. 3) 41–48. [9]GI 278. [10]E.g., L. Ouspensky and L. Lossky, *The Meaning of Icons* (Boston, 1969); L. Ouspensky, *Theology of the Icon* (New York: St. Vladimir's Seminary Press, 1978); P. Evdokimov, *L'art de l'icône, théologie de la beauté* (Paris: Desclée de Brouwer, 1970); P. Galadza, "The Role of Icons in Byzantine Worship," STLTg 21 (1991) 113–135; idem, "Restoring the Icon: Reflections on the Reform of Byzantine Worship," Worship 65 (1991) 238–255; T. Nikolau, "The Place of the Icon in the Liturgical Life of the Orthodox Church," GrOrTR 35 (1990) 317–332. [11]G. Limouris, ed., *Icons Windows on Eternity: Theology and Spirituality in Color:* Faith and Order Paper 147 (Geneva: WCC, 1990).

## NON-CHRISTIAN RELIGIONS

Since Vatican II there has been marked development about the salvation of individuals outside the visible confines of the Church (v. OUTSIDE THE CHURCHES; GS 22; AG 7). The explorations of K. Rahner have been significant and influential in the whole area.[1] But clarity is still lacking on the issue of the salvific signification of non-Christian religions as such, and of their relationship with Christ and the Church. Even the term "non-Christian" is considered problematic by some: especially in dialogue, terms like "believers/ followers of other faiths," or "living faiths," a term used by the World Council of Churches (v. ECUMENI-CAL MOVEMENT), may better indicate that other religions are being considered in themselves, and not merely from a universalist Christian perspective.

Vatican II did make some positive statements about other faiths: "those who have not received the gospel are related to the people of God in various ways. . . . Whatever good and truth is found in them is considered by the Church as a preparation for the gospel" (LG 16; cf. 17; AG 3);[2] truth and grace among peoples are "a secret presence of God, so to speak" (AG 9); "seeds of the Word" *(semina Verbi)* lie hidden in their national and religious traditions (AG 11; cf. 15); "The Catholic Church rejects nothing of those things which are true and holy in these religions" (NA 2). Elements of grace and salvation are therefore attributed to other religions, even though the council does not go so far as to refer to them as "means" or a "way" of salvation.[3]

Almost all religions seek salvation though each conceives it differently.[4] The nature of salvation depends on what is considered to be evil, or how evil is envisaged, e.g., sin, divine perdition, existence itself, death. Some, like K. Barth, followed by H. Kraemer, absolutely deny that there is salvation in non-Christian religions. He distinguishes between revelation which is a divine action and religion which is simply a human activity. All attempts on the part of men and women to know God outside of Jesus Christ are useless; to give a theological meaning to non-Christian religion would be to betray the unique role of Christ.[5] Recently there is, however, some revisionist study of Barth's positions.[6]

Barth's stance may be called Christologically exclusivist. A second view, exemplified among others by the anonymous Christian (q.v.) concept of K. Rahner, can be called Christologically inclusivist: Christ is present outside the visible confines of the Church. A third position is theocentric and, with J. Hicks, abandons any exclusive Christology: all religions, Christianity included, reveal the mystery of God, so that the incarnation may not be considered as normative for salvation.[7] The school of Hicks has proceeded to assert the equal value and significance of all religions and to deny any claim for an exclusive or normative character for Christianity.[8] It is difficult to see how the first and third of these positions can really be compatible with Catholic faith: since the Feeney case (q.v.) in the 1940s, an exclusive emphasis on the Church is no longer tenable (v. OUTSIDE THE CHURCH); Christ must be acknowledged as singular mediator of salvation (1 Tim 2:5; see GS 22). Only some version of the second position would seem to respect the two truths of the universal divine will of salvation, along with the unique mediation of Christ.[9] It does not exclude what is positive in the theocentric insight of Hicks. It holds that God in Christ is the center of all religion, the source of all salvation; Christ has been constituted by the Father as the way, the truth, and the life for all humanity; salvation is ultimately Trinitarian, but in Christ.

There is a growing conviction on the part of theologians that non-Christian religions do have a positive role for salvation.[10] The key question is that of Christ, and secondarily that of the Church.[11] The most common explanations are variants on the patristic theme of the seed of the Word (*Logos spermaticos*): seeds of the Word are found everywhere. In K. Rahner's view the Logos is present in all human reality as possibility for a self-communication of God. The Spirit of Jesus is operating in other religions, indeed wherever there is faith or acceptance of God's self-communication.[12] The difficulty for these views is to see how there is to be a causal relationship with the death and resurrection of Jesus. This problem, and the acceptability or otherwise of their general Christology, will condition one's view of the position of different theologians.[13]

The subsidiary question is to see how the Church is involved in the salvation of non-Christians through their religions. Where the Church is planted, it can be the sacrament of salvation (LG 48; GS 45; AG 1; cf. LG 9) in that place. F.A. Sullivan notes: "As sign and instrument of all salvation, the Church is not merely the goal toward which grace is directed; it is the channel or medium through which grace is given."[14] The way in which the Church is an instrument of salvation, even for those who have never heard of it, is perhaps best seen in terms of the priesthood of its members and in its celebration of the Eucharist.[15]

Ecumenism is becoming more and more concerned with the issue of other religions.[16] With the bewildering variety of religions,[17] their permanence, and the apparent impermeability to Christian mission of the higher religions (Judaism, Islam, Hinduism, Buddhism, and Jainism), intrareligious dialogue (v. DIALOGUE) has come to the fore since Vatican II.[18] John Paul II notes that it is not, however, a substitute for mission which retains its validity and urgency[19] but rather "part of the Church's evangelizing mission" and "one of its expressions."[20] Moreover, "dialogue does not originate from tactical concerns or self-interest but is an activity with its own guiding principles, requirements, and dignity. . . . Other religions constitute a positive challenge to the Church: they stimulate her both to discover and acknowledge the signs of Christ's presence and of the working of the Spirit, as well as to examine more deeply her own identity and to bear witness to the fullness of revelation she has received for the good of all."[21] One of the most promising areas of dialogue is spirituality,[22] for there can be a deep unity in the Spirit when men and women seek the Absolute in unselfish love. The meetings of representatives of various religions in Assisi (1986, 1993) to pray for peace was significant for a recognition of the spiritual unity that exists at the level of prayer and religious experience.[23]

[1]"Christianity and the Non-Christian Religions," ThInvest 5:115-134; "The Christian Among Unbelieving Relations," 3:355-372; "Church, Churches and Religions," 10:30-44; "The One Church and the Universality of Salvation," 16:199-224; "Jesus Christ in the Non-Christian Religions," 17:39-50; "On the Importance of the Non-Christian Religions for Salvation," 18:288-295; "Christianity's Absolute Claim," 21:171-184.   [2]M. Caprioli, "La salvezza dei non cristiani. Note conciliari al n. 16 della Costituzione dogmatica *Lumen gentium*," Teresianum 40 (1989) 479–490; M. Ruokanen, *The Catholic Doctrine of Non-Christian Religions according to the Second Vatican Council.* Studies in Christian Mission (Leiden: Brill, 1992)—but see negative review F.A. Sullivan TS 54 (1993) 201; M. Simon, "Lumen gentium et les non-croyants," RTLv 17 (1986) 38–54.   [3]P. Rossano, "Christ's Lordship and Religious Pluralism in Roman Catholic Perspective," in G.H. Anderson and T.F. Stransky, eds., *Christ's Lordship and Religious Pluralism* (Maryknoll: Orbis, 1985) 193; J. Dupuis, *Jésus Christ à la rencontre des religions* (Paris: Desclée, 1989).   [4]M. Dhavamony, "Today's Challenge:

Salvation Offered by Non-Christian Religions," EuntDoc 41 (1988) 421–438; C.A. Myscofski, "Salvation in the World's Religions," ChicSt 22 (1983) 97–110; N. Smart, "Soteriology," EncycRel 13:418-423; StMiss 30 (1981).    [5]*Church Dogmatics* (New York, 1956) 1/2:1, 329-330, 335, 369; cf. P. Harrison, "Karl Barth and the Non Christian Religions," JEceSt 23 (1986) 207–224; H. Kraemer, *The Christian Message in a Non-Christian World* (Edinburgh, 1947); idem, *Why Christianity of All Religions?* (London, 1962).    [6]R. Boyd, "A Barthian Theology of Interfaith Dialogue," Pacifica 3 (1990) 288–303; D. Lockhead, *The Dialogal Imperative* (London: SCM, 1988).    [7]*God and the Universe of Faiths: Essays in the Philosophy of Religion* (London: Macmillan, 1973); *The Second Christianity* (London: SCM, 1983).    [8]J. Hicks and P.F. Knitter, *The Myth of Christian Uniqueness: Towards a Pluralistic Theology of Religions* (Maryknoll: Orbis, 1987); see A. Russo, "Nel nome di chi siamo salvati? La cristologia non normativa di Paul Knittner," Asp 39 (1992) 341–361.    [9]See G. D'Costa, *Theology and Religious Pluralism* (Oxford: Blackwell, 1986). J. Dupuis, "Pluralisme religieux et mission évangélatrice de l'Église," Spiritus 32/122( 1991).    [10]W.H. Capps, "Towards a Christian Theology of World Religions," CrossC 29 (1979–1980) 156–168, 182; J. Dupuis, "Les religions comme voies de salut?," Spiritus 33/126 (1992) 5–15; Communio 13/4 (1988) 1–127; Concilium 183 (1986); Negative view e.g., L.J. Elders, "The Theological Meaning of Non-christian Religions," DoctCom 42 (1989) 31–41.    [11]L. Richard, *What Are They Saying About Christ and World Religions* (New York: Paulist, 1981).    [12]Rahner, Foundations 311–321; 116–133; cf. J.A. DiNoia, "Implicit Faith: General Revelation and the State of Non-Christians," Thom 47 (1983) 209–241; S.J. Samartha, "The Holy Spirit and People of Other Religions," EcuR 42 (1990) 250–263; F.A. Sullivan, *The Church We Believe In. One, Holy, Catholic and Apostolic* (Dublin: Gill and Macmillan—New York: Paulist, 1988) 124–126, 130–131.    [13]E.g., H. Küng, *On Being a Christian* (New York: Doubleday, 1979); W. Pannenberg, *Jesus—God and Man* (Philadelphia, 1967); idem, *Basic Questions in Theology 1* (London: SCM, 1970); R. Pannikkar, *The Intra-religious Dialogue* (New York: Paulist, 1979); idem, *The Trinity and the Religious Experience of Man* (Maryknoll: Orbis, 1973); cf. R. McBrien, *Catholicism* (London: Chapman, 1984) 267–281.    [14](N. 12) 110.    [15]Ibid., 127–128; see F.A. Sullivan, *Salvation Outside the Church? Tracing the History of the Catholic Response* (New York: Paulist, 1992).    [16]J.H. Pranger, *The Ecumenical Movement and Other Religions*. IIMO Research Publications 35 ('s-Gravenhage: Meinema, 1992).    [17]N. Smart, *The World's Religions* (Cambridge: UP, 1992); S. Sutherland, ed., *The World's Religions* (Boston: Hall, 1988); M. Braybrooke, *Interfaith Organizations 1893–1979: An Historical Directory* (New York—Toronto: Mellen, 1980).    [18]A. Adappur, "The Theology of Inter-Faith Dialogue," VYoti 46 (1982) 485–498; J. Dupuis, "Interreligious Dialogue in the Church's Evangelizing Mission: Twenty Years of Evolution of a Theological Concept," in Latourelle, Vatican II, 3:237-263; M. Fitzgerald, "Panorama du dialogue interreligieux et questions théologiques," Spiritus 126/33 (1992) 92–104; A. Geense, "Der Dialog der Religionen und das Bekenntnis der Kirche," KerDo 26 (1980) 264–276; B. Groth, "From Monologue to Dialogue in Conversations with Nonbelievers, or the Difficult Search for Partners in Dialogue," in Latourelle, Vatican II, 3:184-198; J. Masson, "Le dialogue entre les religions: Deux documents récents," NRT 114 (1992) 726–737; L. Newbigen, "The Basis, Purpose and Manner of Inter-faith Dialogue," ScotJT 30 (1977) 257–270; G. Ragozzino, "Il dialogo con le religioni," Asp 34 (1987) 52–61; R.T. Simpson, "The New Dialogue between Christianity and Other Religions," Theology 92 (1989) 92–102; W. Strolz and H. Waldenfels, eds., *Christliche Grundlagen des Dialogs mit den Weltreligionen*. QDisput 98 (Freiburg—Basle—Vienna: Herder, 1983); L. Swidler, "Interreligious Dialogue—A Christian Necessity:

Who Are Our Partners?," CrossC 35 (1985–1986) 129–147; D. Tracy, *Dialogue with the Other: The Inter-religious Dialogue* (Louvain: Peeters, 1990); JDharma 8 (1983) 225–315.    [19]John Paul II, Ency. *Redemptoris missio*—AAS 83 (1991) 249–340/CathIntern 2/6 (1991) 252–292—nn. 33–36.    [20]Ibid., n. 35.    [21]Ibid., n. 56.    [22]T. Arai and W. Ariarajah, *Spirituality in Interfaith Dialogue* (Geneva: WCC, 1989); P. De Sousa, "Mysticism in Different Religious Traditions," JDharma 13 (1988) 105–115.    [23]BullPont-ConcDialRel 22 (1987) 1–160; M.L. Fitzgerald, "Mission and Dialogue: Reflections in the Light of Assisi 1986," ibid., 23 (1988) 113–120; M. Seckler, "Synodos der Religionen: Das 'Ereignis von Assisi' und seine Perspektiven für eine Teologie der Religionen," TQ 169 (1989) 5–24.

## NOTES OF THE CHURCH

The "Notes of the Church" occupied a major place in post-Reformation polemical ecclesiology. They arose mainly in the context of the question "Where is the true Church?" It became customary to speak of two kinds of notes: positive notes which pointed to the presence of the true Church of Christ; negative notes, the absence of which indicated that a body was not the true Church of Christ.

Though the full elaboration of a theory of notes is a post-Reformation phenomenon,[1] there are earlier indications.[2] Already in St. Augustine we have five signs that justify remaining in the Church: true wisdom, the name "catholic," agreement of the multitude, miracles, the See of Peter, and the succession of bishops.[3] St. Thomas Aquinas' analysis of the four properties of the Church—one, holy, catholic, apostolic—indicated that they are what would later be termed positive notes;[4] they are of course found in the Nicene Creed. Boniface VIII mentions the same four of them in his bull *Unam sanctam* (1302).[5] It was, however, John of Ragusa who first developed what would later become a theology of notes, in his *De ecclesia* (1433–1435).[6] He sought to answer the question "Where is the Catholic Church?" and takes up the signs given by Augustine.

St. Robert Bellarmine (q.v.) would enumerate fifteen notes, which he said could ultimately be reduced to the fourfold: one, holy, catholic and apostolic.[7] These fifteen were: the name Christian; antiquity; uninterrupted duration; multitude and variety of believers; succession of bishops; doctrinal harmony with the ancient Church; unity of members among one another and with the head; efficacious doctrine; holiness of the early Fathers; the glory of miracles; prophecy; admission of adversaries, even pagan; the unhappy lot of those who opposed the Church; and the temporal happiness even of those who defended the Church.[8] These more elaborate notes were contrasted with the Protestant ones. The Augsburg Confession (q.v.) stated that the Church "is the assembly of all believers among whom the Gospel is preached in its purity and the holy sacraments are administered according to the Gospel."[9] Calvin came to a somewhat similar position.[10] The Radical Reformation added other notes, such as obedience to the Cross of Christ, Church discipline which excluded known or public sinners, piety, orthodox confession.[11]

After Bellarmine the manuals presented the notes as leading to discernment of the true Church, e.g., I. Salaverri: "Unity, catholicity, apostolicity, holiness are also notes which belong *(conveniunt)* only to the Roman Church, and therefore point to it as the true Church of Christ."[12] Vatican I (q.v.) presented the credibility of the Church in a way that reflected the theology of notes: "The Church by herself, with her marvelous propagation, eminent holiness, and inexhaustible fruitfulness in everything that is good, with her Catholic unity and invincible stability, is a great and perpetual motive for credibility and an irrefutable testimony of her divine mission."[13]

It is to be regretted that the restricted understanding of one (q.v.), holy (q.v.), catholic (q.v.), and apostolic (q.v.) which served apologetic aims led to a diminishment in the understanding of these qualities of the Church: they were restricted to their visible and empirical aspects.[14] Modern theology of the four qualities of the Church stresses that they are both gift and task *(Gabe—Aufgabe):* the Church will always have these characteristics, but they are also an ideal that is ever to be more fully realized.

[1]G. Thils, *Notes de l'Église dans l'apologétique catholique depuis la Réforme* (Gembloux, 1937). See Y. Congar, *L'Église une, sainte, catholique et apostolique.* Mysterium salutis 15 (Paris: Cerf, 1970); M. Sales, *Le corps de l'Église: Études sur l'Église une, sainte, catholique et apostolique.* Communio (Paris: Fayard, 1989); F.A. Sullivan, *The Church We Believe In: One, Holy, Catholic and Apostolic* (Dublin: Gill and Macmillan, 1988). [2]A. Houssiau, "Images diverses de l'unité de l'Église," RTLv 10 (1979) 131–158. [3]*Contra epist. Manichaei quam vocant fundamenti* 4:5—PL 42:175. [4]*In symbol. apost.* 9. [5]DS 870/ND 804. [6]G. Thils, "Le 'Tractatus de ecclesia' de Jean de Raguse," Ang 17 (1940) 219–244. [7]De controversiis 4:3 (Milan 1857) 109. [8]Ibid., 4:2-18, pp. 106–140. [9]Art. 7—Leith, Creeds 70/Schaff, Creeds 3:11-12. [10]*The Institutes of the Christian Religion* 4:1, 7-9—LCC 21:1021-1024; cf. G. Vincent, "Les marques protestants de l'ecclésialité." RechSR 79 (1991) 191–210. [11]Menno Simons, *Complete Writings* (Scottdale, Penn.: Herald Press, 1956) 741–752. [12]Salaverri, Ecclesia 933; see 933–963. [13]DS 3013/ND 123. [14]Sullivan (n. 1) 4.

## NOVATIANISM

Novatian, a Roman presbyter, refused to have communion with those who defected during the persecution of Decius (249–250), and formed a rigorist sect.[1] Otherwise orthodox, and the author of an important work on the Trinity, Novatian suffered martyrdom 257–258 C.E. under Valerian. Novatianist slogans like "the Church is the people that has not denied the name of Christ and keeps the gospel whole and entire" shows that they maintained a separatist existence in the name of the holiness of the Church. The 8th canon of the Council of Nicaea laid down the conditions for acceptance of the Cathars (q.v.) or Novatians.[2] The exclusivism of the sect ensured its extinction by the 5th–6th centuries, except for isolated communities.

[1]H.J. Vogt, *Coetus sanctorum* (Bonn, 1968); K. Baus, in Jedin-Dolan 1:334-338. [2]Tanner 1:9-10.

# O

## OATHS

See CREEDS AND PROFESSIONS OF FAITH

## OLD CATHOLIC

The term "Old Catholic" is occasionally employed loosely by small sects, but it is used mainly in reference to three groups of small national Churches which have at various times separated from Rome: The Church of Utrecht, which separated from Rome in 1723–1724; the German, Austrian, and Swiss Old Catholic Churches, which refused to accept the dogmas of papal primacy and infallibility at Vatican I (q.v.); some small Slav Churches, viz., the Polish National Church, with four bishoprics in the U.S. and one in Poland, and the Yugoslav Old Catholic Church (Croat).[1]

In the aftermath of Vatican I, disaffected Catholics met in Munich around the historian J.J.I. von Döllinger (1799–1890—q.v.) and formed a group of Old Catholics. Döllinger himself was excommunicated for refusing to accept the teaching of Vatican I. He advised against schism, however, as he foresaw that the group would not expand or prove an alternative over against the Roman Catholic Church. He never joined the Old Catholics,[2] though he did receive the last rites from one of its priests. He worked for reunion and presided over the meetings of Old Catholics with Anglicans, Lutherans, Orthodox, and others in Bonn (1874) which produced Fourteen Theses[3] and a statement on the *Filioque* (q.v.) a year later.[4] These Old Catholics received episcopal succession from the Church of Utrecht in 1874.

The doctrinal positions of the Old Catholics can be found in the 1889 Declaration of Utrecht. It seeks to delineate areas in which there is opposition to the Roman Catholic Church: notably papal primacy and infallibility, the Immaculate Conception, the Syllabus of Pius IX (q.v.). It affirms the ecumenical councils up to 1000 C.E., the sacrificial dimension of the Eucharist, and the Real Presence.[5] Old Catholics allow the marriage of clergy, including bishops. They recognized Anglican Orders (q.v.) in 1925 and entered into full communion with Anglicanism in 1932.

In the last quarter of the 19th century there were discussions with the Orthodox which did not come to conclusions.[6] In the early years of the 20th century there was a growth in agreement with the Russian Church. After the Bonn agreement of Anglican and Old Catholic, an official meeting was held there in Oct. 1931, which desired, but did not achieve, full intercommunion of Old Catholics and Orthodox. The First Pan-Orthodox Conference (Rhodes 1961) recommended an intensification of Old Catholic/Orthodox relations, and this led to official dialogue from 1973.[7] The outcome was the agreed statements on the Doctrine of God (1975), Christology (1975, 1977), ecclesiology (1977–1981).[8] By 1987 there was agreement also on soteriology, sacraments, eschatology, and communion.[9] There are some remaining issues to be resolved before full communion between Orthodox and Old Catholic is possible. The fact of the Old Catholic having full communion with the Anglicans is a difficulty for the Orthodox.[10] There are also dialogues at the national level of Old Catholics with Lutherans, Reformed, and Roman Catholics.

The Old Catholic-Orthodox dialogues are important for the ecumenical movement since they are Eastern and Western, strongly Christological and pneumatological, scriptural and patristic, with an ecclesiology which carefully studies both the universal and local Church.

---

[1]U. Küry, *Die altkatholische Kirche* (Stuttgart: Evangelisches Verlagswerk, ²1978); C.B. Moss, *The Old Catholic Movement: Its Origins and History* (London: SPCK, ²1964). [2]V. Conzemius,

"Aspects ecclésiologiques de l'évolution de Döllinger et du Vieux Catholicisme," RevSR 34 (1960) 247–279; G. Schwaiger, "Ignatz von Döllinger (1799–1890)," in H. Fries and G. Kretschmar, eds., *Klassiker der Theologie*. 2 vols. (Munich: Beck, 1981–1983) 2:127-150. [3]Schaff, Creeds 2:545-551. [4]Ibid., 552–554. [5]Lambeth Conference *Report* (London, 1930) 142–144; P. Amiet, "Zum alt-katholischen Kirchenverständnis," ÖkRu 30 (1981) 47–55; W. Frei, "Altkatholisch, einmal abgesehen von den Papstdogmen," IKZ 74 (1984) 65–84. [6]G. Florovsky, HistEcumMov 1:205-209. [7]H. Meyer and L. Vischer, *Growth in Agreement*. Faith and Order Paper 108 (New York: Paulist—Geneva: WCC, 1984) 390–391. [8]Ibid., 391–419. [9]U. von Arx, ed., "Koinonia auf altkirchlicher Basis: Texte 1975–1985," IKiZ 79/4 (1989)—with trans. French/English; "I documenti di dialogo: Rassegna 1985–1986," StEcum 5 (1987) 145; P. Amiet, "Der altkatholisch-orthodoxe theologische Dialog ist abgeschlossen," IKiZ 78 (1988) 42–62; E. Hämerle, "Old Catholic-Orthodox Dialogue," OneChr 26 (1990) 155–159; G.N. Lempoulos, "Le dialogue théologique entre l'Église orthodoxe et l'Église des vieux-catho-liques," IKiZ 76 (1986) 161–190 G. Papandreou, "Theologischer Konsens und kirchliche Gemeinschaft," IkiZ 79 (1989) 44–52; U. von Arx, "Orthodox-Old Catholic Dialogue: Some Clarifications," OneChr 26 (1990) 282. [10]"Les orthodoxes aux vieux-catholiques: Il faut choisir entre anglicans et nous," UnChrétiens 77 (1990) 39/"Orthodox to Old Catholics: Choose Between Us and the Anglicans," Ecumenical Press Service 56 (1989) 34/10.03.

## OLIVI, Peter John (ca. 1248–1298)

Born in the Languedoc about 1248, Peter John Olivi entered the Franciscan Order at the age of twelve. In time he became a leader of the rigorist party of "Spiritual Franciscans" on the matter of poverty, and gave the whole movement a theological identity.[1] He was one of the forerunners in the area of papal inerrancy (v. INFALLIBILITY).[2] After his death some views ascribed to him on Christology, on the human soul, and on infant baptism were condemned by the Council of Vienne (q.v.), though he was not named.[3]

[1]H. Wolter, in Jedin-Dolan 4:240-246. [2]B. Tierney, "John Peter Olivi and Papal Inerrancy: On a Recent Interpretation of Olivi's Ecclesiology," TS 46 (1985) 315–328 (survey); D. Flood, "Recent Studies on Petrus Johannis Olivi," FranzSt 73 (1991) 262–269. [3]DS 900–904/Tanner 1:360-361. See K.A. Fink in Jedin-Dolan 4:301-302; L. Jarraux, "Pierre-Jean Olivi, sa vie, sa doctrine," ÉtFranc 45 (1933) 521–529; A. Maier, "Per la storia del processo contro Olivi," RivStorChItal 5 (1951) 326–339; C. Partee, "Petrus John Olivi: Historical and Doctrinal Study," FrancStAn 20 (1960) 215–260. See D. Burr, *Olivi and Franciscan Poverty* (Philadelphia UP, 1989).

## ONE

The Nicene-Constantinople Creed used in the liturgy has four epithets about the Church: one, holy, catholic, apostolic. Just as its confession of the divinity is an acknowledgement of the unicity of the persons (a single Father and Son), so the confession of the Creed envisages a single, unique Church rather than being descriptive of its essential nature (unity).[1] "One" as studied in ecclesiology includes both unicity and unity.

The NT clearly proposes only one Church: Jesus is the single shepherd of the one flock (cf. John 10:14-16); Paul knows only one body (q.v.) of Christ (cf. 1 Cor 10:17); the Christian community is one temple (q.v.) of the Spirit (1 Cor 3:16-17; Eph 2:19-22). The parables speak of a single kingdom (q.v.) to which are called the community of the disciples of Christ. The later Pauline and Pastoral Letters perceive one universal Church, the pillar and ground of truth (1 Tim 3:15): Christ is the head of the body, the Church (Col 1:18); the eternal mysterious plan of God is revealed in the Church (Eph 3:9-10). The Church is moving to a still greater unity when God will be all in all (1 Cor 15:25-28).

But in this universal Church there are many local (q.v.) Churches (1 Cor 1:2; 2 Cor 1:1; Gal 1:1—"To the Churches of Galatia"; Rom 16:16—"All the Churches of Christ"). There is a striking address to the divided community at Corinth: "To the Church of God which is at Corinth, to those sanctified in Christ, called to be saints, together with all those who in every place call on the name of our Lord Jesus Christ, both their Lord and ours" (1 Cor 1:2). There is no idea of a prior plan of a federation of these Churches; rather they all belong to the universal Church, with each being fully the Church of God (cf. 1 Cor 1:2—Corinth; 15:9—Jerusalem) in its own place.[2] The word best suited to describe their interrelation is communion (q.v.), which translates *koinônia*. The idea of communion is a rich and variegated notion in the NT. We are concerned here with *koinônia* only insofar as it reflects unity: communion and hence unity through the Eucharist (1 Cor 10:16-17), in apostolic labors and doctrine (Gal 2:2, 7-9—the right hand of *koinônia*), in caring and sharing for the indigent Church of Jerusalem (Rom 15:25-27).[3]

There are two kinds of affirmation about the unity within a local Church: some apply to its particular situation; others apply also to the whole Church. Y. Congar draws attention to the order of the elements of unity resulting from baptism in Acts 2:42; the apostolic teaching leads to fellowship *(koinônia),* thence to the breaking of bread, and the prayers.[4] The primitive community is described later as being of "one heart and soul," and "no one claimed private ownership of any possessions" (Acts 4:32).[5] It is a different story at Corinth, where Paul has to deal with divisions *(schismata)* in this highly charismatically endowed Church (1 Cor 1:10): they are one in *koinônia* of the one Eucharist (1 Cor 10:16-17); the varieties of gifts are from the same Spirit (1 Cor 12:4-11); they are one body (q.v.—1 Cor 12:12, 27); they are to make love their aim (1 Cor 14:1). Elsewhere Paul speaks of the unity in Christ which transcends religious barriers (Jews and Greeks), the social states (slave or free), and the radical difference between persons (male and female—Gal 3:28; cf. Col 3:11). The finest NT expression of the unity of believers is surely Eph 4:1-6, where in Trinitarian terms all are exhorted to live out the consequences of unity in baptism and faith (cf. Phil 2:1-2). Despite tensions (v. PRIMITIVE CHURCH), there is unity between the Jewish and Greek converts (Eph 3:4-6). The same letter indicates that unity is to be pursued and accepted as a gift as well as a task for the believer (Eph 4:3, 13, 15-16).[6]

The Johannine corpus is very conscious of the danger of division in the communities: the prayer in John 17, called the "high-priestly prayer" by David Chytraeus in the 16th century,[7] focuses on the unity of Jesus' disciples (John 17:21, 23); the Johannine letters are written to overcome divisive elements within their communities—fellowship in the community leads to fellowship (again *koinônia*) with God, and all are called to pursue the path of love and truth (1 John 1:3; cf. 2:19; 3:23; 4:11-13; 2 John 8–9).

As we leave NT times the emphasis on unity is, if anything, stronger. The *Didachê* (q.v.) prays twice that the Church be brought together from all parts into the kingdom.[8] The letter of Clement (q.v.) is a plea for ordered unity at Corinth. The letters of Ignatius strongly emphasize unity in doctrine, liturgy, and discipline. He demands unity in doctrine against Judaizing tendencies and Docetism: "Have no truck with the alien herbs of heresy. . . . Flee for your very life from these men; they are poisonous growths with a deadly fruit."[9] He constantly reiterates the need to be at union with the bishop in the celebration of the Eucharist, e.g., "Make certain, therefore, that you all observe one common Eucharist; for there is but one Body of our Lord Jesus Christ, and but one cup of union with his Blood, and one single altar of sacrifice—even as also there is but one bishop, with his clergy and my own fellow-servitors the deacons."[10] All the letters except Romans urge obedience to the bishop: there cannot be a Church without bishop, priests, and deacons.[11] But unity and Church order for Ignatius do not rest with externals. Their purpose is to lead all in imitation of Christ and in living contact with him.[12]

The teaching of the Fathers of the Church about the necessity for unity was unwavering. It is implied in the symbols used about the Church,[13] and especially the seamless robe (see John 19:23-24), which was Christological in the East but ecclesiological in the West, and particularly dear to Augustine.[14] There were also customs which fostered unity:[15] letters of introduction were given by bishops to travelers, which would enable them to be admitted to the Eucharist; there soon emerged formulas of faith for use in baptism; several bishops gathered for the ordination of a new bishop; bishops gathered in local councils to discuss common problems, especially those affecting the faith (cf. LG 22). After the 4th century such councils were seen as affecting the whole Church. Communion with Rome was in time seen to be a major criterion of unity within the Church.

The liturgical evidence is very striking. There was the practice at Rome of sending a particle of the consecrated bread to other Churches: this was placed in the chalice at the Sign of Peace.[16] Moreover, the evidence of the anaphora of various Churches shows that there was intercession for the local community (*Apostolic Tradition*—q.v.), or more commonly, but with an eschatological note, for the Church dispersed throughout the world.[17] These intercessions are still found in the Eucharistic Prayers currently in use in the Latin Church.

At the time of the scholastics the Church was above all the congregation of the faithful, and the Body of Christ—both titles implying unity. St. Thomas Aquinas has several important passages about the unity of the Church: it is a unity in faith, hope, and love;[18] Ephesians speaks of unity such as there is in the human body;[19] the new law has as its distinguishing mark the grace of the Holy Spirit, manifested by faith and working through love;[20] the Church is one Mystical Body whose head is Christ.[21]

The famous bull *Unam sanctam* of Boniface VIII (q.v.) in 1302 laid great stress on the unity of the Church. There are two swords, spiritual and temporal, but the temporal must submit to the spiritual, viz., to the pope, who is called "head of the Church."[22]

At the time of the Reformation and in the succeeding centuries the issue arose about which Church was the true Church, an urgent question in a time when as never before there was religious division in Europe. This question gave rise to the theology of the notes (q.v.) or distinguishing marks of the true Church. The statement of St. Robert Bellarmine (q.v.) was to become classical: "The Church is one and there are not two. This unique and true Church is the assembly of persons united by the one profession of faith and by participation in the same sacraments, under the government of legitimate pastors, and especially the one vicar of Christ on earth, the Roman Pontiff. By this definition it is easy to determine who belongs to the Church and who does not."[23] This definition takes account of the exterior and visible aspects of unity, sufficient to identify the Church, which he says later is "as visible and palpable as the assembly of the people of Rome, the kingdom of France or the republic of Venice."[24] The "note" of unity was variously developed in the succeeding centuries.[25] It was J.A. Möhler (q.v.) who would develop the notion of unity both as a note and as an essential quality of the Church whereby it is Spirit-filled and Spirit-led. The Roman School (q.v.) prepared for Vatican I (q.v.), taking some of the directions of Möhler.

At Vatican I there were schemas prepared on the Mystical Body and on unity, which never reached the aula floor. But the Council stated in its constitution *Pastor aeternus:* "In order, then, that the episcopal office should be one and undivided and that, by the union of the clergy, the whole multitude of believers should be held together in the unity of faith and communion, he set blessed Peter over the rest of the apostles and instituted in him the permanent principle of both unities and their visible foundation."[26] The same council would appeal also to the "catholic unity and unconquerable stability" of the Church as a ground for the credibility of faith.[27]

After this council the theology of the manuals continued to be basically apologetic, but apart from them a dogmatic ecclesiology continued to develop until Vatican II. An important stage was the 1943 encyclical *Mystici corporis* (q.v.) of Pius XII (q.v. and v. BODY OF CHRIST). Here there is asserted an identity between the Mystical Body and the Catholic Church: "If we would define and describe this true Church of Jesus Christ—which is the holy, catholic, apostolic, Roman Church—we shall find no expression more noble, more sublime or more divine than the phrase which calls it 'the mystical Body of Jesus Christ.'"[28] Only those with the triple bond of faith, sacraments, and obedience could truly *(reapse)* be called members of the Church.[29] This identification was repeated in the encyclical, *Humani generis* (1950).[30]

But Vatican II[31] refused to follow this path and instead taught: "[This unique Church of Christ] set up and organized in this world as a society subsists *(subsistit)* in the Catholic Church governed by the Successor of Peter and the bishops in communion with him" (LG 8; cf. UR 4). The word "subsists" (q.v.) has generated some controversy, but one thing is surely clear, viz., the council was distancing itself from the rigid equation "Mystical Body equals Roman Catholic Church"; it deliberately chose the word "subsists in" instead of "is." The council also did not speak of membership (q.v.) of the Church, but used the more traditional biblical and patristic term "communion." The conditions for full communion are spelled out in LG 14: "They are fully incorporated into the society of the Church who, possessing the Spirit of Christ, accept its whole structure and all the means of salvation that have been established within it, and within its visible framework are united with Christ, who governs it through the supreme pontiff and the bishops, by the bonds of profession of faith, the sacraments, ecclesiastical government and communion." We know from the acts of the council that "possessing the Spirit of Christ" means to be in the state of grace or divine friendship.[32] Other Christians are in communion with the Roman Catholic Church to a greater or lesser degree, depending on the bonds that remain intact, such as baptism,

Scripture, Trinitarian faith, etc. (LG 15). The Church is also related to the followers of other religions, to theists, and to those who have not as yet explicit faith in God (LG 16).

In the ecumenical movement (v. ECUMENISM) and generally in ecclesiology there is need for continued reflection on the one Church and the many Churches, on the one Church and the unity of the human race. Allied to these issues is the prime discovery of Vatican II of the theology of the local Church, which for Christians is the immediate if not primary experience of Church.[33] Related questions are the role of ministry (q.v.) in the local Church,[34] and the function of Bishops' Conferences (q.v.) within the local and the universal Church.

The notion of the unity that is sought in ecumenism (q.v.) varies from one confession or groups of confessions to another. Each Church will naturally believe that it is an—if not *the*—authentic manifestation of the Church of Christ.[35] The Catholic assertion of being "the one true Church" means nothing more than institutional fullness: there is no doctrine or structure, e.g., sacrament or Church order, that belongs to the Church of Christ that is missing in the Catholic Church. "One true Church" is not an assertion that the members of the Catholic Church are actually or necessarily holier than those of other Churches (see UR 2–3). Furthermore, in ecumenical dialogues there is some growing acknowledgment that the papacy (q.v.) may—perhaps in some renewed form—be a center and foundation of the Church's external unity.[36]

The theology of unity is clearly Trinitarian. The Church is one through the Holy Spirit, who builds it into the Body of Christ and the people of the Father, whose eternal design the Church is. What is external and institutional serves its interior life of grace and the divine glory manifested in the Church's very weakness (v. KENOSIS). The Church is "a mystery that finds its highest model and source in the unity of the persons of the Trinity: the unity of the one God, the Father and the Son and the Holy Spirit" (UR 2).

Unity of the Church is impaired by heresy (q.v.) and schism (q.v.). Furthermore, a person is to an extent cut off from the unity of the Church through excommunication (q.v.).

The four marks of the Church are intimately interconnected: catholicity is diversity in unity; holiness is a unity with God and with other Christians, indeed humankind; apostolicity has no meaning except through unity.

---

[1]E. Lanne, "L'Église une," Irén 50 (1977) 46–58.    [2]F.A. Sullivan, *The Church We Believe In: One, Holy, Catholic and Apostolic* (Dublin: Gill and Macmillan—Mahwah: Paulist, 1988) 34–37. [3]Ibid., 38–43; cf. R. Schnackenburg, *The Church in the New Testament* (London: Burns & Oates, 1974) 128–132. [4]Congar,

L'Église une 19–20.   ⁵J. Dupont, "L'union entre les premiers chré- tiens dans les Actes des Apôtres," NRT 91 (1969) 898–915. ⁶Schnackenburg (n. 3) 132; J.M. Arroniz, "La unidad de la Iglesia en la Carta a los Efesios," Lumen 30 (1981) 347–368.   ⁷See Cyril of Alexandria, *In Ioan.* 11:8—PG 74:505.   ⁸9:4; 10:5.   ⁹*Ad Trall.* 6:1 and 11:1; cf. 9:1-2; *Ad Philadel.* 2.   ¹⁰*Ad Philadel.* 4; cf. *Ad Eph.* 20:2; *Ad Smyrn.* 6–9.   ¹¹*Ad Trall.* 3:1-2 and passim.   ¹²*Ad Magnes.* 7; 13; *Ad Philadel.* 5:2; *Ad Eph.* 2 and 4.   ¹³H. Rahner, *Symbole der Kirche: Die Ekklesiologie der Väter* (Salzburg, 1964).   ¹⁴M. Aubineau, "La tunique sans couture du Christ: Exégèse patristique de Jean 19, 23-24," in P. Granfield and J.A. Jungmann, eds., *Kyriakon. FS J. Quasten* (Munster: Aschendorff, 1970) 1:99-127. Augustine *Tr. in Ioan.* 118:4—PL 35:1949; cf. 13:13 and 15—PL 35:1499-1500; *En. in ps.* 21:2, 19—PL 36:176.   ¹⁵L. Hertling, *Communio: Church and Papacy in Early Christianity* (Chicago: Loyola UP, 1972). A. Michel, "Unité de l'Église," DTC 15:2172-2230.   ¹⁶A. Chavasse, "A Rome, l'envoi de l'Eucharistie, rite unificateur de l'Église locale," RBén 97 (1987) 7–12.   ¹⁷E. Lanne, "L'Église une dans la prière eu- charistique," Irén 50 (1977) 326–344, 511–555.   ¹⁸*In symbol. apost.* 9.   ¹⁹*In Eph.* 4, lect. 1 (195).   ²⁰ST 1–2ae, q.108, a.1.   ²¹ST 3a, q.8, aa.1, 3, 4, 6.   ²²DS 870/ND 804.   ²³*Disputationes de controversiis christianae fidei adversus huius temporis haereticos* (Ingolstadt, 1588) 3:2, 147.   ²⁴Ibid., 148.   ²⁵A. Houssiau, "Images diverses de l'unité de l'Église," RTLv 10 (1979) 131–158 at 140–145; G. Thils, *Les notes de l'Église dans l'apologétique catholique depuis la ré- forme* (Paris, 1937) 154–211; cf. M. Sales, *Le corps de l'Église: Études sur l'Église une, sainte, catholique et apostolique.* Communio (Paris: Fayard, 1989).   ²⁶Tanner 2:811-812/DS 3051/ND 818. ²⁷Tanner 2:807/DS 3013/ND 123.   ²⁸AAS 35(1943) 199/Carlen 4:39-40/ND 847.   ²⁹Ibid., AAS 202/Carlen 41.   ³⁰AAS 42 (1950) 571/Carlen 4:179.   ³¹W. Kasper, "Die Einheit der Kirche nach dem II. Vatikanischen Konzil," Catholica 33 (1979) 262–277.   ³²ActSyn 3/1:203—Alberigo-Magistretti 446.   ³³J.A. Bracken, "Ecclesiology and the Problem of the One and the Many," TS 43 (1982) 298–311, replying to J.A. Komonchak, "Ministry and the Local Church," CTSAP 36 (1981) 56–82; A. Dulles, "The Church, the Churches and the Catholic Church," TS 33 (1972) 199–234; K. Rahner, "The One Church and the Many Churches," ThInvest 17:183-196; idem, "Unity of the Church—Unity of Mankind," ThInvest 20:154-172.   ³⁴I. Mierzwa, "The Ministry as a Structural Factor of the Unity of the Church," MonEccl 105 (1980) 120–137.   ³⁵P.D.L. Avis, "'The True Church' in Reformation Theology," ScotJT 30(1977) 319–345; P. Chirico, "One Church: What Does It Mean?," TS 28(1967) 659–682. ³⁶G. Alberigo, "L'unité de l'Église dans le service de l'Église romaine et de la papauté (XIe–XXe siècle)," Irén 51 (1978) 46–72.

## OPUS DEI

Opus Dei ("work of God") is a secular institute founded in 1928 by José María Escrivá de Balaguer y Albas, a priest from Barbastro in Northern Spain. He saw that God was asking him to urge men from all walks of life to respond to a specific vocation to seek holiness and carry out an apostolate in the midst of the world through the exercise of their profession or trade, without any change of state. He began in university circles so as afterwards to reach others. Within two years he realized that God wanted him to spread the call to women also. Opus Dei thus consists of two sec- tions: one for men and one for women. There are sev- eral grades of membership, from the fully committed "numeraries," who are celibate, to "associates," who maintain looser links with the organization.

The secular institute (q.v.) was approved by Pius XII in 1940. It has always sought vocations in university milieux, though not exclusively. It runs the University of Navarra at Pamplona, as well as the Santa Croce in Rome. The movement spread rapidly, having 60,000 members of 80 nationalities at the time of its founder's death in 1975. He was beatified in 1992.

The spirituality of Opus Dei centers on the sanctifi- cation of work, and of its members being a leaven in the world. It is strong in the professions, and in some places, notably in Spain, suspected of being deeply involved in politics. Though it claims to be an open in- stitute,¹ it is widely perceived as secretive and manip- ulative in society and the Church; in large measure it attracts both enthusiasm and hostility. Its loyalty to the Church, especially the magisterium, is beyond ques- tion. It has enjoyed special favor from Pius XII and John Paul II. Its ordained members belong to a per- sonal prelature (CIC 294–297—v. PRELATURES, PER- SONAL) established in 1982.²

¹D. le Tourneau, *What Is Opus Dei?* (Cork, Ireland: Mercier, 1987); idem, "L'Opus Dei: Son histoire, sa spiritualité sa nature juridique," EspVie 93 (1983) 561–569, 577–588, 593–599—[a member]; M. Walsh, *The Secret World of Opus Dei* (London: Grafton, 1989)— [hostile]; P.J. Longo, "Escriva's Opus Dei: From Secular Association to Personal Prelature," AmBenR 40 (1989) 190–203—[objective, but critical]. Documentation: G. Rocca, "'L'Opus Dei': Appunti e documenti per una storia," Claret 25 (1985) 5–227.   ² A. de Fuenmayor et al., *L'itinéraire juridique de l'Opus Dei: Histoire et défense d'un charism* (Paris: Desclée, 1992).

## ORIGEN (ca. 185–254)

Origen was born probably at Alexandria about 185.¹ When his father Leonides was martyred in 202 C.E., he supported his family by opening a school of elementary studies. The bishop Demetrius soon put him in charge of catechetics. His manner of life was austere to the point of heroism. He traveled widely: Rome, Palestine, Antioch. Still a layman, he was invited to preach before bishops of Caesarea in Palestine, upon which his own bishop Demetrius protested. When he was ordained in Palestine, his bishop called a council of bishops and ex- pelled him from Egypt for allowing himself to be or- dained in another diocese without permission of his own bishop. He returned to Caesarea, where he wrote and taught. During the Decian persecution he was tor- tured to try to induce him to apostatize. He died soon afterwards in broken health, probably 254 C.E.

A man of prodigious learning, Origen was an astute textual critic and commented on most of the Scriptures. He preached extensively, wrote apologetic, dogmatic, spiritual and speculative works, and a substantial quantity of letters. Only a fraction of his immense out- put has come down to us; because of later controver- sies about his orthodoxy, many of his works were destroyed. H.Urs von Balthasar (q.v.) writes of his own early theological work: "I discovered Origen and recognized with astonishment that he was the most sovereign spirit of the first centuries, who had set his mark for good or ill on the totality of Christian theology."[2]

Origen's importance for ecclesiology would seem to be both indirect and direct.[3] First, we can still learn from him the importance of uniting dogmatic theology and spirituality, of seeing a spiritual meaning as well as a literal one in Scripture.[4] Second, he has ecclesiological insights of great depth, especially his vision of the triple incarnation: the Logos is incarnate in his historical, resurrected, and Eucharistic body, in his ecclesiological body, and in his body of Sacred Scripture.[5] He clearly teaches the Pauline doctrine of the Body (q.v.), with the Logos being its life.[6] He is a witness to the institutions of the Church in his time. Speaking of the *debita* (debts, less accurately "trespasses") in the Our Father he develops: "A widow cared for by the Church has a debt, a deacon another, a presbyter another, and a bishop an extremely heavy debt for which payment is demanded by the Savior of the whole Church and punishment exacted if he does not pay it."[7] The great patristic images of the Church are found at least seminally in Origen: e.g., bride, spouse, city of God, people, believers, Jerusalem.

Origen fell into disfavor in the patristic period for errors which have been called "Origenism," though not all were taught by him. The problems with his writings for later generations were multiple: his novel approach to Scripture, at once literal and spiritual; his penchant for allegory; the tentative nature of his early reflections on what would be differently expressed by later theologians and councils; his speculative genius, which examined possibilities that were subsequently felt to be untenable; the confusion of his philosophical positions with his theology; above all, the misunderstandings both of his writings and of his intentions by those who, like Jerome, read him in a later age and did not take account of his more primitive language and accused him, for example, of Arianism. It has been shown that the anathema against Origen at Constantinople II (q.v.) cannot be attributed to the council.[8] There were certainly flaws in his Trinitarian theology, which would become clear with Nicaea (q.v.). His theory of *apokatastasis,* which held with the ultimate salvation of all, is scarcely firmly based, even though he adduced some scriptural grounds for it.

Origen's varied work is part of the richest inheritance of the Church. At present, he is, after Augustine, perhaps the most widely read of all the ecclesiastical writers of antiquity.[9] To quote von Balthasar again, "Origen was as towering a figure as Augustine and Aquinas."[10]

[1]Bibliog., H. Crouzel, *Bibliographie critique d'Origène* (Steenbrugge—The Hague: Nijhof, 1971); idem, *Supplément 1.* Instrumenta patristica 8 (ibid., 1982); idem, "Chronique origénienne," BLitEc 84 (1983) 115–124; idem, "Les études sur Origène des douze dernières années," ETR 58 (1983) 97–107; idem, "Current Literature on Origen 1970–1988," TS 49 (1988) 499–516. See H. Crouzel, "Origen," EncycEarCh 2:619-623, with bibliog.; Patrology 2:37-101. Texts PG 11–17; many individual texts, e.g., SC; GCS; ANL 10, 23; ANF 4, 9; R.A. Greer, ed. and trans. *Origen: An Exhortation to Martyrdom, Prayer, First Principle Book IV, Prologue to the Commentary on the Song of Songs, Homily XXVII on Numbers.* Classics of Western Spirituality (New York—Ramsey—Toronto: Paulist, 1979). [2]*My Work in Retrospect.* Communio Books (San Francisco: Ignatius, 1993) 11—cf. his *Origen: Spirit and Fire: A Thematic Anthology of his Writings* (Washington, D.C.: The Catholic University of America Press, 1984—German 1938, [2]1953). [3]G. Bardy, *La théologie de l'Église de saint Irénée au concile de Nicée* (Paris, 1947) 128–165; P. Batiffol, *L'Église naissante et le catholicisme* (Paris, [2]1909, Eng. trans. London, 1911; repr. Paris: Cerf, 1971) 355–397; R.P.C. Hanson, "Origen's Doctrine of Tradition," JTS 48 (1948) 17–27; H.J. Vogt, *Das Kirchenverständnis des Origens* (Cologne: Böhlau, 1974). [4]H. de Lubac, *Exégèse médiévale: Les quatre sens de l'écriture. Théologie* 41, 42, 59. 4 vols./2 parts (Paris: Aubier, 1950–1962) 1/1:211-304. [5]Von Balthasar, in Greer (n. 1) xii. [6]*Contra Celsum* 6:48. [7]*De orat.* 28:4—Greer (n. 1) 148. [8]F.X. Murphy and P. Sherwood, *Constantinople II et Constantinople III* (Paris: Ed. l'Orante, 1974) 108–109; H. Crouzel, "Origenism," EncycEarCh 2:623-624. [9]Ibid. [10]In Greer (n. 1) xi.

# ORIGIN OF THE CHURCH

There are many answers to the question "When did the Church begin?" In the Fathers, we have from the time of Augustine the idea of the Church from Abel (q.v.). Hermas (q.v.) speaks of the creation of the Church before all things, e.g., he sees the Church as an old woman: "She was created first of all; that is why she is elderly, and for her the world was created."[1] Other early writers have similar positions.[2] Hundreds of patristic texts speak of the Church being born on Calvary when the New Adam slept on the cross.[3] The liturgy invites us to see the beginning of the Church in the Annunciation itself.[4] Vatican II sees the inauguration of the Church in the preaching of the good news by Jesus (LG 5). But there is a sense in which Pentecost is, if not the birth of the Church, its beginning in power. The Lucan theology in Acts shows the development of the Church through the Spirit.

Until the end of the 19th century, it was generally accepted that Christ intended to, and did, found the Church. With Liberal Protestantism, especially in the person of A. von Harnack, who held that Jesus' aim was to preach the kingdom in people's hearts,[5] we find the first modern challenge to the traditional view. A. Loisy tried to defend on grounds of faith, but not of history, Christ's foundation of the Church. In so doing, he coined the phrase that would henceforth be famous, "Jesus foretold the kingdom, but it was the Church which came."[6] Loisy's views were rejected as Modernist (q.v.), and the oath against Modernism required the statement "I hold . . . that the Church . . . was personally *(proxime)* and directly instituted by the true historical Christ himself during his life among us, and that it is built upon Peter, the prince of the apostolic hierarchy, and upon his successors through the ages."[7]

The difficulty can be stated in two short questions: What is the relationship between the preaching and ministry of Jesus and the post-resurrection community? What is the relationship between the early Church at Jerusalem and Antioch in the 30s and the developed Church we find in the *Letters* of Ignatius (q.v.) about 110? In reply to the first question, the manuals of ecclesiology after the Modernist crisis sought to show the Church developing in three phases: in his lifetime Jesus prepared for the foundation of the Church—he gathered disciples, promised the primacy to Peter, instituted the Eucharist; after the resurrection he instituted the Church—he conferred the actual primacy on Peter, he gave the apostles the power to teach, sanctify, and rule the Church; he promulgated the Church at Pentecost in the sending of the Holy Spirit.[8] But these facts cannot easily be established by historical critical methods.[9] More recently Roman Catholic scholars have a greater openness to the suggestion that Jesus began his mission to Israel, and only gradually realized that it would fail. His establishment of the commemorative meal, the Last Supper, is an indication that he somehow foresaw his followers continuing after his imminent death.[10] The act of Jesus in establishing the Church is now seen as post-resurrectional. Quite clearly such positions seek to be in harmony with traditional ones; they obviously reflect modern Christological concerns which emphasize the limitations of the human knowledge of Jesus. The Church's experience of charism both in the lives of its saints and in recent decades might, however, be expected to leave theologians more open to the suggestion that Jesus may have had profound intuitions and even accurate knowledge about the future. There is the further problem of accepting the limits imposed by the historical-critical method. But as F. Schüssler Fiorenza has shown, "the self-understanding of the early Christian communities expresses strongly that the Church is founded in Christ and is based upon a relation between Christ and the Church"[11] (v. CHURCH, THE TERM EKKLÊSIA).

An examination of the various NT ecclesiologies (q.v.) and especially of the Gospels shows a reception of the words and ministry of Jesus by the communities of the 1st century. This reception, seen in what is chosen to record, points to a continuity between the historical Jesus Christ and the Church, though it is differently specified in each text.[12] It is the very pluriformity of the image of Jesus in the various books of the NT that grounds a new critical certainty that the Church has its true origin in Jesus of Nazareth who became the "Lord and Christ" (Acts 2:36).

[1]*Vis.* 1:2, 2; 2:8—SC 53:80-82, 94-96.  [2]E.g., Ps-Clement, *Second Letter to Corinthians* 14:2—FC 1:74-75/Halton 33; Origen, *In Cant.* 2:62—PG 13:134/Halton 35.  [3]LG 2; cf. Methodius, *Symposium* 3:8—SC 95:108/Halton 47; St. Thomas Aq. *In Ioan.* 19, lect. 5 (2458)—the blood and the water consecrate the Church; S. Tromp, "De nativitate Ecclesiae ex Corde Iesu in Cruce," Greg 13 (1932) 489–527.  [4]See Roman Missal, 25 March. On Birthday of Mary, 8 Sept., and on solemnity of BVM, 1 Jan., the Missal speaks of "the beginning of our salvation."  [5]*What Is Christianity?* (1900. Eng. trans. New York: Harper & Row, 1957) 191. Cf. F. Schüssler Fiorenza, *Foundational Theology: Jesus and the Church* (New York: Crossroad, 1985) 60–64.  [6]*L'Évangile et l'Église* (Paris, 1902) 111.  [7]DS 3540/ND 143.3.  [8]F. Schüssler Fiorenza, op. cit. (n. 5) 72–81. Cf. Salaverri, Ecclesia 1:497-584; P. Ternant, "Church," DBTh 74–76.  [9]Schüssler Fiorenza (n. 5) 81–90; A. Cody, "The Foundation of the Church: Biblical Criticism for Ecumenical Discussion," TS 34 (1973) 3–18; F.J. Cwiekowski, *The Beginnings of the Church* (Mahwah: Paulist—Dublin: Gill and Macmillan, 1988) 38–64.  [10]R. Schnackenburg, *The Church in the New Testament* (London: Burns & Oates, 1974) 12–15; R. McBrien, *Catholicism* (Minneapolis: Winston, 1980) 575–577; K. Rahner, *Foundations of Christian Faith: An Introduction to the Idea of Christianity* (New York: Seabury—London: Darton, Longman & Todd, 1978) 326–335, modified in *A New Christology* (New York: Seabury, 1980) 18–31.  [11]Op. cit. (n. 5) 122–132 at 132.  [12]Ibid., 133–165.

## ORTHODOX CHURCH

The Orthodox Church is the most significant and has the largest membership of the Eastern Churches (q.v.). The term "Orthodox" originally meant soundness in Christology based on the first seven ecumenical councils (*orthos*/right—*doxa*/glory-teaching-opinion).[1] The Orthodox Church has a complex history[2] conditioned by the encounter with the Byzantine Empire,[3] Islam, and Marxist regimes, as well as by estrangement from Rome; this last was a matter not only of doctrine, but also spirituality, politics, and culture, and fundamentally different ecclesiologies.[4] From 1054 the name of the pope ceased to be mentioned in the liturgy—a sign of fracture in communion, and schism began largely because of the insensitivity of the papal legate Cardinal Humbert. Though the 11th century is usually regarded as the beginning of the schism, misunderstandings, distrust, rivalry, and differences had become more marked in the preceding centuries. Despite the attempts at union in the councils of Lyons II (1274—q.v.) and Florence (1439—q.v.), the schism was total by the mid-15th century. This break was in marked contrast with the picture of the first millennium given by Vatican II: "For many centuries the Churches of the East and of the West went their own ways, though a brotherly communion of faith and sacramental life bound them together. If disagreements in faith and discipline arose among them, the Roman See acted by common consent as moderator" (UR 14).

The theological differences between the Orthodox and the Roman Catholic Churches mainly center around the *Filioque* ("and from the Son"—q.v.), the Roman addition to the Nicene Creed, and the role of the primacy and infallibility of the pope. But it would have to be stressed that there are major psychological, social, and historical blockages remaining even after Pope Paul VI and Patriarch Athenagoras I in 1965 lifted the mutual excommunications of 1054.[5] However, ecumenical contact is slowly identifying areas of agreement as well as focusing more clearly the disagreements (v. ECUMENISM, ORTHODOX). The existence of Uniate Churches (q.v.) remains a constant irritant for the Orthodox.

Orthodox Christians regard themselves as belonging to one Church in virtue of a unity of faith, and the Byzantine rite, which includes common liturgical, canonical, and spiritual traditions. The structure of the Orthodox Church is complex. There are four ancient patriarchates (Constantinople, Alexandria, Antioch, and Jerusalem; the fifth patriarchate, Rome, is regarded as being in schism or heresy). There are eleven "autocephalous" Churches (*autos*/self—*kaphalê*/head) which are independent in Church life: four of them are headed by a patriarch (Russia, Romania, Serbia, and Bulgaria), the others have archbishops or metropolitans, except for the Catholicos-Patriarch of Georgia in what was the USSR. Three Churches are quite, but not fully, independent, and are called "autonomous" (Finland, Japan, and China). Churches in other countries depend on one of the above eighteen Churches, except for the disputed autocephalous Orthodox Church in America.

Like all theologies of the Christian East, that of Orthodox Christianity is very much centered on the liturgy[6] and has a fine sense of the local Church being united with other Churches on earth and with the heavenly Church, in a living Tradition that links the Fathers of the Church and the Church living out its life in obedience to the Scriptures.[7] Orthodox ecclesiology is predominantly one of communion: it breathes from the liturgy, but it has some tensions, noted especially by its lay theologians, in the area of hierarchy/authority and laity.[8] But the most abiding characteristic of Orthodox theology is its Trinitarian richness, with a particularly strong pneumatology.[9] Orthodox spirituality has roots going back to Irenaeus (d. ca. 200), and thus to the undivided Church;[10] it has been preserved and developed in schism and is one of the glories of the East. This spirituality is now being deeply appreciated both in the Roman Catholic and Protestant Churches.[11] The Russian Orthodox Church, particularly in its émigré theologians in Paris (Saint Serge) and in the USA, has been to the forefront in Orthodox theology and spirituality in the 19th and 20th centuries.[12] In recent years the importance of the Romanian theologian D. Stanilaoë (q.v.) is being realized in the West.

In the past the Orthodox Church has been criticized for being too inward-looking. The oppression of communism and the hostility of Islam were certainly contributory factors, but the deficiency must not be exaggerated: the Orthodox Church has had a sense of mission and social responsibility which is too often overlooked.[13] The Orthodox Church in this century has become deeply involved in ecumenism (v. ECUMENISM, ORTHODOX) both in the World Council of Churches and in other forums.

---

[1]M. Sesan, "Zur Geschichte des patristischen Wortes 'Orthodox,'" in F. Paschke, ed., *Überlieferungsgeschichtliche Untersuchungen. Texte und Untersuchungen zur altchristlichen Literatur 125* (Berlin: Akademie Verlag, 1981) 525–529.   [2]A. Schmemann, *The Historical Road of Eastern Orthodoxy* (London: Harvell, 1963—Crestwood, N.Y.: St. Vladimir's Seminary Press, 1977); N. Zernov, *Eastern Christendom: A Study of the Origin and Development of the Eastern Orthodox Church* (London, 1961); D. Attwater, *The Christian Churches of the East. Vol 2—Churches not in Communion with Rome* (London, 1961).   [3]J.M. Hussey, *The Orthodox Church in the Byzantine Empire* (Oxford: Clarendon, 1986); J. Meyendorff, *Byzantium and the Rise of Russia: A Study of Byzantino-Russian Relations in the Fourteenth Century* (Cambridge: UP, 1981).   [4]J. Meyendorff, *Byzantine Theology: Historical Trends and Doctrinal Themes* (London—Oxford: Mowbrays, 1974); T. Ware, *The Orthodox Church* (Harmondsworth: Penguin, revised ed. 1983); cf. P. Evdokimov, "Les principaux courants de l'ecclésiologie orthodoxe au XIXe siècle," in AA.VV. *L'ecclésiologie au XIXe siècle.* US 34 (Paris, 1960) 57–76.   [5]AAS 58 (1966) 20–21—Flannery 1:471-473.   [6]D.-I. Ciobotea, "Le rôle de la liturgie dans la formation théologique orthodoxe," Contacts 38 (1986) 198–223.   [7]J.J. Allen, ed., *Orthodox Synthesis: The Unity of Theological Thought* (Crestwood, N.Y.: St. Vladimir's Seminary Press, 1981); S. Bulgakov, *The Orthodox Church* (Eng. trans. 1935, revised, Crestwood, N.Y.: St. Vladimir's Seminary, 1988); L. Cross, *Eastern Christianity: The Byzantine Tradition* (Sydney—Philadelphia: Dwyer, 1988); G.A. Maloney, *A History of Orthodox Theology Since 1453* (Belmont, Mass.: Nordland, 1976); D. Staniloaë, *La génie de l'Orthodoxie: Introduction* (Paris: Desclée de Brouwer, 1985); P.N. Trembelas, *Dogmatique de l'Église Orthodoxe catholique.* 3 vols. (Chevetogne, 1966–1968); C.N. Tsirpanlis, "A Bibliography of Orthodox Theology (1970–1980)," PatByzR 1 (1982) 63–69, 152–155, 235–238; 2 (1982) 87–95; K.[T.] Ware, *The Orthodox Way* (London—Oxford: Mowbray, 1979).   [8]See n. 7 and G.D. Draga, "Orthodox Ecclesiology in Outline," GrOrTR 26 (1981) 185–192; O. Clément, "Orthodox Ecclesiology as an Ecclesiology of Communion," OneChr 6 (1970) 101–122; P. Evdokimov, "The Principal Currents of Orthodox Ecclesiology," EastCR 10 (1978) 26–42; V. Lossky, "Ecclesiology: Some Dangers and Temptations," Sobornost 4 (1982) 22–29; J. Zizioulas, *L'être ecclésial.* Perspective orthodoxe 3 (Geneva: Labor et Fides, 1981); idem, "Le mystère de l'Église dans la tradition orthodoxe," Irén 60 (1987) 323–335—"The Mystery of the Church in Orthodox Tradition," OneChr 24 (1988) 294–303.   [9]W. Hryniewicz, "Der pneumatologische Aspekt der Kirche aus orthodoxer Sicht," Catholica 31 (1977) 122–150 and see works in notes above.   [10]E. Clapsis, "Prolegomena to Orthodox Dogmatics: Bible and Tradition," Diak (USA) 16 (1981) 16–28.   [11]A Monk of the Eastern Church, *Orthodox Spirituality* (London: SPCK, [2]1978); N. Arseniev, *Mysticism and the Eastern Church* (London—Oxford: Mowbray, 1979 from 1st ed. 1926); O. Clément, *The Roots of Christian Mysticism: Text and Commentary* (London: New City, 1993 = French Sources [Paris: Stock, 1982]); T. Špidlík, *The Spirituality of*

*the Christian East: A Systematic Handbook.* Cistercian Studies 75 (Kalamazoo: Cistercian Publications, 1986).    [12]Maloney (n. 6); E. Behr-Sigel, *Preghiera e santità nella Chiesa Russa* (Milan: Ancora, 1984)—*Prière et sainteté dans l'Église russe* (Bégrolles-en-Mauges: Abbaye de Bellefontaine, 1982 reprint of original 1950); L. Bouyer, *A History of Spirituality. Vol. 3—Orthodox Spirituality and Protestant and Anglican Spirituality* (London—Tunbridge Wells: Burns & Oates, reprint 1982) 3–53; T. Špidlík, *La spiritualità russa* (Rome: Studium, 1981); N. Zernov, *The Russians and Their Church* (London: SPCK, [3]1978).    [13]D.-I. Ciobotea, "Les tâches de la théologie orthodoxe aujourd'hui," Contacts 3 (1987) 91–101; G. Lemopoulos, "The Prophetic Mission of Orthodoxy," EcuR 40 (1988) 169–177; N. Palassis, ed., *Saint Nectarios Orthodox Conference—Seattle, Washington—July 22–25, 1980* (Seattle: St. Nectarios Press, 1980); R. Slesinski, "Contemporary Essays in Orthodox Tradition and Life," Diak(USA) 17 (1982) 151–167; A. Schmemann, *Church, World, Mission. Reflections on Orthodoxy in the West* (Crestwood, N.Y.: St. Vladimir's Seminary Press, 1979); T. Špidlík, "El problema de la justicia en la tradición ortodoxa," EstE 55 (1980) 175–193; C.N. Tsirpanlis, "Social and Political Dimensions of Eastern Orthodoxy," PatByzR 3 (1984) 215–222; F. von Lilienfeld, "Die Gabe der Russischen Orthodoxen Kirch an Europa und die Ökumene," UnaSan 42 (1987) 274–290; A. Yannoulatos, "Theology, Mission and Pastoral Care," GrOrTR 22 (1977) 157–180.

## OUTSIDE THE CHURCH

The axiom *Extra Ecclesiam nulla salus* ("outside the Church there is no salvation") could be accurately described by Pius IX as a very well-known Catholic dogma.[1] It certainly has a long and complex history.[2]

There are many quite synonymous expressions in papal and conciliar teaching[3] apart from the explicit statement of the Council of Florence: "(The holy Roman Church) . . . firmly believes, professes and preaches that 'no one remaining outside the Catholic Church, not only pagans,' but also Jews, heretics or schismatics, can become partakers of eternal life; but they will go to the 'eternal fire prepared for the devil and his angels' (Matt 25:41), unless before the end of their life they are received into it."[4] Such texts merely make explicit a strong patristic teaching, quite categorically formulated by Augustine,[5] which also spoke of the Church as the Ark of Noah, or the house of Rahab, where alone salvation was to be found.[6] Texts like "One does not have the love of God who does not love the unity of the Church" abound in Augustine.[7] Behind them lies the doctrine of the necessity of baptism (cf. John 3:5). It is clear that these affirmations both of the Fathers and of the magisterium were made in the context of a presumption of bad faith: those outside the Church were presumed to have knowingly and willingly rejected God's will for them.

With the geographical explorations of the fifteenth and following centuries, it became clear that a multitude, even a majority of humanity, might never have had the chance of hearing about Christ, and so a theology of an implicit desire *(votum)* developed.[8] Thus with

Pius IX we find declarations which at once stress both the necessity of the Church and the possibility of salvation for those invincibly ignorant: ". . . it must be held as a matter of faith that no one can be saved outside the apostolic Roman Church, that the Church is the only ark of salvation, and that whoever does not enter it will perish in the flood. On the other hand, it must likewise be held as certain that those who live in ignorance of the true religion, if such ignorance is invincible, are not subject to any guilt in this matter before the eyes of the Lord."[9] Theologians reconciled this kind of affirmation by positing in the person of good faith an implicit desire for what God would want, in the present case to accept baptism and enter the Church.

When we come to the encyclical *Mystici corporis* (q.v.) it is clear that though Pius XII clarifies the language of previous teaching, he is still in harmony with it.[10] The pope lays down the conditions for membership (q.v.): "Only those are to be accounted really *(reapse)* members of the Church who have been regenerated in the waters of baptism and profess the true faith, and have not unhappily cut themselves off from the structure of the Body, or for very grave crimes have been severed by legitimate authority."[11] But the expressions used have given rise to some difficulty: "It follows that those who in turn are divided in faith and government cannot be living in such a one body, and cannot be living the life of the one divine Spirit";[12] and ". . . he (the Spirit) refuses to dwell by the grace of holiness in members completely severed from the Body."[13] Envisaged in these texts is willful separation from the Church, and/or an exercise of Church authority either expressing or accomplishing such separation. It cannot contradict passages in the encyclical which allow for the salvation of those not united visibly to the Church: "For the salvation of all, especially of the faithful . . . he has the right to be called 'the Savior of all men,' though with St. Paul we must add, 'especially of the faithful' (cf. 1 Tim 4:10)."[14] Again the pope states that "those who do not belong to the visible structure of the Catholic Church" are invited "to extricate themselves from a state in which they cannot be secure of their own eternal salvation" even though "they may be ordered *(ordinentur)* to the mystical Body of the Redeemer by some unconscious yearning and desire *(inconscio quodam desiderio ac voto).*[15] There are two authoritative interpretations of the pope's meaning. First, when a rigorist interpretation of the axiom "Outside the Church there is no salvation" was proposed by L. Feeney (q.v.), a letter was sent by the Holy Office to the archbishop of the place (Boston) explaining that for salvation one must be related to the Church by at least implicit desire, which includes faith and charity; one does not have to be an actual member.[16] Second, in a later encyclical, *Humani generis,* (1950) Pius XII protested against the reduction to an empty formula the necessity of belonging to the true Church.[17] Since it would be totally against the main teaching of the earlier encyclical to speak of two distinct Churches, one visible, the other invisible, it must be held that it is to the visible Church that people must be ordered for their salvation. That did not prevent theologians like K. Rahner speaking of a stratification of membership depending on the bond with the Church a person enjoyed.[18]

Vatican II approached the question in another way. It left aside the concept of membership and spoke instead of "incorporation" (LG 14; v. MEMBERSHIP). It insisted that a willful rejection of the Church which is perceived to be necessary involves exclusion from salvation (LG 14). The Church recognizes that other Christians are joined (*coniunctam*—LG 15), and that others are ordered (*ordinantur*—LG 16) to it in various ways. It then asserts that God will provide the means necessary for salvation to those who have not come to a knowledge of God but who under grace are trying to live aright (LG 16; cf. GS 22; v. NON-CHRISTIAN RELIGIOUS).

The axiom may then be expressed in a positive fashion: those who are saved are saved through the Church. It is a matter for theologians to try to understand how the Church mediates salvation.[19] Since there will always be a multitude with no possibility of encountering the Church as a sign, much less a presence heralding God's grace, the specific activity of mediation would seem to lie in its Eucharistic life and mediation.[20] Moreover, whatever good there may be in other religions is both a shadow of, and a preparation for, the fullness of life which is in the Church (v. ANONYMOUS CHRISTIANS).

[1]DS 2867/ND 814.   [2]Y. Congar, "Hors de l'Église, pas de salut," in *Sainte Église: Études et approches ecclésiologiques.* US 41 (Paris: Cerf, 1963) 417–432; F. A. Sullivan, *Salvation Outside the Church? Tracing the History of the Catholic Response* (New York—Mahwah: Paulist—London: Chapman, 1992); J.P. Theisen, *The Ultimate Church and the Promise of Salvation* (Collegeville: St. John's UP, 1976).   [3]Innocent III—DS 792; Lateran 1V—Tanner 1:230/DS 802/ND 21; Boniface VIII—DS 870, 875/ND 804; Clement VI—DS 1051.   [4]Tanner 1:578/DS 1351/ND 810.   [5]*Serm. ad Caes. eccl. plebem* 6—PL 43:695.   [6]K. Rahner, "Membership of the Church According to the Teaching of Pius XII's Encyclical *Mystici Corporis Christi,* " ThInvest 2:1-88 at 36–38 with nn. 40–43.   [7]*De bapt.* 3:16, 21—CSEL 51:212.   [8]Rahner (n. 6) 42–50; Sullivan (n. 2) 118–122.   [9]Encyc. *Quanto conficiamur*—Carlen 1:370/DS 2865 intro./ND 813; cf. DS 2865–2867/ND 814.   [10]Rahner (n. 6) 51–64; Sullivan (n. 2) 131–135; cf. A. Chevasse, "Ordonnés au Corps Mystique . . . ," NRT 70 (1948) 690–702.   [11]AAS 35 (1943) 203/Carlen 4:41/DS 3802/ND 849.   [12]Ibid.   [13]Ibid.—AAS 220/ Carlen 48/DS 3808/ND 852.   [14]Ibid.—AAS 220/Carlen 49.   [15]Ibid.—AAS 243/Carlen 58/DS 3821.   [16]DS 3866–3873/ND 854–857.   [17]AAS 42 (1950) 571/Carlen 4:179   [18]Art. cit. (n. 6) 77, 86.   [19]Rahner Foundations 347–348; Y. Congar, "Romanité et catholicité: Histoire de la conjonction changeante de deux dimen-

sions de l'Église," RSPT 71 (1987) 161–190 at 177–178 citing LG 14–17 and AG 7–8.   [20]See Sullivan (n. 2) 158–161.

# OXFORD MOVEMENT

The Oxford Movement, which was centered in the English university city of Oxford, lasted only a short time (1833–1845), but it was to be significant for the Anglican Communion and even for other Churches.[1] It was partly reaction to a prevailing liberalism, partly arising from a rediscovery of important elements of the primitive Church.[2] More than an intellectual movement, it was marked by a passion for holiness and truth.[3]

The movement is usually dated from a sermon on "National Apostasy" by J. Keble at Oxford on 14 July 1833. Its members sought to defend the divine institution of the Church of England, its apostolic succession, and the *Book of Common Prayer* as normative for faith. The movement's main platform were the *Tracts for the Times,* begun by J.H. Newman (q.v.) the same year.[4] The other main leader was E.B. Pusey.[5]

The Tractarians asserted the spiritual independence of the Church of England against both liberalism and the state. They tended to bypass the Reformation in seeking the spiritual and theological values of the Church of the first centuries. They regained for the Church of England a doctrine of ministry which would cause tensions within the Church and in ecumenical relations with non-episcopal Churches. The movement was attacked by the liberal wing of the university, by the press, and by the government, which chose bishops from the ranks of those opposed to it.

The movement came to a crisis in 1841 with Newman's *Tract 90,* which was condemned by most of the hierarchy. It was a straight challenge to look seriously at the grounds for a Catholic, rather than a Protestant, interpretation of the *Thirty-nine Articles* (v. ANGLICAN COMMUNION). Shortly afterwards some key figures entered the Catholic Church: Newman, F.W. Faber, and W.G. Ward (1845).

Though afterwards the movement lost its identity and direction, its ideas continued to be influential, especially in worship. The movement also fostered serious theology: the study of the Fathers, with the "Library of the Fathers" edited by Keble, Pusey, and Newman from 1833; the "Library of Anglo-Catholic Theology," comprising classics of 17th-century Anglicanism. Modern Anglo-Catholicism has its origins in the movement.

Keble and Pusey are regarded as saints in some parts of the Anglican world, while the cause of the beatification of Newman is advancing favorably in the Catholic Church.

[1]O. Chadwick, *The Spirit of the Oxford Movement: Tractarian Essays* (New York—Cambridge UK: UP, 1992); G. Rowell, ed.,

*Tradition Renewed: The Oxford Movement. Conference Papers* (London: Darton, Longman & Todd, 1986); M.R. O'Connell, *The Oxford Conspirators: A History of the Oxford Movement 1833–1845* (London: University Press of America, 1991).  [2]P. Nockles, "The Oxford Movement: Historical Background 1780–1833," in Rowell (n. 1) 24–50; idem, *The Oxford Movement in Context: Anglican High Churchmanship, 1760–1852* (Cambridge: UP, 1994).  [3]A.M. Allchin, "The Oxford Movement: Some New Perspectives," OneChr 1 (1965) 43–52; F.H. Borsch, "Ye Shall Be Holy: Reflections on the Spirituality of the Oxford Movement," in Rowell (n. 1) 64–77; A. Louth, "The Oxford Movement, the Fathers and the Bible," Sobornost 6 (1984) 30–45.  [4]I. Ker, *John Henry Newman: A Biography* (New York—Oxford UK: UP, 1988) 81–315.  [5]H.C.G. Matthew, "Edward Bouverie Pusey: From Scholar to Tractarian," JTS 32 (1981) 101–124.

# P

## PAPAL PRIMACY

In the Vatican II Decree on Ecumenism we read: "For many centuries the Churches of the east and west followed their separate ways though linked in a union of faith and sacramental life; the Roman See by common consent acted as guide *(sede Romana moderante)* when disagreements arose between them over matters of faith and discipline" (UR 14). A question that arises in Catholic theology, and most acutely in ecumenical dialogue, is about what actually happened during that period and afterwards: How did Rome achieve a primacy of whatever kind during the first millennium? What changes are legitimate dogmatic development? What are accretions that can and should be discarded, or at any rate not be insisted upon in talks aimed at Christian unity? Other positions are also adopted: J.M.R. Tillard,[1] uses the position of Leo the Great (pope 440-461—q.v.) as a touchstone; P. Granfield,[2] adopts Vatican I but with careful exegesis of its texts and having regard to the way in which Vatican I was received by Vatican II. A survey of the historical development is necessary if we are to understand the papacy for today.[3]

The role of Peter (q.v.)[4] is crucial to an understanding of this development. The text of Matt 16:16-18 has from about the 6th century been one of the key biblical foundations for the Roman Catholic doctrine of the papacy. The first point of interest is the late date at which it was so employed. Earlier, the Fathers saw in the Rock the faith of Peter rather than Peter himself. The second problem associated with the text is its exegesis. No leading contemporary scholar will say that the literal, that is, the inspired, meaning of Matthew's text is the primacy of Peter's successors, much less their infallibility. We can say with confidence, however, that this text, along with such others as Luke 22:31-32 and John 21:15-17, does point to a certain preeminence of Peter among the apostles. The joint Lutheran-Roman Catholic group were agreed on this in their major study on Peter.[5]

The transition from Peter to the popes is a difficult one. It involves the notion of *ius divinum* (q.v.) or divine right. Briefly, the argument is that from quite a number of different structures in the NT, one set became normative by the year 200 in all the Churches of which we have some detailed knowledge. This normative set of structures includes a single bishop in each place, with priests and deacons. It also includes some important position for the bishop of Rome, which is found in two facts: the bishops of Rome acted outside their own territory; other dioceses looked on Rome as having some preeminence. Given the jealousy of the early Churches about their traditions, some with their line of bishops right back to an apostle, as well as the status of civil Rome as a hostile persecuting power, it is improbable that such an evolution could have taken place in so short a time, unless it was under the guidance of the Holy Spirit. Vatican II uses words like "divine institution" or "by divine providence" for this evolution; "Divine right" is common in modern theology. Thus there is an evolution in the Church which has as its basis Matt 16:16-19, etc., but as its operating power the guidance of the Holy Spirit.[6] We see in the NT the college of apostles with Peter in a special position: all of the apostles are a foundation (Eph 2:20; Rev 21:4)—Peter is the only one to whom Jesus gave the name Rock (Matt 16:18); all of the apostles are pastors (Acts 20:28; 1 Pet 5:2)—Peter is the universal pastor (John 21:15-17); all of the apostles—many exegetes say the whole community—receive the keys, the power to bind and loose (Matt 18:18; cf. John 20:23)—Peter received it singularly (Matt 16:19); all of the apostles are witnesses of the risen Christ (Acts 1:8, etc.)—Peter is in the first place (1 Cor 15:5; Luke 24:34); Jesus prays for all (John 17:9, 20)—he prays for Peter for the benefit of the others (Luke 22:32).[7]

The Church at Rome was marked by its association with the two great martyrs Peter and Paul, who in some sense were its foundation, though neither of them was the first to preach the faith there. Peter is the source of unity and authority; Paul, the teacher of authentic doctrine.[8]

It is not at all clear that Peter was Rome's first bishop, or even that there was a single bishop there before the 2nd century.[9] Clement (q.v.) is aware of authority structures going back to the apostles, but we are not in a position to state clearly his own position in Rome. The earliest list of the bishops of Rome is from about 180 C.E.,[10] though some decades earlier a traveler, Hegesippus, testifies to the uniformity of doctrine in the Mediterranean world and to a list of Roman bishops, which he does not cite. It has been suggested that some of the names on the list indicate prominent presbyters who handled relations between the Church of Rome and other Churches without being "bishops" as we would understand the term.[11]

In the period up to Leo the Great (440-461), evidence is rather sparse. We can divide it into two classes: first, action by the Roman Church; second, statements made about the Roman Church. Both of these lines show a development in a sense of the authority of the bishop of Rome, and they result in a cumulative argument for the authenticity of the Roman primacy.

First then, there are the texts that indicate some special position or precedence of the Church of Rome and later of its bishop. Ignatius (q.v.) spoke of the Roman Church as the one "which presides in the country of the land of the Romans" and of its "presiding in love."[12] According to Irenaeus (q.v.) every Church should agree with the Church of Rome because of its more excellent origin (*potior principalitas*—probably Peter and Paul) and the fidelity with which it has retained the apostolic tradition.[13] Tertullian (ca. 200—q.v.) spoke of the authority (prestige?) of the Church founded by Peter and Paul and sanctified by their martyrdom.[14] Cyprian (q.v.) was very anxious that Pope Stephen should agree with him on the rebaptism issue.[15] Cyprian also spoke of the heretics traveling to Rome hoping to get the approval of that Church for their positions.[16] The local council of Sofia (343-344) regarded it as important that its actions be communicated to Pope Julius I. Optatus (ca. 370) spoke of the primacy of the Church founded by Peter, arguing against the Donatists for the importance of being catholic and in communion with Rome.[17] After him similar statements are very common, e.g., in Ambrose (q.v.), Augustine (q.v.), Jerome (q.v.).[18]

Second, there are actions by the Roman Church (not yet always clearly by its bishop) which indicate that this Church had a sense of mission or responsibility towards other Churches. Clement (q.v.) wrote to the dissenters in Corinth (ca. 98) urging acceptance of authority and peace.[19] Pope Victor I threatened to excommunicate Polycrates of Ephesus in the Quartodeciman controversy (q.v.) about 190 C.E.[20] Stephen likewise threatened to excommunicate Cyprian in the rebaptism controversy (after 254) and insisted that Cyprian should follow the line taken by the Roman Church.[21] Julius claimed the right to be informed and to have a say at the time of the deposition of Athanasius (341).[22] A synod of the Roman Church (382) was stated to have objected to the third canon of the Council of Constantinople I (381—q.v.), which placed the bishop of that city second only to Rome in rank.[23] Even as early as Innocent I (ca. 401-417), the bishops of Rome became accustomed to judging cases submitted to them by bishops. The Roman attitude was not one of giving advice but of making decisions, and the Roman way was proposed to, and imposed on, other Churches.[24]

In this history of the first four centuries it is important to note that though Rome was the capital of the empire, it was a persecuting power, the Babylonian prostitute of the Book of Revelation. Constantinople was the first Christian capital, and its bishops soon gained great prestige: the center of imperial authority moved east; papal authority did not, remaining in the ancient pagan capital. The most significant factor is that other Churches allowed their autonomy to be limited by the actions of various popes, and some of these Churches were apostolic sees, founded by an apostle.[25]

The high point of the papacy in the early centuries was the reign of Leo the Great (440-461). His main aim was service of the faith: "We have received from Peter, the Prince of the Apostles, the certainty of possessing the right to defend the truth which brings our peace. No one must be allowed to weaken it, since this truth has so solid a foundation."[26] Leo was the first to articulate clearly the Peter-Pope identity. There is a whole list of occasions where Leo, however, insisted that disputes be settled locally without appeal to Rome.[27] There was no doubt in Leo's mind that he had the power to intervene in doctrinal and judicial matters. He showed himself aware of the power of the papacy.[28] This power was recognized in the famous exclamation at Chalcedon (q.v.), "Peter has spoken through Leo" *(Petrus per Leonem locutus est)*. The history of local and general councils (q.v.) shows that in the early centuries councils considered themselves as autonomous, but the bishops of Rome increasingly regarded themselves as having the role of receiving (v. RECEPTION) and then of approving them, and finally in modern times of being the only one having the authority to summon an ecumenical council.[29]

After the nadir of the papacy in the disastrous 10th century, the idea that reform must come from the "top down" became current through St. Peter Damian (1007-1072) and soon with St. Gregory VII (1073-1085—q.v.).[30] The twenty-seven propositions of the Gregorian *Dictatus papae* (q.v.) are an assertion of near absolute power in the Church. Lay investiture (q.v.) was forbidden by Gregory VII, but the controversy was finally settled at the Concordat of Worms (1122). The reform movement led to much centralization, which began decisively under Alexander II (1061-1073), aided by Hildebrand, the future Gregory VII. Liturgical unification was effected with the elimination of the Greek Rite in the south of Italy, of the Hispanico-Visigothic Rite in Spain, and the refusal to allow the use of the national language in Bohemia.

The ignorance of many bishops in earlier centuries, which led them to submit difficult cases to Rome, brought about a classical case of the power of custom: certain cases were sent to Rome instead of being dealt with locally; Rome became accustomed to dealing with these cases; it became a custom that such cases be sent to Rome; finally, it became a law that only Rome could deal with them—the position of the *Dictatus papae* (q.v.).

In the cause of reform there was a lot of reflection on the notion and on the exercise of power (*potestas*—v. AUTHORITY). Gregory VII commissioned research for documents to bolster up the power of the papacy. The *False Decretals* (q.v.) supplied much material. A notable contribution came from Cardinal Deusdedit (ca. 1084), who nonetheless ensured the transmission of the exclusive clause from Yves of Chartres: The pope is to be judged by no one "unless he be discovered to be deviant in faith" *(nisi deprehenditur a fide devius)*.[31] Again, the titles "Mother" and "Spouse," in the Fathers' Trinitarian and theological statements, became juridical titles, which served to demand obedience.[32] Between Gregory VII and Innocent III (1198–1216), the papal primacy had begun to become a papal monarchy, to be seen in the inflation of the meaning read into in papal titles (q.v.).[33]

In the ecclesiastical order, all power was held to come from the pope. It was seen as an episcopal type of power but superior to any local bishop. Gregory saw power in juridical terms. There was a single end for the two powers, secular and religious, ultimately salvation, and hence the spiritual power was higher. In a sense, one can speak of a hierocracy, but not in the sense that the pope claimed secular government as such.[34]

The rich ecclesiology of St. Thomas Aquinas (q.v.) is much more concerned with theological and spiritual values than with institutional features. With either praise or blame, he is sometimes wrongly credited with originating views on the papacy which are juridic, and in particular with the idea that bishops receive their power (jurisdiction not sacramental) from the pope. The pope has also supreme episcopal power and supreme doctrinal and spiritual power.[35]

The mendicant friar movement was a major source of pro-papal theory in the late 13th and early 14th centuries. Mendicant theologians insisted on the total subordination of parish clergy and bishops to the pope in order to legitimize the papacy's creation of a ministry of friars free from control of bishops and secular clergy.[36]

Centralization continued in the succeeding centuries. The Council of Florence (q.v.), which led to the union of some orientals with the Church, was the strongest affirmation of papal primacy of any council thus far. Though popes had an influence in the appointment of bishops in their area for centuries, it was not until the 14th century that popes began generally to appoint bishops in the West (v. BISHOPS). The Reformation led to still greater centralization and emphasis on papal prerogatives.

At Vatican I (q.v.) there was the desire to strengthen the power of the pope in view of the loss of the papal states and of the attacks on the Church by the Enlightenment and by liberal theorists. During the debate on the primacy, the council fathers clearly lacked both a sufficient general ecclesiology and a theology of the episcopate within which to place the primacy doctrine. In the council debates it was the three words "episcopal, ordinary, and immediate" that would give most cause for concern.[37] The document on the papacy is entitled "The First Constitution *Pastor aeternus* on the Church of Christ."[38] The complementary Second Constitution was not to be issued, owing to the abrupt ending of Vatican I (q.v.).

The prologue of *Pastor aeternus* treated the institution of the Church by Christ, the mission of the apostles, and the function of Peter as permanent principle of the unity of faith and communion and their visible foundation.[39] The first chapter, with its accompanying canons, asserted that a true and proper jurisdiction was conferred on Peter (q.v.).[40] The next chapter taught under anathema that Peter was by divine institution *(iure divino)* to have perpetual successors in the primacy; the pope is the successor of Peter in that primacy.[41]

The key chapter 3 on the primacy[42] is in several parts. Written in very technical juridical language, it needs careful exegesis. It evokes the Council of Florence (q.v.), which had reached a temporary agreement on the primacy with the East. Full power has been given to tend and rule the universal Church. This power is carefully described: it is *episcopal,* that is, similar in the whole Church to the power of a bishop in his diocese;[43] it is *not merely an office of supervision and guidance* but is *full and supreme power of jurisdiction over the whole Church;* it is over both pastors and faithful; it is *immediate,* not therefore mediated by any person or body in the Church but from Christ; it is not restricted to *faith and morals* (q.v.) but covers also *discipline and government;* being *full and supreme,* there is no power in the Church that the pope does not have—though he may not choose to exercise it, or perhaps should not in a particular case; it is *ordinary* power, that is, attached to his office and not delegated; *it does not detract from the power of bishops,* for their power is asserted, supported, and defended by the supreme and universal pastor; there is *no appeal* to any higher power, such as to an ecumenical council.

The notion of episcopal power does not really add anything to that of "ordinary and immediate" power. It is not without roots in tradition: the term "bishop of the whole Church" was ascribed to Leo the Great and was common from the 12th century.[44] Taken together, all the qualifications of the pope's power firmly exclude Febronianism (q.v.) or other positions which would have the pope merely first among equals in the episcopacy *(primus inter pares),* or which would allow him only a power of inspection or supervision and not the fullness of power. The doctrine here is expressed in largely juridical language, which later ages in the Church may express differently while retaining the genuine teaching of the council.

The fourth chapter dealt with the infallibility (q.v.) of the pope. It can and should be seen as an aspect of the apostolic primacy.

There have been two significant ways in which reception (q.v.) of the teaching of Vatican I has occurred. The first was the interpretation of the council in the German bishops' response to Bismarck (v. BISHOPS). The second was Vatican II. Since the Church was founded on the apostles, with Peter as their head, we should with this council approach the papacy through the college of bishops. This is the form of reception of the earlier council. It thus completed the work of Vatican I but within a new perspective. This development (q.v.) was not without some nervousness, as indicated by the repeated insistence in LG 18–25 about the college always acting with its head. But after Vatican II there will never be a fruitful examination of the papacy in the abstract, that is, one not seen in the context of the episcopal college.[45]

The theological question can be asked: How many supreme authorities exist in the Church? It would seem preferable to understand that there is only one subject of supreme power in the Church, the college of bishops, whose head can act independently, though always as a member (head) of the college[46] (v. BISHOPS, COLLEGIALITY).

Since Vatican II there have been important movements in ecumenical discussions about a Petrine ministry.[47] Some Churches, notably the Anglican Communion, already have their own experience of primacy.[48] Among some Protestants[49] and Anglicans[50] there is an openness to accept a center of unity in the pope, with the latter in ARCIC I being open to a pope who would be more than merely first among equals *(primus inter pares),* and with a stress on the service of unity rather than on juridical categories; the position of the Orthodox Churches is mainly one of seeing the Roman bishop as first among equals, though other issues surface in these Churches.[51] While infallibility is a crux, the notion of "full and supreme power" is perhaps the more difficult issue.

The style of John XXIII (q.v.) and Paul VI (q.v.) was very significant in showing a new, less authoritarian face of the papacy. The move, begun by Paul VI, to bring the papacy to the world, has been taken up energetically in more than sixty visits abroad of John Paul II (by 1995), who several times returned again to the same country after a few years.[52] This physical extension of the papacy would seem to strengthen on the part of people a personal esteem for the successor of Peter, a phenomenon very marked from the time of the exceedingly charming and magnetic Pius IX (q.v.).[53] Though the personal qualities as well as much of the teaching of the present pope are widely appreciated, there have been problems arising from people's perceptions of the way in which participated papal authority is exercised by Vatican dicasteries.[54]

In the post-Vatican II period there have been many studies on the meaning of the papacy for the Church.[55] These are often focused on the way in which the papacy is seen in a particular area.[56] The *Code of Canon Law* deals briefly with the papacy (CIC 330-335). It does not break new ground but follows Vatican II.[57] The law provides for the possibility of resignation of a pope (CIC 332 § 2). Though the case of Celestine V (q.v.) is clear, the facts surrounding the few other resignations are not always easy to establish.[58]

The post-Vatican II period has also seen strong anti-Roman sentiments. These are studied in a well-known book by H.U. von Balthasar (q.v.), themes to which he returned shortly before his death.[59] Disaffection with the papacy comes from both the extreme "right" and the "left" of the Church. The former is perhaps the deeper and more problematic; it sees the Church as having gone into theoretical or practical error with Vatican II (v. LEFEBVRE). The latter accepts the council but blames the papacy or Rome with not adapting quickly or wholeheartedly enough, or for not being sensitive enough in current issues, especially in the field of sexual morality, and to a lesser degree bioethics.

But often a problem does not lie so much with Vatican actions, as with their style. In some of the celebrated cases in the 1980s, though the right of Rome to intervene cannot be disputed, it might have been preferable to have had these cases dealt with at a local level. An unfortunate effect is that the time and atmosphere have become inauspicious for humble, loyal, and loving criticism of the papacy or of the Roman Curia (v. VATICAN) such as we find in history, especially among major theologians and saints, like St. Bernard (q.v.) or St. Catherine of Siena (q.v.).[60]

The papacy cannot be very long ignored in any ecumenical dialogue involving the Catholic Church. In the ecumenical movement, theologians are continually studying possible ways of moving forward in this area as in others. A moderate article by A. Dulles[61] is an example of current thinking. It suggests that union and unity with another Church need not await full agreement on all points of doctrine, provided that both Churches accept the legitimacy and harmony with the Scriptures of the doctrines of the other. Going along these lines, one would not, perhaps, have to insist on a detailed or full acceptance of Vatican I as a prior condition for unity. At any rate in ecumenical discussions a careful hermeneutic of this council will be necessary, one that could be greatly helped by the evidence at all times of a beneficent exercise of papal power (v. RECEPTION).

In recent years there is a concentration on seeing the papal primacy not only in relation to the teaching on the episcopacy (v. BISHOPS, COLLEGIALITY)[62] but also in regard to other truths, and to the teaching of Vatican II on the hierarchy of truths (UR 11—q.v.).[63] Other theologians are testing the doctrine of papal primacy to see what elements belong to Christ's permanent gift to the Church through the Spirit and what may be accretions of the ages or time-conditioned positions which were adopted for specific difficulties and may not be normative for all times.[64]

There are no widely received solutions at present, but the coming years can be expected to produce more exploratory work in this direction, work that is crucial for the Marian dogmas and for the Vatican I teaching on the papacy. Central to any future agreement on the papacy will be a recognition of the pope at the service of the unity of the Churches.[65]

---

[1]*The Bishop of Rome* (Wilmington: Glazier, 1983).  [2]*The Limits of the Papacy: Authority and Autonomy in the Church* (London: Darton, Longman & Todd, 1987).  [3]Bibliog. ArHPont 1 (1963–); J.M. Miller, *What Are They Saying About Papal Primacy?* (New York: Paulist, 1982). See B. Carra de Vaux, "Les images de la papauté au cours des siècles," LumièreVie 26/133 (1977) 39–69; W. de Vries, "'Vicarius Petri': Der Primat des Bischofs von Rom im ersten Jahrtausend," StimZ 203 (1985) 507–520; M. Guerra Gómez, "El obispo de Roma y la 'Regula fidei' en los tres primeras siglos de la Iglesia," Burgense 30 (1989) 355–432; J.F. McCue and A.C. Piepkorn, "The Roman Primacy in the Patristic Era," in P.C. Empie and T.A. Murphy, eds., *Papal Primacy and the Universal Church.* Lutherans and Catholics in Dialogue 5 (Minneapolis: Augsburg, 1974) 43–97; M. Maccarrone, ed., *Il primato del vescovo di Roma nel primo millennio: Ricerche e testimonianza.* Atti del symposium storico-teologico, Roma, 9–13 Ottobre 1989 (Vatican, 1991)—multilingual; idem, "Apostolicità, episcopato e primato di Pietro: Ricerche e testimonianze dal II al V secolo," Later 42 (1976) 1–354. P. Stockmeier, "Papsttum und Petrus-Dienst in der frühen Kirche," MüTZ 38 (1987) 19–29. See Y. Congar collected essays, *Église et papauté: Regards historiques* (Paris: Cef, 1994).  [4]P. O'Leary, "New Testament Foundations for Primacy," *Bulletin*—Rome: Centro pro Unione 30 (Fall 1986) 44–51; R. Pesch, *Simon-Petrus: Geschichte und geschichtliche des ersten Jüngers Jesu Christi.* Päpste und Papsttum Bd. 15 (Stuttgart: Hiersemann, 1980).  [5]R.E. Brown et al., eds., *Peter in the New Testament: A Collaborative Assessment by Protestant and Roman Scholars* (London: SCM, 1974).  [6]Y. Congar, "Romanité et catholicité: Histoire de la conjonction changeante de deux dimensions de l'Église," RSPT 71 (1987) 161–190; G. Mastrandrea, "Il principio di apostolicità nella chiesa romana dal I al V secolo: Indagine storica," Nicol 6 (1978) 355–362.  [7]Congar, ibid., 180.  [8]Ibid., 181–182; R.B. Eno, *The Rise of the Papacy.* Theology and Life 32 (Wilmington: Glazier, 1990) 16–18; W.R. Farmer and R. Kereszty, *Peter and Paul in the Church of Rome* (New York—Mahwah: Paulist, 1990); P. Grelot, "Pierre et Paul fondateurs de la 'primauté' romaine," Istina 27 (1982) 228–268; T. Strotmann, "Les Coryphées Pierre et Paul et les autres apôtres," Irén 36 (1963) 164–176; Tillard (n. 1) 74–86, 92–94; J.J. von Allmen, *La primauté de l'Église de Pierre et de Paul* (Fribourg: Ed. Universitaires—Paris: Cerf, 1977)—review E. Lanne, Irén 51 (1978) 186–197.  [9]Eno (n. 8) 28–29.  [10]Irenaeus, *Adv. haer.* 3:3, 3.  [11]Eno (n. 8) 31–34; cf. P. Lampe, *Die stadtrömischen Christen in de ersten beiden Jahrhunderten.* Wiss. Untersuchungen zum NT 2/18 (Tübingen: Mohr, 1987).  [12]*Ad Rom.* prol.  [13]*Adv. haer.* 3:3, 2.  [14]*De praescript. haereticorum* 36.  [15]Eno (n. 8) 61–65.  [16]*Epist.* 59:14—PL 3:818.  [17]*Contra Parmen. Donatist.* 2:2-3—PL 11:947.  [18]Eno (n. 8) 70–86.  [19]*First Letter of Clement.* [20]Eno (n. 8) 40–42.  [21]Ibid., 61–65.  [22]Ibid., 49–51.  [23]Tanner 1:32.  [24]Eno (n. 8) 87–101; K. Baus, in Jedin-Dolan 2:245-269.  [25]K. Baus, in Jedin-Dolan 2:633-636, 816.  [26]*Epist.* 43—PL 54:821; K. Baus, in Jedin-Dolan 2:264-269.  [27]Tillard (n. 1) 222, n. 11; idem, "The Presence of Peter in the Ministry of the Bishop of Rome," OneChr 27 (1991) 101–120.  [28]*Epist.* 14:1—PL 54:668-677.  [29]G. Alberigo, "The Papacy in the Ecumenical Council," Conc 167 (1983) 69–75; H.-J. Sieben, "On the Relation Between Council and Pope up to the Middle of the Fifth Century," ibid., 19–24; J.H. Provost, in Coriden, CIC. 277–281 on canons 338–340.  [30]Congar, Augustin 92–95, 112; cf. H. Wolter, in Jedin-Dolan 4:3-34, 635–643; G. Schwaiger, "Kirchenreform und Reformpapsttum (1046–1124)," MüTZ 38 (1987) 31–51; G.H. Tavard, "The Papacy in the Middle Ages," in Empie and Murphy (n. 3) 98–105.  [31]Congar, Augustin 108–109, 147.  [32]Ibid., 111.  [33]Ibid., 185–188; cf. J.A. Estrada, "La configuración monárquica de primado papal," EstE 63 (1988) 165–188; P. Granfield, *The Papacy in Transition* (Dublin: Gill and Macmillan, 1981) 34–61; W.D. McCready, *The Theory of Papal Monarchy in the Fourteenth Century. Guillaume de Pierre Godin, "Tractatus de causa immediata ecclesiasticae potestatis."* Studies and Texts 56 (Toronto: Inst. Medieval Studies, 1982); C. Morris, *The Papal Monarchy: The Western Church from 1050 to 1250* (Oxford: Clarendon, 1989); P. Prodi, *The Papal Prince: One Body and Two Souls: The Papal Monarchy in Early Modern Europe* (Cambridge: UP, 1988).  [34]Congar, Augustin 105–107.  [35]*Contra impugnantes* 4; *In 4 Sent.* d.7, q.3, a.1, sol. 3c; ST 2–2ae, q.1, a.10;

cf. Congar, Augustin 237–238; *Église et papauté* (n. 3) 211–227; U. Horst, "Kirche und Papst nach Thomas von Aquin," Catholica 31 (1977) 151–167; G. Sabra, *Thomas Aquinas' Vision of the Church.* Tübinger theol. Studien 27 (Mainz: Grünewald, 1987). [36]C. Zuckerman, "Some Texts of Bernard of Auvergne on Papal Power," RechTAncMéd 49 (1982) 174–204; Y. Congar, "Aspects ecclésiologiques de la querelle entre mendiants et séculiers dans la seconde moitié du XIIIe siècle et le début du XIVe," ArHistDoctMA 28 (1961) 35–151. [37]Alberigo, Storia dei concili 386; G. Thils, *Primauté et infaillibilité du Pontife Romain à Vatican I et autres études d'ecclésiologie.* Bibliotheca Ephemeridum theologicarum lovaniensium 89 (Leuven UP—Peeters, 1989). [38]Mansi 52:1330-1334; U. Betti, *La costituzione dommatica "Pastor aeternus" de l Concilio Vaticano I* (Rome: Pont. Athen. Antonianum, 1961) esp. 585–647 = *De doctrina Concilii Vaticani primi. Studia selecta annis 1948–1964 scripta* (Vatican, 1969) 309–360; G. Greshake, "The Pope's Office of Service: The Scope, Significance and Perspectives of the Decisions Made by the First Vatican Council About the Papal Primacy," MilltownSt 31 (1993) 112–143 = UnaSan 34 (1979) 56–78 (German). [39]Tanner 2:812/DS 3051/ND 818; cf. J. Gomis Pomares, "El primado del Papa, fundamento, centro y principio de la unidad de fe y de comunión de la Iglesia, en el Concilio Vaticano I," Burgense 21 (1980) 359–416. [40]Tanner 2:812/DS 3053–3055/ND 819–820. [41]Tanner 2:813/DS 3056–3058/ND 822–824. [42]Tanner 2:813-815/DS 3059–3064/ND 825–830. [43]Betti (n. 38) 617–620 = *De doctrina* 336–338; W.F. Dewan, "'Potestas vere episcopalis' au premier Concile du Vatican," in AA.VV. *L'Épiscopat et L'Église universelle.* US 39 (Paris, 1962) 661–687 = *De doctrina* (n. 38) 361–382; W. Kasper, "Primat und Episcopat nach dem Vatikanum I," TüTQ 147 (1962) 47–83 = ibid., 383–409; cf. G. Colombo, "Il problema dell'episcopato nella costituzione 'De Ecclesia catholica' del concilio Vaticano I," ScuolC 89 (1961) 344–372 = ibid., 410–435. [44]Betti (n. 38) 618, n. 9 = *De doctrina* 336, n. 11. [45]Granfield (n. 2); F.A. Sullivan, "Il Vaticano II e il papato oggi," in AA.VV. *Il vescovo di Roma nella chiesa universale.* Corso breve di ecumenismo 8 (Rome: Centro pro Unione, 1987) 69–77; J.M.R. Tillard, "La juridiction de l'évêque de Rome," Irén 51 (1978) 358–373, 509–520. [46]K. Rahner, in Vorgrimler, Vatican II, 1: 201-204. [47]AA.VV. *Papato e istanze ecumeniche* (Bologna: Ed. Dehoniane, 1984); AA.VV. *Das Papstamt: Dienst oder Hindernis für die Ökumene?* (Regensburg: Pustet, 1985); R. Coppola, "Primato papale ed ecumenismo," Nicol 13 (1986) 3–28; G. Dejaifve, "La papauté, problème oecuménique," NRT 102 (1980) 235–247; P.J. McCord, ed., *A Pope for All Christians? An Inquiry into the Role of Peter in the Modern Church* (New York: Paulist, 1976—London: SPCK, 1977); J. Macquarrie, "The Papacy in a Unified Church," Pacifica 2 (1989) 123–134; M. Thurian, "The Ministry of Unity of the Bishop of Rome to the Whole Church," OneChr 22 (1986) 124–133; R. Zinnhobler, "The Petrine Office and Ecumenism: The State of the Question," TDig 34 (1987) 43–47. [48]P.H.E. Thomas, "The Concept of Primacy in the Anglican Communion," Kanon 9 (1989) 189–195. [49]"Common Statement," 26–34 of Lutherans and Catholics in Empie and Murphy (n. 3) 20–23 = J.A. Burgess and J. Gros, eds., *Building Unity.* Ecumenical Documents 4 (New York: Paulist, 1988) 135–138; G.A. Lindbeck, "Lutherische Theologie und Papsttum," UnaSan 34 (1979) 19–26; W. Loughlin, "Los Angeles Roman-Catholic—Lutheran Dialogue on Papacy," JEcuSt 14 (1977) 565–566; J. Macquarrie, "The Papacy in a Unified Church," Pacifica 2 (1989) 123–134; J. Willebrands, "Roman Catholic/Lutheran Dialog: Papal Primacy," TDig 26 (1978) 129–131 = OneChr 13 (1977) 207–219. [50]"Authority in the Church II," 10–15, *ARCIC Final Report* (London: SPCK—CTS, 1982) 85–88; G.R. Evans, "The Anglican Doctrine of Primacy," AngTR 72 (1990) 363–378; P.H.E. Thomas, "The Concept of Primacy in the Anglican Communion," Kanon 9 (1989) 189–196. [51]E. Clapsis, "The Papal Primacy," GrOrTR 22 (1987) 115–130; A.

Kallis, "Papsttum und Orthodoxie: Der papst und die Kircheneinheit aus orthodoxer Sicht," ÖkRu 30 (1981) 33–46; J. Madley, "Der Papst: Das Problem zwischen Ost und West—Orthodoxe Theologen zu Fragen um Kirche und Primat," Catholica 32 (1978) 131–146; D. Papandreou, "Das Papsttum im Dialog zwischen der römisch-katholischen und der orthodoxen Kirche," UnaSan 34 (1979) 36–43; V. Phidis, "Primus inter pares," Kanon 9 (1989) 181–188; E. Timiadis, "'Tu es Petrus': An Orthodox Approach," PatByzR 2 (1983) 5–26; idem, "La primauté de Pierre dans l'ecclésiologie orthodoxe," Istina 23 (1978) 349–366. [52]J. Bonduelle, "Du prisonnier du Vatican au pape pèlerin," VieSp 144 (1987) 448–461. [53]Y. Congar, "Dévotion au pape aujourd'hui," VieSp 141 (1987) 390–394; M. Albaric, "L'effigie des papes dans les timbres du Vatican," ibid., 462–468; P. Vallin, "La dévotion au Pape dans la Compagnie de Jésus," ibid., 424–437. [54]Examples in Granfield (n. 2) 4–31. [55]E.g., G. Alberigo and A. Riccardi, eds., *Chiesa e papato nel mondo contemporaneo. Storia e società* (Rome-Bari: Laterza, 1990); J.P. Galvin, "Papal Primacy in Contemporary Roman Catholic Theology," TS 47 (1986) 653–667. [56]E.g., B. Cooke, ed., *The Papacy and the Church in the United States* (New York—Mahwah: Paulist, 1989) [57]J.H. Provost, in Coriden CIC 262–275. [58]P. Granfield, "Papal Resignation," Jurist 38 (1978) 118–131. [59]*The Office of Peter and the Structure of the Church* (San Francisco: Ignatius, 1986—German, *Der antirömische Affekt* —1974); idem, "Der antirömische Affekt als Selbstzerstörung der katholischen Kirche," in W. Baier et al., eds., *Weisheit Gottes—Weisheit der Welt.* FS J. Ratzinger. 2 vols. (St. Ottilien: EOS, 1987) 2:1173-1179. [60]E.g., E. de Clermont-Tonnerre, "Sainte Catherine de Sienne et le Pape," Vie Sp 141 (1087) 410–423; B. Häring, "A Letter to the Pope," Tablet (30.6.1990) from *Meine Erfahrung mit der Kirche* (Freiburg-Basel-Vienna: Herder, 1989). [61]A. Dulles, "Paths to Doctrinal Agreement: Ten Theses," TS 47 (1986) 32–47. Cf. G. Ghiberti et al., *Papato e istanze ecumeniche.* Scienze religiose 6 (Trent: Ist. di Scienze Religiose, 1984); P.J. McCord, ed., *A Pope for All Christians: An Inquiry into the Role of Peter in the Modern Church* (New York: Paulist, 1976—London: SPCK, 1977). [62]G. Alberigo, "Istituzioni per la comunione tra l'episcopato universale e il vescovo di Roma," CrNSt 2 (1981) 235–266. [63]B. Mondin, "The Holy Spirit as Legitimation of the Papacy," Conc 128 (1979) 63–71; V.T. Gómez, "El papado en la vida de la iglesia desde el concilio Vaticano I hasta Huan Pablo II," AnVal 8 (1982) 265–290; G.L. Müller, "Der römische Primat: Ein Ansatz zu seiner dogmatisch-theologischen Begründung," MüTZ 38 (1987) 65–85; J.M.R. Tillard, "La primauté romaine," Irén 50 (1977) 291–325; G.B. Winkler, "Kirchenfürst oder Seelsorger? Vom Wandel des päpstlichen Selbstverständnisses," TPQ 134 (1986) 5–12. [64]E.g., G.H. Tavard, "Is the Papacy an Object of Faith?," OneChr 13 (1977) 222–228. [65]G. Alberigo, "L'unité de l'Église dans le service de l'Église romaine et de la papauté (XIe-XXe siècle)," Irén 51 (1978) 46–72; R. Blazquez, "El papa centro de unidad en la Iglesia," Salm 30 (1983) 63–83; P. Granfield (n. 33) 175–195; G. Thils, "Le ministère des Successeurs de Pierre et le service de l' unité universelle,'" RTLv 17 (1986) 61–68.

## PAPAL TITLES

In the Vatican yearbook *Annuario pontificio,* the following titles are found with the frontispiece: Bishop of Rome, Vicar of Jesus Christ, Successor of the Prince of the Apostles, Supreme Pontiff of the Universal Church, Patriarch of the West, Archbishop and Metropolitan of the Province of Rome, Sovereign of the Vatican City. Some of these titles are ancient; not all are of equal significance.

The most common title, "pope," can be examined first. Many papal titles originally belonged to bishops. Thus Cyprian (q.v.) was addressed as "papa" by the Roman Church. From the 7th century the title of "universalis papa" in acts of councils and imperial letters was accepted without protest by the bishops of Rome.[1]

Gregory the Great (q.v.) seems to have been the first to frequently use the title "Servus servorum Dei," (Servant of the Servants of God) though similar phrases had been used by previous popes.[2] Gregory objected to "the head of the Church" at Constantinople calling himself the "Ecumenical Patriarch." Though this might only mean patriarch of the Eastern Empire, it had the possible nuance of "universal" in Greek.[3] He further objected to himself being called "universalem papam."[4]

At the time of the 11th-century Gregorian reform, the two titles "Universal Pope" and "Servant of the Servants of God" were both being used, though there was some opposition to the former. Gratian (q.v.) reacted against the adjective "universal," claiming that it properly belonged only to Christ, but at this stage the adoption of such a title was too well established to be dislodged.[5] At the time of Innocent III the title "Vicar of God" began to be used in addition to the other two.[6]

The title "Vicar of Christ" was originally an episcopal one, dating from about the 3rd century. Perhaps as such it is found in a Roman synod of 495 C.E. but was more frequently used of popes from the 8th century and became common from the time of St. Bernard (q.v.). Innocent III was the first to restrict the title to the pope. It was used formally by the councils of Florence (q.v.) and Vatican I (q.v.) about the pope. In the beginning it had a quasi-sacramental sense of Christ as acting through his vicar, but from the 13th century it took on juridical overtones. It gradually became an exclusive title for popes, in fact the principal one, superseding Vicar of God, and Vicar of Peter.[7] The particular problem with this title, Vicar of Christ, and one not absent from others, too, is that it may give the impression of the pope being above the Church as intermediary between it and Christ. "Vicar of Christ" was used of bishops by Vatican II (LG 27),[8] which in its Acta gave as justification texts of Cyprian and other patristic and medieval usages.[9] Even at a late stage there were objections to this expression in the case of bishops, but the Doctrinal Commission stood firm, though it did allow the addition of "legates."[10]

The title "Pontiff" was also an episcopal one. Originally "Supreme Pontiff" (Pontifex maximus, from Latin "bridge-builder" or Umbrian puntis = "offering") was a pagan title used of the chief priest in Rome. As a Montanist, Tertullian (q.v.) used it satirically about the Roman bishop.[11] Though some authors ascribe it as a papal title to Leo I, recent research

shows it to be a commonly used papal title only from the 15th century.[12]

"Patriarch" was a title in use from the 6th century. Despite the fact that the bishop of Rome has from then been recognized as Western or Latin Patriarch, it has not been a title in common use, though it is occasionally found in all periods. Its significance is studied in another article (v. PATRIARCHS).

The title "Metropolitan and Archbishop of the Roman Province" merely indicates that the diocese of Rome is a principal one and that the bishops in the area around it are suffragans under the presidency of the Roman bishop (cf. CIC 435–436).

The title "Sovereign of the Vatican City" can be seen as a secular one. The Vatican was recognized as being under the jurisdiction of the pope in the Law of Guarantees (1871) which regularized relations between new Kingdom of Italy and the papacy, abolishing the Papal States. This settlement was not acceptable to Pius IX and his successors up to Pius XI, who called themselves "the prisoner[s] of the Vatican." The Lateran Treaty (1929) confirmed the 19th-century dispositions and made clear that the Vatican was also an autonomous state (v. VATICAN).

By far the most ancient title is that of "Bishop of Rome." All the popes have used this title (v. PAPACY), even during the Avignon (q.v.) period when they were absent from the city. It is from this basis that all of the other titles flow. The word "papacy" seems to have appeared in the mid-11th century.[13]

Paul VI signed the documents of Vatican II as follows: "I Paul Bishop of the Catholic Church." By this he seems to have meant "Bishop of the Catholic Church (of Rome)." In so doing, the pope, like all of his predecessors in their use of titles, was saying something about his vision of the papacy and of the Church. The preferred title of John Paul II, except for solemn occasions, is Bishop of Rome, or Successor of Peter.[14] The pope is ultimately a spiritual leader who unifies the Church in communion (q.v.), and titles which suggest this are preferable.

---

[1]S. Kuttner, "Universal Pope or Servant of God's Servants: The Canonists, Papal Titles, and Innocent III," RDroitCan 31 (1981) 109–149 at 110–111; H. Schützeichel, "Die Titel des Papstes" in P. Neuner and H. Wagner, eds., In Verantwortung für die Glauben: Beiträge zur Fundamentaltheologie und Ökumenik. FS H. Fries (Freiburg-Basel-Vienna: Herder, 1992) 217–229. [2]Kuttner (n. 1) 109. [3]Ibid., 110. [4]Epist. 30—PL 77:933. [5]Kuttner (n. 1) 116. [6]Ibid., 129. [7]Congar, Augustin 186–188; G. Corti, Il Papa Vicario di Pietro, contributo alla storia dell'idea papale (Brescia, 1966); W. de Vries, "'Vicarius Petri'—Der Primat des Bischofs von Rom im ersten Jahrtausend," StimZ 203 (1985) 507–520; M. Maccarrone, Vicarius Christi: Storia del titolo papale (Rome: Lateran UP, 1952). [8]P. Goyret, "I vescovi come vicari di Cristo: Analasi di alcuni brani di Lumen gentium n. 27," AnnalT 4 (1990) 369–398. [9]ActaSyn 3/1:254. [10]ActaSyn 3/8:93. [11]De pudicitia 1. [12]Y. Congar, "Titres donnés au pape," Conc (French) 108 (1975) 55–65. [13] See

Y. Congar, "La place de la papauté dans la pieté ecclésiale des ré-formateurs du XIe siècle" in collection *Église et papauté: Regards historiques* (Paris: Cerf, 1994) 93–114 at 109–111 = *Sentire Ecclesiam*. FS H. Rahner (Fribourg in Br.: Herder, 1961) 196–217. [14]*Osservatore Romano* 5/6.3.1984.

## PARISH

The original term for a grouping of Christians was simply *ekklêsia* (church). In the century following the peace of Constantine (313), we find the beginning of diocesan organization.[1] Before that time we had the first rural churches which belonged to the territory of the urban bishop. Such territory was called in Greek *paroikia* (district), in Latin *parochia,* and in the West diocese (Greek *dioikêsis*). It was committed to a chorepiscopus (Greek *chôrepiskopos* or *episkopos tôn agrôn*), a bishop with full episcopal orders but with restrictions on the exercise of power. (This office died out by the 13th century, but it is still a title of honor in the Orthodox and Uniate Patriarchate of Antioch.) In the late 4th-century *Apostolic Constitutions* (q.v.) the district confided to a bishop was called the *paroikia:*[2] it could be small, or it could take in several churches and extend to the countryside around the towns,[3] such as Jerusalem, Rome, Antioch, and Alexandria.[4]

From the 7th century there was a growing usage of the terms "diocese" for the territory of a bishop, and "parish" for a particular community.[5] By the middle of the 6th century there were rural parishes in the entire Christian West.[6] Numerous local councils and synods prescribed a yearly visitation of parishes by the bishop; the early Middle Ages, moreover, saw tensions between the rights of the parish and those of the diocese. Lay investiture (q.v.) in the appointment to, and lay interference in the running of, parishes also became problems. By the time of the medieval councils, concubinage and simony, too, were also serious problems in many parishes.[7] Trent attempted reforms: to overcome the difficulties posed by illiterate pastors or parish priests; to deal with those whose moral behavior was unworthy;[8] to ensure residence in the parish;[9] to secure proper instruction of the people.[10]

Modern reflection on the parish began in the milieu of liturgical reform with an article by A. Wintersig in 1925.[11] The parish is the Church in miniature. The parish being Christ's body and spouse, there is a primary realization of the mystery of the Church in its relation to him. In the 1940s and 1950s there was extensive reflection on the reality of parish: in France it concerned above all its missionary dimension;[12] in Germany there were many studies on can. 216 of the 1917 *Code of Canon Law,*[13] and on the "parish principle" localizing the Church through Eucharistic celebrations.[14]

In Vatican II there was no extensive treatment of parish (see CD 23, 30, 31; OT 2). It did indicate that the local community (evidently the parish) could be called "Church of God" (LG 28). The council's relevance for the theology of parish lies in the difficult hermeneutic of texts that speak of the local/particular Church and in its shift of emphasis from a juridical entity to a community (SC 42; AA 20). The council explicitly speaks of the parish's liturgical celebration as a manifestation of the Church in dependence on the local bishop (SC 24, 42).

Parishes are treated at length in the new *Code of Canon Law* (CIC 515–552). There are some notable changes from the 1917 law.[15] There is a new definition of the parish: "a definite community of the Christian faithful established on a stable basis within a particular Church; the pastoral care of the parish is entrusted to a pastor as its own shepherd under the authority of the diocesan bishop" (CIC 515). The parish priest or pastor "is the proper shepherd of the parish entrusted to him, exercising pastoral care in the community entrusted to him under the authority of the diocesan bishop in whose ministry of Christ he has been called to share; in accord with the norm of law he carries out for his community the duties of teaching, sanctifying, and governing, with the cooperation of other presbyters or deacons and the assistance of lay members of the catholic faithful" (CIC 519). The qualities, rights, and duties of the pastor are spelled out in succeeding canons (521–535), with special emphasis on the office of teaching (528). Team ministry for parishes is possible (CIC 515) and the term of office of a parish priest can be specified with the approval of the conference of bishops (CIC 522). Having consulted with his council of priests, the local bishop may decree that a pastoral council be established in every parish (CIC 536);[16] each must, however, have a finance council. With a priest's supervision non-priests and even non-clerics can function in significant pastoral offices where there is a shortage of priests (CIC 517 § 2). At the age of seventy-five parish priests are to submit their resignations to the ordinary (CIC 538). Curates or parochial vicars are treated in eight canons (CIC 545–552).

Ongoing reflection on the parish stresses the building of community and derives some inspiration also from basic Christian communities (q.v.).[17] It would seem that although the parish alone cannot be the sole experience of Church, the full potential of parish has not yet been exploited (v. LOCAL CHURCH).[18]

In the Orthodox Church there is some tension between a stress on parish which emphasizes a Eucharistic ecclesiology (q.v.) and a stress on the diocese and bishop which ensures unity in teaching and faith.[19]

[1]O. Pasquato, "Organization, Ecclesiastical,"EncycEarCh 2:617–618. [2]2:1, 3—SC 320:144. [3]2:58, 1–2—SC 320:320; 8:47, 35—SC 336:284. [4]8:10, 7 with 46, 2–6—SC 336: 168 with 108. [5]V. Bo, *Storia della parrocchia.* 2 vols. (Rome: Dehoniane, 1988, 1990); L.

Nanni, "L'evoluzione storica della parrocchia," ScuolC 81 (1953) 475–544; H.J. Vogt, "Parrocchie," DPAC 2: 2507-2509; O. Pasquato, "Parrocchia e liturgia nella tradizione," RivLitg 78 (1991) 183–236. [6]H.J. Vogt, "Parish Organization," in Jedin-Dolan 2:644-650.    [7]See Lateran I (1123) c. 7—Tanner 1:191; Lateran II (1139) cc. 1, 7, 10—Tanner 1:197-199; Lateran III (1179) c. 11—Tanner 1:217. [8]Sess 21, c. 6; sess 24, c. 18—Tanner 2:730, 770.    [9]Sess 6, c. 2— Tanner 2:682-683.    [10]Sess 22, Decree; sess 24, c. 18—Tanner 2:737, 770–772.    [11]"Pfarrei und Mysterium," JbLitgW 5 (1925) 136–143 = MaisD 8 (1946) 15–26. See F.G. Brambilla, "La parroc- chia nella chiesa locale: A partire dalla sua dimensione liturgico- sacramentale," RivLitg 78 (1990) 155–182; idem, "La parrocchia nella Chiesa: Riflessione fondamentale," Teologia 13 (1988) 18–44; E. Vecchi, "La vita liturgica alla confluenza della vita pastorale par- rocchiale," RivLtg 78 (1991) 237–268.    [12]Y. Congar, "Mission de la paroisse," in AA.VV. Structures sociales et pastorale paroissiale. Congrès de Lille 1948 (Paris, 1949) 48–65.    [13]F. Coccopalmerio, "Il significato del termine 'parrocchia' nella canonistica susseguente al Codice del 1917," ScuolC 109 (1981) 210–235, 497–531.    [14]H. Rahner, ed., The Parish (Westminster, Md., 1958); K. Rahner, "Peaceful Reflections on the Parochial Principle," ThInvest 2:283- 318; E. Walter, "Die Theologie der Pfarrei," LTK 8:403-406.    [15]E. Barcelon, "Identidad teológico-jurídica de la parroquia en el nuevo Código," CiTom 111 (1984) 551–573; A. Borras, "La notion de curé dans le Code de droit canonique," AnnéeCan 37 (1987) 215–236; T.J. Carlson, "The Parish According to the Revised Law," StCan 19 (1985) 5–14; F. Coccopalmerio, De paroecia (Rome: Gregorian UP, 1991); idem, "Quaestiones de paroecia in novo Codice," Periodica 73 (1984) 379–410, 76 (1987) 47–82; idem, "De paroecia ut com- munitate christifidelium," ibid., 80 (1991) 19–44; J.M. Huet, Les paroisses dans le nouveau Code de droit canonique: Une étude à la lumière de l'ecclésiologie du concile Vatican II. Diss. (Louvain-la- Neuve, 1990); F. Iannone, "La parrocchia nel Codice di diritto canonico: Una normativa in prospettiva pastorale," Asp 38 (1991) 42–60; J.J. Janicki in Coriden, CIC 414–449; J. Passicos, "La paroisse vue par le canoniste," RTLv 13 (1982) 18–30; J.-C. Périsset, La paroisse: Commentaire des canons 515–572. Le nou- veau droit ecclésiale. Commentaire du Code de Droit canonique (Paris: Tardy, 1989); J. Pinzón, "La parroquia y el párroco en la nueva codificación canónica," TXav 34 (1984) 347–364.    [16]W. Dalton, "Parish Councils or Parish Pastoral Councils?," StCan 22 (1988) 169–185.    [17]A.R. Baranowski, Creating Small Faith Communities: A Plan for Restructuring the Parish and Renewing Catholic Life (Cincinnati: St. Anthony Messenger, 1988); T.A. Kleisser, Small Christian Communities (Mahwah: Paulist 1991). [18]B. Evans, "The Rural Parish: A Just and Caring Church," Worship 60 (1986) 399–411; T.P. Ivory, Conversion and Community: A Catechumenal Model for Total Parish Formation (New York: Paulist, 1988); J.J. O'Brien, "Parish Renewal," NDictSacWorship 925–933; T. Philippe, "Les nouvelles paroisses des pauvres," VieCons 58 (1986) 303–314; K. Rahner, "Theology and Spirituality of Pastoral Work in the Parish," ThInvest 19:87-102; M. Searle, "The Notre Dame Study of Catholic Parish Life," Worship 60 (1986) 312–333.    [19]P.N. Tarazi, "The Parish in the New Testament," SVlad 36 (1992) 87–102.

## PARTICULAR CHURCHES

The term "Particular Church" is a fluid one in Vatican II: in the Decree on Bishops it usually means diocese (e.g., CD 3, 6, 28; see AG 27; PO 6, 11); in the Decree for the Eastern Churches it means autonomous Churches with their own rite (e.g., OE 4; see LG 13, 23); in the Decree on Missions it can also mean all of the Churches in a sociocultural area (AG 19–22); in the Constitution on the Church it sometimes means diocese (e.g., LG 23, 27, 45; see AG 19, 20; GS 91), at other times it could be a grouping of dioceses (e.g., LG 13—v. LOCAL CHURCH). There is a tendency to use particular Church when the criterion is theological (CD 11) and to use local Church when geographical and sociocultural criteria are operating so that it means a gathering of more or less particular Churches.[1]

[1]See International Theological Commission, "Select Themes of Ecclesiology" (1984), in Texts and Documents 1969-1985 (San Francisco: Ignatius) 282; H. de Lubac, "Particular Churches in the Universal Church," in The Motherhood of the Church (San Francisco: Ignatius, 1982) 171–190.

## PATRIARCH

A large measure of the misunderstanding between East and West centers on issues concerning patriarchs. Moreover, in recent years the notion of patriarch is seen to have major ecumenical significance. But it re- mains a controverted issue with a complex history.

At the Council of Nicaea (325—q.v.) a certain pre- eminence over neighboring dioceses was acknowl- edged to belong to Alexandria, "just as a similar custom exists with regard to the authority of Rome." It refers also to prerogatives of Antioch and other Churches; these are unspecified but are to be maintained.[1] In the late 4th-century Apostolic Constitutions (q.v.) there are universal prayers at the Eucharist mentioning the four sees: Jerusalem, Rome, Antioch, Alexandria.[2]

The Council of Constantinople I (381—q.v.) speci- fies that bishops are not to intrude beyond their bound- aries, and notes that the bishop of Alexandria "is to administer affairs in Egypt only," with similar state- ments made about the bishops of the East, Asia, Pontus, Thrace.[3] At the same time it laid down: "Because it is the new Rome, the bishop of Constantinople is to enjoy privileges of honor after the bishop of Rome."[4] At Chalcedon (431—q.v.) new privileges were accorded to Constantinople against the voices of the papal legates; Leo I refused to ratify the canon containing them (can. 28), as it was counter to the canons of Nicaea and the privileges of particular Churches.[5]

From that time the title "patriarch," originally per- haps reflecting a Jewish institution, which had been in wider use, was restricted to the great sees of the Roman Empire: Rome (Patriarch of the West), Constantinople, Alexandria, Antioch, and Jerusalem. Outside the em- pire there were Catholicates of Mesopotamia or Persia and Armenia. But as these soon proclaimed themselves autonomous, and with the former becoming Nestorian and the latter Monophysite, they no longer figured in ecumenical councils. The Novella 109 of Justinian in 541 put a break on further extensions of the term: it distinguished the "most holy patriarchs of the whole world" from all other bishops of the empire.

The relationship between Rome and the Eastern patriarchs was characterized many years ago by the historian P. Batiffol: "Precedence of the faith of the Roman Church, canonical autonomy of the East, the need of the East to be in communion with the Roman Church; on these three articles the peaceful relations of the East and Rome, and the attitude of the East towards the Roman primacy rested."[6] The canonical autonomy in the first millennium meant that the East freely chose its patriarchs and regulated everything pertaining to its dioceses; it controlled its liturgy and canonical legislation; it regulated matters regarding its laity and clergy.[7] Rome rarely interfered in these matters.[8]

An important development in the first millennium was the development of the theory of the pentarchy with regard to councils (q.v.): only those which were accepted by the pentarchy could be recognized as truly ecumenical.[9] But from about the time of St. Maximus the Confessor (.q.v), communion within the pentarchy had also been an indication of truth, a point later developed by the Constantinople Patriarch, St. Nicephorus I.[10]

After the Middle Ages both in the East and the West new patriarchates were established, some of them being more or less honorary; Moscow (1593), however, took precedence along with the five ancient patriarchates.[11]

Though the bishop of Rome had the title of patriarch in the Middle Ages, neither Rome nor the Latin Church, as a whole, had any real idea of what the patriarchal system represented in the East. From the early Middle Ages there was a Roman tendency to reduce the preeminence of the patriarchs. The creation of a Latin patriarchate in Constantinople from 1204, later confirmed by Rome, led to untrammelled progression towards a papal *plenitudo potestatis,* making the pope a supreme and universally powerful monarch.[12]

During the Middle Ages, Western theologians and canonists[13] generally regarded the patriarchs as creations of the papacy or derived from Church law, and often saw them on a par with other primates. Roman documents appealed to Ezek 1:5-28 and Rev 4:1-11 as indicating the four patriarchs being subservient to the pope. The fourfold order of precedence was bishops, archbishops, primates or patriarchs, and the pope. Furthermore, the Latin patriarchs nominated in the East during the 11th–12th centuries were in fact primates, not really enjoying patriarchal status. Lateran IV (1215) gave the traditional order of precedence but was mainly concerned with the new *Latin* patriarchs.[14] Even though a formula was agreed upon at Florence (q.v.), giving the traditional order of patriarchs, the concluding phrase "without prejudice to all their privileges and rights" (*salvis videlicet privilegiis omnibus et iuribis eorum*—the *omnibus* [all] being a late addition) was understood differently by Greeks and Latins.[15] A recognition of some patriarchal rights, never clearly specified however, was essential to the work of reconciliation at the Council of Florence.

A thorny issue between Orthodoxy and the Roman Church is the presence of the Uniate Churches (q.v.) and their patriarchs. It would seem that in the second millennium Rome considered these last not a new creation but the legitimate continuation of preexisting institutions, with inherited rights and privileges which on the whole were respected.[16]

Since the Middle Ages the Orthodox Ecumenical Patriarchate of Constantinople has been clarifying its role, especially since the introduction of autocephalous Churches and patriarchates, especially that of Moscow. Such search continues.[17] The East, seeing its vision of Christianity more fulfilled in the Eastern Patriarchates and for many other reasons based on history and theological disputes, is still at times extremely hostile to Rome and its patriarchate.[18]

The key ecumenical issue today concerns not only the position of the Eastern patriarchs but more particularly the concept of the Roman bishop being patriarch of the Latin Church. Patriarch of the West is included in papal titles (q.v.). Although the popes have tended to avoid excessive interference in the canonical affairs of Eastern Churches, they have not seriously considered their patriarchal role in the West: all power is subsumed in the papal primacy. The Churches of the East are much more ready to see the pope as Western Patriarch if only to insist immediately that he is merely *primus inter pares* (first among equals).

Among scholars writing on the Western Patriarch one can detect two attitudes: some play down its importance, seeing the primacy as the more significant thing to emphasize, even considering the title "Patriarch of the West" as without doctrinal foundation.[19] Others would wish to see the two offices of patriarch and primate more carefully distinguished, so that it would be evident that some actions of the bishop of Rome are as patriarch, others as pontiff (and others are only as a local bishop of an admittedly important diocese). Roman centralization is one result of the merging of the two offices. In 1969 J. Ratzinger suggested: "In the future they should be more clearly distinguished."[20]

The ecumenical importance of a conscious separation of the two offices would be an openness to the values of the East and some comfort to those who fear the dogma of Vatican I as oppressive in local Churches. Two different roads seem possible. The more difficult one would be to establish various active patriarchates in the West (unlike the honorary ones of Lisbon and Venice) as proposed by the 5th document of the Dombes Group.[21] That might seem too radical and have little grounding in tradition. But whole Churches newly entering into communion with Rome could be given patriarchal status. In the meantime the Vatican (q.v.) could attempt to act in the Latin Church in a more patriarchal way; at present the style of the Curia is perceived as bureaucratic, and occasionally as autocratic. Legitimate authority cannot afford to ignore even a false perception of itself if it is to be effective and life-giving.

A key text is surely the *Code of Canons of the Eastern Churches* (CCEO).[22] The Eastern law for example provides for a synodal election of the patriarch (cc. 63–69); for encyclical letters to the Church over which he presides (c. 82 § 1); for synodal government of the patriarchate (cc. 82 § 3; 102–113; 115–122; 140–145). The patriarch ensures the discipline of the clergy (c. 89 § 1). There is a synodal election of bishops (cc. 180–187) though from names previously or subsequently approved by the Supreme Pontiff.

The fusion of the canonically, if not indeed theologically, distinct offices of local bishop, Western patriarch, and Supreme Pontiff is perhaps not the best way forward for the renewed papacy that will be necessary if Christian unity is to be fostered. A self-conscious exercise by the bishop of Rome of his office as patriarch of the West could, in appropriate circumstances, only strengthen the patriarchal life of the Eastern Churches and gratify those Eastern Churches not in communion with the bishop of Rome.

[1]Canon 6—Tanner 1:8-9. [2]8:10, 7 with 7:46, 2–6—SC 336:168 and 108. [3]Canon 2—Tanner 1:31. [4]Canon 3—Tanner 1:32. [5]Canon 28—Tanner 1:99-100; A. de Halleux, "Le décret chalcédonien sur les prérogatives de la nouvelle Rome," ETL 64 (1988) 288–323; A. Wuyts, "Le 28e canon de Chalcédoine et le fondement du primat romain," OrChPer 17 (1951) 265–282. [6]*Cathedra Petri.* US 4 (Paris, 1938) 75; cf. 210; W. de Vries, "The 'College of Patriarchs,'" Conc 8/1 (Oct. 1965) 35–43; A. Furioli, "I patriarcati," Nicol 18 (1991) 319–339. [7]G.[W] de Vries, "La S. Sede ed i patriarcati d'Oriente," OrChrPer 27 (1961) 313–361 at 318; M. Van Esbroeck, "Primauté, patriarchats, catholicossats, autocéphalies en orient," in M. Maccarone, *Il primato del vescovo di Roma nel primo millennio: Ricerche e testimonianza.* Atti e documenti 4 (Vatican, 1991) 493–521. [8]De Vries (n. 7) 319–326. [9]H. Marot, "Note sur la pentarchie," Irén 32 (1959) 436–442. [10]P. O'Connell, *The Ecclesiology of St. Nicephorus 1 (758–828) Patriarch of Constantinople: Pentarchy and Primacy,* OrChrAn 194 (Rome: Orientale, 1972). [11]V. Peri, "La dénomination de patriarch dans la titulaire ecclésiastique du IVe au XVIe siècle," Irén 64 (1991) 359–364. [12]Y. Congar, "Church Structures and Councils in the Relations Between East and West," OneChr 11 (1975) 224–265 at 227–229. W. de Vries, *Rom und die Patriarchate des Ostens.* Orbis Academicus (Freiburg-Munich, 1963); idem, "Die Entstehung der Patriarchate des Ostens und ihr Verhältnis zur päpplichen Vollgewalt," Schol 37 (1962) 341–369. [13]M. Thériault, "Le patriarche selon les latins des XIVe et XVe siècles," StCan 22 (1988) 125–146 = Kanon 9 (1989) 113–130; P. Erdö, *L'ufficio del primate nelle canoniste da Graziano ad Uguccione da Pisa* (Rome: Lateran, 1986) = Apoll 54 (1981) 357–397; 55 (1982) 165–193. [14]Constit. 5—Tanner 1:236; cf. Constantinople IV (869–870)—Tanner 1:182. [15]Sess. 6—

Tanner 1:528. [16]G.[W] de Vries (n. 7) 329–361; E. Lanne, "La conception post-tridentine de la primauté et l'origine des Églises unies," Irén 52 (1979) 9–13. [17]P. Meyendorff, "The Ecumenical Patriarchate Seen in the Light of Orthodox Ecclesiology and History," GkOrTR 24 (1979) 227–244, with reply by M. Vaporis 245–247; V.T. Istavridis, "The Authority of the Ecumenical Patriarch in the Life of the Orthodox Church," Nicol 18 (1991) 141–160; G. Tsetsis, "Le patriarch oecuménique en tant que 'protos' dans l'Église orthodoxe," Kanon 9 (1989) 197–206. [18]E.g., J. Cavarnos, "The Five Original Patriarchates Reexamined," PatByzR 2 (1983) 96–106. [19]A. Garauti, *Il papa patriarcha d'Occidente: Studio storico dottrinale.* Collectio antoniana 2 (Bologna: Ed. Francescane, 1990) = Antonian 60 (1985) 42–85; 61 (1986) 274–328; 62 (1987) 184–214; 63 (1988) 485–521; 65 (1990) 23–59; cf. R. Schieffer, "Der Papst als Patriarch von Rom," in Maccarone, ed. op. cit. (n. 7) 433–451. [20]"Primacy and Episcopacy," TDig 19 (1971) 206 (from 1969); Y. Congar, "Le Pape comme patriarche d'Occident: Approche d'une réalité trop négligée," Istina 28 (1983 = collection *Église et papauté: Regards historiques* (Paris: Cerf, 1994) 11–30 = TDig 38 (1991) 3–7. [21]DocCath 68 (1989) 1122–1142, nn. 142–145. [22]Washington, D.C.: Canon Law Society of America, 1991.

## PAUL VI, Pope (1963–1978)

Born in Brescia in 1897, Giovanni Battista Montini[1] was ordained priest in 1920. From 1922 he spent most of his life in the service of the Vatican until becoming archbishop of Milan in 1954. There he was deeply engaged in pastoral work.[2] Becoming cardinal in 1958, he was to be a confidant and close associate of John XXIII (q.v.) in the preparations for Vatican II (q.v.). On the day after he was proclaimed pope (22 June 1963), he stated his intention of reconvoking the council, which had been automatically suspended by the death of his predecessor. In opening its second session (29 Sept. 1963), he clarified the council's agenda under four headings: doctrine on the Church; the renewal of the Church; Christian unity; dialogue with the world.[3] These topics would be programmatic for his pontificate, along with the theme of dialogue (q.v.) emerging in his first encyclical, *Ecclesiam suam.*[4] As well as the encyclical's almost total lack of footnotes, and its personal tone, there are other good reasons to deduce that it was not ghosted, as are most papal documents, but profoundly his own personal work.[5]

As pope he actively supported the work of Vatican II, though like John XXIII he did not take part in its working sessions.[6] In the final stages of some documents he both insisted on modifications and made suggestions, though some of these latter were not accepted by the Theological Commission (v. VATICAN II). In general, his interventions were to help the council towards quasi-unanimous consensus; his actions were thus usually to comfort the conservative minority. Apart from his own convictions,[7] this may have been one of the reasons which prompted him to declare Mary to be Mother of the Church at the close of the 3rd session of the council (21 Nov. 1964).[8]

After the council he pursued its aims with firmness, especially in a series of decrees *motu proprio* (v. VATICAN DOCUMENTS) which set in motion the reforms of Vatican II: he promoted the total revision of the liturgical books in the vernacular and began liturgical renewal immediately, even during the council;[9] he reformed and internationalized the Curia (v. VATICAN); he made permanent the secretariats for Promoting Christian Unity, for Non-Christian Religions, and for Non-Believers; he established norms for the Synod of bishops (q.v.) and summoned it for meetings; he strongly promoted ecumenism,[10] particularly with the East,[11] though he did not neglect the West, especially the Anglican Communion (q.v.), as the Common Statements with the archbishop of Canterbury show.[12]

In the conflictive situations after the council, Paul VI maintained a centrist position and preserved from schism both the extreme right represented by Archbishop Lefebvre (q.v.) and the extreme left, for example, in the Netherlands. The choice of Archbishop G. Benelli, *sostituto* at the Secretariate of State and an utterly loyal associate, for implementing hard decisions was to some a masterly move: it allowed the pope to distance himself from conflicts and to use his papal office in the service of unity.

His magisterium[13] is marked by major documents: on social issues,[14] on the Blessed Virgin,[15] on the regulation of births,[16] and on evangelization—perhaps one of the finest papal documents of the century.[17] His ecclesiology is very much informed by French writers, especially C. Journet (q.v.), H. de Lubac (q.v.), Y. Congar (q.v.), as well as by J.A. Möhler (q.v.).[18]

In the late 1960s, probably under the influence of J. Maritain and due to the stresses of the time—not least the reaction to *Humanae vitae* and the hemorrhage of priestly and religious vocations—his views and actions showed some pessimism. But as the 1970s advanced his assurance grew, and he repeatedly referred to his mission of "strengthening the brethren" (cf. Luke 22:32). His 1975 exhortation on Christian Joy is not at all well known or properly appreciated.[19]

Paul VI was the first modern pope to travel outside Italy: Jerusalem and Bombay (1964), United Nations at New York (1965), Istanbul and Fatima (1967), Bogotá (1968), International Labor Organization and World Council of Churches at Geneva (1969), Uganda (1969), the Far East, Australia, Oceania (1970).

Though in some circles his name remains largely associated with birth control and *Humanae vitae,* his stature among many theologians and others continues to grow.[20] History may well judge him to be one of the more outstanding popes in the history of the Church.

[1]C. Cremona, *Paolo VI* (Milan: Rusconi, 1991); P. Hebblethwaite, *Paul VI: The First Modern Pope* (London: HarperCollinsReligious, 1993). [2]Ambrosius 65 (1989) 3–128; bibliog., T. Kadziński, "Bibliografia di Giovanni Battista Montini Arcivescovo di Milano (1955–1963)," Sales 53 (1991) 521–560; A. Rimoldi, "Bibliografia sull'episcopato milanese del Card. G.B. Montini (1955–1963)," in G.B. *Montini arcivescovo* (Milan: Nouvo Ed. Duomo, 1983) 347–356; P. Arato and P. Vian, *Paulus PP. VI (1963–1978) elenchus bibliographicus* (Brescia: Istituto Paul VI, 1981). [3]ActaSyn 2/1:189-199. [4]AAS 56 (1964) 609–659/Carlen 5:135-160; AA.VV. *"Ecclesiam suam": Première lettre encyclique de Paul VI.* Colloque international Rome 24–26 octobre 1980 (Brescia: Istituto Paolo V1—Rome: Ed. Studium Vita Nova, 1982). [5]Hebblethwaite (n. 1) 380; G. Colombo, "Genesi, storia e significato dell'enciclica 'Ecclesiam suam,'" in AA.VV. *Ecclesiam suam* (n. 4) 133–134; M. O'Carroll, "Pope Paul's First Encyclical," IrEcclRecord 103 (1964) 1–14. [6]Hebblethwaite (n. 1) 333–454; L.-J. Suenens, *Memories and Hopes* (Dublin: Veritas, 1992) 125–156. See J. Grootaers, *I protagonisti del Vaticano II* (Milan: San Paolo, 1994) 51–65. [7]*Profession of Faith*—AAS 60 (1968) 438–439. [8]ActaSyn 3/8:915-918—AAS 56 (1964) 1016–1018. [9]Mp. *Sacram liturgiam*—AAS 56 (1964) 139–144/Flannery 1:41-56 in part. [10]G. Caprile, "Paolo VI e i suoi rapporti con le confessioni non cattoliche," CivCatt 128 (1977) 1:377-386; Y. Congar, "L'oecuménisme de Paul VI," Nicolas 6 (1978) 207–219; E. Lanne, "Hommage à Paul VI: En mémorial d'action de grâce," Irén 51 (1978) 299–311. [11]E.J. Stormon, ed., *Towards the Healing of Schism: The Sees of Rome and Constantinople 1958–1984.* Ecumenical Documents 3 (Mahwah: Paulist, 1987); A. Franquesa, "Paul VI et l'Église orthodoxe," PrOrChr 30 (1980) 179–210. [12]24 March 1966 and 29 April 1977—J.W. Witmer and J.R. White, eds., *Called to Full Unity: Documents on Anglican-Roman Catholic Relations 1966–1983* (Washington, D.C.: U.S. Catholic Conference, 1986) 3–4, 157–159. [13]*Insegnamento di Paulo VI.* 16 vols. (Vatican, 1973–1978); *Indice delle materie contenute nei primi dodici volumi di insegnamenti di Paolo VI 1963–1974* (Vatican, 1977); P. Arató and P. Vian, eds., *Paulus PP. Elenchus bibliographicus* (Brescia: Istituto Paolo V1, ²1981). Cf. R. Guelluy, "Le magistère 'ordinaire' chez Paul VI," RTLv 9 (1978) 407–416. [14]Encycl. *Populorum progressio*—AAS 59 (1967) 257–299/Carlen 5:183-201; Letter to Card. M. Roy, *Octogesima adveniens*—AAS 63 (1971) 401–441. See R. Coste, "L'encyclique 'Populorum progressio' vingt ans après," NRT 109 (1987) 161–181; P. Poupard, "Le père Lebret, Le pape Paul VI et l'encyclique 'Populorum progressio,'" EspVie 97 (1987) 257–264. [15]Encycl. *Christi Matri*—AAS 58 (1966) 745–749/Carlen 5:179-181; Apost. Exhort. *Signum magnum*—AAS 59 (1967) 465–475; Apost. Exhort. *Marialis cultus*—AAS 66 (1974) 113–168. [16]Encycl. *Humanae vitae*—AAS 60 (1968) 481–503/Carlen 5:223-233/Flannery 2:397-416. [17]Apost. Exhort. *Evangelii nuntiandi*—AAS 68 (1976) 1–96/Flannery 2:711-761. [18]AA.VV. *Paolo VI e i problemi ecclesiologici al concilio.* Colloquio internazionale 19–21 settembre 1986 (Brescia: Istituto Paolo VI, 1989)—see G. Caprile, CivCatt 137 (1986) 4:480-490; J.P. Torell, "Paul VI et le cardinal Journet," NVet 61 (1986) 161–174. [19]Apost. Exhort. *Gaudete in Domino*—AAS 67 (1975) 289–322. [20]J. Barrado, "Pablo VI, diez años despues," CiTom 11 (1988) 527–541; cf. A.L. Descamps, "Hommage à Paul VI: Pour un portrait de Paul VI," RTLv 9 (1978) 395–406.

## PAULINE PRIVILEGE

The Pauline Privilege is the dissolution of a natural bond of marriage between non-baptized parties. It arises after one of the parties is baptized and finds that his/her spouse will not live peaceably: the baptized party may then enter a subsequent marriage. This latter marriage dissolves the former one. The privilege is based on an interpretation of 1 Cor 7:12-15 in which Paul advises converts to depart if their non-believing spouses refuse to continue married life in peace.[1]

The Pauline Privilege is treated in CIC 1143–1147. There are four conditions for its exercise: a previous valid marriage of two unbaptized persons; the conversion and baptism (in the Catholic or another Church) of one of the spouses; the physical or moral departure of the unbaptized spouse; interpellation of the unbaptized party. For validity it is required that the non-baptized party must be interrogated on the following points: whether he/she wishes to receive baptism; whether he/she at least wishes to cohabit in peace with the baptized party without insult (contumelia) to the Creator (CIC 1144). A negative response to these questions confirms the "departure" of the non-baptized person and allows for a second marriage to be valid (CIC 1143). The exercise of the Pauline Privilege is not an annulment, as there is no direct intervention on the part of the Church.

If the baptized party is a Catholic, he/she may use the Pauline Privilege to marry a non-Catholic party, baptized or not, observing the canons 1124–1129 on mixed marriages; the permission of the local Ordinary is required in this case (CIC 1147).

The so-called "Petrine Privilege" (q.v.) is considered by some as an extensive interpretation of the Pauline Privilege.

---

[1]T.P. Doyle, "Marriage," in Coriden, CIC 814–819; cf. P. Declau, "The Pauline Privilege: Is It Promulgated in the First Epistle to the Corinthians?," CBQ 13 (1951) 146–152; H. Grenier, "Can We Still Speak of the Pauline Privilege?," Jurist 38 (1978) 158–162.

## PENANCE, SACRAMENT OF

See RECONCILIATION, SACRAMENT OF

## PENTARCHY

See PATRIARCHS

## PENTECOSTAL CHURCHES

Though they appear to have roots in the 19th century, the Pentecostal Churches[1] are generally understood to have originated with the experiences of the Topeka (Kansas) Bible school of Charles Parham on the first day of the 20th century, 1 January 1901; there, speaking in tongues became associated with baptism in the Spirit (v. CHARISMATIC RENEWAL). The movement, or revival, rapidly spread throughout the world, and it is now the fastest growing Christian denomination.

The Pentecostal movement soon encountered opposition from the mainline Churches. Among Protestants

it was perceived as being over-emotional, and even to subordinate Scripture to religious experience. The Pentecostals soon founded their own independent Churches, which P. Hocken distinguishes as being of four categories:[2] Holiness Churches, which add baptism in the Spirit as a third blessing after regeneration and sanctification (e.g., black Church of God in Christ—1907, Pentecostal Holiness Church—1911); two-stage Pentecostals, mostly of Reformed background, holding baptism in the Spirit as a second blessing (e.g., Assemblies of God—1914); the Oneness Church, which rejects the Trinity, affirms a modalist Christology, and baptizes in the name of Jesus (e.g., United Pentecostal Church—origins 1914, with formation in 1945); Churches which focus on the office of apostle and prophet after Eph 4:11 (e.g., Apostolic Church—1918).

Though strong on scriptural reflection, the Pentecostal Churches have been slow to engage in more theological studies on a key issue, which is the integration of Pentecostal experience with the greater traditions of Christianity.[3] Pentecostalism is continually at risk from fundamentalist reading of Scripture and from theological isolation. The new Journal of Pentecostal Theology[4] is a welcome development.

The Pentecostal Churches generally kept aloof from the ecumenical movement, voicing a suspicion of whatever is institution and not clearly from the immediate inspiration of the Spirit. David Du Plessis (1905–1987) was a tireless champion of ecumenical involvement, and he helped to build bridges between Pentecostal Churches and both the WCC and the Catholic Church. Three series of discussions have taken place between Catholics and Pentecostalists.[5]

The Pentecostal Christians have made a limited but highly significant contribution to 20th-century theology and spirituality through alerting other Christian Churches to the experiential dimensions of the Christian faith and to a lived theology of the Holy Spirit.

---

[1]W.J. Hollenweger, The Pentecostals (London: SCM—Minneapolis: Augsburg, 1972); F.A. Sullivan, "Pentecôtisme," DSpir 12:1035-1052—Eng. trans. without notes, Pentecostalism and the Charismatic Renewal (Dublin: Veritas, 1986). [2]"Pentecostals," DictEcumMov 792–794. [3]W.J. Hollenweger, "Creator Spiritus: The Challenge of Pentecostal Experience to Pentecostal Theology," Theology 81 (1978) 32–40. [4]From 1992, by Sheffield Academic Press, UK—Church of God School of Theology, Cleveland. [5]J.L. Sandridge, Roman-Catholic/Pentecostal; Dialogue (1977–1982): A Study in Developing Ecumenism. Studien zur interkulturellen Geschichte des Christentums 4 (Frankfurt a.M.: Lang, 1987); J.A. Radano, "The Pentecostal-Roman Catholic International Dialogue, 1972–1991," Mid-Stream 31 (1991) 26–31; idem, "Roman Catholic/Pentecostal Dialogue," ibid., 33 (1994) 3, 335f.; "Roman Catholic/Pentecostal Dialogue in Venice," JEcuSt 28 (1991) 535–536; "International Roman Catholic/Pentecostal Dialogue," ibid., 29 (1992) 3–4, 500; "Roman Catholic/Pentecostal Dialogue Held in Paris," ibid., 30

(1993) 3–4, 494f.; "Roman Catholic/Pentecostal Dialogue in Switzerland," ibid., 31 (1994) 421.

## PEOPLE OF GOD

Since Vatican II, "People of God" has become for many people a new name for the Church,[1] in some cases displacing Body of Christ (q.v.) as the preferred one. But some authors would seem to have gone beyond the council and developed the idea of "People" in an excessively sociological or political manner.[2] If this problem is to be avoided, one must look at the origin of the concept in recent ecclesiology, at its scriptural roots, and at the actual teaching of the council.

Because it was favored by Reformation theology,[3] the term "People of God" was not common among Catholic theologians in the centuries after Trent. In the 19th century the phrase was occasionally found in the ecclesiology of the "Perfect Society" (q.v.), but there it meant the laity as opposed to the hierarchy.[4] Alongside the theology of the Mystical Body the concept of People of God made steady progress among both Catholic[5] and Protestant[6] scholars from about 1920, though at first in more a sociological than a theological sense. M.D. Koster, asserting that ecclesiology was pre-theological, also attacked the exclusive idea that Body of Christ is the proper name for the Church.[7] But he no less exclusively insisted on the People of God as the "sole, abstract and clear designation of the Church."[8] Later, L. Cerfaux would give important support for the primacy in Pauline ecclesiology of the notion of People.[9] After the publication by Pius XII of the encyclical on the Mystical Body (*Mystici corporis*— 1943 q.v.), which did not mention People of God, Catholic theologians in addition developed the ideas both of the Church as People and the Church as Sacrament (q.v.)[10], while Protestant interest in the notion of People continued apace.[11] The term "People of God" was thus theologically mature when Vatican II opened, though it did not figure much in the first drafts of the Church Constitution (later LG) which, except for a reference to 1 Pet 2:9-10, proposed an ecclesiology based on the Mystical Body with the idea of the Perfect Society also to the fore.

Vatican II did not set out a full exposition of the biblical teaching on the People of God;[12] it gave only an outline in LG 9. Some important points need further emphasis and illustration.[13]

A key to the idea of People is the divine election and covenant;[14] these were at the same time an act of liberation (Deut 7:6-11; 26:5-9). The people promised to obey the Lord (Exod 19:1-8; 24:1-8). The covenant was summed up in the divine promise, "I will be your God and you will be my people" (Lev 26:11-13). The special relationship was underscored by the normal restriction of 'ām (LXX *laos*) for the Lord's People or family, while *gôyîm* (LXX *ethnai*) meant other peoples. There would be a continuing tension between the religious meaning of "People" in terms of covenant and cult and political meanings. The covenant relationship was described in various terms (cf. LG 6): spouse (Isa 54:5-8), indicating God's faithful love and the fickleness of Israel's;[15] vine (Isa 5:1-7), stressing God's care for his crop and the need for it to bear fruit;[16] flock, whose shepherd is God (Ezek 34), highlighting again God's care as well as the frailty of the sheep.[17] Though Israel continued to disobey, God promised a new covenant (Jer 31:31-34).

The new covenant was sealed in the blood of Christ (1 Cor 11:25) and the followers of Jesus become a people. In time they understood that all the promises and endowments of the OT people as now rightfully theirs (see 1 Pet 2:9-10, taking over Exod 19:6 and LXX Isa 43:20-21). But it is not possible to make a single or simple statement about the relationship of the Church to the Israel of old: some authors stress continuity, e.g., Paul sees faith as the means whereby persons become members of the People of God (Gal 3:7, 9, 28-29), and in Rom 9–11 he speaks of the Christians being grafted on (11:17, 24) though he still hopes for the eventual salvation of those cut off (11:25-29);[18] other NT texts speak more of a displacement of the Jews by the Church (e.g., 1 Pet 2:9-10; Eph 2:15); in Matthew and John there is clear evidence of conflict between the Jews and the Church (Matt 4:23; 21:43; John 9:22, 28; 16:2); in Luke the resurrection of Jesus represents a new phase in the history of the people.[19] The issue is still a live one today for dialogue with Jews (q.v.) and for a theological grasp of whatever significance is to be attributed to the state of Israel founded in 1948.[20]

Vatican II used the framework of the People of God to set forth the common priesthood (q.v.) of all believers (LG 10), a priesthood exercised in the sacraments (LG 11), the sense of the faith (*sensus fidei*—q.v.) and charism (LG 12—q.v.). It developed a rich notion of catholicity (v. CATHOLIC) of the Church: its universal diffusion in unity, its diversity in different peoples, in different states and functions in the Church, in different traditions, and in the sharing of resources (LG 13). The question of membership (q.v.) of the Church was considered in terms of full or partial incorporation: Catholics in the state of grace ("possessing the Spirit of Christ") are fully incorporated (LG 14); other Christians are joined to the Church in several ways (LG 15; cf. UR 3, 14–23); non-Christians, especially Jews and Muslims, and all theists are ordered to the People in various ways, as indeed are those who through no fault of their own have not arrived at an explicit knowledge of God (LG

16). Finally the Church has a mission to the whole world (LG 17).

Whereas the 1917 *Code of Canon Law* entitled its second book "Persons," the 1983 revision has as its Book Two "The People of God," in which are treated all the faithful, laity, hierarchy, religious.[21] The faithful are defined in terms of being members of the People: "The Christian faithful are those who, inasmuch as they have been incorporated in the Church through baptism, have been constituted as the People of God; for this reason, since they have become sharers in Christ's priestly, prophetic, and kingly office in their own manner, they are called to become sharers in the mission which God has entrusted to the Church to fulfill in the world in accord with the conditions proper to each one" (CIC 204). The definition here adapts a statement of LG 31 on the laity to cover all the People of God. For the first time in canon law, rights and obligations are explicitly spelled out: those which arise from the basic equality of all the faithful (CIC 208–211); those which ensue from the hierarchical structure of the Church (CIC 212–214); statements relative to the mission of the Church (CIC 215–218). Personal rights are noted (CIC 219–220) and social obligations are stated (CIC 222–223).[22] There is some tendency in the *Code* to revert to pre-Vatican II juridical positions on the Church even within the second part on the People of God (v. LAW).

On the proper interpretation of the People of God, we note that the International Theological Commission observed in 1984: "The Constitution (LG) takes up that term with all the connotations that Old and New Testaments have bestowed on it. In the expression 'People of God,' it is, moreover, the genitive 'of God' that provides the phrase with its own specific determinate significance, by situating it in the biblical context where it appeared and developed. Consequently, any interpretation of the term 'People' of an exclusively biological, racial, cultural, political, or ideological kind must be radically excluded. The 'People of God' derives 'from above,' from the divine plan, that is, from election, Covenant, and mission."[23]

At the 1985 synod of bishops called to commemorate the 20th anniversary of Vatican II, both reports and bishops commented favorably about the impact of the notion of People. But the majority of references would seem to remark on an ideological misuse of the term, on its isolation from other notions, on its use in fostering false oppositions such as communion/institution, popular Church/hierarchical Church. As a result the synod would seem to have come down strongly in support of the notion of communion (q.v.), and in a way to have contributed to some downplaying of the notion of "People" in the post-Vatican II period.[24]

The notion of "People" has rich ecumenical possibilities when compared with the presentation of the Church in *Mystici corporis* (q.v.): it allows for a positive relationship with other Christians. It is a more dynamic concept than Body of Christ and also more historical, giving a sense of the whole Church moving on eschatological pilgrimage. But it cannot replace the notion of Body and Temple (q.v.): each of these has its own contribution to make to a sound Trinitarian ecclesiology:[25] the divine plan is "that the whole human race may form the one People of God, come together as the one body of Christ, and be built into one temple of the Holy Spirit" (AG 7; cf. LG 17; PO 1).

---

[1]D.J. Harrington, "Why Is the Church the People of God?" in L. Richard et al., eds., *Vatican II: The Unfinished Agenda: A Look to the Future* (Mahwah: Paulist, 1987) 47–56.  [2]J. Ratzinger, *Church, Ecumenism and Politics: New Essays in Ecclesiology* (Slough UK: St. Paul—New York: Crossroad, 1988) 21–28; cf. C. Watkins "Organizing the People of God: Social-science Theories of Organization in Ecclesiology," TS 52 (1991) 687–711.  [3]L. Schümmer, "Le Mystère d'Israël et de l'Église, posterité d'Abraham," Irén 61 (1988) 207–242.  [4]Antón 2:678-681.  [5]Ibid., 681–690; cf. R. Schnackenburg and J. Dupont, "Bulletin: The Church as the People of God," Conc 1/1 (Jan. 1965) 56–61.  [6]Antón 2: 690–702; Schnackenburg—Dupont (n. 5) 56–61.  [7]*Ekklesiologie im Werden* (Paderborn, 1940) 15 and passim.  [8]Ibid., 143.  [9]*The Church in the Theology of St. Paul* (New York: Herder & Herder—Edinburgh/London: Nelson, 1959—French [1]1942, [2]1947) 8 and 49–82.  [10]Antón 2:707-724.  [11]Ibid., 724–729.  [12]Y. Congar, "The Church: The People of God," Conc 1/1(Jan. 1965) 7–19 at 8; cf. G.Dejaifve, "L'Église, peuple de Dieu," NRT 103 (1981) 857–871.  [13]In addition to above, see H. Cazelles, "Israel Among the Nations," Pacifica 2 (1989) 47–60; J.F. Craghan, "People of God," NDictT 755–757; M. du Buit, "La sainteté du peuple dans l'Ancien Testament," VieSp 143 (1989) 25–37; P. Grelot, "People," DBT 416–422; J.F. Kobler, "A Phenomenological Hermeneutics of the People of God: Theoretical and Practical Dimensions," ETL 64 (1988) 84–105; P.S. Minear, *Images of the Church in the New Testament* (Philadelphia: Westminster, 1960) 66–104; R. Meyer and H. Strathmann, "Laos," TDNT 4:29-56; K. Rahner, "People of God," SM 4:400-402; W.H. Schmidt, *People of God* in the Old Testament," TDig 34 (1987) 226–231 = GlLer 2/1 (1987) 19–32; R. Schnackenburg, *The Church in the New Testament* (London: Burns & Oates, 1974) 149–157; J. Sharbert, "People (of God)," Bauer 2:651-658; G.S. Worgul, "People of God, Body of Christ: Pauline Ecclesiological Contrasts," BibTB 12 (1982) 24–28.  [14]See C. Focant and A. Wénin, "L'Alliance ancienne et nouvelle," NRT 110 (1988) 850–866 and biblical theologies.  [15]M.-F. Lacan, "Spouse," DBT 576–579.  [16]M.-F. Lacan, "Vine," DBT 629–630; J.F. O'Grady, "The Good Shepherd and the Vine and the Branches," BibTB 8 (1978) 86–89.  [17]C. Lesquivit and X. Léon-Dufour, "Shepherd and Flock," DBT 540–542.  [18]Cf. commentaries on Romans 9–11 and G. Worgul, "Romans 9–11 and Ecclesiology," BibTB 7 (1977) 99–109; D.J. Harrington, *God's People in Christ. New Testament Perspectives on the Church and Judaism* (Philadelphia: Fortress, 1980) 57–66.  [19]J. Dupont, "Note sur le 'peuple de Dieu' dans les Actes des Apôtres," in Commission Biblique Pontificale, *Unité et diversité dans l'Église* (Vatican, 1989) 209–222.  [20]K. Hruby, "Peoplehood in Judaism and Christianity," TDig 22 (1974) 8–12 = EncountToday 7 (1971) 8–36; C. Klein, "Christians and the State of Israel," JES 10 (1973) = TDig 22 (1974) 12–15.  [21]J.H. Provost, in J.A. Coriden CIC 117–159.  [22]Ibid., 136.  [23]International Theological Commission, *Texts and Documents 1969–1985* (San Francisco: Ignatius, 1989) 273.  [24]Final Report in *Synode extraordinaire* (Paris: Cerf, 1986) 559–563. See

J.A. Komonchak, "The Synod of 1985 and the Notion of the Church," ChicSt 26 (1987) 330–345. [25]A. Dulles, *Models of the Church* (Dublin: Gill and Macmillan, [2]1987) 53–59.

## PERFECT SOCIETY

The notion of "perfect society" was present in Greek political theory. As developed in ecclesiology, a perfect society had within it all that was necessary to achieve its ends. Thus a family or a town are not perfect societies, for they depend on others to fulfill their goals. There were in this analysis two perfect societies: Church and State, for both have the means necessary to them. St. Thomas knew the theory of perfect society[1] but did not apply it to the Church.

It began to come into ecclesiology in a discreet way from about the time of R. Bellarmine (q.v.). It was well established by the 19th century and entered into the magisterium. In a schema on the Church never discussed at Vatican I, there was a statement that the Church was a perfect society.[2] A canon was prepared, asserting full judicial and coercive power to belong to the Church.[3] It was found henceforth in papal teaching and became frequent in the encyclicals of Leo XIII (q.v.).[4] It occurred in the opening sentence of the apostolic constitution of Benedict XIII, which promulgated the 1917 *Code of Canon Law*.[5]

In the encyclical on the Mystical Body (*Mystici Corporis*—q.v.).[6] Pius XII presented the Church as both the Body of Christ and as a perfect society, e.g.: "Our union in and with Christ is first evident from the fact that, since Christ wills his Christian community to be a Body, which is a perfect society, its members must be united because they all work together towards a common end."[7]

In the years preceding Vatican II, the view of the Church as perfect society was strongly evident. I. Salaverri, for example, says that it was Catholic faith *(De fide catholica),* since it is proposed to be held by the ordinary universal magisterium. He stated what was to be held: "The Church is a perfect society, and absolutely independent, with full legislative, judicial and coercive power."[8] Another well-known manual by L. Ott was content to state that "the Church is a perfect society," to be certain *(sententia certa).*[9]

The perfect society view of the Church highlights institution (q.v.). It is no longer taught by theologians, but the values that it sought to maintain need to be incorporated into any ecclesiology, viz., the genuine independence of the Church in the pursuit of its goals and the presence in the Church of genuine authority (q.v.). But it is not enough to remain on the juridical level; the juridical dimensions of the Church must be shown to be spiritual, as Pius XII showed in *Mystici corporis,* and theologians such as C. Journet (q.v.) demonstrated. Vatican II successfully included the

vital truths contained in the perfect society theory in its theology of communion (q.v.); communion is both hierarchical or vertical within the Church, and horizontal among its members.

[1]ST 1–2ae, q.90, a.3 ad 3; see A. Michel, "Unité de l'Église," DTC 15:2225-2226. [2]Mansi 51:543. [3]Mansi 51:552. [4]E.g., *Satis cognitum*—ASS 28:724/Carlen 2:396. [5]*Providentissima Mater*—AAS 9 (1917) 5. [6]AAS 35 (1943) 193–248/Carlen 4:37-62. [7]Ibid., AAS 226/Carlen 51. [8]Salaverri, Ecclesia 826–838. [9]*Fundamentals of Catholic Dogma* (Cork, Ireland: Mercier, 1955, from 1952 German) 275–276.

## PERSECUTION

The word "persecution" is derived from the Latin *"persequor,"* which, like the Greek word *diôkô,* can mean simply "to pursue," but can also mean "to persecute." Jesus promised that his disciples would be persecuted (Matt 23:34; Mark 13:9-13),[1] and declared blessed those who are persecuted (Matt 5:10-11; cf. 1 Cor 4:12; 2 Cor 4:9). The response to persecution is to pray for the persecutors (Matt 5:44; Rom 12:14), as did Jesus (Luke 23:34) and Stephen (Acts 6:69), and to pray for boldness (q.v.) to withstand (Acts 4:31).

Paul (as Saul) was one of the first persecutors of the Church (Acts 9:4; Gal 1:13). From 64–313 C.E. there were many persecutions of the Church, traditionally numbered ten,[2] but in reality consisting of about four or five major periods.[3] Persecution was not constant—the years of peace being about equal to those of persecution. Much depended on local circumstances and on the character of local Roman administrators. The official reason for persecutions was social and political as well as, or rather than, religious.[4] Rome tolerated the most diverse cults, provided that their adherents also took part in the worship of Rome and Augustus, which was the key bonding in the empire. The monotheism of the Christians rendered their loyalty to the state suspect in Roman eyes. They were also accused of all kinds of immorality, e.g., incest, cannibalism, superstition,[5] or they were blamed for natural catastrophes. Furthermore, in the 1st century the distinction of Christian and Jew was not very clear to the Romans. While there were some instances of popular hostility and violence against Jews in the Roman world, they were never the object of official persecution. It was when Christianity was recognized as a new religion distinct from Judaism that it lost the legal protection it had previously enjoyed as a Jewish sect.

There were major persecutions under Nero (from 64 C.E.) and Domitian (81–96). The Antonine emperors declared that Christians were not to be sought out, but persecutions took place under Trajan (98–117). There was a period of relative calm under the Severian dynasty (193–235). Decius (248–251) imposed Roman religion, which led to a bitter persecution. Valerius (253–260) did likewise: his was probably the most severe of all persecutions. The emperor Gallienus (253–268) published an edict of tolerance and allowed places of worship (260). The "great persecution" of Diocletian (245–313) lasted in the West from 303–305 and in the East from 303–312. The emperor sought a uniform administration of the empire inspired by the cult of the Roman gods and the practice of the so-called traditional Roman virtues. The persecution was continued under Galerius (305–311), who just six days before his death published an edict of toleration, which was reinforced by the Edict of Milan by Constantine (313—q.v.).

Though the Roman period saw the first great persecutions, every age of the Church has had them and has been glorified with martyrs (q.v.). Particularly in missionary situations, those who brought the faith were often seen as a threat to existing local religions or social and political order. Moreover, persecution takes many forms: it may be a death threat; it often involves loss of property. In the former USSR (up to 1989), though there was officially freedom of religion, Christians were persecuted by imprisonment or death, by being denied education, employment, or civil rights. Baptist Christians (q.v.) were singled out by state authorities for special harassment.

In the late 20th century persecution often follows on the proclamation by Christians of human rights or liberation (as in Latin America and Africa). The exact nature of persecution, as in the past, is often unclear and may be disguised as racism or the ideology of national security. Though the following of Christ often leads to persecution, few authorities will say directly: "I am punishing you because you are a disciple of Jesus Christ." The fact of persecution and concomitant martyrdom is nonetheless real for being hidden under pretexts.

[1]J. Dupont, "La persécution comme situation missionaire (Marc 13:9-11)," in R. Schnackenburg, ed., Die Kirche des Anfangs (Leipzig: St. Benno, 1977) 97–114.    [2]List in OxDCC 1065–1066.    [3]J. Daoust, "Persécutions," Catholicisme 11:14-18; W.H.C. Frend, Martyrdom and Persecution in the Early Church: A Study of a Conflict from Maccabees to Donatus (Oxford, 1965); idem, "Persecutions," EncycEarCh 2:671-674; K. Baus, in Jedin-Dolan, vol. 1 passim; Communio (Paris) 12 (1987) 1–125.    [4]C. Saulnier, "La persécution des chrétiens et la théologie du pouvoir à Rome (Ier–IVe s.)," RevSR 58 (1954) 251–279; R.L. Wilken, The Christians as the Romans Saw Them (New Haven—London: Yale UP, 1984).    [5]L.F. Jannsen, "'Superstitio' and the Persecution of Christians," VigChr 33 (1979) 131–159.

## PETER, St.

The study of Peter since the Reformation has often been oriented by polemics. Roman Catholics sought to discover in Peter the origins of the papal primacy; Protestants resisted such a search and rejected its findings. In modern times a classic study by O. Cullmann allowed that Peter did indeed have some eminence but denied that he was succeeded in his role by those who followed him.[1] Since then, scholarship has been generally marked by greater objectivity.[2]

In the earliest works of the NT, the letters of Paul, we find some evidence of a prominence of Peter: he is a primary resurrection witness (1 Cor 15:5), a leader in Jerusalem, and a guarantee of authentic teaching (Gal 1:18; 2:8), with a special mission to Jews (Gal 2:7-8); Peter's bad example in vacillation was sufficiently serious to merit a public rebuke from Paul (Gal 2:11-14). There is some evidence of the existence of a Peter faction at Corinth (1 Cor 1:12). The story of the early years of the Church could not be told without giving a special plea to Peter (Acts 1–15).

The Synoptic position is significant. There are several elements in the essential presentation of Mark: Peter is given special prominence in six places (1:35-38; 8:27-33; 10:28-30; 14:27-31; 16:7); he is spokesman (8:27-33; 9:2-13; 10:28-30; 11:12-14, 20–22); he is part of an inner group (5:37; 9:2-13; 14:32-42); there is a dark side of weakness and incomprehension (1:35-38; 8:31-33; 9:5-6; 14:27-31, 37–42, 54, 66–72).

With a few significant additions, this basic picture is taken over by Luke and Matthew. Luke, as is his wont, softens the negative features somewhat. He gives also the call of Peter the fisherman, who will henceforth "be catching people" (5:1-11). Jesus prays for Peter who, after his conversion, will strengthen his brothers (22:31-32—NB plural "you" in v. 31 and singular in v. 32). Luke alone of the Synoptics recalls a special apparition of the risen Lord to Peter (24:34).

Matthew records that Jesus saved Peter (14:28-31) and indicates that Peter will have special knowledge in the question of the relations with Judaism (17:24-27). But the key text is, of course, Matt 16:16-19.[3] Simon is given a new name; there is a perfect play on words in Aramaic (kepha-kepha). What is quite unusual is the translation, not transliteration, in the Greek Petros, from petra, rock (e.g., Acts 1:15; Matt 17:1; John 1:42; cf. earlier usage in 1 Cor 15:5; Gal 2:9). Various antecedents for the use of rock, which is a divine attribute in the OT (Deut 32:4), have been suggested:[4] Abraham (Isa 51:1-2),[5] Isaiah (28:16; 54:11-12),[6] and Jesus' own parable of stability (Matt 7:24-28). Since in the OT rock is often a divine attribute (Deut 32:4 and many Pss, e.g., 18:2, 31; 42:9), it can be suggested that Jesus is giving a divine gift of constancy to Peter. He will build his Church on the "rock" of Peter's Christological confession.[7] The "gates of Hades will not prevail" against the Church. Hades, or Sheol, the OT abode of the dead, is normally seen as the power of death—hence the Church will be indefectible; but some exegetes see a suggestion that the powers of evil will not triumph over it.[8] Jesus further promises, "I will give you the keys of the kingdom of heaven, and whatever you bind on earth will be bound in heaven, and whatever you loose on earth will be loosed in heaven." The reference to keys may have Isa 22:15-22 as background (cf. Rev 1:18; 3:7); it suggests authority. The binding and loosing in heaven are in a theological passive, viz., done by God. This, too, implies authority promised to Peter. In rabbinic literature binding and loosing can refer to binding the devil in exorcism, to juridical acts of excommunication, and definitive decision-making.[9]

It is inconceivable that the picture of Peter would be presented in this way by the three Synoptics unless it corresponded to the memory of the Churches in the last quarter of the 1st century.

The picture in John is no different. Despite the important position of the Beloved Disciple, there is still a prominence of Peter, both in the body of the Gospel (John 1:40-42; 6:67-69; 13:6-11, and 13:36-38 with 18:17-18, 25–27), and in the additional final chapter.[10] The Beloved Disciple—idealized figure or actual disciple—has a primacy of love (John 13:23-26; 18:15-16; 19:25-27) and of belief (20:2-10). In John 21, Peter takes the initiative to go fishing, but though the Beloved Disciple recognizes the Lord first (21:1-7), in this same chapter a pastoral office is conferred on Peter by a triple affirmation of the Lord in reply to Peter's threefold confession of love (21:15-17); the words used for the office are significant: *boske/poimaine* = "feed/tend," but the words for loving—*agapas/phileis* —are rather interchangeable in John. The following verses (18–19) point to Peter's martyrdom. The story of Jesus' ministry could not be told at the end of the 1st century without showing Peter to have a prominent place, one that coheres with the Synoptics.

The pseudepigraphy of the late 1 and 2 Peter is a further argument for the importance of Peter. Since they were almost certainly not written by Peter, the author(s) sought to give the prestige of the apostle to the letters, which notably have significant sayings about authority (1 Pet 5:1-4), and about the danger of misinterpreting Paul (2 Pet 3:15-16).

The important Lutheran-Roman Catholic study *Peter in the New Testament* can be summarized as follows: During the ministry of Jesus, Simon 1) was one of the first called, 2) had special prominence, 3) made a special confession of faith, and 4) failed in his understanding of Jesus and his mission. In the early Church Simon 1) was called Cephas, 2) was accorded a special vision of the risen Lord, 3) was the most important of the Twelve, 4) had a missionary career with a special role and authority. The images of Peter in the NT show a plurality: missionary fisherman, pastoral shepherd, martyr, recipient of special revelation, confessor of the true faith, protector of teaching (NB 2 Peter), and repentant sinner.[11] The Anglican-Roman Catholic dialogue (ARCIC) takes a somewhat similar view.[12]

Vatican I defined that an apostolic primacy was conferred on Peter.[13] It sought to eliminate the idea that Peter was only first among equals *(primus inter pares)*. It used the current term for spiritual authority, viz., jurisdiction. Vatican II spoke of Peter's primacy when exposing its teaching on episcopal collegiality (q.v.): ". . . by the Lord's decree, St Peter and the other apostles constitute one apostolic college. . . . The Lord made Simon alone the rock and key bearer of the church (see Matt 16:18–19) and constituted him shepherd of the whole flock (see John 21:15ff). It is clear, however, that this office of binding and loosing which was given to Peter (see Matt 16:19) was also granted to the college of bishops in union with its head (see Matt 18:18; 28:16–20)." It also asserted that the primacy is permanent: ". . . the office that was given individually by the Lord to Peter, the first of the apostles, is permanent and meant to be handed on to his successors . . ." (LG 20).

Among scholars today there is, then, broad agreement about Peter and his prominence among the apostles. Whereas all centrist Catholic theologians would agree that some of the Petrine prerogatives were personal to Peter, they would hold that the primacy invested in him would be transmitted to his successors (v. PAPAL PRIMACY). This claim is vigorously contested in ecumenical dialogue by Protestants in the West and by Orthodox in the East.[14]

In recent years there has been some important study of the joint primacy of Peter and Paul, both pillars of the Church of Rome, even though it was actually not founded by them (Rom 1:11-15.)[15] Such a widening of the notion of primacy to also include Paul should give rise to new ecumenical insights for all of the Churches.

[1]*Peter: Disciple, Apostle, Martyr* (London, [2]1962); cf. O. Karrer, *Peter and the Church: An Examination of Cullmann's Thesis.* QDisput 8 (Freiburg-Edinburgh, 1963).    [2]R.E. Brown et al., eds., *Peter in the New Testament: A Collaborative Assessment by Protestant and Roman Catholic Scholars* (London: SCM, 1974); J.A. Burgess, *A History of the Exegesis of Matthew 16:17-19 from 1781 to 1965* (Ann Arbor: Edwards, 1976); O. Knock, "Petrus im Neuen Testament," in M. Maccarrone, ed., *Il primato del vescovo di Roma nel primo millennio: Ricerche e testimonianze.* Pontificio comitato di scienze storiche—Atti e documenti 4 (Vatican, 1991) 1–52; R. Pesch, *Simon-Petrus: Geschichte und geschichtliche des ersten Jüngers Jesu Christi.* Päpste und Papsttum Bd. 15 (Stuttgart: Hiersemann, 1980); idem, "The Position and Significance of Peter in the Church of the New Testament," Conc 64 (1971) 21–35; B. Rigaux, "St. Peter in Contemporary Exegesis," Conc 7/3 (1967) 72–86; R. Schnackenburg, "The Petrine Office: Peter's Relationship to the Other Apostles," TDig 20 (1972) 148–152; C.P. Thiede, ed., *Das Petrusbild in der neueren Forschung* (Wuppertal: Brockhaus, 1987); T. Citrini, "La ricerca su Simon Pietro: Traguardi e itinerari a trent'anni dal libro di Cullmann,"

ScuolC 111 (1985) 512–556. [3]J. Gnilka, "Tu es Petrus: Die Petrus-Verheißung in Mt 16, 17–19," MüTZ 38 (1987) 7–17; A.J. Nau, *Peter in Matthew: Discipleship, Diplomacy and Dispraise . . . with an Assessment of Power and Privilege in the Petrine Office.* Good News Studies 36 (Collegeville: The Liturgical Press, 1992); J. Ratzinger, "Il primato di Pietro e l'unità della Chiesa," Divinitas 36 (1992) 207–221. [4]C.C. Caragounis, *Peter and the Rock* (New York: De Gruyter, 1990); M. Wilcox, "Peter and the Rock: A Fresh Look at Matthew XVI, 17–19," NTS 22 (1975) 73–88. [5]M.A. Chevallier, "Tu es Petrus, tu es le nouvel Abraham (Mt 16/18)," ETR 57 (1982) 375–389; 58 (1983) 354. [6]J.D.M. Derrett, "Thou art the Stone and upon this Stone," DowR 106 (1988) 276–285. [7]P. Grélot, "Sur cette pierre, je bâtirai mon Église," NRT 109 (1987) 641–654; B. Gherardini, "Pietro, la roccia," Divinitas 23 (1979) 335–345. [8]J. Marcus, "The Gates of Hades and the Keys of the Kingdom (Matt 16:18-19)" CBQ 50 (1988) 443–455. [9]J. Jeremias, TDNT 3:744-753. [10]P.J. Hartin, "The Role of Peter in the Fourth Gospel," Neotestamentica 24 (1990) 49–61. [11]Op. cit. (n. 2) 158–166. [12]"Authority in the Church II," *The Final Report* (London: CTS—SPCK, 1982) 81–83. [13]Tanner 2:812/DS 3053–3055/ND 819–821. [14]J. Meyendorff et al., *The Primacy of Peter* (Leyton Buzzard UK: Faith Press, [2]1973)—cf. P. Benoit RB 69 (1962) 443–445; E. Timiadis, "Saint Pierre dans l'exégèse orthodoxe," Istina 23 (1978) 56–74. [15]W.R. Farmer and R. Kereszty, *Peter and Paul in the Church of Rome: The Ecumenical Potential of a Forgotten Perspective* (Mahwah: Paulist, 1990); E. Lanne, "L'Église de Rome a gloriosissimis duobus apostolis Petro et Paulo fundatae et constitutae ecclesiae (Adv. haer. III, 3, 2)," Irén 49 (1976) 275–322; J.M.R. Tillard, *The Bishop of Rome.* Theology and Life 5 (Wilmington: Glazier, 1983) 101–119; ibid., "La présence de Pierre dans le ministère de l'évêque de Rome," Nicol 19 (1992) 55–76; J.J. von Allmen, *La primauté de l'Église de Pierre et de Paul* (Paris: Cerf—Fribourg: Ed. Universitaires, 1977)—see rev. art. J. Budillon, Istina 25 (1980) 365–387. See J.E. Walsh, *The Bones of St. Peter* (London: Collins Fount, 1982).

## PETRINE PRIVILEGE

The so-called Petrine Privilege is not found in canon law, and is a recent extension of papal power with regard to marriage. The first instance seems to have been in Breslau, Germany, on April 1924.[1] What usually is cited as the first example appeared on 5 November in the same year, the "Helena" case (from the name of a Montana diocese): an unbaptized man had married a baptized woman; after a civil divorce he converted to the Catholic Church and asked for the dissolution of the first marriage. This was granted, and it is sometimes called "Petrine Privilege," since its basis is seen to be the power of the keys granted by Christ to Peter's successors. It is also referred to as "Privilege of the Faith," and it is governed not by the *Code of Canon Law* but by norms of the Congregation of the Doctrine of the Faith,[2] which continues to be the case after the reform of the Curia.[3]

The first dissolutions were given only to baptized non-Catholics who had married non-baptized persons and had later converted to Catholicism and wanted to marry a Catholic. Later it was given to non-baptized persons who wanted to marry Catholics, and finally it was given to either party of a non-sacramental marriage entered into with a dispensation from disparity

of cult.[4] These extended applications of the privilege to non-sacramental marriages mean that the only marriages which cannot be dissolved are those consummated between two Christians. The Petrine differs from the Pauline Privilege (q.v.) in that it involves an act of the pope exercising his supreme authority.

[1]W.H. Woestman, *Special Marriage Cases* (Ottawa: St. Paul University, 1990); "Dissolution in Favor of the Faith," pp. 55–62. [2]6 Dec. 1973—CanLawDig 8:1177-1185. See F. Donnelly,"The Helena Decision of 1924," Jurist 36 (1976) 442–449; I. Gordon, "De processu ad obtinendam dissolutionem matrimonii non sacramentalis in favorem fidei," Periodica 79 (1990) 511–576; J. Kunz, "The Petrine Privilege: A Study of Some Recent Cases," Jurist 28 (1968) 486–496; L.G. Wrenn, "Some Notes on the Petrine Privilege," Jurist 43 (1983) 394–405. [3]*Pastor bonus* n. 53—AAS 80 (1988) 874. [4]T.P. Doyle, "Marriage," in Coriden, CIC 819.

## PHILIPS, Gérard (1899–1972)

One of the leading theologians at Vatican II, Gérard Philips was born in Limbourg in 1899. He studied at the Gregorian University, Rome, and presented a thesis on evil in the works of St. Augustine. He became professor of dogma at Liège in 1927, where he taught until becoming professor at Louvain from 1944–1969. He died in 1972.

His very extensive writings concentrated on questions of Trinity, Christology, ecclesiology, and Mariology.[1] His theology was marked by a speculative thrust always allied to the most representative witnesses of tradition.

He was a main architect of Vatican II's Constitution on the Church: it was his particular genius to be able to find a way forward amid conflicting views to a consensus which was in no way a compromise. He was also author of a substantial amount of the actual text. Given his role in the composition of the document, his commentary on *Lumen gentium* is particularly authoritative.[2]

[1]Bibliog. in AA.VV., *Ecclesia a Spiritu Sancto edocta. Lumen gentium, 53.* FS G. Philips. Bibliotheca Ephemeridum theologicarum lovaniensium 27 (Gembloux: Duculot, 1970) xvii–xxxv. [2]*L'Eglise et son mystère au IIe Concile du Vatican.* 2 vols. (Tournai Paris: Desclée, 1967, 1968).

## PISTOIA, Synod of (1786)

The Synod of Pistoia can be understood only in the context of Jansenism, a set of positions which arose from extreme Augustinian views of grace and is associated with Cornelius Jansen (Jansenius—1585–1638).[1] Jansenism spread after his death and the publication of his life's work *Augustinus* (1640). Jansenist errors were condemned in 1653.[2]

Jansenism spread to Italy in the 18th century, where it advocated not only suspect doctrines, but also genuine desires for reform of the Church. A diocesan synod in Pistoia, Tuscany (1786), passed a large number of acts, eighty-five of which were later condemned in varying degrees by Pius VI (1794).[3]

The synod was genuinely concerned with the holiness of the Church (v. HOLY); its approach to reform was too extreme, however, and tainted with numerous errors. The lasting significance of the synod was twofold: its condemnation effectively marked the end of Jansenism as a force in the Church, though Jansenistic ideas would still be found well into the following century; but the synod itself opened up questions about the relationships of parish/diocese/Rome, which would only find answers in the Vatican Councils I and II.

---

[1]L. Cognet, in Jedin-Dolan 6:24-56. [2]DS 2001–2007, 2010–2012. [3]DS 2600–2700; O. Köhler, in Jedin-Dolan 6:534-535; cf. A. Burlini Calapaj, "Per una rilettura del sinodo di Pistoia," RivLtg 75 (1988) 713–720; P. Hersche, "Zum zweihundertsten Jahrestag der Synode von Pistoia," IKiZ 78 (1988) 243–251; C. Lamioni, ed., *Il Sinodo di Pistoia del 1786.* Atti del Convegno Internazionale per il secondo centenario: Pistoia-Prato (Rome: Herder, 1991); M. Rosa, "Italian Jansenism and the Synod of Pistoia," Conc 7/2–17 (1966) 19–26.

## PIUS IX, Pope (1846–1878)

Giovanni Maria Mastai-Ferretti is a strange, enigmatic figure. Hostile biographers like A.B. Hasler stress his unstable personality and his intrigue and manipulation at Vatican I,[1] but his life and activity are too complex to be easily explained or summarized.[2]

Giovanni Maria was born of a noble family in Ancona, and later studied at Viterbo and Rome. It seems probable that his childhood epilepsy was cured, and he was ordained priest in 1819. After serving in a papal mission in Chile (1825–1827), he was archbishop of Spoleto and later of Imola (1827–1840). At his election as pope in 1846 he was viewed as a moderate progressive.

Though he started some reform in the Papal States, his temporal rule was a history of disasters. He showed some sympathy to early attempts at Italian unification but had to call on French aid for the protection of Rome. By the end of his life, all of the former papal states were annexed except the Vatican State and some buildings, mostly in the center of Rome.

If politically his reign was a disappointment, his pastoral care was much more productive: he established over 200 dioceses and vicariates apostolic, restored the hierarchy in England (1850) and Holland (1853), and entered into concordats with several states. In 1875 he consecrated the Church to the Sacred Heart, whose feast he had extended in 1856 to all the Latin Church. Two years earlier he had proclaimed the dogma of the Immaculate Conception.[3]

But Pius IX is best remembered for being the pope of Vatican I (q.v.) and of the *Syllabus of Errors* (1864).[4]

Due to political disappointments, his liberal tendencies slipped away, and he was determined to strengthen the Church against attacks. He added to his encyclical *Quanta cura* a list of 80 errors of the time. Some of these condemned propositions seem strange to our ears, e.g., "the Church is to be separated from the state, and the state from the Church" (n. 55), "The Roman Pontiff can, and should, reconcile himself and agree with progress, liberalism and modern civilization" (n. 80). But these *Errors* have to be seen in their context of liberalism, continuing much of the anti-religious feeling of the Enlightenment. Furthermore, they are to be judged by the hermeneutic appropriate to each of the various types of papal documents from which they were abstracted.[5]

In his private life there was much evidence of holiness; the cause of his beatification was introduced, and the title "Venerable" was accorded in 1985 as official recognition of heroic virtue. In public his great charm and obvious personal piety aroused much enthusiasm.[6] In addition, his many sufferings in the papacy led to sympathetic feelings towards him, so that by some he was regarded almost as a martyr for the faith. His espousal of Ultramontane (q.v.) positions left the papacy stronger, but his narrow view of society and the emerging world of politics, science, and scholarship left the Church ill-prepared for the radical critiques which would follow in the half-century after his death. However, one must not ignore his achievements as a pastor who oversaw a deepening of the spiritual life of the Church.

---

[1]*Pius IX (1846–1878), Päpstliche Unfehlbarkeit und I. Vatikanisches Konzil.* Päpste und Papsttum 12/1–2. 2 vols. (Stuttgart: Hiersemann, 1977). Abridged Eng. trans., *How the Pope Became Infallible* (London: Sheldon, 1981); G. Denzler, "Bulletin: The Discussion About Bernhard Hasler's Publications on the First Vatican Council," Conc 148 (1981) 81–86. [2]R. Aubert, *Le pontificat de Pie IX—1846–1878* (Paris, 1963); idem, in Fliche-Martin 21: 262-503; idem, "Pius IX," NCE 11:405-408; J.N.D. Kelly, *The Oxford Dictionary of Popes* (Oxford: UP, 1986) 309–311; G. Martina, *Pio IX.* Misc. Hist. Pont. 38, 51, 58. 3 vols. (Rome: Gregorian UP, 1974, 1986, 1990); Jedin-Dolan vol. 8 passim. [3]O'Carroll, Theotokos 179–182. [4]DS 2901–2980. [5]A. Schönmetzer, in DS Introd. preceding 2901; R. Aubert, in Jedin-Dolan 8:293-299. [6]B. Horaist, "La dévotion populaire française rendue à Pie IX," VieSp 14 (1987) 438–447; A. Pedrini, "Studi in onore del venerabile Pio IX," Divinitas 30 (1986) 184–186.

## PIUS X, Pope St. (1903–1914)

Giuseppe Sarto was born in 1835 in Upper Venetia of parents of modest means.[1] Ordained priest in 1858, he spent some years in parish life and in the seminary of Treviso as spiritual director, before becoming an energetic bishop of Mantua, a diocese then in poor condition. Nine years later, in 1893, he became patriarch of

Venice. There he showed pastoral zeal and a certain political acumen in opposing the socialists through an alliance of Catholics and moderate liberals. In 1903 he became pope in a conclave that sensed that a different style of papacy was desirable after what were perceived to be the political strategies of Leo XIII; he took up again the name Pius and chose as his motto "To restore all things in Christ" (Eph 1:10).

In contrast with Leo XIII's attempt to appease secular states, Pius X reacted strongly when he saw that the Church's interests were at stake. But, above all, he is remembered for his work within the Church. He reformed the Roman Curia.[2] He began the revision of canon law, committing it to Cardinal Gasparri, who had almost completed it by the pope's death, though it would not be published until 1917. He urged frequent, even daily, reception of Holy Communion and admitted children to the sacrament at the "use of reason."[3] He fostered liturgical reform, especially in Church music;[4] he instigated a reform of the divine office and the liturgical year.[5] His initiatives in these areas would in time lead to a deep movement of liturgical renewal (v. LITURGY). His pastoral concerns also reached the reform of seminaries, catechetics, and the beginnings of Catholic Action (v. APOSTOLATE).[6]

But his pontificate is nowadays mostly remembered for his implacable opposition to Modernism (q.v.). He had already encountered it in Venice. Soon after he became pope, many of the works of the leading French Modernist, A. Loisy, were placed on the *Index* (v. CENSORSHIP). Two early encyclicals were warnings against the dangers of the new ideas then circulating.[7] The decrees of the Biblical Commission (created in 1902) gradually became more reactionary. In 1907 the Holy Office published the decree *Lamentabili sane exitu*,[8] containing a list of sixty-five errors, almost fifty being explicit or implicit condemnations of Loisy. Later that year the encyclical *Pascendi* was issued;[9] it was a generalized exposition of the errors of the age, describing Modernism as "the meeting place of all heresies." The third weapon against Modernism was the mp. *Sacrorum antistitum* of 1910,[10] which contained an oath against Modernism required of all clergy up to 1967.[11]

The outcome was that while Pius X achieved success in his opposition to modernism, the atmosphere in the Church became poisoned with suspicion and accusations: theologians and ecclesiastics were removed without either being able to defend themselves or even knowing the nature of the charges that had been brought against them. Integralism (q.v.) flourished, with the active support of the Vatican and the undoubted knowledge of the pope himself. It would take Benedict XV's first encyclical[12] to call a halt to the rancor and hostility which were the result of the means used in the successful fight against Modernism.

Though one can disapprove of the methods allowed by Pius X, his personal goodness and holiness were beyond doubt. He was beatified in 1951 and canonized three years later. Since his death, and especially after Vatican II, there has been a tendency by those of the extreme right in the Church to invoke his memory or use his name in support of their causes.

[1]Lives: earlier unsatisfactory—; see list Salm 11 (1964) 353–354; R. Bazin, *Pie X* (Paris, 1928); E. Varcesi, *Il pontificato di Pio X* (Milan, 1935); H. Dal-Gal, *Saint Pius X* (Dublin, 1954); G. Romanato, *Pio X: La Vita di Papa Sarto* (Milan: Rusconi, 1992). Studies: Jedin-Dolan vol. 9 passim, esp. R. Aubert 394–480; OxDPopes 313–314. [2]*Sapiente consilio* (1908)—AAS 1 (1909) 7–19. [3]*Quam singulari*—AAS 2 (1910) 577–583. [4]*Tra le sollectitudini* ASS 36 (1904) 329–332. [5]*Divino afflatu*—AAS 3 (1911) 631–636. [6]Aubert (n. 1) 413–419. [7]*Ad diem illum*—ASS 36:449-462/Carlen 3:5-18; *Iucunda sane accidit*—ASS 36:513-529/Carlen 3:19-28. [8]ASS 40 (1907) 470–470/DS 3401-3466. [9]ASS 40:593-650/Carlen 3:71-97/in part DS 3475–3500. [10]AAS 2 (1910) 655–680. [11]DS 3537–3550/ND 143:1-13; see AAS 59 (1967) 1058. [12]*Ad beatissimi*—AAS 6 (1914) 565–581/Carlen 3:143-151/in part DS 3625–3626.

## PIUS XI, Pope (1922–1939)

Achille Ratti was born near Milan in 1857, son of a silk-factory manager.[1] Ordained in 1879, he obtained three doctorates in Rome, taught at the seminary at Padua (1882–1888), and was assigned to the Milan Ambrosian Library (1888–1911). He later moved to the Vatican Library (1911) and became its prefect (1914–1918). He was appointed to diplomatic missions in Eastern Europe (1918–1921) and became Cardinal Archbishop of Milan (1921) He was elected pope the following year.

The first scholarly pope since Benedict XIV (1740–1758), Pius XI fostered the sciences by founding the Pontifical Academy of Sciences (1936), and he strongly promoted ecclesiastical learning.[2] But above all, he was concerned to see the Church inserted into, not divorced from, society. He opened the Vatican Radio in 1931. His motto was *Pax Christi in regno Christi* ("Christ's peace in Christ's kingdom"). He explained it in his first encyclical, in which he commended Catholic Action (v. APOSTOLATE);[3] and he further developed it in his encyclical on the kingship of Christ, a feast he established in 1925.[4] He was a strong promoter of Catholic missions (q.v.), stressing the development of an indigenous clergy and bishops.

He was attentive to a wide range of Church matters, writing encyclicals on a variety of topics: Christian marriage, in which he condemned contraception;[5] social matters, in continuity with but developing Leo XIII's innovative *Rerum novarum* (1891), and other teaching;[6] St. Thomas Aquinas, called the "Guide to Studies";[7] Christian education.[8]

Faced with totalitarian ideologies of Socialism/ Communism, Fascism, and National Socialism (Nazism), he devoted an encyclical to each.[9] Planning a powerful protest against the ecclesiastical policy of fascist Italy, he died the previous evening, 10 February 1939.

His work in Church-State relations was significant:[10] he concluded concordats (q.v.) with twenty states; he ended the negative relations between the papacy and Italy with the Lateran Treaty (1929) establishing the Vatican as an independent neutral state, and recognizing the Italian state.

Though he favored the Uniate Churches (q.v.), especially by encouraging study of the Eastern traditions, he was cool towards ecumenism with Protestants: on the occasion of the Conferences at Lausanne and Stockholm (v. ECUMENICAL MOVEMENT), he warned against vague formulas of unity; he effectively put an end to public Catholic ecumenism for two decades with his encyclical *Mortalium animos*.[11]

The pontificate of Pius XI represented an important stage in the opening up of the Catholic Church to the world; it would be left to Pius XII (q.v.) and to Vatican II (q.v.) to further this development.

[1]H. Jedin, in Jedin-Dolan 10:23-29, 809; P. Hughes, *Pius XI* (London, 1937); G. Schwaiger, "Pius XI," NCE 11:411-414 with bibliog. OxDPopes 316-318.  [2]*Deus scientiarum*—AAS 23 (1931) 241–284 with encyc. on priesthood *Ad catholici sacerdotii*—AAS 28 (1936) 5–51/Carlen 3:497-516.  [3]*Ubi arcano*—AAS 14 (1922) 673–700/Carlen 3:225-238.  [4]*Quas primas*—AAS 17 (1925) 593–610/Carlen 3:271-279.  [5]*Casti conubii*—AAS 22 (1930) 539–592, 604/Carlen 3:391–414.  [6]*Quadragesimo anno*—AAS 23 (1931) 177–228/Carlen 3:415-441.  [7]*Studiorum ducem*—AAS 15 (1923) 309–326/Carlen 3:249-257.  [8]*Rappresentati in terra*—AAS 21 (1929) 723–762/*Divini illius magistri* 22 (1930) 49–86/Carlen 3:353-371.  [9]*Divini Redemptoris*—AAS 29 (1937) 65–106 [Italian 107–138]/Carlen 3:537-554 (Communism); *Non abbiamo bisogno*—AAS 23 (1931) 285–312/Carlen 3:445-458 (Fascism); *Mit brennender Sorge*—AAS 29 (1937) 145–167/Carlen 3:525-535 (Nazism).  [10]G. May, in Jedin-Dolan 10:177-198; K. Repgen ibid., 35–77;  [11]AAS 20 (1928) 5–16/Carlen 3:313-319.

## PIUS XII, Pope (1939–1958)

Eugenio Pacelli was born into a family of Roman jurists in 1876.[1] After studies in Rome he was ordained priest in 1899, and, entering the papal service in 1902, he became a key assistant to Cardinal Gasparri (1904–1916) in the codification of canon law (q.v.). He was appointed nuncio to Munich in 1917. He was engaged in preparing concordats (q.v.) with Bavaria (1924) and Prussia (1929). Becoming a cardinal in 1929, he was appointed secretary of state the following year. He was elected pope in 1939 and immediately set about urging peace. Throughout the war he continually spoke about peace. Afterwards he was severely criticized for not having been more forthright in condemning Nazi atrocities, especially the persecution of the Jews (q.v.). In his defense, the following are usu-ally stressed: his strong belief in the value of diplomacy, which was deeply ingrained through his training and early life; his belief that explicit condemnations would only make matters worse; his repeated denunciations, though in general terms, of racial extermination; the enormous help he gave to Jews as refugees within the Vatican state, a fact acknowledged by Jews themselves after the war.[2] During the war he organized vast relief works through the Pontifical Aid Commission, and succeeded in having Rome declared an open city, thus sparing it material destruction.

Pius XII regarded Marxism as an even greater threat to humanity and the Church than Nazism. As Bishop of Rome/Pope he intervened strongly in Italian postwar elections in order to have the communists excluded, and in 1948 the Christian Democrats came into power. Thus began an informal alliance of influential Church leaders with this party in Italian politics which lasted into the 1980s. An excommunication was published the following year for adherence to, or furthering of, communism.[3]

He notably internationalized the Curia, creating thirty-two cardinals in 1946 and twenty-four in 1953. But his rule tended to be authoritarian, a fact that grew more noticeable in the closing years of his pontificate; he appointed no secretary of state after 1944, preferring to run the office himself with pro-secretaries. He died in 1958.

At this distance it is possible to place in perspective the remarkable pontificate of Pius XII. He was certainly responsible for an opening out of the Church to the world. In an enormous number of carefully prepared addresses he explained Christian dimensions of their work to groups of every kind: jurists, politicians, doctors, scientists, midwives, journalists, and many others.

At the same time, he did not allow the war to interrupt magisterial teaching of a more solemn kind, as in the encyclicals on the Mystical Body, *Mystici Corporis* (q.v.),[4] and on modern biblical scholarship, *Divino afflante Spiritu,* show.[5] After the war he continued to take very important actions and to make influential statements: he clarified and determined the essence of the sacrament of orders;[6] he wrote an encyclical which would be the *magna charta* for the liturgical movement;[7] he modified the Eucharistic fast to encourage more frequent communion;[8] he restored the liturgy of Holy Week, including the Easter Vigil.[9] Perhaps best remembered by some for his Marian pronouncements, he proclaimed the dogma of the Assumption in 1950[10] and wrote some Marian encyclicals, one for the Marian year he proclaimed for 1954,[11] and one when he established the feast of the queenship of Mary.[12] In his multifaceted magisterium one should also note the encyclicals on the Sacred Heart,[13] on the media,[14] and on the missions.[15]

In 1950, using some of the material which had been prepared during an exploration of the possibility of reopening Vatican I (v. VATICAN II), he issued a rather conservative encyclical warning against the "New Theology" and a recrudescence of Modernism.[16] Though he did not name anyone, others were quick to do so, and a persecution of some of the outstanding theologians of the time followed, e.g., H. de Lubac (q.v.), Y. Congar (q.v.), K. Rahner (q.v.), M.-D. Chenu.

From his training in canon law, Pius XII made a number of important changes in Church discipline,[17] especially in the area of the sacraments, sacramentals, in Eastern canon law, in religious life, as well as the founding charter for secular institutes (q.v.).

It is common nowadays to think more of the statements of Pius XII that were not followed by Vatican II than of the significant contribution he actually made to ecclesiology.[18] Not only the three great encyclicals, on the Mystical Body (1943), Scripture study (1943), and liturgy (1947), for which he is best remembered, but many other allocutions and addresses give a very rich ecclesiology.[19] At heart he would probably most associate with the vision of Vatican I when it spoke of the Church as a motive of credibility.[20] He seems to have had a deep sense of the malaise of modern society and culture: the world is torn by ideologies while the Church remains a haven of truth—indeed, of civilization.

For reasons internal to the council, Vatican II frequently cited Pius XII in its documents (v. VATICAN II). Though the council did not always follow the precise line of this pope, he can be said to have opened the way for many of its initiatives, or helped the minority at the council to accept them. Notwithstanding the fact that in recent years his reputation has suffered some eclipse, his influence on the council was significant and generally very positive.

[1]H. Jedin, in Jedin-Dolan 10:30-34, bibliog. 812–813; OxDPopes 318–320; A. Riccardi, ed., *Pio XII* (Rome—Bari: Laterza, 1984) with bibliog. 5–29; M. O'Carroll, *Pius XII. Greatness Dishonoured. A Documented Study* (Dublin: Laetare Press, 1980); N. Padellaro, *Portrait of Pius XII* (London, 1956). [2]Critical, e.g., C. Falconi, *The Silence of Pius XII* (London: Faber & Faber, 1970) and J.F. Morley, *Vatican Diplomacy and the Jews During the Holocaust 1939–1945* (New York: KTAV Publishing House, 1980). But cf. *Actes et documents du Saint Siège relatifs à la seconde guerre mondiale.* 8 vols. (Vatican, 1965–1978); C. De Celles, "The Importance of Dialoguing with the Holocaust," AmBenR 33 (1982) 75–101 esp. nn. 59–61; R.A. Graham, "La Santa Sede e la difesa degli ebrei durante la seconda guerra mondiale," CivCatt 141 (1990) 3:209-226; id., *Il Vaticano e il nazismo* (Rome: Cinque Lune, 1975); F.J. Weber, "Witness for Pius XII," AmBenR 26 (1975) 227–230; O. Chadwick, *Britain and the Vatican During the Second World War* (Cambridge UK: UP, 1986). [3]Holy Office decree 28 June/1 July 1949—AAS 41 (1949) 334/DS 3865. [4]AAS 35 (1943) 193–248/ Carlen 4:37-62. [5]AAS 35 (1943) 297–326/Carlen 4:65-78. [6]*Sacramentum ordinis*—AAS 40 (1948) 5–7/DS 3858–3861/ND 1737 [7]*Mediator Dei*—AAS 39 (1947) 521–595/Carlen 4:119-153. [8]AAS 45 (1953) 15–24. [9]S. Cong. Rites AAS 43 (1951) 128–137. [10]*Munificentissimus Deus*—AAS 42 (1950) 753–773/DS 3900–3904/ND 713–715. [11]*Fulgens corona*—AAS 45 (1953) 577–592/Carlen 4:231-238/in part DS 3908–3910 [12]*Ad caeli reginam*—AAS 46 (1954) 625–640/Carlen 4:271-278/in part DS 3913–3917. [13]*Haurietis aquas*—AAS 48 (1956) 303–353/Carlen 4:291-312. [14]*Miranda prorsus*—AAS 49 (1957) 765–805/Carlen 4:347-364. [15]*Evangelii praecones* AAS 43 (1951) 497–528/Carlen 4:189-202; *Fidei donum*—AAS 49 (1957) 225–248/Carlen 4:321-332. [16]*Humani generis*—AAS 42 (1950) 561–578/Carlen 4:175-183/in part DS 3875–3899. [17]G. May, in Jedin-Dolan 10:156-158. [18]Antón 2:566-612. [19]Alloc. *Vous avez voulu*—AAS 47 (1955) 672–682; *Pousées par le désir*—49 (1957) 906–922; *Six ans se sont*—49 (1957) 922–937; *La elevetezza*—38 (1946) 141–151; *C'est bien volontiers*—48 (1956) 210–216; encyc. *Ad Sinarum gentem*—47 (1955) 5–14/Carlen 4:265-269. [20]Tanner 2:807-808/DS 3013/ND 123.

## PLURALISM

"Pluralism" is a term in frequent use since Vatican II, but its meaning is not always immediately clear. In itself it means that a multitude is not reduced to one ultimate principle. There is clearly pluralism in cultures, in politics, in religion. Even within a stance of openness to the fact of pluralism, one will not necessarily accept that all views are equally legitimate. Thus a Christian will be aware of other religions, and even maybe agree that the Holy Spirit is working in them, without being required to accept that all religions are equal (v. NON-CHRISTIAN RELIGIONS).

Pluralism was to be found in NT times even within Judaism: Sadducees, Pharisees, and the Qumran community had a variety of views about what authentic living according to the covenant might involve. Today, too, there are still various ways of being Jewish: Orthodox, Conservative, Reformed, etc. Again, there is a pluralism in the theology of the NT books themselves, quite notably on matters which involve the Church (v. NEW TESTAMENT ECCLESIOLOGIES).

Though one associates the pre-Vatican II period with uniformity rather than with pluralism, there has always been a striking pluralism in Catholic theology. One has only to think of the medieval schools following Augustinian, Aristotelian, or Platonic principles, the schools of spirituality throughout the centuries, the diversity of liturgical rites.

With regard to theology and the life of the Church, there are several grounds for pluralism.[1] There are different mentalities in differing cultural milieux, e.g., the Latin, Greek, and Syriac Fathers (q.v.). Different basic philosophies give rise to pluralism, e.g., the Aristotelianism of Thomas Aquinas or the Nominalism of the Reformers. The various schools and religious orders arise from differing intuitions and initial preoccupations, e.g., Benedictine and Dominican schools. There are different theological perspectives, e.g., Christologies and ecclesiologies "from above" and "from below," or theocentric, Christocentric, and anthropological approaches. More profoundly, theological pluralism arises from the insufficiency of any human language to communicate fully divine realities: expressions of divine truth can be further perfectible.[2] We have to note with Vatican II: "There is a difference between the deposit or truths of faith and the manner in which—with their sense and meaning being preserved—they are expressed" (GS 62).

At Vatican II there was genuine pluralism in theology, so that one can detect several theologies at work even in a single document like *Lumen gentium*.[3] But this pluralism was hard-won: the preparatory documentation was generally in neo-scholastic form and needed drastic transformation, one that was in no small part due to the presence of bishops from various parts, especially the East, of the observers from other Churches and of the broadly based panel of experts who were eventually called to serve the council. Part of the problem affecting the post-Vatican II Church is the fact that instead of the pluralism of the council, Vatican documents again appear in a Roman theology which does not always sit easily with people elsewhere in the Church. The council on the other hand had firmly embraced pluralism in liturgy and theology (SC 37, 40; AG 22; LG 13, 23; UR 17). In UR 4e there is an extended exposition of the traditional tessera *"in necesariis unitas, in dubiis libertas, in omnibus caritas"* (unity in essentials, freedom in doubtful matters, in all things love), inspired by Augustine, promulgated in Anglican and Lutheran circles, and canonized by John XXIII.[4]

Pluralism is normal outside the Catholic Church. The Anglican Communion (q.v.) prides itself on its comprehensiveness, which involves not only diverse theologies but also differing understandings of what the Church and its doctrines really are, as well as different ways of being Anglican, ranging from the High Church Catholic wing to an extremely Low Church Evangelical wing which can tend towards fundamentalism (q.v.). The Eastern Churches (q.v.), many of which are in communion with one another, have a bewildering pluralism in theology, rites (q.v.), and structures.

An extreme form of pluralism makes ecumenism impossible, or rather irrelevant: it would involve a decision to agree to differ, a judgment that differences do not really matter;[5] it would be implicit indifferentism.

Like the diversity in catholicity (v. CATHOLIC) of which it is an expression, pluralism is always in tension with necessary fundamental unity. The boundary of pluralism is revelation as expressed in the sense of faith (q.v.) of the Church and propounded by the magisterium (q.v.). Some authors prefer to use the word "pluralism" in a negative sense for what destroys unity, while reserving "pluriformity" for legitimate diversity.

[1]Y. Congar, *Diversity and Communion* (London: SCM, 1984); H. Fries, "Theological Reflection on the Problem of Pluralism," TS 28 (1967) 3–26; R. Latourelle, *Christ and the Church: Signs of Salvation* (New York: Alba House, 1972) 143–144; H. Löwe, Über Pluralismus und Pluralität in der Kirche: Chancen und Grenzen," KerDo 24 (1978) 18–31; International Theological Commission, "Theological Pluralism (1972)," *Texts and Documents 1969–1985* (San Francisco: Ignatius, 1989) 89–92; idem, commentaries *Die Einheit des Glaubens und der theologischer Pluralismus* (Einsiedeln: Johannes Verlag, 1973; Italian—Collana Nouvi Saggi 3, Bologna: Dehoniane, 1974; Spanish—Madrid: BAC, 1976); G. Philips, "A propos du pluralisme en théologie," ETL 46 (1970) 149–169; K. Rahner, "Pluralism in Theology and the Unity of the Creed in the Church," ThInvest 11:3-23.   [2]W. Henn, "Pluralism," NDictT 772; cf. K. Rahner, "Reflections on Dialogue within a Pluralistic Society," ThInvest 6:31-42; idem, "A Small Question Regarding the Contemporary Pluralism in the Intellectual Situation of Catholics and the Church," ThInvest 6:21-30; H.U. von Balthasar, *Truth is Symphonic: Aspects of Christian Pluralism* (San Francisco: Ignatius, 1987); J. Meijer, "La legittimità di diverse tradizioni e usi nella Chiesa secondo il Concilio di Constantinopoli 879–880," Nicol 16 (1989) 87–106; See. T.R. Stinnett, "Lonergan's 'Critical Realism' and Religious Pluralism," Thom 56 (1992) 97–115.   [3]A. Acerbi, *Due ecclesiologie: Ecclesiologia giuridica ed ecclesiologia di comunione nella "Lumen gentium"* (Bologna: Dehoniane, 1975).   [4]Encyc. *Ad Petri cathedram* (1959)—AAS 51 (1959) 513/Carlen 5:12. See for history Y. Congar, "Unité, diversité et divisions," in *Sainte Église*. US 41 (Paris: Cerf, 1963) 118, n. 3.   [5]G.H. Tavard, "Pluralism or Ecumenism," OneChr 6 (1970) 123–134.

## PNEUMATOLOGY AND ECCLESIOLOGY

A Vatican II vignette by Y. Congar has since become classical: "During the discussion of the schema *De ecclesia* at the second session of the council, we were speaking one day with two friends who were Orthodox observers, Fr. Nissiotis and Fr. Alexander Schmemann. They said to us: 'If we had to write a *De ecclesia* we would write one chapter on the Holy Spirit and one chapter on Christian man. Then we would stop. We would have said what was essential.'"[1] Even though such an ecclesiology might be as one-sided as what Congar elsewhere described as Christological monism,[2] it strikingly illustrates a dimension that was weak in Catholic ecclesiology prior to the council, viz., a developed pneumatology or theology of the Holy Spirit. The council itself has 258 references to the Spirit, but it can be asked whether these are, as it were, scattered throughout the conciliar texts, or in fact constitute a veritable pneumatology.

The years after the council have seen extraordinary interest in pneumatology from many different points of view:[3] general works,[4] scriptural,[5] patristic,[6] spirituality,[7] charism (q.v.), liberation,[8] liturgy,[9] ecumenical,[10] and especially from the viewpoint of the Eastern Churches,[11] and including the issue of the *Filioque* (q.v.). Vatican II has also given rise to substantive literature,[12] as have various ecclesiological themes.[13]

The Spirit was gradually revealed throughout the Scriptures.[14] In the OT there are 378 references to the feminine *ruah* (to which eleven Aramaic instances could be added); it is translated 279 times by neuter *pneuma* in the LXX (which in later tradition becomes a Latin masculine, *Spiritus*.) The OT usages of "the Spirit of God" can be seen as fourfold: it is a charismatic force seen for example in the judges (Judg 3:10); it is a power coming on kings ( 1 Sam 16:13); it is associated with prophecy (Hos 9:7; Mic 3:8); it is messianic (Isa 42:1-7; 61:1-3) and eschatological (Ezek 36:26-28; Joel 3:1-2). On the threshold of the NT there is a clear association of spirit and wisdom (Wis 1:6; 7:7; 9:17). There was notable interest in the spirit of God in intertestamental literature (over 200 references in Qumran texts alone). This range of life-giving activities in the OT sensitizes us to his full coming in power on the NT Church.

In the NT there are 379 references to *pneuma*. In these we find that though the OT meanings continue to be found, there is an increasing awareness of the Spirit being personal, especially in Luke (11:13; 12:12) and in John (14–16). In particular the Spirit is associated with Jesus (Luke 1:35; 3:22; 4:1, 14, 18). Paul develops a rich pneumatology (Rom 8).

From the ecclesiological perspective, which is our concern here, the Spirit is both conferred by Jesus (John 20:22) and promised by him (John 16:13-15; Luke 24:49 with Acts 1:4-5, 8). The early Church received the Spirit at Pentecost (Acts 2; cf. 4:31) and was conscious of being inhabited (Acts 5:3) and guided by the Spirit (Acts 13:2, 4; 15:28; 16:7). The Spirit was also given through prayer and the imposition of the hands of the apostles (Acts 8:15-17; 19:6). The community (1 Cor 3:16) and the Christian are a temple (q.v.) of the Spirit (1 Cor 6:19); the believer is sealed by the Spirit (Eph 1:13). Access to the Father is through the Spirit (Eph 2:18). It is the Spirit who gives charisms (q.v.) and builds up the unity of believers (Eph 4:3; cf. 1 Cor 12:13).

The development of the theology of the Spirit took place over several centuries.[15] One can outline it in several stages: a period when the Spirit was affirmed and experienced in the life of the Church (1st—2nd century); the beginnings of theological systematization (3rd century); the definition of Constantinople (381—q.v.); the 5th-century synthesis; the divergence of East and West over the *Filioque* (q.v.). These various developments both concerned the ecclesial activity of the Spirit and affected how people understood that activity.

There is some limited value in observing that the West begins with the unity and unicity of God before going on to affirm the plurality of Persons, whereas the East begins with the Persons as a first datum and proceeds to their unity of nature; it gives an initial orientation but cannot be pressed too far. Throughout the patristic period there was not only speculation about the inner life of the Trinity but continual exploration of the economic Trinity, or the double mission of the Son, and of the Spirit to the Church and the believer. We can illustrate the ecclesial mission by a characteristic author from the East and the West,[16] Sts. Basil and Augustine.

The work of the easterner Basil, *On the Holy Spirit*, can be dated 374–375 C.E.[17] His *Letter* 159 written shortly before contains much of the same doctrine.[18] Though for prudential reasons, mainly to avoid problems similar to those which broke out after the Council of Nicaea (q.v.), Basil never explicitly said "the Spirit is God"; he insisted on the fact that the Third Person is similarly to be adored and glorified as the Father and the Son, which clearly is equivalent. Basil constantly appealed to the Church's life and liturgy as evidence of its faith in the person and working of the Spirit;[19] indeed, he invokes non-written tradition about the Spirit whose power is well-known in the Church.[20]

St. Augustine can be taken as characterizing a Western approach. Like Basil, he, too, in his great work *De Trinitate*, begins from Scripture.[21] Though he is clearly more concerned with the inner life of the Trinity, he nonetheless clearly speaks of the Spirit as sent to the Church,[22] as, indeed, being the communion in the Church, as he is in the Trinity.[23] One of Augustine's most notable assertions was that the Spirit brings about in the Mystical Body of Christ what the soul brings about in our body.[24]

The Western medieval synthesis can be seen in St. Anselm, Richard of St. Victor, St. Bonaventure, and St. Thomas Aquinas, each of whom develops aspects of the rich synthesis of St. Augustine. St Thomas develops from Augustine the notion of procession and mission;[25] he sees Gift *(Donum)* as a proper name for the Spirit,[26] and asserts a genuine mission;[27] he develops beautifully the notion of the Spirit as Friend;[28] he states that it is the Spirit who characterizes the New Law[29] and grants his charisms to the Church.[30]

In the later Middle Ages there were many movements claiming a special anointing of the Spirit, and the term "spiritual" often implied some fanaticism.[31] Some, like Joachim of Fiore (q.v.), seemed to look forward to a final age of humankind, that of the Spirit. Present in some of these movements was an anti-institutionalism: they opposed their sense of being directed by the Spirit to structures which they perceived as being not thus vitalized. Even at the time of the Reformation such tensions continued. Luther and other reform leaders saw themselves as embattled on two fronts: the Catholics crying "Church" and the enthusiasts crying "Spirit."[32] Though basically not sympathetic, R.A. Knox's, study of enthusiasm illustrates the continuance of extreme spiritual movements in the times after the Reformation.[33]

There was a good deal of awareness of the work of the Holy Spirit in spiritual writers after Trent. But in the ecclesiology of the Counter-Reformation and later, though references to the Holy Spirit were not absent, they did not occupy any central position. There were exceptions, such as the work on the unity of the Church by J.A. Möhler (q.v.) and incisive passages in M.J. Scheeben (q.v.).[34]

Pneumatology comes to the fore in ecclesiology from the time of J.A. Möhler (q.v.). In the magisterium one might well wish to date the rediscovery of pneumatology in ecclesiology with the encyclical of Leo XIII on the Holy Spirit in 1897.[35] The letter is heavily dependent on Augustine and Thomas Aquinas. The pneumatocentric spirituality of the encyclical needs to be read from a perspective that recognizes the Christocentric hierarchology of the earlier encyclical *Satis cognitum*.[36] It reiterates the notion of the Spirit being the soul of the Church, and speaks of the Spirit being the source of the Church's abiding in truth and of its sacramental life, as well as inhabiting the souls of the just. It is quite a comprehensive account of the Spirit's role in the Church. After Leo XIII theologians mined from his works statements about the Spirit but did not develop any significant pneumatological ecclesiology.

Though the encyclical of Pius XII (q.v.) on the Mystical Body, *Mystici Corporis* (q.v.),[37] was predominantly Christological, it gave a significant place to the Holy Spirit: the Church was promulgated at Pentecost; Christ willed that it be enriched with the Spirit's gifts; the Church is animated by the Spirit, which is its soul; there is, however, no incompatibility "between the invisible mission of the Holy Spirit and the juridical office which pastors and teachers have received from Christ." But apart from the encyclical, pneumatology does not much enter into the extensive ecclesiological teaching of Pius XII.[38]

There was, however, a growing awareness, even if not always systematically developed,[39] of the importance of pneumatology, both in the Catholic and Protestant Churches in the decades preceding Vatican II.

It can be shown that Vatican II devoted increasing attention to pneumatology in the entire evolution of its texts. The first draft of the Vatican II Constitution on the Church was in the tradition of Pius XII's encyclical on the Mystical Body.[40] It did have thirty-one references to the Spirit, mainly as soul of the Body and as the Spirit of truth, but the idea of the Spirit guiding the Church is also present. Thirteen of these references would remain in the promulgated text of LG.

The council clarified the analogy of the soul of the Church. In LG 7 it stated: "The Spirit gives life, unity and movement to the whole body, so that the fathers of the Church could compare his task to that which is exercised by the life-principle, the soul *(principium vitae seu anima),* in the human body." In the following article the complementary analogy with the Incarnation is developed, "For just as the assumed nature serves the divine Word as a living instrument of salvation inseparably joined with him, in a similar way *(non dissimili modo)* the social structure of the Church serves the Spirit of Christ who vivifies the Church towards the growth of the body."[41] The delicate path trodden here is the avoidance of ecclesial Monophysitism; the council uses the words "social structure" *(socialis compago)* and "serves" *(inservit)* to reduce the range of the analogy and thus avoid any suggestion of a hypostatic union with the Church.

In the final version of LG there is a rich pneumatology. The Constitution begins with a Trinitarian exposition (LG 2–4), as does the later Decree on Missions (AG 2–4). A significant new notion is that of Pentecost[42] and the important development of the teaching about charisms (q.v.). The teaching of both documents (LG 4; AG 4) shows why the early creeds confessed together the Holy Spirit and the Church, so that St. Thomas Aquinas explains the Creed as belief in the Spirit sanctifying the Church *("Credo in Spiritum Sanctum sanctificantem Ecclesiam").*[43]

One can speak of a pneumatology of the council if it can be shown that there is a central insight that unifies both the various references to the Spirit and the council's ecclesiology. Such a central insight would seem to be the statement that "the Holy Spirit was sent to sanctify the Church continually and so that believers would have through Christ access to the Father in one Spirit (see Eph 2:18)"—LG 4; cf. 9). The underdeveloped notion of temple (q.v.) as a third Trinitarian image along with People and Body (LG 17) can be seen to unify and explicitate the teaching of the constitution. With the council's arrival at its penultimate text, we find a development of this intuition in the Decree on the Missions: the Spirit vivifies and unifies the whole Church in all its activities (see AG 4; cf. LG 64). Since these assertions are verified, operative, and developed throughout the council's documents, they are solid grounds for stating that Vatican II has a genuine pneumatology.

Though it has six references to the Spirit (SC 2, 5, 6, 43), the Constitution on the Liturgy is quite weak pneumatologically. The subsequent revision of the liturgical books made good this deficiency (v. LITURGY). A characteristic of all the new Eucharist Prayers and of the various sacramental rites is the presence of an *epiclêsis* (q.v.).

The pneumatology of Vatican II was carried forward by the third encyclical of John Paul's Trinitarian trilogy, "The Holy Spirit in the Life of the Church and of the World."[44] The encyclical is at once both a more extensive treatment of the Spirit's mission and also less focused on ecclesiology. The pope does note that "in a certain way the grace of Pentecost is perpetuated in the Church" through the sacraments of orders and confirmation.[45] Further, "the teaching of Vatican II is 'pneumatological': it is permeated by the truth about the Holy Spirit as the soul of the Church."[46]

The second part of the encyclical expounds the difficult text of John 16:7-8 about the Spirit convincing the world concerning sin:[47] it is both the action of the Spirit in the human conscience and the assurance of redemption.[48] The Spirit, moreover, strengthens each individual and manifests the Church as sacrament.[49] He is the foundation of the Church's eschatological hope;[50] he is in summary "Counsellor, Intercessor, Advocate."[51]

The huge amount of writing on the Spirit and the Church in the past three decades,[52] as well as the teaching of Vatican II and the beneficent influence of Eastern theologians, have set a path for ecclesiology: it cannot regress but only go forward in the exploration of pneumatology, in seeking to understand the mission of the One described, in the haunting phrase of H. U. von Balthasar, "The Unknown beyond the Word."[53]

[1]"The Church the People of God," Conc 1/1 (Jan. 1975) 7–19 at 13. [2]"Pneumatologie ou 'christomonisme' dans la tradition latine?," ETL 46 (1969) 394–416. [3]W.E. Mills, *The Holy Spirit: A Bibliography* (Peabody, Mass.: Hendrickson, 1988). [4]AA. VV. *Credo in Spiritum Sanctum.* Atti del congresso teologico internazionale di pneumatologia, Roma 22–26 marzo 1982. 2 vols. (Vatican, 1983)—multilingual; H.U. von Balthasar, *Explorations in Theology. III Creator Spirit* (San Francisco: Ignatius, 1993); F. Bourassa, "'Dans la communion de l'Esprit saint': Étude théologique 1–3," ScEsp 34 (1982) 31–56, 135–149, 239–268; Y. Congar, *I Believe in the Holy Spirit.* 3 vols. (New York: Seabury—London: Chapman, 1983 from French 1979–1980); F.X. Durrwell, *The Holy Spirit: An Essay in Biblical Theology* (London: Chapman, 1986); B. Gaybba, *The Spirit of Love: Theology of the Holy Spirit.* Chapman Theological Library (London: Chapman, 1987); M. O'Carroll, *Veni Creator Spiritus: A Theological Encyclopedia of the Holy Spirit* (Collegeville: Glazier—The Liturgical Press, 1990); F. Lambiasi, *Lo Spirito Santo: mistero e presenza: Per una sintesi di pneumatologia.* Corso di teologia sistematica 5 (Bologna: Ed. Dehoniane, 1987); K. McDonnell, "A Trinitarian Theology of the Holy Spirit?," TS 46 (1985) 193–220; idem, "The Determinative Doctrine of the Holy Spirit," TTod 39 (1982) 142–161; J. Richard, "Pour une théologie de l'Esprit-saint," LavalTP 36 (1980) 47–75; Communio (Milan) 85 (1986). [5]T.D. Horgan, "Who Is the Holy Spirit? A Biblical Survey," OneChr 25 (1989) 322–332; A. Milano, "La pneumatologia del NT: Considerazioni metodologiche," AugR 20 (1980) 429–469; H. Paprocki, "Les fondements bibliques de la pneumatologie," Istina 33 (1988) 7–21. [6]J.P. Burns and G.M. Fagin, *The Holy Spirit.* Message of the Fathers of the Church 3 (Wilmington: Glazier, 1984); S. Felici, ed., *Spirito Sancto e catechesi patristica.* Biblioteca di scienze religiose 54 (Rome: LAS, 1983); A. Hamman, "El Espíritu Santo en la vida de la Iglesia durante los tres primeros siglos," EstTrin 9 (1975) 273–292; T. Marsh, "The Holy Spirit in Early Christian Teaching," IrTQ 45 (1978) 101–116; A. Quacquarelli, "Accenti popolari alla catechesi pneumatologica dei primi secoli," VetChr 19 (1982) 5–23. [7]Conc 99 (1974); AA.VV. *Viens Esprit Saint: Rencontre spirituelle et théologie 1987.* Centre Notre Dame de Vie. Spiritualité 4 (Verasque: Ed. du Carmel, 1988); J. Galot, "L'Esprit Saint, milieu de vie," Greg

72 (1991) 671–688; S.J. Kilian, "The Holy Spirit in Christ and in Christians," AmBenR 20 (1969) 99–121; K. Rahner, "Experience of the Holy Spirit," ThInvest 18:189-210. [8]J. Comblin, *The Holy Spirit and Liberation.* Liberation and Theology 4 (Maryknoll: Orbis—Tunbridge Wells UK: Burns & Oates, 1989). [9]Bibliog., C. Magnoli, "Quarant'anni di letteratura liturgica attorno al tema pneumatologico," ScuolC 117 (1989) 77–103; M.J. Francisco, "Lo Spirito sancto e i sacramenti—Bibliografia," Notitiae 131–132 (1977) 326–335. See AA.VV. *Le Saint-Esprit dans la liturgie.* Conférences Saint-Serge 16. Bibliotheca *Ephemerides liturgicae* subsidia 8 (Rome: Ed. Liturgiche, 1977); A.M. Triacca, "Presenza e azione dello Spirito Santo nell'assemblea liturgica," EphLtg 99 (1985) 349–382; A. Verheul, "Les symboles de l'Esprit saint dans la bible et la liturgie," QLtg 69 (1988) 67–95; QLtg 67 (1986) 81–179. [10]EcuR 41 (July 1989) 324–467; "The Holy Spirit: Papers Prepared for the Roman Catholic-World Methodist Joint Commission," OneChr 16 (1980) 169–224; G. Cottier, "L'oecuménisme et le mystère du Saint Esprit," NovVet 57 (1982) 180–187; L. Fischer, *La théologie du saint Esprit dans le dialogue oecuménique.* Document Foi et Constitution 103 (Paris: Centurion—Les Presses de Taizé, 1981); W. Hollenweger, "Creator Spiritus: The Challenge of Pentecostal Experience to Pentecostal Theology," Theology 679 (1978) 32–39; P.J. Rosato, *The Spirit and Lord: The Pneumatology of Karl Barth* (Edinburgh: Clark, 1981); J. Thompson, "The Holy Spirit and the Trinity in Ecumenical Perspective," IrTQ 47 (1980) 272–285; H. Wells, "The Holy Spirit and the Theology of the Cross: Significance for Dialogue," TS 53 (1992) 476–492. [11]G. Bentivegna, "L'effusion de l'Esprit-Saint chez les pères grecs," NRT 113 (1991) 690–707; O. Clement, "Quelques approches pneumatologiques de l'Église," Contacts 39 (1983) 17–30; Mgr. Damaskinos, "La disponibilité au Saint Esprit et la fidelité aux origines d'après les pères grecs," Istina 19 (1974) 49–64; P. Evdokimov, *Présence de l'Esprit Saint dans la tradition orthodoxe* (Paris: Cerf, 1977); M.A. Fatula, "The Holy Spirit in East and West: Two Irreducible Traditions," OneChr 19 (1983) 379–386; M.M. Garijo Gueme, "La pneumatología en la moderna teología orthodoxa," EstTrin 9 (1975) 359–383; W. Hryniewcz, "Der pneumatologische Aspekt der Kirche aus orthodoxer Sicht," Catholica 31 (1977) 122–150; J.A.J. Meijer, "L'Esprit Saint dans la liturgie orientale," QLtg 67 (1986) 128–142; P. O'Leary, "The Holy Spirit in Orthodox Theology," IrTQ 46 (1979) 177–184; H. Paprocki, "Le Saint Esprit dans la théologie orthodoxe," Istina 32 (1987) 214–224; C.N. Tsirpanlis, "Pneumatology in the Eastern Church," Diak (USA) 13 (1978) 17–26; J.D. Zizioulas, "Cristologia, pneumatologia e istituzioni ecclesiastiche: Un punto di vista orthodosso," CrNSt 2 (1981) 110–127. [12]J.B. Anderson, *A Vatican II Pneumatology of the Paschal Mystery: The Historical-Doctrinal Genesis of Ad gentes 1, 2–5.* AnGreg 250 (Rome: Gregorian UP, 1988); M.C. Boulding, "The Doctrine of the Holy Spirit in the Documents of Vatican II," IrTQ 51 (1985) 253–267; Y. Congar, "Les implications christologiques et pneumatologiques de l'ecclésiologie de Vatican II," in G. Alberigo, ed., *Les Église après Vatican II: Dynamisme et prospective.* Théologie historique 61 (Paris: Beauchesne, 1981) 117–130 = CrNSt 2 (1981) 97–110; P. J. Mullins, *The Teaching of* Lumen gentium *on the Holy Spirit: The Holy Spirit was Sent at Pentecost in order that He Might Continually Sanctify the Church.* Diss. exc. (Rome: Gregorian, 1991), full text Ann Arbor: UMI, 1991, thesis n. 3266. [13]G. Bassarau, "Das Wesen des Heiligen Geistes in Kirche und Welt," FreibZ 30 (1983) 27–41; C. Dagens, "L'Esprit Saint et l'Église dans la conjoncture actuelle," NRT 96 (1974) 225–245; B. Forte, "La Trinità e la 'pericoresi': Lo Spirito come vita e come forza," StEcum 9 (1991) 245–267 = UnaSan 46 (1991) 9–21; M.M. Garijo-Gueme, *Gemeinschaft der Heiligen Geist: Grund, Wesen und Struktur der Kirche* (Dusseldorf: Patmos, 1988); W. Kasper, "Esprit—Christ—Église" in *L'expérience de l'Esprit.* FS E. Schillebeeckx (Paris: Beauchesne, 1976) 47–69; H. Mühlen, *Una mystica persona: Die Kirche als das Mysterium der*

*Indentität der H. Geistes in Christus und den Christen—Eine Person in vielen Personen* (Munich—Vienna: Schöningh, [2]1967); idem, "El Espíritu y la iglesia," EstTrin 9 (1975) 385–399; K. Rahner, *The Spirit in the Church* (New York: Seabury, 1979); idem, "Do Not Stifle the Spirit," ThInvest 7:72-87; idem, "The Church as the Subject of the Sending of the Spirit," ThInvest 7:186-182; idem, "The Spirit that Is Over All Life," ThInvest 7:193-201; M. Semararo, "Per una ecclesiologia pneumatologica: Linee e orientamenti nel magistero della Chiesa cattolica," Nicol 13 (1986) 243–264; G. Wainwright, "The Holy Spirit in the Life of the Church," GrOrTR 27 (1982) 441–453; J.H. Wright, "The Church: Community of the Holy Spirit," TS 48 (1987) 25–44. [14]See n. 5 and H. Cazelles et al., "Saint Esprit," SuppDictBib (1991) 11:126-398. [15]See n. 6 and J.N.D. Kelly, *Early Christian Doctrines* (San Francisco: Harper, [5]1978). [16]J.D. Zizioulas, "The Teaching of the 2nd Ecumenical Council on the Holy Spirit in Historical and Ecumenical Perspective," in *Credo in Spiritum Sanctum* (n. 4) 1:29-54. [17]B. Pruche in SC 17bis, 41–57; text PG 32:68-217. [18]PG 32:620-621. [19]*On the Holy Spirit* 16— SC 17bis:384-386. [20]Ibid., chs. 27 and 29—SC 478–490, 500. [21]Bks. 1–4—PL 42:819-912/CCL 50:27-205/trans. E. Hill (Brooklyn, N.Y.: New City Press, 1990) 65–96. See Y. Congar (n. 4) 3:80-95; I. Chevalier, "La doctrine de S. Augustin sur l'Esprit Saint à propos du 'De Trinitate,'" RechTAncMéd 2 (1930) 365–387; 3 (1931) 5–19. [22]*De Trinitate* 15:21/CCL 50A: 517–519. [23]*De Trinitate* 6:5, 7—CCL 50:235; *Serm.* 71:33 in P.P. Verbraken, "Le sermon LXXI de saint Augustin sur le blasphème contre le Saint-Esprit," RBén 75 (1965) 54–108 at 102. See F. Genn, *Trinität und Amt nach Augustinus* (Einsiedeln: Johannes, 1986) 86–88; J. Ratzinger, "Der Heilige Geist als communio—Zum Verhältnis von Pneumatologie und Spiritualität bei Augustinus," in C. Heitmann and H. Mühlen, eds, *Erfahrung und Theologie des Heiligen Geistes* (Hamburg: Agentur des Rauhen Hauses—Munich: Kösel, 1974) 223–238. [24]See 83 texts/references in S. Tromp, *De Spiritu Sancto anima Corporis mystici. 2: Testimonia selecta a Patribus latinis* (Rome, 1952). After the patristic period there was the rise of the *Filioque* (q.v.) controversy. [25]ST 1a, qq. 27–43; see Congar (n. 4) 3:116-127. [26]ST 1a, q.38. [27]ST 1a, q.43, aa.6–8. [28]*Summa c. gentiles* 4:21-22; cf. *In Ioan.* 14, lect. 6 (1952–1960); G. Ferraro, "La pneumatologia di san Tommaso d'Aquino nel suo commento al quarto vangelo," Ang 66 (1989) 193–263. [29]ST 1–2ae, q.106, aa.1–2. [30]ST 2–2ae, qq. 171–182; see H.U. von Balthasar's edition, *Besondere Gnadengaben und die zwei Wege menschlichen Lebens* (Heidelberg and Graz-Vienna-Salzburg: Kerle—Pustet, 1954). [31]H. Wolter, in Jedin-Dolan 4:240-246. [32]Congar, Augustin 352–353. [33]*Enthusiasm. A Chapter in the History of Religion with Special Reference to the XVII and XVIII Centuries* (Oxford, 1950). [34]*The Mysteries of Christianity* (St. Louis, Mo.—London, 1946) 544–557. [35]*Divinum illud munus*—ASS 29 (1896–1897) 644–658/Carlen 2:409-417; see Antón 2:488-490; A. Durante, *La missione dello Spirito Sancto: Commento all'enciclica Divinum illud munus di Leo XIII* (Lucca: Ist. di S. Zita, 1975); A. Huerga, "L'Enciclica de León XIII sobre el Espíritu Santo," in *Credo in Spiritum Sanctum* (n. 4) 1:507-516. [36]ASS 28 (1895–1896) 708–739/Carlen 2:387-404. [37]AAS 35 (1943) 193–248/Carlen 4:37-62; see Antón 2:566-653. [38]Antón 2:573. [39]See, however, Y. Congar, *Le Pentecôte* (Paris, 1956). [40]ActaSyn 1/4:12-91/Alberigo Magistretti 3–70, 90–191, 209–225, 295–340 [41]H. Mühlen, "Das Verhältnis von Inkarnation und Kirche in den Aussagen des Vatikanum II," TGl 55 (1965) 270–289; S.J. Kilian, "The Holy Spirit in Christ and Christians," AmBenR 20 (1969) 99–121. [42]P. Mullins, "Pentecost and Ecclesiology in Vatican II's *Lumen gentium*," MilltownSt 31 (1993) 53–78; idem, "The Theology of Charisms: Vatican II and the New Catechism," MilltownSt 33 (1994) 123–162. [43]ST 2–2ae, q.1, a.9 ad 5; see F.A. Sullivan, *The Church We Believe In: One, Holy, Catholic and Apostolic* (Dublin: Gill and Macmillan, 1988) 5–7, 10. [44]*Dominum et Vivificantem*—AAS 78 (1986) 809–900; *Lasciatevi muovere dallo Spirito: Lettera enciclica sullo Spirito Santo di Giovanni Paolo II—Commenti di H.U. von Balthasar e di Y. Congar. Giornale di teologia* 167 (Brescia: Queriniana, 1986). [45]*Dominum et Vivificantem*, n. 25. [46]Ibid., n. 26. [47]Ibid., 27–48. [48]Ibid., 31. [49]Ibid., 55–60 and 64. [50]Ibid., 66. [51]Ibid., 67; cf. C.C. Mitchell, "The Holy Spirit's Intercessory Ministry," BiblSac 139 (1982) 230–242. [52]E.g., works in nn. 4, 7–9, 11–13; Mullins two arts. (n. 42). [53]"The Unknown Lying Beyond the Word," in *Creator Spirit* (n. 4) 105–116; see Y. Congar, *The Word and the Spirit* (London: Chapman, 1986).

## POLITY

Polity is a term used by Protestants to denote the way a Church or denomination structures its organization and carries out its practice. Thus there are three main polities: hierarchical (Anglican, Orthodox, and Roman Catholic); presbyterial (Presbyterian Churches); and congregational (Baptist, United Church of Christ, Disciples of Christ).

## POLYCARP, St. (ca. 69–155)

At the time of his martyrdom, Polycarp, bishop of Smyrna, claimed that he had been serving the Lord for 86 years. As his martyrdom has been usually dated 155 C.E., his life stretches right back to the age of the apostles;[1] recent studies give his death as 23 February 167.[2] Indeed, his own and the testimony of others point to his having known John and people who had seen the Lord; indeed, there is a tradition recalled by Tertullian that he was appointed bishop by John.[3] We know from Eusebius that he visited Rome about the controversy on the date of Easter (v. QUARTODECIMAN).[4] Apart from Eusebius we know Polycarp indirectly through the letter written to him by Ignatius (q.v.), his own letter to the Philippians, and the *Acts* of his martyrdom. There are several ecclesiological themes in these texts. The letter of Ignatius gives the younger man advice: to protect the unity of the Church; to spend time in prayer and preaching; to protect widows; to hold services more often and to beware of heretics. Polycarp's own letter to the Philippians shows extensive acquaintance with nearly all the books of the NT, but little with the OT. He warns them against avarice and shows the office of bishop to be a profoundly pastoral one in leading all to avoid sin and dedicate themselves to holiness. The structure of that Church is clearly that of presbyters and deacons, with a single bishop implied. While it is customary to comment on the pedestrian nature of this letter, one should not ignore its pastoral zeal, its concern for the recipients, its voice of encouragement and hope. The *Acts* of the martyrdom of Polycarp is the earliest account of Christian martyrdom outside the NT. It was clearly seen as having a significance apart from the Church of Smyrna, as copies were sent to other Churches. Notable themes are the following: there is an implied parallel with the death of the Lord—the Upper Room, riding on an ass, the prayer before his death; the martyrdom is according to the Gospel, not a matter of volunteering;[5] the Church at Smyrna greets the "catholic" Church, which here means "universal,"[6] though elsewhere it has the sense of "true" as against the heretics;[7] the date of his martyrdom will be celebrated as his birthday—an early indication of a (liturgical?) commemoration;[8] there is a sense of intercession for all the Churches.[9] These texts of, and about, Polycarp are an important witness to the life of the Church; the prominent place he is given by Eusebius[10] is further evidence of the significance of one who probably knew the apostles and lived into the middle of the 2nd century.

---

[1]On dating, cf. R.M. Grant, *The Apostolic Fathers*. Vol. 1 (London: Nelson, 1964) 64–71; S. Tugwell, *The Apostolic Fathers*. Outstanding Christian Thinkers (London: Chapman 1989) 129 and 134, n. 1. For texts, cf. M. Staniforth and A. Louth, *Early Christian Writings* (Harmondsworth UK: Penguin, [2]1987); W.R. Schoedel, *The Apostolic Fathers*. Vol. 5 (London: Nelson, 1967); M.S. Shepherd, LCC 1:121-158; F.X. Glimm, FC 1:131-163; B. Dahandschutter, "A 'New' Text of the Martyrdom of Polycarp," ETL 66 (1990) 391–394. [2]P. Brind' Amour, "Le date du martyr de Polycarpe (le 23 fév. 167)," AnBoll 98 (1980) 456–462. [3]*De praescript. haer.* 32:2. [4]*Eccl. hist.* 5:24, 8. [5]*Martyrdom* 1:1-2, 1; 4:1; cf. *Ad Phil.* 8:2. [6]*Martyrdom* preface. and 19:2. [7]Ibid., 16:2; 23:2. [8]Ibid., 18:3. [9]Ibid., 5:1; 8:1; [10]*Hist. eccl.* 4:14, 6–7; 5:20, 7; 5:24:16.

## POOR

There are two interrelated issues in ecclesiology under the word "poor": the poverty that the Church should practice; the Church's attitude to the poor. Both are crucial for several reasons: they will stake out areas of reform for the Church; they will provide a framework in which viable liberation theologies (q.v.) can be worked out; they move the issue of evangelical poverty away from a merely personal matter to structures and the working of institutions in the Church; they indicate for us one of the "signs of the times" (GS 4—q.v.) and hence a source for theological reflection (*locus theologicus*, v. THEOLOGICAL SOURCES).

Given the importance of the topic, it would seem to be particularly important that its biblical basis be carefully established. Yet in the post-Vatican II literature there is no unanimity about the meaning, or more seriously the implications, of the biblical message. The reasons are not hard to find: given the urgency, and the very challenging nature of the call to poverty, it is natural that there will be both a maximalist and a minimalist approach to key texts, as well as partial readings of very difficult and nuanced teaching in the Bible. Due account must be taken of the socio-economic picture of the Eastern Mediterranean in NT times, in which "rich" very often referred to an attitude of greed rather than the amount of goods accumulated by or for a person. Since land and other goods were limited, there could be a presumption that wealth was acquired or inherited at the expense of others. In this view "poor" would refer to the socially impotent.[1]

Behind the NT attitudes lies the picture of the OT *anâwîm*.[2] The spirituality of poverty goes back to the 7th-century Zephaniah (cf. 3:12-13), with the two figurative personages, Job and the Servant of the Lord (Isa 42:1-9 [-7?]; 49:1-6; 50:4-11 [-9?]; 52:13–53:12).[3] The poor were less a social class than a category of persons who placed their full trust in the Lord. Poverty provided an ideal condition in which humility and faith could grow into a mystique, so that in the NT the kingdom was fruitfully proclaimed to those disposed to listen, mostly the humble ones, the poor of the Lord.[4] Jesus' attitude reflected not only God's predilection for the poor but his concern with the salvation of the rich, whose very abundance of possessions made their salvation ambivalent.[5] However, we do not find Jesus presented in the NT tradition as a social reformer: he did not condemn riches as such, but warned of their danger. Furthermore, he had friends and disciples of substantial means: women disciples who cared for his and the apostles' needs (Luke 8:1-3); Mary, who poured ointment worth a year's wages on his feet (John 12:3-5); Nicodemus, who provided 100 pounds of spices to anoint Jesus' dead body (John 19:39); Joseph, who owned a new tomb (Matt 27:60). Jesus associated, and had table-fellowship, with the rich (tax collectors, as well as other "sinners," Matt 9:11par). He was nonetheless presented as living austerely, with no place to lay his head (Matt 8:20) and demanding renunciation from his followers (Luke 14:33). Luke had a special interest in the poor and the weak, and in several places he gave indicators of Jesus' position: Jesus' background was shown to comprising *anâwîm* figures (Zechariah, Elizabeth, shepherds, Simeon and Anna—Luke 1–2); he praised the generosity of the widow (21:1-4); he warned against a heart divided between God and wealth, advising that wealth be used in such a way as to ensure one's salvation (Luke 16:9, 11, 13; 12:16-21); he gave unconditional blessings to the poor and woes to the rich and self-satisfied (Luke 6:20-26); but it is important to note in the case of Zechariah that Jesus set the poor of Jericho free by converting the tax collector (cf. Luke 19:1-10). In the Synoptic tradition we have a triangle of the poor, little ones and disciples all with faith in Jesus.[6] This complexity of the picture of Jesus and his ministry arises from his enigmatic proclamation of the kingdom (q.v.). The kingdom is a transformation of human values; it is at the same time good news especially for the poor. When we ask who the poor in the Gospels were, we can describe them as those materially destitute and those who were outcasts (like Samaritans and rich tax collectors); the poor were, and still are, the "have nots," and the "are nots." We must beware of reducing the full biblical teaching to the few favorite texts of liberation theology: the Exodus, in which God hears the cry of the poor (Exod 3:7; cc. 14-15), prophetic denunciations of injustice, and the judgment scene in Matt 25:31-46. We must also avoid a Reductionist Christology and soteriology which would see the death of Jesus solely, or even primarily, as the consequence of his identification with the situation of the poor or powerless. There is an eschatological dimension to the teaching and practice of the NT on poverty that must be integrated into our understanding of the poor and of poverty.[7]

In Acts and Paul there is an insistence on the fact that nobody should be in need (Acts 4:34); there is to be a sharing with the poor at the Eucharist (1 Cor 11:22); the Corinthians, most of whom were not wealthy or powerful, were most receptive to God's call (1 Cor 1:26); Paul wished to express fellowship with the Jerusalem Church through the collection he arranged for the needy in Jerusalem (1 Cor 16:1-4; 2 Cor 8; Rom 15:30-31). We find a new teaching and a new set of values being proposed to the early Church (cf. Gal 3:28; 1 Cor 7:22; 12:13).[8] Paul gives as a model his own indifference to riches or poverty (Phil 4:9-12).

When we move from NT times into the patristic period, the ambiguity of wealth does not lessen. Thus preaching the good news to the poor is in the early centuries seen more as a messianic sign than as a call to serve the socially poor.[9] From the beginning the patristic writers emphasize almsgiving as a duty incumbent on all. However, it is at times donor-oriented, seen as a spiritual benefit for the giver, with some depersonalization of the actual poor people.[10] Thus an early text of Hermas (q.v.) proposes that the rich support the poor and the poor serve the rich by their prayers: "Both fulfill their function in this way: The poor man makes intercession—these are his riches—and gives back to the Lord who supplied him; in the same way the rich man unhesitatingly puts the riches he has received from the Lord at the disposal of the poor. This is a great and acceptable work in the sight of the Lord."[11] However, the record of the Church in the centuries leading up to the Middle Ages is impressive: there was an infrastructure of service around the bishop or in the parish; monasteries were centers where there was genuine caring for the poor. From the end of the 11th century to the middle of the 14th we find a double activity: spiritual movements, often predominantly lay, which sought an evangelical poverty; a new awareness of the gospel demand of care for the poor.[12] The most successful and durable of these were the mendicant orders, especially the Fransciscans.[13] After the Reformation hundreds of congregations of priests, brothers, sisters, and laity were founded to take care of the poor in their multifaceted needs. They provided medical, social, and educational means before these became organized by state agencies, and still do today in many countries where there continues to be poverty of any kind. Added to that, there is the uncountable instances of neighborly help and charitable assistance given by Christians to one another. Two points need to be made. The definition of the poor person is not just one who is destitute enough to have to beg, but a person who cannot cope without help from others. Second, in all the imposing history of the Church's care for the poor, there is little realization of the structural causes of poverty inbuilt into various societies. For this latter insight in the Church we have to await the last hundred years of social teaching, during which the awareness of social justice and the causes of poverty have continually grown.[14]

Vatican II made some important statements on poverty, inspired by, among others, Cardinal Lercaro.[15] The most significant is LG 8. It treats firstly of Christ's poverty, and then of his attitude to the poor: "Just as Christ carried out the work of redemption in poverty and persecution, so the Church is called to follow along the same way in order that it may communicate to humanity the fruits of salvation." The council then presents the *kenôsis* of Christ (Phil 2:6-7; 2 Cor 8:9) as the radical self-emptying and poverty of Christ himself. The council concludes that the Church likewise is "not set up to seek earthly glory, but to spread humility and self-denial." Next the text cites two passages illustrative of the mission of Christ to the poor: Luke 4:18, the fulfillment of the messianic prophecy (Isa 61:1-2; 58:6); the salvation brought to the house of Zacchaeus (Luke 19:10). It then states: "In the same way the Church surrounds with love all who are afflicted with human infirmity, indeed in the poor and suffering it recognizes the face of its poor and suffering founder, it endeavors to relieve their need and in them it strives to serve Christ." Noteworthy here is the wide sense of poor; it is not limited to social deprivation.

Following the council the major focus shifts to Latin America. Drawing on the inspiration of the council, the Conference of Latin American Bishops (CELAM) at their second meeting at Medellín (1968) made an important statement stressing solidarity with the poor.[16] This represents a major turning point from the optimism of the 1960s with their stress on development (q.v.). In the years between Medellín and the 3rd CELAM Conference at Puebla (1979), the theology of liberation (q.v.) developed. It was inspired by, and in dialogue (occasionally conflictual) with, the political theology of J.B. Metz, J. Moltmann, and other European theologians. Puebla deepened and gave standing to the insights of the preceding decade and produced its highly influential document on "The Preferential Option for the Poor and Youth." [17] The fourth CELAM, at Santo Domingo (1992), continued some of the themes of Puebla.[18]

In the years immediately preceding and following Puebla, there has been substantive writing on the Church's mission to the poor.[19] The question is not only for Christian charity or pastoral strategy but concerns the very nature of the Church. Can we speak of a kenotic Church (*kenôsis,* self emptying—q.v.)? The text in LG 8 cited above points in that direction, though a radical pessimism about the Church must not be taken on board from Lutheran sources.[20] In another way we should consider the Cross as central for the intelligibility of the Church: the Church is the *Kreuzgemeinde*—community of the Cross.[21] G. O'Collins observes: "A genuine theology of the cross would call into question much talk about a 'successful' church, a 'well-run' diocese, a 'flourishing' congregation, a parish 'in good shape.' The Christian community in its different groupings should be reminded of the principle 'power made perfect in weakness' (cf. 2 Cor 12:9)."[22] The Church lives under the shadow of the Cross and in its power even while already signs of resurrection are to be seen breaking through in its structures and the lives of its members.

In its living of poverty and its care for the poor, the Church has the eschatological sign of the vowed life (LG 44; PC 13; v. RELIGIOUS LIFE).[23] Poverty, freely chosen, enhances rather than destroys Christian and psychological maturity.[24]

The Church and the Poor, the Church and Poverty are clearly major themes for ecclesiology, also in the East.[25] But there is not yet agreement whether poverty (and liberation) are theologies in the proper sense of the word, thus affecting many aspects of dogmatics and morality, including ecclesiology. Latin American theologians speak about the hermeneutics of the poor: the poor have a new way of reading the Scriptures; the Church must not only serve the poor; it needs to be enlightened by the poor about profound riches of revelation and theology; though the Church evangelizes the poor, in a most profound sense the whole Church needs to be evangelized by the poor.[26] Another alternative, not less exciting, is that we are living through a time of doctrinal development in the whole area of poverty and the poor, a theme which henceforth must have its own special place in ecclesiology.

[1]B.J. Malina, "Wealth and Poverty in the New Testament and Its World," Interp 41 (1987) 354–367; see A. de la Fuente, "El problema de la pobreza en la Biblia," RET 49 (1989) 431–448; M. Hengel, *Property and Riches in the Early Church: Aspects of a Social History of Early Christianity* (Philadelphia: Fortress, 1974). [2]E. Bammel, "Ptôchos," TDNT 6:885–915; S. Légasse, "Pauvreté chrétienne. 1.—Écriture," DSpir 12:614-634; L. Roy, "Poor," DBT

436–438; T.R. Hobbs, "Reflections on 'The Poor' and the Old Testament," ExpTim 100 (1988–1989) 291–294. [3]A. Gelin, *Les pauvres de Yahwé* (Paris, 1953). [4]L. Sabourin, "'Evangelise the Poor' (Lk 4:18)," RelStB 1 (1981) 101–109; cf. J. Dupont, *Les béatitudes.* 3 vols. (Paris, 1954–1973); A. O'Leary, "The Role of Possessions in the Journey Narrative of Luke 9:51–19:27," MilltownSt 28 (1991) 41–60; R.F. O'Toole, "Poverty and Wealth in Luke-Acts," ChicSt 16 (1991) 29–41. [5]Sabourin (n. 4) 104; cf. A. de la Fuente, "El problema de la pobreza en la biblia," RES 49 (1989) 431–448; D. Mealand, *Poverty and Expectation in the Gospels* (London: SPCK, 1980). [6]E. Herando García, "Los pobres y la palabra de Dios en el Nuevo Testamento," Burgense 22 (1981) 9–43 at 20. [7]M. Hengel (n. 1); A. Tosato, "Cristianesimo e capitalismo: il problema esegetico di alcuni passi evangelici," RivBib 35 (1987) 465–476; J.M.R. Tillard, "Le propos de pauvreté et l'exigence évangélique," NRT 100 (1978) 359–372. [8]A. Böckmann, "What Does the New Testament Say About the Church's Attitude to the Poor?," Conc 104 (1977) 36–47. [9]E. Peretto, *"Evangelizare pauperibus* (Lc 4, 18; 7, 22–23) nella lettura patristica dei secoli 11–111," AugR 17 (1977) 71–100; A. Solignac, "Pauvreté chrétienne. 11—Pères de l'Église et moines des origines," DSpir 12:634-647. [10]B. Ramsey, "Almsgiving in the Latin Church: The Later Fourth and Early Fifth Centuries," TS 43 (1982) 226–259 at 251–255; cf. L.Wm. Countryman, *The Rich Christian in the Church of the Early Empire: Contradictions and Accommodations* (New York—Toronto, 1980); R.H. Weaver, "Wealth and Poverty in the Early Church," Interp 41 (1987) 368–381. [11]*Simil.* 2:7 (51). [12]M. Mollat, "Poverty and Service of the Poor in the History of the Church," Conc 104 (1977) 48–55. [13]W. Hellmann, "Poverty: the Fransciscan Way to God," TDig 22 (1974) 339–345; M. Mollat, "Pauvreté chrétienne. 111.—Moyen âge," DSpir 12:647-658; M. Mollat, ed. *Études sur l'histoire de la pauvreté. Moyen Âge—XVIe siècle.* 2 vols. (Paris: Sorbonne, 1974). A. Rotzetter, "Franz von Assisi und die Kirche der Armen," GeistL 56 (1983) 252–261. [14]J.M.R. Tillard, "Pauvreté chrétienne. IV.—Vingtième siècle," DSpir 12:658-689. [15]M.-D. Chenu, "Vatican II and the Church of the Poor," Conc 104 (1977) 56–61; J. Dupont, "L'Église et la pauvreté," in Baraúna-Congar, L'Église 2:339-372; AA.VV. *Église et pauvreté.* US 57 (Paris: Cerf, 1965). [16]A.T. Hennelly, ed., *Liberation Theology: A Documentary History* (New York: Orbis, 1990) 114–119; cf. Met. Geevarghese Mar Osthathios, "Solidarity with the Poor, but How?," IndTS 18 (1981) 323–331. [17]*Puebla: Evangelization at Present and the Future of Latin America.* "Conclusions." Official English Edition (Slough UK: St. Paul— London: CIIR, 1980; Washington, D.C.: National Conference of Catholic Bishops, 1979) 178–186; Hennelly (n. 16) 253–258. Cf. J.-Y. Calvez, "L'option préférentielle pour les pauvres, dans l'Église, récemment," VieCons 59 (1987) 269–284; F. Oz. de Urtaran, "La opción por los pobres. Un poco de historia," Lumen 36 (1987) 216–246; F. Pastor, "De optione praeferentiali pro pauperibus iuxta hodiernum magisterium Ecclesiae," Periodica 77 (1988) 195–217. [18] Numbers 161, 167, 169, 178–180, 196; see 85, 90, 95. [19]Concilium 104 (1977); D.S. Amalorpavadass, "The Poor with No Voice and No Power," Conc 146 (1981) 45–52; J. de Santa Ana, ed., *Towards a Church of the Poor* (Geneva: WCC, 1979); F. Houtart, "The Global Aspects of Dependence and Oppression," Conc 144 (1981) 3–10; E. Granger, "Ceux qui manquent à l'Église," LumièreV 35/177 (1986) 5–19; S. Maggiolini, "Les pauvres et les nouveaux pauvres," NRT 106 (1984) 537–548; J. O'Brien, "Theologians on the Side of the Poor," IrTQ 55 (1989) 59–70; K. Rahner, "The Unreadiness of the Church's Members to Accept Poverty," ThInvest 14:270-279; idem, "On the Theology of Poverty," ThInvest 8:168-214; idem, "Reflections on the Theology of Renunciation," ThInvest 3:47-57. [20]H. Urs von Balthasar, "Kenose (de l'Église)," DSpir 8:1705-1711. [21]S. Cipriani, "'Teologia crucis' ed ecumenismo," Asp 27 (1980) 355–358; P. Delhaye, "Il mistero della croce nei testi del Vaticano II," *La sapienza della croce oggi.* Atti del congresso internazionale Roma 13/18 ottobre 1975. 2 vols. (Turin: Elle Di Ci—Leumann, 1975) 1:332-343; M.P. Green, "The Meaning of Cross-Bearing," BiblSac 140 (1983) 117–133; J. Moltmann, "Ecumenismo sotto la croce," *La sapienza . . .* 1:526-537; L. Sartori, "La croce principio di vera riforma ecclesiale e di dialogo ecumenico," *La sapienza . . .* 1:485-507.  [22]"Towards a Theology of the Cross," in G. O'Collins et al. *The Cross Today: An Evaluation of Current Theological Reflection on the Cross of Christ* (Rome—Sydney: Dwyer, 1977) 30–47 at 46–47.  [23]S. Decloux, "Pauvreté chrétienne et pauvreté religieuse," VieCons 62 (1990) 315–330; G.R. Grosh, "Models of Poverty," RevRel 45 (1986) 119–127; B. Ramsey, "The Centre of Religious Poverty," RevRel 42 (1983) 534–544.  [24]W. Au, "Christian Poverty and Psychological Development," ChicSt 28 (1989) 175–189.  [25]V. Harrison, "Poverty in the Orthodox Church," SVlad 34 (1990) 15–47.  [26]I. Berten, "Les pauvres à l'étroit dans l'ecclésiologie romaine," LumièreV 35/177 (1986) 75–89 = TDig 34 (1987) 154–158; P. Frostin, "The Hermeneutics of the Poor—The Epistemological 'Break' in Third World Theologies," StTheol 39 (1985) 127–150 = TDig 34 (1987) 114–115; Communio (French) 11/5 (1986) 1–85.

## POPES

The word pope is derived ultimately from the Greek *papas/pappas,* a child's word for father. It was used of bishops from the 3rd century but reserved to the bishop of Rome from the 6th century. It is by far the most common title for the bishop of that city (v. PAPAL TITLES).

In early centuries the bishop of Rome was elected like other bishops, that is, by the clergy with the approval of the people of the diocese and with the endorsement of neighboring bishops who agreed to consecrate or ordain him. From the 4th to the 11th centuries temporal rulers became more involved. In the 11th century we see the beginning of the papal conclave, or meeting of cardinals (q.v.), to elect the pope. Recent revisions in the method of electing popes were made by Pius XII (1945), John XXIII (1962), and Paul VI (1975).[1] The practice of the pope taking a new name is ancient: the first pope to do so was Mercurius, who changed this name of a Roman god for John II (533); the second was Octavian, who become John XII (955); after that it became common, and later customary.

In the history of the papacy there have been over 30 anti-popes, i.e., invalid and/or rival claimants to the bishopric of Rome. The number of popes is not exactly agreed upon among scholars, in view of the difficulty of determining the exact status of the early bishops of Rome. A major revision was made in the list of popes for the *Annuario pontificio* in 1947,[2] and there has been significant scholarly enquiry since.[3] It is customary to call John Paul II (pope from 1978) the 263rd pope.

During the long history of the papacy there have been plenty of scandals and numerous unworthy popes, but the picture is at times painted in overly dark colors.[4] An argument can be made for the divine insti-tution of the Church in that it has survived despite very unworthy occupants of the See of Peter. On the other hand, over 70 popes are saints, and eight have been named blessed. In ecclesiology the papacy is treated under several heads, viz., Papal Primacy (q.v.), Infallibility (q.v.), Vatican I (q.v.), Vatican II (q.v.). (See also articles cross-referenced in these entries.)

[1]J.H. Provost, in Coriden, C.I.C. 270–271.  [2]A. Mercati, "The New List of Popes," MedSt 9 (1947) 71–80.  [3]J.N.D. Kelly, *The Oxford Dictionary of Popes* (Oxford: UP, 1986).  [4]Thus P. de Rosa, *Vicars of Christ: The Dark Side of the Papacy* (London: Bantham Press, 1988—Corgi Books, 1989)

## POPULAR RELIGIOSITY, CHRISTIAN

Until recent decades there was not a wide academic interest in popular religiosity, also called "popular piety," "popular faith." For the ecclesiologist it was a fringe manifestation of the Church. In Latin America it was seen as channeling people away from the *lucha* or struggle for liberation (v. LIBERATION THEOLOGIES). Since the Latin American Bishops Conferences (CELAM) at Medellín, and more particularly Puebla, followed by Santo Domingo, popular religiosity has been seen as much more central to, indeed a component of, the indigenous Christianity of Latin America, and a serious re-evaluation has taken place. Since then an extensive literature has grown up, especially in the Romance languages.[1] Serious theological studies are now appearing.[2]

Popular religiosity has a long history in Christianity. It is often found at the intersection of the newly embraced faith and a well-rooted indigenous culture. It can then take on characteristics that last for many centuries. Such is the popular religiosity that is found in many places in Latin America, in Africa, and in Asia, especially the Philippines. Or it may arise from a religious movement. In the Middle Ages the Benedictines, particularly Cluny, fostered devotions to saints, to the names of Jesus and Mary, and Masses for the dead. Shortly afterwards we have the Franciscan movement (v. FRANCIS OF ASSISI), a profound spiritual renewal which led to the popularization of devotions to the passion of Christ, the stations of the cross, the crib. In an age where liturgy, apart from great cathedral occasions, was becoming more and more remote and cerebral, popular devotions touched people in their affectivity and drew them to a faith commitment through a wide variety of symbols.[3]

Popular religiosity is difficult to define; depending on the stance of the observer one or more of the following will seem the most important: sociological, anthropological, psychological, cultural, ethnological, folkloristic, or religious. At the 1974 Synod of Bishops, Cardinal E. Pironio gave a broad, useful description: "The way in which Christianity is incarnated in different cultures and ethnic states, is lived out, and is manifested in the people."[4]

Its essential characteristics can be outlined.[5] It is "popular" not so much as contradistinguished from words like cultivated, critical, official, uncommon, mature, elite, etc., but rather in the sense of the Latin languages *(populaire, popular, popolare)* where it means "of the people." As such it is very often associated with the poor and the marginalized, and it appeals to many whose formal religious education may in some respects be shallow. But there is another meaning of "people" which is a whole nation with a common culture and a common history. Popular religiosity is intuitive, symbolic, and imaginative; it is mystical in the sense of stretching religious experience beyond the ordinary; it is festive, theatrical, spontaneous, and celebratory; it is unsystematic and often unarticulated; above all, it is communal, involving a group of people who gather and who are bound together by some bond, e.g., confraternity, guild, association, village, or town dwellings. Sometimes it is also political in keeping alive a people's identity in the struggle for dignity or liberty.[6] Though popular religiosity marks a departure from daily occupations and problems, it is not to be too easily labeled escapist; penance and conversion are very marked, especially in connections with shrines.

G. Mattai outlines the wide variety of manifestations associated with popular religiosity: magical or superstitious practices or beliefs, some unrelated to Christian rites, e.g., sorcery, evil eye; elaborate celebrations of the Virgin or saints, often with prolonged festivities; pilgrimages to sanctuaries; observances and worship that are quasi-sacramental, especially to celebrate rites of passage; extraliturgical cult of persons who are dead or still living, to whom are attributed special powers.[7] The symbols of popular religion can be seen as consisting of three kinds: need-based for human and social needs; socio-structural for the construction and maintenance of the community; transcendent and oriented to God.[8]

Popular religiosity holds in tension two vital truths: God and the saints are far beyond us in their holiness; they are, however, close, powerful, and benevolent in the presence of human misery. Trusting, confident prayer is generally evident in popular religiosity. Though some people with very little relationship to institutional Church values such as Sunday Mass may be enthusiastic about popular devotions, a negative judgment is not necessarily opportune. Popular religiosity addresses people where they are; the pastoral challenge is to bring them more deeply into the life of the Church. From an ecclesiological point of view, it is to follow the position taken up by Vatican II: the Church "takes nothing away from the temporal well-being of any people. On the contrary, it takes up and encourages the riches,

resources, and customs of people insofar as they are good; and in taking them up it purifies, strengthens and raises them up" (LG 13). One of the areas that can need purification is where a certain magical mentality is often present whenever there is an attempt to manipulate God by some specific religious or other practice; except for the sacraments, we can never expect certain or automatic responses to prayers or rites. The area of healing in popular religion can be ambiguous, and needs to be discerned on a case by case basis.

In judging popular religiosity we have, of course, to be alert to erroneous elements such as the blasphemous idea that some mercy can be obtained through Mary which Jesus would refuse. But popular religiosity is extremely conservative, and deviant emphases cannot always be corrected according to critical theological norms. Moreover, in some places popular religiosity is a lay manifestation and in practice will not tolerate clerical interference; even if a spectacle calls for some negative evaluation, it may thus not be very open to correction. But a smudged window can let in a lot of light. Popular religiosity almost always has a profound openness to the transcendent. Its stubborn perseverance in so many places may give significant opportunity for evangelization.[9]

In the past the attitude of Church authority has varied: it has promoted popular religiosity; it has also tolerated, condemned, or sought to control it. An interesting example of such control has been the substitution of a Christian meaning for a pagan one; thus sacred wells were often dedicated to a saint so that it would be through Christian intercession that a cure would be sought. After Trent there was a reaction by many pastors against popular manifestations.

At Vatican II the subject was not seriously studied, though two articles of the Constitution on the Liturgy are significant (SC 12–13). The first states that "the spiritual life has more to it than sharing in the liturgy." The second praises popular devotions provided that they conform to Church law; they should also be adapted to liturgical seasons. However, after the council, often through excessive multiplication of Masses, there has been a widespread demise of devotional life.[10] Historically, there have been tensions between liturgy and devotional life; there should not be conflict, for both are necessary.[11]

The attitude of the universal and local magisterium has shown great development since Vatican II.[12] Already at the Conference of Latin American Bishops (CELAM) at Medellín (1968) there were positive statements about popular religiosity.[13] But it was Paul VI in his apostolic exhortation on evangelization who firmly charted the way for popular religiosity.[14] He notes the ambiguity and error that can be present in popular religiosity, but then goes on to indicate the great values that it can enshrine: "It may be productive of great good. For it does indicate a certain thirst for God such as only those who are simple and poor in spirit can experience. . . . It can develop in the inmost depths of a person habits of virtue rarely to be found otherwise in the same degree, such as patience, acceptance of the Cross in daily life, detachment, openness to others and a spirit of ready service." Paul VI prefers to call it "popular piety" or "the religion of the people" rather than "religiosity." He strongly emphasizes its potential for evangelization.

The CELAM meeting at Puebla reiterated the papal teaching and developed a pastorale: its values are acknowledged, and various indications are given to foster it and to keep it healthily integrated in the Church.[15] After Puebla the post-synodal exhortation of Pope John Paul II on catechesis[16] spoke of the value of prayers and practices that may have to be purified but have the potential to open people out to deeper mysteries of the faith.

The Santo Domingo meeting of CELAM dealt briefly with popular religiosity: it is multiplying in the Church and is an inculturation of faith; it has alien elements that may need purification; it is to be oriented towards conversion.[17]

Popular religiosity belongs to the integral life of the Church. Though it has ambiguities, it can touch people in their hearts, at the core of their being, where the encounter with God can take place. Though not completely absent in Protestantism, it is most fully manifest in both the Orthodox and Catholic Churches. In an age which seeks spirituality through such movements as New Age (v. MOVEMENTS, NON-CHRISTIAN), the Church has in popular religiosity great riches from which to draw in offering people a privileged means of experiencing the great truth of the Communion of Saints (q.v.).

[1]Bibliog., B.M. Bosatra, "Recenti miscellanee sulla religiosità popolare," ScuolC 110 (1982) 67–84, 300–313, 451–472; 11 (1983) 450–475; 113 (1985) 546–547; 115 (1987) 48–83; 117 (1989) 487–525; See AA.VV., *Religiosidad popular.* Materiales 13 (Salamanca: Sígueme, 1976); S. Galilea, "Popular Christian Religiosity," EncycRel 11:440-442; G. Mattai, "Religiosità popolare," NDizSpir 1316–1331 (extensive bibliog.); Conc 186 (1986); MaisD 122 (1975). [2]F. Bolgiani, "Religione popolare," AugR 21 (1981) 7–75; S. Galilea, *The Challenge of Popular Religiosity* (Manila, 1983); M.-M. Labourdette, "Religion populaire et sainteté," RThom 82 (1982) 120–149; cf. AA.VV. *Foi populaire, foi savante.* Cogitatio fidei 87 (Paris: Cerf, 1976). [3]R. and C. Brook, *Popular Religion in the Middle Ages* (London: Thames & Hudson, 1984); E. Delaruelle, *La piété populaire au moyen-âge* (Turin: Erasmo, 1980). [4]Cited G. Agostino, "Pietà popolare," NDizMar 1111–1122 at 1113. [5]G. Thils, "La 'religion populaire': approches, définition," RTLv 8 (1977) 198–210; L. Maldonado, "Popular Religion: Its Dimensions, Levels and Types," *Sedos Bulletin* (Rome) 20 (1988) 317–324. [6]A.J. Büntig, "Catolicismo popular y aporte a la liberación," in *Religiosidad popular* (n. 1) 149–157. [7]Mattai (n. 1) 1318. [8]M. Amaladoss,

"Popular Religion: Some Questions," VYoti 53 (1989) 357–369. [9]"Evangelization and Popular Religiosity," in *Sedos* (Rome) 21/5 (1989) 144–182. [10]B. Fischer, "Relation entre liturgie et piété populaire après Vatican II," MaisD 170 (1987) 91–101; S. Rosso, "Religiosità popolare," EphLtg 105 (1991) 77–84. [11]B. Neunheuser, "Liturgia e pietà popolare," Notitiae 260 (1988) 210–217; B. Carra de Vaux Saint-Cyr, "Religion populaire et mutations liturgiques," MaisD 125 (1976) 110–126. [12]A. Verwilghen, "La religiosité populaire dans les documents du Magistère," NRT 109 (1078) 521–539; see J. Thornhill, "Popular Religion and Post-Conciliar Catholicism," AustralCR 69/1 (1992) 3–13. [13]*The Church in the Present-Day Transformation of Latin America in the Light of the Council.* 2 vols. (Bogotá, 1970–1973). [14]*Evangelii nuntiandi* 48—AAS 68 (1976) 37–38/Flannery 2:731-732. [15]CELAM, Puebla: Evangelization at Present and in the Future of Latin America. Conclusions (Washington, D.C.: Conference of Catholic Bishops, 1979—Slough UK: St. Paul, 1980) nn. 444–469, 910–915, 959–963. [16]*Catechesi tradendae* n. 54—AAS 71 (1979) 1321–1322/Flannery 2:795. [17] Articles 18, 36, 38, 39, 53, 240.

## PRAGMATIC SANCTIONS

"Pragmatic Sanction" was originally a term limiting the powers of a prince. After Constantinople II (q.v.) the emperor Justinian in 554 rewarded Pope Vigilius with a Pragmatic Sanction which gave much of Italy and various privileges to the Church.[1] The Pragmatic Sanction of Bourges is also significant in ecclesiology.[2] French clergy issued it on 7 July 1438 during the Council of Basle (q.v.). It stated the right of the French Church to administer its temporal property independently of the pope and rejected papal appointments to vacant benefices. It was an early form of Gallicanism (q.v.), and it lasted until the Concordat of Bologna in 1516.

[1]OxDPopes 62–63. [2]Text—S.Z. Ehler and J.B. Morall, eds., *Church and State Throughout the Centuries* (London, 1954) 112–121; R. Hedde, "Pragmatique sanction II," DTC 12:2781-2786.

## PREACHING

Since Vatican II an extensive literature has built up on preaching.[1] But concern with preaching is nothing new in the Church. The ministry of Jesus himself and the one he committed to his apostles was to preach and heal (Mark 1:15; Matt 10:7-8; 28:19; Mark 16:15-18). In the NT there is much about various forms of teaching (v. TEACHERS). Provided we do not make the distinction too binding, it is possible to speak about two main forms of discourse: proclamation *(kerugma)* and instruction *(didaskalia)*. The former is aimed at announcing the good news of Jesus and invites faith and conversion; the latter is information about the message, aimed at increasing knowledge and understanding of the mystery. Again proclamation was the chief but not exclusive aim of the catechumenate (q.v.) leading to baptism; catechesis was the mystagogia that follows on the reception of the sacrament. This broad distinction is carried over in patristic times. But there are other forms also based on the NT that cannot be ignored, e.g., exhortation and rebuke.

As early as the *Didachê* (q.v.),[2] Justin (q.v.),[3] and the *Apostolic Tradition* (q.v.),[4] we have evidence of regular preaching or instruction also at liturgical assemblies. In the early Church, as in the Jewish synagogue (Luke 4:16-21), preaching was linked to the reading of Scripture. Indeed, the most common form in which the teaching of the Fathers (q.v.) comes to us is in commentaries on Scripture or homilies based on the Bible. This preaching operated in various ways. Preachers like Origen carefully considered their audience.[5] They also made varied use of Scripture. Though they did seek what we would call the literal meaning, viz., the sense intended by the sacred writer, they were on the whole much more concerned with the spiritual meaning, which came to life through the Holy Spirit. Throughout the patristic era we find extensive use of allegory and all the techniques of rhetoric in service of the Word. In this first millennium, preaching was the main way in which the bishop exercised his pastoral office.

In the Middle Ages the friars were most of the important bearers of the Word.[6] Usually better educated than the parish clergy, and often stricter in their Christian observance, they made a deep impression, though they stirred up hostility on the part of bishops by reason of their papal exemption (q.v.) and resentment on the part of the parochial clergy who saw them as rivals. Though they sometimes collaborated with the parish clergy, the friars were not always fully sensitive in the areas which the secular clergy regarded as parochial. On the whole, popes and councils sided with the friars on account of the fruits they saw through their preaching and ministrations.

Medieval councils in reaction to abuses, ignorance, and decadence emphasized preaching; the fact that preaching so often appears in local synods and councils is an indication that it was not being done effectively. Some general councils made strong recommendations: Lateran IV (1215—q.v.),[7] Vienne (1311–1312 —q.v.),[8] Constance (1414–1418—q.v.) against Wycliffe and Huss,[9] and Lateran V (q.v.).[10] The Council of Trent (q.v.) in one of its early sessions gave an elaborate decree on preaching[11] and later spoke of the obligations of bishops in this regard;[12] it pronounced specifically about preaching on the Mass.[13]

The focus of the preaching suggested by the decrees of these councils was generally in the area of instruction and morals. There was some condemnation of preaching of worthless ideas, over-concentration on miracles rather than on teaching of the Church. Preaching was seen as a important element in the reform of the Church. The content was variously described, very often as the Word of God. But one does not get the impression that medieval sermons arose out of the

Word to the same degree as did patristic preaching. The councils of Lateran V and Trent insist on the upright behavior and exemplary life that preachers should live.

After Trent there was an improvement in preaching,[14] with both old orders and new ones, such as the Jesuits, being prominent in answering the need.[15] The *Catechism of the Council of Trent* (v. CATECHISMS and TRENT) was designed to help parish priests with their preaching. The Jesuits continued to emphasize preaching alongside their new apostolate of education, and other new congregations[16] like the Redemptorists, Passionists, and the Congregation of the Mission (Vincentians), also devoted themselves to extensive preaching in both rural and urban areas. They developed in time the parish mission, a week or more of intensive preaching and renewal. The style tended to be evangelistic, calling for conversion.

In the decades preceding Vatican II there was frequent preaching at Mass, but this was not everywhere observed. Devotions, novenas, other pious exercises and shrines often gave opportunity for preaching.

Vatican II laid great emphasis on preaching: it expounded a theology of the Word; it laid down norms about preaching. It set up the example of Christ and the apostles who preached the Word (LG 5, 19; DV 7, 9–10, 17; AG 1, 8; UR 2; CD 2). According to the council's teaching, the Church has the duty of preaching the gospel (DH 13; GS 43). It is a primary duty of bishops and priests (LG 24–25; CD 2; PO 2, 4–5). It is within the context of the Eucharist, "source and summit of the Christian life," (LG 11) that preaching finds its most profound meaning. From proclamation people come to faith, faith leads to sacraments, and sacraments lead to active charity (SC 9; PO 2; AG 13–14).

A very significant element of conciliar teaching is the importance of the homily, which is part of the liturgical event (SC 35 § 2, 52), a point reiterated in the reformed *Roman Missal*[17] and made obligatory in the *Code of Canon Law* (CIC 767; see 528, 836). The *Missal* and *Code* are not very explicit about the nature of the homily: "The homily is strongly recommended as an integral part of the liturgy and as a necessary part of nourishment of Christian life. It should develop some point of the readings or of another text from the Ordinary or the Mass of the day. The homilist should keep in mind the mystery that is being celebrated and the needs of the particular community."[18]

The purpose of the homily is indicated by the council: it is a proclamation "of the wonderful deeds of God in the history of salvation, the mystery that is Christ, always present and at work in and among us, especially in liturgical celebrations" (SC 34 § 2). Though the main stress is on the Eucharist, homilies are advocated on other liturgical occasions also.

A huge literature grew up after Vatican II about the nature of the homily,[19] about how to preach it, and books of homilies began to appear. Liturgists and homilists are generally agreed that the homily should arise from the Word of God in the light of the living experience of the congregation. They look with disfavor on the homily being structured in a series of systematic catechetical instructions.[20] They suggest that the people's need for instruction in the faith should be catered to in some other way, but there is little light about how this necessary goal is to be achieved. The wide variety of the Lectionary—weekday readings arranged over a two-year cycle, and Sunday ones over three years—does ensure that many topics of the faith will indeed be covered,[21] but a particular congregation might never hear a homily that would deal with some important elements of the faith, e.g., the sacraments of confirmation or reconciliation, the implications of the commandments, ecumenism, or social justice. This gap can occur despite the desire of the *Code* that "in the homily the mysteries of the faith and the norms for Christian living are to be expounded from the sacred text throughout the course of the liturgical year" (CIC 767 § 1).

While the Missal expresses a preference for the homily being given by the celebrant, canon law makes no specification in this matter.[22] The law does prescribe that the homily, being part of the liturgy itself, is reserved to the priest or deacon. This brings up the whole question of lay preaching on which there is a considerable amount of literature.[23] There is little problem in a variety of circumstances, as the U.S. Bishops' Guidelines observe:[24] retreats, special occasions, meetings, etc. The crunch is with the homily. However, at Children's Masses, if the priest finds it difficult to adapt to the mentality of children, an adult may speak to the children after the Gospel. The word "homily," though, is avoided in the *Directory on Children's Masses.*[25]

The canonical issue here is not easy to grasp. It centers around the core meaning of the word "homily," and there is a danger of manipulating words. Is the homily the explanation of the Scripture given after the Gospel by the priest or deacon? In this case the homily is specified by the homilist, who cannot therefore be lay. Can there be other preaching that occurs after the reading of the Gospel at Mass that is not a homily? Where because of a shortage of priests there are liturgical celebrations other than Mass, lay people are allowed to preach after the reading of the Gospel. One would seem to respect both the essentially negative position of the law and emerging situations in which permission has been given by saying that one can envisage that exceptionally, on rare occasions, the homily may be replaced by preaching given by a lay person. This interpretation applies only to the Eucharist; other liturgical situations need not be so strictly viewed.[26]

The *Code of Canon Law* gives other important canons about the role of preaching and preachers in the Church (CIC 762–772); preaching is only one form of the ministry of the Word (CIC 756–761).[27]

The relationship between hermeneutics and preaching is a serious issue.[28] The homily should not contradict the literal meaning of the text, viz., its inspired sense. Neither can it be restricted to the findings of historical-critical exegetes. It would seem that the rediscovery of the medieval *Lectio divina* has much to offer the preacher. It proceeds in four steps: *Lectio* (reading—what does the text mean?); *Meditatio* (reflection—what does the text mean to me?); *Oratio* (response—prayer on the basis of what is read); *Contemplatio* (resting—allowing oneself to be drawn by, and into, the Word).

Another problem arises when we seek to relate theology and the ambo. There are close connections: the theologian is reflecting on the faith of the Church, one that is preached; the preacher must be theologically literate, presenting the faith in a way that does justice both to the subject matter and the circumstances in which the preaching occurs. K. Rahner makes useful observations in seeking to explain the difference. It is not that people should be shielded from theology, nor that the pulpit is only for the simple faith of the uneducated. The real reason for excluding theologizing from a sermon is that the pulpit is the place where God's Word is encountered as guiding and life-giving, as touching people's conscience and changing their lives. It is thus God's truth, and not human problems with this truth.[29] Therefore disputed matters, theological subtleties, private theological opinions may not be imposed by the preacher. The French proverb gives a guideline: "Theology should be in the preacher, but not in the homily."

There is some, but perhaps not enough, emphasis on prayer that should accompany preaching. The need for prayer arises from the very nature of preaching, which demands charism (q.v.). If the Holy Spirit had not touched both Peter and his hearers at Pentecost, there would not have been the response of several thousand baptisms (Acts 2:14-41). A theology of preaching today needs to take account of the charism, called by St. Thomas Aquinas the "charism of speech." It involves a triple moment: the preacher instructs the intellect by teaching; the hearer is moved to delight in what is said, and is finally moved to respond *(flectat).*[30] Preaching can also be seen within the charism of prophecy—the prophet speaks the Word received. God can touch the preacher with his truth, with insight into the mysteries. But since it is a transient charism, one cannot determine the reception of a prophetic touching but can prepare oneself through prayer.[31] Aquinas' notion, which he shared with the medievals, that God is the principal cause in preaching and the preacher is only an instrument, is still valid.[32] If the Holy Spirit is not concelebrating with the preacher and the congregation, then nothing of worth will be achieved. In preaching, it is the Word of God that is received, not a human word. Preachers as instruments will retain all of their humanity in speech, accent, learning, and so forth. But they must try to ensure that they do not hinder the listeners' encounter with God, who speaks through them. Preachers need the experience of the Word coming alive for themselves before they can be true ministers and servants of that same Word to others.[33]

The Church in the late 20th century still lacks what G. Sloyan has called "a biblical culture." People are not yet at home enough with the Scriptures to make the necessary connections between their lives, salvation history, and the Word of God. For all its impressive achievements, the revival of preaching is still in its infancy.

[1]E.g., in English: W.J. Burghardt, *Preaching: The Art and Craft* (New York—Mahwah: Paulist, 1987); J. Burke, *A New Look at Preaching.* Good News Studies 7 (Wilmington: Glazier, 1983); T.K. Carroll, *Preaching the Word.* MessF 11 (Wilmington: Glazier, 1984); H. Rahner, *A Theology of Preaching* (New York: Herder & Herder, 1968); D.G. Hunter, *Preaching in the Patristic Age.* FS W.J. Burghardt (New York—Mahwah: Paulist, 1989); R. Siegfried and E. Ruane, *In the Company of Preachers* (Collegeville: The Liturgical Press, 1993); see nine arts. in NDictSacWorship 967–1003; Conc 33 (1968). [2]Chs. 11, 13. [3]*Apol.* 1:67. [4]Ch. 35. [5]Carroll (n. 1) 42–62. [6]H. Wolter, in Jedin-Dolan 4:172-183; H.-G. Beck 4:574-578; see J. Longère, *La prédication médiévale* (Paris: Études augustiniennes, 1983). [7]Constit. 10—Tanner 1:239-240. [8]Decree 10—Tanner 1:365-369. [9]Tanner 1:412/DS 1163-1164 and 1:430/DS 1217. [10]Sess. 11—Tanner 1:634-638. [11]Sess. 5—Tanner 2:667-670. [12]Sess. 24, can. 4—Tanner 2:763 [13]Sess. 22, can. 8—Tanner 2:735. [14]H. Jedin, in Jedin-Dolan 5:559-563. [15]Ibid., 5:446-455, 567–574 [16]W. Müller, in Jedin-Dolan 6:554-557. [17]GI 41–42. [18]GI 41. See J.F. Baldovin, "Biblical Preaching in the Liturgy," StLTg 22 (1992) 100–118; E. Henau, "L'homélie comme forme de communication: Ses limites, ses possibilités," QLtg 73 (1992) 53–65. [19]See *Worship* and other journals since Vatican II. [20]W.J. Burghardt, *Preaching: the Art and the Craft* (New York—Mahwah: Paulist, 1987), see idem, NDictSacWorship 967–975. [21]P.H. Biddle, "Preaching the Lectionary," NDictSacWorship 978–983; R.H. Fuller, *Preaching the Lectionary* (Collegeville: The Liturgical Press, revised ed., 1984). [22]Cf. GI 41 with CIC 767. [23]E.g., J.A. Coriden in Coriden, CIC 552–553; N. Foley, ed., *Preaching and the Non-Ordained* (Collegeville: The Liturgical Press, 1983); J. Fox, "The Homily and the Authentic Interpretation of Canon 767 § 1," Apoll 62 (1989) 123–169 = EphLtg 106 (1992) 3–37; P.F. Norris, "Lay Preaching and Canon Law: Who May Give a Homily?," StCan 24 (1990) 443–454; J.H. Provost, "Brought Together by the Word of God (Canons 762–772)," StCan 23 (1989) 345–371; J.A. Wallace, "Preaching by Lay Persons," NDictSacWorship 975–978. [24]Origins 18 (1988) 402–404. [25]DOL 682. [26]See J.H. Provost (n. 23) 362; contrary view, W. Brandmüller, "Annuncio della parola e ordinazione: Il problema della predicazione dei laici alla luce della storia della Chiesa," Divinitas 31 (1987) 144–185. [27]J.M. Huels, "The Ministry of the Divine Word (Canons 756–761)," StCan 23 (1989) 325–344. [28]D. Senior, "Scripture and Homiletics: What the Bible Can Teach the Preacher," Worship 65 (1991) 386–398; W. Vogels, "Biblical Exegesis and the Homily: Two Decades in Retrospect and Prospect," ScEsp 34 (1982) 289–314. [29]K. Rahner, "Heresies in the Church Today," ThInvest 12:117-141 at 138–140. [30]ST 2–2ae, q.177, a.1c. See M.C. Hilkert, "Preaching, Theology of," NDictSacWorship 996–1003. [31]See ST 2–2ae, q. 171. [32]*In Rom.* 10, lect. 2 (837–842); *In I Thess.* 2, lect. 2 (39–40). [33]J.J. von Allmen, "Le prédicateur, témoin de l'Évangile," Irén 49 (1976) 333–349, 453–485.

## PRELATURES, PERSONAL

The possibility of having personal prelatures goes back to Vatican II, which spoke of them as giving *priests* greater flexibility in answering specialized pastoral needs and exercising different forms of the apostolate (PO 10). Paul VI in *Ecclesiae sanctae* (1966) laid down some norms for the erection of such prelatures.[1] In 1982 Pope John Paul established Opus Dei (q.v.) as a personal prelature, and the Congregation for Bishops laid down norms.[2]

In the drafting of the *Code of Canon Law* there was discussion as to whether personal prelatures constituted a particular Church. The canons relating to them (CIC 294–297) were not, however, placed with those on particular Churches (CIC 368–572); such prelatures are not then particular Churches in the sight of the law. Supporters of Opus Dei, and some others, are very favorably disposed to this innovation in law; others are less enthusiastic.[3]

The present canon law follows *Ecclesiae sanctae* but extends it. Canon 294 states: "Personal prelatures which consist of presbyters and deacons of the secular clergy can be erected by the Apostolic See, after consulting the conferences of bishops involved, in order to promote an appropriate distribution of presbyters or to perform particular pastoral or missionary works for various regions or different social groups." A personal prelature is governed by statutes of the Holy See; prelatures may have seminaries and promote candidates to orders for service of the prelature (CIC 295). Lay persons can dedicate themselves to the apostolic work of the prelature by agreements entered into with the prelature (CIC 296). This last canon makes clear that lay people, though committed to work for the prelature, do not form its "people"; they remain part of the diocese in which they live. The prelature mainly therefore concerns priests and deacons.

It is important to see that a personal prelature is not a diocese within a diocese; the permission of the local bishop is required for the prelature to exercise its pastoral or missionary works (CIC 297). It is still too early to judge whether personal prelatures will be a significant feature of the Church's life in the future, or merely a juridical arrangement helpful for particular groups like Opus Dei.

[1]Mp. *Ecclesiae sanctae* I, 4—AAS 58 (1966) 760–761/Flannery 1:594-595. [2]Apost. Const. *Ut sit* AAS 75 (1983) 423–425; norms

464–468; see D. Le Tourneau, "L'Opus Dei Prélature personnelle: dans le droit fil de Vatican II," RevSR 57 (1983) 295–309.   [3]P. Rodriguez, *Particular Churches and Personal Prelatures: A Theological Study of a New Canonical Institution* (Dublin: Four Courts, 1986 = *Iglesias particulares y prelaturas personales* (University of Navarra, 1985); J.-P. Schouppe, "Les prélatures personnelles: Réglementation canonique et contexte ecclésiologique," RTLv 17 (1986) 309–328; D. Le Tourneau, "Les prélatures personelles vues par la doctrine," RevSR 60 (1986) 235–260; less positive G. Ghirlanda, "Natura delle prelature personali e posizione dei laici," Greg 69 (1988) 299–324; idem, "De differentia praelaturam personalem inter et ordinariatum militarem seu castrensem," Periodica 76 (1987) 219–251. W. Stetson and J. Hervada, "Personal Prelatures from Vatican II to the New Code: A Hermeneutical Study of Canons 294–297," Jurist 45 (1985) 379–418.

## PRESBYTERIAN CHURCHES

Presbyterianism is a form of Church polity (q.v.) which holds with government of the Church by presbyters, which from the time of the Reformation was seen as a return to NT models. Nowadays some Presbyterians will acknowledge that the NT also attests to congregational and episcopal structures.

In the United Kingdom and Ireland the structure of the Presbyterian Churches is a hierarchy of bodies but with a parity of ministers: the Kirk Session of the local congregation is composed of the minister and elders; the Presbytery is made up of presbyters/ministers and elected elders from an area; Synods are members of several presbyteries; the General Assembly is the supreme body, and it is composed of ministers and elders in equal numbers. There are two views of the elders: they are seen on the basis of 1 Tim 5:17 as ordained for ruling in the Church; others see them in the role of helpers of the minister as in 1 Cor 12:28.[1] The minister is elected by the congregation and ordained by the Presbytery. Some see an apostolic succession through presbyters as an important feature, while others reject such a notion.

The doctrine of Presbyterian Churches is typically Calvinist, with a major emphasis on hearing and preaching the Word of God. The Apostles' and Nicene Creeds are widely accepted; in the United Kingdom and Ireland the subordinate standard of belief is the *Westminster Confession* (1647),[2] though the mode of subscription to it varies. On the Church it states: "The catholic or universal Church, which is invisible, consists of the whole number of the elect, who have been, are, or shall be gathered into one, under Christ the head thereof; and is the spouse, the body, the fullness of him that filleth all in all. . . . The visible Church, which is also catholic or universal under the gospel . . . consists of all those, throughout the world, that profess the true religion . . . and is the kingdom of the Lord Jesus Christ, the house and family of God. . . . This catholic Church hath been sometimes more, sometimes less visible. And particular churches, which are members

thereof, are more or less pure, according as the doctrine of the gospel is taught and embraced, ordinances administered, and public worship performed more or less purely in them."[3] Weekly Communion services are rare, as are merely twice-yearly celebrations; the majority frequency lies between these two. The main emphasis in Presbyterian teaching has been the sovereignty and authority of God, the lordship of Jesus Christ and the Scriptures as a rule of faith and rule of life. In the past there was an insistence on the depravity of sinners and the total dependence on the divine saving initiative.

Attitudes to ecumenism and to the World Council of Churches vary in Presbyterian Churches, e.g., the Presbyterian Church in Ireland withdrew from membership of the WCC. Presbyterian Churches have been involved in Church unions: United Church of Canada (1925), the Churches of South and North India (1947 and 1970), the United Reformed Church in England (1972). International dialogues take place under the banner of the World Alliance of Reformed Churches (v. REFORMED CHURCHES), which by the 1970s many Presbyterian Churches had joined. A significant contribution of Presbyterian Churches to the ecumenical movement is their insistence on clarity and soundness of theology, as well as their distaste of authoritarianism in Church government.

[1]W.B. Lane, ed., *The Presbyterian Elder: Based on the Books of Order, 1985–1986 Presbyterian Church USA* (Philadelphia: Westminster, 1986).   [2]Schaff, Creeds 3:598-673.   [3]Ch. 25—Ibid., 657–658.

## PRIEST—PROPHET—KING

In the OT priests[1], prophets,[2] and kings[3] were God's special instruments and representatives.[4] The people were built up through their ministries (Deut 17:14–18:22). In the NT Jesus receives all three titles: *priest* (Heb 4:14-16; cf. John 19:23; Rev 1:13); *prophet— nabi* (Luke 24:19); *king* (John 6:15; 18:33-37—ambiguous, but see in all four Gospels his regal messianic entry to Jerusalem, Matt 21:1-11par., and inscription on cross Matt 27:37-42 par.). The early Christian community was kingly and priestly (v. PRIESTHOOD), with a prophetic function of declaring God's wonderful deeds (1 Pet 2:9-10).

The trilogy[5] is found in the *Apostolic Tradition* (q.v.) for the blessing of oil: kings, priests, and prophets.[6] Later it is found in patristic texts and used in a Christological sense by Eusebius of Caesarea (d. ca. 340). It appears also in medieval times[7] but is not a dominant theme until the Reformers, especially Calvin.[8] In Catholic circles it begins to appear in the 17th century, becoming more frequent in the 19th (v. NEWMAN). A key Catholic study was by J. Fuchs in 1941.[9] Y.

Congar had begun to use it as an ecclesiological principle from the 1930s and made it an organizing principle for his classic work on the laity.[10] The trilogy in the form of teacher, king, and priest was applied to Christ by Pius XII in the encyclical *Mystici corporis*.[11] G. Philips used it also in his study of the laity.[12] It was thus mature at the time of Vatican II.

The council applied it to Christ, to the laity, and to ordained ministers.[13] In the case of the latter it followed the order teacher, priest, and pastor/king (LG 25–27; CD 12–16; PO 4–6), whereas for the laity it used priest, prophet, king (LG 34–36). Perhaps its most important function is as an indication of the radical equality in dignity of all Christians: "There is, therefore, one chosen People of God: 'one Lord, one faith, one baptism'(Eph 4:5); there is a common dignity of members deriving from their rebirth in Christ. . . . Although by Christ's will some are established as teachers, dispensers of the mysteries, and pastors for the others, there remains, nevertheless, a true equality between all with regard to the dignity and activity which is common to all the faithful in the building up of the Body of Christ" (LG 32).

There is a difference between the common priesthood (v. PRIESTHOOD) of the faithful and the ministerial or hierarchical priesthood, one that is essential and not a matter of degree (*essentia et non gradu tantum* LG 10). The ministerial priest has a distinct function of service in the community but is not, for all that, necessarily any holier than a lay person. In *Lumen gentium* we need also to look for the key elements that shows a priesthood of the laity that is essentially different from the priesthood of the ordained, as well as what is common.

All are consecrated so that their works are true spiritual sacrifices (Rom 12:1) and a witness to others (LG 10). This common priesthood is exercised in the sacramental life of the Church (LG 11). This life of sacrifice on the part of the laity is "spiritual" (= under the Holy Spirit): Christ associates the laity "intimately in his life and mission and has also given them a share in his priestly office of offering spiritual worship so that God may be glorified and human beings be saved. . . . For all their works, if done in the Spirit, become spiritual sacrifices acceptable to God through Jesus Christ: their prayers and apostolic work, their married and family life, their daily work, their mental and physical recreation, even life's troubles if patiently borne (see 1 Pet 2:5). In the Eucharistic celebration these are offered with very great piety to the Father along with the offering of the body of the Lord" (LG 34).

We know from the *Acta* of the council that LG 12 gives an account of the prophetic role of the whole people:[14] it is a share in Christ's own prophetic role; it consists of witness, praise, confession of faith, and the

*sensus fidei* (v. SENSE OF THE FAITH). Later, LG 35 develops the prophetic function of the laity: established as witnesses, provided with the *sensus fidei* and the grace of the word "so that the power of the gospel may shine out in daily life of family and society," and thus they are heralds of hope, not hiding their hope, so that "even when occupied with temporal cares, the laity can and must perform the valuable task of evangelizing the world. . . . The laity, have a duty to try diligently to deepen their knowledge of revealed truth and earnestly to pray to God for the gift of wisdom."[15] In treating of bishops, *Lumen gentium* 25 stresses the preaching of the gospel as preeminent; they are also authoritative teachers (v. MAGISTERIUM). The proclamation of the gospel is the first charge of priests, who have also an extensive ministry of the Word (PO 4).

The kingly office is not so fully exposed as the other two offices in LG chapter 2 as common to all the baptized but as exercised by the bishops (LG 27 called the "pastoral office," v. BISHOPS) and by the laity (LG 36; for priests see PO 6 on pastoral care). For the latter it is a share in the lordship of Jesus for he "therefore desires that the faithful laity also should extend his kingdom: 'the kingdom of truth and life, the kingdom of holiness and grace, the kingdom of justice, love and peace.' . . . The faithful have, therefore, a duty to acknowledge the inner nature and the value of the whole of creation and its orientation to the praise of God. . . . In the universal fulfillment of this task the laity have the principal role. . . . Moreover, the laity should even band together to improve those secular structures and conditions which constitute an inducement to sin, in such a way that all these things are brought into harmony with the rules of justice. . . . They will imbue human work and culture with a moral value. . . . The faithful must learn carefully to distinguish between the rights and duties which are theirs in so far as they are members of the Church, and those which belong to them as members of human society. They are to labor carefully that both of these work harmoniously together . . ." (LG 36). The pastoral office of bishops (LG 27) and of priests (PO 6) is a special sharing in the kingly office of Christ. They care for the people in a comprehensive way, never as domineering, but always as serving.

There is some problem about the use of "king" today: people in many parts of the world do not have an experience of kings or queens that in any way reflects biblical usage. For the hierarchy, "pastor" is generally preferable. In the case of Christ it is perhaps better to use the primitive credal formula of "Lord" (1 Cor 12:3; Rom 10:9) so that the laity can be said to share in his lordship.

How many offices are there? Vatican II never says three but speaks of a triple office *(triplex munus)* or of the prophetic, priestly, and kingly office. The view which would see one office, viz., priestly, with consequences for a prophetic and kingly role, would seem to have much to commend it. This priestly office is both God-facing and world-facing: it is a mediatorial role. Such a view accounts for the apparent overlap of the Vatican II texts, e.g., witness is said to belong to the priestly office (LG 10) and the prophetic one (LG 35). One may also note the interaction of the three functions: the kingly one is priestly and prophetic; the priestly is kingly and prophetic, and the prophetic is priestly and kingly. But Christ is model for all.[16]

The *Code of Canon Law* begins its exposition of Book II with a statement on all the Christian faithful, which is a modification of LG 31, which refers to the laity's sharing in the priestly, prophetic, and kingly office of Christ (c. 204). The rest of the *Code,* however, does not give any profound or extensive elaboration of how the laity actually exercise this ministry.[17] But the triple office influenced somewhat the structure of its central books: II—The People of God; III—The Teaching Office of the Church; IV—The Office of Sanctifying in the Church.

[1]G. Bornkamm, "Presbus," TDNT 6:651-683; A. George, "Priesthood," DBT [4]59–464; G. Schrenk, "Hierus etc." TDNT 3:247-283; A. Stöger, "Priest(hood)," in Bauer 2:700-709.   [2]P. Beauchamp, "Prophet," DBT 468–467; R. Rendtorff et al., "Prophêtês etc.," TDNT 6:796–861; J. Schildenberger, "Prophet," in Bauer 2:716-722.   [3]P. Grelot, "King," DBT 288–292; H. Kleinknecht et al., "Basileus," TDNT 1:564-579.   [4]R. de Vaux, *Ancient Israel: Its Life and Institutions* (London: Darton, Longman & Todd, 1961).   [5]See Y. Congar, "Prêtre, roi, prophète," Seminarium 34 (1983) 71–82; idem, "Sur la trilogie: prophète-roi-prêtre," RSPT 67 (1983) 96–115, in which he praises and expands L. Schick, *Das dreifache Amt Christi und der Kirche: Zur Entstehung und Entwicklung der Theologien* (Frankfurt/M—Bern: Lang, 1982); J.H. Crehan, "Priesthood, Kingship and Prophecy," TS 42 (1981) 216–231; A. Fernandez, *Munera Christi et munera ecclesiae: Historia de una teoría* (Pamplona: EUNSA, 1982).   [6]Botte SC 11bis:5, pp. 18–19/Dix 5:2, in 5th-cent. Latin text.   [7]E.g., St. Thomas, *In Heb.* 1, lect. 4 (64).   [8]*Institutes of the Christian Religion* 2:15—LCC 20:494-503.   [9]*Magisterium, ministerium, regimen* (Bonn diss. 1941) cf. French RSPT 53 (1969) 185–211.   [10]*Jalons pour une théolgie du laïcat* (1953, Eng. trans., *Lay People in the Church,* London, 1957 and 1965).   [11]AAS 35 (1943) 200/Carlen 4:40/ND 848.   [12]*Le rôle du laïcat dans l'Église* (Paris, 1954).   [13]P.J. Drilling, "The Priest, Prophet and King Trilogy: Elements of Its Meaning in *Lumen gentium* and for Today," EglT 19 (1988) 179–206.   [14]ActaSyn 3/1: 198/Alberigo-Magistretti 444.   [15]N. Weis, *Das prophetische Amt der Laien in der Kirche.* Analecta Gregoriana 225 (Rome: Gregorian UP, 1981).   [16]See Congar, "Prêtre, roi, prophète" (n. 5) 80.   [17]See CIC 759, 765, 774, 834, 837. F. McManus, "Laity in Church Law: New Code, New Focus," Jurist 47 (1987) 11–31.

## PRIESTS, MINISTERIAL

Vatican II teaches that ministerial priesthood is essentially different from the common priesthood (q.v.) of the baptized. Other related issues are apostles (q.v.), bishops (q.v.), deacons (q.v.), and the notion of priest-prophet-king (q.v.). This article concentrates on the second level of the sacrament of orders.[1]

The NT reserves the word *hiereus* (priest) for Jewish or pagan priests, and for Christ (Hebrews); it does not employ *hiereus* for Church officials. Instead there is a wide range of words: *proistamenoi* (those who preside—1 Thess 5:12), *prophêtai* (prophets—q.v.), *didaskaloi* (teachers), *leitourgos* (minister—Rom 15:16), *oikonomoi* (stewards—1 Cor 4:1), *presbeuô* (to be ambassador—2 Cor 5:20; Eph 6:20), *hêgoumenoi* (leaders—Heb 13:7), *sunergos* (fellow worker—Rom 16:3, 9, 21), and especially *episkopoi* (overseers—v. BISHOPS) and *presbuteroi* (elders). To avoid anachronism when dealing with the early Church, it is preferable to refer to these last two as *episkopoi* and *presbuteroi/*presbyters even in English. The above multiplicity of terms is sometimes applied to apostles or to their helpers, and they can imply some authority, e.g., Stephanus in 1 Cor 16:15-18. The two crucial titles or offices, *episkopoi* and *presbyteroi,* are at times interchangeable, e.g., Acts 20:17, 28; Titus 1:5, 7. Both may have Jewish origins, the former from Qumran and the latter from the synagogue.[2] Both *episkopoi* and presbyters were helpers of the apostles or apostolic workers, and they shared in something of the apostles' ministry.

There is no clear indication about who presided at the Eucharist at the time of the Pauline writings.[3] There are indications in the *Didachê* (q.v.) that a prophet could do so (10:7; 13:3; 15:1-2). This document from about the end of the 1st century, and probably from Syria, represents a Church whose structures are in transition. Shortly afterwards (ca. 110) the letters of Ignatius (q.v.) show a clear organization of one *episkopos,* a group of presbyters, and of deacons. This constitution became universal during the 2nd century. In other words, from a fluid and evolving situation in NT times, it was the model of the Pastoral Epistles rather than the charismatic model at Corinth which became normative and would remain so thenceforth. As the *Didachê* shows, one directly chosen by God through being charismatically gifted as a prophet could be a proper minister of the Eucharistic celebration; soon the community would be led to place at the Spirit's disposition specified individuals who were set apart, usually by the laying on of hands. Catholic theology will generally assert that such an essential disposition of the Church must have been through the guidance of the Spirit and be of divine right (*ius divinum*—q.v.).[4] Many Protestant theologians do not find this argument to be compelling; some Catholics, e.g., E. Schillebeeckx, have read the evidence rather differently.[5]

There are rapid developments in the early patristic period.[6] In the letters of Ignatius the *presbyteroi* are grouped around the bishop. Ignatius does not specify their tasks, but they almost certainly celebrated baptism and the Eucharist if appointed by him.[7] From the 3rd century the word "priest" (Greek *hiereus*/Latin *sacerdos*) came frequently to be applied to bishops and later to presbyters.[8]

The *Apostolic Tradition* (q.v.) has an ordination rite of presbyters.[9] With the imposition of hands, the bishop prays for the candidate that he may receive the "spirit of grace and counsel that he may share in the presbyterate and govern thy people in pure heart" and may "minister to thee praising thee in singleness of heart." It is explicitly stated that the presbyter cannot ordain a deacon.[10]

From the 3rd century it became common for bishops to assign outlying areas (*tituli*/*paroikia*—later parishes—q.v.) to the care of presbyters. There were two restrictions on their ministry: they could not ordain, nor in the West confirm.[11] Even in the pre-Nicene period presbyters could be seen to have three roles: they celebrated the sacraments, instructed others in sound doctrine, and they cared for those committed to them —all in dependence on the local bishop, the chief pastor of what was soon to be called a diocese.

After Nicaea there would be little development, though there is a significant body of writing on the qualities that should adorn priests. One dogmatic question surfaces, namely, the nature of the distinction between bishop and presbyter, an issue that will only be resolved fully at Vatican II (v. BISHOPS). In the patristic period presbyters, and indeed bishops, were generally chosen by the local community, at times against the wishes of the one nominated.

One of the best-known patristic works on the priesthood is St. Gregory of Nazianzus' defense of his temporary flight from sacerdotal responsibilities—he had earlier been ordained priest against his will by his father.[12] It is a veritable treatise on the nature and responsibilities of the priesthood. St. John Chrysostom took it as a model for his *Six Books on the Priesthood;*[13] it also inspired St. Gregory the Great's *Pastoral Rule.*[14] In these classics we see several themes recurring: awe at the holiness of the priestly ministry, and the holiness to be cultivated by the priest; teaching and preaching as primary priestly tasks; wonder at the Eucharistic mystery; humility, prayer, ascesis, and charity as marks of the priest's life; the need to avoid all immorality.

There would not be much development about priesthood in the East until modern times. In the West there was a lot of reflection on priestly ministry during the Middle Ages. Treatises on priestly vestments were written; they were tracts on the virtues that the priest should have. Celebration of Mass was given as the reason for seeking holiness. St. Thomas Aquinas can be taken as a high point in scholastic reflection of priesthood, even though his *Summa theologiae* breaks off before he treats of this sacrament. He sees the Eucharist as the ultimate reason for all Church law,[15] and its celebration as the priestly task par excellence.[16] The priest consecrates the Eucharist in the person of Christ *(in persona Christi).*[17] The Eucharistic focus on the priesthood is emphasized further in the view current at the time that the sacrament was conferred by the handing over of the "instruments," viz., chalice and paten, with the words, "Receive the power of offering the Sacrifice in the Church for the living and the dead. In the name of the Father. . . ." This teaching of Thomas was taken up by the Council of Florence (q.v.).[18] The sacramental characters of baptism, confirmation, and order(s) are understood by St. Thomas as different participations in the priesthood of Christ, each one giving a particular deputation to worship.[19] Priests have a care of souls in the area assigned to them by the bishop.[20]

From earliest times the minister of the sacrament of ministerial priest was a bishop; there is, however, evidence in the 14th and 15th centuries that some popes allowed abbots to ordain members of their monasteries.

The Reformation leaders rejected all priestly mediation. They strongly proposed the priesthood of the baptized and would not allow that orders was a sacrament, though they acquiesced in having ministers or pastors in the Church. Trent focused narrowly on the disputed issues and defined the sacramental nature of priestly orders and the traditional teaching in eight canons.[21] Again there was here a primary stress on the relation of priesthood to Eucharist; the former makes possible the celebration of the latter.[22] Other passages of the council spoke of pastoral care and especially preaching.[23] Another contribution of Trent to the priesthood was the injunction to establish seminaries;[24] up to then, priestly training had been more or less on an apprenticeship basis, with only some, mostly religious, attending universities. The growth of seminaries was slow, not fully taking root until the 19th century, and they are still an issue, as Vatican II (OT 4–7) and the 1990 Synod of bishops (q.v.) show.[25]

After the patristic period the most significant teaching on priestly spirituality was the French School of spirituality, notably P. de Bérulle (1575–1629) and J.-J. Olier (1608–1657), who proposed that the priesthood should be seen in relation to the Incarnation. The whole issue of priestly spirituality remains even today seriously underdeveloped;[26] questioning of priestly identity has been an additional cause of unsureness about the correlative spirituality.

Before Vatican II, Pius XII wrote significantly on the priesthood.[27] He also reformed the sacrament of orders (1947) by laying down its essential rite, which was henceforth to be imposition of hands (q.v.), and the core of the preface which immediately follows.[28]

Vatican II devoted one article of the Church Constitution (LG 28) to priests, mainly in the context of their being collaborators of the bishop.[29] This idea of brotherly cooperation is found elsewhere in the council (CD 28–32; PO 7); it finds an institutional expression in the presbyterial council or council of priests (v. SYNODS AND COUNCILS, LOCAL). LG 28 reiterated the idea of the priest acting *in persona Christi,* which had been important in the medieval tradition and later endorsed by Pius XII.[30] Here and elsewhere the council avoided using the expression *alter Christus* (another Christ) which was found in an earlier tradition applied to priests, the Church, and the Christian.[31] The text of LG 28 also implicitly took up the idea of sharing in the office of Christ as priest-prophet-king (q.v.), which had been used by Pius XII in *Mystici corporis* (1943—q.v.).[32]

The Decree on Priestly Ministry, which is quite a comprehensive treatment of priesthood, develops this point in detail (PO 4–6): the ministry of the Word, of sacraments, and of governing. It gives a fine account of priestly spirituality (PO 12). Priests are called to holiness on several accounts, especially their ministry *in persona Christi.* They are primarily sanctified by their ministry (PO 12), but other practices are needful: celibacy (q.v.), humility, obedience, poverty, and a life of prayer with assiduous study of the Scriptures (PO 13, 15–18).

Vatican II can be shown to undergird several theologies of the ministerial priest. In an article aligning models of the priesthood with models of the Church, A. Dulles notes various central insights and approaches.[33] Some have taken the basic function of priests as preaching (PO 4).[34] Others proceed from a cultic vision of the ministerial priesthood (PO 2, 5; AG 39),[35] a view that can be seen to have some support in papal reflections.[36] Others again see the controlling idea to lie in pastoral ministry.[37] None of these is exclusive, and there is a danger in seeing the priest only in terms of his function, whereas the priest's consecration to Christ for the sake of the Church is the radical grounds for all ministerial services.

The new *Code of Canon Law* deals with the conditions for conferring the sacrament and its effects (CIC 1008–1054). It draws on the 1917 *Code* but incorporates changes of Vatican II and legislation coming from Paul VI.[38]

In the ecumenical context[39] there are important developments about ministry in the Lima document, *Baptism, Eucharist, Ministry:*[40] questions of ministry are to be examined from the perspective of the calling of the entire people of God (Ministry I:6; cf. II:12, 16, 26); ministers are a focus of unity (II:8); the Church has always had persons holding specific authority and responsibility (II:9); as heralds and ambassadors, ordained ministers are representatives to the community of Jesus Christ, priest, prophet, and pastor (II:11, 13); ministers and the community share in the priesthood of Christ; the former "may appropriately be called priests because they fulfill a particular priestly service by strengthening and building up the royal and prophetic priesthood of the faithful through word and sacrament, through their prayers of intercession, and through their pastoral guidance of the community" (II:17); after dealing with the threefold ministry of bishops, priests, and deacons (III:19–25), the document says that presbyters "are preachers and teachers of the faith, exercise pastoral care, and bear responsibility for the discipline of the congregation to the end that the world may believe and that the entire membership of the Church may be renewed, strengthened, and equipped in ministry" (III:30). A significant new context for a consideration of ordained ministry is charism (III:32–33—q.v.); the charismatic gifts of the community must not be hindered by ministry, itself a charism. These notable points of convergence have been variously received by the Churches (v. RECEPTION). The Catholic position would be to accept the positive matters agreed but to look for further clarification on topics on which there has been solemn teaching at Trent or at Vatican II, especially the sacramental nature of orders in its three degrees of bishop, priest, and deacon, and the relation of ordained ministry to the Eucharist (II:14). Ministry is also treated in many of the official ecumenical dialogues between the Churches.

Ongoing reflection on orders among Catholic theologians is concerned with certain neuralgic points.[41] The important writings of K. Rahner are an example of the difficulty of speaking about priesthood in the Church today.[42] Quite clearly one's view of the Church and one's positions on Christology will determine one's theology of the priesthood. The questions posed about the priesthood are not slight or peripheral. Given the emergence of a theology of the lay faithful, what is the identity of the priest? Should the sacrament be approached from above (its relationship to Christ) or from below (its relationship with the community)? In other words, is a man primarily priest of Christ or priest of the Church, and how are these connected? Is not a Trinitarian basis necessary to ground and unite all affirmations about priesthood?[43] How are the roles of the priest as pastor and as cultic functionary related?[44] How intrinsic are celibacy (q.v.) and maleness to ministerial priesthood (v. WOMEN, ORDINATION OF)?

[1]D. Donovan, *What Are They Saying about the Ministerial Priesthood?* (New York—Mahwah: Paulist, 1992); G. Greshake, *The Meaning of Christian Priesthood* (Westminster, Md.: Christian Classics, 1989 = *Priestersein* 1982); A. Nicols, *Holy Order: The Apostolic Ministry from the New Testament to the Second Vatican Council.* Oscott Series 5 (Dublin: Veritas, 1990); K. Osborne,

*Priesthood: A History of the Ordained Ministry in the Roman Catholic Church* (New York: Paulist, 1988); R. Wister, ed., *Priests: Identity and Ministry* (Wilmington: Glazier, 1990). [2]R.E. Brown, *Priest and Bishop: Biblical Reflections* (New York: Paulist, 1970—London: Chapman, 1971) 67–68. [3]H.-M. Legrand, "The Presidency of the Eucharist According to the Ancient Tradition," Worship 53 (1979) 413–438. [4]D. Senior, "Biblical Foundations for the Theology of Priesthood," in Wister (n. 1) 11–29; A. Vanhoye, *Prêtres anciens, prêtre nouveau selon le Nouveau Testament* (Paris: Ed. du Seuil, 1980). [5]*Ministry: A Case for a Change* (London: SCM, 1981). See critical reviews, P. Grelot, *Église et ministères:Pour un dialogue critique avec Edward Schillebeeckx* (Paris: Cerf, 1983) and A. Vanhoye and H. Crouzel, "The Ministry in the Church," CleR 68 (1983) 155–174 = NRT 104 (1982) 722–748 = U.S. Bishops' Conference, *Review of Contemporary Perspectives on Ministry* (Washington, D.C., 1983); L. Sabourin, "Questions on Christian Priesthood," RelStB 2 (1982) 1–15; Cf. E. Schillebeeckx, *The Church with a Human Face: A New and Expanded Theology of Ministry* (London: SCM, 1985). [6]A. Cunningham, in Wister (n. 1) 30–53; Nicols (n. 1) 35–66. [7]*Ad Smyrn.* 8:1-2. [8]P.-M. Gy, "Vocabulaire antique du sacerdoce," in *Études sur le sacrement de l'ordre.* Lex orandi 22 (Paris, 1957) 125–145. [9]Botte 7/Dix 8. [10]Botte 8/Dix 9. [11]Innocent I—DS 215/ND 1406. [12]*Orat. 2 Apologeticus de fuga*—PG 35:407-514. [13]PG 47: 623-692. For texts and trans. Quasten, *Patrology* 3:462. [14]PL 77:11-128/ACW 11. [15]M. Useros Carretero, *"Statuta ecclesiae" y "Sacramenta ecclesiae," en la eclesiología de St. Tomas.* Analecta Gregoriana 119 (Rome: Gregorian UP, 1962). [16]*Summa c. gentiles* 4:75; ST 3a, q.65, a.3; q.67, a.2. [17]ST 3a, q.82, aa. 1, 3, 5. [18]*De art. fid. et Eccl. sac.* 2 (626)/DS 1326/ND 1705. [19]ST 3a, q.63, aa.3, 6. [20]ST 2–2ae, q.184, a.6 ad 2; *Summa c. gentiles* 4:76; cf. D.N. Power, *Ministers of Christ and of His Church* (London, 1969) 119–120. [21]Tanner 2:743-744/DS 1771–1778/ND 1714–1721. [22]Tanner 2:742/DS 1764/ND 1707. [23]Sess. 5 and sess. 24, can. 7—Tanner 2:667-670, 764; see Nicols (n. 1) 100–102. [24]Sess. 23 on reform, canon 18—Tanner 2:750-753; J. O'Malley, "Diocesan and Religious Models of Priestly Formation: Historical Perspectives" in Wister (n. 1) 54–70. [25]See post-synodal exhortation, *Pastores dabo vobis*—AAS 84 (1992) 657–804; J. O'Malley, "Priesthood, Ministry and Religious Life: Some Historical and Historiographical Considerations," TS 49 (1988) 223–257. K. Rahner, "Reflections on the Contemporary Intellectual Formation of Future Priests," ThInvest 6:113-138. [26]Bibliog., F. Urbina, "Models of Priestly Holiness: A Bibliographical Review," Conc 129 (1979) 88–98; M. Caprioli, "Spiritualità sacerdotale: Valutazione della bibliografia 1965–1990," Teresianum 42 (1991) 435–473. See F. Morlot, "Consécration sacerdotale et consécration par les conseils," NRT 94 (1972) 290–308; K. Rahner, "The Spirituality of the Secular Priest," ThInvest 19:103-116; idem, "The Spirituality of the Priest in the Light of His Office," ThInvest 19:117-138; idem, "Priestly Existence," ThInvest 3:239-262. [27]Apost. Exhort. *Menti nostrae*—AAS 42 (1950) 657–702. [28]AAS 40 (1948) 5–7/DS 3858–3861/ND 1737. [29]J. Giblet, "Les Prêtres," in Baraúna-Congar, L'Église 3:915-941. [30]Ency. *Mediator Dei*—AAS 39 (1947) 553–554/Carlen, 4:134/DS 3850. [31]R. Gerardi, "'Alter Christus': la Chiesa, il cristiano, il sacerdote," Later 47 (1981) 111–122. [32]AAS 35 (1943) 200/Carlen 4:40/ND 848. [33]A. Dulles, "Models for Ministerial Priesthood," Origins 20/18 (1990) 284–289. [34]K. Rahner, "What Is the Starting Point for a Definition of the Priestly Ministry?," Conc 43 (1969) 80–86. [35]O. Semmelroth, "The Priestly People of God and Its Official Ministers," Conc 31 (1968) 87–100. [36]John Paul II, *Dominicae cenae,* "The Mystery and Worship of the Holy Eucharist," AAS 72 (1980) 113–148—trans. in E. Kilmartin, *Church, Eucharist and Priesthood* (New York: Paulist, 1981) 69–101. [37]W. Kasper, "A New Dogmatic Outlook on the Priestly Ministry," Conc43 (1969) 20–33; T.F. O'Meara, "Towards a Roman Catholic Theology of the Priesthood,"

HeythJ 10 (1972) 390–404; cf. D. Donovan, "Priest," NDictT 798–801. [38]E.J. Gilbert, in Coriden, CIC 713–737. [39]J. Vercruysse," Il ministero ordinato nel dialogo ecumenico," RasT 29 (1988) 445–459. [40]Faith and Order Paper 111 (Geneva: WCC, 1982) 20–32. [41]J. Crehan, "Ministerial Priesthood: A Survey of Work Since the Council," TS 32 (1971) 489–499; A. Marranzini, "La teologia del sacerdozio dopo il Vaticano II," Asp 28 (1991) 117–154; L. Örsy, "The Mission of the Church and the Ministerial Priesthood," ChicSt 20 (1981) 101–113; K. Rahner, "How the Priest Should View His Official Ministry," ThInvest 14:202-219. [42]See above (nn. 25, 26, 34) and: "Priest and Poet," ThInvest 3:294-317; "The Renewal of Priestly Ordination," 3:171-176; "Pastoral Ministries and Community Leadership," 19:73-86; "Theological Reflections on the Priestly Image of Today and Tomorrow," 12:39-60; "The Point of Departure in Theology for Determining the Nature of the Priestly Office," 12:31-38. [43]Greshake (n. 1) 9–101; A. Rouet, "Réflexions sur la relation, le prêtre et l'Église," Supp 138/34 (1981) 369–384. [44]D.L. Gelpi, "Priesthood" in NewDictSac Worship 1013–1018.

## PRIESTHOOD

Priests are to be found in most religions; they are the experts in the sacred.[1] Another article deals more specifically with ministerial priests (v. PRIESTS, MINISTERIAL) and with the trilogy priest, prophet, king (q.v.).

In the OT[2] priesthood had a long evolution, with a clear organization discernible after the Exile, though many features can be detected earlier. Priests were, above all, associated with places of cult (1 Sam 1–3; 21–22), particularly Jerusalem after the reform of Josias in 621 B.C.E. Several functions were given to priests: interpretation of the divine mind by the lot of the Urim and Thummim (e.g., 1 Sam 14:36-42; cf. Judg 18: 5–7), and by the Torah (Deut 33: 8–11; Hos 4:6; Jer 18:18); offering of sacrifice and blessing of the people (Sir 43:6-26). The priests were inaugurated by sacred ceremonies (Lev ch. 8; Num 3:3); after the Exile they were all from the tribe of Levi (cf. Deut 18:1-8), though not all Levites were priests. The priests were regarded as especially holy, and there were special laws of purity for them (Lev 21:1–22:9); only they could enter the inner part of the Temple (2 Chr 23:6).

Jesus is the great high priest, merciful and compassionate (Heb 4:14–5:10), of the order of Melchizedek (7:1-28), offering one eternal sacrifice (8:1–10:39). The term priest, *hiereus,* is not applied to officials of the Christian community but is reserved to Jesus. A notable development is that the Christian community takes over, and applies to itself, the priestly character of the Israelite people (cf. Exod 19:16 LXX with 1 Pet 2:5, 9; Rev 1:6; 5:10) so that Christians are seen corporately as a body of priests.[3] They are to offer their bodies as a living sacrifice (Rom 12:1; cf. 1 Pet 2:5).

In the patristic period we find these biblical themes reechoed, e.g., St. John Chrysostom: "We are made priests offering our bodies for a sacrifice";[4] and generally in the context of baptism.[5] The medievals were faithful to the early tradition[6] but developed it; e.g., St. Thomas: baptism is a sharing in the priesthood of Christ;[7] spiritual priesthood belongs to the laity;[8] the essential act *(proprium officium)* of priesthood is mediation.[9]

At the time of the Reformation, Luther and others insisted on the priesthood of all the baptized.[10] But because the way they made this point involved the denigration of the ministerial priesthood, there would henceforth be a certain caution in the Catholic Church in speaking about the priesthood of all the faithful. Pius XII gave impetus to reflection on the priesthood of the laity even though his presentation of their role is very carefully qualified.[11] For him, the foundation of the difference between the ministerial priesthood and that of the faithful lay in the former alone being able to offer the Eucharistic sacrifice in the name of Christ.[12]

At Vatican II there was much discussion, even concerning the most apt language to use about the priesthood of the baptized: "some" *(quoddam),* "spiritual," "improper" *(improprium),* "universal," "analogical," "incipient" *(inchoativum),* and "common" were all used in texts and debates before the last was finally chosen.[13] The main teaching of the council is in the Church constitution (LG 10, 34).[14] Earlier drafts already spoke of the particular way *(suo perculiari modo)* in which ministerial and universal priesthood flow from the priesthood of Christ. The technical term "participate" *(participant)* was later added; it is to be understood with the help also of LG 62 as analogous: the eternal priesthood of Christ finds limited and temporal expressions in the modes of hierarchical and universal priesthood. Moreover, the ministerial and common priesthood "differ in essence and not just in degree" *(essentia et non gradu tantum differant),* but they are ordered to each other. The hierarchical priesthood exists for the common priesthood.

The council does not define priesthood, but it does specify some of the activities of each priesthood. The common priesthood is found in the consecration of the people, the spiritual sacrifices of daily living, prayer and praise, witness, offering of the Eucharist, and the reception of the sacraments (LG 10, 11, 34). The hierarchical priesthood is described in the same text of LG 10, as well as in LG 26 and CD passim (bishops) and in LG 28, PO and OT passim (priests). It is still possible with St. Thomas to see mediation as the essential act of the common priesthood: all of these priestly activities of the people relate either to God or to the world on God's behalf.

The post-synodal exhortation on the laity, *Christifideles laici* (1988), reiterates the teaching of Vatican II. Notable is the indication that the sharing in the threefold mission of Christ as Priest, Prophet, and King finds "its source in the anointing of baptism, its further

development in confirmation, and its realization and dynamic sustenance in the Holy Eucharist" (n. 14).

An open question in theology is the relation between priest-prophet-king (q.v.) in the participated mission of Christ. There are some indications in Vatican II which would lean in the direction of seeing one office—priesthood, which has two special modalities of prophecy and kingship.

The Faith and Order Lima document distinguishes several instances of priesthood: "Jesus Christ is the unique priest of the new covenant. Christ's life was given as a sacrifice for all. Derivatively, the Church as a whole can be described as a priesthood. All members are called to offer their being 'as a living sacrifice' and to intercede for the Church and the salvation of the world. Ordained ministers are related, as are all Christians, both to the priesthood of Christ, and to the priesthood of the Church. But they may appropriately be called priests because they fulfill a particular priestly service by strengthening and building up the royal and prophetic priesthood of the faithful through word and sacrament, through their prayers of intercession, and through their pastoral guidance of the community."[15] This passage can be interpreted as reflecting Catholic doctrine in the matter, though it needs further elaboration.

Finally, it can be seen that the rights and duties of all the faithful and of the laity in the *Code of Canon Law* (cc. 204, 208–231) have their foundation at least partly in the common priesthood.[16]

[1]W.G. Oxtoby et al., "Priesthood," EncycRel 11:528-550.  [2]A. Cody, NJBC 1253–1259.  [3]G. Bornkamm, "Presbus etc.," TDNT 6:651-683; P.J. Cordes, "Il sacerdozio comune dei fedeli: Richiami biblici per una comprehensione," Later 47 (1981) 44–52; P. Grelot, "La sacerdoce commun des fidèles dans le Nouveau Testament," EspVie 94 (1984) 138–144; A. Stöger, "Priest(hood)," in Bauer 2:716-722.  [4]*Hom 3, in 2 Cor* 3:3, 5—PG 61:411/Halton, Church 71.  [5]E.g., Ambrose *De sacramentis* 4:1—PL 16:435-437/Halton, Church 72–73.  [6]Y. Congar, *Lay People in the Church* (London, [2]1965); C. Eastwood, *The Royal Priesthood of the Faithful: An Investigation of the Doctrine from Biblical Times to the Reformation* (London, 1963).  [7]ST 3a, q.63, a.3 with a.6c.  [8]ST 3a, q.82, a.1 ad 2.  [9]ST 3a, q.22, 1c.; q.26, a.1; q.82, 3c.  [10]H.M. Barth, "'Il sacerdozio universale' secondo Martin Lutero," StEcum 6 (1988) 9–31; F. Bravo, *El sacerdocio común de los creyentes en la teología de Lutero* (Vitoria, 1964).  [11]Encyc. *Mediator Dei* (1947) AAS 39 (1947) 552–562/Carlen 3:133-137/partly in DS 3849–3853/ND 1734–1736.  [12]Alloc. *Magnificate Dominum* (2.11.1954) AAS 46 (1954) 669.  [13]ActaSyn 3/1:194-195/Alberigo-Magistretti 442–443.  [14]A. Acerbi, "Observazioni sulla formula *Essentia et non gradu tantum* nella dottrina cattolica sul sacerdozio," Later 47 (1981) 98–101; M. Adinolfi, *Il sacerdozio comune dei fedeli*. Spicilegium Pont. Athen. Antonianum 23 (Rome: Antonianum, 1983); G. Chantraine, "Synodalité, expression du sacerdoce commun et du sacerdoce ministériel," NRT 113 (1991) 340–362; J. de Smedt, "Le sacerdoce des fidèles," in Baraúna-Congar, L'Église 2:411-424; P.J. Drilling, "Common and Ministerial Priesthood: *Lumen gentium* Article Ten," IrTQ 53 (1987) 81–95; A. Fernandez, *Sacerdocio común y sacerdocio ministerial* (Burgos: Aldecoa, 1979); M.

Löhrer, "'Seipsos hostiam viventem, sanctam, Deo placentem exhibeant' (Rm 12,1): Nota alla questione del rapporto fra culto e vita cristiana nel contesto del sacerdozio comune," Later 47 (1981) 102–110; T. Guarino, "The Priesthood and Analogy: A Note on the Formation and Redaction of *Lumen gentium*, 10," Ang 67 (1990) 309–327; A. Moran, "Sacerdocio común de los fieles y sacerdocio ministerial," EstE 52 (1977) 332–353; G. Philips *L'Église et son mystère au deuxième Concile du Vatican.* 2 vols. (Paris, 1967) 1:36-37, 142–147; J. Rézette, "Sacerdoce commun et sacerdoce ministériel selon Vatican II: Exégèse d'un texte conciliaire," Antonian 52 (1977) 221–230; P. Rosato, "Priesthood of the Baptized and Priesthood of the Ordained: Complementary Approaches to their Interrelation," Greg 68 (1967) 215–265; D. Sartore, "Premese alla lettura di LG 10: Annotazioni su alcuni sviluppi del magistero ecclesiastico," Later 47 (1981) 80–86; A. Vanhoye, "Common and Ministerial Priesthood," TDig 25 (1977), cf. NRT 97 (1975) 193–207. [15]*Baptism, Eucharist, and Ministry.* Faith and Order Paper 111 (Geneva: WCC, 1982) n. 17, p. 23. [16]D. Le Tourneau, "Le sacerdoce commun et son incidence sur les obligations et les droits des fidèles en général et des laïcs en particulier," RDroitC 39 (1989) 155–194.

## PRIMITIVE CHURCH

By the primitive Church we mean the Church in NT times. Evidence for its concerns is the NT corpus and also the *Didachê* (q.v.) and the *Letter* of Clement (q.v.) to the Corinthians. In this period we have various ecclesiologies (v. NEW TESTAMENT ECCLESIOLOGIES), the first indications of apostolic succession (q.v.), and in general the beginnings of Early Catholicism (v. CATHOLICISM, EARLY). The Churches that can be studied with some detail are those of Jerusalem, Corinth, Antioch, and Rome,[1] though a careful reading of other NT books allows us to make some deductions about other places too.

Writing perhaps about 85 C.E., Luke gives us a picture, surely idealized, of the first Christians in Jerusalem. The followers of Jesus were anointed with the power of the Holy Spirit (Luke 24:49; Acts 1:8; 2:1-4; v. PNEUMATOLOGY); they were baptized, and his charisms (q.v.) were abundantly present in the community. Their life is described in three pericopes: "They met constantly to hear the apostles teach and to share the common life, to break bread and to pray" (Acts 2:42; cf. 4:32-37; 5:12-17). Luke's theology would seem to impose an importance on the order given here: the kerygma about the death/resurrection/lordship of Jesus led to their coming together in a shared life (*koinônia*, v. COMMUNION), out of which came Eucharist and shared prayer.[2] A concern for preaching (q.v.) and for adherence to true doctrine characterizes the local communities. The Jerusalem community soon knew sin (Acts 5:1-11—v. HOLY) and persecution by the Jewish authorities (Acts 4:5-30; 5:17-42). An imminent expectation of the parousia was evidenced in the early books of the NT (1 and 2 Thess; cf. Acts 3:20; 2 Pet 3:12). This expectation gradually faded.

At first Christians lived in Christian communities in various places (v. CHURCH, THE WORD EKKLÊSIA, and LOCAL CHURCH). In the beginning they in no sense felt themselves to be a new religion distinct from Judaism. They saw themselves simply as Judaism fulfilled, the beginning of eschatological Israel.[3] Having begun as a sect within Judaism, the followers of Jesus were soon, however, perceived to be a threat: it was Stephen, the Church's first theologian and martyr, who initially realized that there was a need for independence from temple worship and the law (cf. Acts 6:13-14). His opponents, including Saul, saw him as a menace, and had him killed. It was somewhat later that the Gentile world made any distinction between Jews and Christians,[4] a stage reached in 64 C.E. with Nero's explicit persecution of Christians. The rebellion of the Jews against Rome in 66 C.E. would also hasten the process of Christians' insisting on their own identity as a religion. In time they would take over the promises made to the Israelites and so assert that they alone were the authentic People of God (see Rom 11–13; 1 Pet 2:4-10). Matthew's Gospel would harden statements in Mark against Jews, especially against Pharisees,[5] but though it has important insights, R. Ruether's thesis that the NT is essentially anti-Semitic is not to be followed.[6]

In these early days a problem, if not perhaps a split, arose between the Hellenists and the Hebrews in the Church of Jerusalem: the solution was to appoint a group, called the Seven, to provide for the former (Acts 6:1-6). At least two of them, Stephen and Philip, became highly effective preachers (Acts 6:9; 8:4-40; 21:8), which would belie the apparent reason for their appointment, viz., material service of widows (Acts 6:1). It seems clear that a structure was established in which in a wide sense the Seven cared for the Hellenists, but under the authority of the apostles who laid hands on these leaders (Acts 6:6). Diversity was retained within unity.[7] Traces of a double form of leadership—the Twelve and the Seven—may be detected in the gospel tradition (cp. Matt 14:20; Mark 6:42—twelve baskets, and Matt 15:37; Mark 8:8—seven baskets). In time Paul would be the Apostle of the Gentiles after his mission to the Hellenist Jews proved unavailing (Gal 2:8; Acts 13:46).

The relationship of the primitive Church with its mother Judaism is extremely complex. Four different parties, or at least approaches, have been detected in the first Christian communities: some, consisting of Jewish Christians and their Gentile converts, insisted on full observance of the Mosaic law, including circumcision, for those who believed in Jesus (cf. Acts 11:2; 15:5; Gal 2:4); another group, consisting of Jewish Christians and their Gentile converts, did not insist on circumcision, but did require converted Gentiles to keep some Jewish observances (cf. Gal 2:9; Acts 15:20; e.g., Jas); a third group of Jewish Christians and their Gentile converts did not insist on circumcision and did not require observance of Jewish food laws (cf. Gal 2:11-14; 1 Cor 8; e.g., Paul); a fourth group, consisting of Jewish Christians and their Gentile converts, did not insist on circumcision or on the observance of Jewish food laws and saw no abiding significance in Jewish cult and feasts (John; Hebrews).[8] It is thus unhelpful to speak of Jewish Christianity without further specifications,[9] and, indeed, more subtle divisions than the above can be made.

The tensions of these groups are vividly illustrated if one tries to compare Acts and Galatians. It does not seem possible to reconcile four accounts without forcing the texts of either/both Galatians and Acts:[10] Paul's statements in Gal 1–2; the meeting in Acts 11:1-18 in which Peter was dominant; Acts 15, the meeting in Jerusalem where James was dominant and Paul was apparently present (vv. 2, 12, 22); the interview with James and the elders in Acts 21:17-25. It may well be that Paul's fears that the collection for the poor in Jerusalem would not be accepted were justified (Rom 15:31), a collection by which he set great store as a mark of unity—how else can we account for the silence in Acts about the principal purpose of Paul's visit to Jerusalem? There is some important evidence to show that there was a split in the Church between those who supported Paul and those who were more Jewish (cf. 1 and 2 Cor, and Gal 2, which does not seem like a victory of Paul over Peter, who is held in tradition to have been bishop there[11] after Paul's departure with Silas, but significantly not with Barnabas, Acts 15:36-40). What we can be sure about is that relations between former Jews and convert Gentiles would not be smooth for perhaps 100 years after the resurrection: the problems were not only theological, but moral and psychological as well. There is insufficient evidence to document in detail the evolution from Pentecost into the 2nd century. But we see the Gospels of Matthew and John as important indicators: the first was written for moderate Jewish Christians and the author tries to steer a middle path between antinomianism (q.v.) and excessive legalism;[12] John was written from a perspective that is generally hostile to Judaism, but the evangelist is careful to present Jesus as its fulfillment.[13]

With the evolution of the Church in the 2nd century the conservative Jewish Christians were left behind and became heterodox. They were of several kinds, though the generic name Ebionites was given to them. These were characterized by faithful adherence to the law, an exaltation of James and denigration of Paul, adoptionist Christology (Jesus was only the greatest of the prophets), this last being the most significant and the identifying mark of unorthodox sects.[14]

Along with Jewish Christianity we also have Hellenistic Christianity, comprising both Jews of the Diaspora or otherwise only Greek-speaking, and Greek Gentile converts. We have already seen the Hellenists in Jerusalem, whose leader was Stephen. The persecution that broke out after his death was probably only of Hellenists; otherwise it is difficult to explain why the apostles, the leaders of the new faith, were left alone (Acts 8:1, 4). We have perhaps a double view of Hellenists: the Christian Hellenists were less attached to the Temple and the law; the Hellenist Jews were noted for a zeal for their ancestral institutions—hence their readiness to debate with Stephen (Acts 6:9-10), and the fierce persecutions by Saul and others (Acts 8:1-3; 9:1-2).[15] The visit of Peter and John to the highly successful mission of Philip in Samaria need not imply any deficiency in Philip's preaching, but a superintendence of the new mission by the Jerusalem mother Church (Acts 8:17).[16] Antioch would become for a time the center of the Hellenizing mission.[17] Again the mother Church sent a representative, Barnabas, who saw the grace of God at work there (Acts 11:19-30). Paul and Barnabas were sent on a mission to the Gentiles from there (Acts 13:1-3 with 9:15). In Antioch there were perhaps three stands of Hellenistic Christianity: those looking to the inspiration of Stephen, of Peter, and of Paul.[18] Further evidence of Hellenizing influences in the primitive Church are the activity of Apollos in 1 Cor 1–4 and Acts 18:24-28, and possibly the composition of the Letter to the Hebrews.[19] In recent years scholars have been very much more cautious in retrojecting what is known about 2nd-century Gnosticism into the concerns of Colossians, Ephesians, the Pastorals (1 and 2 Tim, Titus), or the Johannine corpus.[20]

In the very fluid situation of the developing primitive Church, many outcomes were theoretically possible. From the letters of Paul and James, Acts, and Revelation we can see the frailty and sin present in the Church even in its early days. Threatened by sin and division from within and by persecution from without, it was the model of the Pastoral Epistles rather than the more charismatic model at Corinth (or some other) that would become ever more dominant. The *Didachê*, though not fully developed, was a stage towards the institutions that find fuller expression in the letters of Ignatius (q.v.), and which would be stable by the end of the 2nd century.[21] Catholic theology holds that this development was guided by the Holy Spirit and that in its main essentials it is irreversible (v. IUS DIVINUM). Indeed, for all its weakness and defects, the primitive Church has a continual drawing power and inspirational force to encourage the Church to renew itself in every age.

[1]M. Mullins, *Called To Be Saints: Christians Living in First-Century Rome* (Dublin: Veritas, 1992); cf. T.J. Harrington, "The Local Church at Rome in the Second Century: A Common Cemetery Emerges Amid Developments in this 'Laboratory of Christian Policy,'" StCan 23 (1989) 167–188. [2]Congar, L'Église une 19–22; B. Michaels, "The 'Model of Church' in the First Christian Community of Jerusalem: Ideal and Reality," LouvSt 10 (1984–1985) 303–323. [3]J.D.G. Dunn, *Unity and Diversity in the New Testament: An Inquiry into the Character of Earliest Christianity* (Philadelphia: Westminster, 1977) 239. [4]M.J. Cook, "The New Testament and Judaism: An Historical Perspective on the Theme," RExp 84 (1987) 183–199 at 187 citing Suetonius, *On the Life of the Caesars,* "Claudius" 25. [5]Ibid., 191–196. [6]*Faith and Fratricide: The Theological Roots of Anti-Semitism* (New York: Seabury, 1974). See rather D.J. Harrington, *The Gospel of Matthew.* Sacra Pagina 1 (Collegeville: Glazier—The Liturgical Press, 1991) 1–22. [7]R.J. Dillon, NJBC in loc.; R.E. Brown, "Early Church," NJBC 1341–1342; F.F. Bruce, *Men and Movements in the Primitive Church* (Exeter UK: Paternoster, 1979) 49–85; J. Leinhard, "Acts 6:1-6: A Redactional View," CBQ 37 (1975) 228–236. [8]R.E. Brown, in R.E. Brown and J.P. Meier, *Antioch and Rome: New Testament Cradles of Catholic Christianity* (London: Chapman—Mahwah: Paulist, 1983) 2–8; idem, "Early Church," NJBC 1342–1343; C.C. Hill, *Hellenists and Hebrews: Reappraising Division within the Earliest Church* (Minneapolis: Fortress, 1992); K. Neith, "The Background of the New Testament: Diversity in First Century Judaism and Its Contemporary Implications," LouvSt 17 (1992) 131–151; R. Murray, "Defining Judeo-Christianity," HeythJ 15 (1974) 303–310; R. Penna, "Configurazione giudeo-cristiana della chiesa di Roma nel I secolo," Later 50 (1984) 101–113; S.K. Riegal, "Jewish Christianity: Definitions and Terminology," NTS 24 (1978) 410–415; J.M. Velasco and L. Sabourin, "Jewish-Christianity of the First Centuries," BibTB 6 (1976) 5–26. [9]R.E. Brown, "Not Jewish Christianity and Gentile Christianity, But Types of Jewish/Gentile Christianity," CBQ 45 (1983) 74–79; cf. J.B. Agus, "Judaism and the New Testament" GkOrTR 22 (1977) 80–97, 596–613; J.E. Taylor, "The Phenomenon of Early Jewish-Christianity: Reality or Scholarly Invention," VigChr 44(1990) 313–334. [10]P.J. Achtmeier, "An Elusive Unity: Paul, Acts, and the Early Church," CBQ 48 (1986) 1–26. But cp. J.A. Fitzmyer, "Galatians," NJBC in Gal 1:12–2:17, pp. 783–785; idem, "Paul," NJBC 1334–1335 with bibliog.; R.J. Dillon, "Acts of the Apostles," NJBC in Acts 11:1-18, p. 747, in Acts 15:1-35, pp. 751–752, and in Acts 21:15-26, p. 759; L.T. Johnson, *The Acts of the Apostles.* Sacra Pagina 5 (Collegeville: Glazier—The Liturgical Press, 1992) 258–281, 373–380; F. Matera, *Galatians.* Sacra Pagina 9 (Collegeville: Glazier—The Liturgical Press, 1992) 1–26, 57–92. [11]G. Orioli, "Le origini della chiesa di Antiochia e la sua fondazione petrina nella documentazione fino al secolo V," Apoll 60 (1987) 645–649. [12]Dunn (n. 3) 245–251; A.F.J. Klijn, "Ebionites," EncyEarCh 1:258-259. [13]T.M. Dowell, "Jews and Christians in Conflict: Why the Fourth Gospel Changed the Synoptic Tradition," LouvSt 15 (1990) 19–37. [14]Dunn (n. 3) 239–242, 261–266. [15]R.J. Dillon, "Acts of the Apostles," NJBC 739–740, 742; M. Hengel, *Between Jesus and Paul* (Philadelphia: Fortress, 1983) 1–29 esp. 4–11. [16]Bruce (n. 7) 57–60. [17]Meier, in Brown and Meier (n. 8) 11–86; P. Grech, "Gerusalemme ed Antiochia: Il ruolo di due chiese nella soluzione di un problema teologico," Later 50 (1974) 77–85; W. Meeks and R. Wilken, *Jews and Christians in Antioch* (Missoula, Mont.: Scholars Press, 1978). [18]Meyer (n. 17) 61 following C.K. Barrett. On Paul cf. J.A. Fitzmyer, "Pauline Theology," NJBC 1385–1386. [19]Meier (n. 17) 79–83, but cp. M.M. Bourke, "Hebrews" in NJBC 921. [20]P. Perkins, "Gnosticism," NJBC 1350–1353. [21]A. Cunningham, "Developing Church-forms in the Post Apostolic Period," Conc 144 (1981) 34–39.

## PRISCILLIANISM

Priscillianism was a heresy from 4th–5th centuries, perhaps begun c. 370 by Priscillian, who despite being condemned at Saragossa, became bishop of Avila. His doctrine was a conglomerate of Manichee ideas (matter is evil and created by the devil) along with Docetic (Christ had only an apparent body) ones. The Priscillian's Trinitarian theology was Sabellian or modalist and tending to monarchianism (the Son is only a mode of the Father, not a distinct divine Person).[1] They thus denied the pre-existence of Christ and also did not ascribe a true humanity to him. They opposed marriage and had a complex set of behaviors, notably centering on fasting when the Church celebrated feasts to which they were opposed, e.g., the Christmas-Epiphany cycle. On Priscillian's appeal to the emperor against a condemnation at a synod at Bordeaux, he was instead tried for sorcery and executed along with some followers. This is the first instance of the secular arm inflicting the death penalty on a heretic. The movement finally died out after condemnation at the provincial Council of Braga in 563.[2]

[1]A. Orbe, "Doctrina trinitaria del anónimo priscilianista *De Trinitate fidei catholicae,*" Greg 49 (1968) 510–562. [2]Works ed. G. Schepss CSEL 18 (1889); G. Bardy, "Priscillien," DTC 13:391-400; K. Baus, in Jedin-Dolan 2:129-136; H. Chadwick, *Priscillian of Avila: The Occult and the Charismatic in the Early Church* (Oxford: Clarendon, 1976).

## PROPHETS

Prophets are known in many religions.[1] The fundamental idea is not so much foretelling the future, but forth-telling, that is, the mediation and interpretation of the divine mind.[2] In Israel there were ecstatic prophets (from *ex-stasis* = "being displaced") from early times (cf. Num 11:24-30; 1 Sam 10:6-13). We also refer to the classical prophets, who are quite distinctive when compared with Near East prophetism; they are mostly those whose names appear at the head of OT books. They were called by God, sent to speak his word, his judgment on events and moral behavior—often in poetic form. Quite crucial in the whole period of Israel's prophetic history was the discernment of true from false prophets (eg., Jer 23:9-40; 28:1-17). There was not in theory a conflict between prophets and priests in the OT, though tensions did exist between institutionalized religion and the prophetic word (e.g., Amos 5:4-7, 21–27).

The NT sees previous prophecy culminating in the mission of Jesus (Matt 25:56; Acts 3:17-24). The prophets (*hoi prophêtai* with article) are the OT prophets who prophesied until John (Matt 11:13). The NT also knows living prophets who with the apostles are the foundation of the Church (cf. Eph 2:20) and are named immediately after the apostles in lists of charismatics (1 Cor 12:28-29; Eph 4:11).[3] Paul's attitude to prophecy was extremely positive: "Strive for the spiritual gifts, especially that you may prophesy" (1 Cor 14:1; see vv. 3–5, 39). The 14th chapter of 1 Cor is largely devoted to questions about prophecy: prophets have a public function in the community, which Paul regulates; the prophecy here is not ecstatic but intelligible—unlike glossolalia, which needed interpretation; the task of discernment, which had already arisen ca. 50 C.E. in 1 Thess 5:19-21, is important and is a function of the other prophets. We find in Matthew a reference to false prophets; in this case the discernment is based on doing the will of the Father and on their fruits (cf. Matt 7:15-21).

Prophecy will come to an end in eschatological times (*to teleion,* 1 Cor 13:10). Meanwhile we see the NT Church being gifted by the charism (q.v.) of prophets and being guided by it (cf. Acts 11:27-28; 13:1; 21:9-11; Rev 1:10-11; 2–3; 19:10). In the Pastoral Letters the prophetic word is also a criterion for activity, and demands a response (1 Tim 1:18; 4:14).

Prophets continue to have a role in the Churches in the years immediately after the NT writings. In the *Didachê* (q.v.) it is envisaged that there may be prophets in the community: these are to be discerned by their behavior and not therefore by their doctrine or by charismatic discernment as in 1 Cor (11:3-12); they are not to be bound by the same rules as others in celebrating the Eucharist or praying at the community meal (10:7); they are to be supported (13:1-7). But there is already a hint that *episkopoi* and *diakonoi* are beginning to take their place (15:1-2), a step that will be hastened in Ignatius (q.v.). The only reference he has to prophecy is an account of a prophecy he himself received.[4] Prophets are also known to Hermas (q.v.), and discernment between true and false ones is through their behavior: false prophets seek money, engage in divination, shun meetings of holy people.[5] Polycarp (q.v.) is called a "prophetic" teacher and bishop.[6] Though the early Fathers, except Origen, presumed that the prophetic gift would remain in the Church, the role of prophecy was gradually assumed into the episcopal office, a transition that was fairly complete by the time of Montanism (q.v.).[7] Nonetheless, the late 4th-century *Apostolic Constitutions* (q.v.) deals with prophets but with a tendency to downplay them: they are not to consider themselves higher than their brethren;[8] those who are prophets might not be holy;[9] true prophets, be they men or women, are to be humble.[10]

As with other charisms, the dispensationalist view largely prevailed about prophecy: it was something exceptional, to be found perhaps in the lives of great saints, but it was not a regular feature of the Church's life. In the Middle Ages St. Thomas struggled to relate what he read in Scripture with his contemporary experience of the Church. He deals extensively with prophecy, grouping under it all the charisms concerned with knowledge.[11] Prophecy is concerned with communicating what is known only to God.[12] The revelation of future contingent acts is most characteristic of prophecy *(ad prophetiam propriisime pertinet).*[13] There is continuing prophecy in the Church, not to produce new doctrines but to direct human acts.[14] St. Thomas also makes the important points that the persons may not know with certainty that they are being divinely illuminated[15] and that prophecy is not a habit to be exercised at the will of the recipient but is a transient illumination from God.[16]

Before Vatican II there was renewed interest in the prophetic dimension of the Church and in the trilogy priest-prophet-king (q.v.), especially in Y. Congar and K. Rahner.[17] This theology was thus mature and entered the council. From its *Acts* we know that LG 12 deals with the prophetic office of the Church:[18] "The holy people of God has a share, too, in the prophetic office of Christ, when it renders him a living witness, especially through a life of faith and charity, and when it offers to God a sacrifice of praise, the tribute of lips that honor his name." The remainder of the paragraph speaks of the *sensus fidei,* the supernatural instinct of the faith (v. SENSE OF FAITH) by which the people "receives the word of God . . . adheres indefectibly to [it] . . . penetrates more deeply . . . and applies it more fully to life." It can be argued that the second paragraph of LG 12 dealing with charism is still considering the prophetic office of the whole people. These ideas are taken up and developed in LG 35, dealing with the prophetic office of the laity,[19] a key feature being evangelization. All members of the Church are bound to render witness to Jesus "by the spirit of prophecy" (PO 2). The laity share in the priestly, prophetic, and kingly office of Christ (AA 2).

After the council there was a reawakening of prophecy in the Charismatic Renewal (q.v.).[20] There, prophecy is found to have most of the characteristics found in St. Paul's treatment of the charism.

Prophecy, either explicit or unconscious, belongs to the nature of the Church: each age needs prophets to be "a tester of the people" (Jer 6:27) and "a sentinel" (Ezek 3:17) to make known the will of God by their words and their deeds; each community in the Church needs also to pray that it be given prophets for "upbuilding and encouragement and consolation" (1 Cor 14:3).[21] As in biblical times, the discernment of genuine prophecy will always be a difficult task in the Church.[22]

[1]G.T. Sheppard and W.G. Herbrechtmeier, "Prophecy," EncycRel 12:8-14.  [2]P. Beauchamp, "Prophet," DBT 468–474; J. Blenkinsopp, *A History of Prophecy in Israel* (London: SCM, 1983); R. Collins et al., eds. *Israel's Prophetic Tradition.* FS P.R. Ackroyd (Cambridge: UP, 1982); G. Couturier, "L'Esprit de Yahweh et la tradition prophétique en Israël," ScEsp 42 (1990) 129–165; K. Koch,

*The Prophets.* 2 vols. (London: SCM, 1982–1984); J. Lindblom, *Prophecy in Ancient Israel* (Philadelphia, 1962); D.P. Reid, *What Are They Saying About the Prophets?* (New York: Paulist, 1980); R. Rendtorff et al., "Prophêtes," TDNT 6:796-861; J. Schildenberger, "Prophet," Bauer 2:716-722; B. Soucek, "Prophecy in the New Testament," TDig 12 (1964) 201–202; B. Vawter, "Introduction to Prophetic Literature," JBC 1:223-237 at 224—NJBC 186–200; R.M. Wilson, "Biblical Prophecy," EncycRel 12:14-23; R.R. Wilson, *Prophecy and Society in Ancient Israel* (Philadelphia: Fortress, 1980). [3]É. Cothenet, "Prophétisme dans le Nouveau Testament," SuppDictBib 8:1222-1237; idem, "Prophétisme et ministère d'après le Nouveau Testament," MaisD 107 (1971) 29–50; F.D. Farnell, "Is the Gift of Prophecy for Today?: 1. "The Current Debate About NT Prophecy," BiblSac 149 (1992) 277–303, "2. The Gift of Prophecy in the Old and New Testaments," ibid., 387–410; C. Perrot, "Prophètes et prophétisme dans le Nouveau Testament," LumièreV 22/115 (1973) 25–39; F.A. Sullivan, *Charisms and the Charismatic Renewal: A Biblical and Theological Study* (Ann Arbor: Servant Books—Dublin: Gill and Macmillan, 1982) 91–119. [4]*Phil* 7:1. [5]*Mand.* 11 (43). Cf. J. Reiling, *Hermas and Christian Prophecy: A Study of the Eleventh Mandate* (Leiden: Brill, 1973). [6]*Martyrdom of Polycarp* 16:2. [7]J.L. Ash, "The Decline of Ecstatic Prophecy in the Early Church," TS 37 (1976) 227–252; F.E. Greenspahn, "Why Prophecy Ceased," JBL 108 (1989) 37–49. [8]8:1, 17—SC 336:134. [9]8:2, 1–3—SC 336:134-136. [10]8:2, 7-10. [11]ST 2–2ae, q.171 prol. Cf. qq.171–174; *In 1 Cor* 14, lect. 1–7 (807–887); *In Rom* 12, lect. 2 (977–979). [12]ST 1–2ae q.111, a.4; In 1 Cor 12, lect. 2 (728); *Summa c. gentiles* 3:154; ST 2–2ae q.171, a.3 ad 3. Cf. E. Bini, "La profezia nella Chiesa secondo S. Tommaso d'Aquino," Divinitas 36 (1992) 38–51; R. Faricy, "The Charism of Prophecy in the Church," in *Atti dell'VIII Congresso tomistico internazionale. Vol 4: Prospettive teologiche moderne.* Studi tomistici 13 (Vatican, 1981) 371–380; B. McCarthy, "El modo del conocimiento profético y escriturístico en San Tomás de Aquino," ScripTPamp 9 (1977) 425–484; M. Reeves, *Prophecy in the Middle Ages* (London, 1969). [13]ST 2–2ae, q.171, a.3c. Cf. *In 1 Cor* 12, lect. 2 (728). [14]ST 2–2ae, q.174, a.6c and ad 3. [15]"Quidam instinctus propheticus"; cf. 2–2ae, q.173, a.4c with q.171, a.5. [16]ST 2–2ae, q.171 a.2. [17]Cf. Y. Congar, *Lay People in the Church* (Westminster, Md., 1965—French 1953); K. Rahner, *The Dynamic Element in the Church.* Quaestiones disputatae 12 (Freiburg: Herder—London: Burns & Oates, 1964—German 1957); D. Lowry, *The Prophetic Element in the Church as Conceived in the Theology of Karl Rahner* (London: University Press of America, 1990). [18]ActaSyn 3/1: 198/Alberigo-Magistretti 444. [19]N. Weis, *Das prophetische Amt der Laien in der Kirche: Eine rechtstheologische Untersuchung anhand drier Dokumente des Zweiten Vatikanischen Konzils.* AnGreg 225 (Rome: Gregorian UP, 1981). [20]Sullivan (n. 3); B. Yocum, *Prophecy* (Ann Arbor: Servant Books, 1976). [21]J.J. Castelot, "The Spirit of Prophecy: An Abiding Charism," CBQ 23 (1961) 210–217; J. Panagopoulos, ed., *Prophetic Vocation in the New Testament and Today* (Leiden: Brill, 1977); K. Rahner, *Visions and Prophecies.* QDisput 10 (Freiburg—London, 1963). [22]H. Bacht, "Wahres und falsches Prophetentum," Bib 32 (1951) 237–262; J.D.G. Dunn, "Discernment of Spirits," in W. Harrington, ed., *Witness to the Spirit* (Dublin: Irish Biblical Association, 1979) 79–96; M. Krämer, "Hütet euch vor den falschen Propheten," Bib 57 (1976) 350–377; K. Rahner, "Prophetism," SM 5:110-113; K.V. Truhlar, "Discernment of Spirits," SM 2:89-91; W. Vogels, "Comment discerner le prophète authentique?," NRT 99 (1977) 681–701.

## PROSELYTISM

In Acts 2:10 we find "proselytes" (Greek *prosêlutoi*), that is, converts to Judaism. The word can still be used of any new convert to a faith. Any organized attempt to induce people to change their faith could be called "proselytism." But the word has nowadays a uniquely negative connotation: it is used only for a perversion of witness "through secret or open improper persuasion such as bribery, intimidation, or external coercion."[1]

Charges of proselytism are often made when a significant number of people change from one Church to another; it is often leveled at the Catholic Church by the Orthodox Churches who resent the Uniate Churches (q.v.) in their midst.[2] Though extreme proselytism is easy to detect, there are a number of grey areas in which it is difficult to distinguish the entirely legitimate witness or evangelization from the evil deed of proselytism. Again, charitable works are correct and rightful, but they may sometimes include an element of bribery.

Sensitivity to proselytism arose only from the mid-20th century, even though at all times a Church which lost members to another Church often decried the fact. The New Delhi meeting of the World Council of Churches (WCC—v. ECUMENISM AND THE WCC) in 1961 received and commended the document on "Christian Witness, Proselytism and Religious Liberty."[3] Shortly afterwards Vatican II implicitly condemned proselytism in the Declaration on Religious Freedom (DH) in 1965: "Religious communities are entitled to teach and give witness to their faith publicly in speech and writing without hindrance. But in propagating their religious belief they must always abstain from any kind of action that savors of undue pressure or improper enticement, particularly in regard to the poor and uneducated. Any such course of action must be held as an abuse of their own rights and an infringement of the rights of others" (DH 4). Again, "The Church severely forbids forcing anyone to embrace the faith, or to persuade or attract him by unbecoming pressures" (AG 13). In 1970 the Catholic Church and the WCC Joint Working Group issued a study document on "Common Witness and Proselytism."[4]

Though rejected by all the mainline Churches, proselytism is still a problem in areas in which sects are active. There can be scarcely any Church that has not in the past engaged in proselytism at some level; caution and honesty in this matter will always be needed.

[1]P. Löffler, "Proselytism," DictEcumMov 829. See N.A. Horner, "The Problem of Intra-Christian Proselytism," InterRMiss 70 (1981) 304–313. [2]Cf. Vavouskos, "Le prosélytisme," Kanon 8 (1987) 157–161. [3]*Evanston to New Delhi* (Geneva: WCC, 1961). [4]EcuR 23 (1971) 9–20.

## PURGATORY

In various religions there is a sense that a person's earthly life may not bring one to ultimate perfection. In the East the notion of reincarnation embodies the idea that another chance is given. Islam knows an intermediate state, b*arzakh*,[1] in which the blessed have a foretaste of the glory which awaits them, and the wicked see the torments they will have to endure. There is also punishment for those who do not respond correctly to the interrogating angels Munkar and Nakîr. But only a few, like the mystic Al Ghazâlî (d. 1111), hold repentance after death.

There is no clear teaching on purgatory in the Scriptures. But tradition, especially in the West, developed a theology of purgatory based on a few texts: 2 Macc 12:39-46 (the sacrifice offered by Judas Maccabeus for soldiers killed while wearing idolatrous objects); 1 Cor 3:11-15 (salvation "through fire" for those who have built inadequately on Christ the foundation); 1 Cor 15:29 (the enigmatic "baptism on behalf of the dead"); 2 Tim 1:16-18 (prayer for Onesiphorus who seems to be dead); Luke 12:48 (lighter punishment for some); Matt 5:26 (escape only on paying the last penny).

Though J. Le Goff appears to be correct in finding the first use of the word "purgatory" to indicate a place in Peter Comestor (Peter Manducator—he devoured books!) between 1170 and 1180,[2] the notion of purgation after death is much earlier. A key series of texts in many of the Fathers support the idea of prayers for the dead. Along with this we find the idea of purgatorial fire/punishments/places *(ignis purgatorius/poenae purgatoriae/loca purgatoria)*. Though some indications of fuller forgiveness and or punishment after death are found as early as Clement of Alexandria (ca. 150—ca. 215) and Origen (ca. 185—ca 254), it is only with Augustine[3] that there is a clear expression of what would later, through development of dogma, culminate in conciliar definitions: there is purification after death of smaller sins;[4] according to what "has been handed down by the Fathers and is upheld by the custom of the universal Church," souls are helped by the saving sacrifice and by the good works of the faithful; they are commemorated in the *anaphora*.[5]

After him various writers, especially Gregory the Great,[6] and the liturgy developed the idea of purgation after death, with the possibility that the prayers of the living could be of value for the departed. At least from the 8th century a commemoration of the dead is to be found in the Roman Canon, though perhaps not used for all Masses (especially Sundays) or in every place.[7] A commemoration of the dead is found in several ancient liturgies Eastern and Western.[8] Archaeological remains from early centuries also give evidence of the conviction that the prayers of the living could in some way assist the departed.[9]

The first conciliar teaching is found in Lyons II (q.v.): the souls of those who die in charity "before having satisfied by worthy fruits of penance for their sins of commission and omission . . . are cleansed after death by purgatorial and purifying penalties *(poenis purgatoriis seu cartharteriis)*. . . . To alleviate such penalties the acts of intercession *(suffragia)* of the living benefit them, namely the sacrifice of the Mass, prayers, alms, and other works of piety."[10] Later, the Council of Florence (q.v.) would make a similar statement, again in the context of the non-acceptance of purgatory by Greeks.[11] Since the Orthodox still generally reject the Western doctrine of purgatory,[12] the meaning of their commemoration of the dead in the liturgy is not, therefore, clear.

The doctrine of purgatory is reaffirmed by Trent against Protestant rejections but with a warning against exaggerations and superstition.[13] Vatican II did not use the word purgatory, but it referred to "others who have departed this life are being purified" (LG 49, 51), and endorsed prayers for the dead (LG 50). The post-Vatican II Eucharistic Prayers have a commemoration of the dead. The Congregation for the Doctrine of the Faith in an instruction (1979) stated: "(The Church) believes in the possibility of a purification for the elect before they see God, a purification altogether different from the punishment of the damned."[14]

The only defined teaching on purgatory is the existence of a state of purification and the efficacy of prayer for the deceased. Theological speculation revolves around several questions: the duration of purgatory, the nature of the purification, the state of those being purified. St. Thomas represents the medieval discussion on these topics, though we do not have any extensive treatment from his mature period: he teaches the value of prayer for the dead;[15] he likens the pain of purgatory to that of hell but lasting for a limited time only; the pains of purgatory are unequal according to the state of those being purified; the object of purgatory is venial sin and the remains of sinfulness that can persist after a sin has been forgiven; those being purified can be aided by indulgences.[16] Dante would soon place purgatory in a prominent position of Christian consciousness in the *Divine Comedy,* which continued to influence many who never read his text.

In the post-Tridentine period there was much speculation about purgatory, and an increase in devotion: prayers were multiplied for the Holy Souls; their intercession was sought;[17] the Augustinian St. Nicolas of Tolentino (1245–1305) became acknowledged as the patron of the souls in purgatory.

Modern writing on purgatory[18] seeks to purify the doctrine from imaginative and fantastic elements as well as unfounded visions and pseudo-revelations. At the same time there is a growing awareness of the value of the insights of the mystics. Reflecting on their own experience of darkness in the search for God, they consider purgatory from the perspective of love, for example, St. Catherine of Genoa and St. Thérèse of Lisieux. Purgatory is seen not as punishment but purifying and healing love.[19] The doctrine of purgatory is one that makes sense even at a rational level: people would need to be purified of envy before they could enjoy heaven! Full purification can come about through holiness of life or through terminal illness, but for others there will be loving healing after death. Purgatory is best considered within the wider teaching of the Communion of Saints (q.v.). The Church militant on earth and the Church triumphant in heaven are united in love and care for the Church suffering in purgatory. Purgatory is also to be seen in the light of the renewed understanding of indulgences (q.v.).[20]

[1]E.L. Ormsby, "Purgatory, Islamic Concept of," DMA 10:214-215. [2]PL 171:741 (wrongly attributed to Hildebert of Lavirdan); see J. Le Goff, *The Birth of Purgatory* (Chicago: UP, 1984—Aldershot UK: Scholar Press, 1990) 154–159, 362–364. [3]J. Ntedika, *Évolution de la doctrine du purgatoire chez saint Augustin* (Paris: Études augustininnes, 1966); H. Kotila, *Memoria mortuorum: Commemoration of the Departed in Augustine.* Studia Ephemeridis "Augustinianum" (Rome: Inst. Patristicum Augustinianum, 1992). [4]*City of God* 26:13 cf. 24—CCL 48:778-779 cf. 789–793. [5]*Serm.* 172:2, 2—PL 38:936. [6]*Dialogi* 4:39-41—PL 77:393-400/SC 265:140-156; see R.R. Atwell, "From Augustine to Gregory the Great: An Evolution of the Emergence of the Doctrine of Purgatory," JEH 38 (1987) 173–186; J. Ntedika, *L'Évolution de l'au-delà dans la prière pour les morts: Études de patristique et de liturgie latines (IVe-VIIIe s.)* (Louvain: Nauwelaerts, 1971). [7]M. Andrieu, *Les "Ordines romani" du haut moyen âge.* Specilegium sacrum lovaniense 23 (Leuven, 1948) 2:274-281; idem, "L'insertion du Memento des morts au canon romain," RevSR 1 (1921) 151–154; C. Mohrmann, "Locus refrigerii lucis et pacis," QLtg 39 (1958) 196–214. [8]R.C.D. Jasper and G.J. Cuming, *Prayers of the Eucharist: Early and Reformed* (New York: Pueblo, [3]1987)—texts at 49, 62, 72, 78, 86, 98, 133, 137, 165; A. Canizzaro, "Il nome del defunto nella preghiera eucaristica," Liturgia 25 (1991) 301–307. [9]N.M. Denis-Boulet, "Les cimetières chrétiens primitifs," in *Le mystère de la mort et sa célébration.* Lex orandi 12 (Paris, 1951). [10]DS 856/ND 26. [11]Tanner 1:526-527/DS 1304/ND 2308. [12]J. Meyendorff, *Byzantine Theology: Historical Trends and Doctrinal Themes* (London—Oxford: Mowbrays, 1975) 96, 110–112, 220–222; P.N. Trembelas, *Dogmatique de l'Église orthodoxe.* 3 vols. (Chevetogne—Paris, 1968) 3:435-455; cf. M. Jugie, "Purgatoire dans l'Église Gréco-Russe après le Concile de Florence," DTC 13:1326-1351. [13]Sess. 25—Tanner 2:774/DS 1820/ND 2310. [14]*Recentiores episcoporum synodi*—AAS 71 (1979) 942/Flannery 2:502. [15]ST Supp q. 71, aa. 2–3, 6, 11. [16]*In 4 Sent.* d.21, q.1; d.45, q.2; In 1 Cor. lect. 2 (164–169). [17]C. de Seyssel, "Purgatoire," DSpir 12:2666-2676. [18]Y. Congar, "Le purgatoire," *Le mystère de la mort.* Lex orandi 12 (Paris, 1951) 279–336; E. Klinger, "Purgatory," SM 5:166-168; E. Lanne, "The Teaching of the Catholic Church on Purgatory," OneChr 28 (1992) 13–30 = Irén 64 (1991) 205–229; A. Michel, "Purgatoire," DTC 13:1163-1326; B. Moriconi, "Il purgatorio soggiorno dell'amore," EphCarm 31 (1986) 539–578; G.L. Müller, "Purgatory," TDig 34 (1987) 31–36 = TQ 166 (1986) 25–39; K. Rahner, "Purgatory," ThInvest 19:181-193; K. Reinhardt, "Das Verständnis des Fegfeurs in der neueren Theologie," TrierTZ 96 (1987) 111–122; R.J. Schreiter, "Purgatory: In Quest of an Image," ChicSt 24 (1985) 167–179. [19]E.g., St. Catherine of Genoa, *Purgation and Purgatory*—LCC 13:392-413/Classics of Western Spirituality (New York: Paulist, 1979); St. John of the Cross, *Dark Night of the Soul* 2:6, 6; 7, 7; 10, 5; 12; Philippe de la Trinité, *La doctrine de S. Thérèse de l'Enfant Jésus sur le purgatoire* (Paris, 1950). [20]Paul VI, *Indulgentiarum doctrina,* AAS 59 (1967) 5–24/Flannery 1:62-79.

# Q

## QUAKERS/RELIGIOUS SOCIETY OF FRIENDS

The Religious Society of Friends which gathered around George Fox (1624–1691) was based on the insight of John 15:14—"You are my friends." Originally, "Quaker" was a term of ridicule, but it is now used by members of the Society themselves. Pennsylvania was founded in 1682 on a Quaker basis by W. Penn (1644–1718), author of the Quaker classic *No Cross, No Crown*. The early work in Latin of Robert Barclay, *Apology of True Christian Theology* (1676), sets out the religious positions of the Friends.[1] From the central doctrine of the "inner light" came the refusal of all sacraments and of any set worship, since Christ, believed to be present where "two or three are gathered" (Matt 18:20), can use any man or woman as a minister. Quakers believe in spiritual baptism and spiritual communion but do not accept the external rites. Their rejection of oaths and military service has often led to harassment and persecution,[2] especially where pacifism is socially or politically unacceptable.

Quakers have been involved in ecumenism according to their convictions: there were Quakers at the foundation of the World Council of Churches, and a Quaker observer at Vatican II. Some have found that the Faith and Order Lima document on Baptism, Eucharist, and Ministry (1982) failed to make allowance for their positions. The major contribution of Quakers to the ecumenical movement lies in their outstanding witness to peace, to social and educational endeavors, and in their deep spirituality allied to an openness to the charisms of the Holy Spirit.

---

[1]Schaff 3:789-798. [2]E.B. Castle, *Approach to Quakerism* (London: Bannisdale, 1961); L.S. Kenworthy, ed., *Friends Face the World: Some Continuing and Current Quaker Concerns* (Kenneth Square, Penn.: Quaker Publ. 1987); H. Loukes, *The Quaker Contribution*

(London: SCM, 1965); D.V. Steere, ed., *Quaker Spirituality: Selected Writings* (New York: Paulist, 1984); D.E. Trueblood, *The People Called Quakers* (New York: Harper, 1966).

## QUARTODECIMAN CONTROVERSY

Ostensibly a dispute about the correct date for the celebration of Easter, the 2nd-century Quartodeciman controversy raised important issues. Some Christians in Asia Minor celebrated Easter on the 14th ("quartodeciman" = 14) day of the Jewish month of Nisan. Other Jewish practices may have been involved as well. Polycarp (q.v.) visited Rome to confer with Anicetus, bishop of Rome (ca. 155—ca. 165). Their visit was amicable, but Anicetus did not agree to establish the date for Easter celebration according to the Jewish mode: every Sunday was for his Church a resurrection celebration.[1] A successor, Victor (189–198), insisted that Asia Minor conform with Roman practice and excommunicated Polycrates of Ephesus, a move deplored by Irenaeus.[2] The controversy shows a self-confident Roman bishop attempting to exclude Polycrates not only from communion with the Roman Church but from the rest of the Church as well. It is also very early evidence both of particular councils and of the Roman predilection for uniformity according to its own mode of action.[3]

---

[1]N. Box, "The Conflict Between Anicetus and Polycarp," Conc 1/8(Jan. 1972) 37–45; OxDPopes 10–11; K.Baus, in Jedin-Dolan 1:268-272. [2]Eusebius *Hist. eccl.* 5:23-24. [3]N. Brox, "Tendenzen und Parteilichkeiten im Osterfeststreit des zweiten Jahrhunderts," ZKG 83 (1972) 291–324; J. Fischer, "Die Synoden im Osterfeststreit des 2. Jahrhunderts," AHC 8 (1976) 15–39.

## QUEEN, Church as

It may not seem an appropriate theme to develop after Vatican II, but the idea of the Church as Queen is found in liturgy, iconography, and in patristic as well as later writings.[1] St. Augustine interpreted the Song of Solomon as the nuptials between Christ-King and Church-Queen.[2] But before him there was already a tradition for interpreting Psalm 44 (45) in an ecclesial sense. Justin (q.v.) used the text to show that the Church is the daughter of the king (vv. 7, 13).[3] The theme is taken up by Jerome (q.v.)[4] but more especially by Augustine (q.v.) in commenting on this psalm.[5] The theme of the Church as Queen continues to emerge in the late patristic and medieval period in the context of Ps 44, e.g., Cassiodorus,[6] Paschasius Radbert,[7] Peter Lombard,[8] Thomas Aquinas,[9] and Bonaventure, who combines mother, nurse, and queen.[10] The theme of queen is frequently associated with that of spouse (q.v.); it still has a place in an integral ecclesiology, one which takes due account of the beauty of the Church.

[1]É. Lamirande, "*Astitit regina a dextris tuis:* L'Église-reine chez Augustin," in *Études sur l'ecclésiologie de saint Augustin* (Ottawa: UP, 1969) 21–31 at 31. [2]*De civ.* Dei 17:20—PL 41:556. [3]*Dialogue* 63:4-5—PL 6:622; see Eusebius of Caesarea, *Comm. in ps.* 44:10—PG 23:401. [4]*Epist.* 65—PL 22:634. [5]*Enarr. in ps.* 44:24—PL 36:509; 44:28—PL 36:512; 44:33—PL 36:513-514; De civ. Dei 17:16—PL 41:549/CSEL 48:581. [6]*Expos. in ps.* 44:10—PL 70:324. [7]*Expos. in ps.* 44:3—PL 120:1039. [8]*Comm. in ps.* 44:11—PL 191:443. [9]*In ps. Davidis expos.* 44:7—ed. Parma 14:324.7. [10]*Apologia pauperum.* Ed. Quaracchi 8:315.

## QUINISEXT, COUNCIL OF

See TRULLO, COUNCIL OF

# R

## RAHNER, Karl (1904–1984)

One of the most important and prolific theologians of the 20th century, Karl Rahner was born in Freiburg in Breisgau in 1904.[1] He became a Jesuit in 1922 and subsequently studied philosophy in Feldkirch and Pullach, where he encountered the work of J. Maréchal. After ordination in 1932 he went to Freiburg where his professors included M. Heidegger. His doctoral thesis on St. Thomas Aquinas was rejected by his director, M. Honecker. Rahner published it in 1937.[2] His doctoral thesis in theology at Innsbruck was on the typological, ecclesial interpretation of John 19:34, and was completed in 1936. During the 1939–1945 war he worked in a pastoral institute in Vienna. After the war he became professor at Innsbruck, later moving to Münster (1963), to Munich (1964), and back to Münster (1967), retiring from teaching in 1971. He died in 1984 just after his eightieth birthday.

Rahner was under a cloud in Rome from 1951–1962 due to several articles that later proved to be ahead of their time. He had only a minor role in the preparations of Vatican II, but after his appointment as *peritus* in 1962, his influence on the council was immense.[3] A symbol of his prestige was the fact that at the Central Commission meetings one of the two microphones was soon permanently left in front of him. The council documents have many favorite Rahnerian themes. Though not its main author, his input into the Constitution on the Church was most important and included the Church as sacrament (q.v.), its eschatological character, bishops' collegiality (q.v.), local Church (q.v.), the ecclesial dimension of the sacraments, salvation of non-Christians (q.v.), the diaconate, Mary's membership of the Church. He also had a major input into the constitutions on Divine Revelation and the Church in the Modern World, and into the Decree on Adaptation of Religious Life. For a decade after the council he remained extremely optimistic; he identified as traces of new or renewed theology those matters on which the Congregation for the Doctrine of the Faith found it necessary to speak defensively; but from about 1980 he began to speak publicly of a wintertime *(eine winterlichen Zeit)* that had fallen on the Church of Rome.[4]

There are several bibliographies of Rahner's immense corpus;[5] there are also ones of the secondary literature about him, which appears to grow daily.[6] On first acquaintance he is notoriously difficult to read, but continuous familiarity makes his work more comprehensible. The language is frequently tortuous. The bulk of his work consists of essays and lectures in which he reflects on, and speculatively explores, a huge range of theological issues. But his customary lack of footnotes makes it difficult to identify the immediate springboards of his always fertile thought. Though a speculative theologian of immense range and depth, he is also significantly pastoral in his approach; theology, he feels, must say something that ministers to salvation. He is not afraid to be tentative in seeking out new implications, in breaking the mold of a narrow, neo-scholastic manual theology.[7] Along with H.U. von Balthasar (q.v.), he is probably the most successful of the 20th-century theologians in integrating spirituality and theology. His many works on spirituality, including speculative essays, meditations and sermons, and some of his writings on Mary,[8] are more immediately accessible.

But the difficulty with Rahner also lies in his transcendental Thomism, which underlies all his work. Central to his theology is the self-communication of the Mystery to humankind in its existential situation; the fact that all persons are thus addressed by Ultimate Reality engenders its own epistemology and ontology.

We cannot explain the ground of our being without reference to the incomprehensible Absolute Mystery which is already a given in our search for truth. Except for one important large-scale volume,[9] his later work though not systematic is, however, consistent.

It is difficult to indicate what works of Rahner pertain to ecclesiology; almost all of his output is in some way addressed to, and is relevant for, the Church and its self-understanding. Each reader might differently assess his most significant contribution to ecclesiology: it may lie in his pneumatology,[10] his awareness of the universality of the Spirit's guiding the whole Church through office, magisterium, and charism—especially prophecy[11]—and bringing all of humanity into a saving encounter with the Absolute, which is Three in unity: the Church would then be the explicit manifestation (sacrament) of grace that is offered to all. An important contribution was his grappling with the problem that the Church with a worldwide mission does not seem to be growing as a percentage of humanity. In very many of his writings he developed the idea of the Church in diaspora, of it being a "little flock" (Luke 12:32; cf. Matt 26:31), like a leaven in society (Matt 13:33).[12] Others would see various stages in his ecclesiological concerns, even if there is a fairly steady pattern in them.[13] In any event, his preparedness to tackle all of the burning issues of the day makes him a model for the contemporary ecclesiologist.

He himself surveyed Vatican II from an ecclesiological point of view in 1968.[14] Afterwards he devoted a lot of attention to pastoral issues, both as an editor of *Handbuch der Pastoraltheologie* (1964–1972) and in a provocative book, *The Shape of the Church to Come.*[15] While one could claim that all of his ecclesiological writing was ecumenical, the number of articles explicitly dealing with Christian unity is small. But in a book written with H. Fries just before his death, he showed a bold ecumenical vision very far ahead, indeed, of the current policy and practice of the official Church.[16]

In the post-Vatican II period Rahner devoted much attention to some topics which continually occupied him as early as his essays on the salvation of non-believers (v. ANONYMOUS CHRISTIANS): the relation of the Church to the world—the modern and secularized world; issues relating to fundamental theology.

An evaluation of his contribution to the Church and to ecclesiology would be incomplete without reference to his editorship of Denzinger (q.v.), the ten-volume *Lexikon für Theologie und Kirche* (1955–1967), the *Concise Theological Dictionary,*[17] of the *Quaestiones disputatae* series (begun in 1961 and now numbering over 100 volumes), and of the theological encyclopedia *Sacramentum mundi.*[18]

[1]J.A. DiNoia, "Karl Rahner," in D.F. Ford, ed., *The Modern Theologians.* 2 vols. (Oxford: Blackwell, 1989) 1:183-204; W.V. Dych, *Karl Rahner.* Outstanding Christian Thinkers (London: Chapman, 1992); H. Vorgrimler, *Understanding Karl Rahner: An Introduction to His Life and Thought* (New York: Crossroad—London: SCM, 1986); idem, *Karl Rahner: His Life, Thought and Works* (London: Burns & Oates, 1965—Glen Rock, N.J.: Paulist, 1966). [2]*Geist in Welt;* Eng. trans. *Spirit in the World,* from 2nd edition by J.B. Metz (New York, 1968). [3]K.H. Neufeld, "Theologen und Konzil: Karl Rahners Beitrage zum Zweiten Vatikanischen Konzil," StimZ 202 (1984) 156–166; H. Vorgrimler, "Karl Rahner: The Theologian's Contribution," in A. Stacpoole, ed., *Vatican II by Those Who Were There* (London: Chapman, 1986) 32–46. [4]Vorgrimler (n. 3) 45–46; P. Imhof and H. Biallowons, eds., *Faith in a Wintry Season: Conversations and Interviews with Karl Rahner in the Last Years of his Life* (New York: Crossroad, 1990). [5]Main works are in collected *Theological Investigations.* 22 vols. (London: Darton, Longman & Todd—U.S.A various, 1961–1991); see G.A. McCool, ed., *A Rahner Reader* (New York: Seabury—London: Darton, Longman & Todd, 1975). [6]R. Bleistein and E. Klinger, *Bibliographie Karl Rahner 1924–1969* (Freiburg: Herder, 1969); R. Bleistein, *Bibliographie Karl Rahner* (Freiburg: Herder, 1974); C.J. Pedley, "An English Bibliographical Aid to Karl Rahner," HeythJ 25 (1984) 319–365; idem, "Supplement," HeythJ 28 (1985) 310; A. Tallon, "In Dialogue with Karl Rahner: Bibliography of Books, Articles and Selected Reviews 1939–1978," TDig 26 (1978) 365–385; idem, "Rahner Studies 1939–1989. Part II—1974–1989," TDig 37 (1990) 17–41; idem, "Rahner Bibliography Supplement," TDig 38 (1991) 131–140; see in H. Vorgrimler, ed., *Wagnis Theologie: Erfahrungen mit der Theologie Karl Rahners* (Freiburg-Basel-Vienna, Herder, 1979)—P. Imhof and H. Treziak, "Bibliographie Karl Rahner 1974–1979": 579–597; A. Raffelt, "Karl Rahner: Bibliographie der Secundärliteratur 1948–1978": 598–622. [7]"Some Clarifying Remarks About My Own Work," ThInvest 17:243-248; "Reflections on Methodology in Theology," Th Invest11:68-114. [8]"Bibliografia mariana di K. Rahner," EphMar 34 (1984) 356–357. [9]*Foundations of Christian Faith: An Introduction to the Idea of Christianity* (London: Darton, Longman & Todd, 1978). [10]J. Losada Espinosa, "La eclesiología pneumatológica de Karl Rahner," EstTrin 21 (1987) 133–168. [11]D. Lowry, *The Prophetic Element in the Church: As Conceived in the Theology of Karl Rahner* (Lanham, Md.—London: University Press of America, 1990). [12]"A Theological Interpretation of the Position of Christians in the Modern World," in *Mission and Grace: Essays in Pastoral Theology,* vol. 1 (London: Sheed & Ward "Stagbooks," 1963) 3–55. [13]L.J. O'Donovan, J.P. Schineller, J.P. Galvin, and M.A. Fahey, "A Changing Ecclesiology in a Changing Church: A Symposium on Development in the Ecclesiology of Karl Rahner," TS 38 (1977) 736–762; cf. Dych (n. 1) 82–101. See R. Lennon, *The Ecclesiology of Karl Rahner* (Oxford: Clarendon, 1995); P.J. Lynch, "Servant Ecclesiologies: A Challenge to Rahner's Understanding of Church and World," IrTQ 57 (1991) 277–298. [14]"The New Image of the Church," ThInvest 10:3-29. [15]London: SPCK, 1974. [16]*Unity of the Churches: An Actual Possibility* (Philadelphia: Fortress—New York—Ramsey: Paulist, 1985 from German 1983). [17]With H. Vorgrimler (Freiburg: Herder—London: Burns & Oates, 1965; German [10]1975). [18]6 vols. (New York: Herder & Herder—London: Burns & Oates, 1968–1970).

## RATZINGER, Cardinal Joseph (1927– )

Joseph Ratzinger was born in Bavaria in 1927. His studies were interrupted by World War II and by brief service in the German defense forces. Ordained a priest in 1951, he soon completed his doctorate on Augustine[1] and his *Habilitationsschrift,* or professorial dissertation, on the theology of history in St. Bonaventure.[2] Teaching posts at Bonn, Münster, Tübingen, and Regensburg followed. Cardinal Frings brought him to Vatican II as his advisor, and he became one of the youngest *periti* at the Council. In 1977 he was named archbishop of Munich-Freising, and cardinal. In 1982 he was brought to Rome to be prefect of the Congregation for the Doctrine of the Faith (CDF).

His theological output is very substantive and wide–ranging, consisting of sixty books and several hundred articles,[3] with a secondary literature on his thought steadily accumulating. It would be generally recognized that at least on a superficial level the thought of Cardinal Ratzinger has changed over the years; he may well see it as a harmonious development, but his earlier writings were a good deal more open and venturesome than his more recent ones. The responsibility of being prefect of the CDF inevitably could contribute to a more cautious and conservative approach. It is not easy now to distinguish the official views of the CDF from the theological positions of its prefect. One can detect some pessimism (Augustinian?) in his widely published interview on the state of the Church.[4]

Ratzinger's present ecclesiology stresses above all communion;[5] a communion ecclesiology is also now the dominant one emanating from the CDF.[6] Fearing a splintering of the Church, the cardinal tends to emphasize the universal over the local Church: he is less than enthusiastic about the significance of bishops' conferences (q.v.); he stresses the importance of papal and other magisterial teaching without, perhaps, giving sufficient attention to the creative role of theology. He is widely seen as a watchman for orthodoxy, as the cases of C. Curran, L. Boff (q.v.), H. Küng (q.v.), and E. Schillebeeckx (q.v.) have shown. His Congregation has shown much circumspection in the area of ecumenism, possibly again reflecting its prefect (v. ANGLICANISM AND ECUMENISM).[7] His ecclesiology shows a concern for spirituality as well as institution, and this is seen especially in his views on post-Vatican II liturgy. His deeply thought-out soteriology and anthropology,[8] in which is evident the currently less popular vertical approach to theology and spirituality, can be shown to underlie his reservations (sometimes exaggerated by his critics, sometimes overharshly articulated) about liberation theology, and about modern society.

[1]*Volk und Haus Gottes in Augustins Lehre von der Kirche* (Munich, 1954). [2]*Die Geschichtstheologie des heiligen Bonaventura* (Munich, 1959)—*The Theology of History in St. Bonaventure* (Chicago: Franciscan Herald, 1971). [3]Bibliog., H. Hofl, in W. Baier et al. eds., *Weisheit Gottes—Weisheit der Welt.* FS J. card. Ratzinger. 2 vols. (St. Ottilien: EOS, 1987). 2:1*—77* = A. Nichols, *The Theology of Joseph Ratzinger: An Introductory Study* (Edinburgh:

Clark, 1988) 297–332. [4]*The Ratzinger Report: An Exclusive Interview on the State of the Church* with V. Messori (San Francisco: Ignatius, 1985). [5]*Zur Gemeinschaft gerufen Kirche heute verstehen* (Freiburg-Basel-Vienna: Herder, 1991). [6]"The Church as Communion" CathIntern3 (1992) 761–767. [7]J. Ratzinger, *Church Ecumenism and Politics: New Essays in Ecclesiology* (Slough UK: St. Paul—New York: Crossroad, 1988). [8]Cf. J. Corkery, *The Relationship Between Human Existence and Christian Salvation in the Theology of Joseph Ratzinger.* Diss. (Washington, D.C.: The Catholic University of America, 1991).

## READERS

The office of Reader, which has been revived in recent decades, is an ancient one in the Church. In the 3rd-century *Apostolic Tradition* (q.v.), it was stated that a reader *(lector/anagnôstês)* did not receive the imposition of the hand (q.v.) but was instituted by being given the Book (11/12). *The Statutes of the Apostles/ Apostolic Church Order*[1] of the early 4th century allowed that a bishop might be illiterate but that the lector must be educated and of ready speech (*diêgêtikos* —able to give homilies?), for he takes the place of an evangelist.[2] The late 4th-century *Apostolic Constitutions* (q.v.) seemed to envisage lectors receiving some support from the Church,[3] and affirmed that the office of lector is of apostolic institution along with priests, deacons, and subdeacons (q.v.).[4] In the Middle Ages, lector was a lower or minor order,[5] and at Trent it was largely seen as a step on the road to the priesthood.[6]

In 1972 the office was renewed by Paul VI: he declared that it is a ministry, not an order; readers are to be "instituted" rather than "ordained"; it is a ministry open to laity in the Church and no longer merely a step towards priestly ordination; the ministry is of reading the Scriptures (except the Gospel) at liturgy, and it also entails instruction of the congregation with a view to more perfect celebration of the liturgy; the office according to ancient tradition is reserved to men—a stipulation later repeated in the *Code of Canon Law* (CIC 230); the ministry is conferred by the Ordinary (bishop, or for his subjects by a major religious superior); the conferring of ministries does not bring with it the right to support or remuneration from the Church.[7] The *Rite for the Institution of Readers* stresses service of the Word and the instruction of children and adults in the faith as well as evangelization. A central theme of this rite is also the reader's obligation himself to meditate upon the Word he proclaims.[8]

There can be some confusion arising from the fact that in many, if not most, parishes those deputed to read at the liturgy, both men and women, are normally not people who have been instituted formally as readers.

[1]OxDCC 75; Patrology 2:119-120. [2]*Statutes of the Apostles*— Saidic text 16,19/Ethiopian 15—G. Horner, trans. and ed., *The Statutes of the Apostles or Canones ecclesiastici* (London, 1904—

Oxford 1915) 134–135, 301, 303; cp. text in A. Faivre, "Clerc/laïc: histoire d'une frontière," RevSR 57 (1983) 202–204. ³2:28, 5; 8:31, 2—SC 320:244; 336:234. ⁴8:46, 13—SC 336:270. ⁵St. Thomas, *Summa c. gentiles* 4:75; *Suppl.* q.37, a.2. ⁶Tanner 2:743/DS 1772/ND 1715. ⁷*Ministeria quaedam*—AAS 64 (1972) 529–534/DOL 2922–2938/Rites 2:98-103. ⁸Rites 2:104-106.

# RECEPTION

There is a very substantial literature on reception in recent decades.[1] But the reality of reception and the use of the words "reception/receive" are very ancient.

The recognition of the scriptural canon by Jews and Christians was a process of reception.[2] At the time of Jesus the Sadducees received as God's word only the Pentateuch; the Pharisees, the Hebrew Scriptures; Jews at Alexandria had other books, though one cannot say that they had any rigid notion of canonicity. The Christian canon was slow in forming. Some biblical books were not accepted in some Churches, e.g., in the West, Hebrews, in the first centuries; other books at one time were considered scriptural in some Churches, e.g., *Didachê* (q.v.), and works by Clement (q.v.) and Hermas (q.v.). There is no scholarly agreement about the detailed process of this crucial reception. Even today some Eastern Churches accept as canonical works that are not accepted as such by either Catholics or Protestants, viz., 3 Esdr, 3 Macc, and Ps 151; most Protestants do not accept the deuterocanonical books (Tob, Jdt, Wis, Sir, Bar, 1–2 Macc, and additional chs. in Dan and Esth). The first conciliar definition on the canon of Scripture had to await Florence (q.v.),[3] and the matter was controverted enough for Trent (q.v.) to reinforce the earlier council.[4]

Even within the Scriptures there is evidence of reception. Second Peter notes a collection of Pauline writings (3:15-16). Paul himself talks about teaching which he himself had "received"—probably in short catechetical formulas (1 Cor 15:3-7); elsewhere he speaks about receiving from the Lord (1 Cor 11:23). More profoundly, Jesus speaks of the command he has received from the Father (John 10:18). Jesus himself must be received (John 1:12, 14; Col 2:6). Receiving is a crucial notion in the NT: the Spirit is received (Acts 1:8; Rom 8:15) as is salvation (Jas 1:12), so that Paul can ask, "What have you that you have not received?" (1 Cor 4:7). Receiving is at the heart of NT soteriology. What is received in the first place and in the final analysis is the love of God the Father made incarnate in the Son and given in the Spirit.[5] These meanings were carried into patristic literature; Church Fathers, like Justin (q.v.) speak of learning, of receiving, and of what is handed down.[6]

In time we encounter what is today referred to as the classical or technical sense of reception. It is mainly concerned with councils and creeds which were accepted by the whole Church and given a special status as a norm of belief or of behavior. But they were never mere formulas: through them the Church encounters its Lord in the Spirit. The process of this reception is not always clear; there were hesitations over various councils which were not accepted by some Churches for a long time. In time seven councils would be called "ecumenical." They were adjudged by the Church to mirror its faith and to moderate its life. Some councils which set out to be ecumenical were not received as such, e.g., the Robber Council ("Latrocinium") at Ephesus (449), the Council of Sardica (343–344). Other local councils were accepted as orthodox expressions of the faith, e.g., Carthage XV/XVI in 418, or the Second Council of Orange (529), forgotten for centuries and used by Trent and ever since as an authentic statement of the Church's faith. Again, only the first seven councils are accepted by the East as ecumenical; the Catholic Church generally adopts twenty-one up to Vatican II (v. COUNCILS).

The reception of the seven great councils was not a matter merely of subsequent papal approval; more profoundly operative was the sense of the faith (q.v.) whereby the bishops of the local Churches and their people welcomed them into their liturgy and life. The reception into liturgy is very significant, for liturgy covers many expressions of faith: Scripture, hymns, art, music, symbols, prayers, all of which together are incomparably richer than mere dogmatic statements.[7]

Reception in this classical sense is communitarian; it is a work of the Spirit in the communion (q.v.) within and among the local Churches; it recognizes a special role for the bishop as witness to tradition and judge of the authenticity of faith.[8] But it also involves the laity who accept and find life-giving what their pastors acknowledge as authentic. As a work of the Spirit in the whole community, reception is not the same as a plebiscite or a modern Gallup poll.[9]

The seven great councils achieved a twofold consensus: one that could be called "vertical," with Scripture and Tradition, and a "horizontal" one with the rest of the Church.[10] But this reception was sometimes slow and partial, and it did not follow predetermined patterns:[11] the explicit reception of Nicaea II (786–787—q.v.) was delayed for a long time in the West,[12] and seems only to have been explicitly received as one of the great councils by a pope (Leo IX) in 1053,[13] even though earlier popes gave it some approval; the Copts for a long time refused Chalcedon; the minority bishops at Vatican I immediately received its teaching on the papacy, the Old Catholics did not. After nearly all the councils there were groups who did not accept the councils which condemned them, at least in the beginning.

But Catholic theology would not accept the position of Russian Orthodox theologians that reception constitutes ecumenicity; Eastern theologians have, nonetheless, contributed much to the formulation and understanding of reception, beginning with Khomiakov (q.v.).[14] The Catholic Church also rejected Gallican (q.v.) theses on the necessity of reception. Reception is a sign that the council or a pope has taught definitively.[15] As in the case of papal infallibility (q.v.), the cause of the orthodoxy of councils can only be the Holy Spirit.

Liturgy provides examples of various kinds of reception. Thus, certain feasts became celebrated in the whole Church, sometimes slowly, as in the case of Mary's Assumption. But a feast of the Precious Blood, though promoted by Pius XI in 1934 and encouraged by John XXIII,[16] never attained popularity and was quietly demoted in the 1968 revision of the calendar. In liturgy we look not only to the feast itself being received but also to its content and focus. Again, in some places a particular saint's feast is profoundly acknowledged, e.g., St. Januarius at Naples, but it may have no particular resonance for the rest of the Church; other saints, like St. John the Baptist, are celebrated by East and West.

More important, though, is the fact that liturgy shows that reception demands inculturation (q.v.). A doctrine, a canonical practice is received by a local Church according to its life and times and finds its expression there. The principles of Catholic social teaching are differently received in communities which view theology through the prism of liberation (v. LIBERATION THEOLOGY).[17]

Again, we can see how liturgy can receive doctrinal teaching. The post-Vatican II Church received the Eastern emphasis on pneumatology (q.v.) in its careful insertion of the *epiclêsis* (q.v.) in the new Eucharist Prayers.

Though Vatican II did not deal extensively with reception in an explicit way, it has important teaching that helps us to grasp the meaning of the process of reception. The whole Constitution on Divine Revelation (DV) can be said to be about the reception by the Church of divine truths contained in Scripture and Tradition. Moreover, the teaching on the sense of the faith (LG 12, 35—q.v.) shows us how the Church receives divine truth. It is not a passive acceptance of static formulas, but "through this sense of faith which is *aroused and sustained by the Spirit of truth,* the people of God, under the guidance of the sacred magisterium . . . receives no longer the words of human beings, but truly the word of God; it (the people) *adheres* indefectibly to the faith once for all delivered to the saints, it *penetrates* more deeply into that same faith by right judgment, and *applies* it more fully to life" (LG 12 with italics added). In LG 25, speaking about infallible teaching, the council stresses that the assent of the Church is through the Holy Spirit, "by

which the whole flock of Christ is preserved in the unity of faith and makes progress."

The instance of non-reception is an extremely difficult one. It is found in relation to doctrinal[18] and canonical enactments.[19] It also raises all the issues connected with dissent (q.v.). We can point to elements of *Unam sanctam* of Boniface VIII (q.v.)[20] which, for all its solemn language, were not received. A more recent example is John XXIII's *Veterum sapientia* (1962), which imposed Latin as the vehicle of theological instruction. Still more recent is the virtual non-reception by many theologians and a large percentage of the laity in some countries of *Humanae vitae* on contraception (1968).[21] When there is non-reception of magisterial teaching, we can look for an explanation in one or more of several directions. The teaching may be false in whole or in part. It may be badly expressed or be stated in language that makes it difficult for a particular culture to accept. It may be mistimed or otherwise misjudged. It may belong only to one era of the Church's life—hundreds of pages of the decrees of the medieval councils are of little interest today. It may have no real message for the Church in a particular place, or even universally. It may be smothered or overlooked because, for example, the inflation of papal teaching since Pius XI makes assimilation, even for professional theologians, well-nigh impossible. Finally, it may be the misunderstanding, blindness, hardness of heart, or sinful perversity of the people that leads to non-reception. Serious questions must always be asked when there is non-reception; but we may not always be immediately able to account for non-reception; it may take time for the truth of the situation to emerge, just as it takes time for reception to become a reality.

As for Vatican II itself, one must admit that its reception has been partial, the reasons for which must be sought in the council itself (v. VATICAN II).[22] The 1985 Synod of Bishops (q.v.) was an examination of how Vatican II had been received in its four Constitutions (SC, LG, DV, GS).

Another use of reception is in the context of ecumenism.[23] There, it has an apparently precise meaning, but one which in practice is not always easy to determine. This is a recent usage; it did not figure at the World Conference of Faith and Order (1963) or at Vatican II when dealing with ecumenism. But a few years later, at Oxford and Bad Gastein (1965, 1966), the idea of reception took hold when Faith and Order brought together historians and patrologists to discuss the early councils. At the Faith and Order Commission meeting in 1972, it was employed in a more decisive way.

We can speak of mutual reception of Churches as the aim of the ecumenical endeavor. This global reception would operate in various areas: the expression of doctrine would be accepted as mutually coherent;

the rites of each Church would be acknowledged as valid; ministry would be admitted as a an authentic form of *episkopê,* one faithful to the apostolic tradition. This reception could only be the fruit of a long process; it would culminate in a juridical or canonical act by Church leaders.[24] J.M.R. Tillard has drawn attention to the need not only for a juridical reception but for what he terms a "theological reception," which includes a "recognition" and which demands a conversion process in eventually taking into the life of the Church some aspect of the divine Mystery.[25]

As instances of partial reception, one could cite many of the responses to the Faith and Order Lima statement (1982) on the part of Churches,[26] or the Vatican response to ARCIC II (v. ANGLICANISM AND ECUMENISM). In the formal ecumenical dialogues the participants represent as faithfully as they can the traditions of their own Church, and may be appointed by its leader. But they must then submit their agreements to their Churches with a view to reception.[27]

Tradition involves the continuous process of re-reception of truths in different ages and cultures.[28]

[1]M.J. Himes, "The Ecclesiological Significance of the Reception of Doctrine," HeythJ 33 (1992) 146–160; E.J. Kilmartin, "Reception in History: An Ecclesiological Phenomenon and Its Significance," JEcuSt 21 (1984) 34–54; E. Lanne, "La 'réception,'" Irén 55 (1982) 199–213; M. O'Gara, "Karl Rahner and the Nature of Reception," OneChr 25 (1989) 75–83; P.O'Leary, "Authority to Proclaim the Word of God and the Consent of the Church," FreiZ 29 (1982) 239–251; T.P. Rausch, "Reception Past and Present," TS 47 (1986) 497–508. [2]R.E. Brown and R.F. Collins, "Canonicity," NJBC 1034–1054; B. Dupuy, "Réception des Écritures et fixation du canon: Recherches et perspectives nouvelles," Istina 36 (1991) 131–159. [3]Tanner 1:572/DS 1335/ND 208. [4]Tanner 2:663-664/DS 1502–1503/ND 211–212 [5]J.D. Zizioulas, "The Theological Problem of 'Reception,'" OneChr 21 (1985) 187–193. [6]*1 Apol.* 10, 12, 43, 44, 45, 66 . . . [7]J.M.R. Tillard, "Reception—Communion," OneChr 28 (1992) 307–322 at 314; Zizioulas (n. 5) 191–192. [8]Zizioulas (n. 5). [9]E. Timiadis, "Reception, Consensus, and Unity," GkOrTR 28 (1991) 47–61. [10]F.A. Sullivan, *Magisterium: Teaching Authority in the Catholic Church* (Dublin: Gill and Macmillan, 1983) 85 following, H.J. Sieben, *Die Konzilsidee der alten Kirche* (Paderborn: Schöningh, 1979); see H. Chadwick, "Un concetto per la storia dei concili: la ricezione," CrNSt 13 (1992) 475–492. [11]Y. Congar, "La 'réception' comme réalité ecclésiologique," RSPT 56 (1972) 369–403 = collection *Église et papauté: Regards historiques* (Paris: Cerf, 1994) 229–266; abbreviated "Reception as an Ecclesiological Reality," Conc 77 (1972) 43–68. [12]J.E. Lynch, "The Reception of an Ecumenical Council: Nicaea II a Case in Point," Jurist 48 (1988) 454–482. [13]DS 686. [14]P.P. O'Leary, *The Triune Church. A Study in the Ecclesiology of A.S. Xomjakov* (Dublin: Dominican—Freiburg: UP, 1982) 144–152. [15]Sullivan (n. 10) 106, 109–117. [16]*Inde a primis*—AAS 52 (1960) 545–550. [17]L. Boff, "Eine kreative Rezeption des II. Vatikanums aus der Sicht der Armen: Die Theologie der Befreiung," TJb 1987: 167-188. [18]P. Granfield, *The Limits of the Papacy: Authority and Autonomy in the Church* (New York: Crossroad—London: Darton, Longman & Todd, 1987) 147–158. [19]J.M. Huels, "Nonreception of Canon Law by the Community," NTRev 4/2 (1991) 47–61; see J.A. Coriden, "The Canonical Doctrine of Reception," Jurist 50

(1990) 58–82. [20]DS 870–875/in part ND 804. [21]J.A. Komonchak, "*Humanae vitae* and Its Reception: Ecclesiological Reflections," TS 39 (1978) 221–257. [22]G. Alberigo et al., eds., *The Reception of Vatican II* (Washington, D.C.: The Catholic University of America, 1987); A. Antón, "La 'recepción' del Concilio Vaticano II y de su eclesiología," RET 48 (1988) 291–319; L. Richard et al., eds., *Vatican II: The Unfinished Agenda* (New York—Mahwah: Paulist, 1987); J.M.R. Tillard, "Haben wir das Zweite Vatikanum 'rezipiert'?," TGegw 29 (1986) 65–72. [23]W.G. Rusch, *Reception: An Ecumenical Opportunity* (Geneva: LWF—Philadelphia: Fortress, 1988); M. Tataryn, "Karl Rahner and the Nature of Reception," OneChr 25 (1989) 75–83. [24]Tillard (n. 7). [25]Ibid., 310–318. [26]M. Thurian, *Churches Respond to BEM.* 6 vols. (Geneva: WCC, 1986–1989). [27]AA. VV. *Les dialogues oecuméniques hier et aujourd'hui:* Les études théologiques de Chambésy 5 (Chambésy—Geneva: Ed. du Centre Orthodoxe du Patriarchat Oecuménique, 1955); H. Meyer, "Les présupposés de la réception ecclésiale ou le problème de la 'recevabilité'—Perspectives luthériennes," Irén 59 (1986) 5–19; R.L. Stewart, "'Reception': What Do the Churches Do with Ecumenical Agreements?," OneChr 21 (1985) 194–203 = StEcum 4(1986) 9–26. J. Willebrands, "Ecumenical Dialogue and Its Reception," Diak (USA) 19 (1984–1985) 118–128; OneChr 21 (1985) 217–225. [28]Tillard (n. 7) 312–313.

## RECONCILIATION, SACRAMENT OF

In the NT we have several important teachings about dealing with sin. Power to remit sins was given by the risen Lord (John 20:21-23; Matt 18:18; cf. 16:19). Mutual forgiveness was central to the teaching of Jesus (Matt 6:12; 18:21-35) and to the primitive community (Col 3:13). There was, too, a confession of sins to one another (Jas 5:16). The Church also excluded sinners from its midst (1 Cor 5:3-5; 1 Tim 1:19-20), itself a form of excommunication (q.v.).[1]

Several centuries would be needed to tease out the full implications of the power given by Jesus to his Church.[2] Here we are concerned principally with the ecclesial dimension of the sacrament, and additional matters are to be sought in other sources.[3]

As early as the *Didachê* (q.v.) there were several injunctions about handling sin in the community: almsgiving (4:6), confession of sins (4:14; 14:1), repentance (10:6). The actual practices are not fully clear, but the implication remains that sin and its forgiveness are not a mere private matter between a person and God.[4] For several centuries there would be two tendencies: a rigorist and a more pastoral one. The former limited the possibility of reconciliation in the case of certain sins and restricted multiple reception of reconciliation.

The tension is already visible in the 2nd-century Hermas (q.v.), who is very important in having been the first to give theological reflection on reconciliation, though his positions are not plain on all points.[5] Hermas represents the first theological reflection on reconciliation. He would seem to be reacting to a rigorism in the early part of the 2nd century. This rigorism appears to have some foundation in Heb 6:4-8; 10:26-31; 12:16-17, but these texts can be interpreted as pastoral urgency about conversion. He speaks of conversion on the part of the sinner and pardon effected by God.[6] Some authors see in Hermas a proclamation of a jubilee, before which the sinner must repent.[7] But it is also possible to see Hermas as being influenced by a sense of imminent eschatology: repentance is pressing; it is envisaged therefore as possible only once. Detached from its eschatological context in Hermas, the notion of a single reconciliation would spread throughout the West, and in the East be found in Alexandria.[8] For Hermas, the Church is being built up, and stones which are not acceptable in building up the tower, which is the Church, need to be purified if they are not to be definitively cast aside.[9]

Hermas is not fully clear on whether all sins can be forgiven: he does not know the three unforgivable Montanist sins. There would appear, however, to be a doubt about forgiveness for apostasy. One explanation is to see Hermas as considering the sin unforgivable not because of its gravity but because of the nature of this sin which renders a person closed to grace.[10] If one turns from such sins, then one can be forgiven. Hermas is clearly trying to steer a centrist path between rigorism and a laxism which would disregard the seriousness both of sin and of the means of repentance. Hermas is not explicit about any role for the Church in the process of reconciliation.[11]

The attitude of Hermas was not universally held. There is evidence of rigorism in Tertullian: single reconciliation;[12] from his Montanist time, unforgivable sins, including but not restricted to the triad of idolatry, fornication, murder.[13] But about the same time Dionysius of Corinth (fl. 170), writing to the Church at Amastris, gives a directive "that those who returned to the fold after any kind of lapse, whether improper conduct or heretical error, should be warmly welcomed."[14] The *Didascalia apostolorum* (v. APOSTOLIC COLLECTIONS) is also a witness to a non-rigorist practice.[15]

At least from the 3rd century we find the institution of penance.[16] The exact form varied from one Church to another; we are best informed about the African Church through the writings of Tertullian, Cyprian (q.v.), and Augustine (q.v.). The developed form known to Cyprian is in many ways the clearest to grasp.[17]

In the preceding centuries, from as early as the *Apostolic Tradition* (3:5—q.v.), the role of the bishop was central. Those who committed grave sins confessed them to him, and he gave what Augustine called *correptio,* God's word about the sin, and an exhortation to penance. In Cyprian the penitential process proper, the *exhomologesis,* then began. It may have been preceded by a time of more private penance. The bishop also decreed what the penance would be; it was usually public and lasted for months or even years. This first stage of penance was a form of "excommunication," (q.v.) as the person was separated from the communion of the Church, especially the Eucharist. Afterwards the person was reconciled usually on Holy Thursday at a liturgical ceremony which included an imposition of hands (q.v.) on the part of the bishop, and in the East an anointing—which last would in time give rise to confusion with confirmation (q.v.).[18]

The whole Church was involved in the process of penance: the Church prayed incessantly for the reconciliation of penitents.[19] The renewal of Church fellowship, the *pax,* had real effects with regard to Church membership and to eternal life.[20]

The question of the role of martyrs (q.v.) and confessors, (q.v.) with regard to the reconciliation of those who had fallen away in time of persecution *(lapsi)* at Carthage, is very involved.[21] Even the word *libellus* (letter) had two meanings: it was the certificate that Christians received from the Roman authorities after they had claimed to have offered pagan sacrifice—those who obtained such a document by bribery without attending the sacrifice were called *libellatici;* the word *libellus* was also the name for the letter given by martyrs before their death, or by confessors after their suffering, in favor of those who had fallen away. The *lapsi* sought letters of peace from those who had confessed to facilitate their re-entry into the community. Cyprian was at least trying to bring Church discipline and the restoration of the *lapsi* under the control of the bishop. He acknowledged the position *(praerogativa)* which the martyrs and confessors had with God as in some way effective on behalf of the *lapsi.*[22] He frequently argued that the martyrs can, indeed, promise peace to the *lapsi,* but must refer them to the bishop. But in *extremis* a presbyter or deacon can absolve when a martyr has given a *libellus.* Cyprian never suggested that the practice of the *libellus* was against the custom of his Church.

In the West there was wider evidence of the rigorism we noted in Tertullian: during these early centuries there was the possibility of reconciliation only once;[23] penance was hence postponed until near death.

After the 6th century there were notable developments. The number of sins that were considered to require public reconciliation with the Church increased, so that the norm of single penance became less realistic. Though probably not unique, the contribution of Celtic monks from Ireland and Britain was substantial;[24] they reconciled people without public penance, and such reconciliation was repeatable. The monks also were responsible for a "tariff system," whereby various sins had an established penance attached. Books called "penitentials" multiplied;[25] they laid down the exact penance for each sin. They, too, would lead to an increase in the number of sins requiring reconciliation.

In the early centuries it was clear that the Church intervened in reconciling the sinner with God; it was not merely enough for the sinner to ask God's mercy in private prayer. Grave sins were seen to alienate a person from "communion" so that one had to be reconciled with the Church. Though this ecclesial role was still found in the Middle Ages,[26] more and more the sacrament of reconciliation is seen as a reconciliation of the individual with God through priestly absolution. The deeper ecclesial sense of the sacrament greatly faded. In the late Middle Ages period the patristic emphasis on the role of the bishop in the sacrament was clarified: priests could absolve, provided they had jurisdiction (q.v.) from the bishop. The notion of jurisdiction indicates that the priest is not *sui iuris* in absolution but that he acts by authority which comes from the Church.[27]

The Council of Florence (q.v.) served to heighten the individualist sense of the sacrament, though it did refer to the necessity of authority to absolve.[28] The Council of Trent faced several problems. It proceeded against the perceived errors of the Reformers. The early Reformers were not against a ritual of reconciliation in itself, though they did not accept it as sacramental in the sense understood in the Catholic Church. In the decrees of Trent there was great stress on conversion from, and contrition for, sin; faith was also central to the sacrament. The role of the priest was seen under two images: medical doctor and judge.[29] The need for integrity of confession is probably to be seen in this context: the priest had to know the number and kinds of sin in order to pronounce the judicial sentence of absolution and to prescribe appropriate satisfaction and remedies.[30] The ecclesial aspect of the sacrament did not come very much to the fore; the necessity of jurisdiction was, however, strongly stated. It is also clearly taught that the Church has the power to forgive sins, though the effects of sin are presumed to lie in the relation of the sinner to God.

In the 20th century new historical studies of the sacrament, notably by B.M. Xiberta and B. Poschmann,[31] led to a rediscovery of the ecclesial dimension of the sacrament. Not only are sinners reconciled with God, but they must also be reconciled with the Church; Xiberta indeed asserted that it is through reconciliation with the Church that they are reconciled with God. The new ecclesial insights would be mature in time for Vatican II.

The council called for a revision of the rites and formulas of penance "in such a way that they express more clearly what the sacrament is and what it brings about" (SC 72). In the context of the common priesthood, it stated: "Those who approach the sacrament of penance, through the mercy of God obtain pardon for any offense committed against him, and at the same time are reconciled with the Church which they have wounded by their sin and which strives for their conversion through charity, example and prayers" (LG 11).[32]

The postconciliar revision of the rites of penance shows the achievement of Vatican II.[33] The preferred name of the sacrament is in many places now "reconciliation" rather than "penance" or "confession," even though the new *Code of Canon Law* and the liturgical books retain the term "penance" generally used by the council.[34] Instead of the Tridentine "judging" and "juridical act," referred to only three times in the *General Instruction,* the emphasis now is on healing and conversion, terms which are found over twenty times in the same document. The ecclesial dimension is strongly accented: "The celebration of this sacrament is thus always an act in which the Church proclaims its faith, gives thanks to God for the freedom with which Christ made us free, and offers its life as a spiritual sacrifice in praise of God's glory as it hastens to meet the Lord Jesus."[35]

The formula of absolution also has a pneumatological and ecclesial reference within the parameter of the paschal mystery and salvation history: "God the Father of mercies, through the death and resurrection of his Son has reconciled the world to himself and sent the Holy Spirit among us for the forgiveness of sins; through the ministry of the Church may God give you pardon and peace, and I absolve you from your sins in the name of the Father, and of the Son and of the Holy Spirit."

The revision also presents three rites: a rite for penitent and priest alone; a rite for reconciliation of several penitents, with individual confession and absolution; rite for reconciliation of several penitents, with general confession and absolution. The third of these has restrictions about its use: its celebration depends on the local bishop in accordance with norms laid down by the episcopal conference (CIC 961).[36]

Though the liturgical revival has stressed the ecclesial dimension of the sacrament of reconciliation, the view of the sacrament is still somewhat individualistic in the Church; the new ecclesial insights into sin and forgiveness/reconciliation have not yet taken deep root in the Church at large. The teaching of important recent documents has not yet been sufficiently appreciated, e.g., the 1984 post-synodal apostolic exhortation on reconciliation and penance,[37] preceded by the 1982 document of the International Theological Commission.[38]

The discovery of the full richness of the ecclesial dimension of the sacrament of reconciliation probably depends on an increased awareness of the social dimension of sin and its anthropological as well as theological aspects.[39] It is a constant in tradition that the daily sins that afflict all Christians are removed by many means, such as personal penance, prayer, almsgiving, acts of charity. Some care needs to be taken about the penitential rite at the beginning of Mass: as the *Confiteor* suggests, it is an acknowledgement of sinfulness rather than a rite of reconciliation.[40] Nonetheless, the Eucharist itself is the great sacrament of reconciliation, even though in the case of grave sin one must be reconciled with the Church before participating fully in it.[41]

The Orthodox Churches practice the sacrament of penance,[42] more frequently in the monasteries than elsewhere. They very much stress the healing aspect of the sacrament. Though the sacrament of penance is found at times in the Anglican Communion[43] being envisaged in the Prayer Books, the ecumenical interest in the sacrament is not great. Most Protestants see dealing with sin as falling within pastoral care rather than belonging to the area of sacrament.[44]

[1]E. Cothenet, "Sainteté de l'Église et péchés des chrétiens: Comment le nouveau testament envisage leur pardon," NRT 96 (1974) 449–470; L. Sabourin, "La rémission des péchés: Écriture sainte et pratique ecclésiale," ScEsp 32 (1980) 299–315, cf. TDig 29 (1981) 123–126; L. Roy, "Reconciliation," DBT 479–480. [2]P. Galtier, L'Église et la remission des péchés aux premiers siècles (Paris, 1932); B. Poschmann, Penance and Anointing of the Sick (New York: Herder & Herder, 1964); idem, Paenitentia secunda: Die kirchliche Busse im ältesten Christentum bis Cyprian und Origenes (Bonn, 1940); K. Rahner, "Penance in the Early Church," ThInvest 15:1-451. [3]E.g., R.A. Duffy, "Reconciliation," NDictT 830–836; M.F. Mannion, "Penance and Reconciliation," NDictSac Worship 934–936; M.K. Hellwig, Sign of Reconciliation and Conversion: The Sacrament of Penance for Our Times. Message of the Sacraments 4 (Wilmington: Glazier, 1982). [4]Cf. W. Rorsdorf, "La rémission des péchés selon la Didachè," Irén 46 (1973) 283–297. [5]K. Baus, in Jedin-Dolan 1:321-324; S. Folgado Flórez, Teoría eclesial en el Pastor de Hermas (La Escorial: Bib. La Ciudad de Dios, 1979) 1–38 = "Sentido eclesial de la penitencia en el 'Pastor' de Hermas," CiuD 191 (1978) 3–38; R. Joly, SC 53:22-30; L. Pernveden, The Concept of the Church in the Shepherd of Hermas. St. Theol. Lundensia 27 (Lund: Gleerup, 1966) 223–265; K. Rahner, "The Penitential Teaching of the Shepherd of Hermas," ThInvest 15:57-113; S. Tugwell, The Apostolic Fathers. Outstanding Christian Thinkers (London: Chapman, 1989) 47–88 at 50–56. [6]Simil. 8:11, 3 (77)—SC 53:286. [7]Mand. 4:2 (30). See Joly SC 53:22-30; E. Amann, "Penitence," DTC 12:759-763. [8]Rahner (n. 2) 8 with nn. 25–27. [9]Simil. 9:8 (85); 9:13, 6–14, 3 (90–91). [10]Vis. 6:7, 2 (15); Simil. 8:6, 2; 9:19, 1 (96); Tugwell (n. 5) 84–86. [11]R. Joly, SC 53:28–30; cf., however, Poschmann, Galtier and Rahner (n. 2) above. [12]De paenitentia—ANL 11:257-278/ANF 3:657-666; Patrology 2:299-302, with bibliog. [13]De pudicitia—ANL 18:56-122/ANF 4:74-101; Patrology 2:312-315. See K. Rahner (n. 2) 125–151; K. Baus, in Jedin-Dolan 1:324-330. [14]Eusebius, Hist. eccl. 4:23, 6. [15]6 and 25; see Quasten 2:149; K. Rahner (n. 2) 225–245. [16]J. Favazza, The Order of Penitents (Collegeville: The Liturgical Press, 1987). [17]K. Rahner (n. 2) 152–222. [18]Ibid., 156–171. [19]Cyprian, De lapsis 16, 32 and 36—CSEL 3/1: 248-249, 260–261, 263–264. [20]Cyprian, Epist. 18:1; 20:3—PL 4:272-273, 277–278; De eccl. un. 6—PL 4:502-504. See M. Bévenot, "The Sacrament of Penance and Cyprian's De lapsis," TS 6 (1955) 175–213; Rahner (n. 2) 191–196. [21]K. Baus, in Jedin-Dolan 1:330-338. [22]See Epist. 18:1—PL 4:272-273; cf. Epp. 15–20; 27; 33; 36—PL 4:264-279, 298–300, 317–320, 326–327. [23]Augustine, Epist. 153:3, 7—PL 33:655-656; Siricius Epist. 1:5—PL 13:1137; cf. Ambrose, De paenit. 2:9-11—PL 16 516–522. [24]K. Dooley, "From Penance to Confession: The Celtic Contribution," Bijd 43 (1982) 390–411; W. Cosgrave, "How Celtic

Penance Gave Us Personal Confession," DoctLife 41 (1991) 412–422. [25]V. Saxer, "Penitence. III.—Penitential Books," Encyc EarCh 2:669, with bibliog.; F. Clancy, "The Irish Penitentials," MilltownSt 21 (1988) 87–109. [26]St. Thomas Aquinas, Supp. q.8, a.2 ad 3; a. 5 ad 4. [27]St. Thomas, Supp. q.8, aa. 4–5; Summa c. gentiles 4:72. [28]Tanner 1:548/DS 1623/ND 1612. [29]Sess 14, 1551—Tanner 2:703-709, 711–713/DS 1667–1693, 1701–1715/ND 1614–1634, 1641–1655; B. de Margerie, "La mission sacerdotale de retenir les péchés en liant les pécheurs: Intérêt actuel et justification historique d'une exégèse tridentine," RevSR 58 (1984) 300–317; 59 (1985) 34–50, 119–146; H. McSorley, "Luther and Trent on Faith Needed for the Sacrament of Penance," Conc 61 (1971) 89–98. [30]Cf. C. Peter, "Auricular Confession and the Council of Trent," Jurist 28 (1968) 280–297; idem, "Integral Confession and the Council of Trent," Conc 1/7–61 (1971) 99–109; V. Siret, "Les fondements bibliques de l'obligation de la confession des péchés pour les pères du concile de Trente," RThom 88 (1988) 421–429; StMor 21 (1983) 3–202. [31]B.M. Xiberta, Clavis ecclesiae (Rome, 1922); Poschmann (n. 2); K. Rahner, "Forgotten Truths Concerning Penance," ThInvest 2:135-174; idem, "Penance as an Additional Act of Reconciliation with the Church," ThInvest 10:125-147. [32]J. Dallen, The Reconciling Community: The Rite of Penance (New York: Pueblo, 1986) 205–209; A.J. Golias, Reconciliation with the Church as an Immediate Effect of Penance: Historical Review and Theological Debate. Diss. exc. (Rome: Gregorian, 1986). [33]A. Biazzi, "Le citazioni nei 'Praenotanda' dell' Ordo Paenitentiae: Natura e significato," EphLtg 106 (1992) 81–116; P. Gervais, "Le sacrement de la réconciliation selon le nouveau rituel," NRT 102 (1980) 879–899; L. Hamelin, Reconciliation in the Church: A Theological and Pastoral Essay on the Sacrament of Penance (Collegeville: The Liturgical Press, 1980); R.J. Kennedy, ed., Penance: The Continuing Agenda (Collegeville, The Liturgical Press, 1987); L. Örsy, The Evolving Church and the Sacrament of Penance (Denville, N.J.: Dimension, 1978); D.N. Power, "The Sacramentalization of Penance," HeythJ 18 (1977) 5–22; idem, "Confession as Ongoing Conversion," HeythJ 18 (1977) 180–190; J. Vellian, "The New Rite of Penance: Understanding Its Newness from the Eastern Tradition," Diak—USA 12 (1977) 24–30; AA.VV. The Rite of Penance. Commentaries. 3 vols. (Washington, D.C.: Liturgical Conference, 1975, 1978). [34]P. de Clerck, "Célébrer la pénitence, ou la réconciliation? Essai de discernement théologique à propos du nouveau Rituel," RTLv 13 (1982) 387–424; C. Wackenheim, "Le sens de la réconciliation ecclésiale," RDroitC 34 (1984) 349–360. [35]GI 7b)—Flannery 2:39. [36]See F.R. McManus, in Coriden, CIC, 678–679. [37]Reconciliatio et paenitentia—AAS 77 (1985) 185–275. [38]International Theological Commission, Texts and Documents 1969–1985 (San Francisco: Ignatius, 1989) 225–250. [39]G. Celada, "Proclamación de la reconciliación en la comunidad," CiTom 74 (1983) 433–468; J. Comblín, "O tema da reconcilação e a teologia na América Latina," REBras 46 (1986) 272–314; P. de Clerck, "Pénitence, confession, réconciliation: Une problématique, après le Synode de 1983," RDroit 34 (1984) 167–184; R. Russo, "Comunione e riconciliazione nella chiesa," Asp 30 (1983) 143–171; M. Seybold, "Die ekklesiale Dimension des Heils, der Schuld und der Vergebung," in K. Baumgartner, ed., Erfahrungen mit dem Busssakrament. 2 vols. (Munich: Wewel, 1978) 2:118-165. [40]GI 29. See P.F. de Bethune, "Rite pénitentiel, rite de conversion," Communautés et Liturgies 62 (1980) 269–280. [41]L. Longobardo, "Eucaristia e riconciliazione nei padri," Asp 30 (1983) 131–141. [42]P. Meyendorff, "Penance in the Orthodox Church Today," StLtg 18 (1988) 108–111; idem, Byzantine Theology (London—Oxford: Mowbrays—Fordham UP, 1974) 195–196; P.M. Trembelas, Dogmatique de l'Église orthodoxe catholique. 3 vols. Textes et études théologiques (Chevtogne—Desclée de Brouwer, 1966–1968) 3:255-303. See F. van de Paverd, "La pénitence dans le rite byzantin," QLtg 54 (1973) 191–203. [43]D.R. Holeton, "Penance in the

Churches of the Anglican Communion," StLtg 18 (1988) 96–102; J.T. McNeil, *A History of the Care of Souls* (San Francisco: Harper & Row, 1951) 218–246.    44O. Jordan, "The Practice of Penance in the Lutheran Church," StLtg 18 (1988) 103–107; A.R. George, "The Ministry of Reconciliation in the Evangelical Tradition," ibid., 112–116; cf. G. Siegwalt, "L'acte ecclésial de réconciliation: Point de vue systématique (protestante)," RDroitC 34 (1984) 322–335.

# REFORMED CHURCHES

The name "Reformed" is usually given to Churches in continental Europe which are Calvinist, occasionally Zwinglian, rather than Lutheran (*Églises Réformées, reformierte Kirchen*). Even before the end of the 16th century, *ecclesiae reformatae* was being applied to Calvinist Churches. Today they are mostly Presbyterian (q.v.) in polity (q.v.). The Reformed Churches, though valuing the Reformation, see the Church in constant need of reform. Their criterion of reform, as well as of life, is the Word of God.

The Presbyterian Churches came to have a world body in 1875, and the Congregational in 1891; these united to form the World Alliance of Reformed Churches (WARC) in 1970.[1] This body sponsors ecumenical dialogue at the international level. Apart from the tripartite talks on interchurch marriages (q.v.) with the Lutherans and Roman Catholic Church, there are several significant bilateral conversations, such as those with the Anglican Communion (v. ANGLICANISM AND ECUMENISM), with Baptists (q.v.), Disciples of Christ (q.v.), Lutherans (q.v.), and Methodists (q.v.).

The first phase of international dialogue with the Roman Catholic Church began from 1970–1977, leading to a statement on *The Presence of Christ in the World.*[2] There was agreement on some essential foundational truths: "There was a complete agreement in presenting ecclesiology from a clear christological and pneumatological perspective in which the Church is the object of declared faith and cannot be completely embraced by a historical and sociological description."[3] Due partly to the wide range of Reformed positions, the Report is not so much a consensus document as a clear exposition of points of agreement and of difference. The second phase produced *Towards a Common Understanding of the Church* (1990). It deals with the past, with a recognition of the need for a "reconciliation of memories." It moves to some consensus on central issues in ecclesiology but has to note divergence arising from two different conceptions of the Church: the Reformed "creation of the Word" and the Catholic "sacrament of grace." It looks forward to further growth in fellowship and mutual understanding and unity.[4]

An important contribution which the Reformed Churches make to ecumenical dialogue is a theology of the Word of God allied to a critical stance towards the Church which needs continual renewal (LG 8).

[1]*The World Alliance of Reformed Churches* (Geneva: World Presbyterian Alliance, 1964).    [2]H. Meyer and L. Vischer, eds., *Growth in Agreement.* Faith and Order Paper 108 (New York: Paulist—Geneva: WCC 1984) 434–463.    [3]Ibid., 437.    [4]L. Vischer and A. Karrer, eds., *Reformed and Roman Catholic in Dialogue* (Geneva: WRAC, 1988); A.D. Falconer, "Towards Reconciling Reformed and Roman Catholic," DoctLife 43 (1993) 274–286.

# RELIGIOUS LIFE

Religious life as a general concept is found under various names in different religions.[1] It is usually a countercultural seeking of the transcendent by persons of a group. In many religions these are called monks (Greek *monos* = "alone"). In Judaism the Essenes clustered around Qumran. In Christianity the instinct was first manifested by hermits (q.v.), many of whom soon gathered together under a charismatic leader like St. Anthony (251–356) or Pachomius (early 4th century).[2] It was the latter who first developed a primitive rule and demanded obedience. The early form was either of hermits living in separate dwellings but as monks, or living together in common; both were called cenobites (Greek *koinobios* = "common" + "life"). Soon rules came to be written, the best known being by St. Basil (ca. 330–379—q.v.)[3] and St. Benedict (ca. 480–ca. 550).[4] After them there was a great flowering of monastic life, which by the time of St. Bernard (ca. 1090–1153—q.v.) was in serious need of reform.

Religious institutes multiplied in the Middle Ages, the mendicant movement of the friars being particularly important. But the increase was so great that Lateran IV (q.v.) forbade the founding of new orders; new foundations were to take their rule from an already approved order.[5] Rivalry between friars and seculars in the universities sharpened theological thought about the meaning of religious life.

St. Thomas dealt with religious life of his time under the heading states of perfection.[6] The state of perfection is one in which a person obliges himself or herself permanently and with some solemnity to seek what pertains to perfection. People who are not in the state of perfection can be perfect, and not all in that state are perfect.[7] Bishops and religious belong to the state of perfection, the former through their pastoral charge to lay down their lives for others, the latter through their vows.[8] Aquinas treated of institutes dedicated to works of the active life, to military acts, to preaching and confession, to study.[9] About mixed institutes, those dedicated to both contemplation and activity, he asserted: "It is a higher thing to give what is contemplated to others than solely to engage in contemplation."[10]

In the later Middle Ages there was constant need for reform of religious life, a topic echoed in the medieval councils. By the time of the Reformation, many monasteries and religious institutes were seriously degenerate, and Trent (q.v.) laid down extensive norms of reform.[11] The following centuries saw major reforms in most institutes and a huge increase in the numbers of religious institutes, especially in the 19th century.

At the time of Vatican II there was still a very large number of vocations to religious life and much internal vitality. But many institutes had moved away from the original inspiration of their founders, and sometimes under the influence of Church authority, had taken on excrescences particularly from monastic life. The council took two steps: it made a theological statement on religious life in the heart of its major document (LG ch. 6); it produced the Decree on the Appropriate (accommodata) Renewal of Religious Life (PC).

During the council there was much discussion concerning the term to use about those to be treated in chapter 6 of LG. In a 1962 draft the Thomistic title "The Evangelical States for Acquiring Perfection" was used. The problem with it was that all are called to holiness through baptism, and all in some way are bound by the evangelical counsels. Thus other titles were excluded: "Those who Profess the Evangelical Counsels"; "Consecrated Life." Eventually "Religious" was chosen but given a broader meaning than in the 1917 Code. Another question to surface was whether religious life was of the Church (part of its divine constitution), or in the Church (a non-institutional gift). It was decided that there is not an intermediate state of the "divine and hierarchical constitution" of the Church, but that from both clergy and laity people are called by God "that in the life of the Church they would enjoy a special gift and in their own way foster the Church's divine mission."[12] Canon law would later insist that the consecrated life by its very nature is neither clerical nor lay, but its members are drawn from both states (CIC 588).

The council had developed the evangelical counsels in the previous chapter 5 (LG 42); they were further developed in the next one (LG 43, 46). Chapter 6 on religious life stressed several important features of this gift: Christological (LG 46); ecclesial (LG 43, 44, 45); sign and testimony (LG 44); eschatological (LG 44); relation to authority of Church and liturgy (LG 45).

When there was a move to speed up the procedures of the council and to reduce its work and aims, a schematic, rather abstract document on the renewal of religious life was produced; it was debated briefly in the 3rd session, meeting with hostile reception from some key bishops and cardinals. It was radically rewritten and easily passed by the council on 11 October 1965. Its title is significant: "Decree on the Appropriate (Sensitive/Adapted/Suitable/Up-to-date—accommodata) Renewal of Religious Life" (PC). The very conservative Cardinal Ruffini already warned in 1964 that this decree would evoke what he called "extravagant" desires for reform. The ambiguity inherent in its title—accommodata—certainly gave occasion for very diverse viewpoints after the council.

The decree is a renewal document concerned with practical norms, but these are placed in quite a rich theological context. After a strong assertion of the place of religious life in the Church, the decree notes that it applies, with due allowance for their special character, to societies of common life without vows (v. SOCIETIES OF APOSTOLIC LIFE) and secular institutes (q.v.). The important second article laid down the principles for reform. Some are unexceptional: the following of Christ, the Church's endeavors in various fields, human society which religious are to serve, spiritual renewal (PC 2). But the norm which would lead to very rich fruit and occasionally confusing or contradictory views was "the constant return to the sources of the Christian life in general, and the original genius of religious foundations (fontes primigeniamque institutorum inspirationem) in particular. . . . Each (religious foundation) must, therefore, reverence and embrace the genius and directives of its founders, its authentic traditions, the whole heritage indeed of the religious body" (PC 2). This norm was reiterated by Paul VI in his postconciliar exhortation Evangelica testificatio.[13]

The rest of the decree dealt with all of the key elements of religious life, for example: updating and renewal (PC 3–6); various kinds of institutes (PC 7–9); the need to combine contemplation with apostolic love (PC 10); vows (PC 12–14); community (PC 15); apostolates (PC 20).

The years after the council saw at once a serious, in places a catastrophic, fall-off in vocations, and an enormous amount of work for renewal. Religious studied their founding charism and the ways in which it could be incarnated into today's world. A suggestion made by Cardinal Döpfner would prove equivocal: How in today's changed circumstances would the founders have responded if they were still alive?[14] But confusion arose when there was not a careful enough distinction between the personal charisms of the founders and the charismatic institutions that they bequeathed to the Church.[15]

Again, new constitutions were written, only to be revised again in the light of the 1983 new Code of Canon Law. In the huge amount of writing on religious life,[16] some questions keep recurring: all aspects of the vows; the theological basis for religious life;[17] its relationship to, and role within, the Church;[18] its identity vis-à-vis the lay vocation, its role in the world;[19] the relationship between doxology and service/vertical and horizontal dimensions.[20] Journals dealing with consecrated life have carried numerous articles on various aspects of community life.[21]

Another issue is the relationship with the hierarchy, which was considered by a document of the then Sacred Congregation for Religious and Secular Institutes.[22] There have been other significant documents from the Holy See on religious life: on contemplative life,[23] on human values,[24] on law and apostolic institutes,[25] and on formation.[26] The 1994 Synod of Bishops on the topic of religious life[27] gave rise to a post-synodal exhortation, *Vita Consecrata* ("On Consecrated Life"—1996).

When we come to canon law in relation to religious life,[28] a major difference between the 1917 and the 1983 *Code*s is that the former was quite detailed, leaving only more minor matters for proper law or constitutions, whereas the latter generally lays down broader principles and leaves much more leeway to the proper or particular law of congregations. The second title of Book Two, "The People of God," part three, "Institutes of Consecrated Life and Societies of Apostolic Life," deals with religious institutes (CIC 607–709), beginning with a definition: "A religious institute is a society in which members, according to proper law, pronounce public vows either perpetual or temporary . . . and lives a life in common as brothers and sisters" (CIC 607 § 2). Furthermore, the house in which the community lives should have the Eucharist celebrated and reserved (CIC 608). Though the authority and duties of superiors are strongly asserted (CIC 618–619), there is a welcome emphasis on shared responsibility through councils (CIC 627), chapters, and organs of participation (CIC 631–633). The theology of religious life in the law is strongly influenced by Vatican II, though it is also traditional: "Religious are to have as their highest rule of life the following of Christ as proposed in the gospel and expressed in the constitutions of their institute" (CIC 662); "Contemplation of divine things and assiduous union with God in prayer is to be the first and foremost duty of all religious" (CIC 663 § 1); "The apostolate of all religious consists first in their witness of a consecrated life, which they are bound to foster by prayer and penance" (CIC 673); "Institutes which are wholly ordered to contemplation always retain a distinguished position in the mystical Body of Christ" (CIC 674); "In institutes dedicated to the apostolate, apostolic action pertains to their very nature" (CIC 675 § 1). Exemption (q.v.) is retained (CIC 591), but there are important matters concerning the rights and role of the local Ordinary (CIC 611, 678–679, 681, cf. 394).

Monastic life is an important feature of the Christian East,[29] and along with other forms of religious life has its own legislation in the Uniate Churches (CCEO cc. 410–553).

There are several negative aspects of the postconciliar period: fall-off in vocations; a sometimes unhealthy emphasis on human development and values, with an exclusion of the Cross; excessive activism; insecurity and crisis of identity. However, positive features are also found in recent years: the focus on issues of justice and peace in most institutes;[30] greater attention to genuine human and Christian values in structures and interpersonal relations; adaptability in seeking new apostolates; the enormous increase in vocations in the young Churches of Africa and Asia. The insights of feminism are usually a positive contribution but at times prove ambiguous. A most important development is the search for new forms of community living, new expressions of the charism of each institute, along with the notion of association (q.v.)[31] to an institute by those who are related to it, but not by vows. Religious life is in a process of rapid evolution in which both new visions and traditional values are in tension.[32] Mistakes and false tracks are inevitable but are not to be unduly feared; much greater danger lies in trying to stand still.

[1]P.J.M. Kitagawa, "Religious Communities," EncycRel 12:302-308; G. Weckman, "Monasticism," 10:35-41; M. Collcutt, "Monasticism. Buddhist," 10:41-44. [2]L. Bouyer, *A History of Spirituality*. 3 vols. (London, 1968) 1:303-394. [3]*Regulae brevius tractatae*—PG 31:620-625; *Regulae fusius tractatae* PG 31: 1080-1305/English FC 9. [4]SC 181, 186A; T. Fry et al, eds, *The Rule of St. Benedict in Latin and English with Notes* (Collegeville: The Liturgical Press, 1981). [5]Constit. 13—Tanner 1:242. [6]ST 2-2ae, qq. 184, 186-189; A. Motte, "La définition de la vie religieuse selon saint Thomas d'Aquin," RThom 87 (1987) 442-453. [7]ST 2-2ae, q. 184, a.4c; cf. q.186, a.1c. [8]Ibid., a.5; cf. a.7. [9]Ibid., q.188, a.2-5 [10]Ibid., q.188, a.6. [11]Sess. 25 Decree on Regulars and Nuns—Tanner 1:776-784. [12]LG 43; cf. ActaSyn 3/1:316-317; P. Molinari and P. Gumpel, *Chapter VI of the Dogmatic Constitution "Lumen gentium" on Religious Life. The Doctrinal Content in the Light of the Official Documents* (Rome: Gregorian UP, 1987 = Italian "Quaderni di vita consecrata 9." Milan: Ancora 1985) 14-32; R. Schulte, J. Daniélou and G. Huyghe in Baraúna-Congar, L'Église 3:1139-1190. [13]AAS 63 (1971) 497-526/Flannery 1:680-706, n. 11. [14]J.M.R. Tillard, "Les grands lois de la rénovation de la vie religieuse," in AA.VV. *Vatican II: L'Adaptation et la rénovation de la vie religieuse*. US 62 (Paris, 1968) 101-102. [15]AA.VV. *The Spirit of Founders and Our Religious Renewal* (Ottawa: Canadian Religious Conference, 1977); J.M. Lozano, "Founder and Community. Inspiration and Charism," RevRel 37 (1978) 214-236; C. O'Donnell, "Ongoing Renewal in the Spirit of the Founder," MilltownSt 4 (1979) 24-41. [16]P. Arrupe, *Challenge to Religious Life Today: Letters and Addresses* (St. Louis: Institute of Jesuit Sources—Anand, India: Gujarat Sahitya Prakash, 1979); J.M. Lozano, *Discipleship: Towards an Understanding of Religious Life* (Chicago: Claret Center for Resources in Spirituality, 1980); idem, *Life as Parable: Reinterpreting Religious Life* (New York—Mahwah: Paulist, 1986); J. Murphy-O'Connor, *What Is Religious Life? A Critical Appraisal* (Dublin: Dominican Publications, n.d.) = Supplement to DoctLife 11 (1973) 5-69; J.M.R. Tillard, *A Gospel Path: The Religious Life* (Brussels: Lumen Vitae, 1977); K. Rahner, *The Religious Life Today* (New York: Seabury, 1976); S. Schneiders, *New Wineskins: Re-Imaging Religious Life Today* (New York: Paulist, 1986). [17]L. Renwart, "Théologie de la vie religieuse. Bulletin bibliographique," VieCons 49 (1977) 48-63; 54 (1982) 112-124; 55 (1983) 45-61; 61 (1989) 32-53; R. Soullard, "Chronique de la vie consacrée," AnnéeCan 32 (1989) 325-333; 33 (1990) 179-185; J.M. Lozano, "Discipleship: New Testament and Religious Life," Claret 19 (1979) 127-164; T. Mattura, "Références

bibliques de la vie religieuse," NRT 105 (1983) 47–68; P.J. Rosato, "Towards a Vision of Religious Life," RevRel 36 (1977) 501–513. [18]A. Bandera, "Eclesiología de la vida religiosa: ¿Hacia un retroceso?," Ang 66 (1989) 577–602; G. Ghirlanda, "Ecclesialità della vita consecrata," VitaCons 12 (1976) 283–293, 410–420, 598–607; 13 (1977) 26–32, 231–237; L. Örsy, "A Theology of the Local Church and Religious Life," RevRel 36 (1977) 666–682; AA.VV. *Religious in the Local Church.* Donum Dei 27 (Ottawa: Canadian Religious Conference, 1981). [19]L. Byrne, *Sharing the Vision: Creative Encounters Between Religious and Lay* (London: SPCK, 1989); F.E. Crowe, "Rethinking the Religious State: Categories from Lonergan," ScEsp 40 (1988) 75–90; D.C. Maldari, "The Identity of Religious Life: The Contribution of Jean-Marie Tillard Critically Examined," LouvSt 14 (1989) 325–345; E. Pironio, "La vie religieuse dans l'Église et dans le monde," VieCons 54 (1982) 67–80; M. Vidal, "Les laïcs séculiers et la vie religieuse dans l'Église," VieCons 59 (1987) 259–265. See P.F. Walters, "Religious Life in Church Documents," RevRel 51 (1992) 550–561. [20]J.M.R. Tillard, "Significato teologico dell'evoluzione dells Congregazioni religiose dopo il Concilio," VitaCons 13 (1977) 65–75. [21]Claret, RelLifeR, RevRel, Sisters Today, VieCons, VitaCons, etc. [22]*Mutuae relationes* AAS 70 (1978) 473–506/Flannery 2:209-243; cf. J. Jukes, "A Commentary on the *Notae directivae* for the Mutual Relations Between Bishops and Religious in the Church," CleR 63 (1978) 472–477; 64 (1979) 21–31. [23]S. Cong. Religious and Secular Institutes, *The Contemplative Dimension of Religious Life* (1980)—Origins 10 (1981) 550–555/Flannery 2:244-259. [24]Idem, *Religious and Human Promotion* (1980)—Origins 10 (1981) 529–541/Flannery 2:260-284. [25]Idem, *Essential Elements in the Church's Teaching on Religious Life as Applied to Institutes Dedicated to Works of the Apostolate* (1983)—Origins 13 (1983) 133–142; cf. S. Euart, "A Canonical Analysis of *Essential Elements* in Light of the 1983 Code of Canon Law," Jurist 45 (1985) 438–501; S.L. Holland, "The Code and *Essential Elements,*" Jurist 44 (1984) 304–338. [26]Cong. for Instit. of Consec. Life and Soc. of Apostolic Life, *Directives on Formation in Religious Institutes* (1990)—Origins 19 (1990) 677–699/AAS 82 (1990) 470–532. [27]A. Flannery, ed., *Towards the 1994 Synod of Bishops* (Dublin: Dominican Publications, 1993). [28]S. Ardito, "Vita consecrata e vita religiosa nel nuovo Codice di Diritto Canonico," Sales 47 (1985) 529–554; J. Beyer, "Vie consacrée et vie religieuse de Vatican II au Code de Droit canonique," NRT 110 (1988) 74–96; T. Doyle, "The Canonical Status of Religious Institutes," Ang 63 (1986) 616–638; J.F. Gallen, "Canon Law for Religious After the New Code," RevRel 45 (1986) 78–112; S.H. Holland et al., in Coriden, CIC 453–542. [29]J. Beyer, "De vita consecrata in iure utriusque codicis orientalis et occidentalis," Periodica 81 (1992) 283–302; F. Haddad, "Orthodox Spirituality: The Monastic Life," EcumR 38 (1986) 64–70; J. Meyendorff, *Byzantine Theology: Historical Trends and Doctrinal Themes* (London—Oxford: Mowbrays, 1974) 54–78. [30]J.M.R. Tillard, *Dilemmas of Modern Religious Life: Work for Justice an Integral Part of the Apostolate.* Consecrated Life Series (Dublin: Dominican Publications—Wilmington: Glazier, 1986—French 1978); S. García Badía, "La vida consagrada en el documento de Puebla," Claret 23 (1983) 119–179. [31] D. Gottemoeller, "Looking at Associate Membership Today, RevRel 50 (1991) 390–397. [32]G.A. Arbuckle and D.L. Fleming, eds., *Religious Life: Rebirth Through Conversion* (Slough UK—Staten Island, N.Y.: St. Paul, 1990); D. Steinberg et al., eds., *The Future of Religious Life* (Collegeville: The Liturgical Press, 1990).

## RENEWAL MOVEMENTS, PRE-VATICAN II

Vatican II, intended by John XXIII and Paul VI to be a renewal council, was itself the result of a convergence of several renewal movements, some of which had their origins in the previous century. Not all of them were equally developed by the opening of the council, but many left their mark on the Church's self-understanding as enunciated by the documents of the council.

The biblical renewal movement began in the last century as linguistics developed, in addition to other methods and skills, such as textual criticism, a grasp of literary forms, archaeology, historical method. These and other discoveries radically changed the approach and the possibilities open to Scripture scholars. Leo XIII, in his encyclical *Providentissimus Deus* (1893), recognized both the danger and the potentiality of the new approaches. The precursor of modern Scripture scholarship in the Catholic Church was M.-J. Lagrange (1855–1938),[1] who was instrumental in founding the École Biblique and the influential *Revue biblique.* Another early landmark was the *Dictionnaire de la bible* (1891–1912); its *Supplément* from 1926 brings the early work more in line with modern scholarship. In the Modernist period (q.v.) the Biblical Commission, founded in 1902, produced a series of very cautious, and even repressive, decrees.[2] The turning point was the encyclical of Pius XII (q.v.), *Divino afflante Spiritu* (1943), which strongly encouraged Catholic biblical scholars to use the best scientific tools available. From the point of view of ecclesiology, the period from 1930–1960 produced many major studies on such themes as the Body of Christ (q.v.) and the People of God (q.v.).

Another renewal movement was patristics (v. FATHERS OF THE CHURCH). Intensive study of the Fathers had been begun in the 18th and early 19th centuries by J.A. Möhler (q.v.) and others. It was greatly fostered by the very complete editions of the *Patrologia graeca* and the *Patrologia latina* of J.-P. Migne.[3] Important for ecclesiology are the studies of early Christianity by P. Batiffol[4] and others in response to the liberal Protestant critique exemplified by A. von Harnack (1851–1930). With critical editions appearing, and especially the important *Sources chrétiennes* (from 1942), the decades immediately before Vatican II saw the emergence of the rich ecclesiology of the Fathers, which contrasted with the rather arid institutional ecclesiology of the contemporary manuals.

A third renewal movement was the liturgical one, usually traced back to P. Guéranger (1805–1875).[5] His pioneering work would in time be greatly developed by the editing and study of early liturgical texts, by subsequent liturgists who had a more pastoral concern, by the profound speculative theology of O. Casel (q.v.), and by cross-fertilization from catechetics. Again it was Pius XII who gave this renewal a new impetus and direction with his encyclical *Mediator Dei* (1947). Liturgy points to important aspects of the Church's life which are of vital concern for a full ecclesiology.

A further renewal movement might be called missionary. Though mission (q.v.) has been a central feature of the Church from its very beginnings, a new awareness of the nature of mission began to develop after the publication of the then startling book by A. Godin, *La France Pays de mission?* (1943). Mission was to be seen not only in terms of proclaiming the gospel to peoples who had never heard of Christ but also as evangelizing in countries that were at least nominally Christian. The missionary impetus and fresh thinking was inserted into a profound Trinitarian theology at Vatican II (AG 2–4), and it gave a certain urgency to many of its documents.

We could think of the area of history as a fifth renewal. There were several matters at issue here. One was the rise of historical consciousness and of the philosophies and theories of both history itself and its writing, which date from the beginning of this century. Another was the more objective and less polemical writing of Church history by scholars such as H. Jedin (1900–1980—q.v.). In ecclesiology we find the fruits of such scholarship in more accurate and balanced assessment of the Catholic Church's past, and of other Christians and their Churches as well. Important also is the sense of the pilgrim Church going through history to its eschatological destiny.

Finally, we need to be alert to the significance of the ecumenical movement (v. ECUMENISM). It is usual to date the birth of modern ecumenism with the International Missionary Conference at Edinburgh in 1910. The Catholic Church was slow to take part in ecumenism, the first official opening being the letter of the Holy Office, *Ecclesia Catholica* (1949), which allowed Catholics to take some limited part in ecumenical activities.[6] The following decade saw great theological interest in ecumenism, and the establishment of the Secretariat for Unity in 1960 paved the way for many of the ecumenical gestures and affirmations of Vatican II. Under the heading of ecumenism we can note not only direct work for Christian unity but a rediscovery by Catholic theologians of rich theological veins in Protestant and Lutheran theology and, above all, in the theology of the East. This last was facilitated by the establishment of theological schools by émigrés from the Communist East and by centers such as the Abbey at Chevetogne, Belgium, and the Pontifical Oriental Institute in Rome.

All of the major writers on ecclesiology from the 1920s were profoundly influenced by renewal in the above mentioned areas. Though we can trace these movements before Vatican II, it is now also important to see how, after the council, each of them has become interlinked with the others. All of them are of vital importance in building up an integral ecclesiology, one which must also take account of the insights of the post-Vatican II period.

[1]See F.M. Braun, *The Work of Père Lagrange* (Milwaukee, 1963); A. Paretsky, "M.-J. Lagrange's Contribution to Catholic Biblical Studies," Ang 63 (1986) 509-531.    [2]See DS from 3372 to 3630. [3]A.G. Hamman, *Jacques–Paul Migne: Le retour aux pères de l'Église*. Le point théologique 16 (Paris: Beauchesne, 1975). [4]*L'Église naissante et le catholicisme* (Paris, [2]1909 and Cerf, 1971). [5]L.C. Sheppard, "Liturgical Movement, Catholic," NCE 8:900-905. [6]AAS 42 (1950) 142–147.

## RITES

Though since Vatican II there is a preference for speaking about Churches rather than rites, the latter notion is still important as well as being complex and often confused. The word "rite" applied to a Church or group of Churches refers not only to their liturgy but also to their jurisprudence and spirituality (OE 3; UR 14).[1] We can leave aside as sufficiently well known the Latin Rite of the West. In the East there were originally five rites: the Alexandrian, Antiochene, Armenian, Chaldean, and Byzantine. Except for the Armenian, they also have derived rites or canonical and liturgical variations. Since the 13th century there has been an insistence on these rites being preserved, and there have been canonical impediments concerning change of rite by individuals or Churches (cf. OE 4). By baptism a person not only becomes a Christian but acquires a membership of a canonical rite. In the Catholic Church eighteen canonical rites are recognized, but the number of liturgical rites is much fewer: the number depends on the criteria used for distinguishing them.

The Antiochene Rite is found in the patriarchate of Antioch and among some Syrians.[2] It is perhaps the most ancient rite, giving rise to all of the others, partly on account of the prestige of the Church at Antioch (Acts 9–11). In the 4th century there was a concern that the liturgy be written down to prevent corruptions and heterodox elements. The Antiochene Rite is sometimes called the West Syrian Rite (to distinguish it from the East Syrian or Chaldean Rite). In the Catholic Church it is often called simply the Syrian Rite. The structure of its liturgy resembles somewhat the Roman revised liturgy except for frequent litanies, more extended prayers, and the *epiclêsis* (q.v.) following the consecration.

The Antiochene Rite was said to have been brought to Egypt by St. Mark, where it became the Alexandrine Rite.[3] In turn this was the origin of the various Coptic liturgical rites in Egypt and Ethiopia. The Alexandrine Rite is important for its monastic tradition, going back to St. Anthony in the desert.

The Armenian Rite has its origin in St. Gregory the Illuminator in the 4th century, though Christianity was found earlier in Armenia. In the 4th and 5th centuries, Scripture and patristic books were translated into

Armenian. For centuries the Armenian Patriarchate was Monophysite at least nominally. The Uniate Armenians have had a codified canon law since their council in 1911.[4] The elaborate liturgy uses only one anaphora (Eucharistic Prayer of Latin Rite); it would seem to have been derived from the liturgy of St. Basil but with a lot of Latin accretions which were removed in the last century.

The Chaldean Rite looks to the 5th century, when its *katholikos* became independent of the Church of Antioch. Earlier the Church in East Syria had produced a doctor (q.v.) of the Universal Church, St. Ephraem. The Church became Nestorian, at least nominally, but attempts at establishing union with Rome go back to the 13th century. The liturgical rite before the 5th century is hard to determine, but it seems to go back to the Antiochene Rite. It is virtually unchanged since the 7th century. It has three anaphoras: the most frequently used one of the apostles Addai and Mari; the seldom used liturgies of St. Theodore of Mopsuestia and of St. Nestorius are for obvious reasons called the "Second" and "Third" anaphoras by Catholics of the Rite. The Liturgy of the Apostles is distinctive in that it is addressed to the Son and not, as in almost all liturgies, to the Father. Furthermore, the Nestorius Liturgy has, to the puzzlement of liturgists, no narrative of the institution of the Eucharist.[5]

The Byzantine Rite is by far the most widespread of the traditional rites: to it belong over 100 million Catholic and Orthodox believers.[6] It evolved from the 4th to 10th century and today is found in many modern and ancient liturgical languages. There are two anaphoras: the Liturgy of St. Basil used ten times annually, and the Liturgy of St. John Chrysostom; there is a Liturgy of the Presanctified for use in the ferias of Lent. Apart from Easter, "the Feast of Feasts," there are twelve great feasts of the Orthodox Church whose liturgical year begins on 1 September: The Nativity of the Mother of God (8 Sept.), The Exaltation of the Honorable and Life-giving Cross (14 Sept.), The Presentation of the Mother of God in the Temple (21 Nov.), The Nativity of Christ (25 Dec.), The Baptism of Christ in the Jordan (6 Jan.), The Presentation of Our Lord in the Temple (2 Feb.), The Annunciation of the Mother of God (25 March), The Entry of Our Lord into Jerusalem (one week before Easter), The Ascension of Our Lord Jesus Christ (40 days after Easter), Pentecost or Trinity Sunday (50 days after Easter), The Transfiguration of Our Savior Jesus Christ (6 Aug.), The Falling Asleep of the Mother of God (15 Aug.).

The attitude of the Roman Church with regard to rites has varied throughout the centuries. It seems that the first usage of the word "rite" in a papal document to designate usages proper to the Orientals was by Celestine III (1191–1198).[7] At the Lateran IV Council it was formally laid down that those in the East, principally Greeks, could have liturgical celebrations according to their own rites and customs *(ritus et mores).*[8] At the Council of Florence the word "rite" seems to have the meaning of "faith,"[9] a usage that would scarcely lead to the encouragement of rites other than the Latin Rite/faith.

The notion of rite was developed especially after Trent to take account of situations in which some Eastern Christians became reconciled with Rome and were living alongside or in Latin dioceses while seeking to maintain their ancient heritage. But, especially in the 18th century, there was a tendency to regard the Latin Rite as having preeminence *(praestantia).*[10] The principle of *praestantia* was rejected by Leo XIII in 1893,[11] but its spirit and attitude lingered until Vatican II.

In 1990 the reform of Eastern canon law (v. LAW) was completed, a task which had been initiated by Pius XI in 1927, partially effected *motu proprio* (v. VATICAN DOCUMENTS) by Pius XII (1949–1957),[12] and further modified later to take account of Vatican II and subsequent developments.

Each of the rites has its own spiritual authors, some well known and shared by the Universal Church, others particular and local. Rites also have their own saints and varying ways of determining how a person is so venerated. Finally, all the rites have both Uniate (q.v.) Churches and Churches not in communion with Rome (v. EASTERN CHURCHES, ORTHODOX CHURCH).

[1]M.M. Wojnar, "Rites, Canonical," NCE 12:514-518; A. Herman, "De 'ritu' in iure canonico," OrChr 32 (1933) 96–158; idem, "De conceptu 'ritus,'" Jurist 2 (1942) 333–345; A.A. King, *The Rites of Eastern Christendom.* 2 vols. (London, 1950); P. Sherwood, "Sense of Rite," EChurchQ 12 (1957) 112–125. Liturgical texts, R.C.D. Jasper and G.J. Cuming, *Prayers of the Eucharist: Early and Reformed* (New York: Pueblo, [3]1987). [2]D. Attwater, *The Christian Churches of the East.* 2 vols. (London, [2]1961) 1:147-172; M.H. Sheperd, Jr., "The Formation and Influence of the Antiochene Liturgy," DumbO 15 (1961) 25–44. [3]Attwater (n. 2) 1:128-146. [4]J. Kaftandjian, "The Armenian Rite," NCE 1:834-837; Attwater (n. 2) 1:173-187; F.C. Conybeare, *Rituale Armenorum, being the Administration of the Sacraments and the Breviary Rite of the Armenian Church* (Oxford, 1950). [5]R. Rabban, "Chaldean Rite," NCE 3:427-430; C.K. von Euw, "Chaldean Rite, Liturgy of," NCE 3: 430-432; Attwater (n. 2) 1:188-208. [6]G.A. Maloney, "Byzantine Rite," NCE 2:1000-1011; Attwater (n. 2) 1:38-54; D. Gelsi, "Byzantine Liturgy," EncycEarCh 1:134-136, with bibliog. [7]E. Lanne, "La conception post-tridentine de la Primauté et l'origine des Églises unies," Irén 52 (1979) 5–33 at "II: L'évolution de la notion de 'rite,'" 19, n. 3. [8]Canons 4 and 9—Tanner 1:235-236, 239. [9]J. Gill, *Eugenius IV, Pope of Christian Union* (Westminster, Md., 1961) 183–184, cited E. Lanne (n. 7) 19, n. 1. [10]A. Petrani, "An ansit ritus praestantior?," Apoll 6 (1933) 74–82; E. Herman, "De 'ritu' in jure canonico," OrChr 32 (1933) 96–158. [11]Lit. apost. *Orientalium dignitas*—ASS 27 (1894–1895) 257–264. [12]*Crebrae allatae*—AAS 41 (1949) 89–119; *Sollicitudinem nostram*—AAS 42 (1950) 5–120; *Postquam apostolicis*—AAS 44 (1952) 65–152; *Cleri sanctitati*—AAS 49 (1957) 433–603. See V.J. Pospishil, "Oriental Codes," NCE 10:763-767; M.M. Wojnar, "The Code of

Oriental Canon Law: *De ritibus orientalibus* and *De personis*," Jurist 19 (1959) 212–245, 277–299, 413–464.

## ROMAN CATHOLIC

The use of the term "Roman" became common after the split with the Orthodox, and especially at the Reformation, when the Catholic Church insisted on its Roman center.[1] The presence of the qualifying "Roman" is important in dealing with the notion of the Church being "Catholic" (q.v.) and with the papacy (q.v.). By the end of the 4th century there are references to the Roman Church *(Ecclesia Romana)*. Thus at the provincial council of Carthage (419 C.E.) Faustinus is described as the legate of the Roman Church.[2] Almost contemporary is the statement of Innocent I to Decentius of Gubbio: "That which has been given by the prince of the apostles, Peter, to the Roman Church and up to now has been preserved, must be held by all."[3] In the 5th and 6th centuries we find "the catholic Church of the city of Rome" *(urbis Romae),* of the Romans *(Romanorum),* or of the Roman Church *(Romanae ecclesiae).* In 515 C.E. there comes with Pope Hormisdas an assertion that, slightly modified, will be commonplace in the Middle Ages, viz., the Church of Rome has never erred: *"in Sede Apostolica immaculata est semper catholica servata religio"* (in the Apostolic See the catholic religion has always been kept inviolate).[4] But in the early stages it is not clear what is meant here by the Roman Church: in the first centuries it seems to have been the Christian community at Rome; later the prayer of Jesus, "I have prayed for you that your faith fail not" (Luke 22:32), would be applied to the Church personified by the pope.[5] Again, we have the sense of the Roman Church's feeling that it somehow summarizes in itself the whole Church: Hadrian I speaks of "our holy, catholic and apostolic universal Roman Church."[6] In the medieval reunion councils and papal statements the phrase "return to Mother Church" is to be found in connection with the Roman See (v. MOTHER).[7]

The adjective "Roman" was normally added to professions of faith.[8] This became necessary as the Reformers accepted the fourfold description of the Church of the "Nicene" Creed, which had the word "catholic." Later the Anglican Communion would increasingly adopt this term "catholic." Vatican I avoided giving any support to the Branch Theory by using the title "the holy, catholic, apostolic Roman Church."[9] But though Vatican II in LG frequently speaks of the Roman Pontiff, it does not use "Roman Church."

The question arises as to whether there is a doctrinal importance attached to the adjective "Roman." The expression "chair of Peter" *(cathredra Petri)* is from Cyprian, and indicates both the episcopate founded in Peter and the episcopal chair of Rome.[10] It is in unity with the bishop of Rome that full and authentic catholicity and apostolicity are found in the Church.[11] The pope is also said to be the successor of Paul: Peter is the source of unity and authority; Paul, the teacher of authentic doctrine.[12] Theologians are generally agreed that the pope should be bishop of Rome. Even during the Avignon stay (1307–1377) the popes retained the title of bishop of Rome. In modern theology "Roman Catholic" is a term to refer to the body of Church in communion with Rome.

What causes much misunderstanding both in Church law and in theology is the failure to distinguish the three offices in the one person of the pope: he is local bishop of the diocese of Rome; he is patriarch (q.v.) of the West; he is supreme pontiff (v. PAPAL TITLES). Among the consequences of unclear thinking on this matter is excessive Latinization, from which the Eastern Churches have often suffered. Evidence of this kind of thinking is found in such apparently small matters as liturgical books noting that the celebration of a saint had been extended to the universal Church when, in fact, it pertains only to the Latin patriarchate.[13] More seriously, it is probably only with more careful attention to these distinctions that the theology of local church (q.v.) will be translated into practice, and the teaching of Vatican I on the papacy will reflect the spirit of Vatican II's Decree on Ecumenism 14: "For many centuries the churches of the east and west followed their separate ways though linked in a union of faith and sacramental life; the Roman see by common consent acted as guide when disagreements arose between them over matters of faith and discipline."

[1]Y. Congar, "Romanité et catholicité: Histoire de la conjonction changeante de deux dimensions de l'Église," RSPT 71 (1987) 161–190; A. Dulles, "The Center of Catholicity: Roman Primacy," in *The Catholicity of the Church* (Oxford: Clarendon, 1985) 127–146. [2]Congar (n. 1) 163–164. [3]PL 20:552, quoted ibid., 164. [4]DS 363; cf. DS 217/ND 801. [5]St. Thomas, ST 2–2ae, q.2, a.6 ad 3. [6]K.F. Morrison, *Tradition and Authority in the Western Church 308–1140* (Princeton, 1969) 156, cited Congar (n. 1) 166; cf. Congar (n. 1) 171–173; B. Tierney, *Foundations of the Conciliar Theory: The Contribution of the Medieval Canonists from Gratian to the Great Schism* (Cambridge, 1955) 41–46. [7]Congar (n. 1) 169–170. [8]Formula for Waldensians—DS 792; for Michael Palaeologus—DS 855, 860, 861; Pius IV "Tridentine" Profession of Faith—DS 1868. [9]DS 3001/Tanner 2:805; Congar (n. 1) 175. [10]*Epist.* 43:5, 2 and 59:14 cited Congar (n. 1) 179. [11]P. Duprey, "Profil de l'Église catholique," PrOrChr 31 (1981) 117–122 at 120. [12]Cf. W.R. Farmer and R. Kereszty, *Peter and Paul in the Church of Rome* (New York—Mahwah: Paulist, 1990); T. Strotmann, "Les Coryphées Pierre et Paul et les autres apôtres," Irén 36 (1963) 164–176; J.J. von Allmen, *La primauté de l'église de Pierre et de Paul* (Fribourg: UP—Paris: Cerf, 1977). [13]Cf. Congar (n. 1) 188.

## ROMAN SCHOOL

The title "Roman School" is given to a group of theologians, almost all from the Roman Gregorian University, who played a prominent part in the development of ecclesiology in the 19th century.[1] At its head was G. Perrone (1794–1876), not so much an original thinker but more a positive theologian and apologist; his main contribution might be said to lie in his direction of two brilliant pupils, C. Passaglia (1812–1887) and J.B. Franzelin (1816–1886). The former with C. Schrader (1820–1875) published a two-volume unfinished study on the Church, *De ecclesia Christi* (1853–1854), which could be termed neo-scholastic, though with a fine sense of tradition. Important themes are the Body of Christ, the work of the Holy Spirit, and the visible and invisible realities in the Church. Though Passaglia wrote an extensive work on the papacy in 1850, he came to oppose Ultramontanism (q.v.), with which the Roman School was itself tinged. He left the Jesuits and became involved in Italian politics. He was alienated from the Church until just before his death. His friend C. Schrader (1820–1875) incorporated several of his ideas in the schema on the Church prepared for Vatican I. Franzelin took an active part in the preparation of Vatican I and was one of its leading theologians:[2] less profound than Passaglia, he organized and clarified the new biblical and patristic insights in a sober, accurate form. One should also mention P. Kleutgen (1811–1883), one of the progenitors of neo-scholasticism (v. AETERNI PATRIS), who taught not in the Gregorian but in the Germanicum. Like the great scholastics, he did not envisage a separate treatise on the Church, but his ecclesiological ideas are to be found in various tracts of theology.

The Roman School was actively involved in the theological climate which led to the definitions of the papal primacy and infallibility at Vatican I. But they also brought some fresh insights into ecclesiology, which had long been over-concerned with apologetics; their emphasis on Scripture, especially St. Paul, and on the Fathers of the Church, was remarkable for its time. But their enduring lesson may well be that ecclesiology must always be contemporary as well as traditional, confronting the live issues of the day.

[1]Antón 2:287–317; Congar: Augustin 428–435; A. Kerkvoorde, "La théologie du 'Corps Mystique' au dix-neuvième siècle," NRT 67 (1945) 417–430. [2]D. Massimino, "Franzelin e l'ecclesiologia del Vatican I," HoTheol 9 (1991) 61–100; idem, "L'apporto del Franzelin alla stesura della Pastor Aeternus e al dibattito sull'infallibilità," ibid., 157–194.

## ROSMINI-SERBATI, Antonio (1797–1855)

Born at Rovereto, Italy, Antonio Rosmini-Serbati studied at Padua and was ordained in 1821. He was distinguished in philosophy, theology, and Italian patriotism.[1] He founded the Sisters of Providence (1832); earlier in 1828, he had established the Institute of Charity/Fathers of Charity (Rosminians),[2] a congregation now in several countries. Some of its members take an additional vow of obedience to the pope, which reflects Rosmini's life-long loyalty to the Church, apparent in his early and best-known devotional work, *Maxims of Christian Perfection* (1830).[3]

A scholar in many fields, he opted mainly for the study of philosophy, on the advice of Pius VII. He sought a unifying philosophical system and drew from a variety of thinkers: Plato, Sts. Augustine and Thomas Aquinas, Kant, Descartes, and Hegel. His philosophical and theological positions were frequently attacked. Two books of his were placed on the Index in 1848, *A Constitution Based on Social Justice* and the famous *Five Wounds of the Church*.[4] His list of wounds was quite different from that of Innocent IV (v. LYONS I), viz., division between people and clergy in public worship, inadequate education of the clergy, disunity of bishops, nomination of bishops by secular power, and restrictions on the use of ecclesiastical benefices. The two books were removed from the Index without censure a year before Rosmini's death. Nearly twenty years after his death forty propositions taken from his works were condemned under Leo XIII without specific theological censure.[5] But as in all such compilations, it is not easy to determine if a short excerpted proposition is really faithful to the author's mind; many of his followers and others would deny that they accurately reflect his thought.[6]

Always very much a cult figure, mainly in Italy,[7] Rosmini's importance for ecclesiology lies partly in the example of loving and loyal but firm criticism of the Church.

[1]D. Cleary, *Antonio Rosmini: Introduction to His Life and Teaching* (Durham UK: Rosminians, 1992); C. Leetham, *Rosmini, Priest, Patriot and Philosopher* (New York, 1957); P. Zovatto, ed., *Introduzione a Rosmini*. Centro Internazionale di Studi Rosminiani 23 (Trieste: Stresa, 1992). [2]C.J. Emery, *The Rosminians* (London, 1960). [3]London, [4]1889, reprint 1963. [4]London, 1883; Leominister UK: Fowler Wright, 1987. [5]DS 3201–3241. [6]E.g., M. Flick, review of A. Luciani, *L'origine dell' anima umana secondo Antonio Rosmini* (Rome: Gregorium UP, 1958) in Greg 40 (1959) 565–566; A. Staglianò, "Rilettura di proposizioni rosminiane," RasT 28 (1987) 374–401. [7]See *Rivista rosminiana di philosophia e di cultura* from 1906; G. Campanini, "Il pensiero di Rosmini e la cultura cattolica: A cento anni dalla condanna," RasT 28(1988) 578–589; F. Evain, "A. Rosmini centi anni dopo: tradizione e modernità," CivCatt 140 (1989) 2:342-355; L. Mariotti, *La Chiesa, unità sacerdotale in Cristo nel pensiero di A. Rosmini*. Diss. (Rome: Gregorian, 1978).

# S

## SACRAMENT, Church as

In the years preceding Vatican II the notion of the Church as sacrament, a patristic theme, began to be explored again.[1] The way to its application was opened up by J.A. Möhler (q.v.), using the analogy of the Incarnation to show up the visible and invisible natures of the Church. He was followed by M.J. Scheeben (q.v.),[2] but apart from some study by J.H. Oswald at the turn of the century, the idea largely lay dormant until the centenary of Möhler's death in 1939. Notable in the pre-Vatican II period was the insight that Christ, and then in a lesser manner the Church, is the primordial sacrament *(Ursakrament)* on which the whole notion of sacramentality and the seven sacraments depend. The matter was thus mature by the time of Vatican II; since the council the literature is extensive.[3]

The notion that the Church is a sacrament is not explicit in Scripture, but the biblical notion of *mustêrion* is important for an understanding of the Church's sacramentality. In the LXX it has the idea of something that is secret but manifested to a few (Jdt 2:2; Wis 2:22; Dan 2:27-45), an idea found also in the only use of the word in the Synoptics, Matt 13:11—"To you it has been given to know the secrets *[mustêria]* of the kingdom of heaven." In Pauline usage *mustêrion* is the whole of the gospel or a particular aspect like the resurrection from the dead (see 1 Cor 15:51). More profoundly the mystery is Jesus himself (see Col 2:2; 4:3; Eph 3:3-4), "Christ in you, the hope of glory" (Col 1:27), and it is the divine plan hidden for ages and now revealed in Christ (see Eph 1:9; 3:9; 1 Tim 3:16).

There are some important developments in post-apostolic times:[4] in Ignatius, Justin, and Melites of Sardis the word *mustêrion* not only signified the entire person of Christ but had a secondary meaning of events in the life of Christ (cf. "Mysteries" of the Rosary). A further

meaning was that of the prophecies, in which the divine plan can be said to have begun. With Origen there was a final development: the paschal mystery is definitive, but its full effects are still awaited by humanity. In the Latin Church the Greek word *mustêrion* was transliterated in Latin as *mysterium,* and translated as *sacramentum.* Both words were used like *mustêrion* in the earlier period, with the rites of initiation and especially the Eucharist being added. By the Middle Ages the word *sacramentum* was reserved for seven rites of encounter with Christ, and the word *mysterium* generally meant mysteries of the faith.

In theologians prior to Vatican II the use of "sacrament" in relation to the Church was usually to underline its mystery. In Vatican II there are several occurrences of the idea of the Church being a sacrament, but in a slightly different sense. The council does not call the Church sacrament of God or of Christ but develops sacramental ideas in its ecclesiology. The opening article of the Church constitution states that "the Church is in Christ as *[veluti]* a sacrament or instrumental sign of intimate union with God and of the unity of all humanity" (LG 1). The use of the word *veluti* warns us that the council is speaking in an analogous way, or indicating that the Church is "a kind of sacrament." But we are not to see sign and instrument as two: it is by being sign that it is an instrument.[5] It is Christ who is the fundamental sacrament. Like the seven sacraments the Church is an "efficacious sign of grace," that is, a perceptible reality which contains and bestows grace. There is a twofold grace of which the Church is sign and instrument: "intimate union with God" (a vertical dimension) and the "unity of all humanity" (a horizontal dimension).[6]

Later the same document states that Jesus, "the author of salvation and the principle of unity and peace," has "constituted the Church that it may be for one and all *[universis et singulis]* the visible sacrament of this saving unity" (LG 9). There is a footnote here to Cyprian, who was the first of the Fathers explicitly to call the Church a "sacrament."

In LG 48 we find the assertion that Christ on the completion of his paschal mystery sent the Spirit, "and through him he constituted his body which is the Church as the universal sacrament of salvation *[universale salutis sacramentum]*." The idea of universal sacrament of salvation is found again in GS 45 and AG 1. F.A. Sullivan rightly notes that this is an aspect of the catholicity of the Church (v. CATHOLIC). Hence the grace of salvation is not only ordered toward the Church but in some way comes from and through the Church; the Church is the channel or medium through which grace is given.[7] Here we have a positive expression of the axiom "Outside the Church there is no salvation" (q.v.), and of the correlative dogmatic affirmation of the necessity of the Church for salvation (cf. LG 14). Again, Sullivan reflects on the teaching of the council and postconciliar magisterial statements and concludes to the fact that the Church is the "sacrament of integral salvation."[8]

Theological reflection on the Church as sacrament can well begin with the dense and rich statement of LG 8, where we find affirmed the complex reality of a visible, hierarchical, earthly Church which is also at the same time the mystical Body, a spiritual community, a Church enriched with heavenly gifts. The Church is sign and instrument. It is thus visible and knowable by reason. But it is precisely by having Christ as the Head of the Body and by being the Bride of Christ that the Church is a sacrament. Hence the Church's deepest reality can be perceived only by faith.[9]

The notion of the Church as sacrament has not been welcomed with any enthusiasm in Protestant circles. A main reason is the weakness of general sacramental theory in these Churches: key stress is on the Word of God and on preaching which stirs up saving faith, rather than on sacraments being signs containing the grace that they signify.[10] Another reason is the fear of appearing to substitute the Church, the basic sacrament *(Grundsakrament),* for Christ, who is the primordial sacrament *(Ursakrament).* Furthermore, there is the usual Protestant reluctance to see any mediation apart from Christ, and sacrament implies that the Church participates in Christ's mediation at least as instrumental cause.[11] Such Protestant views and more emphasis on Scripture and sound preaching are important, but the main answer will have to be sought in the very nature of the divine economy eternally willed by God and revealed in Christ Jesus. Thus with J.M.R. Tillard we have to assert three truths: The Church is evangelized by God, but it also evangelizes for God

(cf. Rom 10:14-18); the Church is reconciled by God, but it is also the Church which reconciles for God (cf 2 Cor 5:18-20); the Church is gathered by God, but it also gathers for God—*koinônia* (v. COMMUNION) is a gift received and a gift to be shared.[12]

We can with A. Dulles see "sacrament" as a model for the Church, while noting that he no longer regards it as the best model.[13] It does have the power to integrate many truths about the Church, especially the relationship between the visible institution and the communion of grace. Furthermore, it gives good grounds for renewal of the Church so that it will be a more perfect sign and instrument. But it labors under some disadvantages: it is too technical and sophisticated to be available for preaching; it could serve to overemphasize externals or encourage a narcissistic aestheticism not easily reconcilable with a full Christian commitment to social and ethical values.[14] But when due account is taken of the scriptural background of Body, Bride, and *mustêrion,* it is clear that it has a substantive contribution to make in ecclesiology, not least in understanding the statement "Outside the Church there is no salvation." In the end the Church will not attain to its full sacramental reality unless it is both seen to be about the works of God and heard to speak a message of salvation for all peoples.[15]

[1]E.g., H. de Lubac, *The Splendor of the Church* (San Francisco: Ignatius, 1986) ch. 6: "The Sacrament of Christ" 203–235—*Méditation sur l'Église* (1953); O. Semmelroth, *Church and Sacrament* (Dublin 1963)—*Die Kirche als Ursakrament* (1953); K. Rahner, *The Church and the Sacraments.* QDisput 9 (London, 1963); E. Schillebeeckx, *Christ the Sacrament of Encounter with God* (London, 1963). [2]*The Mysteries of Christianity* (St. Louis—London, 1946) 581. [3]J. Alfaro, "Cristo, Sacramento de Dios Padre: La Iglesia, sacramento de Cristo," Greg 48 (1967) 5–27; W. Beinert, "Die Sakramentalität der Kirche im theologischen Gespräch," TJb 1983, 216–362; Y. Congar, *This Church That I Love* (Denville, 1969) 39–61; A. Dulles, *Models of the Church* (Dublin: Gill and Macmillan, [2]1988) 63–75, 190–207; J. Groot, "The Church as Sacrament of the World," Conc 1/4(Jan. 1968) 27–34; R. McBrien, "The Church: Sign and Instrument of Unity," Conc 8/6 (1970) 45–52; T. O'Dea, "The Church as *Sacramentum mundi,*" Conc 8/6 (1970) 36–44; M. Ponce, "Sacramentalidad de la Iglesia y sacramentos," ScripTPamp 16 (1984) 183–201; P. Rodriguez, "Dimensión universal de la sacramentalidad de la Iglesia," Scrip TPamp 14 (1982) 807–828; J. Witte, "L'Église 'sacramentum unitatis' du cosmos et du genre humain," Baraúna—Congar 2:457-492. [4]P. Smulders, "L'Église sacrement du salut," Baraúna—Congar 2:313-338. [5]G. Philips, "L'Église, sacrement et mystère," ETL 42 (1968) 405–414 at 406. [6]F.A. Sullivan, *The Church We Believe In: One, Holy, Catholic and Apostolic* (Dublin: Gill and Macmillan—Mahwah: Paulist, 1988) 10; fuller treatment 109–151; G. Canobbio, "La Chiesa sacramento di salvezza," RClerIt 73 (1992) 342–359. [7]Sullivan (n. 6) 110. [8]Ibid., 132–151; idem, *Salvation Outside the Church? Tracing the History of the Catholic Response* (New York: Paulist, 1992) 156–161. [9]H. de Lubac (n. 1) 215–217; G. Martelet, "De la sacramentalité propre à l'Église ou d'un sens de l'Église inséparable du sens du Christ," NRT 95 (1973) 25–42 = TDig 22 (1974) 62–67. [10]See A. Birmelé, "La sacramentalité de l'Église et la tradition luthérienne," Irén 59 (1986) 482–507. [11]Protestant view in E. Jüngel, "Die Kirche als Sakrament," ZTK 80 (1982)

432–457. [12]J.M.R. Tillard, "Church and Salvation: On the Sacramentality of the Church," OneChr 20 (1984) 290–314 = NRT 106 (1984) 656–685. [13]Op. cit. (n. 3) 206; cf. idem, *The Catholicity of the Church* (Oxford: Clarendon, 1985) 106–126; International Theological Commission, "Select Themes of Ecclesiology," (1984) sect. 8 in *Texts and Documents 1969–1985* (San Francisco: Ignatius, 1989) 294–297. [14]Dulles, op. cit. (n. 3) 73–75. [15]Martelet (n. 9) 37–41; see DV 2.

# SAINTS

Saints, or holy persons, are known in many religions.[1] The primitive Church looked to the great figures of the OT for inspiration (Heb 11:4–12:1). But there is no evidence of seeking their intercession. A common name for the followers of Jesus was the "saints" (Acts 9:13, 32, 41; Rom 16:2), in the sense that they were set apart and gifted by God (v. HOLY).[2]

In the early centuries there was a cult of martyrs, often with a Eucharistic celebration on the anniversary of their deaths, especially at the place of their death or burial. From about the 4th century a cult of confessors (q.v.) also grew up. Soon other outstandingly holy persons were venerated. Bishops and councils controlled cultus in the local Church. But the cultus often spread beyond the diocese associated with the saint. Bishops allowed veneration, but a determining factor was often the *vox populi,* the fame of the holy persons, and the veneration with which they were held by the people. Gradually bishops approved veneration,[3] and Rome was sometimes asked to acknowledge the diocesan decision.

In time it would be Rome which canonized, the first attested case being that of Ulrich of Augsburg by Pope John XV in 993.[4] In the late 12th century, veneration of saints without the approval of Rome was forbidden. However, before the 12th century and frequently until the 17th century, local bishops beatified persons for veneration in their own diocese. Since then beatification usually takes place in the presence of the pope: it is a formal presentation to him of a servant of God; the pope does not state definitively that the blessed person is in heaven. Beatification is usually followed by cultus only in a particular country, diocese, church, or religious family.

Canonization originally meant insertion into the list of saints in the Canon of the Mass (Eucharistic Prayer I). Nowadays it takes place at a pontifical celebration during which it is definitely asserted that the canonized person is in glory. The person is henceforth called "saint." There are various ways in which the saint is honored: an annual feast is celebrated; there is an approved Mass and office; churches may be dedicated to the saint; the relics of the saint may be publicly honored. These distinctions between the limited cultus of blessed and the universal one of saints reflect the 1917 *Code of Canon Law* (CIC 1277, 1278, 1287 § 3) which, though not reenacted by the 1983 *Code,* are still current practice (cf. 1983 CIC 1187).

The painstaking and complex process leading to canonization has been gradually established in the Church from the Middle Ages.[5] There have been several important stages in this development: the work of Urban VIII (1623–1644); the study of beatification and canonization by Prospero Lambertini, before he became Benedict XIV (1740–1758);[6] the 1917 *Code of Canon Law* (CIC 1999–2141); the formation of the Vatican Congregation for Causes of Saints in 1969, when the Congregation of Rites was reorganized.[7] The new Congregation is responsible for beatifications and canonizations. There are two main sections in the Congregation: one is concerned with causes of those recently deceased in whose cases there are living witnesses; the other is for causes more remote in history.

The process was simplified in 1983.[8] It begins in the diocese in which the person died and is under the supervision of the bishop.[9] After preliminary enquiries in the diocese, all the documentation is sent to Rome and a postulator is appointed, normally a person resident in Rome. With permission of the Congregation the cause is introduced and a formal investigation begins in the diocese: all documents are again examined, witnesses are questioned. Another examination takes place about a miraculous action, usually a cure, which came about through the intercession of the servant of God.[10] The results of this process are sent to Rome, which in time issues a decree about heroic virtue or martyrdom. After this decree the person can be called "venerable." A further decree is about the miracle. One miracle is required for beatification. Historians and theologians are consulted at each stage of the cause, and particularly before it is finally judged by the Congregation's cardinals and bishops. An essential norm is purity of doctrine in the writings or other works of the person. The final decision about beatification rests with the pope. Before canonization a further miracle, taking place after the beatification, is required. There is, however, no investigation about heroic virtue at this stage. The verdict about canonization again rests with the pope, on the advice of the Congregation.

Several theological issues are raised by the veneration of saints. First is the requirement of martyrdom (v. MARTYR) or heroic virtue. Martyrdom must be for the faith or arise through *odium fidei* or enmity of the faith. Particularly, but not only, in recent history there can be political motivations as well as commitment to God involved in a person's death; careful investigations must therefore take place to establish the fact of genuine martyrdom, the supreme act of love of God and of the Church. In the case of others there must be heroic virtue so that the person is judged to have lived profoundly Christian love towards God, men, and women, and to have practiced all Christian virtues in a perfect, exemplary, and heroic manner. These norms show that the point of beatification and canonization is to provide models of holiness for the Church.

A second theological point is the certitude that lies behind canonization. Until recently, manual theology gave the canonization of saints as an instance of papal infallibility;[11] theologians do not generally retain this position today.[12]

A third point concerns the veneration of saints. The Tridentine profession of faith stated that "saints reigning together with Christ should be venerated and invoked. . . . They offer prayers to God for us, and their relics should be venerated."[13] Trent in its 25th session had laid down important norms: people were to be carefully instructed about the proper veneration of the saints; saints help us through their intercession; Christ is, however, the sole redeemer and one mediator; the veneration of images is legitimate because we thus adore Christ and venerate the saints themselves; such veneration of images is to be encouraged, taking care to avoid all abuses.[14] Already at Nicaea II (787—q.v.), the veneration of images of saints was solemnly approved[15] and reiterated at Constantinople IV (869–870—q.v.);[16] it was recalled again by John Paul II on the occasion of the twelfth centenary of Nicaea II.[17]

The positions of Vatican II on veneration are reflected in the *Code of Canon Law* (CIC 1186–1187), which has a special emphasis on devotion to the Virgin Mary. Its Liturgy Constitution presents a modern theology of veneration: "The Church has also put commemorations of martyrs and other saints into the cycle of the (liturgical) year. These people were brought to their full potential through the grace of Christ active in many different ways; and they already possess eternal salvation. They are singing perfect praise to God in heaven, and are interceding for us. By celebrating the days on which the saints died, the Church proclaims the Easter mystery as found in the holy ones who have suffered for Christ and been glorified with him, puts the example of these people before believers as models to attract all women and men to the Father through Christ, and begs God for favors through what they have gained" *[eorumque meritis Dei beneficia impetrat]* (SC 104).[18]

A fourth point concerns the nature of the veneration of the saints. St. Augustine proposed the Greek term *latreia* for adoration of God.[19] The term *dulia* as honor of the saints is from the Carolingian period;[20] later the term *hyperdulia* emerged for the special form of *dulia* appropriate to the Virgin Mary.

It is clear, then, that veneration of the saints involves strong belief in the Communion of Saints (q.v.), a vision of the Church that takes in heaven as well as earth (see Vatican II, Church ch. 7).[21]

It can be seen that saints throughout the ages give various models for the Church, and reflect different aspects of spirituality, from the ascetics in the desert to the heroic ordinariness of St. Thérèse of Lisieux. The saints are, in the phrase of K. Rahner, "creators of new styles of Christianity."[22] Saints are to be seen and venerated only from within a healthy sense of Church.[23] Indeed their writings and lives are now seen as a *locus theologicus* (v. THEOLOGICAL SOURCES, FATHERS).

The liturgical celebration of the saints has been simplified in the post-Vatican II reforms. The number of celebrations for the universal Church was drastically pruned to give more emphasis to the temporal cycle; saints of more local interest were either deleted from the universal calendar or made optional memorials. Local calendars give prominence to saints of a particular diocese, region, church, or religious family.[24] The liturgy remains the prime form of veneration of the saints; it also instructs us in their role for us in the Church.[25]

Hagiography, or writings about saints—especially biographies—is found from early centuries. There is always a temptation to exaggerate and to accept legends, particularly since one expects to find the miraculous associated with the saints. There has, nonetheless, always been evidence of a desire of popes, theologians, and important writers to present the truth about the saints. From the 17th century the Church has been well served in this regard by the Bollandists, Jesuit followers of John van Bolland (1596–1665), who set new standards for historical accuracy.[26]

In modern times there is some criticism of Roman canonization procedures: the choice of who should be canonized seems to favor predominantly Latins and religious;[27] the monetary cost of the complicated process is very high, though it is commonly believed to include a "tax" on canonizations from the northern hemisphere to support the causes of persons in the southern hemisphere. The sheer number of recent beatifications and canonizations could have the effect of escalation—and there are over 1,000 causes still under consideration by the Congregation.[28]

The Eastern Churches (q.v.) are conspicuous for their veneration of the saints. More than the West they hold in honor, liturgically as well as on the iconostasis, the saints of the OT. The Eastern Churches not in communion with Rome have added very many saints, many of whom are local, but some are of more universal significance, e.g., St. Gregory Palamas (ca. 1296–1359—canonized 1368).[29] The Orthodox Church places great trust in the saints and mystics as guardians and interpreters of tradition and the faith.

The Anglican Communion in the English *Alternative Service Book* and the American *Book of Common Prayer* has given the title saint to important figures and celebrates feasts in their honor, e.g., William Law (1686–1761—9 April), George Herbert (1593–1633 —27 Feb.), John Keble (1792–1866—29 March), Edward Pusey (1800–1882—18 Sept.).[30]

In an ecumenical context there is some study and some convergence about saints, though intercession is still ruled out by most Protestants.[31] Vatican II acknowledged the existence of great holiness outside the Catholic Church, especially in martyrs (LG 15; cf. DH 14; UR 15, 17, 23).[32]

[1]R.L. Cohn, "Sainthood," EncycRel 13:1-6; S. Wilson, ed., *Saints and Their Cults: Studies in Religious Sociology, Folklore and History* (New York: Cambridge UP, 1984). [2]O. Procksch and K.G. Kuhn, "Hagios," TDNT 1:88-115. [3]A. Amore, "Culto e canonizzazione dei santi nell'antichità cristiana," Antonian 52 (1977) 38-80; idem, "La canonizzazione vescovile," ibid., 230–266. [4]See DS 675. [5]L. Hertling, "Materiali per la storia del processo di canonizzazione," Greg 16 (1935) 170–195; P. Molinari, "Canonization of Saints (History and Procedure)," NCE 3:55-59. [6]*De servorum Dei beatificatione et beatorum canonizatione* (1734–1738). [7]AAS 61 (1969) 257–305/CanLawDig 7:238-245. [8]*Novae leges pro causis sanctorum;* Constit. apost. *Divinus perfectionis Magister; Normae servandae in inquisitionibus ab episcopis faciendis in causis sanctorum; Decretum generale de servorum Dei causis quarum iudicium in praesens apud Sacram Congregationem pendet* (Last three in one volume, Vatican, 1983). *Regolamento della Sacra Congregazione per le cause dei santi* (Vatican, 1983). See E. Apeciti, "Le nuove norme per les cause di canonizzazione," ScoulC 119 (1991) 250–278; A. Eszer, "La Congregazione delle Cause dei Santi," in P.A. Bonnet and C. Gullo, *La Curia romana nella Cost. Ap. "Pastor Bonus."* Studi giuridici 21 (Vatican, 1990) 309–329; J.L. Gutiérrez, "La normativa actual sobre las causas de canonización," IusCan 32 (1992) 39–65; F. Veraja, *Commento alla nuova legislazione per le cause dei santi.* Sussidi per lo studio delle cause dei santi 1 (Rome: S. Cong. per le Cause dei Santi, 1983); K.L. Woodward, *Making Saints: How the Catholic Church Determines Who Becomes a Saint, Who Doesn't and Why* (New York: Simon & Schuster, 1990). [9]R.J. Sarno, *Diocesan Inquiries Required by the Legislator in the New Legislation for the Causes of Saints.* Diss. (Rome: Gregorian UP, 1988); A. Casieri, *Postulatorum Vademecum* (Vatican, [2]1986); R. Rodrigo, *Manual para instruir los procesos de canonización* (Vatican, 1987). [10]J.A. Hardon, "The Concept of Miracle from St. Augustine to Modern Apologetics," TS 15 (1954) 229–257; J.C. Carter, "The Recognition of Miracles," TS 20 (1959) 175–197. [11]E.g., J. Salaverri, De ecclesia 741–743. Cp. E. Piacentini, "L'infallibilità papale nella canonizzazione dei santi," MonEccl 117 (1992) 91–132. [12]E.g., F.A. Sullivan, *Magisterium. Teaching Authority in the Catholic Church* (Dublin: Gill and Macmillan, 1983) 136. [13]DS 1867/ND 35; cf. Profession of Faith of Paul VI (1968)—ND 39/22. [14]Tanner 2:774-776/DS 1821/ND 1255; see F. D'Ostilo, "Il culto dei santi, beati, venerabili servi di Dio: Ciò che è dovuto permesso vietato auspicabile," MonEccl 117 (1992) 63–90. [15]Tanner 1:133-137/DS 600–601/ND 1251-1252. [16]Can. 3—Tanner 1:168/DS 653–654/ND 1253. [17]Apost. Letter, *Duodecimum saeculum* (1987)—AAS 80 (1988) 241–252/ND 1260-1261. [18]L.S. Cunningham, "A Decade of Research on the Saints," TS 53 (1992) 517–533; L. Cunningham, *The Meaning of Saints* (New York: Harper & Row, 1980); Conc 129 (1979). [19]*De civ. Dei* 10:1—CSEL 47:272. [20]St. Thomas ST 2–2ae, q.103, a.3. [21]J. Pascher, "Die 'Communio sanctorum' als Grundgefüge der katholischen Heiligenverehrung," MüTZ 3 (1950) 1–11. [22]K. Rahner, "The Church of the Saints," ThInvest 3:91-104; idem, "Why and How Can We Venerate the Saints?," ibid., 8:3-23; idem, "All Saints,"

ibid., 8:24-29; see "Nouvelles saintetés," VieSp 143 (1989)/n. 687. See H.U. von Balthasar, "Les saints, croix de l'histoire," Communio 4/6 (1979) 29–37. [23]W. Beinert, "Ecclesiologische Aspekte der Heiligenverehrung," Catholica 40 (1986) 187–202; idem. ed. *Die Heiligen heute ehren* (Freiburg-Basel-Vienna: Herder, 1983); P. Brown, *The Cult of the Saints: Its Rise and Function in Latin Christianity* (Chicago: UP—London: SCM, 1981); M. Mallet, *Le culte des saints: Pourquoi et comment* (Paris: De Guibert, 1994); P. Molinari, "Alcuni riflessioni sulla funzione dei santi nella Chiesa," Greg 42 (1961) 63–96; G.L. Müller, "Der theologische Ort der Heiligen: Überlegungen zur ekklesiologischen Ansatz der 2. vatikanischen Konzils," ZkT 108 (1986) 145–154; J. Navone, "Eroi, modelli, santi e 'leader,'" CivCatt 138 (1987) 4:340-352; G. Vodopivec, "Il santo e la canonizzazione dei santi nella chiesa: Segno di salvezza," Communio (Milan) 5 (1973) [325–335] 29–38; see Communio (Paris) 13/1 (1988). [24]*Roman Missal.* "General Norms for the Liturgical Year and the Calendar"; P. Jounel, "Le culte des saints dans l'Église catholique," MaisD 147n(1981) 135–146; "The Litany of Saints—Its Place in the Grammar of Liturgy," Worship 65 (1991) 216–223. [25]A.M. Triacca and A. Pistoia, eds., *Saints et sainteté dans la liturgie.* Conférences Saint-Serge 33. Bibliotheca *Ephemerides liturgicae,* Subsidia 40 (Rome: CLV—Ed. Liturgische, 1987); F. Peloso "Il culto dei santi oggi," EphLtg 105 (1991) 237–262, 418–448; idem, *Santi e santità dopo il concilio Vaticano II: Studio teologico-liturgico delle orazioni proprie dei nuovi beati e santi.* Bibliotheca *Ephemerides liturgicae,* Subsidia 61 (Rome: CLV-Ed. Liturgische, 1991). E. Lodi, *I santi del calendario romano: Pregare con i santi nella liturgia.* Manuali liturgici 2 (Milan: Paoline, 1990). [26]*Acta sanctorum* from 1643; *Analecta bollandiana* from 1882. See the Bollandist H. Delahaye, *The Legends of the Saints: An Introduction to Hagiography* (London: Chapman, [2]1962); revision of *Butler's Lives of the Saints* by H. Thurston and D. Attwater (London, 1953–1954); D.H. Farmer, *The Oxford Dictionary of Saints* (Oxford: UP, [2]1987). [27]P. Delooz, "The Social Function of the Canonization of Saints," Conc 129 (1979) 14–24; J. Evenou, "Les saints et bienheureux proclamés par Jean Paul II (1978–1988)," EspVie 99 (1989) 200–207; J.-P. Jossua, "Sociologie des canonisations," VieSp 143 (1989) 165–171; P. de Laubier, "Sociologie des saints," RThom 91 (1991) 34–67. [28]Yearly *Index ac status causarum* (Vatican). [29]P. Evdokimov, "La santità nella tradizione della Chiesa ortodossa," VitaCons 14 (1978) 234–260, 302–322 = Contacts 73–74 (1971) 119–190; P. de Meester, "La canonizzazione dei santi nella Chiesa russa," Greg 30 (1949) 393–407; S. Hackel, ed., *The Byzantine Saint.* Studies Supplementary to Sobornost 5 (London: Fellowship of St. Alban and St. Sergius, 1981); P. Peeters, "La canonisation des saints dans l'Église russe," AnBoll 33 (1914) 380–420; 38 (1920) 172–176. [30]R. Symonds, *The Post Reformation British People Commemorated by the Church of England* (London: Macmillan, 1989). [31]H.G. Anderson et al., eds., *The One Mediator, the Saints and Mary.* Lutherans and Roman Catholics in Dialogue VIII (Minneapolis: Augsburg, 1992); E.A. Johnson, "May We Invoke the Saints?," TTod 44 (1987–1988) 32–52; M. Lienhard, "La sainteté et les saints chez Luther," VieSp 143 (1989) 521–532; G. Tavard, "The Veneration of Saints as an Ecumenical Question," OneChr 26 (1990) 40–50 = T. Horgan, ed., *Walking Together* (Grand Rapids: Eerdmans, 1990) 118–133; S.A. Rabe, "Veneration of the Saints in Western Christianity: An Ecumenical Issue in Historical Perspective," JEcuSt 28 (1991) 39–62; M. Whalen, "Saints and Their Feasts: An Ecumenical Exploration," Worship 63 (1989) 194–209. [32]Cf. V. Maulucci, *Vi sono santi tra i cristiani non cattolici?* Collectio assisiensis 5 (Assisi: Studio teol. Porziuncula, 1969).

## SCHEEBEN, Matthias Joseph (1835–1888)

Matthias Joseph Scheeben, one of the more important and creative theologians of the 19th century, was born near Bonn in 1835. He studied at the Gregorian University, Rome, where the major theologians of the Roman School (q.v.) were then teaching. He taught at the seminary at Cologne from 1860–1888. He had exceptional knowledge of the Fathers, particularly Greek, and of scholastic theology. His work was boldly speculative, from his first important work on method to his final three volumes on dogma.[1] He had almost completed the revision of his best-known work on the Christian mysteries[2] when he died in 1888; it represents his most mature thought.

This summary work is profoundly Trinitarian, and it is in this context that his ecclesiology is inserted.[3] The Church is a living organism, it is "the body of the God-man; and all who enter it become members of the God-man. . . . As the mystical body of Christ, the Church is his true bride who, made fruitful by his divine power, has the destiny of bearing heavenly children to him and his heavenly Father, or nourishing these children with the substance and light of her bridegroom. . . . In brief, the Church is the most intimate and real fellowship of men with the God-man, a fellowship that achieves its truest and most perfect expression in the Eucharist."[4] In the *Mysteries of Christianity* he significantly places his treatment of the Eucharist after the Incarnation and before dealing with the Church and then the sacraments.

But Scheeben's vision is not merely Christological: "If the Church in all its members is thus the body of Christ and the bride of Christ, the power of its divine head, the Spirit of its divine bridegroom must be gloriously operative in it. In all its members the Church is a temple of the Holy Spirit who dwells in it as the soul in its own body, and manifests his divine and divinizing power in it. . . . With his divine fire he must gloriously change Christ's bride into the image of the divine nature, transform her whole body by adding splendor to splendor, and pervade her with his own divine life."[5]

The key images of the Church are Body and bride; and its organization, even jurisdictional, is seen as maternal.[6] The laity also share in the motherhood of the Church, for "all members of the Church are the brides of Christ and as such are made fruitful by his Spirit."[7]

He was a strong supporter of papal infallibility at the time of Vatican I. His preferred term "mission of teaching" *(Lehrapostolat)* was for him the richest expression for the whole range of teaching that is carried on in the Church.[8] He withstood the distinction emerging in early 19th-century canonists of a tripartite division of functions in the Church: doctrinal, priestly, and pastoral. He retained the scholastic double division: power of jurisdiction and of orders. Teaching was proclaimed by the power of orders and imposed by the power of jurisdiction. But in some sense he anticipated Vatican II not only in his notion of the sacramentality of the Church[9] but in his view that there is a certain infallibility of the learning Church which also transmits the revelation of Christ.[10]

The bridal image, so central to Scheeben's ecclesiology, is carried into his important Mariological writing, in which he takes bridal motherhood as the fundamental principle of Marian theology.[11] Mary (q.v.) is Mother of the Church, and "Mary's motherhood remains the root and soul of that of the Church in such unity that the Church can have and exercises its motherhood only insofar as it contains and acts through Mary's motherhood."[12]

---

[1]*Die Lehre von dem Übernatürlichen* (1860); *Handbuch der katholischen Dogmatik.* 3 vols. (1873–1882).   [2]*The Mysteries of Christianity* (St. Louis—London, 1946).   [3]*Mysteries of Christianity* (n. 2) 539–557; Antón 2:428-447; B. Gherardini, "La visione ecclesiologica di Matthias Joseph Scheeben," Divinitas 32 (1988) 287–295. See AA.VV. *M.J. Scheeben, teologo cattolico d'ispirazione tomista.* Studi tomistici 33 (Vatican, 1988).   [4]*Mysteries* (n. 2) 541–542. See P. Toinet, "L'Eucharistie dans la connexion des mystères," Divinitas 32 (1988) 395–408.   [5]Ibid., 544. See F. Holböck, "Der Heilige Geist als Seele des mystischen Leibes Christi bei M.J. Scheeben," Divinitas 32 (1988) 297–311.   [6]Ibid., 545–557.   [7]Ibid., 555, n. 5.   [8]W. Bartz, "Le magistère de l'Église d'après Scheeben," in AA.VV. *L'ecclésiologie au XIXe siècle.* US 34 (Paris: Cerf, 1960) 309–327.   [9]*Mysteries* (n. 2) 558–566, 581; Antón 2:436-437.   [10]*Mysteries* (n. 2) 552–557; see Antón 2:443-445; Bartz (n. 8) 320–321.   [11]*Mariology.* 2 vols. (St. Louis—London, 1948); see D. Flanagan, "Scheeben and the Basic Principle of Mariology," IrTQ 25 (1958) 367–381; O'Carroll, Theotokos, 318–320.   [12]Mariology (n. 11) 2:250; *Mysteries* (n. 2) 546–547.

## SCHILLEBEECKX, Edward (1914– )

The Flemish Dominican theologian Edward Schillebeeckx was born near Antwerp in 1914.[1] He studied theology at Louvain and was ordained in 1941. He was soon to be given the task of teaching theology. After the war he went to Le Saulchoir where he was very much influenced by Y. Congar (q.v.) and M.D. Chenu. Only the first part of his doctoral dissertation on sacramental theology was published, and then solely in Dutch;[2] later he produced an abbreviated version of both parts, *Christ the Sacrament of the Encounter with God.*[3]

The bibliography of his works is extensive.[4] In the 1960s and early 1970s Schillebeeckx produced significant works on sacraments,[5] Mariology,[6] and revelation.[7] Many of his essays from these years are gathered in the series "Theological Soundings."

In the 1970s he moved from writing which was mainly concerned with inner-Church issues to problems associated with faith in the world of today. He began to be greatly interested in NT exegesis of the historical critical school. This development as well as increased attention to contemporary philosophy and hermeneutics led to two controversial books on Christology[8] and two on ministry.[9] Retiring as professor at Nijmegen in 1983, he completed his Christological trilogy with a work on the Church.[10]

He was investigated by Vatican authorities three times (1968, 1976, 1981), but though asked to clarify his positions, nothing he wrote was condemned.[11] His last book on the Church shows him to be disaffected by the positions and attitudes of Church authorities but still a man of hope, a hope that he sees based on the vibrancy found in the grass-roots Church.[12]

[1]J. Bowden, *Edward Schillebeeckx: Portrait of a Theologian* (London: SCM, 1983); G. Daly, "Schillebeeckx and the Renewal of Catholic Theology," DoctLife 31 (1981) 90–101; P. Kennedy, *Schillebeeckx.* Outstanding Christian Thinkers (London: Chapman, 1993); R. Schreiter and M.C. Hilkert, eds., *The Praxis of Christian Experience: An Orientation to Edward Schillebeeckx* (San Francisco: Harper & Row, 1989). R. Schreiter, "Edward Schillebeeckx," in D.F. Ford, ed., The *Modern Theologians: An Introduction to Christian Theology in the Twentieth Century.* 2 vols. (Oxford: Blackwell, 1989) 1:152-163. [2]*De sacramentele heilseconomie* (Antwerp: Bilhoven, 1952). [3]London: Sheed & Ward, "Stagbooks," 1963. [4]R.J. Schreiter, ed., *The Schillebeeckx Reader* (Edinburgh: Clark, 1983) 297–321 (to 1983). [5]*Eucharist* (London, 1968); *Marriage: Secular Reality and Saving Mystery.* 2 vols. (London, 1965). [6]*Mary, Mother of the Redemption* (London, 1964). [7]*Revelation and Theology.* Theological Soundings 1/1. (London, 1973). [8]*Jesus: An Experiment in Christology* (London: Collins 1979—Dutch 1974); *Christ: The Christian Experience in the Modern World* (London: SCM, 1980) = *Christ: The Experience of Jesus as Lord* (New York: Crossroad, 1980—Dutch 1977). See his *Interim Report on the Books Jesus and Christ* (London: SCM, 1980—Dutch 1978). [9]*Ministry: Leadership in the Community of Jesus Christ* (New York: Crossroad, 1981) = *Ministry: A Case for Change* (London: SCM, 1981); cf. critique by A. Vanhoye and H. Crouzel, "The Ministry of the Church," CleR 68 (1983) 155–174 = NRT 104 (1982) 722–748. See revision, *The Church with a Human Face: A New and Expanded Theology of Ministry* (London: SCM, 1985); cf. critique, P. Grelot, *Les ministères dans le peuple de Dieu* (Paris: Cerf, 1988). [10]*Church: The Human Story of God* (London: SCM, 1990—Dutch 1989). [11]T. Schoof, ed., *The Schillebeeckx Case: Official Exchange of Letters and Documents in the Investigation of Fr. Edward Schillebeeckx, O.P., by the Sacred Congregation for the Doctrine of the Faith 1976–1980* (New York-Ramsey: Paulist, 1984); P. Hebblethwaite, *The New Inquisition?* (San Francisco: Harper & Row—London: SCM, 1980) 129–153; L. Swidler and P. Fransen, eds., *Authority in the Church and the Schillebeeckx Case* (New York: Crossroad, 1982); see "The Magisterium and Ideology," JEcuSt 19 (1982) 5–17. [12]See his *I Am a Happy Theologian: Conversations with Francesco Strazzari* (London: SCM, 1994 from Italian 1993).

## SCHISM

In the *Code of Canon Law* schism is defined as "the refusal of submission to the Roman Pontiff or of communion with the members of the Church subject to him" (CIC 751). The law had previously stated the obligation to remain in communion (CIC 209 § 1). This clarity is not always found in the earlier history, which sometimes used the words heresy (q.v.) and schism interchangeably.[1] In modern usage heresy concerns faith, and schism concerns communion (q.v.) and charity. The latter usually arises from disagreements about Church order and authority.

The word itself (from the Greek *schisma*) means a rent, tear, or division. As such it is used by Paul about the divisions in Corinth (1 Cor 1:10; 11:18; cf. 12:25). In the patristic period schism was seen above all in a rupture of Eucharistic fellowship, "altar against altar."[2] It was also seen as a breakdown in love as in the words of Augustine: "The origin and pertinacity of schism is nothing other than hatred of the brethren."[3] In the scholastic period there are two developments: schism is not seen so much in sacramental terms affecting local Churches, but a sin against the universal Church; it is a sin against charity.[4] Whereas St. Thomas distinguishes heresy and schism so that all heresy is schism but not vice versa, he does teach that schism easily leads to heresy.[5] From the 16th century it became common to see schism as a refusal of unity with the pope, a refusal to be a part of the wider whole of the Church.[6]

Schism can come about through a variety of disputes which lead to a breakdown of communion. The word "schism" is also used about the times of the multiple claimants to the papacy during the period of the Avignon (q.v.) residence (v. SCHISM, GREAT WESTERN, CONSTANCE, COUNCIL OF) called the Great Western Schism (1378–1417). From the 17th century there has been schism in the Russian Orthodox Church (Old Believers—Raskol) resulting from a rejection of liturgical changes; in the Catholic Church the schismatic movement of Archbishop Lefebvre (q.v.) came about through a refusal of Vatican II and its subsequent changes—mostly in worship.

The most serious schism in the history of the Church was that between East and West, which was formalized in 1054 but reflected a separation that had gradually arisen in the previous 200 years. After Vatican II there was a growing rapprochement between Paul VI and the Orthodox patriarchs Athenagoras and Dimitrios I, which led to the lifting of the 11th-century anathemas (7 Dec. 1965).[7]

Though Vatican II spoke about divisions and separations (UR 3, 13), it avoided the word "schism"—likewise "heresy." Formerly the Catholic Church regarded the Orthodox Church as being in schism, but the Protestant Churches as in heresy.

In canon law there are serious penalties for schism (CIC 1364); these apply to schism that is public (CIC 194 § 1, n. 2). Nowadays the presumption would be that almost all of those who are materially in a situation to be judged as schismatic, according to the canons, would be in good faith. However, as the episcopal ordinations by Archbishop Lefebvre showed, canonical penalties can be applied; he was excommunicated. Though short of an actual break with the Church, a schismatical attitude may be found adopted on various issues by individuals or groups.[8]

[1]Thus still, C. Argenti et al., *Le schisme: Sa signification théologique et spirituelle* (Lyon: Mappus, 1967). [2]Congar, L'Église une 70–72; idem, "Schisme," DTC 14:1286-1312; S.L. Greenslade, *Schism in the Early Church* (London, [2]1964), but cf. B.C. Butler, "Schism and Unity," DowR 71 (1953) 353–371. [3]*De bapt.* 1:11, 16—CSEL 51:161. [4]Congar (n. 2) 75–76; see St. Thomas ST 2–2ae, q.39, a.1 with q.14, a.2 ad 4. [5]ST 2–2ae, q.39, a.1 ad 3. [6]Congar, L'Église une 76–79. [7]E.J. Storman, ed., *Towards the Healing of Schism: The Sees of Rome and Constantinople—Public Statements and Correspondence Between the Holy See and the Ecumenical Patriarch 1958–1984.* Ecumenical Documents 3 (New York: Paulist, 1987); V.J. Phidas and J. Ratzinger, "Les conséquences ecclésiastiques de la levée des anathèmes," Istina 20 (1978) 75–99. [8]Cf. K. Rahner, "Schism in the Catholic Church?," ThInvest 12:98-115.

## SCHISM, THE GREAT WESTERN

The legitimacy of the election of Urban VI (1378–1389) was contested; it took place during riots in Rome. Later the pope's mental balance gave cause for concern. The French cardinals withdrew and elected Clement VII (1378), thus inaugurating the Great Western Schism (1378–1417, v. SCHISM).[1] National and other sectional interests determined whether parties gave allegiance to Urban or Clement. Urban's successors were Boniface IX (1389–1404), Innocent VII (1404–1406), and Gregory XII (1406–1415)—these are regarded by historians as the genuine popes. The antipope Clement VII was succeeded by Benedict XIII (1394–1417). The Council of Pisa (1409) deposed both Gregory XII and Benedict XIII, and elected a new pope, Alexander V, another antipope (1409–1410). Both deposed popes continued to push their claims. Alexander V was succeeded by the antipope John XXIII (1410–1415). The Council of Constance (q.v.) ended the schism by deposing John XXIII and Benedict XIII and by receiving the abdication of Gregory XII. It elected Martin V (1417–1431), which effectively put an end to the schism. There would be some antipopes in the succeeding decades, but none of them had much following.

[1]OxDictPopes 227–239; K.A. Fink, in Jedin-Dolan 4:401-415; 448–468; W. Brandmüller, *Papst und Konzil im Großem Schisma 1378–1431.* Studien und Quellen (Paderborn-Munich-Vienna: Schöningh, 1990); M. Maillard-Luypaert, "A propos du grand Schisme d'Occident (1378–1417): Réflexions et approche méthodologique," RHE 82 (1987) 549–553.

## SECULAR INSTITUTES

The main features of secular institutes go back several centuries: consecrated life lived in the world, and not in community. But opinions vary about when secular institutes in the modern sense of the term began. The late 19th and early 20th century for some canonists and theologians seems an acceptable dating with O. Kozminski (1829–1916) in Poland and A. Gemelli (1875–1959), the Italian founder of the Missionaries of the Kingship of Christ. The latter adopted a phrase which would be a constant in magisterial, conciliar, and canonical literature—"working from within the world."

Pius XII (q.v.) formally recognized secular institutes in the apostolic constitution *Provida Mater Ecclesia* and in subsequent documents.[1] Secular institutes then multiplied and the literature relating to them grew (mostly in French and Italian).[2] Studies proliferated especially on their secularity,[3] their vocation in the world,[4] their role in the Church,[5] their distinction from religious life.[6]

Vatican II recognized the particular calling of secular institutes: "Secular institutes differ from religious institutes *[quamvis non sint instituta religiosa];* but they are considered by the Church, nonetheless, to embody an authentic commitment to the gospel counsels in the world. This commitment is a true consecration of life for men and women living in the world, both clerics and laity" (PC 11). They can set up bodies similar to the conferences of major superiors (PC 23); their contribution to missionary activity is acknowledged (AG 40).

The First International Congress of Secular Institutes (Rome, 1970) showed a wide pluralism (q.v.): some were quite like religious congregations in all but in name; others did not wish to accept commitment to the evangelical counsels but wished for a more general consecration.[7]

In canon law secular institutes are treated under the rubric of consecrated life (CIC 573–606), and then with their own canons (CIC 710–730), which open with a definition: "A secular institute is an institute of consecrated life in which the Christian faithful living in the world strive for the perfection of charity and work for the sanctification of the world especially from within" (CIC 710). This canon gives their specific characteristic, consecrated secularity.[8] The particular way in which they live the evangelical counsels is to be determined by constitutions, with the addition: ". . . while always preserving, however, in its way of life the distinctive secularity of the institute" (CIC 712 with cf. 598–601 for counsels). The apostolic aim of secular institutes is expressed in a way that echoes Pius XII: "The members of these institutes express and exercise their own consecration in their apostolic activity and like a leaven they strive to imbue all things with the spirit of the gospel for the strengthening and growth of the Body of Christ" (CIC 713 § 1). The same canon goes on to describe this apostolic mission in terms of LG on the laity (31, 32, 34), even though priests can be members of such institutes (CIC 313 § 3; 715 § 1). The law envisages that members may live alone or in groups (CIC 714). There is an emphasis on formation, both initial and ongoing, for the members (CIC 722; 724). There is the possibility of institutes offering association to others who would not be members in the strict sense (CIC 725); an obvious case is those married (CIC 721 § 1, n. 3) who cannot be bound by the evangelical counsels which constitute secular institutes as a form of consecrated life. In general the law shows a flexibility which is appropriate for a form of Church life which is still evolving.

---

[1]AAS 39 (1947) 114–124; *Primo feliciter*—AAS 40 (1948) 283–286; Instruction *Cum sanctissimis*—AAS 40 (1948) 293–297. [2]F. Morlot, "Bibliographia de institutibus secularibus," ComRelM 54 (1973) 231–297; 64 (1983) 183–253. [3]T.J. Olmsted, *The Secularity of Secular Institutes.* Diss. (Rome: Gregorian, 1981); F. Podimattam, "The Theology of Secular Institutes," JDhara 19 (1989) 439–464; G. Rivron, "La secolarità degli istituti socondo la dottrina degli autori," VitaCons 13 (1977) 33–47; P. Schinetti, "Secolarità consecrata," VitaCons 13 (1977) 238–251, 291–303; F. Zanon, "Gli istituti secolari laicali: Osservazioni sulla secolarità," VitaConc 12 (1976) 294–302. [4]A. Oberti, ed., *Nel mondo per il mondo. Gli istituti secolari oggi* (Rome: AVE, 1972); M. Poma, *La spiritualità e la missione dei laici nell'esperienza degli istituti secolari* (Milan: Ed. O.R., 1987). [5]Paolo VI, *Gli istituti secolari una presenza viva nella Chiesa e nel mondo.* Testo scelti a cura di A. Oberti (Milan: Ed. O.R., 1986); J. Beyer, "Gli istituti secolari: trent'anni di vita ecclesiale," VitaCons 13 (1977) 283–290; A. Oberti, "La vocation des instituts séculiers dans l'Église," VieCons 54 (1982) 171–180, 228–240. [6]J. Beyer, "Religious Life or Secular Institute," WaySupp 7 (1969) 112–132; J. de la Croix Bonadio, "Notes Towards a Definition of the Secular Institutes," WaySupp 12 (1971) 16–23; D.K. O'Connor, "Two Forms of Consecrated Life: Religious and Secular Institutes," RevRel 45 (1986) 205–219. [7]*Actus congressus internationalis institutorum saecularium* (Milan: Op. Regalità, 1971); A. Gutiérrez, "Laicitas et pluralismus institutorum saecularium," ComRelM 52 (1971) 3–24. [8]S.L. Holland in Coriden, CIC 525–539 at 526.

## SENSE OF THE FAITH—SENSE OF THE FAITHFUL

Faith can have two basic meanings: it is the objective content of what is believed (*fides quae);* it is the virtue or act whereby people believe (*fides qua*). The faith of the Church in the first eleven centuries usually meant its objective faith; heresies led the councils and Fathers (q.v.) to insist on orthodoxy or correct belief. In the scholastic period, in connection with infant baptism, the faith of the Church meant also the act of the believing community, which in the sacramental system was communicable to individuals: the faith of the Church supplied for the absence of faith in a baby being baptized or in a heretical minister of sacraments.[1]

In contemporary theology there are three terms which can be confused and are sometimes used almost interchangeably; they should rather be carefully distinguished. The sense of the faith (*sensus fidei* of LG 12) refers to a supernatural instinct for the truth in matters of faith; it thus pertains to the *fides qua* above. The sense of the faithful (*sensus fidelium*) is the belief of the faith; this belongs to the *fides quae,* to what is believed. Finally, the consent of the faithful (*consensus fidelium*) refers to a belief shared by all the faithful. In a brief historical survey it can be seen that these three notions, though distinct, are interconnected. The literature is quite extensive.[2]

In the Scriptures we find indications that a special sensitivity in matters of truth is a gift of the Spirit to the community (cf. 1 Cor 2:6-16; John 14:2-6; 16:12-15; 1 John 2:20-21, 27). They will be taught by God (cf. John 6:45).[3] Teaching (v. TEACHERS) is both a personal office or charism and an activity of the community.[4] In the patristic period there is evidence of the importance of the grasp of the faith by all the faithful. We have only to recall the example adduced by that theoretician of the *sensus fidelium,* J.H. Newman (q.v.): "I see, then, in the Arian history a palmary example of a state of the Church, during which, in order to know the tradition of the Apostles, we must have recourse to the faithful. . . . Their voice, then, is the voice of Tradition."[5] The stress of the 16th-century Reformers on personal Scripture reading, on the Spirit's assistance to the believers who read the Scriptures, and the general downplaying of ministries led Trent to be quite guarded about the *sensus fidelium,* the council preferring other terms.[6] By the 19th century it was little in evidence.[7]

The Marian definition of the Immaculate Conception (1854) and of the Assumption (1950) are two critical examples of the *sensus fidelium.* In each case the popes, Pius IX and Pius XII, consulted with the bishops. They asked the bishops not only for their own judgment as official teachers in the Church but about the belief of the faithful. There was seen to be on these doctrines a *consensus fidelium.*[8] The definitions themselves begin from the universal faith of the Church before giving indications from Scripture and Tradition. The theme of *sensus fidelium* was overshadowed by the definitions of Vatican I on primacy and infallibility. It was only from the 1950s that the issue began to be studied again in depth.[9]

In the Constitution on the Church there is an important statement in the article that deals with the people's share in the prophetic role of Christ; it is explaining the *sensus fidei:* "The universal body of the faithful who have received the anointing of the holy one (see 1 John 2:20 and 27), cannot be mistaken in belief. It displays this particular quality through a supernatural sense of the faith in the whole people when 'from the bishops to the last of the faithful laity' (Augustine, *De praed. sanct.*

14:27), it expresses the consent of all in matters of faith and morals. Through this sense of faith which is aroused and sustained by the Spirit of truth, the People of God under the guidance of the sacred magisterium to which it is faithfully obedient, receives no longer the words of human beings but truly the word of God (see 1 Thess 2:13); it adheres indefectibly to 'the faith that was once for all delivered to the saints' (Jude 3); it penetrates more deeply into that same faith through right judgment and applies it to life" (LG 12; cf. 35 in the context of the prophetic office of laity). The verbs used are important: the sense of faith is aroused and sustained *(excitatur* and *sustentatur)* by the Spirit; it is under the guidance of the magisterium *(sub ductu sacri magisterii);* the people receives *(accipit)* the word of God and adheres to *(adhaeret),* penetrates into *(penetrat),* and applies it *(applicat).*[10] There is a clear role for the magisterium (q.v.), but this passage envisages that all in the Church can teach and all must learn; in chapter 2 of , "The People of God" (not just "Laity"), there is no room for a division in the Church which would have the hierarchy only teaching and the laity only listening, though the particular teaching ministry of the hierarchy is detailed later (LG 25).[11] As witnessed by the earlier tradition, all in their own way teach and learn.[12] In receiving this rich conciliar teaching, the *Code of Canon Law* weakened it to the point of distortion.[13]

A new feature of the late 19th and 20th centuries is a changed role of the Roman magisterium (q.v.). In earlier periods conciliar and papal statements came, usually after some crisis, at the end of a process. Now we have spontaneous teaching offered by the magisterium. An acute problem is how this is received by the Church (v. RECEPTION) and how open it is to examination and criticism.[14]

The sense of the faith *(sensus fidei* of LG 12 above) is clearly crucial in the development of doctrine (q.v.),[15] which eventually shows forth the sense of the faithful or consensus about a particular truth. But a difficult area remains, that of the criteria for this latter *sensus fidelium.* It cannot be a matter of majority voting or some vague appeal to public opinion. Some criteria are: the awareness that all are guided by the Spirit; the practical as well as intellectual elements involved; the activity of both laity and the magisterium in their search for truth; the need for open dialogue and criticism as well as adequate communication; the need for discernment to take place in a spirit of *koinônia* (v. COMMUNION); an examination of the position of those who are judged wrong to detect any true values that are enshrined in their false positions.[16]

Though the Catholic Church has in recent centuries more and more developed institutional and centralized agencies for the defense of orthodoxy,[17] there are lessons to be learned from other Churches. They show

that reliance can be placed in Scripture, liturgy, credal formulas, dialogues, and assemblies to enable the people to remain in truth.[18] Finally, there is a need of patience, for faith, like every living thing grows but also has moments of apparent decline: hope and courage are especially needed when it may appear that many difficulties block the reception of truth or hinder the attainment of truth so that the Church appears for a while to be without a definitive answer to some urgent problems, or its answers seem to be partial. A danger in such circumstances is to think that only the professionals (magisterium and theologians) will arrive at, or supply, the answer;[19] the Spirit may be leading some other members of the People of God into new visions and depths of understanding that subsequently will enrich the whole Church. For all there has to be a desire to think and feel with the Church *(sentire cum Ecclesia)* in the Ignatian sense of a habitual frame of mind *(sentido)* of loyalty and love (v. IGNATGIUS LOYOLA and LOVE FOR THE CHURCH).[20]

[1]M.-T. Nadeau, "Le développement de l'expression *Fides Ecclesiae,"* MaisD 174 (1988) 136–152.  [2]J. Burkhard, "*Sensus fidei:* Meaning, Role and Future of a Teaching of Vatican II," LouvSt 17 (1992) 18–34; R.F. Costigan, "The Consent of the Church: Differing Classical Views," TS 51 (1990) 25–48; B. Sesboüé, "Le 'sensus fidelium' en morale à la lumière de Vatican II," Le Supplément 181 (1992) 153–166; L.M. Fz. de Troconiz, "Recurso al 'sensus fidei' en la teología católica de 1950 a 1960," ScriptVict 27 (1980) 142–183; 28 (1981) 39–75; idem, "La teología sobre el 'Sensus Fidei' de 1960 a 1970," ibid., 29 (1982) 133–179; 31 (1984) 5–54; 32 (1985) 5–39.  [3]J.M.R. Tillard, "Sensus fidelium," OneChr 11 (1975) 2–29 at 12–15.  [4]B. van Iersel, "Who According to the New Testament Has the Say in the Church," Conc 148 (1981) 11–17.  [5]*On Consulting the Faithful in Matters of Doctrine.* Ed. J. Coulson (London: Collins, 1986) 76; P.G. Crowley, "Catholicity Inculturation and Newman's *sensus fidelium,"* HeythJ 33 (1992) 161–174. See G.O'Collins, "Note a proposito della consultazione dei fedeli," CivCatt 138 (1988) 4:40-45  [6]*Sess. 13—sensus Ecclesiae,* Tanner 2:694/DS 1637/ND 1514; *Sess. 21—iudicium Ecclesiae,* Tanner 2:726/DS 1726.  [7]L. Scheffczyk, "*Sensus fidelium:* La force de la communauté," Communio 13/3 (1988) 84–100 at 88–90.  [8]Tillard (n. 3) 5–7; J.L. Heft, "'Sensus fidelium' and the Marian Dogmas," OneChr 28 (1992) 106–125.  [9]R. Camilleri, *The "Sensus fidei" of the Whole Church and the Magisterium: From the Time of Vatican I to Vatican II.* Diss. (Rome: Gregorian, 1987); R.F. Costigan, "The Consensus of the Church: Differing Classic Views," TS 51 (1990) 25–48; G. Thils, *L'Infallibilité du peuple chrétien "in credendo."* Bibliotheca Eph. Theol. Lov. 21 (Louvain, 1963).  [10]F.A. Sullivan, *Magisterium: Teaching Authority in the Catholic Church* (Dublin: Gill and Macmillan—Mahwah: Paulist, 1983) 21–23.  [11]L. Boff, "Is the Distinction Between *Ecclesia docens* and *Ecclesia discens* Justified?," Conc 148 (1981) 47–51; P. O'Leary, "Authority to Proclaim the Word of God, and the Consent of the Church," FreibZ 29 (1982) 239–251; L. Swidler, *"Demo-kratia,* the Role of the People of God, or the *consensus fidelium,"* JES 19 (1982) 226–243.  [12]K.S. Frank, "Bishops and Laity in the Faith Tradition," TDig 34 (1987) 37–41 = Diakonia (Mainz) 17/3 (1986) 149–156.  [13]Can. 750; cf. E. Corecco, "Aspects of the Reception of Vatican II in the Code of Canon Law," in G. Alberigo et al., eds., *The Reception of Vatican II* (Washington, D.C.: The Catholic University of America Press—Tunbridge Wells UK: Burns & Oates, 1987) 267.  [14]G.

Daly, "Which Magisterium Is Authentic," Conc 148 (1981) 52–55. [15]Z. Alszeghy, "The *Sensus Fidei* and the Development of Dogma," in Latourelle, Vatican II, 1:138-156; Metropolitan Emilianus, "Consensus in the Formulation of Doctrine," GrOrTR 25 (1980) 21–36.   [16]L. Sartori, "Matters Requiring Clarification: What Is the Criterion for the *Sensus fidelium*?," Conc 148 (1981) 56–60; idem, "Il 'sensus fidelium' del popolo di Dio e il concorso dei laici nelle determinazioni dottrinali," StEcum 6 (1988) 33–57; J. Kerkhofs, "Le Peuple de Dieu est-il infallible? L'importance du *sensus fidelium* dans l'Église postconciliaire," FreibZ 35 (1988) 3–19; G. Mucci, "L'infallibilità della Chiesa, Magistero e autorità dottrinale dei fedeli," CivCatt 139 (1988) 1:431-442.   [17]G. Alberigo, "Institutional Defence of Orthodoxy," Conc 192 (1987) 84–93.   [18]See six churches in Conc 148 (1981) 18–46; M. Dudley, "Waiting for the Common Mind: Authority in Anglicanism," OneChr 20 (1984) 62–77; P.J. Hartin, "Sensus fidelium: A Roman Catholic Reflection on Its Significance for Ecumenical Thought," JEcuSt 28 (1991) 74–87.   [19]"The Teaching Authority of Believers," Conc 180 (1985) 3–91.   [20] See Ignatius Loyola, *Spiritual Exercises* nn. 352–370; J. Losada, "Las Reglas para un Recto Sentir en la Iglesia: Alcance eclesiológico," MiscCom 49 (1991) 383–412.

## SIGNS OF THE TIMES

The expression "signs of the times" came into current usage about the time of Vatican II. Though appearing earlier in France, it was used by Pope John XXIII in the apostolic constitution *Humanae salutis* convoking Vatican II: "Making our own the warning of Jesus exhorting us to discern 'the signs of the times' (Matt 16:3), we detect in the midst of so much darkness many indications that make us hopeful about the future of the Church and humanity."[1] The context of the pope's use of the term aptly echoes the somewhat apocalyptic character of the original NT usage in Matthew, where "of the times" is *kairôn,* with the sense of significant moments in the divine plan. As the exegete B.T. Vivano notes: "God gives hints of his will in each age. . . . The saying is an invitation to the hermeneutics of history and as such a permanent challenge to the Church."[2]

In the council itself the phrase occurs several times. The best known is in the opening section of the Constitution on the Church in the Modern World, stating that "the Church has the duty in every age of examining the signs of the times and interpreting them in the light of the gospel" (GS 4). Other texts also use the phrase: recognizing the signs of the times should lead to involvement in ecumenism (UR 4); priests are to join with the laity in reading the signs of the times (PO 9); one of the signs of the times is stated to be solidarity between peoples (AA 14); an equivalent to "signs of the times" is found in the Liturgy Constitution, which states that "the current enthusiasm for the encouragement and promotion of the liturgy is rightly seen as a sign of God's providential designs with regard to our times and as a movement of the Holy Spirit within his Church" (SC 43). These five instances in the council all have the same thrust: God is at work in human history and the Church must respond. This same idea is found also in GS 11: "God's people works to discern the true signs of God's presence and purpose in the events, needs and desires which it shares with the rest of modern humanity." The same constitution notes: "It is for God's people as a whole, with the help of the Holy Spirit, and especially for pastors and theologians, to listen to the various voices of our day, discerning them, and interpreting them, and to evaluate them in the light of the divine word" (GS 44). Indeed the whole of this constitution can be seen as an extended exercise in reading the signs of the times.[3]

In reading the signs of the times we need to be aware of the ambiguity of human history: not every movement, no matter how popular or widespread, is a work of the divine Spirit. Human history is not identical with salvation history.[4] Even within movements that are clearly of God there are to be found frailty, even sin. So the theological task of discernment is needed.[5] Movements and events need to be interpreted by faith, or in the words of Vatican II "in the light of the Gospel" (GS 4). The statement current in the World Council of Churches (v. ECUMENISM, WORLD COUNCIL OF CHURCHES) in the 1960s, "The world writes the agenda for the Church," says at once both too much and too little: it is the gospel rather than the world which is the Church's main guide; the situation of the world cannot be ignored by the Church, but in itself it is not enough, for the Church must bring its own gift of the gospel to an interpretation of human reality.

Though liberation theologies (q.v.) do not use the term "signs of the times" very frequently, they are at their best an example of a scrutiny of the signs in the light of the gospel.

In a limited way we can speak of the signs of the times both as a task for theology and as a *locus theologicus* or theological source (q.v.).[6]

[1]25 Dec. 1961—AAS 54 (1962) 6.   [2]NJBC 659.   [3]Cf. M. Chenu, "Les signes des temps," in K. Rahner et al., *L'Église dans le monde de ce temps* (Paris: Mame, 1967) 97–116.   [4]K. Rahner, "History of the World and Salvation History," ThInvest 5:97-114.   [5]R. Roelandt, "Le discernement des signes de notre temps," VieCons 64 (1992) 170–183.   [6]X. Quinza Lleo, "Los signos de los tiempos come tópico teológico," EstE 65 (1990) 457–468; J. Tapia, "Los teólogos en la Iglesia: 'signos de los tiempos' y 'lugares teológicos' (Una meditación teológico sobre la Historia de la Teología y a propósito del teólogo Melchor Cano)," CiTom 117 (1990) 297–320.

## SIMONY

The name "simony" is derived from the sin of Simon the Magician, of Samaria, who tried to buy from Peter the power of conferring the Spirit; Peter regarded it as a grave sin (Acts 8:9-24). After the age of the persecutions it began to be a problem in the Church. The Council of Chalcedon (q.v.) forbade the conferring of orders for money.[1] It subsequently became widespread even in the early Middle Ages, and several of the medieval Councils passed enactments against it, e.g., Lateran III (q.v.).[2] The problem extended to a whole range of matters: selling of ecclesiastical preferments, exacting payment for spiritual services. It was legislated against again at Trent.[3]

There is a certain delicacy in the whole area. It is clearly wrong to sell spiritual things and gifts, according to the Lord's injunction in the framework of healing: "You received without payment; give without payment" (Matt 10:8). But he also said that "the laborer deserves to be paid" (Luke 10:7). The *Code* has several stipulations: "simoniacal provision of an office is invalid by the law itself" (CIC 149 § 3); there are penalties for simony (CIC 1380) and for trafficking in Mass stipends (CIC 1385; cf. 947). It states clearly: "The minister should ask nothing for the administration of the sacraments beyond the offerings defined by the competent authority, always being careful that the needy are not deprived of the help of the sacraments because of their poverty" (CIC 848; cf. on funerals CIC 1181). This canon seeks to provide for the support of pastors (CIC 222), while making all spiritual benefits free for those who are poor. T.J. Green's conclusion, in the context of sacraments, is helpful: "(Simony) means an explicit or implicit and externally manifest agreement whereby one party agrees to confer a sacrament on another in exchange for some temporal good, e.g., money, property, etc. The heart of this offense is the deliberate intent to equalize the spiritual and the temporal, i.e., to deal commercially in sacred things."[4] Other sacred things are included in the offense of simony. The appearance of simony is to be avoided, even when the sin may be absent.

[1]Can. 2—Tanner 1:87-88.  [2]Can. 7—Tanner 1:214-215.  [3]Sess. 24, Reform can. 14.—Tanner 2:215.  [4]Coriden, CIC 925.

## SISTER CHURCHES

"Sister Churches" is a term used in an important brief, *Anno ineunte,* of Paul VI to Patriarch Athenagoras (25 July 1967).[1] Its basis is common filiation of the baptized, leading to common sisterhood and brotherhood (v. BROTHERS AND SISTERS). The phrase is found in Vatican II, *Ecumenism* (UR 14) referring to the bonds between local Churches of the Orthodox: "The concern and care in preserving fraternal bonds in a communion of faith and love in local churches, as between sisters."

The notion of sister is found in a difficult text of 2 John 13 which is variously interpreted. In tradition the language of "brotherhood" is more common than sister; it was meant in a generic manner to embrace sisterhood too. The use of "sister" by Paul VI has

important ecclesiological implications,[2] especially as the pope evoked the contemplative East by allusion to Mary the sister of Martha, "the one thing necessary" (Luke 10:42), along with a citation of Acts 15:18 (cf. UR 18), "we must indeed be careful not to impose anything that is not necessary." The clear implication, also found in the way in which he refers to himself and the patriarch in the brief, is that there is a new moment in the relation between the two Churches and new opportunities to be seized.

Paul VI also used the term "Sister Church" when referring to the Anglican Church.[3]

[1]E.J. Stormon, ed., *Towards the Healing of Schism: The Sees of Rome and Constantinople 1958–1984* (Mahwah: Paulist, 1987) 161–163/AAS 59 (1967) 852–854.  [2]J. Meyendorff and E. Lanne, two arts.: "Églises-soeurs: Implications ecclésiologiques du Tomos Agapis," Istina 20 (1975) 35–46, 47–74.  [3]AAS 62 (1970) 753.

## SOBORNOST'

*Sobornost'* is a Russian word of great importance in Orthodox ecclesiology. The adjective *sobornaia* was used to translate the word *katholikê* (catholic—q.v.) in the Creed. S. Bulgakov suggests that "to believe in a 'sobornaia' Church is to believe in a Catholic Church in the original sense of the word, in a Church that assembles and unites; it is also to believe in a conciliar Church in the sense Orthodoxy gives to the term, that is, in the Church of the ecumenical councils, as opposed to a purely monarchical ecclesiology."[1] *Sobor,* also derived from the verb *sobirat* (to bring together, to assemble), means both "council" and a "cathedral Church." The abstract noun *sobornost'* would seem to have been first used by the archimandrite Porfirij Uspenskij,[2] though it was soon taken up by A.S. Khomiakov (q.v.). It is impossible to render it in English by one word, though various suggestions have been made: conciliarity (S. Bulgakov[3]) has an over-institutional tone, as does collegiality (R. Murray[4]); G. Dejaifve[5] is attracted by togetherness, though Murray sees a deficiency of real meaning in this archaicism/ neologism. P. O'Leary suggests that the beautiful introduction to the Creed in the liturgy of St. John Chrysostom, quoted twice by Khomiakov, may have been its source for him: "Let us love one another so that with one mind we may be able to confess the Father, Son and Holy Spirit."[6]

The fundamental meaning of *sobornost'* is the abiding link that must exist between truth and mutual love in the Church. N.O. Lossky defines *sobornost'* as "the combination of freedom and unity in many persons on the basis of their common love for the same absolute values."[7] For Khomiakov and some of his followers an emphasis on *sobornost'* meant a lessening of interest in the institutional Church, except at the local level, and little emphasis on the magisterium of the hierarchy. Thus S. Bulgakov: "In 'sobornost' understood as 'catholicity' each member of the Church, equally with the assembly of the members, lives in union with the entire Church, with the Church invisible, which is itself in uninterrupted union with the Church visible and forms its foundation. So the idea of catholicity, in this sense, is turned inwards and not outwards."[8] Other Orthodox theologians in the past few decades have been attempting to integrate the riches of the notion of *sobornost'* with the mainline tradition of Orthodoxy. Russian writers in particular point to *sobornost'* as a special characteristic of Orthodoxy, contrasting it with Latin juridicism and Protestant individualism.

[1]*The Orthodox Church* (Crestwood, N.Y.: St. Vladimir's Seminary, 1988 revised from London, 1935) 61 = J. Pain and N. Zernov, eds., *A Bulgakov Anthology* (London: SPCK, 1976) 127.  [2]G. Cioffari, "La *Sobornost'* nella teologia russa: La visione della chiesa negli scrittori ecclesiastici della prima metà del XIX secolo," Nicol 5 (1977) 287 and n. 50; P. Plank, "Paralipomena zur Ekklesiologie A.S. Chomjakovs," OstKSt 3–29 at 5–7; P.P. O'Leary, *The Triune Church: A Study in the Ecclesiology of A.S. Xomjakov* (Dublin: Dominican—Freiburg, Switz., 1982) 89.  [3]Op. cit. (n. 1) ibid.  [4]"Collegiality, Infallibility and *Sobornost'*," OneChr 1 (1965) 19–42 at 39 following Y. Congar and A. Bloom.  [5]"Sobornost ou papauté?," NRT 74 (1952) 355–371, 466–484 at 359.  [6]Op. cit. (n. 2) 89.  [7]Cited O'Leary (n. 2) 91.  [8]Op. cit. (n. 1) Anthology 128— The Orthodox Church 62.

## SOCIETIES OF APOSTOLIC LIFE

After treating institutes of consecrated life (religious institutes—q.v., and secular institutes—q.v.), the *Code* deals with societies of apostolic life (CIC 731–746). In the earlier *Code* they were almost an anomaly. Prior to it they were often called "secular congregations," and in 1917 they were called "institutes of associated apostolic life." Some of the more common societies of this kind are the Oratorians (1575), the Congregation of the Mission (1625), the Missionaries of Africa (White Fathers, 1868), Maryknoll Foreign Mission Society (1911) and, among women, the Sisters of Charity of St. Vincent de Paul (1633). In the case of women's societies, the reason for the choice of this lifestyle was that often the apostolic work they sought to perform was not seen as compatible with the cloister, which was laid down in law for women religious. The 1917 law saw them as "imitating" religious life, and a key mark was their lack of public vows (c. 673). During the writing of the 1983 law there were several positions: some wanted them included under institutes of consecrated life; others, including their members, did not want them under this rubric. Eventually, and at a rather late stage, they were given a special section in the *Code* (CIC 731–746).

The law gives a broad definition: "Comparable to institutes of consecrated life are societies of apostolic life whose members without religious vows pursue the particular apostolic purpose of the society, and leading a life of brothers and sisters in common according to a particular manner of life strive for the perfection of charity through the observance of the constitutions" (CIC 731 § 1). Here there are some key constitutive features: striving for the perfection of charity, an apostolic purpose, no vows, common life, their own proper law or constitutions. The next paragraph states: "Among these are societies in which the members embrace the evangelical counsels by some bond defined in the constitutions" (CIC 731 § 2). The bond may be private vows, promises, or oaths. But as bonds in a public institution, they are not strictly speaking private, which would mean binding only in the internal forum.

The canons which follow are modeled on those of religious institutes with suitable modifications as appropriate (CIC 732–746).[1] But given the variety of such societies, the *Code* places great emphasis on proper law, that is, their constitutions. Even though members of apostolic societies frequently stress that they are not religious, in the popular mind and in Church directories they are often placed alongside, or intermingled with, religious institutes, a fact that does not foster their particular identity in the Church.[2]

[1]S.H. Holland, in Coriden, CIC 534–539.  [2]J. Beyer, "Quaesita et dubia de societatibus vitae apostolicae solvenda," Periodica 76 (1987) 99–120, 447–495; J. Bonfils, "Les sociétés de vie apostolique," VieCons 55 (1983) 213–226; T.J. Finn, "An Old Entity— A New Name: Societies of Apostolic Life," StCan 21 (1988) 439–456; G. Gambari, "Le società di vita apostolica e la vita consacrata," ComRelM 70 (1990) 227–262; M. Legrain, "Les sociétés de vie apostolique," VieCons 61 (1989) 103–110; F. Mascarenhas, "Societies of Apostolic Life: Their Identity and Their Statistics with Regard to Their Consecration," ComRelM 71 (1990) 3–65; A. Sauvage, "Est-il canoniquement possible que des Sociétés de vie apostolique soient instituts de vie consacrée?," ComRelM 70 (1989) 39–48; M.-A. Trapet, "Les dangers d'une réduction de la vie consacrée à la vie religieuse," AnnéeCan 30 (1987) 83–99.

## SOLOV'EV, Vladimir Sergeevich (1853–1900)

See SOPHIOLOGY

## SOPHIOLOGY

Though he and his followers would claim to be adhering to core insights of the great Eastern tradition,[1] V.S. Solov'ev (1853–1900) can be considered the modern originator of sophiology, an insight which became in many ways a theological system seeking to solve the problems of the relation of God to humanity and to the world. He returned to Orthodoxy from atheism and became deeply influenced by a variety of 17th- to 19th-century philosophical and mystical writers, especially J. Böhme.[2] In his writings he tried also to counter both the growing influence of Marxism and rather vague expressions of the thought of Khomiakov (q.v.). Solov'ev had three visions of a divine woman whom he later called Sophia (Wisdom). Sophia became for him the female principle of the cosmos; it is the primordial image of the Church and of the Virgin, and to an extent incarnated in them. The Church of East and West were invisibly united; but he looked forward to a day when the Church would be led by wisdom into the pan-unity which is found everywhere in creation. He also desired a new Christian era, a theocracy, to be brought about by Christ's three earthly vicars: the tsar, the pope, and prophets.

Sophiology was developed and refined by P. Florenskii (d. 1943)[3] and especially by S. Bulgakov (q.v.),[4] and interest in it continues to grow.[5] H.U. von Balthasar said of Solov'ev that "his skill in the technique of integrating all partial truths in one vision makes him perhaps second only to Thomas Aquinas as the greatest artist of order and organization in the history of thought."[6] Sophiology as a system has been criticized both within and outside Orthodoxy; G.A. Maloney rightly notes, "Any intuitional method always lacks clarity of terms."[7] But it remains a rich vein to be explored and integrated into ecclesiology.

[1]E.g., on Wisdom, T. Špidlík, *La sophiologie de S. Basile* (Rome: Orientale, 1961).  [2]T. Schipflinger, "Die Sophia bei Jakob Böhme," UnaSan 41 (1956) 195–210. See S.L. Frank, ed., *A Solovyov Anthology* (London, 1950). See various articles on Solov'ev in Istina 37 (1992).  [3]Z. Kijas, "La sophiologie de Paul A. Florensky," ETL 67 (1991) 36–56.  [4]A. Nichols, "Bulgakov and Sophiology," Sobornost 13/2 (1991) 17–31.  [5]C. Frank, "The Problem of Church Unity in the Life and Thought of Vladimir Soloviev," SVlad 36 (1992) 189–215; M. Gavriloff, "Soloviev était-il catholique ou orthodoxe," NRT 76 (1954) 155–175; M. d'Herbigny, *Vladimir Soloviev: A Russian Newman* (Eng. trans. London, 1918); E. Munzer, *Solovyev, Prophet of Russian-Western Unity* (London, 1956); A. Walker, "Sophiology," Diak(USA) 16 (1981) 40–54; N. Zernov, *Three Russian Prophets: Khomyakov, Dostoievski and Soloviev* (New York, 1944); R. Zuzek, "Una mística para hoy: la visión sofiánica de la realidad," OrChrPer 46 (1980) 161–177.  [6]"Soloviev" in *The Glory of the Lord. III—Studies in Theological Style: Lay Styles* (San Francisco: Ignatius—Edinburgh: Clark, 1986) 279–352 at 284. See Solov'ev's *La Russie et l'Église universelle* (Paris, 1889); idem, "Signification di dogme de Nicée," Istina 37 (1992) 229–232; idem, "Sur les falsifications du Christianisme," ibid., 233–242.  [7]*A History of Orthodox Theology since 1453* (Belmont MA: Nordland, 1976) 65.

## SPOUSE

Spousal symbolism is very significant in OT and NT.[1] As early as the 8th-century Hosea, we find in the image of a prophet's unhappy marriage a symbol of the relations between God and God's people: the prophet loves his unfaithful wife (Hos 1–3). The theme then becomes commonplace in the OT: God loves his sinful people; the prophets look forward to a time when there will be faithful love in place of idolatry often called "adultery" (see Ezek 16; Isa 54:4-8; 61:10; 62:4-5.)

Bridal imagery abounds in the NT. Christ's presence is that of the bridegroom (Mark 2:19par.). The invitation to the kingdom is described in terms of a wedding banquet (Matt 22:1-13), the time of celebration of which is yet uncertain (Matt 25:1-13). Paul describes his ministry as presenting a bride to one husband (2 Cor 11:2). Marriage is a symbol of how Christ loves the Church: "He gave himself up for her" (Eph 5:22-32). In the book of Revelation the elect are called "virgins," unsoiled by idolatry (14:4); the eschatological triumph of the redeemed is described in spousal terms (Rev 19:7-9; 21:2, 9; 22:17).

In the patristic period the theme is developed with great care.[2] The creation of Eve from the side of Adam is seen as symbol of the birth of the Church, the new Eve from the side of Christ as he slept on the cross.[3] Christ assumed sullied humanity and purified it, making it his bride;[4] the Church as bride is nourished by the Eucharist to become one flesh (v. BODY). These ideas are often found in the context of the Song of Solomon.[5] An additional idea already found in the 4th century and developed in the early Middle Ages is that of the bishop being espoused to his Church.[6]

In the medieval period the idea of the Incarnation being an espousal with humanity is retained;[7] the Church, as well as the individual soul, is the spouse of Christ. Thus St. Bernard: "We are all one spouse, all together are one spouse, and the souls of individuals are as one single spouse."[8] Though found in Reformation authors,[9] the theme of spouse does not receive much emphasis, though Calvin remarks: "It is also no common praise to say that Christ has chosen and set apart the Church as his bride."[10]

The notion of spouse was not to the fore in pre-Vatican II ecclesiology, though Pius XII did use it to warn against the tendency to over-identify Christ and the Church: Paul "though he combines Christ and his mystical Body in a marvelous union, yet contrasts the one and the other, as Bridegroom with Bride."[11]

Vatican II takes up the theme in LG 6 in a text elaborated in the final drafts: "The church . . . is described as the immaculate spouse of the immaculate lamb (see Rev 19:7; 21:2 and 9; 22:17), whom Christ 'loved . . . and for whom he delivered himself up so that he might make her holy' (Eph 5:25-27). He has bound the church to himself by an indissoluble covenant and continuously 'nourishes and cherishes' it (Eph 5:24), wanting it cleansed and joined to himself and subject to him in love and fidelity (see Eph 5:4)." The Doctrinal Commission of Vatican II pointed out that by the image of spouse three things were being asserted: the intimate union between Christ and the Church; the distinction between the Church and Christ; obedience to him.[12]

The *Roman Missal* uses the text of Rev 21:2, and in the Common of the Dedication of a Church refers to Christ sanctifying his spouse. In the spouse tradition of Fathers, medievals, and the liturgy, there is occasional blurring of the symbol of spouse applied to the Virgin Mary and to the Church, for the marriage of Christ and humanity was initiated in the womb of the Virgin.[13]

The rich theme of spouse[14] draws attention to the beauty of the Church, to the need to love (q.v.) the Church, to the Church's feminine face, and to its obligation to respond faithfully to the love of Christ.

---

[1]J. Jeremias, "Numphê, numphios," TWNT 4:1099-1106; E. Stauffer, "Gameô, gamos," TWNT 1:648-657; R.A. Batey, *New Testament Nuptial Imagery* (Leiden: Brill, 1971). [2]O. Casel, "Die Kirche als Braut Christi nach Schrift, Väterlehre und Liturgie," *Die Kirche des lebendigen Gottes. Theologie der Zeit* (Vienna, 1936); C. Chevasse, *The Bride of Christ: An Enquiry into the Nuptial Element in Early Christianity* (London, 1940); J.J. Marcelic, *Ecclesia sponsa apud S. Ambrosium.* Corona Lateranensis 10 (Rome, 1967). [3]Augustine, *Tr. in Ioan.* 9:10—CCL 36:96; R. Desjardins, "Le Christ *Sponsus* et l'Église *Sponsa* chez Augustin," BLitEc 67 (1966) 241–256; S. Tromp, "De nativitate Ecclesiae ex corde Jesu in Cruce," Greg 13 (1932) 489–527. [4]Augustine, *Tr. in Ioan.* 8:4—CCL 36:84. [5]E.g., Origen, *In Cant.* 1:2—SC 375:177; Y. Congar, Moyen-Âge 77–81; see A. Feuillet, "La double insertion du Cantique des Cantiques dans la vie de la communauté chrétienne et dans la tradition religieuse de l'Ancien Testament," Divinitas 35 (1991) 3–18, see also 107–113. [6]Congar, Moyen-Âge 79, n. 93; J. Gaudemet, "Le symbolisme du mariage entre l'évêque et son église et ses conséquences juridiques," Kan 7 (1985) 110–123. [7]E.g., St. Thomas, *In ps.* 44 prin. See A.W. Astell, *The Song of Songs in the Middle Ages* (Ithaca, N.Y.: Cornell UP, 1990). [8]*Serm. 2 in dom. post oct. Epiph.* 2—PL 183:158; Y. Congar, Augustin 125–126 with nn; cf. St. Thomas, *In 4 Sent.* d.27, a.3, a.1c; d.49, q.4, a.3, ad 4; *In Eph.* 5, lect. 8 (317–323); lect. 10 (334–335). [9]R. Mumm, "Die Kirche als Braut und Mutter nach dem evangelischen Bekenntnis," in W. Baier et al., eds., *Weisheit Gottes—Weisheit der Welt.* FS J. Ratzinger. 2 vols. (St. Ottilen, EOS, 1987) 2:1087-1108. [10]*Institutes of the Christian Religion* 4:1, 10—LCC 21:1024; cf. 2:12, 7—LCC 20:473-474. [11]Ency. *Mystici corporis* (1943) 2:2—AAS 35 (1943) 234/Carlen 4:54/DS 3816. [12]ActaSyn 3/1:174/Alberigo-Magistretti 438. [13]E.g., St. Thomas, *In Ioan.* 2, lect 1 (338 and 343). [14]G. Baril, *Feminine Face of the People of God: Biblical Symbols of the Church as Bride and Mother* (Slough UK: St. Paul, 1991).

## STĂNILOAE, Dumitru (1903–1993)

The works of Dumitru Stăniloae, one of the most important Orthodox theologians of this century, are only recently becoming available in the languages of Western Europe,[1] and are attracting the attention of scholars in the West.[2]

He was born in Vladenai, Romania, in 1903. A married priest, he has been a theological teacher in various institutes in his own country for most of his life. At first he accepted the somewhat Latinized and scholastic approach then current in the theological writings of the East. By the late 1930s he turned to the Fathers, and particularly to the hesychast St. Gregory Palamas.[3] Thenceforth he was impassioned with the anthropol-

ogy of the Greek Fathers: men and women divinized by grace is a central theme in all his later works; he presents a theology of divinized creation; spirituality, too, becomes central to all his theology. He sees theology as a service to the Church, not so much in being original but in creatively interpreting the past for the present in a language that is accessible to today's world.[4]

The Trinity revealed by the incarnate Son is central to his theology. He blames the Catholic Church's doctrine of the *Filioque* (q.v.) for its failure to develop a full pneumatology (q.v.), becoming instead an impersonal juridical system.[5] As his work becomes more widely known and critically examined in the West, one can expect that his profound Trinitarian intuitions will make a serious contribution to ecclesiology.

---

[1]*Theology and the Church* (Crestwood, N.Y.: St. Vladimir's Seminary, 1980); an Eng. trans. of his three volume *Orthodox Dogmatic Theology* (1978) is forthcoming. Very full bibliog. R.G. Roberson, *Contemporary Romanian Orthodox Ecclesiology: The Contribution of Dumitru Staniloae and Younger Colleagues.* Diss. exc. (Rome: Orientale, 1988). [2]I. Bria, "The Creative Vision of D. Stăniloae: An Introduction to His Theological Thought," EcuR 33 (1981) 53–59; idem., "Pour situer la théologie du Père Stăniloae," RTPhil 112 (1980) 133–137; idem, "Hommage au père Dumitru Staniloae à l'occasion de don soixante-quinzième anniversaire," Contacts 31 (1979) 64–74; M. Brun, "Dumitru Staniloae," UnaSan 39 (1984) 67–69; D.-I. Ciobotea, "Un dogmatique pour l'homme d'aujourd'hui," Irén 54 (1981) 472–484; D. Neeser, "Le monde, don de Dieu, réponse de l'homme. Aspects de la pensée du Père Dumitru Stăniloae," RTPhil 112 (1980) 139–150. [3]"Bréviaire hésychaste," Irén 52 (1979) 54–68, 356–373. [4]"L'acceuil de la Tradition dans le monde d'aujourd'hui," Irén 47 (1974) 451–466. [5]*Theology and Church* (n. 1) 13, 106.

## SUBDEACONS

The order of subdeacon goes back to the early Church.[1] In the 3rd-century *Apostolic Tradition* (q.v.) it is stated that the subdeacon does not receive the imposition of the hand (q.v.), but he is named to follow the deacon (13/14). This passage of the *Apostolic Tradition* is missing in the Latin manuscript, and it is difficult to determine what period it represents (the Egyptian Church post 500?). Subdeacons feature in a list of orders in a letter of Pope Cornelius to Fabian, bishop of Antioch (251).[2] The subdeacon generally cared for the sacred vessels and was a servant of the deacons in the 4th-century *Apostolic Constitutions* (q.v.), which asserted that the order was of apostolic institution.[3]

Until the 13th century subdeacon was a minor order, but it was regarded as a sacred order by the time of St. Thomas Aquinas, who also noted that it carried a vow of continence.[4] In Trent it was seen as a major order and, along with the minor orders, a step towards the priesthood.[5] The subdeacon's role was largely liturgical, and it included proclaiming the first reading at Mass and caring for the sacred vessels.

Pope Paul VI, in his renewal of orders and ministries (1972), abolished the subdiaconate for the Western Church, and he assigned what were the ministries of subdeacon to the reader (q.v.) and acolyte (q.v.). He did allow that, at the discretion of the conference of bishops, the ministry of acolyte could be called "subdeacon."[6] Subdeacons remain in the Eastern Church, and the order has been restored in recent years in some Anglican dioceses after its abolition in the 16th century.[7]

---

[1]H. Leclercq, "Sous-diacre," DACL 15:1619-1626.   [2]Eusebius, *Hist. eccl.* 6:43, 11—DS 109.   [3]8:21; 8:28, 8; 8:46, 13—SC 336:222, 230–231, 270.   [4]*Supp.* q.37, aa. 2–3; *Summa c. gentiles* 4:75.   [5]Tanner 2:742, 743/DS 1765, 1772/ND 1708, 1715.   [6]*Ministeria quaedam*—AAS 64 (1972) 534–540/ND 1747/DOL 2929; cf. Cong. Divine Worship, Notitiae 9 (1973) 34–38.   [7]OxDCC 1318.

## SUBSIDIARITY

The Extraordinary Synod of Bishops (1985) recommended a study "to determine if the principle of subsidiarity in use in human society can be applied to the Church, and to what degree and in what sense such an application could or should be made."[1] But though current in post-Vatican II writings, the meaning of subsidiarity is by no means clear. It first figured in a papal document with Pius XI in *Quadragesimo anno* (1931): "It is a most serious principle of social philosophy, one fixed and immutable, that one should not withdraw from individuals and commit to the community what the individuals can accomplish by their own enterprise and industry. So, too, it is an injustice and likewise a great social evil and a disturbance of right order to transfer to a larger and higher order functions that can be performed and provided for by lesser and subordinate bodies." This idea is found also in two social encyclicals of John XXIII.[2] The context and meaning here is clearly sociological. The higher order can give help to the lower body. Thus the principle of subsidiarity can be stated: Nothing should be done by a higher body if it can successfully be accomplished by a lower one. Pius XII suggested that the principle enunciated by Pius XI could be applied to the Church, since one of the Church's characteristics is surely that of being a society: "These very enlightening words are valid for social life at all levels and also for the life of the Church, without prejudice to the latter's hierarchical structure."[3] Though some would stress only the pope's warning at the end, others see some endorsement of subsidiarity in his statement.[4]

The term was used in Vatican II not, however, in an ecclesiological context but rather as affirming fundamental human rights.[5] At the 1967 Synod of Bishops one of the principles approved for the re-drafting of the new *Code of Canon Law* was "The Necessary Application of the Principle of Subsidiarity" (Principle V).[6]

As used after Vatican II, subsidiarity often does not mean much more than decentralization, whereas its full meaning includes the activity of the higher body supplying for the inadequacies of the lower.[7] At the 1985 Synod there were those who denied that subsidiarity was a theological principle.[8]

If subsidiarity is to be used about the Church, there are important reservations to be made: it must take account of the fact that the Church universal is made present in the local Church; it must respect the difference between pastoral and doctrinal matters; it must respect the reality of the Church as communion (q.v.); it must give due regard to the hierarchical structure of the Church and its Petrine ministry located in the bishop of Rome.

These reservations being granted, there are calls for subsidiarity in the Church from those opposed to excessive centralization and bureaucracy at various levels in the Church, especially the Vatican and bishops' conferences (q.v.). But the situation is evolving and not yet fully clarified. Thus one can find high Church officials not unhappy with Vatican centralization, but negative towards any bureaucracy at the level of bishops' conferences. Properly understood and judiciously applied, there is a role for the principle of subsidiarity in the Church, more in pastoral than in doctrinal matters, however.[9]

---

[1]*Synode extraordinaire: Célébration de Vatican II* (Paris: Cerf, 1988) Conclusion: 11, C, 8, p. 563.   [2]AAS 23 (1931) 203/Carlen 3:428/DS 3738; see also John XXIII, *Mater et magistra*—AAS 53 (1961) 413; *Pacem in terris*—AAS 55 (1963) 294/Carlen 5:122-123.   [3]AAS 38 (1946) 144–145.   [4]A. Dulles, *The Reshaping of Catholicism: Current Challenges in the Theology of the Church* (San Francisco: Harper & Row, 1988) 201–205.   [5]GE 3, 6; GS 86; cf. O. Karrer, "Le principe de subsidiarité dans l'Église," in Baraúna—Congar, l'Église 2:575-606.   [6]Coriden, CIC 6.   [7]J. Beyer, "Principle de subsidiarité ou 'juste autonomie' dans l'Église," NRT 108 (1986) 801–822.   [8]*Synode* (n. 1) 31; cf. 602–604.   [9]See arts. by F.X. Kaufmann, L. Voyé, J.A. Komonchak and J. Losada in Jurist 48 (1988) 275–354; B. de Margerie, "Le principe de subsidiarité vaut-il dans la société ecclésiale?," DoctCom 41 (1988) 76–78; M. Krebs, *Subsidiarität und kirchliches Leben: Die Subsidiaritätsprinzip in Anwendung auf die Kirche nach Pius XII.* Diss. (Rome: Gregorian, 1991).

## SUBSISTS

In the early drafts of the Constitution on the Church (LG) of Vatican II, the identification of the Catholic Church with the Mystical Body propounded by Pius XII was retained (v. ONE).[1] After the rejection of the first draft at the opening session, there was an important addition in the next one: "Many elements of sanctification can be found outside its total structure."[2]

For the right understanding the meaning of LG 8, it is essential to note the fact that the next draft was not content to leave the identification of Church of Christ and the Catholic Church, even with the recognition of many elements of sanctification outside its bounds. It was precisely to explicate this latter point that the Theological Commission substituted *subsistit* for *est* (is): "Some words are changed: in the place of is there is *subsists,* so that the expression might better agree with the affirmation about ecclesial elements that *are present* elsewhere."[3] This modification would eventually be passed, so that the text reads: "This Church (of Christ) . . . subsists in the catholic Church, governed by the successor of Peter and the bishops in communion with him, although outside its structure many elements of sanctification and of truth are to be found" (LG 8).

It is important to determine the meaning of *subsists* and the ecumenical consequences of choosing this word rather than "is." A first step would be to acknowledge that a change was indeed made, and whatever "subsists" means, it does not mean simply "is." The word *subsistit* in Latin has as primary meanings "to stand still, to stay, to continue, to remain," etc. It has been observed that interpretations in line with the warning against positions of L. Boff by the Congregation for the Doctrine of the Faith (CDF)[4] tend to an identification of "subsists" and "is,"[5] and to deny that the Church of Christ subsists in any way outside the Catholic Church.

It seems clear from its Acts that Vatican II wished to affirm that the mystery of the Church "exists in the concrete catholic society under the successor of Peter and the bishops in communion with him."[6] The council was not so much contradicting the assertions of Pius XII as seeking to open these out.[7] The crucial point is therefore to see if it is possible to assert if the Church of Christ subsists in any way, even imperfectly, outside the Catholic Church. The CDF position seems to be a denial; it will see as subsisting only "many elements of sanctification and truth" (LG 8).

A carefully nuanced modification can be proposed.[8] This does not support the radical views of L. Bermejo, who would seem to deny the Church's infallible magisterium on the basis of the substitution of "is" by "subsists".[9] Nor does it seek a solution in terms of some philosophy of subsistence.[10] It looks rather to the Decree on Ecumenism (UR), which Paul VI suggested is a key for the interpretation of *Lumen gentium.*[11] In UR 2 we have the self-understanding of the Catholic Church and of its unity. Then in UR 4 we find, with the words "we believe" having a technical sense, the following: "Christ bestowed this unity on his Church from the beginning. We believe that it subsists in the Catholic Church as something she can never lose." The word "subsists" appears later, referring to the Anglican Communion: "Among those in which catholic traditions and institutions in part continue to subsist, the Anglican Communion occupies a special place" (UR 13). Even though these gifts are present in other Churches, nonetheless, "it is only through Christ's Catholic Church . . . that the fullness of the means of salvation can be attained" (UR 3). But the council also spoke about other "Churches and ecclesial communities": the orthodox Churches are truly called Churches in the full theological sense of the word; the council did not determine which of the other bodies might be called Churches, except to suggest that the full reality of the Eucharist is necessary for a body to be a Church (UR 22).[12]

But a narrow interpretation of "the many elements of sanctification and of truth" existing outside the Catholic Church is difficult to square with the assertion that the Holy Spirit uses not only them, but the institutions in which they are found (UR 3).[13] Taking up the approach of the council, which avoids speaking of membership (q.v.) or not of the Church but talks rather of full communion and an imperfect communion that is ordered to full unity (LG 13–15), we can assert that the Church of Christ truly subsists in the Catholic Church, without, however, that perfection which belongs to the eschaton; the Church of Christ subsists in other Churches and ecclesial communities less perfectly. The significance of such presence of the Church of Christ will vary depending on the various elements to be found: clearly the Eucharist in the Orthodox and Old Catholic Churches means that the Church of Christ subsists in a significant way in them; holy baptism in various Churches betokens some real, if lesser, presence of the Church of Christ.

One must completely agree with the CDF interpretation insofar as it asserts that the Church of Christ most fully subsists in the Catholic Church alone. It is less clear that one must deny that the Church of Christ subsists in some real, though imperfect way, in other Churches and ecclesial communities.

[1]*Mystici corporis*—AAS 35 (1943) 199/Carlen 4:39-40; *Humani generis*—AAS 42 (1950) 571/Carlen 4:179.  [2]ActSyn 2/1:219-220—Alberigo-Magistretti 38.  [3]ActSyn 3/1:177—Alberigo-Magistretti 440. (Emphasis in original.)  [4]AAS 77 (1985) 758–759; cf. U. Betti, "Chiesa di Cristo e chiesa cattolica," Antonian 61 (1986) 726–745; G. Mucci, "Il 'subsistit' nella 'Lumen gentium,'" CivCatt 138 (1987) 4:444-445; M. McGuckian, "The Catholic Church's Claim," DoctLife 38 (1988) 421–427. [5]S.N. Bosshard, "Die Subsistenzlehre des Vaticanum II und ihre Integration in die Theologie vom Leib Christi," MüTZ 38 (1987) 355–367 at 366, n. 74; F. McMurray, "Subsistit in," NBlackfr 71 (1990) 387–390. [6]ActSyn 3/1:180—Alberigo-Magistretti 436.  [7]See J. Willebrands, "Vatican II's Ecclesiology of Communion," OneChr 23 (1987) 179–191. [8]F.A. Sullivan, "The Significance of the Vatican II Declaration that the Church of Christ 'Subsists In' the Roman Catholic Church," Latourelle, Vatican II 2:272-287 = *The Church*

We Believe In: One Holy, Catholic and Apostolic (Mahwah—New York: Paulist—Dublin: Gill and Macmillan, 1988) 23–33 = development of OneChr 22 (1986) 115–123; P. O'Leary, "The Roman Catholic and Other Churches," DoctLife 58 (1986) 182–187; G. Pattaro, "Ecclesia subsistit in ecclesia catholica," StEcum 4 (1986) 27–58 (in Italian). ⁹L.M. Bermejo, *Towards Christian Reunion: Vatican I—Obstacles and Opportunities*. Jesuit Forum Studies 2 (Anand, India: Gujarat Sahitya Prakash, 1984). ¹⁰See G. Baum, "The Ecclesial Reality of the Other Churches," Conc 4/1 (1965) 38; F. Ricken, "Ecclesia . . . universale salutis sacramentum," Schol 40 (1965) 373. ¹¹Closure of 3rd session of Vatican II—AAS 56 (1964) 1012–1013. ¹²ActSyn 3/7:35; 3/2:335. ¹³ActSyn 3/7:36.

## SUENENS, Cardinal Léon Joseph (1904–1996)

Born in Belgium in 1904, Léon Joseph Suenens was an only child whose father died when he was four, leaving his mother to bring him up in reduced circumstances.[1] As a seminarian he was a protegé of Cardinal Mercier. Having studied in Rome, obtaining doctorates in philosophy and theology and a baccalaureate in canon law, he taught philosophy in the seminary at Malines 1930–1940. In 1940 he was transferred to Louvain, where he was acting rector during World War II. He became auxiliary bishop of Malines in 1945, during which time he developed an interest in the lay apostolate and especially in the Legion of Mary, a lay movement of Irish origin; he was influenced by Veronica O'Brien, who was to become a lifelong friend and inspiration in many of his future activities.[2] This friendship was to lead to his first books on the laity and, later, on the Virgin Mary. In 1961 he became archbishop of Malines-Brussels, and soon cardinal; his episcopal motto was *In Spiritu Sancto* (In the Holy Spirit). In the same year John XXIII, with whom he had particularly cordial relationships, appointed him to the Central Preparatory Commission for Vatican II (q.v.). He played a major role at the council and was appointed by Paul VI as one of the four moderators (1963–1965).

After the council he traveled extensively in the cause of ecumenism and met most of the leaders of the various Churches and many of their theologians. He spoke frequently on the council, especially on collegiality (v. BISHOPS, COLLEGIALITY) and co-responsibility. It was after publishing a book on the latter,[3] and giving an interview on the topic to *Informations catholiques* (15 May 1969),[4] that a temporary coolness developed between the cardinal and Paul VI, who was deeply hurt by the criticisms of the papacy.[5] But there was renewed warmth in their relationship from 1972.

The pope committed the youthful Charismatic Renewal (q.v.) to the care of the cardinal.[6] In the years which followed, Suenens was a guide and confidant of the movement, and he either wrote or was instrumental in having published six "Malines Documents" for its direction,[7] as well as a pastoral and theological study of the movement.[8]

After his retirement in 1980, Cardinal Suenens continued to lecture, write, and preach, especially on the three subjects that have most marked his life's work: ecumenism, the Virgin Mary, and the Charismatic Renewal.

¹Autobiography, *Memories and Hopes* (Dublin: Veritas, 1992). See J. Grootaers, *I protagonisti del Vaticano II* (Milan: San Paolo, 1994) 230–243; L.J. Suenens, "A Plan for the Whole Council," in A. Stacpoole, ed., *Vatican II by Those Who Were There* (London: Chapman, 1986) 88–105. ²L.J. Suenens, *The Hidden Hand of God. The Life of Veronica O'Brien and Our Common Apostolate* (Dublin: Veritas, 1994). ³*Co-Responsibility in the Church* (London, 1968). ⁴Text in J. de Broucker, ed., *The Suenens Dossier: The Case for Collegiality* (Dublin: Gill and Macmillan, 1970) 7–45. ⁵P. Hebblethwaite, *Paul VI: The First Modern Pope* (London: HarperCollinsReligious, 1993) 532–535; Suenens' version, op. cit. (n. 1) 208–221. ⁶Op. cit. (n. 1) 266–272, 284–285, 288–294, 320; Hebblethwaite (n. 4) 608–610, 636. ⁷Op. cit. (n. 1) 276–279. ⁸*A New Pentecost?* (London: Darton, Longman & Todd, 1975).

## SULLIVAN, Francis A. (1922– )

Born in Boston in 1922, Francis A. Sullivan was ordained priest in the Society of Jesus in 1951. After a doctoral thesis on Theodore of Mopsuestia,[1] he was professor of ecclesiology at the Gregorian University, Rome, from 1956 until his retirement in 1992. He is author of a number of important studies in ecclesiology;[2] a feature of all his writing is his exact and rigorous reading of texts, especially of the magisterium. Sullivan made an important contribution to the Charismatic Renewal (q.v.) by positive evaluations at its outset in the prestigious *Gregorianum*[3] and, later, by being one of the leading theologians of the movement.[4] Since 1992 he has taught at Boston College.

¹*The Christology of Theodore of Mopsuestia* (Rome, 1956). ²*Magisterium: Teaching Authority in the Catholic Church* (Dublin: Gill and Macmillan—New York: Paulist, 1983); *The Church We Believe In: One, Holy, Catholic and Apostolic* (Dublin: Gill and Macmillan—New York: Paulist, 1988); *Salvation Outside the Church: Tracing the History of the Catholic Response* (New York: Paulist, 1992). *Creative Fidelity: Weighing and Interpreting Documents of the Magisterium* (New York: Paulist, 1996). ³"The Pentecostal Movement," Greg 53 (1972) 237–266; "Baptism in the Holy Spirit: A Catholic Interpretation of the Pentecostal Experience," Greg 55 (1974) 49–68. ⁴*Charisms and Charismatic Renewal: A Biblical and Theological Study* (Ann Arbor: Servant, 1982); "Pentecôtisme," DSpir 12:1035-1052 = *Pentecostalism and the Charismatic Renewal* (Dublin: Veritas, 1986, without notes).

## SYMBOLS

See CREEDS, IMAGES, and MODELS

## SYNOD OF BISHOPS

In ecclesiastical language the word "synod" (Greek *sun-odos* "together-road/way," hence "coming together/ meeting") refers to meetings at various levels to discuss matters concerning the Church. The notion is an ancient one, and it can refer to meetings ranging from diocesan level (v. SYNODS AND COUNCILS) to ecumenical councils (q.v.), which are synods of the universal Church.

During Vatican II (q.v.) there was heated debate on the relationship between the pope and the college of bishops (v. BISHOPS, COLLEGIALITY). At the opening of the 2nd session Paul VI called on the bishops to help him in his office.[1] In that session there were various ideas circulating about how the impetus and experience of the council might be carried forward after its close. There were drafts about a permanent body that might be set up. But before it could be debated, Paul VI issued a mp. *Apostolica sollicitudo* setting up the synod of bishops.[2] The move was variously interpreted at the time: some saw it as preempting the council; others saw it both as providing what the majority wanted and as allaying the fears of the minority. The pope wanted to avoid a bruising encounter on the matter on the council floor. The bishops adopted the idea of the synod into their decree on bishops (CD 5).[3]

The question arises as to whether the synod is an expression of collegiality or a support for the primatial role of the pope. The statement in the *motu proprio* that its members act on behalf of the whole Catholic episcopate supports the former view,[4] though from the evolution of the institution one could also argue in favor of the latter position. The subsequent *Code of Canon Law,* while not directly supporting either side, leans subtly to the latter position.[5] Vatican II can be quoted to support either view (CD 5).

As in other instances, the *Code* does not give a legal definition, which would remove the ambiguity. Rather, in a descriptive statement it leaves the question rather open: "The synod of bishops is that group of bishops who have been chosen from different regions of the world and who meet at stated times to foster a closer unity between the Roman Pontiff and the bishops, to assist the Roman Pontiff with their counsel in safeguarding and increasing faith and morals and in preserving and strengthening ecclesiastical discipline, and to consider questions concerning the Church's activity in the world" (CIC 342). Paul VI had also the idea of gathering information and insights about the inner life of the Church, a notion unfortunately not retained in the law. But in general the *Code* made no substantial changes to Paul VI's document, except for a few modifications in the light of the experience of the first synods (CIC 342–348).[6] The pope has full control over the convocation and agenda of the synod; he may give it deliberative power.

The fact that the Secretariat of the synod (CIC 348) is not part of the Vatican Curia (q.v.) can be interpreted in several ways. It gives the synod independence from those dicasteries of whose area the synod might treat. In practice it could lead to a heightened expression of either of the two controverted views about the nature of the synod: an adjunct of the primacy, or an expression of episcopal collegiality.

Some of the discussion about this point is evidence of people thinking in terms of power rather than of communion (v. AUTHORITY); the attempt to give more standing to the synod may be a desire to have a counterweight to papal power. Neither collegiality nor communion is well served when the synod is seen as pitting episcopal power against the pope's, or is perceived as being manipulative or manipulated.

The procedure of the synod of bishops slowly evolved, with the *Ordo synodi epicoporum celebrandae* of constitutions/statutes governing the synod and its proceedings coming out in three versions (1967, 1969, 1971).[7]

After the first synods, a procedure was established which, with variants, has been followed in most of the subsequent ones. From suggestions made by the Secretariat, the pope decides on the topic. An outline of the theme *(lineamenta)* is first sent to the bishops to be discussed by their conferences with a view to their forwarding suggestions. Other experts or bodies are also consulted. When the results of the consultation have been collated, a working document *(instrumentum laboris)* is prepared by the Secretariat for the synod. Between the bishops elected by their episcopal conferences, those nominated by the pope, and invited experts, synods have generally had upwards of 200 participants. The opening days of the synod are devoted to addresses to the whole body by various members and possibly other experts invited by the Secretariat. The bishops then work in small groups and produce findings. A final statement has sometimes been issued, but the substantial work of the more recent synods usually appears as an apostolic exhortation issued by the pope about a year later. Some of the apostolic exhortations have been very significant and influential documents; others less so.

There is some confusion about the nomenclature of the synods—ordinary/extraordinary/special. The bibliography on the synods is huge. Before and after each synod most theological and pastoral journals have carried articles about it, and a balanced judgment about a synod or the whole synodal process would have to be sought in multilingual sources, as each country and culture views synods somewhat differently. A factual account of the synods has been written by G. Caprile.[8]

The following is an enumeration of the synods up to 1994 with their main topics: The 1st ordinary synod (1967) dealt with matters arising from Vatican II, including work on the revised canon law and on the liturgy. It issued a statement on atheism and proposed the setting up of the International Theological Commission.[9]

The 1st extraordinary synod (1969) was devoted to "Doctrinal Principles and Practical Suggestions for Closer Collaboration Between Episcopal Conferences and the Holy See." It issued a concluding statement.[10]

The 2nd ordinary synod (1971) produced two documents: on priestly ministry and on justice in the world.[11]

The 3rd ordinary synod (1974) rejected by vote a final document. The materials were then handed over to the pope; this became henceforth the usual procedure. The result was one of the finest postconciliar documents (indeed of the papal magisterium in this century), *Evangelization in the Modern World.*[12]

The 4th ordinary synod (1977) dealt with catechetics. Though prepared under Paul VI, the apostolic exhortation *Catechesis in Our Time* would be published by John Paul II.[13]

The 5th ordinary synod (1980) had as its theme the family. There were three results from this synod: the exhortation *The Christian Family in the Modern World;*[14] the establishment of both the Pontifical Council for the Family, which had earlier been a commission set up in 1973 by Paul VI (v. VATICAN CURIA) and the International Institute of Studies on Matrimony and the Family.

The 6th ordinary synod (1983) treated of reconciliation. Its work emerged in the exhortation *Reconciliation and Penance in the Mission of the Church Today.*[15]

The 2nd extraordinary synod (1985) was called to verify the reception (q.v.) of Vatican II. It studied the four constitutions (SC, LG, DV, GS). It called for three things: a universal catechism (q.v.), a strengthening of the theological status of bishops' conferences (q.v.), and the publication as soon as possible of the code of canon law for the Eastern Churches.[16]

The 7th ordinary synod (1987) dealt with the laity and led to the exhortation *The Vocation and the Mission of the Lay Faithful in the Church and in the World,*[17] which announced that a commission had been set up to examine all questions of lay ministries (n. 23).

The 8th ordinary synod (1990) dealt with the formation of priests. Its work was presented in the exhortation *The Formation of Priests in the Circumstances of the Present Day.*[18]

The 9th ordinary synod (1994) had as its topic religious in the Church. It gave rise to a post-synodal exhortation "On Consecrated Life and Its Mission in the Church and in the World" (*Vita Consecrata*—1996).

In addition there have been other synodal meetings. There was a special synod for the Netherlands (Jan. 1980), attended by the seven Dutch bishops, two priests, and six cardinals of the curia. The conclusions were given to Cardinal Willebrands as Metropolitan of the Netherlands. A special synod for Africa and Madagascar was convoked by John Paul II in 1990 and celebrated in April 1994; various preparatory meetings had been held throughout Africa. A post-synodal document was presented to the African Church by Pope John Paul II on his visit there in 1995. In 1991 there was a special assembly for Europe of the Synod of Bishops. There was an opening and closing address by the pope,[19] and a final declaration was made.[20] Much attention was devoted to the newly emerging situations in Eastern Europe.[21]

There continues to be much literature on the synods. In the mind of Paul VI it is to be a permanent institution of the Church, though meeting only when summoned. It is clearly a structure in the Church which is evolving, not so much in theory as in practice, as its current Secretary General clearly acknowledges.[22]

[1]AAS 55 (1963) 849–850.  [2]AAS 57 (1965) 775–780.  [3]R. Trisco, "The Synod of Bishops and the Second Vatican Council," AmER 161 (1967) 145–160.  [4]A. Antón, "Episcoporum synodus: partes agens totius catholici episcopatus," Periodica 57 (1968) 495–527.  [5]A. Calvo Espiga, "El ejercicio de la colegialidad en el gobierno de la Iglesia universal," Lumen 32 (1983) 300–320; D. Foley, *The Synod of Bishops: Its Canonical Structure and Procedures* (Washington, D.C.: The Catholic University of America, 1973); see V. Ferrara, "Il sinodo dei Vescovi tra ipotesi e realtà: Natura teologico-giuridica del Sinodo," Apoll 42 (1969) 491–556.  [6]J.H. Provost, in Coriden CIC 281–286.  [7]AAS 59 (1967) 91–103; 61 (1969) 525–539; 63 (1971) 702–704.  [8]*Il sinodo dei vescovi.* 8 vols. (Rome: Civiltà Cattolica, 1968–1990).  [9]DocCath 64 (1967) 1969–1998, 2055–2078/Flannery 2:662-671.  [10]DocCath 66 (1969) 957–972, 1009–1036.  [11]AAS 63 (1971) 898–942—Flannery 2:672-710.  [12]*Evangelii nuntiandi*—AAS 68 (1976) 1–96/Flannery 2:711-761.  [13]*Catechesi tradendae*—AAS 71 (1979) 1277–1340/Flannery 2:762-814.  [14]*Familiaris consortio*—AAS 74 (1982) 81–191.  [15]*Reconciliatio et paenitentia*—AAS 77 (1985) 185–275.  [16]Texts in *Synode extraordinaire: Célébration de Vatican II* (Paris: Cerf, 1986).  [17]*Christifideles laici*—AAS 81 (1989) 393–521.  [18]*Pastores dabo vobis*—AAS 84 (1992) 657–804.  [19]*In tutte le nazioni*—AAS 83 (1991) 70–80 and *Respice finem*—CathIntern 3 (1992) 209–211.  [20]*Ut testes simus*—CathIntern 3 (1992) 211–222.  [21]CathIntern 3 (1992) 152–187, 207–209.  [22]J.P. Schotte, "The Synod of Bishops: A Permanent Yet Adaptable Church Institution," StCan 26 (1992) 289–306. Cf. G. Alberigo, "I sinodi dei vescovi del 1969 e del 1974: Funzionamento insoddisfacente e risultati significativi," CrNSt 2 (1981) 271–294; J.I. Arrieta, "Lo sviluppo instituzionale del sinodo dei vescodi," IusEccl 4 (1992) 189–213; J.G. Johnson, "The Synod of Bishops: An Exploration of Its Nature and Function," StCan 20 (1986) 275–318; R. Laurentin, "Synod and Curia," Conc 127 (1979) 91–103; T.P. Rausch, "The Synod of Bishops: Improving the Synod Process," Jurist 49 (1989) 248–257.

## SYNODS AND COUNCILS, LOCAL

Synods and councils have been part of the Church's history from the beginning. These reflect the situation of the early centuries, when priests and laity collaborated with the bishop in the life of the diocese.[1] The general concept is that of synodality (Greek *synodos*—*syn* = together; *hodos* = way—a meeting or council), a neologism becoming more widespread in French.[2] A synod is a meeting of Church leaders, more familiar to us now in the institution of the Synod of Bishops (q.v.)

and bishops' conferences (q.v.), which last have strong synodal features. Councils (q.v.) may be at a local level or may involve the Church as a whole, in which case they are called ecumenical councils (v. COUNCILS). Councils and synodal bodies have exterior features laid down in law and a crucial spiritual and juridical feature which is communion (q.v.).

Diocesan synods and pastoral councils are carefully distinguished in the *Code of Canon Law*. The *Code of Canons of the Eastern Churches* has its own bodies: Synod of Bishops of Patriarchal Churches (CCEO 102–133); Patriarchal Assembly (CCEO 140–145); Eparchial Assembly (CCEO 235–242); Presbyteral Council (CCEO 264–271); Pastoral Council (CCEO 272–275).[3]

In the West, diocesan synods go back to the 4th century. They were very frequent in the Middle Ages. Lateran IV (1215—q.v.) required them to meet once a year; it also recalled ancient canonical enactments that required yearly meetings of provincial councils within the metropolitan area.[4]

The 1917 *Code* retained the notion of the diocesan synod and laid down that it should meet every ten years, but this was not generally observed (1917 CIC 356–362); it envisaged purely clerical participation. Though Vatican II did not mention the diocesan synod, compared with previous law, the new *Code* creatively widened its membership and scope (CIC 460–468).[5] It described it thus: "A diocesan synod is a group of selected priests and other Christian faithful of a particular Church which offers assistance to the diocesan bishop for the good of the entire diocesan community." (CIC 460). It must, then, include laity. It is to be called "when circumstances warrant it in the judgment of the diocesan bishop, after he has consulted the presbyteral council" (CIC 461). The law lays down the membership: those who must be members, those who can be invited (CIC 463). The spirit of the law is that it should be widely representative of the diocese, and it may include observers from other Churches (CIC 436 § 3). A main purpose of a synod is to pass decrees. While the bishop is the sole legislator in the diocese, and the decrees must have his approval (CIC 466), he should not lightly go against the advice of the synod (see CIC 127 § 2).[6]

A second local body with considerable potential is the pastoral council in a diocese.[7] Unlike the synod, which meets only when summoned, the pastoral council is a quasi-permanent body. Vatican II strongly recommended one in each diocese (CD 27; cf. CIC 511, which is weaker). In its brief reference, it made clear that the pastoral council is to serve the needs of the entire particular Church; to be a group not separate from, but with, the bishop who presides over it; to be a cross-section of the diocese—clerical, lay, religious; to be an advisory group prepared to make concrete proposals. Within a year of the council's end, Paul VI laid down norms for the implementation of this conciliar recommendation.[8] The *Code* carried forward these norms in four canons (CIC 511–514). The existence of a pastoral council, while highly recommended by the council, is not fully obligatory in the *Code*, though it is to be established "to the extent that pastoral circumstances recommend it" (CIC 511). Since it is to deal with the internal matters of the diocese, only those in full communion with the Church may be members. Like the synod, it is consultative.

It will be seen that both synod and pastoral council depend on the willingness of the bishop to have them. It would seem that there has not been full reception (q.v.) of these canons and Vatican II recommendations in relation to them by all the hierarchy.

Distinct from these, but similar in many ways, is the presbyteral council, usually called "council of priests." Its roots are the Vatican II notion of the single presbyterium of bishop and priests (LG 28), the council's emphasis on a bishop seeking consultation and advice (CD 27), and the direct call to have a group or senate of priests representing the presbyterium (PO 7). Again Paul VI acted quickly to give juridical implementation to this desire of the council. Through *Ecclesiae sanctae* it became mandatory to establish a council of priests in each diocese.[9]

The *Code* treats of the council of priests in seven canons (CIC 495–501): it is obligatory; it must have its own statutes approved by the bishop; its membership is confined to priests (*constituatur . . . sacerdotum*—CIC 495 § 1); about one half of its members are to be elected, and it is to be representative of the priests of the diocese; it is a consultative body which the bishop should listen to on more important matters; it has the role of giving consent to actions of the bishop only in matters so determined in law.[10] The priests' council is both a senate of the bishop, giving its advice and recommendations, and a representative of the priests of the diocese.

A fourth expression of synodality is the chapter of canons (CIC 503–509) which may be erected in a diocese. The legislation allows for freedom in the local Church to establish a chapter of canons according to its needs; the chapter by collegial act is to draw up statutes which must be approved by the bishop.

A final diocesan body is the college of consultors. This body is to consist of at least six and not more than twelve members of the priests' council, chosen by the bishop. This small body can take over the nonliturgical duties of the cathedral chapter; the conference of bishops can, however, determine that this latter group function as the college of consultors (CIC 502). There are some important matters committed to the college of consultors by law (CIC 421 § 1; 272; 413 § 2; 419; 422; 494; 1277; 1292 § 1).[11]

All of these synodal or conciliar bodies are consultative, but that does not make them unimportant.[12] Where they are genuinely accepted, they make for a style of government that is truly collegial and participative in the local Church, even though the bishop retains full authority (q.v.) in the diocese (CIC 391).[13]

These assemblies will operate beneficially only in an atmosphere of communion, of trust, and love on all sides. Given the recent past history of the Church, the bishop initially has to allow consultative bodies to express freely their frustrations, fears, and hopes before constructive work can begin in these bodies which have so much potential for the renewal of the diocese.

---

[1]M. Dortel-Claudot, "L'évêque et la synodalité dans le nouveau Code de droit canonique," NRT 106 (1984) 641–657. [2]C. Vogel, "Communion et Église locale: Primatalité et synodalité durant la périod antéenicéenne," AnnéeCan 25 (1981) 169. [3] W. Aymans, "Synodalen Strukturen im Codex Canonum Ecclesiarum Orientalium," ArcKK 160 (1992) 367–389; E. Eid, "La synodalité dans la tradition orientale," EphIurC 48 (1992) 9–27. [4]Constit. 6—Tanner 1:236-237. [5]J.A. Alesandro, in Coriden CIC 378–382; F.B. Donnelly, *The Diocesan Synod: An Historical Conspectus and Commentary.* Canon Law Studies 74 (Washington, D.C., 1932); idem, "The New Diocesan Synod," Jurist 34 (1974) 396–402; L.J. Jennings, "A Renewed Understanding of the Diocesan Synod," StCan 21 (1987) 319–353; D.M. Ross, "The Diocesan Synod: A Comparative Analysis of the 1917 and 1983 Codes of Canon Law," MonEccl 114 (1989) 560–571. [6]J. Provost, "The Working Together of Consultative Bodies—Great Expectations," Jurist 40 (1980) 257–281. [7]J.A. Alesandro, in Coriden, CIC 410–412. [8]Mp. *Ecclesiae sanctae* (1966) 1: 16-17—AAS 58 (1966) 766–767/Flannery 1:601-602. [9]Ibid., 1:15, 17—AAS 58 (1966) 766–767/Flannery 1:600-602. [10]J. Alesandro, in Coriden, CIC 400–407; see J.W. Purcell, "The Institute of the Senate of Priests," Jurist 38 (1978) 132–152. [11]Alesandro, ibid., 406–407. [12]Provost (n. 6). [13]R. Kennedy, "Shared Responsibility in Ecclesial Decision-making," StCan 14 (1980) 5–24.

# T

## TEACHERS

Teachers and teaching are complex ideas in the NT.[1] The name teacher *(didaskalos)* was frequently given to Jesus in the Synoptics, and in his ministry he is often said to teach *(didaskein).* His teaching is the fulfillment of the law and the prophets (Matt 5:17-20; Luke 16:16). In Matthew the term "rabbi" is given to Jesus by those hostile to him. Luke warns his readers against being corrupted by the Pharisees or rigorist teachers (cf. Luke 12:1-3). Despite the apparent prohibition of the name "rabbi" by Jesus (Matt 23:8), we find in other writings of the NT a group called teachers, listed after apostles and prophets (1 Cor 12:28; cf. Acts 13:1; Eph 4:11). Though it is clear that those who were called teachers were bearers of a charism (q.v.), they also seemed to hold an office or at least to be recognized as a group in the primitive Church (cf. Jas 3:1). It was not, however, always a singular function: the author of 1 Timothy calls himself (or Paul) both apostle and teacher (1:1; 2:7). In the Pastoral Letters the object of teaching is the good news *(parathêkê*—deposit cf. 2 Tim 1:10-14); its source is the apostolic tradition (cf. 2 Tim 1:13; 2:2; 3:10)—Timothy is to devote himself to reading, exhortation, and teaching (1 Tim 4:13; cf. 2 Tim 3:16); the words of the Lord and Scripture are to be preserved (1 Tim 6:3; 2 Tim 2:9; Titus 2:5). The teaching of the Pastoral Letters is at once kerygma, catechesis, and exhortation—in short, it is to lead to the perfection of the Christian faith in its double dimension of doctrine and ethics.[2]

In the *Didachê* (q.v.) an important role of the prophet is to teach (11), even though alongside the prophets there are teachers (13:2; 15:1-2). Therefore the position of H. Küng who, on the basis of NT and other early texts, denies that bishops can be genuine teachers since this would be to monopolize the charisms,[3] cannot be sustained.[4] Nor need we assert

that the "Antiochene trilogy" of apostles, prophets, and teachers (cf. Acts 13:1 with 14:4, 14) represents separate specialized ministries.[5]

For some centuries in various Churches there was an office of teacher, but the role and position is not fully clear in the texts we have.[6] For Ignatius (q.v.) Christ is the great teacher,[7] and his letters show a concern about false teachers,[8] a problem even in NT times (cf. Gal 1:6-8; 1 John 2:21-25). In the *Apostolic Tradition* (q.v.) the teacher *(doctor),* whether cleric *(ekklêsiastikos)* or layman *(laikos),* prays and then lays hands on the catechumens (19). If there is a morning instruction *(katêchêsis),* it should not be missed if a teacher comes (41/35:3): this text implies both that people other than teachers gave instruction, and also the importance of the teacher's ministry. Justin (q.v.) was certainly a teacher as was Origen (q.v.), both heading schools of theology or catechetics. Justin was active before the Church was clearly stratified into clergy and laity. Origen somewhat later became a priest after many years as a lay theologian. Experts are not in agreement as to whether Tertullian was ever a priest.[9] Teachers still figured in the 4th-century *Apostolic Constitutions* (q.v.): they were subordinate to the bishop;[10] women could not be teachers;[11] thanksgiving was to be made for the gift of the teachers of catechumens.[12] Since teachers were also apostles,[13] bishops,[14] and presbyters,[15] it could be that the office of teacher was no longer a separate ministry in some Churches by that time.[16] With the decline of prophecy, teachers became more prominent but eventually they became institutionalized in the clerical state.

In the Middle Ages the notion of magisterium (q.v.) or authoritative teaching of bishops and the pope developed. But it was still recognized that there were many in the Church who teach, e.g., St. Thomas Aquinas in the context of baptism noted bishops, priests, sponsors, lower ministers as giving instruction, or indeed any of the faithful could be an instrument leading a person to conversion.[17] He recognized two teaching chairs, pastoral and academic: the *cathedra pastoralis/pontificalis* of bishops; the *cathedra magisterialis* of the masters of theology (v. THEOLOGIANS).[18]

At Vatican II, teaching is a primary office of bishops (LG 23–25; CD 14) and of priests (PO 4). The laity, in virtue of their sharing in the prophetic office of Christ, have an obligation to teach by witness, verbal profession of faith along with a lived faith, and evangelization (LG 34; cf. AA 6; GS 11). The whole Church, moreover, has a responsibility in teaching: all Christians have a right to a Christian education (GE 3); the responsibility devolves primarily on the family, but it concerns the whole Church (GE 3, 6); the Catholic school is of great importance (GE 5, 8–9); special help is to be given to those attending non-Catholic schools (GE 7); the Church also gives particular attention to higher level education (GE 10), especially faculties of the sacred sciences (GE 11).

This teaching of Vatican II is given specific embodiment in Book Three of *the Code of Canon Law*.[19] After an introduction (CIC 747–755) it has five titles or sections: the ministry of the divine word, which mostly concerns bishops and priests (CIC 756–780); catechetical instruction (CIC 773–780); the missionary action of the Church (CIC 781–792; cf. AG 23 for persons); Catholic education at all levels (CIC 793–821); instruments of social communication, and specifically books (CIC 822–832); profession of faith (CIC 833). The thrust of Vatican II and of the norms of the *Code* are well summed up in canon 761: "The various available means are to be employed to proclaim Christian doctrine, especially preaching and catechetical formation, which always indeed hold a principal place. Other means are to be employed, however, are the exposition of doctrine in schools, academies, conferences, and meetings of all kinds, and its spreading by means of public declarations by legitimate authority made on the occasion of certain events, by the press, and the other instruments of social communication." In other words, all possible means are to be employed in the furtherance of Catholic teaching. Teaching in Eastern law is found under Title XV, "The Ecclesiastical Magisterium," which covers all forms of teaching in the Church.[20]

For other aspects of the question see MAGISTERIUM, THEOLOGIANS, RECEPTION and SENSE OF THE FAITH and related articles. In the end, while teaching is of great importance, it is in the service of believing faith that is salvific.[21]

[1]A. Barucq and P. Grelot, "Teach," DBT 591–593; K.H. Rengstorf, "Didaskô, etc.," TWNT 2:135-165.    [2]J. Schlosser, "La didascalie et ses agents dans les epîtres pastorales," RevSR 59 (1985) 81–94 at 93.    [3]*Infallible? An Enquiry* ch. 4:11 (London: Collins Fontana, 1972) 181–197.    [4]F.A. Sullivan, *Magisterium: Teaching Authority in the Catholic Church* (Dublin: Gill and Macmillan—New York: Paulist, 1983) 35–49.    [5]A. de Halleux, *"Les ministères dans la Didachè,"* Irén 53 (1980) 5–29 at 17–22.    [6]J.K. Coyle, "The Exercise of Teaching in the Postapostolic Church," EglT 15 (1984) 23–34.    [7]E.g., *Ad Magnes.* 9–10; *Ad Eph.* 15.    [8]E.g., *Ad Eph.* 8–9; *Ad Trall.* 6–9.    [9]A. Faivre, "Théologiens laïcs et laïcs théologiens. Positions des problèmes à l'époque paléochrétienne," Irén 60 (1987) 193–217; 350–377 at 199–210.    [10]2:3, 1—SC 320:166.    [11]3:6, 1–2—SC 329:132.    [12]8:6, 11—SC 336:154-156.    [13]8:33, 8—SC 336:242.    [14]2:20, 1; 2:26, 4; 3:19, 7; 8:5, 3; 8:12, 3; 8:47, 80—SC 320:196, 238; 329:164; 336:146, 178, 304.    [15]2:26, 7—SC 320:240.    [16]So M. Metzger SC 329:58.    [17]ST 3a, q.71, a.4 ad 3.    [18]*Quodl.* 3, q.4, a.1 (9); cf. *In 4 Sent.* d.19, q.2, a.2, qa, 2 ad 4.    [19]J.A. Coriden, "The Teaching Office of the Church," in Coriden, CIC 543–589; L.J. Crowley, "The Teaching Power and Mission of the Church," StCan 9 (1975); G. Damizia, "La funzione di insegnare nella Chiesa," Apoll 56 (1983) 601–631; L. Vela, "La función docente de la Iglesia (El libro III del Nuevo Código)," EstE 58 (1983) 217–226.    [20]CCEO 595–666.    [21]Conc 180 (1985).

## TEMPLE

The Trinitarian dimension of the Church is found in its three most important designations in Vatican II: People of God, Body of Christ, and Temple of the Holy Spirit (AG 7; PO 1; LG 17). The third of these, temple, was not so developed as the others at the council and needs to be situated in terms of its OT and NT background.[1] From the time of the OT patriarchs, there were holy shrines to mark places of theophanies or divine communications. The idea of a temple in Jerusalem was firstly David's, but it was his son Solomon who was to build the first temple (ca. 970—ca. 930 B.C.E.; cf. 2 Sam 7:1-12). A post-exilic temple was built after 520 B.C.E. The most sumptuous was Herod's begun in 20 B.C.E., and destroyed in 70 C.E. at the fall of Jerusalem.

Concerning the first temple of Solomon the question already arose: How could the transcendent God be said to be present in a temple? The believer prays in the temple, and God hears the person in heaven (1 Kgs 8:30-40). But there is something more: the "name" of God will be there (1 Kgs 8:29; cf. Jer 7:12). Since "the 'name' represents the personality of its bearer, the 'name of Yahweh' means that God is present in a special sense."[2] God's glory dwells in the temple as over the Ark of old (2 Chr 5:14; cf. Ezek 10:18; 11:23 with 43:4). The temple is also a place where God communicates with a chosen person, e.g., Isaiah (6:1; 66:6). The prophets had a finely nuanced attitude to the temple: they loved it (Isa 2:1-2), prayed in it, but they put justice and interior religion before any merely external worship (Amos 5:12-24; Isa 1:11-13; 66:1-2), and inveighed against any magical reliance on the temple as a talisman that would protect the sinful city of Jerusalem from destruction (Jer 7:4-15).

Jesus showed Jewish temple piety: he went there for feasts and taught there (Luke 2:46; John 7:10, 14);

he cleansed it from profanation (Matt 21:12-13par.; Mark 11:16) and at the same time announced that the barriers erected there between Jew and pagan would cease (Mark 11:17; cf. Eph 2:14-18); he healed at the temple (Matt 21:14); he demanded that offering sacrifice there be done with purity of heart (Matt 5:23-24) and condemned mere formalism (Matt 23:16-22).

In the NT there are two Greek words for temple. There is a tendency, which is not fully consistent, to use *hieron* for the whole temple and its precincts, and to reserve *naos* for the sanctuary or inner part of the temple.[3] Thus when Jesus cleansed the temple the word *hieron* is used (Matt 21:12-13par). But when he spoke cryptically of the destruction of the temple of his body, it is *naos* we find (John 2:19; Matt 26:61par). The prohibition of swearing by the temple because God dwells in it (Matt 23:16, 21) again employs *naos*.

In the Incarnate Word we find summed up the essential features of the OT temple: he is the supreme place of divine communication (cf. John 14:7, 10-11); in him God dwells with his glory (John 1:14); his is the supreme worship of the Father (John 17:4). Further, the Synoptic tradition presents him as being overshadowed by the Holy Spirit (Matt 3:16par. cf. Luke 4:1, 14, 18), thus suggesting perhaps the *shekinah* (cf. Exod 40:35) of God's presence in him—"anointed by the Holy Spirit . . . God was with him" (cf. Acts 10:38 with 7:47; 17:24-25; Col 2:9). At the death of Jesus the veil of the temple *(naos)* was torn from top to bottom (Matt 27:51par), symbolizing a transcending of the ancient worship and a new access to God through the blood of Christ (Heb 9:8-12).

Not only is Christ a temple or sanctuary *(naos)* but so, too, is the Christian community. After Pentecost there is some ambiguity about the temple:[4] the disciples pray there (Acts 2:46; 3:1-11); Stephen in some way glimpses the insufficiency of the temple and the Torah (Acts 6:13-14); Paul continues to show piety towards the temple (Acts 21:26). But the theme of temple takes on a new richness, for now it is the Christian community which is a temple of the Spirit (*naos*—1 Cor 3:16-17; Eph 2:20-22; cf. 2 Cor 6:16). Indeed the individual Christian is also a temple *(naos)* of the Spirit (1 Cor 6:19). The community is, further, a building, which has Christ for its cornerstone (cf. 1 Pet 2:4-5; cf. Acts 4:11; Matt 21:42), it is God's house (Heb 3:3-6).

In the Book of Revelation there seem to be two temples, one heavenly and one below: in heaven the temple is one of eternal praise and glory (Rev 7:15; cf. 5:6-14; 11:19); there is possibly a reference to the temple on earth, the Church, with persecutors in its outer portals (Rev 11:1; cf. 3:12); most profoundly, however, the temple is the Lamb (Rev 21:22).

In the patristic tradition the scriptural notion of the Church as temple is taken up, e.g., Ambrose (q.v.)

"For just as we are a temple of God, so we are a tabernacle of God, in which the feasts of the Lord are celebrated."[5] The Virgin Mary is also a temple, because she carried the Word in her womb,[6] a theme taken up by Vatican II (LG 53). She is the supreme realization of the Church (SC 103), which itself is a temple.

The texts of Vatican II speak of the Spirit dwelling in the Church and in the Christian as in a temple (LG 4, 17, 41; AG 7; PO 1; cf. LG 6, 51), but precedence is given to his dwelling in the Church. The Church is a temple in which God communicates with humanity by his word of revelation. It is, further, the place where God is present, dwelling through the Holy Spirit. It is, finally, the place wherein the Body of the Lord God is most fully worshiped, again through the Holy Spirit. The theology of temple looks to Jesus, to the Church, and to the individual for its fullest exposition.[7] The image of temple complements the other two Trinitarian images of the Church, People and Body, and adds to them the notions of divine communication, pneumatological presence, and authentic worship, for the Holy Spirit has been sent "continually to sanctify the Church" (LG 4).[8]

[1]Cf. J.J. Castelot and A. Cody, NJBC 1259–1266.    [2]W. Kornfeld, "Temple," in Bauer 3:899-903 at 901; cf. F. Amiot, "Temple," DBT 594–597.    [3]Y. Congar, *The Mystery of the Temple* (London: Burns & Oates, 1962—French, 1958); O. Michel, "Naos," TDNT 4:880-890; G. Schrenk, "Hieron," TDNT 3:232-247.    [4]F.D. Weinert, "The Meaning of the Temple in Luke-Acts," BibTB 11 (1981) 85–89.    [5]*De interpell. Job et David* 4:2/7:28—CSEL 32/2: 288-289/FC 65:412.    [6]Ambrose, *De Spiritu sancto* 6:80—PL 16:795; Sedulius, *A solis ortus cardine*—PL 19:764; Isidore, *De ortu et obitu patrum*—67:111—PL 83:148; Andrew of Crete, *Canones et trioda*—PG 97:1313; John Damascene, *In nativitatem* BVM 10—PG 96:677; Ps-Epiphanius, *De laudibus s. Mariae deiparae*—PG 43:488.    [7]J.P. Kenny, "Temple and Temples of the Holy Spirit," HeythJ 2 (1961) 318–332; V. Scaturchio, *Tempio e corporeità: Il significato del corpo del cristiano come tempio dello Spirito Santo in S. Paolo.* Diss. (Rome: Gregorian, 1988).    [8]P. Mullins, *The Teaching of Lumen gentium on the Holy Spirit: The Holy Spirit Was Sent at Pentecost in Order that He Might Continually Sanctify the Church.* Diss. (Rome: Gregorian, 1990), full text Ann Arbor: UMI, 1991, thesis n. 3266.

## TERTULLIAN (ca. 155–ca. 220)

Despite his vast output,[1] and the intensive scholarly work written about him,[2] much of Tertullian's life and doctrines still remain somewhat enigmatic and disputed. He was born about 155 C.E. of pagan parents. He would seem, on his own admission, to have spent a dissipated youth; he married and was converted to Christianity sometime before 197 C.E. Jerome (q.v.) asserts that he was a priest, a fact that cannot otherwise be clearly verified. He was skilled in rhetoric and law; he showed considerable acquaintance with philosophical systems. Much of his writing is apologetic, often written with bitter polemic. From about 207 C.E. he began to show an influence from Montanism (q.v.), a group which he later joined (ca. 212). After his writing on modesty (*De pudicitia*—217–222) he disappeared from sight and there are conflicting or uncorroborated accounts of his later life and death.

He has been called the Father of Latin Theology, which is an excessive tribute. He did not give a balanced or unified account of theology. However, he helped to forge a Latin language for theology and raised many issues crucial for his time and for later theology. He seems to have been the first to use the word *"trinitas,"* and he opened up questions of Trinitarian theology; he also distinguished two substances in the one person of Christ, thereby giving an initial statement of a problem which would be resolved only at Chalcedon (q.v.). He was the author of the first extended theological treatment of baptism.[3]

In his pre-Montanist period he was a caustic opponent of heresy and was much concerned with matters of morals. His Montanist period showed him to be extremely rigorist in ascetical practices,[4] in his rejection of remarriage,[5] in his denial, found in De *pudicitia*,[6] of any forgiveness of very grave sins (idolatry, fornication or murder). In this work he also denies the right of the Church to forgive sins, holding that only (Montanist) "spiritual men"—apostles and prophets—can do so.

His contribution to ecclesiology is significant.[7] Though it must not be exaggerated, there is a contrast between the more objective and ecclesial views of the early Tertullian and the more subjective and spiritual position of the later Montanist.[8] He was probably the first to call the Church "mother" (q.v.), a term he retained even in his Montanist period.[9] It is also the Body (q.v.), developed in terms which reflect Rom 12 and 1 Cor 12; here as elsewhere Tertullian seemed happier with legal and juridical bonds than with Christian love.[10] He saw the Church as being born from the side of Christ on the Cross.[11] He wrote with great beauty and passion on martyrdom (q.v.),[12] though in his Montanist period he denied the probity of fleeing from martyrdom, notwithstanding texts like Matt 10:23 used in a contrary sense in much Christian tradition.[13] But it is in his major work, *De praescriptione haereticorum*,[14] that some of his most significant ecclesiological teaching is found. A *praescriptio* (*prae—scribere*, "to write in advance") was a juridical submission of defense which destroyed a legal suit. Tertullian advanced two such pleas: Christ sent the apostles, and no others should be accepted as preachers; the apostles founded the Churches in which true doctrine is preached. These two statements alone are enough to demolish all heresy.[15] He went on to assert that "We hold communion with the apostolic Churches because our doctrine is in no way different from theirs. This is our witness of truth."[16] The heretics have no right to the Scriptures which belong to the apostolic Churches and in which alone the authentic meaning of the Scriptures is to be found.[17]

Though perhaps in the end Tertullian does not emerge as an attractive figure, his life and works bring us into the deep concerns of the early Church and show the response of one stalwart Christian to the main problems of the time. His embracing of Montanism, more than any intellectual conversion, was perhaps due to his passionate personality which always avoided the least compromise with human frailty, even if his unyielding spirit led him out of the Church which earlier he had so stoutly defended.

[1]Texts PL 1–2; PLS 1, 29–30; CSEL 20, 20, 47, 69–70, 76; CCL 1–2; with many texts SC and trans. ANL 7, 11, 15, 18; ANF 3–4. [2]Bibliog. Patrology 2:246-340; P. Siniscalco, "Tertullian," Encyc EarCh 2:818-820; R.D. Sider, "Approaches to Tertullian: A Study of Recent Scholarship," SecC 2 (1982) 228–260; K. Baus, in Jedin-Dolan 248–252, with 202–203 bibliog. 488–489. [3]De *baptismo*—PL 1:1198-1224/ANL 11:231-256/ANF:3:669-679/SC 35. [4]*De ieiunio adv. Psychicos* (viz., Catholics)—CSEL 20:274-297/ANL 18:123-153/ANF 4:102-114. [5]*De monogamia*—PL 2:929-954/ANL 18:21-55/ANF 4:59-72. [6]CSEL 20:219-273/ANL 18:56-122/ANF 4:74-101. [7]S. Folgado Flóres, "Puntos de eclesiología en Tertuliano," CiuD 192 (1979) 3–33, 127–163; Patrology 2:320-332 with bibliog. [8]K. Adams, *Der Kirchenbegriff Tertullians: Eine dogmengeschichtliche Studie* (Paderborn, 1907). [9]J.C. Plumpe, *Mater Ecclesia: An Inquiry into the Concept of the Church as Mother in Early Christianity* (Washington, D.C., 1943) 45–62. [10]R. Uglione, "'Corpus sumus.' (Tert. Apol. 39)," in S. Felici ed., *Ecclesiologia e catechesi Patristica "Sentirsi Chiesa."* Biblioteca di scienze religiose 46 (Rome: LAS, 1982) 101–111. [11]*De anima* 43—PL 2:723/FC 10:277; see H. Rahner, "Flumina de ventre Christi," Bib 22 (1941) 269–302, 367–403. [12]*Ad martyras*—PL 619–628/ANL 11:1-7/ANF 3:693-696. [13]*De fuga in persecutione* —PL 2:101-120/ANL 11:356-378/ANF 4:116-125. [14]PL 2:10-74/CSEL 70:1-58/SC 46/ANF 3:243-265/ANL 15:1-54/LCC 5:25-64. [15]*De praesc. haer.* 21—PL 2:33/Patrology 1:269-273; C. Munier, "La tradition apostolique chez Tertullian," AnnéeCan 23 (1979) 175–192. [16]*De praescr. haer.* 21—PL 2:33. [17]Ibid., 20–21, 32/PL 2:32-33, 45/ANF 3: 252, 258.

## THEOLOGIANS

A general article on theologians in the Church[1] must take for granted the deep pluralism (q.v.) in theological method that characterizes the post-Vatican II period in all of the Churches. It must also allow for the fact that there is no universally accepted definition of either theology or the theologian. For the purposes of this article, the theologian will be taken as one who seeks to explain and interpret revelation as it is received and lived in the Church. The theologian has a conservative role of explaining the belief of the Church and a creative role of showing and developing the implications of this belief for the Church and society. This double role was largely a shared one in the OT. It was the priest who interpreted the law; the prophet drew attention to the concrete challenge of the divine will in the present or future (Jer 18:18). Both were to have knowledge, an experiential grasp of the divine realities about which they spoke (Jer 14:18; cf. Hos 4:6; Mal 2:7).[2]

In the NT there were several groups of people associated with teaching and the interpretation of the divine mind. The sacred authors were more than theologians, for their reflection formed part of God's revelation to God's People. In addition apostles (q.v.), prophets (q.v.), and teachers (q.v.) were all engaged in a ministry of the Word and of teaching. In the immediate post-NT time, these offices and charisms continued, but with a growing emphasis on the bishop as teacher and upholder of orthodoxy.

In the 2nd century we find people who were not bishops having a role in teaching and reflecting on the mysteries. Examples are St. Justin (q.v.), a layman, and Origen (q.v.), who as a layman had a catechetical school before his ordination to ministerial priesthood. In the patristic period those who taught the faith and reflected on its implications were, however, mostly bishops, though St. Athanasius (d. 373) was present at the Council of Nicaea (q.v.) as a deacon, and St. Ephrem, the only Syrian Doctor (q.v.) of the Church, was a deacon who ran a cathedral school of theology. Another Doctor of the Church, St. Jerome, was a priest.

In the early Middle Ages those who did the work of theologizing were still mainly bishops, but to the 11th century there was an ever-increasing contribution from the monasteries. Theology was also taught in cathedral schools. In the late 12th century the schools at Paris and soon afterwards at Bologna and elsewhere began to be communities of learning, each being a *universitas* of students and a *collegium* of teachers. By 1222 Paris had four faculties: liberal arts, medicine, theology, and the *Decretum* (canon law).

By the mid-12th century the institution of the great universities had taken a form that they would have for centuries. A student of theology would first study the liberal arts and philosophy. Then, after a number of years, he would become a *baccalarius biblicus,* who "ran lightly" (hence *cursor biblicus*) over the text of a scriptural book. In time he progressed to be a *sententiarius,* expounding the *Sentences* of Peter Lombard (d. 1160), the standard manual of theology right up to the Reformation. This position was also one of apprenticeship to a Master. One became a Master by a process of "inception," which was a public examination by other masters stretching over two days. The Master was above all an exegete, *Magister in sacra pagina.* Only a Master could "determine" an issue or the meaning of a passage of Scripture; he gave a definitive answer, a *determinatio,* which in medieval authors like St. Thomas is often introduced by the words *respondeo dicendum* ("I reply that it must be said"). Each university had several magisterial chairs of the-

ology: the secular clergy held several and mendicant orders one or two each. There was rivalry between them, often due to envy of the secular masters.[3]

St. Thomas distinguished a double teaching office (v. MAGISTERIUM), pastoral and academic: that of the *cathedrae pastoralis/pontificalis* of bishops and that of the *cathedrae magisterialis* of the masters of theology. The former, based on charity, is the power to teach and govern; the latter, based on knowledge, gives an opportunity to teach others.[4] It does not seem helpful to use this kind of language today, as it might be seen as setting up a parallel or alternative magisterium (q.v.). The universities also undertook teaching of a more public kind. Like the university of Paris, which in 1497 ranged itself in favor of the Immaculate Conception, they affirmed doctrines; at times universities condemned errors, e.g., the Oxford University condemnations of Wycliffe (q.v.) and Huss (q.v.).

Relations between bishops and theologians have often been uneasy, from the Middle Ages to the present day. There were times of important collaboration, such as the Council of Trent (q.v.), in which the preliminary work was done by theologians and then submitted to the judgment of the council fathers. After Trent and the establishment of seminaries (v. PRIESTHOOD, MINISTERIAL), in addition to lecturing in universities, theologians were teachers of theology for those preparing for ordination. In the whole period from the Middle Ages to Vatican II, almost all theologians were priests or bishops.

Vatican II (q.v.) was a time of fruitful collaboration between theologians and bishops. For the preparatory work of the council, the original theological experts *(periti)* were largely rather conservative and in the Roman mold. Pressure from council members ensured that many of the best theologians in the Church would have a role in the work of the council, either as *periti* and thus usually members of one or more commissions, or as the personal theologians of bishops. The large number of theologians then present in Rome ensured a true pluralism in the debates of the council and notably contributed to the richness of the final texts.

If we take our working description of the theologian as one who explains and interprets divine revelation, it can be argued that every believing Christian is a theologian, operating out of the sense of the faith (LG 12—q.v.). But in the more narrow sense we have two important descriptions of the theologian. In the West it is a person qualified with higher degrees (licentiate/master and frequently doctorate) and who is professionally engaged in theology in a significant way, generally by teaching or writing.

In the East the emphasis is quite other; the key notion is that of one who shares a personal experience of the divine mysteries. The theologian is characterized not so much by learning as by contemplation, especially of the Trinity. Thus their three paradigmatic theologians are: John the Theologian (Evangelist), Gregory Nazianzus (d. 389), and Simeon the New Theologian (d. 1022).[5] Gregory Nazianzus gives as examples of great theologians Moses, Elijah, and Paul. He notes that to become a theologian one must observe the commandments, seek purity of heart, avoid merely human reasoning and techniques, and contemplate heavenly things.[6] P. Evdokimov points out that theology is a work done in the Spirit, and quotes St. Macarius' saying that the theologian is *theodidaktos* ("taught by God") and St. Simeon, who states that it is the Spirit who makes a learned person into a theologian.[7]

In the post-Vatican II period dissent (q.v.) has become an important issue. There would seem to be two problems. Church authorities do not like to see erroneous, nowadays frequently critical, views publicized. This first problem, given modern communications media, is irreversible. Another gravamen of Church authorities is objectionable teaching in theological faculties, schools, and seminaries. Especially at the undergraduate level, Church authorities have a right to insist on orthodox teaching. To ensure this there are several juridical procedures: teachers may have to make a public profession of faith (*professio fidei*—v. CREEDS); some types of books may require ecclesiastical permission (*imprimatur*—v. CENSORSHIP); there can be a warning *(monitum),* usually from the Congregation for the Doctrine of the Faith, about a work. The most important measure is the "licensing" of seminary teachers and members of ecclesiastical faculties: "It is necessary that those who teach theological disciplines in any institute of higher studies have a mandate from the competent ecclesiastical authority" (CIC 812). The institute here would not seem to be a seminary, which has its own legislation: the appropriate bishop(s) appoint and can remove seminary teachers from office (CIC 253). Those who teach in ecclesiastical faculties would still seem bound to have a canonical mission, which was used in documents from the Holy See from the 19th century until as late as 1979,[8] though it has been argued that the legislation on the mandate replaces this need.[9] It should be noted that since the law is restrictive, "theological disciplines" must be strictly, i.e., narrowly, interpreted (see CIC 18): it would seem that it covers systematic or dogmatic theology as well as historical, moral, and sacramental theology, Church history, liturgy, Scripture, and canon law, but not other disciplines.[10]

Canonists have noted several problems: the particular situation in the United States makes these provisions difficult to implement; they are very open to abuse, to stifling academic research, and to problems arising from civil law; they do not sufficiently provide

for due recourse.[11] As in the case of all law, one cannot legislate or provide for wise, just, or prudent application. But the point at issue is crucial: Church authorities have the right to try to ensure that its official teaching is faithfully transmitted.[12] In the case of faculties which through civil law are largely impervious to Church control, or more often when teachers have tenure recognized in civil law, the Roman Congregation may declare that a person is no longer considered to be a Catholic theologian.

The International Theological Commission (q.v.) issued a document in 1975, "Theses on the Relationship Between the Ecclesiastical Magisterium and Theology."[13] Though ignored and superseded in part by later documents from the Holy See, many of its insights maintain their validity. It is arguably richer than the document to which we now turn.

Though probably occasioned by problems of dissent, the Instruction of the Congregation for the Doctrine of the Faith, "On the Ecclesial Vocation of the Theologian,"[14] has many positive features. It develops the qualities required of theology teachers at greater length than does the *Code* (CIC 810; 252; 253–254) and fills a void in Vatican II teaching, which mentioned theologians only in passing (LG 67; GS 44; PO 19; DV 23; UR 11; cf. OT 14, 16; UR 10). It stresses that theology is a common quest for truth (nn. 1, 21); theology is assisted by the Spirit (nn. 5, 6, 17). The theologians are at the heart of the People (n. 6), making an important contribution: "In times of great spiritual and cultural change, theology is all the more important. Yet it is exposed to risks since it must strive to 'abide' in the truth (see John 8:31), while at the same time taking into account the new problems which confront the human spirit. In our century, in particular, during the periods of preparation for and implementation of the Second Vatican Council, theology contributed much to a deeper 'understanding of the realities and the words handed on' (DV 8). But it also experienced and continues to experience moments of crisis and tension" (n. 1). The Instruction notes the multifaceted work of theology: seeking an understanding of the faith (n. 6); communication of faith and hope both within the Church and in its missionary vocation (n. 7); interpretation of revelation (n. 10); using hermeneutical rules to give a correct interpretation to the texts of the magisterium (n. 34). The work of the theologian is also diverse: plumbing the Word of God in Scripture and Tradition (n. 6); uncovering the faith (n. 7); being attentive "to the epistemological requirements of the discipline (of theology), to the demands of rigorous critical standards, and thus to a rational verification of each stage of research" (n. 9); working in an interdisciplinary way (n. 10); engaged in disinterested and patient service within the People of God (n. 11); enjoying a real but circumscribed freedom of research (n. 12); being prepared, in some circumstances, to raise questions about magisterial interventions (n. 24); being animated by love of the Church (n. 31) and interpreting the texts of its magisterium (n. 34). In an important statement it deals with the relation between theology and the magisterium—an issue which underlies the whole Instruction: "To be sure, theology and the magisterium are of diverse natures and missions and cannot be confused. Nonetheless they fulfill two vital roles in the Church which must interpenetrate and enrich each other for the service of the People of God" (n. 40).

It is the task of theology to articulate this relationship better. But some key distinctions seem necessary. The magisterium teaches authoritatively, in a way that demands a religious submission of mind and will (LG 25; v. MAGISTERIUM); unless the theologian is presenting revelation, his or her statements do not impose any obligation of acceptance but are to be judged in the light of arguments adduced. The magisterium is mainly concerned with maintaining the Tradition—a conservative role in the proper sense of the word; it is the theologian's task to be creative. The theologian pursues research and reflects on revelation in terms of contemporary problems, exercising a critical role within the Church; the ultimate judgment of validity on such work belongs to the magisterium—"ultimate" because there is also judgment by theological peers, and more generally in the Church through the sense of faith (q.v.). Theologians operate at best through charism as well as learning,[15] and can be, but are not always, prophetic; the magisterium is usually institutional (v. CHARISM).

Reaction to the Instruction has been mixed.[16] While it is generally welcomed in its positive assertions, there has been criticism of the narrowness of its treatment of dissent (q.v.). In particular, it seems to stress the interpretative and conservative role of the theologian without giving sufficient attention to the creative role of theology. Moreover, it could have given some more positive guidance to those who are involved in magisterial teaching.[17] The document, moreover, seems to convey the impression that, where there are problems, it is most probably the theologian who is at fault. A healthy tension between the magisterium and theologians is probably the optimum situation; if tension is missing, then theologians and/or the magisterium are probably failing in their role.[18]

[1]A. Cirillo, "La teologia e il teologo in recenti scritti," AnnalT 4 (1990) 309–332; 5 (1991) 351–386; C. Dumont, "Qui est théologien?," NRT 113 (1991) 185–204.  [2]J.J. Castelot and A. Cody, NJBC 1254–1256; B. Vawter, NJBC 192–197.  [3]H. Wolter, in Jedin-Dolan 4:95-97, 246–260; A. Piltz, The World of Medieval Learning (Oxford: Blackwell, 1981); J.A. Weisheipl, Friar Thomas d'Aquino: His Life, Thought, and Works. (Washington, D.C.: The

Catholic University of America Press, [2]1983) 53–139.  [4]Quodl. 3, q.4, a.1 (9); cf. In 4 Sent. d.19, q.2, a.2, qa 2 ad 4.  [5]T. Špidlík, The Spirituality of the Christian East. Cistercian Studies 79 (Kalamazoo, Mich.: Cistercian Publications, 1986) ch. 13—327–349; idem, La spiritualité de l'Orient chrétien. 2—La prière. OrChrAn 230 (Rome: Orientale, 1988) 206–208; bibliog. 406.  [6]Orat. 20:12; 26:5; 27:2; 28:2—PG 35:1086, 1233; 36:13, 28.  [7]P.G. Gianazza, Paul Evdokimov cantore dello Spirito Santo. Bibliotecha di scienze religiose 52 (Rome: LAS, 1983) 32.  [8]Sapientia christiana—AAS 71 (1979) 469; cf. F. Marchisano, "La legislazione accademica ecclesiastica: Dalla Constituzione Apostolica Deus scientiarum Dominus ad Costituzione Apostolica Sapientia christiana," Seminarium 32 (1980) 332–352; H. Schmitz, "Mandat et Nihil obstat des Theologieprofessors," TPQ 139 (1991) 265–283.  [9]J.A. Coriden, in Coriden CIC 576.  [10]Ibid., citing CIC 252. See L. Örsy, "The Mandate to Teach Theological Disciplines: Glosses on Canon 812 of the New Code," TS 44 (1983) 476–488.  [11]See J.A. Coriden, in Coriden CIC 575–576; cf. 571–572; also CIC 220–221 with J.H. Provost, CIC 152–156 and Instruction of CDF "On the Ecclesial Vocation of the Theologian" (Vatican City—Slough UK: St Paul, 1990—Origins 20 (1990) 117–120) n. 37, . . ."these procedures can be improved."  [12]A. Dulles, The Craft of Theology: From Symbol to System (Dublin: Gill and Macmillan, 1992) 116.  [13]International Theological Commission, Texts and Documents 1969–1985 (San Francisco: Ignatius, 1989) 129–144 = "The Ecclesiastical Magisterium and Theology," in C.E. Curran and R.A. McCormick, The Magisterium and Morality: Readings in Moral Theology 3 (New York—Ramsey: Paulist, 1982) 151–170; Commentary in F.A. Sullivan, Magisterium: Teaching Authority in the Catholic Church (Dublin: Gill and Macmillan, 1983) 174–218 and T.R. Potvin, "Guidelines for a Working Relationship Between the Pastoral Magisterium and the Theologians in the Church," StCan 15 (1981) 13–43.  [14](N. 11). See R. Tremblay, "'Donum veritatis.' Un document qui donne à penser," NRT 114 (1992) 391–411.  [15]Cf. B. Gherardini, "Teologia: Fedeltà ad un carisma," Divinitas 35 (1991) 55–63.  [16]Dulles (n. 12) 107–116; J.A. Komonchak, "The Magisterium and Theologians," ChicSt 29 (1990) 307–329; M. Lefebvre, "Quelle est la mission du théologien?," EglT 22 (1991) 177–190.  [17]Dulles (n. 12) 116–118; F.A. Sullivan, "The Theologian's Ecclesial Vocation and the 1990 CDF Instruction," TS 52 (1991) 51–68.  [18]S. Cipriani, "Magistero e teologia: un difficile ma ineludibile rapporto," Asp 37 (1990) 41–58; Y. Congar, "Le théologien dans l'Église aujourd'hui," QuatreF 12 (1980) 7–28; ibid., "Reflections on Being a Theologian," NBlackfr 62 (1981) 405–409; J.A. DiNoia, "Authority, Public Dissent and the Nature of Theological Thinking," Thom 52 (1988) 185–207; J. Hoffmann, "Theology and the Magisterium: A 'Model' Deriving from Vatican I," CleR 68 (1983) 3–18; W. Kern, ed., Die Theologie und das Lehramt. QDisput 91 (Freiburg-Basle-Vienna: Herder, 1982); P. Schoonenberg, "The Theologian's Calling, Freedom, and Constraint," JEcuSt 19 (1982) 92–118; F.A. Sullivan, "The Magisterium and Theology," CTSAP 43 (1988) 65–75; J.E. Thiel, "The Theologian in the Eyes of the Magisterium," HeythJ 32 (1991) 383–387.

## THEOLOGICAL CENSURES

See THEOLOGICAL NOTES

## THEOLOGICAL NOTES

Closely associated with theological sources (q.v.) and with the magisterium (q.v.) is the notion of theological notes or theological qualifications. These are an evaluation of the status of a particular statement in relation to revelation, the magisterium, and theological teaching. Their negative expressions are called theological censures, which are a judgment of the level of error contained in a statement or work. The approach of the pre-Vatican II manuals was to lay great emphasis on qualifications and censures. Theologians varied somewhat in the detailed description of notes and censures. We take the two together as they have been understood in standard works up to the council.[1]

In the writings of St. Thomas Aquinas there are various negative judgments, such as *stultum/stultissime, ridiculum, inconveniens,* which are not terms of abuse ("stupid," etc.), but scientific judgments about the absence of the wisdom that should characterize theology.[2] We find theological censures used somewhat later by John XXII (1316–1334) against the Fraticelli,[3] by the Council of Constance (q.v.),[4] and frequently thereafter.[5]

The censure of heresy (q.v.) is appropriate when a statement contradicts something formally revealed and defined (*De fide definita*—"of defined faith") or something formally revealed and taught as infallible by the universal magisterium (*De fide divina et catholica*—"of divine and Catholic faith"). The censure of erroneous applies to statements that contradict a truth that is authoritatively taught by the magisterium (*Doctrina catholica*—"Catholic doctrine") or taught universally by theologians as connected with revelation or logically deduced from revelation (*theologice certum*—"theologically certain"). Other censures are "close to heresy," "open to an heretical interpretation" *(sapiens haeresim),* "temerarious," viz., contradicting a commonly held theological opinion without sufficient grounds, "scandalous," viz., which could lead people astray as in the condemnations of moral laxity by the Holy Office (1679),[6] "offensive to pious ears," "dangerous," etc. The note of "pious opinion" *(pia opinio)* is understood in the Pauline sense of what builds up or edifies.

Though after the council notes and censures largely dropped out of theological textbooks and writings, they retain a value, and the International Theological Commission (q.v.) has recently advocated their renewal.[7]

[1]S. Cartechini, *De valore notarum theologicarum et de criteriis ad eas dignoscendas* (Rome: Gregorian UP, 1951); E.J. Fortman, "Notes, Theological," NCE 10:523-524; idem, "Censure, Theological," NCE 3:394; H. Quilliet, "Censures," DTC 2:2101-2113; Salaverri, 1:800-810. [2]E.g., ST 1a, q.3, a.8; q.103, a.5; cf. *In 1 Cor* 1, lect. 3 (43–47); Y. Congar, *La foi et la théologie.* Le mystère chrétien (Tournai, 1962) 168. [3]DS 916. [4]Tanner 1:432/DS 1235. [5]E.g., DS 2332 (against Jansen); DS 2502 (against Quesnel). [6]DS 1151–2166. [7]"The Interpretation of Dogma" (1989)—DocCath 87 (1990) 489–502 at 493–494. See further F.A. Sullivan, *Creative Fidelity: Weighing and Interpreting Documents of the Magisterium* (New York: Paulist, 1996) passim.

## THEOLOGICAL SOURCES

At various times different descriptions are given of the sources for doctrinal affirmation and theological reflection *(loci theologici).* The classical treatment of the issue is the posthumously published *De locis theologicis* of Melchior Cano (1509–1560).[1] In Book One he takes up the scholastic position that all argumentation and refutation of error is by means of authorities or by reason.[2] In the following ten books he gives seven authorities to which the theologian can appeal on the basis of faith, then three sources founded on reason: firstly, the authority of Scripture, apostolic tradition, the Church, councils (q.v.), the Roman Church (v. PAPACY), the saints, viz., the Fathers (q.v.), scholastic doctors; secondly, reason, philosophers, and human history. In each case he gives the limits and proper use of each source.[3] He concludes with a long book on the use of the sources in scholastic disputation.[4]

Cano's work has been extremely influential, especially in controversial and manual theology. It still gives essential sources for theology. Today, however, it needs to be complemented by others which have not always been clearly seen as significant sources of theology.[5] In dealing with these other *loci* it is important to get beyond the manual attraction for proof texts to prove assertions or to support affirmations of the magisterium. Theological sources are mediations or ways in which God teaches and builds up the Church.

The Fathers of the Church (q.v.) are a source for theology; if it could in a specific case be established, their unanimous consent in doctrinal matter or exegesis would be a certain argument. Similarly, the Doctors of the Church (q.v.) are a source of teaching. In the case of both of these there is not only the value of their witness to the faith and their theological speculation but their comprehension as saints of the sacred mysteries of which they have a vital awareness through prayer, often through mystical experience, and through faith, hope, and love lived to an intense degree. Some theologians today, largely following the lead of H.U. von Balthasar (q.v.),[6] see in the lives and writings of the saints (q.v.) what the Fathers saw to be a living commentary on the gospel,[7] and thus a source for theology.[8] In general, religious experience,[9] not excluding popular religiosity (q.v.), is a theological source. Indeed the Church is becoming more aware of the relevance of spirituality for the rest of theology. The separation of systematic theology from spirituality after the time of St. Thomas has in fact been a serious impoverishment for both.[10]

A primary source of theology is the liturgy (q.v.). But it is not to be used as an arsenal of proof texts. Rather, in liturgy we see and hear the faith of the Church proclaimed; liturgy, especially the sacraments, is an affirmation of faith *(protestatio fidei)*.[11] In the signs of the liturgy "faith is nourished, strengthened and expressed."[12] The Church "completes the formation of the faithful during the various seasons of the liturgical year."[13] Liturgy is then a privileged source for theological reflection; it is also a branch of theology in its own right.[14] For the International Theological Commission there must be a return to the liturgy as "the living and unifying theological source of the faith."[15]

Another frequently used source for theology, but not often articulated as such, is "signs of the times" (q.v.). But the ambiguity of human history means that discernment is needed, for not every human movement or event in history is a work of the Holy Spirit.[16] Indeed, the whole teaching of Vatican II, and not only its Constitution on the Church in the Modern World, can in a sense be seen as theologizing in the light of these signs of the times. Without necessarily opting for a horizontal view, one can see at the very least that the situation of the world poses questions for theology, especially ecclesiology. Indeed, liberation theology (q.v.) usually proceeds from an analysis of the situation to a search in the Bible and Tradition for God's word or judgment on events.

Church law is in a certain sense a source for theology.[17] At one level doctrine and theology are a basis for law; at another level enshrinement in law marks a significant reception (q.v.) of a theological position. However, one cannot necessarily argue from a restrictive law to a theological conclusion. A law which, for example, confines a ministry or office to a priest or male reflects a positive teaching: such can truly be ministers. But one cannot simply conclude from a limitation expressed in law to a permanent exclusion of a contrary position. Theology has the task of exploring other possibilities.

One may also consider as a theological source of some value the classical norm of orthodoxy from St. Vincent of Lérins (d. before 450): universality, antiquity, and unanimity *(Quod ubique, quod semper, quod ab omnibus creditum est)*.[18] Limitations of this norm are the absence of reference to the magisterium (q.v.) and the fact that it may not seem to allow for doctrinal development (q.v.), which is acknowledged elsewhere, however, by Vincent.

Reflection on theological sources is merely a stage preliminary to the presentation of doctrine or the further work of understanding, viz., theology, which in turn leads to a more comprehensive communication of divine truth.[19] In the past, ignorance of sources led to a narrowness of doctrinal affirmation and theological reflection. Today the sheer volume of research in all fields relating to theology threatens to swamp scholars and can lead to a new narrowness arising from excessive specialization.

[1]Salamanca, 1563. See M.D. Chenu, "Les lieux théologiques chez Melchior Cano," in AA.VV. *Le déplacement de la théologie* (Paris: Beauchesne, 1977) 45–50.  [2]Ibid., 1:3, p. 4; cf. St. Thomas, ST 1a, q.1, a.8.  [3]Ibid., Lib. 2–11, pp. 5–384. See A. Gardeil, "Lieux théologiques," DTC 9:712-747.  [4]Lib. 12, pp. 385–518.  [5]Y. Congar, *La foi et la théologie:* Le mystère chrétien (Tournai: Desclée, 1962) 142–165.  [6]*Spiritus Creator* (Einsiedeln, 1967) 67; *Word and Redemption* (New York: Herder & Herder, 1965) 49–86.  [7]Augustine *Contra mend.* 15:26-27—PL 40:506; Gregory the Great, *In Ezech. hom.* 1:10, 38—PL 76:901; cf. St. Thomas, *In Rom.* c. 1, lect 5 (80); c. 12, lect. 3 (1011); *In Heb.* c. 12, lect. 1 (657).  [8]See M.L. Gondal, "La mystique est-elle un lieu théologique?," NRT 108 (1986) 666–684; Pont. Facultas Theol. O.C.D., *Mysterium Ecclesiae in conscientia sanctorum* (Rome, 1967) = EphCarm 17 (1966); W.M. Thompson, *Fire and Light: The Saints and Theology. On Consulting the Saints, Mystics and Martyrs in Theology* (New York—Mahwah, 1987). Examples: G.H. Tavard, "The Christology of the Mystics," TS 42 (1981) 561–579; C. O'Donnell, "Love: An Ecclesiological Theme in Some Carmelite Saints," in P. Chandler and K.J. Egan, eds., *The Land of Carmel*. FS J. Smet (Rome: Institutum Carmelitanum, 1991) 405–417; D. Orsuto, *Saint Catherine of Siena: Trinitarian Experience and Mission in the Church*. Diss. Exc. (Rome: Gregorian, 1989).  [9]K. Rahner, "Experience of the Spirit and Existential Commitment," ThInvest 16:24-34; cf. idem, "Experience of the Spirit," ThInvest 18:189-210.  [10]Cf. H.U. von Balthasar, *Word and Redemption* (n. 6) 87–108.  [11]St. Thomas, ST 3a, q.63, a.4 ad 3; q.72, a.5 ad 2; see J. Gaillard, "Les sacrements de la foi," RThom 59 (1959) 5–31, 270–309.  [12]*General Instr. Roman Missal* 1:1, 5 cf. SC 33. See R.Q. Quilotti, *Aspetti dell'ecclesiologia del "Missale romanum."* Diss. Pont. Athen. S. Anselmi Rome (Bologna, 1990).  [13]*Roman Missal. General Norms for the Liturgical Year* Introd. 2; cf. SC 102–105.  [14]W.M. Baum, "La liturgia luogo teologico per la ecclesiologia," HoTheol 1 (1983) 339–348; B. Capelle, "Autorité de la liturgie chez les Pères," RechTAncMéd 21 (1954) 5–22; C.M. LaCugna, "Can Liturgy Ever Again Become a Source for Theology?" StLtg 19 (1989) 1–13; G. Lukken, "La liturgie comme lieu théologique irremplaçable," QLtg 56 (1975) 97–115; idem, "Plaidoyer pour une approche intégrale de la liturgie comme lieu théologique: Un défi à toute la théologie," QLtg 68 (1987) 242–255; A.G. Martimort, *The Church and Prayer* (London: Chapman, 1987) 1:273-280; H. Vorgrimler, "Liturgie als Thema der Dogmatik," ThJb (1988) 126–136; G. Wainwright, "Der Gottesdienst als 'locus theologicus,' oder der Gottesdienst als Quelle und Thema der Theologie," KerDo 28 (1982) 248–258; L. Walsh, "Liturgy in the Theology of St. Thomas," Thom 38 (1974) 557–583; AA.VV. *L'Église dans la liturgie.* Conferences Saint-Serge 26. Bibliotheca *"Ephemerides liturgicae"* subsidia 18 (Rome: CLV, 1980).  [15]"L'interpretazione dei dogmi," CivCatt 141 (1990) 2:167.  [16]A. Tornos, "Los signos de los tiempos como lugar teológico," EstE 53 (1978) 517–532; X. Quinzá Lleó, "Los signos de los tiempos como tópico teológico," EstE 65 (1990) 457–468.  [17]T.I. Jiménez Urresti, "The Theologian in Interface with Canonical Reality," JEcuSt (1982) 145–175; L. Örsy, *Theology and Canon Law* (Collegeville: The Liturgical Press, 1992).  [18]*Commonitorium* 2—PL 50:639; see J. Madoz, *El concepto de la tradición en S. Vicente de Lerins.* Analecta gregoriana 5 (Rome: Gregorian UP, 1933).  [19]B.J.F. Lonergan, *Method in Theology* (London: Darton, Longman & Todd, 1972).

## THÉRÈSE OF LISIEUX, St. (1873–1897)

Thérèse Martin was born into a middle-class family of great piety in Alençon, France, in 1873. She entered the Carmel at Lisieux at the age of fifteen. Her life was unremarkable. The only responsibility she held was that of assistant to the novice mistress from 1893. She died of tuberculosis in 1897.

She was asked to write her spiritual autobiography by her superiors. Its three parts were published after her death as *The Story of a Soul*.[1] It proved to be enormously popular. Her canonization took place in 1925.

Many recognized the importance of her spiritual teaching and her significance for ecclesiology, including H.U. von Balthasar in 1950.[2] Her contribution to spirituality is her "little way" of responding to divine love through a profound sense of spiritual childhood. Her central intuition into the Church arose when she failed to identify herself among the charisms of 1 Cor 12. A blinding insight led her to see her vocation to be "love in the heart of the Church." She wrote: "I understood that it was Love alone that made the Church's members act, and that if love ever became extinct, apostles would not preach the Gospel, and martyrs would not shed their blood. . . . My vocation is love. . . . O my Jesus I love you! I love the Church my Mother!"[3]

In addition, she was given by her superiors two spiritual brothers: a seminarian and future missionary, Fr. Bellière, and the missionary Fr. Roullard. Her correspondence with them shows her deep appreciation of their vocation, combined with a firm insistence on their being trusting and generous in their commitment.[4] She had aspirations of going to the missions, but her health did not allow it. For about a year and a half before her death, she experienced a mystical total darkness, of which the serenity of her recorded last conversations does not give much indication.[5]

In 1927 Pius XI declared her co-patroness of the Missions alongside that most active of missionaries, St. Francis Xavier.

[1]Best Eng. trans. J. Clarke, *Story of a Soul. The Autobiography of St. Thérèse of Lisieux* (Washington, D.C.: Institute of Carmelite Studies, ²1976). [2]English—*Therese of Lisieux. The Story of a Mission* (London: Sheed & Ward, 1953); new ed., *Two Sisters in the Spirit: Thérèse of Lisieux and Elizabeth of the Trinity* (San Francisco: Ignatius, 1992 = German 1970); idem, "The Timeliness of Lisieux," *Carmelite Studies* (Washington, D.C.) 1 (1980) 103–121. [3]*Story of a Soul*, MS B (ch. 9)—Clarke ed. (n. 1) 192–197; see C. O'Donnell, "Love: An Ecclesiological Theme in Some Carmelite Saints" in P. Chandler and K.J. Egan, *The Land of Carmel*. FS J. Smet (Rome: Institutum Carmelitanum, 1991) 405–417; K.H. Braun, *Ich Habe meinen Platz in der Kirche gefunden: Therese von Lisieux und die nachkonziliare Krise der Kirche* (Leutesdorf: Johannes, 1983); A. Combes, "L'Église pour saint Thérèse de Lisieux," *Divinitas* 13 (1969) 581–622; K. de Meester, "Thérèse contemplative et son sens de l'Église," *Vie Thérésienne* (Lisieux) 11 (1971) 133–144; idem, "Una vita per la Chiesa," *RVSp* 27 (1993) 426–439; C. Journet, "St. Thérèse's Conception of the Church," *Sicut parvuli* (London) 23 (1961) 20–30 = *Annales de sainte Thérèse de Lisieux* (Lisieux) 34 (1958) 39–43; P. Vercoustre, "Le sens de l'Église chez saint Thérèse de Lisieux," *Vie Thérésienne* 15 (1975) 199–206. [4]*Letters of St. Thérèse of Lisieux*. 2 vols. (Washington, D.C.: Institute of Carmelite Studies, 1982, 1988); A. Déclais, "L'éveil missionaire de Thérèse aux Buissonnets," *Vie Thérésienne* (Lisieux) 17 (1977) 87–96; L. Ferrigno, "Dall' esperienza mistica all' esperienza missionaria. S. Teresa di Gesù Bambino patrona delle missioni," *Riflessioni* (Castellarano RE) 1990:23-36, 111-123, 179-193; E. Mura, "Aux sources de l'esprit missionnaire de sainte Thérèse de Lisieux," *Vie Thérésienne* 17 (1977) 18–27; G. Vallejo Tobón, *Santa Teresa de Lisieux: Apóstol y profeta en el corazón de la Iglesia* (Bogotá: Ed. Paulinas, 1992); S. Vrai, *Thérèse de Lisieux et ses frères missionnaires* (Paris: Médiaspaul—Montral: Ed. Paulines, 1992). [5]*St. Thérèse of Lisieux, Her Last Conversations* (Washington, D.C.: Institute of Carmelite Studies, 1977).

## THOMAS AQUINAS, St. (ca. 1225–1274)

Thomas, of the noble Aquino family, was born about 1225 at Roccasecca.[1] His family opposed his joining the Dominican Order, which he eventually entered in 1244. In 1248 he was probably sent to Cologne, where he came under the influence of St. Albert the Great (1206–1280) and imbibed some of the latter's Aristotelianism and attachment to the Pseudo-Dionysius (v. DIONYSIUS, PSEUDO). He was sent to Paris to teach theology at the Dominican convent in 1252, that is, to comment on the *Sentences* of Peter Lombard. At the exceptionally early age of thirty-one he became a Master of Theology in Paris (1256). He lectured there except for the time he spent in Italy (1259–1269 and 1272, until his death in 1274). He was canonized in 1323 and declared a Doctor of the Church in 1567. His theology has been specially commended by popes, Trent, Vatican II, and Church law (v. AETERNI PATRIS).

His works are extensive: twenty-five folio volumes in the Parma edition (1852–1873), thirty-four quarto volumes in the Paris Vivès edition (1871–1882). The critical Leonine edition begun in 1882 comprises about two-thirds of his works, but will hardly be completed until well into the 21st century. The secondary literature on St. Thomas is immense. The bibliographical *Bulletin thomiste* which became the *Rassegna di letteratura tomista* notes and gives a critical abstract of major articles and books.

Like a giant army on the march, Aquinas' thought on the whole range of philosophy and theology continually advanced. But it advanced at a different pace in various areas; some matters are treated only in his earlier writings. There are several reasons for a wide variety of interpretations claiming to be the authentic thought of Aquinas.[2] Though important for any thinker, it is especially crucial with Aquinas to know to what period of his reflection a particular position belongs. Furthermore, many theologians neglect to take account of the nature of his authorship of works that are extant: some he wrote or dictated; others are lecture notes taken down by others, some of which, like the *Commentary on John*, were later corrected by himself. A further difficulty arises from the literary genre of his works, such as commentaries on Scripture, on Aristotle and others, and above all the disputations; one must always be careful to identify St. Thomas' own position amid other opinions that he exposes in the course of argumentation.[3]

As regards the Church, the first thing to notice is that he did not write a comprehensive ecclesiology. But as A. Dulles and others show, he did cover most of the crucial issues of ecclesiology, in many of them taking up positions that are still of interest today.[4]

In considering what might be the central unifying idea of St. Thomas' ecclesiology, there is a divergence among 20th-century writers. Those who are interested in the institutional aspects of the Church see the foundation of his ecclesiology in the passages about states and offices in the Church,[5] or the papacy.[6] Others see the questions on the grace of Christ as head of the Church to be central.[7] But there are dangers of distortion if one attempts to transfer directly into ecclesiology matters that are primarily Christological and soteriological.[8]

A Thomistic ecclesiology has to be sought throughout his works, taking particular account of the contexts in which he expounds the relevant matters. In general one can say that in polemical works and those in which he seeks to defend Catholic doctrine there is greater emphasis on the papacy and on visible aspects of the Church. The pope has a special role in ensuring the unity of the Church;[9] he has plenitude of power;[10] he has power with regard to new versions of the Creed and to all that concerns the whole Church;[11] St. Thomas does not state explicitly that the pope is infallible or that he cannot err, though these may be implicit in his writing.[12]

The first place in which to seek an overview of his ecclesiology is in his late sermons on the Apostles' Creed (1273).[13] Here he is free to expound his views of the Church unconstrained by the structure of the disputation or the exigencies of a text.[14] The main points he chooses to make in this sermon, along with the biblical passages he uses to support his reflection, can thus be expected to give his basic ecclesiology. The Church is a body, whose life-giving soul is the Holy Spirit. It is a gathering *(congregatio)* with four characteristics *(conditiones)*. First, the Church is one (Song 6:8) from a triple cause, oneness of faith (1 Cor 1:10; Eph 4:5), of hope (Eph 4:4), of love (John 17:22; Eph 4:15-16), and is necessary for salvation (Ps 25:5). Second, the Church is holy as the temple of the Spirit (1 Cor 3:17) and through the blood of Christ (Rev 1:5; Heb 13:12) and the anointing by the grace of the Spirit (2 Cor 1:21). It is holy, too, from the inhabitation of the Trinity (Gen 28:16; Ps 92:5) and the invocation of the Lord's name (Jer 14:9). Third, the Church is catholic: it exists throughout the world (Rom 1:8; Mark 16:15); it is in three parts: on earth, in heaven, and in purgatory. It is also catholic in embracing all, male and female (Gal 3:28), and in having begun at the time of Abel and lasting to the end of the ages (Matt 28:20). After the consummation of the ages it will remain in heaven. Fourth, it is firm, having Christ as its principal foundation (1 Cor 3:2); its secondary foundation are the apostles and their doctrine (Rev 21:14) and hence it is called apostolic. Peter is the head *(vertex)* of the Church, which has a firmness that persecutions (Matt 21:44), errors (2 Tim 3:8), and evil (Prov 18:10; Matt 18:18) cannot overcome; it flourishes in the faith of Peter and is free of error (Luke 22:32).

Many of these points are developed in greater depth elsewhere in his works: the earthly Church is a similitude of the heavenly Church,[15] and likewise the kingdom (q.v.) is in two phases, earthly and heavenly;[16] the Church is from Abel (q.v.)[17] and consists also of the angels.[18] Y. Congar sees the dialectical tension between the eschatological good that is to be achieved and the temporal means as fundamental to Aquinas' ecclesiology.[19]

From his earlier writings Aquinas firmly grasped the doctrine of the Mystical Body of Christ;[20] however, influenced by deeper insight into St. John Damascene, he sees with precision in his last work the humanity of Christ being precisely the instrument of grace for the Church.[21] St. Thomas' pneumatology (q.v.) develops throughout his work, though already in his earlier writings he saw the Spirit identical *(idem et unus numero)* in Christ and in us.[22] The Spirit unifies and vivifies the Church[23] and the New Law is so characterized by the Spirit that all externals in the Church are secondary to this interior principle.[24]

The Church is consistently described by St. Thomas as a gathering of the faithful *(congregatio/coetus/collegium/collectio . . . fidelium)*.[25] One might say that the Eucharistic Prayer I of the Latin rite is a true but partial reflection of his ecclesiology. He occasionally uses the idea of the Church being a society, but it is not so central to his vision of the Church.[26] Rather he employs the patristic Genesis typology of the Church being born from the side of Christ on the Cross (see Gen 2:21 with John 19:34).[27]

Thomas frequently states that the Church is constructed/founded/consecrated by faith and sacraments.[28] A. Osuna summarizes well: "A Thomistic ecclesiology . . . cannot prescind from the sacraments, just as it cannot prescind from faith."[29] The Eucharist is clearly central not only in the sacramental theology of St. Thomas[30] but also in his ecclesiology, for "the common spiritual good of the whole Church is substantially contained in the sacrament of the Eucharist itself";[31] the Eucharist is the principle of the Church's unity,[32] and the purpose *(finis)* of all offices in the Church.[33] Indeed, the thesis of M. Useros Carretero is now generally accepted, namely that for Aquinas the primary purpose of Church law is the sacraments, their ordering, and what relates to them.[34]

It is mainly in a sacramental context that Aquinas considers Church hierarchy.[35] As his *Summa theologiae* is incomplete, we lack St. Thomas' mature thought on episcopacy,[36] but main lines are clear from other places: "the bishop is as a leader *(quasi princeps)* in the Church";[37] the purpose of the episcopal office is the service of others;[38] a characteristic word for the bishops' office is care *(cura);*[39] bishops take the place of the apostles;[40] they have a principal office of preaching,[41] of dealing with difficulties concerning the whole people.[42]

Though A. Dulles has given an impressive list of twenty-four Thomistic themes later incorporated into Vatican II,[43] we have to agree that Thomistic ecclesiology is incomplete by modern standards; it lacks our adequate treatment of papal infallibility, the people of God, ecumenism, the sacramental nature and collegiality of the episcopate. But especially in its strong sacramental sense, in its insights into our sharing in the priesthood of Christ for worship taken in a wide sense,[44] in its pneumatology, and in the theorem of the grace of Christ the Head,[45] St. Thomas' teaching displays many of the features that make an ecclesiology "from above" an essential complement to any ecclesiology "from below," which begins with experience. Moreover, with his consistently advancing thought, with his involvement in all the controversies of the day, with his insatiable appetite for new and more accurate texts and theological tools, he would be the last to approve any wooden ecclesiology *ad mentem S. Thomae.*

[1]Critical biography, T.A. Weisheipl, *Friar Thomas D'Aquino: His Life and Works* (New York: Doubleday, 1974); 2nd ed., with corrigenda and addenda (Washington, D.C.: The Catholic University of America Press, 1983). See K. Rahner, "On Recognising the Importance of Thomas Aquinas," ThInvest 13:3-12. [2]M. Chenu, *Toward Understanding St. Thomas* (Chicago, 1964). [3]O. Bird, "How to Read an Article of the Summa," NewSchol 33 (1953) 129–159. [4]A. Dulles, "The Church According to Thomas Aquinas," in *A Church to Believe In: Discipleship and the Dynamics of Freedom* (New York: Crossroad, 1983) 149–169, 186–192; Y. Congar, "Vision de l'Église chez Thomas d'Aquin," RSPT 62 (1978) 523–541; B. Gherardini, "Tematiche ecclesiologico-tomistiche," DoctCom 33 (1980) 194–209 at 201; Congar, Augustin 232–241; G. Sabra, *Thomas Aquinas' Vision of the Church: Fundamentals of an Ecumenical Ecclesiology.* Tübingen theologische Studien 27 (Mainz: Matthias—Grünewald, 1987). [5]ST 2–2ae, q.183, a.2; see S. Tromp, *Corpus Christi quod est ecclesia* (Rome: Gregorian UP, [2]1946) 144. [6]ST 2–2ae, q.1, a.10; see Y. Congar, "Traditio thomistica in materia ecclesiologica," Ang 43 (1966) 405–428 at 416–418. [7]ST 3a, q.8; see E. Mersch, *The Whole Christ* (London, 1938) 458–459; E. Sauras, "Esquema tomista de una teología sobre la 'Iglesia del Espíritu,'" in AA.VV. *Prospettive teologiche moderne.* Studi tomistici 13—Atti dell'VIII congresso

tomistico internazionale IV (Vatican, 1981) 307–326 at 310; cf. R.M. Schmitz, "De nexu Christum inter et ecclesiam iuxta sanctum Thomam," DoctCom 43 (1990) 277–287. [8]Congar (n. 6) 420–421. [9]*S. contra gent.* 4:74. [10]*Qlb.* 4, q.8, a.2 (82); *In 4 Sent.* d.7, q.3, a.1, sol.3 (Moos 172); *C. err. graecorum* II, 32–36; ST 3a, q.72, a.11 ad 1; G. Rocca, "St Thomas and Papal Authority," Ang 62 (1985) 472–484. [11]ST 2–2ae, q.1, a.10. [12]See *Qlb.* 9, q.8, a.1 (194); Y. Congar, "St. Thomas and the Infallibility of the Papal Magisterium (*Summa theol.* II–II, q.1, a.10)," Thom 38 (1974) 81–105. [13]*In symbol. apost.* 9. Eng. trans. *The Three Greatest Prayers* (London, 1937). [14]Y. Congar, "The Idea of the Church in St. Thomas Aquinas," in *The Mystery of the Church* (London, 1960) 97–117. [15]*S. contra gent.* 4:76. [16]*In Matt* 3, lect. 1 (250); *In 4 Sent.* d.49, q.1, a.1, sol. 5; *S. contra gent.* 4:83; *In 1 Cor.* 15, lect. 3 (938); see B.M. Lemeer, "De relatione inter regnum Dei et ecclesiam in doctrina S. Thomae," in *Prospettive* (n. 7) 339–349 at 346. [17]*In ps.* 36:23. [18]ST 3a, q.8, a.4c.; q.80, a.2 ad 2. [19]Art. cit. (n. 6) 424. [20]*In Col.* 2, lect. 4 (129); *In 3 Sent.* d.13, q.2, a.1. [21]ST 3a, q.8, aa.1–2 with q.7, a.9c. See R. Valesco, "La Iglesia en la tercera parte de la Suma de Sto. Tomás," Claret 10 (1970) 109–138. [22]*In 3 Sent.* d.13, q.2, a.1, ad 2 (Moos 78); *De veritate* q.27, a.4c; *In Ioan.* 1, lect. 10 (202). [23]ST 2–2ae, q.183, a.2 ad 3; 3a, q.8, a.1 ad 3. [24]ST 1–2ae, qq.106–108; see G. Ferraro, "Lo Spirito Sancto nel commento di san Tomasso d'Aquino ai capitoli XIV–XVI del Quarto Vangelo," in *Tommaso d'Aquino nel suo settimo centenario.* Atti del Congresso internazionale (Roma—Napoli, 1974). Vol. 4: *Problemi di teologia* 79–91. [25]Congar (n. 6) 410; idem, *"Ecclesia et populus (fidelis)* dans l'ecclésiologie de S. Thomas," in AA.VV., *St. Thomas Aquinas 1274–1974. Commemorative Studies.* 2 vols. (Toronto: Pont. Institute Medieval Studies, 1974) 1:159-173. [26]*In Ps.* 45, n. 3; *In Eph.* 2, lect. 4 (124). [27]*In 4 Sent.* d.18, q.1, sol.1 (Moos 24); ST 1a, q.92, a.3; *In Ioan.* 19, lect. 5 (2458); on this tradition Congar, Moyen-âge 76–79. [28]*In 4 Sent.* d.17, q.3, a.1, sol.5 (Moos 389); ST 2–2ae, q.99, a.1 ad 2; 3a, q.64, a.2 ad 3. [29]"La doctrine de los estadios de la Iglesia en Santo Tomás," CiTom 88 (1961) 77–135, 215–266 at 249. [30]ST 3a, q.65, a.3. [31]ST 3a, q.65, a.3 ad 1. [32]ST 3a, q.73, a.3c. [33]ST 3a, q.65, a.3 ad 2. [34]*"Statuta Ecclesiae" y "Sacramenta Ecclesiae" en la eclesiología de St. Tomás.* AnGreg 119 (Rome: Gregorian UP, 1962). [35]ST 3a, q.83, a.4 ad 8; *De art. fid. et sac.* 2; *S. contra gent.* 4:74. [36]J. Lécuyer, "Les étapes de l'enseignement thomiste sur l'épiscopat," RThom 57 (1957) 29–52. [37]ST 3a, q.65, a.3 ad 2. [38]ST 2–2ae, q.185, a.1c and ad 1. [39]*De perf. spir. vit.* 15; *Qlb.* 3, q.12, a.3 (55). [40]ST 3a, q.72, a.11. [41]ST 3a, q.67, a.2. [42]*S. contra gent.* 4:76. [43]Art. cit. (n. 4) 165–166. [44]ST 3a, q.63 esp. a.3; see J.M. Donahue, "Sacramental Character: The State of the Question," Thom 31 (1967) 445–464; J. Galot, *La nature du caractère sacramentel: Étude de théologie médiévale.* Museum Lessianum 52 (Paris—Louvain, [2]1958) 171–197, esp. 186–190; A. Huerga, "La teología aquina de los carácteres sacramentales en la perspectiva eclesiológico contemporánea," RET 33 (1973) 213–243; W.F. Ryan, "The Teaching of St. Thomas in the Summa Concerning the Baptismal Character," AmER 149 (1963) 361–385; B. Thierry d'Argenlieu, "La doctrine du caractère sacramentel dans la 'Somme,'" RThom 12 (1929) 289–302. [45]ST 3a, q.8; J. Vodopivec, "La *gratia capitis* in San Tomasso in relazione all'ecclesiologia di comunione," in *Prospettive* (n. 7) 320–338.

## THOMAS CHRISTIANS

The St. Thomas Christians of India are divided into eight Churches, two of which are in communion with Rome (v. EASTERN CHURCHES).[1] When the Portuguese came to S.W. India in the 16th century, they found Christian communities claiming their origin from the apostle Thomas. They were in communion with the Assyrian (Nestorian) Church. Latinization by the Portuguese led to schism, resulting in the Malankar Orthodox Syrian Church, but eventually two-thirds were reconciled with Rome in 1662 as a result of Carmelite ministry. These became the Malabar Catholic Church. In 1930 there was a further reunion leading to the Malankar Catholic Church. The Mar Thomas Church which arose in the late 19th century has been in communion with the Anglican Church in India since 1961.[2]

The Thomas Christians are remarkable for their retention of ancient rites and their inculturation with true openness to Hindu religious inspiration in a rich spiritual tradition open in some places to further development.[3]

An example is the Kurisumala Ashram—a monastic community based strictly on the Benedictine Rule, observance of the Syrian liturgical tradition, and Hindu ascetical practices.[4] The Churches of the Thomas Christians are highly literate, both theologically and spiritually.

[1] J. Madoy, "La chrétienté de Saint-Thomas en Inde: Églises catholiques et orthodoxes," Irén 65 (1992) 5–24.  [2] H. Wybrew, "L'Église Mar Thoma en Inde," Irén 65 (1992) 451–461.  [3] T. Aykara and J.B. Chetthimattam, "Church of St. Thomas in India," JDharma 14 (1989) 62–73; X. Koodapuzha, "The Ecclesiology of the Thomas Christians in India," JDhara 8 (1978) 290–308; J. Madey, "La chrétienté de saint Thomas en Inde: Églises catholiques et orthodoxes," Irén 65 (1992) 24–41; A. Manjaly, The Ecclesiology of the St. Thomas Christians in India: A Historico-Theological Study. Diss. (Leuven, 1990); A.M. Mundadan, Sixteenth Century Traditions of St. Thomas Christians (Bangalore: Dharmaran College, 1970); G. Nedungatt, "La spiritualità dei cristiani di San Tomasso o 'Thomaschristians,'" in AA.VV. La spiritualità delle chiese christiane orientali. Corso breve di ecumenismo 7 (Rome: Centro pro Unione, 1986) 90–104; V. Pathikulangara, "St. Thomas Christians and Popular Devotions," JDharma 15 (1990) 259–272; P.J. Podipara, The Thomas Christians (Bombay: St. Paul, 1970); E. Tisserant, Eastern Christianity in India (London—New York—Sydney: Longmans Green, 1957); B. Vadakkekara, India's St. Thomas Christians: Questions of Their Origin—A Historiographical Critique. Diss. (Rome: Gregorian, 1987); H. Wybrew, "L'Église Mar Thoma en Inde," Irén 65 (1992) 451–461.  [4] R.G. Roberson, The Eastern Christian Churches: A Brief Survey (Rome: Orientale, [3] 1986) 4; cf. M. Anikuzhikattil, "The Penitential Life of the St. Thomas Christians in India,"QLtg 71 (1990) 1–11.

## TILLARD, J.M.R. (1927– )

One of the most experienced ecumenists in the Catholic Church, Jean-Marie Tillard was born at Iles Saint-Pierre et Miquelon in 1927. Entering the Dominican Order, he studied at the Angelicum and Le Saulchoir. He has received the highest theological accolade of his order, the Master of Sacred Theology (STM). A very young peritus at Vatican II, he worked on the religious life document and on schema 13, which was to become the Constitution on the Church

in the Modern World. After the council he wrote significantly on religious life[1] and on various issues of sacramental theology.[2]

His two major works of ecclesiology are on the papacy and communion.[3] He has been a Catholic representative of several international and national ecumenical commissions, among others the World Council of Churches (q.v.), Faith and Order and ARCIC (v. ANGLICANISM AND ECUMENISM). He has written irenic and insightful discussion papers for many ecumenical meetings, which show centrist positions and a delicate sense of Catholic doctrines. These foundational papers are found in various journals, especially Irénikon, and occasionally in English in One in Christ. He teaches mainly in Ottawa and at the University of Freibourg.

[1] A Gospel Path: The Religious Life (Washington, D.C.: Lumen Vitae, 1978); There Are Charisms and Charisms: The Religious Life (Brussels: Lumen Vitae, 1977).  [2] E.g., The Eucharist: Pasch of God's People (New York: Society of St. Paul, 1967—French 1964).  [3] The Bishop of Rome (London: SPCK, 1983); Église d'églises: L'ecclésiologie de communion (Paris: Cerf, 1981), not fully satisfactory Eng. trans., Church of Churches (Collegeville: The Liturgical Press, 1992); Chair de l'Église, chair du Christ: Aux sources de l'ecclésiologie de communion (Paris: Cerf, 1992). See M. O'Connor, "The Holy Spirit and the Church in Catholic Theology: A Study in the Ecclesiology of J.-M.R. Tillard," One Chr 28 (1992) 331–341.

## TREASURY OF THE CHURCH

The Church's treasury/treasures (thesauri ecclesiae) has important ecumenical implications. It depends on a theology of the Communion of Saints (q.v.) and it underlies the theology of indulgences (q.v.). It was, indeed, in the context of the latter that the idea of the Church's treasury was developed, perhaps first by Hugh of St. Cher (ca. 1200–1263). It was first used by the magisterium in this context by Clement VI (1342–1352) in his bull extending the Jubilee to each fifty years.[1]

The pope describes the blood of Christ as a great treasure acquired for the Church militant; the merits of Christ are infinite, and to them are added the merits of Mary and of all the just. The treasure has been given to the care of St. Peter, who holds the keys, and to his successors. It is to be applied with compassion (salubriter) for the remission of the temporal punishment due to sin.

Cajetan appealed to this bull in his famous disputation with Luther in 1518.[2] Luther was intransigent and there was a condemnation of propositions representing his views on indulgences, but without a theological specification about individual articles.[3] The first was his rejection of the Treasury: "The treasuries of the Church, from which the pope gives indulgences, are not the merits of Christ and of the saints."

In an apostolic constitution on indulgences, Paul VI changed somewhat the emphasis of previous teaching: now the term "treasury of the Church" is not seen in terms of a material accumulation of merits but rather "the infinite value . . . which Christ's merits have before God"; it refers more to Christ himself "in whom the satisfaction and merits of his redemption still exist and retain their efficacy." He then notes: "This treasury includes as well the prayers and good works of the Blessed Virgin Mary. . . . In the treasury too are the prayers and good works of all the saints." The pope avoids using the word "merits" about either Mary or the saints: he speaks of the value before God of the good works of the Virgin, and observes that she and the saints cooperated in the salvation of their brothers and sisters in the Mystical Body.[4] This teaching is quoted in the new *Catechism* (nn. 1476–1477).

Though usually used in the context of indulgences, one could also perhaps see the treasury of the Church being appealed to at Mass when we pray before Communion: "Look not on our sins but on the faith of your Church." Because of the Protestant sensibilities in the whole area of merits and good works, it is always necessary to speak with discretion and accuracy about the treasury of the Church, emphasizing God's good pleasure in the merits of Christ and his freely given appreciation of the works of his holy people. The only ecumenical way forward in this matter would seem to be through a deepened understanding of the Communion of Saints and of the Body of Christ together, by drawing out the consequences of their interrelatedness.

---

[1]Bull *Unigenitus Dei Filius* (1343)—DS 1205–1207/ND 1681–1683. [2]C.J. Peter, "The Church's Treasures *(Thesauri Ecclesiae)* Then and Now," TS 47 (1986) 251–272.    [3]DS 1467–1472/ND 1685:17-22.    [4]*Indulgentiarum doctrina*—AAS 59 (1967) 5–24/Flannery 1:62-79/ND 1687–1688.

## TRENT, Council of (1545–1563)

Lateran V (1512–1517—q.v.) was an ineffectual reform council. A year after its close Martin Luther threw down his challenge to Church authorities and began to call for a council. He repeated this call in his *Address to the Nobles of the German Nation* (1520). As the Reformation progressed there would be many appeals from Catholics, too, for a council. Some reforms meanwhile were beginning in the Catholic Church. Among the popes at the time, Clement VII (1523–1534) feared the reappearance of conciliarism (q.v.); Paul III (1534–1549) soon began preparations for a council, but it would be eleven years before it opened at Trent in 1545.[1]

One's view of Trent will be conditioned by one's understanding of the Reformation. Faced with the need for change and renewal in the Church, the Reformers saw no hope in the papacy or in other institutions, all of which themselves seemed in need of reform. The Reformers thus took their stand on Scripture, and the principle of *sola scriptura* ("Scripture alone") progressively hardened. Whatever was not clear in Scripture tended to be denied, though the early Reformers were not fully consistent on this point. If a brief summary of the Protestant Reformation's deepest roots were to be asked, one could perhaps state that most profoundly the Reformation involved an insistence on the sufficiency of Scripture and faith along with a denial of developments, especially the medieval ones.[2]

With long intervals, the Council of Trent met in three sittings. The first phase (1545–1548) was at Trent and comprised sessions 1–8 (under Pope Paul III); two sessions (9, 10) took place in Bologna, but no decrees were passed except for ones deciding postponement. The second phase (1551–1552), at Trent, comprised sessions 11–16 (under Pope Julius III). War between the emperor and the Protestants led to its suspension. The third and final phase (1562–1563) was the meetings of sessions 17–25 (under Pope Pius IV).

There were never many members at the council. At the final part there was sporadic attendance of nine cardinals, thirty-nine patriarchs and archbishops, two hundred thirty-six bishops, and seventeen abbots or generals of religious orders. At other times the attendance could be as low as fifty to eighty members. More significant, perhaps, was their origin: Germans, for example, were never very numerous except for the final phase; the vast majority were always Italians. Laity, too, were present but in an ambiguous role: they were the ambassadors of the princes who watched over the council, trying to sway matters in favor of their masters. The papal legates were highly influential: they sought to ensure that a Roman line would be adhered to. Since the general theological culture of the bishops was low—they were mostly canonists—the role of the theologians at Trent was crucial.

The plan eventually adopted by the council was to move in parallel: each session had doctrinal *chapters* and *canons* against the Protestants, as well as *decrees* for reform. The procedure often adopted was a preliminary study of the issues by the theologians and the papal legates. The perceived positions of the Protestants were gathered. One has to qualify their positions with "perceived," since it is not always clear that any Protestant text or author may actually have held the position precisely as condemned. The matter was discussed by the assembly. A draft was drawn up by commissions of qualified bishops with the legates, assisted by the theologians. It was then discussed by the whole assembly and modified until approved at general sessions. In the interpretation of the decrees we have to remember that various schools were represented by both theologians and bishops, notably, Augustinian, Dominican, and Franciscan, among whom some tended to be Nominalists. The council members and theologians were careful not to condemn each other; their aim was to set forth an agreed Catholic position against the perceived errors of the Protestants; they did not decide on differences between Catholics.

The main work of the council was as follows. In the first period (1545–1548) it established the foundations of the Christian life, such as Scripture and Tradition, original sin, justification, sacraments in general, baptism, and confirmation.[3] In reforms it made notable decrees on preaching, on the residence of bishops, and on benefices.[4] The 9th and 10th sessions at Bologna did not issue any document but did have useful discussions.

The second period (1551–1552) was marked by the presence in Trent of some Protestant ambassadors but, though speeches were made, there was no true dialogue. The session also had thirteen German bishops, the highest number up to then. The doctrinal statements defined teaching on the Eucharist, the sacrament of penance, and the sacrament of the sick.[5] The decrees on reform were weak; they were mostly about bishops and religious, matters about trials, ordinations, conferral of monasteries.[6] The council had not embarked on the profound Church reform sought by so many at the time.

In the interim, steps were taken by the pope, Julius III, to begin the reform of the Roman Curia, but what he achieved was judged inadequate. His successor, Marcellus II, was the first reform pope; he pursued reform with energy and conviction but died after only 22 days. He was succeeded by the severe but determined Paul IV (1555–1559) who thought that, like a medieval pope, he could carry through reforms himself without a council. His zeal was undoubted, but there was a lack of wholesomeness in his vision of reform and in his despotic pontificate; he achieved some reform, but he perhaps served best by preparing the ground for his successor, Pius IV (1559–1565), who reconvened the council. The reform of the curia was pursued with vigor by him from 1561.

The final phase (1562–1563) took up again the contentious issue of the residence of bishops and other beneficiaries.[7] It gave teaching and canons on questions of the Eucharist, especially the sacrificial character of the Mass and Communion under both kinds. It dealt with the sacraments of orders and marriage.[8] The council deliberately abstained from any definition on the papacy. It made more decrees about diocesan and parish life[9] and one on the proper celebration of Mass.[10] In the area of marriage, in addition to the dogmatic decree on the sacramental nature of marriage, its indissolubility, and the Church's right to establish impediments, there was the famous *Tametsi,* which determined that the validity of marriage depended on the

Tridentine form, which required that marriage take place before the authorized parish priest and at least two witnesses.[11] Reform decrees about marriage were also enacted.[12] At the very end there were dogmatic statements on purgatory, the veneration of saints, relics and images, and on indulgences.[13] As reform decrees there were additional penalties for non-residence by bishops. There was a call for careful choice of those who were to be clerics, and for the establishment of seminaries for the training of priests.[14] The decree on marriage also demanded that priests should keep proper registers of baptisms and weddings. The reform decrees also laid down norms for nominating bishops, canonical processes of obtaining information for, and proceeding in, judicial cases, synods, episcopal visitations, appointment of parish clergy. Other matters concerned cardinals, clerical concubinage, temporal goods, religious, the reform of the Missal and Breviary and the catechism for parish priests.[15]

At the end of the twenty-fifth and closing session, the decrees from all sessions since 1545 were read and signed, thus unifying the work of the whole protracted council: the council sought confirmation of its work by the pope.[16] The council was approved by Pius IV on 30 June 1564 (antedated 26 Jan.).[17]

H. Jedin summarizes the achievements of Trent as being principally two: it defined the Catholic deposit of faith against current errors; it set up a Catholic reform, not in the medieval sense of "head and members" but in seeking to eliminate the worst abuses at diocesan and parish levels.[18]

A brief summary of the dogmatic results of the council was promulgated on 16 April 1564 and made obligatory for bishops, religious superiors, and theologians.[19]

Even though the Reformation was wholly about the Church, its doctrines and its need of reform, there is little direct ecclesiology in Trent.[20] The threat of episcopalism and Gallicanism prevented a definition of papal primacy. One has to seek for the council's teaching on the Church in various *obiter dicta,* in the vision that underlies the reform decrees. Various traditional formulas are found passim, e.g., Church is founded by Christ and is Body, Spouse, Mother, etc. Several ecclesiological positions are to be found. One is *salus animarum* ("salvation of souls"):[21] the Church operates through sacraments for the salvation of Christians; the Church is the living body of believers who receive the faith handed down in Scripture and Tradition. This sacramental view may be seen as the foundation of all the controversy about bishops being in residence: they are to ensure the spiritual health of their people by preaching, sacraments, and pastoring. The other ecclesiology is more juridical. It surfaced especially in the debate on the origin of episcopal jurisdiction (q.v.):

Does this last come immediately from Christ when the pope assigns a diocese, or is it a power derived from the pope? After Trent the latter view came to dominate and was just another instance of the great centralization that arose in succeeding centuries.

We must not identify the Counter-Reformation, or Catholic reform, with Trent. Trent was an important factor, and in many ways a guide. But the reform began before Trent, e.g., with St. Ignatius Loyola (q.v.), and emerged charismatically after the council in a variety of ways. On an institutional level Pope St. Pius V (1566–1572) set about the implementation of the council with energy.[22] An early fruit of the council was the so-called Roman Catechism (1566—v. CATECHETICS): it was to be the principal means whereby Catholics came to know the orthodox teaching of the Church, especially as expounded by Trent. The revised Breviary appeared in 1568, and the revised Missal in 1570. The revision of the Latin Vulgate Bible appeared in 1592.

The reception of the council was quick in some places, in others slow or sporadic. Various princes already accepted its decrees through their ambassadors at Trent itself. Others, e.g., Philip II in Spain, at first balked at elements of the reform decrees. Elsewhere there were synods that received the council's decrees. St. Charles Borromeo (1538–1584) in Milan was seen by many as a model reform bishop; but his approach was denigrated by others; even Bellarmine (q.v.) at the time of Borromeo's canonization (1610) praised his personal sanctity, without any regard for his zeal for reform or even his being a bishop.[23] The Counter-Reformation saw other means of renewal emphasized, like the restoration of the obligatory *ad limina* visits ("to the thresholds," viz., to venerate the relics of Peter and Paul and visit the pope) imposed on bishops by Sixtus V in 1585; depending on distance from Rome, such visits were from three to ten yearly.

Y. Congar credits G. Alberigo with the coining of the word "Tridentinism," which involved a rather negative, somewhat one-sided, reading of the period from Trent to the eve of Vatican II which saw a Roman version of Trent becoming the norm for Church life: it looked for the center of the Church only in Rome rather than being also in the local Church; it exalted the papacy at the expense of the episcopate, and it revered the clerical over the lay state; it displaced medieval canon law and became almost the sole source for legislation and the practical running of the Church; it led to a static ecclesiology; it lost sight of the need for Church unity; its attitude to Scripture was ambiguous, for despite being praised in session four, the Bible tended to lose its place in the Christian life; it led to the Eucharist becoming more and more a center for personal piety, even though the council had insisted on the sacrificial character of the Mass; it led to an upsurge of piety encouraged by many indulgences but largely divorced from liturgy; in short, it was a complete system taking in every aspect of social and Church life. Nevertheless, one's judgment of Tridentinism has to be moderated by a recognition that reform of the Church probably could not have come about without such centralization; already Gregory VII (q.v.) realized that reform may have to come from the top. Furthermore, even to the extent that the evaluation of "Tridentinism" is valid, it still does not do justice to all the many positive elements in the Church from the 16th to the 20th century.

In a sense, it can be said that the final reception (q.v.) of the council was the *Code of Canon Law* in 1917.[24] It is perhaps the paradox of Trent that while it met because of Protestant, especially Lutheran, doctrines, afterwards the Catholic Church lost interest in Protestantism and became too exclusively centered on itself.

[1]H. Jedin, *Geschichte des Konzils von Trient.* 5 vols. (Freiburg, 1949–1975 with Eng, trans, of first two vols. *A History of the Council of Trent* (London, 1957, 1961); H. Jedin, in Jedin-Dolan 5:433-498, bibliog. 714–721; AA.VV. *Il concilio di Trento e la riforma tridentina.* Atti del convegno storico internazionale Trento 2–6 settembre 1963. 2 vols. (Rome—Freiburg, 1965); R. Bäumer, ed., *Concilium Tridentinum.* Wege der Forschung 313 (Darmstadt: Wissenschaftliche Buchgeschellschaft, 1979); J. Lecler et al, *Latran V et Trente.* 2 vols. Histoire des conciles 10–11 (Paris: Ed. Orante, 1975–1981); M. Venard in Alberigo, Concili 330–367. [2]Congar, Augustin 359. [3]Tanner 2:663-686/DS 1500–1630/ND 210–215, 507–513, 1924–1983, 1310–1323, 1420–1436. [4]Tanner 2:681-683, 686-689. [5]Tanner 2:693-698, 703-713/DS 1635–1719/ND 1512–1536, 1615–1659. [6]Tanner 2:698-701, 714-718. [7]Tanner 2:744-746. [8]Tanner 2:726-728, 732-736, 742-744, 753-755/DS 1725–1812/ND 1537–1563, 1706–1721, 1804–1819. [9]Tanner 2:728-732, 737-741, 742-753. [10]Tanner 2:736-737. [11]Tanner 2:755-757/DS 1813–1816. [12]Tanner 2:757-759. [13]Tanner 2:774-776/DS 1820–1835/ND 2310, 1255–1257, 1686. [14]Tanner 2:750-753. [15]Tanner 2:759-774, 776-796. [16]Tanner 2:798-799. [17]*Benedictus Deus*—in part DS 1847–1850. [18]Jedin-Dolan 5:496. [19]DS 1862–1870/ND 30-38. [20]G. Alberigo, "Die Ekklesiologie des Konzils von Trient" in Bäumer (n. 1) 278–300 = RivStorChItal 18 (1964) 227–242; Congar, Augustin 364–368; J. Rigal, "L'ecclésiologie tridentine," BLitEc 91 (1990) 251–273. [21]G. Alberigo, "Du concile de Trente au tridentinisme," Irén 54 (1981) 192–210 at 199. [22]On post Trent, see H. Jedin, in Jedin-Dolan 499–522 [23]Alberigo (n. 21) 203–204. [24]G. Alberigo, "La 'réception' du Concile de Trente par l'Église catholique romaine," Irén 58 (1985) 311–337.

## TROMP, Sebastian (1899–1975)

Born in Beek in the Netherlands in 1899, the Jesuit Sebastian Tromp taught in the Roman Gregorian University for many years and died there in 1975.[1] He specialized in the theology of the Mystical Body (v. BODY OF CHRIST); along with É. Mersch he was instrumental in the rediscovery of this teaching.[2] In time he became a main author and commentator of *Mystici corporis* (q.v.). The problematic identification of the

Mystical Body with the Roman Catholic Church was his.[3] He edited sermons of Bellarmine[4] and wrote on his views of the Mystical Body.[5]

Tromp was one of the theologians consulted by Pius XII in the 1940s about the possibility of reconvening Vatican I (v. VATICAN COUNCIL II). He was a main author for the first draft of the document on the Church of Vatican II and was responsible for large parts of other rejected drafts. At first he was the only secretary of the Theological Commission of the council; later he was joined by G. Philips (q.v.). He was the theologian behind the very conservative Cardinal Ottaviani who, being a canonist and having impaired sight at the time of the council, depended on him. Tromp was one of the leading theologians of the more conservative group at the council. His earlier contribution to the revival of ecclesiology thus tends to be overlooked.

[1]J.N. Bakhuizen van den Brink, "Discorso in memoria del R.P. Sebastiano Tromp," Greg 57 (1976) 367–372.   [2]*Corpus Christi quod est ecclesia. 1. Introductio generalis. 2. De Christo capite Mystici corporis. 3. De Spiritu Christi anima* (Rome: Gregorian UP, 1937–1960)—Eng. trans. New York: Vantage Press, 1960.   [3]Antón 2:623, 629.   [4]*Opera oratoria postuma 1–9* (Rome 1942–1972).   [5]"De biformi conceptu cum 'Christi mystici' tum corporis Christi mystici' in controversiis Bellarmini," Greg 23 (1942) 474–490.

## TRUCE OF GOD

The origins of the truce of God are obscure.[1] We first encounter it at the French local council of Toulouse (Roussillon) in 1027, and it spread to Spain, Germany, and northern Italy. The truce was an attempt to control the feudal anarchy in the 11th century. Hostilities were forbidden on certain days, e.g., Saturday evening to Monday morning. Lateran II (1139—q.v.) extended the truce to Advent and Lent and from sunset on Wednesday to sunrise on Monday,[2] an ordinance repeated in Lateran III (1179—q.v.).[3] Though never very successful, the truce was a pioneer effort in medieval peace movements.

[1]F. Kempf, in Jedin-Dolan 3:346; OxDCC 1397.   [2]Can. 12—Tanner 1:199-200.   [3]Can. 21—Tanner 1:222.

## TRULLO, Council of (692)

Sitting in the domed room *(trullus)* of the emperor's palace in Constantinople, this meeting of Eastern bishops in 692 C.E. sought to pass disciplinary canons to complete the work of the 5th and 6th general Councils (Constantinople II and III—q.v.), hence its other name "Quinisext." Its 102 canons are largely incorporated in the tradition of Eastern Church law. It approved the 85 Apostolic Canons (v. APOSTOLIC COLLECTIONS), placing them before the canons of Nicaea (q.v.). Papal approval of the council is disputed, but appears improbable; the Syrian Sergius I would seem to have rejected some, if not all, of its canons in 692.[1] At any rate, its canons were never applied in the Western Church.[2]

[1]Davis, Councils 284–286; E. Ewig, in Jedin-Dolan 3:5.   [2]Text: CCO 98–241; Mansi 11:929-1006; cf. OxDCC 1397.

# U

## ULTRAMONTANISM

Though the word "ultramontane" (beyond the mountains, i.e., southward from northern Europe) is found in the 11th century, its main usage is in Church history to describe attitudes which are Rome centered.[1] Ultramontanism is opposed to Gallicanism (q.v.), Josephinism (q.v.), and it developed accordingly as these latter were discredited. Its main emphasis was on centralization of government in Rome, the independence of the Church from any secular authority, and power and authority in the Church. At Vatican I (q.v.) the Ultramontane party hoped that the *Syllabus of Errors* (v. PIUS IX) would be defined; it actively supported the definition of papal infallibility (q.v.). Extreme Ultramontane figures hoped for, but did not get, a statement that the pope is infallible in administrative decisions. In the 19th century some key Ultramontane adherents were Jean Lacordaire (1806–1861), Cardinal Henry Manning (1808–1892), Louis Veuillot (1813–1883), and William G. Ward (1812–1882). Ultramontanism was a form of Romanticism in that it included among other things a nostalgia and hope for an idealized past. It viewed the pope as an ideal father and authority. It gradually died out with the departure of its main proponents, but its spirit can be seen to have reemerged in the 20th century, especially during the Modernist (q.v.) crisis.

---

[1]R. Aubert, in Jedin-Dolan 8:3-9, 304-315; R.F. Costigan, "Tradition and the Beginning of the Ultramontane Movement," IrTQ 48 (1981) 27–46; M. O'Callaghan, "Ultramontanism," NCE 14:380; OxDCC 1405; cf. R. Aubert in Fliche-Martin 21:262-310; H.J. Pottmeyer, "Ultramontanismo e ecclesiologia," CrNSt 12 (1991) 527–552 = StimZ 210 (1992) 449–464.

## UNIATE CHURCHES

The Uniat(e) Churches are Eastern Catholic Churches (q.v.), most of which became reconciled with Rome over the centuries though two, the Maronite Catholic Church (mostly in Lebanon, Syria) and the Italo-Albanian Catholic Church (Southern Italy), were never in schism or heresy.[1] Listed according to their five rites, the twenty-one Uniate Churches are *Alexandrian Rite:* Coptic Church (Patriarchate, q.v.), Ethiopian Church; *Antiochene Rite:* Malankara Church, Maronite Church (Patriarchate), Syrian Church (Patriarchate); *Armenian Rite:* Armenian Church (Patriarchate); *Chaldean Rite:* Chaldean Church (Patriarchate), Syro-Malabar Church; *Constantinopolitan/Byzantine Rite:* the Albanian, Byelorussian, Bulgarian, Greek, Hungarian, Italo-Albanian, Melchite (Patriarchate), Romanian, Russian, Ruthenian, Slovakian, Ukrainian, and Yugoslavian (Croatian) Churches. Their total membership, something over 10 million members of a total of more than 550 million Catholics, bears no relation to their importance. For the Catholic Church they preserve the traditions and rites of the East as part of the heritage of the whole Church (OE 5). They thus enhance the diversity in unity which belongs to the gift of catholicity (v. CATHOLIC) in the Church. It is common for Roman Catholics to see them as bridges to the Orthodox and other Eastern Churches—Vatican II spoke of them as having "a special duty *(peculiare . . . munus)* of fostering the union of all Christians, in particular of Eastern Churches" (OE 24).[2] But the attitude of the Orthodox and other Eastern Churches to them is generally negative;[3] they are seen as unfaithful to Orthodoxy; as betrayed by Rome or Romanized/Latinized; as having lost their true identity; as being a blockage to any true communication between Orthodoxy and Roman Catholicism. These charges are still made despite Vatican II's attempt to deal in an integral and open fashion with the Orthodox and other Eastern Churches in the Decree on Ecumenism (UR 14–18) and in the Decree on the Catholic Eastern Churches

(OE). Particularly resented has been the appointment of Uniate bishops in Eastern Europe after the fall of Communism in 1989; the Roman Catholic Church is perceived as engaging in covert or disguised proselytism (q.v.) by many Orthodox.

The Vatican II Decree on the Catholic Eastern Churches was a major step forward in the Church's understanding and appreciation of its Eastern tradition.[4] Very much influenced by the observers from the Eastern Churches, it was given a guarded welcome by some of them, significantly so, though it was regarded by one distinguished Orthodox theologian as a "Latin text about the Eastern tradition."[5] The document can be seen as having six parts: after an introduction it deals in general (OE 2–4) with the particular Churches or rites (q.v.), clearly stating that "these churches are of equal rank, so that none of them is superior to others because of its rite" (3); the spiritual heritage of the East (OE 5–6) is fostered by their governing themselves according to their own tradition and by ever greater knowledge of their own rite; the patriarchs (OE 7–11—q.v.) are father and head of their patriarchates, and so the Council decreed that "their rights and privileges be restored in accord with the ancient traditions of each church and decrees of the ecumenical councils"; canonical legislation is enacted in relation to the sacraments (OE 13–18), divine worship (OE 19–23), and relations with the Brethren of the Separated Churches (OE 24–29); a conclusion states that the legal enactments are made "in view of present conditions until such time as the Catholic Church and the separated Eastern Churches unite together in the fullness of communion" (OE 30). The Uniate Churches were given a *Code of Canon Law* in 1990 called *The Code of Canons of the Oriental Churches* (abbrev. from Latin CCEO, v. LAW); this law reflects Vatican II and decades of earlier work.

An important development was the legislation about *communicatio in sacris* or sacramental sharing (v. INTERCOMMUNION). Since the usual dangers associated with intercommunion are largely absent between the Catholic Church and the other Churches of the East, a "less rigorous course of action" can be adopted (OE 26): members of other Eastern Churches are to be given the sacraments of penance, Eucharist, and the sacrament of the sick, if they are rightly disposed and spontaneously make such a request; Catholics may ask for these same sacraments from non-Catholic ministers "in whose Church there are valid sacraments, as often as necessary or true spiritual benefit recommends such action, and access to a Catholic priest is physically or morally impossible" (OE 27).[6] This development has not been reciprocated on the Orthodox side.

A major area for renewal is the specifically Eastern form of monasticism which has all but disappeared in some Uniate Churches and/or is displaced by Western-style religious congregations.[7] It will take several decades to learn how valuable the 1990 revision of Eastern Canon Law will be in this and other areas (v. RITES and LAW). But the main challenge facing the Uniate Churches and the Latin West is to bear living witness to the description by Vatican II of the first millennium: "For many centuries the Churches of the East and of the West went their own ways, though a brotherly communion of faith and sacramental life bound them together. If disagreements in faith and discipline arose among them, the Roman See acted by common consent as moderator" (UR 14). The Orthodox Church continually watches to see if this is being reenacted today.

For centuries uniatism was the major strategy of the Catholic Church. In the dialogue between the Orthodox and Roman Catholic Church, the Joint Commission in its Balamand Statement (1993) declared that uniatism "can no longer be accepted either as a method to be followed or as model of the unity our Churches are seeking."[8] Due to the sensitivities of the Orthodox it has been recently suggested that the name "Uniate" be dropped in favor of "Catholic" to denote the Eastern Churches in communion with Rome.[9]

---

[1]D. Attwater, *The Christian Churches of the East. Vol. 1—Churches in Communion with Rome* (Birmingham: Thomas More Books, [2]1961). E. Lanne, "La conception post-tridentine de la primauté et l'origine des Églises unies," Irén 52 (1979) 5–33.68; R.G. Roberson, *The Eastern Christian Churches. A Brief Survey* (Rome: Oriental Institute, [3]1986). See E.F. Fortino, "Aspects ecclésiologiques de l'Église italo-albanaise: Tensioni et communion," Irén 65 (1992) 363–386. [2]R.D. Lee, "The Mission and Witness of the Eastern Catholic Church," Diak (USA) 15 (1980) 159–166; T. Puccini, "Towards an Acceptable Byzantine Catholic Ecclesiology," Diak (USA) 15 (1980) 5–22; D. Salachas, "L'ecumenismo nello Schema del Codice di Diritto Canonico Orientale," Apoll 61 (1988) 205–227. See R.T. Greenacre, "La signification des Églises orientales catholiques au sein de la communion Romaine dans la perspective de l'Église anglicane unie non absorbées," Irén 65 (1992) 339–351. [3]F. Bouwen, "Eastern Catholic Churches," DictEcum Mov 310–311. [4]G.D. Gallaro, "'Orienalium ecclesiarum' Deserves more Attention," Nicol 13 (1986) 293–302; P. O'Connell, *Vatican II: The Decree on the Catholic Eastern Churches* (Dublin, 1965); V. Popishil, *Orientalium Ecclesiarum: The Decree on the Eastern Catholic Churches of the II Council of the Vatican* (New York, 1965); C. Pujol, *Decretum Concilii Vaticani II: "Orientalium Ecclesiarum"* (Rome: Oriental Institute, 1970); M. Wojnar, "Decree on the Oriental Catholic Churches," Jurist 25 (1965) 173–255. [5]A. Schmemann, in Abbot 388. [6]D. Salachas, "La comunione nel culto liturgico e nella vita sacramentale tra la Chiesa Cattolica e le altre Chiese e comunità ecclesiali secondo lo 'Schema Codicis Canonicis orientalis,'" Ang 66 (1989) 403–421. [7]Cf. Lanne (n. 1) 23–31. [8]"L'uniatisme, méthode d'union au passé et la recherche actuelle de la plein communion (Document de Balamand)," Irén 66 (1993) 347–356, n. 12 at 349; B. Bobrinskoy, L'uniatisme à la lumière des ecclésiologies qui s'affrontent," Irén 65 (1992) 423–439. [9]"A Note on Terminology," *Eastern Churches Journal* 1 (1993–1994) 152–153. P. Pallath, ed., *Catholic Eastern Churches: Heritage and Identity* (Rome: Mar Thoma Yogam, 1994).

# V

## VATICAN I, Council of (1869–1870)

The First Vatican Council cannot be understood except in the light of the enigmatic personality of Pius IX (q.v.) and the preceding turbulent decades of the 19th century.[1] Pius IX was determined that the papacy would never be humiliated as it had been in the exiles of Pius VI (1775–1799) and Pius VII (1800–1823). His age was a time in which political and intellectual ferments were seen as resulting from the French Revolution and the previous Enlightenment, and thus as being one hostile to the Church. The loss of temporal power, which we can now judge as a necessary condition for the emergence of the universal spiritual power of the papacy,[2] was perceived at the time as a disaster: Pius IX was convinced to the very end of his life that the papal states were required for the survival of the Church.[3]

There was a Catholic restoration after the Congress of Vienna (1814–1815), but it was Ultramontane (v. ULTRAMONTANISM) in character: power, indeed ecclesiastical studies, were being centralized in Rome; the Eternal City became a center of pilgrimage; there was increasing use of the *Index librorum prohibitorum* (v. CENSORSHIP OF BOOKS); the role and activities of papal nuncios expanded; the Church opposed liberalism, though only Italian liberalism was known to Rome, which nonetheless engaged in a sweeping condemnation of all liberalism and liberal ideas; the *Syllabus of Errors* (1864—v. PIUS IX) seemed to turn the Church defensively away from the present and the future; new errors were seen to attack the very fabric of the faith. As early as 1849, the thought of holding a council was on the mind of Pius IX, and though he referred to it occasionally, it was not until 1868 that he officially convoked it.[4] The orientation in the earliest preparatory work was that the council would give

solemn sanction to the major themes of the magisterium of Pius IX. Early in 1869, the influential periodical *La civiltà cattolica* published early in 1869 French correspondence which expressed the hope that the council would concentrate on three matters: a solemn proclamation of the *Syllabus;* papal infallibility; the Assumption of Mary.[5] The council was to take place in the cultural, spiritual, and ecclesiological framework of a Europe dominated by the restoration of authority and of a Church stressing the search for doctrinal and institutional security. Its main theologians were of the Roman School (q.v.).

The council opened on 8 December 1869 with 744 bishops (40 percent of its members were Italian; 121 fathers were from America, 41 from Asia, 61 of oriental rites, almost all from the Middle East, 18 from Oceania, and only 9 from Africa) It soon became clear that the pope's agenda and rules of procedure would not allow great freedom for the expression of views he did not like. As time went on it became clear that the pope would stoop to manipulation and threats in pursuing his ends. In privately scolding the Dominican Cardinal Guidi, he is reported to have stated, *"La tradizione sono io"* (I myself am tradition). The question must arise as to whether or not the council was really free. The comment of the distinguished historian of Vatican I is judicious: "The Vatican Council, without having a full and perfect liberty, had incontestably enough for the validity of its acts."[6] Again, from the very outset there was a division between the infallibilists and the anti-infallibilists, called "liberals" or even "heretics" by the former.

On 28 December 1869 the Council began work on the document on revelation prepared by the Roman theologian J.B. Franzelin.[7] It was unfavorably received. The council approved a profession of faith on

6 January 1870.[8] It also discussed documents on the clergy[9] and on the opportuneness of a universal catechism (q.v.).[10] Nothing would come of these last two initiatives.

After redrafting by J. Kleutgen, the document on revelation was debated for four weeks beginning 22 March 1870. By then it had four instead of the previous eighteen chapters. It was approved as the constitution *Dei Filius*[11] on 24 April by 667 votes, with neither contrary votes nor abstentions. Its prologue summarized the principal errors that had emerged after Trent: Protestantism, which has collapsed into a multiplicity of sects *(in sectas paullatim dissolutas esse multiplices);* rationalism or naturalism; pantheism, materialism, and atheism. It noted that members of the Church had strayed along these erroneous paths. The prologue in the name of Pius IX referred to the bishops of the entire world as sitting and judging with him. Chapter 1, on God the Creator of all things, reaffirms faith in the one, true God by paraphrasing the Nicene Creed (v. NICAEA and CREEDS). Chapter 2, on revelation, affirmed the knowability of God and the inspiration of Scripture. Chapter 3, on faith, had an important ecclesiological text which stated that "the Church herself by reason of her astonishing propagation, her outstanding holiness and inexhaustible fertility in every kind of goodness, by her catholic unity and her unconquerable stability, is a kind of great and perpetual motive of credibility and an incontrovertible evidence of her own divine mission."[12] It also proposed the distinction between solemn judgment and the ordinary and universal magisterium.[13] Chapter 4 dealt with faith and reason.[14] Eighteen canons under anathema followed, which were aimed at the particular errors treated in these chapters, especially those espoused by G. Hermes (1775–1831) and A. Günther (1783–1863).[15]

In the meantime the issue of infallibility (q.v.) was simmering in the background. Almost from the beginning of the council there were those who wanted to take up the issue of infallibility, and some wanted it passed by acclamation. The *Deputatio de Fide,* the commission which would deal with it, was packed with those favorable to the definition of infallibility. This was the work of Cardinal Manning and of others, several of whom took an oath at the beginning of the council to do their utmost to get it defined.

As early as 21 January the fathers received a schema on the Church by the German K. Schrader, another member of the Roman School (q.v.), consisting of 15 chapters followed by 21 canons.[16] It opened with an affirmation of the Church as the Mystical Body of Christ, but reflected a theology of "perfect society" (q.v.).[17] Significantly, it treated neither of bishops nor of infallibility; it was not well received by the fathers of the council. Numerous observations were made. While these were being processed, and during the attempt to improve the appalling acoustics of the council chamber, there was ample opportunity to attempt a reconciliation or rapprochement between the bitterly divided camps; the will for such did not exist. It was decided at this time to leave aside the rest of the schema on the Church for the time being and to concentrate on the question of papal primacy and infallibility.

On 6 March a text on infallibility was distributed which was to be considered along with the existing chapter 11 on the papal primacy. This latter caused a lot of unease in the way it treated the jurisdiction of the pope over the Church. The minority claimed that not only were their observations not properly considered, but they were not even noted.[18]

On 13 May the fathers began a general debate on the text "The Roman Pontiff" (v. PAPAL PRIMACY). Fourteen meetings were devoted to the general discussion of this draft, the majority of interventions being on the opportuneness or otherwise of a definition of infallibility. On 2 June there was a closure motion, felt by the minority to be a real act of violence.[19] Almost the whole of June and the first days of July were devoted to a detailed examination of the text: the prologue and the first two chapters occupied two meetings; the chapter on the primacy took five meetings, and the rest of the time was spent on the infallibility chapter. Meanwhile the German Jesuit J. Kleutgen was at work drafting "The Second Constitution on the Church," in ten chapters with sixteen canons.[20] But circumstances dictated that it would never be considered by the council, and so the work of the council remained one-sided and incomplete. On 11 July there was an important four-hour discourse by Bishop Vincent Gasser explaining the infallibility text.[21]

Despite this, nearly a quarter of the assembly failed to vote positively on 13 July. The solemn vote took place on 18 July: 533 voted in favor of the Constitution, *Pastor aeternus,* two voted against, possibly through error. Those 61 who opposed had left Rome to avoid the scandal of voting against the known wishes of the pope. All afterwards submitted to the council definitions (v. PAPAL PRIMACY and INFALLIBILITY). A number of Catholics, led by J.J. Döllinger (q.v.), refused to accept and were excommunicated. Some of them, but not he, joined the Old Catholics (q.v.), a schismatic Church. The day after the definitions, the Franco-Prussian war broke out. Though there were some sessions until 20 October, when the council was suspended *sine die,* nothing of significance was achieved.

The council never made a statement on the bishops that would have balanced its teaching on the papacy. Bismarck would later try to stir up the German bishops against the pope, but he failed in the attempt (v. BISHOPS). Both major documents of the council, viz., on revelation and on the papacy, would serve the Church in the Modernist (q.v.) period, giving clear guidance on key issues. Despite its unbalanced ecclesiology, the council did not block the emergence of an ecclesiological renewal which would culminate in the complementary council, Vatican II.

[1]G. Alberigo, "Il concilio Vaticano I (1869–1870)," in idem, ed., Storia dei concili 371–396; R. Aubert, *Vatican I.* Histoire des conciles 12 (Paris: Orante, 1964); idem, in Jedin-Dolan 8:315-330; AA.VV. *De doctrina concilii Vaticani primi: Studia selecta annis 1948–1964 scripta* (Vatican, 1969)—multilingual; J.A. Burgess, "The Historical Background of Vatican I," in P.C. Empie et al., eds., *Teaching Authority and Infallibility in the Church.* Lutherans and Roman Catholics in Dialogue 6 (Minneapolis: Augsburg, 1978) 287–297, 360–366; C. Butler, *The Vatican Council 1869–1870* (London, 1930, reissued London: Collins Fontana, 1962); O. Chadwick, *The Secularization of the European Mind in the Nineteenth Century* (Cambridge: UP, 1975); Y. Congar, "L'ecclésiologie, de la Révolution française au Concile du Vatican, sous le signe de l'affirmation de l'autorité," in AA.VV. *L'ecclésiologie au XIXe siècle.* US 34 (Paris, 1960) 77–114; K. Schatz, *Vaticanum I, 1869–1870.* Vol. 1 (Paderborn: Schöningh, 1992).    [2]Congar (n. 1) 98.    [3]Burgess (n. 1) 289.    [4]Alberigo (n. 1) 371–373.    [5]Ibid., 374.    [6]R. Aubert, Vatican I (n. 1) 246.    [7]Mansi 58:58-119 (v. ROMAN SCHOOL); D. Massimo, "Franzelin e l'ecclesiologia del Vaticano I," HoTheol 9 (1991) 61–100; idem, "L'apporto del Franzelin alla stesura della Pastor aeterns e al dibattito sull' infallibilità," ibid., 157–194.    [8]Tanner 2:802-803.    [9]Mansi 50:517-522.    [10]Mansi 50:699-702; 51:454-456.    [11]Mansi 51:31-38/Tanner 2:804-811/DS 3000–3045/ND 412–418, 113–140.    [12]Tanner 2:807-808/DS 3013/ND 123; cf. R. Schlund, "Zur Quellenfrage der vatikanischen Lehre von der Kirche als Glaubwürdigkeitsgrund," ZKT 62 (1950) 443–459 = *De doctrina* (n. 1) 27–45.    [13]Tanner 2:807/DS 3011/ND 121; cf. M. Caudron, "Magistère ordinaire et infallibilité pontificale d'après la Constitution 'Dei Filius,'" ETL 36 (1960) 393–431; P. Nau, "Le magistère pontifical ordinaire au premier Concile du Vatican," RThom 62 (1962) 341–397 both = *De doctrina* (n. 1) 122–220.    [14]Tanner 2:808-809/DS 3015–3020/ND 131–136; see G. Paradis, "Foi et raison au premier Concile du Vatican," BLitEc 63 (1962) 200–226, 268–292; 64 (1963) 9–25 = *De doctrina* (n. 1) 221–281    [15]Tanner 2:809-811/DS 3021–3043/ND 414–418, 115–117, 125–130, 137–139.    [16]"*Supremi pastoris*"—Mansi 50:539-636.    [17]P. Granfield, "The Church as Societas perfecta in the Schemata of Vatican I," ChurchHist 46 (1979) 431–446.    [18]Alberigo (n. 1) 385. See M. O'Gara, *Triumph in Defeat: Infallibility, Vatican I and the French Minority Bishops* (Washington, D.C.: The Catholic University of America Press, 1988) with reviews ETL 65 (1989) 412–419 (G. Thils) and Greg 70 (1989) 568–570 (F.A. Sullivan).    [19]Ibid., 386.    [20]Mansi 53:308-317.    [21]Mansi 52:1204-1230; J.T. O'Connor, trans. and ed., *The Gift of Infallibility The Official Relatio on Infallibility of Bishop Vincent Gasser at Vatican Council I* (Boston: St. Paul, 1986). See K. McDonnell, "Infallibility as Charism and Vatican I," in Empie (n. 1) 270–286 = OneChr 15 (1975) 21–39.

## VATICAN II, Council of (1962–1965)

Vatican I (q.v.) was suspended *sine die* on 20 October 1870. Some people later wondered if after the decrees on papal primacy (q.v.) and infallibility (q.v.) a council would ever again be necessary.[1] Indeed the decisive actions of Pius X (q.v.) in the Modernist period would lead people to have confidence in the action of the pope alone. The 1917 *Code of Canon Law,* however, did treat of a general council (CIC 222–229).

As early as 1922 Pius XI (q.v.) considered reconvening Vatican I or convoking a new council.[2] When the documents of Vatican I were reexamined, it was thought that there was sufficient material prepared for a council, and the consultors made further suggestions of topics.[3] Pius XI sought the advice of the bishops with a view to having a council on the occasion of the Holy Year in 1925; only a tenth seem to have rejected the idea. But some, especially Cardinal Ehrle, strongly advised the pope against having a council, and the idea was abandoned in 1924.

Several people have gone on record as having advised Pius XII (q.v.) to have a council.[4] The pope decided that investigations about a possible council should be in the hands of a special commission from within the then Holy Office which met in great secrecy from March 1948 until January 1951. A substantial amount of work was done by the commission, which did not seem aware of what had been done in the 1920s. Subcommissions were also nominated and were active. But there were divergent views about the kind of council it should be, and difficulties were foreseen which would seem to have led to Pius XII's abandonment of the idea. However, it was to have had some later influence: the preparatory documents were used by Pius XII, for example, in the encyclical *Humani generis;*[5] John XXIII in 1959 authorized the Antepreparatory Commission for Vatican II to take account of the documents retained in the Holy Office; some of the members of the 1940s commission would play a notable part at the council, e.g., Cardinals Bea, Ottaviani, Parente, and Brown.

There yet is no critical history of Vatican II; a brief account by H. Jedin is perhaps the best available report.[6] There is a valuable Chronicle in Italian, and journalistic accounts in various languages.[7] These, though valuable, have to be read with caution, as they are not always fully accurate and sometimes reflect the emotive reactions at the time; a calmer evaluation of persons and events is often called for.

As is well known, the idea of a council, sprung on the cardinals by John XXIII on 25 January 1959, was coolly received. In general one can say that from the Roman Curia the pope received little enthusiasm and much hindrance (v. JOHN XXIII).[8] Before the council there was in the Church a wide gap between the creative studies in ecclesiology, chiefly from biblical, patristic, and ecumenical perspectives, and what was emerging from the magisterium and being taught in manual theology.[9] There was a determined effort to block the new insights.

An Antepreparatory Commission was established on 17 May 1959. It received 2,812 submissions (*postulate*).[10] Ten Preparatory Commissions were set up on

5 June 1960.[11] On parity with them was the Secretariat for Christian Unity which John XXIII had established in 1960; it would not be until the first session that the Secretariat would reach its potential. Unlike the commission of Vatican I, one half of members of the preparatory commissions were future voting members of the council; 28 percent of them were members of the Roman Curia; the others were bishops from around the world and theologians called "experts" (periti). They sifted the material received and prepared drafts, which were sent to the Central Commission.[12] The seventy-six schemata were rather a summary of previous magisterial positions and had little new theology or insights. Though they would provide a resource for the council, very little of them was approved in the form in which they were first sent to the council members.[13] At this stage the proceedings were very much dominated by curial members and Roman theologians in the various commissions. A number of the outstanding theologians of the Church were at first excluded, only later, at the insistence of bishops and in some cases of the pope, becoming periti. There were signs of tension in the years of preparation: the Roman Synod (1960) was a disappointment in being very traditional; the papal constitution imposing Latin as the vehicle of theological instruction was seen as retrogressive;[14] expectations of the council were high in some countries and people began to look for decisive changes;[15] there was growing interest in the ecumenical dimensions of the council.

When the council opened on 11 October 1962, it became clear that for all its intensive preparation, the working procedures were not geared for their task. The direction of the council was committed to a group of ten cardinals; later four moderators would be appointed to facilitate the running of the council (1963). At its opening there were 2,540 council members, less than one-fifth (379) of whom were Italians: bishops (including cardinals and patriarchs) and heads (generals) of male religious institutes. There were also observers from various other Christian bodies (Protestants being notably stronger than Easterners). From the second session (1963) there were guests (auditores—"hearers") who did not have a right to intervene; from the third session (1964) these included some women.

The official language about the council's activity used a traditional and technical terminology. There were four sessions (11 Oct.–8 Dec. 1962; 29 Sept.–4 Dec. 1963; 14 Sept.–21 Nov. 1964; 14 Sept.–8 Dec. 1965). There were ten solemn (public) congregations: these were liturgical occasions, attended by the pope, and were opening and closing assemblies, and ones for the approbation of documents. The ordinary work of the council consisted of 186 general congregations which were devoted to speeches and voting. A particular feature of the general congregations was the fact that

bishops wishing to speak had to indicate the fact some days in advance. Thus the cut-and-thrust of parliamentary debate did not take place as speaker following speaker delivered a prepared text. Members could also submit written texts for the consideration of the conciliar commissions. All of these speeches and written submissions, as well as all the documentation supplied to the council members, have now been published, but in the Latin, in which practically all the council interventions were made.[16] It should be remembered that the early commentaries on Vatican II did not have this ample material available, and all would need revision in the light of it. Many doctoral theses have been written on the council since this documentation appeared; these cast much light on how the council's teaching developed on particular issues. The time is now ripe for a second generation of commentaries, such as have already appeared on LG, chapter 8.[17]

Most of the individual documents of the council are treated in this work under their topics. What follows is a brief outline of the stages of the council's work.

The council opened with a most significant address by John XXIII (q.v.). The first session had a period of settling in, with procedural matters being important at the beginning; the significant number of non-curial bishops elected to the various conciliar commissions had to find their feet. This was an important time in the council's history as two different groups began to emerge. Words like "conservative/traditionalist/right," "progressive/ecumenical/left" are only of limited use in this context. But the fact remains that there was a group basically representing the views of the Vatican Curia and its theologians, and a larger group which was more open to new ideas.[18] The early days of the council showed that the curial view, reflected in the documentation already received by the council members, was not going to dominate the council. John XXIII, and Paul VI after him, ensured that this minority was not crushed, but it was not, however, allowed to dictate the outcome of the council, which in the end always managed to arrive at consensus on each document.

The first document discussed was on liturgy (q.v.), and it occasioned a clear clash of various views. When the council reached an impasse during its discussion of the document on revelation, John XXIII resolved it by setting up a mixed commission jointly chaired by Cardinals Ottaviani and Bea, each representing strongly held opposed positions; this commission was to revise the document thoroughly. A schema on the means of social communication was better received. The council next considered a schema on the Eastern Churches (q.v.), which was poorly received. Lastly the constitution on the Church was presented (v. LUMEN GENTIUM). This draft, which largely reflected the "perfect society" (q.v.) view of the Church typical of the magisterium of the previous century, was harshly received. All these documents were sent back for revision.

The first session failed to produce any document. But even if the council had never met again, its expression of the evident pluralism (q.v.) existing in the Church was a significant witness. This pluralism indeed scandalized some, who saw it as confusion; but it laid to rest forever the numbing uniformity which had been passing for unity in the Church (v. ONE).

At the end of the first session it was clear that the number of documents would have to be reduced and the procedures of the council streamlined. John XXIII set up a Coordinating Commission, which would be vital for the future work of the council. When he died on 3 June 1963, the council was automatically suspended. But Paul VI (q.v.) lost no time in reconvening it after his election on 21 June.

Paul VI gave the council four clear guidelines at the opening of its second session on 21 September 1963: a doctrinal statement on the nature of the Church; its inner renewal; promotion of unity of Christians; dialogue of the Church with today's world.[19]

The second session began with a consideration of the document on the Church, and the members spent most of October discussing it. The crucial issues were sacramentality and collegiality of the episcopate, the restoration of the diaconate, and whether the council should speak of the Virgin Mary (q.v.) in this document or issue a separate one on her. The constitution was sent back for further revision, as was the decree on ecumenism (v. ECUMENISM, RCC), which was discussed next. This last had chapters on the Jews and on religious liberty (v. FREEDOM, RELIGIOUS) which would become part of different documents. At the end of the session the Constitution on the Liturgy and the Decree on the Media of Social Communication were solemnly approved.

After the second session, Paul VI made a visit to Jerusalem where he met Ecumenical Patriarch Athenagoras, 4–6 January 1964. This move aroused great interest, and helped to focus the ecumenical intent of the council.

The third session opened with a Mass concelebrated by twenty-four council members; it was a symbolic act indicating that the liturgy constitution was already being implemented. The council again considered the Church document; it had test votes, all positive, on its then thirty-nine sections, all of which were positive. There was again discussion as to how the Virgin Mary should be treated. The document on the pastoral office of bishops was discussed, but 1,741 amendments were proposed on its first two chapters, indicating that serious revision was needed. The chapter on religious freedom from the document on ecumenism was sharply debated and sent for further revision. The declaration

on the Jews was also debated, showing how bishops from the Middle East were under pressure from Arab governments not to appear to recognize the State of Israel. The constitution on revelation was, surprisingly, rather calmly debated, but a minority, which though small was influential, objected to the way in which the council appeared to deviate from a line of theological thought which had its origin in Trent. More texts were introduced in this session. All of them received many emendations and were sent back for revision: ministry and life of priests (v. PRIESTS, MINISTERIAL), missions (q.v.) lay apostolate (v. apostolate), renewal of religious life (q.v.), formation of priests, schema 13 on the Church in the World, marriage (q.v.).

There were moves to stifle the document on religious freedom, but after an appeal to the pope, a guarantee was given that it would be treated first in the next session. When the decree on ecumenism was almost ready for voting, it was revealed that Paul VI had suggested forty emendations to the text; only nineteen were accepted by the commission, none of which were substantive.

Both this action of the pope and the fact that not all of his suggestions were accepted were significant indications of the dynamic operating between the pope and council. Added to this was the fact that though the pope had urged the acceptance of the document on the missions in the *aula* (council hall, viz., St. Peter's), it was decisively rejected after blunt criticism, notably by a missionary, Bishop D. Lamont, of the then Southern Rhodesia. Again, the pope judged that a debate on clerical celibacy and contraception were inopportune. The bishops, realizing the complexity of the issues in the document on marriage, passed it over to the pope during the third session. The pope also influenced the council indirectly in several ways: his encyclical *Ecclesiam suam* (1964)[20] encouraged the idea of dialogue with other religions and the world. Further, at the end of the third session, he proclaimed the Virgin Mary "Mother of the Church,"[21] an act which would seem to have arisen both out of his personal conviction as well as out of an attempt to succor those who had been disappointed with chapter 8 of the Constitution on the Church. The activity of the pope during the council was thus both indirect and direct. He took the initiative, or approved suggestions, for the better organization the council's work.[22] He exercised strong direction through the four moderators, Cardinals Agagianian, Doepfner, Lercaro, and Suenens (q.v.), whom he appointed at the beginning of the second session, and who met weekly during the council.[23]

Three decrees were promulgated at the final general congregation of the third session (1964), viz., the Constitution on the Church, the decrees on Ecumenism and on the Oriental Catholic Churches.

The fourth session was marked by an extraordinary amount of voting, with some pauses for the commissions to prepare modified texts. There were still problems with the document on religious freedom and the one on the Jews, the latter becoming a declaration on non-Christian religions and dealing also with faiths other than Judaism. It did, however, state that the guilt for the death of Jesus could not be laid on the Jews living at that time without distinction, nor Jews of today. At the general congregation of 28 October 1965 five texts were promulgated: bishops, religious life, priestly formation, religious education, non-Christian religions. With frenetic work in the commissions, two more documents were ready for promulgation at the solemn congregation of 18 November: revelation, apostolate of the laity. The remaining documents were promulgated on 7 December: religious freedom, missionary activity, priestly ministry, and the Church in the modern world. A document on indulgences dropped out during this session. The council ended with the solemn congregation on 8 December 1965.

From a sociological viewpoint, the council resembled a huge committee which had managed through subcommittees to produce consensus documents. One of the great calls at the council was for decentralization. It is a paradox that much of the postconciliar work depended on renewed centralization. It was left to Paul VI to see to the implementation of much of the council. He quickly moved on liturgy, establishing the Consilium for its implementation and astutely choosing H. Bugnini (q.v.) as its energetic and forceful secretary. Through the apostolic letter mp. *Ecclesiae sanctae,*[24] he laid the ground for renewal in three key areas: bishops and priests, religious, and the missions. Even during the council he began to implement its decrees: he established a pontifical commission for means of social communication;[25] he approved a new secretariat for non-Christians to help the council's work[26]; as early as 15 September 1965 he had laid down the grounds for the establishment of the Synod of Bishops (q.v.).[27] Within a month of the ending of the council he set up five postconciliar commissions: on bishops, religious, missions, Christian education, apostolate of the laity. At the same time he confirmed existing commissions: liturgy, the media, reform of canon law, Christian unity, non-Christian religions, and non-believers.[28] He also soon took steps to begin the reform of the Vatican Curia (v. VATICAN).[29] While at one level one can admire the vigor with which Paul VI set about implementing the council, one can also note that it seems in some ways to have been more in virtue of his primacy rather than as an exercise of collegiality; the fact that so much of the implementation took place *motu proprio* is not without significance, at least symbolic.[30] Tensions, however, already present in the council, soon erupted widely in the

Church. It is surely one of the great achievements of Paul VI that he managed to keep pressing forward with the council's renewal program, while avoiding schism either from the right or the left.

In the thirty-four years since the opening of Vatican II it has been possible to make some evaluations and to indicate some of the council's achievements, failures, and incomplete realization. In the years which followed its conclusion, it suffered from manifold interpretations of its texts and appeals to the spirit of the council to support widely diverging viewpoints. In an insightful article, J.W. O'Malley notes that compared with other reforms in the 11th and 16th centuries, there was a lack of clarity in the council's aims and rhetoric, arising precisely from the decision of John XXIII not to make condemnations: a condemnation by implication always shows clearly the opposite or orthodox position. Moreover, the slogan of updating-renewal, both notions implicit and intended by John XXIII with the word *aggiornamento,* could and would be variously interpreted.[31]

Reflections on the council after twenty/twenty five years in various books and journals make clear the fact that the council was responsible for enormous changes in some areas, but was less effective in others.[32] For every positive achievement it would also be possible to indicate a negative feature. Every area of the Church's life was touched on, but the council has as yet failed to renew the Church deeply. Beneath such superficial observations there lies a deeper problem of the hermeneutic and reception of the council.[33] We have to remember that there was a minority, perhaps 220 bishops of a more traditionalist stance, who had to be satisfied by compromises on the part of the majority, so that the council could reach a consensus in each document.[34] This minority was mollified largely by repeated mention of two previous councils (half of the conciliar references were to Trent and Vatican I) and of earlier papal magisterium (half of the citations of previous popes were to Pius XII). Consensus was not generally achieved by a higher viewpoint which would take up in a richer unity the diverse viewpoints. In some cases, e.g., chapter 8 of LG, the council juxtaposed different viewpoints to gratify the various parties. A hermeneutic of the council has to take account of this procedure and avoid an imposition of one viewpoint in the interpretation of certain texts. Crucial was the inability of the council to go beyond the gains of the theology of the 1950s to the creativity which John XXIII sensed was needed for the spirit of the times. The council at best represented the finest contemporary theology. It also received the teaching of the earlier councils, putting them into wider perspective, e.g., the re-presentation of papal primacy and infallibility within the context of collegiality,[35] or the ecclesial and pneumatological depth (to some extent at least) given to traditional sacramental theology from Florence (q.v.) and Trent.

One of the significant achievements of the council was to open up the rather narrow theology of recent magisterium. This was realized by the presence of theologians and bishops from the whole world refusing to be constricted by the narrow Roman theology of the prepared drafts of council texts. The role of theologians can be exaggerated; Vatican II was a bishops' pastoral council within which the theologians were essential.[36] A feature of the post-Vatican II Church is that now that the bishops and their theologians are no longer gathered together, we are again encountering a restricted theology in magisterial documents coming both from the pope and the Vatican congregations—notwithstanding Paul VI's attempts to internationalize the Curia. Neither the synods of bishops nor the International Theological Commission (q.v.) have always been able to escape what at times appears to be a stranglehold of curial theology.

In the post-Vatican II period there has been a dialectic between the institutional view of the Church and the new openings from the council, especially in LG, UR, and GS. Though neither has emerged victorious,[37] it would seem that in some cases, there is greater weight given to what were the concerns of the minority of the council rather than to new beginnings supported by the will of the majority. Thus, despite the dependence of the new *Code of Canon Law* on the ecclesiology of Vatican II, some have noted in places a certain ambivalence.[38] It must also be said that although some would consider Vatican II as being primarily juridical, from this latter point of view its ecclesiology has, at times, been accused of much unresolved ambiguity,[39] which has led to people choosing what they consider to be the "mind" of Vatican II.

There is not one theology of Vatican II, but several. Since A. Acerbi's often cited book,[40] it has been common to speak of two ecclesiologies of Vatican II. Though he is right in stating that the juridical and communion approaches to ecclesiology have not been resolved in the postconciliar period, one can argue that in the council itself there is already found a resolution of the tension. For this we have to see chapter 2 of LG as being a communion approach, and to note carefully that chapter 3 speaks of a hierarchical communion (v. BISHOPS, COLLEGIALITY). The Holy Spirit is the principle of both communion and hierarchy (LG 4, 10–11).[41] In the post-Vatican II period the selectivity of authors, both magisterial and theological, has faced the Church with a bewildering number of presentations of what has purported to be the authentic mind of Vatican II. Within ecclesiology itself, one can suggest that since the council the Vatican I view of the papacy has, in practice, been quite dominant in the Church,

notwithstanding some attempt to incorporate elements of the reception of this earlier council into Vatican II.

The 1985 Synod (q.v.)[42] was an examination of the reception of the four constitutions of Vatican II: Liturgy, Church, Revelation, Church in the Modern World. The evaluation was overall positive, but several deviations and areas requiring further study were noted. Faced with problems in the use and interpretation of the notion of the People of God (q.v.), the synod spoke rather of communion (q.v.). Indeed the final report notes: "The ecclesiology of communion is a central and fundamental idea in the documents of the council."[43] Though it is clear that the biblical notion of communion (*koinônia*—q.v.), if taken in all its richness, is certainly a profound and overarching notion, it is not, however, clear that all conciliar ecclesiology can easily come under its scope without hopelessly widening the notion of communion so that it loses all specificity. The letter of the Congregation for the Doctrine of the Faith on this question[44] cites an address of Pope John Paul II to the effect that the concept of communion lies "at the heart of the Church's self-understanding";[45] The document seems to portray an anxiety to use communion as a way of stressing Roman primacy and the universal over the local Church and the Roman primacy, and as the preferred expression of the ecumenical movement. It might, however, be accused of representing a partial reading of the council in its failure to integrate the full teaching on the People of God and on the Church in the modern world (GS).

Msgr. P. Delhaye of the International Theological Commission, speaking at the 1985 synod, noted four areas which had been touched on by Vatican II but which had since become crucial: salvation (the Redeemer, the Cross, sin and grace); moral principles; ministerial priesthood; the poor.[46] It would, however, be true to say that without the impulse of Vatican II, it would be most unlikely that we would have seen the rich theologies of liberation (q.v.) and of the basic Christian communities (q.v.) that have emerged since the council. Vatican II has produced rich fruits, and we can await still others.

Some final points should be made. There is a large literature on Protestant and Orthodox evaluations of the council, both by those who were observers and by others.[47] There is also a tiny but extremely vocal minority of Catholics opposed to the council and its subsequent renewal. This group is exemplified by Archbishop Lefebvre (q.v.), but its thinking is by no means confined to his circle.[48] It includes both those who rejected the council outright and those who became worried at the turn events took after the council.[49] Finally, there is an opposite view which states that either the council has been betrayed by the Church's officialdom, which ranges from the highest authorities to local pastors,[50] or that the council only began a process of reflection and *aggiornamento* which must continue to address new questions.[51]

[1]See J. Forget, "Conciles, Nécessité de conciles oecuméniques," DTC 3:669. [2]G. Caprile, "Pie XI et la ripresa del Concilio Vaticano," CivCatt 117 (1966) 3:27-39; idem, "Pio XI, la Curia romana e il concilio: riserve e timori," ibid., 120 (1969) 2:121-133; idem, "Pio XI, la Curia romana e il concilio: pareri favorevoli," ibid., 120 (1969) 2:563-575. [3]F.-C. Uginet, "Les projets de concile générale sous Pie XI et Pie XII," in AA.VV. *Le deuxième concile du Vatican (1959–1965)*. Colloque (Rome 28–30 mai 1986). Collection de l'École Française de Rome 113 (Rome: École Française de Rome, 1989) 65–78. [4]Uginet (n. 3) 75 nn. 20–22; G. Caprile, "Pio XII e un nuovo progetto di concilio ecumenico," CivCatt 117 (1966) 3:209–227; amplified version "Pius XII und das zweite Vatikanische Konzil," in H. Schambeck, ed., *Pius XII: zum Gedächtnis* (Berlin: Duncker & Humblot, 1977) 649–691. [5]AAS 42 (1950) 561–578/Carlen 4:175-184. [6]Jedin-Dolan 10:96-151. [7]G. Caprile, *Il concilio Vaticano II: Chronache del Concilio Vaticano II edite dalla "Civiltà cattolica."* 5 vols. (Rome, 1966–1969); Y. Congar, *Le concile au jour le jour.* 4 vols. (Paris: Cerf, 1963–1966); B. Kloppenburg, *Concílio Vaticano II.* 4 vols. (Petrópolis: Vozes, 1962–1965); R. Laurentin, *L'enjeu du concile.* 5 vols. (Paris: Seuil, 1962–1966); X. Rynne [F.X. Murphy], *Letters from Vatican City., The Second Session., The Third Session., The Fourth Session* (London: Faber & Faber, 1963–1966); *Council Daybook.* 4 vols. (Washington, D.C.: National Catholic Welfare Conference, 1963–1966). [8]A. Indelicato, "La preparazione del Vaticano II," CrNSt 8/2 (1987) 119–133. [9]Y. Congar, "Situation ecclésiologique au moment de "Ecclesiam suam" et passage à une Église dans l'itinéraire des hommes," in *Le concile de Vatican II: Son Église Peuple de Dieu et Corps du Christ.* Théologie historique 71 (Paris: Beauchesne, 1984) 7–32 = AA.VV. *Ecclesiam suam, première lettre encyclique de Paul VI.* Colloque Rome 24–26 octobre 1980 (Brescia: Istituto Paolo VI—Rome: Ed. Studium Vita Nova, 1982) 80–102; G. Martina, "The Historical Context in Which the Idea of a New Ecumenical Council Was Born," in Latourelle, Vatican II, 1:3-73; M. Velati, "Christianity and the Churches on the Eve of Vatican II," CrNSt 12 (1991) 165–175 = REBras 51 (1991) 663–670. [10]*Acta et documenta concilio oecumenico II apparando. Series I, Antepreparatoria.* 4 vols. in 6 parts and 16 tomes (Vatican, 1960–1961). [11]Mp. *Superno Dei nutu*—AAS 52 (1960) 433–437. [12]V. Gómez Mier, "Para una sistematización en los documentos del Concilio Vaticano II," CiuD 202 (1989) 735–746. [13]Acta et documenta concilio Vatican II apparando. Series II, praeparatoria. 3 vols in 7 parts and 7 tomes (Vatican, 1964–1969). [14]*Veterum sapientia*—AAS 54 (1962) 129–135/CleR 47 (1962) 302–306. [15]E.g., K. Rahner, "On the Theology of the Council," ThInvest 5:244-267; H. Küng, *The Council and Reunion* (London—New York, 1961). [16]*Acta synodalia sacrosancti Concilii Vaticani II* (Vatican, 1970–1978). Each of the four sessions has one volume with several parts: 4, 6, 8, 7 respectively. [17]MarSt 37 (1986) 43–164. [18]G. Philips, "Deux tendences dans la théologie contemporaine," NRT 85 (1963) 225–238. [19]ActaSyn 2/1:189-199. [20]AAS 56 (1964) 609–659/Carlen 4:135-160. [21]ActaSyn 3/8:915-918. [22]P. Levillain, "Les choix de Paul VI," in *Le deuxième concile* (n. 3) 463–474. [23]L.J. Suenens, *Memories and Hopes* (Dublin: Veritas, 1992) 125–139. [24]AAS 67 (1966) 757–787/Flannery 1:591-610, 624-633, 857-862. [25]Mp. *In fructibus multis*—AAS 56 (1964) 289–292. [26]AAS 56 (1964) 560, cf. 433, 515, 584. [27]Mp. *Apostolica sollicitudo*—AAS 67 (1965) 775–778. [28]Mp. *Finis concilio*—AAS 58 (1966) 37–40. [29]*Regimini Ecclesiae universalis*—AAS 59 (1967) 885–929 with 881–884. [30]See A. Acerbi, "L'ecclesiologia sottesa alle istituzioni ecclesiali postconciliari," CrNSt 2 (1981) 203–234. [31]"Developments, Reforms and Two Great Reformations: Towards a Historical Assessment of Vatican II," TS 44 (1983) 373–406; see idem, "Reform, Historical Consciousness, and Vatican II's *Aggiornamento,*" TS 32 (1971) 573–601; idem, *Tradition and Transition: Historical Perspectives on Vatican II.* Theology and Life 26 (Wilmington: Glazier, 1989). [32]AA. VV. *Ripensare il concilio.* Collana Cultura e Teologia 2 (Casale Monteferrato: Piemme, 1986); G. Alberigo, ed., *Les Églises après Vatican II: Dynamisme et perspectives.* Théologie historique 61 (Paris: Beauchesne, 1981); G. Alberigo et al., eds., *The Reception of Vatican II* (Washington, D.C.: The Catholic University of America Press—Tunbridge Wells UK: Burns & Oates, 1987); Y. Congar, *Le concile de Vatican II: Son Église Peuple de Dieu et Corps du Christ.* Théologie historique 71 (Paris: Beauchesne, 1984); G.M. Fagin, ed., *Vatican II: Open Questions and New Horizons.* Theology and Life 5 (Wilmington: Glazier—Dublin: Dominican Publications, 1984); A. Falconer et al., eds., *Freedom to Hope: The Catholic Church in Ireland Twenty Years After Vatican II* (Dublin: Columba, 1985); A. Hastings, *Modern Catholicism: Vatican II and After* (London: SPCK, 1991); E. Pérez Delgado et al., *Temas conciliares 25 años despues.* Series Valentina 26 (Valencia: Fac. Teol. S. Vincente Ferrer, 1990); R. Latourelle, ed., *Vatican II Assessment and Perspectives: Twenty-five Years After.* 3 vols—multilingual (Eng. trans. New York—Mahwah: Paulist, 1988); T.E. O'Connell, ed., *Vatican II and its Documents: An American Reappraisal.* Theology and Life 15 (Wilmington: Glazier, 1986); K. Rahner, "The Abiding Significance of the Council," ThInvest 20:90-102; L. Richard et al., eds., *Vatican II: The Unfinished Agenda: A Look to the Future* (New York—Mahwah: Paulist, 1987); M. Simone, ed., *Il concilio venti anni dopo: Le nuove categorie dell'autocomprensione della Chiesa.* Saggi 23 (Rome: A.V.E., 1984); G.H. Tavard, "Vatican II, Understood and Misunderstood," OneChr 27 (1991) 209–221. [33]H.J. Pottmeyer, "A New Phase in the Reception of Vatican II: Twenty Years of Interpretation of Council," in Alberigo, *Reception* (n. 32) 27–43. [34]R.T. Lawerence, "The Building of Consensus: The Conciliar Rules of Procedure and the Evolution of *Dei Verbum,*" Jurist 46 (1986) 474–510. [35]H. Pottmeyer, "Continuità e innovazione nell'ecclesiologia del Vaticano II: L'Influsso del Vatican I sull'ecclesiologia del Vaticano II e la ri-recezione del Vaticano I alla luce del Vaticano II," CrNSt 2 (1981) 71–95; see G. Dejaifve, *Un tournant décisif de l'ecclésiologie à Vatican II.* Le point théologique 31 (Paris: Beauchesne, 1978). [36]See J.F. Kobler, "Were Theologians the Engineers of Vatican II?," Greg 70 (1989) 233–250. [37]N. Nissiotis, "Towards a New Ecumenical Age," EcuR 37 (1985) 326–335; G. Thils, *L'après-Vatican II un nouvel âge de l'Église.* Cahiers de la RTLv 13 (Louvain-la-Neuve: Faculté de Théologie, 1985). [38]E. Corecco, "Aspects of the Reception of Vatican II in the Code of Canon Law," in Alberigo, *Reception* (n. 32) 249–296. [39]K. Walf, "Lacune e ambiguità nell'ecclesiologia del Vaticano II," CrNSt 2 (1981) 187–201. [40]*Due ecclesiologie Ecclesiologia giuridica ed ecclesiologia di comunione nella "Lumen gentium"* (Bologna: Dehoniane, 1975); see B.-D. de la Soujeole, "L'Église comme société et l'Église comme communion au deuxième concile du Vatican," RThom 91 (1991) 219–258. [41]See P. Mullins, *The Teaching of Lumen gentium on the Holy Spirit: The Holy Spirit Was Sent at Pentecost in Order That He Might Continually Sanctify the Church.* Diss. exc. (Rome: Gregorian UP, 1991—full text Ann Arbor: UMI, 1991, number 3266). [42]*Synode extraordinaire: Célébration de Vatican II* (Paris: Cerf, 1986); A. Dulles, *The Reshaping of Catholicism: Current Challenges in the Theology of the Church* (San Francisco: Harper & Row, 1988) 184–206; A. Denaux, "L'Église communion: Réflections à propos du rapport final du Synod extraordinaire de 1985," NRT 110 (1988) 16–37, 161–180; J.A. Komonchak, "The Synod of 1985 and the Nature of the Church," ChicSt 26 (1987) 330–345; Conc 188 (1986). [43]*Synode extraordinaire* (n. 40) 559. [44]"The Church as Communion" (22 May 1992)—CathIntern 3 (1992) 761–767.

[45]Ibid., n. 3.  [46]*Synode extraordinaire* (n. 40) 373–375.  [47]J.M.R. Tillard, "La réception de Vatican II par les non-Catholiques," in G.R. Evans, ed., *Christian Authority.* FS H. Chadwick (Oxford: Clarendon, 1988) 20–39; R. McAfee Brown, *Observer in Rome: A Protestant Report on the Vatican Council* (Garden City, N.Y.: Doubleday, 1964); J. Bosc et al., *Points de vue des théologiens protestantes: Études sur les decréts du concile Vatican II.* US 64 (Paris: Cerf, 1967); J.H. Millar, ed., *Vatican II: An Interfaith Appraisal* (Notre Dame—London: Notre Dame UP, 1966); J. Moorman, *Vatican Observed: An Anglican Impression of Vatican II* (London: Darton, Longman & Todd, 1967); idem, "Observers and Guests at the Council," in A. Stacpoole, *Vatican II by Those Who Were There* (London: Chapman, 1986); A.C. Outler, "'Strangers Within the Gates'" ibid., 170–183; L. Vischer, "The Reception of the Debate on Collegiality," in Alberigo, *Reception* (n. 32) 233–248.  [48]E.g., F. Spadafora, *La tradizione contra il concilio: L'apertura a sinistra del Vaticano 2* (Rome: Ed. Pol—Volpe, 1989).  [49]D. Menozzi, "Opposition to the Council," in Alberigo, Reception (n. 32) 325–348; cf. N. Colaianni, "Criticism of the Second Vatican Council in Recent Literature," Conc 167 (1983) 106–110.  [50]See H. Küng and L. Swidler, eds., *The Church in Anguish: Has the Vatican Betrayed Vatican II?* (San Francisco: Harper & Row, 1987).  [51]L. Richard et al. eds., *Vatican II: The Unfinished Agenda—A Look to the Future* (New York—Mahwah: Paulist, 1987).

## VATICAN CURIA

The word "curia" is taken from lay magistrature or imperial language. It was used of any court, ecclesiastical or lay. It had developed a well-established usage by the pontificate of Urban II (1088–1099). It is unlikely that such a term would have come into use had the Western Church not lost living contact with the East and been so taken up with Latin concerns.[1]

The history of the Curia is clear from the Middle Ages.[2] In the previous centuries, at least from about the time of Gregory I (q.v.), a simple structure existed: the Roman synod met weekly and dealt with matters referred to Rome. Then two bodies developed: the chancellery, which issued documents, and the camera, responsible for taxes and finance. With the reform of Gregory VII (q.v.), there was a growing centralization, and the consistory or group of cardinals gradually became important. Juridical responsibilities were added accordingly as it became more common to appeal to Rome against local judgments.

Even in his time St. Bernard (q.v.) was very concerned about the quality of those who worked in the papal bureaucracy.[3] From medieval times to the Reformation the calls for a reform of the Church "head and members" envisaged not just the pope but more especially the Curia. With Avignon (v. SCHISM, GREAT WESTERN) there was further centralization. The papacy, too, became more highly personalized, so that there were two moral bodies handing down decisions and favors: the pope and the Curia. Moreover, the Curia had to be supported; tariffs were payable for all documents furnished by Rome, and other taxes were imposed. The Curia grew as did nepotism and corruption of various kinds, moral as well as financial. By the time of the Reformation change was badly needed.

Sixtus V reformed the Curia in 1588, setting up fifteen permanent congregations of cardinals. This weakened the consistory as a body: the congregations now had both legislative and administrative functions. The word for a Greek law court, "dicastery," was used for curial bodies. Efficiency resulted from this reform. But the congregations developed a life of their own and became increasingly impervious to any outside influence, even from the pope. John XXIII was not the first pope to have been frustrated by what should have been "his" Curia.

By the 20th century, dicasteries had multiplied; some dealing with the papal states, nonexistent since 1870, were redundant. Pius X reorganized the Curia in 1908.[4] He set up eleven congregations, three tribunals, and five offices; he sought to avoid overlapping. With some modifications this reorganization entered the 1917 *Code of Canon Law* (canons 242–264). Though reconstituted, the mentality of the Curia was unchanged. Even a strong pope like Pius XII (q.v.) had difficulties with the Curia.[5]

At Vatican II many bishops complained about the Curia, especially about the need to have recourse to it in the running of their own dioceses. They sought reform, and the urbane language of CD 9–10[6] covered over a lot of episcopal frustration. Paul VI reformed the Curia in a number of documents centering on *Regimine Ecclesiae universae* (1967).[7] Despite this pope's advantage of having served in the Curia, the reforms were not fully effectual and seem not to have answered the desires of the council.[8] Centralization continued: the Curia, which had 185 officials in 1900, grew to 2,866 in 1967 and 3,146 by 1977 (not all resident in Rome or full-time).[9] The notions of subsidiarity (q.v.) and communion (q.v.) did not find very clear expression in the central administration of the Church.

The revised canon law gave two general canons on the Curia as principles, leaving their implementation to particular law: "The Supreme Pontiff usually conducts the business of the universal Church by means of the Roman Curia, which fulfills its duty in his name and by his authority for the good and service of the Church . . ." (CIC 360). The Apostolic See, or Holy See, in the law applies not only to the pope but also to the dicasteries (CIC 361). There was still another reorganization in 1988 with John Paul II's *Pastor bonus*.[10]It is still too soon to evaluate the latest reforms.

A listing of the bodies with a summary indication of their competence and the date of their first establishment (and reorganization) will give some idea of the structure and complexity of the Roman Curia. This information is expanded in the Vatican yearbook *Annuario pontificio,* which may not always seem to catch in Italian the nuances of distinctive prepositions *pro/de* ("for/on") of the Latin *Pastor bonus*. The Curia comprises congregations, tribunals, councils, offices.

The *Secretariat of State* (1487) immediately assists the Pope. Then follow the congregations. The *Congregation for the Doctrine of the Faith* (1588, formally the Holy Office) deals with questions of faith and morals, with all Vatican documents having implications in these areas having to be cleared by this congregation. The *Congregation for Eastern Churches* (1862) treats issues dealing with Eastern Catholics. The *Congregation for Divine Worship and the Discipline of the Sacraments* (1908, 1969) handles issues of liturgy, as well as processing petitions for marriages *"ratum/non-consummatum."* The *Congregation of the Causes of Saints* (1558) treats of beatifications, canonizations, relics. The *Congregation for Bishops* (1588, 1908) deals with erection/suppression of dioceses, naming of bishops, "ad limina" visits; it has a subsidiary Pontifical Commission for Latin America (1958). The *Congregation for Evangelization of Peoples* (1599; from 1622 called Propaganda Fidei) is responsible for all missionary activity except territories of Eastern Churches. The *Congregation for the Clergy* (1564 as Congregation for the Council) deals with secular priests and deacons, dispensations from clerical state, catechetical work; it has a subsidiary Pontifical Commission for the Preservation of Artistic and Historical Patrimony (1988). The *Congregation for Institutes of Consecrated Life and Societies of Apostolic Life* (1586) handles matters about religious, secular institutes, societies of apostolic life, hermits, virgins, and dispensations relative to these. The *Congregation for Christian Education (of Seminaries and Institutes of Studies)* [the official title retains these parentheses] (1588, 1824, 1908, 1967) treats of education, Catholic schools, seminaries, Catholic universities.

Second, there are the tribunals. The *Apostolic Penitentiary* (12th century) deals with matters of internal forum. The *Supreme Tribunal of the Apostolic Signatura* (13th century) is the highest judicial body in the Church. The *Tribunal of the Roman Rota* (13th century) is the judicial tribunal of first, second, and third instance.

Third, there are several pontifical councils; these were upgraded in 1988 from previously being secretariats and commissions. They have a certain autonomy but are obliged in some cases to relate to one or more congregations. The *Pontifical Council for the Laity* (1967) has the responsibility of promoting the laity in all fields. The *Pontifical Council for the Promotion of the Unity of Christians* (1960) fosters ecumenism; it has a special section, Commission for Religious Relations with Judaism. The *Pontifical Council for the Family* (1973, 1981) treats all aspects of family. The *Pontifical Council on Justice and Peace* (1967) is concerned with justice and peace issues,

human rights, social teaching, while working closely with the Secretariat of State. The *Pontifical Council "Cor unum"* (1971) aids relief work and charitable efforts. The *Pontifical Council for the Pastoral Care of Migrants and Tourists (Itineranti—1970)* deals with questions affecting migrants, refugees, travelers, religious dimension of pilgrimages. The *Pontifical Council for the Pastoral Care of Health Workers* (1985) has an interest in all matters regarding health care and sickness. The *Pontifical Council for the Interpretation of Legislative Texts* (1917) gives authoritative interpretations of universal Church law, assists other dicasteries with legal texts, reviews general decrees of episcopal conferences for legal issues. The *Pontifical Council for Interreligious Dialogue* (1964) promotes dialogue with other religions; it has a special section, Commission for Religious Relations with Islam (1974). *The Pontifical Council for Dialogue with Non-Believers* (1965) studies atheism and dialogue with non-believers. The *Pontifical Commission on Culture* (1982) promotes culture, science, and learning. The *Pontifical Council on Social Communications* (1948) fosters media and Catholic participation in press, cinema, radio, and television.

There are also offices belonging to the Curia. The *Office of Apostolic Camera* (from 11th century, various functions) has a special role when the Apostolic See is vacant. The *Office for the Administration of the Patrimony of the Holy See* (1967) administers the property of the Holy See. The *Office of the Economic Prefecture of the Holy See* (1967) administers goods and funds of the Holy See. The *Prefecture of the Pontifical Household* (1967) administers internal matters of papal household and audiences. Its extremely varied area of responsibility involves a number of departments and officials: Pontifical Chapel; College of Patriarchs, Archbishops, and Bishops Assistants at Throne; College of Consistorial Advocates; Clerics of the Pontifical Chapel; the Theologian of Papal Household; Apostolic Protonotaries; Antechamber Prelates; Honorary Prelates; Chaplains; Papal Preacher; Assistants at the Throne; Gentlemen of his Holiness; College of the Procurators of the Apostolic Palaces; Chapel of Papal Music. The *Office for Liturgical Celebrations of the Supreme Pontiff* (1563) prepares papal ceremonies.

There are, too, Vatican offices which do not belong to the Curia: Press Office; Central Statistics Office; Biblical Commission; International Theological Commission; Pontifical Commission for the Revision and Emendation of the Vulgate; Pontifical Committee for Eucharistic Congresses; Pontifical Commission for Sacred Archaeology; Pontifical Committee for History.

Finally, there are other bodies associated with the Holy See but not part of the Curia: Secret Archives of the Vatican; Vatican Library; Vatican Polyglot Press;

Vatican Press; *L'Osservatore Romano;* Vatican Radio and Television; Institute for the Fabric of St. Peter's Basilica; Apostolic Almoner. Furthermore, there are other civil service departments connected with Vatican City. Well buried among other offices in the papal yearbook is the so-called Vatican Bank, properly called "The Institute for the Works of Religion" *(Istituto per le opere di religione),* which dates from 1942, incorporating an office established in 1887 by Leo XIII. It is surely significant that not belonging to the Curia is the highly influential and significant permanent General Secretariate for the Synods of Bishops: it would seem to report directly to the pope, who names all its members (CIC 348).

Pope John Paul II made it clear that the Vatican Curia directly serves the pope in his supreme pastoral office, and indirectly the whole Church.[11] The undeniable anti-Roman feeling in the Church, which H.U. von Balthasar (q.v.) studied in 1974 and returned to shortly before his death,[12] is not confined to the anti-papal attitude he mostly described. It certainly also includes an antipathy to the Vatican when seen as a faceless bureaucracy. The fact that the Curia can rightly claim to be acting on behalf of the pope makes it imperative that it both be, and be perceived to be, acting pastorally in the service of communion (q.v.).[13] Y. Congar is usually credited with coining the phrase "creeping infallibility." With regard to the Curia, this is found in rather inflated authority claimed for some of its documents and actions (v. PAPAL DOCUMENTS). People can have problems with authoritative statements from various dicasteries on matters which seem far removed from the central mystery of Christ. The admirable pastoral decision of Pope John Paul to travel widely leads to an uneasy feeling that he may not be fully in control of his Curia or civil service, which as history shows, is quick to act with autonomy when not closely supervised. This being said, one should not impugn the Curia too readily,[14] as so many of its members—lay men and women, religious, clerics, bishops, and cardinals—are indeed humble and dedicated servants of the Church.

Finally, the territorial base is called "Vatican City State," a term used only in post and telecommunications; "Holy See" is used in all international relations.

[1]Congar, Augustin 101–102.  [2]G. Alberigo, "Serving the Communion of Churches," Conc 127 (1979) 12–33; L. Pásztor, "L'histoire de la Curie romaine, problème d'histoire de l'Église," RHE 64 (1969) 353–366; J.H. Provost, in Coriden, CIC 292–294; see Conc 127 (1979). See P. Partner, *The Pope's Men: The Papal Civil Service on the Renaissance* (Oxford: Clarendon, 1990).  [3]*Consideration* 3:8 and 13; 4:9, 10, 15, and 17.  [4]*Sapienti consilio*—AAS 1 (1909) 7–19.  [5]Alberigo (n. 2) 20.  [6]K. Mörsdorf, in Vorgrimler, Vatican II, 2:171-175.  [7]AAS 59 (1967) 885–928.  [8]J. Sánchez y Sánchez, "La constitution apostolique *Regimini ecclesiae universae* six ans après," AnnéCan 20 (1976) 33–66.  [9]S. Sanz Villalba, "La curia romana, órgano de administración de la Iglesia," REspDerCan 17 (1972) 772; see G. Zizola, "Le pouvoir romain: centralisation et bureaucratisation dans l'Église catholique," LumièreV 26/133 (1977) 18–36.  [10]AAS 80 (1988) 841–934. See semi-official commentary: P.A. Bonnet and C. Gullo, eds., *La Curia Romana nella Cost. Ap. "Pastor Bonus."* Studi giuridici 21 (Vatican, 1990). Cf. J.I. Arrieta, "La reforma de la Curia Romana (Commentario a la constitución apostolica 'Pastor bonus')," IusCan 57 (1989) 185–204; J. Beyer, "Linee fondamentali dell'attuale riforma della Curia Romana," VitaCons 26 (1990) 582–592; J.H. Provost, "*Pastor Bonus:* Reflections on the Reorganization of the Roman Curia," Jurist 48 (1988) 499–535; Conc 188 (1986).  [11]*Pastor bonus* art. 1.  [12]*The Office of Peter and the Structure of the Church* (San Francisco, 1986—German, *Der antirömische Affekt,* 1974); idem, "Der antirömische Affekt als Selbstzertörung der katholischen Kirche," in W. Baier et al., eds., *Weisheit Gottes—Weisheit der Welt.* FS J. Ratzinger. 2 vols. (St. Ottilien: EOS, 1987) 2:1173-1179.  [13]*Pastor bonus* nn. 1–2.  [14]Cf. P. Hebblethwaite, *In the Vatican* (London: Sidgwick and Jackson, 1986—Oxford: OP paperback, 1987).

## VATICAN DOCUMENTS

Roman papal documents up to the Reformation are an extremely complex study;[1] after that the usage became more standardized, though changes have taken place in this century. The present-day practice is still elaborate.

Documents are distinguished by their inspiration, appearance or production, and name. It is *motu proprio* ("on his own impulse") when it comes through the initiative of the pope himself, who also signs it. Its usage goes back to Innocent VIII (1484–1492). It can be about quite significant matters, such as some documents of Paul VI in implementing Vatican II (q.v.).

There are several different ways in which documents are produced. A *bull* is a very important papal document of particularly solemn appearance, a parchment with a lead seal *(bulla);* Marian definitions were issued in the form of bulls. For less important matters a *brief* is issued, written on parchment and sealed in wax. *Letters* are written on ordinary paper with a stamped seal in ink. *Decrees* and *rescripts* appear in the same form as letters. *Autographed letters/chirographi* are used within the Vatican and as a sign of special favor to an individual: they are handwritten and signed by the pope.

The more important distinction between various documents arises from their contents and authority; these have various names. The most solemn is an *apostolic constitution,* which can be about disciplinary or dogmatic matters. Examples are the Marian definitions in 1848 and in 1950 (which were bulls in appearance) and the convocation of Vatican II (1961).

Papal letters are of various kinds. *Encyclical letters* (Greek *en-kyklos* = "in a circle," hence passed around by bishops) began with Benedict XIV's *Ubi primum* (1740). They were normally addressed to all the bishops in communion with Rome, but through them were meant for the whole Church. Recently the title has often been amplified, e.g., John Paul II's first encyclical

*Redemptor hominis* (1979): "To his venerable brothers in the episcopate, the priests, the religious families, the sons and daughters of the Church, and to all men and women of good will." Modern encyclicals normally deal with doctrinal, social, or moral matters. When addressed to a restricted group of bishops, they can be called *encyclical epistles.*[2]

*Apostolic letters* can be from the pope or from one of the Roman congregations (v. VATICAN CURIA); it is a rather generic term but used normally for specific purposes, e.g., the erection of a diocese or the appointment of a bishop.

An *allocution* is an oral address delivered by the pope.

In recent years popes have been making more use of *apostolic exhortations,* especially in giving a definitive presentation based on the work of a meeting of the Synod of Bishops (q.v.). But Paul VI also issued his Marian document, *Marialis cultus* (1974), as an apostolic exhortation addressed "To all bishops in peace and communion with the Apostolic See." In practice apostolic exhortations resemble encyclicals, though they tend to encourage some specific activity in the Church.

A decree can be made by the pope or by a congregation (CIC 48–58). It is usually administrative or disciplinary and binds those to whom it is addressed. A *rescript* (CIC 59–75) is a reply to a request for some dispensation (CIC 85–93), privilege (CIC 76–84), or other favor. The juridical decision of a tribunal is called a *sentence.* Decrees, rescripts, and sentences can also be issued by superiors of lower level according to their competence, e.g., a bishop in his own diocese.

The nature of *Instructions* is not always easy to determine. The word has a canonical meaning: "Instructions which clarify the prescription of laws and elaborate on and determine an approach to be followed in implementing them, are given for the use of those persons whose concern it is to see that the laws are implemented and oblige such persons in the execution of the laws" (CIC 34). Benedict XV decreed in 1917 that one of the ordinary functions of the sacred congregations was to issue instructions to explain canon law and to see to its effective implementation.[3] However, it would appear that some documents, especially from the Congregation for the Doctrine of the Faith (CDF), are instructions concerned with doctrine and thus are an exercise of participated ordinary magisterium.[4]

The intent of a *directory* is to provide the basic principles of pastoral theology taken from the magisterium of the Church and in a special way from Vatican II, by which pastoral action in the ministry can be more fittingly directed and governed. Thus after the council we have directories on ecumenism (1967, 1970, 1993), and on catechetics (1971). Directories are addressed more particularly to bishops to give them assistance on practical matters.[5]

The more important of all of these documents are usually published in Latin in the *Acta Apostolicae Sedis* (AAS) and the daily *Osservatore Romano.* Less important ones can be found also in the latter and are published in yearly volumes as the *Insegnamenti* (teachings) of the particular pope. English translations of many documents are found in *Origins* (Washington, D.C.), *The Pope Speaks* (Huntington, Ind.), in *The Pope Teaches* (London), and in *Catholic International* (Worcester, Mass.). The French *Documentation catholique* is also quite comprehensive in this matter.

A most serious problem arises concerning the degree of weight one should attach to Vatican documents. In the extremely rare case of infallible teaching, the issue is clear-cut: a Catholic must accept infallible teaching. But with regard to non-infallible teaching, Vatican II gave some guidance. "The religious submission of mind and will *(religiosum voluntatis et intellectus obsequium)* is to be given in a special way to the authoritative teaching authority *(authentico magisterio)* of the Roman Pontiff even when he is not speaking *ex cathedra;* in such a way, that is, that his supreme teaching authority is respectfully acknowledged and sincere adherence is given to the decisions he has delivered, in accordance with his manifest will which is communicated chiefly by the nature of the documents, by the frequent repetition of the same doctrine or by the style of verbal expression" (LG 25). There is clearly an obligation to assent, but an encyclical or apostolic exhortation will carry more weight than the allocution given each Sunday at the Angelus in St. Peter's Square. However, a theological hermeneutic is needed for these texts: the pope may be declaring what is already the faith of the Church, and thus already binding, or he may be evolving a personal theological opinion which would be prestigious, and to be considered seriously, but not decisively binding. The criteria of the "manifest will" of the pope, mentioned in LG 25, cannot easily be applied to documents or a body of teaching in such a way as to give certain guidance in every case.

A further difficulty arises with documents from Roman congregations. A congregation may issue one with its own authority, which can be described as a participation in the authority of the papal magisterium. It may also publish a document which has papal approval. This approval is of two kinds: it can be *in specific form* if the pope commands its publication and makes its contents his own; it can be *in common form* if the pope agrees to the publication but does not make its contents his own. The former of these two could be called papal teaching, the latter cannot. The approval in specific form must be explicit and never to be presumed.[6]

Needless to say, the media cannot be expected to take account of all of these subtleties. Hence we hear of

"Vatican documents," the provenance and standing of which are not always clear. Added to all this is the theological problem of dissent (q.v. and v. MAGISTERIUM).

There is an urgent need for serious study of the hermeneutic for interpreting Vatican documents. Otherwise they will either be given undue weight or not receive the attention, including assent or obedience, that they may warrant.[7]

[1]P. Rabikauskas, *Diplomatica pontificia* (Rome: Gregorian UP, [4]1980). [2]J.T. Catoir, "Documents, Papal," NCE 4:946-947. [3]Mp. *Cum iuris canonici*—AAS 9 (1917) 483–484; J.E. Risk, in Coriden, CIC 48. [4]F.A. Sullivan, "The Theologian's Ecclesial Vocation and the 1990 CDF Instruction," TS 52 (1991) 51–68 at 52–54. [5]F.G. Morrissey, *The Canonical Significance of Papal and Curial Pronouncements* (Washington, D.C.: Canon Law Society of America, [2]1981) 12—French Ottawa: University of St. Paul, 1992. [6]L. Örsy, *The Church: Learning and Teaching. Magisterium—Assent—Dissent—Academic Freedom* (Wilmington: Glazier—Dublin: Dominican Publications—Leominster UK: Fowler Wright, 1987) 51–55 with nn. 6–9. [7]See F.A. Sullivan, *Creative Fidelity: Weighing and Interpreting Documents of the Magisterium* (New York: Paulist, 1996).

## VIENNE, Council of (1311–1312)

The Council of Vienne (near Lyons in France) was the last of the medieval papal councils (v. COUNCILS).[1] Its purpose was to deal with the Knights Templar, a military order founded in 1118. By the 14th century the order was the object of implacable pursuit by Philip IV of France, who prevailed on Pope Clement V (1305–1314) to summon the council and then to disband the order. Historians nowadays are of the view that most of the charges against the Knights as a whole were unfounded.[2] The council also condemned a number of positions of Peter Olivi (q.v.) but without naming him,[3] and it passed a number of disciplinary decrees, mostly about friars and monks.[4] On the question of Franciscan poverty, the council somewhat favored the more rigorous line, though it did not accept the extremes of the "Spiritual Franciscans," who rejected what they saw as compromises contrary to the original spirit of Francis (q.v.). The council did not, as planned, provide for a new crusade. Inspired by Raymond Lull (ca. 1233–ca. 1315), it decreed that there be schools of oriental languages at the Roman Curia and the universities of Paris, Oxford, Bologna, and Salamanca to foster missionary work among Jews and Moslems. Lack of teachers meant that this was never fully implemented. The council did not so much debate issues as receive in a rather passive fashion the papal or commission decrees prepared on various points.

[1]K.A. Fink, in Jedin-Dolan 4:297-304; H. Jedin, *Ecumenical Councils of the Catholic Church* (Freiburg—Edinburgh 1959) 94–104; J. Lecler, *Vienne.* Histoire des conciles 8 (Paris: Ed. de L'Orante, 1964); A. Melloni, in Alberigo, Concili 211–214. [2]Texts, Tanner 1:336-360; cf. M. Barber, *The Trial of the Templars* (Cambridge: UP, 1978, 1993). [3]Tanner 1:360-361/DS 900–904. [4]Tanner 1:362-401; H.J. Schroeder, *Disciplinary Decrees of the General Councils* (St. Louis—London, 1937) 365–442.

## VIGILIUS, Pope (537–555)

Little is known about Vigilius before he became a deacon in 531 C.E. Achieving the papal office in 537 with the questionable help of the Monophysite empress Theodora, Vigilius was immediately embroiled in the Christological questions of the day. He seems to have promised her that he would revoke the Council of Chalcedon (q.v.), which he never did. It was expected that he would also condemn the so-called Three Chapters, viz., the condemnation by the emperor Justinian in 543 of the person and writings of Theodore of Mopsuestia (d. 428) and certain writings of Theodoret of Cyrrhus (d. ca. 458) and Ibas of Edessa (d. 457) on the grounds that they were Nestorian. Vigilius refused to go along with the condemnation, as it might seem to repudiate Chalcedon. He was brought to Constantinople (547) where for seven years he suffered physical and psychological badgering. In this position of extreme vulnerability he condemned the Three Chapters a year later in his first *Judicatum* or "verdict." He was excommunicated by a synod of African bishops and revoked his condemnation. He refused to attend Constantinople II (q.v.), as he would inevitably have been compromised. Under intense pressure from the emperor, Vigilius eventually condemned the Three Chapters in 554, but made it clear that he upheld Chalcedon. He died in 555.

History can judge Vigilius to have been weak and devious. Though he was far from witnessing to the rock-like quality of faith and decisiveness that the Church might expect from the bishop of Rome, he did not deny the faith of Chalcedon. His case was adduced at Vatican I (q.v.) by those who opposed papal infallibility (q.v.). The condemnation of the Three Chapters was certainly inopportune. Some have justified it on the grounds of their Nestorian tendencies.[1]

[1]OxDPopes 60–62; É. Amann, "Vigilius," DTC 15:2994-3005; H.G. Beck, in Jedin-Dolan 2:450-456; Davis, Councils 235–243; F.X. Murphy, "Vigilius," NCE 14:664-667; G. Every, "Was Vigilius a Victim or an Ally of Justinian?," HeythJ 20 (1979) 257–266.

## VIRGINS

Very many religions and cultures have a special place for virgins, though a fully comprehensive study of virginity does not exist.[1] There is not much positive affirmation of virginity in the OT which, belonging to a tribal culture, held marriage and childbearing in high esteem but placed a high value on a woman being a virgin at the time of marriage (e.g., Gen 24:16; Lev 12:7, 15). The daughter of Jephthah requested a stay on her death for two months "to bewail her virginity" (Judg 11:37-38). The rabbis at the time of Jesus considered it almost obligatory to be married and to procreate children. Without very much scriptural foundation the patristic tradition saw in Elijah and Elisha the forerunners of those who would later be called to Christian virginity.[2] The real foreshadowing of NT virginity was in God's making fruitful the barrenness of the patriarchs' wives; in the continence temporarily imposed on the people (e.g., Exod 19:15) or permanently on a person (Jer 16:2); in the espousals between God and his people (Isa 62:5). But "virgin" is also used about the OT people as indicating their barren disobedience to the Lord (e.g., Isa 37:22; Jer 14:17).

In the NT[3] there are several developments: Mary the mother of Jesus is a virgin (Luke 1:27, 34; Matt 1:23); the Church as spouse of Christ is virginal (1 Cor 11:2; cf. Eph 5:25, 27). For Paul the state of virginity is higher than marriage because it is an undivided attachment to the Lord (1 Cor 7:32-35). But virginity is a charism (1 Cor 7:7), and living in perpetual continence is justified in terms of the kingdom (Matt 19:11-12).[4] There is also an eschatological aspect to virginity, and it symbolizes the chosen ones in the heavenly Jerusalem who were faithful to Christ (Rev 14:4; 19:7, 9). Hence infidelity to the covenant or idolatry in the Bible is often called adultery (Hos 2:4; Ezek 23:43-49; Matt 12:39; 16:4).

Soon, perhaps as early as Ignatius (q.v.), the Church had a distinct state of virgins.[5] The idea of preserving virginity in men and women was known to Justin (q.v.)[6] and to the 2nd-century Athenagoras.[7] From the 3rd century we have the idea of a virgin being spouse of Christ. We find clearly a state or order of virgins in the *Apostolic Tradition* (q.v.), which does not, however, allow an imposition of the bishop's hand for entering this state: "The hand is not imposed on a virgin, her decision alone makes her a virgin" (12/13; v. IMPOSITION OF THE HAND); virgins are to fast frequently and to pray for the Church (23/25:1). Up to the 4th century we find references to male and female virgins; after that period the term "anchorites/monks" is applied to men, "virgins" to women.

The late 4th-century *Apostolic Constitutions* (q.v.) deals extensively with virgins: a virgin is to be holy in body and mind as a temple of God, house of Christ, and dwelling of the Holy Spirit;[8] the state is chosen not from disdain of marriage but as a consecration to holiness *(eusebeias).*[9] But the text does not give much information about the virgins' manner of living: they receive some support from the Church,[10] like the widows whom they usually precede in lists;[11] they are like incense;[12] deaconesses (q.v.) are to be chosen from their ranks.[13]

Many of the Fathers wrote treatises on virgins and virginity,[14] two letters of the 3rd- or early 4th-century Pseudo-Clement (q.v.) being of special interest.[15] The author is the first to attack the custom of male and female ascetics living under the same roof *(syneisaktoi/ virgines subintroductae),* which will be common complaint in succeeding centuries.[16] Clement of Alexandria defended marriage against various Gnostics, and though he praised virginity as his own state, he regarded marriage as higher.[17] Origen stressed virginity as imitation of Christ[18] and placed virgins in second place as a state of perfection;[19] Methodius wrote of virginity as a model for the Church, along with motherhood.[20] Novatian exhorted to chastity those who are "temples of the Lord, members of Christ, and dwelling places of the Holy Spirit," and noted three degrees of chastity—virginity, continence, and fidelity to the marriage bond.[21] Tertullian, who disapproved of second marriages, wrote *De exhortatione castitatis* to a man recently widowed.[22] Other Fathers who wrote significant works on virginity were: Athanasius, who wrote several works, some carrying his name being of doubtful authenticity, however, even if highly influential;[23] Basil of Ancyra, now known to be the author of a work from the spurious texts of Basil the Great, which is interesting in dealing with the whole life of the virgin rather than a more narrow perspective;[24] Gregory of Nyssa wrote an extensive *De virginitate* in which he gave as models of virginity both Christ and Mary, and in which he stated the necessity of virginity for a holier life—the purpose of virginity is to contemplate God;[25] Ambrose wrote three authoritative works on virginity;[26] Jerome wrote on virginity with harsh condemnation of luxurious living, which earned him much enmity;[27] Augustine wrote several works on virginity in which he no way slighted marriage,[28] stating further that Mary gave rise to the Christian ideal of virginity[29] even though Joseph was truly her spouse;[30] John Chrysostom wrote a book on virginity which is largely a detailed commentary on 1 Cor 7:38.[31] The heretic Pelagius wrote one or perhaps two tracts of remarkable spiritual depth on virginity.[32]

By the Middle Ages the normal way for women to live consecrated lives was as nuns; Lateran II (1139) forbade them to live in the world without a religious rule.[33] St. Thomas Aquinas, who knew the works of Ambrose and Augustine on virginity, summed up the patristic tradition. He observed that what makes virginity laudable is that the person wishes to be free for God. Virginity is not the highest of the virtues (faith, hope, and love are), but it is the highest form of chastity compared with conjugal or widowed chastity. He placed the essential of virginity in the intention and determination rather than in physical integrity; virginity is, however, destroyed by an act contrary to chastity.[34] Trent defended virginity from attacks by the Reformers, and it taught: "If anyone says that the married state is to be preferred to that of virginity or celibacy, and that it is no better or more blessed to persevere in virginity or celibacy than to be joined in marriage (cf. Matt 19:11-12; 1 Cor 7:25-26; 7:38; Rev 14:4): let him be anathema."[35] This text cannot be taken as asserting that those who are virgins or celibates are holier than the married. But it does hold that the state of virginity or celibacy is higher. It would then seem to mean that the symbolism and meaning of the virgin's direct adhering to the Lord, not mediated through the love of a marriage partner, is a higher vision of the Christian reality.

Modern reflection[36] on virginity draws extensively on the findings of psychology. As it is not good for a person to be alone (Gen 2:18), the virgin needs a deep relationship with God and with others in unselfish love in order to grow in spiritual maturity. It is "being-for" rather than "not-having" in imitation of Christ, and for him; in Augustine's words, "the virgin's joy of Christ, about Christ, with Christ, after Christ, through Christ, because of Christ."[37] Marriage and virginity are two charisms of the Spirit, each complementary and interacting for the upbuilding of the Church.[38] Virginity can always seek ever-deeper meaning in the virginity of Mary.[39]

Vatican II spoke appreciatively of the values of virginity and celibacy for the whole Church (e.g., LG 42, 46; OT 10; PC 12; PO 16). At the same time it called for a revision of the Rite of Consecration of Virgins (SC 80).[40] According to Canon Law (CIC 604), the order of virgins is not religious life but is a consecrated life.[41] This canon also gives reason for consecration: to follow Christ more closely and intimately and to be dedicated to the service of the Church. The restored rite makes clear that there are two conditions for the consecration of virgins: they must not have been married; they must not have lived in public or flagrant violation of chastity.[42] It does not then demand that the person should have lived in unimpaired virginity: some non-public sins against chastity would not prevent such consecration. Admission to this state of public consecration is by the local bishop. It is by way of decision or commitment (propositum), not a vow. The duties of such virgins are to spend time "in works of penance and of mercy, in apostolic activity and in prayer according to their state of life and spiritual gifts."[43] The words of the bishop in the rite make very clear that this consecration of virginity is for the service of the Church: "Help the poor, care for the weak, teach the ignorant, protect the young, minister to the old, bring strength and comfort to widows and all in adversity."[44] The restored rite leaves many unanswered questions, among them: the relationship with the bishop; formation, both initial and ongoing; structures; financial and other supports in this demanding vocation—all issues that will arise in the

years ahead. But this restoration is yet one more example of the Holy Spirit leading the Church to bring forth old things and new (cf. Matt 13:52) from its rich tradition.[45] The apostolic exhortation of John Paul II, "The Dignity of Women" (1988), has a fine section on the perennial values of virginity.[46] Virginity remains one of the most powerful countercultural expressions with which to challenge today's society.

[1]H.J.W. Drijvers, "Virginity," EncycRel 15:279-281. [2]M. Hayek, "Élie dans la tradition syriaque," in AA.VV. Élie le prophète (Bruges, 1956) 165–187; Hervé de l'Incarnation, "Élie chez les pères latins," ibid., 189–190. [3]G. Delling, "Parthenos," TDNT 5:826-837; I de la Potterie, "Virginity," DBT 635–636. [4]P.-R. Côté, "Les eunuques pour le Royaume (Mt 19,12)," EglT 17 (1986) 321–334. [5]Ad Smyrn. 13:1; Ad Polycarp. 5:2. [6]1 Apology 15. [7]Apologia 33—SC 379:198/ANL 2:417-418. [8]4:14, 2—SC 329:192. [9]8:24, 2—SC 336:226. [10]8:30, 2—SC 336:234. [11]E.g., 2:26, 3 and 8—SC 320: 236, 240; 8:10, 10; 8:12, 43-44; 8:14; 8:30, 2—SC 336:168, 202, 210. [12]2:26, 8—SC 320:240. [13]6:17, 4—SC 329:348. [14]J. Mayer, ed., Monumenta de viduis, diaconissis virginibusque tractantia. Florilegium patristicum 42 (Bonn, 1938); J. Joubert, "La virginité ou les vraies noces," RDroitC 40 (1990) 117–133; H. Leclercq, "Vierge," DACL 15:3103; C. Munier, Mariage et virginité dans l'Église ancienne (1er—111e siècles) (Frankfurt: Lang, 1987); F. de B. Vizmanos, Las virgines cristianas de la primitiva Iglesia: Estudio histórico-ideológico y antología patrística. BAC 45 (Madrid, 1949). [15]F. Diekamp, ed., Patres apostolici. Vol. 2/2 (Tübingen, 1913) 1–49; English—B.P. Pratten, ANF 8:51-66. E.S. Cirici, "Las 'Cartas a las vírgenes' atribuidas a Clemente romano," EfMex 8/22 (1990) 71–81; D. Marafioti, "La verginità in tempo di crisi: Le due lettere pseudo-clementine Ad virgines," CivCatt 140 (1989) 4:439-498. [16] See apocryphal Epist. Titi discipuli Pauli de dispositione sanctimonii—ed. D. de Bruyne, RBén 37(1925) 47–72; John Chrysostom, Adversus eos qui apud se habent virgines subintroductas—PG 47:495-514; Quod regulares feminae viris cohabitare non debeant—PG 47:515-532. [17]Stromata 7:12.70—GCS 17:50-51/English ANF 2:543. [18]In Num. hom. 24:2—PG 12:759-761. [19]In Jesu nave hom. 2:1—PG 12:834. [20]The Banquet or On Virginity—GCS 27:1-141/SC 95/ANF 6:309-355. See 2:2, 1-7; 2:7:50 in Quasten 2:130-132. [21]De bono pudicitiae—CSEL 3/3:13-25/ANF 5:587-592; see 2 and 4 in Quasten 2:224-226. [22]CSEL 70: 125-152/ANL 18:1-20/ANF 4:50-58. [23]See Quasten Patrology 2:45-49 [24]PG 30:669-809. [25]PG 46:317-416/SC 119. Cf. M.D. Hart, "Gregory of Nyssa's Ironic Praise of the Celibate Life," HeythJ 32 (1992) 1–19. [26]De virginitate—PL 16:279-316; De institutione virginis—PL 16:319-348; Exhortatio virginitatis—PL 16:351-380; see G.E. Saint-Laurent, "St. Ambrose's Theology of the Consecrated Virgin," RevRel 41 (1982) 356–367; L. Mirri, "Donne e virginità nei Padri Girolamo e Ambrogio," StFrances 88 (1991) 339–362; C. Riggi, "La verginità nel pensiero di S. Ambrogio," Sales 42 (1980) 789–806; H. Savon, "Un modèle de sainteté à la fin du IVe siècle: La virginité dans l'oeuvre de saint Ambroise," ProbHistChrist 19 (1989) 21–31. [27]Epist. 22—CSEL 54:211-214/ACW 33:134-179. [28]De sancta virginitate—PL 40:397-428; De continentia—PL 40:349-372; M.Agterberg, "Saint Augustin exégète de l'Ecclesia Virgo," AugL 8 (1958) 237–366; R.G. Herbert, "Saint Augustin et la virginité de la foi," in AA.VV. Augustinus Magister (Paris: Études Augustiniennes, 1954) 2:645-655. [29]Serm. 51:26—PL 38:344. [30]De nupt. et conc. 1:11-13—PL 44:420-421. [31]De virginitate—PG 48:533-596/SC 125. [32]Epist. de virginitate—CSEL 1:224-250; (contested authenticity) Epistola de castitate—PLS 1:1464-1505; [33]Canon 26—Tanner 1:203. [34]ST 2–2ae, q.152, aa. 1–5. [35]Tanner 2:755/DS 1810/ND 1818. [36]A. Cuva, "Recente letteratura spirituale-liturgica italiana sulla verginità

consecrata," EphLtg 95 (1981) 478–505; J. Hourcade, *L'Église est-elle misogyne? Une vocation antique et nouvelle* (Paris: Téqui, 1989). [37]"Gaudium virginum Christi de Christo, in Christo, cum Christo, post Christum, per Christum, propter Christum."—*De sancta virginitate* 27—PL 40:411. [38]J.B. Fuertes Bildarraz, "Virginitas et matrimonium in processu dialectico status perfectuionis," ComRelM 69 (1988) 285–306. A.M. Sicari, "La verginità 'per il regno,'" RClerIt 61 (1980) 204–210; R. de Tryon-Montalembert, "La vierge consacrée signe de l'amour de l'Église pour le Christ," VieCons 61 (1989) 226–238. [39]A. Caporale, "Il significato della verginità cristiana," RasT 18 (1977) 57–69, 139–151. [40]J. Beyer, "L'ordine delle vergini," VitaCons 24 (1986) 590–602; T. Clements, "Consecrated to Virginity: A Life-style Restored," RelLifeR 29 (1990) 146–153; eadem, "Order of the Consecration of Virgins: Commentary and Bibliography," MilltownSt 24 (1989) 92–112; D.C. Desautels, "An Early Christian Rite Revisited: Consecrated Virgins Living in the World," RRel 49 (1990) 567–580; M.-P. Dion, "La virginité," EglT 17 (1986) 5–39; J.-M Hennaux, "Consécration des vierges et hierarchie," VieCons 61 (1989) 239–242; M.T. Huguet, "La rénovation du rite liturgique de la consécration des vierges: Quelques questionnements et enjeux," NVet 67 (1992) 91–119; A.M. Triacca, "Significato teologico-liturgico della consecrazione cristiana della verginità (anamnesis, epiclesis, methexis)," EphLtg 96 (1982) 154–183. See Hourcade (n. 36); G. Ramis, "Los formularios romanos de las misas de benedición de vírgenes y viudas," in G. Farnedi, ed., *Traditio et progressio.* FS A. Nocent. Studia anselmiana 95 (Rome: Pont. Athen. S. Anselmo, 1988) 437–467. [41]M.-A. Trapet, "Les dangers d'une réduction de la vie consacrée à la vie religieuse," AnnéeCan 30 (1987) 83–89; cf. S.H. Holland on canon 603–604, in Coriden CIC 467–468. [42]GI 5—Rites 2:133. [43]GI 2—Rites 2:132. [44]Address of bishop, Rites 2:140. Cf. Prayer of Consecration Rites 2:143-145; G.R. Miquel, "La oración 'Deus castorum corporum': Teología sobre la virginidad consagrada," EphLtg 100 (1986) 508–561. [45]G. Ramis, "Los formularios romanos de las misas de benedición de vírgenes y viudas," in *Traditio et progressio.* FS A. Nocent—Studia anselmiana 95 (Rome: Pont. Athen. S. Anselmo, 1988) 437–467. [46]*Mulieris dignitatem* n. 20—AAS 80 (1988) 1700–1703.

# VISIBLE

In a dense passage, Vatican II describes the compound nature of the Church: "This society, however, equipped with hierarchical structures, and the mystical body of Christ, a visible assembly and a spiritual community, an earthly Church and a Church enriched with heavenly gifts, must not be considered as two things, but as forming one complex reality comprising a human and a divine element" (LG 8).[1] One can say that what is human in the Church is visible. But one cannot confine what is divine to what is invisible; the sacraments are a divine work, which are both visible in celebration and invisible in their ultimate effects.

The well-known book of A. Acerbi[2] argues that two ecclesiologies were operative in the Constitution on the Church: a juridical one reflecting the Church as a perfect society (q.v.), and an ecclesiology of communion giving due regard to the fact of divine life being historically manifested and communicated in the structures and life of the Church. The above passage, however, may be more helpfully interpreted historically in the light of Pius XII's encyclical *Mystici corporis*

(q.v.). There, the pope was seeking to integrate the juridical and charismatic dimensions of the Church and was setting his face against any exclusive emphasis on the charismatic or internal facets of the Church. He in turn was reflecting the prepared, but never promulgated, schema of Vatican I (q.v.) on the Church. This council, nonetheless, did give an important, if implicit, assertion of visibility when it appealed to the Church as a motive of credibility of the faith: "The Church herself by reason of her astonishing propagation, her outstanding holiness and her inexhaustible fertility in every kind of goodness, by her catholic unity and her unconquerable stability, is a kind of great and perpetual motive of credibility and an uncontroverted evidence of her own divine mission."[3]

We know from LG 14 that visible and invisible bonds are necessary for full communion in the Church: grace, acceptance of its structures, profession of faith, sacraments, ecclesiastical government, and communion (v. MEMBERSHIP). These last three go back to Bellarmine (q.v.). Other indications of the visibility of the Church are the principal manifestation of the local Church in the liturgy (LG 26; cf. SC 41) and the role of the Church in the world (GS passim).

Tradition and the magisterium have always rejected the view that the true Church is invisible, known solely to God, and consisting only of the holy or the predestined.[4] Even though the Reformers may have held that the Church in the truest sense consists only in the holy or elect, they did, nonetheless, insist on the necessity of communing with the visible Church (v. CALVIN). The theology of the notes (q.v.) also implies visibility.

From a theological viewpoint, visibility is necessary for the Church to be a sacrament (q.v.), or sign of God's saving love. It is thus seen as calling on people to enter the community which proclaims the Lordship of Jesus, a community in continuity with the apostolic Church derived from him, and reaching towards the eschatological hope held out for all.

But though the Church is essentially visible, its deepest reality is also spiritual: grace, prayer, the existence of Christians as temples of the Spirit in the wider temple (q.v.) which is the Church. There are bonds which relate the Church to other Christians (v. SUBSISTS), to other theists, and to persons of good will (LG 15–16; cf. GS 22).

[1]Y.-J. Harder, "Un mystère de visibilité," Communio 12/1 (1987) 5–14; A. Houssiau, "L'Église du Christ, réalité visible et invisible," NRT 107 (1985) 814–822; J.P. Rosa, "'Entaissement' ou 'visibilité': Un débat dans l'Église," Études 376 (1992) 239–248. [2]*Due ecclesiologie: Ecclesiologia giuridica ed ecclesiologia di communione nella "Lumen gentium."* Nuovi saggi teologici 4 (Bologna: Ed. Dehoniane, 1975). [3]Tanner 2:807-808/DS 3013/ND 123. [4]Against Huss DS 1201, 1206/ND 808/1, 6; Quesnel DS 2474–2478; Synod of Pistoia DS 2615.

# W

## WALDENSES

Also called "Waldensians" and "Vaudois," the Waldenses are a small Christian community still surviving mainly in Italy with perhaps 20,000 members ("Chiesa Evangelica Valdese"). They originated in the 12th century from the "Poor Men of Lyons" led by Peter Valdès, who lived by mendicant and itinerant preaching. By 1205 there was a schism between the followers of Valdès north of the Alps and the Lombard Waldenses. The former were found in some numbers in Germany, France, and Spain; they were strongly persecuted and eventually destroyed. The latter survived, confined to the valleys around Savoy and Piedmont.

They tended to reject sacraments, especially where they considered the ministers to be unworthy; they lived in communities of workers. They were inclined to deny that sinners were truly members of the Church. All, men and women, who were pure in spirit were priests, ordained by God. Later they would adopt a Presbyterian structure. Their beginnings[1] are overlaid with legend and with 16th-century Reformers' attempts to present them as a pure strain of primitive Christianity, some claiming that they were a community founded by Paul on his way to Spain. They were often seen as precursors of the Reformation.[2] They were favored and courted by some Reformers, particularly Calvinists, but in succeeding centuries were again persecuted. At the time of a massacre in 1655 they published a brief confession of faith in thirty-three articles.[3]

This confession stated that there is only one Church in the world for the salvation of people, and proceeded: "This Church is the company of the faithful, who, having been elected by God before the foundation of the world, and called into a holy calling, unite themselves to follow the Word of God" (art. 25). In an appendix it rejected statements which they claimed were imputed to them by Catholics, including: "That the Church can entirely fail and be destroyed."[4]

In Italy they did not receive religious freedom again until 1848. There, the Waldenses have had a covenanted union with the Methodists, both, however, retaining their specific identities. Outside Italy they are found in South America, again having close relationships with Methodists. Their worldwide membership is probably somewhat in excess of 20,000, but their active involvement in the ecumenical movement in Argentina and Italy is more significant than these figures suggest.[5]

[1]A. Armand-Hugon and G. Gonnet, *Bibliografia valdesi* (Torre Pellice, 1953); D. Christie-Murray, *A History of Heresy* (Oxford: UP, 1989) 102–104; J.-Fr. Gilmont, "Les Vaudois des Alpes: Mythes et réalité," RHE 83 (1988) 69–89; G. Gonnet, "Cathars and Waldenses within the Church of the Middle Ages," Conc 200 (1988) 89–93; G. Leff, *Heresy in the Later Middle Ages.* 2 vols. (Manchester—New York, 1967) 2:445-450, 452-485; G. Leff, "Waldensians," EncycRel 15:327-328; G. Scuderi, "Profili ecclesiologici ed instituzione della Chiesa Valdese," DirEccl 102 (1991) 1:230-288. [2]J. Duvernoy, "Cathares et Vaudois sont-ils des précurseurs de la Réforme?," ETR 62 (1987) 377–384. [3]Schaff, Creeds 3:757-770. [4] Ibid., 769–770, n. 10. [5] See StEcum 11 (1993) 235f., "Testo comune di studio sui matrimoni misti-commissioni valdese-metodista e CEI," *Il Regno* 39/720 (1994) 116–123.

## WESLEY, John (1703–1791)

John Wesley cannot be appreciated without reference to Methodism (q.v.). He was born at Epworth in 1703.[1] He became a fellow at Oxford in 1726, where he had begun to take part in spiritual meetings (v. METHODISM). About this time he was much influenced by the Anglican mystic W. Law (1686–1761) and other spiritual writers. He went briefly on an abortive preaching mission to Georgia, U.S.A. (1735–1737). Coming under the influence of the Moravian P. Böhler, he had a profound religious conversion in 1738. His aim thenceforth became, "to promote as far as I am able vital practical religion and by the grace of God to beget, preserve, and increase the life of God in the souls of men."[2]

The rest of his life was spent in evangelization through the Methodist movement, along with his brother Charles, one of the most gifted hymn-writers in English Christianity. John's strong organizational gifts gave the movement a strength and cohesion which he reinforced by constant journeys.

Wesley's ecclesiology is basically Anglican (q.v.) with some change in emphasis.[3] His ideas are developed in his extensive works, almost all of which are occasional writings, such as sermons, letters, and pamphlets.[4] In his revision of the Anglican *Thirty-nine Articles* for America, he retained the 19th article, numbering it as the 13th: "The visible Church is a congregation of faithful men in which the pure Word of God is preached and the sacraments be duly administered according to Christ's ordinance in all those things that of necessity are requisite to the same."[5] In his revision he omitted the declaration that the Roman and other Churches had erred. We find a development of his ideas in a sermon on the Church (1786).[6] Though his ministry would lead one to suspect that he would emphasize the first part of the Article, he always insisted on the second also. He was not prepared to set limits on where the Church may be found, yet he seemed to exclude public sinners from it. The "real members of the Church" are to "see that they walk holy and unblamable in all things." Elsewhere he indicates three things that the Article says are essential to the visible Church: "First: Living faith; without which, indeed, there can be no Church at all, neither visible or invisible. Second: Preaching, and consequently hearing, the pure word of God, else that faith would languish and die. And, thirdly, a due administration of the sacraments,—the ordinary means whereby God increaseth faith."[7]

The most notable breach with Anglicanism was his controversial ordinations, though there was antipathy to Wesley also at parish level from Anglican priests who disapproved, disliked, or felt threatened by his revival-type preaching. Wesley wished Methodism to remain as a renewal movement within the Church of England; he was, for instance, very careful never to have a Methodist session clashing with a parochial one. But he was unable to obtain ordinations for his preachers from the Church of England. From a study of the early Church in Alexandria he became convinced that he as a priest could ordain and, in what he saw as a dire pastoral situation, he proceeded to do so.

This action was to create a rift with the Church of England, a rift that was already growing to an extent of which Wesley himself was not fully aware. He wished to die as a member of the Church of England. The separation took place after his death.[8]

For his time Wesley was quite ecumenical, as the well-known *Letter to a Roman Catholic* (1749) shows.[9] He wished that love and understanding should prevail between Protestants (Methodists) and Catholics. In itself the letter is a fine example of attempted dialogue. The Wesleyan gifts, from both John and Charles, to the Oikumene are a practical Christianity shown forth in social and charitable commitment, together with a deep devotional life well evidenced in the hymns, which are profoundly embedded in the soul of Methodists.[10] John Wesley was a reformer deeply in touch with the tradition of spirituality, both East and West. He started a series, *The Christian Library,* of classical texts for his preachers. He was greatly enamored with the teaching of the Pseudo-Macarius, a fourth-century Syrian.[11] His life and teaching are an enduring witness that evangelization, reform, and spirituality must be fed from tradition for enduring benefits to accrue to the Church.

[1]No definitive biography: see C.E. Vulliamy, *John Wesley* (London: Epworth, [3]1954); V.H.H. Green, John Wesley (London, 1964); J. Baker, *John Wesley and the Church of England* (London: Epworth, 1970).   [2]OxDCC 1467, with bibliog.; J. Murray Turner, "John Wesley—People's Theologian," OneChr 14 (1978) 328–339; G. Rupp, "John Wesley—Christian Prophet," Conc 7/4 (Sept. 1968) 24–29.   [3]C.W. Williams, *John Wesley's Theology Today* (London: Epworth—Nashville: Abingdon 1960) 141–166. See H. Abelove, *The Evangelist of Desire: John Wesley and the Methodists* (Stanford, Calif.: Stanford UP, 1990); T.A. Campbell, "Christian Tradition: John Wesley and Evangelicalism," AngTR 74 (1992) 54–67.   [4]*The Journal of John Wesley.* Ed. N. Curnock. 8 vols. (London: Epworth, 1938); *The Works of John Wesley.* Ed. T. Jackson. 15 vols. (London, [3]1856–62); *The Letters of John Wesley.* Ed. J. Telford. 8 vols. (London, 1931). New edition of works, gen. ed. F. Baker (Oxford (1975–1983; Nashville 1984– ). See E. Jay, *The Journal of John Wesley: A Selection* (Oxford: UP, 1987); J.R. Tryson, *Charles Wesley: A Reader* (Oxford: UP, 1990).   [5]Schaff, Creeds 3:810; Williams (n. 3) ch. 9.   [6]*Works* (n. 4) 6:392-401; A.C. Coulter, ed., *John Wesley* (New York: Oxford UP, 1964) 308–317.   [7]*An Earnest Appeal* in Works 8:31 cited Williams (n. 3) 142.   [8]R.E. Davies, *Methodism* (London: Epworth, [2]1985) 105–112.   [9]Ed. M. Hurley (London: Chapman—Belfast: Epworth House, 1968); cf. J.M. Todd, *John Wesley and the Catholic Church* (London, 1958); Williams (n. 3) ch. 1.   [10]G.S. Wakefield, *Methodist Devotion* (London: Epworth, 1966).   [11] Idem, "La littérature du Désert chez John Wesley," Irén 51 (1978) 155–170, 295.

## WIDOWS

In the OT, widows were figures of misfortune and poverty (Bar 4:12-16; Isa 47:9), but they were also specially treasured in the eyes of God and protected by God's law (Isa 10:2; Deut 26:12-13; Sir 35:13-15; Ps 94:6-10). In the NT,[1] especially in the Lucan writings, they were seen also to be the recipient of the special affection of Jesus (Luke 7:11-15; 18:3-5; 20:47; 21:2-4). Caring for widows was an important duty of charity (Jas 1:27).

The portrait of Anna in Luke 2:36-38 is in full harmony with the institution of widowhood in the Pastorals,[2] which show a grouping of widows with a special role in the primitive community. In 1 Tim 5:9-10 we see that a widow is not to be enrolled (chêra katalegesthô) until she is 60 years of age, and "she must be well attested for her good deeds, as one who has brought up children, shown hospitality, washed the feet of the saints, relieved the afflicted, and devoted herself to doing good in every way." The "true widow" (1 Tim 5:3, 5, 16) who has been left alone (with nobody to support her?) was one who "has set her hope on God and continues in supplications and prayers night and day" (1 Tim 5:5). The portrait of the "true widow" will in time influence the picture of deaconesses (q.v.) on the part of various Churches. Younger widows are not to be inscribed: they are not mature and will possibly give cause for scandal (1 Tim 5:11-15); it is clear that the author fears the consequences of a widow not living out a permanent commitment to widowhood. But there is biblical advice that it can be preferable for younger widows to remarry (1 Cor 7:39; 1 Tim 5:14). In addition, there is a preference for a widower not to remarry, hence the apparent condition of a single marriage for the officials in 1 Tim 3:2, 12; Titus 1:6, though these texts have been interpreted as fidelity to an existing marriage.

Church history and spirituality of the early centuries show an important place for widows.[3] Though tradition shows a preference for a widow remaining single (1 Cor 7:8, 40), the right of remarriage has always been defended, with a few exceptions: the 2nd- or 3rd-century Athenagoras who referred to remarriage as "decent or veiled adultery";[4] Tertullian, who wrote three works on monogamy;[5] Basil was particularly severe in his views about second marriages but did not condemn them outright.[6] Third or subsequent marriages are almost universally treated with extreme disapproval.[7]

Ignatius (q.v.) has a curious phrase when he greets "the virgins called widows,"[8] which would seem to indicate virgins exceptional in virtue, or single women placed with the widows to obtain charitable relief. To Polycarp he writes: "Take care that widows are not neglected. After the Lord you must be their guardian."[9] In his turn Polycarp (q.v.) has particular injunctions for widows: "Let them be wise in the faith they owe to the Lord; let them make continuing intercession for all; let them avoid all calumny, backbiting, false testimony, love of money, and all evil, knowing that they are the altar of God."[10] The last striking phrase, taken up by other writers, points either to their continual offering and worship of God, or to their living on the offerings of the faithful, part of the offering being given to them for their support.[11]

Several of the canonico-liturgical apostolic collections (q.v.) give norms for widows. In the Apostolic Tradition (q.v.) it is stated that a widow is not ordained but instituted (kathistasthai) by the word, after which she joins the group of widows. She does not receive imposition of the hand (q.v.). Widows are not to be too quickly accepted. They are appointed for prayer, a role common to all,[12] and are to fast frequently.[13] But they do not have a liturgical role.[14] But in the 5th-century Testamentum Domini they have assigned to them nearly all the roles of the deaconesses at baptisms,[15] in visiting the sick and in instruction.[16] This document would seem to envisage widows living together, almost as in a monastery. Similar ideas can be found in the Statutes of the Apostles/Ecclesiastical Church Canons,[17] in the Didascalia Apostolorum.[18] In the Egyptian Canons of Hippolytus, from about 340 C.E., widows are assigned three tasks: frequent prayer, service of the sick, and frequent fasting. There do not seem to have been deaconesses in the milieu where these canons were compiled (Alexandria?).[19] The late 4th-century Apostolic Constitutions (q.v.) take over the material from the Didascalia and other earlier works, but it is not easy to distinguish between what is addressed to all widows and what belongs to the order of widows. The compiler stresses various matters: the widow's role is only to pray for benefactors and for the Church—she is forbidden to instruct anyone except to bear testimony on matters of faith, justice, and hope;[20] like other women she is not to teach in the Church or to baptize;[21] as the altar of God she is to remain fixed in her house;[22] the ideal widow is adorned with all human and spiritual virtues, with special emphasis on obedience to the bishop and the deacons;[23] there are elaborate warnings against various undesirable activities.[24] The general impression one gets is that the Apostolic Constitutions are more restrictive and cautious than earlier works.[25] Their compiler takes a severe line on the matter of second marriages but is thinking of those who have taken the vow of widowhood; only those widows of one marriage could be deaconesses (q.v.);[26] third and subsequent marriages are condemned.[27] For men there is also a negative view: access to the clergy is forbidden to one who is married twice, or to one who marries a widow.[28]

Along with canonico-liturgical writing there are important treatises on, or works addressed to, widows in the Fathers.[29] Origen gives a spiritualized interpretation of the injunction of the Pastoral Epistles' "washing the feet of the saints" (cf. 1 Tim 5:10),[30] but like many writers he insists on monogamy for those widows who have been instituted as such in the Church.[31] There is in the Fathers also a tendency to discourage second marriages for both widows and widowers. A number of them have written tracts on widowhood: Ambrose (q.v.) in his work on widows does not condemn second marriages;[32] Augustine (q.v.) wrote briefly in 414 on the merits of widowhood;[33] the widow was also for him an image of the Church;[34] John Chrysostom has a work consoling a young widow, and one against a second marriage.[35] Common patristic ideas are: Judith and Anna are biblical models; the widow is surrounded by evil in the world; she is to turn to prayer, holy reading (divina lectio) and fasting; she is to raise her mind and heart to God.

By the Middle Ages the Order of Widows gradually gave way to monasticism and other forms of sisterhood (e.g., Beguines) or religious life, though the canonization of widows such as Sts. Elizabeth of Portugal, Monica, Elizabeth of Hungary kept the ideals of widowhood alive in the Church.

For the spirituality and ecclesiology of widowhood, the following themes are frequent and important: the state of widowhood points to the symbol of marriage being faithful and enduring love to Christ's love for the Church; the widow is one of those who are poor, having lost the riches of a life partner—the blessings promised to the poor in spirit can be her expectation; the challenges of widowhood, especially in the rearing of children, make of the widow one who needs to trust deeply in God; just as love lasts into eternity, and death does not break the bond of love, so too, forgiveness can reach beyond the grave to the husband; the widow knows both the possibility of true human love and its happiness, but she knows, too, their fragility. There are threats to a rewarding life of widowhood in boredom and self-centeredness: the former Blessing of Widows sought to point the gaze of the widow beyond her own pain to love and service of others. The Church places before widows a path of holiness (LG 41) which is a continuation of the calling to marriage (GS 48), and looks to them for special service (AA 4).

In recent years there has been renewed interest in the state of widowhood both by the Magisterium[36] and theologians,[37] though developments of associations and groups were too late to have any influence on the Code of Canon Law, which did, however, acknowledge the restoration of the Consecration of Virgins. It would seem appropriate to look for some form of recognition of the gift of widowhood in and for the Church.[38]

[1]P. Sandevoir, "Widows," DBT 652; G. Stählin, "Chêra," TDNT 9:440-446. [2]J.M. Basler, "The Widow's Tale: A Fresh Look at 1 Tim 5:3-16," JBL 103 (1986) 23–41; O. Bangerter, "Les veuves des epîtres pastorales, modèle d'un ministère féminin dans l'Église ancienne," FoiVie 83 (1084) 27–45; R.A. Wild, NJBC in loc.; B.W. Winter, "Providentia for the Widows of 1 Timothy 5:3-16," TyndB 39 (1988) 83–99. [3]H. Leclercq, "Veuvage," DACL 15:3008-3023; J. Mayer, ed., Monumenta de viduis, diaconissis, virginibusque tractantia. Florilegium patristicum 42 (Bonn, 1938); J. Viteau, "L'institution des diacres et des veuves," RHE 22 (1926) 513–537. [4]Plea 33—SC 3:162/LCC 1:337. [5]Ad uxorem—CSEL 70:96-124/ANL 11:279-303/ANF 4:39-49; De exhortatione castitatis—CSEL 70:125-152/ANL 18:1-20/ANF 4:50-58—both in ACW 13; De monogamia—PL 2:929-954/ANL 18:21-55/ANF 4:59-72. [6]Discourse 37:8—PG 36:292; cf. Basil, Epist. 188:4—PG 32:673; 199:24—PG 32:724; 160, 4—PG 32:627. [7]B. Grillet, "Secondes noces dans les premiers siècles de l'Église," SC 138:33-52 at 48, 50; John Chrysostom, Ad viduam iuniorem—SC 138:112-159/LNPF 9:119-128 with De non iterando coniugio—PG 48:399-410/SC 138:161-201. Trans. S.R. Shore, On Virginity: Against Remarriage (Lewiston, N.Y.: Mellen, 1983). [8]Ad Smyrn. 13:1. [9]Ad Polycarpum 4:1. [10]Epist. 4:3; cf. C. Osiek, "The Widow as Altar: The Rise and Fall of a Symbol," SecC 3 (1983) 159–169. [11]Didascalia apostolorum 2:26, 8—R.H. Connolly trans. (Oxford, 1929) 88. [12]10/11:1-5. [13]23/25:1. [14]10/11:5. [15]Testamentum Domini 2:8, 12—J. Cooper and A.J. Maclean, trans, The Testament of Our Lord (Edinburgh, 1902) 127. [16]Ibid., 1:40—Cooper and Maclean (n. 15) 105–107. [17]Ethiopic Statutes 1, 17, 26, 39—G. Horner, trans., The Statutes of the Apostles or Canones Ecclesiastici (London, 1904—Oxford, 1915) 127, 136, 146–147, 161. [18]2:26; 3:5-8—R.H. Connolly (n. 11) 88, 132–140. [19]R.G. Coquin, Les canons d'Hippolytus. PO 31, 2 (Paris, 1966) 318–331, 363. [20]3:5, 3—SC 329:128. [21]3:6, 1-2; 3:9—SC 329:132, 138-140. [22]3:6, 3-4—SC 329:132. [23]3:7, 3–8, 2—SC 329:136-140. [24]3:7; 3:12—SC 329:134-136, 146-148. [25]Cf. M. Metzger, SC 329:61-63. [26]6:17, 4—SC 329:348. [27]3:2, 2—SC 329:124. [28]8:47, 17-19 with 2:2, 3—SC 336:278-280; SC 320:148. [29]B.B. Thursdon, The Widows: A Woman's Ministry in the Early Church (Minneapolis: Fortress, 1989); B. Grillet, "Viduité et secondes noces dans l'oeuvre de Jean Chrysostome," SC 138:54-83. [30]In Ioan. comm. 32:12 (7), ed. GCS 10:1903 p. 444. [31]Hom. in Luc. 17:10—SC 87:263. [32]De viduis—PL 16:233-262—LNPF 10:391-407. [33]De bono viduitatis—PL 40:429-450/LNPF 3, ser. 3. 1:397-413. [34]En. in ps. 131:23, 25—PL 37:1726-1727. [35]Supra (n. 7). [36]Pius XII Address to International Family Group, 16 Sept. 1957, Discorsi e radiomessaggi 19:395-405. [37]J. Beyer, "L'ordine delle vedove," VitaCons 23 (1987) 238–248; idem, "Ordo viduarum," Periodica 76 (1987) 253–269; Renée de Tryon-Montalembert, "La veuve dans l'Église catholique," FoiVie 83/1 (1984) 47–63; G. Ramis, "La benedición de las vírgenes y de las viudas en la liturgia céltica," EphLtg 101 (1987) 145–149; idem, "La benedición de las viudas," EphLtg 104 (1990) 159–175; J.I. Ugarte Grijalba, "Notas para una teología espiritual de la viudez cristiana," RTLim 14 (1980) 165–180. [38]Mère Geneviève de Grandshamps, "La mission de la veuve dans l'Église," FoiVie 83/1 (1984) 65–71.

# WOMEN

See FEMINISM AND THE CHURCH and WOMEN, ORDINATION OF

# WOMEN, ORDINATION OF

The question of the ordination of women is an ecumenical issue, as well as one being discussed within the Catholic Church. Underlying the question are many matters that also concern feminism and the Church (q.v.). Until recent years the ministry of word and sacrament was a male preserve in the main-line Churches. Exceptions were the Anabaptists (q.v.) at the time of the Reformation and various groups of sects throughout history, who were invariably condemned by Church authorities. From the nineteenth century the order of deaconess (q.v.) was restored in many Protestant Churches. The Methodists ordained women to full ministry in the U.S. in 1956, and many other Churches subsequently followed. The Anglican Communion was slower to take this step, Hong Kong being the first Anglican Province to ordain a woman (1971—an individual bishop had ordained a deaconess to priesthood in 1944, but she felt compelled to resign within two years, such was the opposition to her by the province House of Bishops). The first woman Anglican bishop, Barbara Harris, was consecrated in Massachusetts (1989). The Church of England, after much painful heart-searching, decided for the ordination of women in 1993 and implemented the decision in 1994.

The ordination of women has led to severe tensions within the ecumenical movement, especially with Old Catholics, Orthodox Churches, the Catholic Church, and other Churches which have not proceeded with such ordinations themselves.[1] As early as 1975, in an exchange of letters, Paul VI warned Archbishop David Coggan of Canterbury that "the new course taken by the Anglican Communion in admitting women to the ordained priesthood cannot fail to introduce into this [the ARCIC] dialogue an element of grave difficulty."[2] Further correspondence took place between Canterbury and Rome as the Anglican commitment to the ordination of women became firmer.[3]

Though Anglicans who support the ordination of women claim theological support for their position, much strain has been created within their Churches, with some disaffected clergy and laity turning to seek full communion with the Old Catholic, Orthodox, and Catholic Churches. The number of those doing so has up to now been perhaps less than had been expected by some Anglicans, Catholics, and others opposed to such ordinations.

For the Catholic theologian, the key question to be asked is whether the restriction of orders to males is of divine law (hence immutable), or a matter of Church discipline (reversible).[4] An evaluation of the discussion within the Catholic Church must be very carefully nuanced. The importance of the popes' attitude to the question in ecumenical discussions with the Anglicans must bear great weight. Furthermore, there is an authoritative statement of the Congregation for the Doctrine of the Faith, mandated by Pope Paul VI, *Inter insigniores* (1976, henceforth InterIn).[5] While these statements did not carry the irrevocable status of definitive or infallible declarations, they have to be given an appropriate response by Catholics, including theologians. It is not possible to dismiss them out of hand, and assert that the ordination of women will surely come about in time, or that only stubborn intransigence on the part of Rome is blocking an obvious step to be taken. It would, however, seem that neither the arguments for, nor those against, the ordination of women are so apodictic that the future position of the Catholic Church in the matter can be predicted with absolute certainty; it must, however, be stated that the most recent statements of the magisterium do lead one in the direction of seeing an irreformable position against the ordination of women. In the meantime some delicate probing and evaluation of the arguments on both sides may still be possible.

The main ground for the rejection by Rome of the ordination of women, and one shared with the East, is tradition (InterIn 1).[6] This is a very serious basis indeed. The situation of the NT concerning ministry is both unclear, and fluid; we cannot say with certainty who in the primitive Church presided at the Eucharist or by what right. But by the year 200, there was a triple order of deacon, priest, and bishop universally in the Church. This rapid evolution and its persistent form is best explained by it being Spirit-guided; theologians use the concept of *ius divinum* (q.v. and v. PRIESTS, MINISTERIAL to explain this development). Such a constant tradition cited by the document could also be explained in terms of *ius divinum* (see InterIn 4).

The other arguments of the document are less impressive (InterIn 3–5). The attitude of Jesus in choosing only males for apostles is hardly conclusive: the apostles were more than priests; they were to be the foundation of the eschatological Church (see Matt 19:28), and after the substitution for Judas (Acts 1:15-23), it was a closed college; the apostles as such were not afterwards replaced. Moreover, Jesus' choice was only of Israelites, and the Church soon extended beyond this restricted range. The appeal to Jesus and the apostles' example would be more solid if it were applied to bishops (q.v.), not priests. The argument that only a male can truly act *in persona Christi* is not probative. Indeed, if not used carefully, it is open to Nestorian interpretations, for there is only a divine person (neither male nor female) who has a fully human, male nature. But all these arguments, except for the one from tradition, seem to be arguments which lead to an *understanding* of the Church's position, rather than be convincing *proofs;* technically, such arguments *ex convenientia* are an attempt to grasp the inner coherence of a doctrine otherwise established. The document's authors are not unaware of the difficulty and speak of "the profound fittingness" of a solely male ordination in the total sacramental mystery of Christ (InterIn 5). This teaching was reiterated by Pope John Paul II in his apostolic letter on women, *Mulieris dignitatem* (1988, n. 26). The calibre of the theologians who have supported the document is very striking; that alone should make one hesitate before dismissing the declaration; similar reflections by Orthodox writers serve as a significant confirmation.[7]

When we come to the opposite view, there are several approaches. One is an almost simplistic assumption that the non-ordination of women is the result of sinful human patriarchy, and the rectitude of ordaining women is practically self-evident to any unbiased person.[8] Another line of argument is a serious consideration of women's ministry in the NT and tradition, and a weighing of arguments found in InterIn and elsewhere, before coming to the conclusion of the admissibility of women to ministerial priesthood.[9] Some authors combine both approaches.[10] Others take the view that the case against the ordination of women is not proven,[11] while the opposite view is also found, viz., that the case against InterIn is not established.[12] Some give particular weight to the clear exercise of ministries by women in the NT, concluding that this and other NT evidence do not rule out women priests.[13] Others find unconvincing the argument that for the fullness of the sacramental sign, it is necessary for Christ to be represented by a male.[14] It can be pointed out that women are ministers in the sacrament of marriage, and extraordinarily so for baptism in extreme circumstances (CIC 861 § 2).[15] Many conclude that even after the intervention of the Vatican, the discussion must continue.[16]

A further development would seem to have arisen after the letter to the bishops of Pope John Paul II, *Ordinationis sacerdotalis,* on the non-admission of women to ministerial priesthood.[17] The pope reviews briefly the previous teaching by Pope Paul VI, the Declaration, InterIn, and his own statements. He repeats that "the real reason is . . . Tradition—Christ established things in this way" (n. 2). He appeals to the non-ordination of the Virgin Mary as proof that there is no down-grading of women in this position of the Church (n. 3), and stresses the need for women's ministries in the Church (n. 3). He states that, not withstanding the constant and universal Tradition of the Church and the teaching of the magisterium, "in some places it is nonetheless considered open to debate, or the Church's judgment that women are not to be admitted to ordination is considered to have a merely disciplinary force." He therefore concludes: "Wherefore, in order that all doubt may be removed regarding a matter of great importance, a matter which pertains to the Church's divine constitution itself, in virtue of my ministry of confirming the brethren (cf. Luke 22:23), I declare that the Church has no authority whatsoever to confer priestly ordination on women and that this judgment is to be definitively held by all the Church's faithful" (n. 3). This document, and especially its conclusion just cited, is certainly a very solemn exercise of the magisterium when judged by the criteria given by Vatican II (LG 25 § 1). It falls short, however, of being an infallible statement. A close parallel that springs to mind is the statement on Anglican Orders by Leo XIII, *Apostolicae curae* (1896): in both cases the pope wished to put an end to controversy, to close debate (v. ANGLICAN ORDERS), and to settle a question once and for all. But the decision of Leo XIII is now, one hundred years later, rather freely discussed.

On 28 October 1995 the CDF published a *dubium* with a response. This is the traditional way in which Vatican congregations focus clearly on a point of doctrine or discipline. A question is formulated with exactitude, a positive or negative response is given, and an explanation usually follows. In this case we find: "Whether the teaching that the Church has no authority whatsoever to confer priestly ordination on women, which is presented in the apostolic brief *Ordinatio sacerdotalis* to be held definitively, is to be understood as belonging to the deposit of faith." The response was: "In the affirmative." The explanatory paragraph stated: "This teaching requires definitive assent, since, founded on the written Word of God, and from the beginning constantly preserved and applied in the tradition of the Church, it has been set forth infallibly by the ordinary and universal magisterium (cf. Second Vatican Council, Dogmatic Constitution on the Church, *Lumen gentium* 25, 2)." The document also noted that the pope "approved this reply, adopted in the ordinary session of this congregation and ordered it to be published."[18] An unsigned commentary in the *Osservatore Romano* observed that the teaching is *definitive tenenda*. It examined the scriptural foundation of the teaching and its universal character in Tradition and concludes: "In this case, an act of the ordinary papal magisterium, in itself not infallible, witnesses to the infallibility of the teaching of a doctrine already possessed by the Church." The context of the commentary is two truths: first, the non-admissibility of women to orders; second, "an absolutely fundamental truth of Christian anthropology (taught by the Church, namely) the equal personal dignity of men and women, and the necessity of overcoming and doing away with 'every type of discrimination regarding fundamental rights' (Vatican II, *Gaudium et spes* 29." The commentary asserted that ordination is "a service and not a position of privilege or human power over others. . . . Priestly ministry constitutes neither the universal ideal, nor even less the goal of Christian life."[19]

The matter now arises about the situation of the believer or theologian.[20] One is no longer free to assert boldly that women should be ordained (v. DISSENT, THEOLOGIANS). But one may be still free to question the issue. Questions are of two kinds: the *quid sit* question, which is posed in order to understand something; the *an sit* question, which leads to a yes/no answer.[21] Clearly, the first kind of question remains legitimate, especially about the main argument given in the matter, viz., Tradition; theology must always continue to seek understanding. The second question cannot now be asked in an uninhibited way—the pope has asserted that the matter is not "open to debate"; the solemn teaching of the pope must be acknowledged, even if one is examining or probing it—one must attempt a "religious assent of will and intellect" (LG 25). One should not publicly assert that this teaching is false; on the other hand, it cannot be treated as if it were an infallible statement. The Congregation's statement that the magisterium has infallibly taught the non-admissibility of women to priestly ordination is not itself an infallible statement. That is not to say that it is not true. To know whether the Congregation is correct in its assertion that the matter belongs to the deposit of faith, and that it is taught infallibly by the ordinary magisterium, one has to apply the normal criteria for discernment of infallible teaching (v. INFALLIBLE). In an examination of the document, F.A. Sullivan draws attention to canon 749 of the *Code of Canon Law,* which declares that no doctrine is understood to have been defined infallibly unless this fact is clearly established, and suggests that there are sound theological arguments for applying this rule to the present case.[22] He noted three criteria to ensure that it has been taught infallibly by the ordinary and universal magisterium: actual consultation of all the bishops, the universal and constant consensus of Catholic theologians, the common adherence of the faithful. The third criterion can also be seen in terms of the category of reception (q.v.): if the teaching of the CDF is received as being of divine truth and to be definitively held in the universal Church, then in time the Church will be certain that it is irrevocably true. Reception is, however, a slow process. There are several cases of doctrines being accepted as true, even as infallible, which today would not be regarded as such: one thinks of some statements of the Council of Florence (q.v.), Boniface VIII (q.v.), positions on slavery, usury, and Church-State relations.

The attitude of the theologian should be an acceptance that the teaching is almost certainly true, but legitimate questions can still be raised cautiously and respectfully. A wise method would be to remain at the level of deferential and tentative questions; prudence, respect, and the danger of scandal would all suggest that one should not draw conclusions against the papal teaching. This approach would reflect something of best practice by theologians in the past.

Can a Catholic envisage, or even hope for, a change in the Church's position on the ordination of women? The answer can be a guarded affirmative, on the understanding that such a reversal could come about only through the Holy Spirit leading the sense of the faith (q.v.) of the whole Church into a certainty that women can be validly ordained; this would constitute an authentic development of doctrine (q.v.). If such a sense of the faith were to come about, the supreme authority of the Church would in time undoubtedly follow the Spirit's leading. There is no evidence that such a consensus exists and little enough that it may be forming. Hence, it would not be pastorally wise to encourage such hopes. But a statement, however heavily qualified, that it is possible to hope for a change is itself an assertion that at the present time (Dec. 1995) it is not yet absolutely clear that the non-admittance of women to ordination has been irrevocably taught. To believe otherwise, or to hope for a change, might well be judged foolish, misguided, or vain; it would not, however, place one outside the pale of Catholic faith and Church membership. One must also note that a reversal of the current position could not come easily: as A. Dulles wrote recently, the Church would have to be completely certain that the ordination of women was clearly valid before proceeding to a change.[23] In sacramental practice, especially where validity is concerned, the Church always follows the safer course. It would be hard to conceive of such a change coming about quickly, even within a century.

It would then follow that the present practice and the teaching of the magisterium must be followed despite the pain it causes to so many women and not a few men in the Church. But in the meantime, the Catholic Church needs to develop true partnership in ministry between all its members, clerical and lay, and especially with women who, though often the most committed and gifted members in a local Church community, yet have least participation in its decision-making processes and in its clerically monopolized ministries.[24] The request of the German bishops to have the order of deaconess (q.v.) restored is an interesting move in this direction.

If those Anglican Churches having an exclusively male priesthood/episcopacy, urgently need to continue dialogue with Churches that have the ordination of women,[25] no less can be urged on the Catholic Church; ecumenical dialogue is concerned with how the Spirit may be speaking to the Churches (see Rev 2:7, 11 . . .).

The ordination of women in recent literature is often presented as a justice or equity/equality issue; it is certainly a burning one which will not go away in the foreseeable future. We need constantly to keep in mind that the papal and other authoritative statements are an assertion that the Church does not have the power to ordain women; they are not to be judged as arbitrary refusals to allow women to be priests. Moreover, as recent documents imply, the assumptions of secular society about the relations of men and women cannot be the determinant in this question; it cannot be solved in terms of women's rights. But painful and important as this issue of ordination clearly is, it needs to be relativized in a more comprehensive picture of the Church in which it is the Marian, not the Petrine, functions that are most significant (v. ECCLESIOLOGY and MARY AND THE CHURCH),[26] even if many women, nearly all men and most of the clergy, are not yet aware of the enormous and exciting implications of this Marian priority.

[1]M. Tanner, "Ordination of Women," DictEcumMov 752–755. [2]J.W. Witmer and J. R. Wright, eds., *Called to Full Unity: Documents on Anglican-Roman Catholic Relations 1966–1983* (Washington, D.C.: United States Catholic Conference, 1986) 132–135. [3]Pope John Paul II to Robert Runcie, Archbishop of Canterbury 20.12.1984; Response 22.11.1985; Runcie to Card. Willebrands 22.11.1985; Response of Willebrands 17.6.1986—*Women Priests, Obstacle to Unity?* (London: Catholic Truth Society, 1986)/DocCath 1924 (21 Sept. 1986) 800–806/Irén 59 (1986) 352–365/OneChr 22 (1986) 289–299. [4]See bibliog. in G.S. Worgul, Jr. "Ritual, Power, Authority and Riddles: The Anthropology of Rome's Declaration on the Ordination of Women," LouvSt 14 (1989) 38–61. [5]AAS 69 (1977) 98–116/Flannery 2:331-345. [6]R. Maloney, "The Ordination of Women," Fur 32 (1981) 438–448; N. López Martínez, "El sacerdocio de la mujer en la tradición de la Iglesia católica," Burgense 26 (1985) 421–439. [7]AA.VV. *The Order of Priesthood. Nine Commentaries on the Vatican Decree Inter insigniores* (Huntington, Ind.: Our Sunday Visitor, 1978)—from OssRomano Feb.–June 1977; [Ecumenical Patriarchate], "Die Stellung der Frau in der Orthodoxen Kirche und die Frage der Ordination der Frauen," OrthFor 3 (1989) 93–102; G. Barrois, "Women and Priestly Office According to the Scriptures," SVlad 19 (1975) 174–192; D. Connell, "Women Priests; Why Not?," Apoll 59 (1986) 493–511/OssRomano (English) 7 March 1988; J. Galot, "La femme et le sacerdoce: Le problème et les revendications actuelles," Seminarium 30 (1978) 98–118; P. Grelot, "Y aura-t-il 'femmes prêtres' dans l'Église?," NRT 111 (1989) 842–865; T. Hopko, "On the Male Character of Christian Priesthood," SVlad 19 (1975) 147–173, with "A Reply to Criticism," ibid. 21 (1977) 161–167; T. Hopko, ed., *Women and the Priesthood: Essays from the Orthodox Tradition* (Crestwood, N.Y.: St. Vladimir's Seminary Press, 1982); L. Ligier, "La question du sacerdoce des femmes dans l'Église," DocCath 75 (1978) 478–489. [8]D.C. Maguire, "The Exclusion of Women from Orders: A Moral Evaluation," CrossC 34 (1984–1985) 141–152; R.R. Ruether, *Sexism and God-Talk* (London: SCM, [2]1983) 193–213. [9]G. Tavard, "The Ordination of Women," OneChr 23 (1987) 200–211; J. Wijngaards, *Did Christ Rule Out Women Priests?* (Great Wakering UK: McCrimmon's, [2]1986). [10]E. Schüssler Fiorenza, *Discipleship of Equals: A Critical Feminist Ecclêsia-logy of Liberation* (London: SCM, 1993); G. Wilson, *Why No Women Priests?* (Worthing UK: Churchman—Dublin: APCK, 1988); K. Untener et al., "Forum: The Ordination of Women: Can the Horizon Widen?," Worship 65 (1991) 50–59, 256–268, 451–461, 482–508. [11]D. Edwards, "The Ordination of Women and Anglican-Roman Catholic Dialogue," Pacifica 1 (1988) 125–140; H. Legrand, "Traditio perpetuo servanda? The Non-ordination of Women: Tradition or Simply an Historical Fact," Worship 65 (1991) 482–508. Cf. review art. L. Sabourin, "Questions of Christian Priesthood," RelStB 2 (1982) 1–15; A. Stacpoole, "Ordination of Women: Two Traditions," Month 267 (1985) 15–22—re: Anglican-Roman Catholic issues. [12]See S. Butler, "Second Thoughts on Ordaining Women," Worship 63 (1989) 157–163, response by M. Schaefer 467–471 and reply by S. Butler 471–473; A. Rolla, "Il sacerdozio alle donne? Riflessioni sulla Dichiarazione Inter insigniores," Asp 24 (1977) 67–95, 177–187. [13]Catholic Bib. Assoc. of America Task Force, "Women and Priestly Ministry: The New Testament Evidence," CBQ 41 (1979) 608–613; cf. on ministries O. Genest, "Femmes et ministères dans le Nouveau Testament," StRel16 (1987) 7–20; P. Richardson, "From Apostles to Virgins: Romans 16 and the Roles of Women in the Early Church," TorontoJT 2 (1986) 232–261. [14]D. Power, "Representing Christ in Community and Sacrament," in D.J. Goergen ed., *Being a Priest Today* (Collegeville: The Liturgical Press, 1992) 97–123, seriously critiqued by S. Butler in "The Priest as Sacrament of Christ the Bridegroom," Worship 66 (1992) 498–517; an Anglican view: R.A. Norris, "The Ordination of Women and the 'Maleness' of Christ," AngTR—Supp 58 (1976) 69–80. [15]RCIA, GI 16–17/DOL 2266. [16]K. Rahner, "Women and the Priesthood," ThInvest 20:35-47. [17]*Ordinatio sacerdotalis*—AAS 86 (1994) 545–548/CathIntern 5/9 (1994) 412–414. [18]OssRom (English) 22 Nov. 1995/Tablet 25 November 1995. [19]L. Örsy, "Infallibility and the Ordination of Women: A Canon Law Approach, DoctLife (1966) = *America* 9 Dec. 1995. [20]See responses by N. Lash, A. Dulles, H. Küng, and F.A. Sullivan, in Tablet 25 Nov. to 23/30 Dec. 1995. [21]B.J.F. Lonergan, *Method in Theology* (London: Darton, Longman and Todd, 1971) 335–353. [22]*America* 9 December 1995/Tablet 16 December 1995. [23]Tablet 9 Dec. 1995. [24]G. Blaquière, "La mission de la femme dans l'Église," NRT 109 (1987) 345–361; Rolla (n. 12) 183–187; E.E. and J.D. Whitehead, "Women and Men: Partners in Ministry," ChicSt 27 (1988) 159–172. [25]J. Baycroft, "Inclusive Episcopacy and Koinonia," OneChr 24 (1988) 7–11. [26]H.U. von Balthasar, *Neue Klarstellungen* (Einseideln: Johannes, 1979) 109–115; for context, see J. O'Donnell, "Man and Woman as *Imago Dei* in the Theology of Hans Urs von Balthasar," CleR 68 (1983) 117–128. See for Orthodox, Elizabeth Behr-Sigel, *Le ministère de la femme dans l'Église*. Théologies (Paris: Cerf, 1987).

# WORLD

The world could be said to form the backdrop of almost every article in this volume; every aspect of ecclesiology is influenced by the world and our understanding of it. The attitude of the Christian to the world is complex, and one's statements need to be always carefully nuanced.[1] Since the Church is in the world and in history, the relation of the Church to the world will also be time-conditioned, and in some way a history of salvation of a pilgrim Church.

The biblical teaching itself is multifaceted. The world, or "the heavens and the earth" (Gen 1:1), come from God who creates it as good and gives it to men and women to enjoy and subjugate (Gen 1:28-31). The heavens and the earth proclaim the goodness of God (Pss 8; 104) and God's wisdom (Prov 8:22-31). Hebrew thought is far removed from the dualism, pantheism, and other distortions of the surrounding peoples. Towards the end of the OT, the Greek word *kosmos* comes into use, which bears also a sense of beauty and of history.

But the position of humankind in the world was soon distorted by sin, and the world became an instrument of God's wrath and punishment: work was no longer to be solely pleasant (Gen 3:17-19); the earth will be a curse for those who disobey God (Deut

28:15-46). None of the helps God provided for the people through judges, kings, or prophets would suffice. So the final stage of God's plan is put into operation: "God so loved the world *(ton kosmon)* that he gave his only Son" (John 3:16). In the NT[2] the basic optimism of the OT is still to be found (e.g., Acts 17:24; John 1:3-4, 10; Col 1:16). But there is a new dimension as the NT writers develop the notion of the world being under sin (Rom 5:12), and Satan is called the ruler of this world (John 12:31; 14:30); the world of darkness is ruled by evil forces (Eph 6:12). Hence in the Last Supper Discourse—an extended meditation on the Holy Spirit, love and the world—Jesus announces that he is leaving the world (John 16:28); the conviction of the world will be the work of the Spirit (16:8-11); the world will hate his disciples just as it hated him (15:18-19); Jesus prays for his disciples and not for the world (17:9), in which they will have persecution (16:33); they are to have courage, for Jesus has overcome the world (16:33).

The reflection of the primitive Church on the world continues this sense of the world being good and needing redemption (1 Cor 5:10), the place where Christians must perforce live, being in (John 11:11) but not of the world (John 15:19).[3] Jesus warned that it is not an advantage to gain the whole world *(kosmos)* and lose one's life *(psuchên*—Matt 16:20). The world is passing away (1 Cor 7:31), so we must not allow ourselves to be conformed to it (Rom 12:1-2—*aiôn*); indeed the task is "to keep oneself unstained by the world" (Jas 1:27). The traditional enemies of the spiritual life, "the world, the flesh and the devil," are already insinuated in the NT (e.g., 1 John 2:15-18). In the end God will overcome all evil and there will be a new heaven and a new earth (Rev 21:1-5).

The first millennium took up and developed this rich biblical teaching.[4] At first the world was a persecuting power and enemy of the Church and of Christians. But the early Apologetic Fathers such as Justin (q.v.) insisted that Christians were good citizens of the empire. After the Edict of Constantine (q.v.) in 313, the world gradually became friendly towards the Church—too friendly. Members of the Church at all levels from laity to papacy became overcommitted to secular affairs to the detriment of Christian commitment. All attempts at reform in some way or other were concerned with the relationship of the Church and the world.

Christian reflection on the world took many forms. The Church always regarded as heterodox any ontological or material dualism that suggested that matter, the flesh, or the world were evil. But Platonic ideas were quite influential: the world had to be transcended in the ascent to God. But a moderate moral dualism is part of Christian realism: the world is infected by sin and thus a danger. But the ordinary Christian must live in the world; flight from the world *(fuga mundi)* was a possibility only for a minority. Gradually, spiritual teaching became more subtle as writers realized that one can be engrossed in the world even in the desert, and that all must cultivate an inner attitude of such renunciation of the world and of sin as seeking salvation may demand.[5]

A very important work in the West was St. Augustine's extended analysis of the love of God and love of self, *The City of God.* A book of enormous influence in patristic times and in the Middle Ages, it was not always fully understood as being both present and eschatological. It furnished many theological writers, and political figures like Charlemagne, with deep insight into the ambiguity of the world.

The tension between Church and the world continued during the Middle Ages. Thus we have Lotario as a young man writing on the wretchedness of the lot of humanity and the need to flee the world[6]; later, as Innocent III (1198–1216), he would be one of the most energetic and distinguished reform popes of the period, but autocratic, deeply involved in politics, wars, and crusades.

In the period of the Enlightenment, the Church tended to withdraw in the face of hostility, and a chance was missed to dialogue with the emerging modern world.[7] A certain unease with science arose, not unconnected with the Galileo incidents (q.v.), which would last into the 20th century.[8] Nineteenth-century liberalism was seen as a further attack on the Church.[9] Its response was again to retreat or sidestep the world. Missions were developed in far-off places; piety was fostered, and all kinds of intra-Church activities evolved. The citadel mentality was especially strong during the Modernist period (q.v.), in which there was no dialogue, except by a few who were therefore suspect by those in authority.

The pontificate of Pius XII (q.v.) saw an immense attempt to show that the Church had a message for the world. The pope tried, moreover, to address different groups at the level of their situation in the world. But it was not yet dialogue; the pope taught people in the world the message of the Church, which he was so profoundly fashioning throughout his reign. For dialogue we have to wait for Vatican II which, though deeply optimistic, nevertheless recognized that the world has to be recovered from sin and brought under the lordship of Jesus (LG 36), refashioned anew according to God's design (GS 4).

By Vatican II we have the beginnings of reflection on secularism and secularization. The term "secularism" was first used apparently by G.J. Holyoake (d. 1906). It is an attempt to interpret reality independently of God and any future life; as such, it could be an atheistic or agnostic ideology. Secularization was employed to denote the legitimate autonomy of the secular from ecclesiastical control. But this legitimate autonomy can be infected by the reality of sin (GS 36–38). The idea of dialogue with the world was given strong impetus from the first encyclical of Paul VI (q.v.), *Ecclesiam suam* (Aug. 1964). Schema XIII, eventually to become the Pastoral Constitution on the Church in the World of Today *(Gaudium et spes),* was studied in the third session of the Council;[10] it clearly sought to answer one of the desires of John XXIII for the council. Nevertheless it would prove a most difficult document to draft, not least because it was unlike anything ever before attempted by the magisterium. It sought to examine the situation of the world under various headings: condition of humanity today and the deeper human questioning; the dignity of the human person; freedom; atheism; the worldwide human community and activity; urgent problems—marriage and family, the proper development of culture, socio-economic life, life of the political community, peace, international issues. In each case it offered a reflection on the present reality and a response in terms of the message of Christ.

In GS we find that the Church's relationship to the world changes from a juridical conception to an anthropological conception.[11] But the council does not blur the distinction between Church and world. It warns: "Although earthly progress must be carefully distinguished from the growth of Christ's kingdom, nevertheless its capacity to contribute to a better ordering of human society makes it highly relevant to the kingdom of God" (GS 39). The foundation of the Church's secular apostolate is the Church's positive relationship with the world, a relationship which is rooted in the meaning of human dignity, human community, human activity (GS 40–45).[12]

The comment on GS by H. Jedin (q.v.), probably the most distinguished Catholic historian of this century, must inevitably give pause for thought: "[The Constitution] aimed to be a fundamental new definition of the relation of the Church to the world and thereby to orient the Church to the world, and that meant to the spirit of the new epoch, from which it had held itself aloof since a century earlier in the *Syllabus.* This constitution was greeted with enthusiasm, but history has already proved that at that time its significance was greatly overestimated and there was hardly a suspicion of how deeply that 'world' which people wanted to win for Christ would penetrate the Church."[13]

After the council the Church opened up in dialogue with the world in a way that was more confident than at any time since the Middle Ages. The magisterium and theologians took up the ideas of development (q.v.) in the 1960s, liberation theologies (q.v.) from the 1970s, inculturation (q.v.). At the same time there was an involvement in international politics and affairs that was generally open and informed (v. also CONCOR-

DATS).[14] The social teaching of the Church since the 1891 encyclical of Leo XIII, *Rerum novarum,* is yet another rich seam for a theology of the relation of Church and world,[15] as well as the whole Church-State question (v. MURRAY, J.C.).

Another area that also must be the concern of ecclesiology is ecology.[16] The issue has rich ecumenical possibilities. But it is a rather new awareness, often dated from Rachel Carson's *Silent Spring* (1962). It is at once a theological, an ethical, a scientific, an economic, a cultural, and a political issue, with implications for spirituality. Having such a huge literature and very many points of view and of concern, it is especially important to heed the warnings of Vatican II that no one may propose what is deemed to be "the Catholic position," nor can we expect full answers from the magisterium, for indeed it is probably from the laity who are expert in these matters that the richest insights may come (GS 43).

The continual reflection on the laity (q.v.) by magisterium, theologians, and laity (many of whom became theologians in the post-Vatican II period) led to some clarification of the role of the secular for the Church. But this period would also witness a harsh secularism and the new visions of the world and humanity that many will call post-Christian and post-modernity.[17] The publication of the new *Code of Canon Law* (1983) saw reflections on the Church and world from yet another perspective.[18]

There will always be new questions posed to the Church by the world. These must not be avoided, even if we sense that we do not have more than a partial answer at a particular time.[19] A healthy tension in the Church between the vertical and the horizontal dimensions of Christian life and of theology will always be necessary if the needed subtlety in speaking about Church and world is to be achieved.

The Orthodox Church, so long regarded as excessively inward-looking, has in the past decades taken on a new openness to the world,[20] influenced both by its sense of the transfiguration of the world and its cosmic sense of the Eucharist.[21] The Eucharist (q.v.) remains the center of the Church's service of the world, seen in anthropological and ecological terms. When it is authentically celebrated, that is, with the mind of Christ by a community reflecting vertical and horizontal communion (q.v.) and love, the world is brought before God for all its needs, spiritual and temporal.

[1]J.C. Haughey, "World," NDictCSpir 1051–1062.  [2]H. Sasse, "Kosmos," TDNT 3:868-895; idem, "Aiôn," ibid., 1:197-209; C. Lesquivit and P. Grelot, "World," DBT 676–680.  [3]J. Beutler, "In der Welt, nicht von der Welt: Zum Ort der Christen nach dem Neuen Testament," StimZ 206 (1988) 37–46.  [4]T. Špidlík, "World," EncycEarCh 2:882.  [5]T. Špidlík, "Stare nel mondo o fuggire il mondo," VitaCons 13 (1977) 170–177.  [6]*De contemptu mundi*—PL 217:701-746.  [7]Jedin-Dolan, vol. 6.  [8]C.C. Hefling, Jr., "Science

and Religion," NDictT 938–945. [9]Jedin-Dolan, vol. 8. [10]Y. Congar and M. Peuchmaurd, eds., *L'Église dans le monde de ce temps: Constitution pastorale "Gaudium et spes."* US 65a–c (Paris: Cerf, 1967); M. McEntee, "The Way the Church Understands Its Presence and Function in the World Today (Pastoral Constitution par. 2): What Did Vatican II Say?," AustralCR 63 (1986) 236–251; A.M. Oriol, "Sobre la relación Iglesia-Mundo en el Concilio Vaticano," Lumen 35 (1986) 119–146. [11]A. Alvarez-Suárez, "Releyendo la 'Gaudium et spes' de la teología a la antropología," Burgense 33 (1992) 381–420; J. Bryan Hehir, "Church-State and Church-World: The Ecclesiological Implications," CTSAP 41 (1986) 56; cf. J.A. Komonchak, "Clergy, Laity and Church Mission" in *Official Ministry in a New Age,* CanLawSAP 47 (1981) 177–189. [12]See M.D. Place, "'In the Manner of a Leaven': The Lay Mission to the Secular World," Jurist 47 (1987) 86–102 at 93–97. [13]"The Second Vatican Council," in Jedin-Dolan 10:145. [14]E.O. Hanson, *The Catholic Church in World Politics* (Princeton: UP, 1987); M. Merle and C. de Montlos, *L'Église catholique et les relations internationales.* Église et société (Paris: Centurion, 1988); R. Russo, "La Saint-Siège et les organisations internationales," Études 345 (1976/2) 15–31; Conc 193 (1987). [15]See J.A. Dwyer and E.L. Montgomery, eds., *The New Dictionary of Catholic Social Thought* (Collegeville: The Liturgical Press, 1994). [16]R. Berthalot, "Il problema ecologico: Prospettive ecumeniche," StEcum 5 (1987) 483–490; J. Carmody, *Ecology and Religion: Towards a New Christian Theology of Nature* (New York—Ramsey: Paulist, 1983); idem, "Ecological Consciousness," NDictCSpir 330–332; S.R.L. "Christian Responsibility for the Environment," ModChm 25/2 (1985–1986) 24–31; H. Frisch, "Die Sorge um die Umwelt als Aufgabe christicher Gemeinden," StimZ 202 (1988) 112–124; G. Hens-Piazza, "A Theology of Ecology: God's Image and the Natural World," BibTB 13 (1983) 107–110; J. McPherson, "Towards an Ecological Theology,"ExpTim 97 (1985–1986) 230–240; H.E. Maertens, "The Doctrine of Creation in Ecological Perspective," LouvSt 12 (1987) 83–88; S. McDonagh, *To Care for the Earth: A Call to a New Theology* (London: Chapman, 1986); J. Moltmann, *Dieu dans la création: Traité écologique de la création.* Cogitatio fidei 146 (Paris: Cerf, 1988); H.P. Santmire, "Ecology and Ethical Economics," AngTR 59 (1977) 98–114; D. Senior, "The Gospel and the Earth," *The Bible Today* 26 (1988) 141–149. [17]P.L. Berger, "Secular Theology and the Rejection of the Supernatural: Reflections on Modern Trends," TS 38 (1977) 39–56; D. Bourg, "Christianité et déchristianisation," RevSR 59 (1985) 162–175; T. Glebe-Møller, "The Possibility of Theology in a Post Modern World," StTheol 46 (1992) 29–39; P. Gordan, "Kirche in der Welt von heute," TPQ 125 (1977) 102–106, 297–301. [18]L.-E. Ghesquières, "L'Église et l'État dans le droit canonique des origines au nouveau Code," MélSR 44 (1987) 57–69; N. Provencher, "The Church in the World," Jurist 47 (1987) 32–50. [19]See W. Bühlmann, *The Coming of the Third Church* (Slough UK: St. Paul, 1974); idem, *The Church for the Future: A Model for the Year 2001* (Maryknoll: Orbis, 1988); K. Rahner, *The Shape of the Church to Come* (New York: Seabury—London: SPCK, 1974); P. Imhof, H. Biallowons and H. Egan, eds., *Faith in a Wintery Season: Conversations and Interviews with Karl Rahner in the Last Years of His Life* (New York: Crossroad, 1990). [20]A. Schmemann, "The Problem of the Church's Presence in the World in Orthodox Consciousness," SVlad 21 (1977) 3–17. [21]See P. McPartlan, *The Eucharist Makes the Church: Henri de Lubac and John Zizioulas in Dialogue* (Edinburgh: Clark, 1993) passim, and esp. 289–305.

## WYCLIFFE, John (ca. 1330–1384)

Born in North Yorkshire, England, and educated in Oxford, where he later taught,[1] John Wycliffe (Wyclif/Wiclef) began academic writing as a philosopher, in which he returned to Augustinianism in place of the prevailing skepticism. In theology he was influenced by the Bible and the Fathers rather than the schools. His growing disillusionment with Church institutions led to his developing, on the basis of a Platonic philosophy, a view of the Church which distinguished its eternal spiritual ideal from the visible material Church. The latter had no authority which did not come from the former. Later he would apply his ideas to all authority, civil and ecclesiastical. Those who were not in grace lacked authority and could be deposed. These ideas were condemned in 1377 by Gregory XI.[2] Later he taught a form of *sola scriptura* ("Scripture alone"),[3] which led many to see him as a forerunner of the Reformation, though his concerns were different from those of the Reformers. He inspired one of the first translations of the Scriptures into English. His Eucharistic doctrines and his anti-papal views secured him a following, especially in Europe, where his thoughts were taken up by John Huss (q.v.), and in England, where a dwindling number of his disciples were known as Lollards.[4]

Various condemnations based on his voluminous works[5] followed after his death; a comprehensive list of his opinions—drafted in the most pejorative light possible—was condemned at the Council of Constance (1414).[6]

[1]K.A. Fink, in Jedin-Dolan 4:443-448; A. Kenny, ed., *Wycliffe and His Times* (Oxford: Clarendon, 1968); G. Leff, *Heresy in the Later Middle Ages: The Relation of Heterodoxy to Dissent c. 1250–c. 1450.* 2 vols. (Manchester: UP—New York: Barnes & Noble, 1967) 2:494-558; J.A. Robson, *Wycliffe and the Oxford Schools* (Cambridge: UP, 1961); H.H. Workman, *John Wycliffe.* 2 vols. (Oxford, 1926). [2]DS 1121–1139; L.J. Daly, *The Political Theory of John Wycliffe.* Jesuit Studies. (Chicago: Loyola UP, 1962). [3]M. Hurley, *John Wycliffe and Scriptura sola.* Diss exc. (Rome: Gregorian—New York: Fordham UP, 1960); idem, "Scriptura sola: Wycliffe and His Critics," Traditio 16 (1960) 275–352. [4]C. von Nolcken, "Notes on Lollard Citations of John Wycliffe's Works," JTS 39 (19888) 411–437. [5]*Works.* Wycliffe Society. 35 vols. (London, 1883–1914); P. Gradon and A. Hudson, eds, *English Wycliffite Sermons.* 3 vols. (Oxford: Clarendon, 1983–1990); A. Hudson, ed., *The Premature Reformation: Wycliffite Texts and Lollard History* (Oxford: Clarendon, 1988). [6]Tanner 1:411-416/DS 1151–1195/ND 806–808; Christie-Murray, Heresy 113–117; G. Christianson, "Wycliffe's Ghost: The Politics of Reunion at the Council of Basel," AHC 17 (1985) 193–208.

# Z

## ZIZIOULAS, Jean (1931– )

Born in Greece in 1931, Jean Zizioulas belongs to a second generation of Orthodox scholars in Western Europe. He was secretary for three years at the Life and Work department of the World Council of Churches in Geneva, before taking up a professorship at Edinburgh in 1970 and later moving to Glasgow. Nearly all of his work has an ecumenical thrust. He is currently bishop of Pergamon.[1]

Besides being perhaps the main current spokesperson for Orthodoxy in ecumenical dialogues, he has made a significant contribution to ecclesiology by developing the Eucharistic theology of N. Afanas'ev (q.v.), and extending the thought of H. de Lubac (q.v.), with whom he shares central intuitions.[2]

He states clearly that "the Church constitutes the Eucharist while being constituted by it."[3] He seeks to amplify the views of Afanas'ev, especially by insisting on the Eucharist being celebrated in communion with the local Church whose head is the bishop, and in communion also with the universal Church. Though he stresses the notion of the Body of Christ, Zizioulas is rather out of sympathy with Augustine, who was a great proponent of this doctrine.[4]

Zizioulas' ecclesiology is extremely rich and full:[5] at the heart of the Church is Christ, but in the Holy Spirit. Christ institutes, the Spirit constitutes the Church; institution is a fact, something done, constitution engages us in commitment.[6] Zizioulas develops an ecclesiology also of the local Church, one that is at once both anthropological and eschatological. His ecclesiology is best grasped when one considers the full meaning of what is celebrated in liturgy, where the Church is vertically united with the heavenly Jerusalem and is horizontally in communion with other Churches in service of the world.

[1]Bibliog. in P. McPartlan, *The Eucharist Makes the Church: Henri de Lubac and John Zizioulas in Dialogue* (Edinburgh: Clark, 1993) 316–321; G. Baillargeon, *Perspectives orthodoxes sur Église—Communion, L'oeuvre de Jean Zizioulas* (Montreal: Paulines—Paris: Médiaspaul, 1989); idem, "Jean Zizioulas, porte-parole de l'Orthodoxie contemporaine," NRT 111 (1989) 176–193. [2]McPartlan (n. 1). [3]"The Ecumenical Presuppositions of the Holy Eucharist," Nicol 10 (1982) 333–349 at 341. [4]F.G. Clancy, *St. Augustine of Hippo on Christ, His Church and the Holy Spirit: A Study of the De baptismo and the Tractatus in Johannis evangelium*. Diss. (Oxford, 1992). [5]See bibliog. (n. 1); *Being as Communion: Studies in Personhood and the Church* (London: Darton, Longman & Todd, 1985). [6]"Christologie, pneumatologie et institutions ecclésiales: Un point de vue orthodoxe," in G. Alberigo, ed., *Les Églises après Vatican II*. Théologie historique 61 (Paris: Beauchesne, 1981) 131–148. See C. Agoras, "Vision ecclésiologie: À propos d'une lecture de l'oeuvre de Jean Zizioulas," Contacts 43 (1991) 106–123.

## ZWINGLI, Ulrich (1484–1531)

Born in 1484 at Wildhaus in Switzerland, Ulrich (Huldreich/Huldrych) Zwingli was ordained priest in 1506.[1] As a pastor at Glarus he gave himself to humanistic studies, to the study of Greek and some Hebrew, and to the reading of the Fathers of the Church. His visit to the Benedictine shrine at Einsiedeln led to a determination to oppose abuses in the Church. He obtained a preaching post in Zürich in 1518, where he remained until his death.

Zwingli's espousal of Reformation ideals came during his lectures on the NT in 1519. He made the definitive break the following year. Soon afterwards he was writing against the papal and episcopal institutions. He held the sole sufficiency of Scripture and opposed also the invocation of the saints, the sacrifice of the Mass, fasting, clerical celibacy, and images.[2]

Except on the subject of the Eucharist, his theology is broadly a Reformation one,[3] and can be found in summary form in the sixty-seven theses he defended at a public disputation with the Catholic John Faber in 1523.[4] His overmastering idea was the sovereignty of God rather than human sinfulness or justification. He held that the true Church was the whole company of true believers from every age. To this Church he applied the word "invisible," in the sense that it is known only to God. The visible Church contains both true believers and those who are not. The notes (q.v.) of the visible members are the triple ones of preaching the Word, the two dominical sacraments, and Church discipline.[5]

Though as late as 1522 Zwingli held a traditional position on the Eucharist, by 1524/25 he was proposing a purely symbolic presence of Christ and rejecting all other views such as the Catholic transubstantiation or Protestant consubstantiation or companation.[6]

Zwingli was an effective polemicist for the Reformation causes in his native Switzerland, where he also opposed the Anabaptists (q.v.). He was killed during a skirmish in 1531 when acting as chaplain to the forces of Zürich. He was succeeded in Zürich by J.H. Bullinger (1504–1575), under whom Zürich drew close to Geneva and the doctrines of Calvin (q.v.).

[1]R. Dellsperger, "Das Zwinglijahr 1984 und die Zwingliforschung," VerkündForsch 34/2 (1989) 24–38; E. Iserloh, in Jedin-Dolan 156–170, 241–253; E. Koch, "Zwingli im Jubiläumsjahr 1984: Ein Literaturbericht," TLZ 113 (1988) 707–727; J.V. Pollet, *Huldrych Zwingli: Biographie et théologie.* Histoire et société 15 (Geneva: Labor et Fides, 1988); G.R. Potter, *Huldrych Zwingli* (London: Arnold, 1978); W.P. Stephens, *Zwingli: An Introduction to His Thought* (Oxford: Clarendon, 1992). [2]W.P. Stephens, "Zwingli's Reforming Ministry," ExpT 93 (1981–1982) 6–10; idem, "Huldrych Zwingli: The Swiss Reformer," ScotJT 41 (1988) 27–44. [3]Texts: Corpus Reformatorum 88–98, 101–102; *The Latin Works of Zwingli.* 3 vols. (New York, 1912—Philadelphia, 1922, 1929); LCC 24. See Antón 1:621-647; J.-P. Gabus, "Huldrych Zwingli: Théologien de la Réforme (1484–1531) ETR 60 (1985) 527–543; J.V. Pollet, *Huldrych Zwingli et le zwinglianisme: Essai de synthèse historique et théologique mis à jour d'après les recherches récentes.* De Pétrarch à Descartes 52 (Paris: Vrin, 1988); W.P. Stephens, *The Theology of Huldrych Zwingli* (Oxford: Clarendon, 1986). [4]Schaff, Creeds 3:196-207. [5]*An Exposition of the Faith* in LCC 24:265-266; cf. G.W. Bromiley, ibid., 35–36. [6]*An Exposition of the Faith* in LCC 24:254-262; U. Gäbler, "Huldrych Zwingli 1484–1984," UnaSan 39 (1984) 266–277 at 274–276 (Reformed); E. Iserloh, in Jedin-Dolan 5:245-249; V. Limberis, "Symbol and Sanctification: An Orthodox Critique of Zwingli," GrOrTR 20 (1981) 97–112.

# THE AUTHOR

Christopher O'Donnell, O.Carm., a senior lecturer in systematic theology at the Milltown Institute, Dublin, Ireland, holds a doctorate in sacred theology from the Gregorian University in Rome.

Father O'Donnell is the author of four other books (*Life in the Spirit* [Dublin: Dominican Publications, 1981; Wilmington: Michael Glazier, 1981], *Called to Holiness in the Church: An Ecclesial Spirituality* [Dublin: Avila Centre of Spirituality, 1983], *The Ecclesial Dimension of Confirmation: A Study in Saint Thomas and in the Revised Rite* [Rome: Gregorian University, 1987], and *At Worship with Mary: A Pastoral and Theological Study* [Wilmington: Michael Glazier, 1988; Collegeville: The Liturgical Press, 1990]), as well as some two hundred articles on ecclesiology, mariology, spirituality, charismatic renewal, sacramental theology, pastoral ministry, and ecumenism.

*Life in the Spirit and Mary* has been published in Italian (*Maria e la vita nello Spirito* [Milan: Áncora, 1984]) and *At Worship with Mary* in Czech (*Slavími s Marií: Matka Boží v liturgii* [Dačice: Karmelitánské nakladatelství, 1996]).

# SELECT TOPICAL INDEX

This select topical index serves several purposes.

It indicates the 389 main articles, which are given in uppercase, e.g., ADAM, K. An arrow indicates other related articles in which more information may be found, e.g., VATICAN II is treated not only in its own main article, but features in 98 others, e.g., BUDDHISM, which will be found also under VATICAN II.

Over 70 topics which do not have a main entry, but are considered in other articles, sometimes very briefly, are in lower case with an indicative arrow, e.g., Akribeia is found in the article on ECONOMY.

Finally, in cases where there could be confusion, the index indicates where a topic is treated, e.g., Religious Freedom is located at FREEDOM, RELIGIOUS; Mixed Marriage is found under MARRIAGE, INTER-CHURCH.

Being too numerous, citations from Scripture and the *Code of Canon Law* do not appear in this select index.